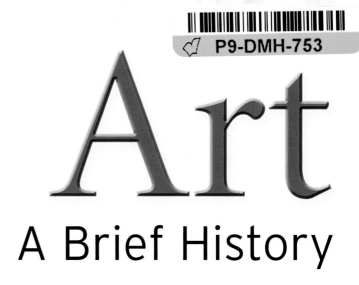

Art
A Brief History

Art

A Brief History

THIRD EDITION

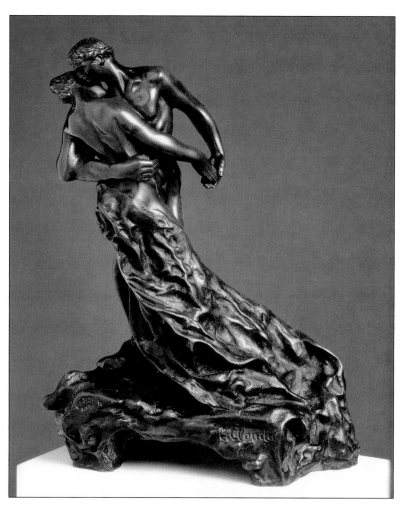

Marilyn Stokstad

EMERITA

THE UNIVERSITY OF KANSAS

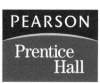

Upper Saddle River, New Jersey 07458

Library of Congress Cataloging-in-Publication Data

Stokstad, Marilyn
   Art: a brief history / Marilyn Stokstad—3rd ed.
     p. cm.
   Abridgment of the author's Art history.
   Includes bibliographical references and index.
   ISBN 0-13-195541-1 (alk. paper)
   1. Art—History. I. Title.

N5300.S923 2006
709—dc22   2005054986

EDITOR-IN-CHIEF: Sarah Touborg
SPONSORING EDITOR: Helen Ronan
EDITORIAL ASSISTANT: Jacqueline Zea
EDITORIAL INTERN: Aiza Keesey
MEDIA EDITOR: Anita Castro
DIRECTOR OF MARKETING: Brandy Dawson
ASSISTANT MARKETING MANAGER: Andrea Messineo
MARKETING ASSISTANT: Victoria DeVita
VP, DIRECTOR OF PRODUCTION AND MANUFACTURING: Barbara Kittle
SENIOR MANAGING EDITOR: Lisa Iarkowski
PRODUCTION LIAISON: Barbara Taylor-Laino
PRODUCTION ASSISTANT: Marlene Gassler
MANUFACTURING MANAGER: Nick Sklitsis
MANUFACTURING BUYER: Sherry Lewis
CREATIVE DESIGN DIRECTOR: Leslie Osher
ART DIRECTORS: Nancy Wells and Amy Rosen
INTERIOR AND COVER DESIGN: BTDnyc
LAYOUT ARTIST: Ximena Tamvakopoulos

LINE ART COORDINATOR: Maria Piper
CARTOGRAPHER: Cartographics
PEARSON IMAGING CENTER: Corin Skidds, Greg Harrison, Robert Uibelhoer, Ron Walko, Shayle Keating, and Dennis Sheehan
SITE SUPERVISOR, PEARSON IMAGING CENTER: Joe Conti
PHOTO RESEARCHER: Emma Brown
DIRECTOR, IMAGE RESOURCE CENTER: Melinda Reo
MANAGER, RIGHTS AND PERMISSIONS: Zina Arabia
MANAGER, VISUAL RESEARCH: Beth Brenzel
MANAGER, COVER VISUAL RESEARCH AND PERMISSIONS: Karen Sanatar
IMAGE PERMISSION COORDINATOR: Debbie Latronica
COVER IMAGE COORDINATOR: Gladys Soto
TEXT EDITOR: Kevin P. Supples
PROOFREADERS: Mary Ellen Wilson and Victoria Waters
PRODUCTION MANAGEMENT AND COMPOSITION: Assunta Petrone/ Prepare, Inc.
COVER PRINTER: Phoenix Color Corporation
PRINTER/BINDER: R. R. Donnelley

Credits and acknowledgements borrowed from other sources and reproduced, with permission, in this textbook appear on the appropriate page within text or on the credit pages in the back of this book.

Cover Photo: Camille Claudel. *The Waltz.* c. 1892-1905. Bronze, 9 $\frac{7}{8}$″ (25 cm). Neue Pinakothek, Munich

Pearson Education Ltd
Pearson Education Australia PTY, Limited
Pearson Education Singapore, Pte. Ltd
Pearson Education North Asia Ltd

Pearson Education, Canada, Ltd
Pearson Educación de Mexico, S.A. de C.V.
Pearson Education-Japan
Pearson Education Malaysia, Pte. Ltd

PEARSON
Prentice
Hall

10 9 8 7 6 5 4 3 2 1
ISBN 0-13-195541-1

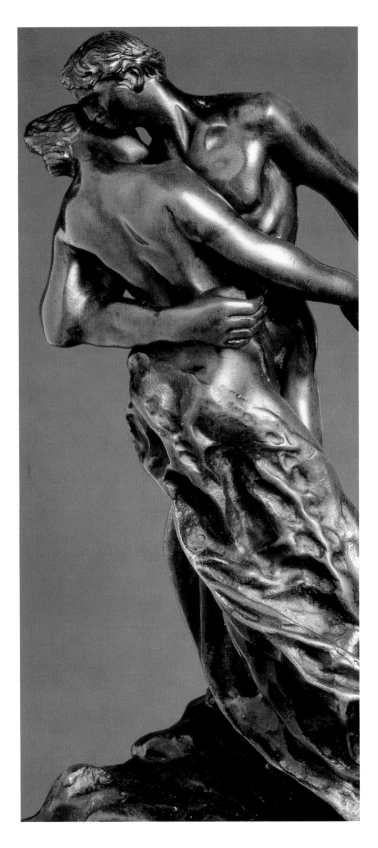

As I expressed in the Second Edition of *Art: A Brief History*, I believe that the first goal of an introductory art history course is to create an educated, enthusiastic public for the inspired, tangible creations of human skill and imagination that make up the visual arts—and I remain convinced that every student can and should enjoy her or his introduction to this broad field of study.

Like its predecessors, this book balances formalist analysis with contextual art history to support the needs of a diverse and fast-changing student population. Throughout the text, the visual arts are treated within the real-world contexts of history, geography, politics, religion, economics, and the broad social and personal aspects of human culture.

So . . . What's New in This Edition?

I strongly believe that an established text should continually respond to the changing needs of its audience—both students and educators. By addressing such needs, an introductory art history text is more likely to make a greater difference in the role that art can and will assume in its readers' lives, both at the time of use and long into the future—indeed, long after the need for the next revision arises.

My goal was to make this revised text an improvement over its earlier incarnations in sensitivity, readability, and accessibility without losing anything in comprehensiveness or in its ability to engage the reader. Incorporating feedback from our many users and reviewers, I believe we have succeeded.

Some highlights of the new edition include the following.

- Every chapter now ends with a summary essay called "Looking Back" accompanied by an illustrated timeline.
- Maps are now included in every chapter, and improved for clarity and accuracy.
- Throughout, black-and-white images have been replaced with color wherever possible and older reproductions of uncleaned or unrestored works have also been updated whenever new and improved images were available. In some instances, details have also been added to allow for closer inspection.
- The treatment of American art has been strengthened, and greater depth has been added to the coverage of work by women and minorities.

- Coverage of Korea and Cambodia has been added to the Asian chapters.
- Several chapters have been reorganized for greater clarity, such as those covering Hellenistic, Romanesque, and Modern art.
- In keeping with this book's tradition of inclusivity, every media is addressed—from tapestries and timber architecture to silver (whether Georgian or Bauhaus) and 21st-century electronic art.

New Scholarship

Over the many years that I've taught art history, I've found it continually inspiring to share new research with both my students and my fellow educators, and I am excited to have the opportunity here of incorporating some of the latest thinking and discoveries—whether this involves recently revised dates for ancient Egyptian art or fascinating recreations of familiar masterworks such as the new "colorful" Augustus of Primaporta. Throughout, I've added to the number of works that cover secular architecture and those that reflect domestic scenes, which provide such significant glimpses into the daily life of the past. Indeed, changes have been made on many levels—from the introduction to the bibliography, and from captions to chapter introductions and conclusions and even, in a few instances, chapter titles. Every change aims to make the text more useful to the instructors and students in today's art history classrooms.

In Gratitude

As its predecessors did, this Third Edition of *Art: A Brief History* represents the cumulative efforts of a distinguished team of scholars and educators. We are grateful to the following academic reviewers for their numerous insights and suggestions for improvement:

Claudia Brown, Arizona State University
Valerie Hedquist, University of Montana
Janet Leblanc, Clemson University
Sara E. Orel, Truman State University
Shannon Pritchard, University of Georgia
Andrea K. Rusnock, Glendale Community College
Donald E. Sloan, University of Wisconsin-La Crosse

Chapter by Chapter Revisions

With different specialists examining each chapter, and an exhaustive peer review process, the many specific revisions to the text are far too extensive to enumerate in detail. Some of the more prominent highlights of this new edition include the following:

INTRODUCTION

A revised Introduction acquaints readers with some key study terms, provides context for the introductory student of art history, and offers an overview of some of the questions about art that will engage students throughout the text.

CHAPTER 1

Additions to the opening chapter include pictographs from Utah's Horseshoe Canyon, the fascinating Bird-Headed Man from Lascaux, and clay figures from Cernavoda.

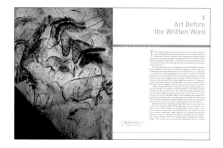

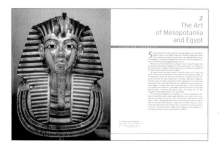

CHAPTER 2

New images here include a portrait of the pharaoh Senusret III, the funerary stele of Amenemhat and his family, and a stunning aerial view of the great Temple at Karnak.

CHAPTER 3

New sections covering the art of Korea and Indonesia are supported by images of the Indonesian Temple of Borobudur and a Korean Seated Matreya. A fascinating model of a house from an ancient Chinese tomb and a detail of an Indian Yakshi figure at Sanchi are also new.

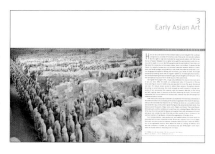

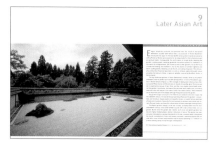

CHAPTER 4

Better quality pictures now illustrate the special boxed features here, and the color of images has been improved throughout, which significantly enhances the sculptural works. More effective images of architecture have also replaced older images.

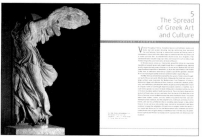

CHAPTER 5

A significant reorganization has moved Hellenistic art to the beginning of the chapter and Etruscan art to the end, where they now serve as bridges to the preceding and subsequent chapters. Additions include coverage of ancient coinage and Hellenistic architecture as well as images of the Temple of Zeus in Athens and the famed theater at Epidauros.

CHAPTER 6

This revised chapter includes expanded coverage of the Celts, a new portrait of Julius Caesar, an image of a lovely Pompeian garden fountain, and the above-mentioned colorized version of the Augustus of Primaporta.

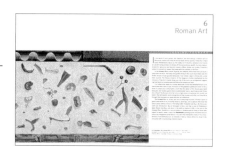

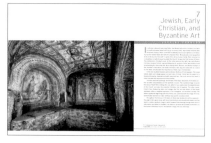

CHAPTER 7

Additions here include a painting that illustrates the interior of St. Peter's, the renowned Ravenna mosaic of Justinian and his attendants, and an illustrated manuscript depicting Rebecca at the Well from the Book of Genesis.

CHAPTER 8

In this chapter, which had been heavily revised in the previous edition, a feature on carpet-making techniques is newly illustrated with an Anatolian rug.

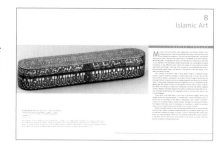

CHAPTER 9

New images include Korean ceramic-ware, and a new section covering Southeast Asia includes an image of the stunning site of Angkor Wat in Cambodia.

CHAPTER 10

Supporting the reorganization of this chapter are new images of Dover Castle, sculptural details from Vezelay and Modena, the wondrous Borgund stave church in Norway, and the interior of Santiago de Compostela.

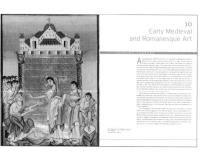

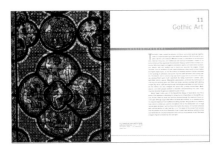

CHAPTER 11

Additions include new images of the glorious rose window at Chartres, newly cleaned sculpture from Amiens, the nave of Salisbury Cathedral, the dazzling *Windmill Psalter*, Lorenzetti's *Allegory of Good Government in the City*, and the charming ivory *Attack on the Castle of Love.*

CHAPTER 12

Enhancing the text here are new images of the Medici Palace; *The Buxheim St. Christopher*, one of the earliest known woodcuts; and a perspective diagram of Perugino's fresco *The Delivery of the Keys to St. Peter.*

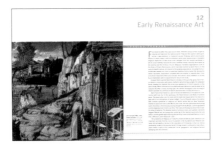

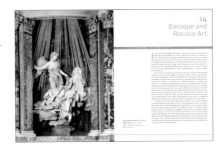

CHAPTER 13

New images of works by Giorgione, Bellini, and Altdorfer illustrate this chapter, which also now includes a Raphael tapestry from the Vatican and an exquisite self-portrait by Sofonisba Anguissola.

CHAPTER 14

This chapter is newly enhanced by a representative painting by Murillo, new images of dramatic works by Artemisia Gentileschi and Caravaggio, and a new photograph showing the famed Garden Façade of Versailles.

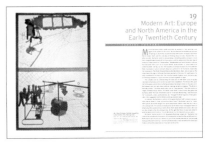

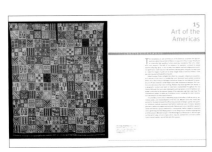

CHAPTER 15

Here, additions include new images of a gold shaman pendant from Costa Rica, a ceramic depicting a Moche lord with a cat, a rare wooden pelican figurehead from Florida, and a remarkable Mandan buffalo hide painting.

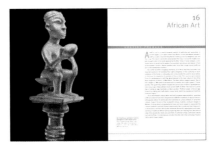

CHAPTER 16

A new photograph from the Smithsonian Institution of a terra-cotta horseman from Mali illustrates this chapter, which also contains a new image of the Great Friday Mosque at Djenné and an image offering a view of the Nankani compound at Ghana.

CHAPTER 17

Additions to this chapter include a display of Georgian silver by women silversmiths; a painting by Théodore Rousseau; and *The Oxbow*, a popular American landscape painting by Thomas Cole.

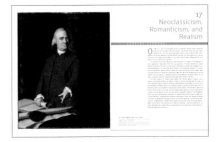

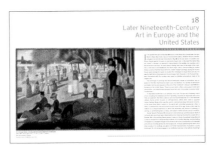

CHAPTER 18

Enhancing this chapter are new images of the Grand Staircase at the Paris Opera; *The Banjo Player*, a sensitive work by Henry O. Tanner; a masterful watercolor, *The Blue Boat* by Winslow Homer; and the 1872 Monet painting *Impression, Sunrise*, which gave the name to the Impressionist movement.

CHAPTER 19

The inclusion of representative works by Klimt, Brancusi, Marsden Hartley, Mondrian, and Jacob Lawrence, as well as a Bauhaus tea and coffee service by Marriane Brandt and the famous *Luncheon in Fur* by Meret Oppenheim, are among the refinements made to this chapter.

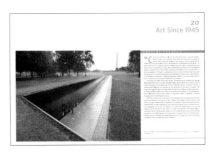

CHAPTER 20

Additions include commentary on the academic enthusiasm for art theory, works by Faith Ringgold and Santiago Calatrava, the California *Running Fence* installation by Christo and Jeanne-Claude, a computer-generated work by Jennifer Steinkamp, and stoneware by Toshiko Takaezu.

KEY FEATURES OF EVERY CHAPTER

Art: A Brief History has always been known for superb pedagogical features in every chapter, many of which have been enhanced for this new edition. These include:

LOOKING FORWARD

Using a compelling work of art as a springboard, this narrative introduction presents the major themes, cultures, and time periods of the chapter.

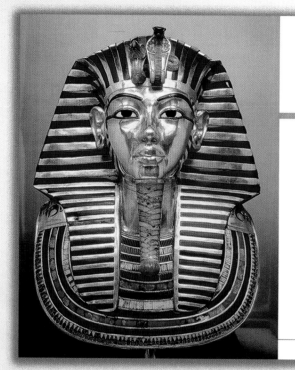

LOOKING BACK/TIMELINE

NEW in every chapter, summaries highlight key pedagogical concepts, and chronologies situate the works of art in their historical era.

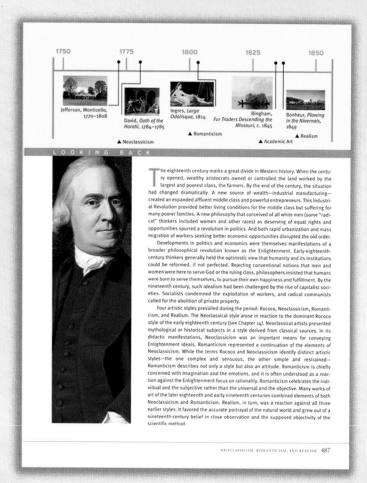

EXTENDED CAPTIONS
These contain complementary historic or intellectual context or additional formal analysis of the work illustrated.

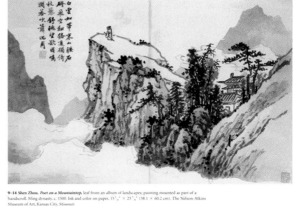

9–14 Shen Zhou. *Poet on a Mountaintop*, leaf from an album of landscapes; painting mounted as part of a handscroll. Ming dynasty, c. 1500. Ink and color on paper, 15¼″ × 23⅝″ (38.1 × 60.2 cms). The Nelson-Atkins Museum of Art, Kansas City, Missouri
PURCHASE, NELSON TRUST (46-51)

The poem at the upper left reads:

White clouds like a belt encircle the mountain's waist
A stone ledge flying in space and the far thin road.
I lean alone on my bramble staff and gazing contented into space
Wish the sounding torrent would answer to your flute.

(Translated by Richard Edwards, cited in *Eight Dynasties of Chinese Paintings*, page 185)

Shen Zhou composed the poem and the inscription, written at the time he painted the album. The style of the calligraphy, like the style of the painting, is informal, relaxed, and straightforward—qualities that were believed to reflect the artist's character and personality.

The contrast between the opulent display and the austere aesthetic ideals of the literati is a defining feature of Ming dynasty (1368–1644) painting. Whereas court painters revived academic traditions of the Song dynasty, many literati painters built on the styles created by their predecessors, the Yuan. One of the major literati artists of the Ming period is Shen Zhou (1427–1509), who spent most of his life in the southern city of Suzhou, far from the court in Beijing. Shen Zhou studied the Yuan painters avidly and tried to recapture their spirit in such works as *Poet on a Mountaintop* (fig. 9–14). Here the poet has climbed a mountain and surveys the landscape. Before his gaze, a poem hangs in the air, like a projection of his thoughts. Like the poem, the landscape is a vehicle for self-expression, having more to do with the artist's response to nature than with the physical world itself. With its perfect synthesis of poetry, calligraphy, and painting, and its harmony of mind and landscape, *Poet on a Mountaintop* represents the very essence of literati painting.

The cities of the south, such as Suzhou, were full of newly wealthy merchants who collected paintings, antiques, and art objects. The court, too, was prosperous and patronized the arts on a lavish scale. In such a setting, the decorative arts thrived.

Like the Song dynasty before it, the Ming became famous the world over for its exquisite ceramics, especially **porcelain**. Porcelain is made from kaolin, an extremely refined white clay, and petuntze, a variety of the mineral feldspar. When properly combined and fired at a high temperature, the two materials fuse into a glasslike, translucent ceramic that is far stronger than it looks.

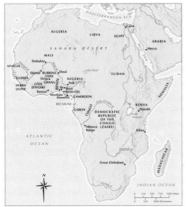

Map 16–1 The African Continent

Africa is a continent of enormous diversity. Geographically, it ranges from vast deserts to tropical rain forests, from flat grasslands to spectacular mountains and dramatic rift valleys. Human diversity in Africa is equally impressive. More than 1,000 major languages have been identified, representing a seemingly infinite variety of cultures, each with its own history, customs, and art forms. Africa is the site of one of the great ancient civilizations, that of Egypt (see Chapter 2), and North Africa later contributed prominently to the development of Islamic art and culture.

The history of African art begins in the Paleolithic era. Like prehistoric people around the world, early Africans painted and inscribed an abundance of images on the walls of caves and overhanging rocks. The mountains of the central Sahara have especially fascinating examples of rock art, with the earliest images dating from at least 8000 BCE. At that time, the Sahara was a great grassy plain, perhaps much like the game-park areas of modern East Africa. Vivid images of hippopotamuses, elephants, giraffes, antelope, and other animals incised into rock surfaces testify to the abundant wildlife that roamed the region.

By 4000 BCE, hunting had given way to herding as the Saharan climate became more arid. Remarkably lifelike paintings on rock surfaces from the herding period show scenes of cattle and the people who tended them. The desiccation of the Sahara coincided with the rise of Egyptian civilization along the Nile Valley to the east. As the Saharan grasslands dried up, some of their inhabitants may have migrated to the Nile Valley region in search of arable land and pasture. Perhaps this migration, by greatly expanding the population of the valley, contributed to the tensions that resulted in the emergence of complex forms of social organization there.

Saharan people presumably migrated southward as well, into the Sudan, the broad belt of grassland that stretches across Africa south of the Sahara desert, bringing with them knowledge of agriculture and animal husbandry. Agriculture reached the Sudan by at least 3000 BCE, and knowledge of ironworking spread across the area toward the middle of the first millennium BCE.

Some of the earliest evidence of iron technology in sub-Saharan Africa comes from the so-called Nok culture, which arose in the western Sudan (present-day Nigeria), as early as 500 BCE. The Nok people were farmers who grew grain and oil-bearing seeds; they were also smelters, using the technology for refining ore. In addition, they created the earliest known sculpture of sub-Saharan Africa, producing accomplished terra-cotta figures of human and animal subjects between about 500 BCE and 200 CE.

The Nok head shown here (fig. 16–2), slightly larger than life-size, originally formed part of a complete figure. The triangular or D-shaped eyes are characteristic of Nok style and appear in Nok animal sculptures. Each large bun of the elaborate hairstyle is pierced with a hole that may have held ornamental feathers. Other Nok figures boast large quantities of beads and other prestige ornaments. Since the original context for these pieces is unknown—none of these sculptures were excavated by archaeologists—it is difficult to hypothesize what their original meaning and function might have been.

MAPS
NEW in every chapter, detailed maps show the places mentioned within the text.

DIVERSE BOXED TEXTS, SUCH AS

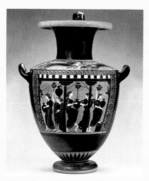

CLOSER LOOK

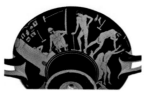

4–22 Priam Painter. *Women at a Fountain House,* black-figure decoration on a hydria. 520–510 BCE. Ceramic, height of hydria 20⅞" (53 cm). Museum of Fine Arts, Boston
WILLIAM FRANCIS WARDEN FUND

Here, the Priam Painter provides an interesting insight into everyday Greek city life as well as a view of an important public building in use (fig. 4–22). Most women in ancient Greece were confined to their homes, so their daily trip to the communal well, or fountain house, was an important event. At a fountain house, in the shade of a Doric-columned porch, three women patiently fill hydriae like the one on which they are painted. A fourth balances her empty jug on her head as she waits, while a fifth woman, without a jug, appears to be waving a greeting to someone. The women's skin is painted white, a convention similar to the pale female figures found in Egyptian and Minoan art. Incising and touches of reddish-purple paint create fine details in the architecture and in the figures' clothing and hair.

The composition of this vase painting finely balances vertical, horizontal, rectangular, and rounded elements. The Doric columns, the decorative vertical borders, and even the streams of water flowing from the animal-head spigots echo the upright figures of the women. The wide black band forming the ground line, the architrave above the colonnade, and the left-to-right movement of the horse-drawn chariots across the shoulder emphasize the horizontal, friezelike arrangement of the women across the body of the pot. This geometric framework is softened by the rounded contours of the female bodies, the globular water vessels, the circular **palmettes** (fan-shaped petal designs) framing the main scene, and the arching bodies of the galloping horses on the shoulder.

vessel with light-colored figures painted with dark-colored details (see fig. 4–24). The greater ease, speed, and flexibility of this technique led artists to adopt it quickly.

An early-fifth-century red-figure **kylix,** or two-handled drinking cup, displays the painter's virtuosity at adapting a scene to the shape of the vessel (fig. 4–23) and in drawing individual figures in action. The artist, known as the Foundry Painter, used the circular underside of the cup to illustrate the workings of a foundry for casting bronze figures. The walls of the pictured workshop are filled with tools and other paraphernalia: hammers, molds of a human foot and hand, and several sketches. A seated helmeted worker attends to a furnace at left, while a second man—perhaps the supervisor—leans on a staff. A third worker assembles the already-cast parts of a leaping figure; the parts are braced against a molded support, and the head lies at the worker's feet. The painter has created a lively scene in an awkward space and also gives us insight into the working methods of sculptors creating large bronze statues.

4–23 Foundry Painter. *A Bronze Foundry,* red-figure decoration on a kylix from Vulci, Italy. 490–480 BCE. Ceramic, diameter of kylix 12" (31 cm). Staatliche Museen zu Berlin, Preussischer Kulturbesitz, Antikensammlung
The painter conveys the mass and energy of the figures and also draws in details of muscles and facial features. The men work in a real space defined by their furnace and other equipment as well as by their foreshortened bodies and limbs, especially the legs of the man tending the furnace.

CLOSER LOOK
A special feature that concentrates on a work of art, providing in-depth historical background as well as an extensive analysis of the work's formal elements.

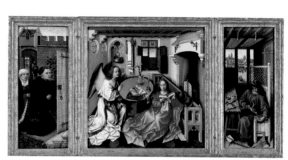

12–3 Robert Campin and assistants. *Mérode Altarpiece (Triptych of the Annunciation)* (open). c. 1425–1428. Oil on wood, center 25¼" × 24⅞" (64.1 × 63.2 cm); each wing approx. 25⅜" × 10⅞" (64.5 × 27.6 cm). The Metropolitan Museum of Art, New York
THE CLOISTERS COLLECTION, 1956 (56.70)

conventions (seen, for example, in the *Petites Heures de Jeanne d'Evreux,* fig. 11–16), which persisted in Northern Renaissance art into the first half of the fifteenth century. These include the missing front wall of the house, removed in order to show the activities inside, the attention to detail, and the high placement of the horizon line. The integration of figures and animals into the landscape has been accomplished within the prevailing Gothic style, but on a more believable scale, with a landscape receding continuously from foreground to middle ground to background.

Throughout most of the fifteenth century, the artists of Flanders (roughly equivalent to the present-day lands of western Belgium, the southwestern Netherlands, and a small area of northern France) were considered the best in Europe, and the art produced there during this period is commonly called *Flemish.* Flanders, which included part of the domain of the duke of Burgundy and the major seaport and commercial center of Bruges, was the commercial power of Northern Europe, rivaling the Italian city-states of Florence and Venice.

The most outstanding exponents of the new Flemish style were Robert Campin, Jan van Eyck, and Rogier van der Weyden. About 1425–1428, Campin (documented from 1406; d. 1444) painted an altarpiece now known as the *Mérode Altarpiece* (fig. 12–3) after the

Technique
Painting on Panel

Painting pictures on wood has an ancient history, and wood panels were particularly favored by European painters and their patrons in the fifteenth century for works ranging from small portraits to enormous altarpieces.

Once the panel was prepared, artists painted in their preferred medium (see "Cennini on Panel Painting," page 297). Italian artists favored tempera, using it almost exclusively for panel painting until the end of the fifteenth century. Northern European artists preferred oil paints, which Flemish painters so skillfully exploited at the beginning of the century. Tempera had to be applied in a very precise manner, because it dried almost as quickly as it was laid down. Shading had to be done with careful overlying strokes in tones ranging from white and gray to dark brown and black. Because tempera is opaque, light striking its surface does not penetrate to lower layers of color and reflect back—the resulting surface is **matte,** or dull. (Varnish gives it a sheen.)

Oil paint, on the other hand, takes much longer to dry, and while it is still wet, changes can be made easily. Oil paint can also be translucent when applied in very thin layers, called glazes. Light striking a surface built up of glazes penetrates to the lower layers and is reflected back, creating the appearance of an interior glow. In both tempera and oil, the desired result in the fifteenth century was a smooth surface that betrayed no brushstrokes.

TECHNIQUE
Illustrations and explanations of processes used by artists.

ELEMENTS OF ARCHITECTURE
A close-up and detailed look at an important architectural topic.

ELEMENTS OF **Architecture**
Mosque Plans

The earliest mosques were **hypostyle halls** at one side of an open courtyard. Rows of closely spaced columns perpendicular to the **qibla** wall support a flat roof. The Great Mosque at Cordoba (see fig. 8–7) is typical.

The **four-iwan** mosque, developed in Persia, is seen in buildings such as the Congregational Mosque at Isfahan (see fig. 8–10). Iwans—vaulted halls with monumental arched openings—faced each other across a central court-

yard, and related structures spread out and behind the iwans.

Central-plan mosques, the last type to develop, were inspired by Istanbul's Byzantine architecture, such as the Church of Hagia Sophia in Istanbul (see figs. 7–11 and 7–13). The Mosque of Selim in Edirne (see fig. 8–19) is characteristic of this style. The large central dome permits the interior space to be uninterrupted by structural supports.

Plans are not to scale

hypostyle mosque
Great Mosque, Cordoba,
after extension by
al-Hakam II

four-iwan mosque
Great Mosque, Isfahan

central-plan mosque
Sultan Selim Mosque, Edirne

many of his subjects. The caliph attempted to answer their objections to paying for such ostentation with an inscription giving thanks to God, who "helped him in the building of this eternal place, with the goal of making this mosque more spacious for his subjects, something which both he and they greatly wanted" (Dodds, page 23).

The renovations to the Great Mosque by Caliph al Hakam II in the tenth century included enlargements and a new *mihrab* with a richly decorated *maqsura*, the protected space for the

ruler. In front of the *mihrab*, melon-shaped, ribbed domes seem to float over intersecting arches (fig. 8–8). The arches are placed diagonally over the corners of a space to provide a base for a dome whose surface is covered with arabesques, geometric motifs, and stylized vegetation and inscriptions. In conscious competition with the Byzantines and the Abbasids, the Cordoban Umayyads employed mosaic decoration. Since the technique was not practiced in Spain, they acquired materials and the artisans from Byzantium to do the work.

---

trying to understand what is happening in the picture piques our interest. At the right, a woman is seated on the ground, nude except for the end of a long white cloth thrown over her shoulders. Her nudity seems maternal rather than erotic as she nurses the baby at her side. Across the dark, rock-edged spring stands a man wearing the uniform of a German mercenary soldier. His head is turned toward the woman, but he appears to have paused for a moment before continuing to turn toward the viewer. X-rays of the painting show that Giorgione altered his composition while he was still at work on it—the woman on the right was originally balanced by another nude woman on the left. The spring between the figures feeds a lake surrounded by substantial houses, and in the far distance a bolt of lightning splits the darkening sky. Indeed, the artist's attention seems focused on the landscape and the unruly elements of nature rather than the figures.

In 1507, Giorgione took on a new assistant, Tiziano Vecellio, who is better known to us today as Titian (c. 1488–1576). The painting called *Pastoral Concert* (fig. **13–15**) is dated to a few years after this time. Perhaps Giorgione began the painting and Titian

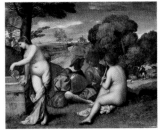

13–15 Titian (formerly attributed to Giorgione). *Pastoral Concert.*
c. 1509–1510. Oil on canvas, 43¹⁄₄" × 54³⁄₄" (109.9 × 132.1 cm).
Musée du Louvre, Paris
PARIS/RMN-RÉUNION DES MUSÉES NATIONAUX, FRANCE, ERICH LESSING/ART RESOURCE, NY

WOMEN PATRONS OF THE ARTS

In the sixteenth century, many wealthy women—both from the aristocracy and from the merchant class—were enthusiastic patrons of the arts. Two English queens, the Tudor half-sisters Mary I and Elizabeth I, glorified their reigns with the aid of court artists, as did most sovereigns of the period. And the Habsburg princesses Margaret of Austria and Mary of Hungary presided over brilliant Humanist courts when they were regents. But perhaps the Renaissance's greatest woman patron of the arts was Isabella d'Esté, Marchesa of Mantua, (1474–1539), who gathered painters, musicians, composers, writers, and literary scholars around her. Married to Francesco II Gonzaga at age 15, she had great beauty, great wealth, and a brilliant mind that made her a successful diplomat and administrator. A true Renaissance woman, her motto was the epitome of rational thinking: "Neither Hope nor Fear." An avid reader and collector of manuscripts and books, she sponsored an edition of Virgil while still in her twenties. She also collected ancient art and objects, as well as works by contemporary Italian artists such as Botticelli, Mantegna, Perugino, Correggio, and Titian. Her grotto, or cave, as she called her study in the Mantuan palace, was a veritable museum for her collections. The walls above the storage and display cabinets were painted in fresco by Mantegna, and the carved-wood ceiling was covered with mottoes and visual references to Isabella's impressive literary interests.

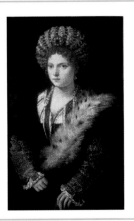

Titian. *Isabella d'Esté.* 1534–1536. Oil on canvas, 40¹⁄₈" × 25³⁄₄" (102 × 64.1 cm). Kunsthistorisches Museum, Vienna

---

OTHER BOXES
Provide contextual information that expands on a theme, idea, or event mentioned in the chapter and offers the student deep background on a variety of topics.

Faculty and Student Resources for Teaching & Learning with *Art: A Brief History*

Prentice Hall is pleased to present an outstanding array of high quality resources for teaching and learning with Stokstad's *Art: A Brief History.* Please contact your local Prentice Hall representative for more details on how to obtain these items, or send us an email at art@prenhall.com.

Digital & Visual Resources

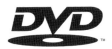 **The Prentice Hall Digital Art Library:** Instructors who adopt Stokstad's *Art: A Brief History* are eligible to receive this unparalleled resource. Available in a two-DVD set or a 10-CD set, The Prentice Hall Digital Art Library contains every image in *Art: A Brief History* in the highest resolution (over 300 dpi) and pixellation possible for optimal projection and easy download. Developed and endorsed by a panel of visual curators and instructors across the country, this resource features over 1,600 illustrations in jpeg and in PowerPoint, an instant download function for easy import into any presentation software, along with a zoom feature, and a compare/contrast function, both of which are unique and were developed exclusively for Prentice Hall.

 OneKey is Prentice Hall's exclusive course management system that delivers all student and instructor resources in one place. Powered by WebCT and Blackboard, OneKey offers an abundance of online study and research tools for students and a variety of teaching and presentation resources for instructors, including an easy-to-use gradebook and access to many of the images from the book.

 Art History Interactive CD-ROM: 800 Images for Study & Presentation is an outstanding study tool for students. Images are viewable by title, by period, or by artist. Students can quiz themselves in flashcard mode or by answering any number of short answer and compare/contrast questions.

Classroom Response System (CRS) In Class Questions: Get instant, class-wide responses to beautifully illustrated chapter-specific questions during a lecture to gauge student comprehension—and keep them engaged. Contact your local Prentice Hall sales representative for details.

 Companion Website: Visit www.prenhall.com/stokstad for a comprehensive online resource featuring a variety of learning and teaching modules, all correlated to the chapters of *Art: A Brief History.*

Fine Art Slides and Videos are also available to qualified adopters. Please contact your local Prentice Hall sales representative to discuss your slide and video needs. To find your representative, use our rep locator at www.prenhall.com.

Prentice Hall Test Generator is a commercial-quality computerized test management program available for both Microsoft Windows and Macintosh environments.

Print Resources

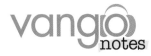 **VangoNotes:** Study on the go with VangoNotes—chapter reviews from your text in downloadable mp3 format. You can study by listening to the following for each chapter of your textbook: Big Ideas: Your "need to know" for each chapter; Practice Test: A check for the Big Ideas—tells you if you need to keep studying; Key Terms: audio "flashcards" to help you review key concepts and terms; and Rapid Review: A quick drill session—use it right before your test. VangoNotes are flexible; download all the material directly to your player, or only the chapters you need.

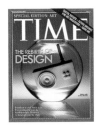 **TIME Special Edition, Art:** Featuring stories such as "The Mighty Medici," "When Henri Met Pablo," and "Redesigning America," Prentice Hall's *TIME Special Edition* contains thirty articles and exhibition reviews on a wide range of subjects, all illustrated in full color. This is the perfect complement for discussion groups, in-class debates, or writing assignments. With *TIME Special Edition,* students also receive a 3-month pass to the TIME archive, a unique reference and research tool.

Understanding the Art Museum by Barbara Beall: This handbook gives students essential museum-going guidance to help them make the most of their experience seeing art outside of the classroom. Case studies are incorporated into the text, and a list of major museums in the United States and key cities across the world is included.

ArtNotes Plus: An invaluable slide and study guide for students, ArtNotes Plus contains all of the images from the book in thumbnail form with caption information to illuminate their "art in the dark" experience. In addition, ArtNotes Plus features study questions and tips for each chapter of the book.

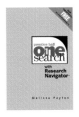 **OneSearch with Research Navigator** helps students with finding the right articles and journals in art history. Students get exclusive access to three research databases: The New York Times Search by Subject Archive, ContentSelect Academic Journal Database, and Link Library.

Instructor's Manual & Test Item File is an invaluable professional resource and reference for new and experienced faculty, containing sample syllabi, hundreds of sample test questions, and guidance on incorporating media technology into your course.

This edition is dedicated to all my students and to my sister,
Karen L. S. Leider, and my niece, Anna J. Leider.

Art: A Brief History is a concise version of *Art History*, which was first published in 1995 by Harry N. Abrams, Inc., and Prentice Hall, Inc. This new edition reflects the changes made in the second revised edition of *Art History*. Everyone who contributed to the original and revised editions of *Art History* deserves to be recognized and thanked for step-parenting *Art: A Brief History*.

Again I worked with my editors at Prentice Hall, Sarah Touborg and Helen Ronan, to create a book that would incorporate effective pedagogical features into a shortened narrative. Helen Ronan, Barbara Taylor-Laino, Assunta Petrone, and Lisa Iarkowski managed the project; Kevin Supples diligently edited the manuscript to the book's lasting benefit. They were ably supported by the skillful editorial assistance of Jacqueline Zea. John McKenna's drawings have brought information and clarity to the discussions of architecture. Designer Beth Tondeau created an intelligent, approachable design of this book; she was supported by the masterful talents of Nancy Wells and Ximena Tamvakopoulos. Much appreciation goes to Brandy Dawson, Director of Marketing, and Andrea Messineo, Assistant Marketing Manager, as well as the entire Humanities and Social Sciences team at Prentice Hall.

Many people reviewed the original edition of *Art History* and their work continues to be reflected in subsequent editions. Margaret Oppenheimer helped me condense *Art History* into the first edition of *Art: A Brief History*. Colleagues wrote chapters for the original book: Stephen Addiss, Chu-tsing Li, Marilyn M. Rhie, and Christopher Roy. For the new (third) edition of *Art: A Brief History*, David Cateforis has helped me update the chapters on modern art, Sally Cornelison has assisted with the Renaissance, and Roger Ward with the Baroque chapters. The late Paul Rehak and John Younger answered my questions on the art of the classical world. And thanks must go to Mary Miller and Helen Evans for their expertise on the Pre-Columbian and Byzantine chapters. Jean Middleton James, a friend from Carleton College days, has read every word in every version of the book.

Others who have tried to keep me from errors of fact and interpretation—who have shared ideas and course syllabi, read chapters or sections of chapters, and offered suggestions and criticism—include: Barbara Abou-elHaj, SUNY Binghamton; Roger Aiken, Creighton University; Molly Aitken; Anthony Alofsin, University of Texas, Austin; Christiane Andersson, Bucknell University; Kathryn Arnold; Julie Aronson, Cincinnati Art Museum; Larry Beck; Evelyn Bell, San Jose State University; Janetta Rebold Benton, Pace University; Janet Berlo, University of Rochester; David Binkley; Sara Blick, Kenyon College; Suzaan Boettger; Judith Bookbinder, University of Massachusetts, Boston; Marta Braun, Ryerson Polytechnic University; Elizabeth Gibson Broun, Smithsonian American Art Museum; Claudia Brown, Arizona State University; Glen R. Brown, Kansas State University; Maria Elena Buszek, Kansas City Art Institute; Robert G. Calkins; April Clagget, Keene State College; William W. Clark, Queens College, CUNY; John Clarke, University of Texas, Austin; Jaqueline Clipsham; Ralph T. Coe; Robert Cohon, The Nelson-Atkins Museum of Art; Bradford Collins, University of South Carolina; Alessandra Comini, Southern Methodist University; Sally Cornelison and Susan Craig, University of Kansas; Charles Cuttler; Patricia Darish; James D'Emilio, University of South Florida; Lois Drewer, Index of Christian Art; Susan Earle, Edmund Eglinski, and Charles Eldredge, University of Kansas; Helen Evans, The Metropolitan Museum of Art; James Farmer, Virginia Commonwealth University; Grace Flam, Salt Lake City Community College; Patrick Frank; Mary D. Garrard, American University; Paula Gerson, Florida State University; Walter S. Gibson; Dorothy Glass; Stephen Goddard, University of Kansas; Randall Griffey, The Nelson-Atkins Museum of Art; Cynthia Hahn, Florida State University; Marsha Haufler, University of Kansas; Sharon Hill, Virginia Commonwealth University; John Hoopes, University of Kansas; Carol Ivory, Washington State University; Marni Kessler, University of Kansas; Alison Kettering, Carleton College; Wendy Kindred, University of Maine at Fort Kent; Alan T. Kohl, Minneapolis College of Art; Ruth Kolarik, Colorado College; Carol H. Krinski, New York University; Aileen Laing, Sweet Briar College; Janet Le Blanc, Clemson University; Charles Little, The Metropolitan Museum of Art; Laureen Reu Liu, McHenry Country College; Loretta Lorance; Brian Madigan, Wayne State University; Janice Mann, Bucknell University; Judith Mann, St. Louis Art Museum; Richard Mann, San Francisco State University; James Martin, The Nelson-Atkins Museum of Art; Elizabeth Parker McLachlan; Amy McNair, University of Kansas; Gustav Medicus, Kent State University; Tamara Mikailova, St. Petersburg, Russia, and Macalester College; Vernon Minor, University of Colorado, Boulder; Anta Montet-White; Anne E. Morganstern, Ohio State University; Robert Mowry, Harvard University; Winslow Myers, Bancroft School; Lawrence Nees, University of Delaware; Amy Ogata, Cleveland Institute of Art; Judith Oliver, Colgate University; Edward Olszewski, Case Western Reserve University; Sarah Orel, Truman State University; Sara Jane Pearman; John G. Pedley, University of Michigan; Michael Plante, H. Sophie Newcomb Memorial College; John Pultz, University of Kansas; Eloise Quiñones-Keber, Baruch College and the Graduate Center, CUNY; Virginia Raguin, College of the Holy Cross; Nancy H. Ramage, Ithaca College; Ann M. Roberts, University of Iowa; Lisa Robertson, The Cleveland Museum of Art; Barry Rubin, Talmudic College of Florida; Charles Sack; Jan Schall, The Nelson-Atkins Museum of Art; Diane Scillia, Kent State University; Tom Shaw, Kean College; Pamela Sheingorn, Baruch College, CUNY; Rachel Smith, Kansas City Art Institute; Lauren Soth; Anne R. Stanton, University of Missouri, Columbia; Michael Stoughton; Thomas Sullivan, OSB, Benedictine College (Conception Abbey); Pamela Trimpe, University of Iowa; Richard Turnbull, Fashion Institute of Technology; Elizabeth Valdez del Alamo, Montclair State College; Lisa Vergara; Monica Visoná, Metropolitan State College of Denver; Roger Ward, Norton Museum of Art; Mark Weil, Washington University, St. Louis; David Wilkins; and Marcilene Wittmer, University of Miami.

Work began on the second edition while I was a resident at the American Academy in Rome, an ideal place for study and writing set in one of the most visually stimulating places in the Western world. Special thanks are due the director and the many scholars who patiently answered my questions. The third edition has been written in Lawrence, Kansas, where the directors and staff of the Kenneth Spencer Research Library and the Helen Foresman Spencer Museum of Art provided research and study facilities, computer back-up, and companionship. I thank them all. Many friends, as well as colleagues, have endured my enthusiasm and despair, but I extend my special thanks to Katherine Giele, Nancy and David Dinneen, Anta Montet-White, Charlie and Jane Eldredge, and Katherine Stannard. Of course, my very special thanks go to my sister, Karen Leider, and my niece, Anna Leider.

If the arts are the ultimate expression of human faith and integrity as well as creativity, then writing and producing books about art—and in so doing to introduce new viewers to the creativity, courage, and vision that artists express—remains a worthy undertaking.

Marilyn Stokstad
Lawrence, Kansas
Winter 2005

Use Notes

The various features of this book reinforce each other, helping the reader to become comfortable with terminology and concepts that are specific to art history.

Starter Kit and Introduction The Starter Kit is a highly concise primer of basic concepts and tools. The outer margins of the Starter Kit pages are tinted to make them easy to find. The Introduction is an invitation to the many pleasures of art history.

Captions There are two kinds of captions in this book: short and long. Short captions identify information specific to the work of art or architecture illustrated:

> artist (when known)
> title or descriptive name of work
> date
> original location (if moved to a museum or other site)
> material or materials a work is made of
> size (height before width) in feet and inches, with meters
>   and centimeters in parentheses
> present location

The order of these elements varies, depending on the type of work illustrated. Dimensions are not given for architecture, for most wall paintings, or for most architectural sculpture. Some captions have one or more lines of small print below the identification section of the caption that gives museum or collection information. This is rarely required reading.

Long captions contain information that complements the narrative of the main text.

Definitions of Terms You will encounter the basic terms of art history in three places:

IN THE TEXT, where words appearing in **boldface** type are defined, or glossed, at their first use. Some terms are boldfaced and explained more than once, especially those that experience shows are hard to remember.

IN BOXED FEATURES on technique and other subjects, where labeled drawings and diagrams visually reinforce the use of terms.

IN THE GLOSSARY at the end of the volume, which contains all the words in **boldface** type in the text and boxes. The Glossary begins on page 601, and the outer margins are tinted to make it easy to find.

Maps and Timelines At the beginning of each chapter you will find a map with all the places mentioned in the chapter. At the end if each chapter, a timeline runs from the earliest through the latest years covered in that chapter.

Boxes Special material that complements, enhances, explains, or extends the text is set off in three types of tinted boxes. Elements of Architecture boxes clarify specifically architectural features, such as "Space-Spanning Construction Devices" in the Starter Kit

(page xxxi). Technique boxes (see "Lost-Wax Casting," page xxx) amplify the methodology by which a type of artwork is created. Other boxes treat special-interest material related to the text.

Bibliography The bibliography at the end of this book beginning on page 607 contains books in English, organized by general works and by chapter, that are basic to the study of art history today, as well as works cited in the text.

Dates, Abbreviations, and Other Conventions This book uses the designations BCE and CE, abbreviations for "before the Common Era" and "Common Era," instead of BC ("before Christ") and AD ("Anno Domini," "the year of our Lord"). The first century BCE is the period from 99 BCE to 1 BCE; the first century CE is from the year 1 CE to 99 CE. Similarly, the second century BCE is the period from 199 BCE to 100 BCE; the second century CE extends from 100 CE to 199 CE.

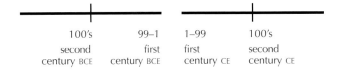

100's	99–1	1–99	100's
second century BCE	first century BCE	first century CE	second century CE

Circa ("about" or "approximately") is used with dates, spelled out in the text and abbreviated to "c." in the captions, when an exact date is not yet verified.

An illustration is called a "figure," or "fig." Thus, figure 6–7 is the seventh numbered illustration in Chapter 6. Figures 1 through 30 are in the Introduction. There are two types of figures: photographs of artworks or of models, and line drawings. Drawings are used when a work cannot be photographed or when a diagram or simple drawing is the clearest way to illustrate an object or a place.

When introducing artists, we use the words *active* and *documented* with dates, in addition to "b." (for "born") and "d." (for "died"). "Active" means that an artist worked during the years given. "Documented" means that documents link the person to that date.

Accents are used for words in French, German, Italian, and Spanish only.

With few exceptions, names of museums and other cultural bodies in Western European countries are given in the form used in that country.

Titles of Works of Art Most paintings and works of sculpture created in Europe and North America in the past 500 years have been given formal titles, either by the artist or by critics and art historians. Such formal titles are printed in italics. In other traditions and cultures, a single title is not important or even recognized. In this book we use formal descriptive titles of artworks where titles are not established. If a work is best known by its non-English title, such as Manet's *Le Déjeuner sur l'Herbe (The Luncheon on the Grass)*, the original language precedes the translation.

Starter Kit

Art history focuses on the visual arts—painting, drawing, sculpture, graphic arts, photography, decorative arts, and architecture. This Starter Kit contains basic information and addresses concepts that underlie and support the study of art history. It provides a quick reference guide to the vocabulary used to classify and describe art objects. Understanding these terms is indispensable since you will encounter them again and again in reading, talking, and writing about art, and you when experiencing works of art directly.

Let us begin with the basic properties of art. A work of art is a material object having both form and content. It is also described and categorized according to its STYLE and MEDIUM.

FORM

Referring to purely visual aspects of art and architecture, the term *form* encompasses qualities of LINE, SHAPE, COLOR, TEXTURE, SPACE, MASS and VOLUME, and COMPOSITION. These qualities all are known as FORMAL ELEMENTS. When art historians use the term *formal*, they mean "relating to form."

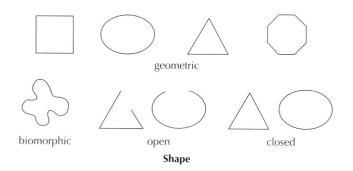

geometric

biomorphic   open   closed

Shape

Line and **shape** are attributes of form. Line is a form—usually drawn or painted—the length of which is so much greater than the width that we perceive it as having only length. Line can be actual, as when the line is visible, or it can be implied, as when the movement of the viewer's eyes over the surface of a work follows a path determined by the artist. Shape, on the other hand, is the two-dimensional, or flat, area defined by the borders of an enclosing *outline*, or *contour*. Shape can be *geometric, biomorphic* (suggesting living things; sometimes called *organic*), *closed,* or *open.* The *outline,* or *contour,* of a three-dimensional object can also be perceived as line.

Color has several attributes. These include HUE, VALUE, and SATURATION.

HUE is what we think of when we hear the word *color*, and the terms are interchangeable. We perceive hues as the result of differing wavelengths of electromagnetic energy. The visible spectrum, which can be seen in a rainbow, runs from red through violet. When the ends of the spectrum are connected

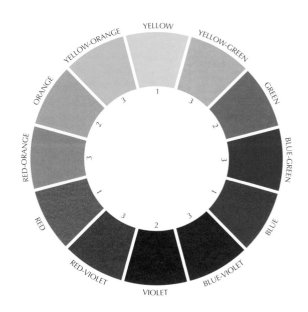

through the hue red-violet, the result may be diagrammed as a color wheel. The primary hues (numbered 1) are red, yellow, and blue. They are known as primaries because all other colors are made of a combination of these hues. Orange, green, and violet result from the mixture of two primaries and are known as secondary hues (numbered 2). Intermediate hues, or tertiaries (numbered 3), result from the mixture of a primary and a secondary. Complementary colors are the two colors directly opposite one another on the color wheel, such as red and green. Red, orange, and yellow are regarded as warm colors and appear to advance toward us. Blue, green, and violet, which seem to recede, are called cool colors. Black and white are not considered colors but neutrals; in terms of light, black is understood as the absence of color and white as the mixture of all colors.

VALUE is the relative degree of lightness or darkness of a given color and is created by the amount of light reflected from an object's surface. A dark green has a deeper value than a light green, for example. In black-and-white reproductions of colored objects, you see only value, and some artworks—for example, a drawing made with black ink—possesses only value, not hue or saturation.

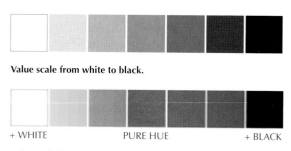

Value scale from white to black.

+ WHITE   PURE HUE   + BLACK

Value variation in red.

SATURATION, also sometimes referred to as INTENSITY, is a color's quality of brightness or dullness. A color described as highly saturated looks vivid and pure; a hue of low saturation may or look a little muddy or dark.

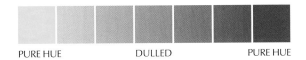

PURE HUE   DULLED   PURE HUE

Texture, another attribute of form, is the tactile (or touch-perceived) quality of a surface. It is described by words such as *smooth, polished, rough, grainy,* or *oily.* Texture takes two forms: the texture of the actual surface of the work of art and the implied (illusionistically depicted) surface of the object that the work represents.

Space is what contains objects. It may be actual and three-dimensional, as it is with sculpture and architecture, or it may be represented illusionistically in two dimensions, as when artists represent recession into the distance on a wall or canvas.

Mass and **volume** are properties of three-dimensional things. Mass is matter—whether sculpture or architecture—that takes up space. Volume is enclosed or defined space, and may be either solid or hollow. Like space, mass and volume may be illusionistically represented in two dimensions.

Composition is the organization, or arrangement, of form in a work of art. Shapes and colors may be repeated or varied, balanced symmetrically or asymmetrically; they may be static or dynamic. The possibilities are nearly endless and depend on the time and place where the work was created as well as the personal sensibility of the artist. PICTORIAL DEPTH (spatial recession) is a specialized aspect of composition in which the three-dimensional world is represented in two dimensions on a flat surface, or PICTURE PLANE. The area "behind" the picture plane is called the PICTURE SPACE and conventionally contains three "zones": FOREGROUND, MIDDLE GROUND, and BACKGROUND.

Various techniques for conveying a sense of pictorial depth have been devised by artists in different cultures and at different times. A number of them are diagrammed below. In Western art, the use of various systems of PERSPECTIVE has created highly convincing illusions of recession into space. In other cultures, perspective is not the most favored way to treat objects in space.

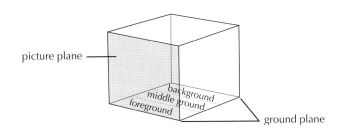

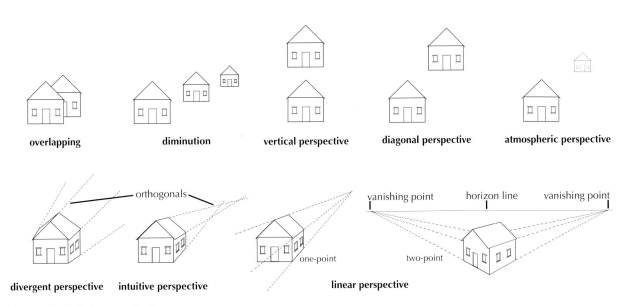

overlapping   diminution   vertical perspective   diagonal perspective   atmospheric perspective

divergent perspective   intuitive perspective   linear perspective

Pictorial devices for depicting recession in space

The top row shows several comparatively simple devices, including OVERLAPPING, in which partially covered elements are meant to be seen as located behind those covering them, and DIMINUTION, in which smaller elements are to be perceived as being farther away than larger ones. In VERTICAL PERSPECTIVE (space in registers), elements are stacked vertically, with the higher elements intended to be perceived as deeper in space. Another way of suggesting depth is through ATMOSPHERIC PERSPECTIVE, which depicts objects in the far distance, often in bluish gray hues, with less clarity than nearer objects and treats sky as paler near the horizon than higher up. In the lower row, DIVERGENT or REVERSE PERSPECTIVE, in which forms widen slightly and lines diverge as they recede in space. INTUITIVE PERSPECTIVE, used in some medieval European art, takes the opposite approach: Forms become narrower and converge the farther they are from the viewer, approximating the optical experience of spatial recession. LINEAR PERSPECTIVE, also called SCIENTIFIC, MATHEMATICAL, ONE-POINT, and RENAISSANCE PERSPECTIVE, is an elaboration and standardization of intuitive perspective and was developed in fifteenth-century Italy. It uses mathematical formulas to construct illusionistic images in which all elements are shaped by imaginary lines called ORTHOGONALS that converge in one or more VANISHING POINTS on a HORIZON LINE. Linear perspective is the system that most people living in Western cultures think of as perspective. Because it is the visual code they are accustomed to reading, they accept as "truth" the distortions it imposes. One of these distortions is the assumption of a single viewpoint. When perspective is applied to a single object it is known as foreshortening.

CONTENT

Content includes SUBJECT MATTER, which is what a work of art represents. Not all works of art have subject matter; many buildings, paintings, sculptures, and other art objects include no recognizable imagery but feature only lines, colors, masses, volumes, and other formal elements. However, all works of art—even those without recognizable subject matter—have content, or meaning, insofar as they seek to convey feelings, communicate ideas, or affirm the beliefs and values of their makers and, often, the people who view or use them.

Content may comprise the social, political, religious, and economic CONTEXTS in which a work was created, the INTENTION of the artist, the RECEPTION of the work by the beholder (the audience), and ultimately the meanings of the work to both artist and audience. Art historians applying different methods of INTERPRETATION often arrive at different conclusions regarding the content of a work of art.

The study of subject matter is ICONOGRAPHY (literally, "the writing of images"). The iconographer asks, What is the meaning of this image? Iconography includes the study of SYMBOLS and SYMBOLISM—the process of representing one thing by another through association, resemblance, or convention.

STYLE

Expressed very broadly, *style* is the combination of form and composition that makes a work distinctive. STYLISTIC ANALYSIS is one of art history's most developed practices, because it is how art historians recognize the work of an individual artist or the characteristic manner of several artists working in a particular time or place. Some of the most commonly used terms to discuss ARTISTIC STYLES include PERIOD STYLE, REGIONAL STYLE, REPRESENTATIONAL STYLE, ABSTRACT STYLE, LINEAR STYLE, and PAINTERLY STYLE.

Period style refers to the common traits detectable in works of art and architecture from a particular historical era. For instance, Roman portrait sculpture created at the height of the Empire is different from sculpture made during the late imperial period, but it is recognizably Roman. It is good practice not to use the words style and period interchangeably. Style is the sum of many influences and characteristics, including the period of its creation. An example of proper usage is "an American house from the Colonial period built in the Georgian style."

Regional style refers to stylistic traits that persist in a geographic region. An art historian whose specialty is medieval art can recognize French style through many successive medieval periods and can distinguish individual objects created in medieval France from other medieval objects that were created in, for example, the Low Countries.

Representational styles are those that create recognizable subject matter. REALISM, NATURALISM, and ILLUSIONISM are representational styles.

> REALISM and NATURALISM are terms often used interchangeably, and both describe the artist's attempt to describe the observable world. REALISM is the attempt to depict objects accurately and objectively. NATURALISM is closely linked to realism but often implies a grim or sordid subject matter.

> IDEAL STYLES strive to create images of physical perfection according to the prevailing values of a culture. The artist may work in a representational style or may try to capture an underlying or expressive reality. Both *The Medici Venus* and Utamaro's *Woman at the Height of Her Beauty* (see Introduction, figs. 6 and 8) can be considered IDEALIZED.

> ILLUSIONISM refers to a highly detailed style that seeks to create a convincing illusion of reality. *Flower Piece with Curtain* is a good example of this trick-the-eye form of realism (see Introduction, fig. 2).

> IDEALIZATION strives to realize an image of physical perfection according to the prevailing values of a culture. *The Medici Venus* is idealized, as is Utamaro's *Woman at the Height of Her Beauty* (see Introduction, figs. 6 and 8).

Abstract styles depart from literal realism to capture the essence of a form. An abstract artist may work from nature or from a memory image of nature's forms and colors, which are simplified, stylized, distorted, or otherwise transformed to achieve a desired expressive effect. Georgia O'Keeffe's *Red Canna* and the Indian bronze statue of *Punitavati* are both abstract representations of nature (see Introduction, figs. 4 and 9). NONREPRESENTATIONAL ART and EXPRESSIONISM are particular kinds of abstract styles.

> NONREPRESENTATIONAL (OR NONOBJECTIVE) ART is a form that does not produce recognizable imagery. *Cubi XIX* is nonrepresentational (see Introduction, fig. 5).

> EXPRESSIONISM refers to styles in which the artist uses exaggeration of form to appeal to the beholder's subjective response or to project the artist's own subjective feelings. Munch's *The Scream* is expressionistic (see fig 18–30).

Linear describe both style and techniques. In the linear style the artist uses line as the primary means of definition, and MODELING—the creation of an illusion of three-dimensional substance, through shading. Is so subtle that brushstrokes nearly disappear. Such a technique is also called "sculptural." Raphael's *The Small Cowper Madonna* is linear and sculptural (fig. 13–4)

Painterly describes a style of painting in which vigorous, evident brushstrokes dominate and shadows and highlights are brushed in freely. Sculpture in which complex surfaces emphasize moving light and shade is called "painterly." Claudel's *The Waltz* is painterly sculpture (see fig. 18–34).

MEDIUM

What is meant by *medium* or *mediums* (the plural we use in this book to distinguish the word from print and electronic news media) refers to the material or materials from which a work of art is made.

Technique is the process used to make the work. Today, literally anything can be used to make a work of art, including not only traditional materials like paint, ink, and stone, but also rubbish, food, and the earth itself. Various techniques are explained throughout this book in Technique boxes. When several mediums are used in a single work of art, we employ the term *mixed mediums*. Two-dimensional mediums include painting, drawing, prints, and photography. Three-dimensional mediums are sculpture, architecture, and many so-called decorative arts.

Painting includes wall painting and fresco, illumination (the decoration of books with paintings), panel painting (painting on wood panels) and painting on canvas, miniature painting (small-scale painting), and handscroll and hanging scroll painting. Paint is pigment mixed with a liquid vehicle, or binder.

Graphic arts are those that involve the application of lines and strokes to a two-dimensional surface or support, most often paper. Drawing is a graphic art, as are the various forms of printmaking. Drawings may be sketches (quick visual notes made in preparation for larger drawings or paintings); studies (more carefully drawn analyses of details or entire compositions); cartoons (full-scale drawings made in preparation for work in another medium, such as fresco); or complete artworks in themselves. Drawings are made with such materials as ink, charcoal, crayon, and pencil. Prints, unlike drawings, are reproducible. The various forms of printmaking include woodcut, the intaglio processes (engraving, etching, drypoint), and lithography.

Photography (literally "light writing") is a medium that involves the rendering of optical images on light-sensitive surfaces. Photographic images are typically recorded by a camera.

Sculpture is three-dimensional art that is CARVED, MODELED, CAST, or ASSEMBLED. Carved sculpture is subtractive in the sense that the image is created by taking away material. Wood, stone, and ivory are common materials used to create carved sculptures. Modeled sculpture is considered additive, meaning that the object is built up from a material, such as clay, that is soft enough to be molded and shaped. Metal sculpture is usually cast (see "Lost-Wax Casting," opposite) or is assembled by welding or a similar means of permanent joining.

Sculpture is either freestanding (that is, not attached) or in relief. Relief sculpture projects from the background surface of which it is a part. High relief sculpture projects far from its background; low relief sculpture is only slightly raised; and sunken relief, found mainly in Egyptian art, is carved into the surface, with the highest part of the relief being the flat surface.

Ephemeral arts include processions and festival decorations and costumes, performance art, earthworks, cinema, video art, and some forms of digital and computer art. All have a central temporal aspect in that the artwork is viewable for a finite period of time and then disappears forever, is in a constant state of change, or must be replayed to be experienced again.

Architecture is three-dimensional, highly spatial, functional, and closely bound with developments in technology and materials. An example of the relationship among technology, materials, and function can be seen in "Space-Spanning Construction Devices" (page xxxi). Several types of two-dimensional schematic drawings are commonly used to enable the visualization of a building. These architectural graphic devices include plans, elevations, sections, and cutaways.

PLANS depict a structure's masses and voids, presenting a view from above—as if the building had been sliced horizontally at about waist height.

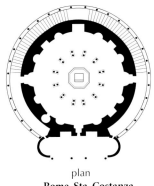

plan
Rome, Sta. Costanza

ELEVATIONS show exterior sides of a building as if seen from a moderate distance without any perspective distortion.

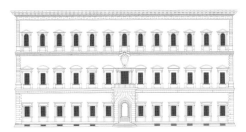

elevation
Rome, Farnese Palace

SECTIONS reveal a building as if it had been cut vertically by an imaginary slicer from top to bottom.

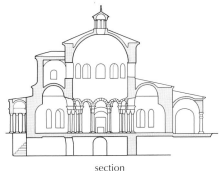

section
Rome, Sta. Costanza

CUTAWAYS show both inside and outside elements from an oblique angle.

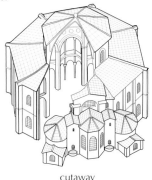

cutaway
Ravenna, San Vitale

TECHNIQUE

Lost-Wax Casting

The lost-wax process consists of a core on which the sculptor models the image in wax. A heat-resistant mold is formed over the wax. The wax is melted and replaced with metal, usually bronze or brass. The mold is broken away and the piece finished and polished by hand.

The usual metal for this casting process was bronze, an alloy of copper and tin, although sometimes brass, an alloy of copper and zinc, was used. The progression of drawings here shows the steps used by the Benin sculptors of Africa. A heat-resistant "core" of clay approximating the shape of the sculpture-to-be (and eventually becoming the hollow inside the sculpture) was covered by a layer of wax having the thickness of the final sculpture. The sculptor carved or modeled the details in the wax. Rods and a pouring cup made of wax were attached to the model. A thin layer of fine, damp sand was pressed very firmly into the surface of the wax model, and then model, rods, and cup were encased in thick layers of clay. When the clay was completely dry, the mold was heated to melt out the wax. The mold was then turned upside down to receive the molten metal, which is heated to the point of liquification. The cast was placed in the ground. When the metal was completely cool, the outside clay cast and the inside core were broken up and removed, leaving the cast brass sculpture. Details were polished to finish the piece of sculpture, which could not be duplicated because the mold had been destroyed in the process.

In lost-wax casting the mold had to be broken and only one sculpture could be made. In the eighteenth century a second process came into use—the piece mold. As its name implies, the piece mold could be removed without breaking, allowing sculptors to make several copies (an edition) of their work.

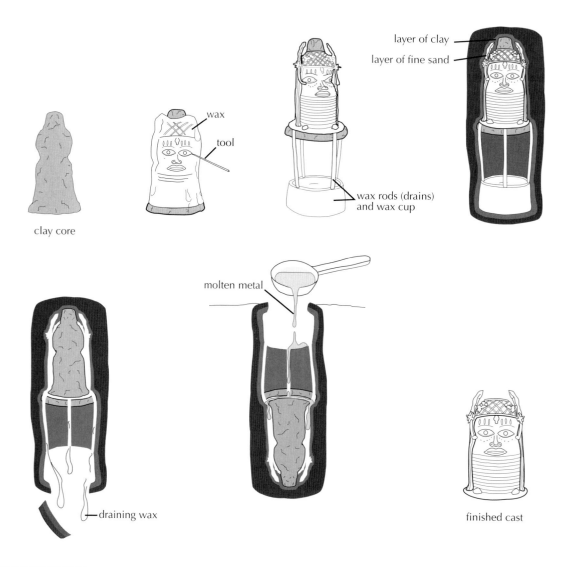

clay core

wax

tool

layer of clay

layer of fine sand

wax rods (drains) and wax cup

molten metal

draining wax

finished cast

ELEMENTS OF Architecture
Space-Spanning Construction Devices

Gravity pulls on everything, presenting great challenges to architects and sculptors. Spanning elements must transfer weight to the ground. The simplest space-spanning device is POST-AND-LINTEL construction, in which uprights are spanned by a horizontal element. However, if not flexible, a horizontal element over a wide span may break under the pressure of its own weight and the weight it carries.

CORBELING, the building up of overlapping stones, is another simple method for transferring weight to the ground. ARCHES, round or pointed, span space. VAULTS, which are essentially extended arches, move weight out from the center of the covered space and down through the corners. The CANTILEVER is a variant of post-and-lintel construction. SUSPENSION works to counter the effect of gravity by lifting the spanning element upward. TRUSSES of wood or metal are relatively lightweight spanners but cannot bear heavy loads. Large-scale modern construction is chiefly steel frame and relies on steel's properties of strength and flexibility to bear great loads. When CONCRETE is REINFORCED with steel or iron rods, the inherent brittleness of cement and stone is overcome because of metal's flexible qualities. The concrete can then span much more space and bear heavier loads. The BALLOON FRAME, an American innovation, is based on POST-AND-LINTEL principles and exploits the lightweight, flexible properties of wood.

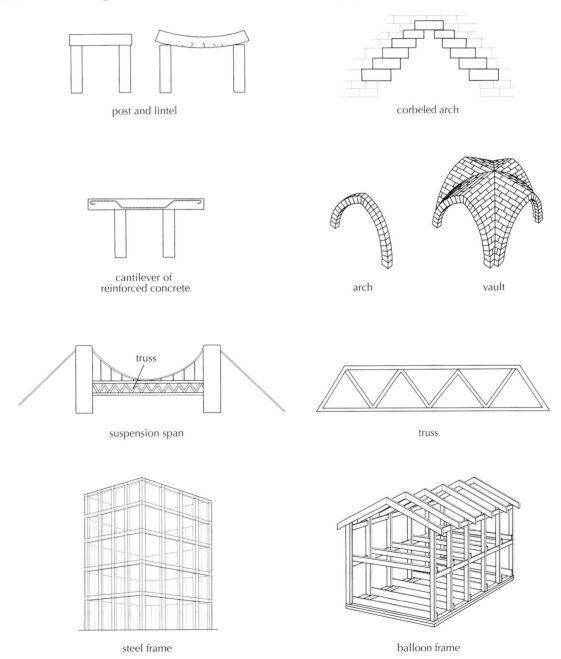

post and lintel

corbeled arch

cantilever of
reinforced concrete

arch

vault

suspension span

truss

steel frame

balloon frame

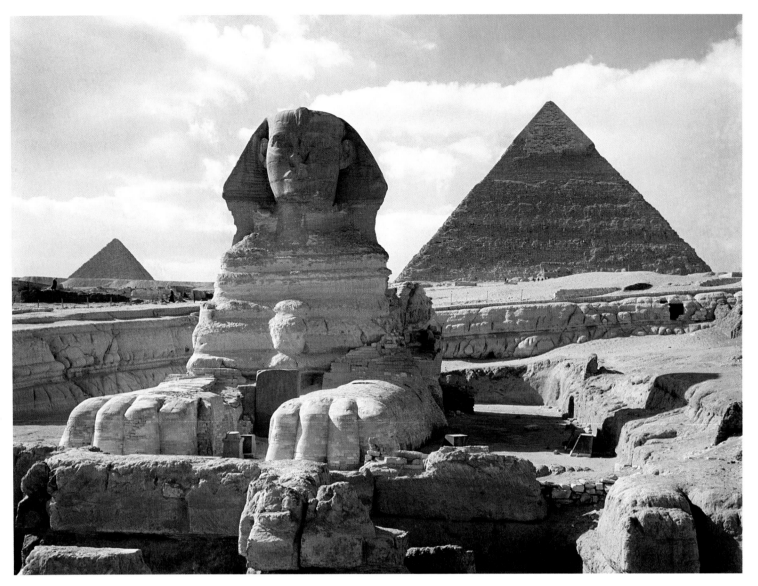

1 The Great Sphinx, Giza, Egypt. Dynasty 4, c. 2613–2494 BCE. Sandstone, height approx. 65′ (19.8 m)

Introduction

Crouching in front of the pyramids of Egypt and carved from the living rock of the Giza plateau, the Great Sphinx is one of the world's best-known monuments (fig. 1). By placing the head of the ancient Egyptian king Khafra on the body of a huge lion, the sculptors joined human intelligence and animal strength in a single image to evoke the superhuman power of the ruler. For some 4,600 years, the Sphinx has defied encroaching desert sands and other assaults of nature; today it also must withstand the human-made sprawl of greater Cairo and the impact of air pollution. The Sphinx, in its majesty, symbolizes mysterious wisdom and dreams of permanence, of immortality. But is such a monument a work of art? Does it matter that the people who carved the Sphinx—unlike today's independent, individualistic artists—followed time-honored, formulaic conventions and the precise instructions of their priests? No matter how viewers of the time may have labeled it, today most people would answer, "Certainly, it is art." Human imagination conceived this amazing creature, and human skill gave material form to the concept of a man-lion. Combining imagination and skill, the creators have produced a work of art. But what is art?

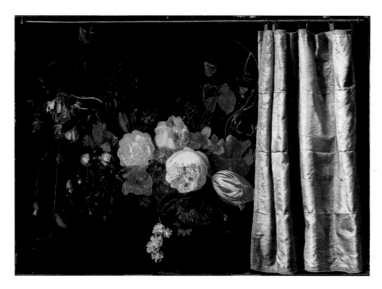

2 Adriaen van der Spelt and Frans van Mieris. *Flower Piece with Curtain.* 1658. Oil on panel, 18¼" × 25¼" (46.5 × 64 cm). The Art Institute of Chicago

What Is Art?

At one time the answer to the question "What is art?" would have been easier than it is today. The severe geometric forms of the Great Sphinx and of the pyramids behind it on the Giza plateau are unquestionably "art." They demonstrate a combination of imagination, skill, training, and observation on the part of their creators, and above all, they appeal to our innate aesthetic sense. Once one might have said, "They please the eye."

Today the definition of art also depends on the intention of both the creator and those who commissioned the work and also on the anticipated role of the creation. It relies, too, on the response of the viewers—both today and at the historical time when the work was made. The role of art history is to answer complex questions—Who are these artists and patrons? What is this thing they have they created? When and how was the work done? Only after we have found answers to practical questions like these can we achieve an understanding and appreciation of the artwork and, answering our earlier question, we can say, "Yes, this is a work of art."

The Relationship Between Nature and Art

Like many people today, the ancient Greeks enjoyed the work of especially skillful artists working in increasingly realistic styles. Their admiration for accurate depiction is illustrated in a famous story about a competition between rival Greek painters named Zeuxis and Parrhasios in the late fifth century BCE. Zeuxis painted a picture of grapes so accurately that birds flew down to peck at them. Then Parrhasios took his turn, and when Zeuxis asked his rival to remove the curtain hanging over the picture, Parrhasios gleefully pointed out that the curtain was his painting. Zeuxis agreed that Parrhasios had won the competition since he, Zeuxis, had fooled only birds, but Parrhasios had tricked an intelligent fellow artist.

Styles of Representation

In the seventeenth century, painter Adriaen van der Spelt (1630–73) and his artist friend Frans van Mieris (1635–1681) paid homage to the story of Parrhasios's curtain with *Flower Piece with Curtain*, their painting of blue satin drapery drawn aside to show a garland of flowers (fig. **2**). More than a tour de force of eye-fooling **naturalism,** the work is an intellectual delight. The artists not only re-created Parrhasios's curtain illusion but also included a reference to another Greek story that was popular in the fourth century BCE, the tale of Pausias, who depicted in a painting the exquisite

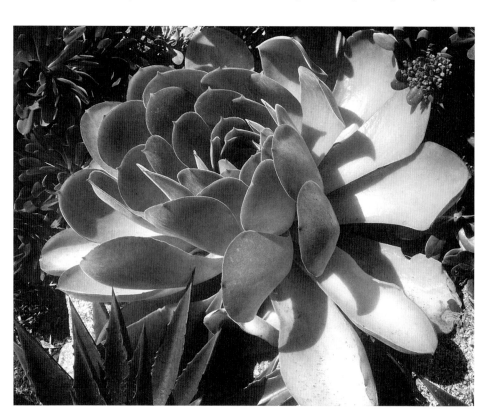

3 Edward Weston. *Succulent.* 1930. Gelatin silver print, 7½" × 9½" (19.1 × 24 cm). Collection Center for Creative Photography, The University of Arizona, Tucson

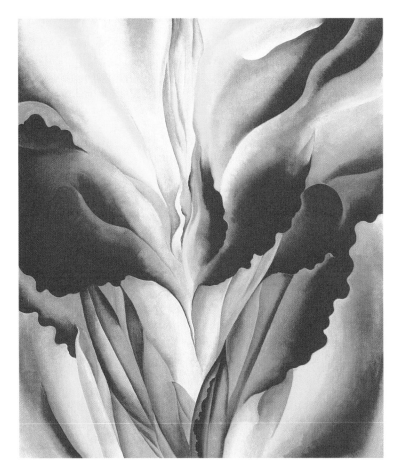

4 Georgia O'Keeffe. *Red Canna.* 1924. Oil on canvas mounted on Masonite, 36" × 29⁷⁄₈" (91.44 × 75.88 cm). Collection of the University of Arizona Museum of Art, Tucson

floral garlands made by a young woman, Glykera. This second story raises the troubling and possibly unanswerable question of who was the true artist—the painter who copied nature in his art or the garland-maker who made works of art out of nature. The seventeenth-century people who bought such popular **still-life** paintings knew those stories and appreciated the artists' classical references as well as their skill in drawing and their ability to manipulate colors on canvas.

Although even today many people think that the manner of representation that we call **naturalism,** or **realism,** represents the highest accomplishment in art, not everyone agrees. The first artist to argue persuasively that observation alone produced "mere likeness" was the Italian master Leonardo da Vinci (1452–1519), who said that the painter who copied the external forms of nature was acting only as a mirror. He believed that the true artist should engage in intellectual activity of a higher order and attempt to capture the inner life—the energy and power—of a subject.

Like van der Spelt and van Mieris, Edward Weston (1886–1958) and Georgia O'Keeffe (1887–1986) studied living plants. In his photograph *Succulent*, Weston used straightforward camera work, without manipulating the film in the darkroom in order to accurately portray his subject (fig. **3**). He argued that although the camera sees more than the human eye, the quality of the image depends not on the camera, but on the choices made by the photographer-artist. When Georgia O'Keeffe painted *Red Canna*, she, too, sought to capture the plant's essence, not its

appearance (fig. **4**) By painting the canna lily's organic energy rather than the way it actually looked, she created a new abstract beauty, conveying in paint the pure vigor of the flower's life force. This **abstraction**—in which the artist appears to transform a visible or recognizable subject from nature in a way that suggests the original but purposefully does not record the subject in an entirely realistic or naturalistic way—is another manner of representation.

Furthest of all from naturalism are the pure geometric creations of polished stainless steel made by David Smith (1906–1965). His *Cubi* works, such as the sculpture in figure **5**, are usually called **nonrepresentational** art—art that does not depict a recognizable subject. With works such as *Cubi XIX*, it is important to distinguish between subject matter and content. Abstract art like O'Keeffe's has both subject matter and content, or meaning. Nonrepresentational art does not have subject matter but it does have meaning, which is a product of the interaction between the artist's intention and the viewer's interpretation. Some viewers may see the *Cubi* works as robotic plants sprung from the core of an unyielding earth, a reflection of today's mechanistic society that challenges the natural forms of trees and hills.

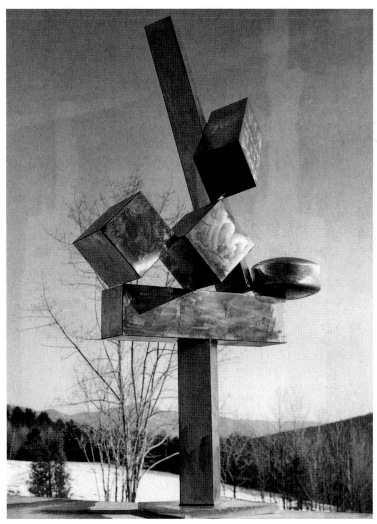

5 David Smith. *Cubi XIX.* 1964. Stainless steel, 9'5³⁄₈" × 1'9³⁄₄" × 1'8" (2.88 × 0.55 × 0.51 m). Tate Gallery, London

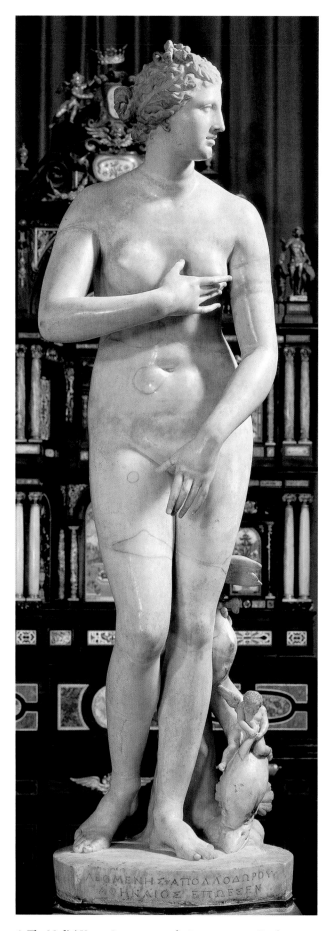

Because meaning can change over time, one goal of art history—a goal that this book exemplifies—is to identify the cultural factors that produce a work, to determine what it probably meant for the artist and the original audience, and to acknowledge that no interpretation is definitive. This approach is known as **contextualism**.

The Human Body as Idea and Ideal

Ever since people first made what we call art, they have been fascinated with their own image and have used the human body to express ideas and ideals. And popular culture in the twenty-first century continues to be obsessed with beautiful people—with Miss Universe pageants and lists of the Ten Best-Dressed Women and the Fifty Sexiest Men, just to name a few examples from "popular culture." Today the *Medici Venus*, with her plump arms and legs and sturdy body, would surely be expected to slim down, yet for generations such a figure represented the peak of female beauty (fig. **6**).

This image of the goddess of love inspired artists and those who commissioned their work from the fifteenth through the nineteenth century. Clearly the artist had the skill to represent a

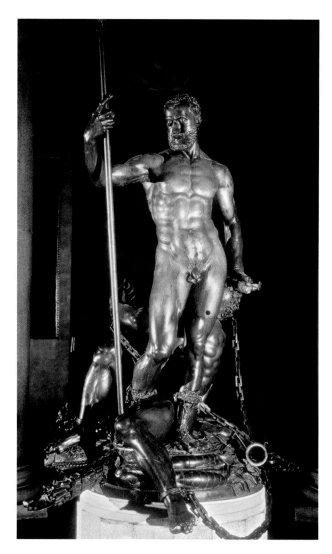

6 *The Medici Venus.* Roman copy of a 1st-century BCE Greek statue. Marble, height 5′ (1.53 m) without base. Villa Medici, Florence, Italy

7 Leone Leoni, *Charles V Triumphing over Fury, without Armor.* c. 1549–1555. Bronze, height to top of head 5′8″ (1.74 m). Museo Nacional del Prado, Madrid

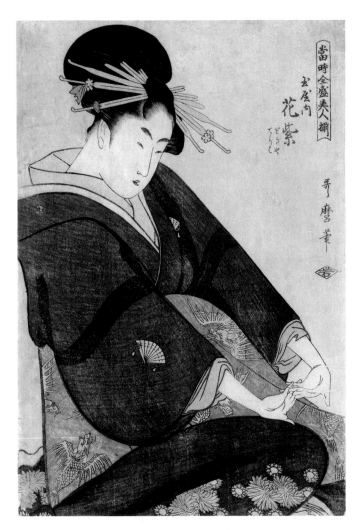

8 Kitagawa Utamaro. *Woman at the Height of Her Beauty.* Mid-1790s. Color woodblock print, 15 $\frac{1}{8}$″ × 10″ (38.5 × 25.5 cm). Spencer Museum of Art, The University of Kansas, Lawrence
WILLIAM BRIDGES THAYER MEMORIAL, (1928.7879)

woman as she actually appeared but instead chose to generalize her form and adhere to the classical **canon** (rule) of proportions. In so doing, the sculptor created a universal image, an ideal rather than a specific woman.

The *Medici Venus* represents a goddess, but artists also represented living people as idealized figures, creating symbolic portraits rather than accurate likenesses. The sculptor Leone Leoni (1509–1590), commissioned to create a monumental bronze statue of Charles V (ruled 1519–1556), expressed the power of this ruler of the Holy Roman Empire just as vividly as did the sculptors of the Egyptian king Khafra, the subject of the Great Sphinx (see fig. 1). Whereas in the sphinx, Khafra took on the body of a vigilant crouching lion, in *Charles V Triumphing over Fury* the emperor has been endowed with the muscular torso and proportions of the classical ideal male athlete (fig. 7). Charles does not inhabit a fragile human body; rather, in his muscular nakedness, he embodies the idea of triumphant authoritarian rule. (Not everyone approved. In fact, a full suit of armor was made for the statue, and today museum officials usually exhibit the sculpture clad in armor rather than nude.)

Another example of ideal beauty is the abstract vision of woman depicted in a woodblock print by Japanese artist Kitagawa Utamaro (1753–1806). In its stylization, *Woman at the Height of*

Her Beauty (fig. 8) reflects a complex society regulated by convention and ritual. Simplified shapes depict the woman's garments and suggest the underlying human forms. The treatment of the rich textiles turn the body into an abstract pattern, and pins turn the hair into another elaborate shape. Utamaro rendered the decorative silks and carved pins meticulously, but he depicted the woman's face and hands with a few sweeping lines. The elaboration of surface detail combined with an effort to capture the essence of form is characteristic of abstract art of Utamaro's time and place, and images of men were equally simplified and elegant.

How different from these ideals of physical beauty can be the perception and representation of spiritual beauty! A fifteenth-century bronze sculpture from India represents Punitavati, a beautiful and generous woman who was deeply devoted to the Hindu god Shiva. Abandoned by her husband because she gave one of his mangos to a beggar, Punitavati offered her beauty to Shiva. Shiva accepted the offering and in taking her loveliness turned her into an emaciated, fanged hag (fig. 9). According to legend, Punitavati, with clanging cymbals, provides the music for Shiva as he keeps the universe in motion by dancing the cosmic dance of destruction and creation. The bronze sculpture, although it depicts Punitavati's hideous appearance, is beautiful both in its formal qualities as a work of art and in its message of generosity and sacrifice.

Today, when images—including those of great physical and/or spiritual beauty—can be captured with a camera, why should an artist or sculptor draw, paint, or chip away at a knob of stone? Does beauty even play a significant role in our world?

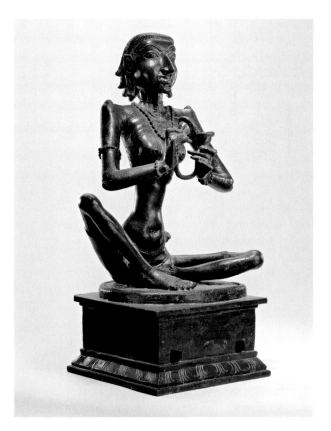

9 *Punitavati (Karaikkalammaiyar),* Shiva saint, from Karaikka, India. c. 1050. Bronze, height 12 $\frac{5}{8}$″ (32.1 cm). The Nelson-Atkins Museum of Art, Kansas City, Missouri
PURCHASE: NELSON TRUST (33-533)

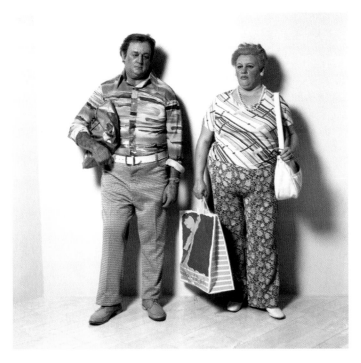

10 Duan Hanson. The Shoppers. 1976. Cast vinyl, polychromed in oil with accessories, life-size. Collection of the Nerman Family
© ESTATE OF DUANE HANSON / LICENSED BY VAGA, NEW YORK, NY

Attempting to answer these and other questions that consider the role of beauty in art is a branch of philosophy called **aesthetics**. In general, aesthetics considers the nature of beauty, art, and taste as well as the creation of beauty and art. A basic example of the type of complex ideas explored by aestheticians would be to compare the Duane Hanson figures of two tourists (fig. **10**) with the figures of the Medici Venus, the portrait of Charles V, and the sculpture of Punitavati. Is Hanson's couple more beautiful or less beautiful than these other works? How do you define beauty? And does it even matter whether any of these works seem beautiful to you?

Whether or not these figural works are beautiful, even a cursory look at the similarities and differences among them can teach us about the time in which they were made and help us explore what each individual artist have may been trying to communicate. Historically, styles often vary from one era to another and from one culture to another. Differing manners of representation—for example, naturalism and abstraction—also may be practiced simultaneously within a single culture. In ancient Greece, for example, the philosophers Aristotle (384–322 BCE) and Plato (428–348/7 BCE) both considered the nature of art and beauty in purely intellectual terms, but the two thinkers arrived at divergent conclusions. Aristotle believed that works of art should be evaluated on the basis of mimesis ("imitation"), that is, on how faithfully artists recorded what they saw in the natural world. According to this approach, Hanson's work of the two tourists might be considered the finest of the three. This approach to defining "What is art?" is a common one. In many societies people hold art in higher regard. But of course, we need to be aware that while artists may work in a realistic or naturalistic style, they also can render lifelike such fictions as a unicorn, a dragon, or a sphinx.

In contrast to Aristotle, Plato looked beyond nature for a definition of art. In his view even the most realistic painting or sculpture was only a shadow or approximation of the material world. Rather than focus on an exact copy of the particular details that one saw in nature, Plato's conclusions regarding art and beauty focused on an ideal, that is, on a representation of a subject that exhibited perfect symmetry and proportion. Thus, in a triumph of human reason over nature, a sculptor should eliminate all irregularities when depicting a subject from nature, ensuring a balanced and harmonious work of art. To achieve Plato's ideal images and represent things "as they ought to be" rather than as they are, classical sculpture and painting established ideals that have inspired Western art ever since. Let us depart from the figures to examine a simple example from architecture: the carved top, or **capital**, of a Corinthian column, a popular type, or **order**, of column that appeared in ancient Greece in the fourth century. The Corinthian capital has an inverted bell shape surrounded by acanthus leaves (fig. **11**). Although this foliage was inspired by the appearance of natural vegetation, the sculptors who carved the leaves eliminated blemishes and created ideally perfect leaves by first looking at nature and then carving the essence of the form, the Platonic ideal of foliage.

The terms *classic* and *classical*, which derive from the style of art in the period in ancient Greek history when this type of **idealism** emerged, have come to define the art of ancient Greece and Rome in general and are used even more broadly as synonyms for the peak of perfection in any period. Today, for example, we commonly use the adjective "classic" when speaking of exemplary films, automobiles, and clothing.

In the past, ideas such as ideal beauty inspired artists and those who commissioned or bought their works, but today, while we admire the achievements of the past, we realize that artists can think and work in very different ways. The anonymous builders of the pyramids would not have said they were creating beautiful works of art. Nor, in the twentieth century, would such artists as James Hampton and Olówè of Isè, whom we will meet later in this Introduction.

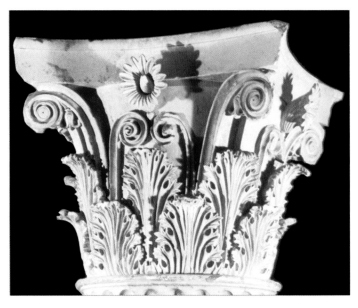

11 Corinthian capital from the *tholos* at Epidaurus. c. 350 BCE. Archaeological Museum, Epidaurus, Greece

Questions (and Answers) About Art

Underlying the assumptions of both those who commission art and those who make works of art—whether in the past or the present—is the idea that art has a message and that it can educate and convince viewers. But what gives an image meaning and expressive power? Why do some images fascinate and inspire us? Why have people treasured some things and not others? These are difficult questions, and even specialists disagree about the answers. Sometimes even the most informed people conclude, "I just don't know."

Studying art history, therefore, may not provide us with definitive answers to such questions, but it can help us better understand the value of asking the questions and also lead us to explore possible answers. Art history is grounded in the study of material objects that are the tangible expression of the ideas—and ideals—of a culture. For example, when we become captivated by the mysteriousness of a striking creation such as the Sphinx, art history can help us understand its particular imagery and meaning. Art history can also help us understand the larger cultural context of the work—that is, the social, economic, and political situation of the historical period in which it was produced.

On their own, exceptional works of art can speak to us over great expanses of time, but sometimes only if the viewer knows something about the **iconography** (meaning and interpretation) of an image does its larger meaning become clear. For example, let's look again at *Flower Piece with Curtain* (fig. 2). The brilliant red and white tulip just to the left of the blue curtain was the most desirable and expensive flower in the seventeenth century; thus, it symbolizes wealth and power. Yet insects creep out of it, and a butterfly—fragile and transitory—hovers above the flower. Consequently, the flowers also symbolize the passage of time and the fleeting quality of human riches. After studying the iconography and cultural context of the painting, we begin to understand that this is more than a simple still life.

So, before we turn to Chapter 1—before we begin to look at, read about, and think about works of art and architecture historically, from the earliest times to our own day—let us consider a few general questions that studying art history *can* help us answer and that we should keep in mind as we proceed: "Why do we need art?," "Who are artists?," "What role do patrons play?," "What is art history?," and "What is a viewer's role and responsibility?" By grappling with such questions, our experience of art can be greatly enhanced.

Why Do We Need Art?

Biologists account for the human desire for art by explaining that human beings have very large brains that demand stimulation. Curious, active, and inventive, we humans constantly explore, and in so doing invent things that appeal to our senses—fine art, fine food, fine scents, fine fabrics, and fine music. Ever since our prehistoric ancestors developed their ability to draw and speak, we have visually and verbally been communicating with each other. We speculate on the nature of things and the meaning of life. In fulfilling our need to understand and our need to communicate, the arts serve a vital function.

Art and the Search for Meaning

Throughout history art has played an important part in our search for the meaning of the human experience. In an effort to understand the world and our place in it, we turn both to introspective personal art and to communal public art. Following a personal vision, James Hampton (1909–1964) created profoundly stirring religious art. Hampton worked as a janitor to support himself while, in a rented garage, he built *Throne of the Third Heaven of the Nations' Millennium General Assembly* (fig. **12**), his monument to his faith. In rising tiers, thrones and altars have been prepared for Jesus and Moses. Placing New Testament

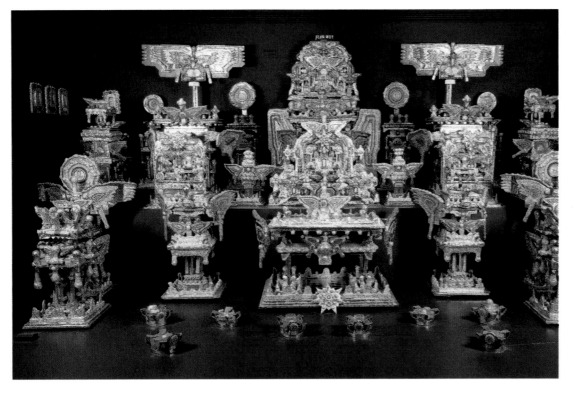

12 James Hampton. *Throne of the Third Heaven of the Nations' Millennium General Assembly.* c. 1950–1964. Gold and silver aluminum foil, colored Kraft paper, and plastic sheets over wood, paperboard, and glass, 10′6″ × 27′ × 14′6″ (3.2 × 8.23 × 4.42 m). Smithsonian American Art Museum, Smithsonian Institution, Washington, D.C.
GIFT OF ANONYMOUS DONORS, (1970.353.1)

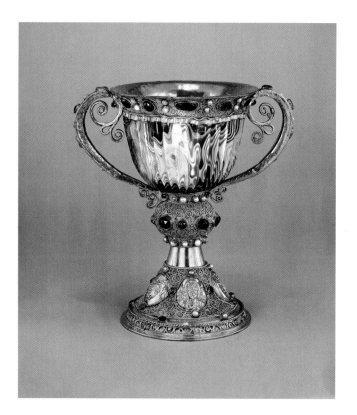

that blood. For both groups the chalice—the vessel for the sacramental wine—plays a central role. In the twelfth century in France, Abbot Suger, head of the monastery dedicated to Saint Denis near Paris, found an ancient agate vase in the storage chests of the abbey. He ordered his goldsmiths to add a foot, a rim, and handles as well as semiprecious stones and medallions to the vase, turning an entirely secular piece—an object of prestige and delight—into a chalice to be used at the altar of his church.

The Yoruba offering bowl, like the chalice, served the Yoruba people of Africa in rituals designed to communicate with their gods (fig. 14). It once held the palm nuts offered at the beginning of ceremonies in which people call on the god Olodumare (or Olorun) to reveal their destiny. Carved by the Yoruba master Olówè of Isè in about 1925, this sculpture appears to be a woman with a child on her back holding an ornate covered cup. Men and women help the woman support the bowl, and more women link arms in a ritual dance on the cover. A bearded head rolls freely in the cage formed by the figures. The child suggests the

13 Chalice of Abbot Suger, from Abbey Church of Saint-Denis, France. Cup: Ptolemaic Egypt (2nd–1st century BCE) or Byzantine 11th century, sardonyx; mounts: France, 1137–1140, silver gilt, adorned with filigree, semiprecious stones, pearls, glass insets, and opaque white glass with modern replacements. $7\,^{1}/_{2}'' \times 4\,^{1}/_{4}''$ (19 × 10.8 cm). National Gallery of Art, Washington, D.C.
PHOTOGRAPH © BOARD OF TRUSTEES, NATIONAL GALLERY OF ART, WASHINGTON, D.C.

imagery on the right and Old Testament imagery on the left, Hampton labeled and described everything. He even invented his own language to express his visions. On one of many placards he wrote his credo: "Where there is no vision, the people perish" (Proverbs 29:18). Hampton made this fabulous assemblage out of discarded furniture, flashbulbs, and all sorts of refuse tacked together and wrapped in gold and silver aluminum foil and purple tissue paper. How can such worthless materials be turned into such an exalted work of art? Today we recognize that the genius of the artist transcends any material.

In contrast to James Hampton, most artists and viewers participate in more public expressions of art and belief. People create rituals hoping to establish ties to unseen powers and also with the past and the future. When they employ special objects in their rituals such as statues, masks, and vessels, these pieces may be seen as works of art by outsiders who do not know about their intended use and original significance. Two ceremonial offering bowls—a European chalice and an African cup—will illustrate our point.

The cup known as the *Chalice of Abbot Suger* was used for the most important ceremony of the Christian religion (fig. 13). For Christians, communication between God and humans becomes possible through the ritual enactment of Jesus's Last Supper with his friends and disciples. For Catholic Christians, a complex rite enacted at a consecrated altar changes ordinary wine into the blood of Christ. For Protestants, the wine remains the symbol of

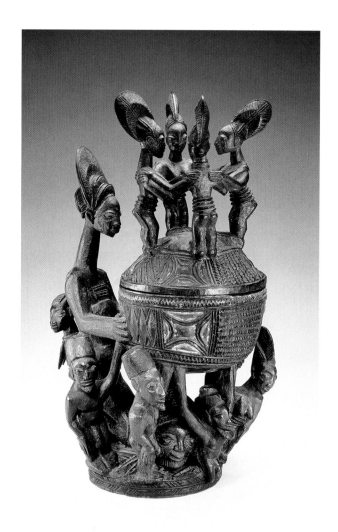

14 Olówè of Isè. Offering bowl, Nigeria, c. 1925. Wood and pigment, height $25\,^{1}/_{16}''$ (63.7 cm). National Museum of African Art, Smithsonian Institution, Washington, D.C.
BEQUEST OF WILLIAM A. MCCARTY-COOPER, (95-10-1)

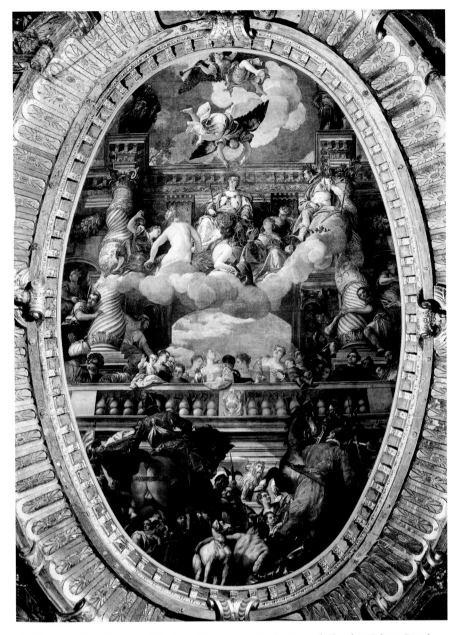

15 Veronese. *The Triumph of Venice,* ceiling painting in the Council Chamber, Palazzo Ducale, Venice, Italy. c. 1585. Oil on canvas, 29′8″ × 19′ (9.04 × 5.79 m)

life-giving power of women and perhaps ultimately of Olodumare. The richly decorative and symbolic wood carving, even when isolated in a museum case, reminds us of all who sought to learn from Olodumare, the god of destiny, certainty, and order.

Today Suger's chalice no longer functions in the liturgy of the Mass and Olówè's cup stands empty. Placed in museums, these ritual vessels take on a new secular life, enshrined as precious works of art. By linking today's viewers with people in the distant past and in faraway places, they serve an educational purpose very different from the original intention of their makers.

Art and Social Context

The visual arts are among the most sophisticated forms of human communication, at once shaping and being shaped by their social context. Artists may unconsciously interpret their times, but they also may be enlisted to consciously serve social ends in ways that range from heavy-handed propaganda (as seen earlier in the portrait of Charles V, for example) to subtle suggestion. From ancient Egyptian priests to elected officials today, religious and political leaders have understood the educational and motivational value of the visual arts.

How governments—that is, civic leaders—can use the power of art to strengthen the unity that nourishes society was well-llustrated in sixteenth-century Venice. There, city officials ordered Veronese (Paolo Caliari, 1528–1588) and his assistants to fill the ceiling of the Great Council Hall in the ruler's palace with a huge and colorful painting, *The Triumph of Venice* (fig. **15**). Their contract with the artist survives, proclaiming their intention. They wanted a painting that showed their beloved Venice surrounded by peace, abundance, fame, happiness, honor, security, and freedom—all in vivid colors and idealized forms. Veronese complied by painting the city personified as a mature, beautiful, and splendidly robed woman enthroned between the towers of the arsenal, a building where ships were built for worldwide trade, the source of the city's wealth and power. Veronese painted enthusiastic crowds of cheering citizens, while personifications of Fame blow

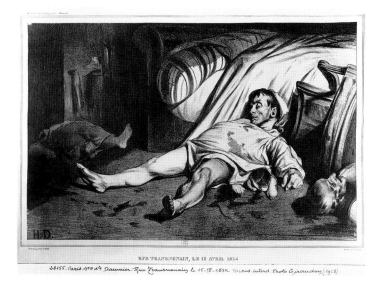

16 Honoré Daumier. *Rue Transonain, Le 15 Avril 1834.* Lithograph, 11″ × 17⅜″ (28 × 44 cm). Bibliothèque Nationale, Paris

trumpets and Victory crowns Venice with a wreath. Supporting this happy throng, bound prisoners and piles of armor attest to Venetian military power. The Lion of Venice—the symbol of the city and its patron, Saint Mark—oversees the triumph. Veronese has created a splendid propaganda piece as well as a work of art. Although Veronese created his work to serve the purposes of his patron, his artistic vision was as individualistic as that of James Hampton, whose art was purely a form of self-expression.

Uncovering Sociopolitical Intentions

Although powerful patrons have used artworks throughout history to promote their political and educational agendas, modern artists are often independent-minded, astute commentators in their own right. For example, among Honoré Daumier's most powerful critiques of the French government is his print *Rue Transonain, Le 15 Avril 1834* (fig. **16**). During a period of urban unrest, the French National Guard fired on unarmed citizens, killing 14 people. For his depiction of the massacre, Daumier used lithography—a cheap new means of illustration. He was not thinking in terms of an enduring historical record, but rather of a medium that would enable him to spread his message as widely as possible. Daumier's political commentary created such horror and revulsion that the government reacted by buying and destroying all the newspapers in which the print appeared. As this example shows, art historians sometimes need to consider not just the historical context of a work of art but also its political content and medium to have a fuller understanding of it.

Another, more recent, work with a powerful sociopolitical message is a reminder to those of us in the twenty-first century who may not know or may have forgotten that American citizens of Japanese ancestry were removed from their homes and confined in internment camps during World War II. In 1978, Roger Shimomura (b. 1939) painted *Diary*, recalling his grandmother's record of the family's experience in one such camp in Idaho (fig. **17**). Shimomura has painted his grandmother writing in her diary, while he (the toddler) and his mother stand by an open door—a door that does not signify freedom but opens on to a field bounded by barbed wire. In this commentary on twentieth-century discrimination and injustice, Shimomura combines two formal traditions—the Japanese art of color woodblock prints (see fig. 8) and American Pop art of the 1960s—to create a personal style that expresses his own dual culture.

Who Are Artists?

We have focused so far mostly on works of art. But what of the artists who make them? How artists have viewed themselves and have been viewed by their contemporaries has changed dramatically over time. In Western art, painters and sculptors were at

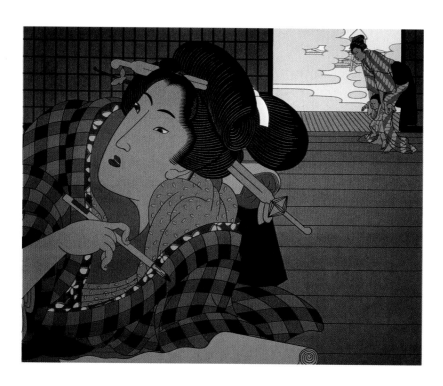

17 Roger Shimomura. *Diary (Minidoka Series #3).* 1978. Acrylic on canvas, 4′11⅞″ × 6′1/16″ (1.52 × 1.83 m). Spencer Museum of Art, The University of Kansas, Lawrence
MUSEUM PURCHASE, (1979.51)

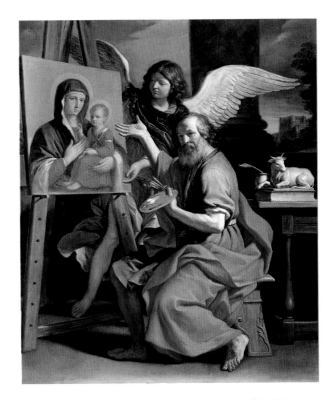

18 Il Guercino. *Saint Luke Displaying a Painting of the Virgin.*
1652–1653. Oil on canvas, 7′3″ × 5′11″ (2.21 × 1.81 m). The
Nelson-Atkins Museum of Art, Kansas City, Missouri
PURCHASE (F83-55)

other artists share in this special power and status. This image of
the artist as an inspired genius has continued into the twenty-
first century.

Even after the idea of "specially endowed" creators emerged,
numerous artists continued to see themselves, as they had in
many historical periods, as craftspeople led by the head of a
workshop, and oftentimes artwork continued to be a team effort.
In the eighteenth century, for example, Utamaro's color woodblock prints (see fig. 8) were the product of a number of people
working together. Utamaro painted pictures, and others transferred the images to blocks of wood to be printed on paper. Nevertheless, Utamaro—as the one who conceived the work—is the
"creative center," the "artist" whose name is associated with the
final product.

The same spirit is evident today in the complex glassworks of
American artist Dale Chihuly (b. 1941). His team of artist-crafts-
people is skilled in the ancient art of glass-making, but Chihuly
remains the controlling mind and imagination behind the works.
Once created, his multipart pieces may be transformed when they
are assembled for display; they take on a new life in accordance
with the will of every owner, who may arrange the pieces to
reflect his or her own preference. The viewer/owner thus becomes
part of the creative team. Made in 1990, *Violet Persian Set with
Red Lip Wraps* (fig. **19**) has twenty separate pieces, and the person
who assembles them determines the composition.

Whether artists work individually or communally, even the
most brilliant ones typically spend years in study and apprenticeship. In his painting *The Drawing Lesson*, Dutch artist Jan
Steen (1626–1679) takes us into an artist's studio where two

first considered artisans or craftspeople. The ancient Greeks and
Romans ranked painters and sculptors among the skilled workers; they admired the creations, but not the creators. The Greek
word for art, *tekne,* is the source for the English word *technique,*
and the English words *art* and *artist* come from the Latin word
ars, which means "skill." People in the Middle Ages went to the
opposite extreme and attributed especially fine works of art to
angels or to Saint Luke. Artists continued to be seen as craftspeople—admired, often prosperous, but not particularly special—
until the Renaissance, when artists such as Leonardo da Vinci
proclaimed themselves to be geniuses with unique God-given
abilities.

Soon after Leonardo's declaration of superiority, the Italian
painter Il Guercino (Giovanni Francesco Barbieri, 1591–1666)
synthesized the idea that saints and angels have miraculously
made art with the concept that human painters have special,
even divinely inspired, gifts. In his painting *Saint Luke Displaying
a Painting of the Virgin* (fig. 18), Guercino portrays the evangelist
who was regarded as the patron saint of artists because Christians widely believed that Luke had painted a portrait of the Virgin Mary holding the Christ Child. In Guercino's work, Luke,
seated before just such a painting and assisted by an angel, holds
his palette and brushes. A book, a quill pen, and an inkpot decorated with a statue of an ox (Saint Luke's symbol) rest on a table,
reminders of his status as an evangelist. Guercino seems to say
that if Saint Luke is a divinely endowed artist, then surely all

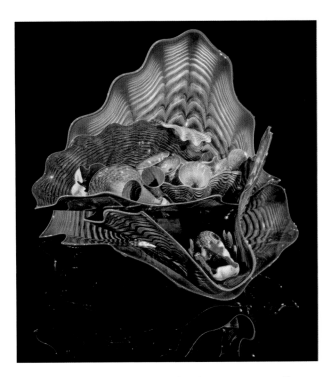

19 Dale Chihuly. *Violet Persian Set with Red Lip Wraps.* 1990. Glass,
26″ × 30″ × 25″ (66 × 76.2 × 63.5 cm). Spencer Museum of Art,
The University of Kansas, Lawrence
MUSEUM PURCHASE: PETER T. BOHAN ART ACQUISITION FUND, (1992.2)

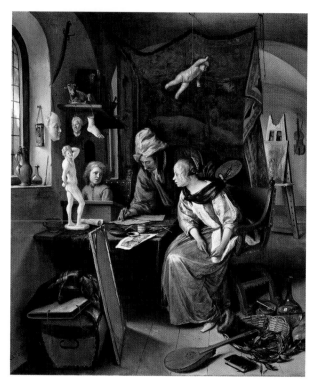

people—a boy apprentice and a young woman—are learning the rudiments of their art (fig. **20**). The pupil has been drawing from sculpture and plaster casts because women were not permitted to work from nude models. *The Drawing Lesson* records contemporary educational practice and is a valuable record of an artist's workplace in the seventeenth century.

Even the most mature artists learned from each other. In the seventeenth century, Rembrandt van Rijn carefully studied Leonardo's painting of *The Last Supper* (fig. **21**). Leonardo turned this traditional theme into a powerful human drama by portraying the moment when Christ announced that one of the assembled apostles would betray him. The men react with surprise and horror to this shocking news, yet Leonardo depicts the scene as a balanced symmetrical composition with the apostles in groups of three on each side of Christ. The regularly spaced tapestries and ceiling panels lead the viewers' eyes to Christ, who is silhouetted in front of an open window (the door seen in the photograph was cut through the painting at a later date).

Rembrandt, working 130 years later in the Netherlands, could only have known the Italian master's painting from a print, since he never went to Italy. Rembrandt copied *The Last Supper* in hard red chalk (fig. **22**). Then he reworked the drawing

20 Jan Steen. *The Drawing Lesson.* 1665. Oil on wood, 19³/₈″ × 16¹/₄″ (49.3 × 41 cm). The J. Paul Getty Museum, Los Angeles, California

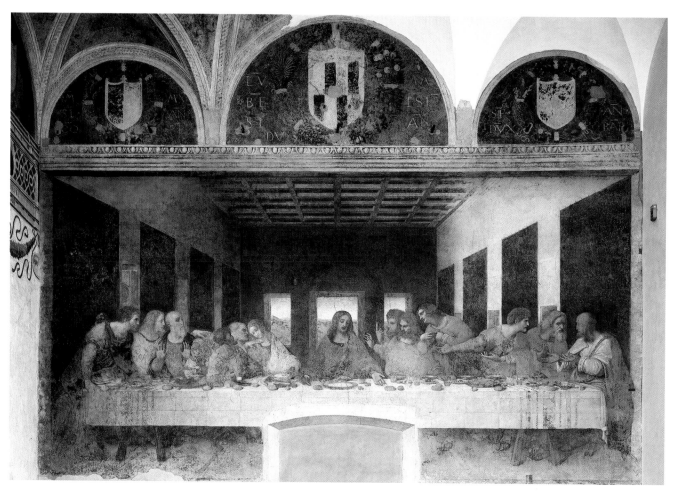

21 Leonardo da Vinci. *The Last Supper,* wall painting in the refectory, Monastery of Santa Maria delle Grazie, Milan, Italy. 1495–1498. Tempera and oil on plaster, 15′2″ × 28′10″ (4.6 × 8.8 m)

in a softer chalk, assimilating Leonardo's lessons but revising the composition and changing the mood of the original. With heavy overdrawing he re-created the scene, shifting Jesus's position to the left, giving Judas more emphasis, and adding a dog at the right. Gone are the wall hangings and ceiling, replaced by a huge canopy. The space is undetermined and expansive rather than focused. Rembrandt's drawing is more than an academic exercise; it is a sincere tribute from one great master to another. The artist must have been pleased with his version of Leonardo's masterpiece because he signed his drawing boldly in the lower right-hand corner.

What Role Do Patrons Play?

As we have seen, the person or group who commissions or supports a work of art—the **patron**—can have significant impact on it. The Great Sphinx (see fig. 1) was "designed" following the conventions of priests in ancient Egypt; the monumental statue of Charles V was cast to glorify totalitarian rule (see fig. 7); the content of Veronese's *Triumph of Venice* (see fig. 15) was deter-

mined by that city's government officials; and Chihuly's glassworks (see fig. 19) may be reassembled according to the collector's wishes or whims.

Although some artists work independently, hoping to sell their work on the open market, throughout art history both individuals and institutions have acted as patrons of the arts. Patrons very often have been essential factors in the development of the arts, but all too often have been overlooked when we study the history of art. Today, not only individuals but also museums, other institutions, and national governments (for example, the United States, through the National Endowment for the Arts) provide support for the arts.

Individual Patrons

People who are not artists often want to be involved with art, and patrons of art constitute a very special audience for artists. Many collectors truly love works of art, but some who collect art do so to enhance their own prestige, creating for themselves an aura of power and importance. Patrons vicariously participate in the creation of a work when they provide economic support to the

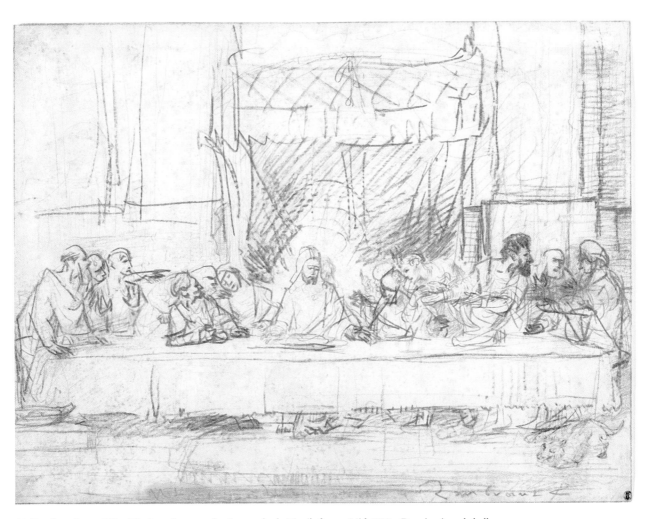

22 Rembrandt van Rijn. *The Last Supper,* after Leonardo da Vinci's fresco. Mid-1630s. Drawing in red chalk, $14\frac{3}{8}'' \times 18\frac{3}{4}''$ (36.5 × 47.5 cm). The Metropolitan Museum of Art, New York
ROBERT LEHMAN COLLECTION, 1975 (1975.1.794)

artist. Such individual patronage can spring from a cordial relationship between a patron and an artist, as is evident in an early-fifteenth-century manuscript illustration in which the author, Christine de Pizan, presents her work to Isabeau, the Queen of France (fig. **23**). Christine, a widow who supported her family by writing, hired painters and scribes to copy, illustrate, and decorate her books. She especially admired the painting of a woman named Anastaise, whose work she considered unsurpassed in the city of Paris. Queen Isabeau was Christine's patron; Christine was Anastaise's patron; and all the women seen in the painting were patrons of the brilliant textile workers who supplied the brocades for their gowns, the tapestries for the wall, and the embroideries for the bed.

Relations between artists and patrons do not always prove to be as congenial as Christine portrayed them. Patrons may change their minds and sometimes fail to pay their bills. Artists may ignore their patron's wishes, to the dismay of everyone. In the late nineteenth century, the Liverpool shipping magnate Frederick Leyland asked James McNeill Whistler (1834–1903), an American painter living in London, what color to paint the shutters in the dining room where he planned to hang Whistler's painting *The Princess from the Land of Porcelain*. The room had been decorated with expensive embossed and gilded leather and finely crafted shelves to show off Leyland's collection of blue-and-white porcelain. Whistler, inspired by the Japanese theme of his own painting as well as by the Asian porcelain, painted the window shutters with splendid turquoise, blue, and gold peacocks. But he did not stop there: While Leland was away, Whistler painted the entire room, covering the gilded leather on the walls with turquoise peacock feathers (fig. **24**). Leyland was shocked and angry at what seemed to him to be wanton destruction of the room. Luckily, he did not destroy Whistler's "Peacock Room" (which Whistler called simply *Harmony in Blue and Gold*), for it is an extraordinary example of total interior design; it is preserved at the Freer Gallery of Art in Washington, D.C.

Institutional Patronage: Museums and Civic Bodies

From the earliest times, people have gathered and preserved precious objects that convey the idea of power and prestige. Today both private and public museums are major patrons, collectors, and preservers of art. Curators of such collections acquire works of art for their museums and often assist patrons in obtaining especially fine pieces, although the idea of what is best and what is worth collecting and preserving often changes from one generation to another. For example, the collection of abstract and nonrepresentational art formed by members of the Guggenheim family was once considered so radical that few people—and certainly no civic or governmental group—would have considered the art worth collecting at all. Today the collection fills more than one major museum.

Frank Lloyd Wright's Solomon R. Guggenheim Museum (fig. **25**), with its snail-like, continuous spiral ramp, is a suitably **avant-garde** (strikingly new or of a radical nature for the time) home for the collection in New York City. Sited on Fifth Avenue, beside the public green space of Central Park and surrounded on the other three sides by quadrangles of city buildings, the Guggenheim Museum challenges and relieves the verticality and right angles of the modern city. The Guggenheim Foundation

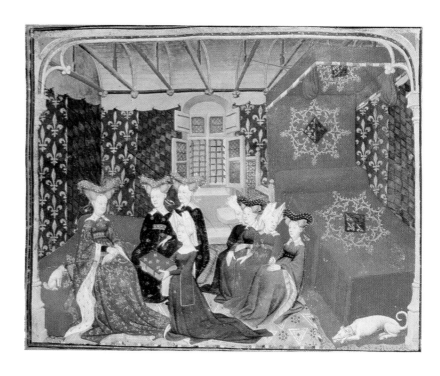

23 *Christine de Pizan Presenting Her Book to the Queen of France.* 1410–15. Tempera and gold on vellum, image approx. $5\frac{1}{2}" \times 6\frac{3}{4}"$ (14 × 17 cm). The British Library, London
MS. HARLEY 4431, FOLIO 3

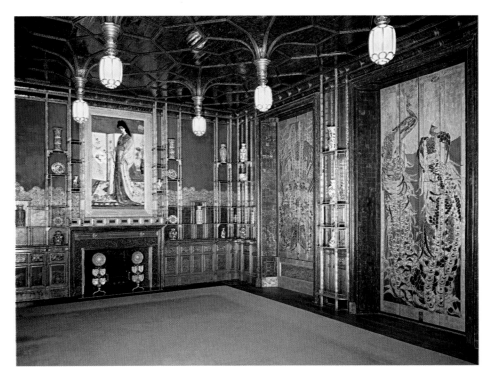

24 James McNeill Whistler. *Harmony in Blue and Gold.* The Peacock Room, northeast corner, from a house owned by Frederick Leyland, London. 1876–1877. Oil paint and metal leaf on canvas, leather, and wood, 13′11⅞″ × 33′2″ × 19′11½″ (4.26 × 10.11 × 6.83 m). Over the fireplace, Whistler's *The Princess from The Land of Porcelain.* Freer Gallery of Art, Smithsonian Institution, Washington, D.C.

recently opened another home for art, in Bilbao, Spain, designed by Frank Gehry, a leader of the twenty-first-century avant-garde in architecture. As both Guggenheim museums show, such structures can do more than house collections; they can be works of art themselves.

Historically, civic sponsorship of art is epitomized by the citizens of fifth-century BCE Athens, a Greek city-state where the people practiced an early form of democracy. Led by the statesman and general Pericles, the Athenians defeated the Persians, and then rebuilt Athens's civic and religious center, the Acropolis, as a tribute to the goddess Athena and a testament to the glory of Athens. In figure **26**, a nineteenth-century British artist, Sir Lawrence Alma-Tadema, conveys the accomplishment of the Athenian architects, sculptors, and painters, who were led by the artist Phidias. Alma-Tadema imagines the moment when Phidias showed the carved and painted frieze at the top of the wall of the Temple of Athena (the Parthenon) to Pericles and a privileged group of Athenian citizens—his civic sponsors.

What Is Art History?

Art history became an academic field of study relatively recently. Many art historians consider the first art history book to be the 1550 publication *Lives of the Most Excellent Italian Architects, Painters, and Sculptors,* by the Italian artist and writer Giorgio Vasari. As the name implies, art history combines two very different special studies—the study of individual works of art

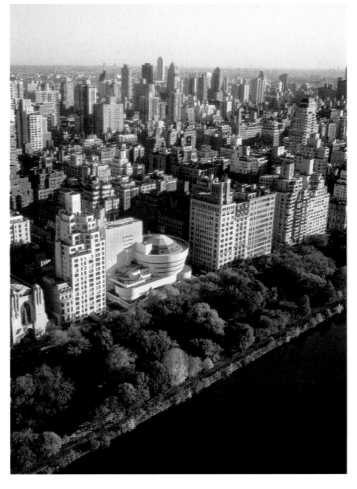

25 Frank Lloyd Wright. Solomon R. Guggenheim Museum, New York City. 1956–1959. Aerial view

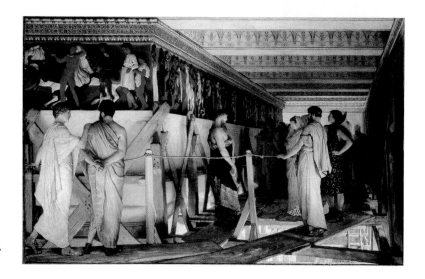

26 Lawrence Alma-Tadema. *Phidias and the Frieze of the Parthenon, Athens.* 1868. Oil on canvas, $29\,{}^{3}\!/_{5}"\times42\,{}^{1}\!/_{3}"$ (75.3 × 108 cm). Birmingham City Museum and Art Gallery, England

outside time and place (formal analysis and theory) and the study of art in its historical and cultural context (contextualism), the primary approach taken in this book. The scope of art history is immense. It shows how people have represented their world and how they have expressed their ideas and ideals. As a result, art history today draws on many other disciplines and diverse methodologies.

Studying Art Formally and Contextually

At the most sophisticated level, the intense study of individual art objects is known as **connoisseurship.** Through years of close contact with and study of the formal qualities that make up various styles in art (such as design, composition, the way materials are manipulated, an approach known as **formalism**), the connoisseur categorizes an unknown work through comparison with related pieces, attributing it to a period, a place, and sometimes even to a specific artist. Today such experts also make use of the many scientific tests available to them—such as X-ray radiography, electron microscopy, infrared spectroscopy, and X-ray diffraction—but ultimately, connoisseurs depend on their visual memory and their skills in formal analysis.

Art history as a humanistic discipline adds theoretical and contextual studies to the formal analysis of works of art. Art historians draw on biography to learn about artists' lives; social history to understand the economic and political forces shaping artists, their patrons, and their public; and the history of ideas to gain an understanding of the intellectual currents influencing artists' work. They also study the history of other arts—including music, drama, and literature—to gain a richer sense of the context of the visual arts. Their work results in an understanding of the iconography (the narrative and allegorical significance) and the context (social history) of the artwork.

When we become captivated by the mysteriousness of a creation such as the Sphinx, art history can help us understand its striking imagery and meaning. We need to know the artwork's total cultural context. We must work with scholars in many other fields; for example, someone has to be able to read Egyptian hieroglyphs to tell us that we are looking at the face of a king. By studying the translations of these hieroglyphs, we study the historical period in which the sculpture was made and learn about the king's earthly power, the culture's belief in an afterlife, and the overwhelming cultural importance of ceremony—all defined and expressed by the monumental Sphinx.

Such intense study of the history of art is also enhanced by the work of anthropologists and archaeologists, who study the wide range of material culture produced by a society. Archaeologists often experience the excitement of finding new and wonderful objects as they reconstruct the social context of the works. They do not, however, single out individual works of perceived excellence for special attention.

Today art historians study a wider range of artworks than ever before, and many reject the idea of a fixed canon of superior pieces. The distinction between elite fine arts and popular utilitarian arts has become blurred, and the notion that some mediums, techniques, or subjects are better than others has almost disappeared. This is one of the most telling characteristics of art history today, along with the breadth of studies it now encompasses and its changing attitude to challenges such as preservation and restoration.

Defending Endangered Objects

Today's art historians are also concerned with past and present natural and human threats to works of art. Even as methodological sophistication and technological advances soar, art historians and other viewers are faced with some special challenges of

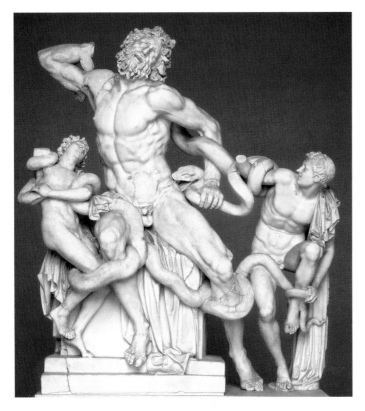

27 Hagesandros, Polydoros, and Athanadoros of Rhodes. *Laocoön and His Sons,* as restored today. Probably the original of 1st century CE or a Roman copy of the 1st century CE. Marble, height 8′ (2.44 m). Musei Vaticani, Museo Pio Clementino, Cortile Ottagono, Rome, Italy

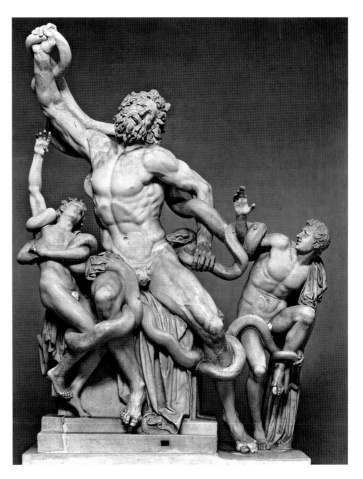

28 Hagesandros, Polydoros, and Athanadoros of Rhodes. *Laocoön and His Sons,* in an earlier restoration

interpretation, especially regarding works that have been damaged or restored, as many of the works in and out of museums around the world (and many of those reproduced in this book) have been. As we try to understand such works of art, we must remain quizzical and flexible; damaged artworks may have had large parts replaced—the legs of a marble figure may have been replaced or a section of wall in a mural painting may have been repainted, for example.

The dangers inherent in restoration are blatantly illustrated by what happened during two restorations, hundreds of years apart, of the renowned sculpture *Laocoön and His Sons.*

Laocoön was a priest who warned the Trojans of an invasion by the Greeks in Homer's account of the Trojan War. Although Laocoön told the truth, the goddess Athena, who took the Greeks' side in the war, dispatched serpents to strangle him and his sons. A tragic hero, Laocoön represents a virtuous man destroyed by unjust forces. In the powerful ancient Greek sculpture, his features twist in agony, and the muscles of his and his sons' superhuman torsos and arms extend and knot as they struggle (figs. **27** and **28**). When the sculpture was discovered in Rome in 1506, artists such as Michelangelo rushed to see it, and it inspired many artists to develop an ideal, heroic style. The pope acquired it for the papal collection, and it can still be seen in the Vatican Museums.

In piecing together the past of this one work, we know that mistakes were made during an early restoration. The broken pieces of the *Laocoön* group first were reassembled with figures

flinging their arms out in the melodramatic fashion seen in figure 28—this was the sculpture the Renaissance and Baroque artists knew. Modern conservation methods, however, have produced a different image and with it a changed mood (fig. 27). Lost pieces are not replaced and Laocoön's right arm turns back upon his body, making a compact composition that internalizes the men's agony. This version speaks directly to a self-centered twenty-first century. We can only wonder if twenty-fifth-century art historians will re-create yet another *Laocoön.*

Restoration of works like *Laocoön* is intended to conserve precious art. But throughout the world, other human acts intentionally or mindlessly threaten works of art and architecture—and this is not a recent problem. Egyptian tombs were plundered and vandalized many hundreds of years ago—and such theft continues to this day. Objects of cultural and artistic value in places including Iraq and Central America are being taken from official and unofficial excavation sites, then sold illegally.

In industrialized regions of the world, emissions from cars, trucks, buses, and factories turn into corrosive rain that damages and sometimes literally destroys the works of art and architecture on which it falls. For art, however, war is by far the most destructive of all human enterprises.

History is filled with examples of plundered works of art that, as spoils of war, were taken elsewhere and paraded and protected. But countless numbers of churches, synagogues, mosques, temples, and shrines have been burned, bombed, and stripped of decoration in the name of winning a war or

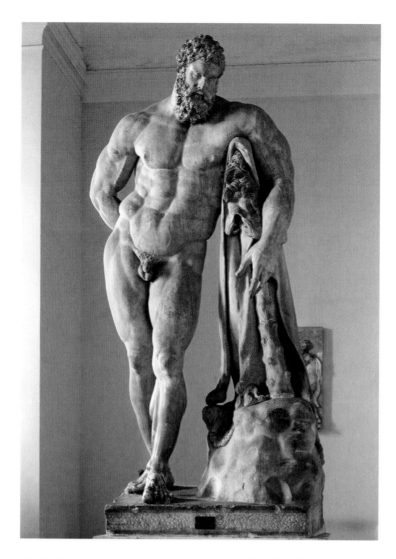

29 The Farnese Hercules, 3rd century BCE. Copy of The Weary Hercules by Lysippos. Found in the Baths of Caracalla in 1546; exhibited in the Farnese Palace until 1787. Marble, $10\frac{1}{2}'$ (3.17 m). Signed "Glykon" on the rock under the club. Left arm restored

confirming an ideology. In modern times, with weapons of mass destruction, so much that is lost is absolutely irrecoverable.

Nature, too, can be equally capricious: Floods, hurricanes, tornadoes, avalanches, mudslides, and earthquakes all damage and destroy priceless treasures. For example, an earthquake on the morning of September 27, 1997, convulsed the small Italian town of Assisi, where Saint Francis was born and where he founded the Franciscan order. It shook the thirteenth-century Basilica of Saint Francis of Assisi—one of the richest repositories of Italian Gothic and Early Renaissance wall painting—causing great damage to architecture and paintings.

In all the examples mentioned, art historians have played a role in trying to protect the treasures that are the cultural heritage of us all. Viewers of art also play a role and also have a distinct responsibility in art history, though it is one that may not be obvious at first.

What Is a Viewer's Role and Responsibility?

We as viewers enter into an agreement with artists, who in turn make special demands on us. We re-create the works of art for ourselves as we bring to them our own experiences, our intelligence, and even our prejudices. Without our participation, artworks are only chunks of stone or paint on canvas. But we must also remember that styles change with time and place. From extreme realism at one end of the spectrum to entirely nonrepresentational art at the other—from van der Spelt and van Mieris's *Flower Piece with Curtain* (see fig. 2) to Smith's *Cubi* (see fig. 5)—artists have worked with varying degrees of naturalism, idealism, and abstraction. The challenge for the student of art history is to discover not only how but also why those styles evolved, and ultimately what of significance can be learned from that evolution.

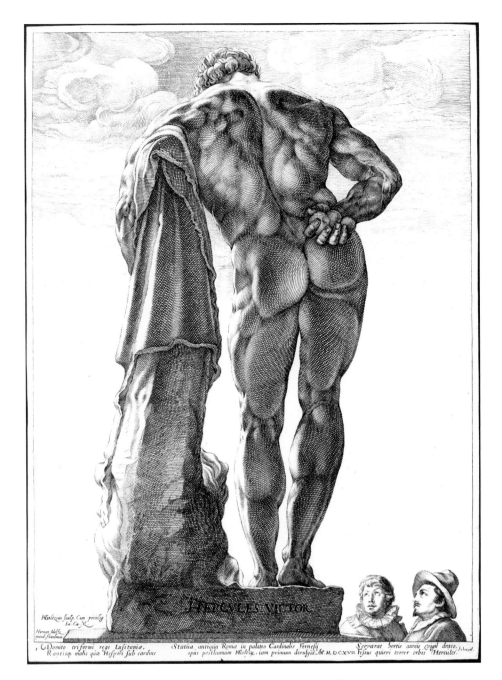

30 Hendrick Goltzius, *Dutch visitors to Rome looking at the Farnese Hercules.* Engraving, c. 1592.
16″ × 11½″ (40.5 × 29.4 cm). After Goltzius returned from a trip to Rome in 1591–1592, he made engravings based on his drawings. The awe-struck viewers have been identified as two of his Dutch friends

Our involvement with art may be casual or intense, naive or sophisticated. At first we may simply react instinctively to a painting or building, or in the case of the sixteenth century Dutch visitors to Rome, to the sculpture (figs. **29** and **30**), but this level of "feeling" about art—"I know what I like"—can never be fully satisfying. Because as viewers we participate in the re-creation of a work of art, its meaning changes from individual to individual, from era to era.

Once we welcome the arts into our lives, we have a ready source of sustenance and challenge that grows, changes, mellows, and enriches our daily experience. This book introduces us to works of art in their historical context, but no matter how much we study or read about art and artists, eventually we return to the contemplation of an original work itself, for art is the tangible evidence of the ever-questing human spirit.

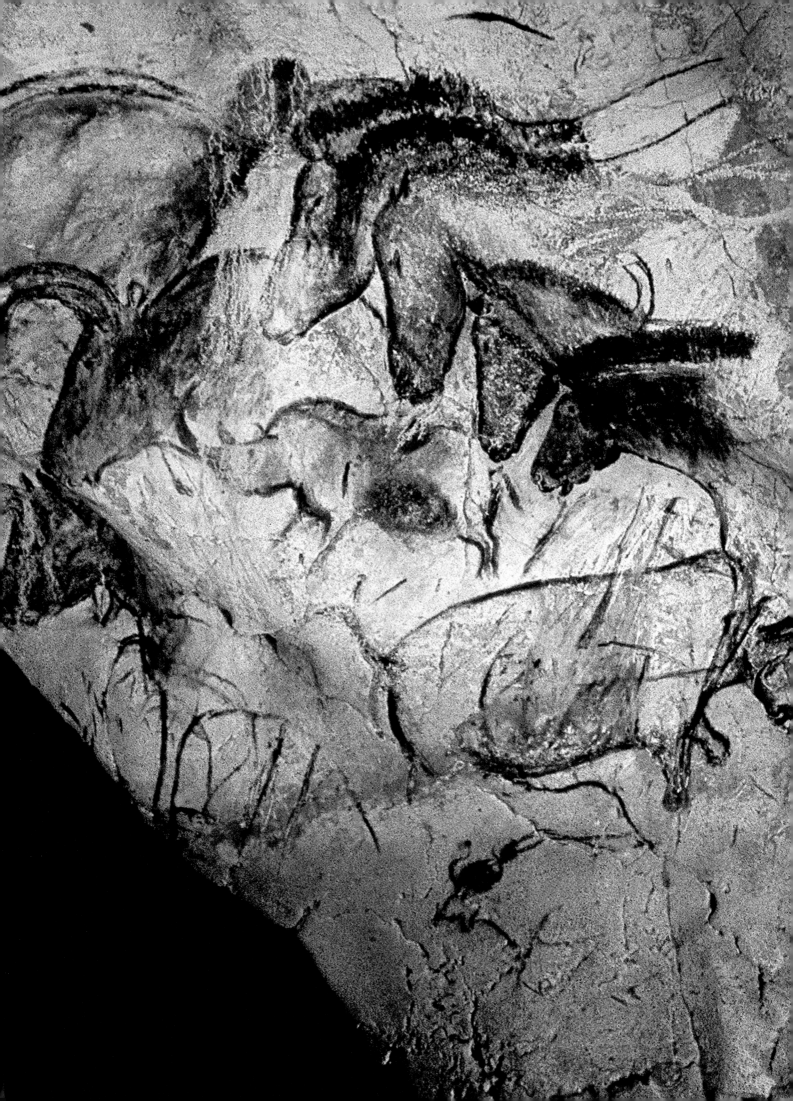

1

Art Before
the Written Word

The first people to explore the painted caves of France and Spain entered an almost unimaginably ancient world. What they found in the deep recesses of these caves—hundreds of yards from the entrances and accessed through long, narrow underground passages—astounded them then and still fascinates us now. The paintings and engravings on the walls and ceilings of these caves record herds of animals seen 30,000 years ago, and they are among the very first images in the history of art.

Scholars of prehistory, such as archaeologists and anthropologists, study every aspect of material culture, whereas art historians usually focus on those objects that to twenty-first century eyes seem superior in craft and beauty. But 30,000 years ago, our ancestors were pounding (flaking) flints into arrows or scrapers. They were not creating works of art, although the forms of their tools appear beautiful to us today. We also assume that the images we see on the walls of Chauvet Cave (fig. 1–1) must have been vitally important to their makers. What we perceive as "art" today was a matter of necessity to these ancient image-makers. The selection of special objects and images and the designation "fine arts" arose late in the history of humankind.

Images of horses, aurochs (extinct ancestors of domestic cattle), and even rhinos cover the cave walls. The animals are easily identifiable, for the painters represent the essence of well-observed animals—their meat-bearing flanks and heads in profile; their powerful legs and dangerous horns as seen from the front for the sake of descriptive clarity and completeness. What a leap of intelligence and imagination we witness here! The painters have turned their memories of moving, three-dimensional figures into fixed, two-dimensional images. Without written words and using only the basic elements of line and color, they communicate with us across the millennia.

Why did early humans make these paintings? Were they recording an event such as a hunt or a successful roundup? Did the images play a role in the education or initiation of their children? Perhaps the paintings express beliefs, imagine a spirit world, or record a complex ritual. Could the makers have been trying to control the forces of nature through these images? Might the act of painting itself have been important as a ritual act, regardless of the image? Frustratingly, we have no answers, only questions. Perhaps in the end the greatest value of studying these mysterious images is their ability to lead us to speculations about what it means to be human.

1–1 Wall painting with four horses, Chauvet Cave, Vallon-Pont-d'Arc, Ardèche Gorge, France. c. 28,000 BCE. Paint on limestone

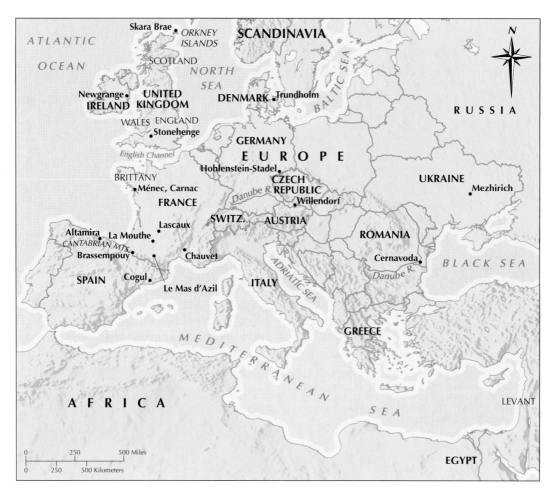

Map 1–1 Prehistoric Europe

Human beings made tools long before they made what today we call "art." *Homo habilis* ("handy human"), who first flaked and chipped (knapped) flint pebbles into blades and scrapers with cutting edges, lived in Africa two million years ago. By 200,000 years ago, *Homo sapiens* ("wise human") had moved into North Africa and Europe, and Asia as far as China. Evolutionary changes continued to take place; by 100,000 years ago, a well-developed type of *Homo sapiens* called Neanderthal inhabited Europe. Neanderthals used many different stone tools and carefully buried their dead with funerary offerings. By 35,000 years ago, they had disappeared as Cro-Magnons inhabited the continent. The Cro-Magnons made tools of reindeer antler and bone as well as very fine chipped-stone implements. Clearly social beings, Cro-Magnons must have had social organization, rituals, and beliefs that led them to create art. They engraved, carved, drew, and painted with colored ochers, earthy mineral oxides of iron that could be ground into pigments. These people are our ancestors, and with their sculpture and painting the history of art begins. This book presents the tangible record of the uniquely human aesthetic spirit.

Scholars began to study prehistory systematically—that is, to examine the thousands of years of human civilization before the invention of written historical records—less than 200 years ago. Struck by the wealth of stone tools, weapons, and figures found at ancient living sites, nineteenth-century archaeologists named the whole period of early human development the "Stone Age." Today's researchers further divide the time span into the Paleolithic, or Old Stone Age (from the Greek *paleo*, "old," and *lithos*, "stone")—which has Lower (earliest), Middle, and Upper phases—and the Neolithic, or New Stone Age (from the Greek *neo*, "new"). In this chapter we will consider the art of the Paleolithic and Neolithic periods and also the earliest age of metals—the Bronze and Iron Ages in Europe.

Upper Paleolithic Art

Our hunter-gatherer ancestors lived in small nomadic groups and created works of art and architecture as early as the Upper (later) Paleolithic period (c. 42,000–8000 BCE). During this time, the glaciers of the last ice age still covered northern stretches of Europe, North America, and Asia. Some of the most ancient examples of Paleolithic art are small figures, or figurines, of people and animals, made of bone, ivory, stone, or clay. These three-dimensional pieces are examples of **sculpture in the round**. Prehistoric carvers also produced **relief sculpture** in stone, bone, or ivory. In a relief sculpture, the surrounding material is carved away, forming a background that sets off the figure.

An early and puzzling example of a sculpture in the round is a human figure with a feline head (fig. **1–2**), made about 30,000–26,000 BCE. Archaeologists excavating at Hohlenstein-Stadel, Germany, found broken pieces of ivory (from the tusk of the now-extinct woolly mammoth) that they realized were parts of an entire figure. Nearly a foot tall, this remarkable statue surpasses in size and complexity most early figurines. Instead of copying what he or she saw in nature, the carver created a unique, imagined creature, part human and part beast. Was the figure intended to represent a person wearing a ritual lion mask? Or has the man taken on the appearance and power of an animal? One of the few indisputable things that can be said about the *Lion-Human* is that it shows the sculptor's highly complex thinking and creative imagination: the ability to imagine and represent a creature never seen in nature.

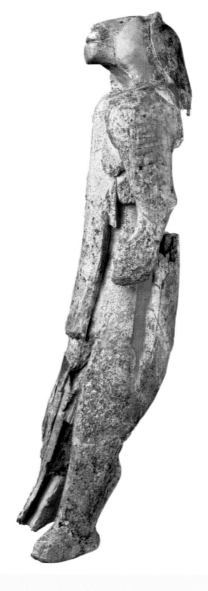

1–2 *Lion-Human,* from Hohlenstein-Stadel, Germany. c. 30,000–26,000 BCE. Mammoth ivory, height 11⅝″ (29.6 cm). Ulmer Museum, Ulm, Germany

C L O S E R   L O O K

Elegant and remote yet warmly human, the *Woman from Brassempouy* (fig. **1–3**) seems to contemplate her world with equanimity, her once-painted pupils made sightless by more than 24,000 years of lying in the soil of central France. The subtle arch of her brows, the graceful lines of her neck and nose, even the neat pattern of her hair or headdress capture the living presence of a mature young woman. Her image in ivory by a long-dead sculptor still speaks to us of our essential humanity, of our need to make images of ourselves and our kind, of our status as the only creatures who both make useful tools (the great apes do that, too) *and* create what we now call works of art. Humans make things of beauty, however we may define such elusive concepts as "art" and "beauty."

We do not know what moved someone to carve this piece, of which only the head survives. Perhaps the maker associated the woman with spiritual or magical powers. Perhaps the figure ensured her tribe's continuity as a fertility figure controlling the abundance of nature; perhaps she presided over some dark unknown world.

Our speculations are fruitless, for the makers of the *Woman from Brassempouy* were prehistoric, leaving behind no written record to share their thoughts and deeds. And therein lies part of our fascination with this mysterious art. New studies of physical remains—from fossils to Stone Age hunting sites—tell us about the physical life, appearance, and capabilities of our distant ancestors, and their painting and sculpture hint at their spiritual and intellectual life. We begin our study of the history of art with many large questions and a mission to understand.

1–3 *Woman from Brassempouy,* Grotte du Pape, Brassempouy Landes, France. c. 22,000 BCE. Ivory, height 1¼″ (3 cm). Musée des Antiquités Nationales, St.-Germain-en-Laye

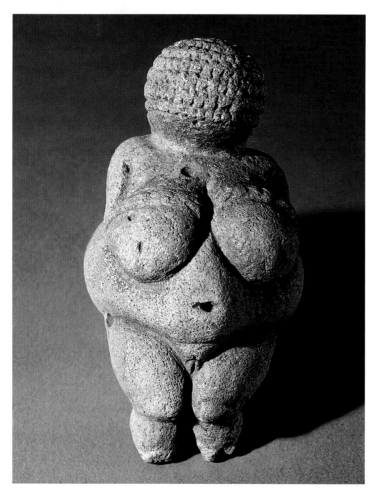

1–4 *Woman from Willendorf,* Austria. c. 22,000–21,000 BCE. Limestone, height 4³⁄₈″ (11 cm). Naturhistorisches Museum, Vienna

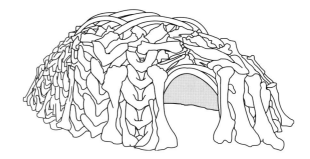

1–5 Reconstruction drawing of mammoth-bone house from Ukraine. c. 16,000–10,000 BCE

Paleolithic sculptors depicted women more frequently than other subjects. The carver of the *Woman from Brassempouy* (fig. 1–3) captured the essence of a head or what psychologists call the "memory image"—those generalized elements that reside in our standard memory of a human head. An egg shape rests atop a long neck, a wide nose and a strongly defined browline suggest deep-set eyes, and an engraved squared patterning may be hair or a headdress. This is an example of **abstraction**, the reduction of shapes and appearances to basic yet recognizable **forms** that are not intended to be exact replications of nature. The result in this case looks uncannily modern to the contemporary viewer. Today, when such a piece is isolated in a museum case or as a book illustration, we enjoy the ivory head as an aesthetic object, but we lose its cultural context.

Another early female figurine, the *Woman from Willendorf* (fig. 1–4), dates from about 22,000–21,000 BCE (see "The Power of Naming," page 26). Carved from limestone and originally colored with red ocher, the statuette's swelling, rounded forms make it seem much larger than its actual 4³⁄₈-inch height. The sculptor exaggerated the figure's female **attributes**, giving it pendulous breasts, a big belly with a deep navel (notably, natural hole in the stone), wide hips, dimpled knees and buttocks, and solid thighs. Sculptures depicting women, from adolescence to

old age, have been found at dozens of sites from France to Ukraine. By carving a woman with a well-nourished body, the artist expresses the condition of health, which could ensure both longevity and the ability to produce strong children, thus guaranteeing the survival of the clan.

Whatever their original significance, Paleolithic works of sculpture show an aesthetic sense and the ability to both pose and solve problems. These faculties are among the characteristics unique to human beings. Similar talents are sometimes revealed in structures of the period, in which builders seem to have had a feel for what we now call architecture—enclosure of spaces with some measure of aesthetic intent—rather than simple constructions.

Some well-preserved examples of Upper Paleolithic dwellings have been found in Russia and Ukraine. The people of those treeless grasslands built settlements of up to 10 houses using the bones and hide of the woolly mammoth (fig. 1–5). One such village, dating from 16,000–10,000 BCE, was discovered near the Ukrainian village of Mezhirich. Its turf-and-hide-covered houses were cleverly constructed with dozens of skulls, shoulder blades, pelvis bones, jawbones, and tusks. The largest house is an impressive 24 by 33 feet, and inside, archaeologists found 15 small hearths containing ashes and charred bones left by its last occupants. Clearly, life revolved around the hearth, the source of light and heat in the dark winter months.

Cave and rock shelter paintings from the Upper Paleolithic period also connect us with our early ancestors. Rock art survives in many places around the world, but the oldest known examples come from western Europe. People began to paint, engrave, draw, and model images in caves and rock shelters about 30,000 years ago. They produced many cave paintings in southern France and northern Spain between about 28,000 and 10,000 BCE. Artists painted images of animals—such as wild horses, bison, mammoths, aurochs—and a few people; many handprints; and hundreds of **geometric** markings, such as **grids**, circles, and dots. In some caves, painters decorated not only large caverns but also tiny chambers and recesses whose natural surfaces inspired images resembling **low-relief sculpture**. They worked in the light of small stone lamps fueled by animal fat, using charcoal and red and brown pigments of ground ochers (see "Prehistoric Wall Painting," page 27).

The oldest securely dated European cave paintings are found in Chauvet Cave in southeastern France, which was discovered in 1994 (see fig. 1–1). These paintings were made around 28,000 BCE, which seems remarkable given the accomplished depictions of the animals. It is impossible to know whether the animals represent the beginnings of early painting or some later stage in early artistic development. Because we know of no images predating this time, we have no way of knowing whether artists had already been practicing for thousands of years. As previously mentioned, the significance of cave paintings is unknown, but many theories have been suggested (see "The Meaning(s) of Prehistoric Paintings," page 28).

The best-known cave paintings today are those at Lascaux, in southern France (figs. 1–6 and 1–7), and Altamira, in northern Spain. The Lascaux paintings of cows, bulls, horses, and deer date from about 15,000–13,000 BCE. The animals appear singly, in rows, face-to-face, tail-to-tail, and even painted on top of one another. To insure a complete image, the horns, eyes, and hooves are shown as seen from the front, while heads and bodies are rendered in profile. The technique is known as "twisted perspective." The painters used the contours of the rock as part of their compositions. This sculptural dimension is seen perhaps most clearly in photographs of the cave ceiling at Altamira (fig. 1–8). The Altamira artists created sculptural effects by painting the bodies of their animals over and around natural protuberances in the cave's walls and ceilings. To produce the herd of bison on the ceiling of the main cavern, they used rich red and brown ochers to paint the large areas of the animals' shoulders, backs, and flanks, then sharpened the contours and added the details of the legs,

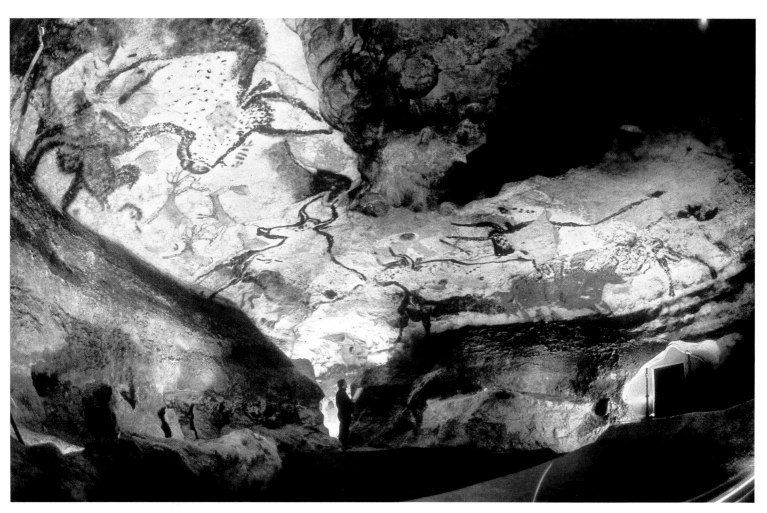

1–6 Hall of Bulls, Lascaux caves. c. 15,000–13,000 BCE. Paint on limestone

Discovered in 1940 and opened to the public after World War II, the prehistoric "museum" at Lascaux soon became one of the most popular tourist sites in France—too popular, for many visitors sowed the seeds of the paintings' destruction in the form of heat, humidity, exhaled carbon dioxide, and other contaminants. The cave was closed to the public in 1963 so that conservators might battle with an aggressive fungus that had attacked the paintings. Eventually the conservators won, but instead of reopening the site, the authorities created a facsimile of it. Visitors at what is called Lascaux II may now view copies of the painted images without harming the precious originals.

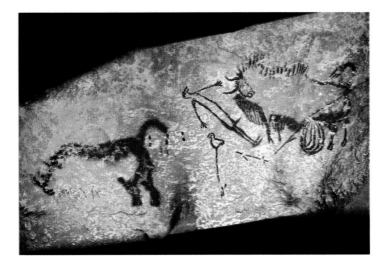

1–7 *Bird-Headed Man with Bison,* Lascaux caves. c. 15,000–13,000 BCE. Paint on limestone, length approx. 9′ (2.75 m)

A figure who could be a hunter, highly stylized but recognizably male and wearing a bird's-head mask, appears to be lying on the ground. A great bison looms above him. Below him lie a staff, or baton, and a spear thrower—a device that allowed hunters to throw farther and with greater force—the outer end of which has been carved in the shape of a bird. The long diagonal line slanting across the bison's hindquarters is a spear. The bison has been disemboweled.

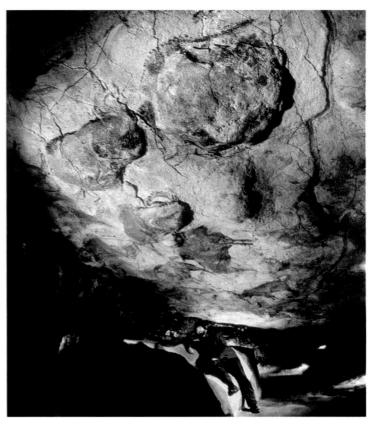

1–8 *Bison,* on the ceiling of a cave at Altamira, Spain. c. 12,000 BCE. Paint on limestone, length approx. 8′3″ (2.5 m)

No one knew of the existence of prehistoric cave painting until one day in 1879, when a young girl exploring with her father on the family estate in Altamira crawled through a small opening in the ground and found herself in a cave chamber whose ceiling was covered with painted animals. Her father searched the rest of the cave, and then told authorities about the remarkable find. Few people believed that these amazing works could have been done by "primitive" people, and the scientific community declared the paintings a hoax. They were accepted as authentic only in 1902, after many other cave paintings, drawings, and engravings had been discovered at other spots in northern Spain and in France.

tails, heads, and horns in black and brown, mixing yellow and brown from ochers with iron to make the red tones and deriving black from manganese or charcoal.

One scene at Lascaux is unusual not only because it includes a human figure but also because it is a rare example of a painting that seems to tell a story (fig. 1–7). But what is this scene telling us? Why did the artist portray the man as only a sticklike figure with a bird's head when the bison was rendered with such accurate detail? It may be that the painting illustrates a myth regarding the death of a hero. Perhaps it illustrates an actual event. The most likely theory is that it depicts the vision of a shaman. As we know shamanism from practitioners today, shamans were people thought to have special

THE POWER OF NAMING

Figures such as the *Woman from Willendorf* (see fig. 1–4) are sometimes termed "goddess" or "Venus" figurines; the statuette discovered near Willendorf, Austria, was originally called the "Venus of Willendorf." Because Venus was the Roman goddess of love and beauty, the use of this name seemed to imply that the statuette was associated with religious belief, that it represented an ideal of womanhood, and that it was one in a long line of images of "classical" feminine beauty. Yet

there is no proof that figures such as the *Woman from Willendorf* had any religious associations. These figures have been interpreted as representations of actual women, fertility symbols, expressions of ideal beauty, erotic images, ancestor figures, or even dolls meant to help young girls learn women's roles. Given the diversity of ages and physical types represented, it is possible that they were any or all of these.

Our ability to understand and interpret works of art is easily compromised by distracting labels. Even knowing that the figure was once labeled the "Venus of Willendorf" influences the way we look at it. And the tradition of a name, no matter how guided by an era's cultural conventions, makes it extremely difficult for members of a later era to challenge accepted or unquestioned belief. Calling a prehistoric figure a "woman" instead of "Venus" frees us to think about it in new and different ways.

In a dark cave, working by the light of an animal-fat lamp, an artist chews a piece of charcoal to dilute it with saliva and water. Then he blows the mixture onto the surface of a wall, using his hand as a stencil. Cave archaeologist Michel Lorblanchet is showing us how prehistoric cave artists worked. By turning himself into a human spray can, he can produce clear lines on the rough stone surface much more easily than he could with a brush. To create the line of an animal's back, with a clean upper edge and a blurry lower one, Lorblanchet blows pigment below his hand, or he places his hand vertically against the wall, holding it slightly curved; to produce the sharpest lines, he places his hands side by side and blows between them. He also uses finger painting, and a hole punched in a piece of leather serves as a stencil. It takes Lorblanchet only 32 hours to reproduce a large painting, his speed suggesting that a single prehistoric artist could have created a painting of similar size (perhaps with the help of an assistant to mix pigments and tend the lamp).

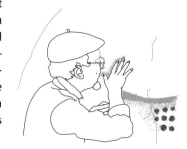

---

powers, an ability to foretell events and assist their people through contact with spirits in the form of animals or birds. Shamans typically make use of trance states, in which they believe they fly and receive communications from their spirit guides. The images they use to record their visions tend to be abstract, incorporating geometric figures and combinations of human and animal forms such as the bird-headed or masked man in this scene from Lascaux or the lion-headed figure discussed earlier (see fig. 1–2).

Early humans were skilled toolmakers. They built scaffolds in order to paint high on cave walls. They made stone pottery and lamps, and simple brushes. Evidence of perishable ropes, string, baskets, and nets exists. And they worked in clay.

Pottery cooking vessels, which first appeared in the Paleolithic period, also display the artistry of early humankind. Recent scientific dating methods have shown that Japanese potters made the oldest-known fired pottery vessels more than 12,000 years ago. The people of the Japanese Jomon culture who made the cooking pots, or *fukabachi*, decorated virtually all their ceramic **wares**, even utilitarian cooking vessels like this one (fig. **1–9**). They pressed slender ribs of clay onto the body of the pot in a diamond pattern, set off above and below with bands of horizontal grooves. The round base of the vessel was probably buried in sand to steady it when cooking food over an open fire. Beginning about 7500 BCE, potters decorated *fukabachi* with *jomon*, or marks of cords pressed into damp clay, a pottery style that gives the Jomon period its name.

Art in the Neolithic Period

Fundamental social and cultural changes mark the beginning of the Neolithic period. These include the development of organized agriculture, the maintenance of herds of domesticated animals (animal husbandry), and the foundation of year-round settlements. These shifts, which took place as the Ice Age ended, occurred in some regions earlier than others. The Neolithic period ended with the introduction of metalworking—the Bronze Age— around 3400 BCE in the Near East and about 2300 BCE in Europe.

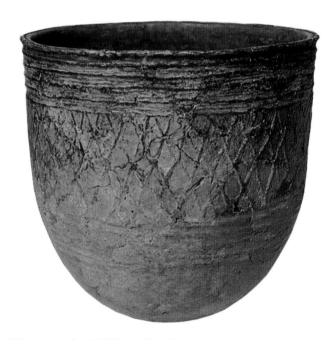

1–9 Jomon vessel, c. 10,000 BCE. Ceramic, reconstructed from sherds. Height 8⅝″ (21.9 cm); mouth diameter 9¼″ (23.5 cm). Yamato-shi Board of Education, Kanagawa-ken

Early Neolithic Communities

The world's first settled farming communities emerged in an area of the ancient Near East long referred to as the Fertile Crescent. Rising along the Mediterranean coast through modern Jordan, Israel, Lebanon, and Syria, this "crescent" arched into central Turkey and descended along the plains of Mesopotamia through Iraq and western Iran to the Persian Gulf. Agriculture first began in this region around 9000 BCE; farming villages formed nearly 4,000 years later.

One of the earliest Near Eastern cities, Jericho, located in the West Bank territory, was home to about 2,000 people by around 7000 BCE. Its collection of houses, made of mud brick

THE MEANING(S) OF PREHISTORIC PAINTINGS

Anthropologists and art historians have put forward countless theories to explain cave painting, often telling us as much about themselves and their times as about the art. Here are two early theories.

In the nineteenth century, the idea that human beings have an inherent desire to decorate themselves and their surroundings—an innate "aesthetic sense"—found ready acceptance. Some artists at the time promoted the idea of "art for art's sake," believing that people create works of art for the sheer love of beauty. However, the effort and organization required to accomplish the great paintings of Lascaux and elsewhere suggest that their creators were motivated by more than simple pleasure.

Early in the twentieth century, scholars rejected the idea of "art for art's sake" as a dated, romantic explanation. Led by Salomon Reinach, who believed that art fulfills a social function, they proposed that prehistoric cave paintings might be the end products of rites performed to enhance the fertility of the animals on which people depended for food. In 1903 Reinach proposed that cave paintings also were expressions of "sympathetic magic." He suggested that the painters may have thought that producing a picture of a bison lying down would ensure that hunters found their prey asleep, or that the symbolic killing of the picture of a bison would guarantee the hunters' triumph over the beast itself.

In the second half of the twentieth century, scholars tended to base their interpretations on rigorous scientific methods and current social theory. French scholars such as André Leroi-Gourhan and Annette Laming-Emperaire dismissed the "hunting magic" theory because debris from human settlements revealed that the animals used most frequently for food were not the ones traditionally portrayed in caves. These scholars discovered that cave images were often systematically organized, with different animals predominating in different areas of a cave. They concluded that cave images are meaningful pictures.

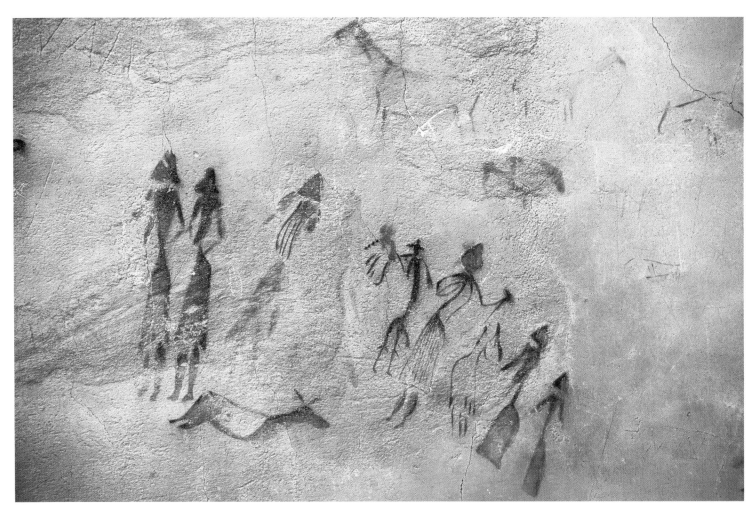

1–10 *People and Animals,* detail of a rock-shelter painting in Cogul Lérida, Spain. c. 4000–2000 BCE. Museo Arqueológico, Barcelona

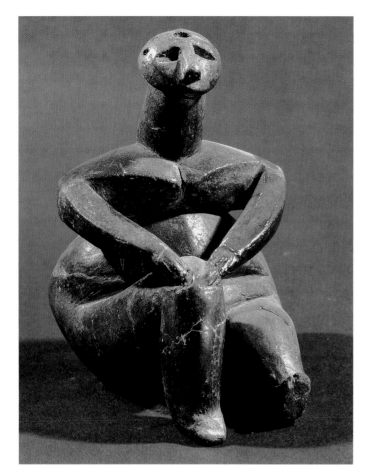
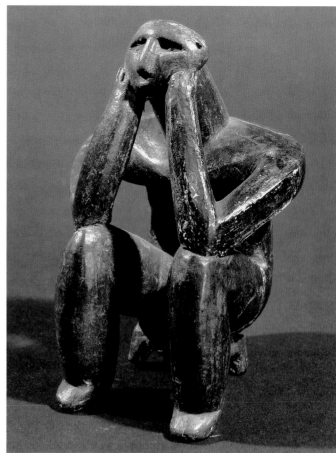

1–11 Woman and Man, Cernavoda, Romania. c. 3500 BCE. Ceramic, height 4¹/₂″ (11.5 cm). National Historical Museum, Bucharest

We can interpret the Cernavoda woman and man in many ways. Depending on how they are displayed, we spin out different stories about them. When placed facing each other we tend to see them as a couple—a woman and man in a relationship. In fact, we do not know what they meant to their makers or owners.

(bricks shaped from clay and dried in the sun), covered six acres, which is an enormous size for that time. Ain Ghazal (Spring of Gazelles), located just outside present-day Amman, Jordan, was even larger. This settlement, which lasted from about 7200–5000 BCE, occupied 30 acres on a slope that was shaped into terraces stabilized by stone retaining walls. Its houses may have resembled the adobe pueblos that native peoples in the southwestern United States began to build more than 7,000 years later (see fig. 15–21). The concentration of people and resources in cities such as Jericho and Ain Ghazal was an early step toward the formation of larger city-states that first arose in Mesopotamia and later became common throughout the ancient Near East.

Much of what we know of daily life comes from material remains of art and architecture. At Cogul, in the province of Lérida in Catalonia, the broad surfaces of a rock shelter are decorated with elaborate narrative scenes involving dozens of small figures—men, women, children, animals, and even insects (fig. **1–10**). The scenes date from between 4000 and 2000 BCE. No specific landscape features are indicated, but occasional painted patterns of animal tracks give the sense of a rocky terrain, like that of the surrounding barren hillsides. In the detail shown here, a number of women gracefully stroll or stand about, and some pairs hold hands. The women's small waists are emphasized by skirts with scalloped hemlines revealing large calves and sturdy ankles, and all the women appear to have shoulder-length hair.

These rock shelters contain so much information that it is tempting to imagine them as records of daily life. But like all early art, they probably served a greater social function. Perhaps they had an educational or religious use, for in some places the images were repainted many times. People were still coming to the sites in Roman times when, scribbling on the walls, they left **graffiti**.

In addition to working in stone, Neolithic artists commonly used clay. Their **ceramics**, or wares made of baked clay—whether vessels or figures of people and animals—display a high degree of technical skill and aesthetic imagination. To produce ceramic works, artists had to add certain substances to the clay—bone ash was a common additive—and then subject the objects formed of that mixture to high heat for a period of time, thus hardening them and creating an entirely new material. Among the ceramic figures discovered at a pottery-production center in the Danube River valley at Cernavoda, Romania, are a seated man and woman (fig. **1–11**). The artist who made them shaped their bodies out of simple cylinders of clay but managed to pose them in ways that make them seem very true to life.

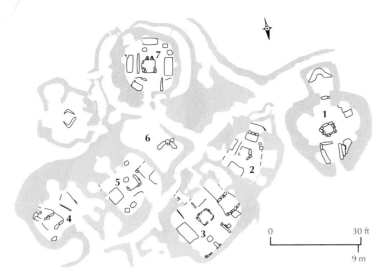

1–12 Plan, village of Skara Brae, Orkney Islands, Scotland. c. 3100 BCE. (Numbers refer to individual houses.)

Architecture

As people adopted a settled, agricultural way of life, they began to build walls, storage spaces, and animal shelters. In Europe, timber became abundant after the retreat of the glaciers, and Neolithic people, like their Paleolithic predecessors, used wood and other plant materials that leave only traces, such as post holes, in the earth. People clustered their dwellings in villages, and they built large tombs and ritual centers outside their settlements. Luckily for us, where timber was scarce, they had to use stone.

A Neolithic settlement preserved in the sea sands at Skara Brae, on the Orkney Islands off the northern coast of Scotland, gives a vivid picture of an early village (fig. **1–12**). The excavated village (occupied 3100–2600 BCE) consists of a compact cluster of stone dwellings linked together by covered passageways. The largest house measures 20 × 21 feet, the smallest 13 × 14 feet. Layers of flat stones without mortar form walls, with each layer, or **course**, projecting slightly inward over the one below. This type of construction is called **corbelling**. At Skara Brae the walls stopped short of meeting, and the remaining open space was covered with a roof of hides or turf. The interiors, such as the one shown (fig. **1–13**), were equipped with space-saving, built-in furniture. Rectangular stone beds, some of them engraved with simple markings, flank the walls on either side of the large rectangular hearth. These boxlike beds would probably have been filled with heather "mattresses" and covered with warm furs. On the back wall is a sizable storage niche and a two-shelf cabinet erected using **post-and-lintel construction**. In this building system, two or more vertical elements (posts) are used to support a bridging horizontal one (**lintel**). The structural principle has been used throughout history, whether for simple framing elements like these shelves or for huge stone monuments such as Stonehenge and the temples of ancient Egypt (Chapter 2) and Greece (Chapter 4).

Megalithic Architecture

Massive tombs and monuments built from huge stones first appeared in the Neolithic period, when human societies became

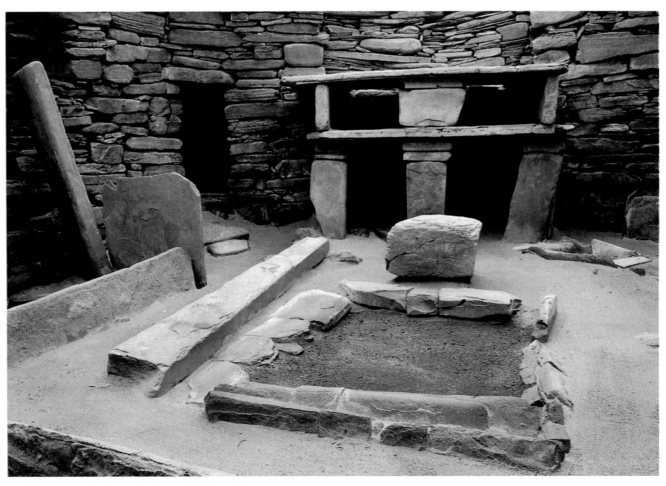

1–13 House interior, Skara Brae (house 7 in fig. 1–12)

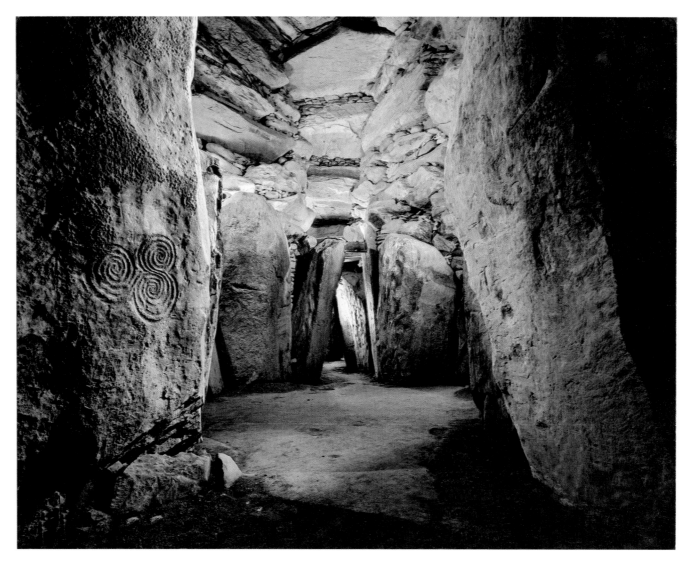

1–14 Tomb interior with engraved stones, Newgrange, Ireland. c. 3000–2500 BCE

more stratified and complex. These structures are known as megalithic architecture, after the Greek terms *megas* for "large" and *lithos* for "stone." Their construction required not only laborers to transport the giant boulders, but also people to devise methods to shape and align the stones. These skilled workers could be considered the predecessors of artists and engineers. In addition to a coordinated workforce to build such edifices, megalithic structures also required powerful political and religious leaders to dictate a society's need for them.

Many megalithic tombs are preserved in Europe, where they were used for both single and multiple burials. In the simplest type, the **dolmen**, a tomb chamber was formed of huge upright stones supporting one or more tablelike rocks, or **capstones**. Smaller rocks and dirt were mounded on top of the chamber to form an artificial hill called a **cairn**. A cairn is any pile of stones that forms a memorial or landmark.

Elaborate burial sites called **passage graves** had one or more corridors leading into a large burial chamber. Many still command the landscape in Ireland and elsewhere. At Newgrange in Ireland a huge complex was constructed about 3000–2500 BCE (fig. **1–14**). Rings, spirals, diamond shapes, and other **linear** designs were engraved on the stones at its entrance and along its entrance passageway. These patterns must have been marked out using strings or compasses, and then carved by pecking at the rock surface with

tools made of antlers and hard stones. A cairn that measured about 280 feet in diameter concealed a chamber with alcoves and a passage. The ritual purpose of Newgrange is still a mystery; however, some powerful solar symbolism must have played a part. The builders oriented the passage to the rising sun in midsummer, at which time the sun shines through a semi-concealed opening down the length of the passage to the tomb chamber and falls on a shallow, scooped out, platter-like stone.

Besides tombs, Neolithic and post-Neolithic cultures built megalithic monuments and sculptures for ritual purposes that are still not fully understood by today's scholars. The best-known of these megalithic constructions, and another solar structure, is Stonehenge in southern England (figs. **1–15** and **1–16**). A *henge* is a circle formed by stones or wooden posts, often surrounded by a ditch with built-up embankments. While Stonehenge is not the largest such circle from the Neolithic period, it is the most complex. Reworked over at least four major building phases between about 2750 and 1500 BCE, Stonehenge must have had extraordinary social and symbolic importance in its region.

The main elements of Stonehenge are illustrated in the accompanying aerial photograph and diagram. The earliest circle was a ditch with a 6-foot embankment, about 330 feet in diameter, with a surrounding circle of white chalk marks in the earth. A single 35-ton sarsen (sandstone) megalith, known today as the

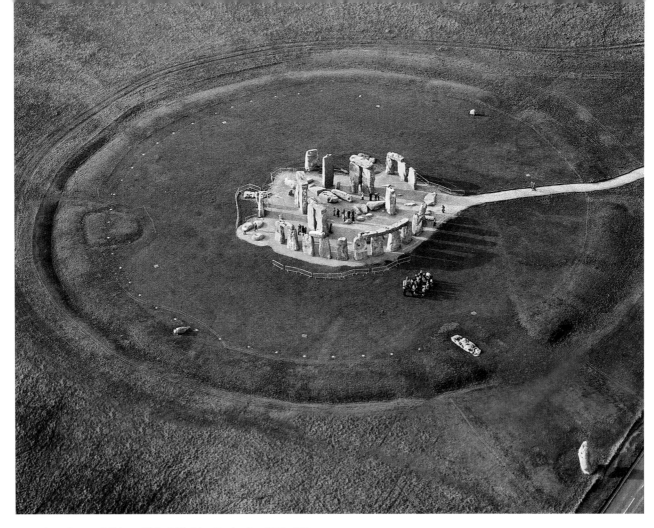

1–15 Stonehenge, Salisbury Plain, Wiltshire, England. c. 2750–1500 BCE

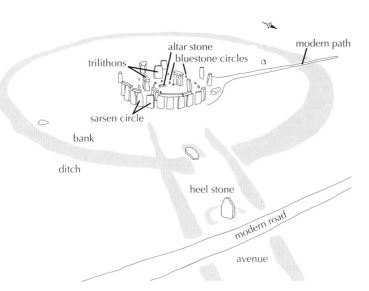

1–16 Diagram of Stonehenge showing elements discussed in text

Heel Stone, was moved from quarries 23 miles away and placed outside the circles. Later generations added a more complex structure. They built a ring of gray sarsen uprights about 20 feet tall and topped by a continuous lintel. Inside the sarsen circle they placed a ring of smaller bluestones, made of a bluish dolerite that they transported from Welsh quarries 150 miles away. These circles surround a horseshoe-shaped arrangement of five trilithons, or pairs of stones topped by lintels (three stones in total), and a second horseshoe of bluestones. The largest of the trilithons stood 24 feet high. At the very center of this complex lies the so-called "altar stone." The actual role of this stone is unknown; designating it as an **altar**, which has religious connotations, is a modern presumption. We have seen the problems modern labels or titles can present as discussed in "The Power of Naming," page 26. The opening of the horseshoe focuses on the Heel Stone, which stands outside the henge to the northeast and connects to the opening by a causeway.

One aspect of this megalithic monument more than any other has captured the public's imagination. Anyone standing at the exact center of Stonehenge on the morning of the summer solstice 4,000 years ago would have seen the sun rise directly over the Heel Stone. The midsummer sunrise still inspires hundreds of people to gather at Stonehenge. Given the relationship between the monument's orientation and the sun, some scholars think Stonehenge may have been a kind of observatory that helped astronomers to track cosmic events. Aside from its possible astronomical significance, anthropologists suspect that Stonehenge was an important site for major public ceremonies, possibly planting or harvest rituals.

Bronze and Iron Ages in Europe

Neolithic culture persisted in northern Europe until about 2300–2000 BCE. Metals had made their appearance about 2300 BCE, although gold and copper had been used in southern Europe and the Near East much earlier. The period that follows the introduction of metalworking is commonly called the Bronze Age.

A remarkable sculpture found in Denmark depicts a horse pulling a wheeled cart laden with a large, upright disk, thought to represent the sun (fig. 1–17). A widespread sun cult seems to have existed in the north, as our discussion of Stonehenge suggests. The horse, with its gleaming load, could have been rolled from place to place in a ritual reenactment of the sun's passage across the sky.

The *Horse and Sun-Chariot* dates from between 1800 and 1600 BCE. The valuable materials from which the sculpture was made attest to its importance. The horse, cart, and disk were cast in bronze and delicately engraved with an abstract design of concentric rings, zigzags, circles, spirals, and loops. A thin sheet of beaten gold was then applied to the bronze disk and pressed into the **incised** patterns. The continuous and curvilinear patterns suggest the movement of the sun itself.

By 1000 BCE, iron technology had spread across Europe, although bronze remained the preferred material for luxury goods. Cheaper and more readily available than other metals, iron was most commonly used for practical items. The blacksmiths who forged the warriors' swords and the farmers' plowshares held a privileged position among artisans, for they practiced a craft that seemed akin to magic as they transformed iron by heat and hammer work into tools. A hierarchy of metals emerged based on each material's resistance to corrosion: Gold, the most permanent and precious metal, ranked first, followed by silver, bronze, and finally practical but rusty iron.

Early Art Outside Europe

Neolithic art was not limited to Europe and the Near East. Painting on rock faces survives in many places around the world, including Africa, Australia, and North America. In Australia, the hunter-gatherer ancestors of today's Aborigines practiced both rock painting and rock engraving (pecking designs into rock with stone tools). They sometimes returned to a single location over many centuries to renew a fading painting or add new images, and the ritual of making the painting may have been more important than the finished work. An ornately decorated rock surface located on the northern coast of Australia in Oenpelli, Arnhem Land, contains two superimposed compositions (fig. 1–18). The first, painted around 16,000–7000 BCE, shows the skinny, sticklike humans that later Aborigines believed had been painted by *Mimis* (ancestral spirits). Long after this imagery was abandoned, the figures were painted over with a kangaroo image in the so-called **x-ray style**, in which the bones and internal organs are drawn inside the silhouetted outline of the animal. Bark painters in Australia today still use the x-ray style.

In North America people also engraved and painted on rock faces. In the Southwest they drew images by scraping through the **desert varnish**, a substance that turned cliff faces into dark glistening surfaces. The Colorado Plateau (extending over parts of Colorado, New Mexico, Utah, and Arizona) has hundreds of images. Created by the "old ones," the Anasazi, as well as later people, they consist of geometric figures, humans, and animals—represented singly and in huge multifigured murals. In the Barrier

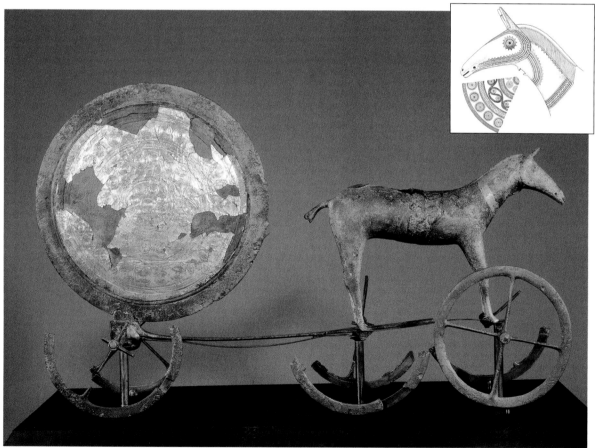

1–17 *Horse and Sun-Chariot* from Trundholm, Zealand, Denmark. c. 1800–1600 BCE. Bronze and gold, length 23 1/4″ (59.2 cm). National Museum Copenhagen. (Insert is a drawing of incised designs.)

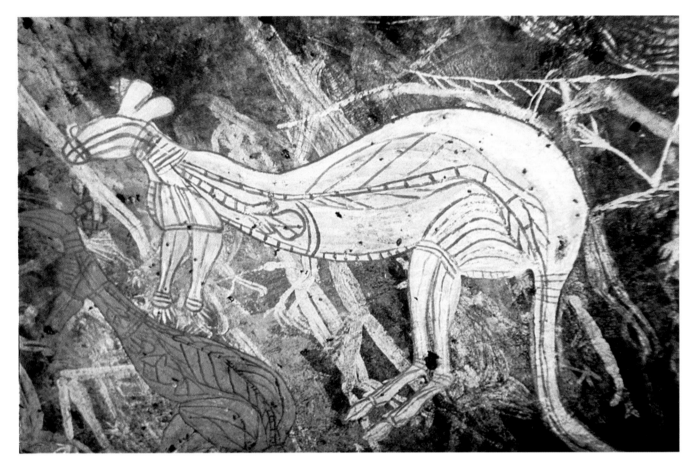

1–18 *Mimis and Kangaroo,* prehistoric rock art, Oenpelli, Arnhem Land, Australia. Older painting 16,000–7000 BCE. Red and yellow ocher and white pipe clay

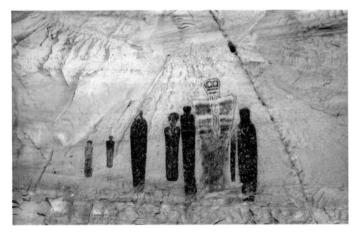

1–19 Anthromorphs, The Great Gallery, Horseshoe Canyon, Utah

The figures may represent shamans and are often associated with snakes, dogs, and other small energetic creatures. Big-eyed anthromorphs may be rain gods. Painters used their fingers and yucca-fiber brushes to apply the reddish pigment made from hematite (iron oxide).

Canyon Style, found at more than 100 sites in Utah and nearby Arizona and Colorado, human figures (called anthromorphs) have long decorated rectangular bodies and knob-like heads. The largest figures are nearly eight feet tall. The tall (fig. **1–19**) wide-eyed figure, popularly known as the "Holy Ghost," is one of 80 anthromorphs found in Horseshoe Canyon's "Great Gallery." Archaeologists have dated the paintings as early as 1900 BCE and as late as 300 CE, but a few scholars now claim that these paintings may be as early as 5400 or even 7500 BCE. The study of the early inhabitants of the Americas is filled with lively debates.

It is so tempting to see history, and art history, as a series of cumulative developments. This perspective goes hand in hand with the notion that human beings have always striven toward progressively more perfect expressions of their artistic and cultural values. Yet there is much evidence to the contrary. Around the globe, significant cultural transitions have often occurred at the same time in geographically unrelated and unconnected places, and conversely, some changes or discoveries have happened in different places at very different times. History does not unfold in neatly packaged categories, and nowhere is the notion of systematic human progress shakier than when dealing with prehistoric periods and cultures. In fact, given how little we know about early art and architecture, we must be prepared to continually revise our theories and update our ideas as new evidence comes to light.

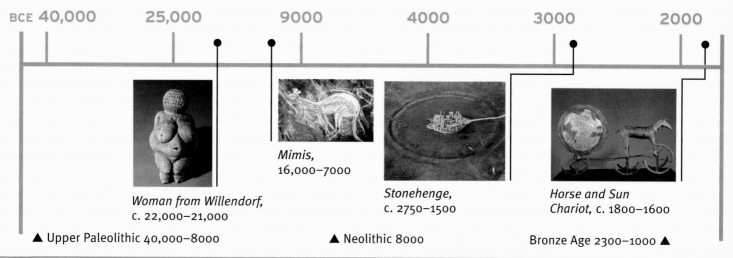

Mimis,
16,000–7000

Woman from Willendorf,
c. 22,000–21,000

Stonehenge,
c. 2750–1500

Horse and Sun
Chariot, c. 1800–1600

▲ Upper Paleolithic 40,000–8000   ▲ Neolithic 8000   Bronze Age 2300–1000 ▲

LOOKING BACK

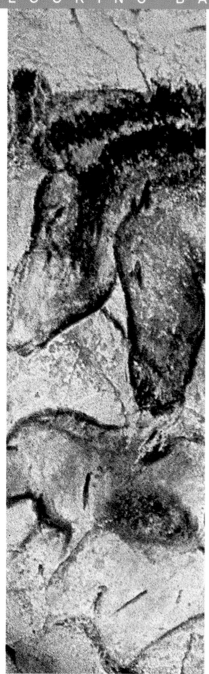

Long before men and women communicated through writing, they made images and objects. Sculpture began as a skillful flaking and chipping of flint tools and later developed into the decoration of bone and horn implements with simple patterns of engraved lines. As early as 30,000 BCE, small figures of people and animals made of bone, ivory, stone, and clay appear in Europe and Asia. Between about 28,000 and 10,000 BCE, many images of animals, geometric figures, and human hands were painted on the walls of caves. In cave paintings in Lascaux (in southwestern France) and Altamira (in northern Spain), artists also created three-dimensional effects using the natural formations of the cave walls. These prehistoric drawn, painted, and engraved images are remarkable for their realism and, when painted, for their rich colors. In the later Neolithic period, the art becomes more abstract, and the technique is often simple line drawing; artists represent people, not only animals, in energetic poses, whether engaged in battle, hunting, or possibly even dancing. These various groups of oldest-known artists were not simply decorating cave walls or applying ornament to utensils in the sense that we use the words *decorating* and *ornament*. They must have believed that what they were doing was essential to their very existence and that of their fellow humans.

An aesthetic sense and the ability to pose and solve problems are among the characteristics unique to human beings. That these characteristics were richly developed in very early times is evident from artifacts of many kinds. Humans have always found ingenious ways of providing themselves with shelter, and constructing even a simple shelter requires a degree of imagination and planning. As people adopted a settled, agricultural way of life, they began to build large structures clustered in villages to serve as dwellings, storage spaces, and shelters for their animals. Eventually, people built large tombs and ritual centers outside their settlements. As we stand awestruck in front of Stonehenge in England, for example, we wonder how human beings could have imagined, and then achieved, such a creation. The builders had to overcome enormous obstacles to move special stones to create and expand this solar structure. But these Neolithic farmers, whose well-being depended on a recurring cycle of sowing, growing, harvesting, and fallow seasons, had compelling reasons to worship the sun and do all they could to assure its regular motion through the year.

Stone Age culture persisted in Northern Europe until about 2000 BCE, until the time when the use of metals makes its appearance. In Southern Europe—especially the Aegean region—copper, gold, and tin had been mined, worked, and traded even earlier than this. The period that follows the introduction of metalworking is commonly called the Bronze Age, after the exquisite objects made of bronze that are frequently found in the settlements and graves of that time.

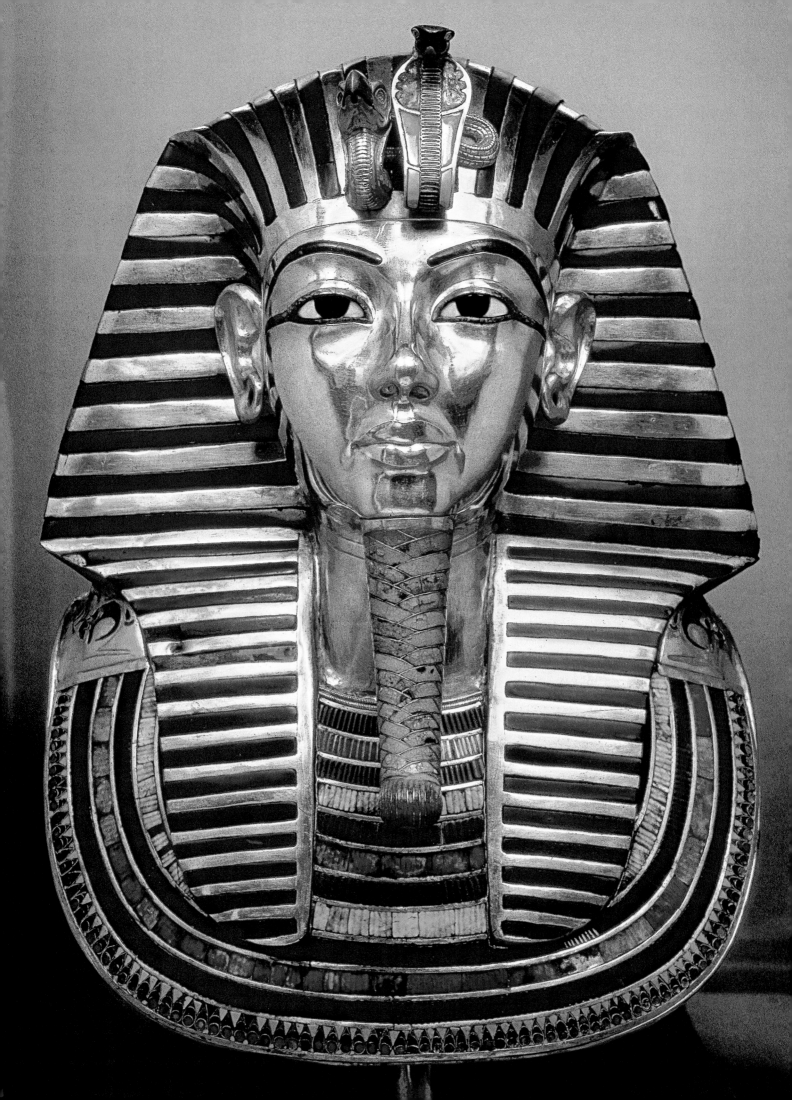

2
The Art
of Mesopotamia
and Egypt

Staring serenely, the funerary mask of the young Egyptian ruler Tutankhamun dazzles us with its royal splendor (fig. 2–1). The British archaeologist Howard Carter's dramatic discovery of the king's tomb in 1922 established the "romance of archaeology" in the public mind. Now the more than 3,500 items from Tutankhamun's tomb are the centerpiece of the Egyptian Museum in Cairo.

Why are we so mesmerized by the art of Egypt? It may be simply the elegant style and exquisite craftsmanship of Egyptian art. Or the reason may lie in our fascination with ancient people's struggle to create an explanation for the transition between life and death and their belief in an eternal hereafter.

As fragile humans, we observe nature's continuous cycle of birth, death, and rebirth, and we come to realize that for all our ingenuity, we cannot escape death. Yet our imaginations recoil at the idea of our own extinction. Through the centuries people have lived with the hope or expectation of a life after death. Ancient Egyptians, from their narrow river valley, observed the constant regeneration of the land through yearly floods. They could easily believe that such regeneration would be granted to human beings, or at least to their rulers, who became gods on earth. Ancient Egyptians thought of the afterlife as a continuation of the life they knew. Thus they made elaborate efforts to preserve their bodies forever, and through the arts, they equipped the dead magnificently for life in the hereafter.

The enchantment of Egyptian art is aesthetic, too. Look into Tutankhamun's eyes. They are beautifully formed, simple shapes. Black discs set in white, they are energized by tiny touches of red at the corners, yet their dark outline lacks the natural detail of lashes. Capturing fleeting moments like the fluttering of lashes during the blink of an eye was of little interest to a people concerned with timeless and eternal visions. By emphasizing clarity of line and color, simplified forms, and the reduction of nature to elemental geometric shapes, ancient Egyptian artists established an unsurpassed standard of technical and aesthetic excellence.

2–1 Funerary mask of Tutankhamun, (ruled 1336/35–1327 BCE). Gold inlaid with glass and semiprecious stones, height 21 $\frac{1}{4}$" (54 cm). Egyptian Museum, Cairo

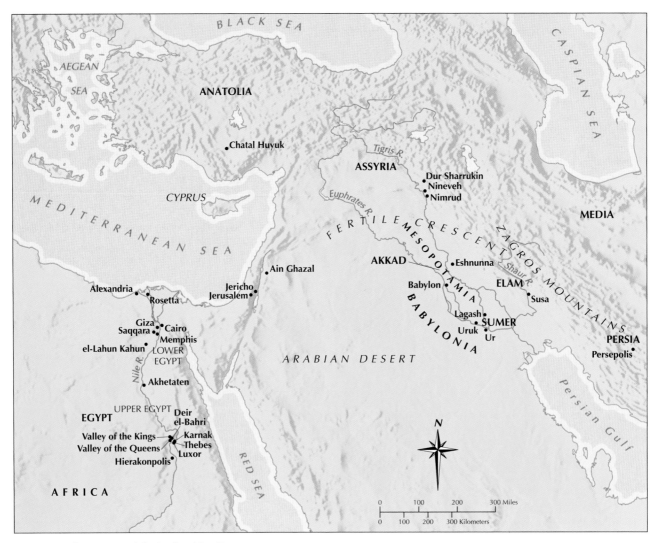

Map 2–1 Ancient Egypt and the Ancient Near East

Earth's great river valleys nourished and united people: Water and waterways made agriculture and a settled way of life possible. The Tigris and Euphrates in Mesopotamia (which means "between the rivers") and the Nile in Egypt—and, as we shall see, the Indus and the Huang He in Asia, the Danube in Europe, and the Mississippi in North America—were among the most important waterways. Rivers also formed transportation corridors linking farmers along the banks (see Map 2–1, above).

More than 5,000 years ago, men and women in the Near East and Egypt laid the foundations for western civilization. Political and religious hierarchies evolved as people banded together in community projects: digging irrigation and drainage ditches, planting and reaping crops, storing and distributing the harvest. The families and clans that had come together in communities eventually created cities, places known today by such fabled names as Jericho and Babylon, Memphis and Thebes. By about 3500 BCE, rulers, priests, and laborers—and eventually artists—lived and worked together in cities in the service of the community and of the gods. Artists and artisans produced weavings, ceramics, **monumental** sculpture, and statuettes. Around 3000 BCE, another important breakthrough occurred in the Near East: Sumerian artists became expert metalworkers. They created bronze, a hard, strong alloy of tin and copper. The Mesopotamian Bronze Age replaced the Stone Age about a thousand years before this development occurred in northern Europe (see fig. 1–17).

In some ways, life in Mesopotamia and Egypt followed similar courses. In both places, agriculture became the basis of wealth. Community leaders consolidated their power until kingship became the dominant form of government. Religion played a central role in both government and daily life. People worshiped many gods, each of whom had distinct powers and features. Rulers often identified closely with the gods, sometimes through symbolic marriage to a god or goddess. The responsibilities of rulers included ceremonial as well as political duties. The priests who honored and communicated with the gods joined the rulers to mediate between these deities and the people. Some individuals, freed from the necessity of daily work in the fields, became administrative assistants to these intermediaries, and eventually people settled into stratified social groups.

Such complex, hierarchical societies could no longer depend on oral communication. People needed records, and this led to the development of writing—first, simple **pictographs** and then a complex standardized system of **hieroglyphic** or **cuneiform** signs. Today these records, and the history and literature that were soon recorded, help us interpret the visual arts produced at that time.

In other ways life and culture in Mesopotamia and Egypt differed. Mesopotamia's wealth and agricultural resources, as well as its few natural defenses, made its people vulnerable to repeated invasions and to internal conflicts. Over the centuries the balance of power in Mesopotamia shifted between north and south and

ORIGINS OF WRITING

The Sumerians developed the first known system of writing when they created records on clay tablets in the late third millennium BCE. The earliest preserved tablets, dating to around 3300 BCE, record an accounting system for products traded at the city of Uruk. The symbols, which were drawn in wet clay with a pointed tool, are simple pictures, or **pictographs**, that each represent a thing or concept. The head of a bull, for example, means "bull." Between 2900 and 2400 BCE, the symbols evolved from pictures into phonograms—representations of the sounds of syllables in the Sumerian language—thus becoming a true writing system. During the same centuries, scribes (specialists in writing and maintaining records) developed a writing instrument called a **stylus**, shaped like a triangular wedge. Mesopotamian writing is termed **cuneiform** (from the Latin "wedge-shaped") after the shape of the marks made by the stylus.

Ancient Egypt developed three types of writing. The earliest system employed symbols called **hieroglyphs**. Like cuneiform, these were either pictographs or phono- grams. Later, scribes evolved **hieratic** writing, a shorthand version of hieroglyphs. The simplified forms, used for record keeping, correspondence, and manuscripts of all sorts, could be written quickly in script on scrolls made of papyrus (a plant that grew along the Nile). The third type of Egyptian writing came into use only in the eighth century BCE, as written communication ceased to be restricted exclusively to priests and scribes. It was less formal and easier to master; the Greeks referred to it as demotic writing (from *demos*, "the people").

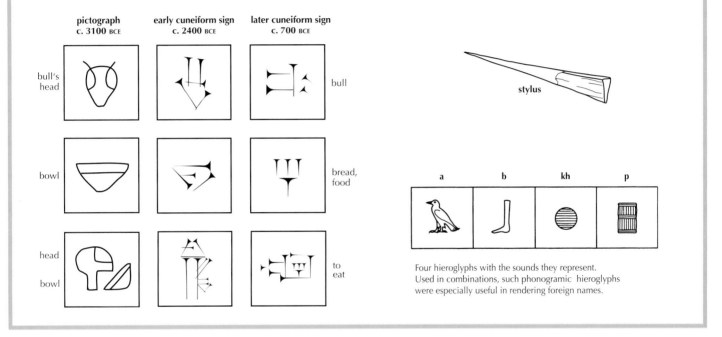

Four hieroglyphs with the sounds they represent. Used in combinations, such phonogramic hieroglyphs were especially useful in rendering foreign names.

between local powers and outside invaders. The rise and fall of cities such as Babylon, Nineveh, and Ur left behind a varied and rich concentration of archaeological remains. Mesopotamian art and architecture continued to be based on the earliest Sumerian traditions, but changed subtly with each successive culture.

In contrast, mountains and deserts protected the Nile Valley. With only a few interruptions, ancient Egypt remained a unified state for some 3,000 years. This cohesion made possible an unprecedented continuity in artistic and cultural development. Strikingly, Egypt's resources were directed toward the decoration and outfitting of tombs, and much of what we know about ancient Egypt today we owe to the survival of its funerary art.

Mesopotamia

The prosperous Mesopotamian cities and their surrounding territories developed around 3500 BCE into independently governed city-states. Eventually the most powerful city-states absorbed their neighbors to form larger kingdoms and empires. One powerful cluster of cities in the southern region was known collectively as Sumer. The Sumerians have been credited with many "firsts": inventing the wagon wheel and the plow, casting objects in copper and bronze, and—perhaps their greatest contribution to later civilizations—inventing a system of writing, known as cuneiform script, between 3300 and 3000 BCE (see "Origins of Writing," above).

In architecture, the Sumerians' most imposing buildings were **ziggurats**, stepped pyramidal structures with a temple or shrine on top. Towering over the flat plains, ziggurats proclaimed the wealth, prestige, and stability of a city's rulers and glorified its gods. The peoples of the ancient Near East were polytheistic; they worshiped many gods and goddesses, attributing to them power over human activities and the forces of nature. Each city had one special protective deity for whom the people worked and from whom they received benefits. Religious specialists, eventually developing into a priest class, controlled rituals and sacred sites, ensuring that the gods were honored properly.

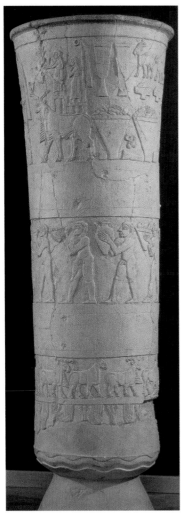
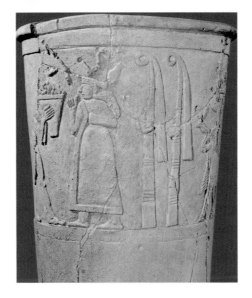
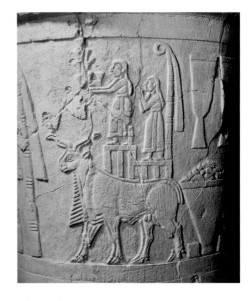

2–2 Carved vase (with two details), from Uruk (modern Warka, Iraq). c. 3500–3000 BCE. Alabaster, height 36″ (91 cm). Iraq Museum, Baghdad

Temple complexes—clusters of religious, administrative, and service buildings—stood in each city's center.

Two large temple complexes at Uruk (modern Warka, Iraq) mark the first independent Sumerian city-state. One complex was dedicated to Inanna, the goddess of fertility; the other probably to the sky god Anu. A tall vase of carved alabaster (a fine, white stone), found near Inanna's temple, shows her accepting an offering from a naked priest (fig. **2–2**). Inanna stands in front of her shrine, indicated by two reed door-poles. Through the doorway her wealth is displayed, and behind the priest come others bearing offerings. Plants and animals in horizontal bands decorate the base of the vase. Medical historians have identified the plants as the pomegranate and the now-extinct silphium, plants used by early people as fertility symbols and to control fertility. The scene is usually interpreted as the ritual marriage between the goddess and a human to ensure the fertility of crops, animals, and people, and thus the continued survival of Uruk.

The Anu Ziggurat, built up in stages over the centuries, ultimately rose to a height of about 40 feet. Around 3100 BCE, the people of Uruk built a temple of whitewashed brick on its top. Modern archaeologists call it the White Temple (fig. **2–3**).

The ziggurat reached its final form (about a thousand years after the completion of the White Temple) in Ur, a city on the Euphrates south of Uruk. The people of Ur built a mud-brick ziggurat dedicated to the moon god Nanna, also called Sin (fig. **2–4**). Here three staircases converge at an imposing entrance gate atop the first platform. Each platform is angled outward from top to base, probably to prevent rainwater from forming puddles and eroding the pavement. The first two levels of the Nanna Ziggurat and their retaining walls were reconstructed in recent times, and little remains of the upper level and the temple. Such temples were known as "the offering table of heaven" and "the waiting room of the gods," but we know nothing of the rituals performed in them.

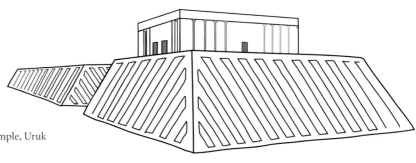

2–3 Reconstruction drawing of the Anu Ziggurat and White Temple, Uruk (modern Warka, Iraq). c. 3100 BCE

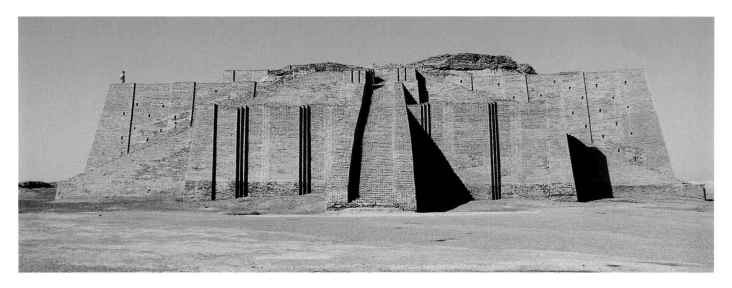

2–4 Nanna Ziggurat, Ur (modern Muqaiyir, Iraq). c. 2100–2050 BCE

Sculpture during this period was associated with religion, and large statues were commonly placed in temples as objects of devotion. In addition, individual worshipers set up **votive** figures, small statues that they sometimes identified as portraits of themselves. Apparently anyone who could afford to might commission a votive figure and place it in the god's shrine. A simple inscription might identify the figure as "one who offers prayers." Larger inscriptions might recount all the things accomplished in the god's honor.

Marble votive statues dating from about 2900–2600 BCE (fig. **2–5**) were found in the ruins of a temple at Eshnunna (modern Tell Asmar, Iraq). The carvers, following the conventions of Sumerian art—that is, the traditional ways of represent-

ing forms—simplified the faces, bodies, and dress to emphasize the cylindrical forms of the figures. The men in this group wear sheepskin kilts, while the tall female figure to the right of center wears a dress wrapped diagonally to expose one breast. Some of the figures hold small vessels, probably similar to those that visitors used during ritual activities. The votive figures stand at respectful attention for all eternity, and their wide, staring eyes indicate communication between them and the god of the temple.

The artists of Ur became accomplished in many arts: music, oral storytelling (which later became literature), work in precious materials, as well as stone sculpture and architecture. A superb example of their skill is a lyre—a kind of harp—from a royal tomb

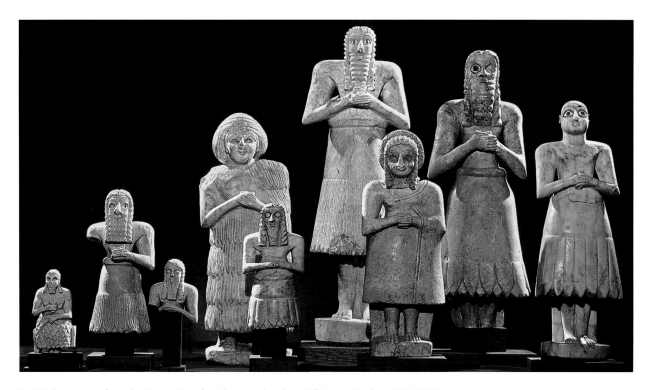

2–5 Votive statues from the Square Temple, Eshnunna (modern Tell Asmar, Iraq). c. 2900–2600 BCE. Limestone, alabaster, and gypsum, height of largest figure approx. 30″ (76.3 cm). The Oriental Institute of the University of Chicago; Iraq Museum, Baghdad

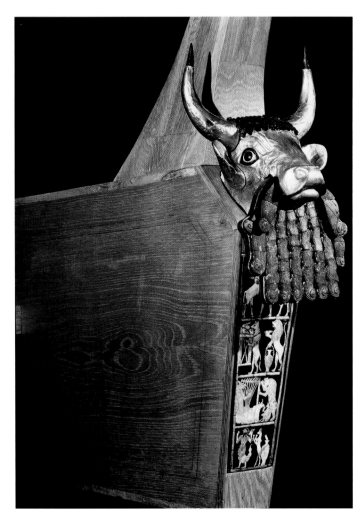

of Ur (c. 2550–2400 BCE), which combines wood, gold, lapis lazuli imported from Afghanistan, and shell (fig. **2–6**). Archaeologists have restored the lost wooden parts of the lyre and reassembled the surviving pieces. On one end of the sound box, surmounting the inlaid shell images of animals (fig. 2–8; see "Closer Look," page 43), sits the head of a magnificent bearded bull created out of gold and the semiprecious gemstone lapis lazuli.

In addition to inventing cuneiform writing, Sumerian temple staff and merchants developed flat stamps and more elaborate **cylinder seals** to secure and identify documents and signify property ownership. Cylinder seals, usually less than 2 inches high, were made of hard and sometimes semiprecious stones with designs **incised** (cut) into the surface. Rolled across a damp clay surface, the seal leaves a mirror image of its design that cannot easily be altered once dry. The seals were used for signing documents or for marking container lids or storage-room doorways. The distinctive design on the stone cylinder seal shown in figure **2–7** belonged only to its owner, like a coat of arms in the European Middle Ages or a modern cattle-rancher's brand. When rolled across soft clay applied to the closure to be sealed—a jar lid, the knot securing a bundle, or the door to a room—the cylinder left a raised image or a band of repeated raised images of the design. Sealing discouraged unauthorized people from secretly gaining access to goods or information.

Animal and human combats such as this one remind us that kings were expected to protect their people from both human and animal enemies. Kings also intervened with the gods to exert control over the natural world. The Akkadians, warring invaders who settled the area north of Uruk near modern Baghdad, are an example of such a hostile group. Unlike the Sumerians, the Akkadians spoke a Semitic language (a language in the same family as Arabic and Hebrew). Under the powerful military and political figure Sargon I (ruled

2–6 Bull lyre, from the tomb of King Meskalamdug, Ur (modern Muqaiyir, Iraq). c. 2500–2400 BCE. Wood with gold, silver, lapis lazuli, bitumen, and shell, reassembled in modern wood support; height of plaque 13″ (33 cm); maximum length of lyre 55½″ (140 cm); height of upright backarm 46½″ (117 cm). University of Pennsylvania Museum of Archeology and Anthropology, Philadelphia

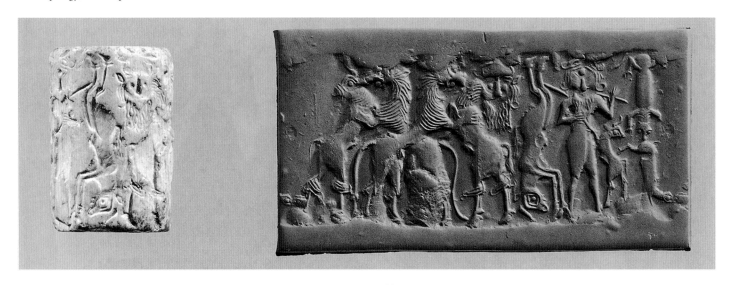

2–7 Cylinder seal from Sumer and its impression. c. 2500 BCE. Marble, height approx. 1¾″ (4.5 cm). The Metropolitan Museum of Art, New York

The scene in figure 2–7 includes rearing lions fighting with a human-headed bull and a stag on the left, and a hunter on the right-perhaps a spoils-of-the-hunt depiction or an example of the Near Eastern practice of showing leaders protecting their people from both human and animal enemies as well as exerting control over the natural world. This stele probably came originally from Sippar, an Akkadian city on the Euphrates River, in what is now Iraq. It was not discovered at Sippar, however, but at the Elamite city of Susa (modern Shush, Iran), some 300 miles to the southeast. Raiders from Elam presumable took it there as booty in the twelfth century BCE.

GIFT OF WALTER HAUSER, 1955 (55.65.4)

As in the animal fables of the legendary Greek author Aesop, the animals in the panels that decorate a very early (c. 2680 BCE) harp from Sumer (fig. **2–8**) personify humans: A donkey, assisted by a bear, plays the harp, accompanied by a fox with a rattle; a lion and a wolf, imitating the upright posture of humans, march in stately procession carrying offerings. The top and bottom registers, or bands, are particularly intriguing because they seem to illustrate scenes found in the *Epic of Gilgamesh*, a 3,000-line epic poem that is Sumer's great contribution to world literature. What is especially interesting is that the poem was first written down nearly 700 years after the harp was decorated, suggesting a very long oral tradition. In the *Epic of Gilgamesh*, the hero, Gilgamesh, undertakes a voyage to the netherworld, the Land of No Return, and declares it a bad place. In the depths of the ocean, Gilgamesh encounters scorpionmen, like the one pictured in the lowest register of figure 2–8. Gilgamesh's story probes the question of immortality and expresses the heroic aim to understand hostile surroundings and the longing to find meaning in human existence.

Notice that the almost-human, bearded figure in the top register of the panel masterfully controls two rearing human-headed bulls—a recurring theme in art of the ancient Near East. So vivid were the imagined hybrid ancestors' strange adventures with fabulous friends and adversaries that early Mesopotamians actually thought they might have to confront these composite creatures during their lifetime. (Other early civilizations also had human-animal composite power figures: sphinxes in Egypt; human-headed bulls and lions in Akkadia, Babylonia, and Assyria; and cat-faced humans in Japan, to name three.) We can analyze the **iconography**, or imagery, of Sumerian works of art with some confidence; thanks to the inscribed clay tablets and decorated seals found at Sumer, we are no longer dealing with the speculations of prehistory.

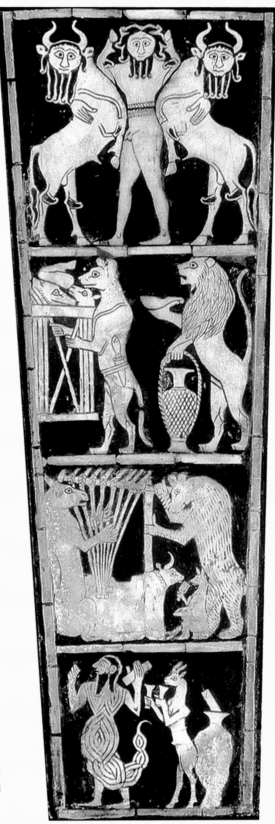

2–8 Mythological figures, detail of the sound box of the bull lyre from the tomb of King Meskalamdug, Ur (modern Muqaiyir, Iraq). c. 2500–2400 BCE. Wood with shell inlay, $12\frac{1}{4}''$ × $4\frac{1}{4}''$ (31.1 × 11 cm). University of Pennsylvania Museum of Archeology and Anthropology, Philadelphia

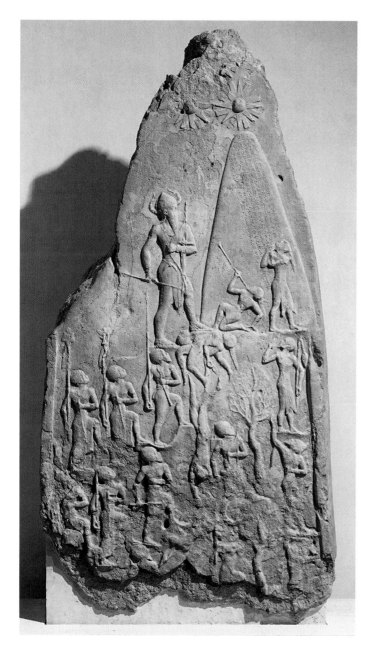

2–9 *Stele of Naramsin,* c. 2254–2218 BCE. Limestone, height 6′ 6″ (1.98 m). Musée du Louvre, Paris

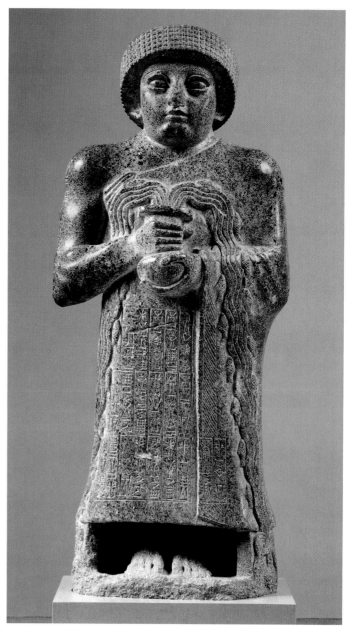

2–10 Votive statue of Gudea, from Lagash (modern Telloh, Iraq). c. 2120 BCE. Diorite, height 29″ (73.7 cm). Musée du Louvre, Paris

c. 2332–2279 BCE), they conquered the Sumerian cities and brought most of Mesopotamia under their control. Sargon I even elevated himself to the status of a god, setting a precedent followed by later Akkadian rulers. Soon after, the Akkadians adopted Sumerian culture.

The *Stele of Naramsin,* from about 2254–2218 BCE (fig. **2–9**), commemorates a military victory of Naramsin, Sargon's grandson and successor. The king, wearing the horned crown associated with deities, stands above his soldiers and fallen foes near the top of the stone. The shape of the **stele** (upright stone slab) is used as a dynamic part of the composition. Its pointed shape accommodates the carved mountain within it. Naramsin is also larger than the other figures. In the art of many peoples, greater

size is an indication of greater relative importance. Art historians call this convention **hieratic scale.**

The Akkadian Empire fell around 2180 BCE to the Guti, a mountain people from the northeast. For a brief time the Guti controlled most of the Mesopotamian plain, except for the city-state of Lagash, which remained independent under its ruler, Gudea. The tradition of votive statues continued in the art of Lagash. About 2100 BCE, Gudea presented votive statues of himself, made of a hard, durable stone called diorite, to many temples he built or restored. The cuneiform inscription on the statue shown here (fig. **2–10**) relates that Gudea dedicated himself, the sculpture, and the temple in which the sculpture resided to the goddess Geshtinanna, the divine poet and interpreter of dreams. Gudea is clothed in a long garment similar to that worn by the female votive figure from Eshnunna (see fig. 2–5), and he holds a vessel from which life-giving water flows in two streams filled with leaping fish.

The land between the rivers remained a much-contested prize. Periods of political turmoil and stable government alternated until the Amorites, a Semitic-speaking people from the Arabian Desert to the west, moved into the area and reunited Sumer under Hammurabi (ruled 1792–1750 BCE). Their capital city was Babylon, and its residents were called Babylonians.

Among Hammurabi's achievements was a written legal code that recorded the laws of his realm and the penalties for breaking them. The code, incised in cuneiform script on a stele, appears under a portrait of the ruler depicted standing before the supreme judge and sun god, Shamash, patron of law and justice (fig. 2–11). In the introductory section of the stele's long cuneiform inscription, Hammurabi declared that with this code of law he intended "to cause justice to prevail in the land to destroy the wicked and the evil, that the strong might not oppress the weak nor the weak the strong." Most of the 300 or so entries that follow deal with commercial and property matters. Only 68 relate to domestic problems, and a mere 20 deal with physical assault. Punishments depended on the gender and social standing of the offender.

Around 1400 BCE the Assyrians rose to dominance in northern Mesopotamia. Known for their military prowess, they controlled most of Mesopotamia by the end of the ninth century BCE. By the early seventh century BCE, they had extended their influence as far west as Egypt. Strongly influenced by Sumerian culture, the Assyrians adopted the ziggurat form and preserved Sumerian texts. The most complete surviving version of the *Epic of Gilgamesh* was found in the library of the powerful Assyrian king Assurbanipal (ruled 669–c. 627 BCE).

The Assyrians built fortified cities and vast palaces decorated with wall paintings and stone reliefs. The capital at Dur Sharrukin (modern Khorsabad, Iraq), built by Sargon II (ruled 721–705 BCE), featured a walled citadel, or fortress, containing 200 rooms, 30 courtyards, and an immense ziggurat. Inside the citadel, a palace complex was raised on a fortified platform about 52 feet high. Deep inside the palace complex, the king's throne room was protected by a stone gate carved with colossal

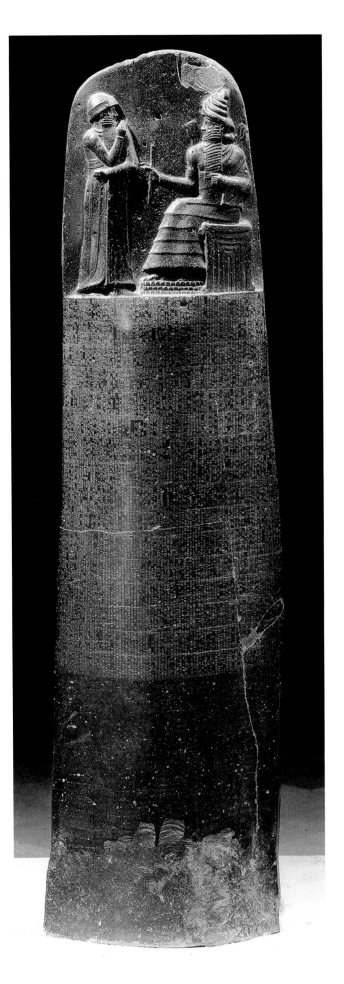

2–11 *Stele of Hammurabi,* from Susa (modern Shush, Iran). c. 1792–1750 BCE. Basalt, height of stele approx. 7′5″ (2.25 m), height of relief 28″ (71.1 cm). Musée du Louvre, Paris

As in the stele of Naramsin, the relative importance of the figures is indicated by hieratic scale. Hammurabi, the earthly law enforcer, is smaller than Shamash, who wears a four-horned headdress that marks him as a deity. Rays of light rise from the god's shoulders as he holds a rod and ring, Babylonian symbols of justice and power.

guardian figures, including the human-headed lion illustrated here (fig. 2–12). These hybrid creatures, ranging from 13 to 16 feet tall, also flanked the gates of the citadel.

Assurbanipal, king of the Assyrians three generations after Sargon II, had his own capital at Nineveh (modern Kuyunjik, Iraq). His palace was decorated with panels of alabaster, carved with a pictorial narrative in low relief. One panel shows the king and queen in a pleasure garden (fig. 2–13). The ruler, reclining on a couch, and his queen, seated, are surrounded by servants bringing trays of food and whisking away flies. The king has taken off his rich necklace and hung it on his couch, and he has laid aside his weapons, seen on the table behind him. This tranquil domestic scene is actually a victory celebration. A grisly trophy, the upside-down severed head of his vanquished enemy, hangs from a tree at the far left.

Assurbanipal's conquests—which stretched as far as Egypt—were short-lived, but soon after Assurbanipal's reign, the Assyrians succumbed to internal weakness and external enemies, and by 600 BCE their empire had collapsed. Before another century passed, Mesopotamia was absorbed by the Persian Empire under Cyrus II, called "the Great" (ruled 559–530 BCE). Under Persian rule, Mesopotamia became part of an empire that eventually stretched from India to Egypt.

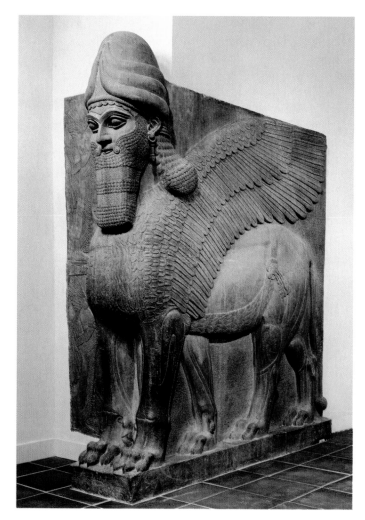

2–12 *Human-Headed Winged Lion (Lamassu),* from the palace of Assurnasirpal II, Nimrud. 883–859 BCE. Limestone, height 10′ 2″ (3.11 m). The Metropolitan Museum of Art, New York

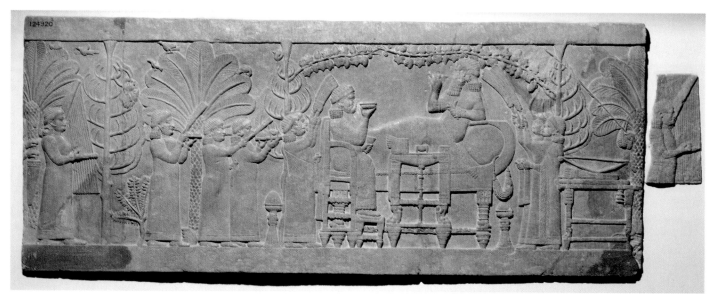

2–13 *Assurbanipal and His Queen in the Garden,* from the palace at Nineveh (modern Kuyunjik, Iraq). c. 647 BCE. Alabaster, height approx. 21″ (53.3 cm). The British Museum, London

THE FIBER ARTS

Fragments of fired clay impressed with cloth have been dated to 25,000 BCE, showing that fiber arts, including various weaving and knotting techniques, vie with ceramics as the earliest evidence of human creative and technical skill. Since prehistoric times, weaving appears to have been women's work—probably because women, with primary responsibility for childcare, could spin and weave no matter how frequently they were interrupted by family needs. Men, as shepherds and farmers, produced the raw materials for spinning and, as merchants, they distributed the fabrics not needed by the family. Early Assyrian cuneiform tablets preserve the correspondence between merchants traveling by caravan and their wives, who were running the production end of the business back home. The women often complain about late payments and changed orders. It is no coincidence that the woman shown spinning in the fragment from Susa is important-looking and adorned with many ornaments. She sits barefoot and cross-legged on a lion-footed stool covered with sheepskin, spinning thread with a large spindle. A fish lies on an offering stand in front of her, together with six round objects (perhaps fruit). A young servant stands behind the woman as she works, fanning her.

The production of textiles is complex. First, thread must be produced. Fibers gathered from plants (such as flax for linen cloth or hemp for rope) or from animals (wool from sheep, goats, and camels or hair from humans and horses) are cleaned, combed, and sorted. Only then can they be twisted and drawn out under tension—that is, spun—into the long, strong, flexible fibers needed for textiles or cords. Spinning tools include a long, sticklike spindle to gather the spun fibers, a whorl (weight) to help rotate the spindle and stretch the thread, and a distaff (a

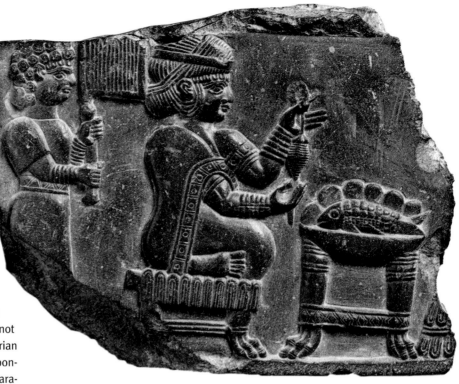

Woman Spinning, from Susa (modern Shush, Iran). c. 8th–7th century BCE. Bitumen compound, 3 5/8″ × 5 1/8″ (9.2 × 13 cm). Musée du Louvre, Paris

word long used to describe women and their work) to hold the raw materials. Because textiles are fragile and rapidly decompose, the indestructible stone- or clay-fired spindle whorls are usually the only surviving evidence of thread making.

Weaving begins on a loom. Warp threads are laid out at right angles to weft threads, which are passed over and under the warp. In the earliest, vertical looms, warp threads were hung from a beam, their tension created either by wrapping them around a lower beam (a tapestry loom) or by tying them to heavy stones (a warp-weighted loom, which the woman from Susa would have used). Although weaving was usually a home industry, palaces and temples had large shops staffed by slave women, who specialized as spinners, warpers, weavers, and finishers.

The fiber arts also include various non-weaving techniques: cording for ropes and strings; netting for traps, fishnets, and hairnets; knotting for macramé and carpets; sprang (a looping technique similar to cat's cradle); and single-hook work or crocheting (knitting with two needles came relatively late).

Early fiber artists depended on the natural color of their materials and on natural dyes from the earth (ochers) and from plants (madder for red, woad or indigo for blue, and safflower or crocus for yellow). Ancient Egyptians seem to have preferred white linen for their garments, which were elaborately folded and pleated. Minoans created multicolored patterned fabrics with fancy edgings, and Greeks perfected pictorial tapestries. The people of the ancient Near East used woven and dyed patterns and developed knotted pile (the so-called Persian carpet) and felt (a cloth of fibers bound by heat and pressure without spinning, weaving, or knitting).

Egypt

At the same time that city-states such as Sumer began to develop in Mesopotamia, a rich civilization arose in Egypt in the fertile valley and delta of the Nile. The Predynastic period, which lasted roughly from 4500 to 3300 BCE, was a time of social and political transformation during which Egypt was unified under a succession of powerful families or dynasties.

In the third century BCE, an Egyptian priest and historian named Manetho collected and recorded the names of Egyptian Kings. He based his work on temple records and inscriptions written in hieroglyphs or hieratic writing (see "Origins of Writing," page 39). Manetho grouped the kings into 30 dynasties that ruled the country between its unification around 3150 BCE and its conquest by Alexander the Great of Macedonia in 332 BCE. Egyptologists have since organized these dynasties into larger time spans reflecting broad historical developments. The Early Dynastic period (c. 3150–2700 BCE, Dynasties 1–2) was followed by three major periods: the Old Kingdom (c. 2686–2181 BCE, Dynasties 3–6), the Middle Kingdom (c. 2055–1795 BCE, Dynasties 11–14), and the New Kingdom (c. 1550–1069 BCE, Dynasties 18–20). These phases alternated with politically turbulent intermediate periods. After the conquest of Egypt by Alexander the Great and the subsequent period of Macedonian rule (332–305 BCE), Greek Ptolemaic rulers (15 rulers in succession were named Ptolemy) reigned until the country became part of the Roman Empire in 31 BCE. The line of Ptolemaic rulers ended with the famous queen Cleopatra. The dating system and the spelling of Egyptian names and places used in this book are those followed by the British Museum.

Early Dynastic and Old Kingdom Egypt

With the start of the Early Dynastic period, Egypt became a consolidated state along the banks of the Nile River. According to Egyptian tradition, the country had previously evolved into two kingdoms: Upper Egypt in the south and Lower Egypt in the north. ("Upper" and "Lower" refer to the flow of the Nile.) An Upper Egyptian ruler, referred to in an ancient document as "Menés king-Menes god," conquered Lower Egypt and first merged the lands into a single kingdom.

Dynasty 1 began with a king named Narmer (ruled c. 3100 BCE), known from the stone *Palette of Narmer* (fig. **2–14**) found in the temple of Horus at Hierakonpolis. **Palettes**, flat stones with a circular depression carved on one side, were used to grind paint that was applied around the eye to reduce the glare of the sun. The *Palette of Narmer* has the same form as these common objects but is much larger and may have been a votive offering.

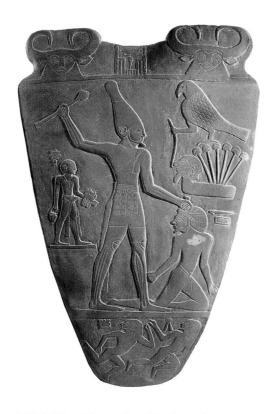
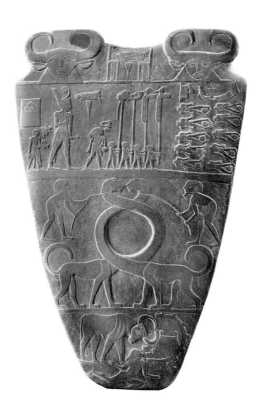

2–14 *Palette of Narmer,* from Hierakonpolis. Dynasty 1, c. 3150–3125 BCE. Slate, height 25″ (63.5 cm). Egyptian Museum, Cairo

ELEMENTS OF **Architecture**

Mastaba to Pyramid

The Egyptian burial structure—the gateway to the afterlife for kings and members of the royal court—began as a low rectangular **mastaba** with an internal room and chapel. Later, mastaba forms of decreasing size were stacked over an underground burial chamber to form a stepped pyramid. The culmination of the Egyptian burial structure is the pyramid, which housed an aboveground tomb and included false chambers, false doors, and confusing passageways to foil potential tomb robbers.

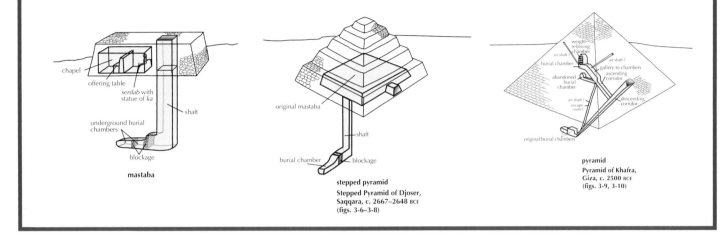

mastaba

stepped pyramid
Stepped Pyramid of Djoser,
Saqqara, c. 2667–2648 BCE
(figs. 3-6–3-8)

pyramid
Pyramid of Khafra,
Giza, c. 2500 BCE
(figs. 3-9, 3-10)

King Narmer dominates the scene on both sides of the palette. His name appears at the top in pictographs: a horizontal fish *(nar)* above a vertical chisel *(mer)* in a stylized palace facade. Following the convention of hieratic scale, he is shown larger than the other human figures to indicate his importance. On one side of the palette (fig. 2–14, left), Narmer, wearing the White Crown of Upper Egypt (see "Egyptian Symbols," page 54), holds the hair of a captive who may be the conquered ruler of Lower Egypt. The god Horus—a falcon with a human hand—holds a rope tied around the neck of a man whose head is attached to the stylized papyrus symbolizing Lower Egypt. This combination of symbols makes it clear that Lower Egypt has been conquered and Narmer now rules both lands. On the other side of the palette (fig. 2–14, right), Narmer is shown at the top left wearing the Red Crown of Lower Egypt. Note that the decapitated bodies of Lower Egyptian warriors have been placed in two neat rows, their heads between their feet.

Many of the figures on the palette are shown in poses that would be impossible to assume in real life. Again the artists use twisted perspective. Heads are shown in profile, to best capture the subject's identifying features, while eyes, most expressive when seen from the front, are rendered in frontal view. Shoulders are represented frontally, but hips, legs, and feet are drawn in profile. These conventions of Egyptian painting and relief sculpture were followed especially in depictions of royalty and other dignitaries, while persons of lesser social rank tended to be represented slightly more **naturalistically** (compare the figure of Narmer with those of his standard-bearers in fig. 2–14, right).

Old Kingdom

The kings of Dynasties 3 and 4, the first dynasties of the Old Kingdom, devoted huge sums to the construction of extensive funerary complexes. Central to ancient Egyptian belief was the idea that every human being had a life force—the *ka,* or spirit. The *ka* lived on after the death of the body, forever engaged in the activities it had enjoyed during its earthly existence. The *ka* needed a body to live in, however, such as a carved likeness of the deceased and/or his or her actual corpse, preserved by mummification (see "Mummies," page 59).

The need to fulfill the requirements of the *ka* led not only to the creation of *ka* statues, but also to the development of elaborate funerary rites and tombs filled with supplies and furnishings that the *ka* might require throughout eternity. In the Early Dynastic period, the most common type of tomb structure in Egypt was the **mastaba**, a flat-topped, one-story structure with slanted walls erected above an underground burial chamber. These structures tended to be grouped together in a **necropolis**—literally, a city of the dead—at the edge of the desert on the west bank of the Nile. This location, where the sun set, was believed to be the land of the dead. Two of the most extensive of these early necropolises are those at Saqqara and Giza, near modern Cairo.

For his tomb complex at Saqqara, King Djoser (Dynasty 3, ruled c. 2681–2662 BCE) commissioned the earliest truly monumental architecture in Egypt. The designer of the complex, a man called Imhotep, laid out Djoser's tomb as a stepped pyramid consisting of six mastaba-like elements placed on

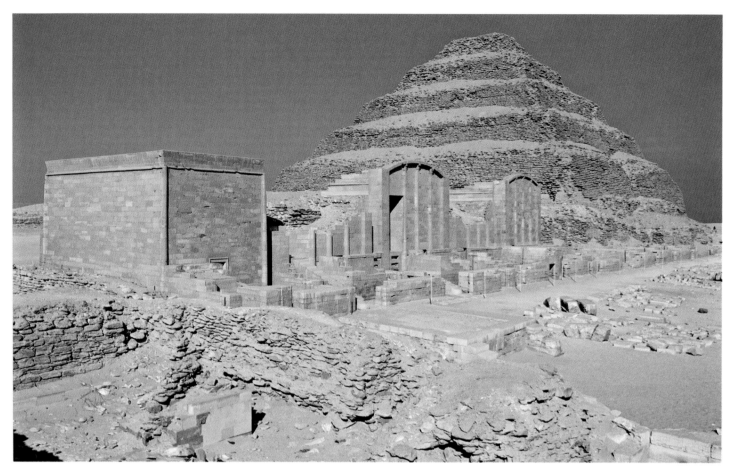

2–15 Stepped pyramid and sham buildings of the funerary complex of Djoser, Saqqara. Limestone, height of pyramid 204′ (62 m)

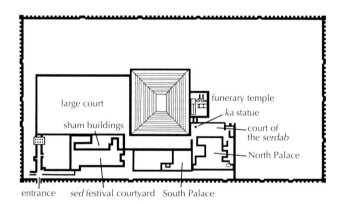

2–16 Plan of Djoser's funerary complex, Saqqara. Dynasty 3, c. 2681–2662 BCE

top of each other and originally covered with a limestone facing, or **veneer** (fig. **2–15**). Although the final structure superficially resembles the ziggurats of Mesopotamia, it differs in both concept and purpose. It is built of finely cut stone, not mud brick; it rises in stages and does not have ramps; and it protects a tomb. From its top, a 92-foot shaft descended to a granite-lined burial vault. Adjacent to the stepped pyramid, a funerary temple was used for continuing worship of the dead king, and sham buildings—simple masonry shells filled with debris—represented chapels, palaces with courtyards, and other structures (fig. **2–16**). Designed as a miniature replica of the king's earthly realm, these buildings were intended for the use of his *ka* in the hereafter.

In three-dimensional sculpture, Egyptian artists were capable of carving lifelike figures. Nevertheless a rigidly frontal, simple conception continued to control sculpted forms. Egyptian sculpture is rectilinear and blocklike, in contrast to the cylindrical forms of early Mesopotamian sculpture. The compactness and solidity of the form relate to a desire to make something without fragile extended limbs that would be easily broken and to the practical difficulties of carving hard stone such as diorite.

An over-lifesize statue from the Old Kingdom of the Dynasty 4 King Khafra (ruled c. 2558–2532 BCE) represents the ruler enthroned and protected by the falcon-god Horus (fig. **2–17**). Horus merges with the king's headdress as he protectively enfolds the king's head at the back with his wings. In

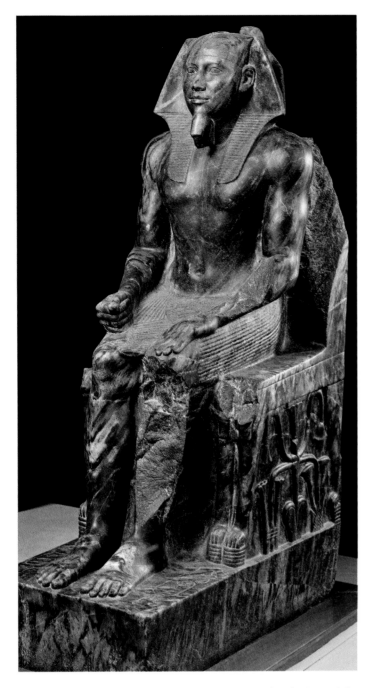

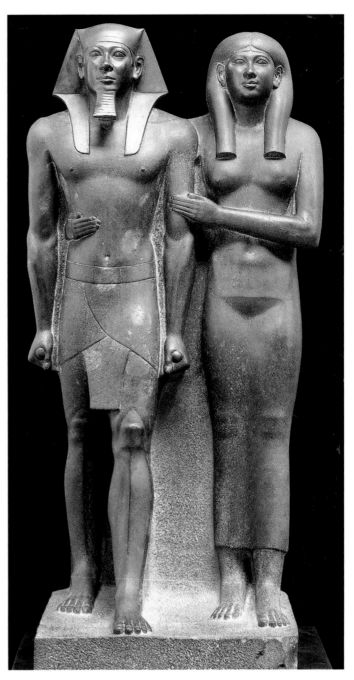

2–17 Khafra, from Giza. Dynasty 4, c. 2500 BCE. Diorite (northosite gneiss), height 5′6 1/8″ (1.68 m). Egyptian Museum, Cairo

The statue was carved in an unusual material, northosite gneiss, imported from Nubia. This stone produces a rare optical effect in sunlight; it glows a deep blue, the celestial color of Horus. In its original location in the valley temple, the sun would have shown through skylights illuminating the alabaster floor and the figure, and creating a blue radiance around the figure.

2–18 Menkaure and His Wife, Queen Khamerernebty, from Giza. Dynasty 4, c. 2500 BCE. Graywacke with traces of red and black paint, height 54 1/2″ (142.3 cm). Museum of Fine Arts, Boston, Harvard University–MFA Expedition

this statue from his valley temple, Khafra wears the traditional royal costume: a short kilt, a false beard symbolic of kingship, and a linen headdress with a *uraeus,* the cobra symbol of the sun god, Ra. Symbols of united Egypt, the lotus and papyrus, decorate the throne. The figure conveys a strong sense of dignity, calm, and above all, permanence; its compactness—the arms pressed tightly to the body, the body firmly anchored in the block—ensured a lasting presence.

A double portrait of Khafra's son, King Menkaure (ruled c. 2532–2503 BCE), and a queen, probably Khamerernebty

(fig. **2–18**), was discovered in the funerary temple built by Menkaure. The figures, carved from a single block of stone, are visually joined by the queen's symbolic gesture of embrace. The king, depicted in accordance with cultural and political ideals as an athletic, youthful figure nude to the waist, stands in a typically Egyptian balanced pose with one foot extended, his arms straight at his sides and his fists clenched. His equally youthful queen mimics his striding pose with a smaller step forward, and her sheer, tight-fitting garment reveals the curves of her body.

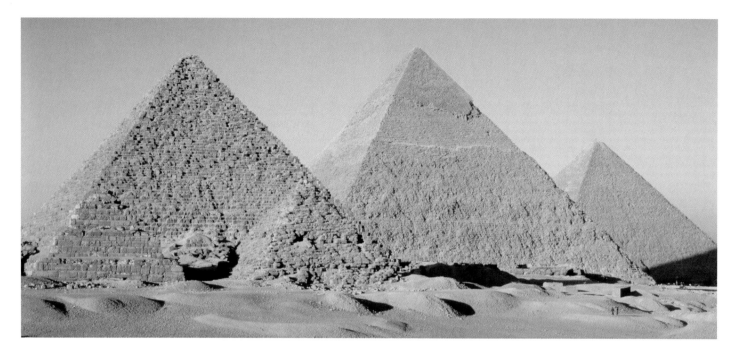

2–19 Great Pyramids, Giza. Dynasty 4, c. 2601–2515 BCE. Erected by (from left) Menkaure, Khafra, and Khufu. Granite and limestone, height of pyramid of Khufu 450′ (137 m)

The designers of the pyramids tried to ensure that the king and the tomb "home" would never be disturbed. Khufu's builders placed his tomb chamber in the very heart of the mountain of masonry, at the end of a long, narrow, steeply rising passageway, sealed off after the king's burial by a 50-ton stone block. Three false passageways, either deliberately meant to mislead or the result of changes in plan as construction progressed, obscured the location of the tomb. Despite such precautions, early looters managed to penetrate to the tomb chamber and make off with Khufu's funeral treasure.

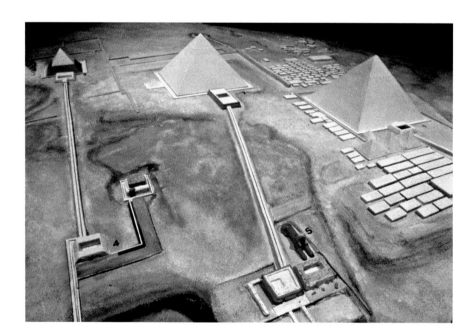

2–20 Model of the Giza plateau, Prepared for the exhibition "The Sphinx and the Pyramids: One Hundred Years of American Archaeology at Giza," held in 1998 at the Harvard University Semitic Museum. Harvard University Semitic Museum, Cambridge, Massachusetts

The Pyramid Complex

The architectural form most closely identified with Egypt is the true pyramid with a square base and four sloping triangular sides (see "Mastaba to Pyramid," page 49). Egypt's most famous funerary structures are the three Great Pyramids at Giza (fig. **2–19**), part of Old Kingdom tomb complexes built by the Dynasty 4 kings Khufu, Khafra, and Menkaure (the three ruled c. 2589–2503 BCE). The oldest and largest of the Giza pyramids is that of Khufu, which covers 13 acres at its base and rises to a height of about 450 feet even in its deteriorated state. It was originally faced with a sheath of polished limestone that lifted its apex some 30 feet above the present summit, to roughly the height of a modern-day, 48-story skyscraper.

Next to each of the three Great Pyramids was a funerary temple connected by a causeway, or elevated road, to a valley temple on the bank of the Nile (fig. **2–20**). When a king died, his body was ferried across the Nile from the royal palace to his valley temple, where it was received with elaborate ceremony. It was then carried up the causeway to the funerary temple and placed in its chapel, where further rites took place. Finally, the body was entombed in a well-hidden vault inside the pyramid.

Although not found within the three Great Pyramids, elaborate paintings and reliefs often decorated the interiors of the tombs of royalty and wealthy individuals. These images frequently show the dead person going about the duties and pleasures of earthly life.

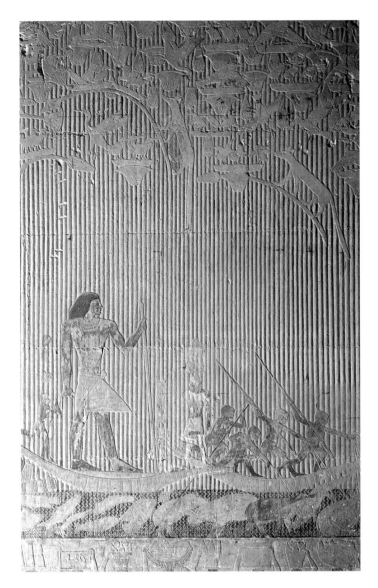

2–21 *Ti Watching a Hippopotamus Hunt,* Tomb of Ti, Saqqara. Dynasty 5, c. 2510–2460 BCE. Painted limestone relief, height approx. 45″ (114.3 cm)

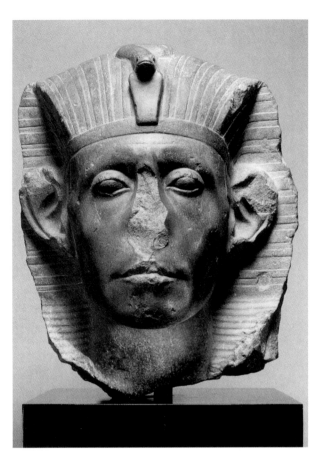

2–22 *Head of Senusret III.* Dynasty 12, c. 1836–1898 BCE. Yellow quartzite, $17^3/_4$″ × $13^1/_2$″ × 17″ (45.1 × 34.3 × 43.2 cm). The Nelson-Atkins Museum of Art, Kansas City, Missouri

PURCHASE: NELSON TRUST (62-11)

The paintings might also have symbolic or religious meanings. A scene in the mastaba of a Dynasty 5 government official named Ti shows him supervising a hippopotamus hunt from a shallow boat (fig. **2–21**). The erect figure of Ti, rendered in the traditional twisted pose, looms over this teeming Nile environment. The actual hunters, being of lesser rank and engaged in more strenuous activities, are rendered more realistically.

In Egyptian art, as in that of the ancient Near East, scenes showing a ruler hunting wild animals illustrated the king's power to maintain order and balance. By dynastic times, hunting had become primarily a showy pastime for the nobility. The hippopotamus hunt, however, was more than simple sport. Hippos tended to wander into fields, damaging crops. Killing them was an official duty of members of the court. Furthermore, it was believed that the companions of Seth, the god of darkness, disguised themselves as hippopotamuses. Tomb depictions of such hunts therefore illustrated not only the valor of the deceased but also the triumph of good over evil.

The Middle Kingdom

About 2055 BCE, Mentuhotep II (Dynasty 11, ruled c. 2055–2004 BCE) finally reunited the country. He and his successors reasserted royal power, but beginning with the next dynasty, about 1985 BCE, political authority became less centralized. Provincial governors claimed increasing power, limiting the king's responsibilities to national concerns such as the defense of Egypt's frontiers, the control of water, and related matters such as agricultural wealth and trade.

Royal portraits from the Middle Kingdom do not always exhibit the idealized formality of earlier examples. Some express a special awareness of the hardship and fragility of human existence. A statue of Senusret III (Dynasty 12, ruled c. 1874–1855 BCE) reflects this new sensibility (fig. **2–22**). Senusret was a dynamic king and successful general who led four military expeditions into Nubia (Egypt's neighbor to the south), overhauled the central administration at home, and did much toward regaining control over the country's increasingly independent nobles. His portrait statue seems to reflect not only his achievements but also something of his personality and inner thoughts. Senusret appears to be a man wise in the ways of the world but lonely, saddened, and burdened by the weight of his responsibilities.

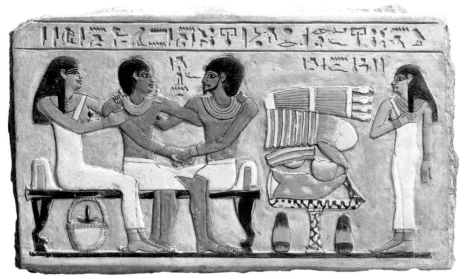

2–23 Funerary Stele of Amenemhat I, from Assasif. Dynasty 11, 2055–1985 BCE. Painted limestone, 11″ × 15″ (30 × 50 cm). Egyptian Museum, Cairo. The Metropolitan Museum of Art, New York
EXCAVATION 1915–16

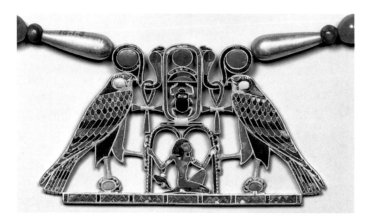

2–24 Pectoral with the name of Senusret II, from el-Lahun. Dynasty 12, c. 1895–1878 BCE. Detail of a necklace. Gold and semiprecious stones, length 3¼″ (8.3 cm). The Metropolitan Museum of Art, New York
PURCHASE, ROGERS FUND AND HENRY WALTERS GIFT, 1916 (16.1.3)

In contrast, the family of Amenemhat presents a united and confident picture. On his funeral stele (fig. **2–23**) a table heaped with food is watched over by a young woman named Hapi. The family sits together on a lion-legged bench. Everyone wears green jewelry and white linen garments, produced by Amenemhat's wife Iji and Hapi (see "The Fiber Arts," page 47). Amenemhat (at the right) and his son Antel link arms and clasp hands while Iji holds her son's arm and shoulder with a firm but tender gesture. Funeral offerings represented in statues and paintings would be available for the deceased's use throughout eternity.

There is little indication of how ancient Egyptians viewed the artists who created portraits of kings and nobles and recorded so many details of contemporary life, but artists must have been admired and respected. Some certainly had a high opinion of themselves, as we learn from an inscription on the tombstone of a Middle Kingdom sculptor: "I am an artist who excels in my art, a man above the common herd in knowledge. I know the proper attitude for a statue [of a man]; I know how a woman holds herself, [and how] a spearman lifts his arm. . . . There is no man famous for this knowledge other than I myself and my eldest son" (cited in Montet, page 159).

The patron's—and the artist's—desire for clarity permeates Egyptian art. A pectoral, or chest ornament on a necklace (fig. **2–24**), incorporates clearly recognizable human and animal imagery. The pectoral suggests the splendor of royal dress and tomb furnishings of the period. Executed in gold and inlaid with perfectly cut and fitted semiprecious stones, it was discovered in the funerary complex of Senusret II (Dynasty 12, ruled c. 1895–1878 BCE), in the tomb of the king's daughter Sithathoryunet. Two Horus falcons and coiled cobras of the sun god, Ra, support a **cartouche**—an oval figure or tablet enclosing the hieroglyphs of the king's name. The cobras wear the *ankh*,

EGYPTIAN SYMBOLS

Crowned figures, symbolizing kingship, are everywhere in Egyptian art. The false beard of a god or god-king is long and braided, and it ends in a knob. A living king is portrayed with a shorter, squared-off beard (see fig. 2–17). The cobra, "she who rears up," was equated with the sun, the king, and other deities.

The god Horus, king of the earth and a force for good, is represented most characteristically as a falcon. The eye of Horus *(wedjat)* was regarded as symbolic of the sun and moon. The *wedjat* here is the solar eye. The *ankh* is symbolic of everlasting life. The scarab (beetle) was associated with the rising sun and the creator-god, Atum.

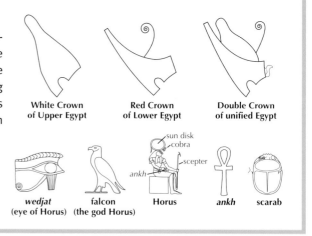

White Crown of Upper Egypt

Red Crown of Lower Egypt

Double Crown of unified Egypt

wedjat (eye of Horus)

falcon (the god Horus)

Horus

ankh

scarab

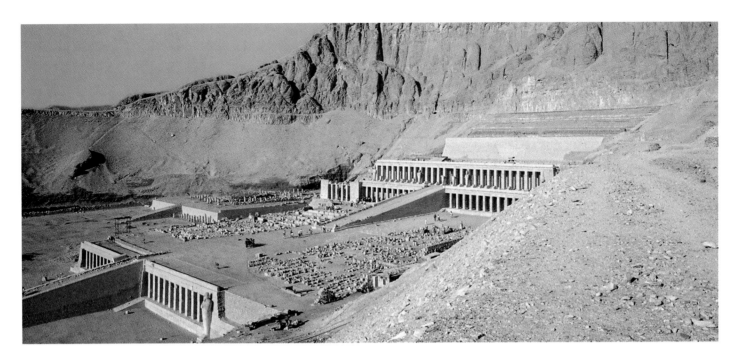

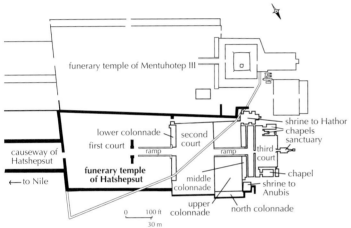

2–26 **Plan of the funerary temple of Hatshepsut,** Deir el-Bahri

the symbol of life, around their necks. Below, a male figure helps to support a double arch of notched palm ribs, a hieroglyph meaning "millions of years." Decoded, the pectoral's combination of images yields the message: "May the sun god give eternal life to Senusret II."

The New Kingdom

During the New Kingdom (1550–1069 BCE), Egypt prospered both politically and economically, its kings surpassing in wealth and power the rulers of Mesopotamia. One of the most dynamic kings of Dynasty 18, Tuthmose III (ruled 1479–1425 BCE), even extended Egypt's influence along the eastern Mediterranean coast as far as modern Syria. Tuthmose III was the first ruler to refer to himself as "pharaoh," a term that simply meant "great house." (Egyptians used it in the same way that people in the United States speak of "the White House" when they really mean the current president.) The successors of Tuthmose III continued to use the term, which ultimately found its way into the Hebrew Bible—and modern usage—as the title for the kings of Egypt.

At the height of the New Kingdom, rulers again undertook extensive building programs. One of the most spectacular surviving architectural complexes is the funerary temple of the female ruler Hatshepsut (Dynasty 18, ruled c. 1473–1458 BCE). Like the temples adjacent to the Old Kingdom pyramids at Giza, the structure—located at Deir el-Bahri across the Nile from the New Kingdom capital city of Thebes—was designed for funeral rites and commemorative ceremonies (fig. 2–25). Hatshepsut's actual tomb was hidden in the hills.

Magnificently positioned against high cliffs, Hatshepsut's temple was constructed on three levels connected by ramps and adorned with rows of columns, or colonnades (fig. 2–26). The colonnade on the top level was fronted by colossal royal statues; behind it was a **hypostyle hall**, a vast column-filled space, with chapels dedicated to Hatshepsut, her father Tuthmose I, and the gods Amun and Ra-Horakhty. At the back of the hall, the temple's innermost sanctuary was cut deep into the cliff. Rare myrrh trees brought from Nubia and pools of water decorated the temple's terraces, and an elevated causeway lined with sphinxes connected the complex to a valley temple on the Nile.

Early in the New Kingdom, the priests of the god Amun in Thebes had gained such dominance that worship of the Theban triad of deities—Amun; his wife, Mut; and their son, Khons—had spread throughout the country. Temples to these and other gods were a major focus of royal art patronage, as were tombs and temples erected to glorify the kings themselves. Two temple districts consecrated primarily to the worship of Amun, Mut, and Khons arose near Thebes—one at Karnak to the north and the other at Luxor to the south.

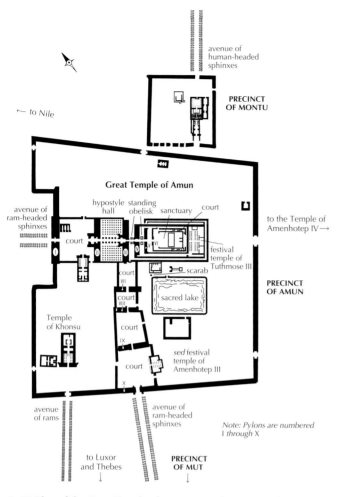

avenue of human-headed sphinxes

PRECINCT OF MONTU

← *to Nile*

Great Temple of Amun

avenue of ram-headed sphinxes

court

hypostyle hall / standing obelisk / sanctuary / court

festival temple of Tuthmose III

scarab

court VII

court VIII

sacred lake

Temple of Khonsu

court IX

court

sed festival temple of Amenhotep III

court X

avenue of rams

avenue of ram-headed sphinxes

to Luxor and Thebes

PRECINCT OF MUT

to the Temple of Amenhotep IV →

PRECINCT OF AMUN

Note: Pylons are numbered I through X

2–27 Plan of the Great Temple of Amun, Karnak, New Kingdom

The Great Temple of Amun at Karnak still dominates the landscape today (figs. **2–27** and **2–28**). The heart of the temple, a sanctuary containing the statue of Amun, was accessed through a huge courtyard, a hypostyle hall, and a number of smaller halls and courts. Massive gateways called **pylons** set off each of these separate elements. Only kings and priests were allowed to enter the sanctuary of Amun. The priests washed the god's statue every morning and clothed it in a new garment. Twice a day, they offered the statue tempting meals. The god was thought to derive nourishment from the spirit of the food, which the priests then removed and ate themselves.

Between Pylons II and III at Karnak stands the enormous hypostyle hall erected in the reigns of the Dynasty 19 rulers Sety I (ruled c. 1294–1279 BCE) and his son Rameses II (ruled c. 1279–1213 BCE) (fig. **2–29**). Called the "Temple of the Spirit of Sety, Beloved of Ptah in the House of Amun," the hall may have been used for royal coronation ceremonies. Rameses II referred to it in more mundane terms as "the place where the common people extol the name of his majesty." The hall is 340 feet wide and 170 feet long. Its 134 closely spaced columns supported a stepped roof of flat stones, the center section of which rose some 30 feet above the rest (fig. **2–30**). The columns supporting the higher part of the roof are 66 feet tall and 12 feet in diameter, with massive lotus flower capitals. Smaller columns on each side have lotus bud capitals. Piercing the side walls of the higher central section was a long row of window openings called a **clerestory**. Filled with stone grillwork, these openings cannot have provided much light, but they did permit a cooling flow of air through the hall. Despite the dimness of the interior, artists covered nearly every inch of the columns, walls, and crossbeams with carved and painted images and hieroglyphics.

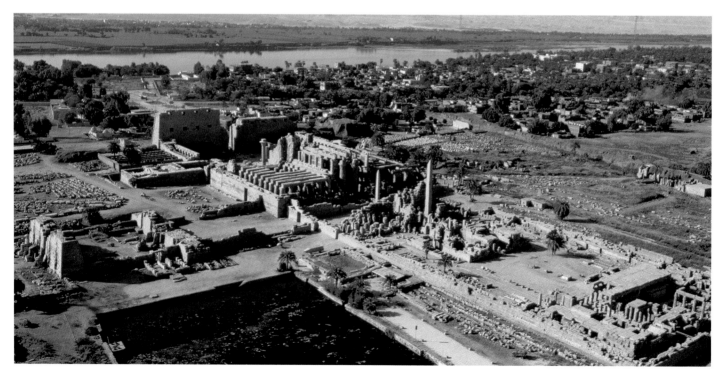

2–28 Aerial view of the ruins of the Great Temple of Amun, Karnak

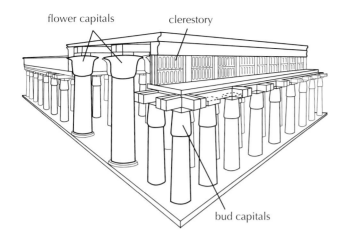

2–29 **Reconstruction drawing of the hypostyle hall,** Great Temple of Amun, Karnak. Dynasty 19, c. 1294–1212 BCE

The tomb of Nefertari, the best known of Rameses II's eight wives, is among the wonders of the Valley of the Queens necropolis, near Deir el-Bahri. In one of the tomb's many beautiful, large-figured scenes, Nefertari offers jars of perfumed ointment to the goddess Isis (fig. **2–31**). The queen wears the vulture-skin headdress of royalty, a royal collar, and a long, transparent white gown. The outline drawing and use of clear colors reflect traditional practices of depicting figures. The artists took particular care in placing the hieroglyphic inscriptions around the figures to create a harmonious overall design.

The veneration of traditional Egyptian deities—and especially the worship of the Theban triad Amun, Mut, and Khonsu, which spread throughout the country during the New Kingdom—was interrupted briefly during the reign of the unusual ruler Amenhotep IV (Dynasty 18, 1352–c. 1348 BCE). This king founded a new religion demanding belief in a single god, the life-giving sun disk Aten, and accordingly in 1348 BCE he changed his own name to Akhenaten ("One Who Is Effective on Behalf of Aten"). Akhenaten built a new capital city along the Nile between Giza and Thebes and called it Akhetaten ("Horizon of the Aten"). Borrowing from the modern name for this site, Tell el-Amarna, historians refer to his reign as the Amarna period.

Akhenaten saw himself as Aten's son, and at his new capital he presided over the worship of Aten as a divine priest. His chief queen, Nefertiti, served as a divine priestess. Temples to Aten were designed as open courtyards, where altars could be bathed in the direct rays of the sun. In art of the Amarna period, Aten is depicted as a round sun disk sending down long, thin rays ending in human hands, some of which hold the *ankh*.

Akhenaten emphasized the philosophical principle of *maat*, or divine truth, and one of his kingly titles was "Living in Maat." Akhenaten's reign, which saw the creation of a new capital, the rise of a new religion, and a concern for truth, found expression in new artistic conventions. In portraits of the king, artists emphasized his unusual physical characteristics: long, thin arms and legs; a protruding stomach; swelling thighs; and a thin neck supporting an elongated skull.

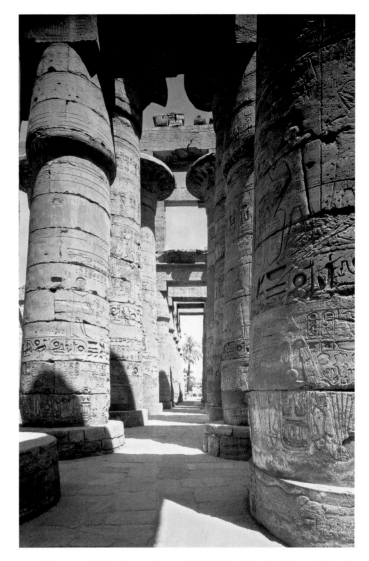

2–30 **Flower and bud columns, hypostyle hall,** Great Temple of Amun, Karnak

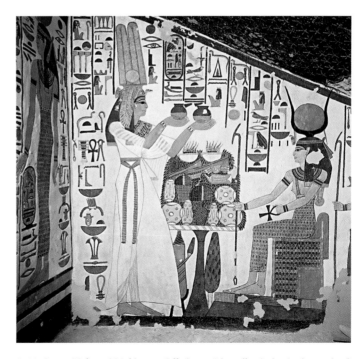

2–31 *Queen Nefertari Making an Offering to Isis,* wall painting in the tomb of Nefertari, Valley of the Queens near Deir el-Bahri. Dynasty 19, c. 1279–1212 BCE

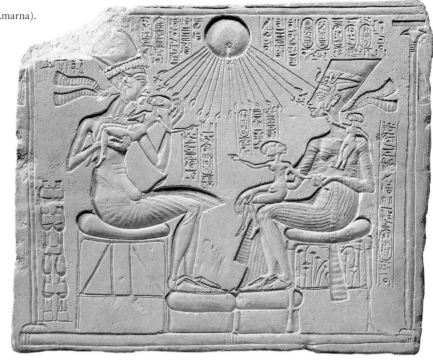

2–32 *Akhenaten and His Family,* from Akhetaten (modern Tell el-Amarna). Dynasty 18, c. 1348–1336/5 BCE. Painted limestone relief, 12¼″ × 15¼″ (31.1 × 38.7 cm). Staatliche Museen zu Berlin, Preussischer Kulturbesitz, Ägyptisches Museum

Egyptian relief sculptors often employed the technique seen here, called sunken relief. In ordinary reliefs, the background is carved away so that the figures project out from the finished surface. In sunken relief, the original flat surface of the stone is the background, and the outlines of the figures are deeply incised, permitting the development of three-dimensional forms within them. If an ordinary relief became badly worn, a sculptor might restore it by recarving it as a sunken relief.

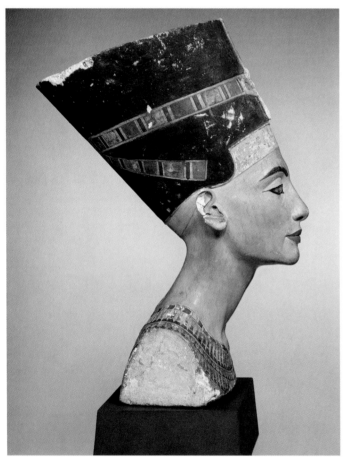

2–33 *Nefertiti,* from Akhetaten (modern Tell el-Amarna). Dynasty 18, c. 1348–1336/5 BCE. Limestone, height 20″ (51 cm). Staatliche Museen zu Berlin, Preussischer Kulturbesitz, Ägyptisches Museum

This famous head was discovered, along with drawings and other items relating to commissions for the royal family, in the studio of the sculptor Thutmose at Akhetaten, the capital city during the Amarna period. Bust portraits, consisting solely of the head and shoulders, were rare in New Kingdom art. Scholars believe that Thutmose may have made this one as a finished model to follow in carving or painting other images of his patron.

A relief of Akhenaten, Queen Nefertiti, and three of their daughters exemplifies the new style (fig. **2–32**). The king and queen sit on cushioned thrones playing with their children. The base of the queen's throne is adorned with the stylized lotus and papyrus, a symbol of a unified Egypt, which has led some historians to conclude that Nefertiti acted as co-ruler with her husband. The royal couple is receiving the blessings of Aten, whose rays ending in hands penetrate the open pavilion.

In a famed portrait of Nefertiti, her refined, regular features, long neck, and heavy-lidded eyes seem almost too perfect to be human (fig. **2–33**). Part of the beauty of this head is the result of the artist's dramatic use of color. The hues of the blue headdress and its colorful band are repeated in the rich red, blue, green, and gold of the jewelry. Nefertiti's beauty may be exaggerated, but phrases used by her subjects to refer to her—"Fair of Face," "Mistress of Happiness," "Great of Love," or "Endowed with Favors"—tend to support the portrait's perfection.

Akhenaten's goals were actively supported not only by Nefertiti but also by his mother, Queen Tiy. She had been the chief wife of Akhenaten's father, Amenhotep III (Dynasty 18, ruled c. 1390–1352 BCE), and played a significant role in affairs of state during Amenhotep's reign. Queen Tiy's personality emerges from a miniature portrait-head that reveals the exquisite bone structure of her dark-skinned face, with its arched brows, uptilted eyes, and slightly pouting lips (fig. **2–34**).

Akhenaten died c. 1348 BCE, and the new religion outlived him by only a few years, at which time the priesthood of Amun quickly regained its former power. The young king Tutankhaten (ruled 1336/35–1327 BCE) returned to traditional religious beliefs, changing his name, which meant "Living Image of the Aten," to Tutankhamun, or "Living Image of Amun." He died young and was buried in the Valley of the Kings, a necropolis used by New Kingdom rulers across the Nile from Thebes and adjacent to Deir el-Bahri. The undisturbed inner chambers of Tutankhamun's tomb, discovered in 1922, contained great treasures: jewelry, textiles, gold-clad furniture, a carved and inlaid throne, four gold chariots, and other precious objects. The king's body lay inside three nested coffins that identified him with Osiris, the god of the dead. The innermost coffin (fig. **2–35**) within the **sarcophagus** (rectangular stone coffin) was made of solid gold, decorated with colored **enamelwork**, semiprecious gemstones, and very finely incised linear designs and hieroglyphic inscriptions. The king holds a crook and a flywhip associated with Osiris, a fertility and vegetation god who presided over the dead and the underworld.

Egyptian funerary practices revolved around Osiris, his resurrection, and a belief in the continuity of life after death by Egyptians of all ranks. The dead were thought to undergo a "last judgment" consisting of two tests presided over by Osiris and supervised by the god Anubis, overseer of funerals and cemeteries, represented as a man with a jackal's head. The deceased were first questioned by a delegation of deities about

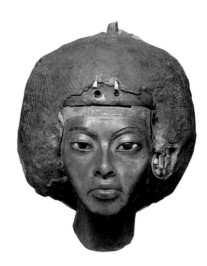

2–34 *Queen Tiy,* from Kom Mendinet Ghurab (near el-Lahun). Dynasty 18, c. 1390–1352 BCE. Boxwood, ebony, glass, gold, lapis lazuli, cloth, clay, and wax, height 33 3/4″ (9.4 cm). Staatliche Museen zu Berlin, Preussischer Kulturbesitz, Ägyptisches Museum

2–35 Inner coffin of Tutankhamun's sarcophagus, from the tomb of Tutankhamun, Valley of the Kings. Dynasty 18, 1336/5–1327 BCE. Gold inlaid with glass and semiprecious stones, height 6′ 7/8″ (1.85 m). Egyptian Museum, Cairo

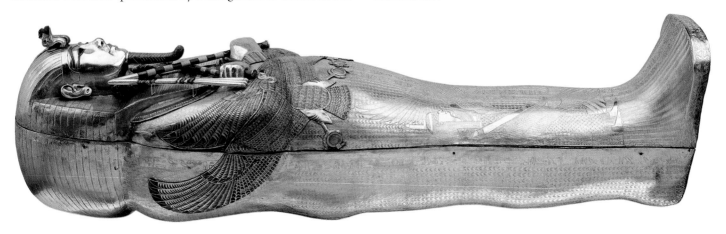

MUMMIES

No actual ancient Egyptian recipes for preserving the dead have been found, but the basic process can be gleaned from several sources, including images found in tombs, the descriptions of later Greek writers, scientific analysis of mummies, and modern experiments. The process was roughly as follows.

The dead body was taken to a mortuary, a special structure used exclusively for embalming. Under the supervision of a priest, embalmers removed the brain, generally through the nose, and emptied the body cavity through an incision in the left side. They then placed the body, together with its major internal organs, in a vat of

natron, a naturally occurring salt. The body was left to steep in this solution for a period of a month or more, which caused the skin to blacken. Once workers retrieved the body from the vat and carefully dried it, they often dyed it to restore something of its color; they used red ocher for a man and yellow ocher for a woman. Embalmers then packed the body cavity with clean linen—provided by the family of the deceased—that had been soaked in various herbs and ointments. They wrapped the major organs in separate packets, either putting them in special containers called "canopic jars" to be placed in the tomb chamber or stuffing them back in the body.

The tedious ritual of wrapping the body could now begin. Embalmers first wound the trunk and each of the limbs separately with cloth strips and then wrapped the whole body in a shroud. They then wound the body in additional strips of cloth, layer after layer, to produce the familiar mummy shape. The linen winders often inserted good luck charms and other small objects among the wrappings. If the family happened to have furnished a Book of the Dead (see fig. 2–36), a selection of magic spells meant to help the deceased survive a "last judgment" and win everlasting life, it was tucked in between the mummy's legs.

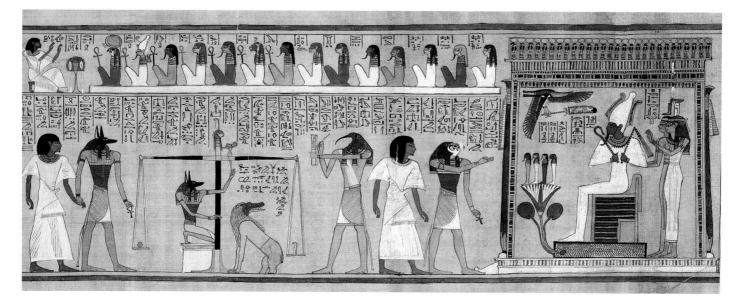

2–36 *Judgment Before Osiris,* illustration from a Book of the Dead. Dynasty 19, c. 1285 BCE. Painted papyrus, height 15⅝″ (39.8 cm). The British Museum, London

their behavior in life. Then their hearts, which the Egyptians believed to be the seat of the soul, were weighed on a scale against an ostrich feather, the symbol of Maat, goddess of truth. A monster named Ammit, the "Eater of the Dead," waited beside the scale to devour those who tipped the balance.

These beliefs gave rise to additional funerary practices especially popular among the nonroyal classes. Family members commissioned papyrus scrolls containing magical texts or spells to help the dead survive and pass the tests (see "Mummies," page 59). Early collectors of Egyptian artifacts referred to such scrolls as Books of the Dead. A scene from a Dynasty 19 example, created for a man named Hunefer, shows him at successive stages in his introduction into the afterlife (fig. **2–36**). At the left, Anubis leads Hunefer to the spot where he will weigh the man's heart in a tiny jar. After passing the test recorded by the ibis-headed god, Thoth, Hunefer is presented by the god Horus to the enthroned Osiris, who holds his usual crook and flywhip. In the top register, Hunefer kneels before the gods of Heliopolis, the sacred city of the sun-god Ra.

The Late Period

Egypt's Late Period (c. 747–332 BCE) saw the country and its art in the hands and service of foreigners. In the eighth century, Piye (747–716 BCE), a Nubian leader of the Kingdom of Kush—ancient Egypt's neighbor to the south—conquered Egypt. The Nubians established capitals at Memphis and Thebes and adopted Egyptian religious practices and architectural forms, including pyramids and sphinxes. The royal sphinx of the Nubian King Taharqo (ruled c. 690–664 BCE) illustrates this continuity of tradition (fig. **2–37**; compare with fig. 1 in the Introduction). Cobras rear up from the royal headdress, while the individual features of the king emerge from a lion's body and gaze out from a lion's mane. The sculpture combines the elegant simplified forms of Egyptian art with portraiture.

Nubian rule of Egypt was followed by the rule of Assyrians, Persians, and Macedonians until the Ptolemies regained control of Egypt after the death of Alexander the Great in 323 BCE (see page 112). In 30 BCE, when the last Egyptian ruler, Cleopatra VII, died from suicide, the Romans added Egypt to their empire. The creativity and accomplishments of the Egyptians had been acknowledged and admired by their contemporaries for many centuries, and even their eventual conquerors showed respect for what the Egyptians had left behind.

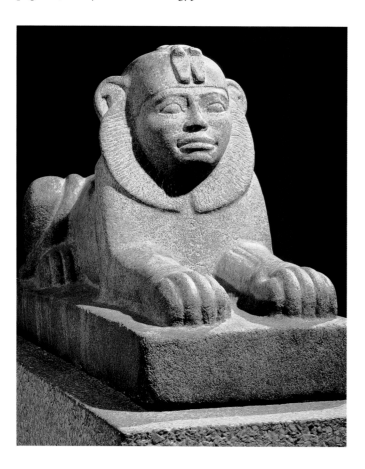

2–37 Sphinx of Taharqo, from Temple T, Kawa, Nubia. Dynasty 25, c. 690–664 BCE. Height 29⅜″ (74.7 cm). The British Museum, London

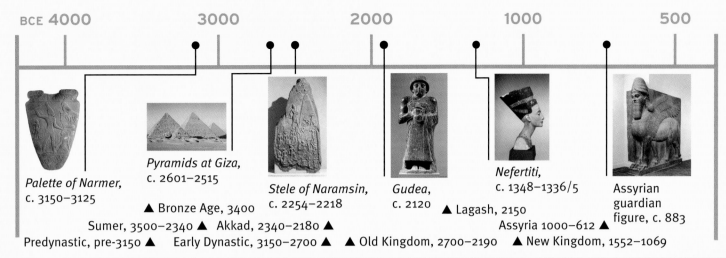

Palette of Narmer,
c. 3150–3125

Pyramids at Giza,
c. 2601–2515

Stele of Naramsin,
c. 2254–2218

Gudea,
c. 2120

Nefertiti,
c. 1348–1336/5

Assyrian
guardian
figure, c. 883

▲ Bronze Age, 3400

Sumer, 3500–2340 ▲   Akkad, 2340–2180 ▲   ▲ Lagash, 2150

Predynastic, pre-3150 ▲   Early Dynastic, 3150–2700 ▲   ▲ Old Kingdom, 2700–2190   ▲ New Kingdom, 1552–1069

Assyria 1000–612 ▲

LOOKING BACK

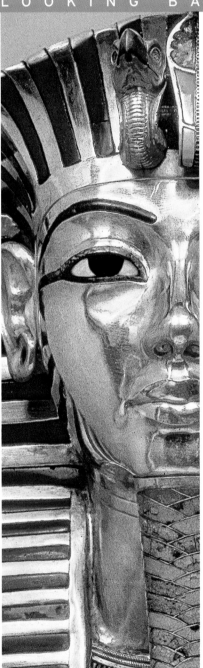

Prehistory came to an end in both Mesopotamia and Egypt when people there developed systems of record keeping and written communication. The thousands of Sumerian tablets left behind document the gradual evolution of writing and arithmetic, as well as an organized system of justice and the world's first epic literature. And the Egyptians, who created hieroglyphic writing (the use of pictures of objects and other signs to represent spoken sounds), also developed a rich tradition of written history and literature known to us today thanks to the many surviving texts carved in stone, written on papyrus, and painted on walls.

Indeed, we know a great deal about these two ancient societies—both from their records and from modern archaeological exploration and excavation. Improved agriculture permitted urban life, and population density gave rise to the development of specialized skills other than those for agricultural work. Soon social hierarchies evolved. As society became highly stratified—as it did in both Mesopotamia and Egypt—individuals assumed special duties and privileges. Priests communicated with the gods, developing religious rituals and ceremonies. Rulers led and governed; warriors defended the greater community and its fields and villages; and artisans and farmers supplied basic material needs. Artists helped define, record, and enhance the power of mortals as well as gods. And art itself became a means of communicating with the gods.

In Mesopotamia large temple complexes—clusters of religious, administrative, and service buildings—developed in each city as centers of worship and also as thriving businesses. Religious and political powers were closely interrelated. In Egypt elaborate funerary practices were another focus. Rulers devoted huge sums to the design, construction, and decoration of extensive funerary complexes, including the famous pyramids and subterranean tombs.

All cultures have agreed on rules for representing both things and ideas, but Egyptian conventions are among the most distinctive in art history. All objects and individual elements are represented from their most characteristic viewpoint; consequently, profile heads are seen on frontal shoulders and stare out at the viewer with eyes drawn in frontal view. These ancient works of art—even those we judge today to be especially fine—are simplified, even geometric, in appearance and often abstract in style.

The artists of Mesopotamia and Egypt created a symbolic visual language, a kind of conceptual art that communicated meaning to its audiences. To understand and use any symbolic language—whether composed of alphabets, shapes, hieroglyphs, or other images—we too must learn the vocabularies and respect the rules. Our own cultural, societal, or individual preferences and prejudices are irrelevant to appreciating the artistic accomplishments of the ancient Mesopotamians and Egyptians or, indeed, the art of any era.

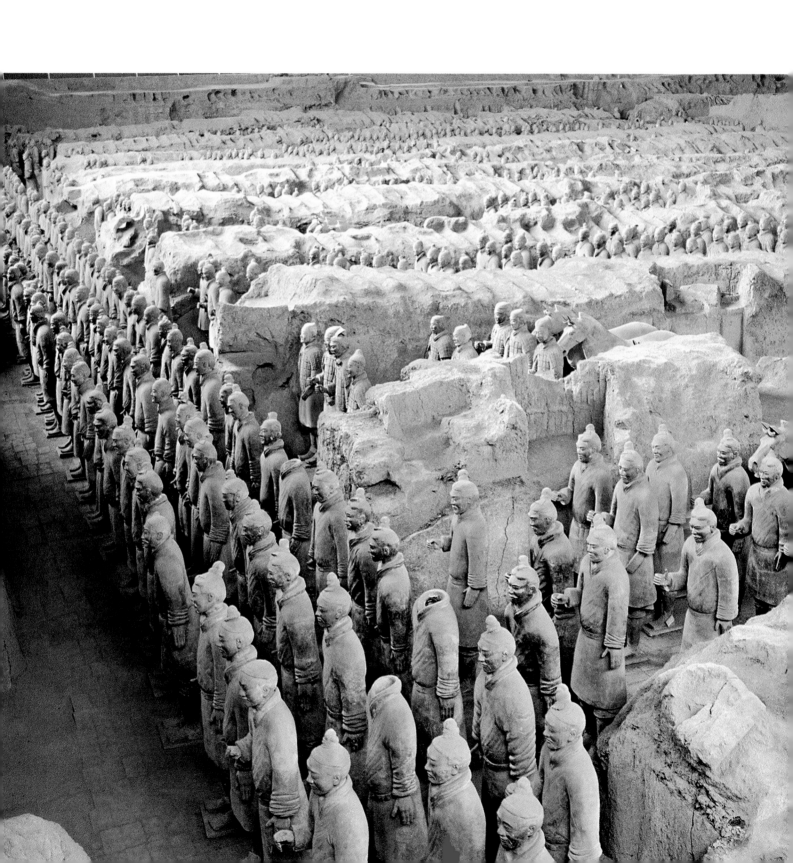

3
Early Asian Art

How can we understand the fierce determination and driving will that could lead a single man to conceive of himself as ruler of the world, of a man who believed that his right to reign was bestowed by supernatural powers and that he was the son of heaven? Between 221 BCE when he brought the warring states under his control until his death in 210 BCE, Qin Shihuangdi turned his vast lands of China into a unified state. His tremendous actions were simple, direct, and brilliant. To govern the Qin Empire, he created a bureaucracy—an intricate, hierarchal network—based on competence, not family heritage, and guided by a code of law. He united his lands with a common language and system of writing and more than 4,000 miles of roads. He brought prosperity by building canals and an irrigation system to increase agricultural production and by facilitating the ease of trade through uniform weights and measures. In fact, the name *Qin* (pronounced "chin") is the source of the name China.

During Qin Shihuangdi's life, a huge army defended his empire (historians write of 300,000 men). After his death, an underground army of thousands of life-size terra-cotta figures stood in battle array and guarded his tomb (fig. 3–1). Disciplined and alert, the statues remain poised to defend their emperor throughout eternity. According to early historians, this tomb beneath an earth mound at Lintong (near modern Xi'an) represented the universe, with the heavens depicted on the ceiling and with rippling rivers of mercury on the floor depicting the earth. The tomb also represented the success behind the bureaucratic universe that Qin Shihuangdi had established before he died.

How could such a vast project have been accomplished? The technical achievement of the artists and artisans is as amazing as the political organization that made the work possible and the worldview that inspired the art. Perhaps as many as 1,000 potters molded and carved the clay, and 85 artists signed the figures. By using standardized molds, they mass-produced thousands of legs, torsos, arms, fingers, and heads. They joined the prefabricated parts and then modeled and carved them into individual figures. After the firing of the clay, the artists painted the figures and supplied them with real weapons of bronze and wood. Just consider the size of the kilns and the quantity of wood necessary to fire such vast numbers of clay figures—let alone the organization of the labor force.

Such standardization, mass production, and prefabrication of modular parts are associated with modern industrial society. Yet ancient cultures, from China to Egypt, fashioned intricate production systems centuries before Europe's Industrial Revolution of the eighteenth century. Here, within the earth at Lintong, we witness more than the confluence of power, art, and bureaucracy: Qin Shihuangdi's tomb represents the human drive for imposing order on chaos.

3–1 **Soldiers,** from the mausoleum of the first emperor of Qin, Lintong, Shaanxi. Qin dynasty, c. 210 BCE. Earthenware, life-size

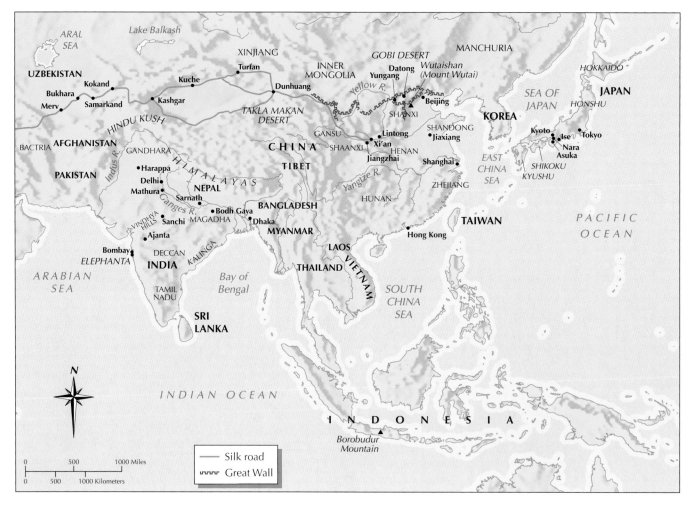

Map 3–1 Early Asia

The civilizations of South and East Asia, among the world's oldest, also rank among the most culturally rich. Together, the South Asian subcontinent and the East Asian lands of China and Japan witnessed the birth of six great, still-active religions and/or philosophies: Buddhism, Hinduism, and Jainism in India; Confucianism and Daoism in China; and Shinto in Japan. The eastward spread of Buddhism—from the Indian subcontinent through Central Asia to the lands of present-day China, Korea, and Japan—united these regions culturally through its philosophy and art. At the same time, the work of Indian, Chinese, and Japanese artists proudly reflects the profound differences among their aesthetic traditions (see Map 3–1, above).

The Indian Subcontinent

The Indian or South Asian subcontinent includes present-day India, southeastern Afghanistan, Pakistan, Nepal, Bangladesh, and the island of Sri Lanka. Throughout the history of the area, these places have been culturally linked. Differences in language, climate, and terrain within India have fostered distinct regional and cultural characteristics and artistic traditions. However, despite such regional diversity, several overarching traits tend to unite Indian

art. Most evident is a distinctive sense of beauty, with voluptuous forms and a profusion of ornament, texture, and color. Visual abundance is considered auspicious, and it reflects a belief in the generosity and favor of the gods. Another characteristic is the pervasive symbolism that enriches all Indian arts with intellectual and emotional layers. Third, and perhaps most important, is an emphasis on capturing the vibrant quality of a world seen as infused with the dynamics of the divine. Gods and humans, ideas and abstractions, are given tactile, sensuous forms, radiant with inner spirit.

The earliest civilization of South Asia arose in the lower reaches of the Indus River (in present-day Pakistan and in northwestern India). This Indus Valley, or Harappan, civilization (after Harappa, the first discovered site) flourished from approximately 2600–1900 BCE, during roughly the same time as Egypt's Old Kingdom and the dynasty of Ur in Mesopotamia. Indeed, with Egypt and Mesopotamia, it is one of the world's earliest urban river-valley civilizations.

Stone seals offer an intriguing window on Indus Valley civilization (fig. **3–2**). More than 2,000 small stone seals and impressions have been found. Many of the images carved on the seals suggest relationships with later South Asian culture. Seal **e** in figure 3–2, for example, depicts a man in the meditative posture

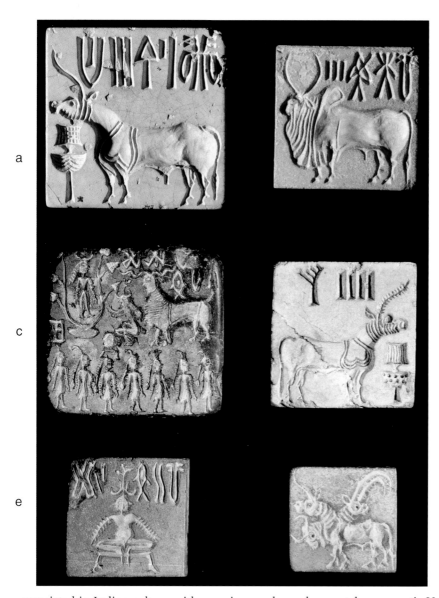

a

b

c

d

e

f

3–2 Seal impressions, from the Indus Valley civilization: **a., d.** horned animal; **b.** buffalo; **c.** sacrificial rite to a goddess (?); **e.** yogi; **f.** three-headed animal. c. 2500–1500 BCE. Seals: steatite, each approx. 1 1/4″ × 1 1/4″ (3.2 × 3.2 cm)

Usually carved from steatite, seals were coated with alkali and then fired to produce a lustrous, white surface. A perforated knob on the back of each may have been for suspending them. The most popular subjects are animals, the most common being a long-horned bovine standing before an altarlike object (a, d). Animals on Indus Valley seals are often portrayed with remarkable naturalism, their taut, well-modeled surfaces implying their underlying skeletal structures.

associated in Indian culture with a yogi, one who seeks mental, physical, and spiritual purification and self-control. In seal **c,** people in a procession walk single file under a kneeling worshiper and a figure, possibly a goddess, standing in a tree. This scene may offer some insight into the religious customs of Indus Valley peoples, whose deities may have been the prototypes of later Indian gods and goddesses. The function of the seals, beyond sealing packets, remains a mystery, and their pictographic script has yet to be deciphered.

Around 1500 BCE, after the Indus Valley civilization declined for unknown reasons, a seminomadic warrior people known as the Aryans entered India from the northwest, bringing with them an Indo-European language called Sanskrit and a hierarchical social order. The Vedic period that followed was named for the Vedas, a body of sacred writings. It lasted from about 1500 BCE until the rise of the first unified empire in the South Asian subcontinent in the late fourth century BCE.

The Vedic period is marked by the development of religiously sanctioned social classes or castes, which became hereditary, and by the beginnings of Buddhism, Hinduism, and Jainism—three of the four great religions of India. (The fourth is Islam.) The metaphysical texts known as the *Upanishads* were also written during this period. Examining the meaning of earlier, more cryptic Vedic hymns, the *Upanishads* focus on the relationship between the individual soul and the universal soul, or *Brahman.* The *Upanishads* advance concepts that became central to subsequent Indian philosophy, including the assertions that the material world is illusory and only the *Brahman* is real and eternal; that existence is cyclical; and that all beings are caught in *samsara,* which is a relentless cycle of birth, life, death, and rebirth. The goal of religious life is to attain *nirvana*—liberation from this cycle—by uniting our individual soul with the eternal, universal *Brahman.* These philosophical ideas are expressed in a more accessible and popular way in India's great literary epics, the *Mahabharata* and the *Ramayana.* Appearing toward the end of the Vedic period, these texts relate stories of gods and humans that later became immensely important in Hinduism.

In addition to Shakyamuni Buddha (see "Buddhism," page 66), a second great teacher helped the Buddhist and Jain religions arise in India: Mahavira (599–527 BCE). Both Shakyamuni Buddha and Mahavira espoused such basic Upanishadic tenets as the cyclical nature of existence and the desirability of escape from it. However, they rejected the authority of the Vedas and the hereditary class structure of Vedic society, with its powerful, exclusive priesthood. Buddhism and Jainism were open to all, regardless of social position.

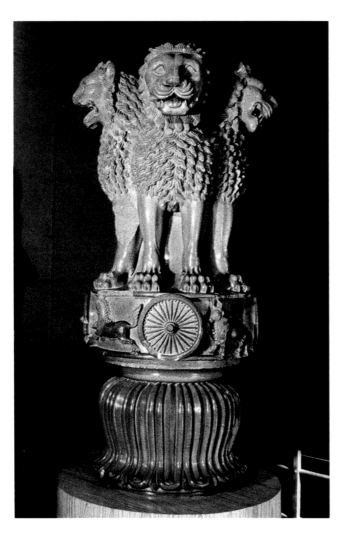

Buddhism provided the impetus for much of the major art created between the third century BCE and the fifth century CE. Under the Maurya Empire (c. 322–185 BCE), whose rule extended over all but the southernmost regions of the subcontinent, Buddhism became the state religion. For many centuries, the painting and sculpture of India were associated with imperial sponsorship of the religion. The Mauryan lion capital (fig. **3–3**), dated to about 250 BCE, is a prime example of one emperor's promotion of Buddhism. This capital once topped a 50-foot-high pillar of highly polished sandstone located on the grounds of the monastery at Sarnath, site of the Buddha's first teaching. One of many so-called Ashokan pillars, it was erected by the king who first sponsored Buddhism as the state religion. The capital rises with a cushion of downturned lotus petals, on which rests a deep, round collar carved with four animals—lion, horse, bull, and elephant—alternating with four wheels called *chakras* (see "Buddhist Symbols," page 71). Four lions stand back-to-back facing the four cardinal directions, emblematic of the universal nature of Buddhism. Their heraldic stance and the strong **stylization** of elements such as leg tendons and veins, claws, manes, and toothy muzzles, endow the lions with almost supernatural presence. When India gained its independence in 1947, this capital became the national emblem.

Between the second century BCE and the early first century CE, Buddhism continued as the main inspiration for art in the region, and some of the most important and magnificent early Buddhist structures were created. In early Buddhist art, the Buddha himself

3–3 Lion capital, from an Ashokan pillar at Sarnath, Uttar Pradesh, India. Maurya Empire, c. 250 BCE. Polished sandstone, height 7′ (2.13 m). Archaeological Museum, Sarnath

BUDDHISM

The Buddhist religion developed from the teachings of Shakyamuni Buddha (traditionally dated c. 563–483 BCE, though some scholars now put his death at c. 400 BCE), who lived and taught in the present-day regions of Nepal and northeast India. Born Prince Siddhartha Gautama in a small kingdom of the Shakya clan, he left his family and home at the age of 29 to live as an ascetic in the wilderness. He was deeply troubled by the inevitable sufferings of the human condition—old age, sickness, and death—and the repetitions of these sufferings through the continual cycle of rebirth. But after six long years of meditation, while sitting under a pipal (bodhi) tree at Bodh Gaya, Siddhartha Gautama attained complete enlightenment, or understanding of true reality, becoming the Buddha (*Buddha* means "enlightened one").

In his teachings, Shakyamuni Buddha expounded the Four Noble Truths, which are the foundation of Buddhism: (1) life is suffering; (2) this suffering has a cause, which is desire; (3) desire can be overcome and extinguished; and (4) the way to overcome desire is by following the eightfold path of right view, right resolve, right speech, right action, right livelihood, right effort, right mindfulness, and right concentration.

The early form of Buddhism, known as Theravada, stresses self-cultivation for the purpose of attaining *nirvana*. In Mahayana Buddhism, which developed later and became popular in northern India, China, Korea, and Japan, the goal was expanded from attaining *nirvana* for oneself to the attainment of buddhahood for all beings. A buddha is not a god but rather one who sees the ultimate nature of the world and is therefore no longer subject to the cycle of birth, death, and rebirth. Compassion for all became a primary motivating force of the religion.

Mahayana Buddhism recognizes not only Shakyamuni Buddha but also numerous other buddhas, such as Maitreya, the Buddha of the Future; and Amitabha (called Amida in Japan), the Buddha of Infinite Light and Infinite Life (that is, incorporating all space and time). Mahayana Buddhism developed the concept of **bodhisattvas**, saintly beings on the brink of buddhahood who have vowed to help others become buddhas before crossing over themselves. The appearance of bodhisattvas in art is based on the princely image of Siddhartha Gautama before he became the Buddha. They wear the princely garb of India, jewelry, and long hair. They are easily distinguished from buddhas, who wear a monk's robe, no jewelry, and have short hair.

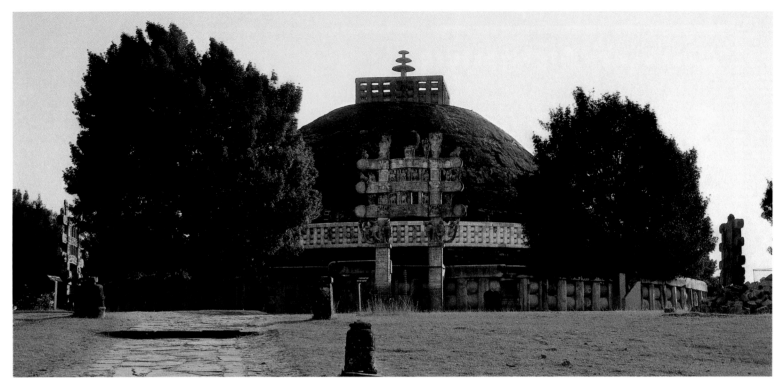

3–4 Great Stupa, Sanchi, Madhya Pradesh, India. Erected 3rd century BCE; enlarged c. 150–50 BCE

is not shown in human form. Instead, he is represented by symbols such as his footprints, an empty "enlightenment" seat, or a **stupa** (see "Stupas," page 68). Perhaps no early Indian monument is more famous than the Great Stupa at Sanchi in central India (fig. **3–4**). Stupas derive from burial mounds and contain **relics,** or material remains associated with a holy person, within their solid, dome-shaped earthen core. The first Buddhist stupas, holding the remains of the Buddha after his cremation, were venerated as his body and, by extension, his enlightenment and attainment of *nirvana*. Rituals of veneration at the stupa included circumambulation of the stupa, or walking around in a clockwise direction, following the sun's path across the sky.

Originally built during the Maurya period and enlarged about 150–50 BCE, the Great Stupa at Sanchi was part of a large monastery complex crowning a hilltop. The stupa's brick dome, once covered with shining white plaster, is topped by a square stone railing symbolizing the domain of the gods atop the cosmic mountain. The railing encloses the top of a mast bearing three stone disks, or "parasols," of decreasing size, which signal high rank and status. The mast itself is an ***axis mundi*** (axis of the world) assumed to connect the cosmic waters below the earth with the celestial realm above it and to anchor everything in its proper place.

An 11-foot-tall stone railing—punctuated by four stone gateways, or **toranas**—rings the entire stupa. As in much religious architecture, the railing provides a physical and symbolic boundary between the inner, sacred area and the outer, profane world. Each gateway is decorated with a profusion of carved incidents from the Buddha's life and past lives, as well as figural sculpture depicting subjects such as *Yakshis,* female spirits associated with the beauty and fertility of nature (fig. **3–5**). The swelling, arching curves of the Yakshi's body evoke this deity's procreative and bountiful essence. Her thin, diaphanous garment is noticeable only by its hems, and

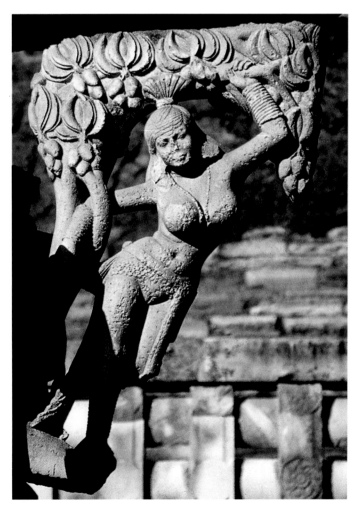

3–5 Yakshi bracket figure, detail from great Stupa, Sanchi, Madhya Pradesh, India

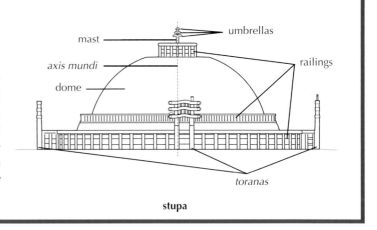
so she appears almost nude. As the personification of the waters, she is also the source of life. Here she symbolizes the sap of the tree, which flowers at her touch.

Gandhara and Mathura Styles

During the first century CE, the regions of present-day Afghanistan, Pakistan, and North India came under the control of the Kushans, a nomadic people from Central Asia. During this period Buddhism underwent profound change resulting in the development of a form of Buddhism known as Mahayana, or Great Vehicle (see "Buddhism," page 66). Closely related to this new movement was the appearance of the first Buddha images. The two earliest styles of Buddha images arose in Kushan-ruled areas: Gandhara in the northwest (present-day Pakistan and Afghanistan) and Mathura in central India. Slightly later, a third stylistic tradition, known as the Amaravati school after its most famous site, developed to the south in the region ruled by the Andhra dynasty.

In images from all three schools and throughout Asian art, the Buddha is readily recognized by certain visual characteristics. He wears a simple monk's robe, and because he had been a prince in his youth and had worn the customary heavy earrings, his earlobes are distended. The top of his head has a protuberance (*ushnisha*), which in images often resembles a bun or topknot, a symbol of his enlightenment. Between his eyes is the *urna*, a tuft of white hair.

A typical image from the Gandhara school portrays the Buddha as a powerful, over-life-size figure (fig. **3–6**). His robe is carved in tight, riblike folds alternating with delicate creases, setting up a clear, rhythmic pattern of deep and shallow lines. This complex pattern of folds resembles the treatment of togas in some sculptural works from ancient Rome (see figs. 6–3 and 6–7), a stylistic influence resulting from the region's long history of contact with the Western world. The Gandhara style, transmitted across Central Asia, also exerted a strong influence on portrayals of the Buddha in East Asia.

At Mathura, the image of Buddha developed within the indigenous sculptural tradition as represented by statues of *yakshas*, the native male nature deities. In one of the finest of the early Mathura images of Buddha (fig. **3–7**), the thin robe is pulled tightly over the body, allowing the fleshy form to be seen

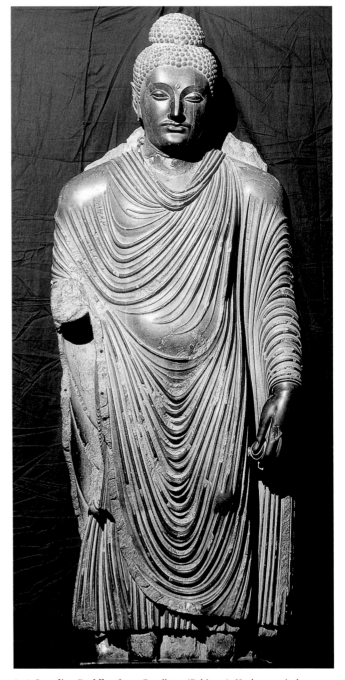

3–6 *Standing Buddha,* from Gandhara (Pakistan). Kushan period, c. 2nd–3rd century CE. Schist, height 7′6″ (2.28 m). Lahore Museum, Lahore

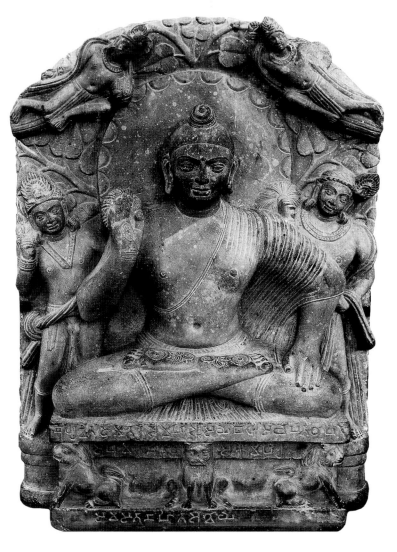

3–7 Buddha and Attendants, from Katra Keshavdev, Mathura, Madhya Pradesh, India. Kushan period, c. late 1st–early 2nd century CE. Red sandstone, height 27¼″ (69.2 cm). Government Museum, Mathura

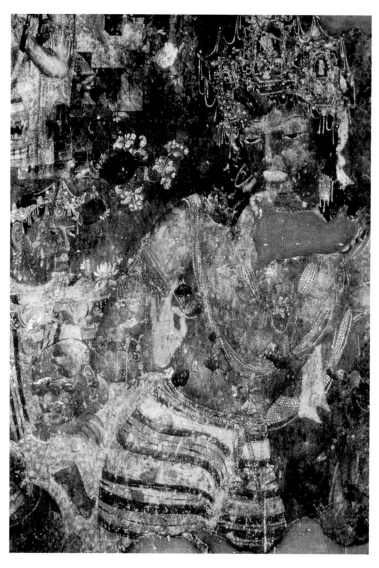

3–8 Bodhisattva, detail of a wall painting in Cave I, Ajanta, Maharashtra, India. Gupta period, c. 475 CE

as almost nude. The Buddha is seated in a yogic posture, and his right hand is raised in a **mudra**, or symbolic gesture, meaning "have no fear." His distinctive features and the impressions of *chakras,* or wheels, on his feet and right hand are all clearly visible (see "Buddhist Symbols," p. 71). In the background are the branches of the pipal, or bodhi, tree, under which the Buddha was sitting when he achieved enlightenment.

Gupta Period

Buddhism reached its greatest influence in India during the Gupta period (c. 320–500 CE), named for the founders of a dynasty that ruled much of India at that time. Some of the finest surviving artworks of the Gupta period are **murals** (wall paintings) from the Buddhist rock-cut temples and halls of Ajanta, in western India (fig. **3–8**). Since ancient times, caves, frequently the abode of holy ones and ascetics, have been considered hallowed

places in India. During the second century BCE, Buddhist monks began to excavate two types of rock-cut halls from the plateaus of the Deccan region. The type known as the *vihara* was used for the living quarters of the monks, and that known as *chaitya,* meaning "sacred," usually enshrined a stupa. Cave I at Ajanta, carved around 475 CE, is a *vihara* with monks' chambers around the sides and a shrine chamber in the back. Flanking the entrance of the shrine are murals of two bodhisattvas. A bodhisattva is distinguishable from a buddha because the former wears princely garments lavishly adorned with delicate ornaments and a crown festooned with pearls, rather than the simple monk's robe (fig. 3–8). The graceful bending posture conveys his sympathetic attitude, while his spiritual power is suggested by his large size in comparison with the surrounding figures. In no other known example of Indian painting do bodhisattvas appear so magnanimous and graciously divine yet at the same time so human.

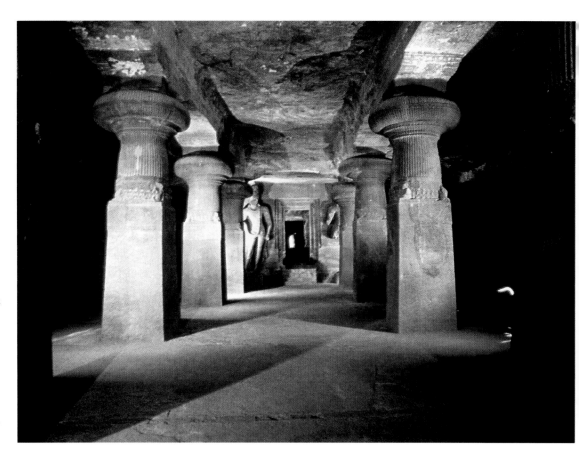

3–9 Cave-Temple of Shiva at Elephanta, Maharashtra, India. Mid-6th century CE. View along the east-west axis to the Shiva shrine

Large pillars cut from the living rock appear to support the beams of the low ceiling, although, as with all architectural elements in a cave-temple, they are not structural. Each pillar has a billowing "cushion" capital. Columns and capitals are delicately fluted, adding a surprising refinement to these otherwise heavy forms. The focus is on the lingam, the phallic symbol of Shiva, shown here at the center of the illustration.

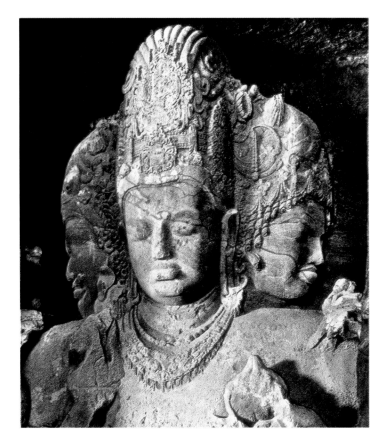

3–10 *Eternal Shiva,* rock-cut relief in the Cave-Temple of Shiva at Elephanta. Mid-6th century CE. Height approx. 11″ (3.4 m)

Even as Buddhism flourished, Hinduism, sponsored by Gupta monarchs, began the ascendancy that led to its eventual domination of Indian religious life (see "Hinduism," page 73). Hindu temples—and sculpture of the Hindu gods—rose with increasing frequency during the Gupta period and the post-Gupta era of the sixth to mid-seventh century.

In the mid-sixth century, a rock-cut cave-temple devoted to the major Hindu god Shiva was carved on the island of Elephanta, off the coast of Bombay in western India (fig. **3–9**). Impressive in its size and grandeur, the cave-temple's interior is designed along two main axes, one running north-south, and the other east-west. The three entrances provide the only source of light, and the resulting cross- and back-lighting effects add to the sense of the cave as a place of mysterious and confusing complexity. A worshiper is thrown off-balance—in preparation for a meeting with Shiva.

Shiva (meaning "the auspicious one") embodies the entire universe and exhibits a wide range of aspects or forms, both gentle and wild (see "Hinduism," page 73). He is the Great Yogi who dwells for vast periods of time in meditation in the Himalaya, the husband par excellence who makes love to the goddess Parvati for eons at a time, the Slayer of Demons, and the Cosmic Dancer.

Many forms of Shiva appear in monumental relief panels adorning the cave-temple at Elephanta. A huge bust of the deity represents his Sadashiva, or Eternal Shiva, aspect (fig. **3–10**). Carved out of the cave wall, three heads are shown

BUDDHIST SYMBOLS

Buddhist symbols have myriad variations. A few of the most important are described here in their most generalized forms.

Lotus flower: Usually shown as a white water lily, the lotus (Sanskrit, *padma*) symbolizes spiritual purity, the wholeness of creation, and cosmic harmony. The flower's stem is an *axis mundi*.

Lotus throne: Buddhas are frequently shown seated on an open lotus, either single or double, which is a representation of *nirvana*.

Chakra: An ancient sun symbol, this wheel symbolizes both the various states of existence (the Wheel of Life) and the Buddhist doctrine (the Wheel of the Law). A *chakra's* exact meaning depends on its number of spokes.

Attributes of a buddha: A buddha is distinguished by 32 physical attributes (*lakshanas*). Among them are a bulge on top of the head *(ushnisha)*, a tuft of hair between the eyebrows *(urna)*, elongated earlobes, and thousand-spoked circles *(chakras)* on the soles of the feet.

Mandala: Mandalas are diagrams of cosmic realms, representing order and meaning within the spiritual universe. They may be simple or complex, three- or two-dimensional, and in a wide array of shapes and forms—such as an Indian stupa (see fig. 3–4).

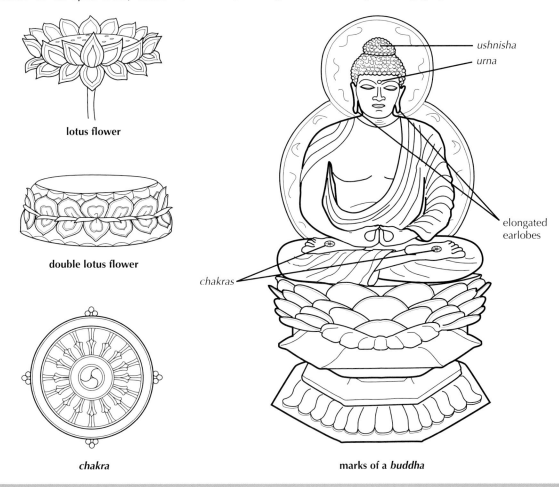

lotus flower

double lotus flower

ushnisha
urna

elongated
earlobes

chakras

chakra

marks of a *buddha*

in the photo resting upon the broad shoulders of the upper body. A fourth head may have faced the stone wall since a four-faced Shiva *(chaturmuk)* is plausible in this setting and also a more common Hindu image. Typically the heads summarize Shiva's fivefold nature as creator (back), protector (left shoulder), destroyer (right shoulder), obscurer (front), and releaser (top). On his left shoulder, his protector nature is depicted as female, with curled hair and a pearl-festooned crown. On his right, the wrathful destroyer nature wears a fierce expression, and in front, the god is shown in deep introspection, with the piled-up hair of a yogi. The releaser contemplates the heavens. Indian artists often convey the many aspects or essential nature of a deity through multiple heads or arms. Their intent is to portray these additions with such convincing naturalism that we readily accept them. Here, for example, the artist has united three heads onto a single body so skillfully that we still relate to the statue as an essentially human presence.

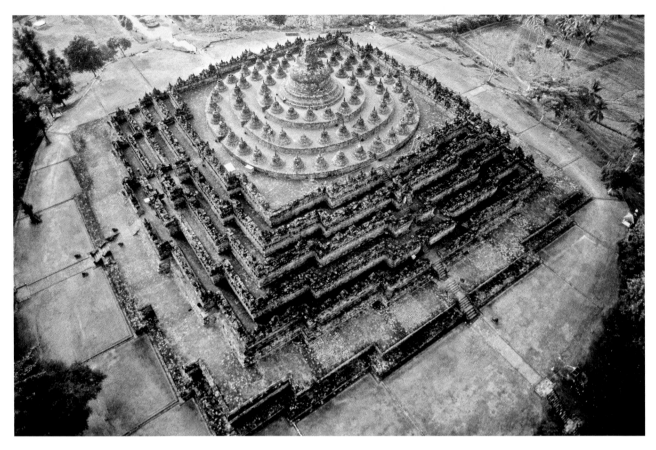

3–11 Buddhist Temple of Borobudur, Java, Indonesia. Sailendra dynasty, 835–60 CE. Lava stone, perimeter of lowest gallery 1,180′, diameter of crowning stupa 52′

Southeast Asia

Indonesia

Buddhism spread rapidly across Asia. At the end of the eighth century in Java, a family of rulers known as the Lords of the Mountains (the Sailendra dynasty) began building a magnificent temple in the form of a sacred mountain at Borobudur (fig. **3–11**). The builders turned a natural hill into a three-step platform, measuring more than 400 feet across and oriented to the four cardinal directions. On this platform, slightly later builders erected five more platforms and covered the walls with relief sculpture. Then they built three round terraces that support 22 small stupas and a large central stupa. The entire complex rises more than 100 feet above the ground. The stupas hold images of the Buddha, and the vertical walls of the three terraces are carved with the Wheel of Life—birth, life, death, and rebirth—the life of the Buddha, and the stages of enlightenment and paradise. The people who came to Borobudur followed the path established by these corridors of sculpture, and circling clockwise they climbed the sacred mountain. They hoped to achieve enlightenment when they reached the stupa on the final platform.

China

Among the cultures of the world, China is distinguished by its long, uninterrupted development, which has been traced back some 8,000 years. Even more remarkably, while rulers have come and gone, the country has been, with only a few breaks, unified since 221 BCE. Geographically, China is notable for its size, occupying a landmass slightly larger than the continental United States.

The country's historical and cultural heart—sometimes called Inner China—is the land watered by its three great rivers, the Huang He (the so-called "Yellow River"), the Yangtze, and the Xiang Jiang. Chinese towns and cities first emerged in the Neolithic period in fertile river valleys, especially around the deep southern bend of the Huang He, nicknamed "China's Sorrow" because of its disastrous floods.

Agriculture based on rice and millet arose independently in East Asia before 5000 BCE. One of the clearest signs of Neolithic culture in China is the vigorous emergence of towns and cities. At Jiangzhai, near modern Xi'an, for example, the foundations of more than 100 dwellings have been discovered surrounding the remains of a community center, a cemetery, and a kiln. Dated to about 4000 BCE, the ruins point to the existence of a highly developed early society.

The first Chinese kingdoms date to the Bronze Age, which began in China before 1600 BCE. Traditional histories tell of three Bronze Age dynasties: the Xia, the Shang, and the Zhou. Modern scholars once dismissed the Xia and Shang as legends, not actual civilizations, but recent archaeological discoveries have now established the historical existence of the Shang (c. 1700–1100 BCE) and point strongly to the historical existence of the Xia as well.

HINDUISM

Hinduism is not one religion but many related beliefs and innumerable sects. It results from the mingling of Vedic beliefs with indigenous, local beliefs and practices. All three major Hindu sects draw upon the texts of the Vedas, which are believed to be sacred revelations set down about 1200–800 BCE. The gods lie outside the finite world, but they can appear in visible form to believers. Each Hindu sect takes its particular deity as supreme. By worshiping gods with rituals, meditation, and intense love, individuals may be reborn into increasingly higher positions until they escape the cycle of life, death, and rebirth. The most popular deities are Vishnu; Shiva; and the Great Goddess, Devi. Deities are revealed and depicted in multiple aspects.

Vishnu is a benevolent god who works for the order and well-being of the world. He is often represented lying in a trance or asleep on the Cosmic Waters where he dreams the world into existence. His symbols are the wheel and a conch shell. A huge figure, he usually has four arms and wears a crown and lavish jewelry. He rides a man-bird, Garuda. Vishnu appears in 10 different incarnations, including Rama and Krishna, who have their own cults. Rama embodies virtue, and—assisted by the monkey king—he fights the demon Ravana. As Krishna, Vishnu is a supremely beautiful, blue-skinned youth who lives with the cowherds, loves the maiden Radha, and battles the demon Kansa.

Shiva, Lord of Existence, is both creative and destructive, light and dark, male and female. His symbol is the lingam, an upright phallus, which is represented as a low pillar. As an expression of his power and creative energy, he is often represented as the Cosmic Dancer, who dances the destruction and re-creation of the world (see fig. 9–4). He dances within a ring of fire, his four hands holding fire, a drum, and gesturing to the worshipers. Shiva's animal is the bull. His consort is Parvati; their sons are the elephant-headed Ganesha, God of Prosperity, and the six-faced Karttikeya, God of War.

Devi, the Great Goddess, controls material riches and fertility. She has forms indicative of beauty, wealth, and auspiciousness, but also forms of wrath, pestilence, and power. As the embodiment of cosmic energy, she provides the vital force to all the male gods. Her symbol is an abstract depiction of female genitals, often associated with the lingam of Shiva. When armed and riding a lion (as the goddess Durga), Devi personifies righteous fury. As the goddess Lakshmi, she is the goddess of wealth and beauty. She is often represented by the basic geometric forms of squares, circles, and triangles.

There are countless other deities, including Brahma, the creator, who once had his own cult. Brahma embodies spiritual wisdom. His four heads symbolize the four cosmic cycles, four earthly directions, and four classes of society: priests (brahmins), warriors, merchants, and laborers.

Central to Hindu practice are *puja* (forms of worship) and *darshan* (beholding a deity), generally performed to obtain a deity's favor and in the hope that this favor will lead to liberation from *samsara*. Because desire for the fruits of our actions traps us, the ideal is to consider all earthly endeavors as sacrificial offerings to the gods. Pleased with our devotion, a god may then grant us an eternal state of pure being, pure consciousness, and pure bliss.

Shang kings ruled from a succession of capitals in the Huang He valley, where archaeologists have found walled cities, palaces, and vast royal tombs. Society seems to have been highly stratified, with a ruling group that possessed the bronze technology needed to make weapons. They maintained their authority in part by claiming power as shamans. Nature and fertility spirits were also honored, and regular sacrifices were made to the spirits of dead ancestors so that they might help the living.

Bronze vessels are the most admired and studied of Shang artifacts. They were connected with shamanistic practices, serving as containers for ritual offerings of food and wine. The illustrated bronze *fang ding,* a square vessel with four legs (fig. 3–12), is one of the largest of hundreds of vessels recovered from royal tombs near the last of the Shang capitals, Yin (present-day Anyang). In typical Shang style, its surface is decorated with a complex array of images based on animal forms. A large **stylized** deer's head *(taotie)* adorns the center of each side; more deer appear on the legs; and the rest of the surface is filled with images resembling birds, dragons, and other fantastic creatures. Such images seem to be related to the hunting life of the Shang, but their deeper significance is unknown.

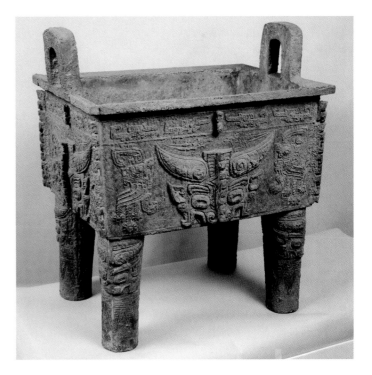

3–12 Fang ding, from the tomb of Lady Hao, Anyang, Henan Province, People's Republic of China. Shang dynasty, c. 1200 BCE. Bronze, height 1′4³/₄″. (42.5 cm) Cultural Relics Bureau, Beijing. Commissioned by Lady Hao or her family

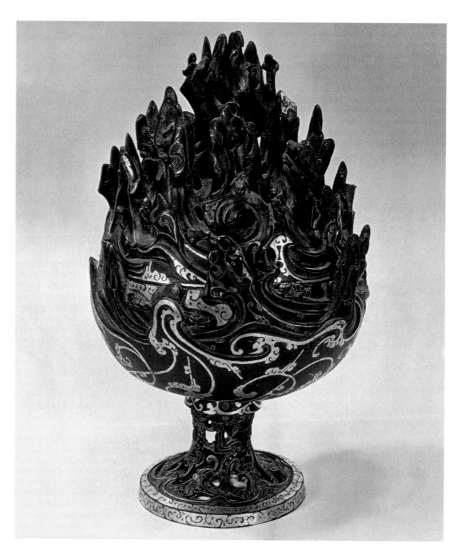

3–13 Incense burner, from the tomb of Prince Liu Sheng, Macheng, Hebei. Han dynasty, 113 BCE. Bronze with gold inlay, height 10½″ (26 cm). Hebei Provincial Museum, Shijiazhuang

In the eleventh century BCE, the Shang were conquered by the Zhou from western China. During the Zhou dynasty (1100–221 BCE), a feudal society developed, with a king and his relatives ruling over numerous small states. The supreme deity became known as Tian, or Heaven, and the king ruled as the Son of Heaven. Tian remained the personal cult of China's sovereigns until the end of imperial rule in the early twentieth century.

Many of China's great philosophers lived during the Zhou dynasty, thinkers such as Confucius, Lao Tzu, and Mozi. During the lifetime of Confucius (551–479 BCE)—a scholar born into an aristocratic family—warfare for supremacy among the various states of China had begun, and the traditional social fabric seemed to be breaking down. Looking back to the early Zhou dynasty as a golden age, Confucius thought about how a just and harmonious society could once again emerge (see "Confucianism," page 75). He never found a ruler who would put his ideas into effect, but his philosophy, Confucianism, eventually became central to Chinese thought and culture.

Toward the middle of the third century BCE, the state of Qin launched military campaigns that led to its triumph over the other Chinese states by 221 BCE. For the first time, China was united under a single ruler, the powerful Qin Shihuangdi (see "Looking Forward," page 63). Anxious to ensure personal immortality, Qin Shihuangdi built his own **mausoleum** (a build-ing used as a tomb) near the city of Xi'an in Shaanxi Province. Archaeologists who began to excavate a pit near the tomb in 1974 were stunned by the vast underground army of soldiers and horses that they found (see fig. 3–1). The Chinese have not yet opened the tomb itself.

Although harsh and repressive as rulers, the Qin emperors established a centralized bureaucracy and administrative framework, aspects of which are still used in China today. The country was divided into provinces and prefectures, the writing system and coinage were standardized, and forts on the northern frontier were connected to build an early form of the Great Wall.

During the peaceful and prosperous Han dynasty that followed (206 BCE–220 CE), the country's borders were extended and secured. Chinese control over strategic stretches of Central Asia led to the opening of the famous Silk Route, actually a network of land and sea routes that linked China by trade to Europe. The philosophies of **Daoism** and Confucianism flourished as well. Daoism emphasizes the close relationship between humans and nature. On a philosophical level, it is concerned with bringing the quiet and humble individual life into harmony with the *Dao*, or Way, of the universe. On a popular level, Daoism developed into an organized religion, absorbing many traditional folk practices such as shamanism and the search for immortality.

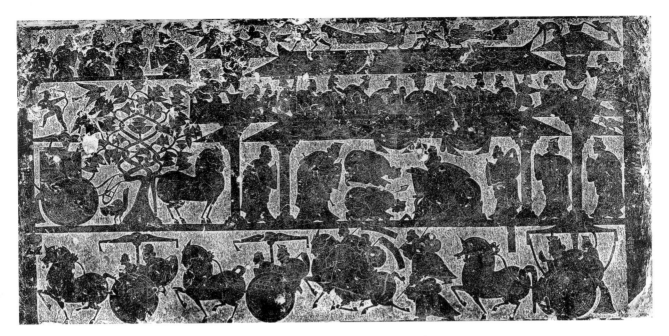

3–14 Detail from a rubbing of a relief in the Wu family shrine, (Wuliangci), Jiaxiang, Shandong. Han dynasty, 151 CE. Stone, 27 $\frac{1}{2}''$ × 66 $\frac{1}{2}''$ (70 × 169 cm)

A popular Daoist legend, which tells of the Isles of the Immortals in the Eastern Sea, is depicted on a bronze incense burner from the tomb of Prince Liu Sheng, who died in 113 BCE (fig. **3–13**). Gold **inlays** on the base outline the stylized waves of the sea. Above them rises the mountainous island, crowded with birds, animals, and people who have discovered the secret of immortality. The techniques used in the manufacturing of this piece represent the ultimate development of the long tradition of bronze casting in China.

In contrast to the metaphysical focus of Daoism, Confucianism is concerned with the human world, and its goal is the attainment of harmony. To this end, it offers an ethical system based on correct relationships among people (see "Confucianism," below). Attracted by this emphasis on social order and respect for authority, the Han emperor Wu (ruled 141–87 BCE) made Confucianism the official philosophy. It remained the state ideology of China until the end of imperial rule in the twentieth century and eventually assumed the form and force of a religion.

Confucian subjects appear frequently in Han art. Among the most famous examples are the reliefs from the Wu family shrines built in 151 CE in Jiaxiang. Carved and engraved in low relief on stone slabs, the scenes were meant to teach such basic Confucian tenets as respect for the emperor, filial piety, and wifely devotion. One relief (fig. **3–14**) seems to depict homage to the first emperor

CONFUCIANISM

Confucianism is based on the teachings of the Chinese scholar Confucius (551–479 BCE). His words have come down to us through a book known in English as the *Analects*, which records sayings of the great philosopher collected by his disciples and their followers. At the heart of Confucian thought is the concept of *ren*, or humanheartedness. *Ren*, which emphasizes morality and empathy as the basic standards for all human interactions, is most fully realized in the Confucian ideal of the *junzi*, or gentleman. Originally indicating noble birth, the term *junzi* was redirected to mean one who through education and self-cultivation becomes a superior person, right-thinking and right-acting in all situations.

Confucius also emphasized the importance of *li*, ritual or etiquette. The formalities of social interaction—scrupulous manners as well as ritual, ceremony, and protocol—choreographed life so that an entire society moved in harmony.

Both *ren* and *li* operated in the realm of the Five Constant Relationships defining Confucian society: ruler and subject, parent and child, husband and wife, elder sibling and younger sibling, and elder friend and younger friend. Deference based on age and sex is built into this view, as is the deference to authority that made Confucianism popular with emperors. Yet responsibilities flow the other way as well: The duty of a ruler is to earn the loyalty of subjects, of a husband to earn the respect of his wife, and of age to guide youth wisely.

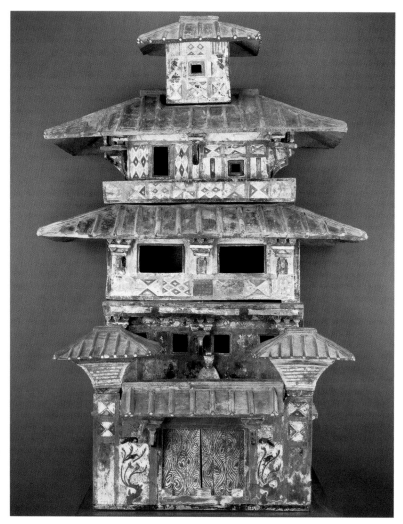

3–15 Tomb model of house.
Eastern Han dynasty, 1st-mid
2nd century CE. Painted
earthenware, 52″ × 33½″ × 27″
(132.1 × 85.1 × 68.6 cm).
The Nelson Atkins Museum of
Art, Kansas City, Missouri

of the Han dynasty, who is sheltered in a two-story building and distinguished by his larger size. Birds and small figures on the roof may represent mythical creatures and immortals, while to the left the legendary archer Yi shoots at one of the sun-crows. (Traditional myths tell how Yi shot all but one of the 10 crows of the 10 suns so that the earth would not dry out.) Across the lower register, a procession brings more dignitaries to the reception.

Contemporary literary sources are eloquent on the wonders of the Han capital but, unfortunately, only ceramic models of Han architecture survive. One model of a house found in a tomb represents a typical Han dwelling (fig. **3–15**). Its four stories are crowned with a watchtower and face a small walled courtyard. Aside from the multilevel construction, the most interesting feature of the house is the **bracketing** system supporting the broad eaves of its tiled roofs. The painting on the exterior walls illustrates structural features such as posts and lintels. Trees with crows in their branches flank the entrance. Literary sources describe the walls of Han palaces as decorated with paint and lacquer and also inlaid with precious metals and stones.

With the fall of the Han dynasty in 220 CE, China splintered into warring kingdoms. A period of almost constant turmoil

broadly known as the period of the Northern and Southern dynasties lasted until 579 CE. Many intellectuals turned to Daoism, which contained a strong escapist element. Yet ultimately it was a new system of belief, Buddhism, that brought the greatest comfort to people of the time. Buddhism spread gradually north from India into Central Asia. With the increased transportation of people, goods, and ideas along the Silk Route during the Han dynasty, Buddhism eventually reached China (see "The Silk Route and the Making of Silk," opposite). To the Chinese of the post-Han period, beset by constant warfare and social devastation, Buddhism offered consolation in life and the promise of life after death.

The most impressive surviving works of Buddhist art from the period of the Northern and Southern dynasties are hundreds of caves carved from the solid rock of cliffs. The rock-cut caves at Yungang in Shaanxi Province, for instance, contain many impressive examples of early Chinese Buddhist sculpture. The monumental seated Buddha illustrated here was carved in the latter half of the fifth century (fig. **3–16**). Because the front part of the cave has crumbled away, the 45-foot statue is now exposed to the open air. The overall effect of this colossus is remote and even austere, less human than the more sensuous expression of

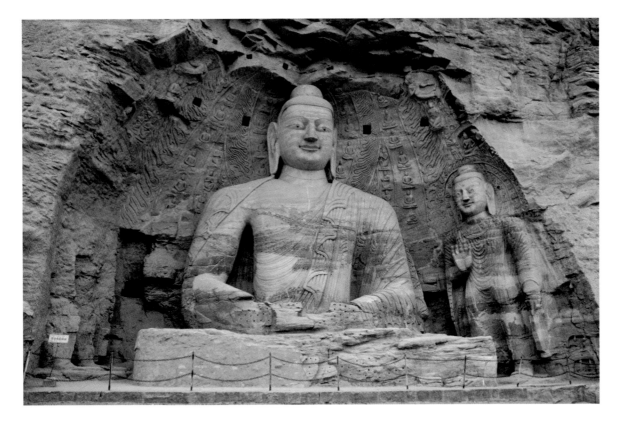

3–16 Seated Buddha, Cave 20, Yungang Datong, Shaanxi. Northern Wei dynasty, c. 460 CE. Stone, height 45′ (13.7 m)

The elongated ears, protuberance on the head (ushnisha), and monk's robe are traditional attributes of the Buddha. The masklike face, massive shoulders, and shallow, stylized drapery indicate a strong Central Asian influence.

earlier sculptures in India. The image of the Buddha became increasingly formal and unearthly as it traveled east from its origins, reflecting a fundamental difference in the way the Chinese and the Indians visualize their deities.

In 581 CE a northern general reunified China and established a short-lived dynasty of his own, the Sui. The Sui paved the way for one of the greatest dynasties in Chinese history, the Tang (618–907 CE). Even today many Chinese living abroad call themselves "Tang people," emphasizing that part of the Chinese character that is strong and vigorous, noble and idealistic, but also realistic and pragmatic. Cosmopolitan and tolerant, too, the Tang were both self-confident and curious about the world.

THE SILK ROUTE AND THE MAKING OF SILK

The fabled trade routes between East Asia and the West, called the Silk Route, were a 5,000-mile-long network of caravan and sea routes stretching from Chang'an to the westernmost point of the Great Wall of China—then all the way to Rome. Caravans carrying Chinese luxury goods to the West—and bringing back gold in payment—passed through some of the most hostile regions in Asia and the Middle East, although no one caravan had to make the entire trip; goods were passed from trader to trader on both the overland and sea routes. The Silk Route's importance fluctuated with the politics of the various regions through which it passed, as did the level of safety for its travelers. Rarely in its long history was it entirely open and comparatively safe.

Among the many precious goods carried along the Silk Route were spices and other foodstuffs, horses for trade, metals, gems, and, of course, silk. The cultivation and weaving of silk had been a closely guarded secret in China since about 2640 BCE, and it was not until about 550 CE—when two Christian missionaries smuggled a few silkworm larvae to Constantinople—that the Chinese lost their virtual monopoly. From as early as the third century BCE, silk cloth was exported to Europe. It was treasured in ancient Greece and Rome. And by the sixth century CE, silk was a protected palace industry in the Byzantine Empire. Eventually, sericulture (the cultivation of silkworms) and luxury textile weaving took hold in southern Europe. For this and many other reasons, the use of the Silk Route declined. By the sixteenth century, it was no longer in use.

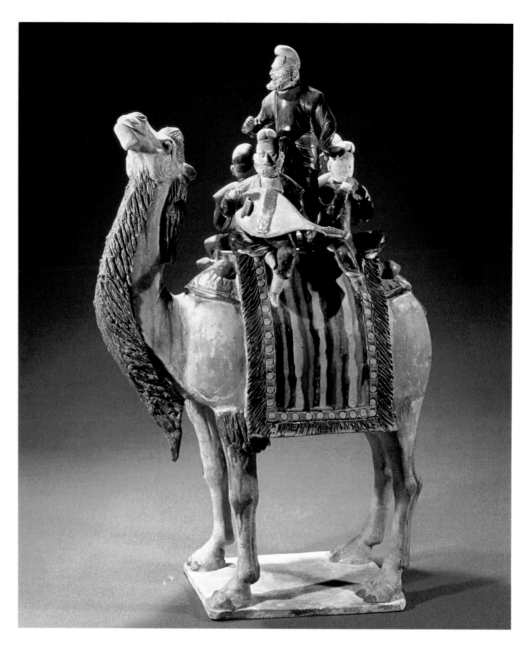

3–17 *Camel Carrying a Group of Musicians* from a tomb near Xi'an, Shaanxi. Tang dynasty, c. mid-8th century CE. Earthenware with three-color glaze, height 26 ⅛″ (66.5 cm). Museum of Chinese History, Beijing

Many foreigners came to the splendid new capital, Chang'an (present-day Xi'an), and the Chinese depicted them in witty detail. A ceramic statue of a camel carrying a troupe of musicians reflects the Tang fascination with the "exotic" Turkic cultures of Central Asia (fig. **3–17**).

Ceramic figurines produced by the thousands for tombs were decorated using a three-color-glaze technique that was a specialty of Tang ceramists. The **glazes**—usually chosen from a restricted palette of amber, yellow, green, and white—were splashed freely and allowed to run over the surface during firing to convey a feeling of spontaneity. Stylistically—compared with the rigid, staring ceramic soldiers of the first emperor of Qin (see pages 63, 74, and fig. 3–1)—the ceramic camel statue shows an interest in naturalistic gesture and expression.

Buddhism flourished in China during the Tang dynasty. The early Tang emperors proclaimed a policy of religious tolerance, and virtually the entire country adopted the Buddhist faith. However, thousands of Buddhist temples, shrines, and monasteries were destroyed and innumerable bronze statues melted down when Confucianism was reasserted during the ninth century and Buddhism was briefly persecuted as a "foreign" religion.

Nanchan Temple, located on Mount Wutai in the eastern part of Shaanxi Province, is not only one of the rare wooden Buddhist structures surviving from the Tang dynasty but also the first important surviving example of Chinese woodframe architecture (fig. 3–18). Constructed in 782 CE, its curved and tiled roof has broad overhanging eaves supported by **brackets** (architectural supports projecting from the walls). Bracketing became a standard element of East Asian architecture, especially in palaces and temples. Also typical is the **bay** system of construction, in which a cubic unit of space, a bay, is formed by four posts and their lintels. The bay functioned in Chinese architecture as a sort of **module**, a basic unit of construction. To create larger structures, an architect multiplied the number of bays. Thus the three-bayed Nanchan Temple, modest in scope, gives an idea of the vast, multistoried, lost palaces of the Tang.

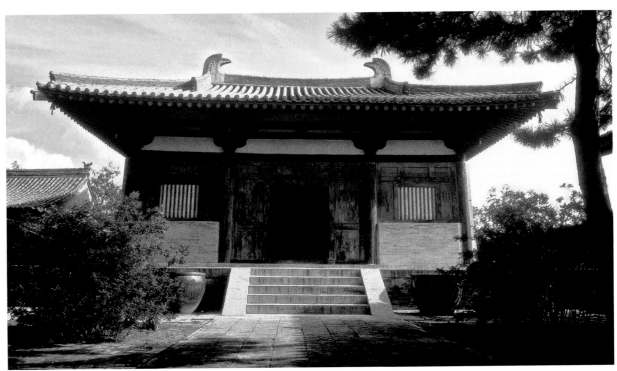

3–18 Nanchan Temple, Wutaishan, Shaanxi. Tang dynasty, 782 CE

The tiled roof, first seen in the Han tomb model (see fig. 3–14) has taken on a curved silhouette that becomes increasingly pronounced in later centuries. The very broad overhanging eaves are supported by a correspondingly elaborate bracketing system.

C L O S E R   L O O K

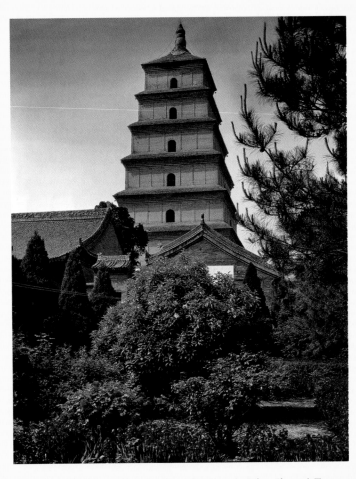

3–19 Great Wild Goose Pagoda of the Ci'en Temple, Xi'an, Shaanxi. Tang dynasty, first erected 645 CE; rebuilt mid-8th century CE

n Xi'an, the ancient capital of China, the Great Wild Goose Pagoda of the Ci'en Temple (fig. **3–19**) rises majestically above small buildings and low foliage. Massive walls, punctuated by roof after horizontal roof, dominate the surroundings with grace and power. The temple was constructed in 645 CE for the famous monk Xuanzang on his return from a 16-year pilgrimage to India. At Ci'en Temple, Xuanzang taught and translated the Sanskrit Buddhist scriptures that he had brought back with him. His dedication to scholarship gave the temple special meaning for his students. Over the years, when students passed their official examinations, they went to the temple and inscribed their names, creating a veritable history of Chinese calligraphy.

Pagodas—towers associated with East Asian Buddhist temples—serve as reminders of the extent and influence of Buddhism. Like the stupas of South Asia, early East Asian pagodas were nearly solid, with small spaces for relics, and they retained *axis mundi* masts. In China the multistoried wooden pagodas with upward-curving roofs supported by elaborate bracketing are much like their prototypes: earlier Han watchtowers. Later pagodas often provided access to the ground floor and sometimes to the upper levels as well. Although modified and repaired in later years (its seven stories were originally five, and a new finial has been added), the Great Wild Goose Pagoda still preserves the essence of Tang architecture in its simplicity, symmetry, proportions, and grace.

The Great Wild Goose Pagoda of the Ci'en Temple in Xi'an, the Tang capital, is another important monument of Tang architecture (see "Closer Look," p. 79). The **pagoda**, or reliquary tower, originated in the Indian Buddhist stupa (see "Stupas," page 68). Chinese builders combined the idea of the stupa reliquary, which developed in India around the first century CE, with traditional Han watchtowers to produce the multistoried pagoda.

Originally built of mud bricks between 645 and 652 CE, and rebuilt at the beginning of the eighth century of brick with wooden floors and steps, the Great Wild Goose Pagoda imitates the forms of wooden architecture of the time. The walls are decorated in low relief to resemble bays, and bracket systems are reproduced under the projecting roofs of each story. The pagoda helps us to visualize the splendor of Tang civilization and the architecture of the great cities of China.

Korea

In the late second century BCE, Emperor Wu Ti of China brought the northern part of the Korean peninsula into the Chinese empire. By this time, the Korean people already had a long tradition as skilled ceramists and metalworkers. Chinese settlers introduced Buddhism into the Korean peninsula and with it a demand for the figurative arts. The Koreans, in turn, transmitted their own blend of Chinese and Korean culture and religion to the Japanese islands at this time. In 552 CE Koreans introduced Buddhism to the Japanese.

The elegant gilded bronze figure of the seated Matreya, or "Buddha of the Future" (fig. 3–20), illustrates the refined and courtly style achieved by Korean artists in the sixth and seventh centuries. The slender figure leans on one knee, striking a pose associated with meditation. The garments cling to the body, the low relief of their folds forming linear patterns—repeated arcs over the legs and sharply pleated folds at the sides. The downcast eyes and the gesture of fingers touching the chin indicate a person lost in deep thought. This sophisticated style of Korean art spread to the Japanese islands, where it became the aesthetic basis for an international style of Buddhist art shared by Korean, Chinese, and Japanese artists.

Japan

Human habitation on the Japanese islands dates back at least 30,000 years, to a time when the islands were still linked to the East Asian landmass and the Sea of Japan was only a lake. Some 15,000 years ago, melting Ice Age glaciers caused the sea level to rise, creating the islands we know today. A distinctive Japanese culture began to emerge during the Jomon period (c. 12,000–300 BCE), which was remarkable for its creation of the world's earliest surviving fired pottery vessels (see fig. 1–9).

From ancient times, indigenous Japanese taste has been distinguished by a respect for and a delight in natural materials. Wooden architecture—farmhouses or Shinto shrines—was often left unpainted, and ceramics frequently were, and are, only partly glazed in order to display the clay bodies underneath. The Japanese aesthetic has a taste for asymmetry, evidenced by paintings and prints that may seem off-balance to Westerners but are actually adroitly composed. In addition, a sense of humor and playfulness sometimes surfaces in unexpected contexts, such as in religious art of great power and depth. Finally, the Japanese have preserved their cultural heritage while welcoming and creatively transforming foreign influences—first from China and Korea and more recently from Europe and North America.

Immigrants from Korea during the Yayoi (c. 300 BCE–300 CE) and Kofun (300–552 CE) periods helped to transform Japan into an agricultural nation, where rice cultivation became widespread. The emergence of a class structure can be dated to the Yayoi period, as can the development of metal technology—first bronze and then iron.

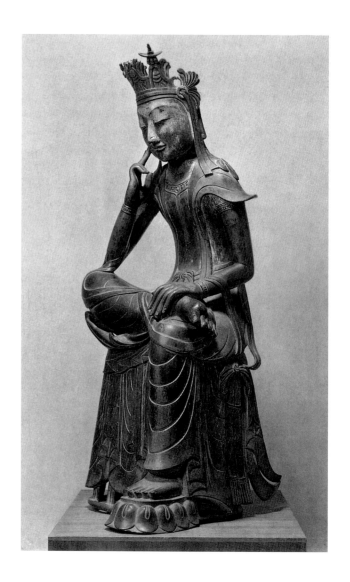

3–20 Seated Matreya. Korea. Three Kingdoms Period, early 7th century. Gilt bronze, height 35 3/4″ (91 cm). National Museum of Korea, Seoul, Republic of Korea

CALLIGRAPHY

The emphasis on expressiveness and structural importance of brush-strokes finds its purest embodiment in calligraphy, from the Greek word for "beautiful writing." In China, calligraphy is regarded as one of the highest forms of artistic expression. For more than 2,000 years, China's literati, all of them Confucian scholars, have enjoyed being connoisseurs and practitioners of this art form. During the fourth century, calligraphy came to full maturity. The most important practitioner of the day was Wang Xizhi (c. 303–361 CE), whose works have served as models of excellence for all subsequent generations.

Calligraphy is based on combinations of strokes, executed with a brush and ink on paper, to create the characters of Chinese writing. Chinese characters, unlike Western letterforms, evolved from pictographs. (A pictograph is a picture or sign representing a thing or concept.) The complex art of calligraphy relies on the stylization of strokes. Chinese calligraphic styles, from which Japanese and Korean calligraphy developed, are based on seven standard strokes, also known as the "Seven Mysteries": a horizontal line, a vertical line, a dot, sharp curves curling either to the left or right, and diagonal strokes executed at various angles, sweeping downward either toward the left or right.

Several styles of calligraphy developed in Asia over the centuries, each with its own unique traits and purpose. The characters in calligraphy used for meditation or poetry, for example, may appear far different from the characters seen in bureaucratic documents or official seals. Depending on the intent of the calligrapher, the width and length of strokes may vary between styles as may the sharpness of edges and corners and the concentration of ink on the page. (Compare, for example, the uniformly placed, compact characters with sharp strokes in figure 9–14 from China to the fluidity and

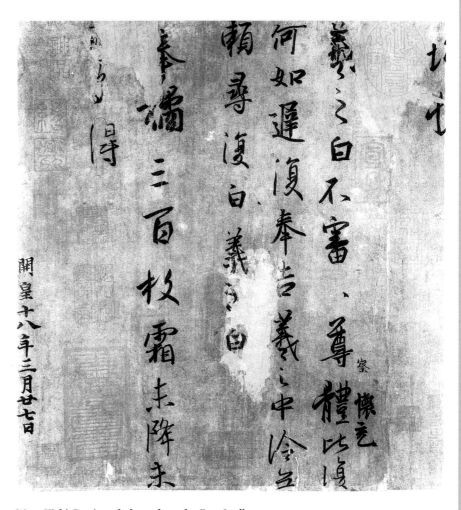

Wang Xizhi, Portion of a letter from the *Feng Ju* album,
Northern and Southern dynasties, mid-4th century CE. Ink on paper,
9$\frac{1}{2}$" × 18$\frac{1}{2}$" (24.7 × 46.9 cm). National Palace Museum Taipei, Taiwan

wild curls that compose the elongated characters in figure 9–19 from Japan.)

The stamped calligraphs that appear on Chinese artworks are seals, or personal emblems. The use of seals dates from the Zhou dynasty, and to this day seals traditionally employ the archaic characters, known appropriately as "seal script," of the Zhou or Qin. Cut in stone, a seal may state a formal, given name, or it may state any of the numerous personal names that China's painters and writers may have adopted throughout their lives. A treasured work

of art often bears not only the seal of its maker but also those of collectors and admirers through the centuries. In the Chinese view, these do not disfigure the work but add another layer of interest and history. This sample of Wang Xizhi's calligraphy, for example, bears the seals of two Song dynasty emperors, a Song official, a famous collector of the sixteenth century, and two emperors of the Qing dynasty of the eighteenth and nineteenth centuries.

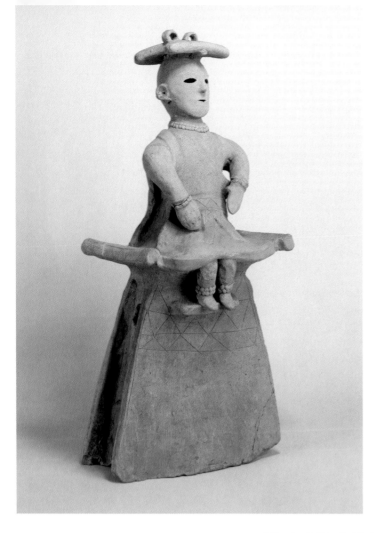

The ensuing Kofun, or "old tombs" period—named for the large royal tombs that were built then—was distinguished by a pattern of veneration of leaders that grew into the beginnings of an imperial system. This system, still in existence today in Japan, eventually equated the emperor (or, very rarely, empress) with the all-powerful sun goddess.

When a Kofun emperor died, chamber tombs furnished with pottery and other grave goods were constructed. Some tomb sites extend over more than 400 acres, with artificial hills built over the tombs themselves. The hills were topped with hollow ceramic works of sculpture called **haniwa** to further distinguish the sites.

The first *haniwa* were simple cylinders that may have held jars with ceremonial offerings. Gradually these cylinders came to be made in the shapes of ceremonial objects—houses, boats, and later, birds and animals. Finally, *haniwa* in human shapes were crafted, of both sexes and all professions and classes. The *haniwa* illustrated here (fig. **3–21**) has been identified as a seated female shaman. Like shamans themselves, *haniwa* figures seem to have served as some kind of link between the world of the dead and the world of the living.

Haniwa figures may also reflect some of the beliefs of Shinto. Shinto, the indigenous religion of Japan, can be characterized as a loose confederation of beliefs in nature deities *(kami). Kami* were thought to inhabit many different aspects of nature, includ-

3–21 *Haniwa* from Kyoto. Kofun period, 6th century CE. Earthenware, height 27″ (68.5 cm). Tokyo National Museum

Haniwa illustrate several characteristics of Japanese taste. They were left unglazed to reveal their clay bodies, and their makers explored the expressive potentials of simple and bold form. Haniwa shapes are never perfectly symmetrical; the slightly off-center placement of the eye slits, the irregular cylindrical bodies, and the unequal arms give them great life and individuality.

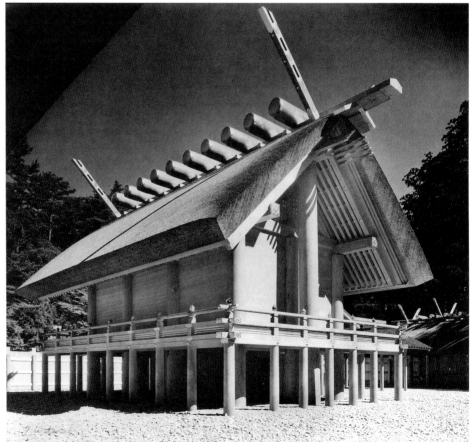

3–22 Inner Shrine, Ise, Mie Prefecture. Early 1st century CE; rebuilt 1993

ing particularly hoary and magnificent trees and rocks, as well as waterfalls, and living creatures such as deer. Shinto also represents the ancient Japanese belief in purification through the ritual use of water. In response to the arrival of Buddhism in Japan in the sixth century CE, Shinto became somewhat more systematized, with shrines, a hierarchy of deities, and more strictly regulated ceremonies.

One of the great Shinto sites is at Ise, on the coast southwest of Tokyo (fig. 3–22). The inner shrine at Ise is dedicated to the sun goddess, the legendary ancestor of Japan's imperial family. A shrine may have been constructed on this ancient sacred spot as early as the first century CE. The building has been ritually rebuilt every 20 years since the seventh century. Stylistically and technically, the shrine is typical of Shinto architecture: The builder used wooden piles to raise the building off the ground and unpainted cypress wood as a construction material; horizontal logs hold a thatched roof in place. These traditional features, which convey a sense of natural simplicity, ultimately derive from the architecture of ancient (first century CE) raised granaries used to store food. The Inner Shrine at Ise houses spiritual rather than corporal nourishment—a sword, a mirror, and a jewel—the three sacred symbols of Shinto.

Buddhism, introduced from China and Korea during the Asuka period (552–646 CE), soon coexisted with Shinto in Japan. During this time of intense cultural transformation, the Japanese also adopted from China a system of writing and a centralized governmental structure. Buddhism, which reached Japan in Mahayana form, with its many buddhas and bodhisattvas (see "Buddhism," page 66), soon became a state religion.

Buddhism introduced not only different gods but also an entirely new concept of religion itself. Where Shinto had found deities in nature, Buddhism introduced a complex pantheon of anthropomorphic gods. The most significant surviving early Japanese temple is Horyu-ji (fig. 3–23), located on Japan's central plain not far from Nara. Founded in 607 CE and rebuilt after a fire in 670, Horyu-ji includes the oldest surviving documented wooden structure in the world.

The main compound of Horyu-ji consists of a rectangular courtyard surrounded by covered corridors. Only two buildings stand within the compound, a large *kondo*, or golden hall, and a slender, five-story pagoda. Both are Chinese-style woodframe buildings with tile roofs. The *kondo* is filled with Buddhist images and is used for worship and ceremonies. The pagoda also serves primarily as a **reliquary** (that is, it holds relics). Other monastery

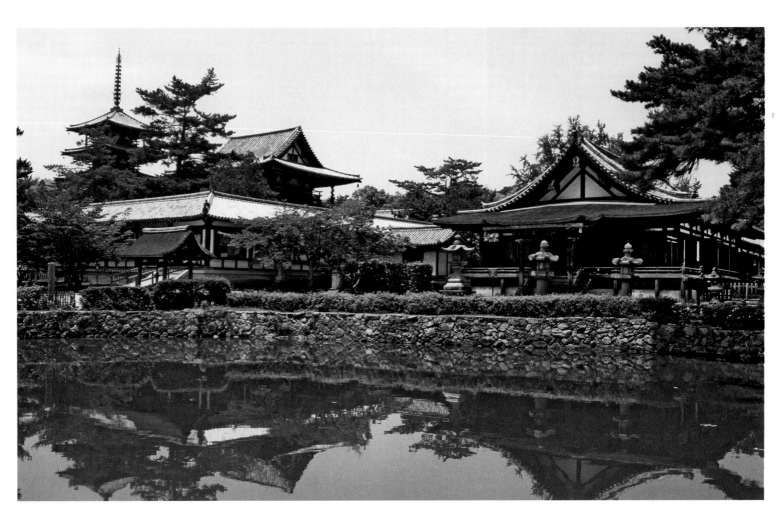

3–23 Main compound, Horyu-ji, Nara Prefecture. Asuka period, 7th century CE

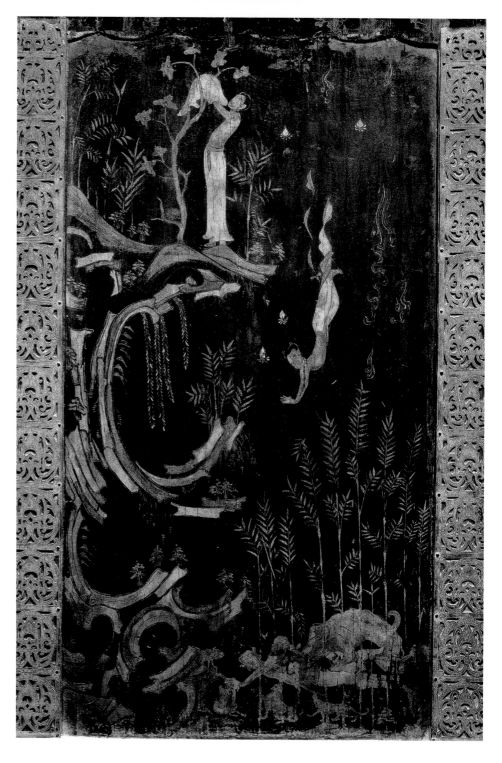

3–24 *Hungry Tigress Jataka*, panel of the
Tamamushi Shrine, Horyu-ji. Asuka period,
7th century CE. Lacquer on wood, height of shrine
7'7³⁄₄" (2.33 m). Horyu-ji Treasure House

buildings, such as a repository for sacred texts and dormitories for monks, lie outside the main compound.

Among the many treasures preserved in Horyu-ji is a miniature shrine decorated with paintings in **lacquer** (a type of hard, glossy varnish) (fig. **3–24**). It is known as the Tamamushi Shrine after the tamamushi beetle, whose iridescent wings were originally affixed to the shrine to make it glitter. The shrine may have been crafted in Korea or Japan, or perhaps by Korean artisans working in Japan, testifying to the international range of Buddhist art at this period.

The paintings ornamenting the Tamamushi Shrine are among the few two-dimensional works of art to survive from the Asuka period. The painting illustrated here tells a story from a former life of the Buddha, who is shown nobly sacrificing his life

in order to feed his body to a starving tigress and her cubs. The tigers are at first too weak to eat him, so he jumps off a cliff to break open his flesh. The elegantly slender rendition of the Buddha's figure, shown three times in the three stages of the story, and the abstract treatment of the cliff, trees, and bamboo, represent a Buddhist style shared during this time by Chinese, Korean, and Japanese artists.

During the seventh and eighth centuries, Buddhism so thoroughly permeated the upper levels of society that an empress wanted to cede her throne to a Buddhist monk. Her advisers intervened, but Buddhism remained the single most significant element in Japanese culture, comfortably coexisting with Shinto, just as it had with Hinduism in India and with Confucianism and Daoism in China.

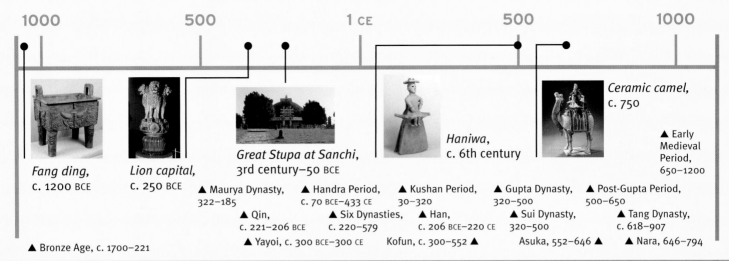

1000	500	1 CE	500	1000

Fang ding,
c. 1200 BCE

Lion capital,
c. 250 BCE

Great Stupa at Sanchi,
3rd century–50 BCE

Haniwa,
c. 6th century

Ceramic camel,
c. 750

▲ Early
Medieval
Period,
650–1200

▲ Maurya Dynasty,
322–185

▲ Handra Period,
c. 70 BCE–433 CE

▲ Kushan Period,
30–320

▲ Gupta Dynasty,
320–500

▲ Post-Gupta Period,
500–650

▲ Qin,
c. 221–206 BCE

▲ Six Dynasties,
c. 220–579

▲ Han,
c. 206 BCE–220 CE

▲ Sui Dynasty,
320–500

▲ Tang Dynasty,
c. 618–907

▲ Bronze Age, c. 1700–221

▲ Yayoi, c. 300 BCE–300 CE   Kofun, c. 300–552 ▲   Asuka, 552–646 ▲   ▲ Nara, 646–794

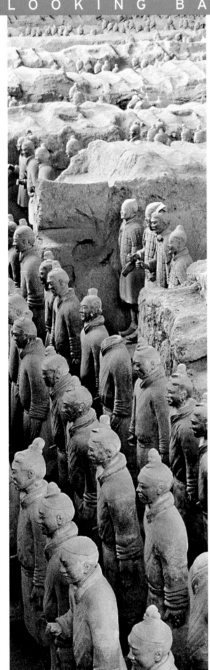

The civilizations of South and East Asia—including those that flourished in what are today the countries of India, China, Korea, Japan, and Indonesia—are among the world's oldest and also rank among the most culturally rich. Early Asian cultures evolved from simple societies into complex ones that were highly organized politically and economically. One famous example—the tomb of the Chinese emperor Qin Shihuangdi—conveys immense power and wealth. A ghostly army, fully human in size and appearance though made of terra-cotta, stood buried underground in timeless battle formation ready for action. The technical achievement of the early artists and artisans behind such a vast project is as amazing as the political organization that made the project possible.

Early Asian societies were also bolstered by belief systems and rituals that evolved into religions that are still widely practiced today. Indigenous beliefs such as Hinduism in India, Confucianism in China, and Shinto in Japan contributed to distinctive styles and subjects of art in the locations where these religions proliferated. The religion of Buddhism, which originated in India, spread throughout the continent. The Buddha became a common subject of Asian art, and art related to Buddhism followed the spread of the religion from India to China, Korea, and Japan. Over time, important traditions of representing the Buddha—linked to a language of symbolic gestures (*mudras*)—evolved in both sculpture and painting.

The rich philosophical and spiritual life of early Asian cultures is also reflected in increasing technical refinement and artistic skill. In China, Korea, and Japan, writing evolved into a complex and stylized pictographic script—calligraphy—in which the image of every character is a miniature work of art. Together with poetry, the mastery of such expressive images came to be considered the highest form of art. Ink painting—often recording images from nature—played a dominant role, too, while porcelain, silk, jade, and finely worked metals such as bronze made early Asian decorative arts especially prized.

Such luxury goods were traded over sea and land along the lengths of the famed Silk Route. And ideas were traded as well. In fact, one example of the flowering that sometimes occurs when ideas are exchanged from place to place can be seen in the type of building perhaps most often associated with Chinese and Japanese architecture: the pagoda. Its progenitors are the distinctive symbolic architectural form of the Indian stupa and the tall multi-roofed structures of the Han Chinese.

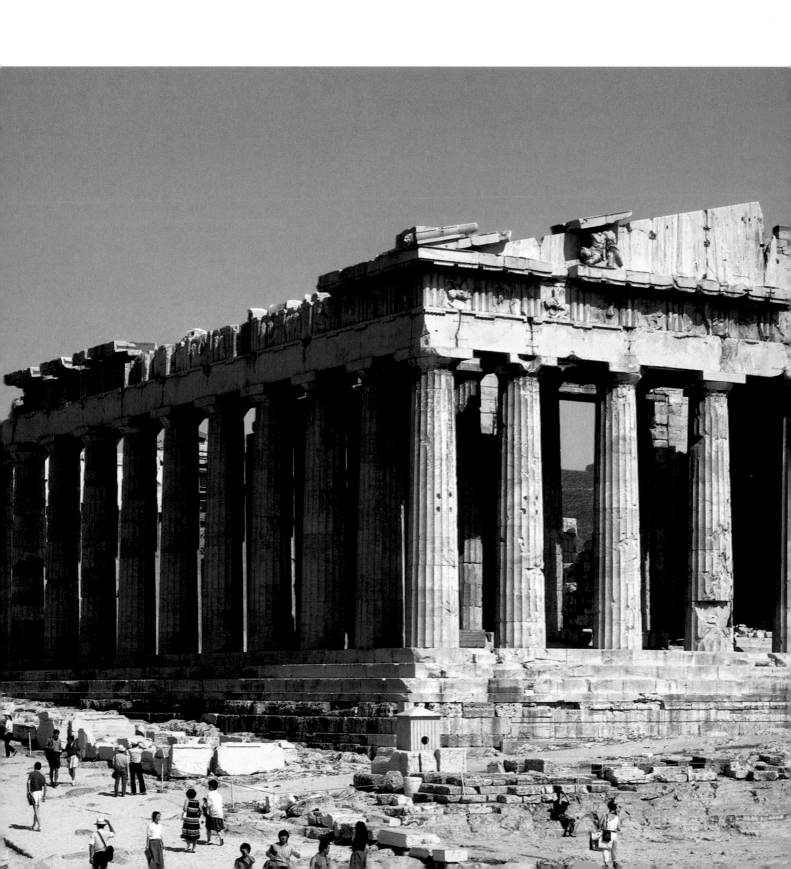

4
Art of Greece and the Aegean World

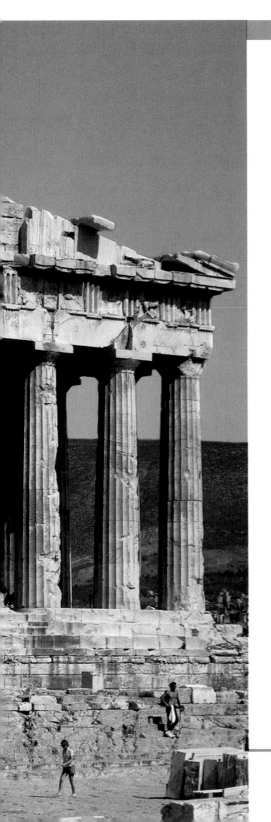

I n contrast to the civilizations of ancient Egypt and China, ancient Greek society focused on the individual—or at least on an elite group of men. "Man is the measure of all things," said one of the Seven Sages of ancient Greece. Here, for the first time, we find a worldview in which greater prominence is given to human beings. Supernatural forces are certainly still at work—Greek gods meddle in, and often control, the affairs of men and women—but the gods themselves have human forms and human foibles. This new focus mirrors a new political system in which democracy replaced one-man, divine rule. And this new view of society required a new art—one centered in the material world, but one that reflected the philosophers' search for the human values of truth, virtue, and harmony.

Ancient Greek art and architecture established an ideal of earthly, physical, and visual perfection. Whether in sculpture, painting, ceramics, metalwork, or architecture, artists sought the essence of forms and combined close observation of nature with generalizations founded in the harmonious beauty of mathematics.

The Greek ideal seems encapsulated in the Parthenon, the Temple of *Athena Parthenos* built nearly 2,400 years ago in Athens (fig. **4–1**). The Parthenon rises triumphantly atop its site, symbolizing Greek independence, self-confidence, and justifiable pride—through the excellence of its materials and craftwork, the rationality of its simple and elegant post-and-lintel structure, and the subtle yet ennobling messages of its sculpture. The great Athenian leader Pericles (c. 495–429 BCE) ordered the construction of this temple about 447 BCE, and it became Athens's most important center for civic and religious celebrations to honor the city's patron goddess.

Isolated like a work of sculpture, the Parthenon is the ideal Doric temple. The building is both an abstract form—a block of columns—and the essence of shelter, an earthly home for Athena. Over the centuries, different people living under a variety of circumstances have found that the design of ancient Greek temples could also express their ideals. They have responded to the harmonious proportions, subtle details, and rational relationship of part to part. As a symbol of the highest standards in art and politics, honesty, heroism, and civic virtue, the Parthenon and its counterparts have become models for national monuments, government buildings, and even private homes throughout the world.

Even today, ancient Greece continues to engage the imagination of artists and architects, who turn to its buildings and sculpture either to rebel against or to emulate the Classical values embodied in its clean lines, simple forms, and mathematical ratios (see "Classic and Classical," page 106).

4–1 Kallikrates and **Iktinos. Parthenon,** Acropolis, Athens. 447–438 BCE. View from the northwest

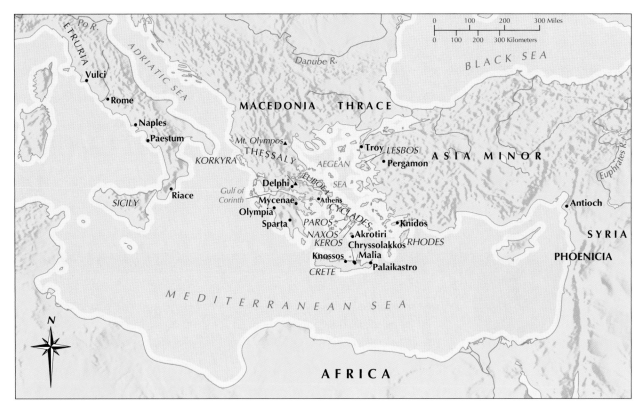

Map 4–1 The Aegean World and Ancient Greece

The Aegean region of Europe is an area composed of mainland Greece, a cluster of nearby islands in the Aegean Sea including the Cyclades, and the large southern island of Crete. Being natives of a rocky peninsula and many islands, Aegean peoples became seafaring and adventurous by necessity. Unlike most of the early civilizations we have already considered, which arose in fertile river valleys, the people of Greece, the Cyclades, and Crete looked to the surrounding seas for both security and resources (see Map 4–1, above). And, beginning in the third millennium BCE and culminating in the Classical art of fifth-century BCE Athens, they created visual arts of striking originality.

Cycladic peoples were established as early as 6000 BCE. However, because they left no written records, the prosperous society they developed in the Bronze Age, about 3000 BCE, is obscure. Their art is one of our main sources of information about them.

South of the Cyclades, on the island of Crete, the culture that modern archaeologists call Minoan took shape. It began at the start of the Aegean Bronze Age, about 3100 BCE, and was marked by the use of **bronze** to make weapons and tools. Strategically located, Minoan Crete became a great sea power, reaching its height between 1750 and 1470 BCE, the so-called New Palace period. Excavations in and around immense architectural com-plexes, built from about 1900 BCE, have revealed the richness of Minoan art and ceremony and have uncovered ceramics, sculpture, wall paintings, and spectacular craftwork in ivory and gold.

Minoan Crete declined after 1500 BCE, although the main center, Knossos, functioned until the mid-thirteenth century BCE. Dominance in the Aegean region then shifted to a mainland Greek culture known as Mycenaean, after one of its major cities, Mycenae. The Mycenaeans, who spoke an early form of the Greek language, built fortified strongholds ruled by local princes or kings, warlords whose exploits were memorialized in later Greek epics such as the *Iliad* and the *Odyssey*.

The Aegean Bronze Age ended about 1100 BCE, when Mycenaean civilization collapsed for unknown reasons. A period of disorganization followed, and not until around 900 BCE did the inhabitants of the Aegean region begin to flourish again. These were the people who came to be called the Greeks. Linked by language—most spoke some form of Greek by then—they lived in self-sufficient, close-knit communities scattered throughout the region, which eventually developed into independently governed city-states.

For at least 700 years, the Greeks were unimaginably creative. We still credit them with groundbreaking experiments in

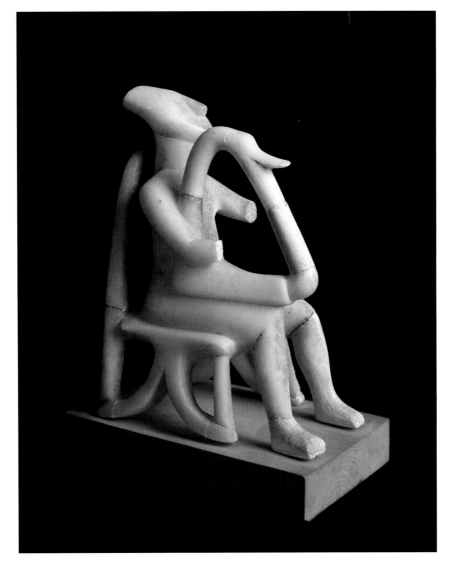

4–2 _Male lyre player,_ from Keros, (Cyclades). c. 2700–2500 BCE. Marble, approx 9″ high. National Archaeological Museum, Athens

science, mathematics, and herbal medicine; for the implementation of a representative government that is a forerunner of modern democracy; and for an astounding legacy of art and architecture that continues to influence the Western world today. The works of Greek poets, dramatists, and philosophers—including Homer, Aeschylus, Sophocles, Euripides, and Plato—have also endured for more than two millennia.

Ancient Greek philosophers sought to define the ideal community, the actions of responsible citizenship, and the meaning of a good life. They asked, "What is the Good, the True, the Beautiful?" Artists responded by trying to capture such intangible concepts as "truth" and "beauty" in the material forms of sculpture, architecture, and painting. "Know thyself" and "Nothing in excess" are maxims inscribed in the sanctuary of the sun god, Apollo, at Delphi in the mountains above the Gulf of Corinth. These words and the ideas they embody and inspire seem to have been imprinted on the heart and hands of every Greek artist: focus on human beings; study the world in which you live; observe the variety found in nature; and strive to simplify and clarify these impressions in order to capture the essence of life.

The Cycladic Islands

During the late Neolithic and early Bronze Ages, the people who lived on the Cyclades—like their contemporaries in the ancient Near East and Egypt (see Chapter 2)—farmed, made utensils, and engaged in trade. They used local stone to build fortified towns and hillside burial chambers, and they produced ceramic pottery and clay figurines of humans and animals.

Human figurines made of a fine white marble, abundant especially on the islands of Naxos and Paros, have been unearthed in and around Cycladic graves. Most of these figurines depict women, although a few male statuettes have been found, including depictions of musicians and acrobats. Now starkly white, the statuettes originally had painted faces and hair. Having been found at grave sites, they may have been used in religious or burial rituals.

The _Seated Harp Player_ is fully developed **sculpture in the round** (fig. **4–2**), yet its body is just as simplified as that of the female figurines. The figure has been reduced to geometric essentials, yet with careful attention to those elements that best characterize an actual musician. The harpist sits on a high-backed

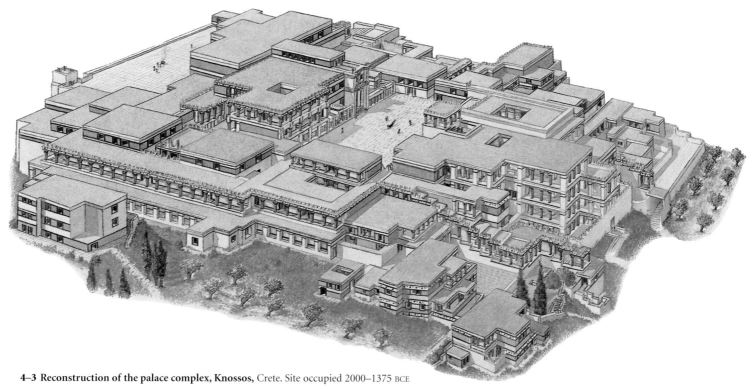

4–3 Reconstruction of the palace complex, Knossos, Crete. Site occupied 2000–1375 BCE

The architectural complex depicted in this drawing is the one built after destructive earthquakes and fires in c. 1700 BCE. From the central courtyard, corridors and stairs led to several levels of suites of rooms and additional smaller courtyards and light-wells. The final destruction of the palace occurred about 1375 BCE.

chair with a splayed base, head tilted back as if singing, knees and feet apart for stability, and arms raised, pluck its strings. So expressive is the pose that we can almost hear the music.

Minoan Crete

The Minoan culture of the island of Crete came into being around 3100 BCE and flourished between c. 1900 and 1375 BCE. The word *Minoan* comes from a Greek legend about King Minos of Crete, who was said to have kept a human-eating monster called a Minotaur (half human and half bull) at the center of a labyrinth, or maze.

Crete, the largest of the Aegean islands, is 150 miles long and 36 miles wide. The earliest Minoans were self-sufficient agriculturally; they produced grains and fruit and raised cattle and sheep, which they traded for various luxury goods and for the copper and tin ores they needed to make bronze. Ancient Minoan traders must have been highly skilled sailors, traveling to ports in places as distant as Egypt, the Near East, and Anatolia (western Turkey).

Relatively little is known about daily life during the Minoan period, although a number of written records have been found. The two earliest forms of Minoan writing, a form of hieroglyphs and a script called Linear A, still defy translation, but surviving documents in a later script, Linear B—a very early form of Greek imported from the mainland—have proved to be invaluable. These documents include administrative records and inventories of animals, olive trees, chariots, and weapons.

Minoan civilization remained very much a mystery until a British archaeologist, Sir Arthur Evans (1851–1941), excavated the buried ruins of an extraordinary building complex at Knossos,

on Crete's north coast, in the early twentieth century. Great complexes such as Knossos—called "palaces" by modern archaeologists—dominated the architecture of Minoan Crete. Safe-guarded by watchtowers and stone walls, they were simultaneously used as administrative, commercial, and religious centers. The builders devised an almost earthquake-proof flexible wall system of timber supports and braces with light, mud-brick fill. Only **facades** and lower walls were faced with **dressed stone** (cut and highly finished).

After a major earthquake about 1750 BCE, several palaces, including Knossos, were repaired and enlarged. The resulting "new palaces"—multistoried, flat-roofed, and with many columns—were designed with staggered levels, open stairwells, and strategically placed air shafts and light-wells to maximize air and light. Residential, manufacturing, and warehouse areas surrounded a large, central courtyard.

During its heyday, the palace complex at Knossos covered 6 acres (fig. 4–3). Its residential quarters had many assets. In addition to sunlit courtyards, there were richly colored murals and an extraordinarily sophisticated plumbing system consisting of bathrooms and a network of terra-cotta pipes laid beneath the palace. Extensive workshops in and around Knossos and other complexes suggest that arts and crafts were officially sponsored, and huge storerooms point to the centralized management of trade in foodstuffs. In a single storeroom at Knossos, excavators found enough large ceramic jars to hold 20,000 gallons of olive oil.

The palace complexes in Crete also included areas for ritual activities. Like many other early cultures, Minoans may have associated their gods and god-rulers with powerful animals, especially the lion and the bull. Priestesses are believed to have overseen the worship of a goddess who controlled the natural

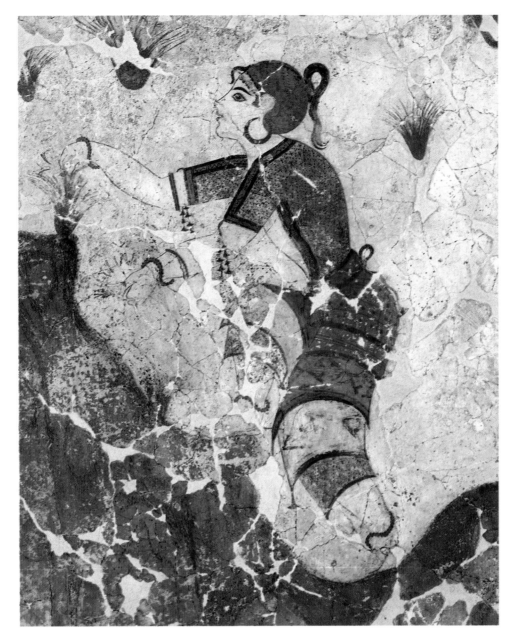

4–4 *Young Girl Gathering Saffron Crocus Flowers,* detail of wall painting, Room 3 of House Xeste, Akrotiri, Thera. Second Palace period, c. 1700–1450 BCE. Thera Foundation, Petros M. Nomikos, Greece

world and who is associated with serpents, bulls, and the double ax. This Aegean deity may have inspired the later Greeks to venerate goddesses such as Artemis and Athena.

Depictions of bulls appear often in Minoan art, rendered with an intensity not seen since the prehistoric cave paintings at Chauvet, Lascaux, and Altamira (see Chapter 1). Horn shapes decorated outdoor altars and also figured in a bull-jumping rite practiced by men and women who must have been trained acrobats (see fig. 4–5). While neither the images nor later myths offer any proof that the Minoans actually worshiped a bull god, the animals apparently were sacrificed.

Minoan wall painting displays elegant drawing, linear contours filled with bright colors, a preference for profile or full-faced views, and a stylization that turns natural forms into decorative patterns, yet keenly observes the appearance of the human body in motion. These conventions can be seen in the vivid murals at Akrotiri, on the island Thíra (also called

Santoríni), located north of Crete and an outpost of Minoan culture. One of the houses at Akrotiri has rooms dedicated to young women's initiation ceremonies. In the detail shown here, a young woman picks the purple flowers of the fall crocus, whose stigmas (also called saffron) were valued for their use as a yellow dye, as a flavoring for food, and as a medicinal plant to alleviate menstrual cramps (fig. **4–4**). The girl wears the typically colorful Minoan flounced skirt with a short-sleeved, open-breasted bodice, large earrings, and bracelets. Notice that she still has the shaved head, fringed hair, and long ponytail of a child. On another wall, not shown here, girls present their flowers to an older seated woman who is flanked by a monkey and a griffin (a mythical half lion and half eagle). Surely the woman is a goddess receiving her devotees, and the room must have had a special ceremonial use.

The palace at Knossos also has wall paintings and painted low reliefs showing bulls. In one painting two women and a man

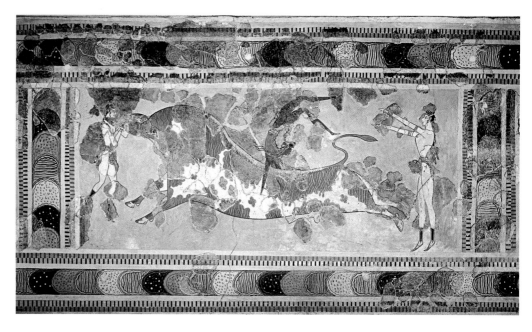

Careful sifting during excavation preserved many fragments of the paintings that once covered the palace walls. The pieces were painstakingly sorted and cleaned by restorers and reassembled into puzzle pictures that still had more pieces missing than found. The next step was to fill in the gaps with colors similar to the original ones. It is therefore obvious which are the restored portions, but the eye can still read and enjoy the image.

engage in the dangerous ritual of bull jumping (fig. **4–5**). (Minoan painters followed the convention of depicting women with pale skin and men with dark skin.) The woman at right is either beginning or finishing her vault, the man is in the midst of his, and the woman at left is grasping the bull by its horns, ready to leap. The painting may show an initiation or fertility ritual, or it may honor a god by displaying human courage.

Painting on a smaller scale decorated ceramics made in palace workshops. A striking vessel from the eastern site of Palaikastro, a bottle known as the *Octopus Flask,* dates from about 1500–1450 BCE (fig. **4–6**). The decoration of sea creatures and plants celebrates Cretan maritime power. Like microscopic life teeming in a drop of seawater, sea creatures float among an

octopus's curling, sucker-lined tentacles. The painter captures the grace and energy of natural forms while presenting them as a stylized design in harmony with the vessel's shape.

The skills of Minoan artists, particularly those of metalsmiths, made their work highly sought after in mainland Greece. Jewelers became adept at decorating their goldwork with minute granules, or balls, of the precious metal fused to the surface, a technique known as **granulation**. This type of ornamentation is visible on a pendant perhaps made for a necklace in about 1700–1550 BCE (fig. **4–7**). The artist arched a pair of bees or wasps around a granulated drop of honey. Their sleek bodies, decorated with parallel rows of granules, are framed by a single pair of outspread wings.

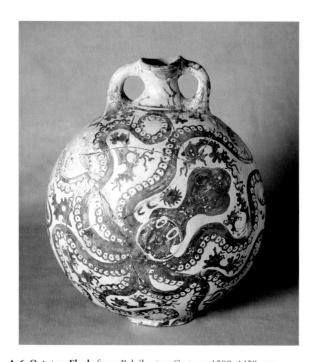

4–6 Octopus Flask, from Palaikastro, Crete. c. 1500–1450 BCE. Ceramic, height 11″ (28 cm). Archaeological Museum, Iráklion, Crete

This bottle was made on a potter's wheel, a technical innovation in use from the early second millennium BCE.

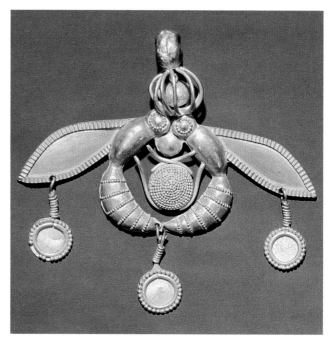

4–7 Pendant in the form of two bees or wasps from Chryssolakkos near Mallia, Crete. c. 1700–1550 BCE. Gold, height approx. $1^{13}/_{16}$″ (4.6 cm). Archaeological Museum, Iráklion, Crete

Human beings are storytellers, and virtually every society has created its own traditional stories that give form to its gods and to explain the unexplained, including the origin of the universe, birth and death, and the existence of good and evil. Throughout the world, mythological characters and their stories are the most frequently represented subjects in the history of art. The main characters of Classical mythology—that of Greek and Roman civilizations—are gods, demigods, heroes, and monsters. The behavior, relationships, and attitudes of such mythical characters mirror the nature and values of the society that created them.

Some myths seem to have originated in actual events. The Greek war against Troy in Asia Minor, for example, is now believed to have happened more than 300 years before it was mythologized in the *Iliad* and the *Odyssey*, by the poet known as Homer, in the eighth century BCE.

Homer tells of a Greek siege of the city of Troy, generally believed to have stood on the site of Hissarlik, in what is now Turkey. Paris, son of the Trojan king, abducted Helen, the most beautiful woman in the world and wife of King Menelaus of Sparta. Menelaus and his brother, King Agamemnon of Mycenae— both sons of Atreus—led the Greek troops against Troy. Human warriors, gods, and goddesses took sides in the 10-year war. It is

not clear whether Helen, Menelaus, or Agamemnon existed, or if the Trojan War actually took place, but the story probably had roots in a real battle or raid. Ancient Greek historians, accepting the Trojan War as history, dated it anywhere from 1334 BCE to 1150 BCE, certainly long before Homer turned it into a legendary combat.

The story of the Trojan War was retold by the Roman poet Virgil (70–19 BCE) in his *Aeneid*, which he wrote to "prove" the lineage of Emperor Augustus back to the heroic era of ancient Greece. The *Aeneid* also includes the story of Laocoön, the Trojan priest whose punishment from the gods was immortalized in a dramatic sculpture from the first century CE (see Introduction, figs. 27 and 28).

Mycenaean (Late Bronze Age) Civilization

At some time about 3000 BCE, Greek-speaking peoples invaded the Greek peninsula. They brought advanced metalworking, ceramic, and architectural techniques and displaced the indigenous Neolithic culture. Archaeologists use the term *Helladic* (from *Hellas*, the Greek name for Greece) to designate this Bronze Age period of mainland Greece. The Helladic period extends from about 3000 to 1000 BCE, overlapping the Cycladic and Minoan cultures. (Dates continue to be debated.) Minoan culture declined after about 1500 BCE, and a late Helladic culture known as Mycenaean became the center of power and cultural influence in the Aegean by 1400 BCE.

Life in the fortified city of Mycenae and other mainland strongholds probably contrasted sharply with life in the open palace complexes on the island of Crete. Mycenaean communities centered around strongholds controlled by local princes or kings. Evidence from shaft graves—deep vertical pits used for burial—dating from between 1600 and 1500 BCE, suggests a society that became increasingly wealthy and stratified. Excavated by the German archaeologist Heinrich Schliemann (1822–1890) in 1876, the magnificent swords, daggers, scepters, jewelry, and drinking cups found within the graves mark the burials of an elite class of warriors.

Three bronze dagger blades found in one of the shaft graves at Mycenae are decorated with inlaid scenes. The artist cut shapes out of different-colored metals—copper, silver, and gold—and inlaid them in the bronze blades, adding fine details in **niello**. In the *Iliad*, Homer's epic poem about the Trojan War, the poet describes similar decoration on Agamemnon's armor and Achilles' shield. The decoration on the blade shown here (fig. **4–8**) depicts a

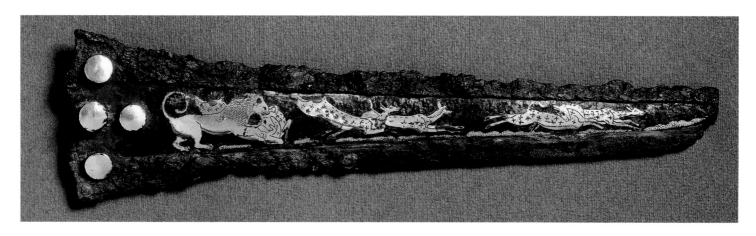

4–8 Dagger blade from Shaft Grave IV Grave Circle A, Mycenae, Greece. c. 1600–1550 BCE. Bronze inlaid with gold, silver, and copper, length 9³⁄₈″ (23.8 cm). National Archaeological Museum, Athens

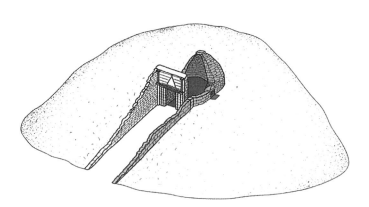

4–9 Cutaway drawing of the beehive tomb called the Treasury of Atreus, Mycenae, Greece. c. 1300–1200 BCE

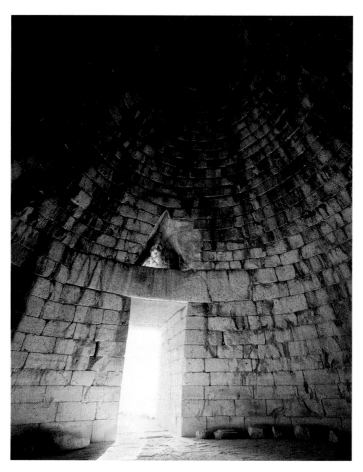

4–10 Corbeled vault, interior of the so-called Treasury of Atreus. Stone, height of vault approx. 43′ (13 m), diameter 47′6″ (14.48 m)

lion attacking a deer with four more terrified animals in full flight. Like the bull in figure 4–5, the animals spring forward in the "flying gallop" pose to indicate their speed and energy.

Other legends tell of a race of giants, the Cyclops, who moved the huge stones and gave the name **cyclopean** to the large-stone masonry seen in Mycenaean citadels and tombs. More than a hundred such tombs have been found on mainland Greece, nine of them in the vicinity of Mycenae. They were constructed for members of Helladic ruling families after shaft graves were no longer used. One tomb, popularly and incorrectly designated as the "Treasury of Atreus," was built around 1300–1200 BCE (fig. **4–9**). It may be close to the likely date of the Trojan War, but most probably it is not connected to Homer's kings of Mycenae.

An uncovered, walled passageway about 120 feet long and 20 feet wide led to the door of a conical structure, the **beehive-shaped** tomb. The circular main chamber is formed by a **corbeled vault:** a **vault** built up in regular **courses** (layers) of dressed stone in overlapping and ever-decreasing rings carefully calculated to meet in a single **capstone** at the peak (fig. **4–10**). The great size of the vaulted chamber—47$\frac{1}{2}$ feet in diameter and 43 feet high—makes the tomb the largest unobstructed interior space built before the Roman Pantheon (see fig. 6–23). Like the Neolithic passage graves constructed in western Europe

(see fig. 1–14), the stone structure was covered by earth to form an artificial mountain.

Megalithic walls, broken by a monumental entrance and one or two secret emergency exits, encircled the fortress of Mycenae (fig. **4–11**). The ruler's residence had a large audience hall called a **megaron**, or "great room." The main courtyard led to a porch, a vestibule, and then to this great room where four large columns around a central hearth supported the ceiling. The roof section above the hearth was either raised or open to admit light and air and to permit smoke to escape. The imposing Lion Gate (c. 1250 BCE) led into the citadel (fig. **4–12**). The gate consists of a post-and-lintel frame that once held massive wood and metal doors, topped by a **relieving arch**, in this case, a corbel arch spanning the open space with layers of stones, each layer projecting over the preceding layer. In the opening over the door, a pair of lions nearly 9 feet tall flank a Minoan-style column that may symbolize the king's inner retreat and audience chamber. The animals have lost their heads, but holes in the stones suggest that the heads were removable and probably fashioned of some precious material. If the lion heads were indeed made of bronze or gold, they must have created an imposing presence. From this gate, a long, stone passageway leads into the citadel, at the center of which stood the king's palace.

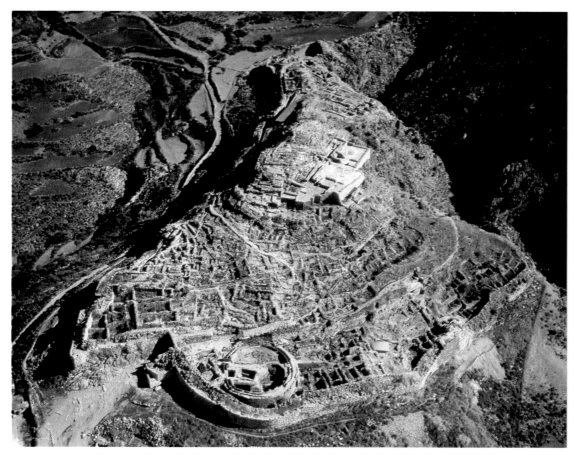

4–11 Mycenae, Greece.
c. 1600–1200 BCE

The citadel's hilltop position and fortified ring wall are clearly visible. The Lion Gate (see fig. 4–12) is at the lower left, approached today by a dirt path. A grave circle is at the lower center. The megaron floor and bases of columns and walls are seen as a light rectangular area at the upper center.

Mycenaean civilization does not have a long history. By 1200 BCE, invaders are believed to have crossed into mainland Greece and taken control of the major cities and citadels. The period between about 1100 and 900 BCE was a "dark age" in the Aegean; marked by political and economic instability and upheaval, it produced very little art. Following this period, however, a new culture emerged—one that looked back to the exploits of the Helladic warrior princes and the glories of a heroic age and at the same time formed the basis of a truly new Greek civilization.

The Emergence of Greek Civilization

In the ninth and eighth centuries BCE, the people we know as Greeks, the offspring of ancient inhabitants of the Aegean region and newer migrants, began to form independently governed

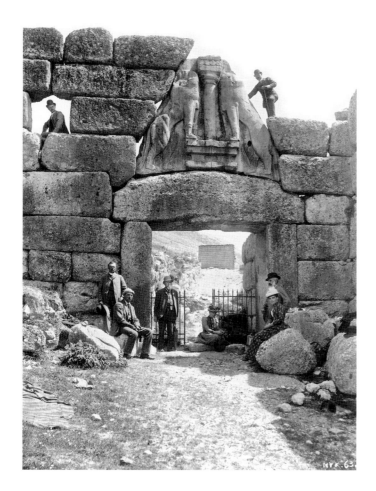

4–12 Lion Gate, Mycenae. c. 1250 BCE. Limestone relief, height of sculpture approx. 9′6″ (2.9 m). Deutsches Archaologisches Institut, Athens

In this historic photograph, Heinrich Schliemann, director of the excavation, stands to the left of the gate and his wife and partner in archaeology, Sophia, sits to the right.

city-states. Whenever possible, cities were built on a hilltop that could be fortified, an **acropolis** (*acro* means "high," and *polis* means "city"). Eventually the hill became a fortified religious sanctuary with the commercial, governmental, and domestic areas constructed in the plain or valley below.

As the Greek population eventually outstripped crop yields, outlying colonies were established to alleviate food shortages. The new communities, like their Bronze Age predecessors, depended on trade with other regions to meet the needs of their growing populations. Many city-states developed merchant fleets that sailed across the Mediterranean and into the Black Sea. They too established colonies, some of which, like Syracuse, became influential commercial centers in their own right.

At first, aristocratic councils ruled the Greek city-states. Then, beginning around 700 BCE and extending into the sixth century BCE, self-appointed leaders called "tyrants" imposed a dictatorial form of rule, often with popular support. At their most beneficent, they fostered urban development at home and sought economic rather than military influence abroad.

The idea that all citizens should share in the rights and responsibilities of government began to emerge in the city-state of Athens in the sixth century BCE, although only a few privileged males were considered citizens. In the late sixth century, a leader called Kleisthenes (d. 508 BCE), often called the father of democracy, instituted reforms that broadened the representative base of Athenian government. Although the system of rulership that Kleisthenes developed was democratic in principle, it was open only to Athenian men. Women took no official part in government, nor did slaves or men born outside Athens.

Athens and the other Greek city-states, in spite of their rivalries, shared a common language and culture and developed a distinctively Greek art. Within a remarkably brief time, Greek artists developed ideals of human beauty and architectural excellence that continue to have a profound influence today. From about 900 BCE until about 100 BCE, they explored new ideas and produced an impressive body of work with clear stylistic and technical characteristics. Periods of the earliest Greek art are named for these styles: Geometric, Archaic, and Classical.

The Geometric Style

The Geometric style became widespread after about 900 BCE and lasted until about 700 BCE. An Athenian vase exemplifies the complex linear decoration of this period (fig. 4–13). Dated about 750 BCE, the vessel, a funerary vase, was a grave marker made to hold offerings. Funerary rituals are recorded in two bands, or registers, of decoration. In the top register, the body of the deceased lies on its side on a platform. Accompanying figures with their hands on their heads may be tearing their hair with grief. Triangles were used to represent torsos; round dots stand for eyes in profile heads, and lines depicting arms and legs swell into bulging thighs and calves. Below, a procession of horse-drawn chariots and foot soldiers, who look like walking shields, recall the athletic competitions or funeral games held to honor dead men. Figures are subtly twisted rather than depicted in fully frontal or full-profile views.

Greek artists of the Geometric period also produced many small figurines of wood, ivory, clay, and especially cast bronze. A tiny bronze of this type, *Man and Centaur,* dates from about 750 BCE (fig. 4–14). Like the painter of the vase discussed above

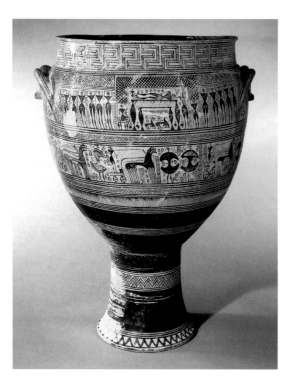

4–13 Funerary vase (Krater), from the Dipylon Cemetery, attributed to the Hirschfeld Workshop, Athens. c. 750–700 BCE. Terra-cotta, height $42\frac{5}{8}''$ (108 cm). The Metropolitan Museum of Art, New York

ROGERS FUND, 1914 (14.130.14). PHOTOGRAPH ©1996 THE METROPOLITAN MUSEUM OF ART

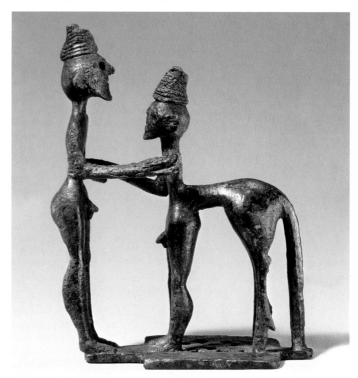

**4–14 *Man and Centaur,* ** perhaps from Olympia. c. 750 BCE. Bronze, height $4\frac{5}{16}''$ (11.1 cm). The Metropolitan Museum of Art, New York

GIFT OF J. PIERPONT MORGAN, 1917, (17.190.2072) PHOTOGRAPH ©1996 THE METROPOLITAN MUSEUM OF ART

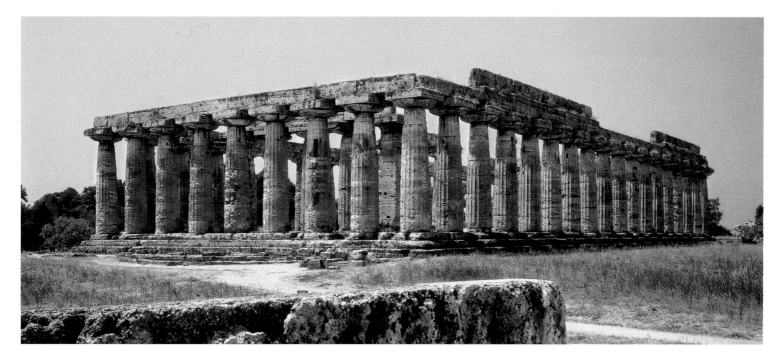

4–15 Temple of Hera I, Paestum, Italy. c. 550 BCE

(see fig. 4–13), the sculptor reduced the body parts to simple geometric shapes. Nevertheless, the figures seem charged with energy. The identity of the two figures is unknown, but they might be the legendary hero Achilles and the centaur Chiron, his teacher. Figurines such as *Man and Centaur,* which possibly served as a votive offering, have been found in sanctuaries, sites sacred to one or more of the Greek gods.

The Archaic Period

The Archaic period lasted from c. 600 to c. 490/480 BCE. Although its name means "old" or "old-fashioned," the Archaic period was a time of great achievement. It was during the Archaic period that Sappho wrote her poetry on the island of Lesbos. Her writing would later inspire the geographer Strabo, near the end of the millennium, to comment: "Never within human memory has there been a woman to compare with her as a poet." Elsewhere the legendary teller of tales, Aesop, captured the imagination with animal fables. Artists shared in the growing prosperity as city councils and wealthy individuals sponsored the creation of sculpture, fine ceramic wares, and civic buildings such as council chambers, public fountains (see fig. 4–22), and temples.

The earliest standing Greek temples date from the Archaic period. A temple was conceived both as an earthly home and as a treasury for its honored god or goddess. It is in effect an idealized shelter. Generally temples have a main room, called the **cella** or **naos**, and a vestibule, called the **pronaos**. This room is surrounded by a single or double row of columns, known as a **peristyle** (see fig. 4–16). The platform or base of the building is called the **stylobate**. Architects developed systems of proportions and ornament known as *orders* for temple plans and elevations—the order defines the arrangement, proportions, and appearance of the temple, especially the posts and lintels. However, the simple posts and lintels we have seen up until now in the history of ancient architecture have become more elaborate **columns** and **entablatures** (see "The Greek Architectural Orders," page 98).

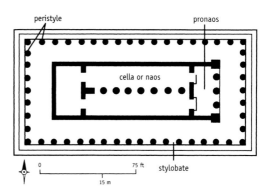

4–16 Plan of the Temple of Hera I, Paestum

Buildings are often better preserved in outlying regions than in the homeland of a culture because they may escape the devastation of years between powerful states. A well-preserved Archaic period temple built about 550 BCE still stands at Paestum (Poseidonia), a Greek colony founded about 50 miles south of the modern city of Naples, Italy. Dedicated to Hera, queen of the gods, the temple (figs. **4–15** and **4–16**) is known today as Hera I to distinguish it from a second temple to Hera built adjacent to it about a century later. The builders used the **Doric order**, the earliest Greek order. Fluted columns without bases, resting directly on the stylobate, rise to unadorned, cushionlike **capitals**. Each capital is formed of a rounded **echinus** and a tabletlike **abacus**. The especially robust columns of Hera I, topped with widely flaring capitals, create an impression of great permanence and stability. But because the columns swell in the middle and contract toward the top (a characteristic known as **entasis**), the building retains a sense of energy and upward lift. Above the columns, a horizontal entablature (composed of **architrave, frieze,** and **cornice**) and the triangular **pediments** (forming the triangular gable ends) support the

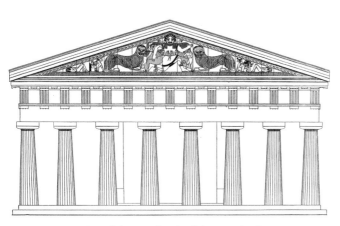

4–17 Reconstruction of the west facade of the Temple of Artemis, Korkyra (Corfu), after G. Rodenwaldt. c. 600–580 BCE

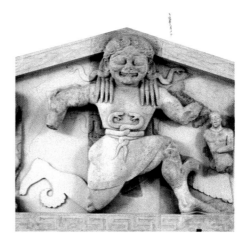

4–18 Gorgon Medusa, detail of sculpture from the west pediment of the Temple of Artemis, Korkyra. c. 580 BCE. Limestone, height of pediment at the center 9′2″ (2.79 m). Gian Beerta Vanni/Archaelolgical Museum, Korkyra (Corfu). Art Resource, NY

temple's roof. In the frieze, flat panels called **metopes** alternate with vertically grooved panels called **triglyphs**.

Sculpture or painting often decorated the metopes of the frieze and the pediments. Perhaps among the earliest surviving examples of Greek pedimental sculpture are fragments of the ruined Temple of Artemis on the island of Korkyra (Corfu), which date from about 600–580 BCE (fig. **4–17**). The figures in this sculpture were carved in high relief on slabs, which were then installed in the pediment

space. At the center is the snake-haired Medusa, a female monster who had the power to turn humans into stone if they looked upon her face (fig. **4–18**). The hero Perseus avoided this fate by looking at her in the mirrorlike surface of his shield as he beheaded her. On either side of Medusa are her offspring: the flying horse Pegasus on the left (only part of his rump and tail remain) and the giant Chrysaor on the right. Flanking them are crouching felines and dying human warriors tucked into the corners of the pediment.

ELEMENTS OF **Architecture**
The Greek Architectural Orders

An *order* is a system of proportions derived from the diameter of a column shaft and used in the ensemble of entablature, capital, column, and base. No element of an order could be changed without producing a corresponding change in the other elements.

The Classical orders are comprised of a system of interdependent parts whose proportions are based on mathematical ratios. The three Classical Greek architectural orders are the Doric, the Ionic, and the Corinthian. The Doric and Ionic orders were well developed by about 600 BCE. The Doric order is the oldest and plainest of the three. The Ionic order is named after Ionia, a region occupied by Greeks on the west coast of Anatolia and the islands off that coast. The Corinthian order, a variation of the Ionic, began to appear around 450 BCE (see Introduction, fig. xx). Later, the Romans appropriated the Corinthian order and elaborated it, as we shall see in Chapter 6.

The basic components of each Greek order are the column and the entablature. All types of columns have a vertical shaft topped by a capital; some also have a base. The column shafts are formed of round sections, or

drums, which are joined inside by metal pegs. The entablature consists of an architrave, frieze, and cornice.

Over the centuries, Western architects have invoked the Greek orders used for temple design to express rationality, restraint, and physical and moral perfection.

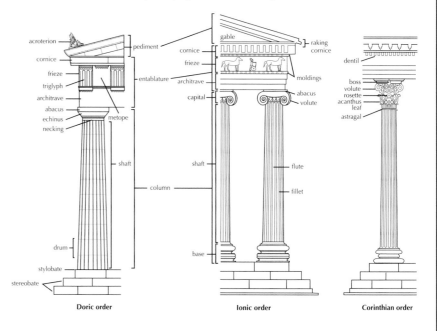

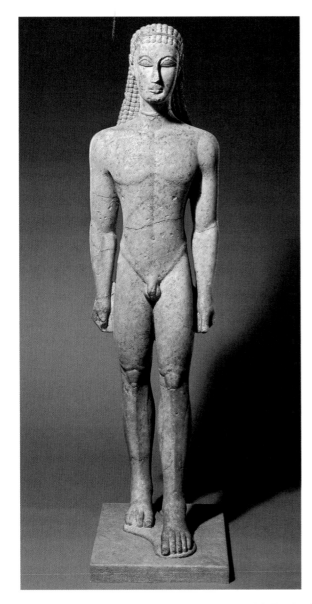

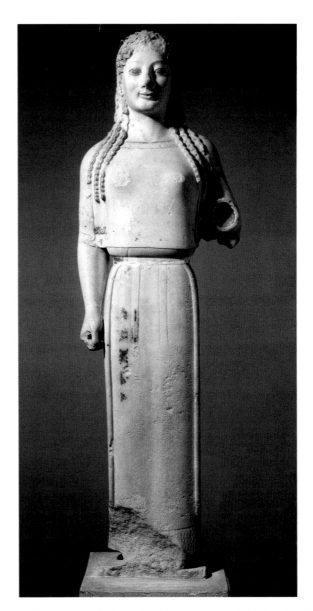

4–19 *Standing Youth (Kouros),* from Attica. c. 580 BCE. Marble, height 6′4″ (1.93 m). The Metropolitan Museum of Art, New York
FLETCHER FUND, 1932 (32.11.1) PHOTOGRAPH © 1997 THE METROPOLITAN MUSEUM OF ART

4–20 *Peplos Kore* from the Acropolis, Athens. c. 530 BCE. Marble, height 48″ (123 cm). Acropolis Museum, Athens

Men, animals, and monster are all depicted in simple **volumetric** forms, once brightly painted in reds and blues.

In addition to carving sculpture for temple exteriors, artists of the Archaic period created freestanding statues. Usually life-size or larger, most Archaic Greek sculptures were made of white marble and originally were painted in bright, naturalistic colors. Some bore inscriptions indicating that they had been commissioned by individual men or women for a commemorative purpose. While some marked graves, most stood in sanctuaries, where they lined the sacred way from the entrance to the main temple in perpetual attendance on the god or goddess.

Traditionally, a female statue of this type is called a **kore** (plural, *korai*), Greek for "young woman," and a male statue is called a **kouros** (plural, *kouroi*), meaning "young man." The Archaic *korai*, wearing long, sleeveless garments and earrings, represented deities, priestesses, or nymphs. The *kouroi*, nearly always nude, have been variously identified as gods, warriors, and victorious athletes. Because the Greeks associated young athletic males with fertility and familial regeneration, the *kouroi* may also have been looked upon as symbolic ancestor figures.

A *kouros* dating from about 580 BCE (fig. **4–19**) exemplifies the early Greek ideal. Superficially reminiscent of standing males in Egyptian sculpture (see fig. 2–18), this young Greek is shown frontally, arms at his sides, fists clenched, and one leg slightly in front of the other. Unlike ancient Egyptian stone statuary, however, is the figure's lithe athletic body, the face, and the way in which the sculptor has freed the arms and legs from the block of stone, making the figure seem light and energetic. He depicted anatomy carefully, although tradition required that the ridges and grooves of bones and muscles form simple, balanced patterns. The eyes are relatively large and wide open, and the mouth forms a characteristic closed smile, known as the Archaic smile, apparently used to enliven the expression of the figure. Unlike his partially clothed Egyptian counterpart, the young Greek wears only a ribbon around his neck and another band on his curly hair. Here, the nudity serves almost to remove the figure from a specific place, time, or social class.

With remarkable rapidity, Greek sculptors perfected the art of creating lifelike human figures. The *Peplos Kore* (fig. **4–20**), dated about 50 years after the youth, exhibits subtly rounded body forms. Her arms and head convey a greater sense of soft flesh covering an anatomically correct bone structure. Her smile and hair seem almost natural, and the original painted colors must have made her seem even more lifelike. She wears the distinctive Athenian garment known as a *peplos*—a draped rectangle of woolen cloth, folded over the top, fastened at the shoulders, and belted to give a bloused effect. She also once wore a metal crown and earrings. Traces of paint on the lower area of the sculpture suggest that the carved *peplos* may have been decorated with a pattern of embroidery, too.

In vase painting, artists presented not just a discrete figure, but a story, or narrative, involving that figure. Abandoning the narrow bands of decoration characteristic of the Geometric period (see fig. 4–13), vase painters, especially in Athens, gradually increased the size of figures until one or two scenes filled the body of the vessel. A mid-sixth-century BCE **amphora**—a large, all-purpose storage jar—illustrates this development (fig. **4–21**). One side shows the suicide of Ajax, an episode from the legends of the Trojan War. Ajax, a Greek warrior, was second only to Achilles in bravery. After the death of Achilles, the Greeks awarded the hero's armor to Odysseus rather than to Ajax; the latter, humiliated, committed suicide. With typical Greek restraint yet

Greek Gods	
Zeus	king of the gods
Hera	Zeus's wife and sister, queen of the gods
Athena	goddess of wisdom and civilization
Ares	god of war
Apollo	god of the sun, creativity, and the fine arts
Aphrodite	goddess of love and beauty
Artemis	goddess of the moon and hunting (twin sister of Apollo)
Hermes	god of commerce; also messenger of the gods
Hades	god of the underworld
Dionysos	god of wine
Hephaestus	god of fire and metalworking
Hestia	goddess of hearth and family
Demeter	goddess of crops and the harvest
Poseidon	god of the sea and earthquakes (brother of Zeus)
Eros	god of love (son of Aphrodite)

Although sometimes worshiped as a god, the hero Herakles, a son of Zeus, is a demi-god known for his physical strength.

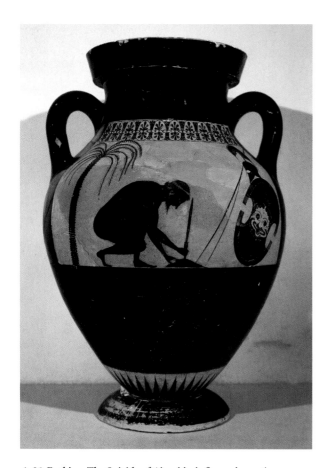

4–21 Exekias. *The Suicide of Ajax,* black-figure decoration on an amphora. c. 540 BCE. Ceramic, height of amphora 27″ (69 cm). Château-Musée, Boulogne-sur-Mer, France

The whole composition focuses the viewer's attention on the head of Ajax and his intense concentration as he pats down the earth to secure the sword. He will not fail in his suicide.

with a sense of drama, Exekias, the potter and painter who signed this vase, captures the impending moment of tragedy rather than the instant of the hero's death. Ajax plants his sword upright in a mound of dirt so that he can fling himself upon it. Two in-curving elements—the tree on the left and the shield and helmet that the warrior has set aside on the right—echo the swelling form of the amphora and the rounding of the hero's back. They also provide a context or setting for the narrative. Thus the painter communicates a complex story in a single scene, whose clear, easily understandable image adds to its solemnity and directness.

In painting this vase, Exekias used a technique known as **black-figure** painting. This technique became the principal mode of Greek vase painting in the sixth century BCE. The painter used **slip** (a mixture of clay and water) to silhouette figures against the reddish, unpainted clay of the background. Details were incised with a sharp tool inside the silhouetted shapes. The color contrast was created in the firing process. On some pieces, touches of white and reddish purple gloss—made of metallic pigments mixed with slip—enhance the black-figure decoration.

Although painters were still creating handsome black-figure wares in the last third of the sixth century BCE, some turned away from this meticulous process to a new technique called **red-figure** decoration. In this technique—so called because red figures stand out against a black background—the painter covered the vase with slip but left figures unpainted to reveal the reddish body of the vessel. Instead of engraving details, the painter drew with a fine brush dipped in the slip. The result was a lustrous dark

Here, the Priam Painter provides an interesting insight into everyday Greek city life as well as a view of an important public building in use (fig. **4–22**). Most women in ancient Greece were confined to their homes, so their daily trip to the communal well, or fountain house, was an important event. At a fountain house, in the shade of a Doric-columned porch, three women patiently fill hydriae like the one on which they are painted. A fourth balances her empty jug on her head as she waits, while a fifth woman, without a jug, appears to be waving a greeting to someone. The women's skin is painted white, a convention similar to the pale female figures found in Egyptian and Minoan art. Incising and touches of reddish-purple paint create fine details in the architecture and in the figures' clothing and hair.

The composition of this vase painting finely balances vertical, horizontal, rectangular, and rounded elements. The Doric columns, the decorative vertical borders, and even the streams of water flowing from the animal-head spigots echo the upright figures of the women. The wide black band forming the ground line, the architrave above the colonnade, and the left-to-right movement of the horse-drawn chariots across the shoulder emphasize the horizontal, friezelike arrangement of the women across the body of the pot. This geometric framework is softened by the rounded contours of the female bodies, the globular water vessels, the circular **palmettes** (fan-shaped petal designs) framing the main scene, and the arching bodies of the galloping horses on the shoulder.

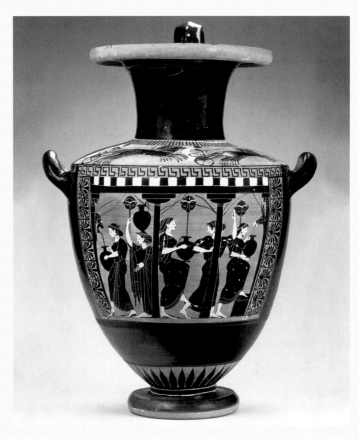

4–22 Priam Painter. *Women at a Fountain House,* black-figure decoration on a hydria. 520–510 BCE. Ceramic, height of hydria 20⁷⁄₈″ (53 cm). Museum of Fine Arts, Boston

WILLIAM FRANCIS WARDEN FUND

vessel with light-colored figures painted with dark-colored details (see fig. 4–24). The greater ease, speed, and flexibility of this technique led artists to adopt it quickly.

An early-fifth-century red-figure **kylix**, or two-handled drinking cup, displays the painter's virtuosity at adapting a scene to the shape of the vessel (fig. **4–23**) and in drawing individual figures in action. The artist, known as the Foundry Painter, used the circular underside of the cup to illustrate the workings of a foundry for casting bronze figures. The walls of the pictured workshop are filled with tools and other paraphernalia: hammers, molds of a human foot and hand, and several sketches. A seated helmeted worker attends to a furnace at left, while a second man—perhaps the supervisor—leans on a staff. A third worker assembles the already-cast parts of a leaping figure; the parts are braced against a molded support, and the head lies at the worker's feet. The painter has created a lively scene in an awkward space and also gives us insight into the working methods of sculptors creating large bronze statues.

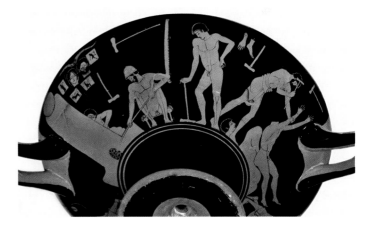

4–23 Foundry Painter. *A Bronze Foundry,* red-figure decoration on a kylix from Vulci, Italy. 490–480 BCE. Ceramic, diameter of kylix 12″ (31 cm). Staatliche Museen zu Berlin, Preussischer Kulturbesitz, Antikensammlung

The painter conveys the mass and energy of the figures and also draws in details of muscles and facial features. The men work in a real space defined by their furnace and other equipment as well as by their foreshortened bodies and limbs, especially the legs of the man tending the furnace.

The Early Classical or Transitional Period

Historically, the early fifth century BCE was marked by a series of invasions from Persia (see Chapter 5). The Greek city-states banded together against their common foe, and by 479 BCE an alliance led by Athens and Sparta had driven out the advancing Persians. Perhaps the Greeks' success against the Persians gave them a self-confidence that accelerated the development of their art. In any event, within 30 years they developed a new style of art. This period of marked change and evolution, called the Transitional or Early Classical period, lasted from the end of the Persian Wars to about 450 BCE.

A red-figured **bell krater** (bell-shaped bowl for mixing wine and water) shows the increasing **naturalism** (resemblance to visible nature) that differentiates the Early Classical from the Archaic style. Here, the painter, called the Pan Painter, depicted *Artemis Slaying Actaeon* (fig. **4–24**). When the hunter Actaeon accidentally saw the goddess Artemis taking her bath, she retaliated by causing his dogs to mistake him for a stag and to tear him apart. Here the hounds swarm over the fallen hunter, whom Artemis prepares to finish off with an arrow. The death seems melodramatic compared with the suicide of Ajax (see fig. 4–21), but the artist's sense of balance and order still successfully adjusts the actions of the figures to the form of the vase.

In freestanding sculpture, the Greeks shifted in only a few generations from the rigid, frontal presentation of the human figure embodied in the Archaic *kouroi* to more natural, lifelike figures such as the so-called *Kritios Boy* (fig. **4–25**). In contrast to the over-life-size Archaic *kouroi* (see fig. 4–19), the *Kritios Boy* originally stood only about 4 feet tall. The solid, rounded body forms, broad facial features, and thoughtful expression—which lacks even a trace of the Archaic smile—give the figure an air of extraordinary solemnity. The easy pose contrasts markedly with the more rigid bearing of Archaic *kouroi*. The boy's weight rests on his left leg (the "engaged" leg), and his relaxed right leg bends slightly at the knee. The curve in his spine counters the slight shifting of his hips and the subtle drop of one shoulder. The sculptor captures the life and movement of the figure, which was only implied in the Archaic *kouroi*.

The technique of modeling and hollow-casting bronze—developed at the end of the Archaic period—made possible more complex action poses, which would be difficult to carve in stone. A life-size bronze *Charioteer* (fig. **4–26**) illustrates the skill of Greek metalworkers. It was found in the Sanctuary of Apollo at Delphi together with fragments of a bronze chariot and horses. An earthquake in 373 BCE toppled the monument with its sculptures and buried them in debris, saving the *Charioteer* from the fate of many ancient bronzes—being melted down. According to its inscription, the sculpture group commemorates a victory by the driver sponsored by King Polyzalos of Gela (Sicily) in the Pythian Games (an event like the Olympics but held at Delphi

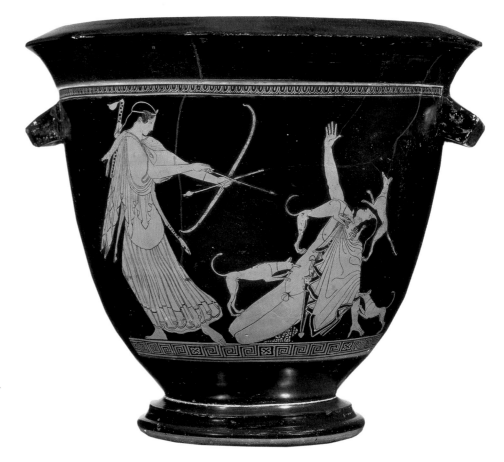

4–24 Pan Painter. *Artemis Slaying Actaeon,*
red-figure decoration on a bell krater. c. 470 BCE.
Ceramic, height of krater 14⁵/₈″ (37 cm).
Museum of Fine Arts, Boston

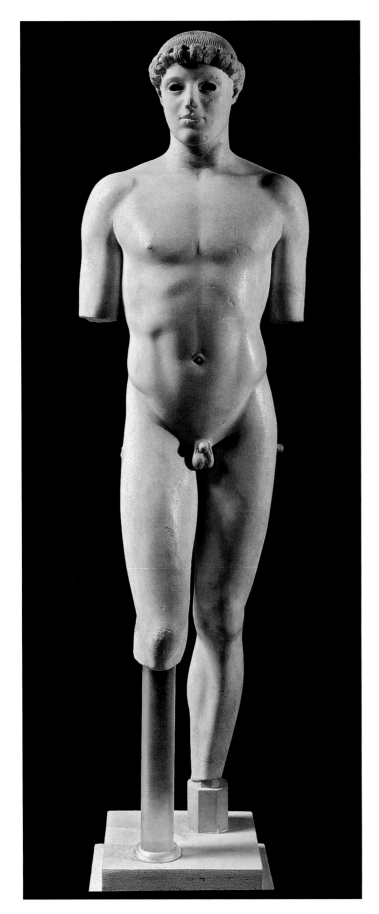

4–25 Kritios Boy. c. 480 BCE. Marble, height 33⁴/₅″ (86 cm). Acropolis Museum, Athens

When the Kritios Boy *was excavated from debris at the Acropolis of Athens, the statue was thought by its finders to be by the Greek sculptor Kritios.*

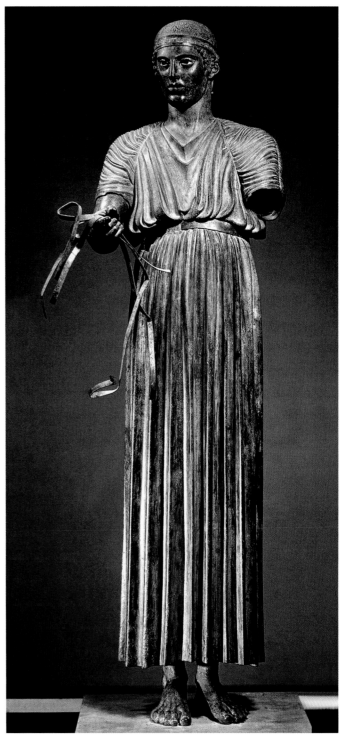

4–26 *Charioteer*, from the Sanctuary of Apollo, Delphi. c. 470 BCE. Bronze, height 5′11″ (1.8 m). Archaeological Museum, Delphi

The setting of a work of art affects our reaction to it. Today, this stunning figure is exhibited on a low base in the peaceful surroundings of a museum, isolated from other works and spotlighted for close examination. Its effect would have been very different in its original outdoor location, standing in a horsedrawn chariot atop a tall monument. Viewers in ancient times, exhausted from the steep climb to the sanctuary, possibly jostled by crowds of fellow pilgrims, could have absorbed only its overall effect, not the fine details of the face, robe, and hand visible to today's viewers.

and honoring Apollo) of 478 or 474 BCE. The idealized features of a handsome youth could almost be those of a particular individual. The single remaining hand and the feet are so realistic that they seem to have been cast from molds made from an actual person. The robe falls neatly into folds, yet the garment seems capable of swaying or rippling from a slight movement or sudden breeze. The lifelike quality of the *Charioteer* calls to mind the report by the Roman historian and naturalist Pliny the Elder (in the first century BCE) that three-time winners in Greek competitions had their features memorialized in statues.

A pair of over-life-size bronze figures known as the *Riace Warriors* illustrates the skill of ancient Greek sculptors in depicting the nude figure. Found by a diver on the seabed near Riace, a town on the eastern coast of Calabria in Italy, the statues may have been thrown from a sinking ship by sailors trying to lighten the load. One of the pair, the so-called *Young Warrior* (fig. **4–27**), dating from about 460–450 BCE, reveals a striking balance between anatomy based on Classical standards of perfection and details corresponding to visible nature. The athletic musculature suggests a youthfulness

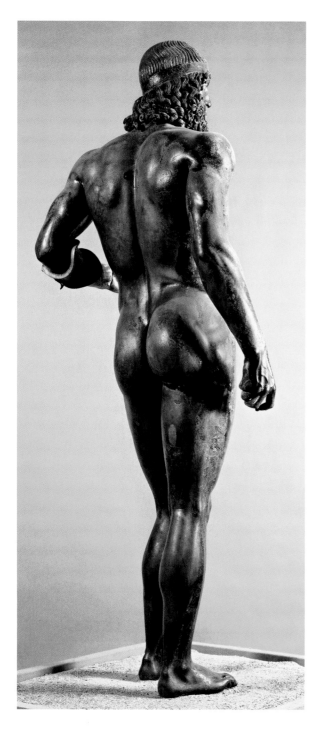 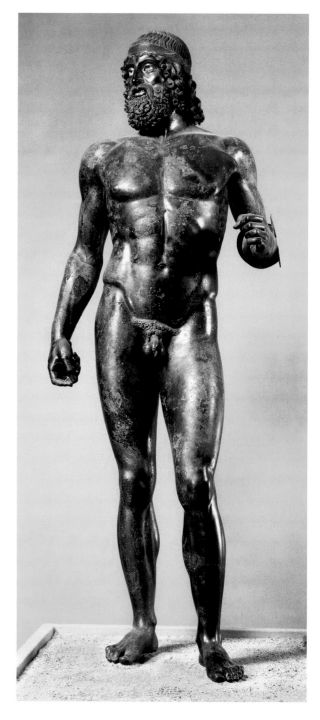

4–27 *Young Warrior* found in the sea off Riace, Italy. c. 460–450 BCE. Bronze with bone and glass eyes, silver teeth, and copper lips and nipples, height 6′8″ (2.03 m). Museo Archaeològico Nazionale, Reggio Calabria, Italy

The man held a shield (parts are still visible) on his left arm and a spear in his right hand. He may have been part of a monument commemorating a military victory, perhaps against the Persians.

belied by the maturity of the heavy beard and almost haggard face. Minutely detailed touches, such as the swelling veins in the backs of the hands, contrast with the idealized smoothness of the rest of the body. The sculptor heightened the lifelike quality of the sculpture by adding eyes of bone and colored glass, silver plating on the teeth, and eyelashes and eyebrows of separately cast strands of bronze. Such intense study of the human figure prepared the way for the achievements of artists in the Classical period.

The "Golden Age" of Art

The Classical period of Greek art lasted only from about 450 to 400 BCE. The period is also known as Greece's "Golden Age," although these decades saw turmoil and destruction resulting from the Peloponnesian War. Sparta and Athens, without a common enemy, turned on each other. Sparta dominated the Peloponnese Peninsula and much of the rest of mainland Greece, while Athens controlled the Aegean and became the wealthy and influential center of a maritime empire. Today we remember Athens more for its cultural and intellectual brilliance and its experiments with democratic government, which reached its zenith in the fifth century BCE under the charismatic leader Pericles, than for its considerable commercial power.

The Parthenon

The Athenian Acropolis, the hill that formed the city's ceremonial center, visually expressed the city's values and its civic pride. The Persians had destroyed the site's earlier buildings and statues in 480 BCE, so the Athenians rebuilt their monuments on the Acropolis during the second half of the fifth century BCE. According to Greek mythology, Athena, goddess of wisdom and civilization, claimed Athens as her city. And a new temple, dedicated to the Virgin Athena (Athena Parthenos in Greek), now rose triumphantly over the city. The Parthenon—designed and built by the architects Kallikrates and Iktinos—dominated the other structures on the hilltop site (fig. 4–28). The builders used the finest white marble on the building, even replacing the customary terra-cotta roof with marble slabs. The renowned sculptor Phidias designed the sculptural decorations and also supervised the entire project of rebuilding the monuments of the Acropolis. The building was completed in 438 BCE, and its sculpture, executed by Phidias and other sculptors in his workshop, was finished in 432 BCE.

In its structure and design, the Parthenon illustrates the refinement of ancient Greek architecture (fig. 4–1). It follows the typical cella and peristyle plan and uses the Doric order. To counteract the optical illusions that would distort its appearance when seen from a distance, the architects made many subtle adjustments. Since long horizontal lines appear to sag in the

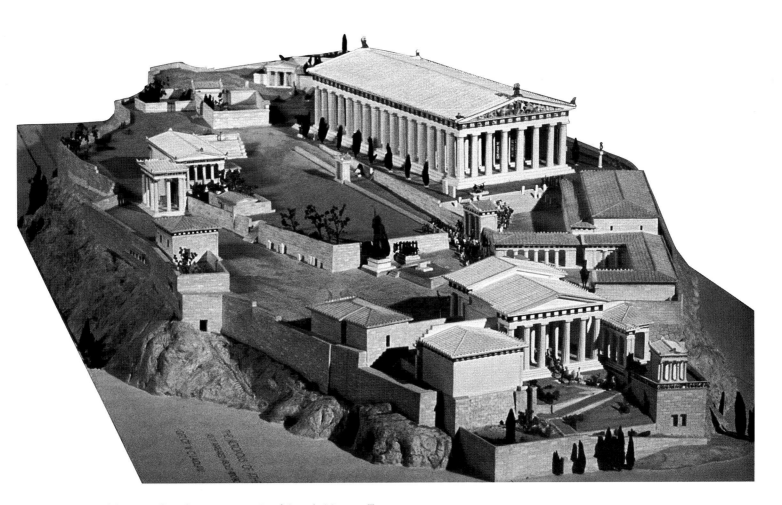

4–28 Model of the Acropolis, Athens, c. 400 BCE. Royal Ontario Museum, Toronto

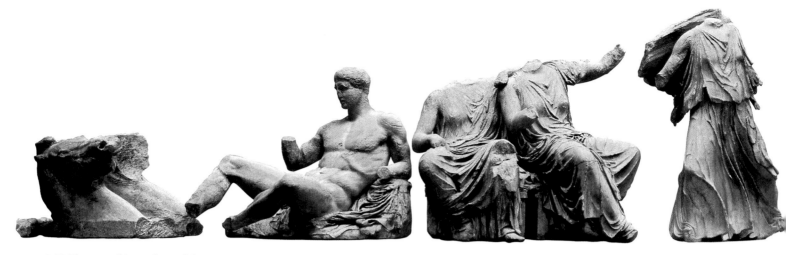

4–29 Photographic mock-up of the east pediment of the Parthenon (using photographs of the extant marble sculpture c. 438–432 BCE). The British Museum, London

© THE BRITISH MUSEUM

The pediment is over 90 feet long; the central space of about 40 feet is missing. Figures were probably destroyed in the fifth century when Christians turned the Parthenon into a church and built an apse at the east end. The figures illustrate the birth of Athena. The statues in the center of the composition probably showed Zeus seated on a throne, and standing next to him, Athena, who according to mythology had emerged fully grown from his head. The male nude, who fits so easily into the sloping pediment, has been identified as the hero Herakles with his lion skin or Dionysos (god of wine) lying on a panther skin. The two seated women may be the earth and grain goddesses, Demeter and Persephone. The running woman is the messenger of the gods, Iris, who is spreading the news of Athena's birth. The three female figures on the right side are probably Hestia (a sister of Zeus and goddess of the hearth), Dione (one of Zeus's many consorts), and her daughter Aphrodite (goddess of love) who reclines to fit into the triangular pediment. The horses' heads represent (at far left) the chariot of the sun god, Helios (Apollo), and (at far right) the moon goddess, Selene.

center, the architects designed both the base of the temple and the entablature to curve slightly upward toward the center. The columns have a subtle swelling, or entasis, and tilt inward slightly from bottom to top. In addition, the corners are strengthened visually by reducing the space between columns at the corners. These subtle modifications in the arrangement of elements give the Parthenon a buoyant organic appearance and prevent it from looking like a heavy, lifeless stone box.

Sculpture carved in the round filled the pediments of the Parthenon. The figures stood on the projecting shelves of the horizontal cornice—the top of the entablature—secured to the pediment wall with metal pins. The sculptor, whether Phidias or someone working in the Phidian style, expertly rendered the human form beneath the draperies. The clinging fabric creates circular patterns rippling over torsos, breasts, and knees. Most of the works of sculpture from the Parthenon have been damaged or lost over the centuries, but using the locations of existing pinholes,

scholars have determined the placement of the surviving statues and can infer the poses of the missing ones (fig. **4–29**). The west pediment sculpture, facing the entrance to the Acropolis, illustrate the contest that Athena won over the sea god, Poseidon, for rule over the Athenians. The east pediment figures, above the entrance to the cella, illustrate the birth of Athena, fully grown and clad in armor, from the brow of her father, Zeus.

At the beginning of the nineteenth century, Thomas Bruce, the British earl of Elgin and ambassador to Constantinople, acquired much of the surviving sculpture from the Parthenon, which was being used for military purposes at the time. He shipped the pieces back to London to exhibit them but, after a financial dispute and other difficulties, he sold them to the British government in 1816. Referred to as the *Elgin Marbles* or the *Parthenon Marbles,* most of the sculpture is now in the British Museum, London. In recent times, the Greek government has tried unsuccessfully to have the *Elgin Marbles* returned.

CLASSIC AND CLASSICAL

Our words "classic" and "classical" come from the Latin word *classis*, referring to the division of people into classes based on wealth. Consequently, "classic" has come to mean "first class," "the highest rank," and "the standard of excellence." Greek artists in the fifth century BCE tried to create ideal images based on perfect mathematical proportions. Since Roman artists were also inspired by these ideals, the term "Classical" in this context refers to the cultures of ancient Greece and Rome. By extension, the word may also mean "in the style of ancient Greece and Rome," whenever or wherever that style is used. In the most general usage, a classic is something—whether a literary work, car, or film—of lasting quality and universal significance.

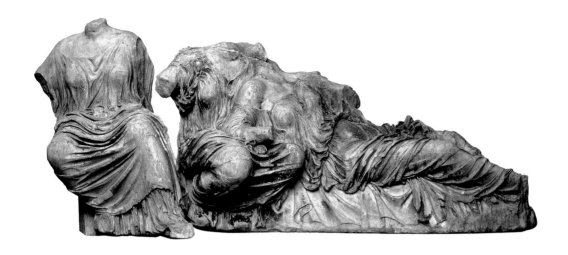
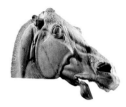

Originally, the Parthenon's white marble columns and inner walls supported bands of brightly painted low-relief sculpture. (Sir Lawrence Alma-Tadema captured the effect in his painting of 1868, entitled *Phidias and the Frieze of the Parthenon, Athens* [see Introduction, fig. 26]). The Doric frieze included carved metopes with scenes of victory. On the south side, the metopes depicted the fight between half-human centaurs and a legendary Greek tribe known as the Lapiths. The Lapith victory over the centaurs may have symbolized the triumph of reason over animal passions. In one relief (fig. **4–30**), what should be a death struggle seems more like a choreographed, athletic ballet, displaying the Lapith's muscles and graceful movements against the implausible backdrop of his carefully draped cloak.

Inside the Parthenon's Doric peristyle, an Ionic frieze (see "The Greek Architectural Orders," page 98) decorated the upper temple wall (fig. **4–31**). Unlike the episodic Doric frieze, the Ionic frieze consisted of a continuous band of sculpture. Here, the 525-foot-long frieze depicted a procession, traditionally believed to celebrate the great Panathenaic festival. The women of Athens carry a new wool *peplos* to the Acropolis sanctuary to clothe an ancient wooden cult statue of Athena housed there. In the frieze,

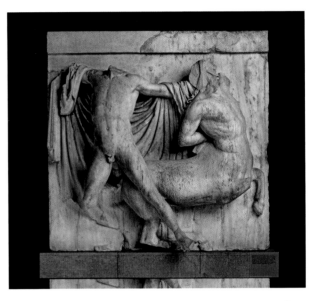

4–30 *Lapith Fighting a Centaur,* metope relief from the Doric frieze on the south side of the Parthenon. c. 440 BCE. Marble, height 56″ (1.42 m). The British Museum, London

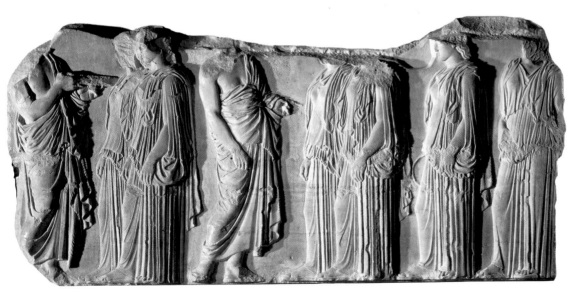

4–31 *Marshals and Young Women*, detail of the *Procession*, from the Ionic frieze on the east side of the Parthenon. c. 438–432 BCE. Marble, height 43″ (109 cm). Musée du Louvre, Paris

The procession culminated with the presentation of a new robe to Athena. The east facade presents a totally integrated program of images: the birth of the goddess in the pediment, her honoring by the citizens who present her with a newly woven peplos, and—seen through the doors—the glorious ivory and gold figure of Athena herself, the cult image.

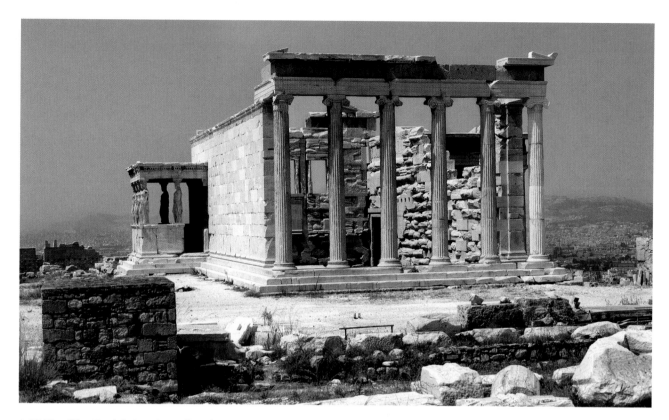

4–32 Mnesikles. Erechtheion, Acropolis, Athens. c. 430–405 BCE. View from the east

carefully planned rhythmic variations enliven the composition: Horses plunge ahead at full gallop; women proceed with a slow, stately step; parade marshals pause to look back at the progress of those behind; and gods and goddesses seated on benches await the arrival of the marchers.

The maidens, who walk with such grace and dignity, represent the Greek ideal of young womanhood, and their procession is an ideal one outside time and place. Each figure fills the space, so maidens and marshals have the same height. The marble sculpture of the frieze was originally painted in dark blue, red, and ocher, and details such as the bridles and reins of the horses were added in bronze. To compensate for the dim lighting inside the peristyle, the top of the frieze band is carved in slightly higher relief than the lower part, tilting the figures outward to catch reflected light from the pavement. The procession of maidens attended by parade marshals, although only a fragment of the architectural decoration, provides an indication of the extraordinary quality of every detail of the temple.

Other Buildings of the Athenian Acropolis

Upon completion of the Parthenon, Perikles commissioned an architect named Mnesikles to design a monumental gatehouse for the Acropolis, the Propylaia. Work began on it in 437 and stopped in 432, with the structure still incomplete. The Propylaia had no sculptural decoration, but its north wing was the earliest known museum (meaning "home of the Muses"), a gallery built specifically to house a collection of paintings for public view.

Mnesikles may also be the designer of the Erechtheion, the second important temple erected on the Acropolis under Pericles' building program (fig. **4–32**). Work began on it in the 430s and ended in 405 BCE, just before the fall of Athens to Sparta. The asymmetrical plan and several levels reflect the building's multiple functions in housing many different shrines, and it also conforms to the sharply sloping terrain on which the temple is located. The Erechtheion stands on the site of the mythical contest between the sea god, Poseidon, and Athena for patronage over Athens. During this contest, Poseidon struck a rock with his trident (three-pronged harpoon), bringing forth a spout of water, but Athena gave an olive tree and won the contest. The Athenians enclosed what they believed to be this sacred rock, bearing the marks of the trident, in the Erechtheion's north porch. Another area housed a sacred spring dedicated to Erechtheus, a legendary king of Athens, during whose reign the goddess Demeter was said to have instructed the Athenians in the arts of growing crops and other vegetation. The Erechtheion also contained a memorial to the legendary founder of Athens, Kekrops, half man and half serpent, who acted as judge in the contest between Athena and Poseidon. And it housed the venerable wooden cult statue of Athena that was the center of the Panathenaic festival.

The Erechtheion—which has porches on the north, east, and south sides—was constructed using the **Ionic order**, and the north and east porches of the Erechtheion epitomize the Ionic form. Taller and more slender in proportion than the Doric, the Ionic order also has richer and more elaborately carved decoration (see "The Greek Architectural Orders," page 98). The

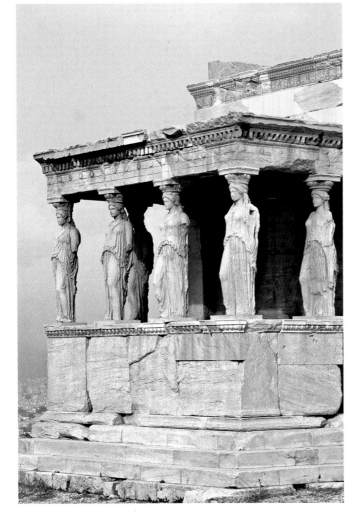

4–33 Porch of the Maidens (Caryatid Porch), Erechtheion, Acropolis, Athens. 421–405 BCE

*Six stately **caryatids** (carved figures functioning as columns) topped with simple capitals stand on a high base and support an Ionic entablature, lightened by eliminating the frieze. Assuming a pose characteristic of Classical figures, each caryatid's weight is supported on one engaged leg, while the free leg, bent at the knee, rests on the ball of the foot. The vertical fall of the drapery on the engaged side resembles the fluting of a column shaft and provides a sense of stability, whereas the bent leg gives an impression of relaxed grace and effortless support, like the entasis of the Doric shaft.*

columns rise from molded bases and end in **volute** (spiral) capitals. The frieze consists of continuous moldings or bands of sculpture. At the west end of the south side, six caryatids (female figures acting as columns) support the entablature of another porch (fig. **4–33**).

A second Ionic temple, dedicated to Athena Nike (Victory), stands near the entrance to the Acropolis precinct. A low wall faced with relief panels of Athena presiding over her winged attendants as they prepared for a victory celebration once surrounded the temple. The female figures (known as Nikes or Victories) contrast with the restrained caryatids of the Erechtheion. One of the most admired panels depicts Nike adjusting her sandal (fig. **4–34**).

The figure bends forward gracefully, causing her ample robe to slip off one shoulder. Though now mostly lost, her large wings, one open and one closed, effectively balance this unstable pose. Unlike the swirls of heavy fabric covering the Parthenon goddesses or the weighty pleats of the robes of the Erechtheion caryatids, the textile covering this Nike appears delicate and light, clinging to her body like wet silk. The artist's vision, and the patron's wish, has changed dramatically since the creation of the *Peplos Kore* (see fig. 4–20).

Just as Greek architects defined and followed a set of standards for temple design, Greek sculptors sought to create ideal human figures (see "The Canon of Polykleitos," page 110). By observing and then eliminating the irregularities they saw in nature and using their knowledge of geometry to find perfect proportions, they created timeless images of men and women. And, to achieve the rhythmic harmony presented in works such as the *Procession* frieze (fig. 4–32)—in which each form is

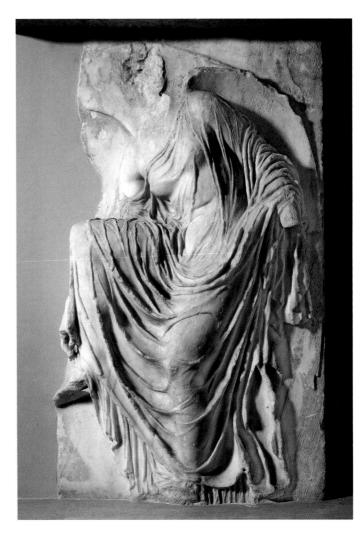

4–34 *Nike (Victory) Adjusting Her Sandal,* fragment of relief decoration from the parapet (now destroyed). Temple of Athena Nike, Acropolis, Athens. 410–407 BCE. Marble, height 42″ (107 cm). Acropolis Museum, Athens

THE CANON OF POLYKLEITOS

Just as Greek architects defined and followed a set of standards for ideal temple design, Greek sculptors sought to represent an ideal of human beauty. Studying human appearances closely, the sculptors of the Classical period selected those attributes they considered most desirable, such as regular facial features, smooth skin, and particular body proportions, and combined them into a single ideal of physical perfection. This quest for the ideal was seen also in fifth-century BCE rationalists' philosophy that all objects in the physical world were reflections of ideal forms that could be discovered through reason.

The best-known art theorist of the Classical period was the sculptor Polykleitos of Argos. About 450 BCE he developed a set of rules for constructing the ideal human figure, which he set down in a treatise called "The Canon" (*kanon* is Greek for "measure," "rule," or "law"). To illustrate his theory, Polykleitos created a larger-than-life bronze statue of Achilles (fig. **4–35**). Neither the treatise nor the original statue has survived, but both were widely discussed in the writings of his contemporaries, and later Roman artists made copies in stone and marble of the Achilles, commonly known as the *Spear Bearer* (*Doryphoros*).

By studying the most exact of these copies, or replicas, scholars have tried to determine the set of measurements that defined the ideal proportions in Polykleitos's canon. The canon included a system of ratios between a basic unit and the length of various body parts. Some studies suggest that his basic unit may have been the length of the figure's index finger or the width of its hand across the knuckles; others suggest that it was the height of the head from chin to hairline. The canon also included guidelines for *symmetria* ("commensurability"), by which Polykleitos meant the relationship of body parts to one another. In the statue he made to illustrate his treatise, he explored not only proportions but also the relationships among weight-bearing and relaxed legs and arms in a perfectly balanced figure. The cross-balancing of supporting and free elements in a figure is sometimes referred to as *contrapposto*.

In true Classical fashion, Polykleitos balanced careful observation and generalization to create an ideal figure. The Roman marble replica of the Greek bronze illustrated here shows a male athlete, perfectly balanced with the whole weight of the upper body supported by the straight (engaged) right leg. The left leg is bent at the knee, with the left foot poised on the ball of the foot, suggesting movement. The pattern of tension and relaxation is reversed in the arrangement of the arms, with the right relaxed on the engaged side and the left bent to support the weight of the (missing) spear. This dynamically balanced body pose—characteristic of Classical standing figure sculpture—differs from that of the *Kritios Boy* (see fig. 4–25) of a generation earlier. The tilt of the hipline in the Achilles is a little more pronounced to accommodate the raising of the left foot onto its ball, and the head is turned toward the same side as the engaged leg.

To Polykleitos and others of the time, the beautiful was synonymous with the good, and sculptors sought a mathematical

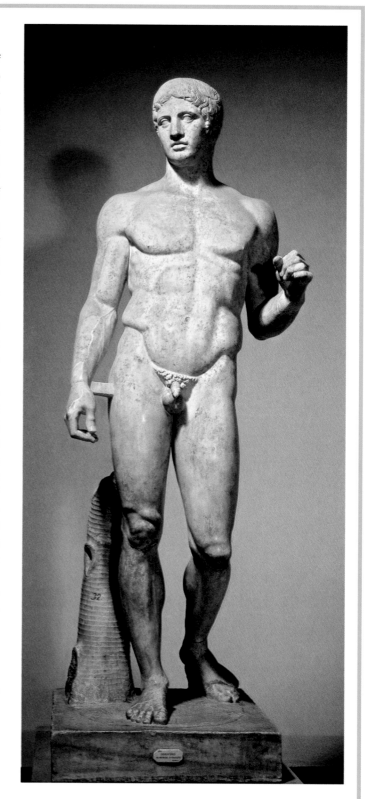

4–35 Polykleitos. *Spear Bearer (Doryphoros), Achilles.*
Roman copy after the original bronze of c. 450–440 BCE. Marble, height 6′6″ (2 m). Museo Archaeològico Nazionale, Naples, Italy

definition of the beautiful as it applied to the human figure, aspiring to make it possible to replicate human perfection in the tangible form of sculpture.

distinct and individual yet all are united into an utterly satisfying whole—the artists must have carefully observed and distilled the incidents of many similar events. This quest to explore the relationship between the actual and the ideal can also be seen in the work of the Greek philosopher Socrates (c. 470–399 BCE) and his disciple Plato (c. 429–347 BCE), both of whom argued that all objects in the physical world were reflections of ideal forms that could be discovered through reason.

Late Classical Art of the Fourth Century BCE

In 404 BCE, the Peloponnesian War concluded with the defeat of Athens by Sparta. Ancient Athens never regained its dominant political and military status, yet Sparta failed to establish a lasting preeminence over the other Greek lands. The quarreling city-states finally fell under the dominance of Philip II of Macedonia in 338 BCE and—after Philip's assassination two years later—his son, Alexander the Great, incorporated the Greek city-states into an empire.

Remarkably, Greek art continued to evolve during this turbulent period. Architects preferred the elegant Ionic order and introduced the even more decorative **Corinthian order** (see "The Greek Architectural Orders," page 98; see also Introduction, fig. 11). In their search for an ideal human form, sculptors, most notably Praxiteles and Lysippos in the fourth century BCE, developed a new canon of proportions for figures. Polykleitos's fifth-century BCE canon had produced a figure 6 1/2 or 7 times the height of the head. Praxiteles, who worked in Athens from about 370 to 335 BCE or later, created figures about 8 or more "heads" tall. A marble sculpture of *Hermes and the Infant Dionysos* (fig. **4–36**)—probably a Hellenistic or Roman copy but so fine that generations of scholars believed it to be an original statue by Praxiteles—has a smaller head and a more youthful and graceful body than Polykleitos's *Spear Bearer* (fig. 4–35). Its off-balance, S-curve pose contrasts sharply with that of the earlier work. The subject is less dignified, too: Hermes teases the infant god of wine with a bunch of grapes. But the soft modulations in the musculature, the deep folds in the draperies, and the rough locks of hair create a sensuous play of light and shadow over the figure's surface.

Around 350 BCE Praxiteles created a daring statue of Aphrodite, the goddess of love. For the first time, a well-known Greek sculptor depicted a goddess as a completely nude woman. The citizens of Knidos in Asia Minor purchased the sculpture and displayed it proudly in a shrine open on all four sides. The original sculpture is lost, but several versions survive in Roman copies; one that was once in the Medici collection profoundly influenced artists in the fifteenth and sixteenth centuries. The goddess is preparing to take a bath. Her hands, posed in a gesture of modesty, paradoxically seem to emphasize her nudity. She leans forward slightly with one knee bent in a seductive pose that emphasizes the swelling forms of her thighs, abdomen, and breasts. According to an old legend, Praxiteles' original statue depicted her so accurately that Aphrodite herself made a journey to Knidos to see it and cried out in shock, "Where did Praxiteles see me naked?"

The other major sculptor of the fourth century BCE whose name and fame come down to us is Lysippos. He became famous for his monumental bronze statues of Zeus and Herakles. He also created portraits of Alexander the Great

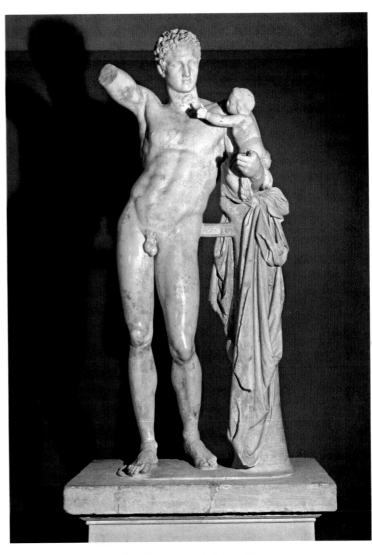

4–36 Followers of Praxiteles. *Hermes and the Infant Dionysos,* probably a Roman copy after an original of c. 300–250 BCE. Marble, with remnants of red paint on the lips and hair, height 7′1″ (2.16 m). National Archaeological Museum, Olympia. Scala / Art Resource, NY

Discovered in the rubble of the ruined Temple of Hera at Olympia in 1875, this statue is now widely accepted as a very good Roman or Hellenistic copy. Support for this conclusion comes from certain elements typical of Roman sculpture: Hermes' sandals, which recent studies suggest are not accurate for a fourth-century BCE date; the supporting element of crumpled fabric covering a tree stump; and the use of a reinforcing strut, or brace, between Hermes' hip and the tree stump.

WOMEN ARTISTS IN ANCIENT GREECE

Although comparatively few artists in ancient Greece were women, there is evidence that women artists worked in many media. Ancient writers noted women painters—Pliny the Elder, for example listed Aristarete, Eirene, Iaia, Kalypso, Olympias, and Timarete. Helen, a painter from Egypt who had been taught by her father, is known to have worked in the fourth century BCE and may have been responsible for the original wall painting of *Alexander the Great Confronts Darius III* at the Battle of Issos (see fig. 5–2). Greek women excelled in creating narrative or pictorial tapestries, and they also worked in pottery-making workshops. The hydria shown here, dating from about 450 BCE, shows a woman and three men painting in such a workshop. In the center Athena, patron of crafts and the arts, holds a wreath, and Nikes crown the men, symbolizing victory in an artistic competition.

The woman sits on a raised dais, painting the largest vase in the workshop. She is isolated from the other artists and is not part of the awards ceremony. Perhaps most women were excluded from public artistic competitions, as they were from men's athletic competitions. Another interpretation, however, is that the woman is the head of this workshop. Athenian women could control property that they gained through inheritance. Secure in her own status, this woman may have encouraged her assistants to enter contests to further their careers and to bring glory to the workshop.

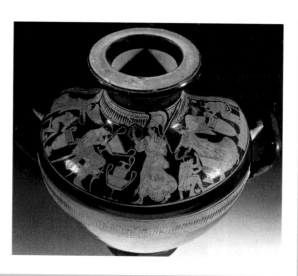

The Leningrad Painter. *A Vase Painter and Assistants Crowned by Athena and Victories*, composite photograph of the red-figure decoration on a hydria from Athens. c. 450 BCE. Private collection, Milan, Italy

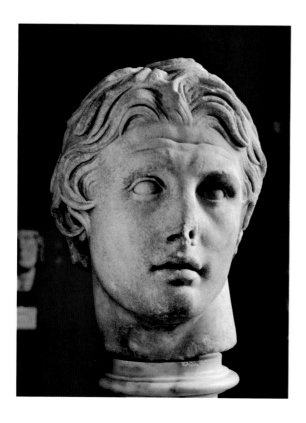

standing and holding a scepter in the same way he is believed to have represented the king of the gods. Not one of his original statues survives. A marble head found at Pergamon (in modern Turkey), once part of a standing figure, is believed to come from one of several copies of Lysippos's portrait (fig. **4–37**). According to the Roman historian Plutarch, the sculptor depicted Alexander with his head slightly turned and his face raised upward toward the sky, a description that fits this head well. The deep-set eyes are gazing upward and the low forehead is lined, as though the ruler, contemplating grave decisions, is waiting to receive divine advice.

Alexander is typically portrayed in Greek art as young and godlike. After establishing an empire that stretched from Greece south to Egypt, and as far east as India, he died of a fever in Babylon at the age of 33 in 323 BCE. Alexander's premature death, and the subsequent breakup of his vast empire, marks the end of the Classical period in Greek art.

4–37 *Alexander the Great,* head from a Hellenistic copy (c. 200 BCE) of a statue possibly after a fourth-century BCE original by Lysippos. Marble fragment, height 16 ⅛″ (41 cm). Archaeological Museum, Istanbul, Turkey

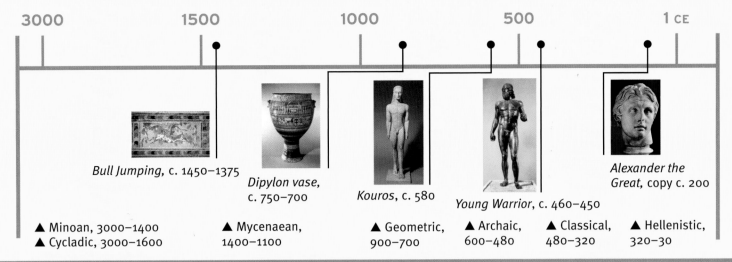

3000	1500	1000	500	1 CE

Bull Jumping, c. 1450–1375

Dipylon vase,
c. 750–700

Kouros, c. 580

Young Warrior, c. 460–450

Alexander the
Great, copy c. 200

▲ Minoan, 3000–1400
▲ Cycladic, 3000–1600

▲ Mycenaean,
1400–1100

▲ Geometric,
900–700

▲ Archaic,
600–480

▲ Classical,
480–320

▲ Hellenistic,
320–30

LOOKING BACK

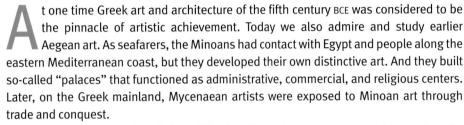

At one time Greek art and architecture of the fifth century BCE was considered to be the pinnacle of artistic achievement. Today we also admire and study earlier Aegean art. As seafarers, the Minoans had contact with Egypt and people along the eastern Mediterranean coast, but they developed their own distinctive art. And they built so-called "palaces" that functioned as administrative, commercial, and religious centers. Later, on the Greek mainland, Mycenaean artists were exposed to Minoan art through trade and conquest.

Greek art between the sixth and the fourth centuries BCE shows evidence that the Greeks had begun studying their surroundings with intense interest, focusing on every detail from the acanthus leaf to the folds of their own clothing. By then, too, temple builders had experimented with the arrangement, proportions, and appearance of their temples until they perfected two distinct designs—the Doric order and the Ionic order to which they added the Corinthian order, a variant of the Ionic.

In the fifth century the Athenians built a new temple to the goddess Athena, a building whose architectural design and sculptural decoration established a Classical ideal. The planning and execution of the Parthenon—perched on a site overlooking Athens—required extraordinary mathematical and mechanical skills and would have been impossible without a large contingent of distinguished architects and builders, as well as talented sculptors and painters, and their patrons. The Parthenon's extensive program of decoration strongly reflects the ancient Greek vision of unity and beauty.

Greek sculptors sought to represent ideal physical beauty in their depictions of men and women. Studying human appearances closely, the sculptors of the Classical period selected those attributes they considered most desirable and combined them into a single ideal of perfection. These idealized figures also expressed profound themes and ideas. The sculpture of the Parthenon, for example, embodies Greek ideals: the triumph of the democratic Greek city-states over Persia's imperial forces, the preeminence of Athens thanks to the favor of Athena, and the triumph of an enlightened Greek civilization over despotism and barbarism. Greek philosophers of the time argued that all objects in the physical world were reflections of ideal forms that could be discovered through reason.

This outburst of intellectual and aesthetic energy in the Greek world of the fifth century is concurrent with the evolution of a new democratic form of government, especially in Athens. This increased importance of the individual may even be linked to a new overall focus on the role that men and women play in the world. Certainly, this new ideal of individual freedom—even one that seems limited by modern standards—created an environment in which new ideas could blossom and flourish.

ART OF GREECE AND THE AEGEAN WORLD   113

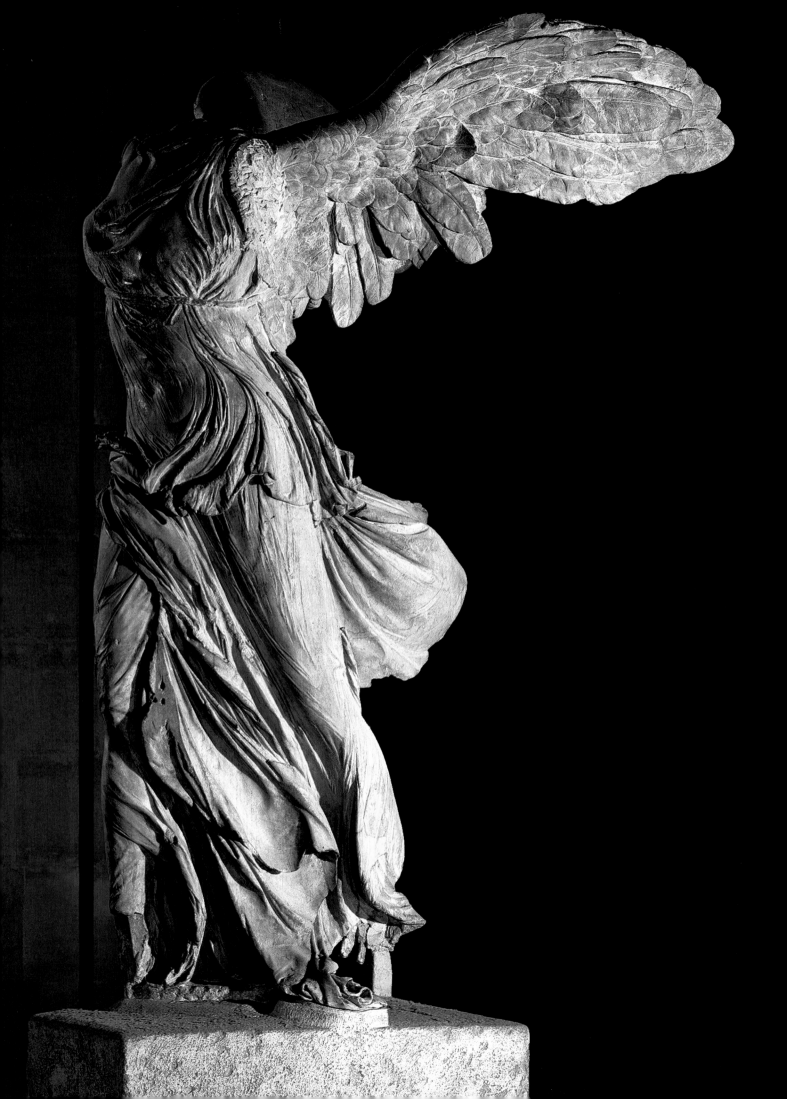

5
The Spread of Greek Art and Culture

Victory! Throughout history, triumphant warriors and athletes, leaders and mobs, men and women—shouting, dancing, embracing—have expressed the joy of winning. Yearning to capture that supreme yet fleeting sense of achievement, victors have often taken steps to commemorate their successes and to make sure that their accomplishments would not be soon forgotten. Their expressions have included songs, epic tales, and monuments such as steles, huge freestanding arches, and memorials—all forms of the arts.

In the late second century BCE, Greek artists personified victory as a supremely beautiful and powerful woman who swept through the air on eaglelike wings, alighting at will to bestow the leafy crown of victory on a chosen mortal. Nowhere was she more magnificently portrayed than in Samothrace, a city on the coast of what is now modern Turkey. Here, to celebrate a naval victory, sculptors captured the goddess's idealized form in an imposing and subtly carved and polished marble sculpture (fig. 5–1).

The *Nike (Victory) of Samothrace* exemplifies the spread of Greek culture throughout much of the ancient world. After the death of Alexander the Great (356–323 BCE), no single political center dominated the Mediterranean. From Pergamon in Turkey to Alexandria in Egypt, and ultimately in Rome, Greek art, architecture, literature, philosophy, and mathematics stimulated the diverse peoples touched by Alexander's march of conquest. Greek art and thought might be accepted, rejected, or modified, but it could not be ignored, not only in the wake of Alexander's triumphant armies, but also in the more mundane reality of seafaring merchants. These merchants dispersed the products of Greek culture across a vast area—from the shores of the Black Sea to the Pillars of Hercules, where the Mediterranean Sea meets the Atlantic Ocean. The people whom Greek soldiers, traders, and also settlers encountered had their own well-developed artistic traditions, but they adapted forms, techniques, and ideas from the Greeks, until over time a Hellenistic (that is, Greeklike) style emerged. In Italy, skilled Etruscan bronze and terra-cotta workers were inspired by monumental Greek figure sculpture, but gave their adaptation of Greek forms an energetic realism that would in turn inspire later Roman art. Far from the Mediterranean lands, herdsmen and farmers coveted Greek silver and gold jewelry and tableware. And in the Near East, the powerful and sophisticated Persians built palaces with columned halls and refined low-relief sculpture.

5–1 *Nike (Victory) of Samothrace,* from the Sanctuary of the Great Gods, Samothrace. c. 190 BCE (?). Marble, height 8′ (2.44 m). Musée du Louvre, Paris

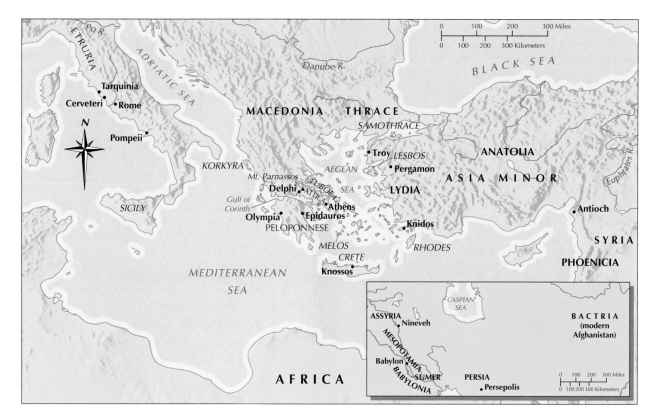

Map 5–1 The Spread of Greek Art and Culture

For much of the first millennium BCE, many states and kingdoms rose and fell in the vicinity of the Mediterranean, playing out a delicate balance of power (see Map 5–1, above). The Greeks (see Chapter 4) ruled far-flung colonies, including southern Italy and Anatolia (western Asia Minor, modern Turkey). From coastal outposts in what is now the Crimean region of Ukraine, the Greeks also traded with the Scythians, nomadic horsemen who lived north of the Black Sea on the semi-arid, grass-covered plains, or steppes.

The Assyrian Empire in Mesopotamia remained a significant force until around 625 BCE (see Chapter 2). Harassed periodically by the Scythians, the Assyrians were overthrown in 612 BCE by an alliance of the southern Mesopotamian state of Babylonia (now Iraq) and an Iranian people known as the Medes. Neo-Babylonia—so-named because it recaptured the splendor that had marked Babylon twelve centuries earlier under Hammurabi—flourished for less than a century before being taken over by the Persians, vassals of the Medes who obtained their independence in 549 BCE.

Beginning in the mid-sixth century BCE, the Persians, who occupied an area that is now southwestern Iran, began a vigorous campaign of military expansion. Under a dynasty of kings known as the Achaemenids, the Persian Empire became the dominant power in an area reaching from Asia Minor to Bactria (modern Afghanistan). They also conquered Egypt, Arabia, and

Syria and attempted, but failed, to overcome mainland Greece (as we learned in Chapter 4) in the early fifth century BCE.

The lands ruled by the Persians were part of the vast region that fell to Alexander the Great in the late fourth century BCE. Under Alexander the Great and his successors, non-Greek people produced Hellenistic (Greeklike) art in Egypt, Asia Minor, and in the lands of the former Persian Empire.

In the western Mediterranean, the Etruscans controlled much of the Italian Peninsula from the seventh century BCE until the rise of Rome in the third century BCE. Renowned both as metalworkers and sailors, the Etruscans maintained close trading relationships with the Greeks and Phoenicians. The Phoenicians, based in the coastal area of modern Lebanon in the eastern Mediterranean, sailed and traded as far as the western coast of Africa. By the eighth century BCE, they had founded colonies in North Africa and Spain.

The Hellenistic Greeks

Alexander's death had left a vast empire with no administrative structure and no appointed successor. Almost immediately, his generals turned against one another, and local leaders tried to regain their lost autonomy. By the early third century BCE, three major powers had emerged from the chaos, ruled by three of Alexander's generals and their heirs: Antigonus, Ptolemy, and

Seleucus. The Antigonids controlled Macedonia and mainland Greece; the Ptolemies ruled Egypt; and the Seleucids controlled Anatolia, Syria, Mesopotamia, and Persia. Each of these regions followed a different political course, but they were unified artistically and culturally by Greek ideas and art. This Hellenistic world would last until the rise of Rome in the second and first centuries BCE.

Artists of the Hellenistic period had a vision discernibly different from that of their Classical Greek predecessors. Whereas earlier artists often sought to capture the ideal and the all-encompassing in art, Hellenistic artists sought to represent the individual and the specific. They turned increasingly from the heroic to the everyday, from aloof serenity to individual emotion, and from serious drama to melodramatic expression. Their works appeal to the senses through lustrous or glittering surface treatments and to the emotions through dramatic subjects and poses (see Introduction, fig. 29). These tendencies, already seen as early as the fourth century BCE, became more pronounced in Hellenistic art.

Hellenistic painting reflects the new taste for dramatic narrative subject matter. Little remains of original Greek wall paintings, but in antiquity later patrons greatly admired Greek murals and commissioned copies in the form of wall paintings or mosaics. The second-century BCE mosaic illustrated in figure **5–2**, showing a battle between Alexander the Great and Darius III of Persia, is a Roman copy of a wall painting of about 310 BCE. The historian Pliny the Elder attributed the original to a Greek painter named Philoxenos of Eretria; a recent theory claims it as a work of Helen of Egypt, one of a number of women painters recorded as having worked in ancient Greece. The **mosaic** was found in a home in the ancient Roman city of Pompeii, a prosperous resort strongly influenced by Greek culture.

The dramatic scene is one of violent action and radical **foreshortening**, both working to elicit a strong response in the viewer. Astride a horse at the left, his hair blowing free and his neck bare, Alexander challenges the helmeted and armored Persian leader, who stretches out his arm in a gesture of defeat and apprehension as his charioteer whisks him back toward safety in the Persian ranks. Presumably in close imitation of the original painting, the mosaicist created the illusion of solid figures through **modeling**, mimicking the play of light on three-dimensional surfaces by highlighting protruding areas and **shading** receding ones.

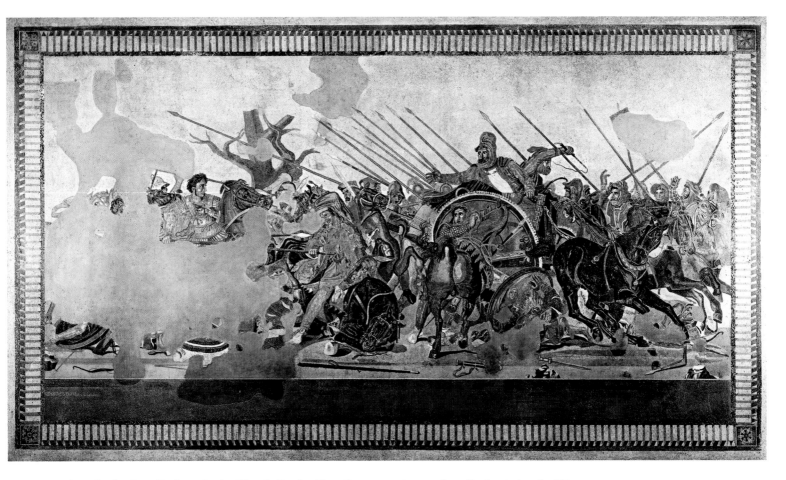

5–2 *Alexander the Great Confronts Darius III at the Battle of Issos,* Roman mosaic copy after a Greek painting of c. 310 BCE, perhaps by Philoxenos or Helen of Egypt. Museo Archeologico Nazionale, Naples

*Roman patrons in the second century BCE and later greatly admired Greek murals and commissioned copies, as either wall paintings or **mosaics**, to decorate their homes. Mosaics are created from **tesserae**, small cubes of colored stone or marble. They provide a permanent waterproof surface that the Romans used for floors in important rooms.*

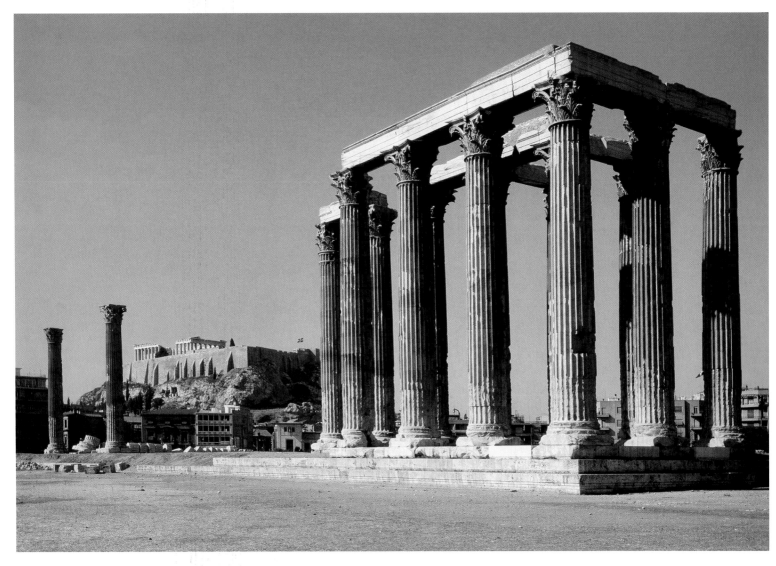

5–3 Temple of the Olympian Zeus, Athens. Building and rebuilding phases: foundation c. 520–510 BCE using the Doric order; temple designed by Cossutius, begun 175 BCE, left unfinished 164 BCE, completed 132 CE using Cossutius's design and Corinthian order. (Acropolis and Parthenon can be seen in the background.)

During the Hellenistic period, there was also increasing innovation in public architecture. For example, a variant of the Ionic order featuring a tall, slender column with an elaborate foliate capital began to challenge the dominance of the Doric and Ionic orders. Invented in the late fifth century BCE, and called *Corinthian* by later Romans, this highly ornate capital had previously been used for interior decorative purposes (see Introduction, fig. 11). But the new Temple of the Olympian Zeus (fig. **5–3**), located in the lower city of Athens at the foot of the Acropolis, used the Corinthian order on a large scale. In the second century BCE—building atop the huge foundation (measuring 135 by 354 feet) of a mid-sixth century BCE Doric temple—the Roman architect Cossutius designed a temple, which was not completed until three centuries later under the Roman emperor Hadrian. The columns and entablature soar 57 feet above the base. Indeed, viewed through the temple's few remaining upright columns, the Parthenon seems almost modest in scale. But for all its height and luxurious decoration, the Temple of the Olympian Zeus followed long-established design norms. It stood on a three-stepped base; it had an enclosed room or series of rooms surrounded by a screen of columns; and its proportions and details followed traditional standards. Quite simply, it is a Greek temple grown very large (see "The Greek Architectural Orders," page 98).

Hellenistic sculptors produced an enormous variety of work in a wide range of materials, techniques, and styles. The period was marked by two broad and conflicting trends. One (sometimes called anti-Classical) led away from Classical models and toward experimentation with new forms and subjects. This radical style was practiced in Pergamon and other eastern centers of Greek culture. The other trend led back to Classical models, with artists selecting aspects of certain favored works by fourth-century BCE sculptors to incorporate into their own works. Many popular sculptors looked back especially to Praxiteles and Lysippos for their models.

ELEMENTS OF **Architecture**

Theaters

In ancient Greece, the theater offered more than entertainment; it was a vehicle for the communal expression of religious and civic beliefs shared through music, poetry, and dance. During the fifth century BCE, the plays performed were primarily tragedies in verse based on popular myths and were written for a festival dedicated to Dionysos. The three great Greek tragedians of the time—Aeschylus, Sophocles, and Euripides—created works that defined tragedy for centuries.

Because ancient theaters were used continuously and were modified frequently over many centuries, no early theaters have survived in their original form. The largely intact theater at Epidauros, however, which dates from the early third century BCE, presents a good example of the characteristics of early theaters. A semicircle of tiered seats built into a hillside overlooks a circular performance area, called the *orkhestra* (from a Greek word meaning "to dance"), at the center of which was an altar to Dionysos. Rising behind the orchestra was a two-tiered stage structure made up of the vertical *skene* (scene)—an architectural backdrop for performances and a screen for the backstage area—and the *proskenion (proscenium)*, a raised platform in front of the *skene* that was increasingly used over time as an extension of the orchestra. Ramps connecting the *proskenion* with lateral passageways *(parodoi;* singular *parodos)* provided access to the stage for performers.

Steps gave the audience access to the rows of seats and divided the seating area into uniform wedge-shaped sections. (At Epidauros, the tiers of seats above the wide corridor, or gangway, were added at a much later date.) This standard design provided uninterrupted sight lines, excellent acoustics, and efficient crowd control for thousands of spectators—a basic plan not greatly improved upon since.

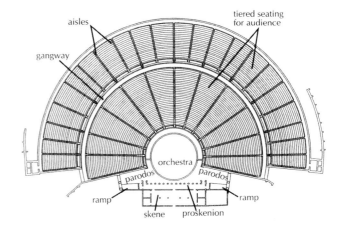

5–4 Plan of the theater of Epidauros

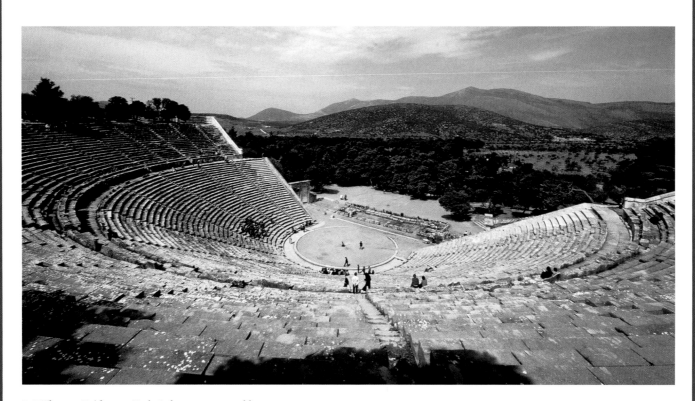

5–5 Theater, Epidauros. Early 3rd century BCE and later

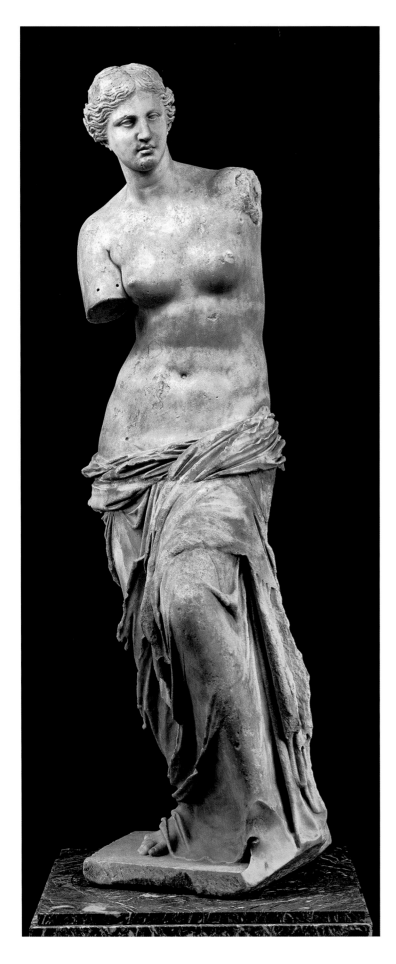

This renewed interest in the style of the fourth century BCE is exemplified by the *Aphrodite of Melos* (fig. **5–6**), found on the Aegean island of Melos by French excavators in the early nineteenth century. The sculpture was intended by its maker to recall the *Aphrodite of Knidos* by Praxiteles, which exists only in later interpretations, including the *Medici Venus* (see Introduction, fig. 6), and indeed the head, with its dreamy gaze, suggests Praxiteles' lost work. But the twisting stance and strong projection of the knee, as well as the rich, three-dimensional quality of the drapery, are typical of Hellenistic art of the third century BCE and later. Moreover, the sensuous juxtaposition of flesh with the texture of drapery, which seems about to slip off the figure, adds an insistent note of erotic tension that is thoroughly Hellenistic in concept and intent.

The idealized beauty of the *Aphrodite of Melos* contrasts sharply with the realistic depiction of an old woman carrying a basket of vegetables and a chicken, also made in the second century BCE (fig. **5–7**). At first glance she seems to be an old market woman; however, the disarray of her dress and her unfocused stare suggest that she represents an aging, dissolute follower of Dionysos, god of wine. We may assume that she is on her way to make an offering, since she seems to step out assertively into the space around her. This representation of people from all levels of society, as well as unusual physical types, became popular during the Hellenistic period.

Even more dramatic in its depiction of action is the *Nike (Victory) of Samothrace* (fig. 5–1). The wind-whipped robe and raised wings of this victory goddess indicate that she has just landed on the prow of the stone ship that formed the original base of the statue. The 8-foot-high Victory originally stood in a hillside niche high above the sanctuary of the Samothracian gods, perhaps drenched with spray from a fountain. The fact that victory in real life does often seem miraculous makes this image of a goddess alighting suddenly on a ship breathtakingly appropriate for a war memorial.

Some of the best-known examples of Hellenistic art were made in the third and second centuries BCE in the kingdom of Pergamon, a Greek state on the west coast of Asia Minor. After gaining independence in the early third century BCE, Pergamon quickly became a leading center of the arts and the hub of a new sculptural style that had far-reaching influence. That style is illustrated by sculpture from a monument commemorating the victory in 230 BCE of Attalos I (ruled 241–197 BCE) over the Gauls, a Celtic people who invaded from the north. These figures, originally in bronze but known today from Roman copies in marble, were mounted on a large pedestal. One of them, with the name

5–6 *Aphrodite of Melos* (also called *Venus de Milo*). c. 150 BCE. Marble, height 6′10″ (2.1 m). Musée du Louvre, Paris

APHRODITE'S ARMS

In the Western world the *Aphrodite of Melos* (see fig. 5–6), better known as the *Venus de Milo*, has traditionally been synonymous with female beauty. Perhaps some of the figure's enduring hold is attributable to her very incompleteness. What was she doing, and where were her hands placed? Was she clutching the drapery slipping so seductively off her hips? Or was she temptingly holding out an apple in her right hand, as fragments of sculpture found near her suggest? When the sculpture was dug up in a field in 1820, many judged the loose fragments to be part of a later restoration and not part of the original statue.

An image of Aphrodite admiring herself in the highly polished shield of her lover, the war god, Ares, became popular in the second century BCE. So the statue may have been holding a shield. If this were the case, a shield would have been positioned at an angle to one side, and probably resting on the goddess's left thigh. Today, many archaeologists compare the statue to the similar image of a Victory writing the name of a hero on a shield. Both these theories offer an explanation for the position of the shoulders, the pronounced S-curve of the pose, and the otherwise unnatural forward projection of the knee.

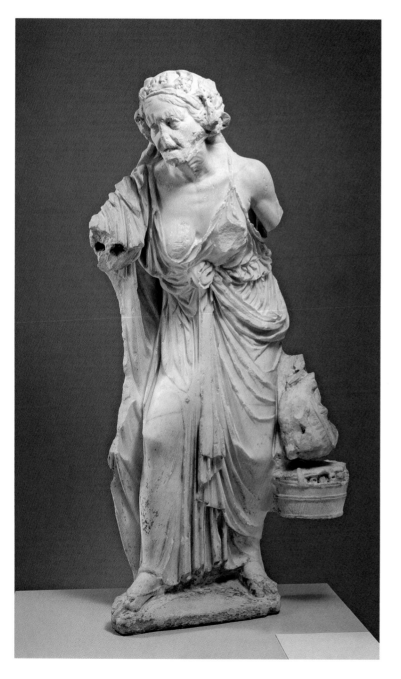

5–7 *Market Woman.* 1st century BCE. Marble, height 49 $\frac{1}{2}$″ (125.7 cm). The Metropolitan Museum of Art, New York

Epigonos inscribed on the base, shows the agonizing death of a wounded soldier-trumpeter (fig. 5–8). His wiry, unkempt hair and neck ring, or torque (reputedly the only item of dress the Gauls wore in battle), identify him as a "barbarian." But the sculpture also depicts dignity and heroism in defeat, and interestingly the artist has sought to inspire the viewer's admiration and pity for his fallen subject. The viewer experiences a sense of arrested motion seeing the trumpeter supporting himself on his right arm, struggling to remain upright. One can see that his elbow is buckling, his body about to collapse. This kind of deliberate attempt to elicit a specific emotional response in the viewer, a form of "expressionism," became another characteristic of Hellenistic art.

The style and approach seen in the monument to the defeated Gauls culminated in the celebrated frieze of the Pergamon Altar enclosure. The frieze wrapped around the base of a huge Ionic colonnade that enclosed an altar to Zeus on a mountainside at Pergamon (fig. 5–9). The frieze was probably executed during the reign of Eumenes II (197–159 BCE). It depicts the battle between the gods and the giants, a mythical struggle used by the Greeks as a metaphor for contemporary conflict—in this case, Pergamon's victory over the Gauls.

The panels, each about 7 $\frac{1}{2}$ feet tall, show Greek gods fighting human-looking giants and grotesque hybrids emerging from the bowels of the earth. In one section of the frieze, the goddess Athena has forced a winged monster to his knees (fig. 5–10). Inscriptions along the base of the sculpture identify the monster as Alkyoneos, a son of the earth goddess, Ge, who rises in maternal wrath from the ground on the right. At the far right, a winged Victory foretells the outcome of this struggle, as she is about to crown Athena the victor.

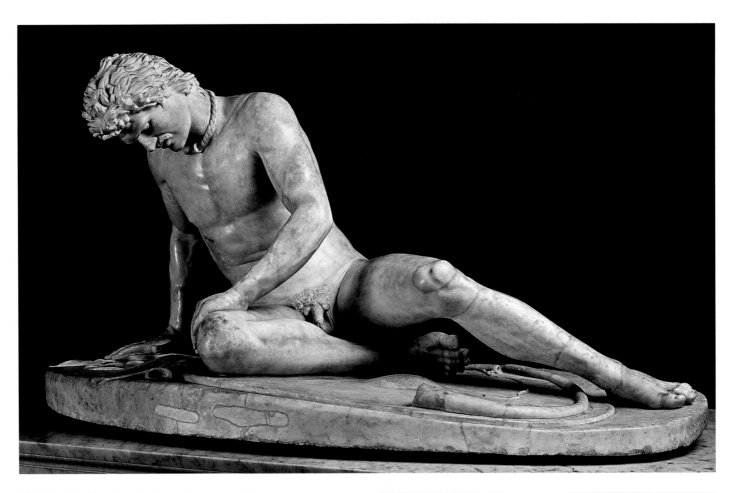

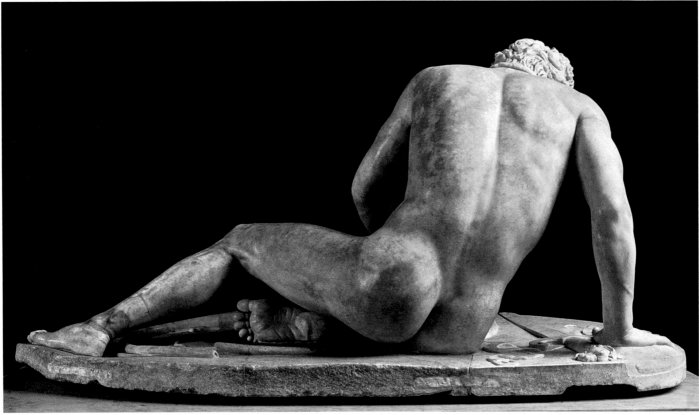

5–8 Epigonos (?). *Dying Gallic Trumpeter,* Roman copy after the original bronze of c. 220 BCE. Marble, life-size. Museo Capitolino, Rome

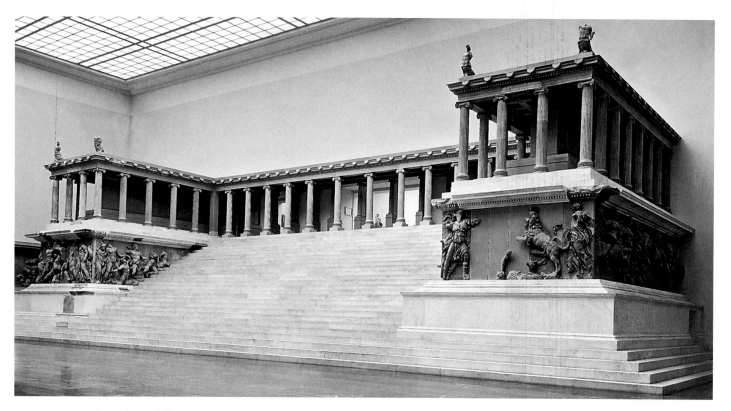

5–9 Reconstructed west front of the altar from Pergamon, Turkey. c. 166–159 BCE. Marble. Staatliche Museen zu Berlin, Preussischer Kulturbesitz, Antikensammlung

The Pergamon frieze is carved in high relief with deep **undercutting** that creates dramatic contrasts of light and shade that play over the complex forms. Compositionally, the Pergamene sculptors sought to balance opposing forces in three-dimensional space along diagonal lines, whereas Greek artists of the fifth century BCE sought equilibrium and control through balanced horizontals and verticals. Some figures in the Pergamon frieze even extend beyond the architectural setting onto the steps, where visitors had to pass them on their way up to the shrine (see sculptural figures at far left, fig. 5–9). Many consider this theatrical and complex interaction of space and form to be another hallmark of the Hellenistic style, just as they consider the balanced restraint of the Parthenon sculpture to characterize the Classical style. Similarly, the emotional composure admired in Classical art gives way in the Hellenistic period to extreme expressions of pain, stress, wild anger, fear, and despair. (All these emotions are also characteristic of the sculpture of *Laocoön and His Sons* already seen in the Introduction, figs. 27 and 28.)

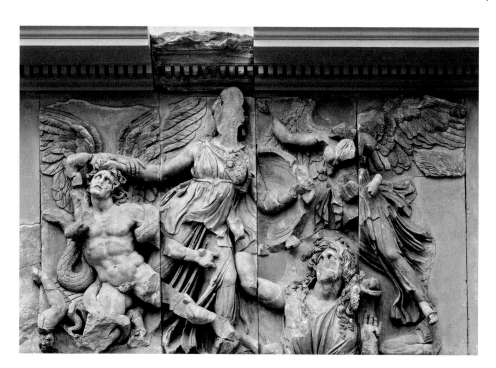

5–10 *Athena Attacking the Giants,* detail of the frieze from the east front of the altar from Pergamon. Marble frieze, height 7′6″ (2.3 m). Staatliche Museen zu Berlin, Preussischer Kulturbesitz, Antikensammlung

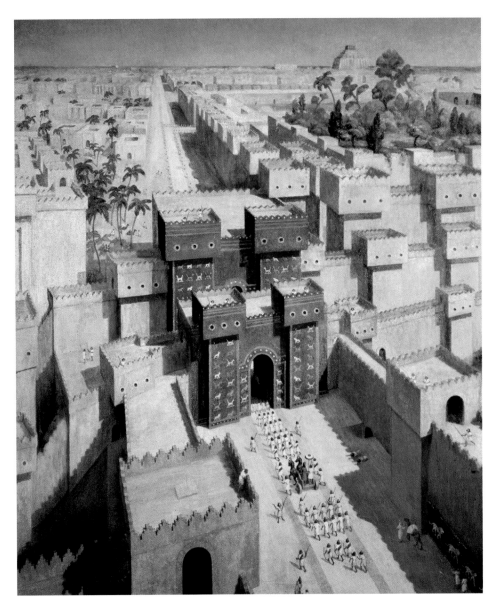

5-11 Reconstruction drawing of Babylon in the 6th century BCE. The Oriental Institute of the University of Chicago

In this view, the palace of Nebuchadnezzar II, with its famous Hanging Gardens, can be seen just behind and to the right of the Ishtar Gate, to the west of the Processional Way. The Marduk Ziggurat looms up in the far distance on the east bank of the Euphrates. This structure was at times believed to be the biblical Tower of Babel—Bab-il was an early form of the city's name.

The Neo-Babylonians

Alexander's battles with the Persians, and his conquest of the Persian Empire, brought what had been the center of ancient Mesopotamian civilization, including lands from Anatolia to India, into the sphere of Greek influence. Centuries earlier, the Babylonians had rebelled against their Assyrian rulers. Joining the Medes (western Iran), in 612 they captured Nineveh, the capital of Assyria. When the dust settled, Assyria was no longer a power, the Medes controlled a large strip of land south of the Black and Caspian seas, and the Neo-Babylonians dominated the lowlands of Mesopotamia.

The most famous Neo-Babylonian ruler was Nebuchadnezzar II (ruled 604–562 BCE). A great patron of architecture, he built

temples throughout his realm and transformed Babylon—the cultural, political, and economic hub of his empire—into one of the most splendid cities of its day. A broad avenue named May the Enemy Not Have Victory—also called the Processional Way because it was the route taken by religious processions honoring the city's patron god, Marduk—crossed the eastern sector of the city (fig. 5–11). Up to 66 feet wide at some points, the avenue was paved with large stone slabs. Colorful glazed bricks faced the walls on both sides along the route. The Processional Way ended at the Ishtar Gate, a main entrance to the city (fig. 5–12). Named after the goddess known as Inanna in Sumer and Ishtar in the Semitic-speaking regions of Mesopotamia, the gate symbolized Babylonian power. Guarded by four **crenellated** (notched) towers, the glazed-brick gate was decorated with tiers of dragons.

Greek tales of the magnificent palaces, temples, and hanging gardens of ancient Babylon still fire the imagination, and biblical accounts of the tyranny and decadence of Babylon's rulers conjure up images of licentious splendor. The Jews had reason to record Babylonian faults, since twice—in 597 BCE and 587 BCE—Babylonian armies destroyed Jerusalem and its temple and carried off the Jews into exile and captivity. In Babylon, one of these exiles, Daniel, survived death in the lion's den to tell his story. The "Babylonian Captivity" became a turning point in Jewish history and prompted the poetic lamentations of the prophets Isaiah and Ezekiel.

Babylon was a huge city covering more than $3\frac{1}{2}$ square miles on both sides of the Euphrates River in what is now Iraq. A wide Processional Way running parallel to the river joined temples and palaces and led to the northern palace complex. A moat, double walls, and gates with double towers defended the city. The northern gate (fig. 5–12) in the royal sector was dedicated to Ishtar, the goddess of Love and War. The deep-blue surfaces of this so-called Ishtar Gate are decorated with alternating rows of bulls with blue forelocks—associated with Adad, the sky and weather god—and dragons, sacred to the city god Marduk. Between 1905 and 1914, German archaeologists excavated the northern palace area. They recovered the brilliant glazed-tile decoration of part of the Processional Way, the Ishtar Gate, and Nebuchadnezzar's throne room, much of which they shipped to Germany, where it was reassembled in Berlin.

Using glazed bricks to decorate these enormous surfaces required careful planning and great technical skill. Just one of the dragons, for example, required as many as 75 to 80 bricks. Since firing caused the bricks to shrink, each brick had to be slightly larger than its allotted space in the final design. To enhance the splendid effect, brilliantly colored glass-based glazes were applied to the reliefs. (When fired, glaze produces a shiny, waterproof surface.)

Seen at right in the photo, an intricate design of striding lions, tall palm trees with blue fronds, and patterns of white and yellow rosettes and palmettes covers the deep blue wall of the panel from Nebuchadnezzar's throne room. The date palm was associated with Ishtar in her role as protectress of the date storehouses. Date palms and lions reminded Ishtar's devotees

that she controlled both food and safety—the physical well-being and survival of her people.

In such a setting, described in the Bible, the Book of Daniel, Nebuchadnezzar could have set up his golden idol, and Belshazzar could have used gold and silver vessels stolen from the Jewish Temple to serve wine at his infamous feast, causing Daniel to proclaim, "You have been weighed in the balance and found wanting!" Indeed Belshazzar's feast was his last, for the Persians entered the gates in 539 BCE—among them the Ishtar Gate—and destroyed Babylon that very night.

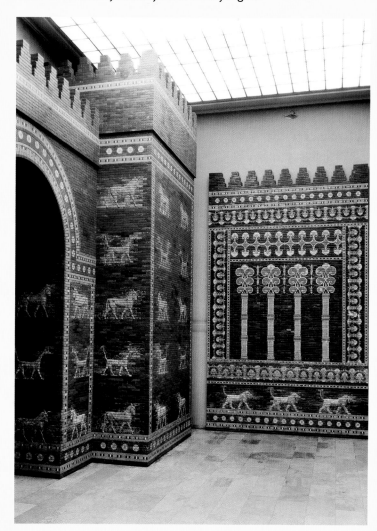

5–12 Ishtar Gate and throne room wall, from Babylon (Iraq). c. 575 BCE. Glazed brick. Staatliche Museen zu Berlin, Preussischer Kulturbesitz, Vorderasiatisches Museum

Technique

Coining Money

Before the invention of coins, people used gold, silver, bronze, and copper as mediums of exchange, but each piece had to be weighed to establish its exact value. The Lydians of western Anatolia began to produce metal coins in standard weights in the seventh century BCE, adapting the use of a seal—a Sumerian invention—to designate each coin's value.

Until about 525 BCE, coins bore an image on one side only. The beautiful early coin here, minted during the reign of the Lydian king Croesus (ruled 560–546 BCE), is stamped with the heads and forelegs of a bull and lion in low relief. The reverse has only a squarish depression left by the punch used to force the metal into the mold.

To make two-faced coins, the ancients used a punch and anvil, each of which held a die, or mold, incised with the design to be impressed into the coin. A metal blank weighing the exact amount of the denomination was placed over the anvil die, which contained the design for the "head" (obverse) of the coin. The punch, with the die of the "tail" (reverse) design, was placed on top of the metal blank and struck with a mallet.

Beginning in the reign of Darius I, a king's portrait appeared on coins, proclaiming the ruler's control of the coin of the realm—a custom that continued throughout much of the world. Because we often know when ancient monarchs ruled, coins discovered in an archaeological excavation can help date the objects found with them.

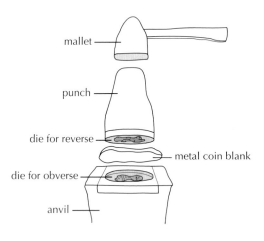

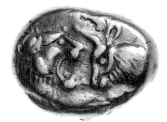 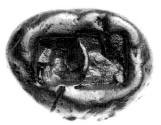

Front and back of gold coin first minted under Croesus, king of Lydia. 560–546 BCE. Heberden Coin Room, Ashmolean Museum, Oxford

---

Now reconstructed in Berlin's Pergamon Museum, the Ishtar Gate is installed next to a panel from the facade of the throne room of Nebuchadnezzar's palace (the so-called Southern Palace) (seen on the right in fig. 5–12). Here, lions also made of molded and glazed brick stride in single file beneath stylized palm trees. Lions were often associated with royal power in the Near East, and Mesopotamian cylinder seals sometimes show the goddess Ishtar resting her foot on a lion.

The Persians

The Persians settled in southwestern Iran at the beginning of the first millennium BCE. Originally subservient to the Medes, the Persians obtained their independence in 549 BCE under Cyrus II, a dynamic leader called "the Great" who ruled 559–530 BCE. Cyrus led the Persians in an astonishing series of conquests. By the time of his death, the Persian Empire included Babylonia, vanquished by Persia in 539 BCE, and stretched from Iran into Anatolia. Cyrus's son Cambyses II (ruled 529–522 BCE) added Egypt and Cyprus to the empire. By the time Darius I (ruled 521–486 BCE) took the throne, he could boast: "I am Darius, great King, King of Kings, King of countries, King of this earth." Darius and his successors were known as the Achaemenid monarchs after a semi-legendary ancestor, Achaemenes. They ruled for nearly two centuries, expanding the Achaemenid Empire both eastward and westward.

When Cyrus the Great defeated the ancient country of Lydia's fabulously wealthy King Croesus (ruled 560–546 BCE) in 546 BCE, Persia gained control over Lydia's gold. (Croesus's name has come down to us in the expression "as rich as Croesus.") The Persians learned from the Lydians to mint coins in standard weights. In addition to their obvious economic function, coins also served as propaganda, carrying a ruler's portrait throughout the land. One type of Persian coin, the gold daric, named for Darius and first minted during his reign, is among the most sought-after rare coins in the world today (fig. **5–13**). Commonly called an "archer," the coin shows the well-armed emperor wearing his crown and carrying a lance in his right hand and a bow in his left: He lunges forward as if he had just loosed an arrow from his bow.

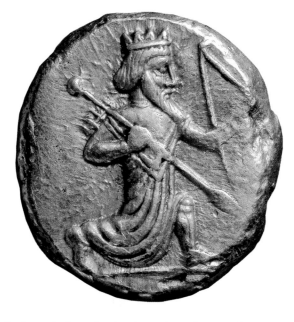

5–13 Daric, a coin first minted under Darius I of Persia. 4th century BCE. Gold. Heberden Coin Room, Ashmolean Museum, Oxford
© ASHMOLEAN ICON MUSEUM, OXFORD, ENGLAND, U.K.

An able administrator, Darius organized the Persian lands into 20 tribute-paying areas under Persian governors, and he often left lesser local rulers in place. This practice, along with a tolerance for diverse native customs and religions, won the Persians the loyalty of many of their subjects. Darius also developed a system of fair taxation, issued a standardized currency (see "Coining Money," page 126), and improved communication throughout the empire.

Like many powerful rulers, Darius created monuments to serve as visible symbols of his authority. About 518 BCE, he began building a new capital in the Persian homeland, today known by its Greek name: Persepolis. He employed materials, workers, and artists from all over his empire. The result was a new style of art that combined many different cultural traditions—Persian, Mede, Mesopotamian, Egyptian, and Greek.

In Assyrian fashion, the imperial complex at Persepolis was set on a raised platform, 40 feet high, and like Egyptian and Greek cities, it was laid out on a rectangular grid. The platform was accessible only from a single ramp made of wide, shallow steps to allow horsemen to ride up rather than dismount and climb on foot. Construction extended over nearly 60 years, and Darius lived to see the erection of only a treasury, the Apadana (Audience Hall), and a small palace for himself.

Darius's Apadana (fig. **5–14**), set above the rest of the complex on a second terrace, had a square hall large enough to hold several thousand people. The sides of the staircases and walls of the platform were covered with sculpture in low relief. On the walls, ranks of warriors seem ready to defend the palace, while on the staircase, lions attack bulls at each side of the Persian generals. These animal combats (a theme found throughout the Near East) emphasize the ferocity of the leaders and their men. The Persian reliefs, like Greek friezes, were once brightly painted, and metal objects, such as Darius's crown, were covered in **gold leaf** (thin sheets of hammered gold). Other reliefs throughout Persepolis depict displays of allegiance or economic prosperity. In one example, Darius holds an audience while his son and heir, Xerxes, listens from behind the throne (fig. **5–15**). During his own reign, Xerxes I (ruled 484–465 BCE) added a sprawling palace complex, enlarged the treasury building, and began a vast new public reception space, the Hall of 100 Columns.

At its height, the empire ruled by Darius and his successors extended from Africa to India. Only mainland Greeks successfully resisted the armies of the Achaemenids, and it was a Greek who ultimately put an end to their rule: Alexander the Great of Macedonia. Alexander crossed into Anatolia and swept through Mesopotamia in 334 BCE, subsequently defeating Darius III and sacking Persepolis in 331 BCE. The lands of Persia then became part of the Hellenistic world.

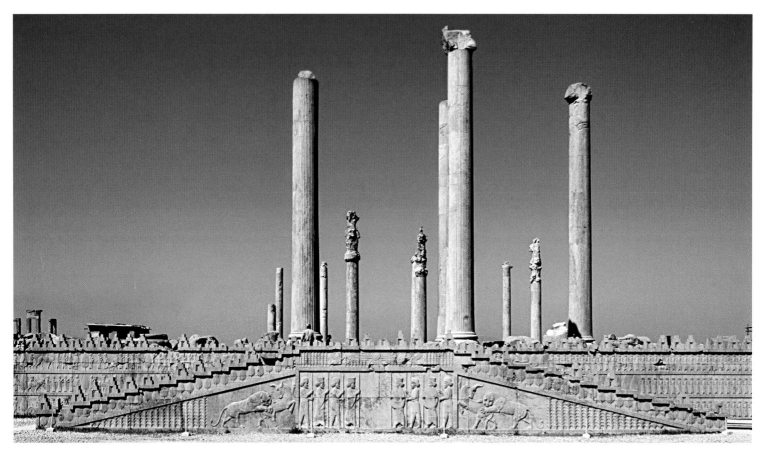

5–14 Apadana (Audience Hall) of Darius I and Xerxes I, ceremonial complex, Persepolis, Iran. 518–c. 460 BCE

The ancient historian Cleiarchus of Alexandria relates that Alexander the Great and his troops accidentally torched the royal compound at Persepolis during a wild banquet in celebration of their victory over the Persians. It is more probable that Alexander had it destroyed deliberately. The site was never rebuilt, and its ruins were never buried. Scholars have been measuring, mapping, and studying what remains of the complex for generations. Various pieces of architectural ornament have been stripped from Persepolis for display in museums around the world.

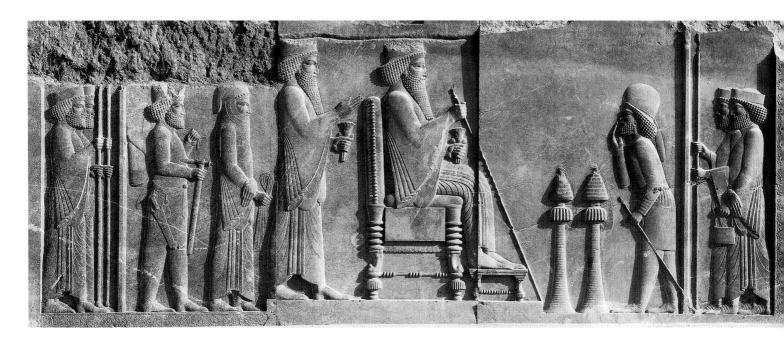

5–15 *Darius and Xerxes Receiving Tribute,* detail of a relief from the stairway leading to the Apadana, ceremonial complex, Persepolis, Iran. 491–486 BCE. Limestone, height 8′4″ (2.54 m). Iranbastan Museum, Tehran
COURTESY OF THE ORIENTAL INSTITUTE OF THE UNIVERSITY OF CHICAGO

The Etruscans

The boot-shaped Italian peninsula, shielded on the north by the formidable Alps, juts into the Mediterranean Sea. In ancient times, the peninsula's inhabitants were exposed to the interplay among Near Eastern, Egyptian, and Greek civilizations. Etruscan society, deeply influenced by the Greek, emerged in the seventh century BCE in Etruria (modern Tuscany). The Etruscans may have descended from a people called the Villanovans, who had occupied the northern and western regions of Italy since the Bronze Age. The Etruscans reached the height of their power in the sixth century BCE, when they formed a loose federation of a dozen cities. The fertile soil of Etruria and its rich lodes of metal ore formed the basis of their wealth.

Etruscan artists excelled at making monumental terra-cotta sculpture, a task requiring great technical and physical skill. Artists had to construct the pieces so that they would not collapse under their own weight while the raw clay was still heavy with moisture. In addition, they had to regulate the **kiln** temperature during the long firing process. The life-size figure of the god Apollo (fig. **5–16**) was made about 500 BCE. Its well-developed body and "Archaic smile" demonstrate that Etruscan sculptors knew Greek Archaic *kouroi* and *korai* (see figs. 4–19 and 4–20). But while the Greeks represented men nude, the Etruscans usually represented them partially clothed. Here Apollo is partly concealed by a robe. Note that the striding pose has a vigor that contrasts with the quieter stance of Archaic Greek figures. The figure was originally placed along the roof ridge of an Etruscan temple at Veii as part of a four-figure scene depicting one of the labors of Herakles. Apollo fought with the hero Hercules for the possession of a deer sacred to Artemis, goddess of the moon and hunting. Two other figures—Artemis and Hermes (Mercury)—watched over the struggle. Apollo looks as if he is stepping over the decorative scroll that helped support the sculpture when it was atop a temple. This quality of energy expressed in purposeful movement is characteristic of both Etruscan sculpture and painting.

According to the Roman architect Vitruvius, Etruscan temples had only a superficial resemblance to those of the Greeks. The Etruscans used the post-and-lintel structure and gable roofs. The columns' bases, shafts (which were sometimes fluted), and capitals resembled those of either the Greek Doric or Ionic order, and the entablature might have a frieze. Vitruvius used the term "Tuscan Order" to describe the variation of an unfluted shaft and simplified base, capital, and entablature (see "Roman Architectural Orders," page 149). The Etruscans built their temples on a high base with a single flight of stairs leading to a

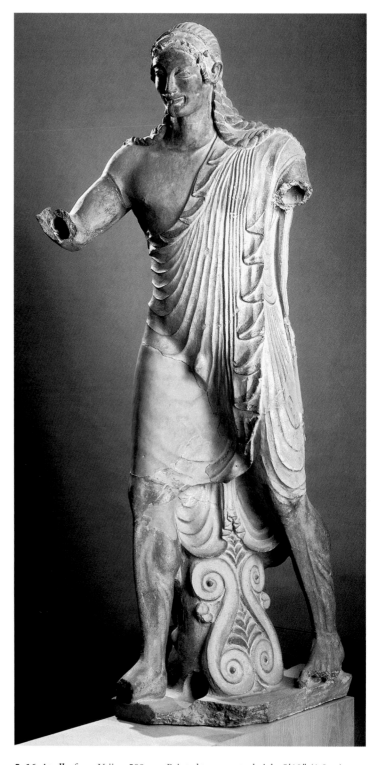

5–16 *Apollo,* from Veii. c. 500 BCE. Painted terra-cotta, height 5′10″ (1.8 m). Museo Nazionale di Villa Giulia, Rome

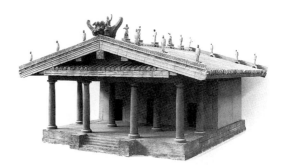

5–17 Reconstruction of an Etruscan temple based partly on descriptions by Vitruvius University of Rome, Istituto di Etruscologia e Antichità Italiche

Although Etruscan temples were simple in form, they were embellished with dazzling displays of painting and terra-cotta sculpture. The temple roof, rather than the pediment, served as a base for large statue groups.

columned porch. The deep porch led in turn to a **cella**, which was divided into three parallel rooms (fig. **5–17**).

The typical Etruscan home was a rectangular mud-brick structure built either around a central courtyard or around an **atrium**, a room with a shallow indoor pool for drinking, cooking, and bathing, fed by rainwater through a large opening in the roof. The burial chamber of the "Tomb of the Reliefs" at Cerveteri (near Rome) was carved to imitate such a house in the third century BCE (fig. **5–18**). The tomb's walls were plastered and painted, and the tomb was provided with a full selection of furnishings, some carved, others simulated in **stucco**, a slow-drying type of plaster that can easily be modeled or molded.

Some tombs were painted not carved. In the "Tomb of the Lionesses" at Tarquinia, a detail of a frieze painted about 480–470 BCE shows a couple energetically dancing to the music of

a double flute beneath a pediment ornamented with a female leopard (fig. **5–19**). The woman is represented on equal footing with her male partner, suggesting that some women were active in Etruscan society. The immediacy of this wall painting is striking. The dancers and musicians seem to be performing for us, not enacting the formal rituals of a remote, long-dead civilization.

Etruscan **sarcophagi** (large carved tomb chests) also provided a domestic touch. Rather than a cold, somber memorial to the dead, sculpted terra-cotta figures of the dead recline comfortably on the lid of a terra-cotta sarcophagus made to look like a couch. Two happy individuals, with slanting almond-shaped eyes and benign smiles, seem to greet the viewer with lively gestures. Their bodies are rendered in sufficient detail to convey contemporary hair and clothing styles (fig. **5–20**). They might almost be attending a banquet or enjoying a performance of music or

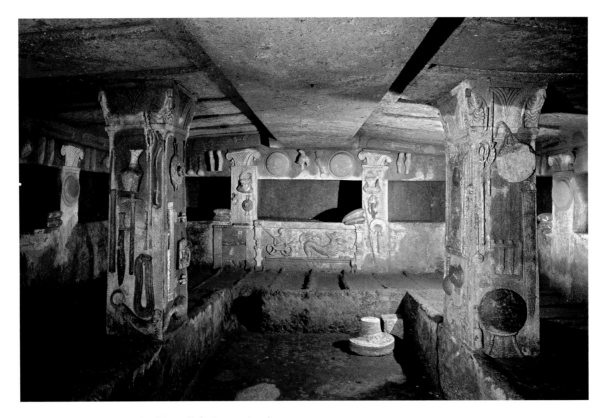

5–18 Burial chamber, Tomb of the Reliefs, Cerveteri. 3rd century BCE

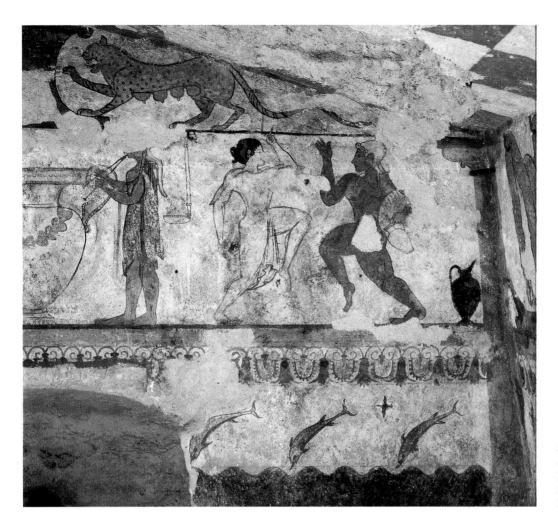

5–19 *Musicians and Dancers,* detail of a wall painting, Tomb of the Lionesses, Tarquinia. c. 480–470 BCE. Soprintendenza Archeologica per l'Etruria Meridionale, Rome, Italy

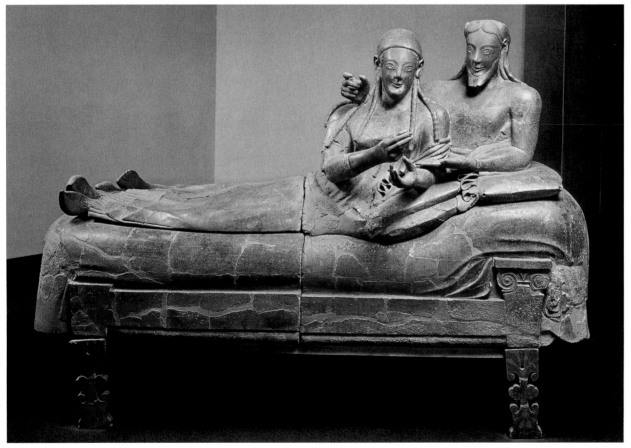

5–20 Sarcophagus, from Cerveteri. c. 520 BCE. Terra-cotta, length 6′7″ (2.06 m). Museo Nazionale di Villa Giulia, Rome

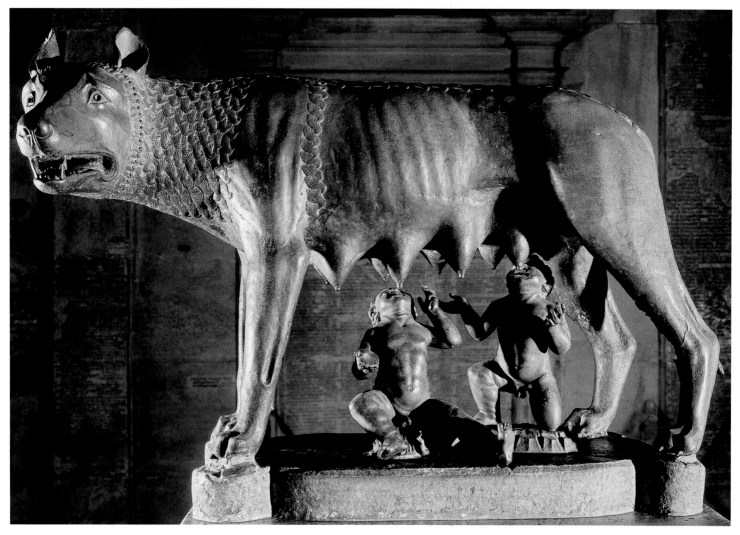

5–21 *She-Wolf.* c. 500 BCE. Bronze, glass-paste eyes, height 33 ½" (85 cm). Museo Capitolino, Rome. The children are later additions

Although this sculpture was almost certainly the work of an Etruscan artist, it has long been associated with Rome. According to an ancient Roman legend, twin infants named Romulus and Remus, who had been abandoned on the banks of the Tiber River by a wicked uncle and left there to die, were suckled by a she-wolf that had come to the river to drink. The twins were raised by a shepherd, and when they grew up, they decided to build a city near the spot where they had been rescued by the wolf. They quarreled, however, about its exact location. Romulus killed Remus and then established a small settlement that would become the great city of Rome, an event that, according to tradition, occurred in 753 BCE.

dance, examples of convivial festivities recorded in paintings on Etruscan tomb walls.

The skill of Etruscan bronzeworkers was widely known in ancient times. Unfortunately, only a few examples of large-scale cast-bronze sculpture in the round have survived the wholesale recycling of bronze objects over the centuries. One such sculpture, which dates to about 500 BCE, portrays a she-wolf with heavy, milk-filled teats—evidence that she has recently given birth (fig. **5–21**). The naturalistic rendering of the animal's body contrasts with the stylized rendering of the tightly curled ruff of fur around the neck. Remarkable realism combined with decorative stylization is a characteristic of Etruscan art. The sculpture may represent the legendary she-wolf who nurtured the twins Romulus and Remus, the founders of Rome. The bronze twins were added to the sculpture during the Renaissance period.

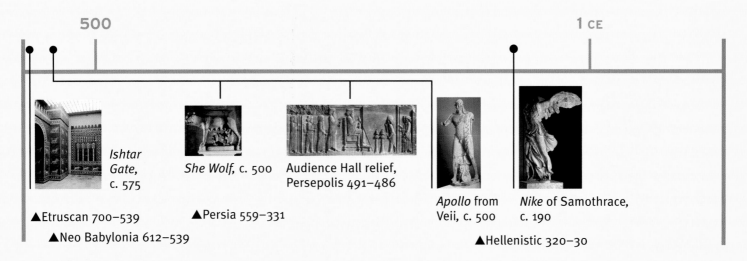

500   1 CE

Ishtar Gate, c. 575

She Wolf, c. 500

Audience Hall relief, Persepolis 491–486

Apollo from Veii, c. 500

Nike of Samothrace, c. 190

▲Etruscan 700–539

▲Neo Babylonia 612–539

▲Persia 559–331

▲Hellenistic 320–30

LOOKING BACK

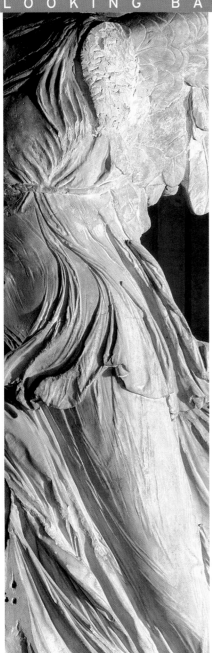

Changing political conditions never seriously dampened the Greek creative spirit and its influence. Although later artists continued to observe the basic Classical approach to composition and form, they no longer adhered rigidly to its conventions. Despite the instability of the fourth century BCE, Greek city-states undertook innovative architectural projects. Architects developed variations on Classical ideals in urban planning, temple design, and the construction of monumental tombs and altars. In contrast to the fifth century, much of this activity took place outside of Athens and even in areas outside of mainland Greece, notably in Asia Minor.

Earlier Greek artists had sought to capture the ideal and often focused on the heroic. Hellenistic artists sought to represent the specific and turned increasingly to the everyday. A trend introduced in the fourth century BCE—the appeal to the senses through surface treatments and to the emotions through drama—became more pronounced. Even the architecture of the Hellenistic period largely reflected the contemporary taste for high drama.

Persians, Etruscans, and others adapted Greek techniques and aesthetics and integrated them into their own traditions. Greek material culture and ideas spread to these people through trade, colonies, and conquest—especially throughout the lands conquered by Alexander the Great. The multicultural composition of imperial Persia, for example, is evident in the varied appearance of its art, notably at Persepolis where architecture and sculpture reflect design ideas from Near Eastern, Egyptian, and Greek sources.

Although Etruscan artists also patronized Greek artists and drew inspiration from Greek and Near Eastern sources, they never slavishly copied what they admired. Instead, they assimilated these influences, combining them with their own traditions to create distinctive styles of architecture, including new temple plans, bronze and terra-cotta sculpture, and wall painting.

Why did so many people in different times and places turn to the Classical art of Greece for inspiration? Perhaps in part because each in his or her own way respected and admired a tradition of art that was grounded in an intense study of nature and the human condition.

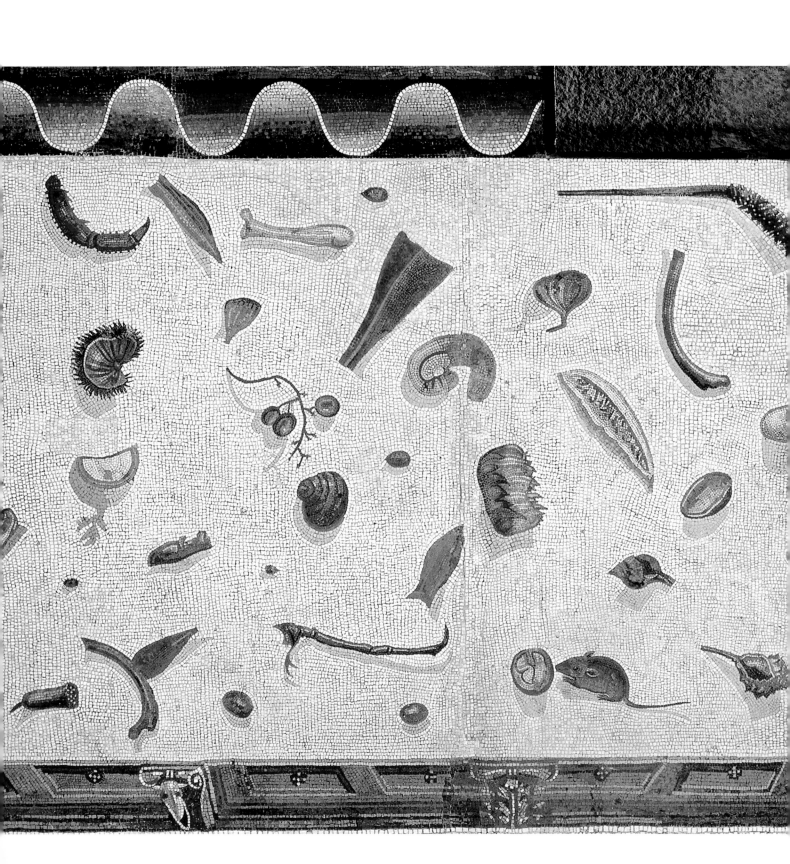

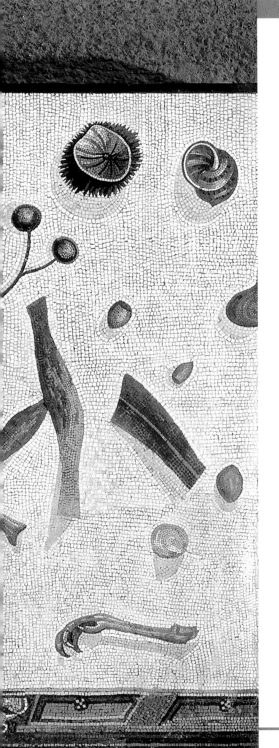

I n his work of comic genius, the *Satyricon*, the first-century CE Roman satirist Petronius created one of the all-time fantastic dinner parties, Trimalchio's Feast (*Cena Trimalchionis*, Book 15). The newly rich Trimalchio entertains his friends at a lavish banquet where he shows off his extraordinary wealth, but also demonstrates his ignorance and boorish manners. When dishes are broken, Trimalchio orders his servants to sweep them away with the rubbish on the floor.

In the *Unswept Floor* mosaic (fig. **6–1**), the remains of fine food from just such a party litter the floor. The family and guests dining in this room would have seen the fictive remains of past gourmet pleasures—from lobster claws to cherry pits—under their couches. The literary character of the imagery is further emphasized by the inclusion of six actor's masks along one side of the room—an arrangement suggesting that theatrical entertainment will follow the sumptuous feast.

If art reflects the ideals of a society, what does it mean that wealthy Romans commemorated their table scraps in mosaics of the greatest subtlety and skill? Is this a form of conspicuous consumption, proof that the owner of this house gave lavish banquets and hosted guests whose sophisticated humor would appreciate Trimalchio's Feast? The Romans did in fact place a high value on displaying their wealth and taste in the semi-public rooms and gardens of their houses and villas, and they did so through their possessions, especially their art collections.

The Unswept Floor is, in fact, just one of a very large number of Roman copies of great Greek works of art, including mosaics, paintings, and sculptures. We know that Julius Caesar owned a version of the *Dying Gallic Trumpeter* (see fig. 5–8); that a *Laocoön* (see Introduction, fig. 27) belonged to Nero; and that a copy of Polykleitos's *Spear Bearer* (see fig. 4–36) stood in the baths at Hadrian's Villa. In the case of *The Unswept Floor*, Heraklitos, a second-century CE Greek mosaicist living in Rome (who signed his work), made a copy of an **illusionistic** painting by the renowned second-century BCE Pergamene artist Sosos. It is a work that exemplifies many of the characteristics of ancient Roman art: an interest in history, literary allusions, visual tricks, and great skill in representing material objects.

6–1 Heraklitos. *The Unswept Floor,* mosaic variant of a 2nd-century BCE painting by Sosos of Pergamon. 2nd century CE. 13'3 $\frac{1}{2}$" (4.05 m). Musei Vaticani, Museo Gregoriano Profano, ex Lateranese, Rome

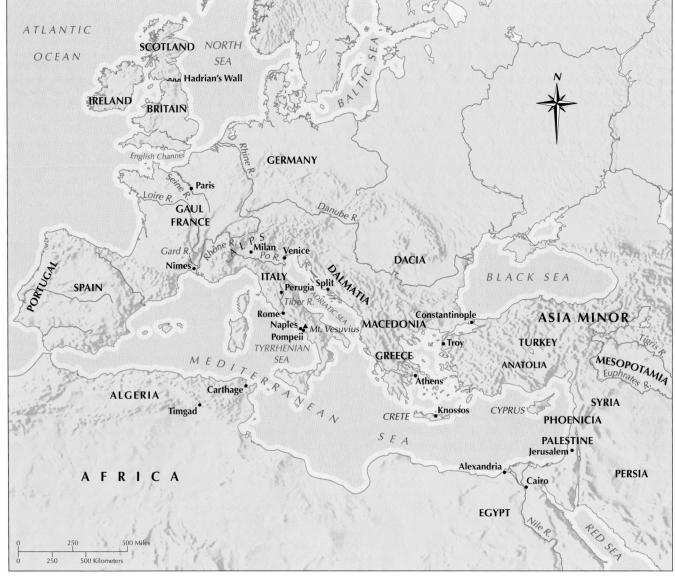

Map 6–1 The Roman Republic and Empire

As early as the Iron Age, small groups of people who spoke a common language, Latin, settled in central Italy south of the Tiber River. They also built small settlements on a group of seven hills near the Tiber. These hilltop villages eventually grew in size and joined to become the city of Rome. By the sixth century BCE, Rome had developed into a major transportation and trading center. At this time, central Italy was also home to the Etruscans (see Chapter 5). But the Romans soon challenged the Etruscan presence, and by the first century BCE they ruled the peninsula.

At the height of their power—in the early second century CE—Romans ruled all the lands around the Mediterranean Sea, which they proudly referred to as *mare nostrum*, or "our sea." Their empire stretched east to the Euphrates, south to Egypt, and northwest as far as Scotland.

To spur growth and to simplify administration of this vast empire, the Roman government undertook building programs of unprecedented scale and complexity, constructing central administrative and commercial centers (**forums** and **basilicas**),

racetracks, theaters, public baths and water systems, apartment buildings, and even entire new cities. To speed communication and to facilitate commerce and the movement of troops, the Romans built a vast and sophisticated network of roads between their capital and the empire's farthest reaches. In fact, many modern European highways still follow the routes laid down by ancient Roman engineers, and Roman-era foundations underlie the streets of many European cities.

Culturally, the Romans borrowed heavily from Greece and the larger Hellenistic world. They incorporated Greek orders into their architecture, imported Greek art, and employed Greek artists. Like the Etruscans, they also adopted the Greek gods and heroes as their own, giving them Latin names (see "Roman Counterparts of Greek Gods," page 138). In Western Europe, the sophisticated legal, administrative, and cultural systems that the Romans imposed on the people they conquered endured for some five hundred years. And in the eastern Mediterranean, the Classical traditions and styles of ancient Rome survived into the fifteenth century as important elements of Byzantine art.

The Republican Period

Early Rome was governed by a series of kings and an advisory body called the Senate, made up of upper-class citizens. The last kings of Rome were overthrown in 509 BCE, marking the beginning of what is known as the period of the Republic (509–27 BCE). Rome's conquest of lands outside the Italian peninsula strained its political system, weakening the authority of the Senate and leading to a series of civil wars among powerful generals. In 49 BCE Julius Caesar invaded Italy from his post in France and in 46 BCE the general—who had been co-ruler of Rome with Pompey and Crassus in the First Triumvirate—emerged victorious over his rivals. He ruled Rome as dictator until his assassination in 44 BCE.

Artists of the Republican period sought to create believable images based on careful observation. For example, we know what Julius Caesar looked like because a coin issued in 44 BCE bears his portrait (fig. 6–2). This tiny relief sculpture reproduces the ruler's careworn features and growing baldness. This new idea of placing a living ruler's portrait on one side of a coin and a symbol of the country or an image that recalls some important action or event on the other was adopted by Caesar's successors. Consequently, Roman coins give us an unprecedented and personal view of Roman history.

The convention of rendering accurate and faithful portraits of individuals, called naturalism, may have been derived from the practice of making death masks of deceased relatives. In any case, during the Republican period patrons clearly admired veristic portraits, and they often turned to skilled Etruscan artists to execute them. The life-size bronze portrait of *Aulus Metellus*—the Roman official's name is inscribed on the hem of

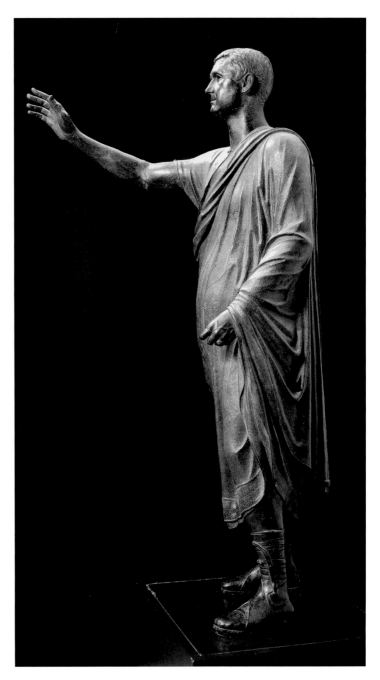

6–3 **Aulus Metellus,** found near Perugia. Late 2nd or early 1st century BCE. Bronze, height 5′11″ (1.8 m). Museo Archeològico Nazionale, Florence

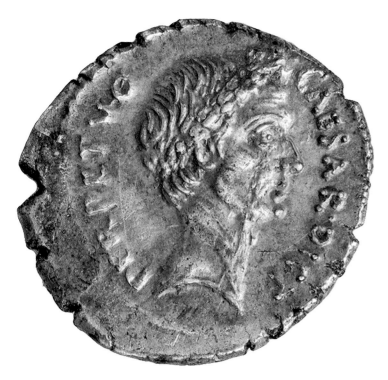

6–2 *Denarius* **with portrait of Julius Caesar.** 44 BCE. Silver, diameter approximately ³/₄″ (1.9 cm). American Numismatic Society, New York

his garment in Etruscan letters (fig. 6–3)—depicts the man addressing a gathering, his arm outstretched and slightly raised, a pose expressive of authority and persuasiveness. The orator wears the folded and draped garment called a toga, which would become characteristic of a Roman official. According to Pliny the Elder, large statues like this were often placed atop columns as memorials to the individuals portrayed.

Art and architecture during the Republic initially reflected both Etruscan and Greek influences. In religious architecture, the Romans favored urban temples set, in the Etruscan manner, in the midst of congested commercial centers. An early example is a small, rectangular temple built in the late second century BCE beside the Tiber River in Rome, perhaps dedicated to Portunus, the god of harbors and ports (figs. 6–4 and 6–5). The structure

Roman Counterparts of Greek Gods	
ROMAN NAME	**GREEK NAME**
Jupiter	Zeus
Juno	Hera
Minerva	Athena
Mars	Ares
Apollo	Apollo (also Phoebus)
Venus	Aphrodite
Diana	Artemis
Mercury	Hermes
Pluto	Hades
Bacchus	Dionysos
Vulcan	Hephaistos
Vesta	Hestia
Ceres	Demeter
Neptune	Poseidon
Cupid or Amor	Eros
Hercules	Herakles (a demi-god)
Distinctively Roman Gods	
Fortuna—Goddess of Fate (Fortune)	
Priapus—God of Fertility	
Janus—God of Beginnings and Endings (his two faces look forward and back)	
Terminus—God of Boundaries	

rests on a raised platform, or podium. It has a rectangular cella and a colonnaded porch at one end approached by a broad stair. The Romans also applied the Greek Ionic order here. However, in contrast to a Greek temple, the Ionic columns on the porch are freestanding and those around the cella are engaged (attached to the wall). The entablature above the porch columns continues around the cella as a frieze. This design was to become the standard for Roman temples.

As city dwellers, Romans also devoted their ingenuity and resources to secular architecture. In fact, public building projects related to the transport and storage of food and water made Roman cities viable. In many areas of Europe, especially around the Mediterranean, impressive examples of Roman engineering still stand. The Pont du Gard near Nîmes in southern France (fig. **6–6**), spanning 900 feet, was designed to carry water over the Gard River. This **aqueduct**, as such structures with water conduits are called, was part of a system that brought water to Nîmes from springs 30 miles to the north. At the time it was built, probably about 20 BCE, the aqueduct could provide 100 gallons of water a day for every person in Nîmes.

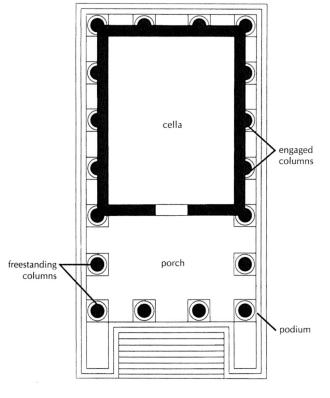

6–5 Plan of the temple, perhaps dedicated to Portunus

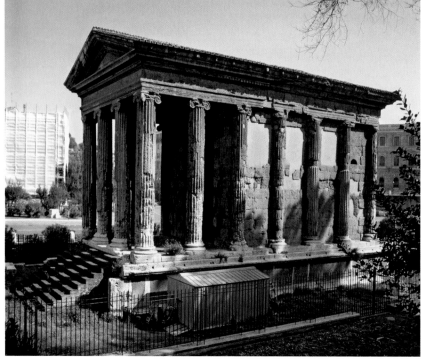

6–4 Temple, perhaps dedicated to Portunus, Forum Boarium (cattle market), Rome. Late 2nd century BCE

ELEMENTS OF Architecture

Arch and Vault

The round arch is a basic unit of Roman architecture. It is designed to displace most of the weight above it to its curving sides, and from there to the ground through supporting upright elements (**piers**, columns, or door or window **jambs**). Within a succession of arches, the unit made up of one arch and its supports is called a **bay**. Wall areas adjacent to curves of an arch are called **spandrels**. In the illustration at right, arrows indicate the outward thrust and downward gravity pull (weight) of the arch or vault.

A simple round arch can be lengthened to form a cylindrical **barrel vault**. In a barrel vault, however, the outward pressure exerted by its long curving sides usually requires added external support, called **buttressing**. When two barrel-vaulted spaces intersect each other at right angles, the result is a **groin vault**. The round arch and barrel vault were known and put to limited use by the ancient Mesopotamians, Egyptians, and Greeks. And they were employed more extensively by the Etruscans. But it was the Romans who realized the potential strength and versatility of these architectural elements and who exploited them to the fullest degree.

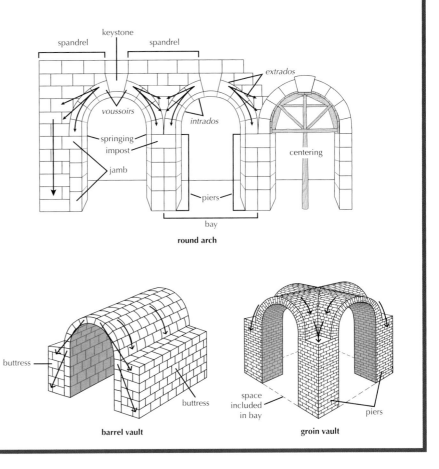

round arch

barrel vault

groin vault

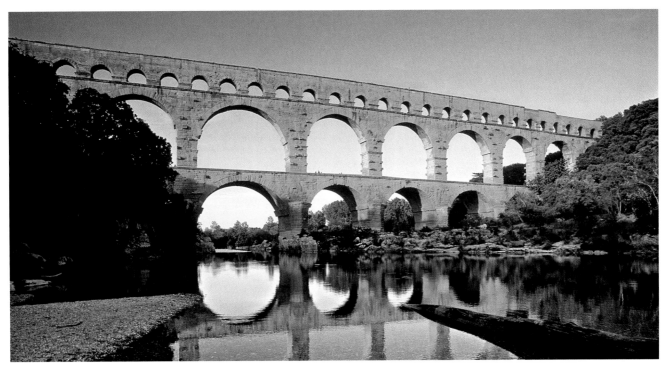

6–6 Pont du Gard, Nîmes, France. Late 1st century BCE

The three arcades of the aquaduct rise 160 feet (49 m) above the river. They exemplify the simplest use of the arch as a structural element. The thick base arcade supports a roadbed approximately 20 feet wide. The arches of the second arcade are narrower than the first and are set at one side of the roadbed. The narrow third arcade supports the water trough, 900 feet long on 35 arches, each of which is 23 feet (7 m) high.

The first Roman emperor was born Octavius (Octavian) in 63 BCE into a minor branch of the Caesar family. When he was only 18 years old, Octavian was adopted as son and heir by his brilliant great-uncle, Julius Caesar, who recognized qualities in him that would make him a worthy successor. Early in 44 BCE, Julius Caesar refused the Roman Senate's offer of the imperial crown, which amounted to his refusing to be the first Roman emperor. By March 15 of that year he was dead, murdered by a group of conspirators. Octavian stepped up. Over the next 17 spectacular years, as general, politician, statesman, and public relations genius, Octavian vanquished warring internal factions and brought peace to fractious provinces. By 27 BCE, the Senate conferred on him the title Augustus (meaning "exalted, sacred"). Augustus led the state and the empire for another 41 years of peace and prosperity—a period known as the great *Pax Romana*, or Roman Peace. Upon his death in 14 CE, Augustus left behind a legacy that defined the concept of empire and imperial rule for later Western rulers.

A statue found in the villa of Augustus's wife, Livia, at Primaporta near Rome embodies the man's complex character and creative conservatism (figs. **6–7** and **6–8**). We see Augustus as he wanted to be seen and remembered, an image depicting him in his prime and inspired by heroic Greek figures such as the *Spear Bearer* (see fig. 4–36). Augustus's staggering accomplishments are evoked through this work of art, which is one of history's most successful imperial images. The emperor extends his hand in an orator's gesture, as if convincing his people through his superior intellect rather than commanding them by force of arms. Yet imperial power is evident in the idealization of the figure, in the bare feet (a sign of divine status) and in the parade armor with its defeated "barbarians" and scenes of victory. At the same time, the image is skillfully rendered in naturalistic representation, as demanded by the Roman public and patrons of the time. Recently it has been suggested that the marble sculpture was made after Augustus's death in 14 BCE and copied an earlier bronze figure. The marble was originally painted.

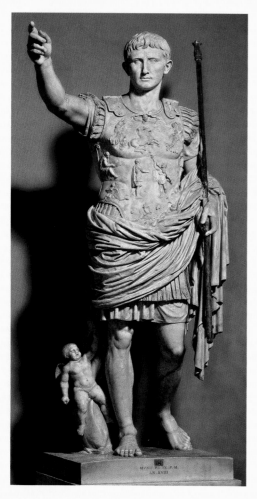

6–7 *Augustus of Primaporta.* Early 1st century CE (perhaps a copy of a bronze statue of c. 20 BCE). Marble, height 6'8" (2.03 m). Musei Vaticani, Braccio Nuovo, Rome

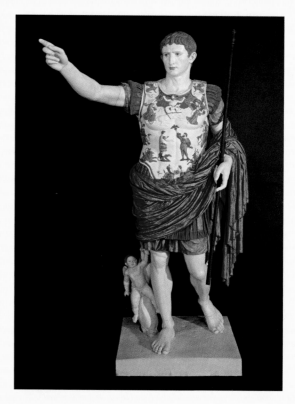

6–8 *Augustus of Primaporta,* copy with color restored. Vatican Museum, Rome.

A reproduction of the Augustus of Primaporta was made based on the research of scholars in the Ny Carlsburg Glyptotek of Copenhagen, Denmark and the Munich Glyptotek, Germany. Vincenz Brinkmann of Munich researched the use of color on ancient sculpture in the 1980s using ultraviolet rays to find traces of color. Color heightened the effect of ancient sculpture, sometimes to a shocking degree.

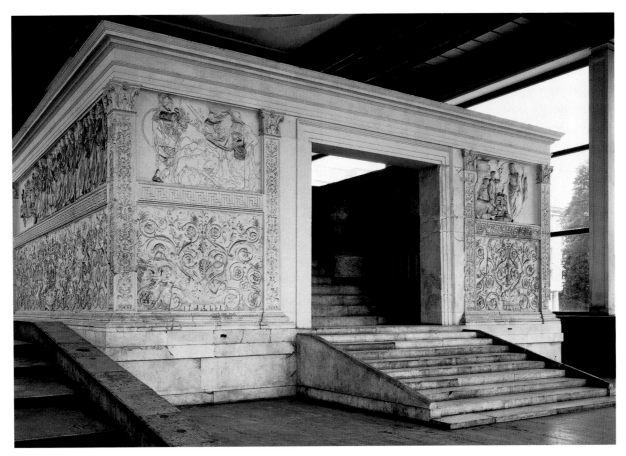

6–9 *Ara Pacis.* 13–9 BCE. Marble, approx. 34'5" (10.5 m) × 38' (11.6 m). Rome. The actual altar stands at the top of the stairs, visible through the door in the enclosure wall.

The Pont du Gard was constructed of precisely cut stones from a nearby quarry. It consists of three **arcades** (series of regularly spaced arched openings). The top arcade supports the water trough. The fundamental element of all three arcades is the round **arch** (see "Arch and Vault," page 139), formed by fitting together wedge-shaped pieces, called **voussoirs**, which are locked together at the top center by a final piece, called a **keystone**. A utilitarian structure, the aqueduct was left undecorated, and the projecting blocks that supported scaffolding during construction were left to provide easy access for repairs. Nevertheless, the Pont du Gard and other Roman aqueducts convey a sense of proportion and rhythm and seem to harmonize with their settings.

The Age of Augustus

After Julius Caesar's death and a period of renewed fighting, his great-nephew and adopted son, Octavian, assumed power. Although Octavian kept the forms of Republican government, he retained the real authority for himself, and his ascension marks the end of the Republic. Under Augustus Caesar, as Octavian was titled in 27 BCE, the Romans began to use imperial por-

traiture as political propaganda. An over-life-size statue of the emperor, the *Augustus of Primaporta* (fig. 6–7), exemplifies the form. Augustus wears a cuirass (body armor) and holds a commander's baton, but his feet are bare, suggesting to some scholars that the work was made after his death to commemorate his **apotheosis**, or elevation to divine status. After Augustus, all Roman emperors were deified, in part to unify the culturally diverse populations that had come under Roman rule. Thus the worship of ancient gods became mingled with homage to past rulers and oaths of allegiance to living ones.

Roman sculptors contributed unabashedly to imperial propaganda by recording contemporary events on commemorative arches, columns, and tombs. One monument erected by Augustus, the *Ara Pacis*, or Altar of Augustan Peace (fig. **6–9**), was as famous in its day as the *Vietnam Veterans Memorial* is in ours (see fig. 20–1). The altar, begun in 13 BCE and dedicated in 9 BCE, commemorates Augustus's triumphal return to Rome after establishing Roman rule in Gaul. The walled rectangular enclosure with an altar inside is approached by a flight of steep stairs. The altar's decoration is a thoughtful union of portraiture and allegory, religion and politics, and the public and the private. Relief panels along the exterior of the north and south sides

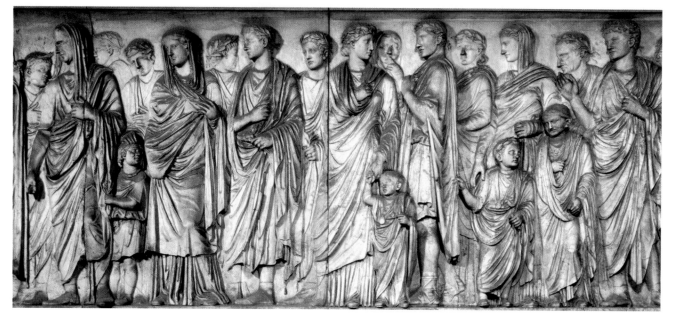

6–10 Imperial Procession, detail of a relief on the *Ara Pacis.* Height 5′2″ (1.6 m)

The middle-aged man with the shrouded head at the far left is Marcus Agrippa, who would have been Augustus's successor had he not died in 12 CE, the year after the Ara Pacis *was dedicated. The bored but well-behaved youngster pulling at Agrippa's robe—and being restrained gently by the hand of the man behind him—is probably Agrippa's son, Gaius Caesar. The heavily swathed woman next to Agrippa on the right is probably Augustus's wife, Livia, followed by the elder of her two sons, Tiberius, who would become the next emperor. Behind Tiberius is Antonia, the niece of Augustus, looking back at her husband, Drusus, Livia's younger son. She grasps the hand of Germanicus, one of her younger children. Behind their uncle Drusus are Gnaeus and Domitia, children of Antonia's older sister, who can be seen standing quietly beside them. The depiction of children in an official relief was new to the Augustan period and reflects Augustus's desire to promote private family life.*

depict senators and members of the imperial family who would have attended the victory celebrations (fig. **6–10**).

Unlike the Greek sculptors who created an ideal procession for the Parthenon frieze (see fig. 4–32), the Roman sculptors of the *Ara Pacis* depicted actual individuals participating in a specific event at a known time. To suggest a double line of marchers in space, they varied the depth of the carving, with the closest elements in high relief and those farther back in increasingly lower relief. In part, the design draws us, as spectators, into the event by making the feet of the nearest figures project into our space. In contrast to the *Augustus of Primaporta*, which displays a more idealized style of portraiture, the *Ara Pacis* procession represents a continuation of the naturalistic, or realistic, tradition that had developed during Rome's Republican period, influenced at that time by Etruscan models.

The marriage of Augustus and Livia was childless, so the emperor's successor was Tiberius, one of Livia's two sons by her first marriage to Tiberius Claudius Nero. A large onyx cameo (a gemstone carved in low relief) known as *Gemma Augustea* carries the scene of the apotheosis of Augustus after his death (fig. **6–11**). The emperor, crowned with a victor's wreath, sits at the center right of the upper register. He has assumed the identity of Jupiter, king of the gods; an eagle, sacred to Jupiter, stands at his feet. Sitting next to him is a personification of Rome that has Livia's features. The sea goat in the roundel between them may represent Capricorn, the emperor's zodiac sign. At the left, Tiberius, the adopted son of Augustus, holds a lance and steps out of a chariot. Returning victorious from the German front, he will assume the imperial throne as the designated heir of Augustus. Below this realm of godly rulers is the earth, where Roman soldiers are raising a trophy—a post or standard on which armor captured from a defeated enemy is displayed. The cowering, shackled barbarians on the bottom right wait to be tied to this trophy. The *Gemma Augustea* brilliantly combines idealized, heroic figures of a kind characteristic of Classical Greek art with recognizable portraits, the dramatic action of Hellenistic art, and a purely Roman realism in the depiction of historical events.

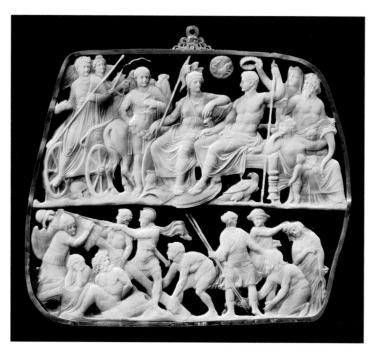

6–11 *Gemma Augustea.* Early 1st century CE. Onyx, 7½″ × 9″ (19 × 23 cm). Kunsthistorisches Museum, Vienna

The Roman House and Its Decoration

In large cities, most Romans lived in two- or three-story apartment buildings with shared walls, and in towns, they often lived in houses behind or above rows of shops. The nature-loving Romans softened the regularity of their homes with beautifully planted gardens even in towns and cities. Most urban gardens served a practical function, being planted with fruit- and nut-bearing trees. Wealthy people built gracious private residences with one or more gardens (fig. **6–12**). These large, elegant houses had rooms opening onto a central atrium, an unroofed space with a pool for catching rainwater. In dry climates, the rainwater coming through the open roof might instead be drained into a deep cistern.

Many fine examples of private residential dwellings can be seen at Pompeii, near modern Naples. Located near Mount Vesuvius, Pompeii was buried in volcanic ash after the eruption of 79 CE and remained remarkably well preserved until its rediscovery in the eighteenth century. The so-called House of the Silver Wedding is typical (fig. **6–13**). Behind the atrium and its surrounding rooms lay a second open area known as a peristyle court, an interior garden courtyard surrounded by a colonnaded

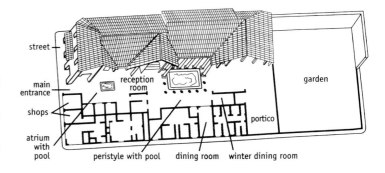

6–12 Reconstruction drawing and plan of the House of Pansa, Pompeii. 2nd century BCE

6–13 Atrium, House of the Silver Wedding, Pompeii. Early 1st century CE

Ancient Roman houses excavated at Pompeii and elsewhere are usually simply given numbers by archaeologists or (if known) named after the families or individuals who once lived in them. This house received its unusual name as a commemorative gesture. It was excavated in 1893, the year of the silver wedding anniversary of Italy's King Humbert and his wife, Margaret of Savoy, who had supported archaeological fieldwork at Pompeii.

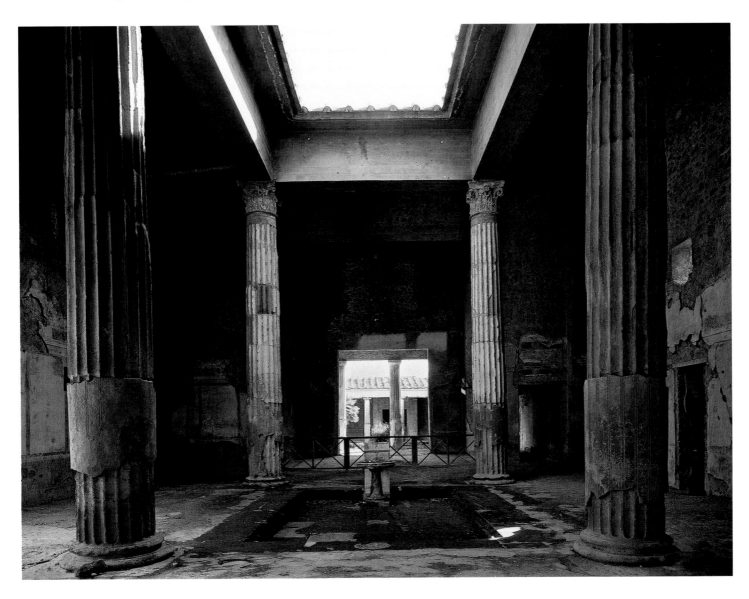

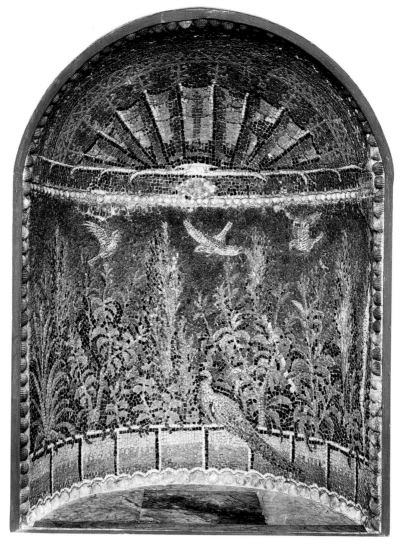

6–14 Wall niche, from a garden in Pompeii. Mid-1st century CE. Mosaic, 43 3/4″ × 31 1/2″ (111 × 80 cm). Fitzwilliam Museum, University of Cambridge, England

walkway or portico. The mild climate of Pompeii permitted gardens to flourish year-round, and an aqueduct provided a reliable water supply. The more private family quarters, such as the bedrooms, dining room, and servants' quarters, were usually entered through the peristyle court. This courtyard functioned as an outdoor living room with painted walls, sculpture, and fountains. In one mosaic fountain niche (fig. **6–14**), an artist created the illusion of being on a porch or pavilion looking out over a low fence into an orchard of heavily laden fruit trees. These trees and flowering shrubs are filled with a variety of wonderfully observed birds. Through the mosaic workers' art, the wall has been turned into an extension of the garden.

Mosaics became popular as decoration for Roman floors and fountains, where durability and waterproofing were desired. Mosaic designs were created with pebbles or with small, regularly shaped pieces of marble, other stones, and sometimes pottery. The individual cube like pieces, which could be black, white, colored, or even clear, are called *tesserae*. Some mosaicists were so accomplished that they created works that resemble paintings. In fact, at the request of patrons, they often copied well-known paintings, employing a technique in which very small tesserae created subtle shadings and color changes. The "Alexander mosaic" (see fig. 5–2), once the floor of a house in Pompeii, is a superb example. And as we have seen in *The Unswept Floor* mosaic (fig. 6–1), Heraklitos adapted the design of an earlier Hellenistic painter named Sosos. Sosos's painting had included a *trompe l'oeil* ("fool the eye") representation of a floor littered with droppings from a table. Heraklitos's mosaic version, made three centuries later, even shows a mouse among the table scraps. Bones of fish and foul, fruit, and nuts are all recreated in meticulous detail, even casting shadows on the floor.

Realistic effects are also pronounced in the paintings with which Romans decorated the walls of the important rooms of their homes. The interior walls of Roman houses were smooth plaster surfaces with few architectural features. On these invitingly plain surfaces, artists painted decorations using pigment in a solution of lime and soap, sometimes with a little wax. In the earliest paintings, beginning about 200 BCE, artists created the illusion of thin slabs of colored marble covering the walls. They also modeled shallow architectural moldings and columns in plaster. By about 80 BCE, painters began to extend the space of a room visually with scenes of figures on a shallow platform or with a landscape or cityscape. Architectural details such as columns were painted rather than modeled from plaster. As time passed, such illusionistic architecture became increasingly fanciful. Solid colored walls were decorated with slender, whimsical

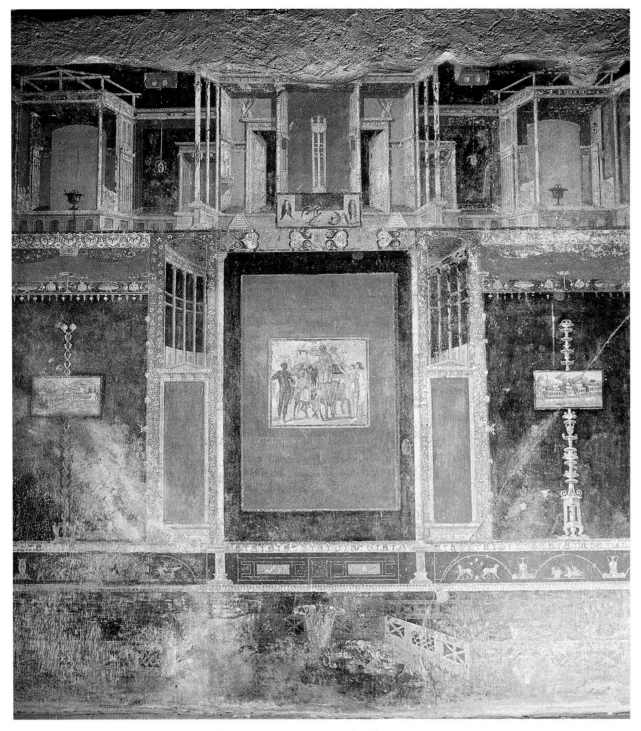

6–15 Detail of a wall painting in the House of M. Lucretius Fronto, Pompeii. Mid-1st century CE

architectural and floral details and small, delicate vignettes. The wall surfaces seem to recede or even disappear behind a maze of floating architectural forms that create purely visual effects.

Artists used two different conventions to create the illusion of space: **intuitive perspective** and **atmospheric perspective**. In intuitive perspective, the architectural details follow diagonal lines that the eye interprets as parallel lines receding into the distance. Objects meant to be perceived as far away from the surface plane of the wall are shown slightly smaller than those intended to appear nearby. The artist created the illusion of looking out over a low, paneled wall, thus "painting away" the wall surface above. In atmospheric perspective, the colors become slightly grayer in the far background, reproducing the tendency of distant objects to appear hazy.

In the House of M. Lucretius Fronto in Pompeii, from the mid-first century CE (fig. **6–15**), the artist painted a room with panels of black and red, bordered with architectural moldings. These architectural elements have no logic and for all their playing with perspective, they fail to create any significant illusion of great depth. The scene with figures, at the center, seems to be mounted on the large red panel. It is flanked by two small simulated window openings protected by grilles. Above the red panel a small still life of fish appears to float. Two small pictures of villas in landscapes appear to be held up by intricate bronze easels.

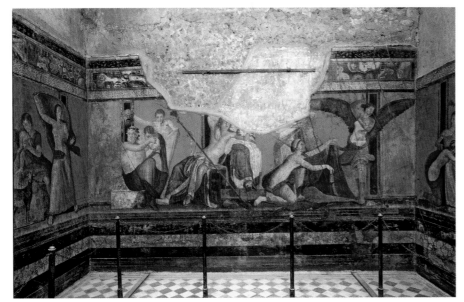

6–16 Wall painting, Villa of the Mysteries. c. 50 BCE. Pompeii

One of the most famous painted rooms in Roman art is in the so-called Villa of the Mysteries at Pompeii (fig. **6–16**). The rites of mystery religions were often performed in private homes as well as in special buildings or temples, and this room, at the corner of a suburban villa, must have been a shrine or a meeting place for such a cult. A reminder of the wide variety of religious practices tolerated by the Romans, the murals depict initiation rites—probably into the cult of Bacchus, who was the god of vegetation and fertility as well as wine, and was one of the most popular deities in Pompeii. The entirely painted architectural setting consists of a "marble" dado (the lower part of a wall) and, around the top of the wall, an elegant frieze supported by **pilasters** (engaged shafts). The action takes place on a shallow stage along the top of the dado, with a background of brilliant, deep red that was very popular with Roman painters—and has come to be called "Pompeian red." The scene unfolds around the entire room, depicting a succession of events that culminate in the acceptance of an initiate into the cult.

The Empire

The sequence of related Roman rulers that follows Augustus, beginning with Tiberius, is known as the Julio-Claudian dynasty (14–68 CE). It ended with the reign of the despotic and capricious emperor Nero. A powerful general named Vespasian seized control of the government after Nero's death. The dynasty he founded, the Flavian, ruled from 69 to 96 CE. The Flavian emperors, Vespasian (ruled 69–79 CE), Titus (ruled 79–81 CE), and Domitian (ruled 81–96 CE), restored imperial finances and stabilized the empire's frontiers. Five very competent rulers succeeded the Flavians: Nerva (ruled 96–98 CE), Trajan (ruled 98–117 CE), Hadrian (ruled 117–138 CE), Antoninus Pius (ruled 138–161 CE), and Marcus Aurelius (ruled 161–180 CE). Known as the "Five Good Emperors," they oversaw a long period of stability and prosperity. Under Trajan, the Roman Empire reached its greatest extent, annexing Dacia (roughly, modern Romania) in 106 CE and expanding the empire's boundaries in the Near East.

Imperial Art and Architecture

Romans were huge fans of sports events, and the Flavian emperors catered to their taste by building enormous arenas, including the Colosseum, one of Rome's most influential monuments (fig. **6–17**). Construction began in 72 CE during the reign of Vespasian, and the Colosseum—originally called the Flavian Amphiteatre—was dedicated by Titus in 80 CE, after Vespasian's death. (The name "Colosseum," by which it came to be known, derived from the Colossus, a bigger-than-life statue of Nero

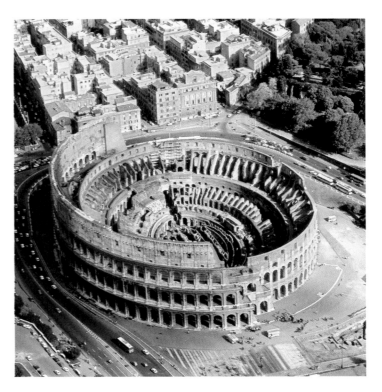

6–17 Colosseum, Rome. 72–80 CE

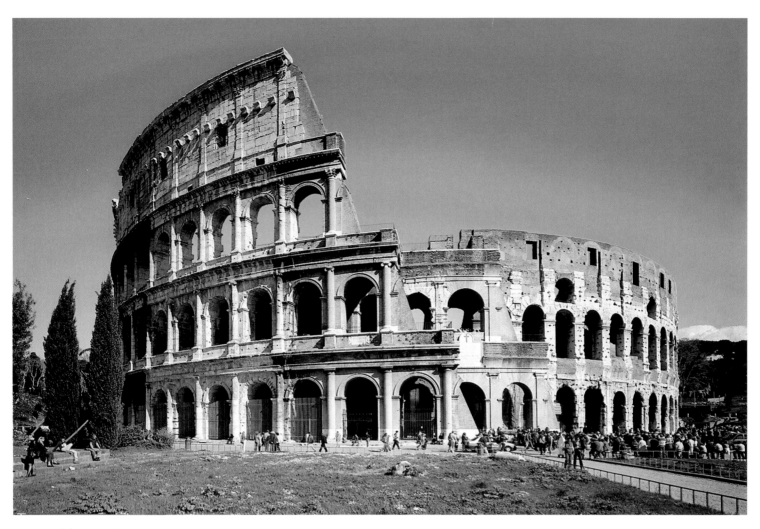

6–18 Colosseum, Rome. 72–80 CE

standing next to it.) The Flavians erected the arena to bolster their popularity in Rome, and in this enormous entertainment center, audiences watched blood sports and spectacles. Popular events included animal hunts, fights to the death between gladiators or between gladiators and wild animals, performances of trained animals and acrobats, and even mock naval battles, for which the arena could be flooded by a built-in mechanism. The opening performance in 80 CE lasted 100 days, during which time, it was claimed, 9,000 wild animals and 2,000 gladiators died. For its ease of crowd movement and unobstructed views, the design of the Colosseum—which held about 50,000 spectators—has never been improved upon. Architects still copy features of it today.

The Colosseum was built entirely of masonry—travertine and tufa blocks and **concrete** faced with stone. Eighty barrel vaults built to cover corridors and stairs radiate from the arena's center. These form groin vaults where they intersect the barrel ring vaults that cover the passageways around the perimeter (see "Arch and Vault," page 139). These complex curved shapes could be formed of concrete faster and more cheaply than of stone blocks, which have to be cut by trained masons. The concrete consisted of stone rubble (*caementa*) in a binder made from volcanic sand and water. This rough but strong core was faced with finer, worked stone. (In very fine buildings, the core might be covered with a travertine or marble veneer or other facing.)

A canopy, operated by a team of 1,000 sailors, could be extended to shield spectators from the sun. The curving outer wall of the Colosseum consists of three levels of arcades surmounted by a wall-like top, or **attic story** (fig. **6–18**). Every arch in the arcades is framed by engaged columns, which support friezes that mark the division between levels. Each level uses a different architectural order, and the levels become increasingly decorative as they rise. The ground floor is ornamented with columns in the Tuscan order (generally similar to the Greek Doric order except that the columns have bases). The Ionic order is used on the second level, the Corinthian on the third, and flat Corinthian pilasters adorn the fourth story. All these elements are purely decorative and serve no structural function. The systematic use of the orders in a logical succession from sturdy Tuscan to decorative Corinthian follows a tradition inherited from Hellenistic architecture. It is still popular today as a way of articulating and organizing the facades of large buildings.

When Domitian became emperor in 81 CE, he immediately commissioned a triumphal arch to honor his brother and deified predecessor, Titus (fig. **6–19**). The Arch of Titus—which commemorates Titus's capture of Jerusalem in 70 CE—is essentially a large freestanding arch, the interior of which is a short barrel-vaulted passageway. The exterior of the arch is ornamented with engaged Composite columns (see "Roman Architectural Orders," above).

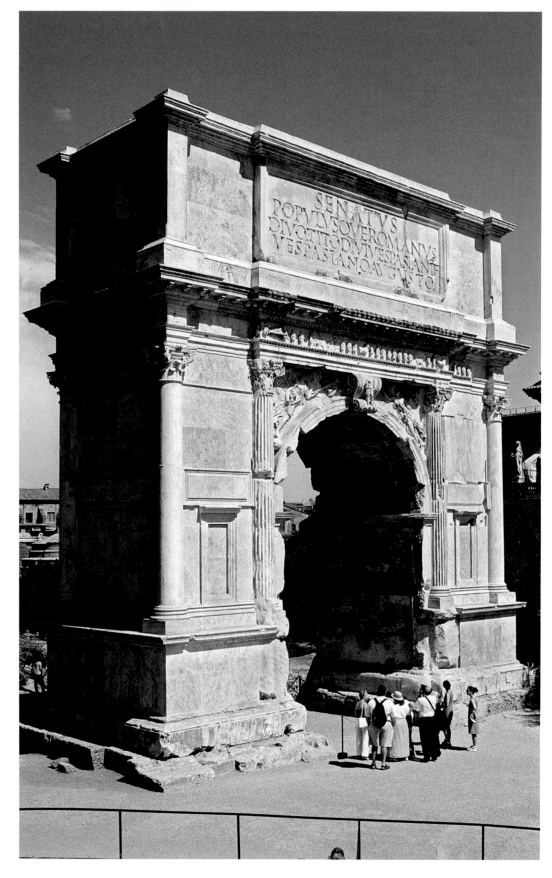

6–19 Arch of Titus, Rome. c. 81 CE. Concrete and white marble, height 50′ (15 m)

The dedication inscribed across the tall attic story above the arch opening reads: "The Senate and the Roman People to the Deified Titus Flavius Vespasianus Augustus, son of the Deified Vespasian." The Romans typically recorded historic occasions and identified monuments with solemn prose and beautiful inscriptions in stone. The sculptors' use of elegant Roman capital letters—perfectly sized and spaced to be read from a distance and cut with sharp terminals (serifs) to catch the light—established a standard that calligraphers and alphabet designers still follow.

ELEMENTS OF **Architecture**
Roman Architectural Orders

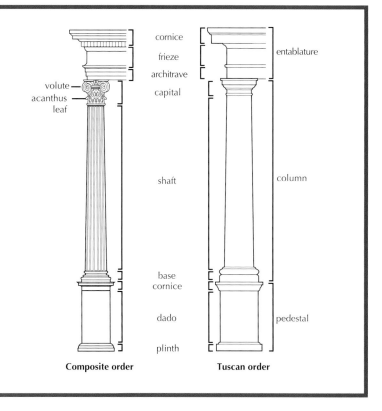

The Etruscans and Romans adapted Greek architectural orders to their own tastes and uses. For example, the Etruscans modified the Greek Doric order by adding a base to the column. The Romans created the Composite order by combining the volute of the Greek Ionic capital with the acanthus leaves of the Corinthian order. The sturdy, unfluted Tuscan order combined the Greek Doric order and Etruscan models. In this diagram, the Roman orders are shown on pedestals, which consist of a plinth, a dado, and a cornice. The Romans often used the orders as applied (low-relief) decoration on a wall.

Composite order

Tuscan order

Originally the 50-foot-tall arch served as a giant base for a statue of a four-horse chariot and driver, a typical Roman triumphal symbol.

Titus's capture of Jerusalem ended a fierce campaign to crush a revolt of the Jews in Palestine. His troops looted and destroyed the Second Temple of Jerusalem and carted off its sacred treasures. These spoils were displayed in Rome during Titus's triumphal procession. According to the Jewish eyewitness and historian Flavius Josephus, the prizes included "the law of the Jews," a gold table, and a seven-branched lamp stand, or menorah.

The reliefs on the inside walls of the arch depict Titus's soldiers carrying this booty through the streets of Rome (fig. **6–20**). Viewing them, the observer can easily imagine the boisterous

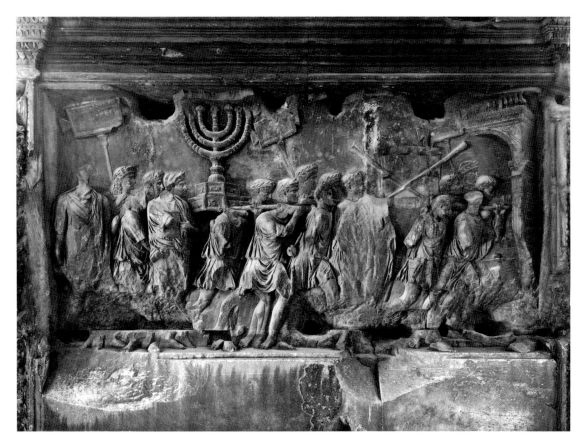

6–20 *Spoils from the Temple of Solomon, Jerusalem,* relief in the passageway of the Arch of Titus, Rome. Marble, height 6′8″ (2.03 m)

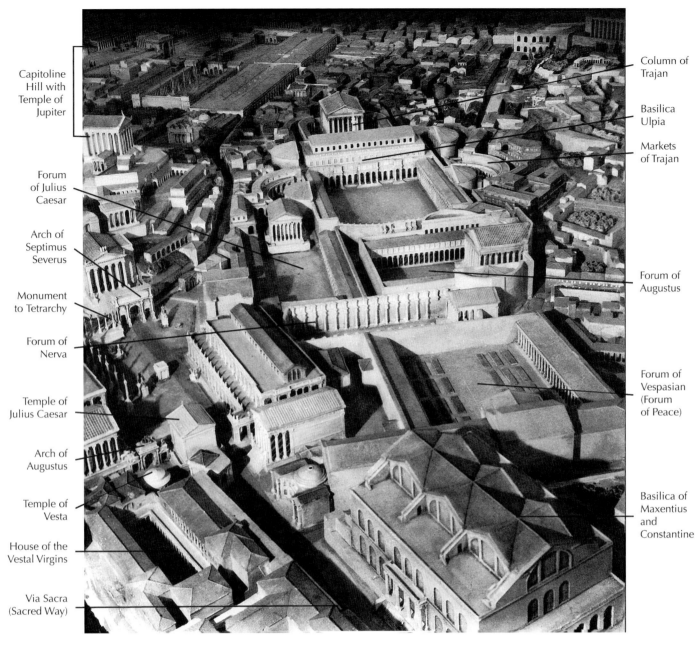

Capitoline Hill with Temple of Jupiter

Forum of Julius Caesar

Arch of Septimus Severus

Monument to Tetrarchy

Forum of Nerva

Temple of Julius Caesar

Arch of Augustus

Temple of Vesta

House of the Vestal Virgins

Via Sacra (Sacred Way)

Column of Trajan

Basilica Ulpia

Markets of Trajan

Forum of Augustus

Forum of Vespasian (Forum of Peace)

Basilica of Maxentius and Constantine

6–21 Model of the Forum Romanum and Imperial Forums, Rome. c. 46. BCE–325 CE

scene. The artist creates a window on the world through which we observe the crowd. The varying depth of the relief elements creates the impression that the marchers are moving toward the viewer and then turning to move away through a distant arch. Spatial relationships, achieved by rendering close elements in higher relief than more distant ones, also produce a clear sense of deeper space. This illusion of depth is more complex and convincing than that depicted in the reliefs of the *Ara Pacis*.

As mentioned earlier, Romans built throughout the empire. Projects such as the imperial forums of the capital were repeated elsewhere on a smaller scale. A **forum**, the civic center, consisted of a large open square generally surrounded by colonnades leading to a temple and sometimes a basilica. A general-purpose

administrative structure, a basilica could be adapted to many uses. They served as imperial audience chambers, army drill halls, courts of law, or schools. The spacious and adaptable interior made the basilica form attractive to Christians, who would later appropriate it for churches.

Three basilicas can be seen in figure **6–21**: the Basilica Aemilia in the early Forum Romanum, the Basilica Ulpia in Trajan's Forum, and the vaulted Basilica of Maxentius and Constantine. The Basilica Ulpia a typical basilica, was entered through several doors on the long sides of the building facing the open square of the Forum of Trajan. A court of law dedicated in 113 CE, the Basilica Ulpia was named for the family to which Trajan belonged. It was a large, rectangular building with a rounded extension, called

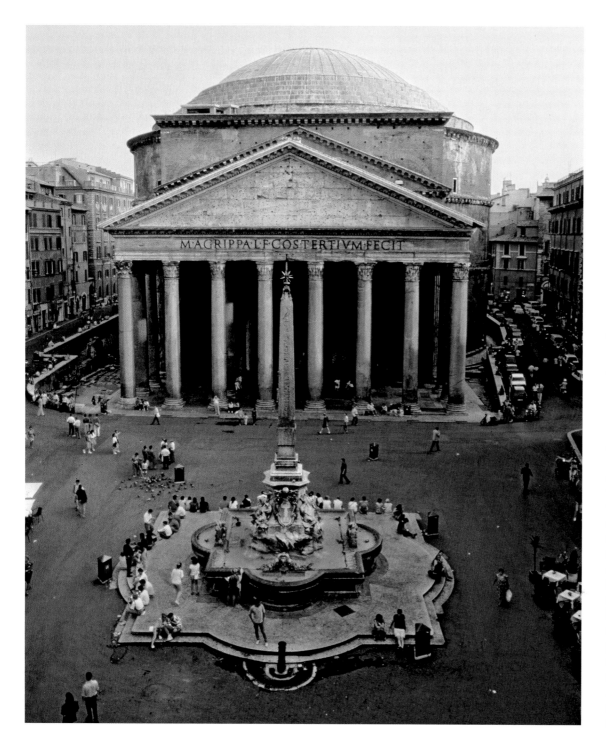

6–22 Pantheon, Rome.
125–128 CE

It is not clear what the early Romans themselves thought of this architectural monument, so well known to travelers and students today, because it was rarely mentioned by any contemporary writers. An exception was Ammianus Marcellinus, who described it in 357 CE with restrained praise as being "rounded like the boundary of the horizon, and vaulted with a beautiful loftiness." In the foreground of the photograph is a monumental fountain by G. della Porta, 1578. In 1711 Pope Clement XI added the obelisk (from the Temple of Isis).

an apse, at each end. The interior space was partitioned into a large central area bordered by two lower colonnaded **aisles**. This tall central space was able to accommodate a **clerestory**, or an upper wall with a row of windows, that extended above the abutting aisle roofs and brought light into the interior. A timber-raftered roof covered the space. The semi-circular vaulted apses gave the building an overall length of about 330 feet and provided imposing settings for judges when the court was in session.

Beyond the Basilica Ulpia stood two libraries, one for Greek texts and the other for Latin. Trajan's tomb, surmounted by a column carved with reliefs depicting his victory over the Dacians, stood between these libraries. Later the forum complex was completed with a temple to the deified emperor. A great

market was built into an adjacent hillside. The collective structures and spaces that make up the Forum of Trajan exemplify the finest in imperial city planning, satisfying both the needs of the citizens and the imperial desire for impressive public works and propaganda.

Trajan's successor, Hadrian, was well educated and widely traveled. His admiration for Greek culture spurred new building programs throughout the empire. To the splendid architecture of Rome itself, he added the remarkable temple to the Olympian gods known as the Pantheon ("all the gods"), built between 125 and 128 CE (fig. **6–22**). The entrance porch, made to resemble the facade of a typical Roman temple, was raised on a podium (now mostly buried under centuries of dirt, debris,

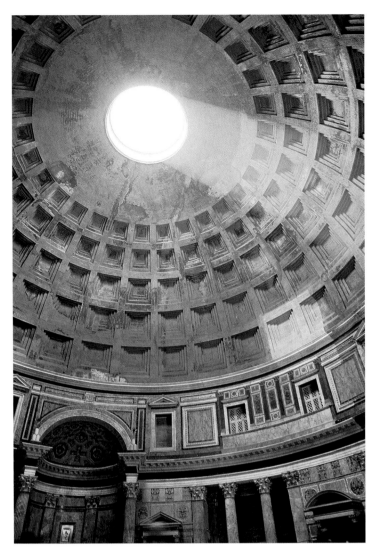

6–23 Dome of the Pantheon with light from oculus on its coffered ceiling

and street construction). Behind this porch, a giant **rotunda** (circular room) is surmounted with a huge, bowl-shaped dome, 143 feet in diameter and 143 feet from the floor to its summit (figs. **6–23** and **6–24**).

Although the Pantheon has inspired hundreds of copies, variants, and eclectic borrowings, only recently has the true complexity of its construction been fully understood. The circular wall, or **drum**, of the rotunda, which supports and buttresses the dome, is formed of brick arches and concrete. These structural elements are hidden beneath a marble veneer. Structurally, a dome works as an arch pivoted 360° around the top of the drum. In the Pantheon, the usual keystone is replaced by a central circular opening, or oculus, which was a daring concept. The repetition of square against circle, established on a large scale by juxtaposing the rectilinear portico against the circular rotunda, is found throughout the building's ornamentation. Seven interior niches, rectangular alternating with semicircular, originally held statues of the gods. Inside the dome, square, boxlike coffers (sunken ceiling panels) help lighten the weight of the masonry and may once have contained gilded bronze rosettes or stars suggesting the heavens.

Inside, the eye is drawn upward over the pattern made by the coffers to the light entering through the 29-foot-wide oculus (see fig. 6–23). Clouds can be seen moving across this opening on some days; on others, rain falls through and then drains off as planned by the original engineer. Occasionally, a bird flies in.

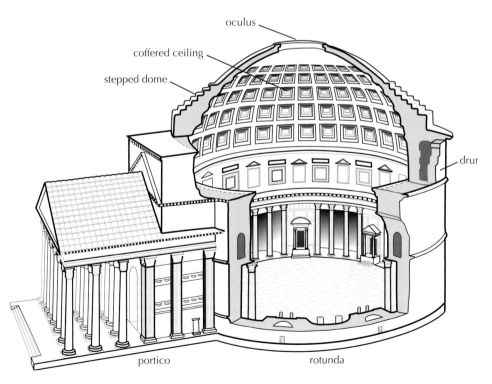

6–24 Reconstruction drawing of the Pantheon

oculus
coffered ceiling
stepped dome
drur
portico
rotunda

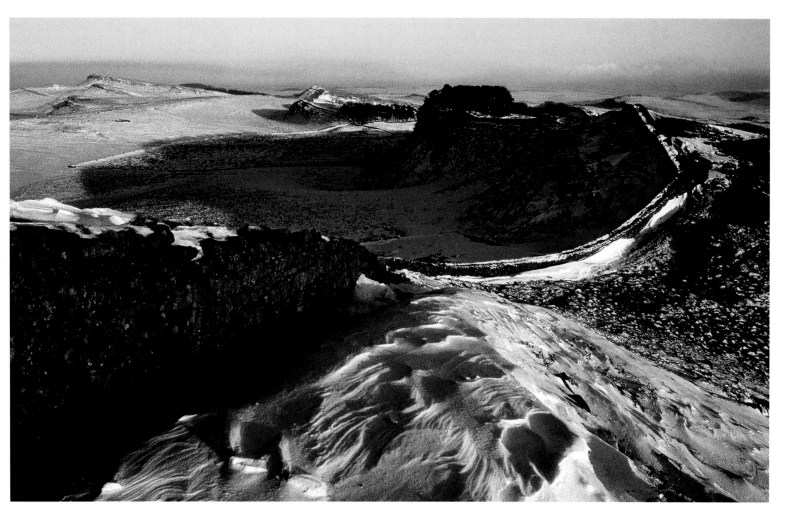

6–25 Hadrian's Wall, seen near Housesteads, England. 2nd century CE

This open, luminous space imparts the sense that one could rise buoyantly upward to escape the spherical hollow of the building and commune with the gods above.

During his rule, Hadrian consolidated the empire's borders and imposed far-reaching social, administrative, and military reforms. He ordered the construction of a monumental stone wall in England to protect his northern frontier. Known as Hadrian's Wall, this barrier stretches from coast to coast across a 73 $\frac{1}{2}$-mile-wide strip of England (fig. **6–25**). Some 8 to 10 feet thick and 20 feet high, it created a symbolic as well as a physical boundary between Roman territory and that of the Picts and Scots to the north. Towers were located at every mile mark. Seventeen larger camps housed auxiliary forces ready to respond to any trouble the sentries might spot. These camps were laid out in a grid pattern, like Roman cities, with main streets dividing them into blocks. At the center were a hospital, granaries, and the commander's house and administrative headquarters. Surrounding these structures were barracks. Similarly designed camps were built from one end of the Roman Empire to the other, wherever military troops were quartered.

Reigns of Significant Roman Emperors
Augustus, 27 BCE–14 CE
Nero, 54–68 CE
The Flavians, 69–96 CE
Trajan, 98–117 CE
Hadrian, 117–138 CE
Marcus Aurelius, 161–180 CE
Constantine, 306–337 CE

Portraits in Sculpture and Painting

Hadrian used monumental sculpture as well as architecture to vaunt his accomplishments. Several large circular reliefs, or **roundels**—originally part of a monument that no longer exists—contain images designed to affirm his imperial stature and right

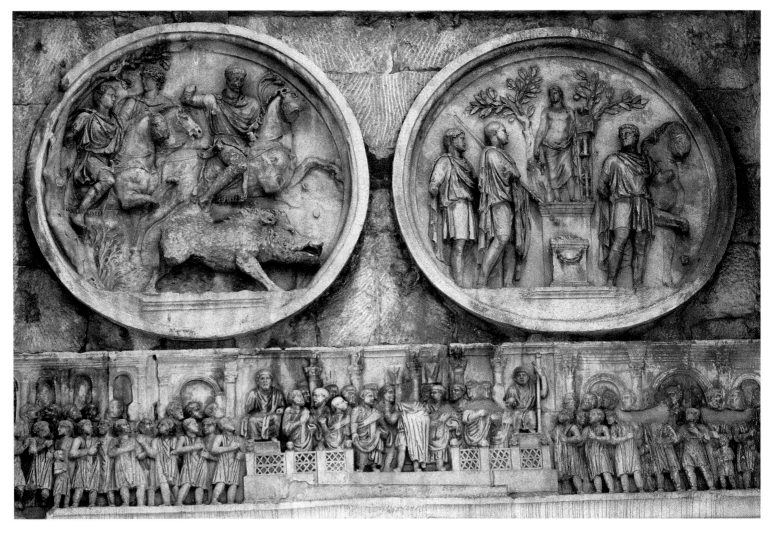

6–26 Hadrian Hunting Boar and Sacrificing to Apollo. Roundels made for a monument to Hadrian and reused on the Arch of Constantine. Sculpture c. 130–38 CE. Marble, roundel diameter 40″ (102 cm)

In the fourth century CE, *Emperor Constantine had the roundels removed from the Hadrian monument, had Hadrian's head recarved with his own or his father's features, and placed them on his own triumphal arch (see fig. 6–34, p. 160).*

to rule (fig. **6–26**). In the scene on the left, he demonstrates his courage and physical prowess in a boar hunt. At the right, in a show of piety and appreciation to the gods for their support of his endeavors, Hadrian makes a sacrificial offering to Apollo at an outdoor altar. The sculptors of these roundels included elements of a natural landscape setting but kept them relatively small, using them to frame the proportionally larger figures. The idealized heads, form-enhancing drapery, and graceful yet energetic movement of the figures owe a distant debt to the works of Praxiteles (see fig. 4–37) and Lysippos (see fig. 4–38), but the well-observed details of the features and the bits of landscape are typically Roman.

The development of art in Rome depended on private as well as public patronage. For their homes, wealthy individuals might commission wall paintings, mosaics, or portraits in marble or bronze. Roman patrons usually demanded accurate likenesses in their portraits. Sometimes, however, they preferred some idealization of the sitter. The portrait of a *Young Flavian Woman*, whose identity is not known (fig. **6–27**), exemplifies the idealized portrait type, in the manner of the *Augustus of Primaporta* (see fig. 6–7). The well-observed, recognizable features—a strong nose and jaw, heavy brows, deep-set eyes, and a long neck contrast with the smoothly rendered flesh and soft lips. The hair is piled high in an extraordinary mass of ringlets in the latest court fashion. Executing the head required skillfull chiseling and **drillwork**, a technique for rapidly cutting deep grooves with straight sides, as was done here to render the holes in the center of the curls. The overall effect, especially from a distance, is very lifelike. The play of natural light over the more subtly sculpted marble surfaces gives the illusion of being reflected off real skin and hair.

Portraits were also popular in wall paintings. A late-first-century CE **tondo** (circular panel) from a house in Pompeii contains a portrait known as *Young Woman Writing* (fig. **6–28**). Perhaps, like some Roman women, she was a professional writer. In a convention popular among women patrons, she is shown

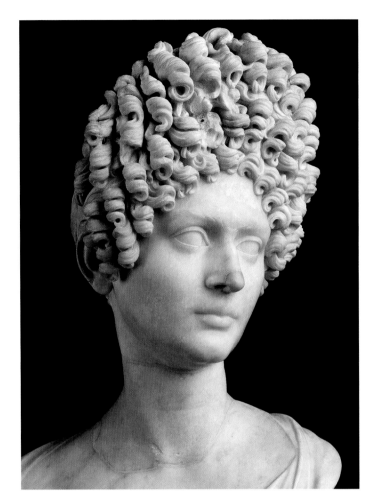

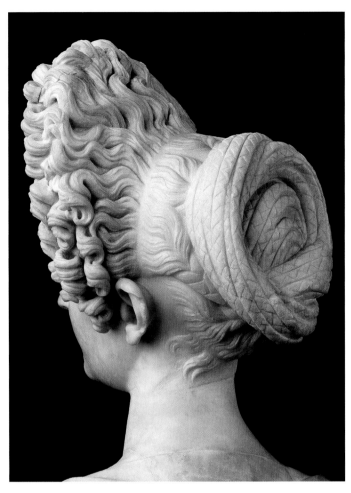

6–27 *Young Flavian Woman.* c. 90 CE. Marble, height 25″ (65.5 cm). Museo Capitolino, Rome

The typical Flavian hairstyle seen on this woman required a patient hairdresser handy with a curling iron and with a special knack for turning the back of the head into an intricate basketweave of braids. Male writers loved to scoff at the results. Martial described the style precisely as "a globe of hair." Statius spoke of "the glory of woman's lofty front, her storied hair." And Juvenal waxed comically poetic: "See her from the front; she is Andromache (an epic heroine). From behind she looks half the size—a different woman you would think" (cited in Balsdon, page 256).

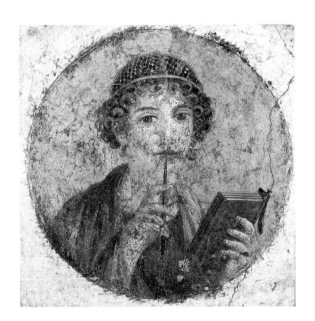

with the tip of a writing stylus raised to her lips. She holds a set of wood tablets coated with wax that were used in much the same way that we might use a small chalkboard or pad of paper; letters engraved in soft wax with a stylus could be smoothed over and rewritten. When a text or letter was considered ready, it was copied onto expensive papyrus or parchment. As in a modern studio photograph, with its careful lighting and retouching, the young woman in this painting is portrayed in an idealized fashion.

6–28 *Young Woman Writing,* detail of a wall painting from Pompeii. Late 1st century CE. Diameter 14⅝″ (37 cm). Museo Archeològico Nazionale, Naples

The fashionable young woman seems to be pondering what she will write about with her stylus on the beribboned writing tablet that she holds in her other hand. Romans used pointed styluses to engrave letters on thin, wax-coated ivory or wood tablets in much the way we might use a hand-held computer; errors could be easily smoothed over. When a text or letter was considered ready, it was copied onto expensive papyrus or parchment. Tablets like these were also used by schoolchildren for their homework.

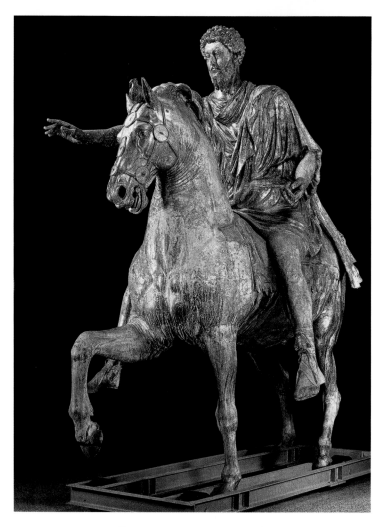

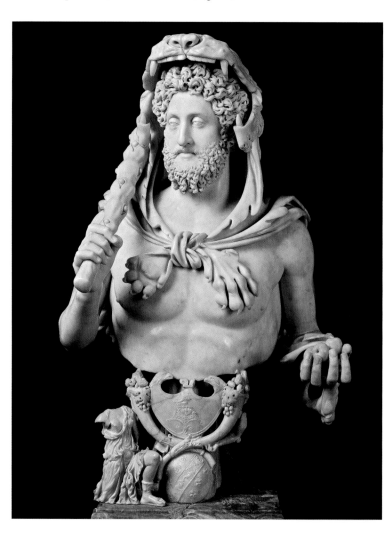

Hadrian's successor, Marcus Aurelius, was renowned for both his intellectual and military achievements. In a gilded bronze equestrian statue, the emperor appears as a commander dressed in a tunic and short, heavy cloak (fig. **6–29**). The raised foreleg of his horse is poised to trample a defeated foe (now lost). The emperor wears no armor and carries no weapons; like the Egyptian kings, he conquers effortlessly by the will of the gods. And like his illustrious predecessor Augustus (see fig. 6–7), he assumes a gesture symbolic of addressing an assembly. In a lucky error or twist of fate, this statue came mistakenly to be revered during the Middle Ages as a portrait of Constantine, the first Christian emperor. Consequently, it escaped being melted down, a fate that befell many other bronze statues from antiquity.

Marcus Aurelius was succeeded by his son Commodus, a man without political skill, administrative competence, or intellectual distinction. During his unfortunate reign (180–192 CE), Commodus devoted himself to luxury and frivolous pursuits. He did, however, attract some of the finest artists of the day for his commissions. A marble bust of Commodus (fig. **6–30**) conveys the illusion of life and movement, but it also captures its subject's vanity and weakness through the grand pretensions of his costume. In this portrait, the emperor is shown in the guise of Hercules, adorned with references to the hero's legendary labors: his club, the skin and head of the Nemean Lion, and the golden apples from the gardens of the Hesperides (see Introduction, fig. 29).

6–29 *Marcus Aurelius.* 161–180 CE. Bronze, originally gilded, height of statue 11′6″ (3.5 m). Capitoline Museum, Rome

6–30 Commodus as Hercules, from Esquiline Hill, Rome. c. 191–192 CE. Marble, height 46 ½″ (118 cm). Palazzo dei Conservatori, Rome

The emperor Commodus was not just decadent—he was probably insane. He claimed at various times to be the reincarnation of Hercules and the incarnation of the god Jupiter, and he even appeared in public as a gladiator. He ordered the months of the Roman year to be renamed after him and changed the name of Rome to Colonia Commodiana. When he proposed to assume the consulship dressed and armed as a gladiator, his associates, including his mistress, arranged to have him strangled in his bath by a wrestling partner.

THE CELTS

During the first millennium BCE, Celtic peoples inhabited most of Central and Western Europe. Ousted by migrating people and then by Roman armies, they settled in the northwesternmost parts of the continent—Ireland, Cornwall, and Brittany. Their wooden sculpture and buildings and colorful woven textiles have disintegrated, but their protective **earthworks** such as the embankments fortifying their cities and funerary goods such as jewelry, weapons, and tableware have survived.

An **openwork** box lid illustrates the characteristic abstract Celtic style. Solid metal and open space play equal roles in the design, which consists of a pair of flaring, diagonally symmetrical trumpet-shaped spirals surrounded by a lattice pattern. Shapes inspired by compass-drawn spirals—and perhaps even by stylized vines or serpentine dragons—seem to change at the blink of an eye, for the artist has eliminated any distinction between figure and background. The openwork trumpets—the forms defined by the absence of material—catch the viewer's attention, yet at the same time the delicate tendrils of solid metal are equally compelling. In Celtic hands, pattern becomes an integral part of the object itself, not an applied decoration.

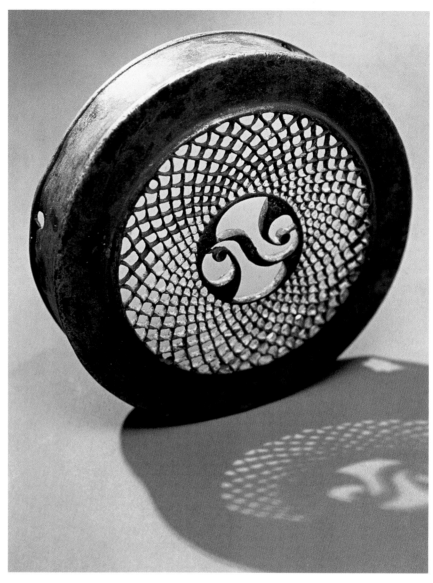

Openwork Box Lid. Cornalargh, County Monaghan, Ireland. La Tène period, c. 1st century BCE. Bronze, diameter 3″(7.5 cm)

PHOTO: NATIONAL MUSEUM OF IRELAND, DUBLIN

The Late Empire

The reign of Commodus marked the beginning of a period of political and economic decline. During the rule of the Severan emperors (193–235 CE) who succeeded Commodus, migrating peoples from the north and east began to cross Rome's frontiers, disrupting provincial government. Imperial rule became increasingly autocratic, and soon the army controlled the government.

During the turmoil of the third century, Roman artists lost interest in representing the natural world, emphasizing instead the symbolic or general characters of their subjects and expressing them in increasingly simplified, geometric forms. But the simplification of natural forms to geometric shapes, the disregard for basic human proportions, and the emphasis on message or idea are also characteristics of Roman art made by the end of the third century. By the beginning of the fourth century, a new style of abstract art appeared in Rome.

The anarchy of the mid-third century ended with the rise to power of the emperor Diocletian (ruled 284–305 CE). This brilliant politician and general reversed the empire's declining fortunes, but he also initiated an increasingly dictatorial government, eventually dividing the empire among four rulers known as the Tetrarchy. In 305 CE Diocletian abdicated his rule of the eastern portion of the empire and forced his fellow Tetrarch, Maximian, to do so, too. The orderly succession that Diocletian had hoped for failed to occur, and a struggle for position and advantage almost immediately ensued. Thereafter, two main

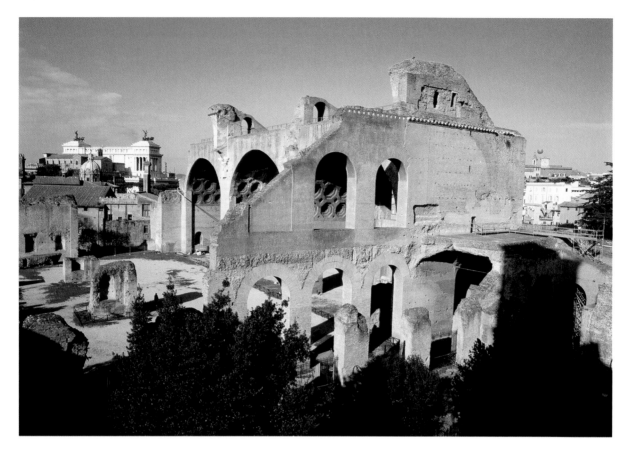

6–31 Basilica of Maxentius and Constantine, Rome. 306–313 CE

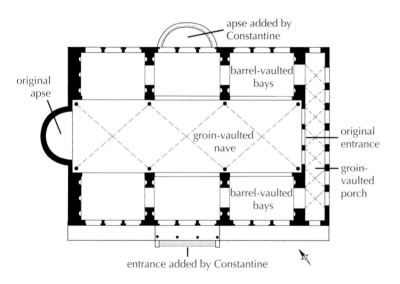

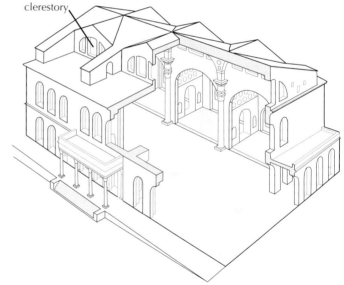

6–32 Plan and isometric reconstruction of the Basilica of Maxentius and Constantine, Rome (constructed 306–313 CE)

contenders—both sons of Tetrarchs—emerged in the western part of the empire: Maxentius, who controlled the Italian peninsula, and Constantine.

Although Rome had declined in importance at this time, building did not end altogether. Maxentius (ruled 306–312 CE) ordered the repair of many buildings in Rome and had others built there during his short reign. His most impressive undertaking in Rome was a huge new basilica called the Basilica Nova, or

New Basilica (figs. **6–31** and **6–32**). Now known as the Basilica of Maxentius and Constantine because Constantine's architects modified and completed it, this was the last important imperial government building erected in Rome itself. It functioned as an administrative center and provided a magnificent setting for the emperor when he appeared as supreme judge. Three brick-and-concrete barrel vaults of the side aisle still loom over the streets of modern Rome (fig. 6–31). The central hall was covered with

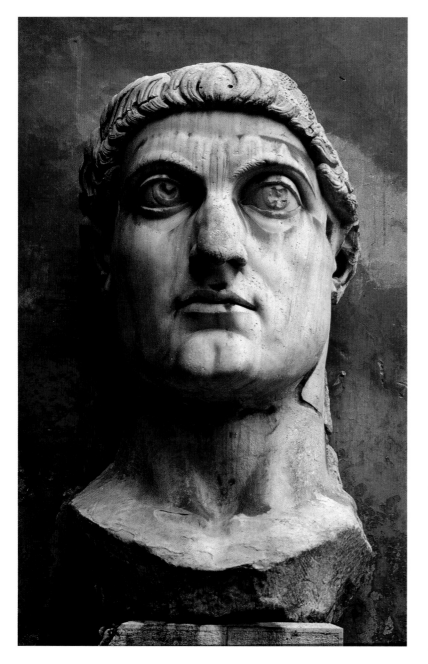

6–33 Constantine the Great, from the Basilica of Maxentius and Constantine, Rome. 325–326 CE. Marble, height of head 8′6″ (2.6 m). Palazzo dei Conservatori, Rome

This fragment came from a statue of the seated emperor. The original sculpture combined marble and probably bronze supported on a core of wood and bricks. Only a few marble fragments survive— the head, a hand, a knee, an elbow, and a foot. The body might have been made of either colored stone or of bronze on a scaffold of wood and bricks sheathed in bronze. The complete statue must have been awe-inspiring. Constantine was a master of the use of portrait statues to spread imperial propaganda.

groin vaults (see "Arch and Vault," page 139). The side aisles were covered with barrel vaults that acted as buttresses, or projecting supports, for the central groin vault and allowed generous window openings in the clerestory areas of the central aisle. A groin-vaulted porch extended across the short side and sheltered a triple entrance to the central hall. At the opposite end of the long axis of the hall was an apse nearly as wide as the nave, which acted as a focal point for the interior. The directional focus along a central axis from the entrance to the apse emphasized the imperial presence of the emperor, or at least his statue. A monumental portrait of Constantine (fig. **6–33**), found in the basilica, evidently served as a stand-in for the emperor and a reminder of his imperial power.

After defeating Maxentius at the Battle of the Milvian Bridge in 312 CE, at the entrance to Rome, Constantine ruled in the west (306–337). According to tradition, Constantine had a vision the night before the battle in which he saw a flaming cross in the sky bearing these words: "In this sign you shall conquer" (*in hoc signo vinces*). The next morning he ordered that his army's

shields and standards be inscribed with the monogram XP (the Greek letters *chi* and *rho* for Christos or Christ, but also an abbreviation of the Greek word *chrestos,* meaning auspicious). In 313 CE, Constantine issued the Edict of Milan granting freedom to all religious groups, not just Christians.

One of the last major pre-Christian Roman monuments to be constructed was a triumphal arch to commemorate Constantine's defeat of Maxentius. This memorial, placed next to the Colosseum in Rome, took the form of a huge triple arch (fig. **6–34**) that dwarfs the nearby Arch of Titus (see fig. 6–19). Three barrel-vaulted passageways are flanked by columns on high pedestals and surmounted by a large attic story bearing a laudatory inscription indicating that the arch was dedicated to Constantine by the Senate and the Roman people. Some of the sculpture decorating the arch came from other monuments made for Constantine's illustrious predecessors, the "good emperors" Trajan, Hadrian, and Marcus Aurelius. The reused items in effect transferred to Constantine the virtues of strength, courage, and piety associated with these earlier emperors.

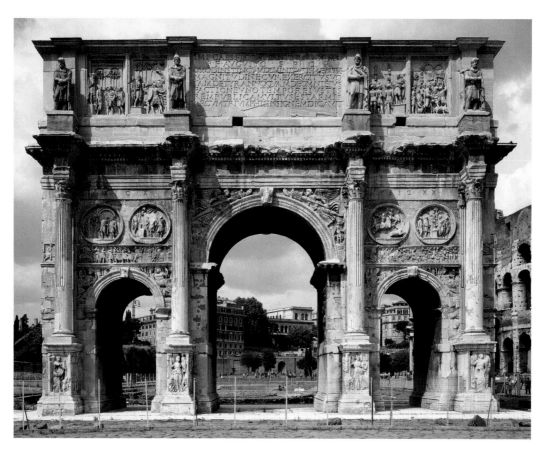

6–34 Arch of Constantine, Rome. 312–315 CE (dedicated July 25, 315 CE)

This massive, triple-arched monument to Emperor Constantine's victory over Maxentius in 312 CE is a wonder of recycled sculpture. On the attic story, flanking the inscription over the central arch, are relief panels taken from a monument celebrating the victory of Marcus Aurelius over the Germans in 174 CE. On the attached piers framing these panels are large statues of prisoners made to celebrate Trajan's victory over the Dacians in the early second century CE. On the inner walls of the central arch (not seen here) are reliefs also commemorating Trajan's conquest of Dacia. Over each of the side arches are pairs of giant roundels taken from a monument to Hadrian (see fig. 6–26). The rest of the decoration is contemporary with the arch.

New reliefs made for the arch recount the story of Constantine's victory and remind viewers of his power and generosity. A rectangular panel above one arch (below the two roundels) depicts Constantine's first public speech after defeating Maxentius (see fig. 6–26). Toward the center of the panel, the emperor (his head is missing) stands on a temporary speaker's platform. He is flanked by standing officials and seated statues of Marcus Aurelius and Hadrian. In the background, the Basilica Julia and the Arch of Tiberius are to the left and the Arch of Septimius Severus is to the right, identifying the site of the speech as the Republican Forum.

Although the new reliefs reflect the long-standing Roman fondness for depicting important events with realistic detail, in style and subject matter they contrast with the reused elements in the arch. The stocky, mostly frontal figures, each one resembling the next, are compressed into the foreground plane. The participants below the standing Constantine look so uniform that they seem to isolate "the new Augustus" and connect him visually with his illustrious predecessors on each side of him. This two-dimensional, hierarchical approach, with its emphasis on authority, ritual, and symbolism rather than on outward form, was adopted by the emerging Christian Church.

After 324 CE, Constantine—who had earned the epithet "the Great"—ruled as sole Roman emperor of the reunited empire until his death in 337. He made the port city of Byzantium the new capital and renamed it Constantinople (modern Istanbul, Turkey). After Constantinople was dedicated in 330, Rome, which had earlier ceased to be the seat of government in the west, further declined in importance.

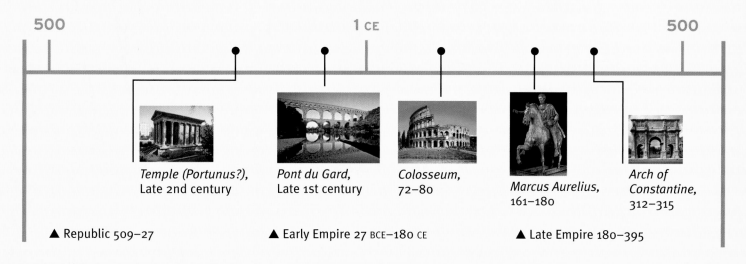

500   1 CE   500

Temple (Portunus?),   Pont du Gard,   Colosseum,   Marcus Aurelius,   Arch of
Late 2nd century   Late 1st century   72–80   161–180   Constantine,
                                                                              312–315

▲ Republic 509–27   ▲ Early Empire 27 BCE–180 CE   ▲ Late Empire 180–395

LOOKING BACK

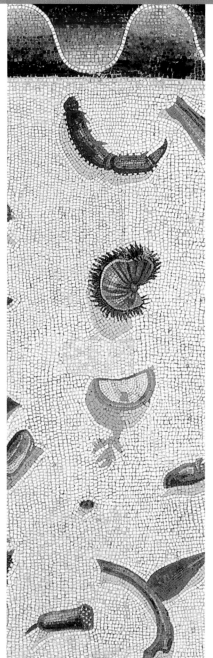

The ancient Romans conquered and ruled a vast territory around the Mediterranean Sea. As the empire absorbed the peoples it conquered, it imposed on them a legal, administrative, and cultural structure that endured for some five centuries—leaving a lasting mark on the later civilizations that emerged in Europe and surrounding regions.

The Romans, whose empire had supplanted the Greeks, appreciated Greek art and adapted it to their own uses, but they also had their own strengths, such as efficiency and a practical genius for organization. As sophisticated visual propaganda, Roman art served the state and imperial authority. Creating both official images and representations of private individuals, Roman sculptors enriched and developed the art of portraiture. They also recorded contemporary historical events on commemorative arches, columns, and mausoleums erected in public places.

Roman artists covered the walls of private homes with paintings, too. Sometimes fantastic urban panoramas surround a room, or painted columns and cornices, swinging garlands, and niches make a wall seem to dissolve. Some artists created the illusion of being on a porch or in a pavilion looking out into an extensive landscape. Such painted surfaces are often like backdrops for a theatrical set.

Roman architects relied heavily on the round arch and masonry vaulting. Beginning in the second century BCE, they also relied increasingly on a new building material: concrete. In contrast to stone, the components of concrete are cheap, light, and easily transported, and imposing and lasting concrete structures could be built by a large, semi-skilled work force directed by one or two trained and experienced supervisors.

Drawing artistic inspiration from their Etruscan and Greek predecessors and combining this with their own traditions, Roman artists made a distinctive contribution to the history of art, creating works that formed an enduring ideal of excellence in the West. And as Roman authority gave way to local rule, the newly powerful "barbarian" tribes continued to appreciate and even treasure the Classical learning and art that the Romans left behind.

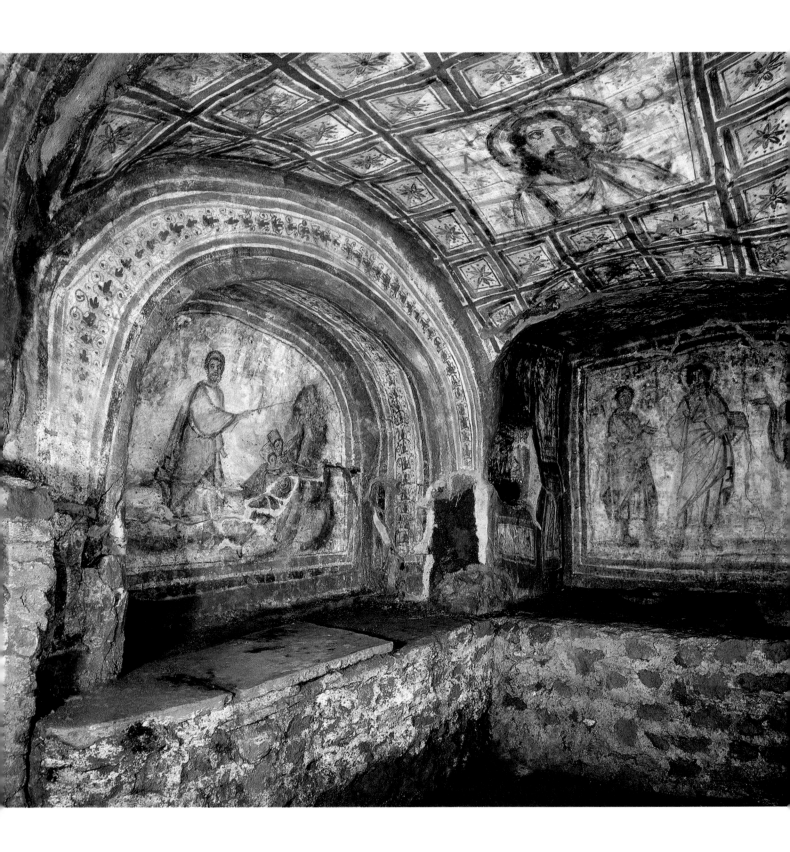

7
Jewish, Early Christian, and Byzantine Art

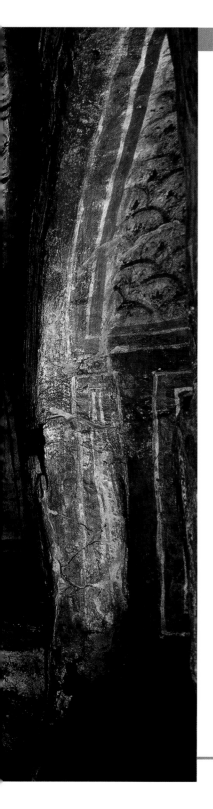

I n a Roman catacomb painting, Peter, like Moses before him, strikes a rock with his staff and water flows forth (fig. **7–1** scene at left). Imprisoned in Rome after the arrest of Jesus, Peter converted his fellow prisoners and jailers to Christianity, but he needed water with which to baptize them. Miraculously a spring gushed forth at the touch of his staff. In spite of his all too human frailty, Peter became the rock *(petrus)* on which Jesus founded the Church. He was the first bishop of Rome, the predecessor of today's pope. In the niche seen on the right, two early Roman Christian martyrs, Felix (d. 274) and Adauctus (d. 303) join Christ, who holds a book emphasizing his role as teacher. By including Peter, Romans, and Roman martyrs in the chamber's decoration, the early Christians, who dug this catacomb as a place for the dead, emphasized the importance of their city in Christendom.

In the star-studded heavens painted above, the face of Christ appears. The Greek letters alpha and omega appear on each side of Christ. Christ has the aspect of a Greek philosopher, bearded and with long dark hair. The circle around his head (a halo) indicates his importance and his divinity.

In these catacomb paintings, we see two of the major directions of Christian art— the narrative (educational) and the symbolic (iconic). The narrative image recounts the story of Saint Peter striking the rock, which in turn symbolizes the establishment of the Church and also the essential Christian rite of baptism. The other scene, Christ's face flanked by alpha and omega—the first and last letters of the Greek alphabet—offers a tangible expression of an intangible, non-narrative concept. The letters signify the beginning and end of time, and, combined with the image of Christ, symbolically represent an idea—without any specific narrative intent.

Throughout the history of Christian art these two tendencies will be apparent— the urge to tell a good story, with moral implications and educational values, and the need to create a symbolic image in which viewers find meaning through their store of information and belief. In the West, the didactic narrative will achieve prominence; in the Eastern Orthodox Church, the symbolic image, the icon, will reign.

7–1 Cubiculum of Leonis, Catacomb of Commodilla, near Rome. Late 4th century

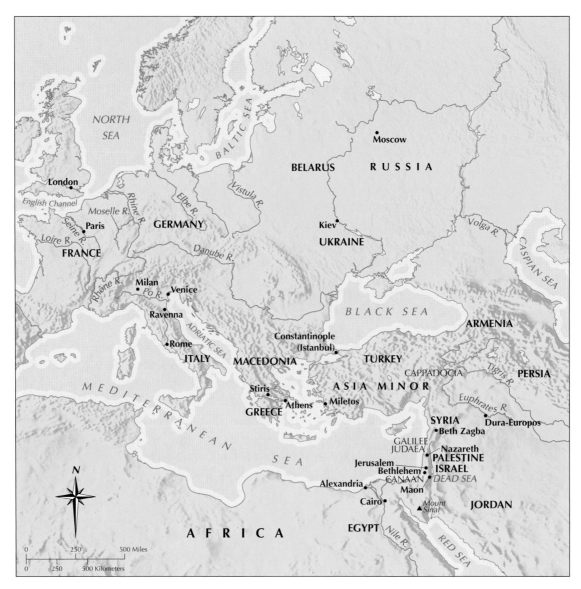

Map 7–1 The Early Jewish, Christian, and Byzantine World

Three ancient religions that arose in the Near East continue to inspire people's spiritual life in the Western world today: Judaism and Christianity, discussed in this chapter, and Islam, treated in Chapter 8. All three religions are monotheistic, meaning that their followers believe that only one god created and rules the universe. They are known as "religions of the book" because they have written records of God's will and words: the Hebrew Scriptures; the Christian Bible, which includes both the Hebrew Scriptures as its Old Testament and the Christian New Testament; and the Muslim Koran, the word of God (Allah) revealed through the angel Gabriel to the prophet Muhammad. Each religion builds on the beliefs and traditions of the earlier one. Traditional Jews believe that God made a covenant, or pact, with their ancestors and that they are God's chosen people. They await the coming of a savior, the Messiah, "the anointed one." Traditional Christians maintain that Jesus of Nazareth was that Messiah (the title *Christ* is derived from a Greek word meaning "Messiah"). They believe that God took human form, preached among men and women, was put to death on a cross, and then rose from the dead and ascended into heaven, having estab-

lished the Christian Church under the leadership of the apostles (his closest disciples). The followers of Islam, called Muslims, while accepting the Hebrew prophets and Jesus as divinely inspired, believe Muhammad to be Allah's last and greatest prophet, through whom Islam was revealed some six centuries after Jesus's earthly lifetime.

Jewish, Christian, and Muslim art combine in varying degrees Greek, Roman, and Near Eastern themes and forms. Jews and Christians use the visual arts to educate their followers through narratives and symbols and to glorify their religious services through ornamental enrichment of buildings and books. Muslims also use ornamental forms and abstract styles but prefer to convey meaning through words rather than through images (see Map **7–1**, above).

Jewish Art

The Jewish people trace their ancestry to a Semitic people called the Hebrews, who lived in the land of Canaan. Canaan, known from the second century CE by the Roman name of Palestine, was located between the Mediterranean Sea and the Jordan River.

According to the Torah (the first five books of the Hebrew Scriptures), God promised the patriarch Abraham that Canaan would be a homeland for the Jewish people (Genesis 17:8), a belief that remains important among Jews to this day.

Jewish settlement of Canaan probably began sometime in the second millennium BCE. According to Exodus, the second book of the Torah, the prophet Moses led the Hebrews out of slavery in Egypt to the promised land of Canaan. At one crucial point during the journey, Moses climbed alone to the top of Mount Sinai, where God gave him the Ten Commandments, the cornerstone of Jewish law. These commandments, inscribed on tablets, were kept in a gold-covered wooden box, the Ark of the Covenant.

In the tenth century BCE, the Jewish king, Solomon, built a temple in Jerusalem to house the Ark of the Covenant. The Temple consisted of courtyards, a porch, a hall, and the holy of holies housing the Ark with its guardian **cherubim**. King Solomon sent to nearby Phoenicia for cedar, cypress, and sandalwood, and for a master craftsman to supervise the Temple's construction (II Chronicles 2:2–15). The Temple was the spiritual center of Jewish life.

In 586 BCE, the Neo-Babylonians, under King Nebuchadnezzar II, conquered Jerusalem (see Chapter 5). They destroyed the Temple, exiled the Jews, and carried off the Ark of the Covenant. When Cyrus the Great of Persia conquered Babylonia in 538 BCE, the Jews were permitted to return to Jerusalem and build the Second Temple, but from that time forward Canaan, existed primarily under foreign rule and eventually became part of the Roman Empire. In 70 CE Roman forces led by the future emperor, Titus, destroyed the Second Temple and Jerusalem (see Chapter 6, figure 6-20).

Jews continued to live in dispersed communities throughout the Roman Empire. Most of the earliest surviving examples of Jewish art date from the Hellenistic and Roman periods. Six Jewish **catacombs**, or underground burial chambers, discovered just outside the city of Rome and in use from the first to the fourth century CE, display wall paintings with Jewish themes. In one example, from the third century CE, two **menorahs**, or seven-branched lamps, flank the long-lost Ark of the Covenant (fig. **7–2**). The conspicuous representation of the menorah looted from the Second Temple of Jerusalem on the Arch of Titus in Rome kept the memory of these treasures alive. The menorah form probably derives from the ancient Near Eastern Tree of Life, symbolizing both the end of exile and the paradise to come.

Judaism has always emphasized religious learning. Jews gather in synagogues for study and worship; a synagogue can be any large room where the Torah scrolls are kept and read publicly. The destroyed Temple in Jerusalem had been a special, central holy place for all Jews, but synagogues could be constructed in any Jewish community. Some Jewish places of worship were located in private homes or in buildings originally constructed as homes. Far less Jewish art than Christian or Islamic art has survived, but a number of synagogues have been discovered or excavated. Their architecture and ornament reflect late Roman artistic traditions melded with specifically Jewish symbols.

In the Roman city of Dura-Europos, in modern Syria, excavators discovered a Jewish **house-synagogue**, or synagogue built within a private home. The first Dura-Europos synagogue consisted of an assembly hall, a separate alcove for women, and a

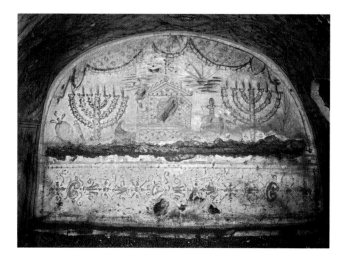

7–2 *Menorahs and Ark of the Covenant,* wall painting in a Jewish catacomb, Villa Torlonia, Rome. 3rd century. 3′11″ × 5′9″ (1.19 × 1.8 m)

courtyard. After a remodeling of the building, completed in 244–45 CE, men and women shared the hall, and residential rooms were added. Two architectural features distinguished the assembly hall: a bench along its walls and a niche for the Torah scrolls (fig. **7–3**). Scenes from Jewish history cover the walls. The story of Moses unfolds in a continuous narrative around the room. The vivid scenes follow the Roman tradition of historical representation; however, the frontal poses, strong outlines, and flat colors are pictorial devices associated with Near Eastern art.

Jews also built synagogues designed on the model of the ancient Roman basilica. A typical basilica synagogue had a central nave with aisles; a semicircular apse in the wall facing Jerusalem; and perhaps an atrium (courtyard) and a porch, or narthex. A Torah was kept in a shrine in the apse.

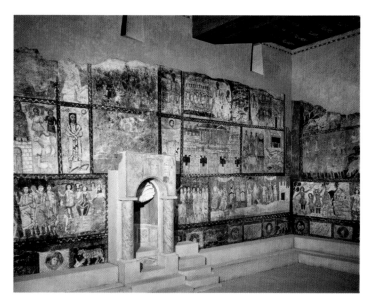

7–3 Wall with Torah niche, from a house-synagogue, Dura-Europos, Syria. 244–245. Tempera on plaster, section approx. 40′ (12.19 m) long. Reconstructed in the National Museum, Damascus, Syria

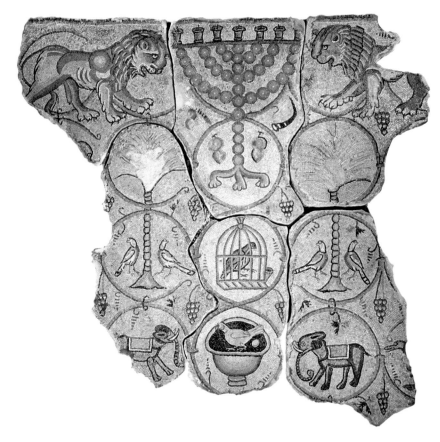

7–4 Synagogue floor, Maon (Menois). c. 530. Mosaic. Collection of the Israel
Antiquities Authority/Israel Museum, Jerusalem

Synagogues contained almost no **representational** sculpture because Jewish law forbade praying to images or idols. Paintings and mosaics, on the other hand, often decorated walls and floors. A fragment of a mosaic floor (fig. **7–4**) from a sixth-century synagogue at Maon (Menois) features traditional Jewish symbols along with a variety of stylized plants, birds, and animals. Two lions of Judah flank a menorah. Beside it is a *shofar*, or ram's horn, blown on ceremonial occasions, and three gourd-shaped *etrogs*, or citrons, used to celebrate the harvest festival of Sukkot. The etrog symbolizes the bounty of the earth and the unity of all Jews. Two palm trees refer to another Sukkot emblem, the *lulav*, a sheaf of palm, myrtle, and willow branches. The variety of placid birds and elephants may symbolize the universal peace as prophesied by Isaiah (11:6–9; 65:25). The pairing of images around a central element, such as the birds flanking the palm trees or the lions facing the menorah, is characteristic of Near Eastern art. In contrast, the grapevine, stylized until it is almost unrecognizable, forms circular **medallions** that frame the images.

In 395 the Roman Empire split permanently in two, becoming the Western (Roman) Empire, which collapsed in 476, and the Eastern, or Byzantine, Empire, which lasted until 1453, when it fell to the Ottoman Turks. By this time most Jews lived outside Palestine, in communities spread across the Near East, North Africa, and Europe. Because their religious practice set them apart, and their numbers made them a minority, they faced special taxes, restrictions on the occupations they could enter, and sometimes violent persecution. The history of Jewish art is fragmented because many artworks were destroyed when Jewish homes and synagogues were attacked and burned. The artworks that survive reflect the interplay of many styles, centuries, and regions.

Early Christianity

Christianity began with the life and teachings of Jesus of Nazareth, a Jew born sometime between 8 and 4 BCE and crucified at age 33. Christians believe that Jesus was the son of God; born in a human body to a virgin woman, Mary; and resurrected after death. Most Christians believe in one God manifest in three Persons, a Trinity of Father (God), Son (Jesus Christ), and Holy Spirit. In later years Christians also began to acknowledge saints—devout individuals connected with verifiable miracles and canonized, or officially honored, by the Church for upholding and practicing Christian beliefs, often at the cost of martyrdom (execution). Worshipers may ask saints to intercede for them with God, but saints are not worshiped as gods in their own right.

The Christian New Testament describes the life of Jesus in its first four books, known as the Gospels (the Good News). The Gospels relate that Jesus was a descendant of the Jewish royal house of King David and that he was born in Bethlehem in Judaea, where his mother, Mary, and her husband, Joseph, had gone to be registered in the Roman census. He grew up in Nazareth in Galilee, where Joseph was a carpenter. At age 30, Jesus began his public ministry. He gathered about him a group

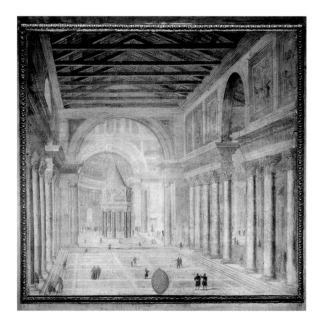

7–5 Interior of St. Peter's

The sixteenth-century depiction of Old St. Peter's in the church of S. Martino ai Monte, Rome, shows columns supporting a straight lintel and an open timber roof, but omits the clerestory windows. Light streams into the transept and illuminates the high altar with its tower-like baldacchino. The giant pinecone at the lower edge of the painting stood in the atrium.

of disciples, male and female; he preached love and charity, a personal relationship with God, the forgiveness of sins, and the promise of life after death. From his followers, he chose 12 apostles to carry on his work after his death (see "Iconography of the Life of Jesus," pages 168–169).

Jesus limited his ministry primarily to Jews; his apostles—including Paul, who joined the group later—took Jesus's teachings to non-Jews. Despite sporadic persecutions, Christianity persisted and spread throughout the Roman Empire. The Roman emperor Constantine (see Chapter 6) permitted the Christians freedom of worship with the Edict of Milan in 313 CE. By the end of the fourth century, Christianity had become the official religion of the empire and non-Christians became the targets of persecution.

In Rome, even before their religion was recognized, Christians met in private houses for worship. Several private patrons also owned cemeteries and funeral basilicas. The congregations used the burial grounds as places to gather for worship, commemorative meals, and funeral rituals. They also excavated underground cemeteries, or catacombs, consisting of narrow passages and small burial chambers lined with rectangular burial niches (fig. 7–1). These niches were filled with stone sarcophagi or sealed with tiles or stone slabs. The painted walls and ceilings of such catacombs provide some of the earliest examples of Christian art. The ceiling of a **cubiculum,** or small room, in the fourth-century catacomb of Commodilla is painted with a central medallion showing the face of Christ.

The era of religious toleration, which began with the Edict of Milan and Constantine's active support of Christianity, spurred the building of Christian churches and shrines. Constantine ordered a monumental basilica constructed at the place where Christians believed Saint Peter, the leader of the apostles, to be buried. Peter (d. c. 64 CE) had established the first Christian community in Rome. As the city's first bishop (spiritual and administrative leader of the Church), he was later recognized as the precursor of the popes—the heads of the Christian Church in the West. Old Saint Peter's Church (called "old" because it was completely replaced by a new building in the sixteenth century, see below) became the pope's church and came to signify his authority over all Christendom.

Old Saint Peter's Church (see "Basilica-Plan and Central-Plan Churches," page 171, and fig. 7–5) included architectural elements arranged in a way that has characterized Christian basilica-plan churches ever since it was built. It also had four side aisles, two on each side of the nave, and the nave was lined with columns supporting an entablature (fig. 7–6). Because of its size and double aisles, the columns of the side aisles supported a series of round arches. A **transept**—a wing that crossed the nave and aisles at a right angle—met the need for more space near the tomb of the saint. A large number of clergy and pilgrims gathered near the altar and tomb for elaborate rituals. Christians believed that Saint Peter's bones lay beneath the high altar; indeed early Christian and pagan catacombs did lie under the

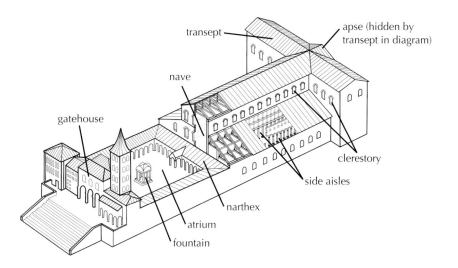

7–6 Reconstruction drawing of Old Saint Peter's, Rome, c. 320–327; atrium added in later 4th century. For plan see "Basilica-Plan and Central-Plan Churches," page 171

transept

apse (hidden by transept in diagram)

nave

gatehouse

clerestory

side aisles

narthex

atrium

fountain

ICONOGRAPHY OF THE LIFE OF JESUS

conography is the study of subject matter in art. It involves identifying both what a work of art represents—what it depicts—and the deeper significance of what is represented—its symbolic meaning. Stories about the life of Jesus, grouped in "cycles," form the basis of Christian iconography. What follows is an outline of those cycles and the main events of each.

THE INCARNATION CYCLE AND THE CHILDHOOD OF JESUS (events surrounding the conception and birth of Jesus)

The Annunciation: The archangel Gabriel informs the Virgin Mary that God has chosen her to bear his son. A dove represents the Incarnation, her miraculous conception of Jesus through the Holy Spirit.

The Visitation: The pregnant Mary visits her older cousin Elizabeth, pregnant with the future Saint John the Baptist. Elizabeth is the first to recognize and acknowledge the divinity of the child Mary is carrying.

The Nativity: Jesus is born to Mary in Bethlehem. The Holy Family—Jesus, Mary, and her husband, Joseph—is shown in a house, a stable, or, in Byzantine art, a cave.

Annunciation to the Shepherds and Adoration of the Shepherds: An angel announces Jesus's birth to humble shepherds, who hurry to Bethlehem to honor him.

Adoration of the Magi: Wise men from the East follow a bright star to Bethlehem to honor Jesus as King of the Jews, presenting him with precious gifts—gold (symbolizing kingship), frankincense (divinity), and myrrh (death). In medieval Europe, the Magi were identified as three kings.

Presentation in the Temple: Mary and Joseph bring the infant Jesus to the Temple in Jerusalem, where he is presented to the high priest. It is prophesied that Jesus will redeem humankind and that Mary will suffer great sorrow.

Massacre of the Innocents and Flight into Egypt: An angel warns Joseph that King Herod—to eliminate the threat of a newborn rival king—plans to murder all male babies in Bethlehem. The Holy Family flees to Egypt.

Jesus Among the Doctors: In Jerusalem to celebrate Passover, Joseph and Mary find the 12-year-old Jesus in serious discussion with Temple scholars, a sign of his coming ministry.

THE PUBLIC MINISTRY CYCLE (in which Jesus preaches and performs miracles, signs of God's power)

Marriage at Cana: At his mother's request Jesus turns water into wine at a wedding feast, his first public miracle. Later the event was interpreted as prefiguring the Eucharist.

Cleansing of the Temple: Jesus, in anger, drives moneychangers and animal traders from the Temple.

The Baptism: At age 30, Jesus is baptized by John the Baptist in the Jordan River. He sees the Holy Spirit and hears a heavenly voice proclaiming him God's son. His ministry begins.

Jesus and the Samaritan Woman at the Well: Jesus rests by a spring called Jacob's Well. Contrary to Jewish custom, he asks a local Samaritan woman for a drink of water.

Miracles of Healing: Jesus performs miracles of healing the blind, possessed (mentally ill), paralytic, and lepers; he also resurrects the dead.

Miraculous Draft of Fishes: At Jesus's command, Peter lowers the nets and catches so many fish that James and John have to help bring them into the boat. Jesus promises that the men soon will be "fishers of men."

Jesus Walking on the Water; Storm at Sea: The disciples, in a storm-tossed boat, see Jesus walking toward them on the water. Peter tries to go out to meet Jesus, but begins to sink; Jesus saves him.

Calling of Levi/Matthew: Passing the customhouse, Jesus sees Levi, a tax collector, and says, "Follow me." Levi complies, becoming the disciple Matthew.

Raising of Lazarus: Jesus brings his friend Lazarus back to life four days after death. Lazarus emerges from the tomb wrapped in a shroud.

Jesus in the House of Mary and Martha: Mary (representing the contemplative life) sits listening to Jesus while Martha (the active life) prepares food. Jesus praises Mary.

The Transfiguration: Jesus reveals his divinity in a dazzling vision on Mount Tabor in Galilee as his closest disciples—Peter, James, and John—look on. A cloud envelops them, and a heavenly voice proclaims Jesus to be God's son.

Tribute Money: Challenged to pay the temple tax, Jesus sends Peter to catch a fish, which has the required coin in its mouth.

Delivery of the Keys to Peter: Jesus designates Peter as his successor, symbolically turning over to him the keys to the kingdom of heaven.

THE PASSION CYCLE (events surrounding Jesus's death and resurrection. *Passio* is Latin for "suffering.")

Entry into Jerusalem: Jesus, riding an ass, and his disciples enter Jerusalem in triumph. Crowds honor them, spreading clothes and palm fronds in their path.

The Last Supper: During the Jewish Passover seder, Jesus reveals his impending death to his disciples. Instructing them to drink wine (his blood) and eat bread (his body) in remembrance of him, he lays the foundation for the Christian Eucharist (Mass).

Jesus Washing the Disciples' Feet: After the Last Supper, Jesus humbly washes the disciples' feet to set an example of humility. Peter, embarrassed, protests.

The Agony in the Garden: In the Garden of Gethsemane on the Mount of Olives, Jesus struggles between his human fear of pain and death and his divine strength to overcome them (*agon* is Greek for "contest"). The apostles sleep nearby, oblivious.

Betrayal (The Arrest): Judas Iscariot (a disciple) accepts a bribe to point Jesus out to his enemies. Judas brings an armed crowd to Gethsemane and kisses Jesus (a prearranged signal). Peter futilely attempt to defend Jesus from Roman soldiers who seize him.

Denial of Peter: Jesus is taken to the Jewish high priest, Caiaphas, to be interrogated for claiming to be the Messiah. Peter follows and three times denies knowing Jesus, as Jesus predicted.

Jesus Before Pilate: Jesus is taken to Pontius Pilate, Roman governor of Judaea, and charged with treason for calling himself King of the Jews. He is sent to Herod Antipas, ruler of Galilee, who scorns him. Pilate proposes freeing Jesus but is shouted down by the mob, which demands Jesus be crucified. Pilate washes his hands before the mob to signify that Jesus's blood is on their hands, not his.

The Flagellation (Scourging): Jesus is whipped by his Roman captors.

Jesus Crowned with Thorns (Mocking of Jesus): Pilate's soldiers torment Jesus. They dress him in royal robes, crown him with thorns, and kneel before him, hailing him King of the Jews.

Bearing of the Cross (Road to Calvary): Jesus bears the cross from Pilate's house to Golgotha, where he is executed. This event and accompanying incidents came to be called the Stations of the Cross: 1) Jesus condemned to death; 2) Jesus picks up cross; 3) Jesus falls; 4) Jesus meets his grieving mother; 5) Simon of Cyrene forced to help Jesus carry cross; 6) Veronica wipes Jesus's face with her veil; 7) Jesus falls again; 8) Jesus admonishes women of Jerusalem; 9) Jesus falls a third time; 10) Jesus is stripped; 11) Jesus is nailed to cross; 12) Jesus dies on cross; 13) Jesus taken down from cross; 14) Jesus entombed.

The Crucifixion: The earliest representations show either a cross alone or a cross and a lamb. Later depictions include some or all of these details: two criminals (one penitent, one not) are crucified alongside Jesus; the Virgin Mary, John the Evangelist, Mary Magdalen, and others mourn at the foot of the cross; Roman soldiers torment Jesus—one extends a sponge on a pole with vinegar instead of water for him to drink, another stabs him in the side with a spear, others gamble for his clothes; a skull identifies the execution ground as Golgotha, "the place of the skull," where Adam was buried (symbolizing the promise of redemption).

Descent from the Cross (The Deposition): Jesus's followers take his body down from the cross. Joseph of Arimathea and Nicodemus wrap it in linen with myrrh and aloe. Also present are the grief-stricken Virgin, John the Evangelist, and sometimes Mary Magdalen, other disciples, and angels.

The Lamentation/Pietà: Jesus's sorrowful followers gather around his body. An image of the Virgin mourning alone with Jesus across her lap is known as a pietà (from Latin *pietas*, "pity").

The Entombment: Jesus's mother and friends place his body in a nearby sarcophagus, or rock tomb. This is done hastily because the Jewish Sabbath approaches.

Descent into Limbo (Harrowing of Hell): No longer in mortal form, Jesus, now called Christ, descends into limbo, or hell, to free deserving souls, among them Adam, Eve, and Moses.

The Resurrection (Anastasis): Three days after death, Christ walks from his tomb while soldiers guarding it sleep.

The Marys at the Tomb (Holy Women at the Sepulchre): Christ's female followers—usually including Mary Magdalen and Mary the mother of the apostle James—discover his empty tomb. An angel announces Christ's resurrection. Soldiers guarding the tomb look on, terrified.

Noli Me Tangere ("Do Not Touch Me"), The Supper at Emmaus, and The Doubting of Thomas: Christ makes a series of appearances to his followers in the 40 days between his resurrection and ascension—first to Mary Magdalen, as she weeps at his tomb. She reaches out to him, but he warns her not to touch him. At Emmaus, Christ and his disciples share a meal. Christ invites Thomas, who doubts his resurrection, to touch the wound in his side to convince him.

The Ascension: Christ ascends to heaven from the Mount of Olives, disappearing in a cloud. His apostles, often accompanied by the Virgin, watch.

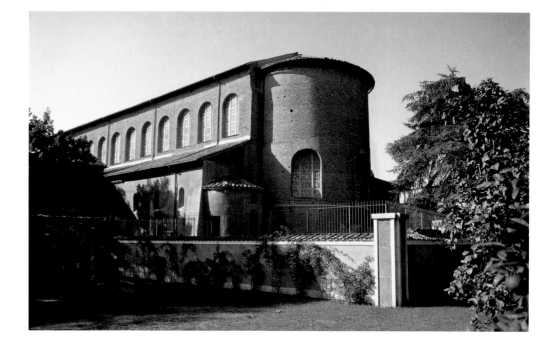

7–7 Church of Santa Sabina, Rome. 422–432

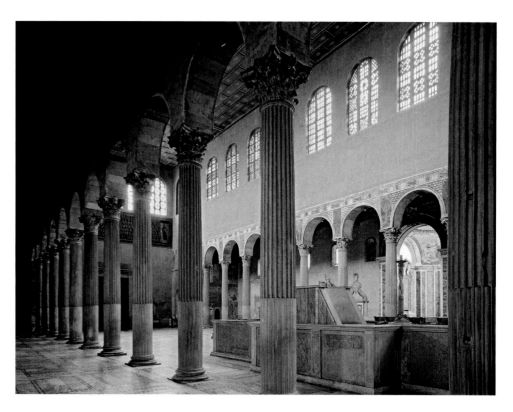

7–8 Interior, Church of Santa Sabina. View from side aisle, across the nave toward the entrance. The choir enclosure stands at the lower right

church. Clearly, Old Saint Peter's had to serve a variety of functions; it was a burial place, a pilgrimage shrine containing the relics of Saint Peter, and a congregational church. Old Saint Peter's could hold at least 14,000 worshipers, and it remained the largest of all Christian churches until the eleventh century.

Old Saint Peter's is gone, but some idea of a typical basilica can be gained from the Church of Santa Sabina, a fifth-century basilica in Rome. The basilica, constructed by Bishop Peter of Ilyria between 422 and 432, appears much as it did when first built (fig. **7–7**). The basic elements of the basilica church are clearly visible inside and out: a nave lit by **clerestory** windows, and side aisles that end in a rounded apse (compare Roman secular basilicas, such as the Basilica Ulpia or Basilica Aemilia [fig.

6–21]). Santa Sabina's exterior, typical of the time, is severe brickwork. In contrast, the interior displays a wealth of marble veneer and 24 fluted marble columns with Corinthian capitals acquired from a second-century building (fig. **7–8**). The columns support arches creating a **nave arcade** (in contrast to a **nave colonnade**, which has no arches above). The **spandrels** are inlaid with marble images of the chalice and paten (the plate that holds the bread)—the essential equipment for the **Eucharistic** rite that took place at the altar. The **triforium**, the blind wall between the arcade and the clerestory, typically had paintings or mosaics with scenes from the Old Testament or the Gospels. The decoration of the upper walls here has been lost. A paneled ceiling covers a pitched rafter roof.

ELEMENTS OF **Architecture**
Basilica-Plan and Central-Plan Churches

The forms of early Christian buildings were based on two **classical** prototypes: rectangular Roman basilicas (see fig. 6–22) and round-domed structures—rotundas—such as the Pantheon (see figs. 6–23, 6–24, 6–32). As in Old Saint Peter's in Rome (see fig. 7–6), **basilica-plan** churches are characterized by a forecourt, the **atrium**, leading to a porch, the **narthex**, which spans one of the building's short ends. Doorways—known collectively as the church's portal—lead from the narthex into a long central area called a **nave**. Rows of columns separate the high-ceilinged nave from the aisles on either side. The nave is lit by windows along its upper story, called a **clerestory**, that rises above the side aisles' roofs. At the opposite end of the nave from the narthex is a semicircular projection, the **apse**. The apse functions as the building's focal point where the altar, raised on a platform, is located. Sometimes there is also a **transept**, a wing that crosses the nave in front of the apse, making the building T-shaped; this is known as a *tau* plan. When additional space (a choir) comes between the transept and the apse, the plan is known as a Latin cross.

Central-plan buildings were first used by Christians as tombs, baptism centers, and shrines to martyrs. (The **Greek-cross plan**, in which two similarly sized "arms" intersect at their centers, is a type of central plan, fig. 6–9.) Like basilicas, central-plan churches generally have an atrium, a narthex, and an apse. But instead of the longitudinal axis of basilican churches, which draws worshipers forward toward the apse, central-plan churches such as Ravenna's San Vitale (see figs. 7–14, 7–15) have a more vertical axis. This makes worshipers focus on the dome, which functions as a symbolic "vault of heaven." This space where the liturgy is performed, containing the central dome, sanctuary, and apse, is called the naos.

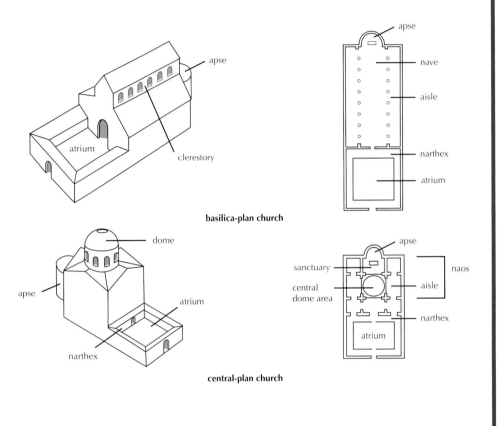

basilica-plan church

central-plan church

The beauty and richness of Early Christian church interiors, with their encrustation of mosaics and colored marbles, can still be experienced in several fifth- and sixth-century buildings in Ravenna. By the time the Roman church of Santa Sabina was completed, Rome had lost its political, although not its spiritual, importance. The capital of the Western (Roman) Empire was moved to Milan in the late fourth century and then to Ravenna at the beginning of the fifth century. Ravenna had an important naval base, Classis (modern Classe), and offered direct access by sea to Constantinople, the capital of the Eastern, or Byzantine, Empire.

One of the earliest surviving Christian structures in Ravenna is a small, cross-shaped building once attached to the church of the imperial palace. It is called the Mausoleum of Galla Placidia after one of the most remarkable women of the fifth century (although she was not buried there). Galla Placidia was the daughter of the Western Roman emperor, the wife of a Gothic king, the sister of Emperor Honorius, and the mother of Emperor Valentinian. As regent for her son after 425, she ruled the Western Empire. The upper walls and vaults of the tiny chapel are richly decorated with mosaics, and panels

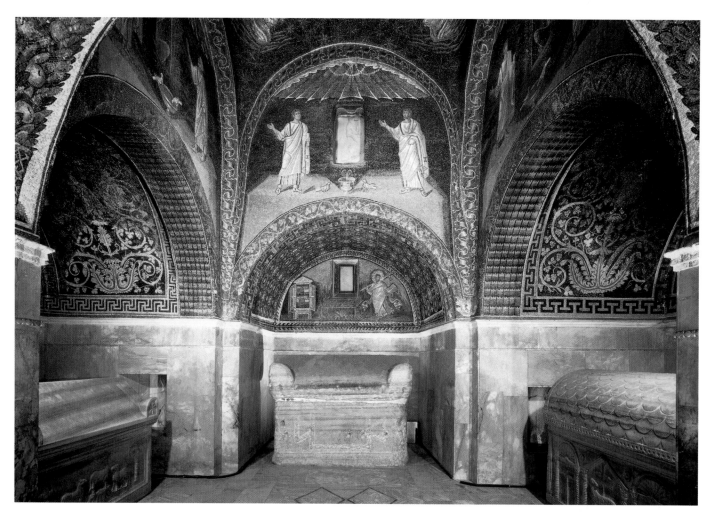

7–9 Mausoleum of Galla Placidia, Ravenna, Italy c. 425–426. View from entrance. Three of the four arms of the cross-shaped building hold sarchophagi. Lunette mosaic, the *Martyrdom of Saint Lawrence;* upper walls, apostles

of veined marble cover the walls below (fig. **7–9**). Patterns including floral designs derived from funeral garlands decorate the four central arches, and the walls above them are filled with the figures of standing apostles gesturing like orators. Saint Lawrence, to whom the building was probably dedicated, is represented in the central **lunette** filling the arm of the cross. The saint holds a cross and gestures toward the metal grill on which he was literally roasted. Left of the grill stands a tall cabinet containing the books of the Gospels, signifying the faith for which Lawrence was martyred.

Another lunette depicts the *Good Shepherd* (fig. **7–10**). In this mosaic, Jesus is a young adult wearing imperial robes. There is a halo, or circle of light, behind his head—a device artists used to distinguish rulers and holy personages from ordinary people. The rocky band at the bottom of the scene, resembling a cliff face riddled with clefts, separates the divine image from worshipers. This visual device illustrates an increasing tendency in Christian art to differentiate the sacred and secular worlds.

Early Byzantine Art

During the fifth and sixth centuries, the Italian peninsula was invaded by the Visigoths, Vandals, and Ostrogoths—Germanic

peoples from the north. Rome was sacked twice, in 410 and 455. The Western (Roman) Empire collapsed in 476, and Italy fell to the Ostrogoths.

During the same period, the Eastern Empire and its capital city of Constantinople flourished. Byzantine political power, wealth, and culture reached its height in the sixth century, under Emperor Justinian I (ruled 527–565), ably seconded by Empress Theodora (c. 500–548). At the height of its powers under Justinian, the Byzantine Empire included the lands that are now Greece, the Balkans, and Turkey; the Levant from Syria south to Arabia; Egypt; part of Spain; and a long strip along the Mediterranean coast of Africa. Justinian also reconquered Italy and Sicily, establishing Ravenna as the administrative capital of Byzantine Italy.

In Constantinople, Justinian began a campaign of building and renovation, but little remains of his architectural projects or of the old imperial city. The Church of Hagia Sophia (Holy Wisdom) is a magnificent exception (fig. **7–11**). Designed by two scholar-theoreticians, Anthemius of Tralles and Isidorus of Miletus, it embodies both imperial power and Christian glory. Anthemius was a specialist in geometry and optics, and Isidorus was a specialist in physics who had studied vaulted construction. Their crowning achievement was the original dome of Hagia

Few images have such great appeal as the Good Shepherd, with its associations of loving, caring, protectiveness, and strength (fig. **7–10**). Originating in agrarian societies, the theme of the shepherd watching over a flock of sheep or carrying home a weak or lost lamb became a powerful and positive image even in urban cultures. Today the Good Shepherd may be thought of as a Christian symbol, but it was not conceived as such. Ancient Greeks and Romans sometimes represented Hermes as a shepherd carrying a lamb or calf, and Orpheus was believed to have charmed flocks with his music. Jewish patriarchs measured their wealth in herds of sheep and camels, and one of the best known of the songs of King David envisions God as an all-providing shepherd (Psalm 23). Not surprisingly, Christians adopted this imagery for Jesus, who used it himself in his parables as an effective way to make God's love understandable to his listeners (Luke 15:3–7 and Matthew 18:12–14). According to John (10:10–11), Jesus called himself the good shepherd who lays down his life for his sheep. And so the imagery communicated a common theme for Jews and Christians alike in both the West and the East.

By the fifth century—with Christianity relatively secure as an established religion—an artist might add, or a patron might request to include, specifically Christian symbols in a work. In this mosaic from Ravenna, Jesus sits with his sheep in a luxuriant landscape, like a young Orpheus. But his shepherd's crook has become a golden cross. Not dressed as a simple peasant, Jesus wears imperial robes of purple and gold and embodies the Byzantine ideal of majesty. At the time this mosaic was made, Christianity had been the official state religion for 45 years, and nearly a century had passed since the last official persecution of Christians. The patrons of the mosaic chose to assert the glory of Jesus Christ in mosaic, the richest medium of decoration known, and to present Jesus in the guise of a young emperor, an imperial image still imbued with pagan spirit but now glorying in the triumph of the new faith.

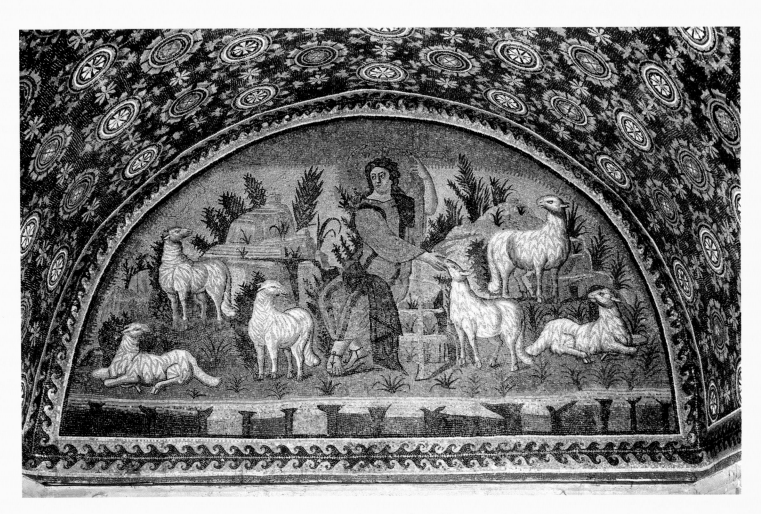

7–10 *Good Shepherd,* mosaic in the lunette over the west entrance, Mausoleum of Galla Placidia, Ravenna, Italy c. 425–426.
This mosaic is behind the viewer in fig. 7–9

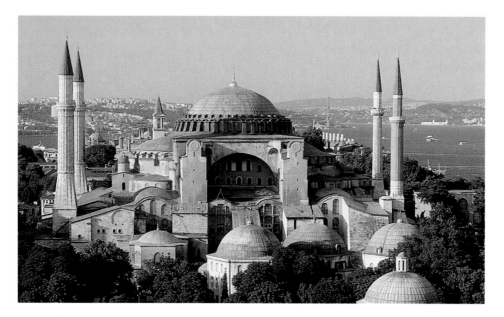

7–11 Anthemius of Tralles and Isidorus of Miletus. Church of Hagia Sophia, Istanbul, Turkey. 532–537. View from the southwest

Sophia, which provided a golden, light-filled canopy high above a processional space (fig. **7–12**). Procopius of Caesarea, who chronicled Justinian's reign, claimed poetically that the dome seemed to hang suspended on a "golden chain from heaven." It was rumored that Hagia Sophia was constructed by angels, but mortal builders achieved the feat in only five years (532–537) (see "Pendentives and Squinches," page 176).

Hagia Sophia is based on a central plan with a dome inscribed in a square (fig. **7–12**). To form a longitudinal nave, **conches**—semidomes—expand outward from the central dome to connect with the narthex on one end and the sanctuary apse on the other. This central core, called the **naos** in Byzantine architecture, is flanked by side aisles; above the aisles, **galleries** overlook the naos. The Byzantine church required galleries to accommodate female worshipers, who were not allowed to stand directly on the church floor.

The main dome of Hagia Sophia is supported on pendentives, triangular curving wall sections built between the four huge arches that spring from **piers** (large masonry supports) at the corners of the dome's square base (fig. **7–13** and "Pendentives and Squinches," page 176). The origin of the dome on pendentives, which became the preferred method for supporting domes in Byzantine architecture, is obscure, but Hagia Sophia represents its earliest use in a major building. Unlike the Pantheon's dome, which rises as a solid form from a circular drum and opens with an oculus at the top (see fig. 6–24), the dome of Hagia Sophia has a band of forty windows around its base. This daring concept challenged architectural logic by weakening the integrity of the masonry, but it created the all-important circle of light that makes the dome appear to float.

Among the sixth-century Byzantine churches built outside Constantinople, the Church of San Vitale in Ravenna was one of the most important structures. It was commissioned by a local bishop, Ecclesius, when Italy was under Ostrogothic rule, but it was only completed after Justinian's conquest of Ravenna. The church was dedicated in 547 to the fourth-century Italian

martyr, Saint Vitalis. Its design is basically a dome-covered octagon extended by eight **exedrae,** or semicircular niches (fig. **7–14**), one of which is extended to form the sanctuary. The rectangular sanctuary is flanked by circular rooms. A narthex once led to the palace.

The floor plan of San Vitale only begins to convey the effect of the complex, interpenetrating interior spaces of the church. The dome rests on eight large piers that frame the

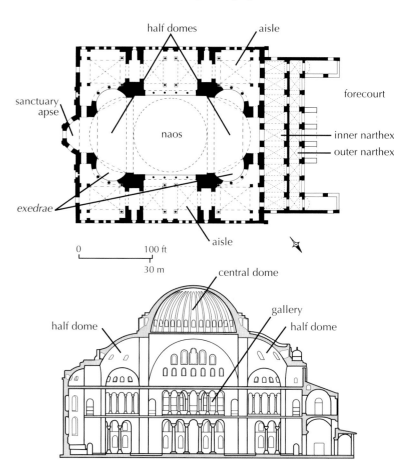

7–12 Plan and section of the Church of Hagia Sophia

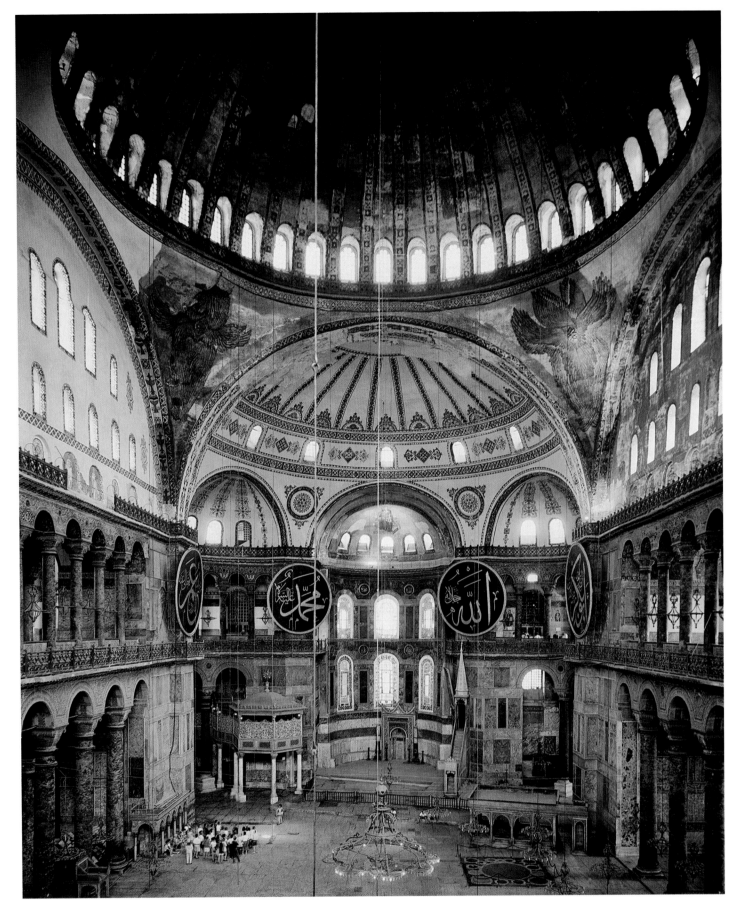

7–13 Church of Hagia Sophia

Hypatius of Ephesus, writing in the mid-sixth century, justified decorating churches in a luxurious manner as a means to inspire piety in the congregation. He wrote: "We, too, permit material adornment in the sanctuaries, not because God considered gold and silver, silken vestments and vessels encrusted with gems to be precious and holy, but because we allow every order of the faithful to be guided in a suitable manner and to o be led up to the Godhead, inasmuch as some men are guided even by such things towards the illegible beauty, and from the abundant light of the sanctuaries to the intelligible and immaterial light" (cited in Mango, page 117). The large medallions were added by the Ottoman Turks when they turned the church into a mosque.

Elements of Architecture

Pendentives and Squinches

Pendentives and squinches are two methods of supporting a round dome or its drum over a square space. Pendentives are spherical triangles between arches that rise to form a circular opening on which the dome sits. Squinches are lintels supported on bracketlike constructions placed across the walls' upper corners. Because squinches create an octagon, which is close in shape to a circle, they provide a solid base for the dome. Byzantine builders experimented with both pendentives (as at Hagia Sophia, see fig. 7–13) and squinches. Elaborate squinch-supported domes became a hallmark of Islamic interiors.

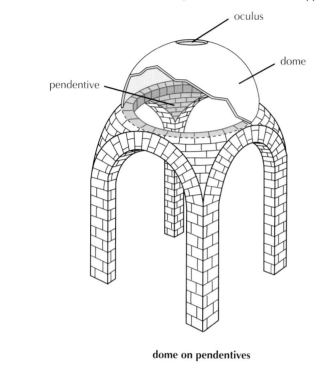

dome on pendentives

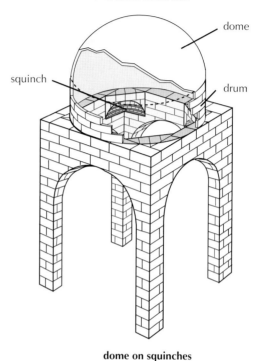

dome on squinches

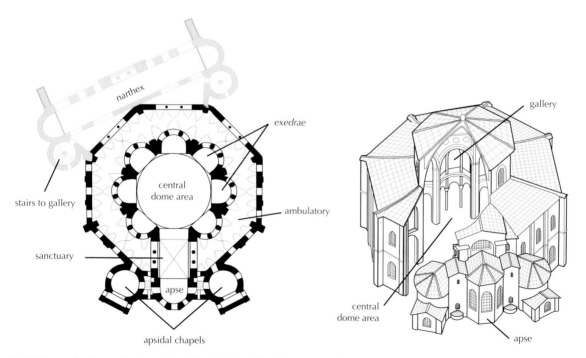

7–14 Plan and cutaway drawing of the Church of San Vitale, Ravenna, Italy. 526–547

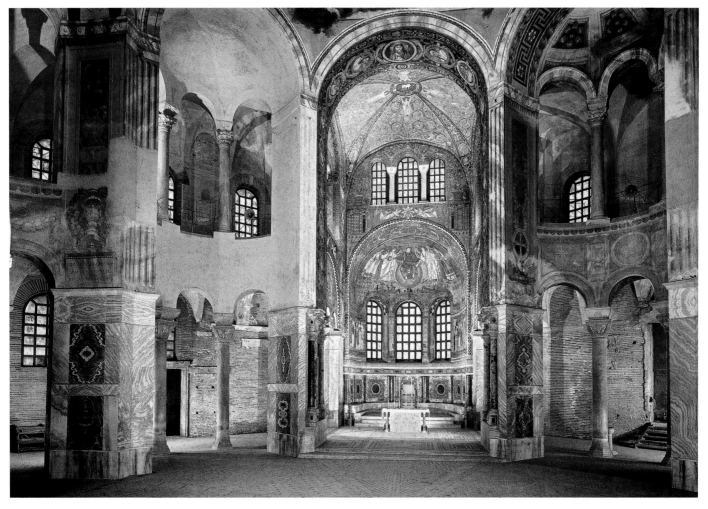

7–15 Church of San Vitale. View across the central space toward the sanctuary apse with mosaic showing Christ enthroned and flanked by Saint Vitalis and Bishop Ecclesius

exedrae and the sanctuary. These two-story exedrae open through arches into outer aisles on the ground floor and into galleries on the second floor. They expand the circular central space and create an airy, floating sensation, reinforced by the liberal use of colored veined marble veneer, colored glass, and gold tesserae in the surface decoration. In the vault over the altar, angels support the Lamb of God, and in the conch of the sanctuary apse, an image of Christ enthroned is flanked by Saint Vitalis and by Bishop Ecclesius, who presents a model of the church to Christ (fig. **7–15**).

SAINT PETER'S, NOTRE-DAME, AND SANTA MARIA MAGGIORE (TRADITIONAL USAGE AND ABBREVIATIONS)

Christian churches always have a dedication—for example, Saint Peter's Church or the Church of Saint Mary. Even when we omit the word *church*, we should add an apostrophe *s* to the saint's name; thus, Saint Mary's. Mary is often called Our Lady (*Notre-Dame* in French). Although many churches are dedicated to Our Lady, the words alone now usually refer to the Cathedral of Paris.

In English, *Saint* is abbreviated *St.*; *Sta.* is used for female saints and *S.* for male saints (plural *SS.*) in Italian; and *Ste.* or *St.* (and joined to the name with a hyphen) is used in French. Relics are material remains or objects associated with the saint to whom the church is dedicated. Relics lie in, on, or under the main altar of the church. The church of Santa Maria Maggiore in Rome has as its chief relic a piece of wood believed to be from the manger where the infant Jesus was born.

The domain of a bishop is called a diocese. Only one church in each diocese can be called a **cathedral**. It is the bishop's primary church and has his throne (in Latin, *cathedra*). Other churches within the diocese, regardless of their size or splendor, are simply called churches. The Lateran Basilica, (dedicated to the two Saint Johns) where the pope presides as the bishop of Rome—not Saint Peter's—is the Cathedral of Rome.

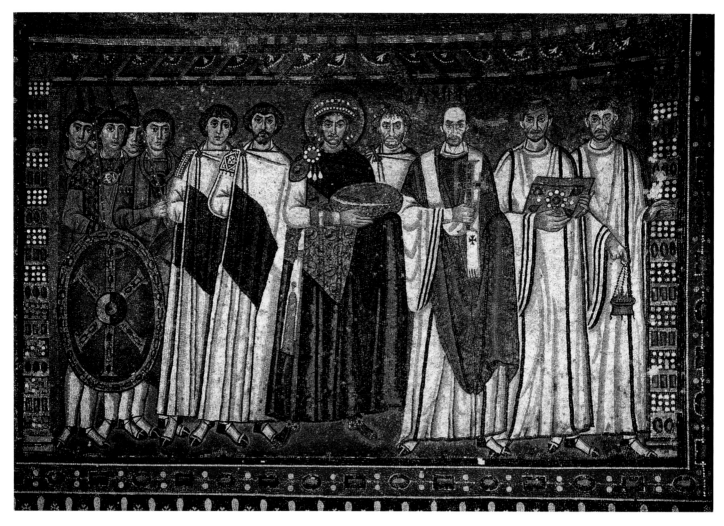

7–16 *Emperor Justinian and His Attendants,* mosaic on north wall of the apse. Church of San Vitale, Ravenna, Italy c. 547. 8'8" × 12' (2.64 × 3.65 m)

As head of state, Justinian wears a huge jeweled crown and a purple cloak; as head of the Church, he carries a large golden paten for the Host. The archbishop at his left holds a jeweled cross and another churchman holds a jewel-covered book. Government officials stand at his right and Justinian's soldiers stand behind a shield decorated with the Chi Rho monogram of Christ. On the opposite wall, Empress Theodora, also dressed in royal purple, offers a golden chalice for the liturgical wine.

Justinian and Theodora may never have set foot in Ravenna, but two large mosaic panels that face each other across the apse make their presences known. In one panel, Justinian (fig. 7–16), accompanied by the bishop and a general, leaders of the church and state, presents the paten (platter) to hold the host. In the other, Theodora, followed by her sisters and ladies of the court, carries a huge golden chalice studded with jewels (fig. 7–17). The rulers present these gifts as precious offerings to Christ—

THE DEPICTION OF SPACE

In Western European art, the picture space appears to open out behind the picture plane (the image-bearing surface). In Byzantine art, images seem to move forward, away from the picture plane, rather than exist within a fictive space behind it (figs. 7–16 and 7–17). The picture space thus lies between the image and the viewer, that is, in front of the wall, panel, or parchment. It is an active space through which sight lines—like beams of light—move, joining image and viewer. This concept forces artists to create so-called "reverse perspective," in which lines perpendicular to the picture plane seem to spread apart. This sense of intimate contact between the viewer and image gives Byzantine art great immediacy and power.

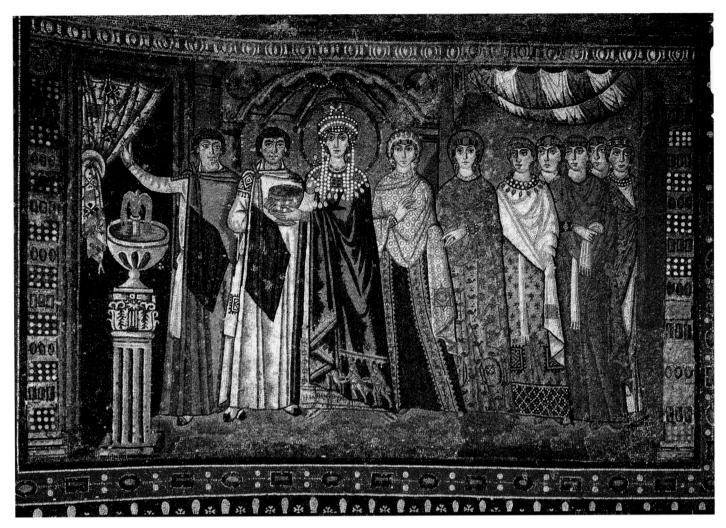

7–17 *Empress Theodora and Her Attendants,* mosaic on south wall of the apse, Church of San Vitale. c. 547. 8′8″ × 12′
(2.64 × 3.65 m)

*Theodora and her ladies wear the rich textiles and jewelry of the Byzantine court. Both men and women dressed in linen or
silk tunics and cloaks. The men's cloaks are fastened on the right shoulder with a fibula (brooch) and are decorated with a rectangular embroidered panel (tablion). Women wore a second full, long-sleeved garment over their tunics and a large rectangular shawl. Like Justinian, Theodora wears imperial purple. Her elaborate jewelry includes a wide collar of embroidered and
jeweled cloth. A crown, hung with long strands of pearls (thought to protect the wearer from disease), frames her face.*

emulating the Magi, wise kings from the East, whom Christians
believe brought valuable gifts to Jesus at his birth. Note that the
three Magi are depicted in the embroidered panel at the bottom
of Theodora's purple cloak. The chalice and paten—holding the
bread and wine—also represent the offering during the Mass, the
religious ceremony performed during communal Christian worship. At the central core of the Mass, the ritual of Eucharist identifies the body and blood of Christ with the substances of bread
and wine, which Jesus had instructed his followers to eat and
drink in remembrance of him.

The group stands beside a fountain at the entrance to the
women's gallery. The open doorway and curtain are classical illusionistic devices, but here the mosaicists deliberately avoided
making them space-creating elements and instead turned them
into flat two-dimensional patterns. Notice, too, that the figures

cast no shadows but stand in pools of yellow light. By the sixth
century, the early interest Christian artists had shown in capturing the appearance of the material world had given way to a
newer, hieratic style: a formal, stately, and static mode of presenting religious imagery with which artists sought to convey a
timeless, supernatural world.

Christians required large numbers of books for religious
services, for public education, and for personal study and meditation. Recall the cabinet holding the four gospels in the Saint
Lawrence lunette (fig. 7–9). A book with a jeweled cover is also
one of Justinian's gifts to San Vitale in figure 7–16. Until the
invention of printing, all books were **manuscripts**—that is, they
were written by hand on **parchment,** specially prepared animal
skin. If they were decorated or illustrated, today we call them
illuminated. During the Byzantine period and the European

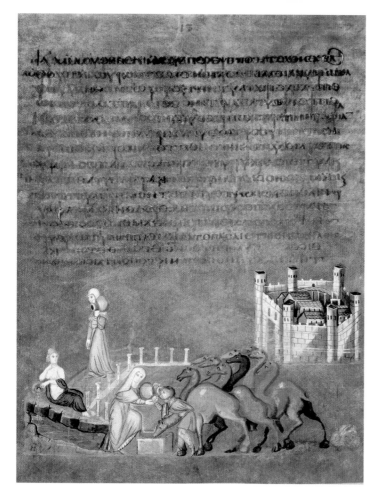

7–18 Page with *Rebecca at the Well,* from *Book of Genesis*, probably made in Syria or Palestine. Early 6th century. Tempera, gold, and silver paint on purple-dyed vellum, 13¹/₂″ × 9⁷/₈″ (33.7 × 25 cm). Österreichische Nationalbibliothek, Vienna

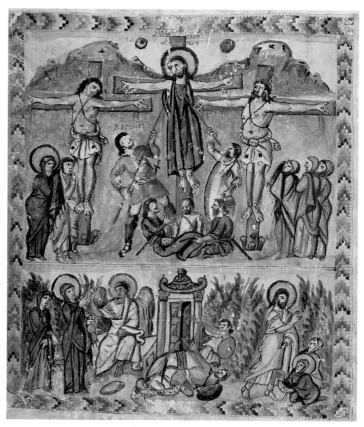

7–19 Page with *The Crucifixion,* from the *Rabbula Gospels,* from Beth Zagba, Syria. 586. 13¹/₄″ × 10¹/₂″ (33.7 × 26.7 cm). Library Medicea Laurenziana, Florence. ms. Plut. 1.56, BML - Settore Riproduzioni, c. 13r
COURTESY OF MINISTERO PER I BENI E LE ATTIVITÀ CULTURALI

Middle Ages, many illuminated manuscripts were made in monasteries and convents, religious communities where devout men and women (monks and nuns) withdrew from the secular world to devote their lives to study and prayer.

The manuscript page (called a **folio**) illustrated in figure **7–18** comes from a book in codex form, written in Greek on purple vellum. The purple color indicates that it may have been done for an imperial patron. Costly purple dye, made from the shells of murex mollusks, usually was restricted to imperial use. Illustrations appear below the text at the bottom of the pages. The story of *Rebecca at the Well* (Genesis 24) appears to be a single scene, but the painter actually mimics the continuous narrative techniques used in scrolls. Events that take place at different times in the story follow in succession. Rebecca, the heroine of the story, appears at the left walking away from the walled city of Nahor with a large jug on her shoulder. She goes to fetch water. A colonnaded road leads to a spring, personified by a reclining pagan water nymph holding a flowing jar. In the foreground, Rebecca, her jug now full, encounters a thirsty camel driver and offers him a drink. He is Abraham's servant Eliezer who is searching for a bride for Abraham's son, Isaac. Her generosity leads to her marriage with Isaac. Although the realistic poses and rounded, full-bodied figures in this painting reflect an earlier Roman painting tradition, the unnatural purple of the

background and the glittering metallic letters of the text remove the scene from the mundane world.

More appropriate to the codex form are the illustrations seen in a Gospel Book signed by a monk named Rabbula and completed in February 586, at a monastery in Beth Zagba, Syria (fig. **7–19**). It depicts crucial events from the life of Jesus. Both upper and lower illustrations are examples of a conventional narrative form. The upper illustration tells the story of the Crucifixion. Jesus was said to be crucified in the company of two criminals, one penitent and the other not. As he died, he was tormented by Roman soldiers: one extending a sponge on a pole with vinegar instead of water for him to drink, another stabbing him in the side with a spear, and others gambling for his clothes. Jesus is dressed in a long purple robe, called a colobium, signifying royal status in the Byzantine world. Jesus's mother, the Virgin Mary, and Saint John the Evangelist watch the Crucifixion at the left.

In the lower register, Jesus's empty tomb stands with open doors, proving that Christ rose from the dead. The soldiers guarding his burial place have fallen asleep. At left, an angel announces the Resurrection to the Marys, and at right, Jesus appears to female followers who came to his tomb. The events take place in an otherworldly setting that is indicated by lush foliage and glowing bands of color in the sky.

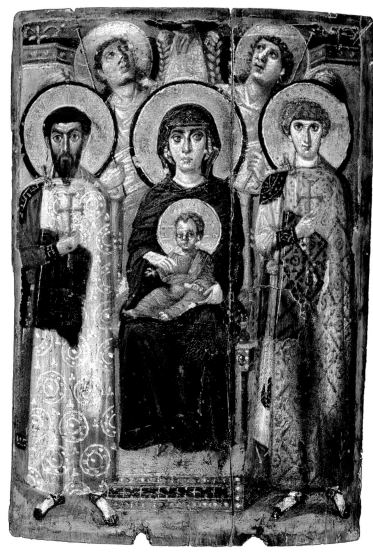

7–20 *Virgin and Child with Saints and Angels,* icon, Monastery of Saint Catherine, Mount Sinai, Egypt. Second half of 6th century. Encaustic on wood, 27″ × 18⁷⁄₈″ (69 × 48 cm)

Icons and Iconoclasm

Many Eastern Christians prayed to Christ, Mary, and the saints while looking at images of them in manuscripts or on painted panels known as **icons.** Church doctrine toward the veneration of icons distinguished between idolatry—the worship of images—and the veneration of an idea or holy person depicted in a work of art. Icons were thus accepted as aids to meditation and prayer; the images were thought to act as intermediaries between worshipers and the holy personages they depicted.

Early icons are rare. Among the finest is the *Virgin and Child with Saints and Angels* (fig. **7–20**). The humble, earthly mother of Jesus, the Virgin Mary was viewed as a powerful intercessor, or go-between, who could appeal to her divine Son for mercy on behalf of repentant Christians. She was called *Theotokos,* bearer of God. She was also called the Seat of Wisdom, and many images of her show her holding Jesus on her lap in a way that suggests that she

has become an imperial throne for her son. In this icon, the Virgin Mary is flanked by the Christian warrior-saints Theodore (left) and George (right), two legendary figures said to have slain dragons. Symbolically the warrior-saints represent the triumph of the Church over the "evil serpent" of paganism. The artist who painted the Christ Child, the Virgin, and the angels worked in an illusionistic, Roman-derived manner and created almost realistic figures. The male saints are more stylized, and the artist barely hints at real bodies beneath the richly patterned textiles of their cloaks.

In the eighth century, in a reaction against the veneration of images known as **iconoclasm,** conservative churchmen ordered icons to be destroyed. A few icons survived in isolated places such as Mount Sinai, Egypt. But icons had played such an important role in popular worship and in people's lives that iconoclasm did not last. In 843 the ruling empress Theodora reinstated the veneration of images, and icons play an increasingly important role in later periods.

Later Byzantine Art

After the defeat of the iconoclasts, a second golden age of Byzantine art began, in 867, under the leadership of an imperial dynasty from Macedonia. The period lasted until Christian Crusaders from the West occupied Constantinople in 1204. The westerners were soon expelled, however, and Byzantine culture flourished once more in the fourteenth and early fifteenth centuries until Muslim Ottoman Turks conquered Constantinople in 1453. At that time Constantinople was renamed Istanbul.

During the tenth, eleventh, and twelfth centuries, artists also produced luxury items for the Byzantine church and court, using precious materials such as silver and gold, jewels and **enamels**, and working them with impeccable skill and aesthetic sensibility. One of the prizes the Crusaders carried to Venice in 1204 was a silver gilt-and-enamel icon of the archangel Michael (fig. **7–21**). The angel's head and hands are executed in relief in the **repoussé** technique (pounded out from the back of the plate). Halo, wings, and garments are detailed in delicate **cloisonné** enamel, and the framing borders are inset with enamel roundels. (Cloisonné is produced by soldering fine wires in the desired pattern to a metal plate and then filling the cells—**cloisons**—with powdered colored glass. When the object is heated, the glass powder melts and fuses onto the surface of the metal to create small, jewel-like sections.) The angel is portrayed as a timeless youth, but the halo and the stylized and dazzling patterns of the wings and bodice remove the image from our physical world. The sheer artistry of this icon seems to lift the image to a plane where light and color supplant form, and material substance becomes pure spirit.

While little Byzantine art survives from Constantinople, the northeastern Italian city of Venice holds many rich treasures of middle and late Byzantine art. At the end of the tenth century, Constantinople granted Venice a special trade status that allowed its merchants to control much of the commercial exchange between Western Europe and the Eastern Empire. With untold wealth flowing into the city's coffers, Venice's ruler, the doge, in 1063 commissioned a splendid church to replace an older chapel holding the relics of the martyred patron saint of Venice, Saint Mark the Apostle. Venetian architects looked to Byzantine domed churches for inspiration, especially the Church of the Holy Apostles in Constantinople. This important church—commemorating Constantine as well as the Apostles—had a Greek cross plan surmounted by domes. The church of St. Mark, as it appeared in the fifteenth century with elaborate portals and tall outer domes, can be seen in Bellini's painting of a procession honoring a miracle-working relic (fig. **7–22**).

The builders of Saint Mark's adopted the plan and covered each of the five square units with a dome on pendentives

---

CHRISTIAN SYMBOLS

Symbols have always played an important part in Christian art. Some were devised just for Christianity, but most were borrowed from pagan and Jewish traditions and adapted for Christian use. The Old Testament **dove** is a symbol of purity, representing peace when it is shown bearing an olive branch. In Christian art, a white dove is the symbolic embodiment of the Holy Spirit. The **fish** was one of the earliest Christian symbols. The first letters of "Jesus Christ, Son of God, Savior" spelled "fish" in Greek. Because of its association with baptism in water, it came to stand for all Christians. The **lamb**, an ancient sacrificial animal, symbolizes Jesus's sacrifice on the cross as the Lamb of God. A flock of sheep represents the apostles—or all Christians—cared for by their Good Shepherd, Jesus Christ. The evangelists who were believed to have written the New Testament Gospels are traditionally associated with the following winged creatures:

Saint Matthew, a man (or angel); Saint Mark, a lion; Saint Luke, an ox; and Saint John, an eagle.

The Cross. The primary Christian emblem, the cross, symbolizes the suffering and triumph of Jesus's crucifixion and resurrection as Christ. It also stands for Jesus Christ himself, as well as the Christian religion as a whole. Crosses have taken various forms. The Latin cross has a long stem; the Greek cross has arms of equal length.

Monograms. Alpha (the first letter of the Greek alphabet) and omega (the last) signify God as the beginning and end of all things. The initials *I* and *X* are the first letters of Jesus and Christ in Greek. The Greek letters *XP* (chi rho) were the first two letters of the word *Christos*. These emblems are sometimes enclosed by a halo or wreath of victory.

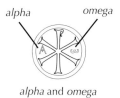

alpha and *omega*

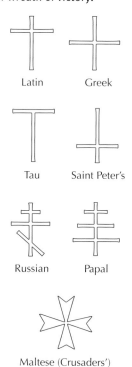

Latin   Greek

Tau   Saint Peter's

Russian   Papal

Maltese (Crusaders')

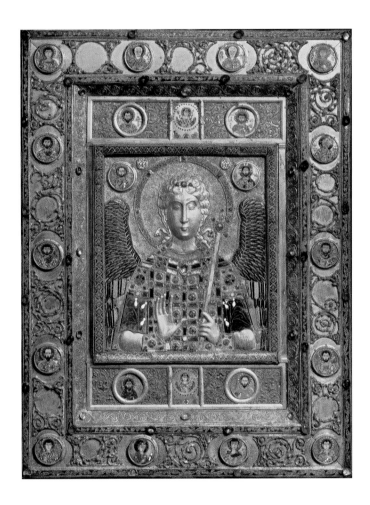

7–21 *Archangel Michael*, icon, 10th century. Silver gilt and enamel, 19″ × 14″ (48 × 36 cm). Treasury of the Cathedral of San Marco, Venice

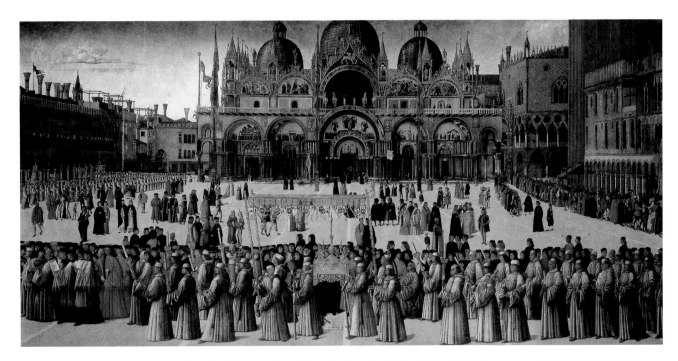

7–22 Gentile Bellini. *Procession of the Relic of the True Cross before the Church of Saint Mark.* 1496. Oil on canvas, 12′ × 24′5″ (3.67 × 7.4 m). Galleria dell'Accademia, Venice

Every year on the Feast of Saint Mark (April 25), the Confraternity of Saint John the Evangelist carried a miracle-working relic of the True Cross in a procession through the square in front of the church. The facade and domes of the church of Saint Mark, as they appeared in the fifteenth century, can be seen in the background of Bellini's painting. The choir leading the procession is followed by marchers carrying giant candles, and the relic in a gold reliquary under a canopy. City officials including the Doge (the ruler) bring up the rear.

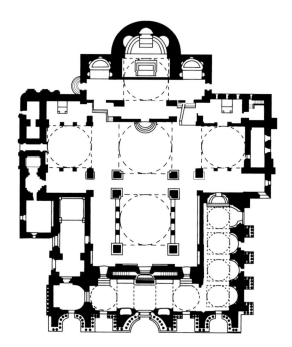

7–23 Plan of the Cathedral of San Marco,
Venice. Begun 1063

(fig. **7–23**). To construct several smaller domes involved less risk than attempting one grand dome. Inside the church, these domed compartments, separated by barrel vaults and lit by circles of windows, produce a complex space in which each individual dome vies for attention in seeming competition with the high altar and choir (fig. **7–24**). The result is that Saint Mark's, and the Holy Apostles before it, lacks the powerful focus of Hagia Sophia, with its sweeping upward and forward movement created by the unity of the single dome. But nevertheless the intricate compartmentalized space of Saint Mark's appealed to later Byzantine builders, and the Greek cross five dome plan was readily adopted as far away as Greece and Ukraine.

Greece lay within the Byzantine Empire in the tenth and eleventh centuries. Two churches of the Monastery of Hosios Loukas (near Stiris) there are excellent examples of later Byzantine architecture (fig. **7–25**). The Katholikon (the major church) is a compact, central-plan structure. Pendentives fill the corners of the cubical core of the building; squinches over

7–24 Cathedral of San Marco, Venice. Present building begun 1063

This church is the third one built on the site. It was both the palace chapel of the doge and the martyrium *that stored the bones of the patron of Venice, Saint Mark. This great multidomed structure, consecrated as a cathedral in 1807, has been reworked continually to the present day.*

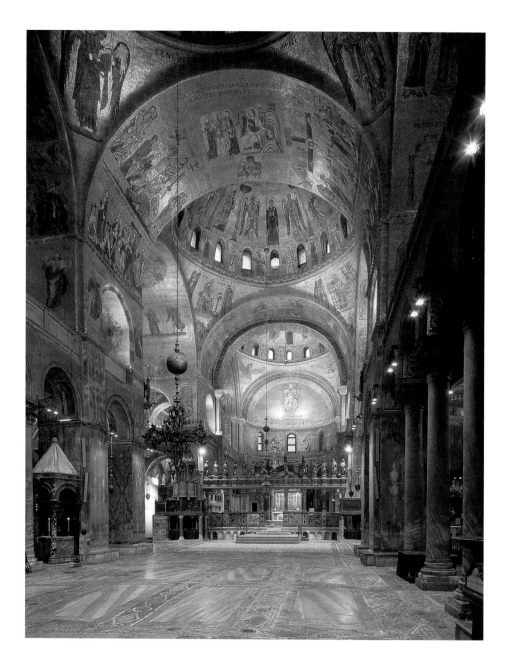

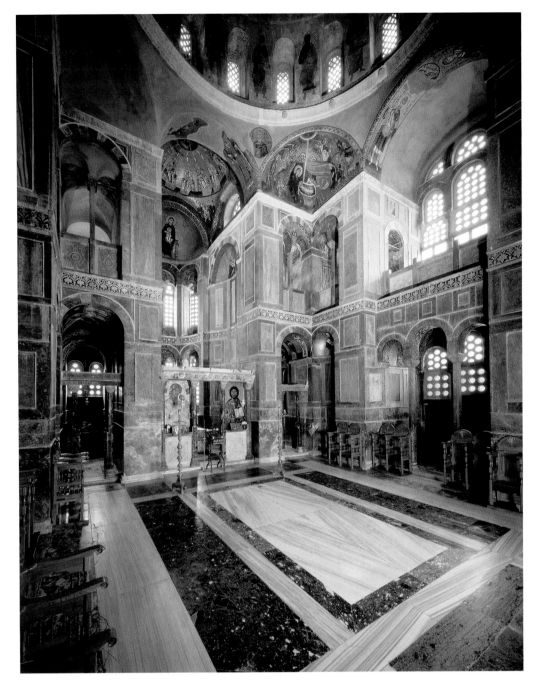

7–25 Central dome and apse, Katholikon, Monastery of Hosios Loukas, near Stiris, Greece. Early 11th century and later

the pendentives and barrel vaults form an octagonal base for the dome. The high central space carries the eye of the worshiper upward into the main dome, which soars above a ring of tall arched windows. The builders of the Katholikon at Hosisos Loukas seem to revel in the complexity. Single, double, and triple windows create intricate and unusual patterns of light. An icon screen (iconostasis) separates the sanctuary from the congregation. The decorative program of mosaics and marble veneers further complicates the space. Visible in figure 7–25 are images of the Virgin and Child in the apse, the Lamb of God surrounded by the Twelve Apostles in the sanctuary dome, and the Nativity in the pendentive (the mosaic of the Pantokrator in the central dome fell and was replaced by a painting).

Ukraine and Russia

The rulers of the Rus (modern Ukraine, Belarus, and Russia) also fell under the spell of Constantinople and adopted Orthodox Christianity. These lands had been settled by Eastern Slavs in the fifth and sixth centuries, but later were ruled by eastern Scandinavian Vikings (the Rus) who established headquarters in the upper Volga regions and in the city of Kiev. The first Christian member of the Kievan ruling family was Princess Olga (c. 890–969), who was baptized in Constantinople by the patriarch himself, with the Byzantine emperor as her godfather.

In the eleventh century, Grand Prince Yaroslav (ruled 1019–1054) founded the Cathedral of Santa Sophia in Kiev (fig. **7–26**). The increasing complexity seen in Greek Byzantine structures culminates in the Ukrainian and Russian churches. In Kiev,

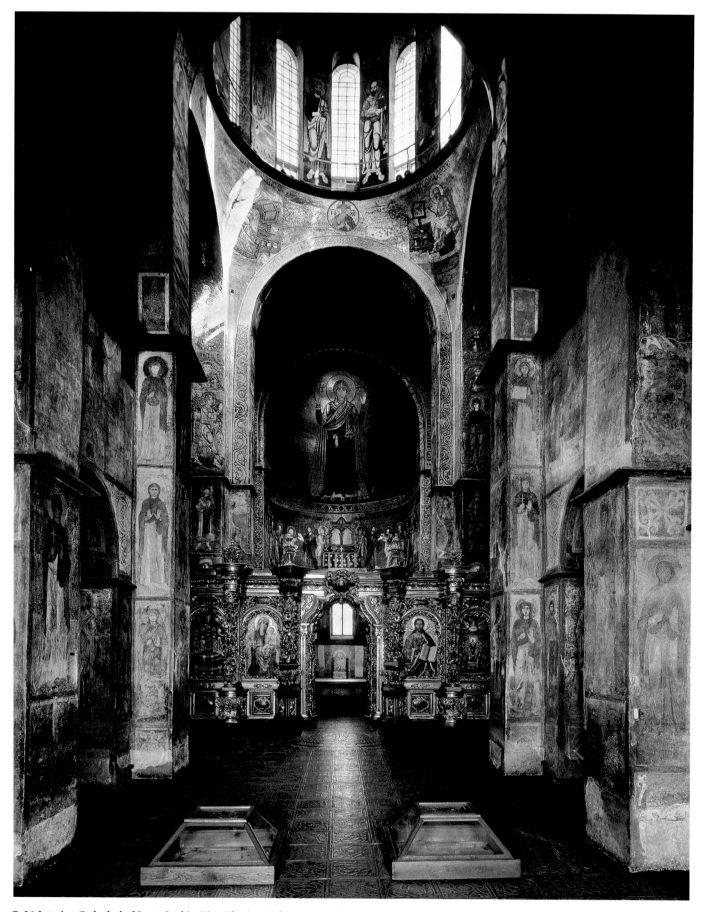

7–26 Interior, Cathedral of Santa Sophia, Kiev, Ukraine. 11th century and later

The view under the dome and into the apse does not convey the quality of the interior as an agglomeration of tall narrow spaces divided by piers whose architectural function is disguised or ignored by elaborate paintings.

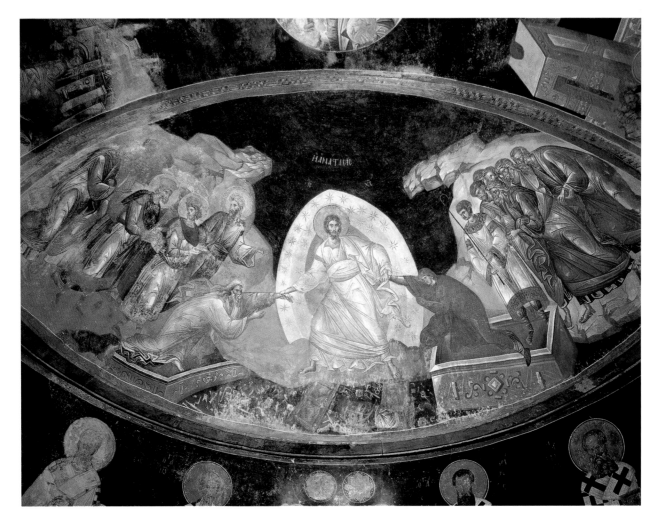

7–27 Anastasis. Painting in the apse of Church of the Monastery of Christ in Chora (now Kariye djami, Istanbul, Turkey). c. 1315–21.
SWAAN PHOTOGRAPH COLLECTION, (96.P.21)

the finished building had double side aisles, five apses, a large central dome, and twelve smaller domes. The small domes were said to represent the twelve apostles gathered around Christ the Pantokrator, symbolized by the central dome. The central domed space of the **crossing** calls attention to the nave and the main apse. The many individual bays, each of which is an almost independent vertical unit, create an often confusing and compartmentalized interior. The interior walls glow with lavish decoration: Mosaics glitter from the central dome, the apse, and the arches of the crossing, and the remaining surfaces are painted with scenes from the lives of Christ, the Virgin, the apostles Peter and Paul, and the archangels.

The design established an iconographical system that came to be followed in Russian Orthodox churches. The *Pantokrator* fills the center of the dome (not visible above the window-pierced drum in figure 7–26). At a lower level, the apostles stand between the windows of the drum, with the Four Evangelists in the pendentives. The Virgin Mary, arms raised in the traditional pose of prayer (an orant figure), seems to float in a golden heaven, filling half dome and upper wall of the apse. In the mosaic on the wall below the Virgin, Christ, appearing not once but twice, accompanied by angels who act as deacons, celebrates Mass at an altar under a canopy, a theme known as the Communion of the

Apostles. He distributes communion to six apostles on each side of the altar. With this extravagant use of costly mosaic, Prince Yaroslav made a powerful political declaration of his own—and the Kievan church's—importance and wealth.

A last great age of Byzantine art began after Crusaders, who occupied Constantinople in 1204, were expelled from the city in 1261. The patronage of emperors, wealthy courtiers, and the Church stimulated renewed church building and renovation. In the early fourteenth century, an elaborately painted funerary chapel was added to the former Church of the Monastery of Christ in Chora, Constantinople (later a mosque and now a museum, Kariye Muzesi). A painting symbolic of the Resurrection of Christ, known as the *Anastasis*, is situated in the apse (fig. **7–27**). Artists in Western Europe usually depicted the Resurrection as the triumphant Christ emerging in glory from his tomb. The Eastern Church instead depicts Christ descending into hell to rescue Adam and Eve and other devout people from Satan. As we see in this example, Christ, dressed in white, is backed by a star-studded **mandorla**, or almond-shaped light. He has trampled down the doors of hell; tied Satan into a helpless bundle; and shattered locks and chains, which lie scattered over the ground. He drags the elderly Adam and Eve from their open sarcophagi with such force that their bodies almost seem airborne.

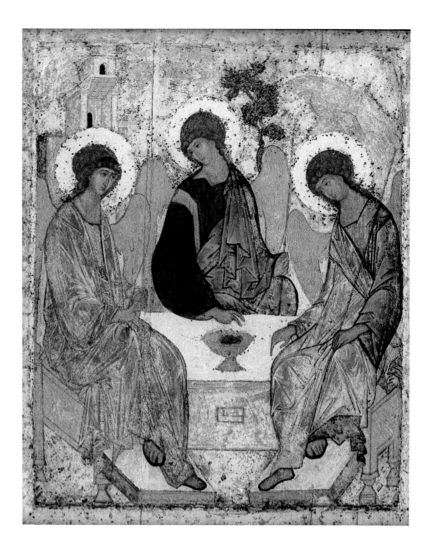

7–28 Andrey Rublyov. *The Old Testament Trinity (Three Angels Visiting Abraham)*, icon. c. 1410–1420 Tempera on panel, 55 ¹/₂″ × 44 ¹/₂″ (141 × 113 cm). Tretyakov Gallery, Moscow

The Late Byzantine period was a time of close commercial ties between the Eastern Empire and Russia. In fact, after Constantinople's fall to the Ottoman Turks in 1453, leadership of the Orthodox Church shifted to Russia. Russian rulers declared Moscow to be the third Rome and themselves the heirs of Caesars (czars).

The practice of venerating icons continued in the Late Byzantine period. Many icons were believed to have been created miraculously and were thought to have magical protective and healing powers. A remarkable icon from this time is *The Old Testament Trinity (Three Angels Visiting Abraham)*, a large panel created between 1410 and 1420 by the famed Russian artist-monk Andrey Rublyov (fig. **7–28**). It was commissioned in honor of the abbot Sergius of the Trinity-Sergius Monastery, near Moscow. The theme represents the dogma of the Trinity, which is a great challenge for artists. One solution used in late medieval works was to show three identical divine individuals—here, three angels—to suggest the idea of the Trinity. The subject was inspired by an Old Testament story of the Hebrew patriarch Abraham and his wife, Sarah, who entertained three strangers who were in fact God represented by three divine beings in human form (Genesis 18). Tiny images of Abraham and Sarah's home and the oak of Mamre can be seen above the angels; on the table, the food they offered to strangers becomes a chalice on an altarlike table. Rublyov conveys a sense of spirituality in this work by using Byzantine conventions, including simple contours, elongation of the body, and a focus on a limited number of figures.

Rublyov's icon clearly illustrates how Late Byzantine artists relied on mathematical conventions to create ideal figures, as did the ancient Greeks, thus giving their work remarkable consistency. Unlike the Greeks, who based their formulas on close observation of nature, however, Byzantine artists invented an ideal geometry to express a heavenly realm and depicted human forms and features according to it. Here, as elsewhere, the circle—most apparent in the haloes—is the basic underlying structure for the composition. Despite the formulaic, somewhat uniform approach, Rublyov—and other talented artists like him—managed to create a personal expressive style. He relied on typical conventions such as simple contours, elongation of the body, and a focus on a limited number of figures to capture the sense of the spiritual in his work, yet he distinguished his art by imbuing it with a sweet, poetic ambience. In his hands, the Byzantine style took on new life.

The Byzantine tradition continues in the art of the Eastern Orthodox Church until today. But in Constantinople, the last of the three golden ages of Byzantine art—and the empire itself—came to a decisive end in 1453 when the forces of the Ottoman sultan Muhammad II overran the capital. The Eastern Empire then became part of the Islamic world, which absorbed aspects of the Byzantine art tradition into a very rich aesthetic heritage of its own.

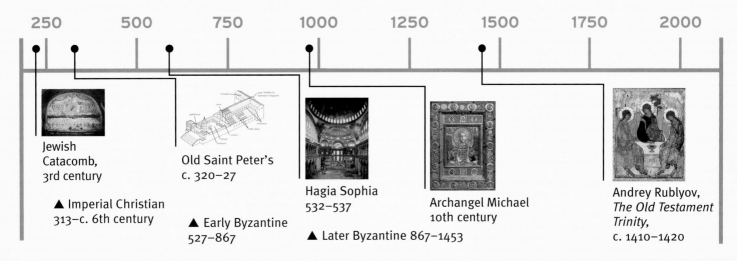

| 250 | 500 | 750 | 1000 | 1250 | 1500 | 1750 | 2000 |

Jewish
Catacomb,
3rd century

Old Saint Peter's
c. 320–27

Hagia Sophia
532–537

Archangel Michael
10th century

Andrey Rublyov,
*The Old Testament
Trinity,*
c. 1410–1420

▲ Imperial Christian
313–c. 6th century

▲ Early Byzantine
527–867

▲ Later Byzantine 867–1453

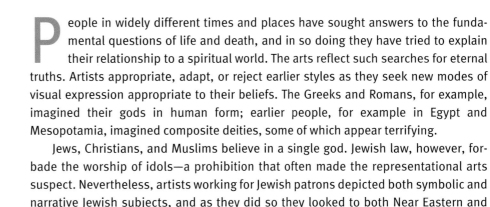

People in widely different times and places have sought answers to the fundamental questions of life and death, and in so doing they have tried to explain their relationship to a spiritual world. The arts reflect such searches for eternal truths. Artists appropriate, adapt, or reject earlier styles as they seek new modes of visual expression appropriate to their beliefs. The Greeks and Romans, for example, imagined their gods in human form; earlier people, for example in Egypt and Mesopotamia, imagined composite deities, some of which appear terrifying.

Jews, Christians, and Muslims believe in a single god. Jewish law, however, forbade the worship of idols—a prohibition that often made the representational arts suspect. Nevertheless, artists working for Jewish patrons depicted both symbolic and narrative Jewish subjects, and as they did so they looked to both Near Eastern and classical Greek and Roman art for inspiration. Christians adopted the Jewish scripture as their Old Testament, and thus Christian artists also respected "the book." Believing that God came to earth as a man, Jesus Christ, they created a powerful figurative art using human beings as expressive symbols. Early Christians were Romans, and their art and architecture was essentially Roman in style and technique. In their earliest art, seen in the Roman catacombs, they depicted scenes of miracles and symbols of salvation. And they began to use the visual arts to instruct the laity as well as to glorify God.

Byzantine art had three "golden ages." The Early Byzantine period, most closely associated with the reign of Emperor Justinian I (527–565), the Middle Byzantine period from the ninth century until 1204, and the Late Byzantine period from 1261 until the empire's fall to Ottoman Turks in 1453. In their painting, Byzantine artists invented an ideal geometry for the depiction of human forms and features, and the Byzantine elite sponsored major scriptoria, or writing rooms, where scribes produced handwritten books.

The rites associated with a religion naturally prompt the development of special buildings—and also specialized books, utensils, and other items. Jewish artists, for example, sometimes converted existing structures into synagogues. Early Christians constructed basilicas covered by simple wooden rafters for their congregations, and they built baptisteries. And the architects of the Byzantine era perfected churches in which glittering domes formed vast, light-filled canopies. Regardless of appearance, the final product in each case is a reflection and an expression both of the spiritual beliefs and of the worldly aspirations of the people who oversaw its construction and who gathered within its walls.

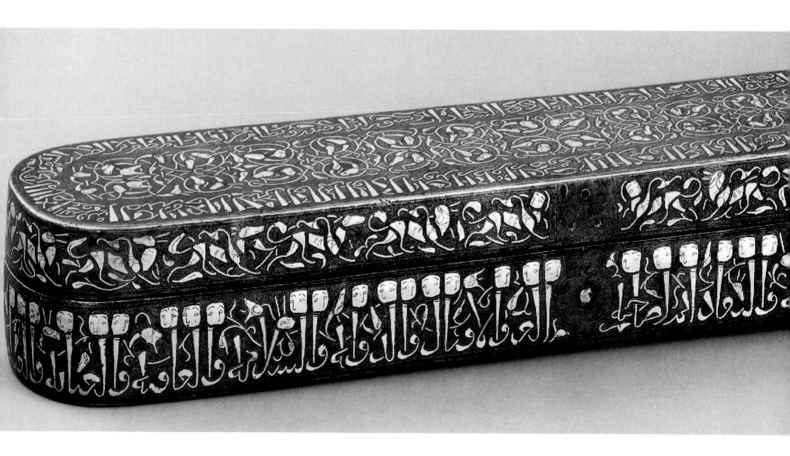

8–1 Shazi. Pen box, from Persia (Iran). 1210–1211. Brass inlaid with silver,
copper, and black organic material, height 2″, length 12 $\frac{5}{8}$ ″, width 2 $\frac{1}{2}$ ″
(5 × 31.4 × 6.4 cm). Freer Gallery of Art, Smithsonian Institution
Washington, D.C.

PURCHASE (F1936.7)

*The inscriptions on the box include some twenty honorific phrases extolling its owner, Majd al-Mulk al-Muzaffar. The inscription in naskhi script on
the lid calls him the "luminous star of Islam." The largest inscription, written in animated naskhi (an animated script is one with human or animal
forms in it), asked twenty-four blessings for him from God. Shazi, the designer of the box, signed and dated it on the side of the lid, making it one of the
earliest signed works in Islamic art. Majd al-Mulk enjoyed his box for only ten years; he was killed by Mongol invaders in 1221.*

8
Islamic Art

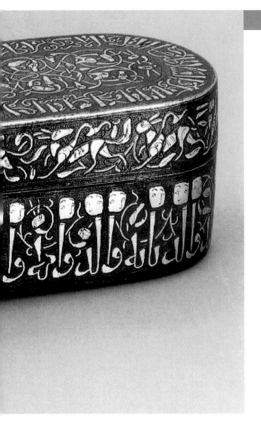

LOOKING FORWARD

Muslim artists and patrons held calligraphy in the highest esteem. Even writing equipment could be wonderfully decorated, and a pen box could be a prestigious possession. This pen box of polished brass, richly inlaid with precious silver, attests to the sophistication and wealth of its owner, Majd al-Mulk al-Muzaffar, a statesman and scholar and the governor of Khorasan, who died in 1221 (fig. **8–1**). The artist Shazi created exceptionally clear and elegant animated inscriptions in two different scripts—kufic and *naskhi*. To some letters he added duck heads and foliage; in the rest of the inscription, he embellished the vertical elements with human heads. Inscriptions on this pen box extol the virtues of the owner and wish him well.

As a "People of the Book"—that is, those whose religion is revealed through sacred scriptures—Muslims (followers of Islam) had cause to honor fine writing. Since the Koran (Qur'an) is believed to be the word of God brought to Muhammad by the angel Gabriel, the words must be accurately preserved and deserve to be embellished. Consequently, calligraphy became the highest form of art in the Muslim world. Writing was not limited to books and documents but was used to adorn surfaces, from walls of buildings to curving brass candlesticks, and from silk textiles to glazed ceramics. Mystics sometimes equated the creation of letters by scribes with the creation of human beings by God, and calligraphy can be so intricate that it seems to be a secret language.

Formal kufic script (after Kufa, a city in Iraq) is blocky and angular, with strong upright strokes and long horizontals. In "foliated kufic," leaves and flowers seem to sprout from the terminals of the letters. Calligraphers later created "animated" scripts, first by adding heads to upright strokes, and later by forming entire letters from figures. Kufic was used for inscriptions on buildings, on metal and wooden objects, and on textiles as well as for writing in ink on paper or vellum.

By the thirteenth century, scribes had developed several forms of cursive writing. Of the six major styles, one extraordinarily beautiful form, known as *naskhi*, was said to have been revealed and taught to scribes in a vision. Even those who cannot read Arabic can enjoy the beauty of the forms. The materials used by the scribes, especially the pens and the inks, had to be as perfect as the script, and thus a pen box became a symbol of scholarly attainment.

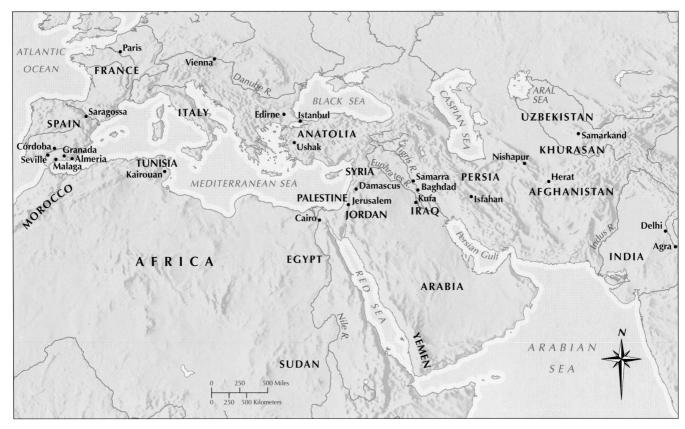

Map 8–1 The Islamic World

The religion called Islam (meaning "submission to [God's will]") originated in Arabia in the early seventh century. Under the leadership of its founder, the Prophet Muhammad (c. 570–632), and his successors, Islam spread rapidly, encompassing much of Africa, Europe, and Asia. Under four of Muhammad's closest associates, who assumed in turn the title of caliph (successor), Muslim armies conquered Persia (Iran), Egypt, and the Byzantine provinces of Syria and Palestine. The last of these caliphs, Ali (ruled 656–661), was succeeded by a rival, Muawiya (ruled 661–680), who founded the Umayyad dynasty. By the early eighth century, the aggressively expansionist Umayyads had reached India, conquered all of North Africa and Spain, and penetrated Europe to within 100 miles of Paris in France before being turned back. Today Islam is the world's fastest growing religion (see Map 8–1, above).

At first, Islamic art reflected local traditions in art and architecture as diverse as Roman, Byzantine, and Persian. Because conservative Muslims discouraged the representation of figures, particularly in religious contexts, artists living in Islamic lands developed a rich vocabulary of nonfigural ornament, including complex geometric designs and the scrolling vines known outside the Islamic world as **arabesques**. Artists excelled in surface decoration, manipulating an infinite variety of highly controlled patterns, and often highlighting the interplay between nonrepresentational designs and organic shapes and forms. For some people, nonrepresentational designs help free the mind from the contemplation of material form, opening the mind to the enormity of divine presence.

Art During the Early Caliphates

Arabic language and script have always held a unique place in Islamic society. As the language of the Koran (Qur'an), Arabic is a powerful unifying force within Islam. From the eighth through the eleventh centuries, Arabic was the universal scholarly language in both Muslim and Christian lands. Reverence for the Koran as the word of God extends by association to the act of writing, and **calligraphy**—the art of fine writing—is one of the glories of Islamic art.

Kufic—the earliest formal script—was angular and probably evolved from inscriptions on stone monuments. A page from a ninth-century Koran exemplifies a style of kufic writing common from the eighth to tenth century (fig. **8–2**). Red diacritical marks (pronunciation guides) accent the dark brown ink. Horizontal strokes are elongated, and fat-bodied letters are emphasized. This Koran is written on vellum, an especially fine parchment (prepared animal skin). Paper, a Chinese invention, was made in the Islamic world by the mid-eighth century but did not fully replace parchment until after the year 1000 (see "Indian Painting on Paper," page 221).

Under caliphs of the Umayyad dynasty (661–750), the political center of the Muslim world moved from the Arabian peninsula to the city of Damascus, in modern Syria. Inspired by the Roman and Byzantine architecture of the eastern Mediterranean, the Muslims became enthusiastic builders of shrines, **mosques**, and palaces. After Mecca and Medina, Jerusalem was the holiest site in Islam. In the center of the city rises the Haram al-Sharif (the Jewish

ISLAM AND THE PROPHET MUHAMMAD

Islam originated in the Arabian peninsula in the seventh century. According to Islamic belief, God (Allah) revealed his message to the archangel Gabriel who transmitted it to an Arab merchant, Muhammad. These revelations form the basis of the Islamic religion. Believers (Muslims) are those who submit to God and acknowledge Muhammad as their Prophet. Muslims also recognize earlier prophets—Moses, Abraham, Jesus—and share with Jews and Christians the belief in one God. Originally God's revelations were committed to memory and passed down orally, but after Muhammad's death an official transcription was made.

The Prophet Muhammad was born about 570 in Mecca, a city in west-central Arabia. Mecca was the site of the Kaaba, an ancient, cube-shaped stone building believed to be the house Abraham built for God. Muhammad received his first revelations in 610 and soon thereafter was accepted as the Prophet of God by his friends and family. After failing to convert the local population, Muhammad and his companions were forced to emigrate in 622 to the oasis of Yathrib, which was renamed Medina, "the [Prophet's] City." It is to this event, called the *Hegira* (emigration), that Muslims date the beginning of their history.

Muhammad regained control of Mecca in 630, and the inhabitants eventually accepted the new religion. The Kaaba in Mecca became Islam's sacred center, toward which Muslims around the world still face when praying. Muhammad died in Medina in 632. Only after his death was the Koran written down and assembled in 114 chapters, or *surahs*, each divided into verses, which make up the sacred scripture of Islam.

Muslims believe in a single, all-powerful God and in Muhammad as the last in the succession of true prophets. Islam also requires Muslims to follow the Five Pillars of Islam, sometimes symbolized by an open hand with five extended fingers. The most important pillar is the statement of faith, "There is no god but God and Muhammad is his messenger."

The second pillar is ritual worship five times a day. (Muslims establish a direct, personal relationship with God through worship. The faithful prostrate themselves facing the Kaaba in Mecca.) The remaining pillars are charity to the poor, fasting during the month of Ramadan, and if possible, a pilgrimage to Mecca. Muslims participate in congregational worship and listen to a sermon at a **mosque** (prayer hall) on Fridays.

A sixteenth-century painting shows Muhammad traveling to a fair, accompanied by his father-in-law, Abu Bakr, and the warrior Ali, the husband of his daughter Fatima. After Muhammad's death, Abu Bakr became the first caliph, or successor to the Prophet. Ali became the fourth caliph. The power struggle that ended in Ali's death led to the division of Islamic communities into Sunni (traditional) and Shi'ite (followers of Ali) Muslims.

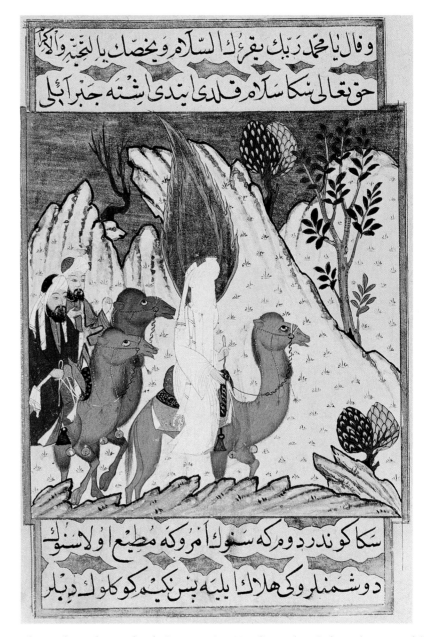

The Prophet Muhammad and His Companions Traveling to the Fair, from a later copy of the *Siyar-i Nabi (Life of the Prophet)* of al-Zarir (14th century), Istanbul, Turkey. 1594. Pigments and gold on paper, 10⅝" × 15" (27 × 38 cm). New York Public Library, New York
SPENCER COLLECTION

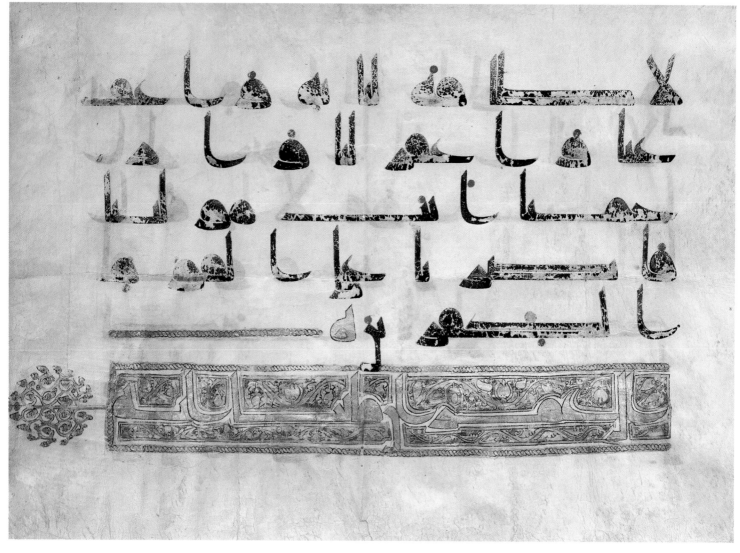

8–2 Page from the Koran (*surah* II: 286 and title *surah* III) in kufic script, from Syria or Iraq. 9th century. Ink, pigments, and gold on vellum, $8\frac{5}{16}'' \times 11\frac{1}{2}''$ (21.1 × 29.2 cm). The Metropolitan Museum of Art, New York

ROGERS FUND, 1937 (37.99.2). PHOTOGRAPH © 1994 THE METROPOLITAN MUSEUM OF ART, NEW YORK

Temple Mount), a rock outcrop that Muslims identify as the place from which Muhammad ascended to the presence of God on the Night Journey mentioned in chapter 17 of the Koran. The same rock face is also associated with the creation of Adam; the place where the patriarch Abraham prepared to sacrifice his son, Isaac, at the command of God; and the site of the temple of Solomon, making it important to Jews and Christians, as well as Muslims.

In 692 the Umayyads constructed a shrine over the rock (fig. **8–3**) using Syrian artisans trained in the Byzantine tradition. The Dome of the Rock is the oldest surviving Islamic building and is decorated on the interior with a mosaic frieze containing the earliest written text of the Koran. Its centralized octagonal plan is derived from both Byzantine and local Christian architecture. Muslim patrons and builders, however, delighted in complex mathematical forms; for example, the plan of the octagonal structure is based on the eight-pointed star, formed by two intersecting squares. The central space is covered by a dome on a tall drum supported by an arcade. Two concentric aisles enclose the rock (fig. **8–4**).

Marble veneer at ground level and glass mosaics above decorate the building's exterior. Originally, glass mosaics also covered the upper half of the octagon's outer walls, but they deteriorated over time. The lower part of the octagon walls retains its original white marble facings, inset with patterns in colored stone. In the sixteenth century the Ottoman Sultan Suleiman ordered the mosaics replaced with magnificent, colorful ceramic tiles, and the Persian and Turkish builders of that time used colorful tiles with consummate skill.

A broad mosaic frieze on the inner wall depicts thick, symmetrical vine scrolls and trees in turquoise, blue, and green, embellished with imitation jewels, over a gold ground. The mosaics are thought to represent both the gardens of Paradise and trophies of Muslim victories offered to God. The focal point of the building, remarkably enough, is not the decorative program—or even something that can be seen. From the entrance one sees only pure light streaming down to the unseen rock, surrounded by color and pattern (fig. **8–5**). After penetrating the space, the viewer/worshiper realizes that the light falls on the

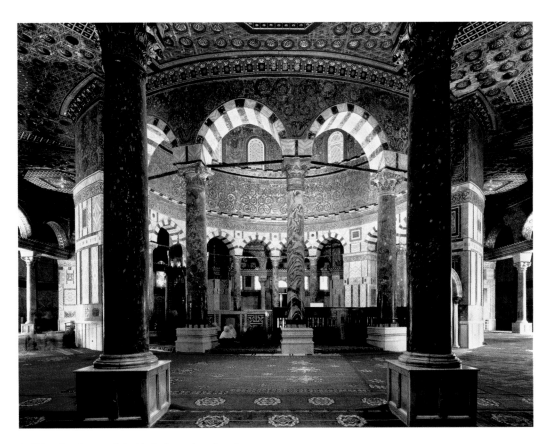

8–3 Dome of the Rock, Jerusalem, Israel. Begun 692

8–4 Cutaway drawing of the Dome of the Rock

8–5 Interior, Dome of the Rock, Jerusalem, Israel

*Concentric **aisles (ambulatories)** permit the devout visitor to circumambulate the rock. Inscriptions from the Koran interspersed with passages from other texts and commentaries, including information about the building, form a frieze around the inner wall in gold mosaic on a turquoise-green ground. The pilgrim must walk around the central space first clockwise and then counterclockwise to read the inscriptions. The carpets and ceiling are modern but probably reflect the original patrons' intention.*

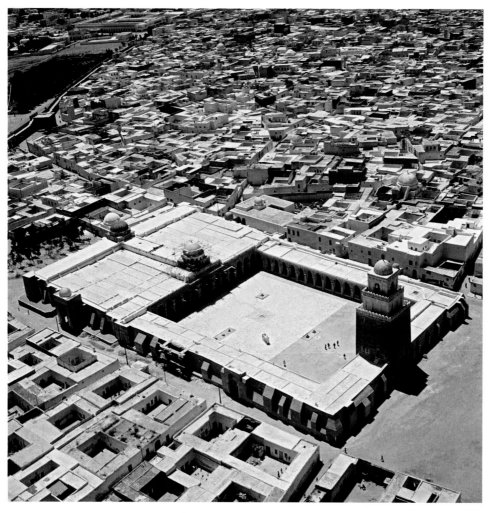

8–6 The Great Mosque. Kairouan, Tunisia. 836–875

precious rock, and in a sense re-creates the passage of Muhammad to the heavens.

The Dome of the Rock is a special shrine. Mosques, in contrast, provide a place for regular public worship. Mosques (in Arabic, *masjid*, a "place of prostration") may have several different plans (see "Mosque Plans," page 198), but they are usually entered through a courtyard, and they must have a large covered space to accommodate the community at Friday prayers. Mosques are oriented in the direction of Mecca *(qibla)*, and worshipers arrange themselves in rows to pray facing Mecca. A niche called a ***mihrab*** identifies the *qibla* wall. The origin and significance of the *mihrab* are debated. A niche signifies a holy place in many religions: niches frame the sculpture of gods or ancestors in Roman architecture, form the shrine for the Torah scrolls in a synagogue, or the apse in a Christian Church. The *maqsura*, an enclosure in front of the *mihrab* for the ruler and other dignitaries, became a feature of the principal congregational mosque after an assassination attempt

on a ruler. The *minbar*, or pulpit/throne, stands by the *mihrab* as a raised platform for the prayer leader and a symbol of his authority (for a fourteenth-century example, see fig. 8–12). The faithful gather for Friday prayers and listen to a sermon in the principal mosque of the city, called the Great Mosque or Friday Mosque (examples can be seen in figs. 8–6 and 8–7).

The earliest mosques were very simple, modeled on Muhammad's house with its courtyard and porticoes. The Prophet spoke to his followers from his raised seat. The Great Mosque of Kairouan, Tunisia (fig. 8–6), although built in the ninth century, reflects the early form of the mosque. Its large rectangular plan is divided between a courtyard and a hypostyle prayer hall with a flat roof. The system of repeated bays and aisles can easily be extended as the congregation grows in size. A huge tower (the **minaret**, from which criers call the faithful to prayer) rises opposite the *mihrab*. Later, one or more minarets came to symbolize Islam's presence in a city.

In 750, the Abbasids overthrew the Umayyads. Abbasid caliphs ruled the central and eastern lands of Islam until 1258 from their capitals at Baghdad and Samarra (in modern Iraq). Their long reign saw great achievements in medicine, mathematics, the natural sciences, philosophy, literature, music, and art.

While the Abbasids ruled the Muslim heartland, the Umayyads controlled the far western lands of Islam. In 750, when the Abbasid caliphs took power, a survivor of the Umayyad dynasty, Abd al-Rahman I, fled across North Africa into southern Spain (known as al-Andalus in Arabic). He established himself there as the provincial ruler, or emir (ruled 756–788). From a new capital at Cordoba, the Umayyads governed al-Andalus until 1031, first as emirs and then, beginning with Abd al-Rahman III (ruled 912–961), as caliphs. Iberian Umayyads set themselves up as equals to the Abbasids. Their court at Cordoba became a renowned center for scholars, scientists, poets, and musicians. They maintained close contacts not just with the Islamic world but also with European and Byzantine rulers.

The finest surviving example of Spanish Umayyad is the Great Mosque of Cordoba. This sprawling structure was begun on the site of a Christian church in 785 and was repeatedly enlarged. The marble columns and capitals in the first hypostyle prayer hall (fig. **8–7**; see also "Mosque Plans," page 198) were recycled from the ruins of classical buildings in the region, formerly a wealthy Roman province. Two tiers of arches, one above the other, surmount the columns. The double-tiered design increases the height of the interior space, stiffens the structure, and creates a light and airy impression. The distinctively shaped horseshoe arches—a form known from ancient Roman times—came to be closely associated with Islamic architecture in the west. At the Great Mosque in Cordoba, these arches are distinguished by the alternation of pale stone voussoirs (wedge-shaped stone blocks) and red bricks. While the alternating colors and textures are decorative, the use of contrasting materials is also functional. The stone gives strength, and the brick lends flexibility and ease in achieving the circular form of the arch. Roman and Byzantine builders also used the technique, but usually in utilitarian structures like defensive walls. The Muslims saw the decorative possibilities of the technique and utilized it for purposes of ornamentation.

In the final century of Umayyad rule, Cordoba emerged as a major commercial and intellectual hub and a flourishing center for the arts. It surpassed Christian European cities economically and in science, literature, and philosophy. Al-Hakam II (ruled 961–76) made the Great Mosque a focus of his patronage, commissioning costly and luxurious renovations that disturbed

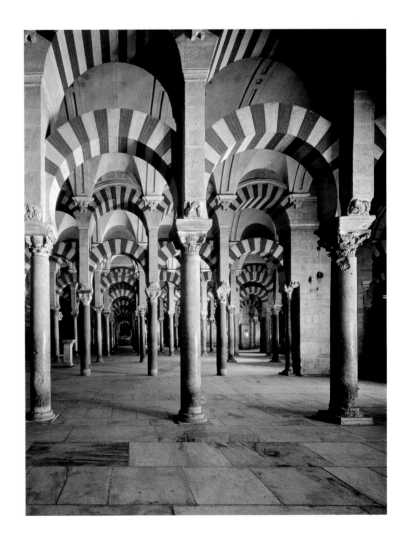

8–7 Prayer hall, Great Mosque, Cordoba, Spain. Begun 785–786

ELEMENTS OF **Architecture**
Mosque Plans

The earliest mosques were **hypostyle halls** at one side of an open courtyard. Rows of closely spaced columns perpendicular to the *qibla* wall support a flat roof. The Great Mosque at Cordoba (see fig. 8–7) is typical.

The *four-iwan* mosque, developed in Persia, is seen in buildings such as the Congregational Mosque at Isfahan (see fig. 8–10). *Iwans*—vaulted halls with monumental arched openings—faced each other across a central court-yard, and related structures spread out and behind the *iwans*.

Central-plan mosques, the last type to develop, were inspired by Istanbul's Byzantine architecture, such as the Church of Hagia Sophia in Istanbul (see figs. 7–11 and 7–13). The Mosque of Selim in Edirne (see fig. 8–19) is characteristic of this style. The large central dome permits the interior space to be uninterrupted by structural supports.

Plans are not to scale

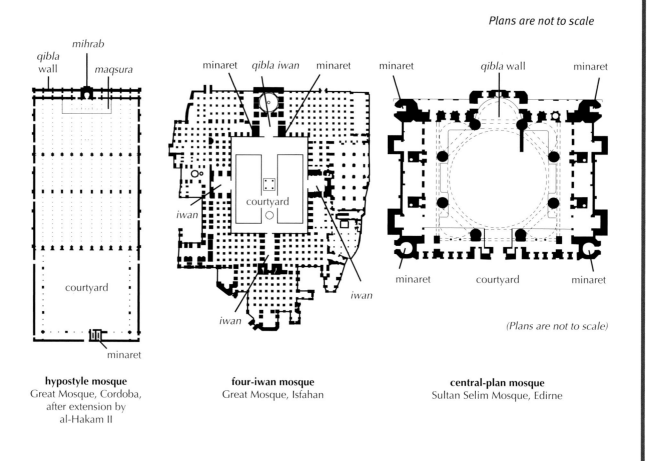

hypostyle mosque
Great Mosque, Cordoba,
after extension by
al-Hakam II

four-iwan mosque
Great Mosque, Isfahan

central-plan mosque
Sultan Selim Mosque, Edirne

(Plans are not to scale)

many of his subjects. The caliph attempted to answer their objections to paying for such ostentation with an inscription giving thanks to God, who "helped him in the building of this eternal place, with the goal of making this mosque more spacious for his subjects, something which both he and they greatly wanted" (Dodds, page 23).

The renovations to the Great Mosque by Caliph al Hakam II in the tenth century included enlargements and a new *mihrab* with a richly decorated *maqsura*, the protected space for the ruler. In front of the *mihrab*, melon-shaped, ribbed domes seem to float over intersecting arches (fig. 8–8). The arches are placed diagonally over the corners of a space to provide a base for a dome whose surface is covered with arabesques, geometric motifs, and stylized vegetation and inscriptions. In conscious competition with the Byzantines and the Abbasids, the Cordoban Umayyads employed mosaic decoration. Since the technique was not practiced in Spain, they acquired materials and the artisans from Byzantium to do the work.

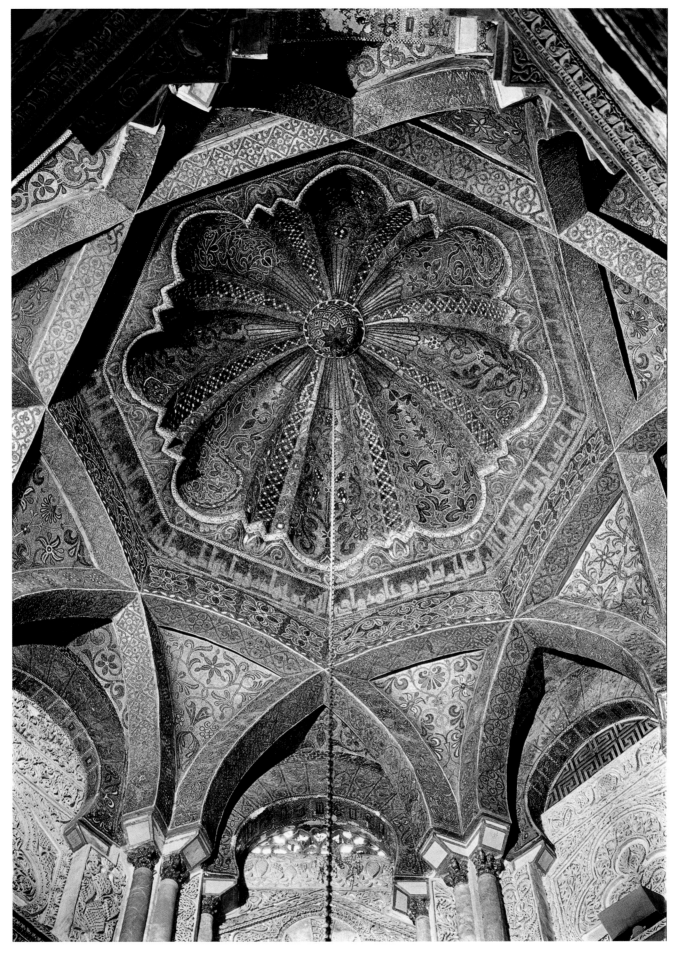

8–8 Dome in front of the *mihrab*, Great Mosque. 965

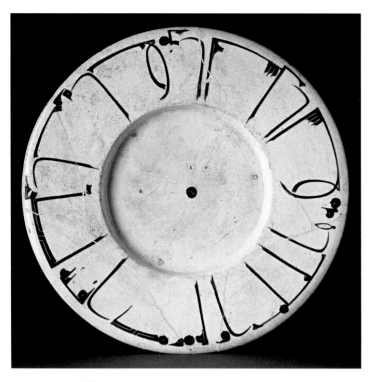

8–9 Bowl with kufic border, Samarkand, Uzbekistan. 9th–10th century. Earthenware with slip, pigment, and glaze, diameter 14 ¹/₂″ (37 cm). Musée du Louvre, Paris

The white ground of this piece imitated prized Chinese porcelains made of fine white kaolin clay. Samarkand was connected to the Silk Route (see Chapter 3, page 77), the great caravan route to China, and was influenced by Chinese culture.

Muslims in Spain had closer commercial and diplomatic associations with local Christians than with those in far-off Byzantium. After the Muslim conquest of Spain, Christians and Jews who did not convert to Islam but acknowledged the authority of the new rulers and paid the taxes required of non-Muslims were usually left free to follow their own religious practices. Christians in the Arab territories were called Mozarabs (from the Arabic *mustarib*, meaning "would-be Arab"). The conquest resulted in a rich exchange of artistic influences between the Islamic and Christian communities. Christian artists adapted many features of Islamic style to their traditional designs, creating a unique, colorful new style known today as Mozarabic.

Calligraphy remained a major form of decoration for architecture, manuscripts, and on all kinds of functional objects, such as bowls and platters. Kufic-style letters decorate the ceramics made in the ninth and tenth centuries, even in distant centers like Nishapur (in modern northeastern Iran) and Samarkand (in modern Uzbekistan in Central Asia). Now known as Samarkand ware, these pieces are characterized by a clear lead glaze applied over a black inscription on a white, slip-painted ceramic ground (fig. **8–9**). The script has been elongated to fill the bowl's rim, stressing the letters' verticality. The inscription translates: "Knowledge, the beginning of it is bitter to taste, but the end is sweeter than honey." Inscriptions on Samarkand ware provide a storehouse of such popular sayings and folk wisdom.

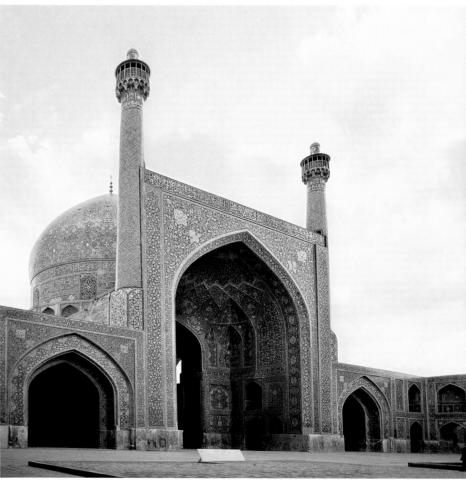

8–10 Courtyard, Masjid-i Jami (Great Mosque), Isfahan, Persia (Iran). 11th–18th century. View from the northeast

Later Islamic Art

In the eleventh century, power in the Islamic world fell into the hands of more or less independent regional rulers. As the Abbasid caliphate disintegrated, one branch of the Seljuks, a Turkic people who converted to Islam in the tenth century, rose to power. The kingdoms gained control of Persia in 1038–40 and took over the Abbasid capital city of Baghdad in 1055, where the Abbasids survived as token rulers until 1258. In 1071 Seljuk Turks defeated the Byzantine army and soon held most of the eastern Mediterranean including Anatolia (modern Turkey). In the west, Umayyad Spain broke up into small kingdoms centered around major cities such as Saragossa, Málaga, Granada, and Seville. They engaged in constant warfare with Christian armies, determined to expel them from the Iberian peninsula. This military action (or reconquest as the Christians call it) continued over a 400-year period, ending only in 1492 with the overthrow of the Nasrid dynasty in the Kingdom of Granada.

The Seljuk rulers proved themselves enlightened patrons of the arts. They built on a grand scale—mosques, *madrasas* (schools for advanced study), palaces, and hostels and trading stations for merchants. They adopted the Persian *iwan*, a vaulted open room (see "Mosque Plans," page 198), and they perfected a mosque/madrasas plan in which four *iwans* are arranged around a courtyard. The Great Mosque in the Seljuk capital of Isfahan (modern Iran) has a four-iwan plan (fig. **8–10**). The *qibla iwan* on the south was vaulted with *muqarnas* (niche-like cells) in the fourteenth century. The tall, slender minarets and brilliant blue tiles were added in the seventeenth century.

Tile work—another highlight of Islamic art—can be seen in a fourteenth-century tile mosaic *mihrab* originally from a *madrasa* in Isfahan (fig. **8–11**). More than 11 feet tall, the *mihrab* was made by painstakingly cutting each piece of tile,

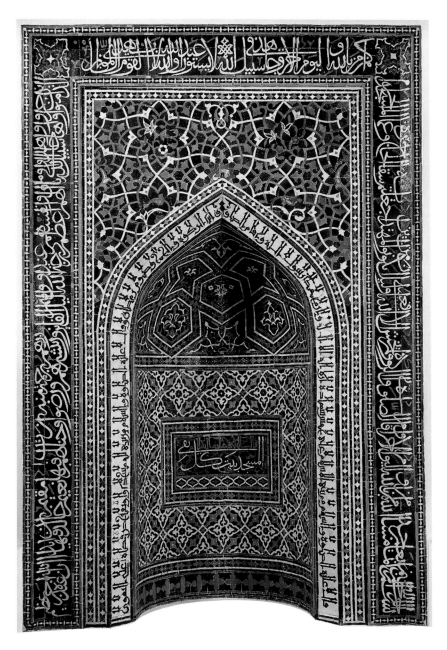

8–11 Tile mosaic *mihrab*, from the Madrasa Imami, Isfahan, Persia (Iran). c. 1354 (restored). Glazed and cut ceramic, 11'3" × 7'6" (3.43 × 2.29 cm). The Metropolitan Museum of Art, New York
HARRIS BRISBANE DICK FUND (39.20). PHOTOGRAPH © 1982 THE METROPOLITAN MUSEUM OF ART, NEW YORK

One of the three Koranic inscriptions on this mihrab *dates it to approximately 1354. Note the combination of decorated kufic (inner inscription) and cursive* muhaqqaq *(outer inscription) scripts. The outer inscription tells of the duties of believers and the heavenly rewards for the builders of mosques. The next (kufic) gives the Five Pillars of Islam. The center panel says: "The mosque is the house of every pious person."*

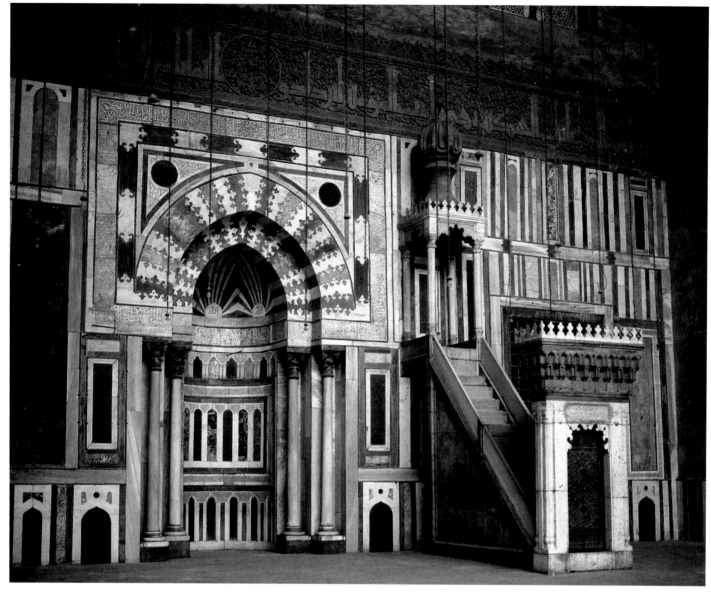

8–12 *Qibla* **wall with** *mihrab* **and** *minbar,* main *iwan* (vaulted chamber in a mosque), Sultan Hasan madrasa-mausoleum-mosque, Cairo, Egypt. 1356–1363

including the pieces making up the calligraphy on the curving surface of the niche, and setting them in mortar. The harmonious, dense patterns include organic and geometric forms that contrast with the inscriptions. The colors—white against turquoise and cobalt blue with accents of dark yellow and green—are characteristic of Islamic tilework art.

In a madrasa-mausoleum-mosque complex built in the mid-fourteenth century by the Mamluk Sultan Hasan in Cairo, Egypt, *iwans* functioned as classrooms with students housed in neighboring rooms (fig. **8–12**). The largest of the four iwans serves as the mosque for the complex, and Hasan's domed tomb lies behind the *qibla* wall. The walls and vaults inside the mosque are plain except for a wide stucco frieze. Originally painted, this frieze combines calligraphy and intricate carved scrollwork. Marble panels cover the *qibla* wall and a double-arched *mihrab*. Slender

columns support pointed arches. Marble inlays create blue, red, and white stripes on the voussoirs, a fanciful echo of the brick and stone voussoirs of Umayyad architecture. The throne-like *minbar* at the right of the *mihrab* is of carved stone, although the door is elaborately carved wood.

Muslim architects also created luxurious palaces set in beautiful gardens, such as the well-preserved medieval palace in Granada, Spain: the Alhambra. A fortified hilltop palace complex, it was the home of the Nasrids, who ruled the provinces of Almería, Málaga, and Granada from 1232 to 1492. The Alhambra gained its present form in the fourteenth century. The builders combined a fortress, royal residences, and city, including mosques, baths, servants' quarters, barracks, stables, workshops, and a mint. The Alhambra extends for about half a mile along the crest of a high hill overlooking Granada.

An especially luxurious section of the palace is the Palace of the Lions, a private retreat built by Muhammad V (ruled 1362–1391). At its heart is the rectangular Court of the Lions (fig. **8–13**), named for a fountain whose basin is supported by stylized stone lions. The patio is surrounded by small, richly decorated rooms. Although the central courtyard is filled with gravel today, it was originally a sunken garden with raised fountains and waterways. Aromatic shrubs, flowers, and small citrus trees were planted between the water channels that radiate from the fountain—evocative of the rivers of paradise—and divide the courtyard into quarters. The architectural focus of the Alhambra was largely directed inward, toward these lushly planted courtyards, which embody the Muslim vision of paradise as a well-watered, walled garden. Indeed, the English word *paradise* comes from *pairidiz*, the old Persian term for an enclosed park.

Pavilions used for dining and the performance of music and poetry open onto the Court of the Lions. One of these, the so-called Hall of the Abencerrajes, on the south side (probably a music room) is covered by a spectacularly intricate ceiling

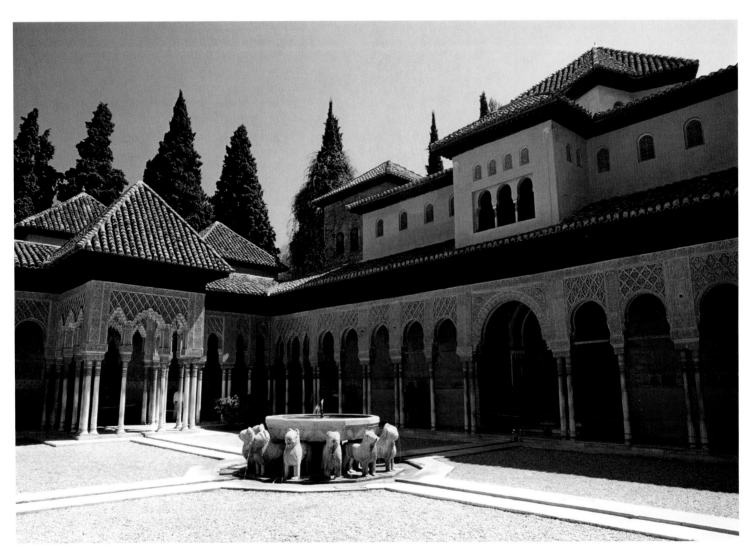

8–13 Court of the Lions, Palace of the Lions (*Palacio de los Leones*), Alhambra, Granada, Spain. Begun c. 1380

Granada, with its ample water supply, had long been known as a city of gardens. The twelve stone lions in the fountain in the center of this court were salvaged from the ruins of an earlier palatial complex on the Alhambra hill. The earlier structure was begun in the late eleventh century by a high Granadan official of Jewish heritage named Samuel ibn Naghralla and completed by his son Yusuf in the early twelfth century. Commentators of the time praised this complex, with its pools, fountains, and gardens. No doubt it was a source of inspiration for the builders of the later palaces.

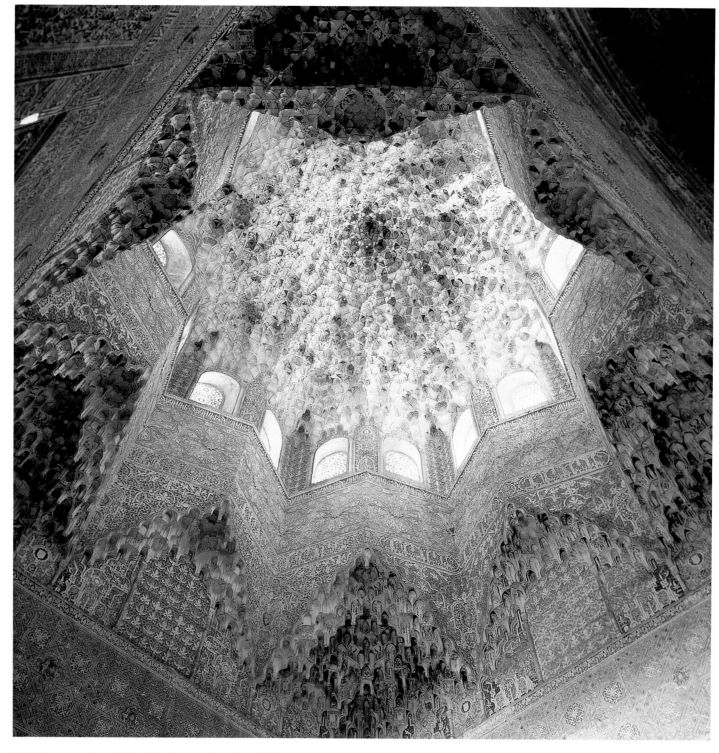

8–14 *Muqarnas* dome, Hall of the Abencerrajes, Palace of the Lions, Alhambra, 1354–1391

*Structurally, **muqarnas** are small nichelike components unique to Islamic architecture. Muqarnas are used in multiples as interlocking load-bearing, vaulting units. Over time they became increasingly ornamental and appeared as intricately faceted surfaces. They are frequently used to vault* mihrabs *and, on a larger scale, to support and to form domes.*

(fig. **8–14**). The eight-pointed-star–shaped dome rests on clusters of small squinches, or niche-like cells *(muqarnas)*, and a honeycomb of *muqarnas* also covers the dome. The effect is like architectural lace. Here the material form becomes an immaterial illusion of heavenly light.

In this cosmopolitan Islamic society, not only palaces but portable objects made with exquisite craftsmanship were valued for their beauty and usefulness, and for the status they bestowed on their owners. Glass, made with the most ordinary ingredients—sand and ash—becomes the most ethereal of materials.

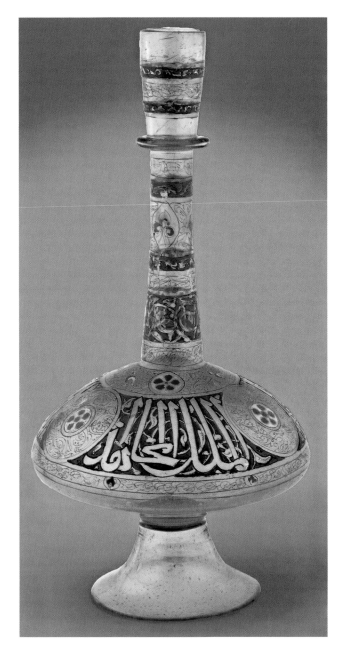

8–15 Bottle, from Syria. Mid-14th century. Blown glass with enamels and gilding, $19\frac{1}{26}'' \times 9\frac{3}{4}''$ (49.7 × 24.8 cm). Freer Gallery of Art, Smithsonian Institution, Washington, D.C.
PURCHASE, F1934.20

According to the twelfth-century poet al-Hariri, glass is "congealed of air, condensed of sunbeam motes, molded of the light of the open plain, or peeled from a white pearl" (Jenkins, page 3). Glassmakers generally adapted earlier practices to new forms because the tools and techniques of making glass have changed very little since ancient times. A tall, elegant enameled bottle from the mid-fourteenth century exemplifies their skill in the application of enameled decoration in gold and various colors (fig. **8–15**). Probably made in a Syrian workshop, it bears a large inscription in cursive script naming and honoring its owner, a sultan from Yemen. The five-petaled red rosette is an insignia of the Yemeni dynasty.

Educated leaders administering the lands for caliphs and emirs commissioned pieces in glass, metal, ivory, and precious stones. Like glassmakers, metalworkers inherited the techniques of their Roman, Byzantine, and Sassanian predecessors, applying their artistic heritage to new forms. Personalized containers for pens, ink, and blotting sand became emblems of the educated

class. One such container is the inlaid brass box belonging to Majd al-Mulk al-Muzaffar (see fig. 8–1). An artist named Shazi cast, engraved, embossed, and inlaid the box with consummate skill. Scrolls, interlacing designs, and human and bird heads enliven its calligraphic inscriptions. All these elements, animate as well as inanimate, seem to be engaged in a lively exchange. That a work of such quality was made of brass rather than a costlier metal may seem surprising. A severe silver shortage in the mid-twelfth century may have prompted the development of inlaid brass pieces like this one that used the more precious metal sparingly. Humbler plain brass ware would have been available in the marketplace for those of more modest means than the vizier.

Rugs and mats have long been used for Muslim prayer, which involves repeatedly prostrating oneself (kneeling and touching the forehead to the floor) before God. Many mosques were literally "carpeted" with wool-pile rugs received as pious donations; wealthy patrons gave large prayer rugs. Since the late Middle Ages, carpets have been the Islamic art form best known

Technique

Carpet Making

Because textiles, especially floor coverings, are destroyed through use, very few carpets from before the sixteenth century have survived. There are two basic types of carpets: flat-weaves and pile, or knotted. Both can be made on either vertical or horizontal looms. The best-known flat-weaves today are Turkish kilims, which are typically woven in wool with bold, geometric patterns and sometimes with embroidered details. Kilim weaving is done in a tapestry technique called slit tapestry (see diagram a).

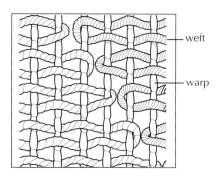

a. Kilim weaving pattern used in flat-weaving

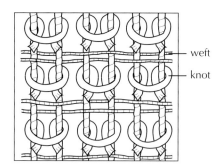

b. Symmetrical knot, used extensively in Iran

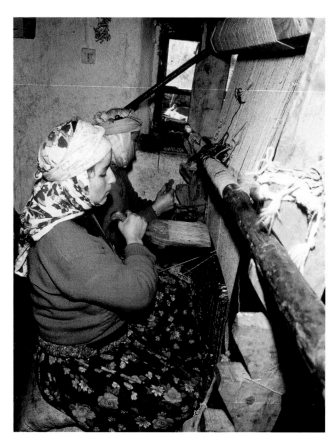

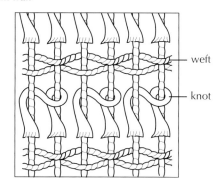

c. Asymmetrical knot, used extensively in Turkey

in Europe. Rugs from Persia, Turkey, and elsewhere were highly prized among Westerners, who often displayed them on tables rather than floors.

A carpet from Ushak in western Anatolia (modern Turkey), created in the first half of the sixteenth century, retains its wonderful colors (see box above). Large, deeply serrated quatrefoil medallions establish the underlying star pattern, but arabesques flow in every direction. This "infinite arabesque", as it is called by experts (the pattern repeats infinitely in all directions), is characteristic of Ushak carpets. Carpets were usually at least three times

as long as they were wide; the asymmetry of this carpet may indicate that the carpet was shortened.

The art of book production also flourished in Muslim countries. Islam's emphasis on the study of the Koran created a high level of literacy among both women and men in Muslim societies. Books on a wide range of secular as well as religious subjects were available, although even books copied on paper were fairly costly. Libraries, often associated with *madrasas*, were endowed by members of the educated elite. Books made for royal patrons had luxurious bindings and highly embellished

Knotted carpets are an ancient invention. The oldest known example, excavated in Siberia and dating to the fourth or fifth century BCE, has designs evocative of Achaemenid Persian art, suggesting that the technique may have originated in Central Asia. In knotted carpets, the pile—the plush, thickly tufted sur-face—is made by tying colored strands of yarn, usually wool but occasionally silk for deluxe carpets, onto the vertical elements (warp) of a yarn grid (b or c). These knotted loops are later trimmed and sheared to form the plush surface of the carpet. The wefts (crosswise threads) are shot horizontally, usually twice, after each row of knots is tied, to hold the knots in place and to form the horizontal element common to all woven structures. The weft is usually an undyed yarn and is hidden by the colored knots. Two common tying techniques are the symmetrical knot extensively used in Iran (including Sehna, the name usually given to this knot) which works well for straight-line designs (b), and the asymmetrical knot used extensively in Turkey, useful for rendering curvilinear patterns (c). The greater the number of knots, the shorter the pile. The finest carpets have up to 2,400 knots per square inch, each one tied separately by hand.

Although royal workshops produced the most luxurious carpets, most knotted rugs have traditionally been made in tents and homes. Carpets were woven by either women or men, depending on local custom. The photograph in this box shows two women, sisters in Çanakkala province in Turkey, weaving a large carpet in a typical Turkish pattern. The woman in the foreground pushes a row of knots tightly against the row below it with a wood comb called a beater. The other woman pulls a dark red weft yarn against the warp threads before tying a knot. Working between September and May, these women may weave five carpets, tying up to 5,000 knots a day. A Çanakkala rug will usually have only 40–50 knots per square inch. Generally, an older woman works with a young girl, who learns the art of carpet weaving at the loom and eventually passes it on to the next generation.

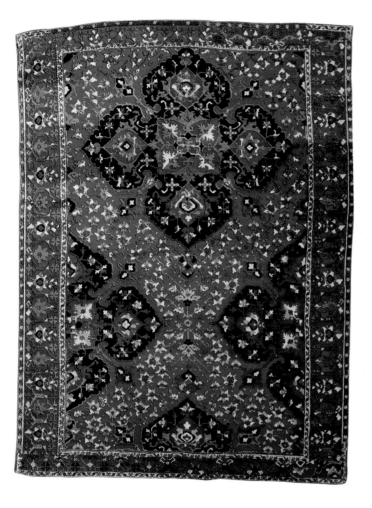

Medallion Rug, **Variant Star Ushak style.** Anatolia (modern Turkey). 16th century. Wool, 10′3″ × 7′6¼″ (313.7 × 229.2 cm). Saint Louis Art Museum

JAMES F. BALLARD COLLECTION/Z. PERKINS

pages, the result of workshop collaboration between noted cal-ligraphers and illuminators. New scripts were developed for new literary forms.

In addition to religious works, scribes copied and recopied famous secular texts—scientific treatises, manuals of all kinds, fiction, and especially poetry. Painters supplied illustrations for these books, and they later created individual small-scale paint-ings—miniatures—that were collected by the wealthy and placed in albums. One of the great royal centers of miniature painting was at Herat (in modern Afghanistan). A school of painting and calligraphy was founded there in the early fifteenth century under the cultured patronage of the Timurid dynasty (1370–1507).

Prince Baysonghur held court in Herat. A great patron of painting and calligraphy, he commissioned superb illuminated manuscripts. The story of the Sassanian prince Bahram Gur, who married seven princesses, one for each night of the week, had been told in poems by the twelfth-century Persian mystic poet Nizami. The painting of *Bahram Gur with the Indian Princess in Her Black Pavilion* illustrates the lyrical idealism that

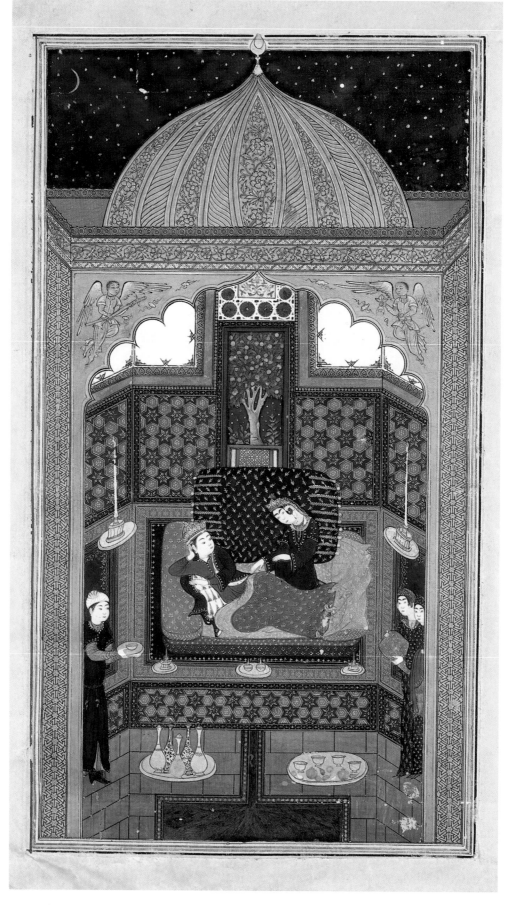

8–16 Bahram Gur with the Indian Princess in Her Black Pavilion. Folio 23 from a *Haft Paykar (Seven Portraits)*, by Nizami. Herat Afghanistan. c. 1426. Color and gilt on paper, 8⅝″ × 4⅝″ (20.9 × 11.7 cm). The Metropolitan Museum of Art, New York

characterized the Timurid style (fig. 8–16). Although the scene takes place at night, the colors are clear and bright without a trace of shadow. The night sky with stars and moon and the two tall candles in the pavilion signal to the viewer that night has fallen. The interior of the black pavilion is decorated with brilliant blue tiles, and through a central opening a garden in bloom can be seen. In the foreground a stream of silver water runs into a silver pool (however the silver has now tarnished to black). Note that the viewpoint shifts; the pavilion, tiled walls and step, the huge pillow, and the items on trays are seen straight on, while the floor, pool, platform, and bed are seen from a **bird's-eye view**. Obviously, the artists delighted in the representation of intricate decorative details, especially the tiles, fabrics, and the garden foliage architectural border. The amorous couple and their servants with their round, impassive faces become part of the idealized world of Persian miniatures.

The Mughal Empire

Islam first touched the Indian subcontinent in the eighth century, when Arab armies captured a small territory near the Indus River. In the eleventh century, the Turks began a war of conquest, and—by the beginning of the thirteenth century—Turkic dynasties ruled portions of the subcontinent from the northern city of Delhi. Although these early dynasties left their mark, it was in the sixteenth and seventeenth centuries that the Mughals made a lasting impression on Indian art.

The Mughals originally came from Central Asia. The first Mughal emperor, Babur (ruled 1526–1530), conquered an empire stretching from Afghanistan to Delhi. Later Akbar (ruled 1556–1605), the third ruler, extended Mughal control over most of northern India. His grandson Shah Jahan (ruled 1628–1658) unified the empire.

Probably no one had more impact on the arts than the emperor Akbar. Known as a dynamic, humane, and just leader, Akbar loved the arts, especially painting. He created an imperial workshop of painters, which he placed under the direction of two artists from the Persian court. Learning from these masters, the Mughal painters soon transformed the lyrical, idealized Persian styles into a vigorous, naturalistic style.

One of the most famous and extraordinary works produced in Akbar's **atelier** is an illustrated manuscript of the *Hamza-nama*, a Persian classic about the adventures of Hamza, uncle of the Prophet Muhammad. Painted on cotton cloth, each illustration is 30 inches high. The entire project gathered 1,400 illustrations into 12 volumes and took 15 years to complete.

One illustration shows Hamza's spies scaling a fortress wall and surprising some men as they sleep (fig. **8–17**). One man climbs a rope, another has already beheaded a figure in yellow and lifts his head aloft—realistic details characteristic of Mughal painting. The architecture, viewed from a slightly elevated vantage point, provides a three-dimensional setting, yet the sense of depth is boldly undercut by the flat geometric patterns of the tile work. The energy exuded by the large human figures is also characteristic of painting under Akbar—even the sleepers seem

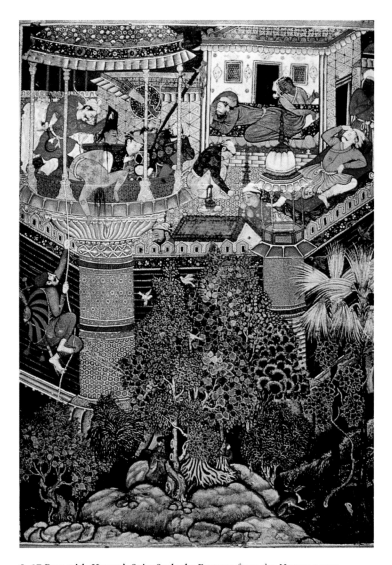

8–17 Page with *Hamza's Spies Scale the Fortress,* from the *Hamza-nama,* North India. Mughal period, Mughal, reign of Akbar, c. 1567–1582. Gouache on cotton, 30″ × 24″ (76 × 61 cm). Museum of Applied Arts, Vienna

active. This robust naturalistic figure style contrasts with the decorative linear qualities derived from Persian painting.

Nearly as prominent as the architectural setting with its vivid human adventure is the sensuous landscape in the foreground, where monkeys, foxes, and birds inhabit a grove of trees that shimmer and glow against the darkened background. The treatment of the gold-edged leaves at first calls to mind the patterned geometry of the tilework, but a closer look reveals a skillful naturalism born of careful observation. Each tree species is carefully distinguished by the shape of its trunk and leaves and its overall form. Pink and blue rocks with lumpy, softly outlined forms add still further interest to this painting, whose every inch is full of intriguing details.

Mughal architects were the heirs to a 300-year-old tradition of Islamic building using arches and domes. (Earlier architecture in the subcontinent used primarily post-and-lintel construction.)

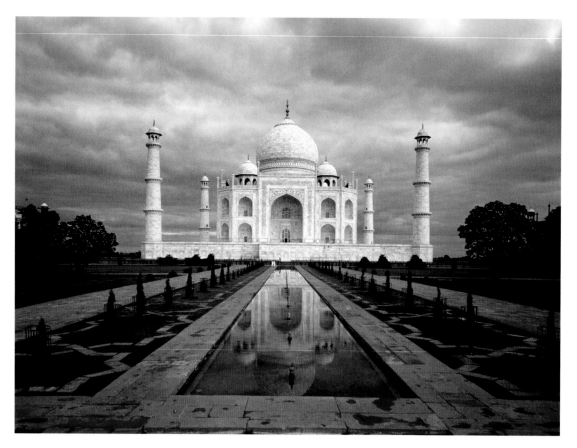

8–18 Taj Mahal, Agra, India. Mughal period, Mughal, reign of Shah Jahan, c. 1632–1648

Inside, the Taj Mahal invokes the hasht behisht, *or "eight paradises," a plan named for the eight small chambers that ring the interior—one at each corner and one behind each* iwan, *a vaulted opening with an arched portal. In two stories (for a total of 16 chambers), the rooms ring the octagonal central area, which rises the full two stories to a domed ceiling that is lower than the outer dome. In this central chamber, surrounded by a finely carved octagonal openwork marble screen, are the exquisite inlaid cenotaphs of Shah Jahan and his wife, whose actual tombs lie in the crypt below.*

The Mughals also benefited from the native virtuosity in stone carving. The Mughal style culminated in the most famous of all Indian Islamic structures: the Taj Mahal (fig. **8–18**). The Taj Mahal is sited on the river bank at Agra in northern India. Built between 1632 and 1648, it was commissioned by the emperor Shah Jahan as a mausoleum for his wife. Shah Jahan may have taken a major part in overseeing the tomb's design and construction.

Visually, the Taj Mahal never fails to impress. As visitors enter through a monumental, hall-like gate, the tomb looms before them across a spacious garden set with long reflecting pools. Measuring some 1,000 by 1,900 feet, the garden is unobtrusively divided into quadrants planted with trees and flowers and framed by broad walkways of stone inlaid in geometric patterns. In Shah Jahan's time, fruit trees and cypresses—symbolic of life and death—lined the walkways, and fountains played in the shallow pools. Truly, the senses were beguiled in this earthly evocation of paradise.

A lucid geometric symmetry pervades the entire design. Each facade of the main structure is identical, with a central *iwan* flanked by two stories of smaller *iwans.* By creating voids in the facades, these *iwans* contribute to the building's sense of weightlessness. The dome rises gracefully on its drum, allowing the swelling curves and lyrical lines of its beautifully proportioned,

surprisingly large form to emerge with perfect clarity. Four minarets surround the central structure, each crowned with a pavilion. Traditional embellishments of Indian palaces, these pavilions quickly passed into the vocabulary of Islamic architecture in India. Four more pavilions, this time on the roof, create a visual transition from the minarets to the lofty dome.

The pristine surfaces of the Taj Mahal are embellished with utmost subtlety. The sides of the platform are carved in relief with a blind arcade motif, and carved relief panels of flowers adorn the base of the building. The portals are framed with verses from the Koran inlaid in black marble, while the spandrels are decorated with floral arabesques inlaid in colored semiprecious stones. Not strong enough to detract from the overall purity of the white marble, the embellishments enliven the surfaces of this impressive yet delicate masterpiece.

The Ottoman Empire

In the early fourteenth century, the Ottoman Turks replaced the Seljuks in northwestern Anatolia. The Ottomans eventually conquered most of the eastern Mediterranean, Egypt, and the Sudan, as well as the Balkans in Eastern Europe. In 1453 they captured Constantinople (renaming it Istanbul) and brought the

Byzantine Empire to an end. The Church of Hagia Sophia (see fig. 7–11) became a mosque framed by graceful Ottoman minarets. The church's mosaics were destroyed or whitewashed over. The huge discs with the names of God, Muhammad, and the early caliphs were added to the interior in the mid-nineteenth century (see fig. 7–13). At present, Hagia Sophia is neither a church nor a mosque, but a state museum.

Inspired by this great Byzantine structure, Ottoman architects developed the domed, central-plan mosque (see "Mosque Plans," page 198). The finest example of this new form was the work of the architect Sinan (c. 1489–1588). Sinan began his career in the army and was chief engineer during the Ottoman campaign and siege of Vienna (1526–1529). He rose through the ranks to become, in 1528, chief architect for Suleiman I, known as "the Magnificent," the tenth Ottoman sultan (ruled 1520–1566). Suleiman's reign marked the height of Ottoman power, and the sultan sponsored a building program on a scale not seen since the days of the Roman Empire. Sinan's crowning accomplishment, completed about 1579, when he was over eighty years old, was a

mosque he designed in the provincial capital of Edirne for Suleiman's son Selim II (ruled 1566–1574) (fig. 8–19). The gigantic hemispheric dome that tops this structure is more than 102 feet in diameter, larger than the dome of Hagia Sophia, as Sinan proudly pointed out. The dome crowns a building of great geometric complexity on the exterior and complete coherence on the interior, a space at once soaring and serene. In addition to the mosque, the complex housed a *madrasa* and other educational buildings, a burial ground, a hospital, and charity kitchens, as well as the income-producing covered market and baths. Framed by the vertical lines of four minarets and raised on a platform at the city's edge, the Mosque of Selim dominates the skyline.

A combination of abstract setting and realistic figures and details characterizes Ottoman manuscript painting. Painters often combined the decorative aspects of the painting with an intense religious feeling, as in the painting of Muhammad (see "Islam and the Prophet Muhammad," page 193) where the Prophet appears as a white, wraithlike shadow under a flaming "halo," riding a realistic camel through a stylized landscape. At

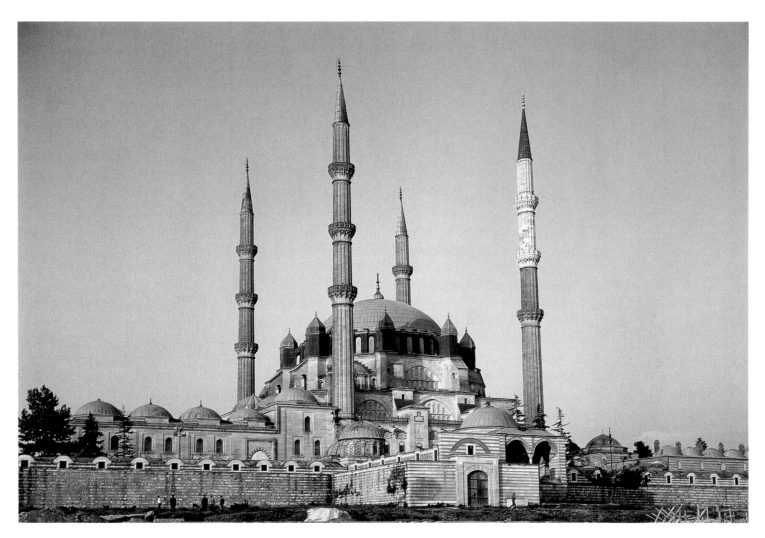

8–19 Sinan. Sultan Selim Mosque, Edirne, Turkey. 1570-74

The minarets that pierce the sky around the prayer hall of this mosque, their sleek, fluted walls and needle-nosed spires soaring to more than 295 feet, are only 12 $\frac{1}{2}$ feet in diameter at the base, an impressive feat of engineering. Only royal mosques were permitted multiple minarets, and more than two was highly unusual.

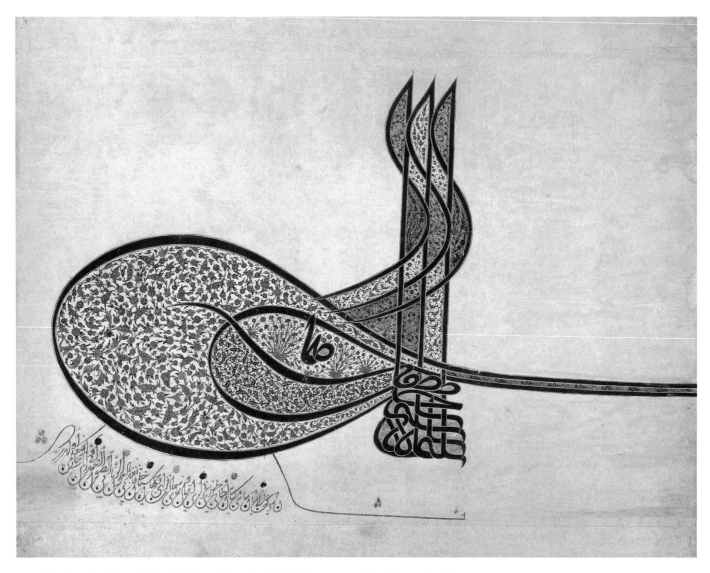

8–20 Illuminated *tughra* of Sultan Suleiman I, from Istanbul, Turkey. c. 1555. Ink, colors, and gold on paper, removed from a *firman* (official document) and trimmed to $20\frac{1}{2}$″ × $25\frac{3}{8}$″ (52.1 × 64.5 cm). The Metropolitan Museum of Art, New York

ROGERS FUND, 1938 (38.149.1)

the Ottoman court of Suleiman I in Istanbul, the imperial workshops produced even more remarkable illuminated manuscripts.

Following a practice begun by the Seljuks and Mamluks, the Ottomans put calligraphy to political use, developing the design of imperial ciphers—*tughras*—into a specialized art form. Ottoman *tughras* combined the ruler's name with the title Khan ("lord"), his father's name, and the motto "Eternally Victorious" into a monogram. Symbolizing the authority of the sultan, *tughras* appeared on seals, coins, and buildings, as well as on official documents. Suleiman issued hundreds of edicts, and a high court official supervised specialist calligraphers and illuminators who produced documents that required particularly elaborate *tughras*. The *tughra* shown here (fig. **8–20**) is from a document endowing a charitable institution in Jerusalem that had been established by Suleiman's wife, Sultana Hurrem.

Tughras were drawn in black or blue ink with three long, vertical strokes (*tug* means "horsetail") to the right of two concentric horizontal teardrops. Decorative foliage patterns fill the spaces. *Tughras* required great skill to execute. The sweeping, fluid lines had to be drawn with perfect control according to set proportions, and a mistake meant starting over. The color scheme of the delicate floral **interlace** enclosed in the body of the *tughra* may have been inspired by Chinese blue-and-white ceramics, and similar designs appear on Ottoman ceramics and textiles. The Ottoman *tughra* is a sophisticated merging of abstraction with naturalism, boldness with delicacy, political power with informed patronage, and function—both utilitarian and symbolic—with adornment.

For many years the largest and most powerful political entity in the Islamic world, the Ottoman Empire lasted until the end of World War I. It was not until 1918 that the modern country of Turkey was founded in Anatolia, the former heart of the empire, and that the Arabic script used by the Ottomans was replaced by the Latin alphabet.

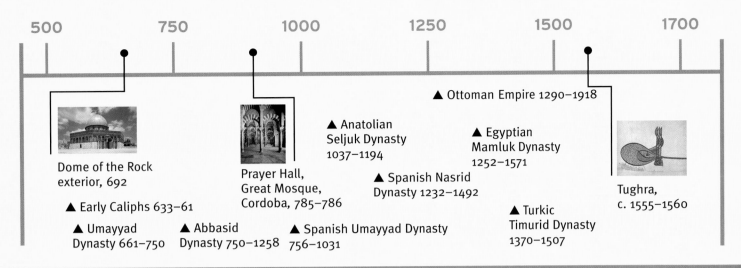

500	750	1000	1250	1500	1700

▲ Ottoman Empire 1290–1918

▲ Anatolian
Seljuk Dynasty
1037–1194

▲ Egyptian
Mamluk Dynasty
1252–1571

Dome of the Rock
exterior, 692

Prayer Hall,
Great Mosque,
Cordoba, 785–786

▲ Spanish Nasrid
Dynasty 1232–1492

Tughra,
c. 1555–1560

▲ Early Caliphs 633–61

▲ Turkic
Timurid Dynasty
1370–1507

▲ Umayyad
Dynasty 661–750

▲ Abbasid
Dynasty 750–1258

▲ Spanish Umayyad Dynasty
756–1031

LOOKING BACK

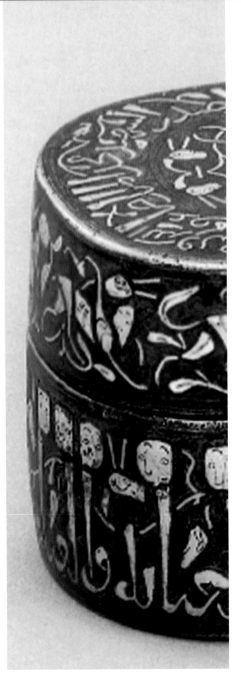

For Muslims, God's word, rather than a likeness, held a position of primary importance. They were among the "People of the Book," the Koran. Muslim artists raised the art of calligraphy to a level of exquisite sophistication and expressiveness. Only in Islamic culture, and in China, Korea, and Japan, was this pure and abstract art given such attention. In all these societies those who mastered the difficult art of beautiful writing, that is, transferring thoughts and sounds into permanent form often using the simplest materials and equipment, became the most admired artists. In Islamic art, calligraphy can be found everywhere from monumental architectural inscriptions, seen as early as the Dome of the Rock, to manuscripts. It is found in every medium from the simple clay—whether in a tile mosaic *mihrab* or a glazed earthenware bowl—to the most valuable gold work and from fragile glass lamps and bottles to durable brass or steel that has been engraved and inlaid with silver, like the pen box in fig. 8–1. Calligraphy captures the words of God and the prayers of the people, as well as mundane accounts, letters, and histories.

Islamic art includes painting and architecture as well as the more ephemeral but related arts of carpets and gardens. Painting is usually associated with the art of the book, in examples such as the stories of Prince Bahram Gur from Ancient Persia or in the Mughal arts of India. Courts were centers for the production of luxury manuscripts.

In architecture, builders adapted the columned halls and the vaults and domes of Roman and Byzantine architecture to build the prayer halls of their mosques, like the Great Mosques in Cordoba, Spain, or Kairouan in Tunisia, and the halls and chambers of palaces like the Alhambra. While using impermanent and inexpensive materials such as brick and timber for the underlying structure, they sheathed the walls with brilliantly colored glazed tiles and carved stucco veneers to create opulent effects. They added to the luxury by covering the floors with carpets. The textile arts, especially the knotted carpet, became almost synonymous with Islamic art and design in Europe and the United States—the ubiquitous so-called Oriental rugs collected by our great grandparents.

In Islamic palaces and houses, such as the Alhambra in Granada, enclosed gardens cross the line between secular and sacred art. Envisioned as gardens of paradise, these gardens include fountains, waterways, and formally organized trees, shrubs, and flowers grown for perfume as well as color. Islamic gardens profoundly influenced the development of garden design in their emphasis on symmetrical, geometric design in both permanent structures and plantings. But here—as often happens in the study of art—we can only imagine the original beauty and opulence of the work.

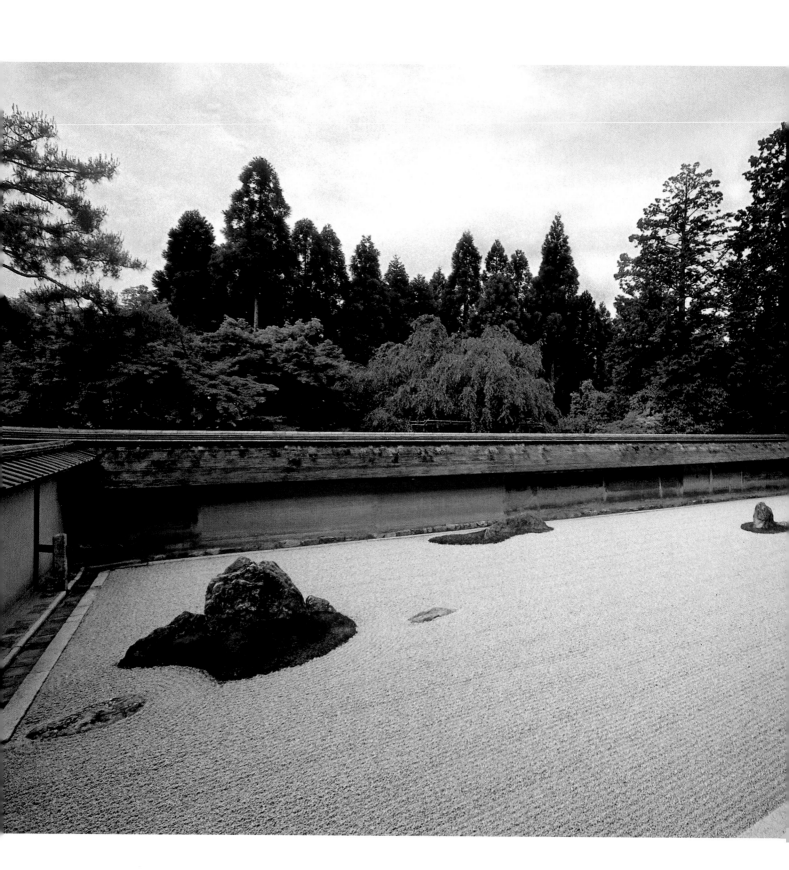

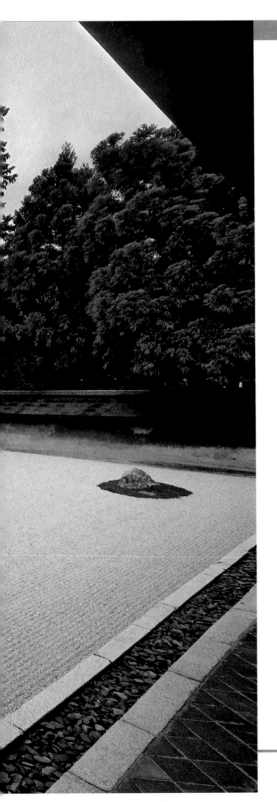

Later Asian Art

Elegant simplicity—profound and personal—was the result of disciplined meditation coupled with manual labor, as practiced in the Zen Buddhism introduced into Japan in the late twelfth century. Zen monasteries aimed at self-sufficiency. Monks were expected to be responsible for their physical as well as spiritual needs. Consequently, the performance of simple tasks—weeding the garden, cooking meals, mending garments—became occasions for meditation in the search for enlightenment. Zen monks turned to their gardens, not as the focus of detached viewing and meditation, but as the objects of constant vigilance and work—pulling weeds, tweaking unruly shoots, and raking the gravel. This philosophy profoundly influenced Japanese art, and an intimate relationship with nature pervades the later art of Asia, in general, whether inspired by Buddhist, Hindu, or Shinto belief.

The dry landscape gardens of Japan (*karesansui*, literally "dried up mountains and water") exist in perfect harmony with Zen Buddhism. In front of the abbot's quarters in the Zen temple of Ryoan-ji, a flat rectangle of raked gravel, about 30 by 70 feet, surrounds fifteen stones of different sizes in islands of moss (fig. **9–1**). The stones are set in asymmetrical groups of two, three, and five. Low, plaster-covered walls establish the garden's boundaries, but beyond the perimeter wall, maple, pine, and cherry trees add color and texture to the scene. Called "borrowed scenery," these elements are an important part of the design although they grow outside the garden.

Dry gardens began to be built in the fifteenth and sixteenth centuries in Japan. By the sixteenth century, Chinese landscape painting influenced the gardens' composition, and miniature clipped plants and beautiful stones re-created famous paintings of trees and mountains. Especially fine and unusual stones were even stolen and carried off as war booty—such was the cultural value of these seemingly simple gardens.

This Kyoto garden's design, as we see it today, probably dates from the mid-seventeenth century, since earlier written sources refer only to cherry trees, not to a garden. By the time this garden was created, such stone and gravel gardens had become highly intellectualized, abstract reflections of nature. This garden has been variously interpreted as representing islands in the sea, mountain peaks rising above the clouds, constellations of stars and planets, and even a swimming tigress with her cubs. All or none of these interpretations may be equally satisfying—or irrelevant—to a monk seeking clarity of mind through contemplation.

9–1 Stone and gravel garden, Ryoan-ji, Kyoto. Muromachi period, c. 1480

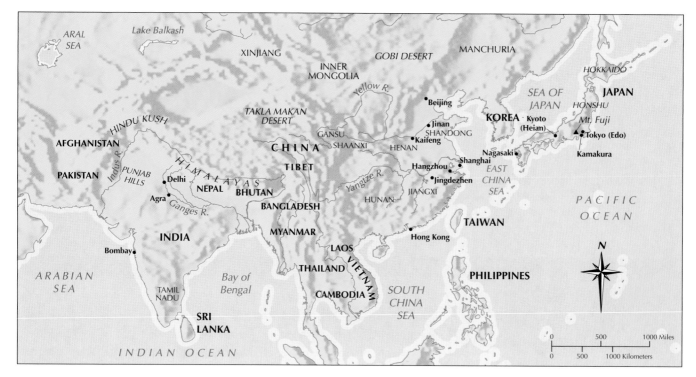

Map 9–1 Later Asia

The long Indian Medieval period (c. 650–1526) was a time of transition in the South Asian subcontinent (see Map 9–1, above). Buddhism declined as a cultural force, while artistic achievements under Hinduism soared. The monumental architecture of Hindu temples was rich in symbolism and ritual function, with each region of India developing its own variation. Later Turkic people carried Islam to the subcontinent, and Muslim art added to the rich mix of styles there, especially in the north. Islamic influence reached its height under the Mughals (1526–1857).

During roughly the same period that Hinduism began to displace Buddhism in India, Buddhism reached its height in China under the Tang dynasty (618–907) (see Chapter 3). Reaction to this flowering of a foreign religion on Chinese soil began during the late Tang and continued under the Song dynasty (960–1279), when openness to foreign influence gave way to greater cultivation of China's own traditions, including the revival of Confucianism. Landscape emerged as a very important subject and was used to express both philosophical and personal concerns.

Introduced from India by way of China and Korea, Buddhism was an important force in Japanese culture by the beginning of the Heian period (794–1185). New forms of Buddhism evolved—first Esoteric Buddhism and Pure Land Buddhism, and later, Zen. By the end of the fourteenth century, Zen Buddhism began to influence many aspects of Japanese life and culture, and soon Zen beliefs were expressed in sophisticated painting and calligraphy.

The South Asian Subcontinent

As Hinduism with its many gods and varied sects, flourished in the Indian subcontinent, temple architecture developed rapidly. Local rulers rivaled each other in the building of temples to their favored deities—Shiva, Vishnu, and Devi the Great Goddess—until the middle of the thirteenth century when Hindu temples reached unparalleled heights of grandeur and complexity.

A typical Hindu temple is the so-called northern type (figs. **9–2** and **9–3**), exemplified by the Kandariya Mahadeva

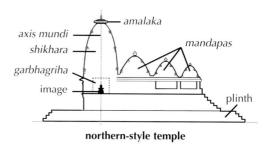

9–2 Schematic drawing of one of the main Indian temple forms: the northern style

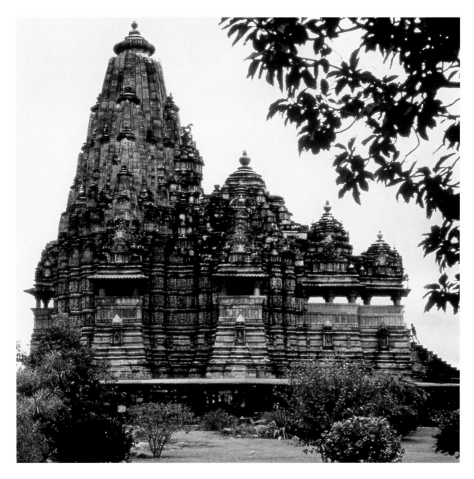

9–3 Kandariya Mahadeva temple, Khajuraho Madhya Pradesh, India. Chandella dynasty, early Medieval period, c. 1000 CE
ASIAN ART ARCHIVES/UNIVERSITY OF MICHIGAN.

temple (c. 1000 CE) dedicated to the god Shiva at Khajuraho in central India, chiefly distinguished by a superstructure called a **shikhara**. The *shikhara* rises as a solid mass above the flat, stone ceiling of a windowless sanctuary, which houses an image of the temple's "resident" deity. Crowning the temple is a circular, cushionlike element, known as an *amalaka*. A **finial** leads the eye to the point where earthly and cosmic worlds are thought to join. An imaginary *axis mundi* (line connecting the center of the earth to the heavens) runs from the finial down through the temple and the image of the deity into the ground below. In this way the temple becomes a conduit between celestial realms and the earth, a concept familiar from Buddhist stupas. At the Kandariya Mahadeva temple, the *shikhara* is bolstered by the addition of many smaller *shikhara* motifs bundled around it. Below, the body of the temple is surrounded by porches on the sides and back. In the front (to the right in figure 9–3), a steep flight of stairs leads to a series of three halls, known as *mandapas*, preceding the sanctuary. The halls serve as a place for rituals, such as dances performed for the deity, and for the presentation of offerings. The halls symbolically represent the second or Subtle Body stage of Shiva's threefold emanation—from Formless One (state of being), to Subtle Body (the world), to Gross Body (assistance for living beings). The surface of the temple is so decorated with architectural motifs (miniature *shikharas)* and sculptured gods and goddesses that the lines of the architecture are almost obscured.

During the Early Medieval period (c. 650–1200), when these temples were built, two major religious movements affected Hindu practice and its art: the tantric, or esoteric, movement primarily in the north and the *bhakti*, or devotional, movement primarily in the south. The *bhakti* movement, based on ideas expressed in ancient texts, especially the Bhagavad-Gita, is concerned with the ideal relationship between humans and deities. *Bhakti* involves an intimate, personal, and loving relationship with god, and the complete devotion and giving up of oneself to god. The movement profoundly influenced the Chola dynasty, rulers in the far south of India from the mid-ninth into the late thirteenth century. Inspired by *bhakti*, southern artists produced some of India's greatest and most humanistic worksof art—the bronze sculptures.

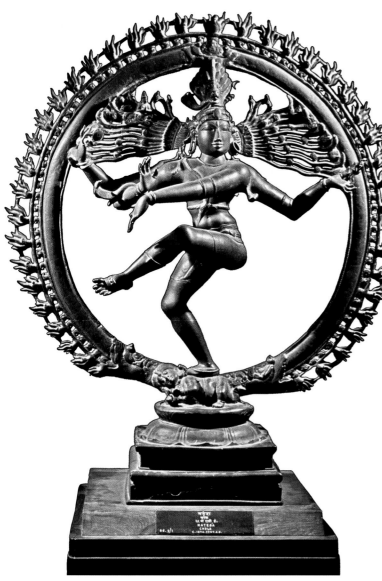

9–4 *Nataraja: Shiva as Lord of Dance.* Chola bronze of Tanjore. 12th Century, South India, height 32″ (81.25 cm). National Museum of India, New Delhi, India

The fervent religious devotion of the bhakti *movement was fueled in no small part by the sublime writings of a series of poet-saints who lived in the south of India. One of these poet-saints, Appar, who lived from the late sixth to mid-seventh century, wrote this tender, personal vision of the Shiva Nataraja. The ash the poem refers to is one of many symbols associated with the deity. In penance for having lopped off one of the five heads of Brahma, the first created being, Shiva smeared his body with ashes and went about as a beggar.*

If you could see
the arch of his brow,
the budding smile
on lips red as the kovvai fruit,
cool matted hair,
the milk-white ash on coral skin,
and the sweet golden foot
raised up in dance,
then even human birth on this wide earth
would become a thing worth having.

(Translated by Indira Vishvanathan Peterson)

Chola bronzes, such as this *Nataraja: Shiva as Lord of Dance* (fig. **9–4**), express the *bhakti* movement at its most fervent. No longer does the deity appear self-absorbed and introspective (see fig. 3–10). Instead, he generously displays himself to the devotee in full awareness of his benevolent powers. Dancing within a ring of fire, Shiva's extended left hand holds a spray of flames, emblematic of the destruction of the universe as well as of our ego-centered concepts. Shiva's back right hand holds a drum, whose ceaseless beat represents the unstoppable rhythms of creation and destruction, birth and death. With his right front hand, he makes the "have no fear" gesture. His left front arm, gracefully stretched across his body with the hand pointing to his raised foot and leg, symbolizes the promise of liberation. The earlier Hindu emphasis on ritual and the depiction of the gods' heroic feats are here subsumed into a pervasive and humanizing quality of grace.

The Hindu successors of the Chola continued the tradition of bronze sculpture in South India. The Shiva saint, discussed in the Introduction, page 5 (see Intro. fig. 9), demonstrates the high level of achievement of the later artists.

The *bhakti* movement spread to North India during the ensuing Late Medieval period (c. 1200–1526) and flourished in the courts of local Hindu princes such as the Rajputs. This period also witnessed the incursion of Islam. The Muslim conquerors introduced Islamic architectural design to the subcontinent, but it was the Mughal dynasty that made the most lasting Islamic contribution to the art and architecture of India in painting (see fig. 8–17) and in buildings such as the Taj Mahal (see fig. 8–18).

Rajput Painting

Outside of the Mughal strongholds at Delhi and Agra, much of northern India was governed by local Hindu princes, descendants of the Rajput warrior clans, who were allowed to keep their lands in return for allegiance to the Mughals. Like the Mughals, Rajput rulers frequently established painting workshops at their courts. In Kangra, a large Rajput kingdom in the Punjab Hills (foothills of the Himalayas north of Delhi), a strong school of painting developed in the middle of the eighteenth century.

Inspired by a revival of the emotional *bhakti* movement, poets wrote of the love of the god Vishnu for human beings, metaphorically expressed as the love of Krishna for the cow maiden Radha. *The Hour of Cowdust* (fig. **9–5**) depicts Krishna, who is living with the cowherds to escape the demons. Wearing his peacock crown, garland of flowers, jewelry, and yellow garment, the blue-skinned god plays his flute as he returns to the village with his fellow cowherds and their cattle. All eyes are upon him, for his music enchants all who hear it. Women with water jugs on their heads turn to look; others lean from windows to watch and call out to him. We follow the path of the cattle as they move along a diagonal, through the gate and into the courtyard. Pink walls and white houses create a sense of space where we glimpse other villagers going about their work or peacefully sitting in their houses. A rim of dark trees softens the horizon, and a rose-tinted sky completes the aura of enchanted

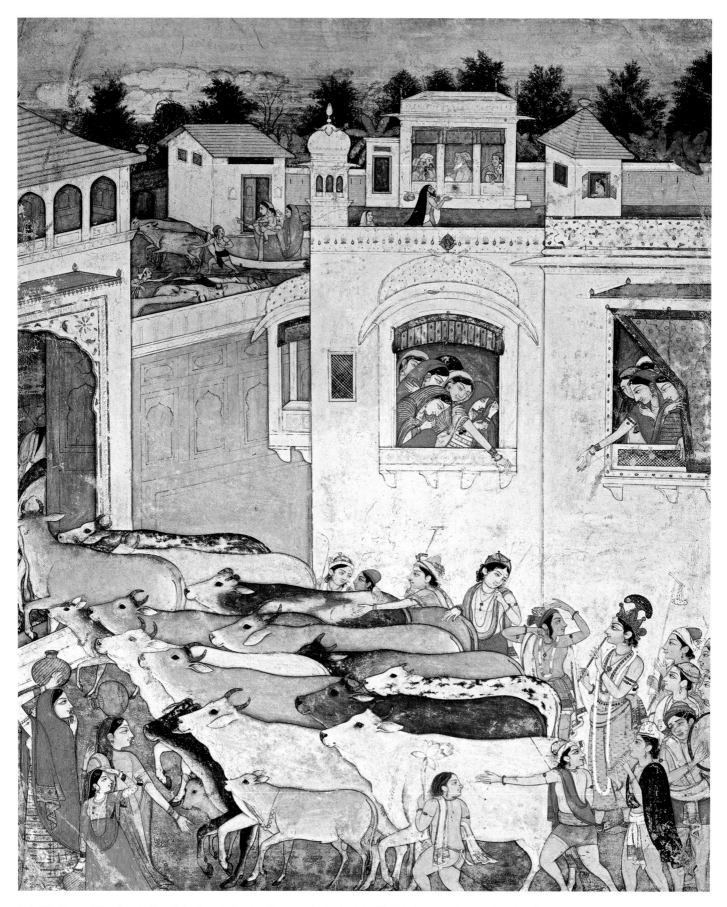

9–5 *The Hour of Cowdust.* Indian, Pahari, c. 1810–1815. Kangra school, Punjab Hills, Northern Indian. Attributed to the
Family of Nainsukh. Opaque watercolor and gold on paper, $14\frac{15}{16}''$ × $12\frac{9}{16}''$ (38 × 31.9 cm). Museum of Fine Arts, Boston

Luxury Arts

The decorative arts of India represent the height of opulent luxury. Ornament embellishes even the invisible backs of pendants and bottoms of containers. Technically superb and crafted from precious materials, the tableware and jewelry, furniture, and containers once enhanced the prestige of their owners and gave visual pleasure as well. Metalwork and work in rock crystal, agate, and jade, carving in ivory, and intricate jewelry are all characteristic Indian arts. Because of the intrinsic value of their materials, however, pieces were disassembled, melted down, and reworked, making the study of Indian luxury arts very difficult. Many pieces, like the carved ivory panel illustrated here (fig. 9–6), have no date or records of manufacture or ownership.

Frozen in timeless delight, carved in ivory against a golden ground where openwork, stylized vines with spiky leaves weave an elegant arabesque, loving couples dally under the arcades of a palace courtyard, the thin columns and cusped arches of which resemble the arcades of the palace of Tirumala Nayak (reigned 1622–1662) in Madurai (Tamil Nadu). Their huge eyes under heavy brows suggest the intensity of their gaze, and the artist's choice of the profile view emphasizes their noses and lips. Their hair is tightly controlled; the men have huge buns, and the women have long braids hanging down their backs. Are they divine lovers? After all, Krishna lived and loved on earth among the cow maidens. Or are we observing scenes of courtly romance?

The rich jewelry and well-fed bodies of the couples indicate a high station in life. Men as well as women have voluptuous figures—rounded buttocks and thighs, and tummies hanging over jeweled belts. The sharply indented slim waists of the women emphasize seductive breasts. Smooth flesh contrasts with diaphanous fabrics that swath plump legs, long arms and elegant gestures seem designed to show off ribbons and rich jewelry—bracelets, armbands, necklaces, and huge earrings. Such amorous couples symbolize harmony as well as fertility.

The erotic imagery suggests that the box illustrated here might have been a container for personal belongings such as jewelry, perfume, or cosmetics. In any event, the ivory relief is a brilliant example of South Indian secular arts.

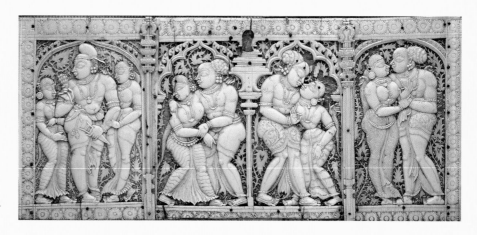

9–6 Panel from a box. Tamil Nadu, India, late 17th–18th century. Ivory backed with gilded paper, 6″ × 12³⁄₈″ × ¹⁄₈″ (15.2 × 31.4 × 0.3 cm). Virginia Museum of Fine Arts

THE ARTHUR AND MARGARET GLASGOW FUND. 80.171. KATHERINE WETZEL © VIRGINIA MUSEUM OF FINE ARTS, RICHMOND.

naturalism. The scene embodies the sublime purity and grace of the god, even in a humble setting, and the gentle, lyrical movement complements the idealism of the setting.

South India had a rich and distinguished architectural and sculptural tradition, represented by the bronze dancing Shiva (see fig. 9–4). One of the most important southern states was Tamil Nadu in the eastern coastal plain. Inhabited by Tamil speakers (a Dravidian language, unlike the Sanskrit-based languages of the north), the region developed its own distinctive character with few outside influences.

The arts of Tamil Nadu are characterized by curvilinear rounded forms and the use of **gilding**, as seen here in an ivory panel (fig. 9–6). The panel must have decorated a box—note the keyhole and the marks of nails in the borders. The delicate columns and pointed and scalloped arches of the architectural frames recall the inner courtyard of the palace in the capital city, Madurai, built in the mid-seventeenth century. Here, Tirumala Nayak (1622–1662) lived and governed Tamil Nadu. The Nayak rulers commissioned sculpture and painting, but wood and ivory carving ranks among their artists' highest achievements. The high quality of Indian luxury arts—work in rock crystal, ivory and mother-of-pearl, metalwork, and jewelry—made them renowned even outside India, and beginning in the sixteenth century, objects were made for export as well as for local sale. Although such fine pieces were very important in daily life, little scholarly work has been devoted to studying India's decorative arts. Sikhs took over the kingdom in 1826, and the British followed in 1846, effectively putting an end to the distinctive local styles.

Cambodia

Cambodia lies between India and China geographically and culturally. Buddhism and Hinduism supplanted local religions, and the Khmer people eventually developed a distinctive synthesis of beliefs that evolved into a state religion under a divine king. The concept of the World Mountain—Mount Meru—whether natural or human-made, underlaid the design of the monuments they built. In Angkor (meaning "the capital city"), every king added to existing buildings or created new and more splendid monuments (fig. **9–7**).

Suryavarman II (reigned c. 1112–1153) built Angkor Wat as his mausoleum and dedicated it to Vishnu. Amazing in its size and magnificence, the site replicates the world mountain, home of Vishnu, and axis of the world. Originally, the visitor approached the building over a bridge across a wide moat and, after passing through a monumental gateway, continued up a long avenue between two water-filled tanks to the building itself. The building has a simple plan of squares within squares defined by galleries surrounding a tall central tower with four lesser towers. Additional towers at the outer corners define the extent of the huge complex.

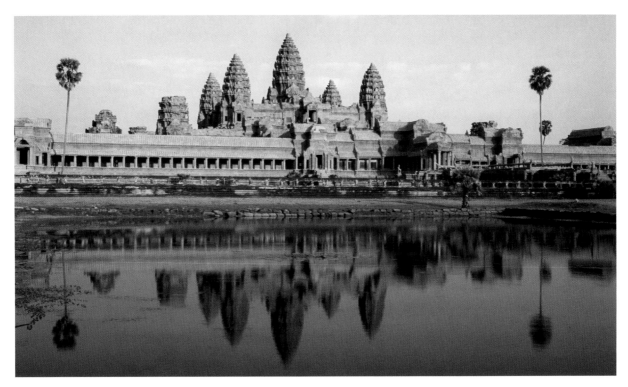

9–7 Angkor Wat, Kampuchea (Cambodia), west entrance. c. 1120–1150. The temple wall is 3,363′ × 2,625′ (1025,042 × 800,1 m) and the moats are 623′ (189,89 m) wide

Corbelled vaults with steep roofs cover galleries, rooms, and towers and emphasize the tall proportions of the structures.

Sculpture covers every possible surface, depicting the many incarnations of the god Vishnu in overwhelming detail. After the Siamese conquered the Khmer Kingdom in 1437, the buildings of Angkor fell into neglect. By the time they were rediscovered in the nineteenth century, the jungle had covered them. Although Angkor Wat is now under the protection of UNESCO, twentieth century wars and twenty-first century thieves continue to imperil the existence of the site.

China

A period of confusion followed the fall of the Tang dynasty in 907. The Liao dynasty (907–1125) exerted some semblance of power, but in fact was soon replaced by the Song dynasty (960–1279). In 1126, invaders from Manchuria defeated the Song and sacked the Song capital at Bian (present-day Kaifeng) and occupied much of the northern part of the country. Song forces withdrew southward and established a new capital at Hangzhou. The dynasty from this point on is known as Southern Song (1127–1279). The earlier years are called Northern Song (960–1126).

In spite of changing political fortunes, artists continued to create splendid works. No hint of chaos or despair intrudes on the sublime grace and beauty of the *Seated Guanyin Bodhisattva* (fig. **9–8**). Bodhisattvas are enlightened beings who return to earth to help others achieve salvation; Guanyin is the Bodhisattva of Infinite Compassion. Bodhisattvas are represented as young princes wearing royal garments and jewelry that represent their worldly but virtuous lives. Guanyin appears in many guises; in this case, as the Water and Moon Guanyin, he sits on rocks by the sea, in the position known as "royal ease." His right arm rests on his raised and bent right knee and his left arm and foot hang down, the foot touching a lotus blossom. The wooden figure was carved in the eleventh or twelfth century; the painting and gilding, however, date from the sixteenth century.

During the Song period, the martial vigor of the Tang and Liao gave way to a culture of increasing refinement and scholarship. It was a great period for the study of history, literature, and philosophy. Song philosophers revived Confucianism, drawing on

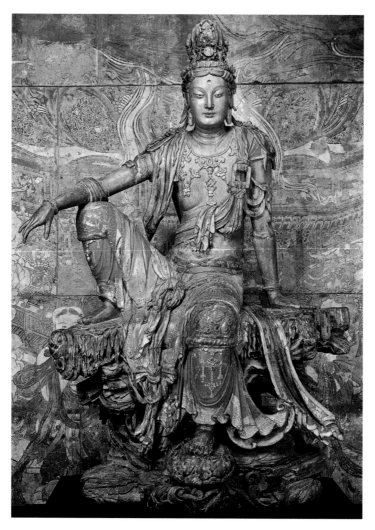

9–8 Seated Guanyin Bodhisattva. Liao dynasty, 11th–12th century. Wood with paint, height 95″ (241.3 cm). The Nelson-Atkins Museum of Art, Kansas City, Missouri
PURCHASE, NELSON TRUST

both Buddhism and Daoism to provide Confucianism with a metaphysical basis, an all-embracing explanation of the universe. This new system of thought is called Neo-Confucianism. It teaches that the universe consists of two interacting forces known as *li* (principle or idea) and *qi* (matter). All pine trees, for instance, consist of an underlying *li* that we might call the "pine tree idea," brought into the world through *qi*, the living tree. All the *li* of the universe, including humans, are but aspects of an eternal first principle known as the Great Ultimate. The task of humans is to rid our *qi* of impurities through education and self-cultivation so that our *li* may achieve its oneness with the Great Ultimate.

Neo-Confucian ideas found visual expression in landscape painting. Northern Song artists studied nature closely to master its varied appearances—the way each species of tree grew, the distinctive character of rock formations, the changing of the seasons, and the myriad kinds of birds, blossoms, and insects. This study was the artist's form of self-cultivation; mastering outward forms showed an understanding of the principles behind them. Yet despite the convincing representation of individual forms, the paintings do not record specific views. The artist's goal was to paint the eternal aspect of a mountain, for example, not to reproduce the particular appearance of a mountain. Over the centuries, landscape also became a vehicle for conveying human emotions, even for expressing one's deepest feelings.

One of the first great masters of Song landscape was Fan Kuan (active c. 990–1030), whose *Travelers Among Mountains and Streams* is generally regarded as one of the great monuments in the history of Chinese art (fig. **9–9**). The composition unfolds in three stages, comparable to the three acts of a drama. A low-lying group of rocks at the bottom establishes the extreme foreground, anticipating, on a small scale, the shape and substance of the mountains to come. In the middle ground, travelers and their mules enter from the right. We realize the discrepancies in relative scale—how small we are, how vast nature is! This middle ground, like the second act of a play, shows variation and development. Instead of a solid mass, the rocks here are separated into two groups by a waterfall. At right, the rooftops of a temple stand out above the trees.

Mist veils the transition to the background, so the mountain seems to loom up suddenly. This background area, almost twice as large as the foreground and middle ground combined, is the climactic third act of the drama. As our eyes begin their ascent, the mountain solidifies, its ponderous weight increasing as it billows upward. The whole painting summons the feeling of climbing a high mountain, leaving the human world behind to come face-to-face in a spiritual communion with the Great Ultimate.

The ability of Chinese landscape painters to let us wander freely through their recorded sites is closely linked to the absence of linear perspective as it has been understood in the West since the fifteenth century. Fifteenth-century European painters developed a "scientific" system for recording exactly the view that could be seen from a single, fixed vantage point (see "Renaissance Perspective Systems," pages 328 and 329). The goal of Chinese painting is to show a totality beyond what we are normally able to see. If the ideal for a naturalistic Western

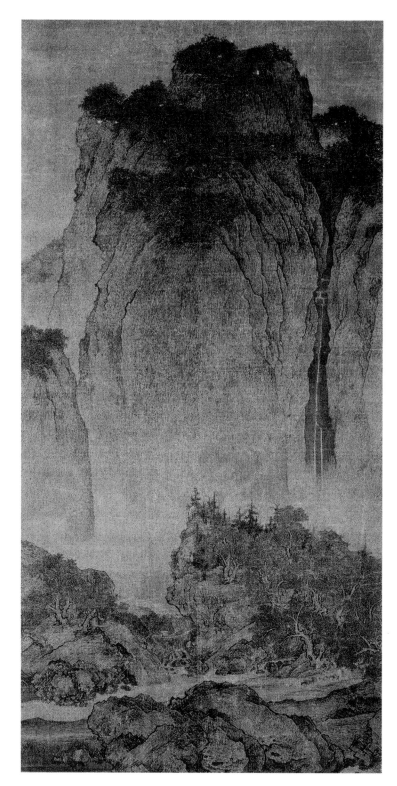

9–9 Fan Kuan. *Travelers Among Mountains and Streams.* Northern Song dynasty, early 11th century. Hanging scroll, ink and colors on silk, height 6′9 1/4″ (2.06 m). National Palace Museum, Taipei, Taiwan

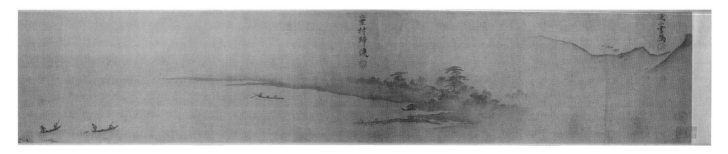

9–10 Xia Gui. Detail of *Twelve Views from a Thatched Hut*. Southern Song dynasty, early 13th century. Handscroll, ink on silk. Height 11″ (28 cm), length of extant portion 7′7 1/4″ (2.31 m). The Nelson-Atkins Museum of Art, Kansas City, Missouri

A few deft brushstrokes suffice to indicate the details showing through the mist—the grasses growing by the bank, the fishermen at their work, the trees laden with moisture, and the two bent-backed figures carrying their heavy load along the path that skirts the hill.

painting is to be like a photograph that shows only what can be seen from a fixed spot, the ideal for a Chinese painting to be like a video camera floating aloft in a balloon: distant, all-seeing, mobile, and capturing a combination of viewpoints.

Chinese landscape painting took a very different course after the fall of the Northern Song and the removal of the court to Hangzhou. The work of Xia Gui (c. 1180–1230), a member of a reestablished imperial painting academy, is representative of this change. His *Twelve Views from a Thatched Hut* (fig. **9–10**)—in sharp contrast to the majestic, austere landscapes of the Northern Song painters—presents an intimate and lyrical view of nature. In the surviving four of the twelve views that originally made up this long hand-scroll (narrow, horizontal painting), subtle ink washes describe a landscape veiled in mists. Simplified forms, stark contrasts of light and dark, asymmetrical compositions, and great expanses of blank space suggest a fleeting world that can be captured only in glimpses.

This development in Song painting from the rational and intellectual to the emotional and intuitive had a parallel in philosophy. During the late twelfth century, a new school of Neo-Confucianism called the School of the Mind insisted that self-cultivation could be achieved through contemplation, which might lead to sudden enlightenment. The idea of sudden enlightenment may have come from Chan Buddhism, better known in the West by its Japanese name, Zen. Chan Buddhists used meditation and techniques designed to "short-circuit" the rational mind. Xia Gui's painting seems also to follow this intuitive approach.

The highly cultivated audience that appreciated the subtle and sophisticated paintings of the Song was equally discerning in other arts, such as ceramics. Of the many types of Song ceramics, one of the most prized was Guan ware, made mainly for imperial use (fig. **9–11**). The form of this graceful vase flows without interruption from base to lip, but the potter intentionally allowed a pattern of irregular, spontaneous cracks to develop in the lustrous off-white glaze. This piece, with its careful inter-play of ordered and unplanned elements, has an understated quality as eloquent as the blank spaces in Xia Gui's painting.

Closely related to the Chinese Guan ware is the Korean celadon made during the Koryu Dynasty (918–1392). At first the Korean potters copied Chinese ceramics, but soon they

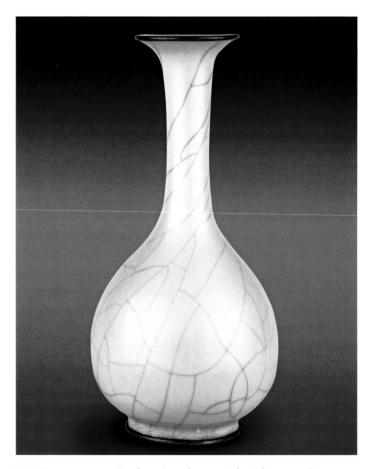

9–11 Guan ware vase. Southern Song dynasty, 12th–13th century. Stoneware with crackled glaze, height 6 5/8″ (18 cm)

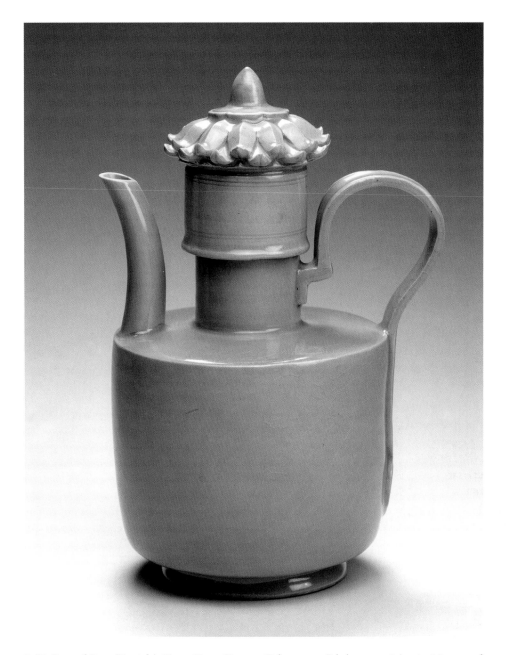

9–12 Covered Ewer (Ru style), Korea. Koryu Dynasty, 12th century, Celadon ware. Asian Art Museum of San Francisco

Ru ware was made for the court, where antiquarian scholars appreciated its resemblance to earlier pieces as well as admired its svelte form and color. The glazes were meant to imitate jade.

developed distinctive forms and a soft, muted green glaze (fig. **9–12**). The body of the vessel might have an incised decoration or might be incised and inlaid, an extremely difficult technique perfected by Korean potters, who managed to create a feeling of spontaneity in spite of the challenge presented by the material. Over time, an appreciation of slight imperfections arose, and Korean ceramists and connoisseurs developed a preference for works that exhibit tiny flaws, which they believe enhance the beauty of a piece.

In 1279, the Southern Song dynasty fell to the armies of the Mongol leader Kublai Khan, and China became part of the vast Mongol Empire. Kublai Khan founded the Yuan dynasty

(1279–1368), setting up his capital in the northeast, in what is now Beijing. The center of Chinese culture remained in the south, however, and southern Chinese scholars found themselves alienated from the Mongol court. Denied normal access to the government positions for which they were educated, these scholars, the literati, searched for other outlets for their talents, including the arts.

The southerner Zhao Mengfu (1254–1322), a descendant of the imperial line of Song, is typical in this regard; a painter, calligrapher, and poet, he produced works for cultivated southern literati. Unlike many of his southern contemporaries, though, he eventually served the Yuan government in Beijing and was made

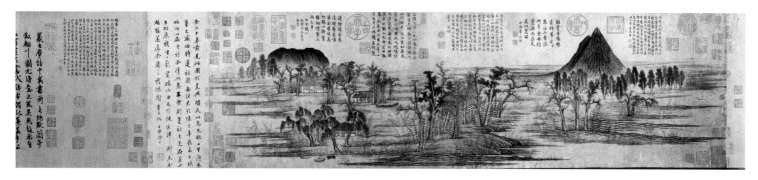

9–13 Zhao Mengfu. Section of *Autumn Colors on the Qiao and Hua Mountains.* Yuan dynasty, 1296. Handscroll, ink and color on paper, 11 1/4″ × 36 3/4″ (28.6 × 93.3 cm). National Palace Museum Taipei, Taiwan

a high official. Zhao painted *Autumn Colors on the Qiao and Hua Mountains* (fig. **9–13**) for a friend living in the south. The painting supposedly depicts the friend's ancestral home, Jinan, the present-day capital of Shandong province, in the north. The mountains are not painted in the naturalistic mode perfected before Zhao's time but rather in an archaic yet oddly elegant manner that recalls the art of the much earlier Tang dynasty. Through his painting, Zhao evoked a feeling of nostalgia, not only for his friend's distant homeland, but also for China's past.

This educated taste for archaic styles became an important aspect of **literati painting** in later periods. Also typical of the literati tradition are the unassuming brushwork, the subtle colors sparingly used, and even the intended audience—often a close friend. The literati painted not for public display but for each other. They favored **hand-scrolls**, **hanging scrolls**, or **album leaves**, which could easily be transported to show to friends or small gatherings (see "Formats of Chinese Painting," below).

Technique

Formats of Chinese Painting

Aside from wall paintings that decorated palaces, temples, and tombs, most Chinese paintings were done in ink and water-based colors on silk or paper. Finished works were usually mounted on silk as hand-scrolls, hanging scrolls, albums, or fans.

An album comprises a set of paintings of similar size, and usually of related subject matter, mounted in an accordion-fold book. Typically the paintings are square or rectangular, but fan paintings were sometimes collected in albums. Album-size paintings could also be mounted as a hand-scroll, a horizontal format generally about 12 inches high and anywhere from a few feet to dozens of feet long. More typically, however, a hand-scroll would be a single continuous painting, generally preceded by a panel giving the work's title and often followed by a long panel bearing colophons—inscriptions, such as poems, in praise of the work or comments by its owners over the centuries. Hand-scrolls were not meant to be displayed all at once, the way they are commonly presented today in museums. Rather, they were kept rolled up and only occasionally taken out for viewing. The viewer would unroll the scroll a few feet at a time, moving gradually through the entire scroll from right to left, lingering over favorite details.

Like hand-scrolls, hanging scrolls were not displayed permanently but were taken out for a limited time, whether a day, a week, or a season. Unlike a hand-scroll, however, the hanging scroll was viewed as a whole, unrolled and put up on a wall, with the wooden roller at the lower end acting as a weight to help the scroll hang flat.

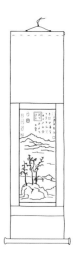

hanging scroll

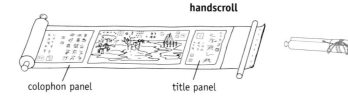

handscroll

colophon panel   title panel

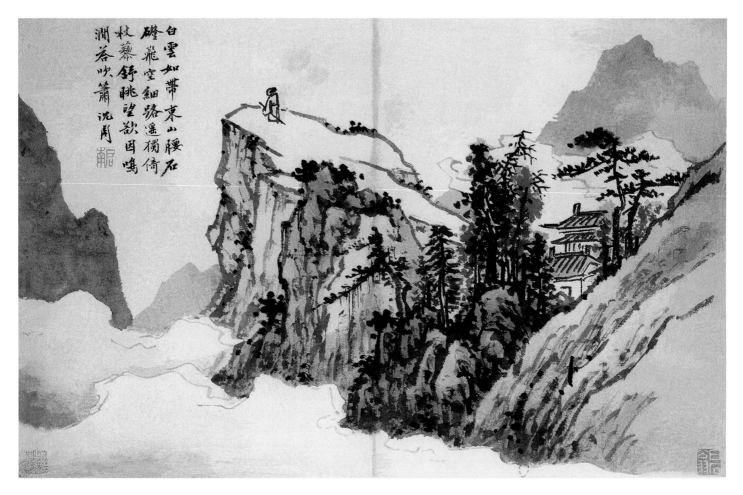

9–14 Shen Zhou. *Poet on a Mountaintop,* leaf from an album of landscapes; painting mounted as part of a handscroll. Ming dynasty, c. 1500. Ink and color on paper, 15 $\frac{1}{4}$″ × 23 $\frac{3}{4}$″ (38.1 × 60.2 cm). The Nelson-Atkins Museum of Art, Kansas City, Missouri

The poem at the upper left reads:

> White clouds like a belt encircle the mountain's waist
> A stone ledge flying in space and the far thin road.
> I lean alone on my bramble staff and gazing contented into space
> Wish the sounding torrent would answer to your flute.

> (Translated by Richard Edwards, cited in *Eight Dynasties of Chinese Paintings*, page 185)

Shen Zhou composed the poem and the inscription, written at the time he painted the album. The style of the calligraphy, like the style of the painting, is informal, relaxed, and straightforward—qualities that were believed to reflect the artist's character and personality.

The contrast between the opulent display and the austere aesthetic ideals of the literati is a defining feature of Ming dynasty (1368–1644) painting. Whereas court painters revived academic traditions of the Song dynasty, many literati painters built on the styles created by their predecessors, the Yuan. One of the major literati artists of the Ming period is Shen Zhou (1427–1509), who spent most of his life in the southern city of Suzhou, far from the court in Beijing. Shen Zhou studied the Yuan painters avidly and tried to recapture their spirit in such works as *Poet on a Mountaintop* (fig. **9–14**). Here the poet has climbed a mountain and surveys the landscape. Before his gaze, a poem hangs in the air, like a projection of his thoughts. Like the poem, the landscape is a vehicle for self-expression, having more to do with the artist's response to nature than with the physical world itself. With its perfect synthesis of poetry, calligraphy, and painting, and its harmony of mind and landscape, *Poet on a Mountaintop* represents the very essence of literati painting.

The cities of the south, such as Suzhou, were full of newly wealthy merchants who collected paintings, antiques, and art objects. The court, too, was prosperous and patronized the arts on a lavish scale. In such a setting, the decorative arts thrived.

Like the Song dynasty before it, the Ming became famous the world over for its exquisite ceramics, especially **porcelain**. Porcelain is made from kaolin, an extremely refined white clay, and petuntze, a variety of the mineral feldspar. When properly combined and fired at a high temperature, the two materials fuse into a glasslike, translucent ceramic that is far stronger than it looks.

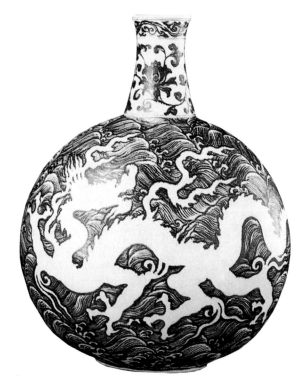

9–15 Porcelain flask with decoration in blue underglaze. Ming dynasty, c. 1425–1435. Palace Museum, Beijing

Dragons have featured prominently in Chinese folklore from earliest times—Neolithic examples have been found painted on pottery and carved in jade. In Bronze Age China, dragons came to be associated with powerful and sudden manifestations of nature, such as wind, thunder, and lightning. At the same time, dragons became associated with superior beings such as virtuous rulers and sages. With the emergence of China's first firmly established empire during the Han dynasty, the dragon was appropriated as an imperial symbol, and it remained so throughout Chinese history. Dragon sightings were duly recorded and considered auspicious. Yet even the Son of Heaven could not monopolize the dragon. During the Tang and Song dynasties the practice arose of painting pictures of dragons to pray for rain, and for Chan (Zen) Buddhists, the dragon was a symbol of enlightenment.

The porcelain flask in figure **9–15** came from the imperial kilns in Jingdezhen, in Jiangxi province, the most renowned center for porcelain in Ming China. The blue decoration—made from cobalt oxide, finely ground and mixed with water—was painted directly onto the unfired porcelain vessel in a technique known as **underglazing**. Next, the painter applied a clear glaze over the entire surface. The piece was then fired, emerging from the kiln with its blue decoration set sharply against snowy white, in this case with the dragon reserved in white against a background of blue patterning. The subtle form, the refined yet vigorous decoration of dragons writhing in the sea, and the flawless **glazing** embody the high achievement of Ming artisans.

Ming ceramists were not alone in their creativity and technical skill. Ming architects created the most important surviving example of traditional Chinese architecture: the Forbidden City, the imperial palace compound in Beijing (fig. **9–16**). The basic plan of Beijing was the work of the Mongols, who laid out their capital city according to Chinese principles, creating a walled rectangle with gates oriented to the four cardinal directions and streets running north-south and east-west arranged as a grid. The palace enclosure occupied the center of the northern part of the city. Under the Ming dynasty Emperor Yongle (who ruled 1402–1424), the Forbidden City was rebuilt as we see it today.

Visitors to the Forbidden City entered on the south and passed through the South Gate, the monumental U-shaped gate seen in figure 9–16. Inside the gate, a bow-shaped canal spanned by five arched marble bridges crosses a broad courtyard. On the north side of the courtyard is the Gate of Supreme Harmony, opening into the larger Outer Court. This area houses three ceremonial halls raised on a broad platform. Classic examples of Chinese palace architecture, with brilliant terra-cotta tile roofs and red lacquered columns, are the Halls of Supreme Harmony, Central Harmony, and Protecting Harmony. In the first and largest, the Hall of Supreme Harmony, the emperor sat on his throne during important state occasions. He faced south,

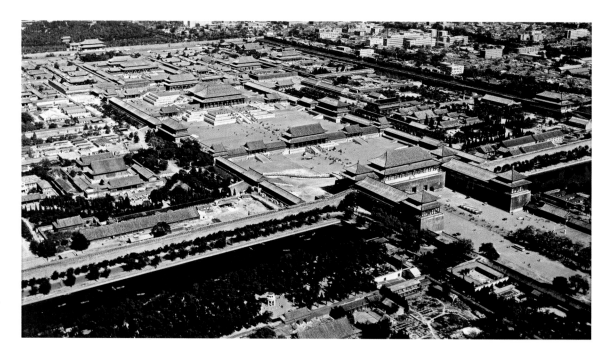

9–16 The Forbidden City, now the Palace Museum, Beijing. Mostly Ming dynasty. View from the southwest

looking out toward his city and, by extension, his realm. His back was to the north, the source of evil spirits, not to mention military threats from non-Chinese peoples beyond the Great Wall. Continuing on to the north in the Forbidden City, the visitor encounters the secluded and smaller Inner Court, which also has a progression of three buildings. This is where the emperor lived and conducted more private business affairs.

In its directional orientation and symmetrical arrangement, the plan of the Forbidden City reflects ancient Chinese beliefs about the harmony of the universe and emphasizes the emperor's role as the Son of Heaven, whose duty was to maintain the cosmic order from his throne in the middle of the world.

Japan

In Japan, by the Heian period (794–1185), Buddhism was practiced throughout the land, although it did not completely supplant the country's indigenous religion, Shinto. Buddhism offers paradisiacal realms and enlightenment, whereas Shinto offers the intercession of the gods in the affairs of this world. Since these two ideals did not fundamentally clash, modes of mutual accommodation were found. To this day, most Japanese see nothing inconsistent about having Shinto weddings and Buddhist funerals.

The generally peaceful Heian period was marked by a new cultural self-reliance on the part of the Japanese. Ties to China were severed in the mid-ninth century, and the imperial government was sustained by support from aristocratic families. During these four centuries of splendor and refinement, two new schools of Buddhism became prominent: first, Esoteric (secret) Buddhism and later, Pure Land Buddhism.

In Esoteric Buddhism, the historical Shakyamuni Buddha became less important. Teaching centered instead on a universal or cosmic Buddha (in Japanese, *Dainichi*, "Great Sun") of whom all other buddhas are emanations. Esoteric Buddhism gave rise to a huge pantheon of buddhas, bodhisattvas, and fierce guardian deities. The leisured aristocracy favored Esoteric Buddhism, whose network of deities, hierarchy, and ritual found a parallel in the elaborate social divisions of the Heian court.

Pure Land Buddhism came to prominence in the latter half of the Heian period, when a rising military class threatened the peace and tranquility of court life. In those uncertain years, many Japanese were ready for a form of Buddhism that would offer a means of salvation more direct than through the elaborate rituals of the Esoteric sects. Pure Land Buddhism taught that the Western Paradise (the Pure Land) of Amida (Amitabha) Buddha could be reached through faith alone. In its ultimate form, Pure Land Buddhism held that the mere chanting of a mantra—the phrase *Namu Amida Butsu* ("Hail to Amida Buddha")—would lead to rebirth in Amida's Pure Land. This doctrine, spread by traveling monks who took the chant to all parts of the country, has made Pure Land Buddhism the most popular form of Buddhism in Japan.

One of the most beautiful temples of Pure Land Buddhism is the Phoenix Hall at the Byodo-in (built c. 1053), located by the Uji River southeast of Kyoto (fig. **9–17**). Originally the summer retreat of a powerful aristocrat, it was later converted into a temple. The hall and its garden combine to evoke the palace of Amida in the Western Paradise. The lightness of its thin columns gives the Phoenix Hall a sense of airiness, as though the entire structure could easily rise up through the sky to the Western

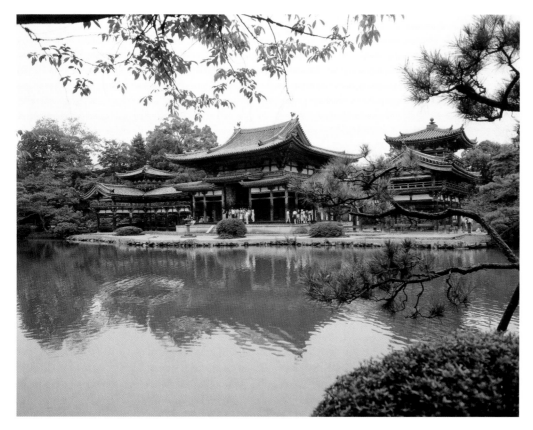

9–17 Byodo-in, Uji, Kyoto Prefecture. Heian period, c. 1053

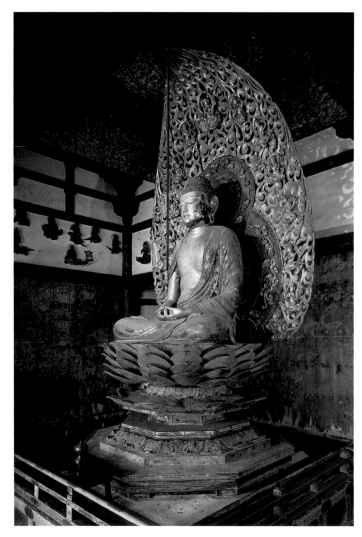

9–18 Jocho. *Amida Buddha.* Byodo-in. Heian period, c. 1053. Gold leaf and lacquer on wood, height 9′8″ (2.95 m)

Paradise. In front of the hall is an artificial pond created in the shape of the Sanskrit letter *A*, the sacred symbol for Amida.

The Phoenix Hall's central image of Amida (fig. **9–18**) was constructed of individually carved blocks of wood by the master sculptor Jocho (d. 1057). This **joined-wood sculpture** method, developed by Jocho, allowed sculptors to create sculpture larger but lighter than those carved from a single block of wood. Reflected in the water of the pond in front of it, the Amida image, heightened with gold leaf and **lacquer** (a hard, glossy surface varnish), seems to shimmer in its private retreat. The Buddha sits on an open lotus, a Buddhist symbol of purity. The flower's stem is an *axis mundi*, connecting the earthly and celestial realms. This timeless image exemplifies the compassion of the Buddha, who welcomes the souls of all believers to his paradise, nirvana.

While Buddhism dominated the Heian era, a refined secular culture also arose at court; it has never been equaled in Japan. A new system of writing in Japanese developed, known as *kana* script (see "Writing, Language, and Culture," page 232). With its simple, flowing symbols interspersed with more complex Chinese characters, *kana* allowed Japanese writers to create a distinctive calligraphy quite unlike that of China.

Kana was used during the Heian period to write down a large body of literature, including many *tanka*, or five-line love poems. The poems of one famous Heian anthology, the *Thirty-Six*

Immortal Poets, are still familiar to educated Japanese today. This anthology was produced in sets of albums, the *Ishiyama-gire*, which display elegantly written *tanka* on high-quality papers decorated with painting, **block printing**, scattered gold and silver, and sometimes paper **collage** (pasted colored papers).

The page shown here reproduces two *tanka* by the courtier Ki no Tsurayuki (fig. **9–19**). Both poems express sadness for the loss of a lover, the first lamenting:

> Until yesterday
> I could meet her,
> But today she is gone—
> Like clouds over the mountain
> She has been wafted away.
> (Translated by Stephen Addiss)

The spiky, flowing calligraphy, the patterning of the papers, the rich use of gold, and the suggestion of natural imagery epitomize courtly Japanese taste.

The world's first known novel, *The Tale of Genji*, written in Japanese at the beginning of the eleventh century by Lady Murasaki, immortalizes the lifestyle of the Heian court. Underlying the story of the love affairs of Prince Genji and his companions is the Japanese conception of fleeting pleasures and ultimate sadness in life, an echo of the Buddhist view of the vanity of earthly pleasures.

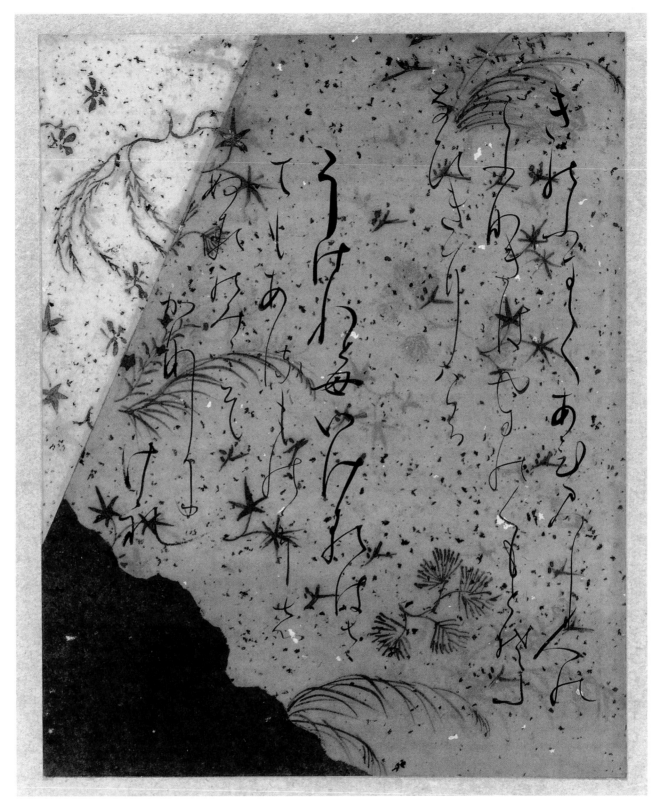

9–19 Album leaf from the *Ishiyama-gire*. Heian period, early 12th century. Ink with gold and silver on decorated and collaged paper, 8″ × 6⅜″ (20.3 × 16.1 cm). Freer Gallery of Art, Smithsonian Institution, Washington, D.C.

Although the style of Japanese calligraphy such as that in the Ishiyama-gire *was considered "women's hand," it is not known how much of the calligraphy of the time was actually written by women. It is certain, however, that women were a vital force in Heian society. Although the place of women in Japanese society was to decline in later periods, they contributed greatly to the art at the Heian court.*

WRITING, LANGUAGE, AND CULTURE

Written Chinese was the international language of scholarship in East Asia, much as Latin was in Medieval Europe. Educated Koreans, for example, wrote almost exclusively in Chinese until the fifteenth century. In Japan, Chinese continued to be used for certain kinds of writing, such as philosophical and legal texts, into the nineteenth century.

When the Japanese first began to write, they borrowed Chinese characters, which they refer to as *kanji*. However, differences between the Chinese and Japanese languages made this system extremely unwieldy, so during the ninth century the Japanese developed two syllabaries *(kana)*, *katakana* and *hiragana*, to transcribe the sounds of their own language. (A syllabary is a system in which each symbol stands for a syllable.) *Katakana*, now generally used for foreign words, consists of mostly angular symbols, while *hiragana*, which is used for Japanese words, has graceful, cursive symbols.

Below is a stanza of a poem written three ways. At the right, it appears in *katakana* glossed with the original phonetic value of each symbol. (Modern pronunciation has shifted slightly). In the center, the stanza appears in flowing *hiragana*. At left is the mixture of Chinese characters and *kana* that eventually became standard. This alternating rhythm of simple *kana* symbols and more complex Chinese characters gives a special flavor to Japanese calligraphy. In all three versions of the stanza, the text is written, like Chinese, in columns from top to bottom and across the page from right to left. Chinese and Japanese hand-scrolls also read from right to left.

常ならむ
我世誰ぞ
散りぬるを
色は匂へど

つねならむ
わかよたれそ
ちりぬるを
いろはにほへと

ツネナラム
ワカヨタ
チリヌルヲ
イロハニホヘト

kanji and *kana*   *hiragana*   *katakana*

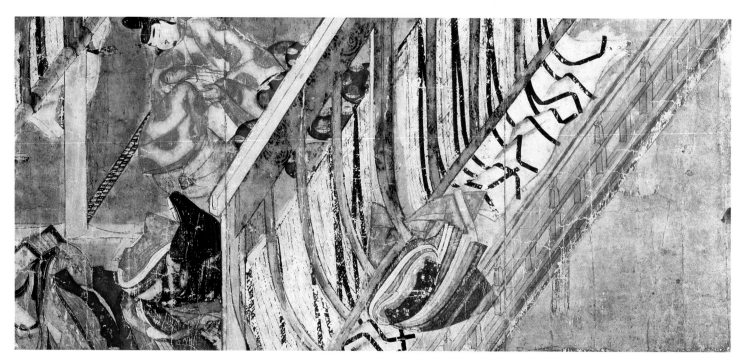

9–20 Scene from *The Tale of Genji*. Heian period, 12th century. Hand-scroll, ink and colors on paper, $8\frac{5}{8}'' \times 18\frac{7}{8}''$ (21.9 × 47.9 cm). Tokugawa Art Museum, Nagoya

Paintings seem to have been produced by a team of artists. One was the calligrapher, most likely a member of the nobility. Another was the master painter, who outlined two or three illustrations per chapter in fine brushstrokes and indicated the color scheme. Next, colorists went to work, applying layer after layer of color to build up patterns and textures. After they had finished, the master painter returned to reinforce outlines and apply the finishing touches, among them the details of faces.

Among the earliest extant secular paintings from Japan are illustrations of *The Tale of Genji*, done in the twelfth century by unknown artists in a style sometimes described as "women's hand." This style was characterized by emphasis on shapes rather than lines, strong if sometimes muted colors, and asymmetrical compositions in which interiors of buildings are viewed from above through invisible, "blown-away" roofs. The painters convey feelings by colors and poses rather than through movement or facial expressions. One evocative scene portrays a seemingly happy Prince Genji holding a baby boy borne by his wife, Princess Nyosan (fig. **9–20**). In fact, the baby was fathered by another court noble. Since Genji himself has not been faithful to Nyosan, who appears in profile below him, he cannot complain; meanwhile the true father of the child has died, unable to acknowledge his only son. The irony is even greater because Genji himself is the illegitimate son of an emperor. Thus what should be a joyous scene has undercurrents of sorrow. This is underscored visually by the muted colors of Genji's clothing, which contrast with the bright colors around him, and by the uncomfortable space he occupies.

The courtiers of the Heian era became so engrossed in their own search for refinement that they neglected their responsibilities for governing the country. Clans of warriors, known as samurai, grew increasingly strong, and samurai leaders soon became the real powers in Japan. The Kamakura era (1185–1392) began when the samurai Minamoto Yoritomo (1147–1199) assumed power in Japan as shogun (general-in-chief). He established a military capital at the seaside town of Kamakura, far from Kyoto. While paying respects to the emperor, Yoritomo kept both military and political power for himself. He thus began a tradition of rule by shogun that lasted in various forms until 1868.

Toward the latter part of the Kamakura period, Zen Buddhism reached Japan from China. In some ways, Zen resembles the original teachings of the historical Buddha in stressing that individuals must achieve their own enlightenment through meditation, without the devotional practices or elaborate rituals promoted by other schools of Buddhism.

An abbot named Kao at an early Zen temple was a pioneer in a kind of rough and simple painting in black ink that so directly expresses the Zen spirit. In a remarkable portrait of a monk sewing his robe (fig. **9–21**), we are drawn into the activity of the painting rather than merely sitting back and enjoying it as a work of art. The almost humorous compression of the monk's face, coupled with the position of the darker robe, focuses our attention on his eyes, which then lead us out to his hand pulling the needle.

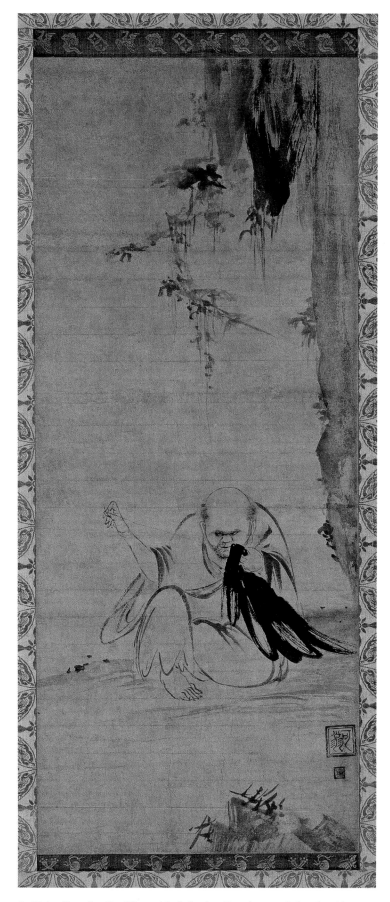

9–21 Attributed to Kao Ninga. *Monk Sewing.* Kamakura period, early 14th century. Ink on paper, $32\frac{7}{8}$" × $13\frac{3}{4}$" (83.5 × 35.4 cm). The Cleveland Museum of Art

JOHN L. SEVERANCE FUND, 62.163

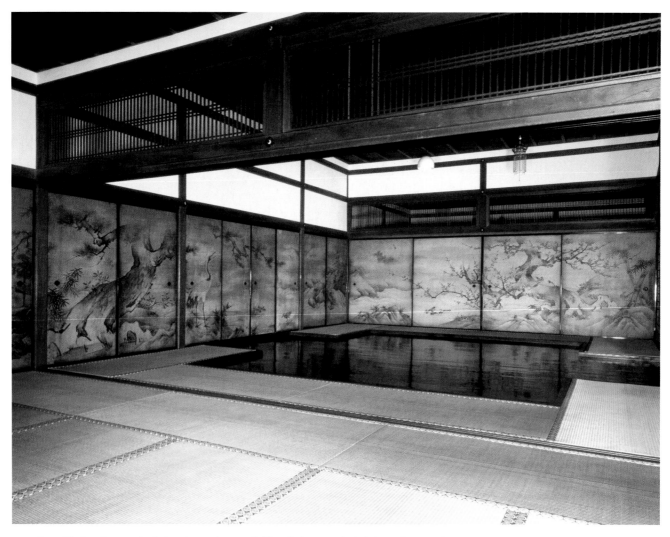

9–22 Kano Eitoku. *Fusuma* depicting pine and cranes (left) and plum tree (right), from the central room of the Juko-in, Daitoku-ji, Kyoto. Momoyama period, c. 1563–1573. Ink and gold on paper, height 5′9 ⅛″ (1.76 m)

By the beginning of the Muromachi period (1392–1568), Zen dominated many aspects of Japanese culture. One of the most renowned Zen creations in Japan, built during the Muromachi era, is the "dry landscape garden" at the temple of Ryoan-ji in Kyoto (see fig. 9–1). There is a record of a famous cherry tree at this spot, so the completely severe nature of the garden may have come about some time after its original founding in the late fifteenth century. Nevertheless, the garden—which is only a part of the larger grounds of Ryoan-ji—is today celebrated for its serene sense of space and emptiness.

During the Momoyama period (1568–1603), civil wars swept through Japan, fought among samurai loyal to their own feudal lords rather than to the central government. Portuguese explorers and traders arrived, and with them European muskets and cannons, which soon changed the nature of Japanese warfare. In response to the new weapons, monumental fortified castles were built in the early seventeenth century. Many were sumptuously decorated, offering artists

unprecedented opportunities to work on a grand scale. Large murals on *fusuma*—paper-covered sliding doors—were particular features of Momoyama design, as were folding screens with gold-leaf backgrounds. Temples, too, commissioned large-scale decorative paintings for rebuilding projects after the devastation of the civil wars.

Daitoku-ji, a celebrated Zen monastery in Kyoto, has a number of subtemples that are treasure troves of Japanese art. One, the Juko-in, features *fusuma* by Kano Eitoku (1543–1590). Eitoku was one of the most brilliant painters from the Kano school, a professional school of artists patronized by government leaders for several centuries. The illustration here shows two of three walls of *fusuma* panels painted when the artist was in his mid-twenties (fig. **9–22**). The subject to the left is a popular Kano-school theme of cranes and pines, both symbols of long life; to the right is a great gnarled plum tree, a symbol of spring and renewal. An island situated where two walls meet in a corner provides a focus for the outreaching trees. Ingeniously, it belongs to both compositions at the same time, thus uniting them into a single organic whole.

During the Momoyama period, there continued to be interest in the quiet, the restrained, and the natural. This introspective mood found expression in the tea ceremony. "Tea ceremony" is an unsatisfactory characterization of *cha no yu*, the Japanese ritual of preparing and drinking of tea, for which there is no counterpart in Western culture. The most famous tea master in Japanese history, Sen no Rikyu (1522–1591), conceived of the tea ceremony as an intimate gathering in which a few people would enter a small, rustic room, drink tea carefully prepared in front of them by their host, and quietly discuss the tea utensils or a work of art displayed for their enjoyment.

The age-old Japanese admiration for the natural and the asymmetrical is reflected in certain types of tea ceramics. A teabowl would be judged by such factors as how well it fit into the hands, how subtly its shape and texture appealed to the eye, and who had previously used and appreciated it. If a bowl had been given a name by a leading tea master, it was especially treasured by later generations. One of the finest teabowls extant was crafted by Hon'ami Koetsu (1558–1637). Named *Mount Fuji* after Japan's most sacred peak (fig. **9–23**), it is an example of *raku*—a hand-built, low-fired ceramic developed especially for use in the tea ceremony. With its small foot, straight sides, slightly irregular shape, and crackled texture, this bowl exemplifies the entire ceremony. Merely looking at it suggests the feeling one would get from holding it, warm with tea, in one's hands.

Korean Painting

In Korea, the Chosun dynasty (1392–1910) bridged the centuries and the cultural change from domination by China to entry into the modern world. In the seventeenth and eighteenth centuries, intellectual life revived. A new creativity appeared in the arts, especially in literature and painting. Buddhism gave way to Confucian religious belief and practice. In Korea as well as Japan an admiration for natural effects and practical solutions emerged. In the eighteenth century, Korean painters turned to their own landscape for inspiration, and both writers and painters used Korean themes. Genre paintings were also popular at the time. With an energy and pride that recall the seventeenth-century Dutch Republic or nineteenth-century America, Korean artists had found inspiration in their own lives and country.

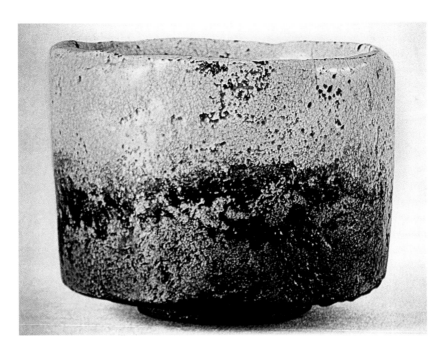

9–23 Hon'ami Koetsu. Teabowl, called *Mount Fuji*. Edo period, early 17th century. Raku ware, height 3⅜″ (8.5 cm). Sakai Collection, Tokyo. Sunritz Hattori Museum of Arts, Japan

A specialized vocabulary developed to allow connoisseurs to discuss the subtle aesthetics of tea. A favorite term was sabi, *which summoned up the particular beauty to be found in stillness or even deprivation.* Sabi *was borrowed from the critical vocabulary of poetry, where it was first established as a positive ideal by the early-thirteenth-century poet Fujiwara Shunzei. Other virtues were* wabi, *conveying a sense of great loneliness or humble and admirable shabbiness, and* shibui, *meaning plain and astringent.*

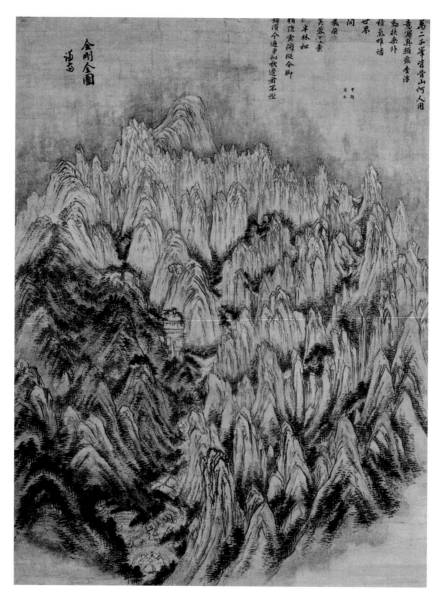

9–24 Chu Son (or Chong Son). *Twelve Thousand Peaks of Mt. Keemgang (Diamond Mountains).* Chosun dynasty. 1734. Hanging scroll. Ink and colors

Typical of this turn to Korean themes is the landscape painting of Chong Son (1676–1759). Inspired by the Chinese scholar-painters of the Ming dynasty, Chong Son used traditional techniques and media as he recorded actual appearances. The so-called *Diamond Mountains* scroll (fig. **9–24**), for example, presents a unique and even fantastic landscape where dozens of sharp jagged peaks emerge from the mist, recalling America's Bryce Canyon. The free and spontaneous quality of Chong Son's brushwork became a Korean characteristic. Just as potters emphasized their perfection with a tiny blemish, so Chong Son self-consciously denied his own skill. Even the inscription on the painting is a matter-of fact-statement—"The Diamond Mountains rise on the far side of the East Sea."

Pictures of the Floating World

During the Edo period (1603–1868), when the *Mount Fuji* bowl was made, peace and prosperity came to Japan at the price of an increasingly rigid and often repressive form of government. Zen Buddhism was replaced as the prevailing intellectual force by a form of Neo-Confucianism, the philosophy formulated in Song dynasty China that emphasized loyalty to the state. The government discouraged foreign ideas and foreign contacts, forbidding Japanese from traveling abroad and barring outsiders from Japan, with the exception of small Chinese and Dutch trading communities on an island off the southern port of Nagasaki.

Across Japan, and especially in the bustling new capital of Edo (modern Tokyo), people savored the delights of their peaceful society. Wealthy merchants patronized painters in the middle and later Edo periods, and even artisans and tradespeople could purchase less costly works of art—above all, **woodblock prints**.

Ukiyo-e ("pictures of the floating world"), as these woodblock prints are called in Japanese, represent the combined expertise of three people: the artist, the carver, and the printer. The artist supplied the master drawing for the print, executing its outlines in ink on tissue-thin paper. The carver pasted the drawing face-down on a hardwood block and cut around the lines with a sharp knife. The rest of the block was chiseled away, leaving the outlines standing in relief. This block, which reproduced the master drawing, was called the **key block**. If the print was to have several colors, the carver made a separate block for each color. A printer brushed water-based ink or color over the blocks, beginning with the key block; placed a piece of paper on top; and then rubbed with a smooth, padded device called a *baren* to make an impression. A publisher coordinated and funded the endeavor and distributed the prints to stores or itinerant peddlers.

The first artist to design **polychrome** prints was Suzuki Harunobu (1724–1770). One print that displays the charm and wit of Harunobu's art is *Geisha as Daruma Crossing the Sea* (fig. **9–25**), in which a gracefully robed young woman is shown floating across the water on a reed. This is a playful reference to one of the legends about Bodhidharma, a semi-legendary Indian monk, known in Japan as Daruma, and recognized as the founder of the Zen tradition in China. Many paintings were made of this monk standing on a reed to cross the Yangtze River. To see a young woman rather than a grizzled Zen master peering ahead to the other shore must have greatly amused the Japanese populace. There was also another layer of meaning in this image

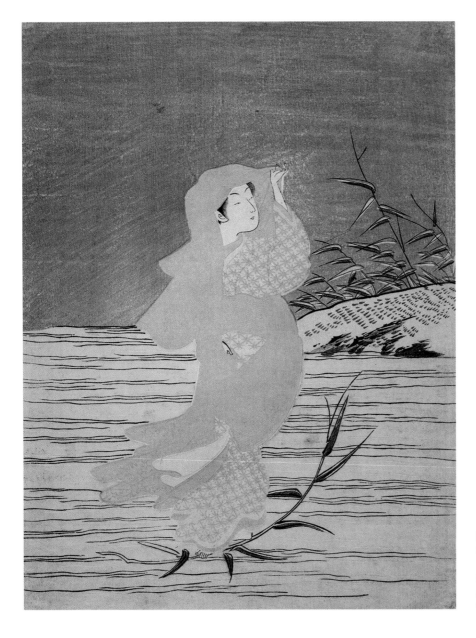

9–25 Suzuki Harunobu. *Geisha as Daruma Crossing the Sea.* Edo period, mid-18th century. Color woodcut, $10\frac{7}{8}$" × $8\frac{1}{4}$" (27.6 × 21 cm). Philadelphia Museum of Art

GIFT OF MRS. EMILE GEYELIN, IN MEMORY OF ANNE HAMPTON BARNES

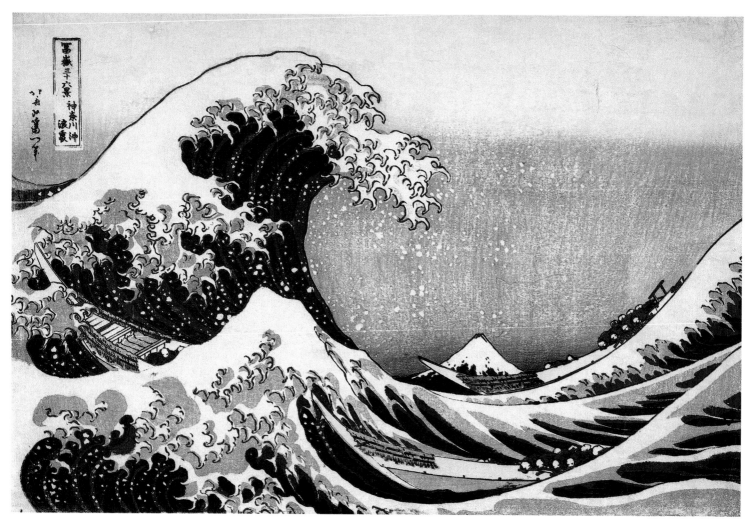

9–26 Katsushika Hokusai. *The Great Wave Off Kanagawa.* Edo period, c. 1828. Polychrome woodblock print on paper, $9\frac{7}{8}''\times14\frac{5}{8}''$ (25 × 37.1 cm). Honolulu Academy of Arts, Honolulu, Hawaii
THE JAMES A. MICHENER COLLECTION. (HAA 13,695).

The great wave rears up like a dragon with claws of foam, ready to crash down on the figures huddled in the boats below. Far in the distance rises Japan's most sacred peak, Mount Fuji, whose slopes, we suddenly realize, swing up like waves and whose snowy crown is like foam—comparisons the artist makes clear in the wave nearest us, caught just at the moment of greatest resemblance.

because geishas (meaning "artists," traditional Japanese entertainers) were sometimes compared with Buddhist teachers or deities in their ability to bring earthly pleasure, akin to enlightenment, to humans.

Popular *ukiyo-e* subjects included courtesans and actors. One of the finest practitioners of the art at the end of the eighteenth century was Kitagawa Utamaro (1753–1806), whose *Woman at the Height of Her Beauty* has been discussed in the Introduction (see fig. 8). Beginning in the nineteenth century, landscapes, such as *Thirty-Six Views of Fuji* by Katsushika Hokusai (1760–1849), also became a popular subject for the makers of colored woodblock prints. The blocks were printed again and again until they were worn out. Then they were recarved and printed again.

The Great Wave Off Kanagawa (fig. **9–26**) may be the most famous scene from the series *Thirty-Six Views of Fuji*. Hokusai was already in his seventies, with a 50-year career behind him,

when he designed this image. Such was his modesty that he felt that his Fuji series was only the beginning of his creativity, and he wrote that if he could live until he was 100, he would finally learn how to become an artist.

When first seen in Europe and America, these and other Japanese prints were immediately acclaimed, and they strongly influenced late-nineteenth- and early-twentieth-century Western art (see "Japonisme," page 507). Not only was the first book on Hokusai published in France, but the value of these prints as collectible works of art was recognized in the West before it was in Japan. Only within the past 50 years or so have Japanese museums and **connoisseurs** fully recognized the value of this originally "plebeian" form of art. In the twentieth century artists such as Roger Shimomura (see Introduction, fig. 17) have rediscovered the power of such prints and incorporated references to such designs in their own work.

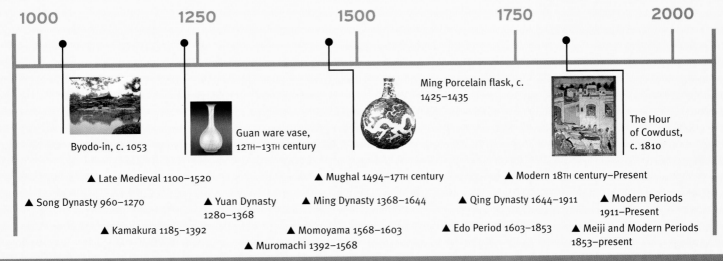

1000   1250   1500   1750   2000

Byodo-in, c. 1053

Guan ware vase, 12TH–13TH century

Ming Porcelain flask, c. 1425–1435

The Hour of Cowdust, c. 1810

▲ Late Medieval 1100–1520   ▲ Mughal 1494–17TH century   ▲ Modern 18TH century–Present

▲ Song Dynasty 960–1270   ▲ Yuan Dynasty 1280–1368   ▲ Ming Dynasty 1368–1644   ▲ Qing Dynasty 1644–1911   ▲ Modern Periods 1911–Present

▲ Kamakura 1185–1392   ▲ Momoyama 1568–1603   ▲ Edo Period 1603–1853   ▲ Meiji and Modern Periods 1853–present

▲ Muromachi 1392–1568

LOOKING BACK

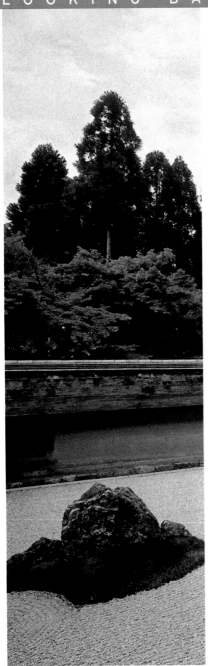

Asian art combines material splendor and spiritual depth with an affinity for nature. Artists aim to give material form to the invisible world of the spirit, creating an art that is centered more in nature than in human activity. To be sure, wealthy rulers devoted resources to create spectacular architectural complexes—temples in India and Angor Wat, or the Forbidden City in Beiying. Nevertheless we associate the finest later Asian art with more intimate things, such as small bronzes in India or ink painting in China, Korea, and Japan, and with that most ephemeral of the arts, gardening. Shiva, the essence of energy, danced to set the world in motion, and the purity of the divine enters and coexists with the human world.

In China, scholar-painters steeped in the classical texts of philosophy, literature, and history shared a common bond in education and outlook. Their lives typically moved between government service and private retirement, and the philosophical poles of Confucianism and Daoism. When they finally retreated from society in order to come to terms with nature and the universe, they wrote poetry, painted landscapes, and built gardens. In their calligraphy and landscape painting they expressed their philosophical and personal concerns. They disguised their skill in apparently spontaneous but completely controlled brushwork. Excellence depended on expressive power of the brushwork not on the resemblance to the scene painted, and they often based their art on earlier art. Today, China's painters still seek spiritual communion with nature through their art as a means to come to terms with human life and the world. Japanese painters carried ink painting to an unimagined level of austere sophistication, expressing the very essence of Zen Buddhism. Profound and personal simplicity resulted from disciplined meditation. Manual dexterity and hard work as well as expressive imagination were required to produce both ink brush painting and the private scholars' and temple gardens.

The ultimate expression of the conversion of base natural material into works of art—in fact, of nature spiritualized—is the ceramic art. Ceramics are among the most prized of Asian art forms, whether Chinese porcelain, Korean celadon, or Japanese tea ceremony wares. Using earth and fire, the artists skillfully create the most refined and delicate forms and colors. As Chinese and Korean artists reached ever-greater levels of sophistication, Japanese potters reversed the process. In ceramics made for the rituals associated with tea, modesty and rusticity characterize both the ritual and the utensils. Through deliberately created imperfect shapes and accidental effects of glaze, the tea bowls appealed to the sense of touch as well as sight.

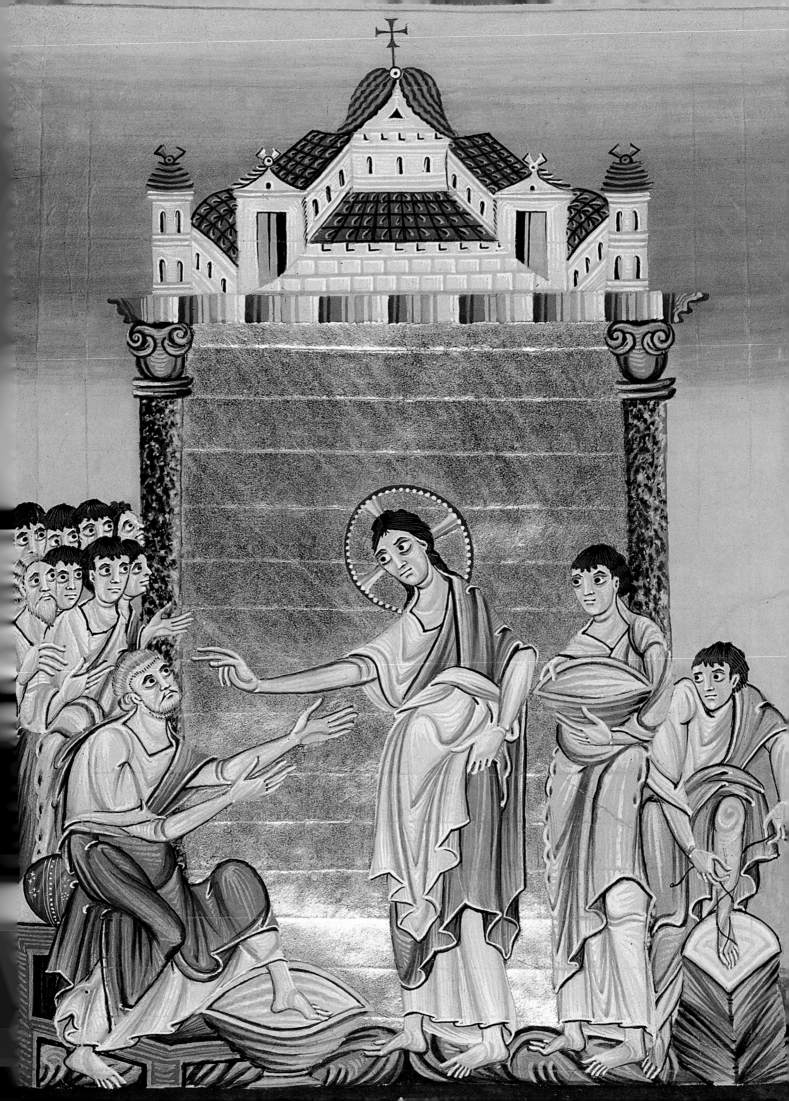

10

Early Medieval and Romanesque Art

A dazzling golden light fills the interior of a fantastic building whose towers, basilicas, and domes balance precariously on a pair of green Roman columns (fig. 10–1). Framed within the columns, tall slender men gesture dramatically with long thin fingers. The scene depicts the moment when Jesus performs the ancient ritual of hospitality by washing the feet of his disciples, a humble courtesy described by Saint John (13:1–17). On the night before the Jewish feast of the Passover, Christ and his disciples gathered in Jerusalem. Rising from the meal (referred to by Christians as the Last Supper) and tying a towel around himself, Jesus washed their feet. As he performed this act of subservience and brotherly love, Peter tried to stop him. In the image shown here, Peter has one foot reluctantly poised over the basin while Jesus explains to him the necessity of an act that will come to symbolize the forgiveness of sins and to foreshadow Christ's ultimate sacrifice on the cross. Herein lies the foundation of Christian belief and salvation: God humbled himself to become a man and to suffer and die like one for the salvation of humankind. And yet, the cruciform halo and the lavish use of gold remind us of the Christian belief that Christ is God and lord.

By the time this miniature was painted in a Gospel book around the year 1000, the Washing of Feet had come to symbolize the sacrament of Baptism and was associated with the sacrament of the Eucharist. The disciple on the far right undoing his sandal symbolizes the putting aside of sin and also recalls the traditional removing of shoes in the presence of divinity. The disciple next to him holds a large basin of water, emphasizing the rite of purification. These two men give visual expression to Christ's example.

The iconography of this painting stresses the importance of humility in Christian belief—that is, the subjugation of one's will and reason to God. Consequently, the ritual of the washing of feet came to be seen as a foundation of monastic spiritual life. Millennial fever, prompted by the coming of the year 1000, may have inspired the production of images of subjugation and forgiveness. But during the 200 years that followed—the Romanesque period—emperors, kings, popes, and abbots lavished their material resources on churches, altars, and liturgical equipment in an attempt to glorify God and to recreate an image of the heavenly Jerusalem on Earth.

10–1 Page with *Christ Washing the Feet of His Disciples, Gospels of Otto III.* c. 1000. Staatsbibliothek, Munich

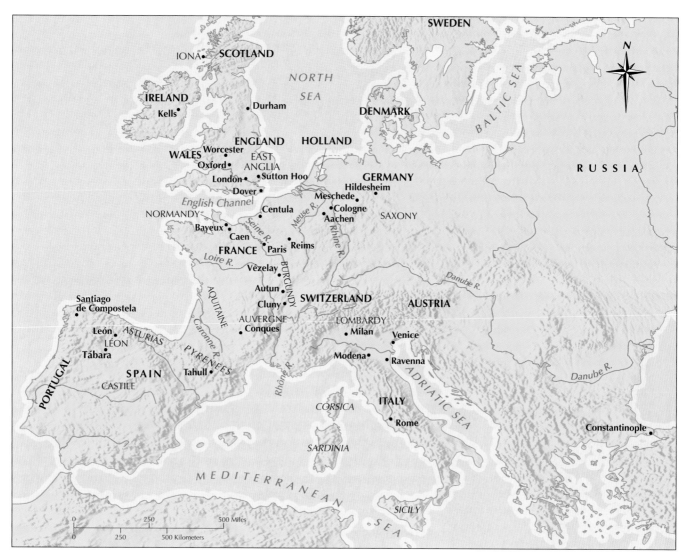

Map 10–1 Europe in the Middle Ages

As Roman authority crumbled at the outset of the Middle Ages, political power in Western Europe passed to the bishops as well as to secular lords. The Christian Church, as the repository of tradition and learning, provided intellectual as well as spiritual leadership. As patrons of the arts, the clergy sponsored the building of churches and the creation of equipment for use in rituals, including crosses, **reliquaries** (shrines for holy relics), and copies of sacred books. Secular leaders built manor houses and castles and commissioned the making of secular works of art such as jewelry, textiles, and armor, little of which survives. Stylistically, early medieval art reflects the fusion of the Germanic and late Roman traditions of the former Western Empire, as well as the influence of both pre-Christian art from Northern Europe and the Islamic art of Spain (see Map 10–1, above).

The fall of the Western Roman Empire in the fifth century left the Germanic peoples—including the Ostrogoths, Visigoths, Alemani, Angles, Saxons, and Franks—in control of many former Roman territories. Germanic artists often worked in abstract geometric patterns inherited from the Bronze and Iron Ages (see "The Celts," page 157), and they also created the fantastic creatures seen in the animal style. The Gummersmark brooch (fig. **10–2**), a large silver-gilt pin made in Denmark in the sixth century, displays an impressive array of generally symmetrical designs, emphasizing fantastic animal forms. Probably one of a pair, it was used to fasten a cloak around the wearer's shoulders. Individual **motifs** include spirals, birds, humans, and dragonlike animals so interlaced that one has to look carefully to identify them.

Christianity gained steadily in strength in the vacuum left by the collapse of the Roman Empire. The Church helped unify Europe's heterogeneous population, and Christianity spread into lands far from its Mediterranean origins, such as Ireland and eventually Scandinavia, which had never been ruled by Rome. In the late eighth and early ninth centuries, the Frankish king—and later emperor—Charlemagne sought to revive the glory of the imperial Rome and to reestablish an explicitly Christian regime in the West.

Western Europeans in this early medieval period looked with dismay on the rapid advance of Islam. The Muslims were also "People of the Book." Monotheistic, they accepted Judaism and Christianity as forerunners of their own prophet, Muhammad. But western and northern European leaders were rarely so

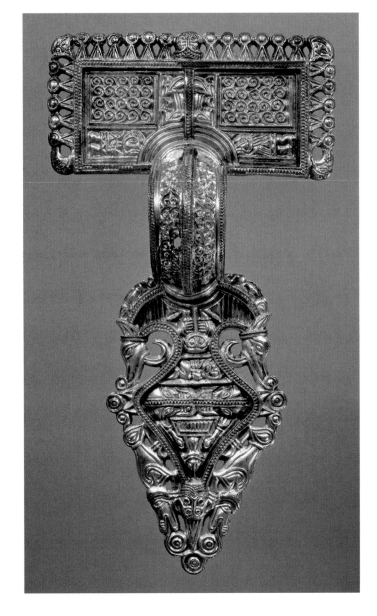

10–2 Gummersmark brooch, Denmark. 6th century. Silver gilt, height 5 3/4″ (14.6 cm). Nationalmuseet, Copenhagen

The faceted surface of this pin seems to seethe with abstract human, animal, and grotesque forms such as the eye-and-beak motif that frames the headplate (at top), the man compressed between dragons just below the bridge element (at bottom center), and the pair of monster heads and crouching dogs with snapping tongues that frame the foot plate (at bottom).

broad-minded. They viewed Muslims not only as unwanted foreigners but also as dangerous infidels. The presence of Muslims in Spain from the eighth century on raised fears among Christians of further Islamic inroads into Europe. Muslim rulers were often tolerant of Christians and Jews in their territories. The Franks beat back the Muslim armies in the eighth century and so secured Europe to develop as a Christian land. By the end of the eleventh century, Christians were on the offensive, mounting Crusades against the Muslims in return.

Early Medieval Art in the British Isles and Scandinavia

Another clash of cultures had occurred in the British Isles (see page 153). The Romans subjugated the native Celtic inhabitants of Britain in 43 CE but did not invade Ireland. During the period of Roman rule, which lasted until the beginning of the fifth century,

Christianity took root in Britain and spread to Ireland. After the fall of the Roman Empire in the fifth century, British chieftains took control, vying for dominance with the help of soldiers from continental Europe, thus giving rise to the legends of King Arthur and the Round Table. The Angles, Saxons, and Jutes from the Continent soon established kingdoms of their own, and the people under their rule adopted Anglo-Saxon speech and customs. Over the next 200 years, a new Anglo-Saxon and Hiberno-Saxon culture (*Hibernia* was the Roman name for Ireland) formed out of a fusion of these Celtic, Germanic, and Romanized British traditions.

Metalworking is one of the glories of Anglo-Saxon art. References to splendid jewelry and military equipment decorated with gold and silver fill Anglo-Saxon literature, such as the epic poem *Beowulf*. An early-seventh-century burial mound, excavated in the English region of East Anglia at a site called Sutton Hoo (*hoo* means "hill") concealed a hoard of such treasures. The grave's still unidentified occupant was buried in an 86-foot-long ship. The vessel held

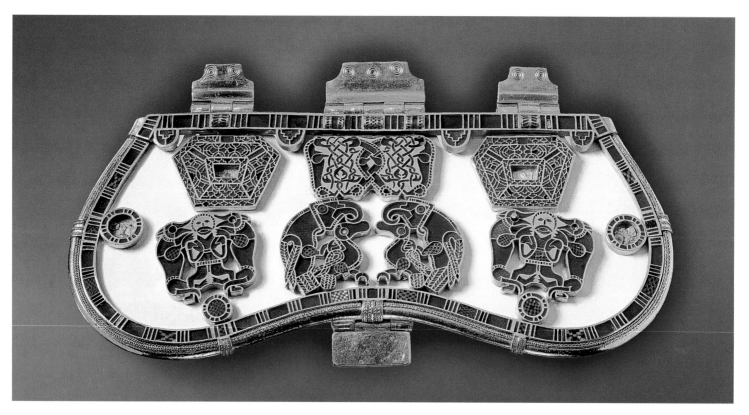

10–3 Purse cover, from the Sutton Hoo burial ship, Suffolk, England. c. 615–625. Cloisonné plaques of gold, garnet, and checked millefiore enamel, length 8″ (20.3 cm). The British Museum, London

Only the decorations on this purse cover are original. The lid itself, of a rich tan-colored ivory or bone, deteriorated and disappeared centuries ago, and the white backing is a modern replacement. The leather pouch also disintegrated, but the coins in the purse survived.

weapons, armor, other equipment for the afterlife, and such luxury items as an exquisitely worked lid for a purse (fig. **10–3**).

The purse lid is decorated with intricate **cloisonné** enamel, whose designs come from wide-ranging sources. **Animal interlace** forms the central piece at top. Growing out of the animal style popular in Scandinavia, animals (here two pairs of quadrupeds) stretch out into interwoven serpentine ribbons (compare with fig. 10–2). The pairs of animals flanking human figures at the lower right and left recall the "animal combat" theme prevalent throughout the ancient Near East (see fig. 2–8). In another combat depicted in the two central pieces at bottom, Norse hawks with curved beaks and square eyebrows attack Celtic ducks. The rich blend of motifs on the purse represent a complex style that flourished in England and Ireland during the seventh and eighth centuries.

As Christianity spread through the islands, Hiberno-Saxon scribes adapted pagan styles for large, lavishly decorated gospel books (see "The Medieval Scriptorium," page 254). The *Book of Kells*, one of the most original and inventive of the surviving Hiberno-Saxon Gospels, was probably made in the late eighth century in a monastery on Iona, an island off the west coast of Scotland. The most celebrated folio (manuscript page) in the *Book of Kells* may be the one from the Gospel of Matthew that begins the account of Jesus' birth (fig. **10–4**). The Greek letters *chi, rho,* and *iota* dominate the page. The letters create an irregular shape that resembles a cluster of gold and enamel brooches. At first glance, the page seems filled with completely abstract ornament, but hidden in the dense thicket of spirals and interlaces are human and animal forms. The spiral of the *rho* at the lower-right center of the page ends in the head of a red-headed youth, possibly representing Christ. At left center, three angels hold the left vertical edge of the *chi*. At bottom center, just at right of the end of the longest stroke, two cats each capture a mouse, and to their right an otter catches a salmon. The cat-and-mouse scene signals the triumph of good (embodied in the cats) over evil (embodied in the mice who try to eat the host—the Communion wafer, the mystical body of Christ).

Even as monks finished the *Book of Kells*, Hiberno-Saxon culture came under threat from abroad. At the end of the eighth century, seafaring bands of western Scandinavians known as

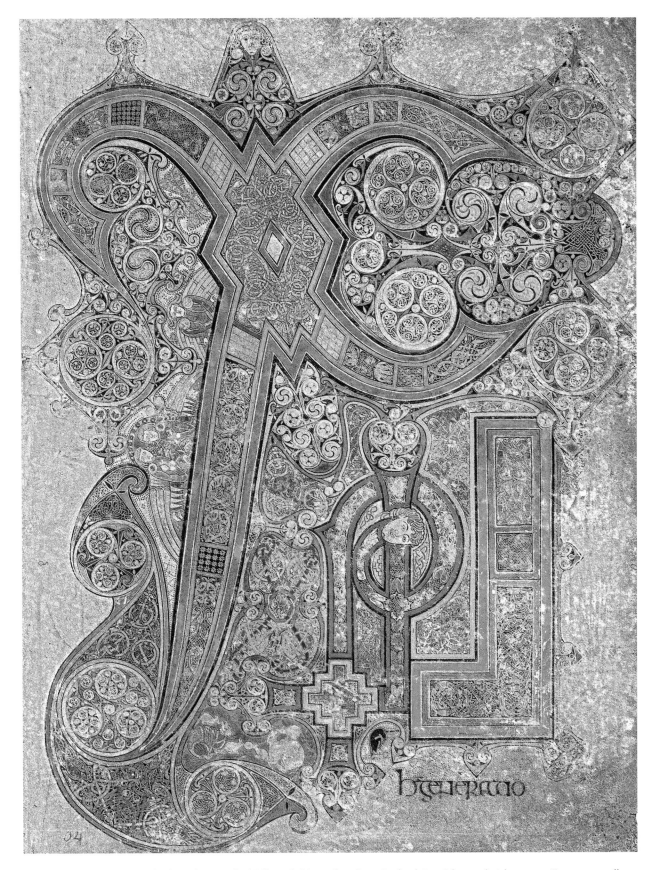

10–4 *Chi Rho Iota* page, Book of Matthew, *Book of Kells,* probably made at Iona, Scotland. Late 8th or early 9th century. Tempera on vellum, 13″ × 9 ¹/₂″ (33 × 24 cm). The Board of Trinity College, Dublin

MS 58 (A.1.6.), FOL. 34V

The Greek letters chi rho iota (XPI, *or* chri) *form the abbreviation for* Christi, *the first word in the Latin sentence* Christi autem generatio, *meaning: "Now this is how the birth of Jesus Christ came about" (Matthew 1:18). The word* autem *appears as another Latin abbreviation resembling an* h, *which is followed by* generatio *written out. The text continues on the next page. Medieval scribes had to learn a long list of standard abbreviations for Latin words, which were used like modern shorthand to save time and space in transcribing long documents or copying texts. Scribes in the courts of popes and secular rulers were even given the official title of "abbreviator."*

Vikings began to appear on the coasts of the British Isles, lured by the wealth of church treasuries and fertile land. The monks of Iona retreated, taking their precious Gospels to the inland Irish monastery of Kells. The Vikings soon descended on much of the rest of Europe. Intermittently looting and destroying coastal and inland river communities, they were a terrifying presence for nearly 300 years. Viking bands settled in what is now Iceland, Greenland, Ireland, England, France, Scotland, and Russia. About 1000, they even established a short-lived outpost in eastern North America.

Carolingian Art

The Franks had settled in northern Gaul (modern France) by the end of the fifth century. In 732 Frankish warriors turned back the Muslim invasion of Gaul, and their leaders established a dynasty of rulers known as the Carolingians, after their greatest member Charles the Great, called Charlemagne (ruled 768–814). Charlemagne consolidated an empire in continental Europe during the second half of the eighth century, which at its greatest extent encompassed modern France, western Germany, Belgium, Holland, Luxemburg, and northeastern Spain. Charlemagne imposed Christianity, sometimes brutally, throughout this territory and promoted church reform through his support of the Benedictine order of monks and nuns. In 800, Pope Leo III (ruled 795–816) granted Charlemagne the title of emperor, declaring him the rightful successor to the first Christian Roman emperor, Constantine. This event served to reinforce Charlemagne's authority over his realm and strengthened the bonds between the papacy and secular government in the West.

To visually proclaim the glory of the new empire, Charlemagne's architects, painters, and sculptors turned to the two former Western imperial capitals, Rome and Ravenna, for inspiration. The chapel of Charlemagne's palace at Aachen (in Germany) had several functions; it served as the emperor's private chapel, as the church of his imperial court, as a martyrium to house the precious relics of saints, and, after Charlemagne's death, as his mausoleum. Perhaps the builders were inspired by buildings they saw in Italy. The building has a central octagonal plan (fig. **10–5**), as does the Church of San Vitale in Ravenna (see fig. 7–14); however, it lacks San Vitale's sophisticated structure. The core of the chapel building is a soaring octagon (fig. **10–6**), surrounded at the ground level by an **ambulatory** (passage) and, on the second floor, ringed by a **gallery** (opening overlooking the nave). In the gallery, bays divided by diaphragm arches (arches supporting walls) support transverse barrel-vaulted bays. Columns and railings at the gallery level form a screen and reemphasize the flat, pierced walls of the octagon. These features create a powerful sense of vertical movement from the floor of the central area to the top of the vault.

A new architectural feature created by Carolingian architects is the **westwork**, or monumental entrance. At Aachen above a projecting porch, a throne room and chapel face the apse, giving the emperor an unobstructed view of the ceremonies at the high altar, and at the same time ensuring his privacy and safety. Twin stair towers flank this entrance complex and create a distinctive western facade. The vertical emphasis of the western towers and the equally upward rising thrust of the interior were northern contributions to Christian architecture, in marked contrast to the more horizontal forms of Roman and Early Christian basilicas.

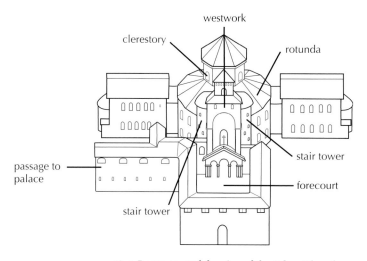

10–5 Reconstructed drawing of the Palace Chapel of Charlemagne, now the Cathedral of Aachen, Germany. Constructed 792–805

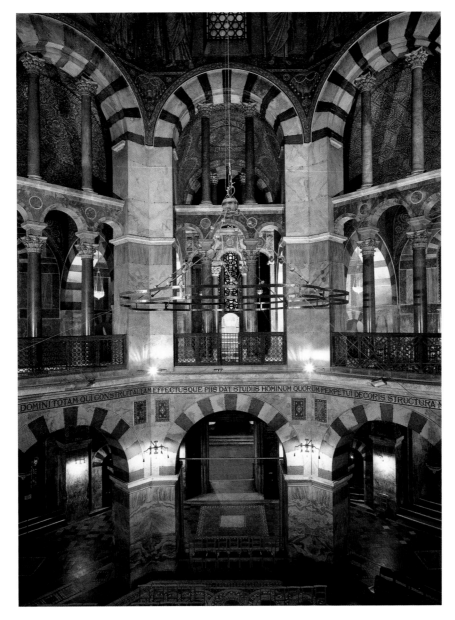

10–6 Palace Chapel of Charlemagne, interior view, Aachen (Aix-la-Chapelle), Germany. 792–805

Although the chapel retains its original design and some fittings, including the bronze railings, much of its decoration either has been restored or dates from later periods. The ivory chair seen through the center arches at the gallery level is reputed to be the throne of Charlemagne. An enormous "crown of light" chandelier—presented to the church by Emperor Frederick Barbarossa in 1168—was once suspended over the central space. Extensive renovations took place in the nineteenth century, when the chapel was reconsecrated as the cathedral of Aachen, and in the twentieth century, after it was damaged in World War II.

The Carolingian Basilica and Timber Architecture

Charlemagne's biographer, Einhard, reported that the ruler, "beyond all sacred and venerable places . . . loved the church of the holy apostle Peter at Rome." Not surprisingly, Charlemagne's architects turned to Constantine's basilica of Saint Peter, with its long nave and side aisles ending in a transept and projecting apse

(see fig. 7–6), as a model for his own churches. The Abbey Church of Saint Riquier at the monastery at Centula in northern France illustrates the Carolingian reworking of the basilican plan at the end of the eighth century. Repeatedly destroyed by Vikings and rebuilt, St. Riquier's no longer stands but is known today from archaeological evidence and a seventeenth-century engraving (fig. 10–7). For the abbey's more than 300 monks, the enclosure between the church and two freestanding chapels may have

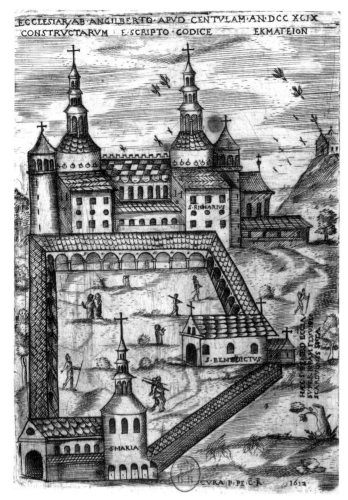

10–7 **Abbey church of Saint Riquier, Monastery of Centula,** France. Dedicated 799. Engraving dated 1612, after an 11th-century drawing. Bibliothèque Nationale, Paris

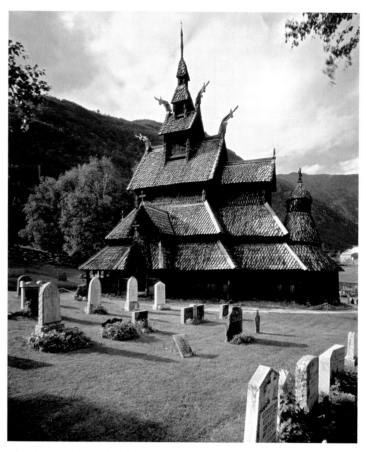

10–8 **Borgund stave church, Sogn,** Norway. c. 1125–1150

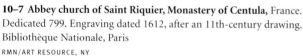

The two tall, multi-storied towers seen at St. Requier (fig. 10–7) must have been timber constructions. Above the cylindrical base supported by the crossing of nave and transepts, three stories of decreasing size rise to form towers. The stave church in Borgund, Norway (fig. 10–8), suggests the appearance and construction technique of such structures. At Borgund the builders used six levels of steeply sloped roofs–the first three cover usable space (outside galleries, aisles, nave), and the upper three create a soaring spire formed by units stacked one on top of the other. Towers and towerlike forms emphasize the importance of building.

served as a cloister. A cloister is an arcaded courtyard that often encloses a garden and a well. The cloister links the church and the buildings of the monastic community.

The Church of Saint Riquier had a nave and side aisles joining complex east and west ends. The western entrance (at the upper left of the drawing) consists of a multistory westwork including paired towers, a transept, and a crossing tower. The eastern end of the church (at the upper right) also has a crossing tower over the transept and an extended choir and apse. The two tall crossing towers would have been the building's most striking feature. They soar from cylindrical bases through three arcaded levels to cross-topped spires. This verticality contrasted dramatically with the horizontality of the Roman basilicas. The Carolingian "double ended" church would have dominated the landscape with towers visible from far away.

A church in the fjord country of western Norway, although built in the twelfth century, suggests the appearance of Carolingian timber buildings. The great forests of Northern Europe provided the materials for timber buildings of all kinds. Subject to decay and fire, wooden buildings rarely survive. However, medieval timber churches can still be found in Norway. They are known as stave churches, from the four huge timbers (staves) that form the structural core of the building. Borgund stave church, built about 1125–1150, is one of the finest (fig. **10–8**). Four corner staves support the central roof, and the stacked wooden stages of the tower, while a rounded apse, also covered with a tower, is attached to the choir (the towers at St. Riquier may have looked like this). A steep-roofed gallery rings the entire building, and wooden shingles cover the roofs and some walls. The steeply pitched roofs protect the walls from the rain and snow. On all the gables either crosses or dragon heads protect the church and its congregation. The same basic wooden structure was used for almost all building types—on a large scale for palaces, assembly halls, and churches; on a small scale for domestic shelters which people shared with their animals.

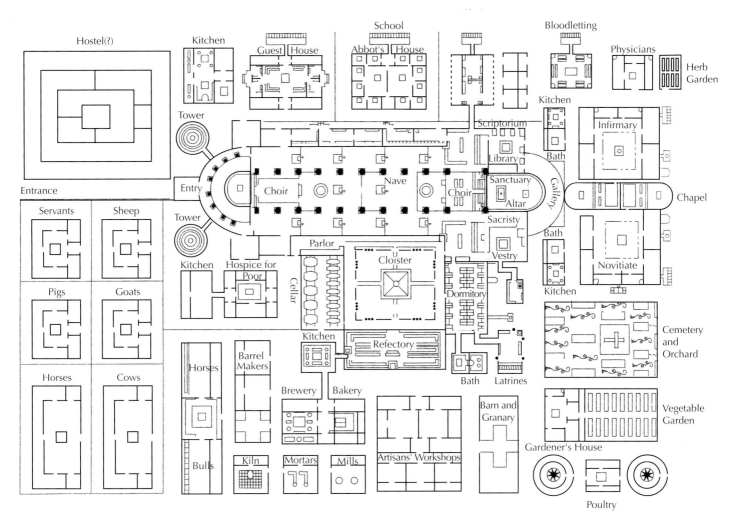

10–9 Plan of the Abbey of Saint Gall, (redrawn). c. 817. Original in red ink on parchment, 28″ × 44½″ (71.1 × 112.1 cm). Stiftsbibliothek, St. Gallen, Switzerland, Cod. Sang. 1092

The Monastery

Charlemagne turned to the Church to help stabilize his empire through religion and education. He looked to the Benedictine monks whom he called his "cultural army." The monks followed the *Rule for Monasteries,* written by Saint Benedict of Nursia (c. 480–c. 547), a set of practical guidelines for community life that combined work, prayer, and participation in religious services. To house such a community, in the ninth century, Abbot Haito of Reichenau developed an ideal plan for the layout of monasteries, which survives in the library of the Abbey of Saint Gall in modern Switzerland (fig. **10–9**). The Saint Gall plan shows a basilican church with towers and—assuming the church would have been orientated—both eastern and western apses to house altars and relics. The cloister and monks' quarters lie at the south, with dormitory, refectory (dining room), and work-

rooms; at the east are the cemetery, hospital, and school for young monks and novices; and at the north stand the abbot's residence, guest quarters, and a hospice for the poor. Buildings for lay farm workers and shelter for animals surrounded this central core. So efficient and functional was this plan that Benedictine monasteries often still follow the layout today.

Although their principal duties consisted of prayer and liturgical services, monks and nuns also spent hours producing books. Scrupulously edited versions of key religious texts, written in a new, clear script based on ancient Roman forms, are among the lasting achievements of the Carolingian period. The monasteries of northeastern France became centers of book production during the reign of Louis the Pious (ruled 814–840), Charlemagne's son and successor. A portrait of Saint Matthew, from a gospel book made for Archbishop Ebbo of Reims at the Abbey of Hautevillers near Reims, demonstrates

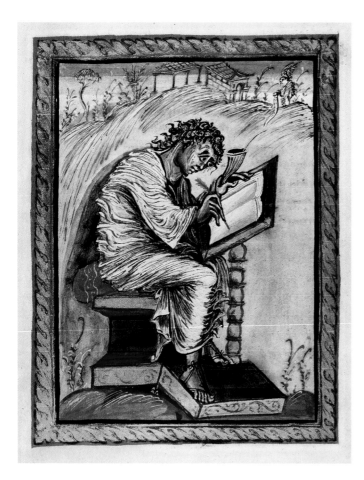

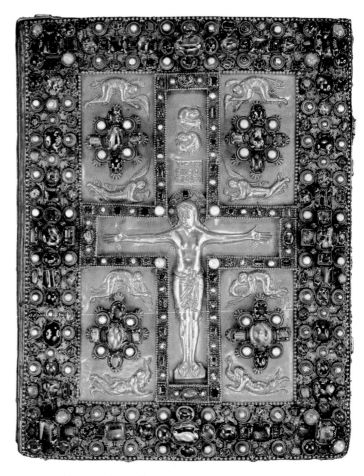

10–10 Page with *Matthew the Evangelist.* Book of Matthew, *Ebbo Gospels.* c. 816–840. Ink and colors on vellum, 10 1/4″ × 8 3/4″ (26 × 22.2 cm). Bibliothèque Municipale Epernay, France
MS 1, FOL.18V

Following an ancient tradition, a "portrait" of the author introduces each Gospel, as a photograph on a book jacket flap may introduce the author to the reader today.

10–11 *Crucifixion with Angels and Mourning Figures,* outer cover, *Lindau Gospels,* c. 870–880. Gold, pearls, and gems, 13 3/4″ × 10 3/8″ (34.9 × 26.7 cm). The Pierpont Morgan Library, New York

the unique style that emerged there (fig. **10–10**). The figure seems to vibrate with intensity. Even the acanthus leaves in the frame seem blown by a violent wind. The rapid, calligraphic style focuses attention on the evangelist's spiritual excitement as he hastens to transcribe the Word of God delivered by the angel (Matthew's symbol), who is almost lost in the upper-right corner. As if to echo the saint's turbulent emotions, the footstool tilts precariously, and the top of the desk seems about to detach itself from the pedestal.

Manuscripts such as the *Ebbo Gospels* represent an enormous investment of time, talent, and materials. Only a wealthy monastery could afford to slaughter the hundreds of sheep required for the parchment on which the books were written. Books were protected with heavy, leather-covered wooden, and sometimes jeweled, covers. One of the richest of these covers (fig. **10–11**)—probably made between 870–880 at one of the shops working for Charles the Bald (ruled 840–877), the son of Louis the

Pious—combines jewels, pearls, and sculpture in gold. (Sometime before the sixteenth century, the cover was added to a late-ninth-century Carolingian manuscript known as the *Lindau Gospels.*)

The Crucifixion scene on the front cover features gold figures in relief. The figures are formed by the repoussé technique, which we saw in the Byzantine icon of the archangel Michael (see fig. 7–21). Angels hover above the arms of the cross, and mourners twist in agony below. Over Jesus's head figures representing the sun and moon hide their faces. In contrast to these agitated figures, the artist modeled Jesus in a rounded, naturalistic style that suggests a classical source. Christ stands in front of the cross—straight and wide-eyed with outstretched arms, announcing his triumph over death and welcoming believers into the faith. The jewels, polished to form cabochons (polished, not faceted, stones), are raised on tiny feet that allow light to penetrate, thus enhancing their luster. Such glowing colored jewels reminded medieval believers of descriptions of the Heavenly Jerusalem.

Painting in Christian Spain

The Christian and Islamic worlds met in medieval Spain. When Muslim armies arrived in the early eighth century, Spain was governed by the Visigoths, a Germanic people who had ruled over the indigenous Spanish population since the fall of the Western Roman Empire. The Islamic conquest of Spain in 711 ended Visigothic rule. With some exceptions, the Muslims allowed Christians and Jews to follow their own religious practices. Christian artists adapted many features of Islamic style to fit their traditional themes and developed a hybrid style known today as Mozarabic.

Writing biblical commentaries to refute heretical beliefs became a major task of the monasteries of northern Spain. Antagonisms among Muslims, orthodox Christians, and the followers of various heretical Christian beliefs provided fertile material for Spanish theologians. Beatus, the abbot of a monastery in the kingdom of Asturias on the northern coast, compiled an influential commentary on the Apocalypse, which describes the final and fiery destruction of the world before the Last Judgment and triumph of Christ. The scribe named Senior made a copy of Beatus's *Commentary on the Apocalypse* in the late tenth century at the Monastery of San Salvador at Tábara, in the Spanish kingdom of León. The illustrators were a monk named Emeterius and a nun named Ende, who signed herself "painter and servant of God."

A full-page painting from this book (fig. **10–12**) illustrates Beatus's metaphorical description of the triumph of Christ over Satan. According to the text next to the illustration, a bird with a powerful beak and beautiful plumage (Christ) covers itself with mud to trick the snake (Satan). Just when the snake decides the bird is harmless, the bird swiftly attacks and kills it. **Allegories** such as this were popular among artists, writers, and theologians in the Middle Ages. Because allegories translate abstract ideas into concrete events and images, they communicate directly with people of almost any level of education. The painters followed a time-honored Christian tradition, for Jesus himself spoke to the people in parables.

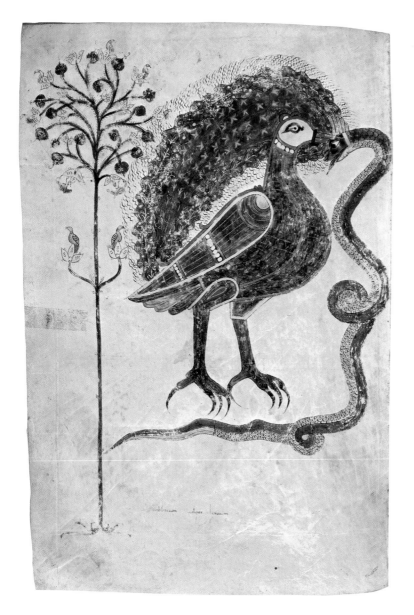

10–12 Emeterius and Ende, with the scribe Senior. Page with ***Battle of the Bird and the Serpent,*** *Commentary on the Apocalypse* by Beatus and *Commentary on Daniel* by Jerome, made for Abbot Dominicus, probably at the Monastery of San Salvador al Tábara, León, Spain. Completed July 6, 975. Tempera on parchment, 15 3/4" × 10 1/4" (40 × 26 cm). Cathedral Library, Gerona, Spain MS7 [11], FOL. 18V

10–13 *Christ Enthroned with Saints and Emperor Otto I,* one of a series of nineteen ivory plaques, known as the *Magdeburg Ivories.* German or North Italian. c. 962–973. Ivory plaque, 5″ × 4¹⁄₂″ (12.7 × 11.4 cm). The Metropolitan Museum of Art, New York

GIFT OF GEORGE BLUMENTHAL, 1941 (41.100.157)

During the reign of Otto I, Magdeburg was on the edge of a buffer zone between the Ottonian Empire and the pagan Slavs. In the 960s, Otto established a religious center there, from which the Slavs could be converted.

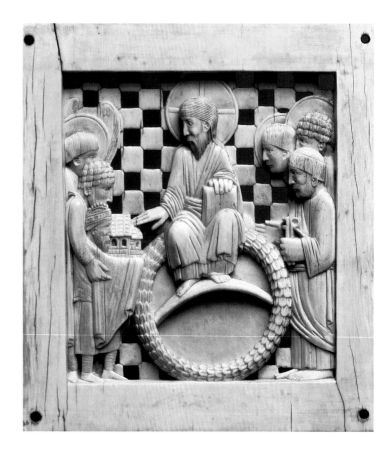

The Ottonian Period

The heirs of Louis the Pious divided the Carolingian Empire into three parts, setting the stage for the modern divisions of Europe. The western portion eventually became France. In the tenth century, control of the eastern portion of the empire, which corresponded roughly to modern Germany, Switzerland, and Austria passed to a dynasty of Saxon rulers known as the Ottonians, after its three principal figures, Otto I (ruled 936–973), Otto II (ruled 973–983), and Otto III (ruled 983–1002). Otto I gained control of Italy in 951, and the pope crowned him emperor in 962. Thereafter Otto and his successors dominated the papacy and appointments to other high Church offices.

An ivory panel shows Otto I presenting a model of the cathedral of Magdeburg to Christ (fig. **10–13**). For all his earthly power, Otto is a tiny figure in the company of Christ and the saints, who include Saint Peter, holding the keys to heaven, and Saint Maurice, who presents Otto to Christ. Saint Maurice was a third-century Roman Christian commander of African troops who is said to have suffered martyrdom for refusing to worship in pagan rites. In the Middle Ages, he was often represented as a dark-skinned African. Christ, seated on a heavenly wreath, his feet on the arc of the earth, graciously extends his hand to receive the offering.

In the tenth and eleventh centuries, Ottonian artists in Northern Europe, drawing on Roman, Byzantine, and Carolingian models, began a new tradition of large sculpture in wood and bronze that would have a significant influence on later medieval art. An important patron of architecture and sculpture was Bishop Bernward of Hildesheim, Germany, who was himself a skilled goldsmith. A pair of bronze doors made under his direction for his Abbey Church of Saint Michael represents the most ambitious and complex bronze-casting project since antiquity (fig. **10–14**). The inscription in the band running across the center of the doors states that Bishop Bernward installed them in 1015.

The doors, standing more than 16 feet tall, are decorated with Old Testament scenes on the left and New Testament scenes on the right. The Old Testament scenes read down from the top to the bottom panel; the New Testament narrative continues on the right, upward from the bottom panel (the Annunciation) to the top *(Noli me tangere)* (see "Iconography of the Life of Jesus," pages 168 and 169). In each pair of scenes, the Old Testament event can be interpreted as a prefiguration of the New Testament event. Such elaborate parallels characterize the Christian use of images. The third panel down on the left, for example, shows Adam and Eve picking the forbidden fruit of Knowledge in the Garden of Eden and thus bringing down on humankind the evils of sin, suffering, and death. This scene is paired on the right with the Crucifixion of Jesus, whose sacrifice was believed to have atoned for Adam and Eve's Original Sin. At the center of the doors, six panels down—between the door pulls—Eve (left) and Mary (right) sit side by side, holding their sons. Cain (who murdered his brother) and Jesus signify the opposition of evil and good, damnation and salvation. Other telling pairs are the murder of Abel with the Annunciation—the first sin and the beginning of salvation—and the passing of blame from Adam and Eve to the serpent paired with Pilate washing his hands.

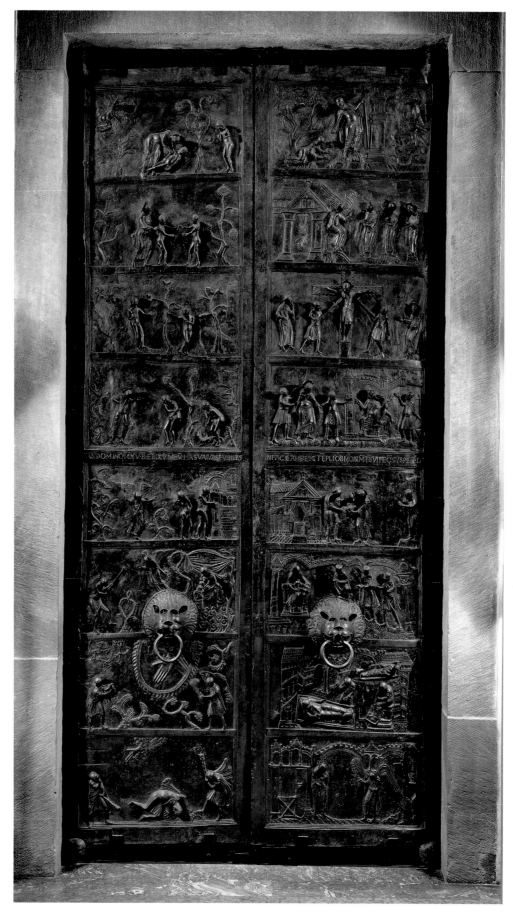

10–14 Bishop Bernward Doors, made for the Abbey Church of Saint Michael. Cathedral Museum, Hildesheim, Germany. 1015. Bronze, height 16′6″ (5 m)

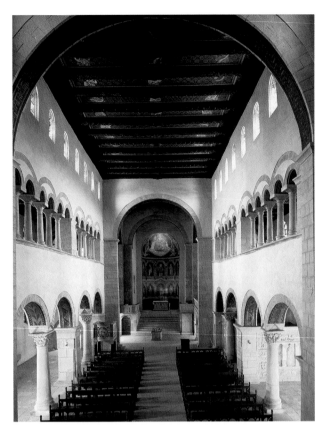

10–15 Nave, Church of Saint Cyriakus, Gernrode, Germany. Begun 961, consecrated 973

During the Ottonian Empire, aristocratic women often held positions of authority, especially as abbesses (leaders of religious communities). When Margrave Gero (the provincial military governor) founded the convent of Saint Cyriakus, he made his widowed daughter-in-law the convent's first abbess, following the Ottonian policy of appointing relatives and close associates to important church offices. The margrave began building the church of Saint Cyriakus (fig. **10–15**) in 961. Like a Carolingian basilica (see figs. 10–7, 10–9), the church has a nave and side aisles with a three-part elevation (nave arcade, gallery, and clerestory). The masons based the plan on a square module, two squares for the nave, and one each for the crossing and choir. Square piers and short walls define the bays (units of space). The rectangular piers and walls alternating with round columns in the nave arcade create a rhythmic effect that is more interesting than the uniform colonnades seen in earlier buildings. At the gallery level, pairs of openings are framed by larger arches and then grouped in threes. The central pier also divides the space vertically with two large arches of the nave arcade surmounted by three pairs of arches at the gallery level. The small, evenly spaced windows and the wooden raftered ceiling do not continue this pattern and instead reinforce the continuous movement toward the choir and altar. This seemingly simple design, with its rhythmic alternation of heavy and light supports, its balance of rectangular and rounded forms, and its combination of horizontal and vertical movements, found full expression in the architecture of the succeeding Romanesque style.

Like their Carolingian predecessors, monks and nuns of the Ottonian Period created richly illuminated manuscripts, often subsidized by secular rulers. Styles varied from place to place, depending on the traditions of the local scriptorium and the models available in each library.

Elaborate architecture provides the setting for the unusual presentation page of a Gospel book made for Abbess Hitda (d. 1041) of Meschede, near Cologne, in the early eleventh century (fig. **10–16**). The abbess offers her book to Saint Walpurga, her convent's patron saint. The artist has arranged the architectural lines of the convent in the background to frame the figures and draw attention to the transaction. The size of the buildings underscores the abbess's position of authority. The foreground setting—a rocky, uneven strip of landscape—is meant to be understood as holy ground, separated from the rest of the world by golden trees and the huge arch-shaped aura that silhouettes Saint Walpurga. The simple contours of the stately figures give them a monumental quality that recalls Byzantine art.

THE MEDIEVAL SCRIPTORIUM

Today, presses can produce hundreds of thousands of identical copies of any book. In medieval Europe, however, before the invention of printing from movable type in the mid-1400s, books were made by hand, one at a time, with pen, ink, brush, and paint. Each one was a time-consuming and expensive undertaking.

At first, medieval books were usually made by monks and nuns in a workshop called a scriptorium (plural, scriptoria), usually in a monastery or convent. As the demand for books increased, rulers set up palace workshops of both religious and lay scribes, supervised by scholars.

Before paper came into common use in the early 1400s, books were written on prepared animal skin called parchment or vellum, which was a fine calfskin. The skins were cleaned and scraped to create a smooth surface for writing and painting. Ink and paint also required time and experience to prepare, and many pigments—particularly blues and greens—were made from costly semiprecious stones. In very important manuscripts, artists also used gold in the form of gold leaf or gold paint.

Work on a book was often divided between scribes, who copied the text, and one or more artists, who painted illustrations, large initials, or other decorations.

Although most books were produced anonymously, scribes and illustrators sometimes signed their work or provided background information in a colophon (notes on the book's production at the end of the manuscript).

The earliest books, scrolls, were made of sheets pasted or stitched together and were kept rolled up for protection and storage. Today, the most common kind of book is the *codex*, in which a number of folded sheets are stitched or glued together. About 400 CE, the codex began to assume greater favor than other book forms in Europe. The scroll remained popular in Asia.

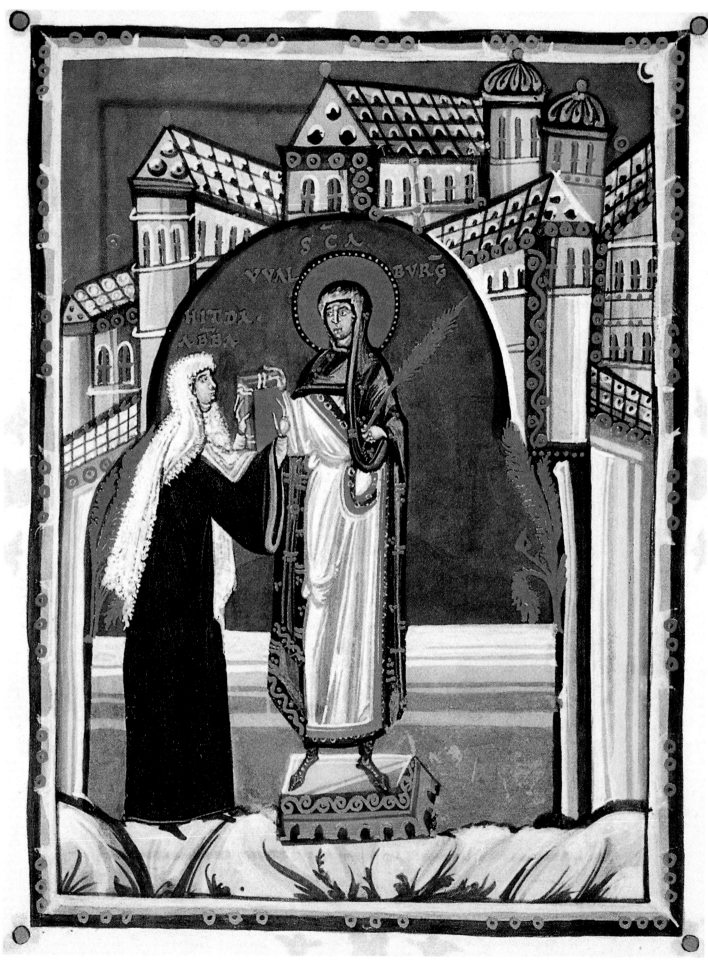

10–16 Presentation page with Abbess Hitda and Saint Walpurga, *Hitda Gospels*. Early 11th century. Ink and colors on vellum, 11⅜″ × 5⅝″ (29 × 14.2 cm). Hessische Landesund Hochschulbibliothek, Darmstadt, Germany

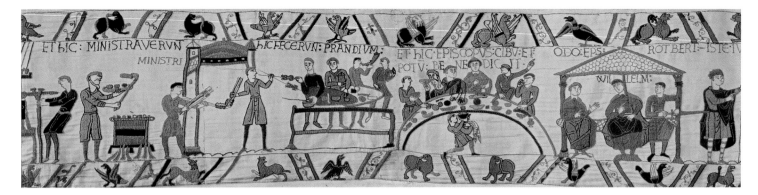

10–17 *Bishop Odo Blessing the Feast,* sections 47–48 of the *Bayeux Tapestry*, Norman-Anglo-Saxon embroidery from Canterbury, Kent, England, or Bayeux, Normandy, France. c. 1066–1082. Linen with wool embroidery, height 20″ (50.8 cm). Centre Guillaume le Conquérant, Bayeux, France, by special permission of the City of Bayeux

A text running above the scenes describes the action. In this section servants (identified as ministri*) are preparing the meal by roasting meat on spits over a grill. They pass the food to the warriors seated at a table made by placing shields on trestles. At the head table Bishop Odo blesses the food, attended by a servant holding a basin and towel. At the right William the Conqueror (Willelm) confers with his two half-brothers, Bishop Odo (Odo epsi) and Robert (Rotbert), who holds a sword.*

The *Gospels of Otto III* (see fig. 10–1), made in a German monastery about 1000, shows the inspiration of Byzantine art in the use of clear outline drawing, rich colors, and lavish amounts of gold. Otto III abandoned his German homeland, preferring to live in Rome. From his palace on the hill near the Early Christian Church of Santa Sabina (see fig. 7–7), he could look out over the ruins of ancient Rome. The theme of Christian charity and humility represented by Christ washing his disciples' feet contrasts with Otto's dream of imperial glory as well as the richness of the illuminated manuscript. The grandeur evoked by this intensely expressive style makes Ottonian painting one of the most splendid in all medieval art.

The incorporation of parts of Italy into the Ottonian Empire, which had begun under Otto I, came to be known in the twelfth century as the Holy Roman Empire. (The Holy Roman Empire formed the basis of the later Habsburg Empire.) The Ottonian court in Rome gave northern artists access to the artistic heritage of Italy, which they reinterpreted in light of their own local materials and techniques. From this groundwork during the early medieval period emerged the arts of European Romanesque culture.

The Romanesque Period

As the first millennium drew to a close, European society began to change. In theory much of the land in medieval Europe belonged to kings and lords, who held the territory in trust for God. In turn, the kings and lords might grant some of this property to their supporters, lesser noblemen called vassals. In exchange, vassals promised to help render justice and provide defensive military service in the form of knights. In some regions, this system of allegiances evolved into a formal "feudal system." The economy was based on the labor of landless but free peasants who lived in villages and worked on the estates (manors).

But in the eleventh century, life changed from a largely agricultural economy controlled by a landholding aristocracy to one where craft industries and trade allowed greater personal freedom and well-being. As various inventions started to make farming more efficient and the population increased, people began to move from agricultural villages into burgeoning towns and cities. Cities populated by merchants and artisans remained outside the feudal system. Rulers sometimes granted charters to cities in exchange for the money they needed to form an independent power base.

The nations we know today did not exist in medieval Europe. In what is now Germany and Italy, local rulers and towns resisted attempts by the successors of the Ottonian emperors to impose a central authority. The Holy Roman Empire existed more in theory than in fact. The pope in Rome and the patriarch in Constantinople continued to be important players in European politics, often forging fruitful alliances with the political rulers. In much of what is now France, where the feudal system prevailed, powerful dukes controlled the richest lands. Kings slowly consolidated their personal territory around Paris, and—by the end of the twelfth century—they had laid the foundation for a powerful national monarchy. Southern French lands retained their own linguistic and cultural traditions, while across the Pyrenees, the Iberian Peninsula was a battleground of Christians and Muslims during this period of "reconquest."

Normandy, a peninsula on the northern coast of Europe that had been settled by Vikings, became a powerful feudal duchy. In 1066, William, Duke of Normandy (1035–1087) invaded England and, as William the Conqueror, he became that country's king. William's victory is recorded in the *Bayeux Tapestry* (fig. **10–17**). William replaced the Anglo-Saxon nobility with Norman nobles, and England began to emerge as the nation it is today.

By the twelfth century, popular mass movements such as pilgrimages and the Crusades began to end European

During the late Middle Ages, people in Western Europe once again began to travel in large numbers as traders, soldiers, and Christians on pilgrimages. Pilgrims throughout history have journeyed to holy sites—the ancient Greeks to Delphi, early Christians to Jerusalem and to Rome, Muslims to Mecca—but in the eleventh century, pilgrimages to the holy places of Christendom dramatically increased.

As difficult and dangerous as these journeys were, rewards awaited the courageous travelers along the routes, even before they reached their destination. Pilgrims could stop along the way to venerate local saints by visiting their relics and the places where miracles were believed to have taken place. Relics—bodies of saints, parts of bodies, or even things owned by saints—were thought to have miraculous powers, and they were kept in richly decorated containers called reliquaries.

Having and displaying the relics of saints so enhanced the prestige and wealth of a community that people went to great lengths to acquire them, not only by purchase but also by theft. In the ninth century, for example, the monks of Conques stole the relics of the child martyr Saint Faith from her shrine at Saint-Agens. Such a theft was called holy robbery, for the new owners insisted that the saint had encouraged them because she wanted to move. The monks of Conques encased their relic—the skull of Saint Faith—in a jewel-bedecked gold statue whose head was made from a Roman parade helmet (fig. **10–18**).

To accommodate the faithful and instruct them in church doctrine, many monasteries on the major pilgrimage routes built large new churches and filled them with sumptuous altars, crosses, and reliquaries. Sculpture and paintings on the walls illustrated important religious stories and doctrines, and served to instruct as well as fascinate the faithful. These awe-inspiring works of art and architecture, like most of what has come down to us from the Romanesque period, had a Christian purpose. One monk wrote that by decorating the church "well and gracefully," the artist showed "the beholders something of the likeness of the paradise of God" (cited in Theophilus, page 79).

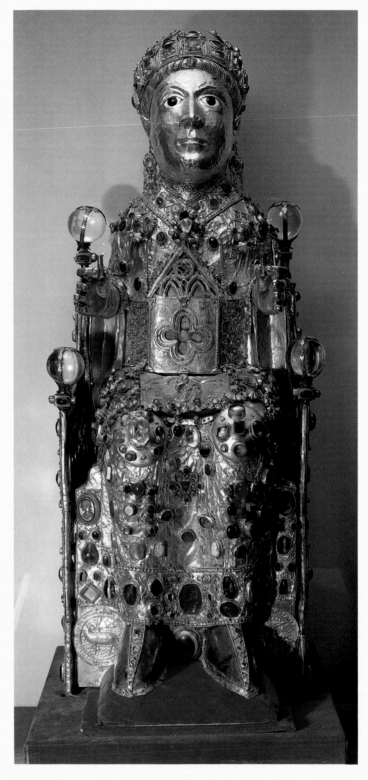

10–18 Reliquary statue of Saint Faith (French: Foy; Latin: Fides), made in the Auvergne region, France, for the Abbey Church of Conques, Rouergue, France. Late 9th to first half of 10th century. Gold repoussé and gemstones over wood core (incorporating a Roman helmet and Roman cameos; later additions 12th–19th centuries), height 33″ (85 cm). Cathedral Treasury, Conques, France

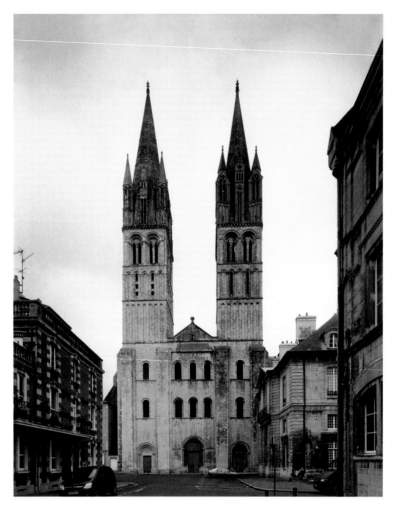

10–19 Church of Saint-Étienne, Caen, Normandy, France. Begun 1064; facade late 11th century; spires 13th century

isolation. In 1095, Pope Urban II called for the first of several Crusades ostensibly to "free" Jerusalem and the Holy Land from Islamic rule. Although the Crusades were for the most part military failures, the Western crusaders' encounters with the sophisticated Byzantine and Islamic cultures introduced new technology and ideas into Europe and created a demand for new products and luxury goods. Despite encountering dire material and physical hardships on their journeys, people from all levels of society traveled on pilgrimages to the holy places of Christendom. The three major shrines were the tomb of Christ (the Holy Sepulchre) in Jerusalem and the tombs of St. Peter in Rome and St. James in Santiago de Compostela, but there were many local pilgrimage sites as well (see fig. **10–19**). Travel and trade led to the rise of an increasingly knowledgeable and urban society, and foreign contacts helped to nourish a period of intellectual and artistic ferment.

The art produced during the period of the eleventh and twelfth centuries is called *Romanesque* ("in the Roman manner"). Historians first used the word to describe architecture that had the solid masonry walls, rounded arches, and masonry vaults characteristic of ancient Roman building. A remarkable variety of artistic traditions, including Roman, Carolingian, Mozarabic, and Italo-Byzantine, blended with local styles to form the Romanesque style. The term *Romanesque* is now applied to all the arts produced from roughly the mid-eleventh through the twelfth century.

Architecture

By the eleventh and twelfth centuries, improving agricultural methods and increased prosperity provided the resources for increased building activity in Europe. The need to provide for personal security in a period of constant local warfare and political upheaval, as well as the desire to glorify the house of the Lord and his saints, meant that builders used much of their resources for castles and churches. Halls, houses, barns, and monasteries were also built. The buildings that still stand—despite the ravages of weather, vandalism, neglect, and war—testify to the technical skills of the builders and the power, local pride, and religious faith of the patrons.

In the twelfth century, Dover Castle (see fig. **10–20**), safeguarding the coast of England from invasion, illustrates the way in which a key defensive position developed over the centuries. The Romans had built a lighthouse on the point, to which the Anglo Saxons added a church (both can be seen surrounded by earthworks in the upper center of the illustration). Earthworks topped by wooden walls provided a measure of security, but the

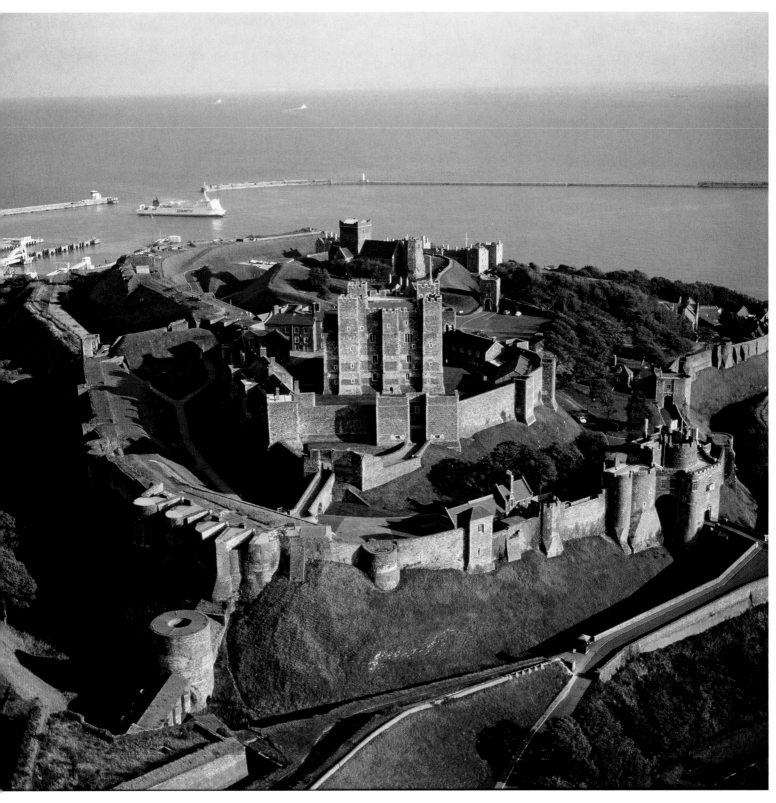

10–20 Dover Castle, air view overlooking the harbor and the English Channel. Center distance: Roman lighthouse tower and rebuilt Anglo Saxon church. Center: square Norman Great Tower in center, surrounding earthworks and walls, 12th century. Outer walls, 13th century. Modern buildings (red tile roofs). The castle still played a role in World War II.

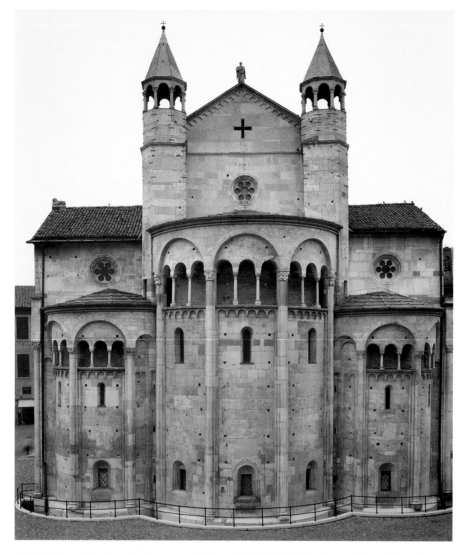

10–21 Modena Cathedral, view from east. Modena, Emilia, Italy. Building begun 1099, mainly 12th century

advantage of building fire-resistant walls was obvious. In the twelfth and thirteenth centuries, military engineers replaced the walls with stone and added the massive stone towers we see today. The Great Tower, as it was called in the Middle Ages (but later known as a *keep* or *donjon*), had a courtyard (*bailey*) surrounded by additional walls. Ditches added to the height of the walls; in some castles, ditches were filled with water to form moats. The castle yard was filled with buildings. A great lord had a hall used for feasts and ceremonial occasions. Timber buildings housed troops, servants, and animals. Barns and workshops, ovens and wells were also needed since the castle had to be self-sufficient. A gatehouse—perhaps with a drawbridge—controlled the entrance. If enemies broke through the outer walls, the castle's defenders retreated to the Great Tower. In the thirteenth century, the walls at Dover were doubled and strengthened with towers although the castle's position on cliffs overlooking the sea made scaling the walls nearly impossible. A castle's garrison could be forced to surrender only by starving its occupants. Dover is well preserved, but in most places broken walls and ruined towers stand as grim reminders of long sieges and the precariousness of medieval life.

If the castle of the secular lord was to be an imposing masonry structure, the house of God was equally powerful and

impressive. As one medieval monk put it, the world was "clothed everywhere in a white garment of churches" (Radulphus Glaber, cited in Holt, page 18). Romanesque churches, like their early medieval predecessors, are often basilicas modified in significant aesthetic and structural ways. Designs varied from place to place, depending on how the master builder solved the problems associated with each project. The master's own knowledge and experience and the wishes of the patrons who provided the funding also influenced the results. Consequently, there is no such thing as a single typical Romanesque church. Although timber remained a common building material, especially in northern Europe, Romanesque builders used masonry when conditions permitted. They and their patrons appreciated the greater strength and fire resistance of masonry. Masonry vaults enhanced the acoustical properties of a building and the effect of the Gregorian chants sung inside. Stone barrel vaults or four-part groin vaults (see "Arch and Vault," page 141) reinforced by powerful supporting arches called ribs—a medieval innovation—covered aisles and even the nave. These new ribbed vaults permitted builders some flexibility in laying out interior space. **Buttresses** (thick masses of masonry) reinforced walls at critical points and made taller buildings and masonry vaults possible. Towers emphasized both the **crossing** (where the nave and transept intersect) and the west facade, which contained the principal entrance to the church. The portal was the entrance to the City of God, the Heavenly Jerusalem.

Across the Channel from Dover, Norman builders created a vertical-towered design for a west facade. The abbey church dedicated to St. Stephen (Saint-Étienne) in Caen (fig. 10–19), was founded by William the Conqueror in 1064, and the facade was built between 1096 and 1100. Massive buttresses divide the walls of the facade into three vertical sections, and small stringcourses (unbroken moldings) at each window level suggest the three stories of the building's interior (nave arcade, triforium gallery, and clerestory). The vertical lines of the buttresses lead to two tall towers whose spires were added later in the Gothic style (see Chapter 11). This two-towered west facade recalls a fortified gateway. It marks the entrance into the church and consequently functions as a symbolic gateway to Paradise.

In Romanesque churches, the portal—which is sometimes preceded by a narthex, or entrance porch—opens into a nave and aisles that lead to the sanctuary. When a large congregation or many clergy required that the sanctuary be expanded, two plans evolved for the east end of a church. At Modena, Italy, the cathedral (fig. 10–21) illustrates the triple apse plan, sometimes called "Benedictine." A large apse housing the high altar is flanked by a smaller apse at each side. A horizontal arcade, or external gallery, composed of large arches enclosing three smaller arches, circles the building at the top of the wall and gives a geometric unity to the design. A pair of slender turrets provides external accents.

The second plan answered the need for additional altars for relics and space for pilgrims as well as clergy. Pilgrimage churches had to accommodate huge crowds of pilgrims and permit them to move from shrine to shrine without disrupting regular church services. Additional altars and chapels were needed as collections of relics grew. Romanesque builders solved the problem by adding chapels to a wide transept and by adding an ambulatory, or walkway, that circled the apse and led to many chapels housing additional altars and relics (fig. 10–22). This new plan permitted the pilgrims to move freely from chapel to chapel. On entering a church like the Cathedral of Santiago de Compostela, the viewer's attention is focused on the principal

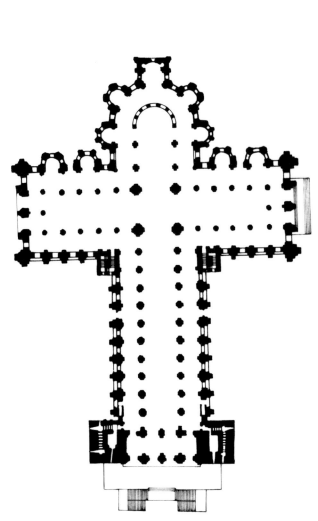

10–22 Plan of Cathedral of Saint James, Santiago de Compostela, Galicia, Spain. c. 1078–1122, with later additions

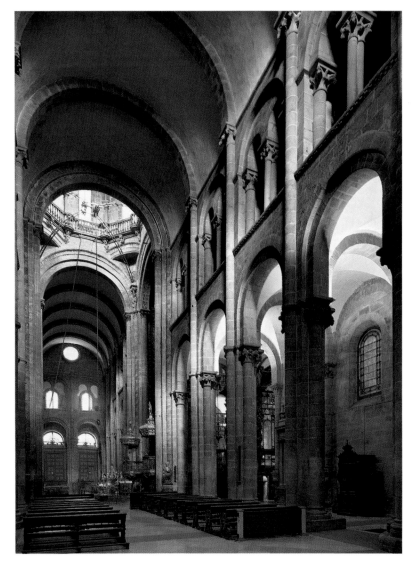

10–23 Transept, Cathedral of Saint James, Santiago de Compostela. Looking from the south transept portal toward the crossing. c. 1078–1122

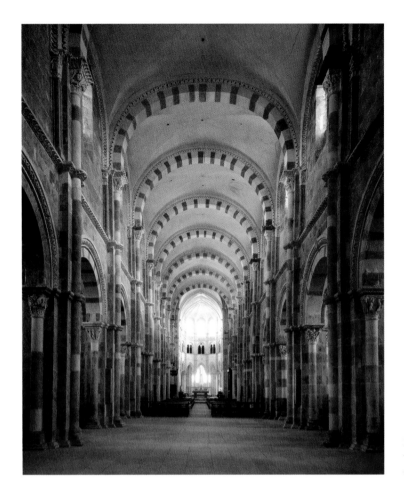

10–24 Church of Mary Magdalene. Vézelay, Burgundy, France. Before 1132. The nave dates to the consecration of 1132, but the choir was rebuilt in early gothic style in the second half of the twelfth century

altar but is also to some extent drawn upward (fig **10–23**). A ribbed barrel vault covers the high nave; the ribs continue the vertical line of the piers. Groin vaults cover the aisles, and in the upper-level galleries, half-barrel vaults, called quadrant vaults, help strengthen the building by carrying the outward thrust of the nave vault to the outer walls and buttresses. Above the church's square crossing, a windowed, octagonal lantern tower admits daylight. The light streaming in from the lantern and apse windows acted as a beacon, directing the worshipers' attention to the altar. The piers supporting the nave arcade have attached half-columns on all four sides, and for this reason they are known as compound piers. Compound piers and ribbed vaults create spatial units or bays. The sculptural form they give to church interiors was a major contribution of Romanesque builders to architectural structure and aesthetics.

The builders of the Church of Mary Magdalene at Vézelay in Burgundy (fig. **10–24**) strove to bring light into the church. They created a spacious well-lit interior by using widely spaced compound piers, eliminating triforium galleries, and inserting large clerestory windows under the slightly depressed vault that approaches a groin vault in form. The transverse ribs become a decorative system of reddish brown and white voussoirs that

recalls Islamic architecture (see Cordoba, page 197), perhaps a reference to the crusading role of the church. In 1050 the Pope had authenticated the relics of the Magdalen, and pilgrims began to come to the shrine. After a fire, the monks rebuilt the church and dedicated it in 1132. (The choir was rebuilt in an early Gothic style in the second half of the twelfth century). A major cultural center, Vézelay saw the beginning of both the second and third Crusades.

Norman builders working in the far north in Durham made what proved to be very significant structural innovations (fig. **10–25**). Strategically located on England's northern frontier with Scotland, Durham grew after the Norman conquest into a fortified complex with a castle, cathedral, monastery, and village. The count-bishop held both secular and religious power. His cathedral is one of the most impressive of all medieval buildings as well as one of the most original. Between 1093 and 1133, the Durham builders developed a system of vaulting that was carried to the Norman homeland in France.

The masons at Durham developed a new system of vaulting. Enormous compound piers alternating with circular piers support the nave arcade, gallery, and vaults. The round piers are carved with chevrons (inverted Vs), spiral fluting,

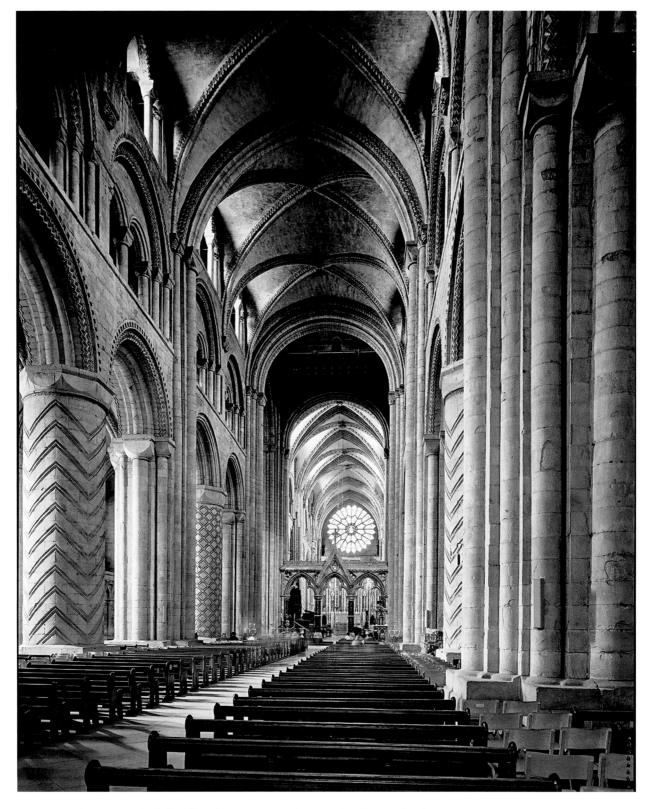

10–25 Nave of Durham Cathedral. Early 12th century. Original apses replaced by a Gothic choir, 1242–c. 1280. Vault height 73′ (22.2 m). View from the west

and diamond patterns, and end in scalloped capitals. All of this ornamentation was originally painted. Above this impressive nave the masons modified the Romanesque ribbed groin vault by using two pairs of crisscrossing ribs in each bay. The complex patterns created by the ribs are visually compelling, and the diagonal lines of the ribs and the uniform height of the vaults unify the individual bays. The architects also experimented with rectangular rather than square bays. Masons perfected this vault and by system as the foundation of Gothic architecture.

The Romanesque Church Portal

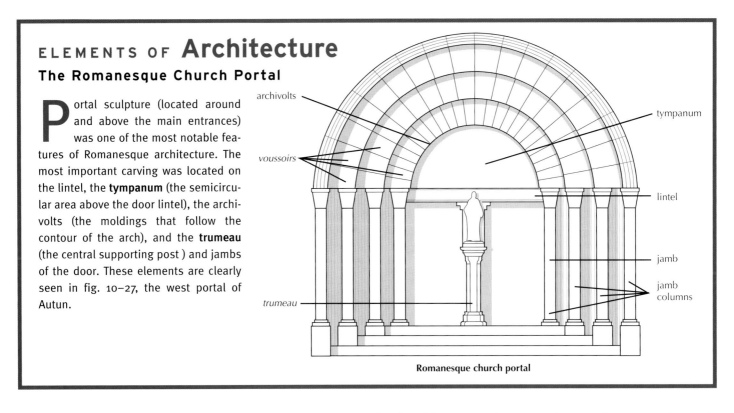

Portal sculpture (located around and above the main entrances) was one of the most notable features of Romanesque architecture. The most important carving was located on the lintel, the **tympanum** (the semicircular area above the door lintel), the archivolts (the moldings that follow the contour of the arch), and the **trumeau** (the central supporting post) and jambs of the door. These elements are clearly seen in fig. 10–27, the west portal of Autun.

archivolts

voussoirs

tympanum

lintel

jamb

jamb columns

trumeau

Romanesque church portal

Architectural Decoration: Sculpture and Painting

Romanesque architectural sculpture was used primarily on the facade and entrance of a church and on the capitals of interior and exterior columns. The sculpture was painted, and the interior walls of the churches were also covered with paintings. Both sculpture and painting carried educational and inspirational messages. People arriving at the church, whether pilgrims from afar or the local parish or monastic community, must have stopped to study the sculpture. At the beginning of the eleventh century, Bishop Bernward had used the bronze doors of his church at Hildesheim to instruct (see fig. 10–14). Now the sculpture and painting on the walls of the buildings themselves added to the instruction.

At Modena Cathedral, the spirit of ancient Rome pervades the sculpture (fig. **10–26**). Horizontal bands of relief on the west facade are among the earliest narrative portal sculpture in Italy (c. 1106–1120). An inscription reads: "Among sculptors, your

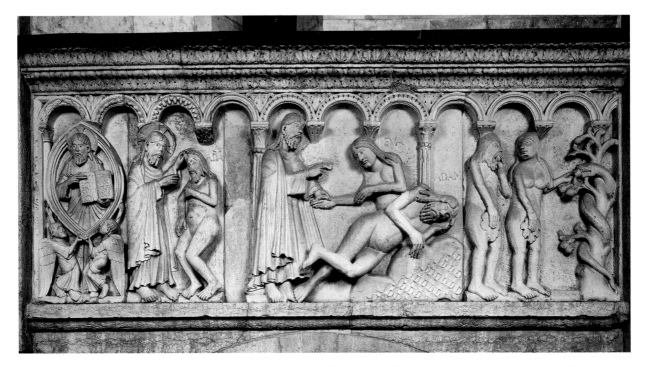

10–26 Wiligelmus. *Creation and Fall of Adam and Eve.* Modena Cathedral, west façade. 1106–1120. Height approx. 3′ (92 cm)

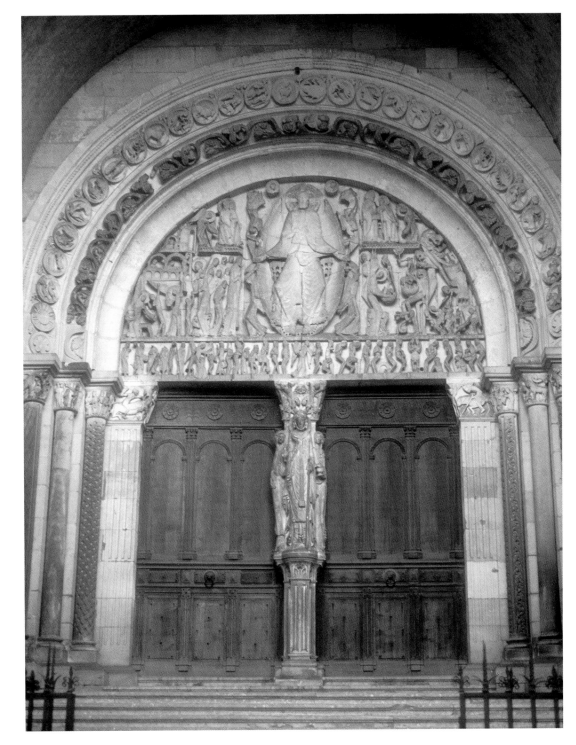

10–27 Gislebertus. *The Last Judgement.* West portal, Cathedral (originally abbey church) of Saint-Lazare, Autun, Burgundy, France. c. 1120–1135/40

In a letter to fellow cleric William of Saint-Thierry, Bernard of Clairvaux, leader of the Cistercian order (led 1125–1153), objected to what he felt was excessive sculptural decoration of churches and cloisters. "So many and so marvelous are the varieties of diverse shapes on every hand," he wrote, "that we are more tempted to read in the marble than in our books, and to spend the whole day in wondering at these things rather than in meditating the law of God. For God's sake, if men are not ashamed of these follies, why at least do they not shrink from the expense?" (cited in Davis-Weyer, page 170)

work shines forth, Wiligelmus." Wiligelmus, the sculptor, must have seen the sculpture of ancient sarcophagi. He took his subjects from the Old Testament Book of Genesis and included events from the Creation to the Flood. This panel shows the *Creation and Fall of Adam and Eve.* On the far left is a half-length God with a cruciform halo, indicating two persons—father and son—framed by a mandorla (almond-shaped nimbus) supported by two angels. The scene to the right shows God bringing Adam to life. Next, he brings forth Eve from Adam's side. On the right, Adam and Eve cover their genitals in shame as they greedily eat the fruit of the forbidden tree, around which the serpent twists.

Wiligelmus's deft modeling and undercutting give these low-relief figures a strong three-dimensionality. While most Romanesque sculpture seems controlled by a strong frame or architectural setting, Wiligelmus used the arcade to establish a stagelike setting. Rocks and a tree add to the impression that figures interact with stage props. Wiligelmus's figures, although not particularly graceful, have a sense of life and personality, and they convey the emotional depth of the narrative. Bright paint, now almost all lost, must have increased the impact of the sculpture.

The tympanum above the west portal of the Cathedral of Saint-Lazare at Autun in France depicts the Last Judgment (fig. **10–27**). Christ, enclosed in a mandorla, presides in judgment over the cowering, naked figures of the resurrected humans at his feet. To those about to enter the church, the message is clear. The damned writhe in torment on Christ's left (the "sinister" side, on the viewer's right) while the saved, praying, reach toward heaven on Christ's right (the viewer's left). On the lintel, angels help other souls rise from their graves, while a pair of giant, pincerlike hands descends at the far right to snatch one of the damned into hell. Above these hands, in a scene reminiscent of the Egyptian Book of the Dead (see fig. 2–36), the archangel Michael oversees the weighing of souls on the scales of good and evil. In a band beneath Christ's feet is an inscription identifying the tympanum as the work of Gislebertus.

Gislebertus, or sculptors working for him, have no interest in depicting the mundane visual world. In an expressive and abstract style they created images of suffering and hopeful human beings surrounded by unseen but psychologically present angels and demons.

Gislebertus may also have carved the pilaster capitals lining the nave and aisles of the church. The creation of lively narrative scenes within the geometric confines of column capitals (the "historiated capital") was an important Romanesque contribution to architectural decoration. One capital depicts the sleeping Magi (fig. 10–28). According to the Gospels, Three Magi, or wise men, traveled from the East to bring gifts to the newborn Jesus and acknowledge him as King of the Jews. Medieval tradition indentified the Magi as kings, and gave them the names Caspar, Melchior, and Balthasar. Gislebertus represents the eldest, Caspar, as bearded, Melchior with a mustache, and Balthasar, the youngest, as clean-shaven. The Magi and the head of the bed are viewed from above, whereas the angel and the foot of the bed are viewed from the side. The angel awakens the Magi and points, thus communicating the key elements of the story with wonderful economy and clarity. This capital, one of a series illustrating events related to the birth of Jesus, may have reminded worshipers that they were embarking on a metaphorically parallel journey to find Christ.

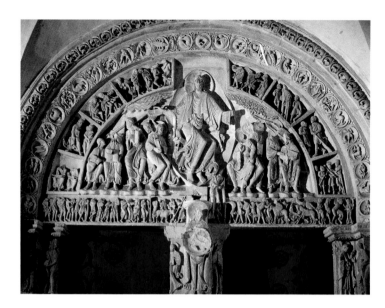

10–29 Detail of *Christ of the Pentecost.* Saint Madeleine Cathedral. Vézelay, France. c. 1135–1140. Stone

An entirely different mood permeates the dramatic sculpture of Vézelay (fig. 10–29). About 1135–1140 the master mason added a huge tympanum representing Pentecost or Christ's mission to the apostles, a theme unique in Christian art of the time. The style of the sculpture has all the energy one would expect in a church associated with Christian crusading warfare. Dynamic angular forms fill the tympanum where the architecture hardly seems able to contain them. Christ is the motivating force, twisting into a compressed zigzag position, a pose enhanced by the spiral patterns of drapery at hip and knee joints. The apostles seem to squirm in their eagerness to set off on their mission to spread the good news, the Gospel. The dynamic linear movement seems closer to the penwork seen in manuscript painting or fine metalwork than to the more restrained rhythms of stone sculpture.

Much as we admire the fine masonry of walls laid bare by centuries of neglect or ill-advised cleaning, we must remember that people in the Middle Ages expected their churches to be filled with colorful and meaningful painting, mosaics, or textiles. An apse painting from the Church of San Clemente (fig. 10–30) in Tahull, in the Catalonian Pyrenees of northern Spain, shows these influences. The Romanesque artist has re-created an almost Byzantine Pantokrator—Christ as ruler and judge of the world. Byzantine features include the figure's frontal pose, the modeling of forms through the use of repeated colored lines of varying width and shades, and such iconographical features as the alpha and omega (the first and last letters of the Greek alphabet) and the depiction of Christ holding a book inscribed in Latin, *ego sum lux mundi* ("I am

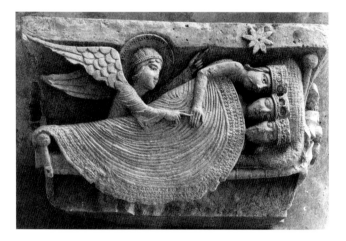

10–28 *The Magi Asleep,* capital from the nave, Cathedral of Saint-Lazare. c. 1120–1132. Musée Lapidaire, Autun

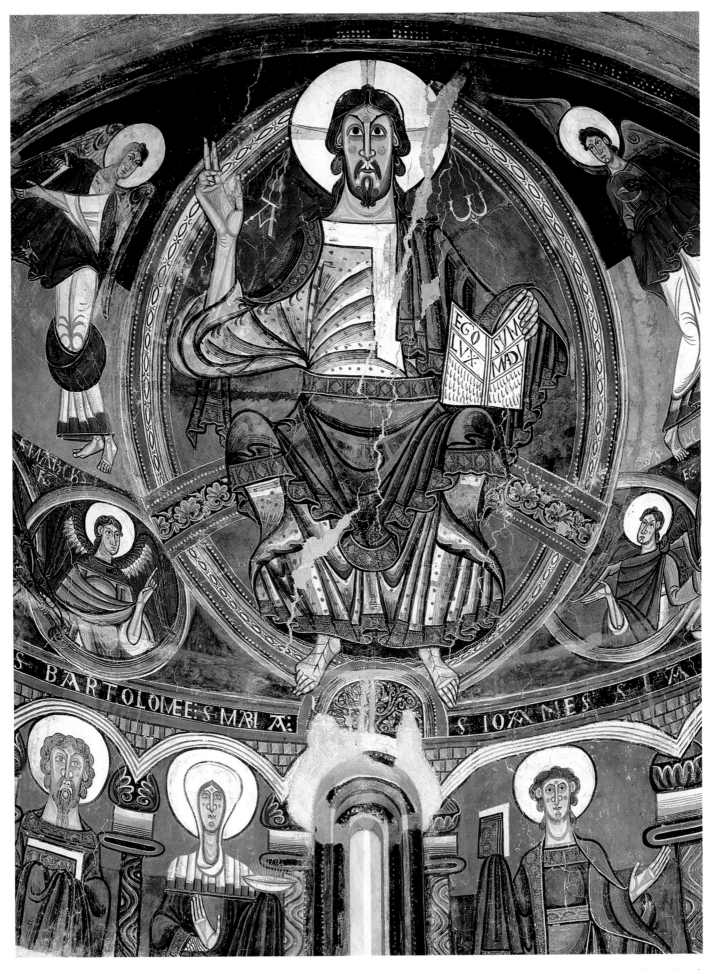

10–30 *Christ in Majesty,* detail of apse painting from the Church of San Clemente, Tahull Lérida, Spain. c. 1123. Museo Nacional d'Art de Catalunya, Barcelona

CALVERAS/MERIDA/SAGRISTA ©MNAC, 2001

the light of the world"; John 8:12). The San Clemente Master, as the otherwise anonymous Tahull painter is known, borrowed elements from several styles. He adapted the Byzantine style to the local taste for geometry and simplicity of form, turning facial features and draperies into elegant patterns. The background of wide stripes of color is Mozarabic. The inventive detailing of the draperies with their crinkles and loops, as well as the mosaiclike intensity of the colors built up from many thin coats of paint, produce a refreshing decorative feeling often found in Carolingian painting. The expressive figures of Evangelists, pointing toward Christ or interacting directly with the viewer, may have been inspired by southern French art, transmitted to the Pyrenees over pilgrimage routes. Bishop Ramon dedicated the church in 1123.

The Cloister Crafts

The most precious and admired arts of the Middle Ages are those that later critics called the "decorative arts." Artists in the eleventh and twelfth centuries were often monks and nuns. They worked as calligraphers and painters in the scriptorium to produce the books that were vital to the Christian mission. They created the metal-, enamel-, and jewel-work used in the church services. And they embroidered the vestments, altar cloths, and wall hangings. Increasingly secular workshops supplied the aristocratic and royal courts with textiles, tableware, books, and weapons. Some of the finest work has survived in church treasuries.

Elaborate textiles, including embroideries and tapestries, enhanced a noble's status. The *Bayeux Tapestry* (see fig. 10–17) chronicles the events leading to Duke William's conquest of England in 1066. Harold, who had sworn an oath of allegiance to William on the relics of Bayeux Cathedral, succeeded to the English throne after the death of King Edward the Confessor. Harold defended his claim at the Battle of Hastings, during which he was killed by William. The section illustrated depicts William and his brothers Odo and Robert, with the Norman troops feasting before the battle. The images depicted on this long embroidered band may have been drawn by a Norman participant, and either Normans or Anglo-Saxons did the actual embroidery. The completed work may have been a gift to Bayeux Cathedral by Bishop Odo, William's brother. The *Bayeux Tapestry* was displayed around the walls of the cathedral on the feast of the relics; however, it represents the kind of secular art that must once have been part of every royal court.

The *Bayeux Tapestry* is an excellent, eleventh-century historical document. Another—the earliest known illustrated history book, *The Worcester Chronicle* (fig. **10–31**)—was written in the

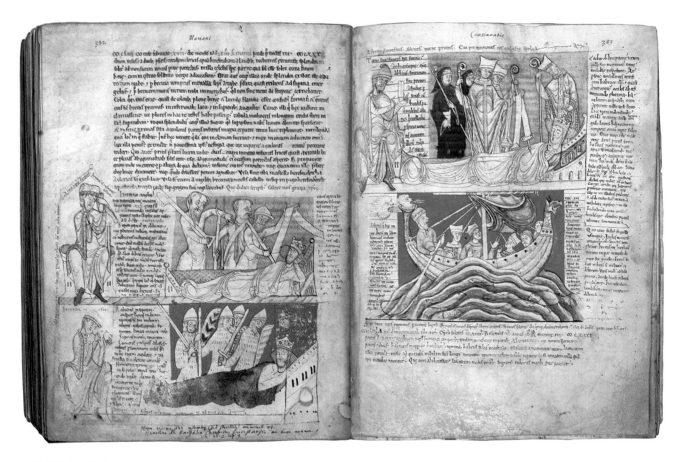

10–31 John of Worcester. Page with *Dream of Henry I, Worcester Chronicle,* Worcester, England. c. 1140.
Ink and tempera on vellum, each page $12\frac{3}{4}$" × $9\frac{3}{8}$" (32.5 × 23.7 cm). Corpus Christi College, Oxford

A remarkable depiction of "current events," the Worcester Chronicle *shows the three classes of society in characteristic dress and carrying their equipment. Historians look at these illustrations for information about life in twelfth-century England, just as they study the* Bayeux Tapestry *to learn about the eleventh century.*

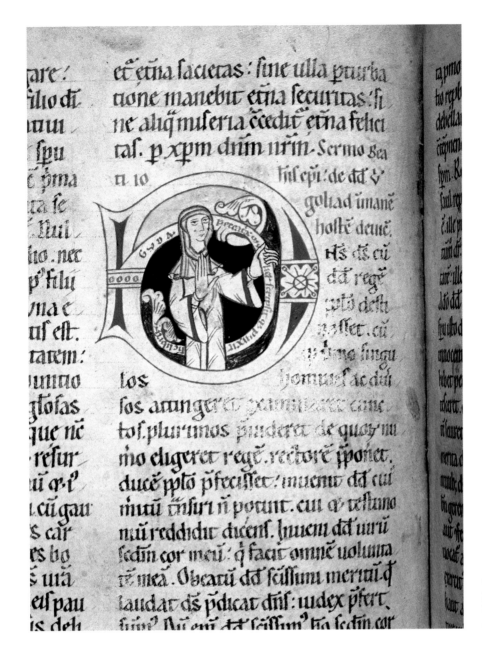

10–32 **Page with self-portrait of the nun Guda,** *Book of Homilies.* Early 12th century. Ink on parchment. Stadtund Universitäts-bibliothek Frankfurt, Germany

twelfth century by a monk named John. The pages shown here concern Henry I (ruled 1100–1135), the second of William the Conqueror's sons to sit on the English throne. The text relates a series of dreams the king had in 1130, in which his subjects demanded tax relief. The artist depicts the king's dreams with energetic directness. On the first night, angry farmers confront the sleeping king; on the second, armed knights surround his bed; and on the third, monks, abbots, and bishops present their case. In the fourth illustration, the king travels in a storm-tossed ship and saves himself by promising God that he will rescind the tax increase for seven years. The author of *The Worcester Chronicle* assured his readers that this story came from a reliable source, the royal physician Grimbald, who appears in the margins next to three of the scenes. The angry farmers capture our attention today because we seldom see working men with their equipment and simple clothing depicted in painting from this time. Although chancery (government) scriptoria existed, it was in monastic scriptoria that most books were produced. While we often study the most spectacularly beautiful manuscripts, the majority of books were functional items with few or no illustrations.

In the Romanesque period, as earlier in the Middle Ages, women were involved in the production of books as authors, scribes, painters, and patrons. The Abbess Hitda (see fig. 10–16) had been a patron; the nun Guda, from Westphalia, was both a scribe and painter. In a book of homilies (sermons), Guda inserted her self-portrait into the letter D and signed the image "Guda, a sinful woman, wrote and illuminated this book" (fig. **10–32**). A simple drawing with colors only in the background spaces, the importance of Guda's self-portrait lies in its demonstration that women were far from anonymous workers. Guda and other nuns played an important role in the production of books in the twelfth century, and this image is the earliest signed self-portrait by a woman in Western Europe.

Among the richest cloister crafts was the art of the metalsmith. The products of the smith's skill might become a special kind of treasure when jewels donated by pilgrims were attached

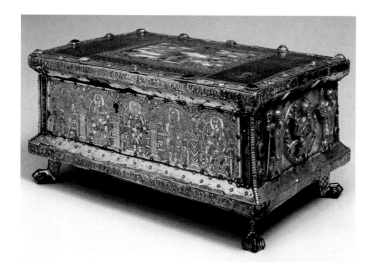

10–33 Roger of Helmarshausen, *Portable altar of Saints Liborius and Kilian,* from the Abbey, Helmarshausen, Saxony, Germany. c. 1100, with later additions. Silver and gilt bronze, with niello and gemstones, $6\frac{1}{2}'' \times 13\frac{5}{8}'' \times 98\frac{3}{8}''$ (16.5 × 34.5 × 21 cm). Erzbischofliches Diozesan-museum und Domschatzkammer, Paderborn, Germany

Some scholars identify Roger, a monk, with "Theophilus," the pseudonym used by a monk who wrote an artist's handbook, On Diverse Arts, *about 1100. The book gives detailed instructions for painting, glassmaking, and goldsmithing. "Theophilus" assured artists that "God delights in embellishments" and that artists worked "under the direction and authority of the Holy Spirit." He wrote, "most beloved son, you should not doubt but should believe in full faith that the Spirit of God has filled your heart when you have embellished His house with such great beauty and variety of workmanship. ... Set a limit with pious consideration on what the work is to be, and for whom, as well as on the time, the amount, and the quality of work, and, lest the vice of greed or cupidity should steal in, on the amount of the recompense" (Theophilus, page 43). The last admonishment is a worldly reminder about fair pricing.*

to a piece. One such piece is the reliquary statue of St. Faith in Conques. Reworked over the centuries, it is a repository of gems from many periods. (See "Closer Look," page 257.)

Although most medieval artists remain anonymous, some additional names survive as well. According to the account books of the Abbey of Helmarshausen in Saxony, an artist named Roger was paid on August 15, 1100, for a portable altar dedicated to Saints Kilian and Liborius (fig. **10–33**). This box made from precious metals, gemstones, and niello supporting a beautiful altar stone was found preserved in the treasury of the cathedral. On one end, in high relief, are two standing saints flanking Christ in Majesty, enthroned on the arc of the heavens. On the front are five apostles, each posed differently, executed in engraving and niello. Saint Peter sits in the center, holding his key. Roger adapted Byzantine figural conventions to his personal style, and he gave his subjects a sense of life despite their formal setting. He was clearly familiar with classical art, but his geometric treatment of natural forms, his use of decorative surface patterning, and the linear clarity of his composition are departures from the classical aesthetic.

Not every church could afford works in precious metals and jewels. Wooden sculpture also satisfied the need for devotional images. Statues of the Virgin Mary holding the Christ Child on her lap, a type known as the Throne of Wisdom, became

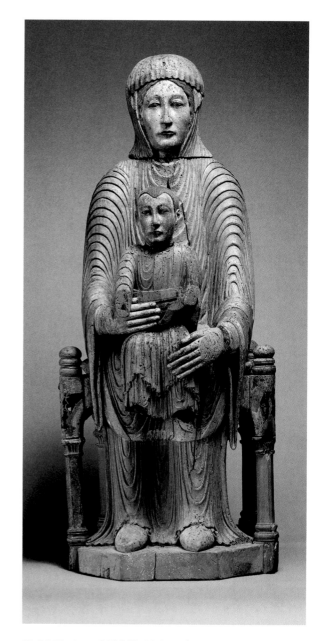

10–34 *Virgin and Child in Majesty,* from Auvergne region, France. c. 1150–1200. Linen, gesso, and polychromy on walnut, height 31″ (78.7 cm). The Metropolitan Museum of Art, New York

increasingly popular (fig. **10–34**). Here, Mary is seated on a thronelike bench symbolizing the lion throne of Solomon, the Old Testament king and symbol of wisdom. She supports Jesus with both hands. Mother and Child are depicted frontally and erect, as rigid as they are regal. The small but adult Jesus once held a book—the Word of God—in his left hand and raised his right hand in blessing. To the medieval believer, Christ represented the priesthood, humankind, and God. In Christ, the Wisdom of God became human; in the medieval scholar's language, he is the Word Incarnate. Mary represented the Church. And Mary, as earthly mother and God-bearer (Theotokos), gave Jesus his human nature and forms a throne on which he sits in majesty. As a fourteenth-century member of the clergy wrote, "The throne of the true Solomon is the Most Blessed Virgin Mary, in which sat Jesus Christ, the true Wisdom" (trans. Forsyth, page 27).

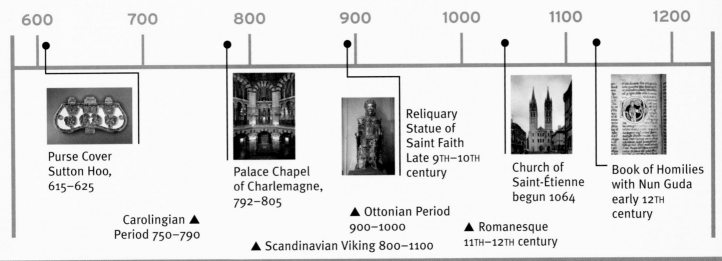

600	700	800	900	1000	1100	1200

Purse Cover
Sutton Hoo,
615–625

Palace Chapel
of Charlemagne,
792–805

Reliquary
Statue of
Saint Faith
Late 9TH–10TH
century

Church of
Saint-Étienne
begun 1064

Book of Homilies
with Nun Guda
early 12TH
century

Carolingian ▲
Period 750–790

▲ Ottonian Period
900–1000

▲ Romanesque
11TH–12TH century

▲ Scandinavian Viking 800–1100

LOOKING BACK

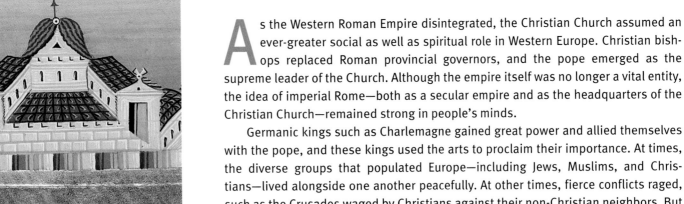

As the Western Roman Empire disintegrated, the Christian Church assumed an ever-greater social as well as spiritual role in Western Europe. Christian bishops replaced Roman provincial governors, and the pope emerged as the supreme leader of the Church. Although the empire itself was no longer a vital entity, the idea of imperial Rome—both as a secular empire and as the headquarters of the Christian Church—remained strong in people's minds.

Germanic kings such as Charlemagne gained great power and allied themselves with the pope, and these kings used the arts to proclaim their importance. At times, the diverse groups that populated Europe—including Jews, Muslims, and Christians—lived alongside one another peacefully. At other times, fierce conflicts raged, such as the Crusades waged by Christians against their non-Christian neighbors. But whether prompted by violence or cooperative interaction, exchanges of intellectual and artistic influences took place, leading to an extraordinary amalgam: ancient Classical forms blended with the Celtic and Germanic styles found in the hinterlands of the Roman Empire; and the abstract modes of Near Eastern art mixed with the Western tradition, leading to the development of a new narrative and figurative art that was also richly decorative and expressive.

The most important functions of Christian art were to glorify God and to teach a largely illiterate populace. From its start, the Church recognized the educational and persuasive power of the visual arts. Carved portals and facades decorated church exteriors, often with terrifying scenes of the Last Judgment. To the medieval man or woman who could not read, art clearly communicated heaven's rewards and the horrors of hell. The elect rejoice in heaven with the angels; the damned suffer, tormented by demons.

Romanesque churches have a remarkable variety of sculpture and painting. Christ Enthroned in Majesty may be carved over the entrance or painted in the half-dome of the apse. Biblical scenes and the lives of the saints may cover the walls, and depictions of Old Testament stories foretell events in the New Testament.

Artists such as Gislebertus of Autun, the nuns Ende and Guda, and many anonymous women and men of the 11th and 12th centuries created a new art—in what we now call the medieval style—that focused on human beings, their stories, and their beliefs. Whether working on a minute or a monumental scale, these artists emphasized the spiritual and intellectual concerns of the Christian Church, but they also began to observe and record what they saw around them. In so doing, they were laying the groundwork for the art of the Gothic period that followed.

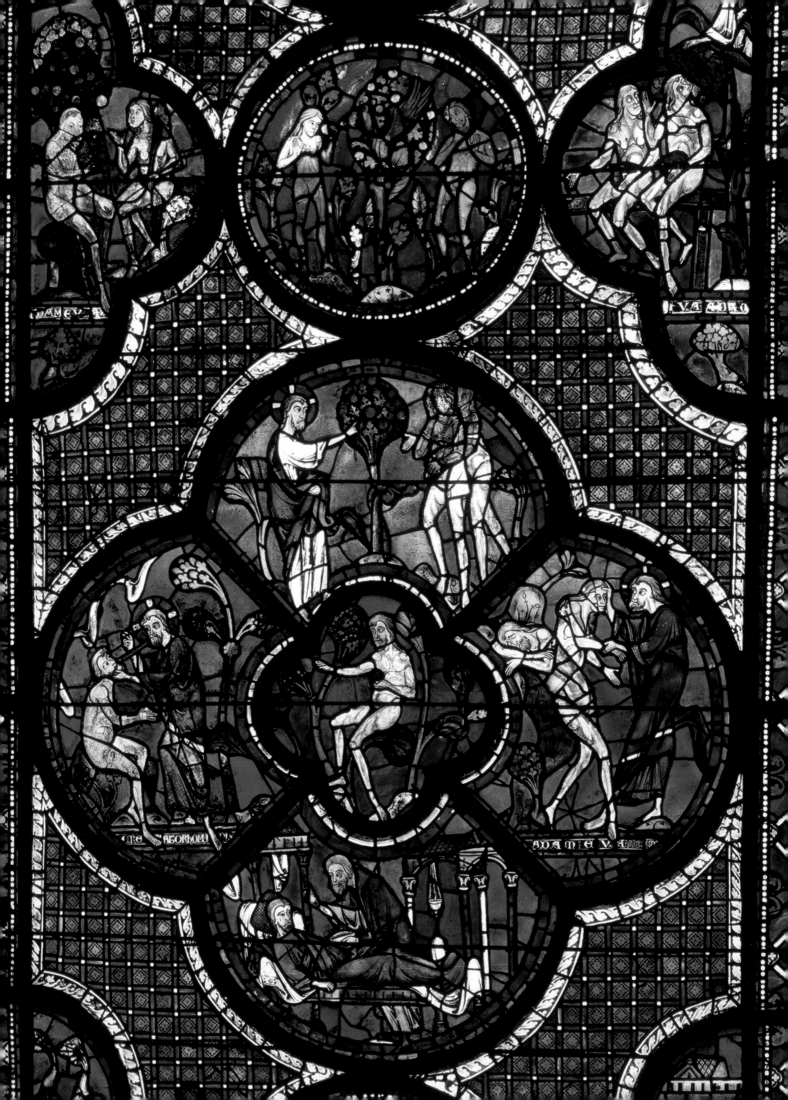

11
Gothic Art

The Gothic style created by patrons, architects, and artists working together toward a supermundane goal dominated the aesthetic life of Europe for 400 years. By mid-12th century in Western Europe, a combination of technological skill, material resources, and intellectual and spiritual motivation created an art and architecture that expressed the dedicated religious belief of the Christian community. Reformers might rant against ostentation, waste, and materialism but bishops, abbots, and civic leaders vied to build and decorate the largest, richest churches. Just as residents of 20th-century American cities raced to erect higher and higher skyscrapers, so too the bishops of medieval western Europe competed in the building of cathedrals and parish churches with tall naves and soaring towers. The masons' skill in constructing high vaults supported on piers and in designing window-filled walls—both stabilized by flying buttresses—created open, light-filled interior spaces. Meanwhile, glassmakers perfected the techniques of coloring and painting glass and filled ever-larger window openings with glowing images (fig. 11–1). Light passing through stained-glass windows not only illuminated the interior but also changed the space into a many-colored haze. Walls, objects, and even people seemed to dissolve—dematerializing into color. Truly, churches became the glorious jeweled houses of God.

Abbot Suger (1081–1151) of the Benedictine Abbey of Saint-Denis near Paris wrote of his experience rebuilding his abbey church of Saint Denis in the twelfth century. He described his visual and spiritual journey through the medium of pure colored light. Although Suger died before the work was finished, he is remembered for his inspired departure from traditional building practice. His goal was to to achieve a truly radiant architecture, and his innovations led to the widespread use of large stained-glass windows, such as those that bathe the interior of Chartres Cathedral with sublime washes of color (see fig. 11–1). This detail of the scenes from Genesis and the parable of the Good Samaritan from a south aisle window reminds us that such windows are actually transparent and luminous monumental murals filled with energetic figures activated by color and light.

11–1 Scenes from *Genesis* and the *Parable of the Good Samaritan,* Chartres Cathedral, aisle window, detail. c. 1210. Stained and painted glass

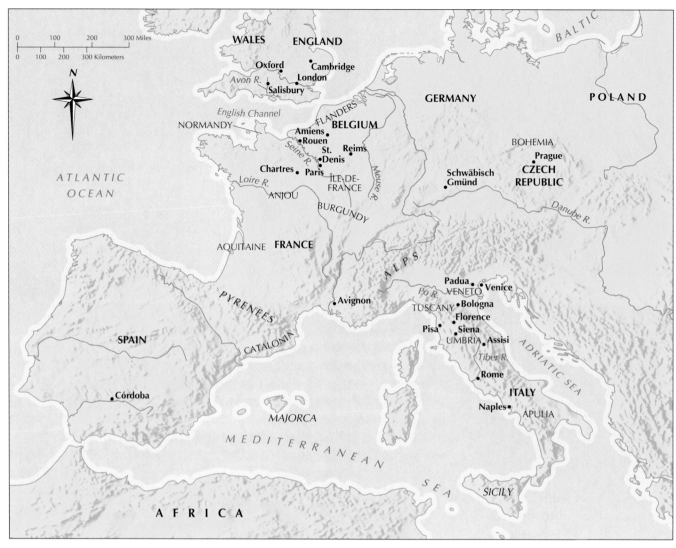

Map 11–1 Europe in the Gothic Era

In the middle of the twelfth century, while builders throughout Europe were working in the Romanesque style, a distinctive new architecture known today as Gothic emerged in the Île-de-France, the French king's domain around Paris. The appearance there of a new style and building technique coincided with the emergence of the monarchy as a powerful centralizing force in France. From there the Gothic style spread, and it prevailed in Western European art until about 1400, lingering for another century in some regions.

Unprecedented resources were devoted to Christian art in the late Middle Ages. Within 100 years an estimated 2,700 churches were built in the Île-de-France region alone. These new churches shimmered with stained glass, sumptuous altars, sculpture, crosses, and reliquaries, paid for by clergy, monarchs, aristocrats, and wealthy merchants. Private patrons commissioned innumerable other works of art for personal use as well, such as luxurious clothing, jewels, armor, and castles.

The term *Gothic* was introduced in the sixteenth century by the Italian artist and historian Giorgio Vasari, who disparagingly attributed the style to the Goths, the Germanic invaders who had destroyed the classical civilization of the Roman Empire that he and his contemporaries so admired. In its own day the Gothic style was simply called "modern art" or the "French style." As it spread from the Île-de-France, it gradually displaced Romanesque forms

but took on regional characteristics inspired by those forms. England developed a distinctive national style, which also influenced architectural design in continental Europe. The Gothic style was slow to take hold in Germanic lands but ultimately endured there well into the sixteenth century. (Italian lands proved more resistant to French Gothic elements, and by 1400, Italian artists and builders sought a return to classical traditions.) In the late fourteenth century, the various regional styles of Europe coalesced into what is known as the International Gothic style. Gothic architecture's elegant, soaring, light-filled interiors were adapted to all types of structures, including town halls, market buildings, residences, and Jewish synagogues, as well as Christian churches.

During the flowering of the Gothic style in the twelfth and thirteenth centuries, Europe enjoyed a period of vigorous growth. Towns gained increasing prominence, becoming important centers of artistic patronage and intellectual life. Urban universities and cathedral schools supplanted rural monastic schools as centers of learning. The first European university, at Bologna, Italy, may have begun in the eleventh century, and soon important universities were established in Paris, Cambridge, and Oxford. Two new religious orders arose to serve the new urban populations, the Franciscans and the Dominicans. The friars, as these monks were called, went out into the world to preach and minister to those in need, rather than confining themselves to monasteries.

Crusades and pilgrimages continued throughout the thirteenth century. One of the benefits of the resulting contact with the Byzantine and Islamic worlds was the European discovery of many literary works from classical antiquity. These writings, particularly those of Aristotle, promoted rational inquiry rather than faith as the path to truth, which, at first, seemed incompatible with Christian emphasis on faith and spirituality. The thirteenth-century scholar Thomas Aquinas finally brought together faith and reason—traditional belief and the new logic—in Scholastic philosophy, which has endured as a basis of Catholic thought to this day.

Artists and master builders of the time, like the Scholastic thinkers, saw divine order in geometric relationships and expressed these in their art. Unlike their Romanesque predecessors, who used stylization and distortion to achieve emotional impact, thirteenth-century sculptors created more naturalistic forms that reflected the idealism and reasoned analysis of Scholastic thought. Gothic religious imagery, like Romanesque imagery, aimed to instruct and persuade the viewer; however, its effects are more varied and subtle, and it incorporates a wide range of subjects drawn from the natural world. In the Gothic church, Scholastic logic and the new naturalism intermingle with the mysticism of light and color to create for the worshiper a direct, emotional, ecstatic experience of the church as the embodiment of God's house, filled with divine light.

Gothic Art in France

As previously mentioned, the birth of the Gothic style took place in France against the backdrop of the growing power of the French monarchy. Europe's first Gothic structure is arguably the Abbey Church of Saint-Denis, which had great symbolic significance for the French crown. Located a few miles north of central Paris, it housed the tombs of many French kings, the royal regalia, and the relics of Saint Denis, the patron saint of France.

Construction began on the new church in the 1130s under the supervision of Abbot Suger, who was familiar with the latest architecture and sculpture of Romanesque Europe through his travels in France, the Rhineland, and the Italian peninsula. He also turned for inspiration to the authority of Church writings, including treatises erroneously attributed to a first-century follower of Saint Paul named Dionysius, who identified radiant light with divinity. Through the centuries, Dionysius had become confused with Saint Denis, so Suger, not unreasonably, adapted Dionysius's concept of divine luminosity to the redesign of the Abbey Church of Saint-Denis. When he began work on the choir—after completing a magnificent Norman-inspired and structurally innovative façade—he created "a circular string of chapels" so that the whole church "would shine with the wonderful and uninterrupted light of most luminous windows, pervading the interior beauty" (cited in Panofsky, page 101).

The plan of the choir, built 1140–1144, superficially resembles that of a Romanesque pilgrimage church (fig. **11–2**); that is, a semicircular or polygonal sanctuary is surrounded by an ambulatory from which radiate seven chapels of uniform size. All the architectural elements of the choir had already appeared in Romanesque buildings, including pointed arches, ribbed groin vaults springing from cylindrical piers, and buttresses to relieve stress on the walls and to permit larger window openings. The dramatic achievement of Suger's master mason was to combine these features into a fully integrated architectural whole that emphasized open, flowing space (fig. **11–3**). Sanctuary, ambulatory, and chapels open into

11–2 Plan of the Abbey Church of Saint-Denis. 1140–1144

■ 12th Century
▨ 13th Century
▧ 14th Century
▨ 15th Century

11–3 Ambulatory and choir, Abbey Church of Saint-Denis, Saint-Denis, Île-de-France, France

Visible in this photograph are the ambulatory and chapels built by Abbot Suger between 1140 and 1144, as well as the upper choir, part of the thirteenth-century building campaign (1231–1281).

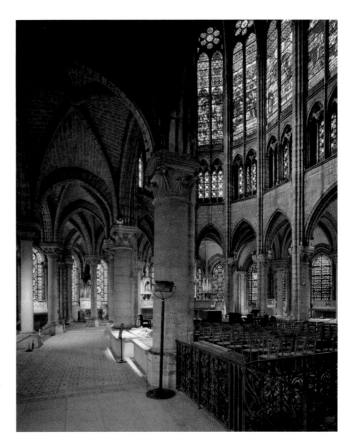

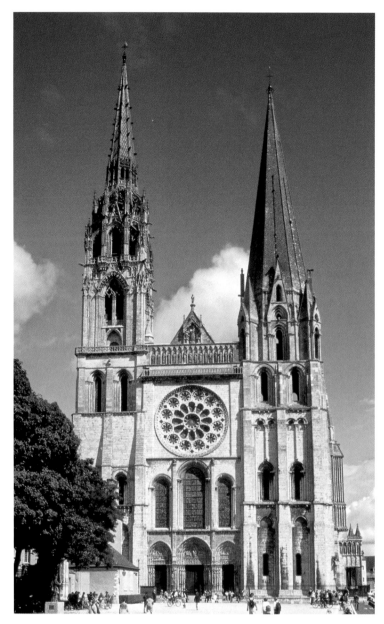

11–4 West façade, the Cathedral of Notre-Dame (Chartres Cathedral),
France. c. 1134–1220; south tower c. 1160; north spire 1507–1513

one another, and the walls give the impression of being made of stained glass rather than masonry, allowing light to flood the interior with color. Suger saw light and color as a means of illuminating the soul and uniting it with God.

The Abbey Church of Saint-Denis initiated a period of competitive experimentation in the Île-de-France and surrounding regions that resulted in ever-taller churches enclosing increasingly larger interior spaces walled with ever-greater expanses of colored glass. At the Cathedral of Notre-Dame in Chartres (Chartres Cathedral) (fig. 11–4), southwest of Paris, masons built on the concepts pioneered at Saint-Denis. Chartres Cathedral, constructed in several stages beginning in the mid-twelfth century and extending into the mid-thirteenth,

illustrates both the early and the mature Gothic style. The west façade survived a fire in 1194 and consequently represents a design contemporary with the portal of Saint-Denis. Its three doors—the so-called Royal Portal (fig. 11–5)—show Christ enthroned in majesty on the central tympanum, supported by his Old Testament precursors in the jambs below. Mary and the Christ Child and the Nativity story fill the right portal; and the Ascension appears at the left. The sculptors pose their high-relief figures naturally and comfortably in the architectural setting. At each side of the doors erect, frontal **column statues**, with their elongated proportions and vertical drapery, echo the cylindrical shafts from which they seem to emerge. Their heads are finely rendered with idealized features.

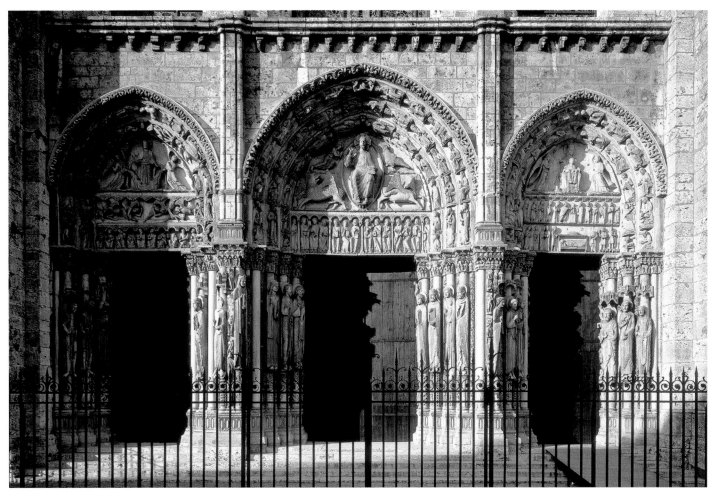

11–5 Royal Portal, west façade, Chartres Cathedral. c. 1145–1155

In the rest of the building, constructed after 1194 (fig. **11–6**), the master mason and his men brought together what were to become the typical Gothic structural devices: pointed arches and ribbed groin vaults rising from **compound piers** over rectangular bays, supported by exterior flying buttresses. This system permitted the masons to introduce huge windows into the upper walls (see "The Gothic Church," page 283). The triforium (series of arched openings under the clerestory) became a midlevel passageway overlooking the nave through an arcaded screen, rather than a flat wall (as in a basilica) or a full gallery. The elegant glass-and-masonry shell of Chartres encloses an enormous open space. The building has one of the widest naves in Europe ($45\frac{1}{2}$ feet) and vaults that

11–6 Plan of Chartres Cathedral. c. 1194–1220

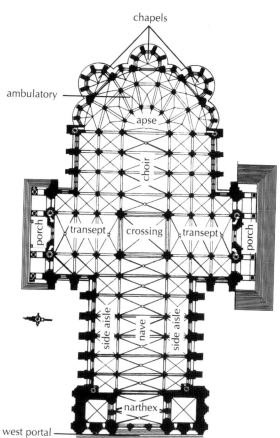

ELEMENTS OF **Architecture**
Rib Vaulting

One of the chief technical contributions of Romanesque and Gothic builders was rib vaulting. Rib vaults are a form of groin vault (see "Arch and Vault," page 141), in which the ridges (groins) formed by the intersecting vaults may rest on and be covered by curved moldings, called ribs. These ribs were usually structural as well as decorative, and they strengthened the joins and helped channel the vaults' thrust outward and downward. The ribs were constructed first and supported the scaffolding necessary to build the vault. Ribs developed over time into an intricate masonry "skeleton" filled with an increasingly lightweight masonry "skin," the web of the vault, or webbing. Sophisticated variations of the basic rib vault created the soaring interiors for which Gothic churches are famous.

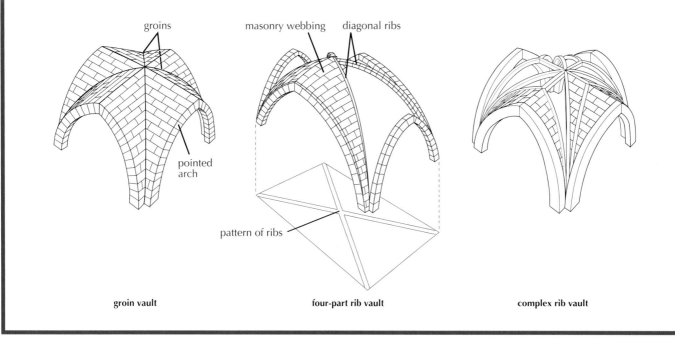

groins

masonry webbing   diagonal ribs

pointed arch

pattern of ribs

groin vault   **four-part rib vault**   **complex rib vault**

soar 118–120 feet above the floor (fig. 11–7). The large and luminous clerestory is filled by tall, arched windows, composed of a pair of **lancets** surmounted by circular windows, called oculi. In a Romanesque church, the worshiper's gaze is mainly drawn forward toward the apse; at Chartres it is drawn upward as well, to the clerestory windows and the soaring vaults overhead.

Chartres is unique among French Gothic buildings in that most of its stained-glass windows have survived. The cathedral was famous for its glassmaking workshops, which by 1260 had installed about 22,000 square feet of stained glass. Although some twelfth century glass (fig. 11–8) survived the 1194 fire, most of the glass dates from between about 1210 and 1250.

The Good Samaritan window illustrates the complexity of Gothic narrative art with an allegory on sin and salvation (see fig. 11–1). The window illustrates a biblical story about a traveling Samaritan who happens upon a stranger, beaten, robbed, and left for dead by thieves along the side of a road. The Good Samaritan is an allegory for Christ's redemption of humanity's sins. Adam and Eve's fall, as described in the Old Testament, introduced sin into the world, but Christ (the Good Samaritan) rescues humanity (the traveler) from sin (the thieves). Christ leads sinners into the Church just as the Good Samaritan takes the wounded man to an inn (as seen in the bottom portion of the window). Other windows tell of saints and heroes, like Charlemagne.

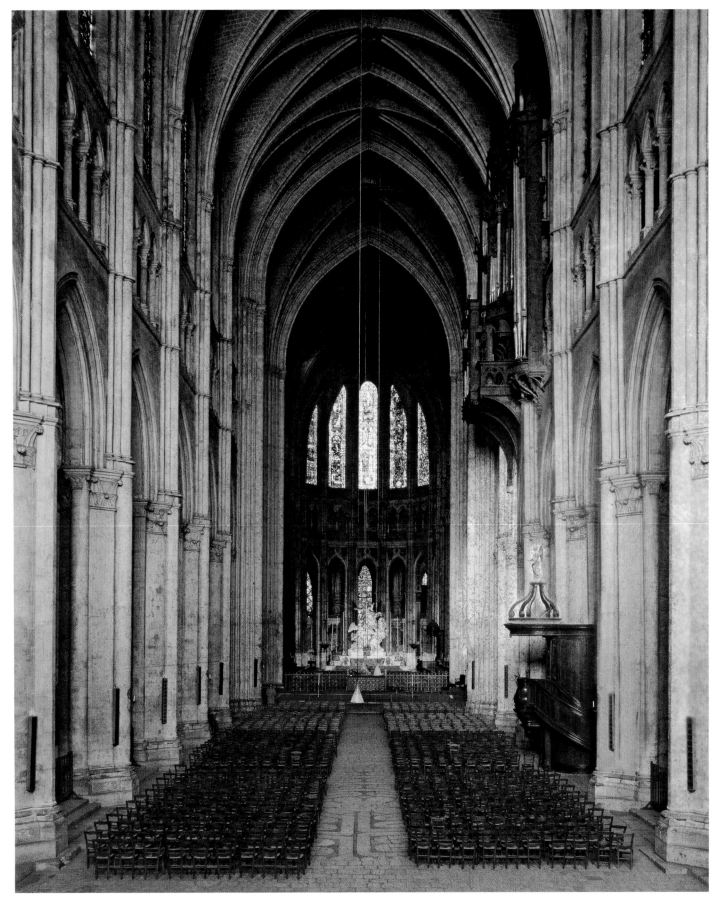

11–7 Nave, Chartres Cathedral. c. 1200–1220

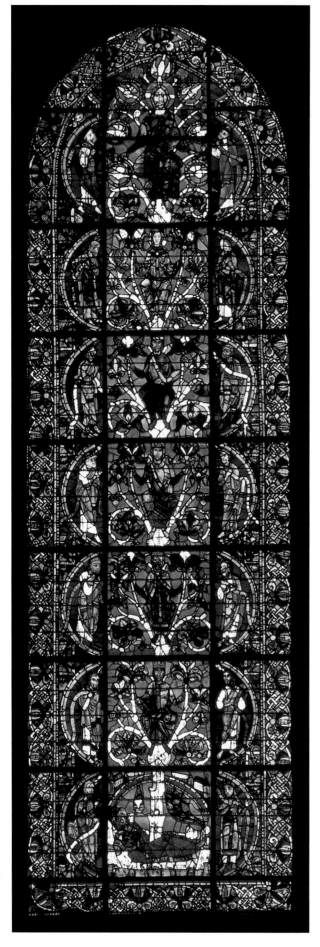

The older *Tree of Jesse* window in the west façade of the cathedral dates from the mid-twelfth century, 1150–1170 (fig. **11–8**). Jesse was the father of King David, who, according to the Gospels, was an ancestor of Mary and therefore of Jesus. A family tree literally connects Jesus with the house of David. At Chartres, Jesse is shown recumbent with the tree trunk growing from his body. In the branches above him appear four kings of Judea (Christ's royal ancestors), then the Virgin Mary, and finally Christ himself. Fourteen prophets stand in the half-moons flanking the tree. The glass is set within a rectilinear iron armature, visible as silhouetted black lines that increase the intensity of the gleaming blues and reds.

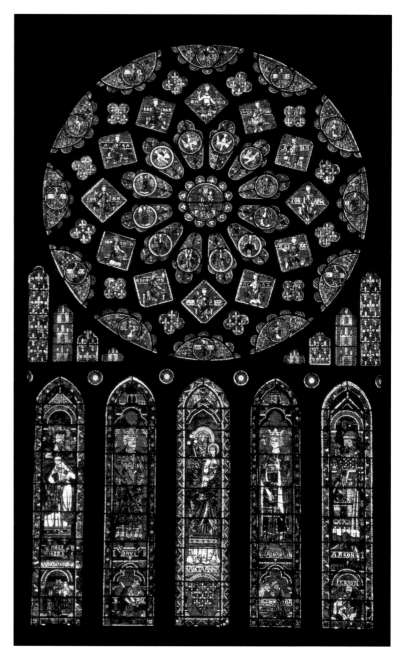

11–8 *Tree of Jesse,* west façade, Chartres Cathedral c. 1150–1170. Stained glass

11–9 Rose and lancets, north transept, Chartres Cathedral

Technique

Stained-Glass Windows

The basic technique for making colored glass has been known since ancient Egypt. It involves the addition of metallic oxides—cobalt for blue, manganese for red and purple—to a basic formula of sand and ash or lime that is fused at high temperature. Such "stained" glass was used on a small scale in church windows during the Early Christian period and in Carolingian, Ottonian, and Romanesque churches. The art form reached its height of sophistication and popularity in the cathedrals and churches of the Gothic era.

Making a stained-glass image was a complex and costly process. A designer first drew a composition on a wood panel the same size as the opening of the window to be filled, noting the colors of each of the elements in it. Glassblowers produced sheets of colored glass. Artisans then cut individual pieces from these large sheets and laid them out on the wood template. Painters added details with enamel emulsion, and the glass was reheated to fuse the enamel to it. Finally, the pieces were joined together with narrow lead strips called **cames**. The assembled pieces were set into iron frames that had been made to fit the window opening.

The colors of twelfth-century glass—mainly reds and blues with touches of dark green, brown, and orange yellow—were often quite dark, and early uncolored glass was full of impurities. But the demand for stained-glass windows stimulated technical experimentation to achieve new colors and greater purity and transparency. Gothic artisans developed a clearer material onto which elaborate narrative scenes could be drawn, and the Cistercians adorned their churches with grisaille windows, painting foliage and crosses onto greenish gray glass. **Grisaille** is a technique of monochromatic painting using shades of gray.

By the thirteenth century, methods to make many new colors were discovered, some accidentally, such as a sunny yellow produced by the addition of silver oxide. Flashing, in which a layer of one color was fused to a layer of another color, produced an almost infinite range of colors. In the same way, clear glass could be fused to layers of colored glass in varying thicknesses to produce a range of values from light to dark. The deep colors of early Gothic stained-glass windows gave them a saturated and mysterious brilliance. The richness of some of these colors, particularly blue, has never been surpassed. Pale colors and large areas of grisaille glass became increasingly popular from the mid-thirteenth century on, making the windows of later Gothic churches bright and clear by comparison.

A rose window—or any stained glass—must be seen and experienced from inside the building. At Chartres the window called the "Rose of France," together with its supporting lancets, fills the upper wall of the north transept (fig. **11–9**). The stained glass is dedicated to Mary and her family. In the central lancet, St. Ann holds her daughter, the baby Mary, and is flanked by Melchizedek, David, Solomon, and Aaron. Above, in the very center of the rose, Mary and Jesus are enthroned; Mary is now queen of heaven. Doves and angels surround mother and child, and Old Testament kings and prophets fill most of the remaining space. The windows may have been a royal gift from Queen Blanche of Castile (the Spanish princess who became the queen of France and ruled as regent, 1226–1234), since her heraldic Spanish golden castles join with the French fleur-de-lis in the smaller lancets that pierce the masonry below the great circle (over 42 feet, 12.8 meters, in diameter). Deep blues and reds dominate and combine to create a hazy purple atmosphere in the soft light of the north side of the building. On a sunny day the masonry and the people moving within the space may seem to dissolve in color.

The bishop of Paris could not be outdone by his fellow churchmen at the Abbey of Saint-Denis or the Cathedral of Chartres. The Benedictine abbey just north of Paris guarded the relics of Saint-Denis, the apostle to the Franks, but Paris was the preferred residence of the kings themselves as well as the administrative center of the diocese. As the location of the royal court and therefore the capital of France, Paris deserved an imposing, modern cathedral building. On a small island in the Seine River, where earlier churches already stood, Pope Alexander III set the cornerstone for the new cathedral—known today as simply Notre-Dame—in 1163, and the building was essentially finished during the next hundred years (see "Closer Look," fig. **11–10**).

The soaring Cathedral Church of Notre-Dame (Our Lady) of Paris that we see today (fig. **11–10)** began as an early Gothic building bridging the period between Abbot Suger's Abbey Church of Saint-Denis and the thirteenth-century Chartres Cathedral. Begun in 1163, construction on Notre-Dame was far enough along for the altar to be consecrated twenty years later. The nave, rising to 115 feet, dates to 1180–1200. The west façade, erected between 1200 and 1250, incorporated an earlier portal dedicated to Mary (Our Lady). By this time, the massive walls, buttresses, and six-part vaults, adopted from Norman Romanesque architecture, must have seemed very old-fashioned.

After 1225, a new master modernized and lightened the building by reworking the clerestory with the large double-lancet and rose windows we see today. Notre-Dame may have had the first true flying buttresses (experts are still arguing) although those seen at the right of the photograph, rising dramatically to support the high vault of the choir, result from later remodeling. (The 290-foot spire over the crossing is the work of the nineteenth-century architect Eugene Emmanuel Viollet-le-Duc, who followed the tradition of placing a tower or spire in this location.)

For all its spiritual and technological glory, Notre-Dame barely survived the French Revolution. The revolutionaries decapitated the statues associated with deposed nobility and transformed the cathedral into a secular "Temple of Reason" (1793–1795). Still, traditional Christians who continued to believe that Mary's church would be restored to her proved to be right, as Notre-Dame was soon returned to religious use. Napoleon crowned himself emperor at its altar in 1804, and Parisians gathered there to celebrate the liberation of Paris from the Nazis in August 1944. Today, boats filled with tourists glide under bridges that link the island where the cathedral stands with the Left Bank, the traditional students' and artists' quarter. Notre-Dame so resonates with life and history that it has become more than a house of worship and work of art; it is a symbol of Paris and part of the shared culture of humankind.

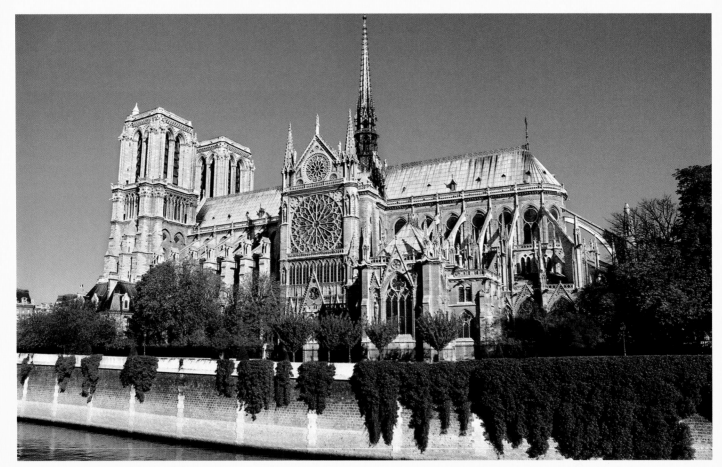

11–10 Cathedral of Notre-Dame, view from the southeast. Paris, France. Begun 1163

The cathedral was restored in the sixteenth century and again in the nineteenth, twentieth, and twenty-first centuries. During World War I it withstood bombardment by some 3,000 shells and a terrible fire, an eloquent testimony to the skills of its builders.

ELEMENTS OF **Architecture**

The Gothic Church

Most large Gothic churches in Western Europe were built on the Latin-cross plan, with a projecting transept marking the transition from nave to **sanctuary**. The main entrance portal was generally on the west, with the choir and apse on the east. A western narthex led to the nave and side aisles. An ambulatory with radiating chapels circled the apse and facilitated the movement of worshipers through the church. Above the nave were a triforium passageway and windowed clerestory. Narthex, side aisles, ambulatory, and nave usually had **rib vaults** in the Gothic period. **Flying buttresses** help support the high rib-vaulted naves by carrying the outward thrust of the nave vaulting over the aisles to massive wall buttresses, which are freestanding above the aisle roofs. Church walls were decorated inside and out with arcades of round or pointed arches, engaged columns and colonnettes, and horizontal moldings called **stringcourses**. The roof was supported by a wooden framework. A spire or crossing tower above the junction of the transept and nave was usually planned, though often never finished. The **apsidal** chapels ringing the apse were often visible on the exterior, as were the buttress piers and flying buttresses that countered the outward thrusts of the interior vaults. Portal façades were customarily marked by high, flanking towers or gabled porches ornamented with **pinnacles** and finials. Architectural sculpture covered each portal's tympanum, **archivolts**, and **jambs**. A magnificent stained-glass rose window typically formed the centerpiece of the portal façades. Stained glass also filled the tall, pointed **lancets**.

Chartres Cathedral

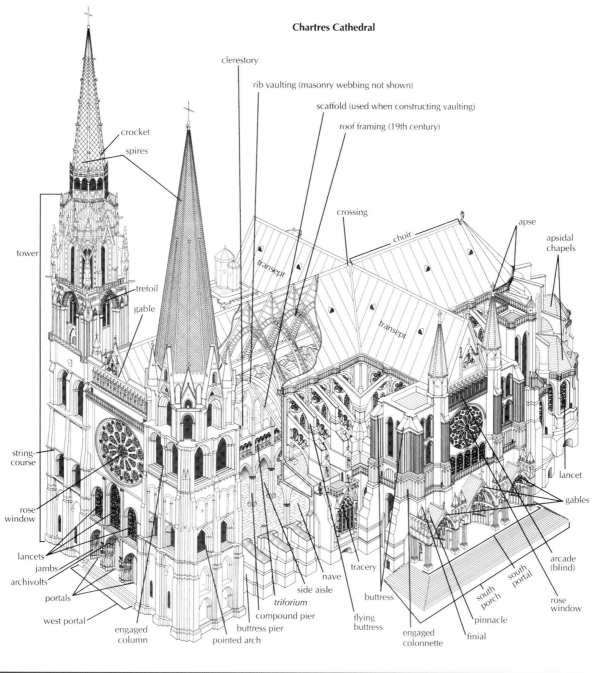

- clerestory
- rib vaulting (masonry webbing not shown)
- scaffold (used when constructing vaulting)
- roof framing (19th century)
- crossing
- choir
- apse
- apsidal chapels
- crocket
- spires
- tower
- trefoil
- gable
- transept
- transept
- string-course
- rose window
- lancets
- jambs
- archivolts
- portals
- west portal
- engaged column
- buttress pier
- pointed arch
- nave
- side aisle
- *triforium*
- compound pier
- flying buttress
- tracery
- buttress
- engaged colonnette
- finial
- pinnacle
- south porch
- south portal
- lancet
- gables
- arcade (blind)
- rose window

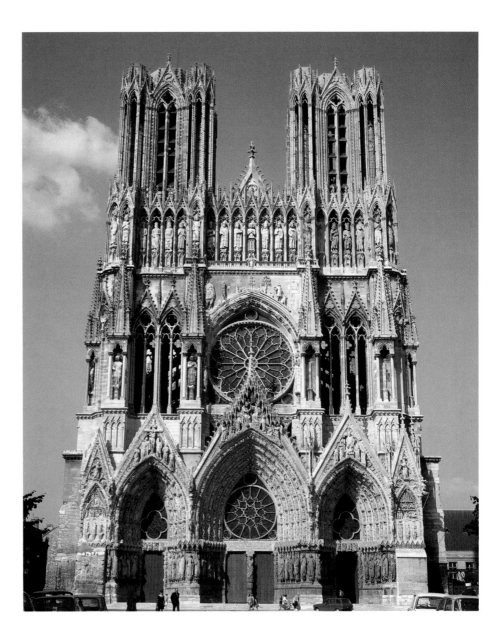

11–11 West façade, Reims Cathedral.
1230s–1260; towers mid-15th century

The cathedral was restored in the sixteenth century and again in the nineteenth and twentieth centuries. During World War I it withstood bombardment by some 3,000 shells, an eloquent testimony to the skills of its builders. It was recently cleaned.

Important buildings were also being constructed at Reims and Amiens (fig. **11–11**). The Cathedral of Reims was the coronation church of France while Amiens was an important commercial center and had relics of John the Baptist. Construction began at Reims Cathedral in 1211 and continued throughout the century. Amiens Cathedral was begun after a fire in 1218. Artisans at each site borrowed from and influenced each other. In each, the nave, like Chartres, has a ribbed vault and a three-part elevation composed of a tall arcade, a triforium, and a clerestory. In the west wall, the great rose window at the clerestory level, a row of lancets at the triforium level, and windows over the portals replace the traditional stone of wall and tympana. A technique known as bar tracery, perfected at Reims, made possible this remarkable expanse of glass. In bar tracery, thin stone strips, called **mullions**, form a lacy frame for the glass, replacing the older practice in which glass was inserted directly into window openings. In Reims's western wall, the glass is anchored visually by a masonry screen around the doorway. Here, ranks of carved Old Testament prophets and ancestors of Christ serve as moral guides for the newly crowned monarchs, who faced them after coronation.

The magnificent west façade at Reims has massive gabled portals with soaring peaks as well as large stained-glass windows that fill the portal tympana. In a departure from tradition, the imagery of the central portal focuses on Mary rather than Christ, a reflection of her growing popularity. An enormous rose window, the focal point of the façade, fills the entire clerestory level. The towers were later additions, as was the row of statues (the so-called Kings' Gallery) stretching across the façade at the base of the towers. The spires were never completed.

Different workshops and individuals worked at Reims for many decades, and a group of four figures from the central portal of the western front illustrates three of the styles of sculpture found there (fig. **11–12**). The subject of the pair on the right is the *Visitation*, in which Mary (left), pregnant with Jesus, visits her older cousin, Elizabeth (right), who is pregnant with Saint John the Baptist. These figures' sculptors, from the so-called Classical Shop, active in Reims about 1230–1235, drew on ancient sources. The heavy figures have the same solidity seen in Roman sculpture (see fig. 6–10), and Mary's full face, wavy hair, and heavy mantle recall imperial

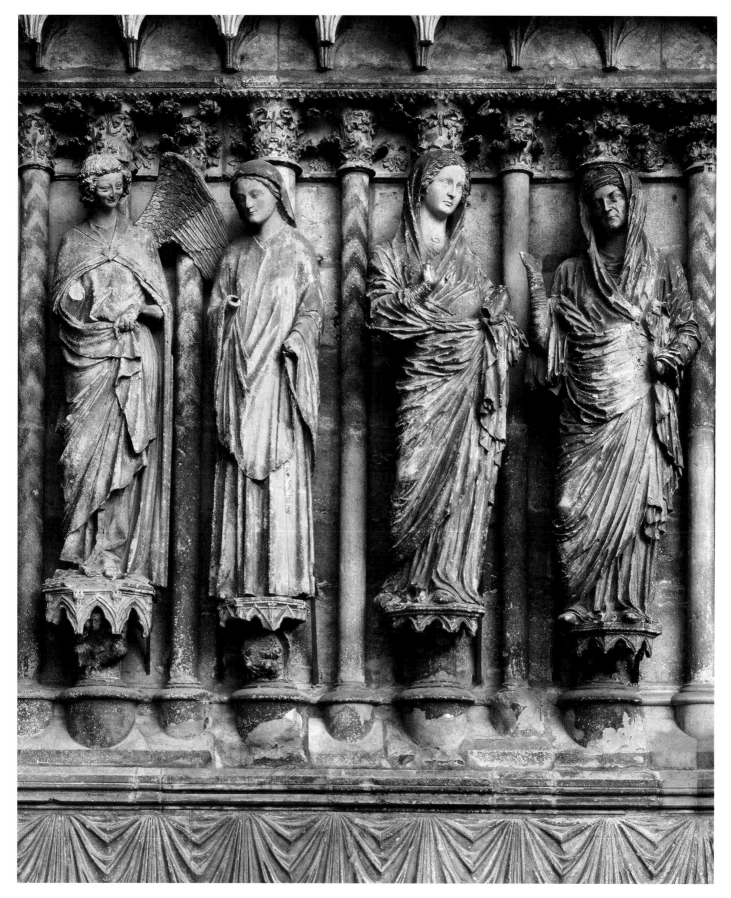

11–12 *Annunciation* (left pair: archangel Gabriel c. 1255, Mary c. 1245) and *Visitation*
(right pair: c. 1230), right side, central portal, west façade, Reims Cathedral

portrait statuary. The figures seem to turn toward each other as if in conversation, their weight shifted to one leg creating a swaying posture.

The pair on the left in figure 11–12 illustrates the *Annunciation*, in which the archangel Gabriel announces to Mary that she will bear Jesus. Mary's slight body, restrained gesture, and delicate features, already the work of a different master, contrast markedly with the bold tangibility of Mary in the Annunciation scene next to her. The angel Gabriel (at the far left) is the work of an artist known today as the Master of the Smiling Angels or the Saint Joseph Master, after his most famous sculptures at Reims. This artist, whose work began to appear in the middle of the thirteenth century, created tall, gracefully swaying figures whose aristocratic refinement became a guiding force in later Gothic sculpture and painting.

The west front of Amiens Cathedral reflects several stages of construction. The lower levels, designed by Robert de Luzarches, are the earliest, dating to about 1220–1236, but building continued over the centuries. The towers date to the fourteenth and fifteenth centuries, and the tracery in the rose window is also from this later date. The sculptural program of the west portals at Amiens presents an almost overwhelming array of images. The sculpture was produced rapidly by a large workshop in only 15 years or so (1220–c. 1236), making it stylistically more uniform than that of many cathedrals. Worshipers approaching the main entrance encountered figures of apostles and saints lined up along the door jambs and projecting buttresses, as were seen at Chartres.

A sculpture of Christ as the *Beau Dieu* ("noble, or beautiful, God")—the kindly teacher-priest bestowing his blessing on the faithful—adorns the **trumeau** of the central portal at Amiens (fig. **11–13**). This exceptionally fine sculpture may have been the work of the master of the Amiens workshop himself. The broad contours of the heavy drapery wrapped around Christ's right hip and bunched over his left arm lead the eye up to the Gospel book he holds and past it to his face, which resembles that of a young king. He stands on a lion and a dragon-like creature called a basilisk, symbolizing his kingship and triumph over evil and death. With its clear, solid forms, elegantly cascading robe, and interplay of close observation with idealization, the *Beau Dieu* embodies the Gothic spirit.

By the middle of the thirteenth century builders had thoroughly mastered the principles and techniques of Gothic architecture and could devote their attention to refining the elements of the style. They made larger windows, disguised walls behind carved bundles of moldings and shafts, and focused on the linear quality that ribs gave to vaults. The architects of the royal palace chapel in Paris, called the Sainte-Chapelle (built 1243–1248), took the use of stained glass and interior sculpture to new heights. Constructed to house the French king Louis IX's prized collection of relics, the Sainte-Chapelle resembles a giant reliquary itself, one made of stone and glass instead of gold and gems. Built in two stories, it has a ground-level chapel accessible from a courtyard and a private upper chapel entered from the royal residence. Entering this upper chapel is like emerging into a glowing jewel box

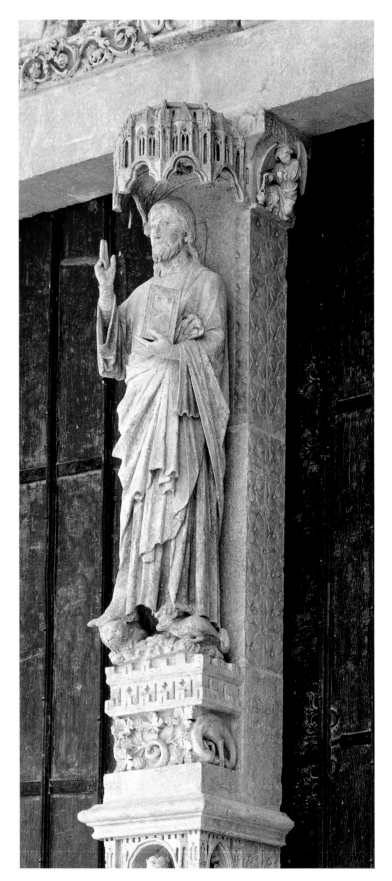

11–13 Amiens Cathedral. *Christ, known as the "beautiful God," Beau Dieu,* trumeau, central portal, west façade, Amiens Cathedral, France. c. 1220–1236

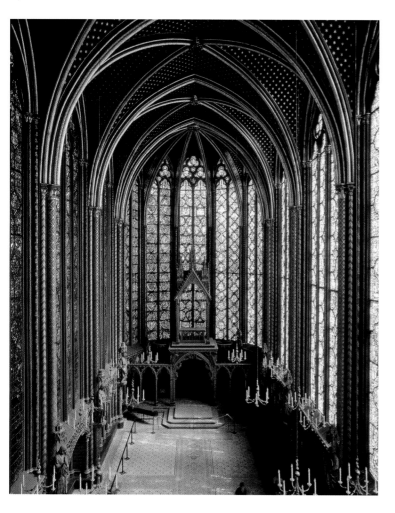

11–14 Interior, upper chapel, the Sainte-Chapelle, Paris. 1243–1248

Louis IX avidly collected relics of the Passion of Christ, some of which became available in the aftermath of the Crusaders' sack of Constantinople. Relics that Louis acquired were supposedly the crown of thorns that had been placed on Jesus's head before the Crucifixion, a bit of the metal lance tip that pierced his side, the vinegar-soaked sponge offered to wet his lips, a nail used in the Crucifixion, and a fragment of the True Cross. In the Sainte-Chapelle's stained glass, the king is depicted walking barefoot to demonstrate his piety and humility as he received his treasures in Paris.

11–15 Page with *Louis IX and Queen Blanche of Castile,* Moralized Bible, from Paris. 1226–1234. Ink, tempera, and gold leaf on vellum, 15″ × 10½″ (38 × 26.6 cm). The Pierpont Morgan Library, New York

M.240, F.8

Thin sheets of gold leaf were painstakingly attached to the vellum and then polished to a high sheen with a tool called a burnisher. Gold was applied to paintings before pigments. The Parisian court style had enormous influence throughout Northern Europe. Artists flocked to Paris, where they joined workshops affiliated with the guild of Saint John. University officials supervised the guild and controlled the production and distribution of manuscripts.

(fig. **11–14**). The ratio of glass to stone is higher here than in any other Gothic structure, for the walls have been reduced to clusters of slender painted colonnettes framing tall windows filled with brilliant colored glass. The stained glass illustrates narrative and symbolic scenes, including the Nativity and Passion (sufferings) of Christ, the life of Saint John the Baptist, and the story of King Louis's acquisition of his relics. This exquisite structure epitomizes a new Gothic style known as *Rayonnant* (a French term meaning "radiant" or "radiating") because of its radiating bar tracery. The style is also sometimes called Court Style because of its association with the royal courts of Paris and London.

France gained renown in the thirteenth and fourteenth centuries not only for the new Gothic architecture and sculpture but also for painting and illustrated books. Books ranged from practical manuals for artisans to elaborate devotional works illustrated with exquisite miniatures. The production of high-quality manuscripts flourished in Paris during the reign of Louis IX, whose royal library was renowned. Queen Blanche of Castile, Louis's mother, served as regent of France (1226–1234) until he came of age. She and the teenage king appear on the dedication page (fig. **11–15**) of a Moralized Bible—one in which selected passages of the Old and New Testaments are paired to give an allegorical, or moralized, interpretation. The royal pair sits

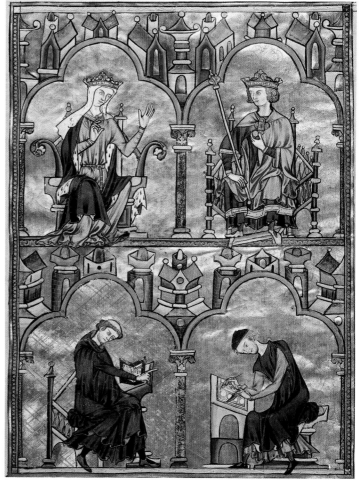

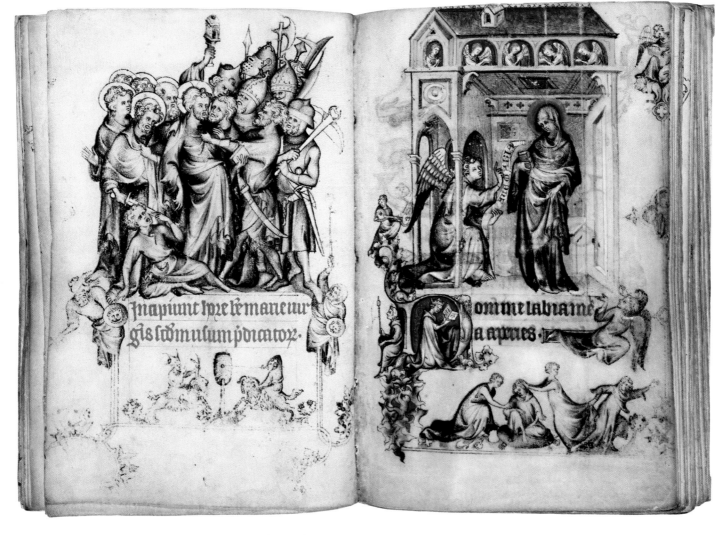

11–16 Jean Pucelle. Pages with *Betrayal and Arrest of Christ,* folio 15v. (left) and *Annunciation,* folio 16r. (right). *Petites Heures of Jeanne d'Evreux*, from Paris. c. 1325–1328. Grisaille and color on vellum, each page 3 $\frac{1}{2}$" × 2 $\frac{1}{4}$" (8.2 × 5.6 cm). The Metropolitan Museum of Art, New York

This book was precious to the queen, who mentioned it in her will. She even named its illuminator, an unusual tribute.

against a solid gold background under trilobed arches. Below them a scholar-monk dictates to a scribe. The ornate thrones of Louis and his mother and the buildings atop the arches suggest that the figures sit inside a royal palace, and in fact it would not have been unusual for the queen to have housed the scholar, scribe, and illuminator while they were executing her commission. Interestingly, only the slightly oversized heads of the queen and king preserve a sense of hierarchical scale. The scribe, in the lower right, is working on a page with a column of roundels for illustrations. This format of manuscript illustration—used on the pages that follow the Bible's dedication page—derives from stained-glass lancets with their columns of images in medallions (see fig. 11–1). The illuminators also show their debt to stained glass in their use of glowing red and blue and reflective gold surfaces.

Beginning in the late thirteenth century a new kind of book, private prayer book, became popular among those who could

afford them. Such books came to be called **Books of Hours** because they contained special prayers to be recited at the eight canonical "hours," literally around the clock. Books of Hours were most commonly devoted to the Virgin, but they could be personalized for individual patrons with prayers to patron saints, a calendar of saints' church festivals, and other offices, such as those said for the dead.

A tiny, exquisite Book of Hours given by King Charles IV of France (ruled 1322–1328) to his wife, Queen Jeanne d'Evreux, shortly after their marriage in 1325 is the work of an illuminator named Jean Pucelle (fig. **11–16**). Instead of the intense colors used by earlier illuminators, Pucelle worked in grisaille—with delicate touches of color added. The pages shown here are part of a narrative cycle juxtaposing scenes from the Infancy and the Passion of Christ, a form known as the Joys and Sorrows of the Virgin. Here, the "joy" of the *Annunciation* on the right is paired with the "sorrow" of the *Betrayal and Arrest of Christ* on the left.

In the *Annunciation*, Mary receives the archangel Gabriel in her Gothic-style home, as rejoicing angels look on from windows under the eaves. Queen Jeanne appears in the initial below the Annunciation, kneeling before a lectern and reading from her Book of Hours. This inclusion of the patron in prayer within a scene, a practice that continued in monumental painting and sculpture in the fifteenth century, conveyed the idea that the scenes were "visions" inspired by meditation rather than records of historical events. In the Betrayal scene on the left page, the traitorous disciple Judas Iscariot embraces Jesus, thus identifying him to soldiers who have come to seize him and setting in motion the events that lead to the Crucifixion. The spoof of military training sketched below, showing "knights" riding goats and jousting at a barrel stuck on a pole, is perhaps a comment on the lack of valor of the soldiers assaulting Jesus.

Both pages show Pucelle adapting the sculptural style of the French court to manuscript illustration. Softly modeled, voluminous draperies are gathered around tall, elegantly curved figures with curly hair and broad foreheads. Jesus on the left and Mary on the right stand in the swaying S-curve pose typical of Court Style works, such as the *Virgin and Child* from Saint-Denis, commissioned by the same queen (see fig. 11–17). Note, too, that the earnest face of the *Annunciation* archangel resembles that of the angel Gabriel at Reims (see fig. 11–12).

Besides carving the sculptural ornament for churches, Gothic sculptors also found a lucrative new outlet for their work in a growing demand for small religious statues intended for homes and personal chapels or as donations to favorite churches. Among the treasures of the Abbey Church of Saint-Denis is the silver-gilt image, slightly more than 2 feet tall, of a standing *Virgin and Child* (fig. **11–17**). An inscription on the base bears the date 1339 and the name of Queen Jeanne d'Evreux. The Virgin holds her son in her left arm, and supports her weight on her left leg, creating the graceful S-curve pose that was a stylistic signature of the period (see fig. 11–12). She holds a scepter topped with an enameled and jeweled lily, the heraldic fleur-de-lis of French royalty, and she originally had a crown on her head. The statue served as a reliquary for hairs said to come from Mary's head. Despite this figure's clear association with royalty, the Virgin's simple clothing and sweet, youthful face anticipate a type of the ideally beautiful mother that emerged in the later fourteenth and fifteenth centuries in northern France, Flanders, and the Germanic lands.

Secular Art

Although we have studied the Gothic style in religious architecture, it is also seen in such secular structures as castles, town halls, and manor houses. Castles evolved during the Romanesque and Gothic periods from enclosed strongholds to elaborate fortified residential complexes (see Chapter 10, Dover Castle, page 259). The ruined towers and walls seem rather romantic and picturesque today, but castles and castle-like residences—which established an aura of power and wealth for a family—had both a

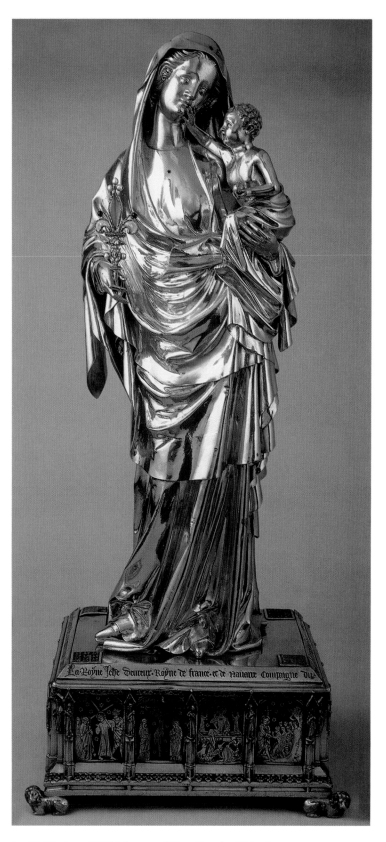

11–17 *Virgin and Child,* from the Abbey Church of Saint-Denis. 1339. Silver gilt and enamel, height 27 1/8″ (69 cm). Musée du Louvre, Paris
PHOTOGRAPHY © 1991. THE METROPOLITAN MUSEUM OF ART

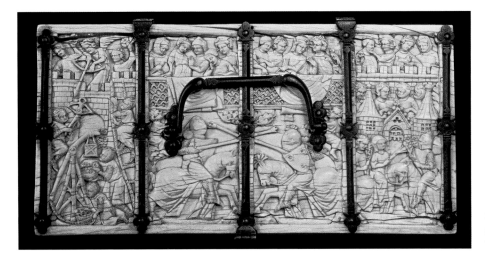

11–18 **Attack on the Castle of Love.** Ivory. Paris, c. 1330–1350 panel $4\frac{1}{2}'' \times 9\frac{1}{16}''$ (11.5 × 24.6 cm). Walters Art Gallery, Baltimore

military and a political function. Even so, by the end of the Middle Ages castles became luxurious residences, their military aspect often more symbolic than real. Private rooms for the ladies, for example, were added to the great hall. One manuscript illumination shows the queen of France in a room with tapestry-hung walls, painted woodwork, and glass windows as well as magnificent furniture (see Introduction, fig. 23). Woven and embroidered textiles provided both insulation and enrichment. The use of heraldry (a symbolic language defining lineage) highlighted an owner's power and feudal rights. Although little secular art survives, embroideries such as the Chichester-Constable chasuble (a priest's vestment) (see fig. 11–23) suggest the finery worn by the queen and her ladies in the painting.

The lid of an ivory box depicts a tournament taking place in front of castle walls (fig. **11–18**). Such mock battles were once intended to keep knights fit for war, but they became a popular aristocratic sporting event. In fact, during the twelfth and thirteenth centuries, the military ideal can be seen giving way to a new ideal of romantic love in literature and music as well as in the visual arts. In the scene on this box, the tournament represents an allegorical battle of love. In the center panel, elegant ladies and gentlemen watch two jousting knights, who—with visors down and lances set—charge to the blare of trumpets played by young boys. In the scene on the left, ardent knights assault the Castle of Love, firing roses from crossbows and the deadly trebuchet (the most powerful medieval siege weapon) and climbing a scaling ladder, while women pelt the men with roses. The God of Love joins the fray and aims his arrows at the attackers. The action concludes in the scene on the right, where the tournament's victor and his lady love meet in a playful joust of their own, and other couples engage in flirtations on the castle walls. This miniature castle has the characteristic crenellated walls and towers that became the symbol of an aristocratic residence. The massive gateway is defended by towers with conical roofs and the portal itself has a sliding iron gate called a portcullis.

Beginning in the late thirteenth century, France began to suffer from overpopulation and economic decline. A great plague, the so-called Black Death, followed in the fourteenth century, along with a devastating conflict with England known as the Hundred Years' War. Large-scale cathedral construction generally ceased,

although the Gothic style continued to develop in smaller churches, municipal and commercial buildings, and private residences.

Gothic Art in England

As the Gothic style spread outside of France, it not only became an international style in Europe but—in the thirteenth and fourteenth centuries—also took on innovative regional forms. In England, for instance, cathedral builders were less concerned with height than were their French counterparts, and they constructed long, broad naves, Romanesque-type galleries, and clerestory-level passageways. The English builders focused their decorative efforts on the cathedral walls, which retained a Romanesque solidity.

Salisbury Cathedral, because its principal structure was built in a relatively short period of time (1220–1258), has a consistency of style that makes it an ideal representative of English Gothic architecture (fig. **11–19**). Typically English is the parklike

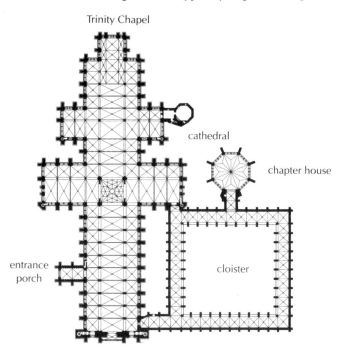

11–19 **Plan, Salisbury Cathedral,** 1220–1258, with a later cloister and chapter house

setting (the cathedral close, or precinct) and attached cloister and chapter house for the cathedral clergy (fig. **11–20**). Tier upon tier of blind tracery and arcaded niches underscore the width of the massive west façade. In contrast to French cathedral façades, which suggest the entrance to paradise with their mighty towers flanking deep portals, English façades like the one at Salisbury suggest a jeweled wall around paradise.

Many English churches were completed with splendid towers and spires in the fourteenth century, and at Salisbury Cathedral, about 1320–1330, Master Richard of Farleigh built a crossing tower with a spire rising to the extraordinary height of 400 feet. Taller than anything visualized by the original builders, the spire required extra buttressing and the builders added flying buttresses. The spire has such harmonious proportions that it seems the logical, and indeed inevitable, focal point of the architectural composition.

Typical of English cathedrals, Salisbury has wide projecting transepts (double transepts, in this case), a square apse, and a spacious sanctuary (fig. **11–21**). The interior reflects enduring Norman traditions, with its heavy walls and tall nave arcade surmounted by a short gallery and a clerestory with simple lancet windows. The emphasis on the horizontal movement of the arcades, unbroken by colonnettes in the unusually restrained nave, directs worshipers' attention forward to the altar, rather than upward into the vaults. Reminiscent of Romanesque interiors is the use of color in the stonework: The shafts supporting the four-part rib vaults are made of a darker stone that contrasts with the lighter stone of the rest of the interior. The stonework was originally painted and gilded as well as carved.

Like the French, the English also made richly decorated books. The dazzling artistry and delight in ambiguities that had marked manuscript illumination as early as the Book of Kells (see fig. 10–4) appeared in the *Windmill Psalter* (c. 1270–1280). The letter *B*, the first letter of Psalm 1—which begins with the words *Beatus vir qui non abit* ("Happy those who do not follow the counsel [of the wicked]")—fills the left page and outlines a

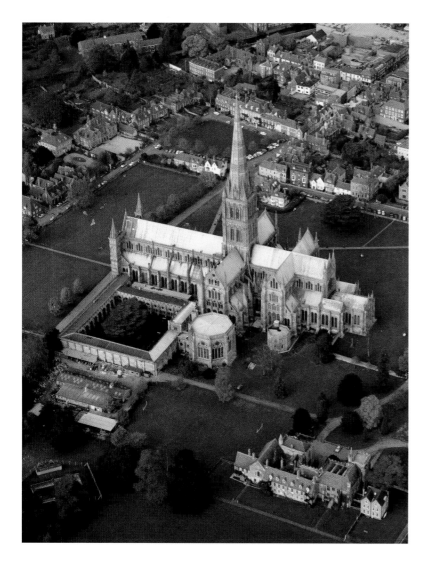

11–20 West façade, Salisbury Cathedral, Salisbury, Wiltshire, England. 1220–1258; west façade 1265; spire c. 1320–1330

The original cathedral had been built inside the hilltop castle of a Norman lord. In 1217, Bishop Richard Poore petitioned the pope to relocate the church, claiming the wind howled so loudly there that the clergy could not hear themselves say Mass. He must have wanted to escape the lord's control. After the cathedral was under way, the bishop laid out the town of Salisbury (from the Saxon Searisbyrig, *meaning "Caesar's burg," or town). Material carted down from the old church was used in the new cathedral, along with dark, fossil-filled Purbeck stone and limestone from Caen. The church was abandoned and vandalized during the Protestant Reformation. In the eighteenth century, the English architect James Wyatt, nicknamed "the Destroyer" subjected it to radical renovations, during which the remaining stained glass and sculptured tombs were removed or rearranged.*

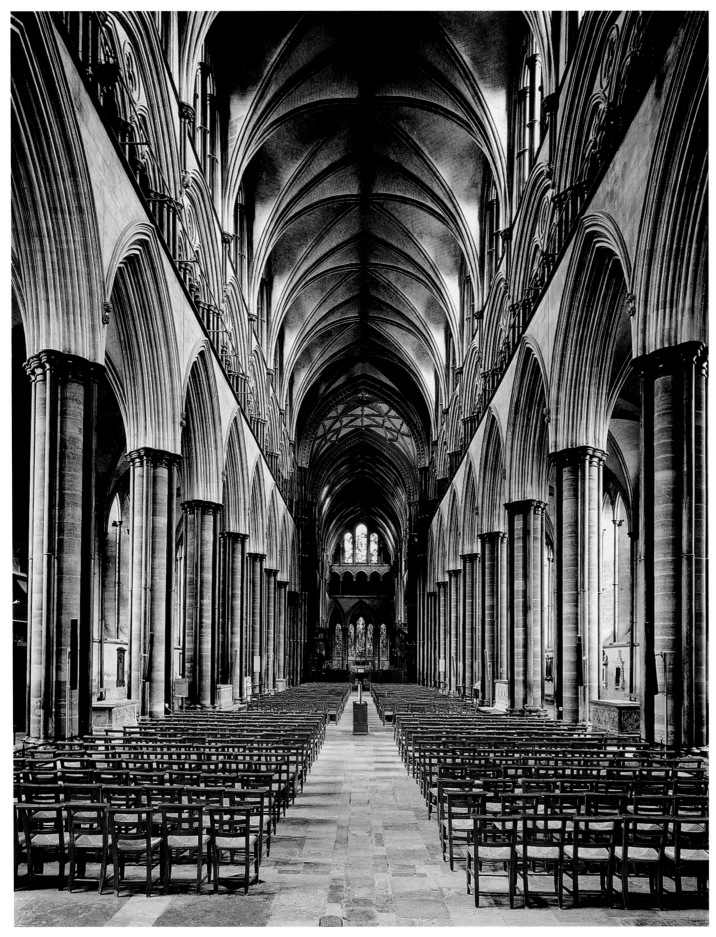

11–21 Nave, Salisbury Cathedral. 1220–1258. Looking east toward the high altar

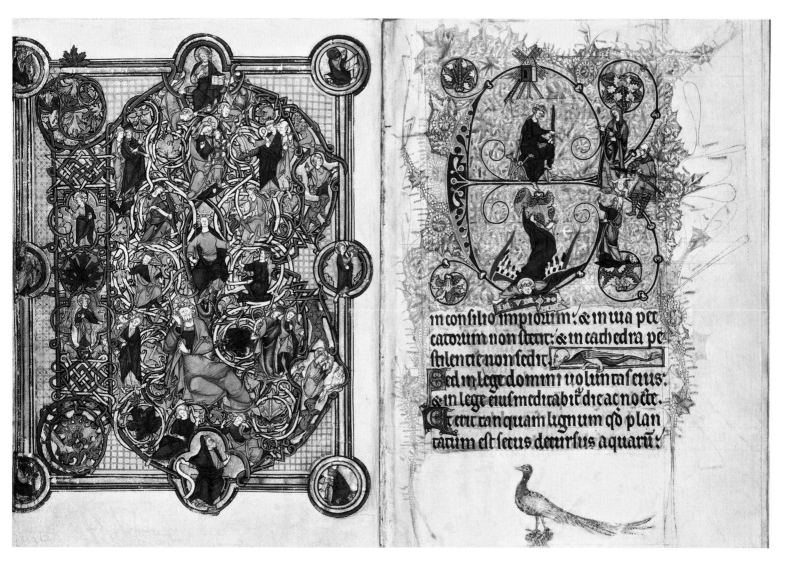

11–22 Page with *Psalm 1 (Beatus Vir)*, *Windmill Psalter,* from London. c. 1270–1280. Ink, pigments and gold on vellum, each page 12 3/4″ × 8 3/4″ (32.3 × 22.2 cm). The Pierpont Morgan Library, New York

M. 102, F. IV-2

densely interlaced Tree of Jesse (fig. **11–22**). An *E*, the second letter, occupies the top of the right page and is formed from large tendrils that escape from delicate background vegetation to support characters in the story of the Judgment of Solomon. The rest of the opening words appear on a banner carried by an angel at the bottom of the E. The story, seen as a prefiguration of the Last Judgment, relates how two women (at the right), claiming the same baby came before King Solomon (on the crossbar) to settle their dispute. The king ordered a guard to slice the baby in half with his sword and give each woman her share. This trick exposed the real mother, who hastened to give up her claim in order to save the baby's life.

Realistic and surprising images appear among the pages' foliage, many of the images visual puns on the text. For example, the large windmill at the top of the initial *E* (which gives the Psalter its name) illustrates the statement in the psalm that the

wicked would not survive the Judgment but would be "like chaff driven by the wind" (Psalm 1:4). Imagery such as this would have stimulated contemplation of the inner meanings of the text's familiar messages.

The English also became renowned throughout Europe for their pictorial needlework, using colored silk and gold thread to create images as detailed as the painters produced in manuscripts. The art came to be called *opus anglicanum* (English work). The names of several prominent embroiderers are known, but in her own day no one surpassed Mabel of Bury St. Edmunds, who worked for King Henry III. She created both religious and secular pieces, and the grateful king paid her in money and rich gifts.

None of Mabel's work has been identified, but it must have resembled the embroidery seen on a chasuble—a garment worn by priests while celebrating the Mass—known as the

Chichester-Constable chasuble (fig. **11–23**). Here, the images are formed by fine gradations of colored silk as subtle as the finest painting. Three Marian scenes—the Annunciation, the Adoration of the Magi, and the Coronation of the Virgin—are arranged in three registers framed by cusped, crocketed S-shaped arches and twisting branches sprouting oak leaves with seed-pearl acorns. This vestment would have glinted in the candlelight amid the other treasures of the altar. So heavy did such gold and bejeweled garments become that their wearers often needed help to move.

Gothic Art in the Germanic Lands

In the Germanic lands, a new type of Gothic church, the hall church, developed in the thirteenth century in response to the increasing importance of sermons within church services. The hall church featured a nave and side aisles with vaults of the same height, creating a spacious and open interior that could accommodate the large crowds drawn by charismatic preachers.

In the fourteenth century, Germanic architects—and especially the Parler family—perfected the hall church. Heinrich Parler designed and began the Church of the Holy Cross in Schwäbisch Gmünd, Swabia, in 1317. In 1351 his son Peter (c. 1330–1399), the most brilliant architect of this talented family, joined the shop to design the choir (fig. **11–24**). Peter turned the building into a hall church whose triple-aisled form was enlarged by a ring of deep chapels between the buttresses of the choir. The unity of the entire space was enhanced by the complex web vault—a veritable web of ribs created by eliminating transverse ribs and ridge ribs. The flexible design of these "great halls" was also widely adopted for civic and residential buildings and even by Jewish architects. Charles IV recognized Peter's talent

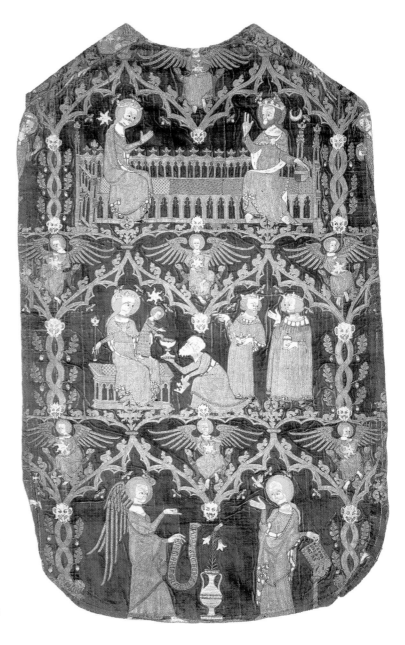

11–23 *Life of the Virgin,* **Chichester-Constable chasuble** back from a set of vestments embroidered in *opus anglicanum,* from southern England. 1330–1350. Red velvet with silk and metallic thread; length 5′ 1/2″ (1.64 m), width 30″ (76 cm). The Metropolitan Museum of Art, New York

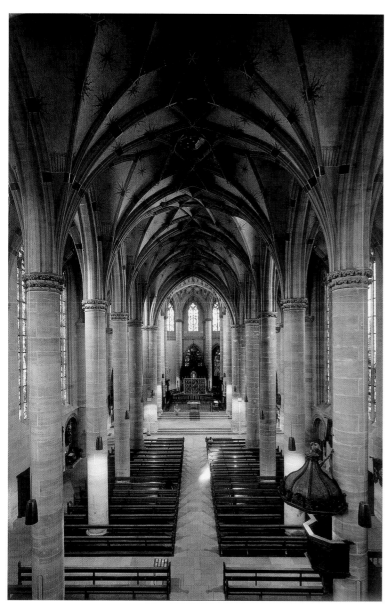

11–24 Heinrich and Peter Parler. Choir, Church of the Holy Cross, Schwäbisch Gmünd, Germany. Begun 1317; choir 1351; vaulting completed 16th century

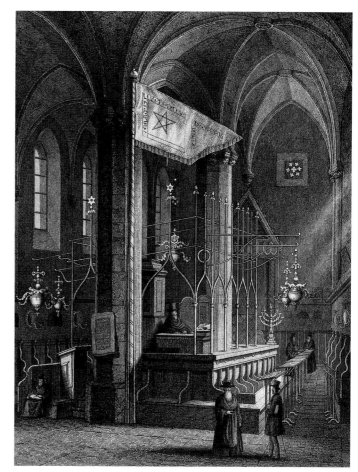

11–25 Interior, Altneuschul, Prague, Bohemia (Czech Republic). c. late 13th century; later additions and alterations. Engraving from *Das Historisches Prag in 25 Stahlstichen,* 1864

and in 1353 called on him to build the Cathedral of Prague, Charles's capital city. Henceforth Peter Parler and his heirs were the most influential architects in the Holy Roman Empire.

Also built in the style of a Gothic great hall is the oldest functioning synagogue in Europe, Prague's Altneuschul (Old-New Synagogue), probably built in the late thirteenth or early fourteenth century (fig. **11–25**). As in a hall church, the vaults of the synagogue are all the same height. But unlike a church, with its nave and side aisles, the Altneuschul has two central aisles with six bays. The bays have four-part vaulting with a decorative fifth rib.

The synagogue has two focal points, the *aron,* or shrine for the Torah scrolls, located on the east wall, toward Jerusalem, and a central raised reading platform called the *bimah.* The *bimah* can be seen straddling the two central bays. The interior of the synagogue was originally richly adorned with murals. Men worshiped and studied in the principal space; women were sequestered in annexes.

Gothic Art in Italy

The thirteenth century was a period of political division and economic expansion for the Italian peninsula and its neighboring islands. The papacy had emerged from its conflict with the Holy Roman Empire as a significant international force, but its temporal success weakened its spiritual authority and brought it into conflict with the growing power of the kings of France and England. In 1309, after the election of a French pope, the papal court moved from Rome to Avignon, in southern France. During the Great Schism of 1378 to 1417, there were two rival lines of popes, one in Rome and one in Avignon, each claiming legitimacy.

The prolonged conflict between the papacy and the empire created two political factions: the pro-papacy Guelphs and the pro-imperial Ghibellines. Northern Italian lands were dominated by several independent and wealthy city-states controlled by a few powerful families. Consequently, these cities were subject to chronic internal factional strife as well as conflict with one another.

Nevertheless, great wealth and a growing individualism promoted arts patronage in northern Italy. Artisans began to emerge as artists in the modern sense, both in their own eyes and the eyes of patrons. Although their methods and working conditions

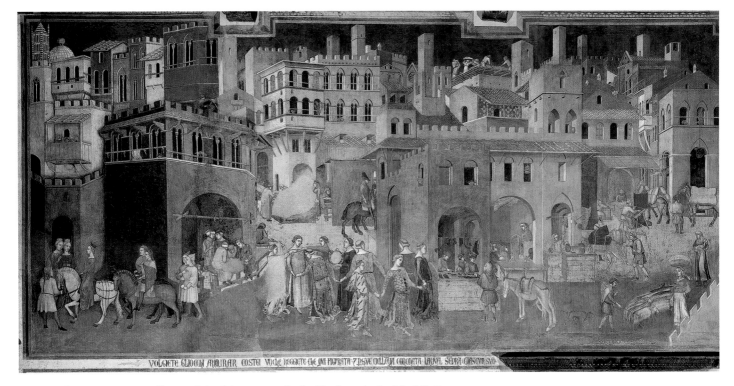

11–26 Ambrogio Lorenzetti, *Allegory of Good Government in the City,* fresco in the Sala della Pace, Palazzo Pubblico, Siena, Italy. 1338–1340. (Left half of mural showing good government in the country and city.)

remained largely unchanged, they now belonged to powerful urban guilds and contracted freely with wealthy townspeople and nobles and with civic and religious bodies. Their ambitious, self-aware art reflects their economic and social freedom.

In 1338 the Siena city council commissioned Ambrogio Lorenzetti to paint a room called the Sala della Pace (Chamber of Peace) in the city hall. The theme chosen for the walls was the contrast between the effects on people's lives of good and bad government (fig. **11–26**). For the *Allegory of Good Government in the City*, and in tribute to his patrons, Ambrogio created a recognizable portrait of Siena. The cathedral dome and the distinctive striped campanile (its freestanding bell tower) are visible in the upper left-hand corner. Ambrogio's achievement in this fresco was twofold. First, he maintained an overall visual coherence despite the shifts in vantage point and scale, helping to keep all parts of the flowing composition intelligible. Second, he created a feeling of accurate scale in the relationship between figures and environment. From the women dancing to a tambourine outside a shoemaker's shop, to the travelers and merchants, to the masons on a scaffold, the work conveys a powerful vision of an orderly society, of peace and plenty. Sadly, famine, poverty, and the horrible Black Death overcame Siena just a few years after this work was completed.

Sculpture

In the first half of the thirteenth century, Holy Roman Emperor Frederick II had fostered a classical revival at his southern Italian court, a revival that stimulated a trend toward greater naturalism in Italian Gothic sculpture. A leading early exemplar of the trend was Nicola Pisano (active c. 1258–1278), who moved from the south to Tuscany at mid-century. An inscription on a freestanding marble pulpit (fig. **11–27**) in the Pisa Baptistry identifies

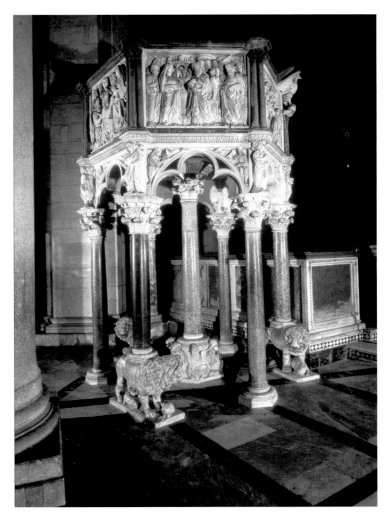

11–27 Nicola Pisano. Pulpit, Baptistry, Pisa. 1260. Marble, height approx. 15′ (4.6 m)

Cennino Cennini's *Il Libro dell'Arte (The Handbook of the Crafts)*, a compendium of early-fifteenth-century Florentine artistic techniques, includes step-by-step instructions for making panel paintings. The wood for these paintings, he specified, should be fine-grained, free of blemishes, and thoroughly seasoned by slow drying.

The first step in preparing a panel for painting was to cover its surface with clean white linen strips soaked in a gesso made from gypsum, a task best done on a dry, windy day. Gesso provides a ground, or surface, on which to paint. Cennini specified that at least nine layers should be applied, with a minimum of two-and-a-half days' drying time between layers, depending on the weather. The gessoed surface should then be burnished until it resembled ivory. The artist could now sketch the composition of the work with charcoal made from burned willow twigs. At this point, advised the author, "When you have finished drawing your figure, especially if it is in a very valuable [altarpiece], so that you are counting on profit and reputation from it, leave it alone for a few days, going back to it now and then to look it over and improve it wherever it still needs something . . . (and bear in mind that you may copy and examine things done by other good masters; that it is no shame to you)" (cited in Thompson, page 75).

The final version of the design, he directed, should be inked in with a fine squirrel-hair brush, and the charcoal brushed off with a feather. Gold leaf was to be affixed on a humid day over a reddish clay ground called bole, and the tissue-thin sheets carefully glued down with a mixture of fine powdered clay and egg white and burnished with a gemstone or the tooth of a carnivorous animal. Punched and incised patterning was to be added later.

Italian painters at this time worked in a type of paint known as tempera, powdered pigments mixed most often with egg yolk, a little water, and an occasional touch of glue. Apprentices were kept busy grinding and mixing paints according to their masters' recipes, setting them out for more senior painters in wooden bowls or shell dishes. Cennini claimed that panel painting was a gentleman's job, but given its laborious complexity, that was wishful thinking. The claim does, however, reflect the rising social status of painters.

Cennini specified a detailed and highly formulaic painting process. Faces, for example, were always to be done last, with flesh tones applied over two coats of a light greenish pigment and highlighted with touches of red and white. The finished painting was to be given a layer of varnish to protect it and enhance its colors. Reflecting the increasing specialization that developed in the thirteenth century, Cennini assumed that an elaborate frame would have been produced by someone else according to the painter's specifications and brought fully assembled to the studio.

Nicola as a supremely self-confident sculptor. The inscription reads: "In the year 1260 Nicola Pisano carved this noble work. May so gifted a hand be praised as it deserves." The six-sided structure, open on one side for a stairway, is supported by columns topped with leafy Corinthian capitals. Standing figures and an angel flank Gothic trefoil arches. Three columns rest on the back of a shaggy-maned lion guarding its prey and the center column stands on crouching figures. The pulpits' panels illustrate New Testament subjects, each treated as an independent composition unrelated to the others. The sculptural treatment of the deeply cut, full-bodied forms is almost classical, as are the heavy, placid faces; the congested layout and the use of hierarchical scale are not. The format, style, and technique of Roman sarcophagus reliefs—readily accessible in the burial ground near the cathedral—may have inspired the carving.

Italian Panel and Mural Painting

The elegant Court Style seen in manuscript illustrations and embroideries also influenced Gothic panel painting (see "Cennini on Panel Painting," above). Large-scale paintings on wood panels, altarpieces made to stand behind and above the altar, began to appear in the twelfth century and proliferated throughout Europe in the thirteenth century.

Two very important schools of Italian Gothic painting emerged in Siena and Florence, rivals in this as in everything else. Siena's foremost painter was Duccio di Buoninsegna (active 1278–1318), whose synthesis of Byzantine and northern Gothic influences transformed the tradition in which he worked. Between 1308 and 1311, Duccio and his studio assistants painted a huge altarpiece for Siena Cathedral known as the *Maestà*

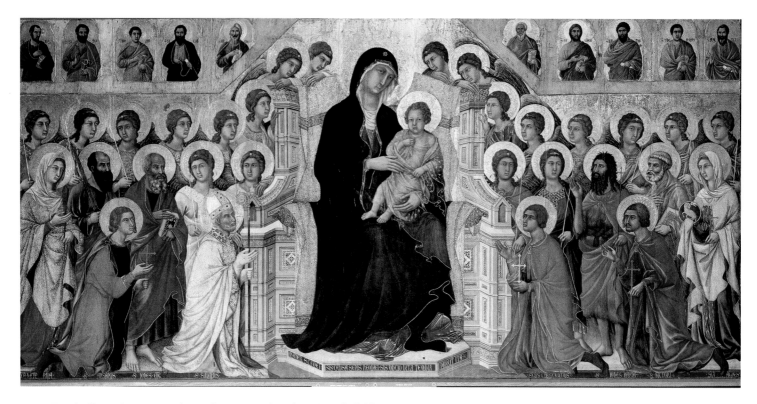

11–28 Duccio di Buoninsegna. Conjectural reconstruction of Virgin and Child in Majesty (Maestà). Original location Siena Cathedral. 1308–1311. Tempera and gold on wood. Main panel, 7′ × 13′ (2.13 × 4.12 m) and many small panels now in Museo dell'Opera del Duomo, Siena

Duccio's altarpiece was moved to the cathedral in a formal civic procession. It must have resembled the procession around St. Mark's Square in Venice painted by Gentile Bellini (fig. 7–22).

(Majesty) Altarpiece. Creating this altarpiece was an arduous undertaking. The work was large—the central panel alone was 7 by 13 feet—and it had to be painted on both sides because the main altar stood in the center of the sanctuary.

Because the *Maestà* was broken up in the eighteenth century, its power and beauty can only be imagined from scattered parts. The main scene, depicting the *Virgin and Child in Majesty* (fig. **11–28**), was once accompanied above and below by narrative scenes from the life of the Virgin and the infancy of Christ. On the back were scenes from the life and Passion of Christ. In this altarpiece, Duccio has combined a softened Italo-Byzantine figure style (an Italian adaptation of later Byzantine art) with the linear grace and easy relationship between figures and their settings that is characteristic of French Gothic art. This subtle blending of northern and southern elements can be seen in the haloed ranks around Mary's architectonic throne (which represents both the Catholic Church and its specific embodiment, Siena Cathedral). The central, most holy figures retain an iconic Byzantine solemnity and immobility, but those adoring them reflect a more naturalistic, courtly style that became the hallmark of the Sienese school for years to come. The ornate punchwork, or tooled designs in gold leaf, is also characteristically Sienese.

The enthusiasm with which the citizens of a city greeted a great painting or altarpiece demonstrates the power of the images it represented as well as the association of those images with the glory of the city. Only rarely was such enthusiasm a testimony to the skill or fame of the artist. Duccio's completed altarpiece for Siena Cathedral was carried from his workshop in a joyous procession:

> On the day that it was carried to the [cathedral] the shops were shut, and the bishop conducted a great and devout company of priests and friars in solemn procession, accompanied by . . . all the officers of the commune, and all the people, and one after another the worthiest with lighted candles in their hands took places near the picture, and behind came the women and children with great devotion. And they accompanied the said picture up to the [cathedral], making the procession around the campo [square], as is the custom, all the bells ringing joyously, out of reverence for so noble a picture as is this (cited in Holt, page 69).

In Florence the transformation of the Italo-Byzantine style began somewhat earlier than in Siena. Duccio's Florentine counterpart was an older painter named Cenni di Pepi (active c. 1272–1302), better known by his nickname, Cimabue. Cimabue is believed to have painted the *Virgin and Child Enthroned* (fig. **11–29**) in about 1280 for the main altar of the Church of the Santa Trinità (Holy Trinity) in Florence. At more than 12 $\frac{1}{2}$ feet

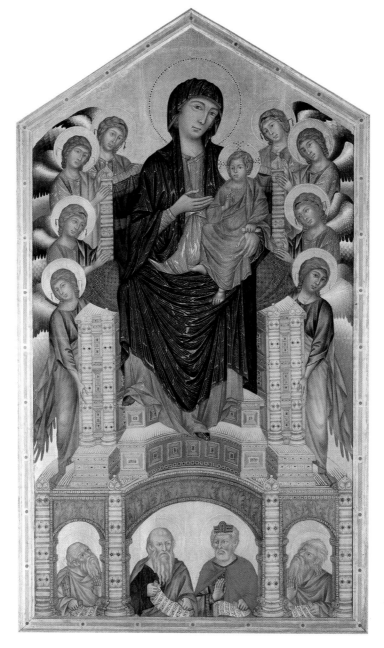

11–29 Cimabue. *Virgin and Child Enthroned,* from the Church of Santa
Trinità, Florence. c. 1280. Tempera and gold on wood, 12′7 $\frac{1}{2}$″ × 7′4″
(3.9 × 2.2 m). Galleria degli Uffizi, Florence

high, this enormous panel painting seems to have set a precedent
for monumental altarpieces. Surrounded by saints, angels, and
Old Testament prophets, Mary holds the infant Jesus in her lap
and points to him as the path to salvation.

Cimabue employed Byzantine formulas in determining the
proportions of the figures, the placement of their features, and
even the tilts of their haloed heads. To render the draperies (and
to suggest divinity), he used the Byzantine technique of highlighting the base color with thin lines of gold. Mary's huge
throne, painted to represent gold with inset enamels and gems,
provides an architectural framework for the figures. The mixture
of vantage points suspends the viewer in space in front of the
image, simultaneously looking down on the projecting elements
of the throne and Mary's lap, but straight at the prophets at the

base of the throne and the splendid winged seraphim who appear
one above another on either side. These spatial ambiguities, as
well as subtle asymmetries throughout the composition, the Virgin's thoughtful gaze, and the well-observed faces of the old men,
are all departures from tradition that serve to enliven the picture.

According to the sixteenth-century chronicler Giorgio
Vasari, Cimabue discovered a talented shepherd boy, Giotto di
Bondone, and taught him how to paint. Then, "Giotto obscured
the fame of Cimabue, as a great light outshines a lesser." Vasari
also credited Giotto (active c. 1300–1337) with "setting art upon
the path that may be called the true one [for he] learned to draw
accurately from life and thus put an end to the crude Greek [i.e.,
Italo-Byzantine] manners" (trans. J. C. and P. Bondanella). The
painter and commentator Cennino Cennini (c. 1370–1440)

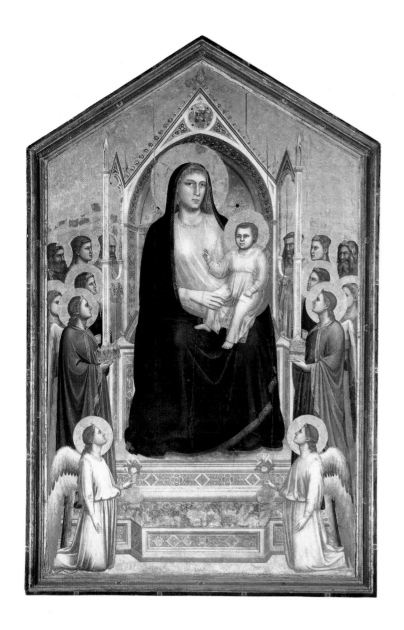

11–30 Giotto di Bondone. *Virgin and Child Enthroned,* from the Church of the Ognissanti, Florence. c. 1310. Tempera and gold on wood, 10′8″ × 6′8¼″ (3.53 × 2.05 m). Galleria degli Uffizi, Florence

(see "Cennini on Panel Painting," page 297), writing in the late fourteenth century, was struck by the accessibility and modernity of Giotto's art, which, though it retained traces of the "Greek manner," was moving toward the depiction of a humanized world anchored in three-dimensional form.

Giotto shared his teacher's concern for spatial volumes, solid forms, and warmly naturalistic human figures. Giotto's 1310 painting of the *Virgin and Child Enthroned* (fig. **11–30**) for the Church of the Ognissanti (All Saints) in Florence reflects Cimabue's influence in its largely symmetrical composition, the rendering of the angels' wings, and Mary's Byzantine facial type. Gone, however, are the Virgin's modestly inclined head and delicate gold-lined drapery; instead, light and shadow play across her substantial form. Figures even peer through openings in the throne canopy. This colossal Mary seems to overwhelm her slender Gothic throne. Despite Giotto's retention of hierarchical scale and the formal, enthroned image type, he has created the sense that his figures are fully three-dimensional beings inhabiting real space.

Giotto's masterpiece is the frescoed interior of the Scrovegni family chapel in Padua *(Cappella degli Scrovegni)*, painted about 1305 (fig. **11–31**). The chapel (also known as the Arena Chapel

because of its location near an ancient Roman arena) is a simple, barrel-vaulted room. Giotto covered the entrance wall with the *Last Judgment* and the sanctuary wall with the *Annunciation.* He subdivided the side walls with a dado of allegorical grisaille paintings of the *Virtues and Vices,* from which rise vertical bands containing quatrefoil portrait medallions. The medallions are set within a framework painted to resemble marble inlay and carved relief. The central band of medallions spans the vault, crossing a brilliant lapis blue, star-spangled sky in which large portrait disks float like glowing moons. Set into this framework are rectangular narrative scenes juxtaposing the life of the Virgin with that of Jesus. Both the individual scenes and the overall program display Giotto's genius for distilling a complex narrative into a coherent visual experience.

Both Giotto's narrative skills and his use of **typology**—in which earlier events presage later ones—are apparent in the paintings on the side walls (fig. **11–32**). Events in the life of the Virgin Mary and in the ministry of Jesus are depicted in three registers that circle the room. In the section illustrated here, the Old Testament images at the top tell the story of the selection of Joseph to be Mary's earthly spouse. In the second register the

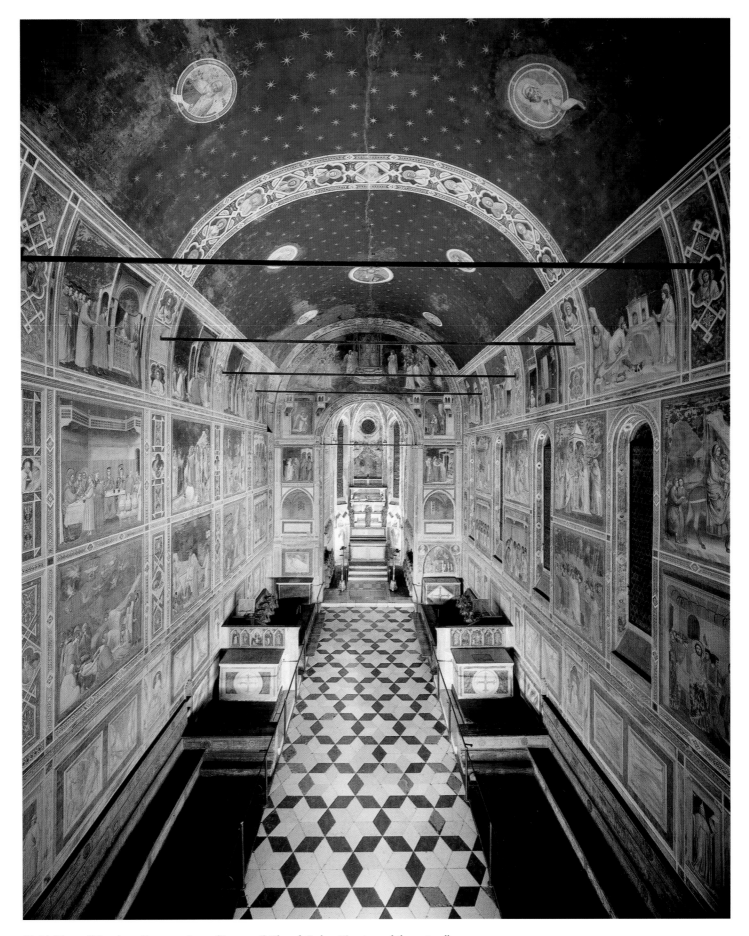

11–31 Giotto di Bondone. Frescoes, Arena (Scrovegni) Chapel, Padua. View toward the east wall, consecrated 1305

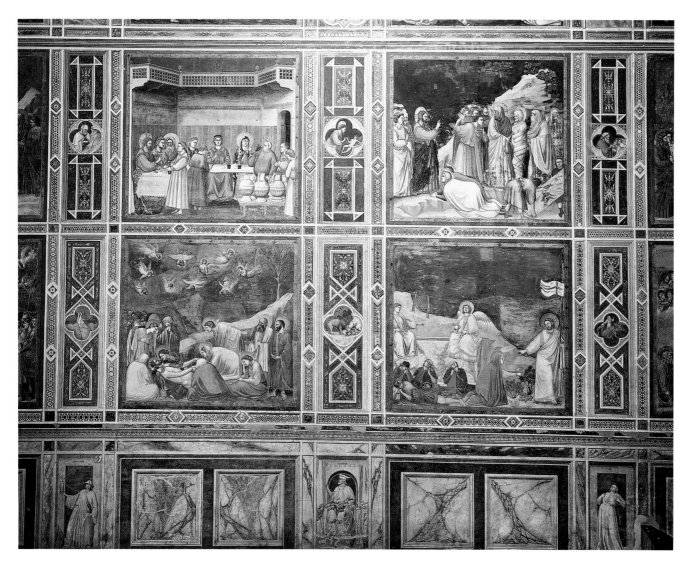

11–32 Giotto di Bondone. *Marriage at Cana, Raising of Lazarus, Lamentation, Resurrection,* and *"Noli Me Tangere,"* (from top left), frescoes on north wall of Arena (Scrovegni) Chapel, Padua (see fig. 11–31, left–hand wall). 1305–1306

first miracle, the event of Jesus's changing water to wine at the wedding feast at Cana (recalling that his blood will become the wine of the Eucharist, or communion), is followed by the raising of Lazarus (a reference to the Resurrection). Below, the lamentation over the body of Jesus by those closest to him leads to the Resurrection, indicated by angels at the empty tomb. Giotto rendered his bulky figures as pure color masses by painting the deepest shadows with the most intense hues and highlighting shapes with lighter shades mixed with white. These sculpturally modeled figures enabled Giotto to convey a sense of depth in both landscape and architectural settings. In his paintings Giotto conveys real human emotions that draw viewers into the scenes. This direct emotional appeal and the simplicity of the forms embody the new Franciscan values of personal devotion and service.

Sienese painting was a key contributor to the development of the mainstream of Gothic art in Europe, but Florentine painting, in the style originated by Giotto and kept alive by his pupils and their followers, was fundamental to the development of Italian Renaissance art over the next two centuries. With Italian Gothic art, artists moved toward the depiction of a humanized world anchored in three-dimensional form.

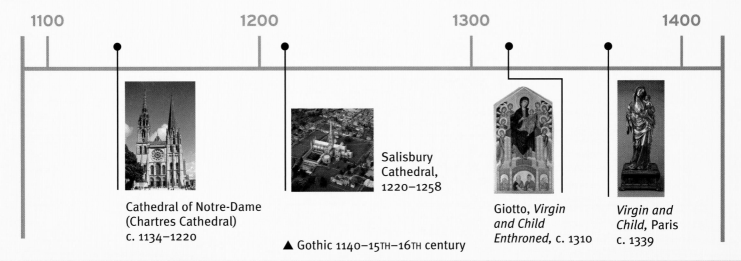

Salisbury Cathedral, 1220–1258

Cathedral of Notre-Dame (Chartres Cathedral) c. 1134–1220

▲ Gothic 1140–15TH–16TH century

Giotto, *Virgin and Child Enthroned,* c. 1310

Virgin and Child, Paris c. 1339

LOOKING BACK

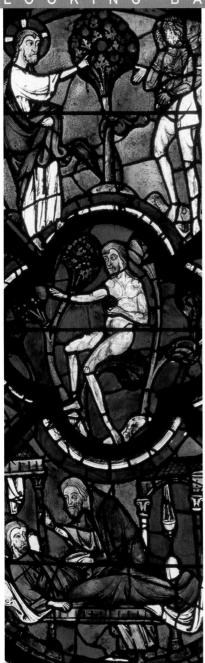

nspired by biblical accounts of the jeweled walls of heaven and the golden gates of paradise, Christian patrons and builders labored to erect glorious dwelling places for God and the saints on Earth. To create effects of light and color, they constructed ever-larger buildings with higher vaults and thinner walls that permitted the insertion of huge windows. The glowing, back-lit colors of stained glass and the soft sheen of mural paintings dissolved the solid forms of masonry, while within the church the reflection of gold, enamels, and gems on altars and gospel book covers, on crosses and candlesticks, captured the splendor of paradise on Earth. Subtle light and dazzling color created a mystical visual pathway to heaven as artists fulfilled their mission and gave tangible form to the unseen and unknowable.

Using a great diversity of media—from bronze to ivory, and enamel to tempera paint—and creating work ranging in size from tiny book illustrations to enormous stained-glass windows, Gothic artists proclaimed the Christian message. These works were both didactic and decorative, and even priestly vestments worn at the altar carried embroidered messages to the congregation.

From its beginnings in France and England, Gothic art spread throughout Europe, becoming a true international style. Architectural forms were based on a highly adaptable skeletal framework constructed from buttressed perimeter walls and an interior vaulting system of pointed-arch masonry ribs. As it evolved, Gothic taste favored increasingly sculptural, ornate façades and intricate window tracery. Deep porches were encrusted with sculpture. The great number of master masons and visual artists, often working for decades on their projects, created a remarkable variety within the Gothic style. Increasing attention to realistic surface detail, combined with underlying geometry of form, produced a kind of Gothic idealism.

At the beginning of the fourteenth century, artists working in Rome, Florence, Padua, and Siena transformed the art of mural and panel painting. Giotto, Duccio, and others created images of a world filled with human actors. They synthesized Byzantine formulas for figures and settings with the linear grace and the surface realism of later Gothic art. Giotto, especially, seemed inspired by the world around him. Even though his architectural and landscape settings remain miniaturized in medieval fashion, he created massive sculptural figures that inhabit a stage-like space. Giotto's work may lack the realistic detail to be found in northern Gothic art, but he created human beings who exhibit a wide range of emotions and interactions and his art heralds a new and worldly age.

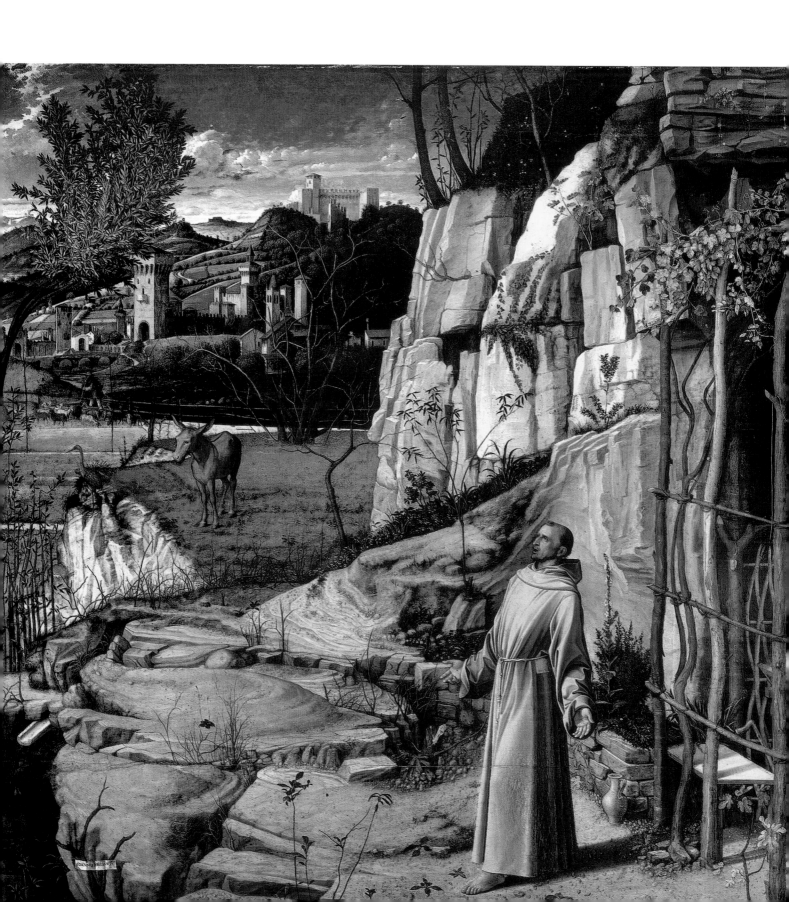

Early Renaissance Art

Fascinated by what they saw around them, fifteenth-century artists sought to observe and represent the material world. They and their patrons were guided by a new emphasis on Humanist secular thinking, which placed great value on science, reason, and the individual, while never abandoning an intangible religious mysticism. A new social order emerged from this secular worldview in which social mobility replaced the static medieval feudal hierarchy dominated by the nobility and the Christian Church. Religious charitable organizations such as the Order of Friars (Franciscans), which had been started by Saint Francis in the early thirteenth century, ministered to the growing populations, including the multitudes who moved into cities to make their livelihood and a better life. Among the Italian city-states, populations competed with one another to beautify their cities and attract important artists and scholars. And overall, many members of society found themselves with increased time for leisure and study.

Giovanni Bellini painted *Saint Francis in Ecstasy* in the 1470s (fig. **12–1**). Saint Francis stands in communion with nature, bathed in early morning sunlight, his outspread hands showing the stigmata (the miraculous appearance of Chirst's wounds on the saint's body). Bellini observed and recorded landscape elements in precise detail as he captured the effect of early morning light. His intense investigation and recording of nature illustrates his command of realism associated with the early Renaissance.

Saint Francis had moved to a cave in the barren wilderness in his search for communion with God, but in this landscape, the fields blossom and flocks of animals graze. The grape arbor over his desk and the leafy tree toward which he directs his gaze add to an atmosphere of sylvan delight. True to fifteenth-century fascination with complex symbolism in religious art, Bellini unites Old and New Testament themes to associate Francis with Moses and Christ: the tree symbolizes the burning bush; the stream, the miraculous spring brought forth by Moses; and the grapevine and the stigmata recall Christ's sacrifice. The crane and donkey represent the monastic virtue of patience. The detailed realism, luminous colors, and symbolic elements suggest Flemish art, but perspective rendering of the reading stand and arbor are Italian, and the golden light suffusing the painting is associated with Venice, a city of mist, reflections, and—above all—color.

The prevalence of religious art made for private as well as public devotion is an important reminder that the rise of Humanism in the fourteenth and fifteenth centuries did not signify a decline in the importance of Christianity. In fact, an intense spirituality, as well as the popular belief in things unseen, continued to inspire European artists in spite of the intellectual, social, geographic, and religious ferment sweeping over the continent.

12–1 Giovanni Bellini. *Saint Francis in Ecstasy.* 1470s. Oil and tempera on wood panel, 49″ × 55⅞″ (125 × 142 cm). The Frick Collection, New York

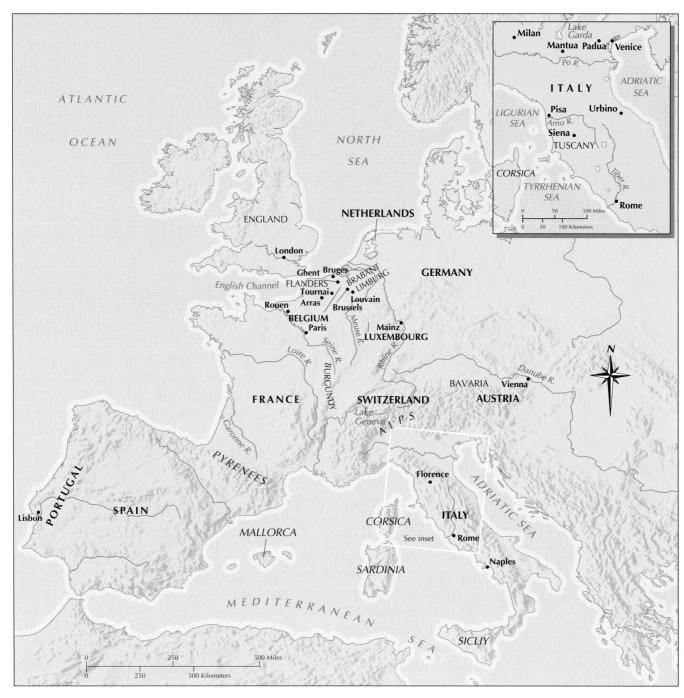

Map 12–1 Early Renaissance Europe

Discovery, not just physical but also intellectual, was the guiding theme of Europe's Renaissance, or "rebirth." During the Middle Ages, European scholars had studied the work of Greek and Roman philosophers, poets, rhetoricians, and historians. In the fifteenth and early sixteenth centuries, a group of scholars of antiquity, known as Humanists, rediscovered the equally remarkable accomplishments of ancient mathematicians, astronomers, geographers, physicians, naturalists, artists, and architects. Encouraged by these examples, Renaissance scholars and artists tried to understand, describe, and reproduce the appearance of the natural world in a rational and scientific way. Italian Renaissance artists developed a system known as linear perspective, which allowed them to represent three-dimensional space convincingly. In Northern Europe, painters often relied on intuitive and atmospheric perspective (see "Renaissance Perspective Systems," pages 328 and 329).

Italian architects revived features of classical architecture, including the classical orders, and borrowed designs and decorative motifs from ruins of Roman temples, triumphal arches, and tombs. In the north, builders continued to work in the Gothic style. Renaissance painters and sculptors tried to portray the human body accurately, and they even depicted nude human beings in secular art for the first time since classical antiquity. Their methods of observing and reproducing the visual world prevailed across Europe into the nineteenth century, and aspects of the Renaissance viewpoint even survive today in the conventions of "realistic" and popular art.

Northern Renaissance Art

In Northern Europe, where the Gothic style had emerged from native traditions, artists came to the Renaissance by way of an

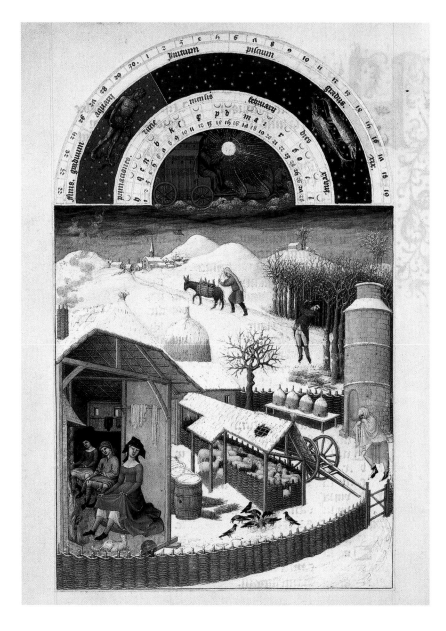

12–2 Paul, Herman, and Jean Limbourg. Page with *February, Très Riches Heures.* 1413–1416. Colors and ink on parchment, $8^7/_8''$ × $55^3/_8''$ (22.5 × 13.7 cm). Musée Condé, Chantilly, France

intense interest in the natural world. Gothic artists in France, the Germanic lands, and the Low Countries (present-day Belgium, the Netherlands, and Luxembourg) had depicted birds, plants, and animals with breathtaking accuracy in manuscript painting, textiles, and sculpture. They enlarged on these developments in the fourteenth century by accurately portraying such things as reflections on water, steamy breath on a cold winter's day, and the sheen of a metal basin. In the fifteenth century, they learned to place these details in scenes that convincingly replicate the material world. Similarly, fifteenth-century portraits seem astonishingly lifelike (see fig. 12–5), and even in religious paintings, saints and angels often seem to have distinct personalities (see fig. 12–8).

Renaissance art followed slightly different paths in the Italian peninsula and north of the Alps (see Map 12–1, page 306). The French Gothic style had never taken deep root among Italian artists, who continued to be influenced by Byzantine art and were surrounded by the ruins of Roman antiquity. Thus, the Italian Renaissance was less a reaction to the Gothic past than a return to a classical tradition that had never been completely forgotten.

At the beginning of the fifteenth century, the most famous illuminators of Northern Europe were three brothers, Paul, Herman, and Jean, commonly known as the Limbourg brothers because they came from the region of Limbourg in the Low Countries. At the time, people generally did not have family names, but were known instead by their first names, often followed by a reference to their place of origin, parentage, or occupation. For instance, the name *Jan van Eyck* means "Jan from [the town of] Eyck."

The Limbourg brothers are first recorded as apprentice goldsmiths in Paris about 1390. About 1404, they entered the service of the duke of Berry, for whom they produced their major work, the so-called *Très Riches Heures (Very Sumptuous Hours)*, between 1413 and 1416. This Book of Hours included a calendar section with full-page paintings introducing each month. The subjects alternated between peasants' labors and aristocratic pleasures. In the *February* page (fig. 12–2), farm people relax before a blazing fire. Although many country people at this time lived in hovels, this farm looks comfortable and well maintained, with timber-framed buildings, a row of beehives, a sheepfold, and woven fences.

Most remarkably, the details of the painting convey the feeling of the cold winter weather: the leaden sky, the bare trees, the soft snow, and the breath of the bundled-up worker turning to steam as he blows on his hands. The painting clearly shows several Gothic

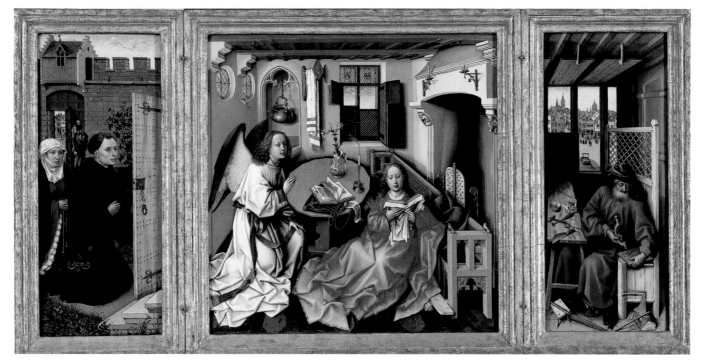

12–3 Robert Campin and assistants. *Mérode Altarpiece (Triptych of the Annunciation)* (open).
c. 1425–1428. Oil on wood, center 25 1/4″ × 24 7/8″ (64.1 × 63.2 cm); each wing approx. 25 3/8″ × 10 7/8″
(64.5 × 27.6 cm). The Metropolitan Museum of Art, New York

conventions (seen, for example, in the *Petites Heures of Jeanne d'Evreux*, fig. 11–16), which persisted in Northern Renaissance art into the first half of the fifteenth century. These include the missing front wall of the house, removed in order to show the activities inside, the attention to detail, and the high placement of the horizon line. The integration of figures and animals into the landscape has been accomplished within the prevailing Gothic style, but on a more believable scale, with a landscape receding continuously from foreground to middle ground to background.

Throughout most of the fifteenth century, the artists of Flanders (roughly equivalent to the present-day lands of western Belgium, the southwestern Netherlands, and a small area of northern France) were considered the best in Europe, and the art produced there during this period is commonly called *Flemish*. Flanders, which included part of the domain of the duke of Burgundy and the major seaport and commercial center of Bruges, was the commercial power of Northern Europe, rivaling the Italian city-states of Florence and Venice.

The most outstanding exponents of the new Flemish style were Robert Campin, Jan van Eyck, and Rogier van der Weyden. About 1425–1428, Campin (documented from 1406; d. 1444) painted an altarpiece now known as the *Mérode Altarpiece* (fig. 12–3) after the

Technique

Painting on Panel

P
ainting pictures on wood has an ancient history, and wood panels were particularly favored by European painters and their patrons in the fifteenth century for works ranging from small portraits to enormous altarpieces.

Once the panel was prepared, artists painted in their preferred medium (see "Cennini on Panel Painting," page 297). Italian artists favored tempera, using it almost exclusively for panel painting until the end of the fifteenth century. Northern European artists preferred oil paints, which Flemish painters so skillfully exploited at the beginning of the century. Tempera had to be applied in a very precise manner, because it dried almost as quickly as it was laid down. Shading had to be done with careful overlying strokes in tones ranging from white and gray to dark brown and black. Because tempera is opaque, light striking its surface does not penetrate to lower layers of color and reflect back—the resulting surface is **matte**, or dull. (Varnish gives it a sheen.)

Oil paint, on the other hand, takes much longer to dry, and while it is still wet, changes can be made easily. Oil paint can also be translucent when applied in very thin layers, called glazes. Light striking a surface built up of glazes penetrates to the lower layers and is reflected back, creating the appearance of an interior glow. In both tempera and oil, the desired result in the fifteenth century was a smooth surface that betrayed no brushstrokes.

name of its former owners. Its relatively small size—slightly more than 2 feet tall and about 4 feet wide with the wings open—suggests that it was made for a private chapel. Campin portrayed the Annunciation as if the Virgin lived in a Flemish home. Into this contemporary setting he brought normal household objects that could also be seen as religious symbols. The lilies on the table, for example, were a traditional element of Annunciation imagery symbolizing Mary's virginity. The hanging water pot and towel in the niche refer to Mary's purity and her sacred role as the vessel for the Incarnation of Christ. Such objects are often referred to as "hidden" symbols because they are treated as a normal part of the scene, but their religious meanings would have been understood by most contemporary viewers.

In the left-hand panel of the *Mérode Altarpiece*, the altarpiece's donors kneel in front of the open door of the house where the Annunciation takes place, suggesting that the scene is a vision induced by their prayers. Such a presentation, often used by Flemish artists, allowed the donors of a religious work to appear in the same space and time, and often on the same scale, as the religious figures represented. In the right-hand panel, the view out Saint Joseph's window depicts a realistic Flemish street scene. Note the mousetraps in Joseph's carpentry shop. They are a reference to a passage written by the theologian Saint Augustine, referring to Christ as the bait in a trap set by God to catch Satan.

The complex treatment of light in the *Mérode Altarpiece* is an example of the innovation of the Flemish painters. The strongest **illumination** comes from an unseen source at the upper left in front of the **picture plane** (picture surface), apparently the sun entering through the miraculously transparent wall that allows the viewer to observe the scene. More light comes from the rear windows, and a few rays from the round window at left are a symbolic vehicle for the Christ Child's descent. Jesus seems to slide down the rays of light joining God and Mary, carrying the cross of human salvation. The light falling on the Virgin's lap emphasizes this connection.

Jan van Eyck (c. 1370/90–1441), Campin's contemporary, was a court painter to Philip the Good, Duke of Burgundy, who was the uncle of the king of France and one of the wealthiest and most sophisticated men in Europe. He made Jan one of his confidential employees and even sent him on an embassy to Portugal. The duke was not Jan's only patron. In the Low Countries—where cities were largely independent of the landed nobility—civic leaders, town councils, and rich merchants were also important art patrons.

Jan's *Annunciation* (fig. **12–4**), a small panel that may have been part of an altarpiece, is an excellent example of the Flemish desire to paint more than the eye can easily see and almost more than the mind can grasp. We can enjoy the painting for its visual characteristics—the drawing, colors, and arrangement of shapes—but we need information about the painting's cultural context to understand it fully. The Annunciation takes place in a richly appointed church, not Mary's house, as we saw in Robert Campin's painting. Gabriel, a youth with splendid multicolored wings, has interrupted Mary's reading. The two figures gesture gracefully upward toward a dove flying down through golden beams. As the angel Gabriel tells the Virgin Mary that she will bear Christ, the Son of God, golden letters spell out the angel's greeting, "Hail, full of grace," and Mary's response, "Behold the

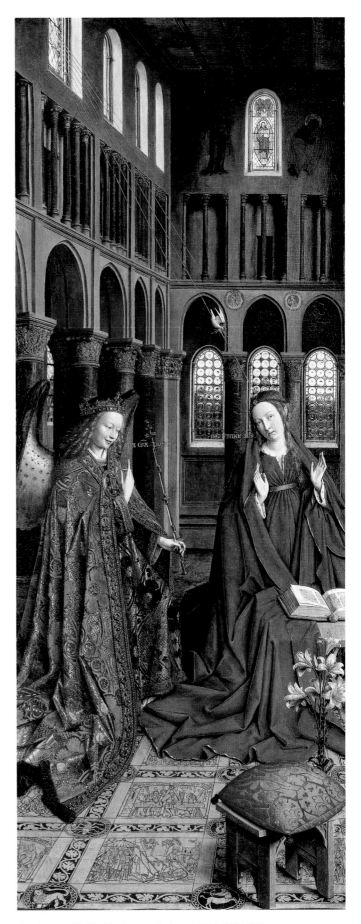

12–4 Jan van Eyck. *The Annunciation.* c. 1434–1436. Oil on canvas, transferred from wood panel, painted surface, $35\frac{3}{8}$″ × $13\frac{7}{8}$″ (90.2 × 34.1 cm). National Gallery of Art, Washington, D.C.
ANDREW W. MELLON COLLECTION (1937.1.39)

WOMEN ARTISTS IN THE LATE MIDDLE AGES AND THE RENAISSANCE

Since most formal apprenticeships were closed to women, medieval and Renaissance women artists learned their trade either from family members or in convents. Despite the obstacles, however, a few highly skilled women received major commissions. In the fourteenth century, Bourgot, the daughter of the miniaturist Jean le Noir, illuminated books for Charles V of France and Jean, Duke of Berry. Christine de Pisan supported herself and her children by writing for these same patrons. She oversaw the production of her books and wrote of one artist named Anastaise, "who is so learned and skillful in painting manuscript borders and miniature backgrounds that one cannot find an artisan who can surpass her . . . nor whose work is more highly esteemed" (Le Libre de la Cité des Dames, I.41.4, translated by Earl J. Richards). Also in the fourteenth century, Jeanne de Montbaston and her husband, Richart, worked together as book illuminators under the auspices of the University of Paris. After Richart's death, Jeanne continued the workshop and was sworn in as a libraire (publisher) by the university in 1343.

In the fifteenth century, women were admitted to the artists' guilds (professional organizations) in some cities, including the Flemish towns of Ghent, Bruges, and Antwerp. The painter Agnes van den Bassche of Ghent, for example, operated a painting workshop with her artist husband and became a free master of the painters' guild after his death. A study of the painters' guild of Bruges has shown that by the 1480s one-quarter of its members were female.

The position of women artists in Italy was not as strong as in Flanders. The Humanists' emphasis on academic study rather than apprenticeship for artists, the tie between mathematics and the new linear perspective, and the emphasis on anatomical study—forbidden to women—and realistic figure drawing prevented women from following careers in painting. Some women nevertheless learned from their fathers or husbands and helped in the family business.

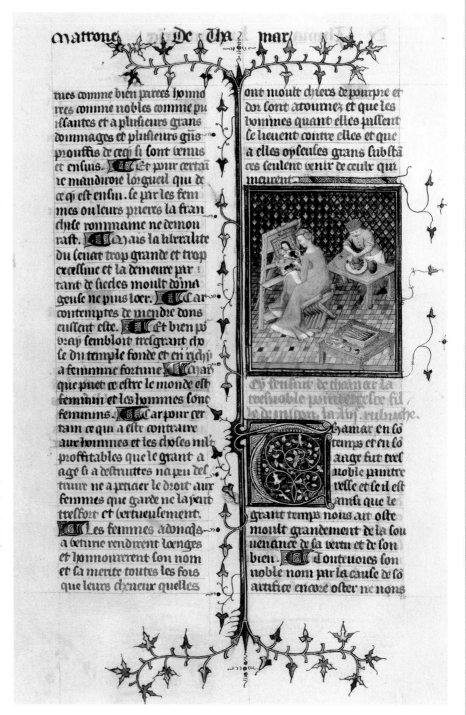

Page with Thamyris from Giovanni Boccaccio's *De Claris Mulieribus (Concerning Famous Women)*. 1402. Ink and tempera on vellum. Bibliothèque Nationale, Paris

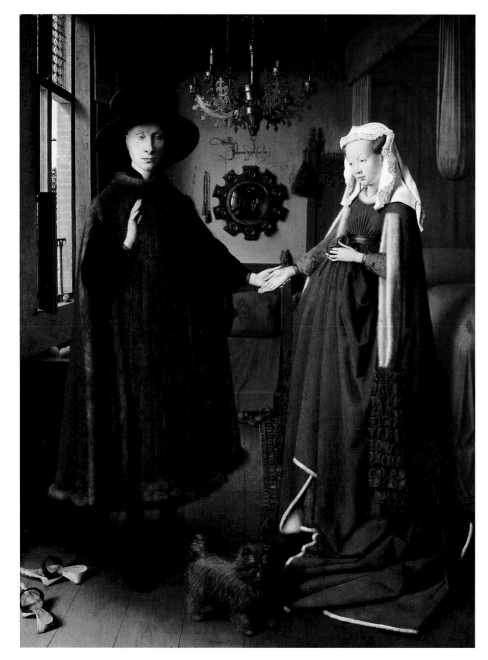

12–5 Jan van Eyck. *Portrait of Giovanni Arnolfini (?) and His Wife, Giovanna Cenami (?).* 1434. Oil on panel, 33″ × 22 ½″ (83.8 × 57.2 cm). The National Gallery, London

A beautifully furnished room containing a large bed hung with rich draperies was often a home's primary public space, not a private retreat. Since the merchant class copied the fashions of the court, the woman wears an aristocratic costume, a fur-lined overdress with a long train. Fashion dictated that the robe be gathered up and held in front of the abdomen, giving an appearance of pregnancy. This ideal of feminine beauty emphasized women's potential fertility. According to a later inventory description of this painting, the original frame (now lost) was inscribed with a quotation from Ovid, a Roman poet known for his celebration of romantic love.

handmaiden of the Lord." The words in the painting are upside down, for God to read. The story is recounted in the Gospel of Luke (1:26–38). In the painting every detail has a meaning. The dove symbolizes the Holy Spirit, the white lilies are symbols of Mary, and the signs of the zodiac in the floor tiles indicate the traditional date of the Annunciation, March 25. The stained-glass window representing God rises above three windows that enclose Mary and represent the Trinity of Father, Son, and Holy Spirit.

Jan's best-known painting today is an elaborate double portrait of a couple, traditionally identified as Giovanni Arnolfini and his wife, Giovanna Cenami (fig. **12–5**). Early interpreters suggested that this fascinating work represents a wedding or betrothal. Above the mirror on the back wall, the artist inscribed the words: *Johannes de eyck fuit hic 1434* ("Jan van Eyck was here

1434"). Normally, the signature on a work of art in fifteenth-century Flanders would have read, "Jan van Eyck made this," but the phrase "was here" suggests that Jan served as a witness. New research has shown that Arnolfini married in 1447, long after the date on the wall and Jan van Eyck's death. The painting evidently represents some form of formal contract since the mirror reflects two witnesses, but its true meaning remains a mystery.

The people stand in the principal room of a house filled with impressive furniture, including a luxurious bed. (Recall the bed in the Queen of France's chamber in the Introduction, figure 23. The modern idea of rooms performing a single specific function did not yet exist.) The furnishings in Jan's painting may have hidden significance. The crystal prayer beads on the wall suggest the couple's piety; the dog is a symbol of fidelity; and the single candle and the round mirror signify the presence of God.

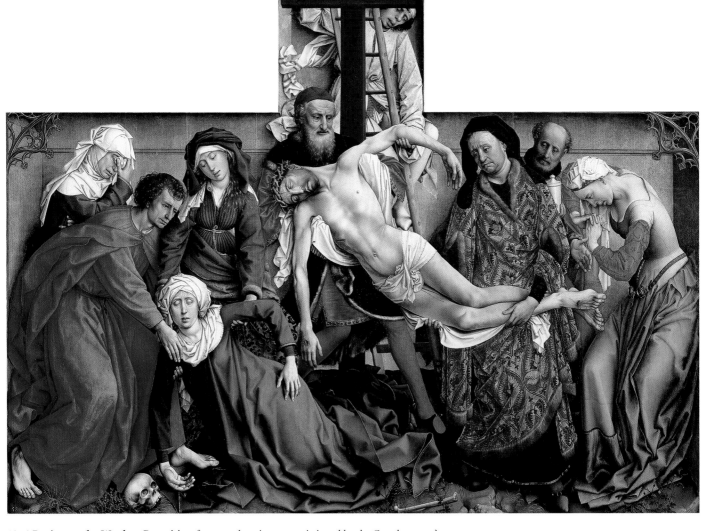

12–6 Rogier van der Weyden. *Deposition,* from an altarpiece commissioned by the Crossbowmen's Guild, Louvain, Brabant, Belgium. c. 1442. Oil on panel, 7′2⅝″ × 8′7⅛″ (2.2 × 2.62 m). Museo del Prado, Madrid

Rogier van der Weyden (c. 1399–1464), an artist slightly younger than Jan, maintained a large workshop in Brussels, attracting apprentices and assistants from as far away as Italy. Nevertheless, not a single existing work of art bears his name. To establish the thematic and stylistic characteristics for Rogier's work, scholars turn to a large panel painting (more than 7 by 8 feet) that depicts the Deposition, or removal of Christ's body from the cross (fig. **12–6**). This was the central panel of an altarpiece, commissioned by the Louvain Crossbowmen's Guild sometime around 1442, that once included other panels representing the Four Evangelists and Christ's Resurrection.

The Deposition was a popular theme in the fifteenth century because of its dramatic, personally engaging subject. In Rogier's painting, Jesus's suffering and death are made palpably real by the display of the life-sized corpse at the center of the composition. Rogier has arranged the figure in a graceful curve, framed by jarringly angular arms. Both the curve of the body and the angular arms are echoed by the form of the

fainting Virgin. The highly emotional treatment of both mother and son encourages the viewer to identify with both of them. Red and white color accents focus attention on the main subject. The whites of the winding cloth and the tunic of the youth on the ladder set off Jesus's pale body, as the white veil wrapped like a turban and shawl emphasizes the ashen face of Mary. The solid, three-dimensional figures, compressed in a shallow space in front of a gilded wood backdrop, press toward the viewer, allowing no escape from their expressions of intense grief.

Many scholars see the emotional quality of Rogier's work as a tie with the Gothic past, but the intense feelings evoked by his painting can also be interpreted as an example of fifteenth-century Humanistic concern for the individual. Although united by their sorrow, the mourning figures react in personal ways, from the intensity of Mary Magdalen wringing her hands in anguish at the right, to Saint John the Evangelist looking sorrowfully down at the Virgin, whom he supports on the left.

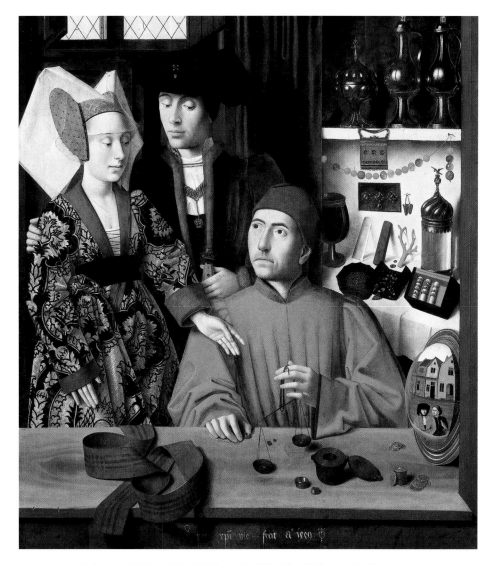

12–7 Petrus Christus. *A Goldsmith in His Shop, Possibly Saint Eligius.* 1449. Oil on wood, 38⅝″ × 33½″ (98 × 85 cm). The Metropolitan Museum of Art, New York

ROBERT LEHMAN COLLECTION, 1975 (1975.1.110)

The artist signed and dated his work on the house reflected in the mirror.

Second Generation Painters

The extraordinary achievements of Robert Campin, Jan van Eyck, and Rogier van der Weyden attracted many followers. Petrus Christus (documented from 1444; d. c. 1475), who worked in Bruges, probably came from the northern duchy of Brabant (now part of the southern Netherlands and north-central Belgium). In 1449, Christus painted one of his most admired works, *A Goldsmith in His Shop* (fig. **12–7**). According to Christian legend, Eligius, a seventh-century ecclesiastic, goldsmith, and mintmaster for the French court, used his wealth to ransom Christian captives. Here he weighs a ring to determine its value, as a handsome couple looks on. The young people are dressed in the height of Burgundian court fashion. The woman wears a rich Italian brocade gown and jeweled headdress; the man wears fur-lined black wool. A box of rings and other trea-sures rest on a shelf in the background, affording us a remark-able view of a fifteenth-century goldsmith's wares.

As in Jan van Eyck's double portrait (see fig. 12–5), a convex mirror extends the viewer's field of vision, in this case showing two men on the street outside. The emphasis on everyday details is so strong that the presence of the saint seems more a pretext for a secular subject rather than an integral part of a religious scene. In fact, this painting provided the precedent for a long line of clearly secular pictures showing business people in their shops, which persisted well into the sixteenth century.

The painter Hugo van der Goes (c. 1440–1482) brought together the intellectual challenge posed by Jan van Eyck and the emotional intensity of Rogier van der Weyden in an entirely new style. Hugo's major work was an exceptionally large altarpiece, more than 8 feet tall, commissioned by Tommaso Portinari for the family chapel in Florence and probably painted between 1474 and

1476 (fig. **12–8**). Portinari, a Florentine living in Bruges, was the local manager of the bank owned by the powerful Medici family. He and his wife, Maria Baroncelli, are seen kneeling with their three eldest children, accompanied by patron saints, on the wing interiors. The central panel represents the Adoration of the newborn Jesus by Mary and Joseph, a host of angels, and a few shepherds who have rushed in from the fields. The monumental figures of Joseph, Mary, and the shepherds dominating the central panel are the same size as the patron saints on the wings; the Portinari family and the angels are small in comparison.

In the center of the composition, the Christ Child rests naked and vulnerable on the ground with rays of light emanating from his body. The source of this image was the visionary writing of the medieval Swedish mystic Bridget (declared a saint in 1391). Saint Bridget described Mary kneeling to adore the Child immediately after giving birth. The glass vessel in the foreground still life alludes to Christ's entry into Mary's womb without destroying her virginity, the way light passes through glass without breaking it. The three red carnations in the glass (just visible at the bottom center) may refer to the Trinity; the seven blue columbines symbolize the Virgin's future sorrows; and the violets scattered on the ground symbolize humility. The majolica (glazed earthenware) *albarelo,* or drug jar, a luxury ceramic imported from Spain, holds three irises—white for purity and purple for Christ's royal ancestry—and a red lily, representing the blood of Christ.

Hugo's artistic vision goes far beyond formal religious symbolism. Although the brilliant palette and meticulous accuracy recall Jan van Eyck, and the intense but controlled feelings suggest the emotional content of Rogier van der Weyden's works, the composition and interpretation of the altarpiece are entirely Hugo's. The shepherds, for example, who stand in unaffected awe before the miraculous event, are among the most sympa-

thetically rendered images of common people to be found in the art of this, or any, period.

The work of Hugo and other Nothern Renaissance painters was a startling contrast to contemporary Florentine art. Michelangelo criticized the detailed realism of Flemish art, but others were fascinated. In fact, Flemish art was so admired in the fifteenth century that many artists visited Flanders to study the work. Only at the end of the century did European patrons begin to favor the new styles of art and architecture developing in Italy.

Books and Tapestries

In France, the Flemish style was particularly influential in manuscript illumination, a field in which women excelled (see "Women Artists in the Late Middle Ages and the Renaissance," page 310). Anastaise for example, who worked for the poet and scholar Christine de Pisan, gained considerable renown. The painting of Christine presenting her manuscript to the Queen of France also serves to illustrate the luxurious woven and embroidered textiles in the royal apartments (see Introduction, fig. 23).

The importance of textiles in the fifteenth century cannot be overemphasized. Major weaving centers arose in Brussels, Tournai, Arras, and in the Loire Valley, where Flemish and French artists produced outstanding tapestries that served both as sumptuous wall coverings and as a form of portable wealth. Indeed, the wealth of individuals can often be judged from the number of tapestries listed in their household inventories. The Christine de Pisan painting gives a good idea of the effect achieved by luxurious wall hangings.

One of the finest examples of Renaissance tapestry is a series of wall-hangings called the Hunt of the Unicorn, which includes *The Unicorn Is Found* (fig. **12–9**). The tapestries might have been made for Anne of Brittany whose initials, AE, hang on a cord from the fountain and at the four corners of the composition. The

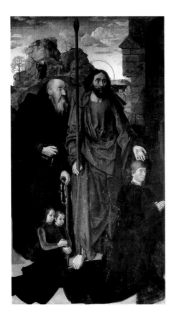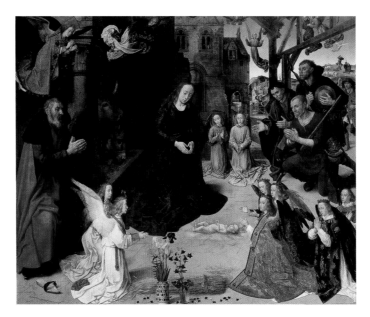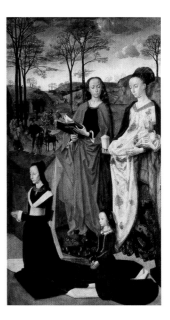

12–8 Hugo van der Goes. *Portinari Altarpiece* (open). c. 1474–1476. Tempera and oil on panel, center
8′3 ¹⁄₂″ × 10′ (2.53 × 3.01 m); wings each 8′3 ¹⁄₂″ × 4′7 ¹⁄₂″ (2.53 × 1.41 m). Galleria degli Uffizi, Florence

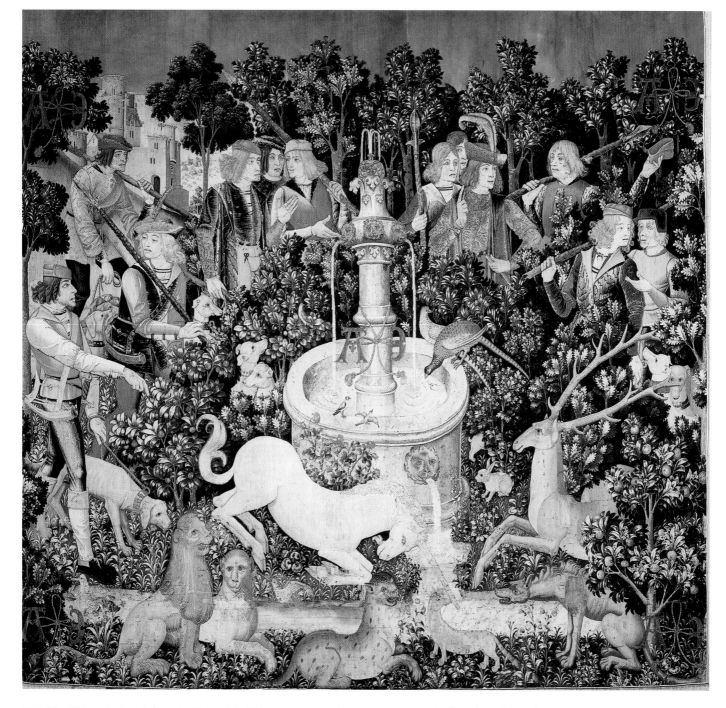

12–9 *The Unicorn Is Found,* from the Hunt of the Unicorn tapestry series. c. 1498–1500. Wool, silk, and metal threads (13–21 warp threads per inch), 12′1″ × 12′5″ (3.68 × 3.78 m). The Metropolitan Museum of Art, New York

The price of a tapestry depended on the materials used. Rarely was a fine, commissioned series woven only with wool; instead tapestry producers enhanced it to varying degrees with colored silk and silver and gold threads. The richest kind of tapestry was one made entirely of silk and gold. Because the silver and gold threads used silk wrapped with real metal, people later burned many tapestries in order to retrieve the precious materials. As a result of this practice, few French royal tapestries have survived. Many existing works show obvious signs that the metallic threads were painstakingly pulled out in order to get the gold but preserve the tapestries.

unicorn, a mythical horselike beast with a single horn, could be captured only by a young virgin, to whom it came willingly. The animal symbolized the Incarnation, with Christ as the unicorn captured by the Virgin Mary; in the secular world, the unicorn hunt became a metaphor for romantic love and a suitable subject for wedding tapestries. The unicorn's horn was believed to be an antidote for poison; thus, the unicorn here is shown dipping its horn into the stream and so purifying the water from the fountain.

The figures in this tapestry appear in a dense forest, filled with flowers, with a distant view of a castle. The many birds and animals shown have symbolic meanings: the lion represents valor and faith; the stag, the Resurrection and protection against

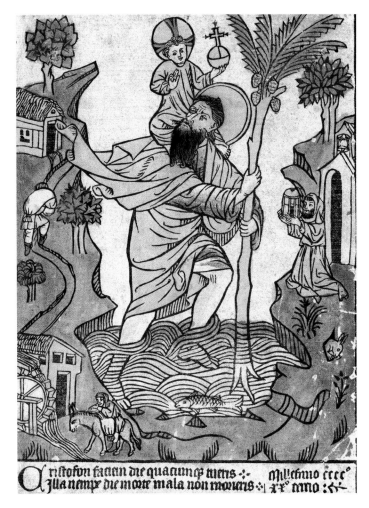

12–10 *The Buxheim Saint Christopher.* 1423. Hand-colored woodcut, The John Rylands University Library. Courtesy of the Director and Librarian, The John Rylands University Library of Manchester, England

evil; rabbits, fertility; and dogs, fidelity. Among the birds, the pair of pheasants perched on the fountain (at right) are emblems of human love and marriage, and the goldfinches (also on the fountain rim) are another fertility symbol. The plants, depicted with botanical accuracy, reinforce the theme of protective and curative powers: the strawberry stands for sexual love, the pansy for remembrance, the oak for fidelity, the holly for protection, and the orange for fertility. The tapestry captures the vision of the biblical Song of Songs (4:12–13): "You are an enclosed garden, my sister, my bride, an enclosed garden, a fountain sealed."

The Graphic Arts

Printmaking emerged in Europe with the wider availability of paper and the development of printing presses at the end of the fourteenth century. The techniques used by printmakers during the Renaissance were **woodcut** and **engraving** (see "Woodcuts and Engravings," page 317).

People had long used **woodblocks** cut in relief to print designs on cloth, but only in the fifteenth century did the printing of images and texts on paper and the production of books in multiple copies begin to replace the copying of each book by hand. Both handwritten and printed books were often illustrated.

Printed books and single-sheet printed images were sometimes hand colored with watercolor paints.

At first, woodcuts were made by woodworkers who had little art training. Soon printers began to hire artists to draw images for the artisans to cut from the block. Simply executed devotional images sold as souvenirs to pilgrims at holy sites became very popular, such is the case with *The Buxheim Saint Christopher* (found in the Carthusian Monastery of Buxheim, in southern Germany), dated 1423 (fig. **12–10**). Saint Christopher, patron saint of travelers, carries the Christ Child across a river; his charitable action is witnessed by a monk and ignored by two workers at a water mill.

Engravings, on the other hand, seem to have developed from the highly skilled metalworking techniques used by goldsmiths and armorers. To record their work and to serve as models, engravers began to make impressions of their work by rubbing lampblack into the engraved lines and pressing paper over the plate. German artist Martin Schongauer (c. 1435–1491), who learned engraving from his goldsmith father, was an immensely skillful printmaker who excelled both in drawing and in the difficult technique of shading from deep black to faintest grays. In his *Temptation of Saint Anthony*, engraved about 1480–1490 (fig. **12–11**), Schongauer illustrated the original

Technique

Woodcuts and Engravings

An artist making a **woodcut** draws a design on a smooth block of wood, then cuts away all the areas around the lines, leaving them in **high relief**. When the block's surface is inked and a piece of paper pressed down hard on it, the ink on the relief areas is transferred to the paper to create a reverse image.

Engraving on metal, in contrast, requires a technique called **intaglio**, in which lines are cut into the plate with tools called gravers or **burins**. Ink is applied over the whole plate and forced down into the lines, after which the surface of the plate is carefully wiped clean. The ink in the recessed lines transfers to a sheet of paper pressed hard against the plate.

Whichever technique is used, the great advantage of printmaking is that woodblocks and metal plates can be used repeatedly to make nearly identical images.

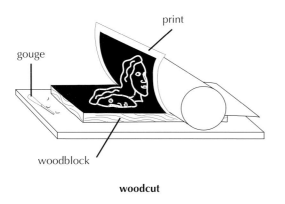

woodcut

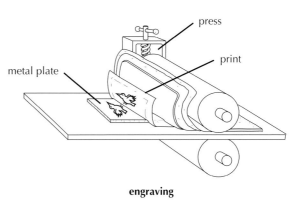

engraving

biblical meaning of temptation as a physical assault rather than a subtle inducement. Wildly acrobatic slithery, spiky demons lift Anthony off the ground to torment and terrify him in midair. The engraver intensified the horror of the moment by condensing the action into a swirling vortex of figures beating, scratching, poking, tugging, and no doubt shrieking at the stoical saint, who remains impervious to all their torments.

The prevalence of religious prints made for private devotion, whether simple woodcuts or highly sophisticated engravings like Schongauer's, are an important reminder that the rise of Humanism did not signify a decline in the importance of Christianity. In fact, an intense spirituality, as well as the popular belief in things unseen, continued to inspire European artists in spite of the intellectual, social, geographic, and religious ferment sweeping over the continent.

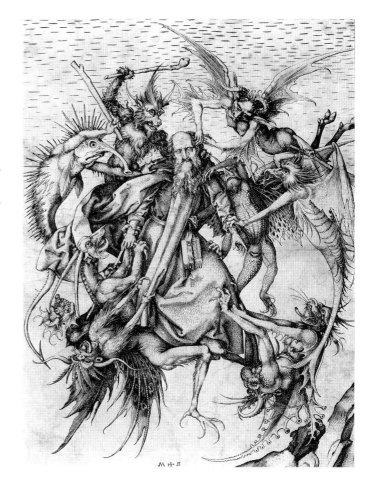

12–11 Martin Schongauer. *Temptation of Saint Anthony.* c. 1480–1490. Engraving, 12 $\frac{1}{4}$" × 9" (31.1 × 22.9 cm). The Metropolitan Museum of Art, New York

ROGERS FUND, 1920 (20.5.2)

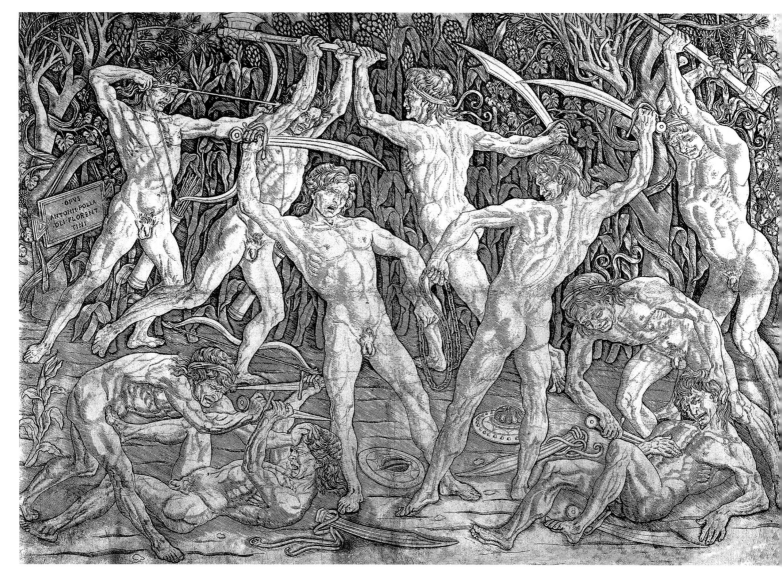

12–12 Antonio del Pollaiuolo. *Battle of the Nudes.* c. 1465–1470. Engraving, $15\frac{1}{8}''\times 23\frac{1}{4}''$ (38.3 × 59 cm).
Cincinnati Art Museum, Ohio

The new Renaissance interest in classical sculpture and anatomical research is illustrated in an engraving by the Florentine goldsmith and sculptor Antonio del Pollaiuolo (c. 1432–1498): *Battle of the Nudes* (fig. **12–12**). Pollaiuolo may have intended this, his only known—but highly influential—print, as a study of the human figure in action. The naked men ferociously fighting against a tapestry-like background of foliage seem to have been drawn from a single model. They strike poses which seem to have been inspired by classical sculpture. Much of our engraving's fascination lies in how Pollaiuolo depicts muscles of the male body reacting under tension. Like their Flemish counterparts, Italian artists moved gradually toward a greater precision in rendering the illusion of physical reality. Italians, however, studied the figure in a more analytical way than the Flemings had, with the goal of achieving correct but perfected generic figures set within a rationally, rather than visually, defined space.

Renaissance Art in Italy

By the end of the Middle Ages, the most important Italian cultural centers were north of Rome at Florence, Milan, Venice, and the smaller duchies of Mantua, Ferrara, and Urbino. Much of the power and art patronage was in the hands of wealthy families: the Medici in Florence, the Visconti and Sforza in Milan, the Gonzaga in Mantua, the Este in Ferrara, and the Montefeltro in Urbino. Cities at the time grew in wealth and independence, and commerce became increasingly important. Money conferred status, and a shrewd business or political leader could become very powerful. Patronage of the arts was an important public activity with political overtones. As one Florentine merchant, Giovanni Rucellai, succinctly noted: He supported the arts "because they serve the glory of God, the honour of the city, and the commemoration of myself" (Baxandall, page 2).

Beginning around 1400, Italian painters and sculptors, like their Flemish counterparts, began to move toward a greater

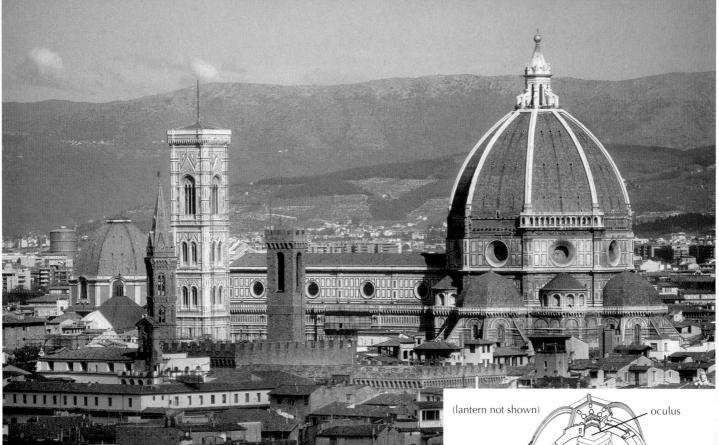

12–13 Filippo Brunelleschi. Dome of Florence Cathedral. 1417–1436; lantern completed 1471

The cathedral dome was a source of immense local pride from the moment of its completion. Renaissance architect and theorist Leon Battista Alberti described it as rising "above the skies, large enough to cover all the peoples of Tuscany with its shadow" (cited in Goldwater and Traves, page 33). While Brunelleschi maintained the Gothic pointed-arch profile of the dome established in the fourteenth century, he devised an advanced construction technique that was more efficient, less costly, and safer than earlier systems. An arcaded gallery he planned to install at the top of the tall drum was never built, however. In 1507 Baccio d'Agnolo won a competition to design the gallery, using supports installed on the drum nearly a century earlier. The first of the eight sections, seen here, was completed in 1515.

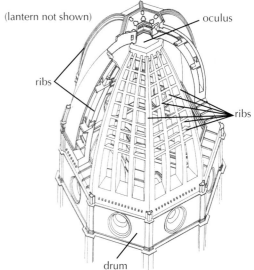

Cutaway drawing of Brunelleschi's dome, Florence Cathedral (drawing by P. Sanpaolesi)

precision in rendering the illusion of physical reality, building on the achievements of the great Florentine artist Giotto (see fig. 11–31). However, rather than replicating the smallest details of appearance with perfect fidelity to nature, as the Flemings did, Italian artists aimed at achieving anatomically correct but idealized figures—perfected, generic types—set within a rationally, rather than intuitively, defined space, organized through the use of linear perspective. At the same time, Italian architects began to use mathematically derived design principles and the classical architectural orders to create buildings expressing the ideals of symmetry and restraint.

Towering figures of early Renaissance art—the architect Brunelleschi, the sculptor Donatello, and the painter Masaccio—came from Florence, the birthplace of the Italian Renaissance.

They visited Rome to study the physical remains of classical antiquity, and they integrated detailed knowledge of the past into their own highly original works.

Architecture

Filippo Brunelleschi (1377–1446), a young sculptor-turned-architect, was one of the major pioneers of Renaissance architectural design in Florence. His design for the vast dome of Florence Cathedral (fig. 12–13) was a great technical accomplishment. The dome is essentially a Gothic construction based on the pointed arch, using ribs to support the vault. It has an octagonal outer shell and a lower inner shell connected through a system of arches and horizontal sandstone rings. Brunelleschi invented an

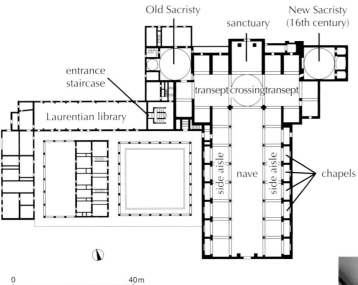

12–14 Plan of the Church of San Lorenzo
including later additions and modifications

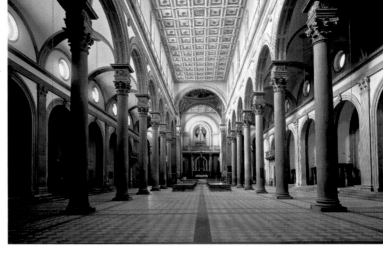

12–15 Filippo Brunelleschi. Nave, Church of San Lorenzo, Florence, begun c. 1421

ingenious structural system by which each portion of the dome reinforced the next one as it was built up layer by layer. When completed, this self-buttressed unit required no external support. The dome is still the source of immense local pride.

Brunelleschi also produced remarkably innovative plans for smaller projects. Between 1419 and 1423, he built the Capponi Chapel in the Church of Santa Felicità (see fig. 13–22). At the same time, around 1421, he was commissioned to rebuild the Church of San Lorenzo in Florence, the parish church of the Medici family (fig. **12–14**). In both, Brunelleschi used classically inspired mouldings and pilasters of pietra serena (a grey stone) against white walls to emphasize the mathematical basis of his design. The Church of San Lorenzo is an austere basilica with a long nave flanked by single side aisles opening into shallow chapels. A short transept forming a square crossing anticipates the square sanctuary. Two **sacristies** (rooms housing ritual attire and vessels) project from the transept. Brunelleschi designed the Old Sacristy as a chapel and mausoleum for the Medici family; the New Sacristy was built in the sixteenth century by Michelangelo.

Brunelleschi, like many Romanesque and Gothic builders before him, worked out his church plans on a module, or basic unit of measure, that could be multiplied or divided and applied to every element of the design. The result was a series of clear, rational interior spaces in harmony with one another. Unlike the Romanesque and Gothic system, however, the result was architecture on a human scale with classical details.

The nave of the church (fig. **12–15**) has a flat ceiling inset with coffers, like a Roman basilica; a hemispherical dome on pendentives covers the crossing. Each nave arch springs from an **impost block**, or section of entablature, resting on slender Corinthian columns. With this arrangement, Brunelleschi managed to bend, without exactly breaking, the rules of classical architecture, in which piers, rather than columns, supported arches, and columns only supported entablatures. In the side aisles, the arched openings to the chapels are surmounted by arched lunettes that mirror the shape of the nave arcade. The Church of San Lorenzo was an experimental building combining old and new elements, but Brunelleschi's rational approach, unique sense of order, and innovative incorporation of classical motifs inspired later Renaissance architects, many of whom learned from his work firsthand by completing his unfinished projects.

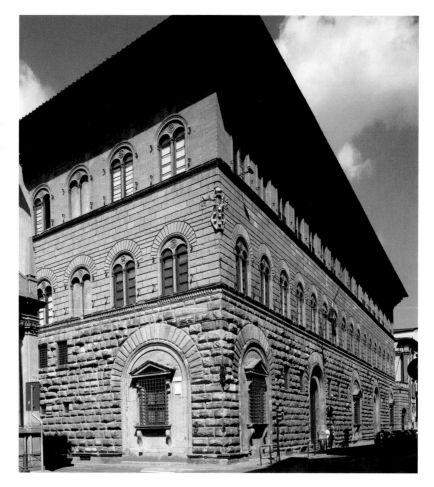

12–16 Attributed to Michelozzo di Bartolomeo. Palazzo Medici-Riccardi, Florence, begun 1446

Cosimo de' Medici the Elder did not decide to build a new palace just to provide more living space for his family. He also incorporated into the plans offices and storage rooms for conducting his business affairs. For the palace site, he chose the Via de' Gori at the corner of the Via Larga, the widest city street at that time. Despite his practical reasons for constructing a large residence and the fact that he chose simplicity and austerity over grandeur in the exterior design, his detractors commented and gossiped. As one exaggerated: "[Cosimo] has begun a palace which throws even the Colosseum at Rome into the shade."

Brunelleschi's role in the Medici Palace in Florence (now known as the Palazzo Medici-Riccardi), begun in 1446, is unclear (fig. **12–16**). According to Giorgio Vasari, the sixteenth-century artist and courtier who wrote the first history of art, Brunelleschi's model for the palazzo (any large house was called a *palazzo*, or palace) was rejected as too grand by Cosimo de' Medici the Elder. Today many scholars believe that Cosimo then hired Michelozzo to design the building. The plain exterior was in keeping with political and religious thinking in Florence, which was strongly influenced by Christian ideals of poverty and charity. Private homes were supposedly limited to a dozen rooms; however, Cosimo acquired and demolished twenty small houses to provide the site for his new residence. In Florence the house was more than a dwelling place; it symbolized the family and established the family's place in society.

Huge in size (each story is more than 20 feet high), the building, nevertheless, has fine proportions and details. On one side, the ground floor originally opened through large, round arches onto the street and provided space for the family business. These arches were walled up in the sixteenth century and windows were designed by Michelangelo. The façade of large **rusticated** stone blocks—that is, blocks with their outer faces left rough—has three stories clearly set off from each other by the change in the stone surfaces from very rough at the ground level to almost smooth on the third story.

The builders followed the time-honored tradition of placing rooms around a central courtyard. Unlike the irregular medieval plans, the Medici Palace courtyard is square with rooms arranged symmetrically (fig. **12–17**). Round arches on

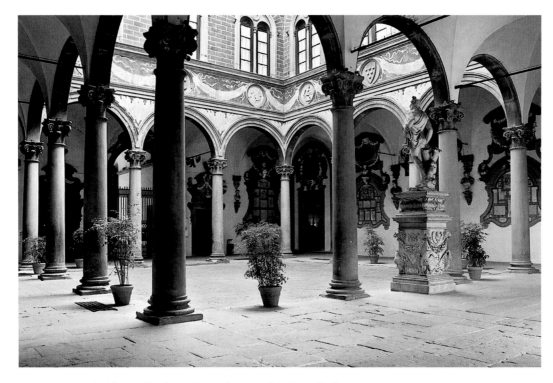

12–17 Courtyard with *sgraffito* decoration, Palazzo Medici-Riccardi, Florence. Begun 1446

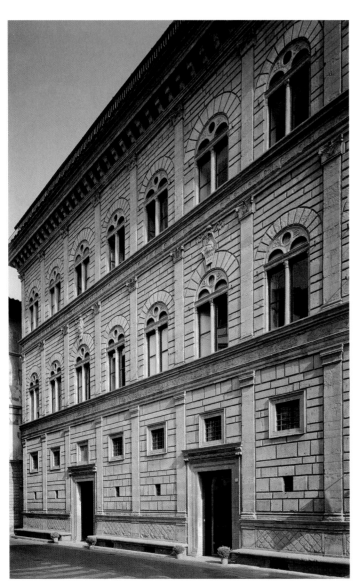

12–18 Leon Battista Alberti. Palazzo Rucellai, Florence. 1455–1470, never finished

slender columns form a continuous arcade and support an enclosed second story. Tall windows in the second story match the exterior windows. The third story was originally a **loggia**, an open covered gallery. Discs bearing Medici symbols surmount each arch in a frieze decorated with swags in **sgraffito** (decoration produced by scratching through plaster or glaze). Such classical elements, inspired by the study of Roman ruins, gave the great house an aura of dignity and stability and undoubtedly enhanced the status of its owners. The Medici Palace inaugurated a new monumentality and regularity of plan in residential urban architecture, and wealthy Florentine families soon copied elements of it in their own houses.

Leon Battista Alberti (1404–1472), a humanist-turned-architect, wrote his now-classic theories on art before ever designing a building. His various writings, including books on painting and sculpture and a ten-volume treatise on architecture, present the first coherent exposition of early Italian aesthetic theory. Like Brunelleschi, Alberti integrated classical forms into his works. In one of his relatively few actual building projects, a palace commissioned by the Rucellai family in Florence, Alberti dealt with one of the continuing challenges faced by Renaissance architects: the relationship (or more often, the lack of one) between a façade and the building behind it. He designed the façade—begun in 1455 but never finished—to be the unify-

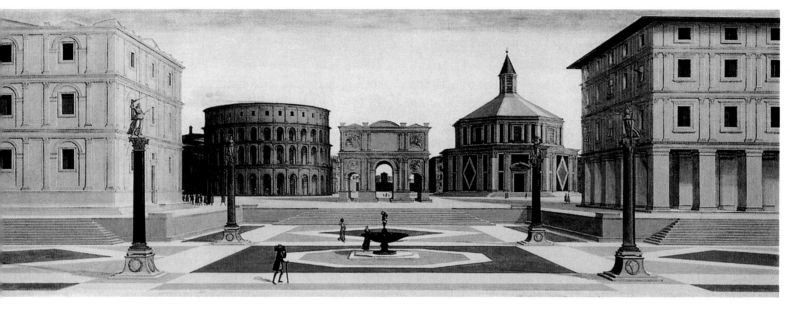

12–19 Anonymous. *View of an Ideal City.* c. 1500. Oil on panel, 30 $\frac{1}{2}$″ × 7′1 $\frac{5}{8}$″ (77.4 cm × 2.17 m). Walters Art Museum, Baltimore

ing front for a planned merger of eight adjacent houses acquired by Giovanni Rucellai (fig. **12–18**). The simple rectangular front suggests a single, cubical three-story building capped with an overhanging cornice. The stone blocks in the façade are lightly rusticated, in a style—derived from fortifications—that was popular in Florentine townhouse exteriors. Possibly inspired by the ancient Colosseum in Rome (see fig. 6–18), Alberti organized the surface of the façade with a pattern of pilasters and architraves superimposed on three levels. Freely interpreting the classical orders, but following the pattern of buildings such as the Colosseum, Alberti adapted the Doric order for use on the ground floor, and the Corinthian order for the third floor, but created a new version of Ionic for the story between them, which used Doric or Tuscan as the base, Ionic on the second story and Corinthian at the top. The Palazzo Rucellai provided a visual lesson for later architects in the use of both classical elements and mathematical proportions.

The intellectual ferment surrounding architecture and urban planning in Renaissance Italy inspired artists to design ideal, and often imaginary, cities. The anonymous central Italian artist who painted an ideal city-center included a triumphal arch and a mini-Colosseum amid contemporary town-houses (fig. **12–19**). The octagonal church or baptistery in the right background suggests the influence of Alberti's theories. In his 1452 treatise *De re*

aedificatoria (On Architecture), Alberti expressed his preference, based on his understanding of classical buildings such as the Pantheon, for churches that were either circular or polygonal, because "most things which are generated, made or directed by Nature are round." The streets in this view are unnaturally wide and clean—surely totally unlike the crowded and twisted alleyways that crisscrossed virtually all fifteenth-century cities. (Note the few tiny figures walking through the ideal city.) The roofs of the houses are the same height, as Alberti recommended in a description of an ideal city. The Four Cardinal Virtues—Justice, Prudence, Patience, and Fortitude—stand on columns in the four corners of the square, a reminder of the dreams of Renaissance theorists, who predicted that ideal surroundings would bring out the best qualities in a city's people.

Sculpture

Donatello, born Donato di Niccolo Bardi (c. 1386–1466), executed each commission as if it were a new experiment. His sculpture is like an encyclopedia of techniques and ideas, with nearly every piece breaking new ground. For example, Donatello's rendition of the biblical hero David, who slew the giant Goliath with a stone from his slingshot, is the earliest known life-size freestanding bronze nude in European art since antiquity (fig. **12–20**).

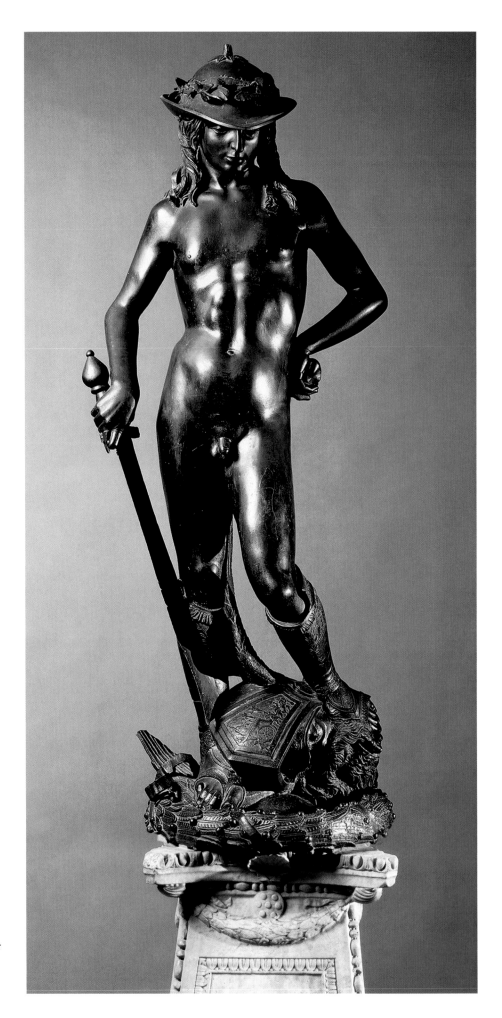

12–20 Donatello. *David.* Dated as early as c. 1420 or as late as the 1460s. Bronze, height 5′2 ¼″ (1.58 m). Museo Nazionale del Bargello, Florence

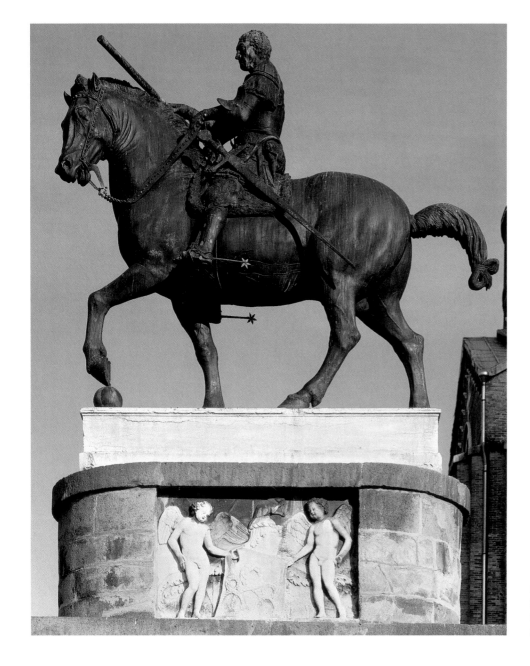

12–21 Donatello. Equestrian monument of Erasmo da Narni (*Gattamelata*), Piazza del Santo, Padua. 1443–1453. Bronze, height approx. 12′2″ (3.71 m)

When Donatello made the sculpture is unknown, but it was first recorded in 1469 in the courtyard of the Medici Palace in Florence. David stood on a base engraved with an inscription extolling Florentine heroism and virtue. Although the work clearly draws on the classical tradition of heroic nudity, this sensuous portrayal of an adolescent boy in a jaunty hat and boots, standing on his enemy's severed head, is utterly original. David's angular pose, his underdeveloped torso, and the sensation of his wavering between childish interests and adult responsibility heighten his heroism in challenging and defeating the giant warrior.

Donatello influenced other artists both in and outside Florence. He worked for a decade in Padua, where he was called in 1443 to execute an equestrian statue commemorating the Venetian general Erasmo da Narni, nicknamed *Gattamelata* (Honeyed Cat) (fig. 12–21). The sources for this statue were two surviving Roman bronze equestrian portraits—one (now lost) in the north Italian city of Pavia, and the other of the emperor Marcus Aurelius (see fig. 6–29), which the sculptor certainly saw and probably sketched during his youthful stay in Rome. The completed *Gattamelata*, installed on a high base in front of the church dedicated to the beloved Franciscan Saint Anthony, was the first life-size bronze equestrian statue since antiquity. Viewed from a distance, this juggernaut of man and animal seems capable of thrusting forward at the first threat. Seen from up close, however, the man's sunken cheeks, sagging jaw, ropey neck, and stern but sad expression suggest a war machine now grown old and tired.

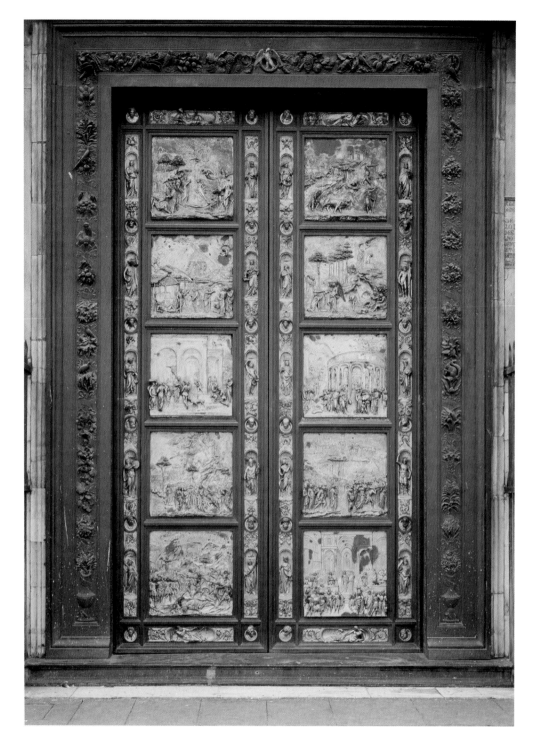

12–22 Lorenzo Ghiberti. Gates of Paradise (East Doors), Baptistery of San Giovanni, Florence 1425–1452. Gilt, bronze, height 15′ (4.57 m). Museo dell'Opera del Duomo, Florence

The door panels, commissioned by the Wool Manufacturers' Guild, depict ten Old Testament scenes beginning with the Creation in the upper left panel. The murder of Abel by his brother, Cain, follows in the upper right panel, succeeded in the same left-right paired order by the Flood and the drunkenness of Noah, Abraham sacrificing Isaac, the story of Jacob and Esau, Joseph sold into slavery by his brothers, Moses receiving the Tablets of the Law, Joshua and the fall of Jericho, David and Goliath, and finally Solomon and the Queen of Sheba. Ghiberti placed his own portrait in the frame beside the Jacob and Esau panel. He wrote in his Commentaries (c. 1450–1455): "I strove to imitate nature as clearly as I could, and with all the perspective I could produce, to have excellent compositions with many figures."

While Donatello was working in Padua, his rival Lorenzo Ghiberti (1378–1455) gained the prestigious commission in Florence for a set of gilded bronze doors to be placed in the baptistery facing the cathedral's west façade. Ghiberti's doors (fig. **12–22**), installed in 1452, were reportedly said by Michelangelo to be worthy of being the Gates of Paradise, a name by which they are still known. Overall gilding unifies the ten large, square reliefs. Ghiberti organized the space depicted within each panel either by a system of linear perspective, approximating the one described by Alberti in his 1435 treatise on painting (see "Renaissance Perspective Systems," pages 328 and 329), or by a series of arches, rocks, or trees leading the eye into the distance. Foreground figures are grouped in the lower third of each panel, while the other figures decrease gradually in size, suggesting deep space. In some panels, the tall buildings suggest ancient Roman architecture and illustrate the emerging antiquarian tone in Renaissance art. Overall, the low-relief settings seem closer to painting than to sculpture.

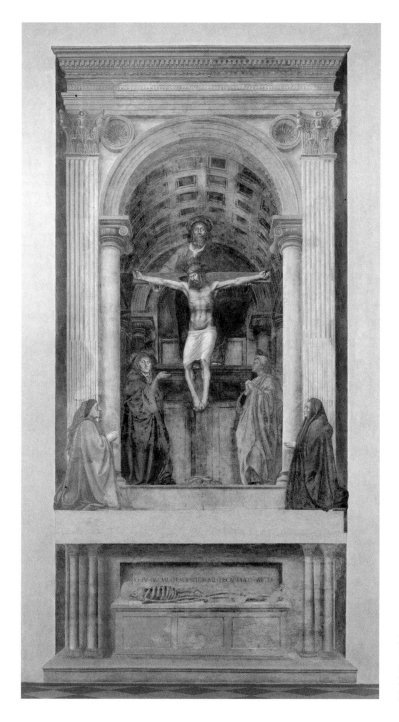

12–23 Masaccio. *Trinity with the Virgin, Saint John the Evangelist, and Donors,* Church of Santa Maria Novella, Florence. c. 1425–1428. Fresco, 21′ × 10′5″ (6.4 × 3.17 m)

Painting

One of the major achievements of Italian Renaissance artists was the convincing integration of human figures into rational architectural settings. This accomplishment can be seen early on in the works of the Florentine artist Tommaso di Ser Giovanni di Mone Cassai (1401–1428), nicknamed Masaccio ("big, ugly Tom"). In his short career of less than a decade, Masaccio established a new direction in Florentine painting, much as Giotto had a century earlier. The exact chronology of his works is uncertain, and his fresco of the Trinity in the Church of Santa Maria Novella in Florence falls sometime between 1425 and 1428 (fig. 12–23).

The *Trinity* fresco was meant to give the illusion of a stone funerary monument and altar table set in a deep **aedicula** (framed niche) in the wall. Masaccio created the appearance of the niche through precisely rendered linear perspective in which the vanishing point lies on a horizon line just above the base of the cross at the eye level of an adult viewer. The niche itself resembles the architecture of San Lorenzo (see fig. 12–15). Thus, the painting demonstrates Masaccio's intimate knowledge of both Brunelleschi's perspective experiments and his architectural style. A consistent illumination, whose "source" seems to lie behind the viewer, models the figures and casts reflections on the coffers, or sunken panels, of the vault.

In Masaccio's painting, God the Father holds the cross on which Jesus hangs, while the dove of the Holy Spirit seems poised in downward flight between Jesus's tilted halo and the

Technique

Renaissance Perspective Systems

Fifteenth-century Italian Humanists developed a system known as **linear,** or **mathematical perspective** that enabled artists to represent the visible world in a convincingly illusionistic way. The architect Filippo Brunelleschi first demonstrated the system about 1420, and the scholar and architect Leon Battista Alberti codified it in 1436 in his treatise *Della Pittura (On Painting)*.

For Alberti, a picture's surface was a flat plane that intersected the viewer's field of vision at right angles. This highly artificial concept presumed a viewer standing dead center at a prescribed distance from a work of art and looking through one eye. From this single fixed vantage point, everything would appear to recede into the distance at the same rate, shaped by imaginary lines called **orthogonals** that met at a single **vanishing point** on the horizon. The use of orthogonals replicated the optical illusion that things appear to grow smaller and closer together as they get farther away from us.

Linear perspective has the advantage of making the pictorial space seem almost like an extension of the real space, creating a compelling, even exaggerated sense of depth (see Perugino, opposite). In the course of the fifteenth century, however, many artists adopted the use of multiple vanishing points, which gave their work a more relaxed and less tunnel-like feeling.

Meanwhile, in the north, artists such as the Limbourg brothers (see fig. 12–2) continued to employ older visual systems known as atmospheric and intuitive perspective. In **atmospheric perspective,** variations in color and clarity convey the feeling of distance. In **intuitive perspective**, artists use visual devices, such as making background figures smaller, to convey spatial depth, but do not follow a consistent mathematical system established by orthogonals. Perugino uses both linear and atmospheric perspective in *Delivery of the Keys to Saint Peter.*

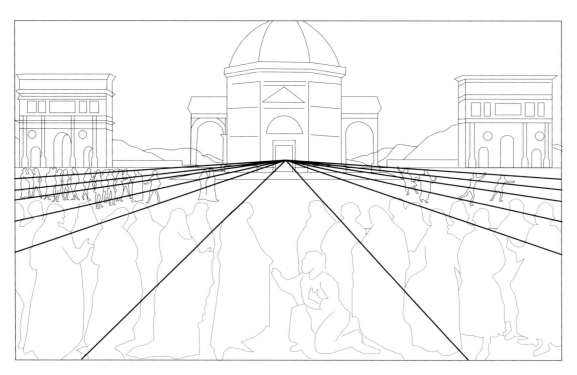

Perugino. *Delivery of the Keys to Saint Peter.* Orthogonals and vanishing point.

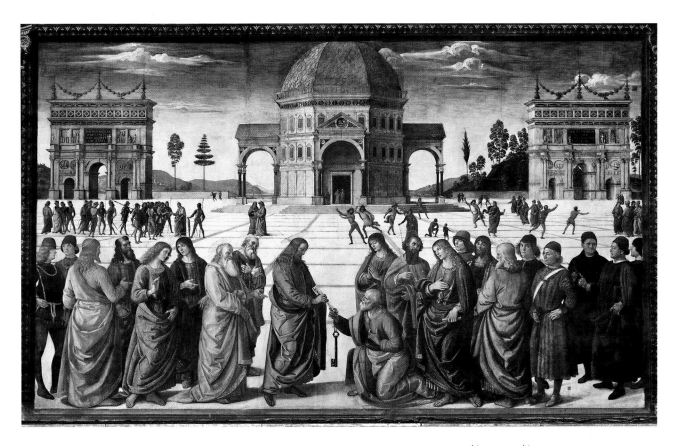

Pietro Perugino. *Delivery of the Keys to Saint Peter.* Sistine Chapel, Vatican, Rome. 1482. Fresco, 11′5 1/2″ × 18′8 1/2″ (3.48 × 5.70 m)

Delivery of the Keys to Saint Peter is a remarkable study in linear perspective (see opposite page). The clear demarcation of the paving stones of the piazza provides a geometric grid against which the figures stand like chess pieces on the squares. The figures and buildings are scaled to size according to their distance from the picture plane and modeled by a consistent light source from the upper left. Horizontally, the composition is divided between the foreground frieze of figures and the widely spaced background buildings, vertically by the open space at the center between Christ and Peter and by the symmetrical architectural forms on either side of this central axis. Perugino's painting is, among other things, a representation of Alberti's ideal city (see fig. 12–19), described in Alberti's treatise on architecture as having a "temple" (that is, a church) at the very center of a great open space raised on a dais and separate from any other buildings that might obstruct its view.

Father's head. Mary and Saint John the Evangelist stand at the foot of the cross, and outside the niche the donors kneel in prayer. Mary gazes calmly out at us, her raised hand presenting the Trinity. Below, in an open sarcophagus, is a skeleton, a grim reminder that death awaits us all and that our only hope is redemption and life in the hereafter through Christian belief. The inscription above the skeleton reads: "I was once that which you are, and what I am you also will be."

Masaccio's brief career reached its height in his collaboration with a painter known as Masolino (c. 1383–after 1435) on the fresco decoration of the Brancacci Chapel in the Church of Santa Maria del Carmine in Florence (fig. **12–24**). The chapel was originally dedicated to Saint Peter and the frescoes illustrate events in his life. In the scene of the *Tribute Money* (fig. **12–25**), Masaccio illustrates an incident in which a collector of Jewish temple taxes demands payment from the apostle Peter, shown in the central group with Jesus and the other disciples (Matthew 17:24–7). Jesus instructs Peter to "go to the sea, drop in a hook, and take the first fish that comes up," which Peter does at the far left. In the fish's mouth, Peter finds a coin worth twice the tax demanded, which he gives to the tax collector at the far right.

The *Tribute Money* is particularly remarkable for its early use of both linear and atmospheric perspective to integrate the figures, architecture, and landscape into a consistent whole. The group of Jesus and his disciples forms a clear central focus from which the landscape seems to recede naturally into the far distance. To create this illusion, Masaccio used linear perspective in the depiction of the house, and then reinforced it by diminishing the sizes of the barren trees and reducing Peter's size at the left. The lines of the house lead the viewer's eye to the head of

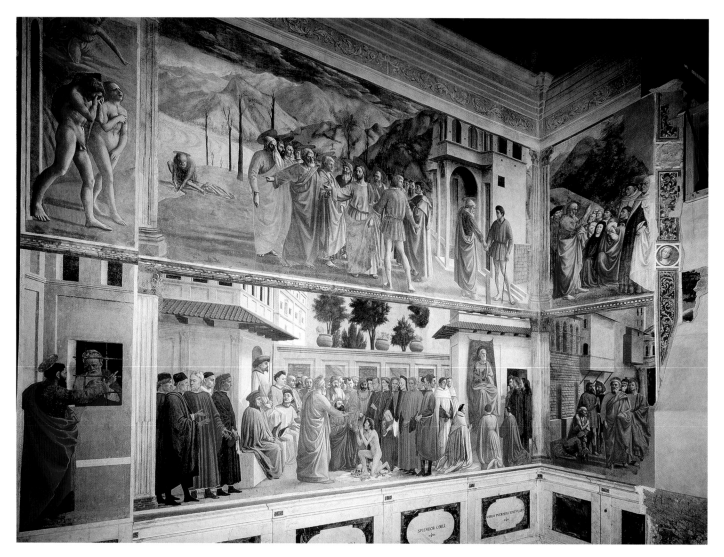

12–24 Masaccio and Masolino (1424–1427) and Filippino Lippi (c. 1482–1484). Interior of the Brancacci Chapel, Church of Santa Maria del Carmine, Florence. Frescoes

Technical study of the painting reveals the speed with which a master painter worked. Reading from left to right in the upper register: The Expulsion of Adam and Eve from Paradise *(Masaccio, 4 giornate or days' work),* Tribute Money *(Masaccio, 32 giornate),* Saint Peter Preaching *(Masolino, 9 giornate); and in the lower register:* Saint Paul Visiting Saint Peter in Prison *(Filippino Lippi, 3 giornate),* Saint Peter Raising the Son of the Ruler of Antioch and Saint Peter Preaching *(Masaccio and Filippino Lippi, 54 giornate), and* Saint Peter Healing with His Shadow *(Masolino, 10 giornate).*

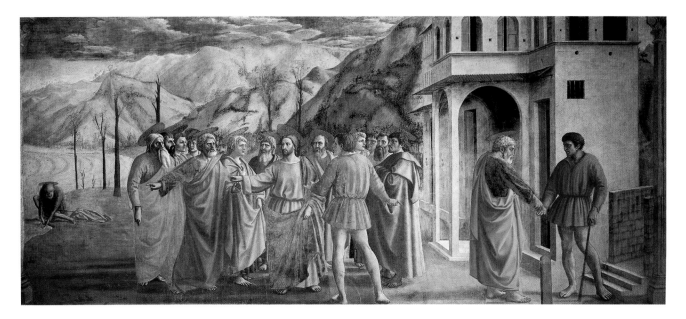

12–25 Masaccio. *Tribute Money,* Brancacci Chapel, Church of Santa Maria del Carmine, Florence. c. 1427.
Fresco, 8′1″ × 19′7″ (2.46 × 6 m)
STUDIO MARIO QUATTRONE

Much valuable new information about the Brancacci Chapel frescoes was discovered during the course of a cleaning and restoration carried out between 1981 and 1991. Art historians now have a more accurate picture of how the frescoes were done and in what sequence, as well as which artist did what. One interesting discovery was that all of the figures in the Tribute Money, *except those of the temple tax collector, originally had gold-leaf halos, several of which had flaked off. Rather than silhouette the heads against flat gold circles in the medieval manner, Masaccio conceived of the halo as a foreshortened gold disk hovering in space above each head.*

Jesus, which the painter has placed at the vanishing point. A second vanishing point determines the position of the steps and stone rail at the right. The cleaning of the fresco revealed that it was done in 32 **giornate** (a giornata is a section of fresh plaster that could be prepared and painted in one day). The cleaning also revealed the subtle colors that Masaccio used to create effects of atmospheric perspective in the distant landscape. The mountains fade from grayish green to grayish white and the houses and trees on their slopes are loosely sketched.

The volumetric solidity of the foreground figures testifies to Masaccio's intimate knowledge of ancient sculpture as well as of earlier Italian painters such as Giotto. Masaccio **modeled** the figures with strong highlights and shadows. The figures cast their long shadows on the ground toward the left, implying a light source at the far right, as if the scene were lit by the actual window in the rear wall of the chapel. Not only does the lighting give the forms sculptural definition, but the colors vary in tone according to the strength of the illumination. Masaccio used a wide range of hues—pale pink, mauve, gold, seafoam green, apple green, and peach—and a sophisticated shading technique in which he used contrasting colors (for example, Andrew's green robe is shaded with red instead of darker green). When restorers cleaned the painting, they also discovered a wealth of linear details, especially in the settings, that had been obscured by dirt and overpainting. The landscape and buildings are much closer in appearance to

the paintings by Masaccio's Northern European contemporaries than previously thought. In contrast to the Flemish artists, however, Masaccio's figures exhibit the artist's study of classical sculpture and the painting of Giotto and his followers, which he could have seen in fifteenth-century Florence.

Stylistic innovations take time to be fully accepted, and Masaccio's genius for depicting weight, volume, and consistent lighting, and for spatial integration was best appreciated by later generations of painters. Many important sixteenth-century Italian artists, including Michelangelo (see Chapter 13), studied and sketched Masaccio's Brancacci Chapel frescoes. In the meantime, painting in Florence after Masaccio's death developed along lines somewhat different from that of the *Tribute Money* or *Trinity*, as other artists such as Paolo Uccello (see "Closer Look," page 333) experimented with their own ways of conveying the illusion of a believably receding space (see "Renaissance Perspective Systems," pages 328 and 329).

The tradition of covering walls with paintings in fresco continued through the fifteenth century. Between 1435 and 1445, the decoration of the Dominican Monastery of San Marco in Florence, where Fra Angelico served as the prior, was one of the most extensive projects. Born Guido di Pietro da Mugello (c. 1395/1400–1455) and known to his peers as Fra Giovanni da Fiesole, Fra Angelico (Angelic Brother) earned his nickname through his piety as well as his painting. He is documented as a painter in Florence in 1417–1418, and he continued to be a very

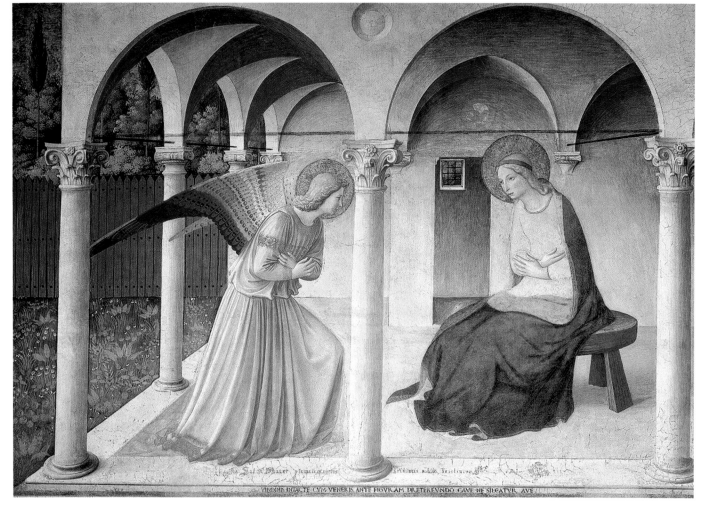

12–26 Fra Angelico. *Annunciation,* Monastery of San Marco, Florence, north corridor. c. 1438–1445. Fresco, 7′1″ × 10′6″ (2.2 × 3.2 m)

The shadowed vault of the portico is supported by a wall on one side and by slender columns on the other, a new building technique being used by Brunelleschi in the very years when the painting was being created. The capitals are creative fifteenth-century adaptations of classical Ionic and Corinthian forms. The edge of the porch, the open door in the back wall, and the grilled window, drawn in linear perspective, establish a complex but ample space for the figures.

active painter after taking his vows as a Dominican monk in near-by Fiesole between 1418 and 1421.

In the Monastery of San Marco, Fra Angelico and his assistants created a painting to inspire meditation in each monk's cell (forty-four in all), and they also added paintings to the chapter house and the corridors. At the top of the stairs in the north corridor, Fra Angelico painted a scene of the Annunciation (fig. **12–26**). Here the monks were to pause for prayer before going to their individual cells. The illusion of space created by the careful linear perspective seems to extend the stair and corridor out into a second cloister, the Virgin's home and verdant enclosed garden, where the angel Gabriel greets the modest, youthful Mary. The slender, graceful figures wearing flowing draperies assume modest poses. The natural light falling from the left models their forms and casts an almost supernatural radiance over their faces and hands. The scene is a vision that welcomes the monks to the most private areas of the monastery and prepares them to continue their meditations.

Pope Eugene IV summoned Fra Angelico to Rome in 1445, and the painter's assistants completed the frescoes in Florence. The pope may have hoped to make the painter a church official, the archbishop of Florence, but finally appointed the vicar of San Marco, Antonino Pierozzi, to the post in January 1446. When Pierozzi was proposed for canonization in the early sixteenth century, several people testified that Pope Eugene's first choice for archbishop had been Fra Angelico, who declined the honor and suggested his Dominican brother Antonino. The world of art was left richer because of the choice, however, for Fra Angelico dedicated the last years of his life to his painting, including the pope's private chapel in the Vatican Palace.

At mid-century, when Fra Angelico was still painting his radiant visions of Mary and Jesus in the monastery of San Marco, a new generation of artists emerged. Thoroughly conversant with the theories of Brunelleschi and Alberti, they had mastered the techniques (and tricks) of depicting figures in a constructed architectural space. The creation of the more subtle nuances of

Under an elegantly fluttering banner, the Florentine general Niccolo da Tolentino leads his men against the Sienese at the Battle of San Romano, which took place June 1, 1432, near Pisa, in Italy. Niccolo holds aloft his baton of command, a sign of his absolute authority. His gesture, together with his white horse and fashionable gold damask turban, ensure that Niccolo dominates the scene. The general's knights charge into the fray, and when they fall, like the soldier at the lower left, they join the many broken lances on the ground—all arranged in conformity with the new mathematical depiction of space called linear perspective.

The battle rages across a shallow stage, defined by the debris of warfare arranged in a neat pattern on the pink ground and backed by a tapestry-like hedge of blooming orange trees and rosebushes. In the cultivated hills beyond, crossbowmen prepare their lethal bolts. An eccentric artist nicknamed Paolo Uccello created this panel painting, now housed in London's National Gallery (fig. **12–27**). Uccello also painted two others like it, which reside in major museums in Florence and Paris. Uccello was fascinated to the point of obsession with the new art and science of linear perspective.

The strange history of these paintings has only recently come to light. Lionardo Bartolini Salimbeni (1409—1479), who headed the Florentine Council of Ten during the war against Lucca and Siena, probably commissioned the paintings. Uccello's remarkable accuracy when depicting armor, heraldic banners, and even fashionable fabrics and crests from the 1430s would appeal to Florentine civic pride. The hedges of oranges, roses, and pomegranates—all ancient fertility symbols—suggest that Lionardo might have commissioned the paintings at the time of his wedding in 1438. He and his wife, Maddalena, had six sons, and two of the brothers inherited the paintings. One of the sons, Damiano, made an official complaint against Lorenzo de' Medici in which he swore that Lorenzo "forcibly removed" the paintings from his house. In any case, Damiano never got his paintings back; instead, Uccello's masterpieces are recorded in a 1492 inventory as hanging in Lorenzo's private chamber in the Medici Palace. There—with their carved and gilded frames—the three paintings would have formed a brilliant and heroic frieze. Perhaps Lorenzo de' Medici, who was called "the Magnificent," saw Uccello's heroic pageant as a trophy more worthy of a Medici merchant prince.

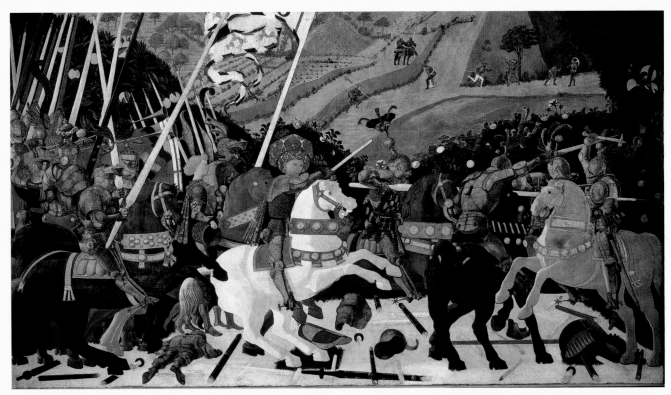

12–27 Paolo Uccello. *The Battle of San Romano.* c. 1430s/1450s. Tempera on wood panel, 6′ × 10′5″ (1.83 × 3.23 m) (later cut down at the top). The National Gallery, London
REPRODUCED BY COURTESY OF THE TRUSTEES

The Florentine forces in the battle against the Sienese at San Romano were led by General Niccolo da Tolentino, a friend and supporter of the Medici, who died in the conflict. In the painting, the general charges onto the field on a white horse, accompanied by his page. He wears a red and gold hat and carries a general's baton; both serve to identify him in this action-packed scene.

landscape came later with the knowledge of Flemish painting and its use of atmospheric or aerial perspective.

Some artists became specialists. The eccentric painter Paolo di Dono (c. 1397–1475), called Paolo Uccello (Paul Bird), devoted his life to the study of linear perspective. Vasari devoted a chapter in his history of art to Uccello, whom he described as a man so obsessed with the study of perspective that he neglected his painting, his family, and even his pet birds. Finally Uccello became, in Vasari's words, "solitary, eccentric, melancholy, and impoverished" (Vasari, *Lives of the Painters*, page 79). According to Vasari, Uccello's wife complained that he sat up drawing all night and when she called to him to come to bed he would say, "Oh, what a sweet mistress is this perspective!"

Contrasting sharply with Uccello's obsession with space is the fluid, linear grace characteristic of the Florentine painter Sandro Botticelli (1445–1510). Botticelli's best-known works are paintings of mythological subjects, among them the *Birth of Venus* (fig. **12–28**). The date of this painting is controversial, but it was probably made around 1484–1486 for the private collection of Lorenzo de' Medici, who had become ruler of Florence in 1469. The central image, a type known as the modest Venus, is based on the antique statue of Venus in the Medici collection (see Introduction, fig. 6). The classical goddess of love and beauty, born of sea foam, floats ashore on a scallop shell gracefully arranging her hands and hair to hide—or enhance—her sexuality. Blown by the wind, Zephyr (and his love, the nymph Chloris), and welcomed by a devotee holding a garment embroidered with flowers, Venus arrives at her earthly home.

The circumstances of this commission are uncertain, but its meaning—and the meanings of Botticelli's other mythological paintings—is probably related to Neoplatonism, a philosophy favored by the Medici. Cosimo de' Medici the Elder (1389–1464) had founded an academy in Florence devoted to the study of classical texts, especially the works of Plato and his followers, the Neoplatonists. Neoplatonism is highly complex, but basically it is characterized by a sharp opposition of the spiritual (the ideal or idea) and the carnal (matter that can be overcome by severe discipline and aversion to the world of the senses). Neoplatonists conceived of Venus, the goddess of love, as having two natures, one terrestrial and the other celestial. The first ruled over earthly, human love and the second over universal or divine love. For the Florentine Neoplatonists, the celestial Venus was a classical equivalent of the Virgin Mary.

An artist who was profoundly influenced by Masaccio was Piero della Francesca (c. 1406/12–1492). Born in the small Tuscan town of Borgo San Sepulcro, Piero worked in Florence in the 1430s. He knew current thinking in art and art theory—including Brunelleschi's system of spatial illusion and linear perspective, Masaccio's powerful modeling of forms and use of atmospheric perspective, and Alberti's theoretical treatises. Piero was one of the few practicing artists who also wrote his own theories of art. Not surprisingly, in his treatise on perspective he emphasized the geometry and the volumetric construction of forms and spaces that were so apparent in his own work.

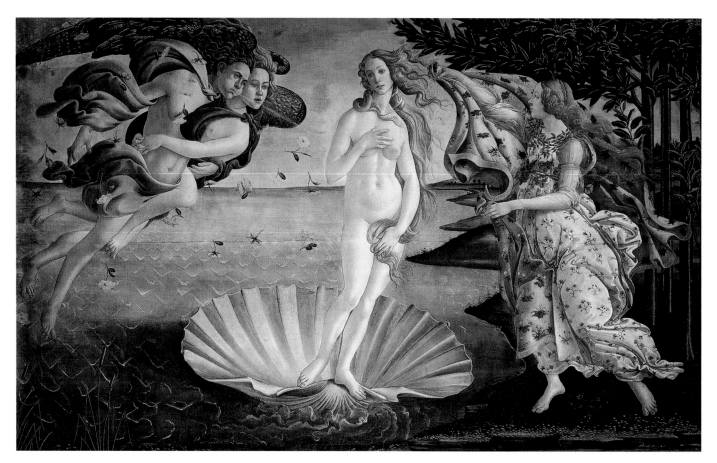

12–28 Sandro Botticelli. ***Birth of Venus.*** c. 1484–1486. Tempera on canvas, 5′8⁷⁄₈″ × 9′1⁷⁄₈″ (1.8 × 2.8 m). Galleria degli Uffizi, Florence

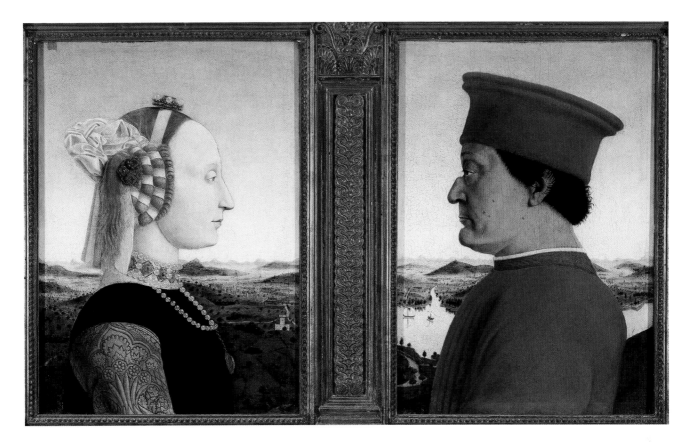

12–29 Piero della Francesca. *Battista Sforza* (left) **and** *Federico da Montefeltro* (right). 1472–1473. Oil on wood panel, each 18 1/2" × 13" (47 × 33 cm). Galleria degli Uffizi, Florence

Commissions took Piero to the court of Federico da Montefeltro at Urbino. There, in 1472–1473, he painted a pair of companion portraits of Federico and his recently deceased wife, Battista Sforza (fig. **12–29**). Like portraits on Roman coins and cameos, the figures are portrayed in strict profile, as remote from the viewer as icons. Piero emphasized the underlying geometry of the forms, rendering the figures with an absolute stillness. At the same time, his use of the northern technique of atmospheric perspective, with the landscape features becoming lighter and paler as they recede, resulted in a highly believable illusion of space. Piero used another Northern European device in the harbor view near the center of Federico's panel: the water narrows into a river and leads the eye into the distant landscape. The portraits may have been joined as a **diptych** (a pair of panels) as they are now framed, since the landscape appears continuous across the two panels. On the back of the panels, the couple rides in triumphant chariots through another continuous landscape.

In the second half of the fourteenth century, a younger generation of artists turned the walls of chapels and palaces into brilliant displays of the good life as it was lived by the rich and powerful citizens of the Italian city-states Florence, Mantua, Urbino, and elsewhere. The subject of the murals might be religious or historical, but patrons wanted to see themselves at work, at prayer, and at play; showing off their jewelry, clothing, and household goods; and surrounded by images of their neighbors, families, servants, fine horses, and dogs. The interest in material possessions, an interest that reformers claimed reached the point of obsession, is apparent in the dazzling display of wealth even in purportedly religious scenes. In his palace in Urbino, Federico da

Montefeltro had a small private room, called a studiolo (a study). There he kept his fine books and art objects and there he could hold private conversations away from the huge halls filled with courtiers. In the studiolo artists worked in intarsia (wood) to achieve remarkable trompe l'oeil ("fool the eye") effects, giving the illusion of pilasters, cupboards with latticed doors, niches with statues, benches, and tables—even the duke's armor, hanging like a suit in a closet. They accomplished these suprising effects by scrupulously applying the rules of linear perspective and foreshortening (a contraction of forms that supports the overall perspectival system) and carefully rendering every detail.

North of Urbino and the Montefeltro court, the Renaissance appeared in Venice and in Padua, where both Giotto (in the fourteenth century) and Donatello (in the mid-fifteenth) had lived and worked. Donatello was in Padua during the formative years of the young artist Andrea Mantegna (1431–1506), who pushed the system of linear perspective used by Donatello to its limits with his radical views and strongly foreshortened figures.

Mantegna's mature style is exemplified by the frescoes of the Camera Picta (Painted Room) in the Ducal Palace of Mantua. The artist decorated this tower chamber between 1465 and 1474 for Ludovico Gonzaga, the ruler of Mantua. On the vaulted ceiling, the artist painted a tour de force of perspective, a viewpoint called *di sotto in sù* (seen directly from below), which began a long tradition of illusionistic ceiling painting (fig. **12–30**). The room appears to be open to a cloud-filled sky through a large oculus in a simulated marble and mosaic-covered vault. On each side of a precariously balanced planter, three young women and an exotically turbaned African man peer over a marble railing. A fourth young woman in

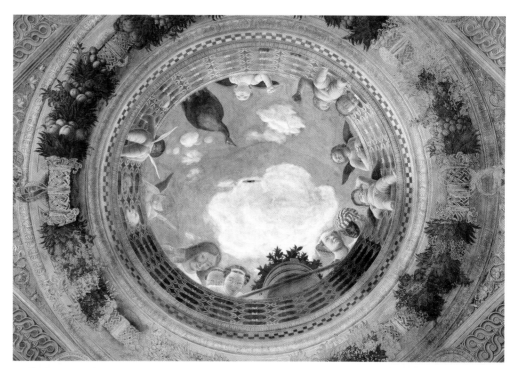

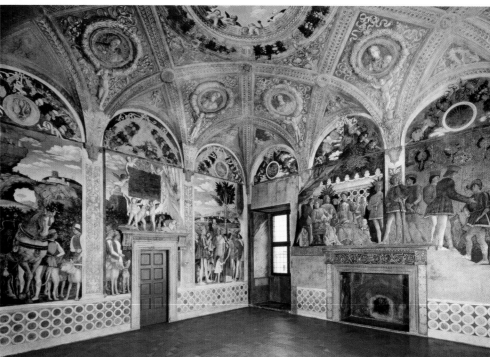

12–30 Andrea Mantegna. Two views of The Camera Picta. Ducal Palace, Mantua. Frescoes. 1465–1474

a veil looks dreamily upward. Joined by a large peacock, several **putti** (a *putto* is a little boy, often shown naked and winged) frolic around the **balustrade** (supports topped by a rail). Mantegna completed the decoration of the room with murals featuring portraits of members of the Gonzaga family.

In the last quarter of the fifteenth century, Venice—once a center of Byzantine art—emerged as a major center of Renaissance painting. From the late 1470s on, Venetian artists embraced the oil medium for works on both panel and canvas. The most important of these painters were members of the Bellini family, Jacopo and his sons Gentile (see Chapter 7, page 183) and Giovanni (see fig. 12–1). Andrea Mantegna was also part of this circle, for he married one of Jacopo Bellini's daughters. Giovanni's career spanned the second half of the fifteenth century, but he produced many of his greatest paintings

in the early years of the sixteenth, when his work matured into a grand, simplified, idealized style (see Chapter 13, page 354).

Late in the fifteenth century, the city of Rome also became a magnet for Renaissance artists. Pope Sixtus IV summoned the finest painters to decorate the walls of his newly built Sistine Chapel, among them Pietro Vannucci, called Perugino (c. 1445–1523). Perugino, who was active in Florence, came from near the town of Perugia in Umbria. In 1482, he painted the *Delivery of the Keys to Saint Peter* (see page 329), an event not actually described in the Bible but suggested in Matthew 16:19. The event provided the justification for the supremacy of papal authority: Christ is shown giving the keys to the kingdom of heaven to the apostle Peter, the first bishop of Rome. With Perugino and other artists working for the papacy, the focus of Italian art shifts to Rome.

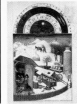

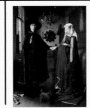

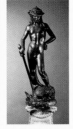

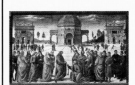

Limbourg Brothers,
Très Riches Heures, 1413–1416

Brunelleschi,
Dome of Florence Cathedral, 1417–1436

Van Eyck,
Portrait of Giovanni Arnolfini (?), 1434

Donatello,
David, after 1428

Perugino, *Delivery of the Keys to Saint Peter*, 1482

▲ Early Renaissance 1400–1500

LOOKING BACK

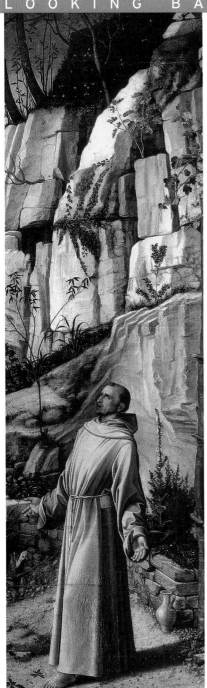

The great fourteenth-century Humanist and poet Petrarch looked back at the thousand years extending from the collapse of the Roman Empire to his own time and determined that history fell into three distinct periods: The ancient classical world, a time of high human achievement, was followed by a purported decline during the Middle Ages, or so-called "dark ages." The third period was the modern world—his own era—a revival, a rebirth, a **renaissance**, when humanity began to emerge from an intellectual and cultural stagnation. For Petrarch and his Italian contemporaries, Humanism embodied a worldview that focused on human beings; an education that perfected individuals through the study of past models of civic and personal virtue; a value system that emphasized personal effort and responsibility; and a physically or intellectually active life that was directed at a common good as well as individual nobility.

The rise of Humanism did not signify a decline in the importance of Christian belief. In fact, an intense Christian spirituality continued to inspire and pervade most European art through the fifteenth century and long after. While wealthy and sophisticated men in the highest ranks of the clergy—bishops, cardinals, and the pope himself—and the royal and aristocratic courts continued to play major roles in the support of the arts, the urban lay public increasingly sought to express personal and civic pride by sponsoring architecture and the arts, including townhouses and portraits of family members. In fact, the commonsense values of the merchants formed a solid underpinning for Humanist theories and enthusiasms.

Art of the time upheld the values and worldview of the new social order in an era that came to be called the Renaissance. Power was no longer the prerogative only of divinely sanctioned elites; it now also lay in the hands of commoners—such as artists, merchants, and bankers—whose wealth was largely earned rather than inherited. Humanist patrons (including the Church) and artists wanted to see themselves and their possessions depicted realistically and placed in the cities and countryside where they worked and played, fought and died. Artists learned to created anatomically correct figures and to reproduce the textures and colors of the natural world, and they tacitly agreed to follow new ways of representing space and visually organizing a scene.

Along with the desire for accurate depiction came a new interest in individual personalities. Fifteenth-century portraits have an astonishingly lifelike quality, combining careful—sometimes even unflattering—description with an uncanny sense of vitality. In a number of religious paintings, even the saints and angels seem to be portraits. Indeed, individuality became important in every sphere. More names of artists survive from the fifteenth century, for example, than in the entire span from the beginning of the Common Era to the year 1400. By the end of the fifteenth century, the visual mastery of the material world seemed complete; the rational and scientific had triumphed in both secular and religious art.

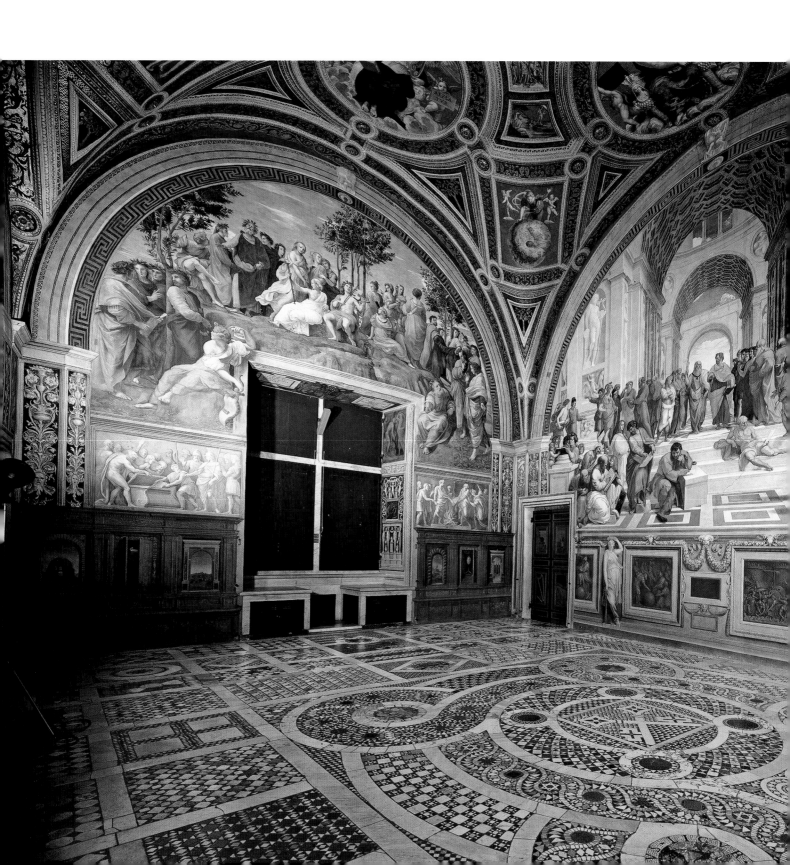

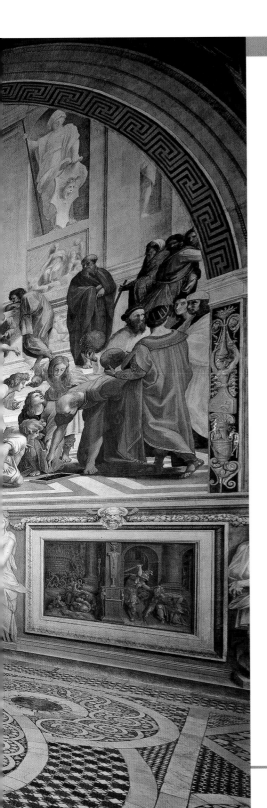

13
Art of the High Renaissance and Reformation

I n a single generation at the beginning of the sixteenth century, the painter Raphael (Raffaello Santi or Sanzio, 1483–1520), together with the architect Bramante, Michelangelo, and a few other artists, established a style often called the High Renaissance. Artists and philosophers, each in their own way, combined Christian belief and ancient philosophy into a balanced, rational, Humanistic system.

Faith in human rationality and perfectibility seems to underlie Raphael's decoration of the private apartment of Pope Julius II, who ruled from 1503 to 1513. Raphael achieved a lofty style in keeping with papal ideals, but when he died at the age of 37 on April 6, 1520, the grand moment was already passing; Luther and the Protestant Reformation were challenging papal authority.

Pope Julius II intended the Stanza della Segnatura, or Room of the Signature, to be his library and study (fig. **13–1**). The paintings in the pope's library proclaimed that all human knowledge existed under the power of Divine Wisdom. Raphael retained the traditional organization of a library into divisions of theology, philosophy, the arts, and justice; and he created allegories to illustrate the themes. Churchmen discussing the sacraments represent theology, while across the room ancient philosophers debate in the *School of Athens* (see fig. 13–5). Poetry and the arts are represented by Apollo and the Muses; and Justice, holding a sword and scales, assigns each his due. Plato and Aristotle lead the *School of Athens*. They carry appropriate books, Plato holding the *Timaeus* and Aristotle the *Nicomachean Ethics*. Ancient representatives of the academic curriculum—Grammar, Rhetoric, Dialectic, Arithmetic, Music, Geometry, and Astronomy—surround them. The poet Sappho is the only woman in the room. She reclines against the (real) window frame among the Muses. Raphael included his own portrait among the onlookers in the *School of Athens* and signed the painting with his initials.

In this all-encompassing iconographic program, Raphael has created an ideal setting for papal activity. In an architectural setting inspired by Roman antiquities, or Bramante's designs for the new church of Saint Peter, or the majestic landscapes with oak trees (a gracious reference to the pope's powerful della Rovere, "of the oak," family), monumental figures move with quiet dignity. Raphael's idealized forms are as grand as the ideas they represent. During his brief career, Raphael established the standard of classical Renaissance art for the future.

13–1 Raphael. Stanza della Segnatura, Vatican, Rome. Right: *Philosophy,* or *School of Athens, with Plato and Aristotle;* left: (over the window) *Poetry and the Arts,* represented by Apollo and the Muses. 1510–1511. Fresco, 19′ × 27′ (5.8 × 8.2 m)

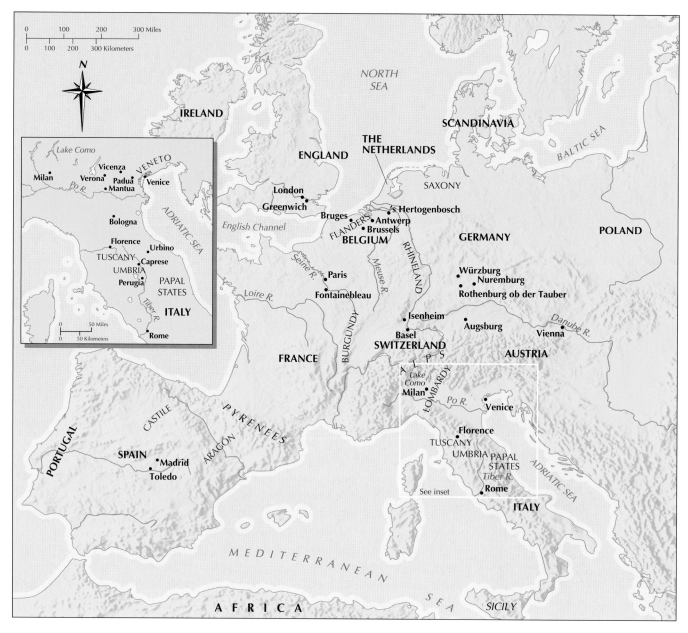

Map 13–1 Europe of the High Renaissance and Reformation

During the sixteenth century, the Humanism of the early Renaissance underwent a radical shift. With its medieval roots and often uncritical acceptance of the authority of classical texts, Renaissance Humanism slowly gave way to an intensified spirit of inquiry. This impulse led scholars to investigate the natural world around them, to conduct scientific and mechanical experiments, to explore lands in Africa, Asia, and the Americas previously unknown to Europeans, and even to question the authority of the pope and the Church hierarchy in a movement known as the Reformation. The influential writings and leadership of important reformers, such as Martin Luther (1483–1546) in Germany, led to the establishment of Protestant churches in Northern Europe (see Map 13-1, above). And in response, at the Council of Trent (1545–1563), the Roman Catholic hierarchy formulated a program to counter the Reformation.

During these centuries, travel in Europe was becoming easier and safer, and artists became increasingly mobile, journeying from city to city and from one country to another; consequently, styles and techniques became less regional and more interna-tional. The materials artists worked with changed, too. Fresco painting was still common, but more and more artists painted with oil on canvas. They could produce oil paintings in their studios and easily transport and install them anywhere. Artists of stature became sought-after international celebrities, and their social status rose as painting, sculpture, and works of architecture came to be seen as liberal rather than manual arts, requiring intellectual activity rather than merely technical skill.

Italian Art

The painting, sculpture, and architecture produced during the early sixteenth century reflect a self-confident Humanism, an abiding admiration for classical forms, and a dominating sense of stability and order. These characteristics are found above all in the work of four towering figures of the Italian Renaissance: Leonardo, Raphael, Michelangelo, and Titian. The achievements of these artists are so remarkable that nineteenth-century scholars called the period in Italy from about 1495 until the death of Raphael in 1520 the High Renaissance.

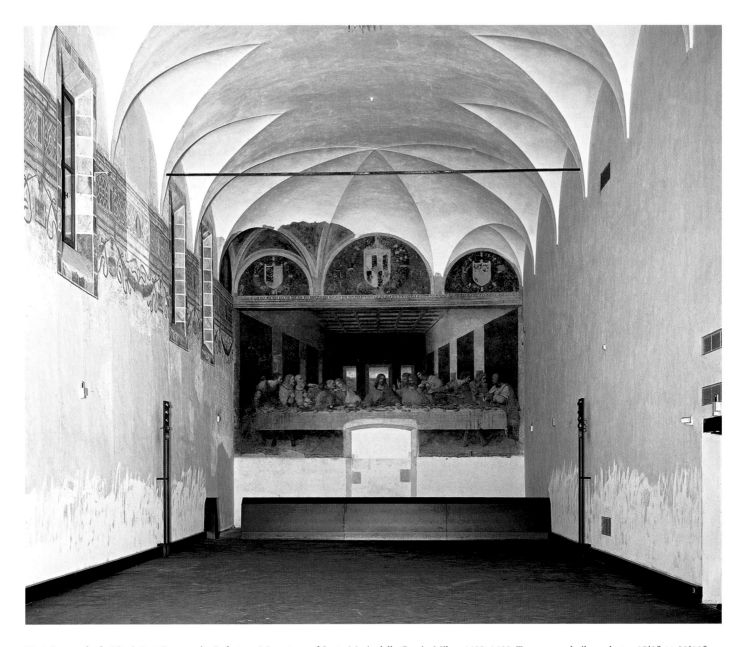

13–2 Leonardo da Vinci. *Last Supper,* the Refectory, Monastery of Santa Maria delle Grazie, Milan. 1495–1498. Tempera and oil on plaster, 15′2″ × 28′10″ (4.6 × 8.8 m). (See Introduction, fig. 21)

STUDIO MARIO QUATTRONE, QUATTRONE, FLORENCE, ITALY

Instead of painting in fresco, Leonardo devised an experimental technique for this mural. Hoping to achieve the freedom and flexibility of painting on panel, he worked directly on dry intonaco—*a thin layer of smooth plaster—with an oil tempera paint whose formula is unknown. The result was disastrous. Within a short time, the painting began to deteriorate, and by the middle of the sixteenth century its figures could be seen only with difficulty. In the seventeenth century, the monks saw no harm in cutting a doorway through the lower center of the composition. Since then the work has barely survived, despite many attempts to halt its deterioration and restore its original appearance. The painting narrowly escaped complete destruction in World War II, when the refectory was bombed to rubble around its heavily sandbagged wall. The most recent restoration was completed in May 1999.*

Leonardo da Vinci (1452–1519) received his training in Florence in the workshop of the painter and sculptor Verrocchio. Leonardo's fame as an artist is based on only a few known works of art, for his fertile mind jumped from one subject to another, and he seldom finished his projects. He had a passion for the study of mathematics, science, and engineering, and he compiled volumes of detailed drawings and notes on anatomy, botany, geology, meteorology, architectural design, and mechanics (see "The Vitruvian Man," page 342). At the court of Duke Ludovico Sforza of Milan, where Leonardo worked from 1482 or 1483 until 1498, he spent much of his time on military and civil- engineering projects, including an urban renewal plan for the city. But at Duke Ludovico's request, Leonardo also created one of the defining monuments of Renaissance art: an image of the Last Supper painted on the wall of the refectory (dining room) in the Monastery of Santa Maria delle Grazie in Milan (fig. **13–2**; see also Introduction, fig. 21).

THE VITRUVIAN MAN

Artists throughout history have turned to geometric shapes and mathematical proportions to seek the ideal representation of the human form. Leonardo, and before him the first-century BCE Roman architect and engineer (Marcus) Vitruvius (Pollio), equated the ideal man with both circle and square.

In his ten-volume *De architectura (On Architecture)*, Vitruvius wrote: "For if a man be placed flat on his back, with his hands and feet extended, and a pair of compasses centered at his navel, the fingers and toes of his two hands and feet will touch the circumference of a circle described therefrom. And just as the human body yields a circular outline, so too a square figure may be found from it. For if we measure the distance from the soles of the feet to the top of the head, and then apply that measure to the outstretched arms, the breadth will be found to be the same as the height" (Book III, Chapter 1, Section 2). Vitruvius determined that the ideal body should be eight heads high. Leonardo added his own observations—in the reversed writing he always used for his notebooks—when he created his well-known diagram for the ideal male figure, called the *Vitruvian Man*.

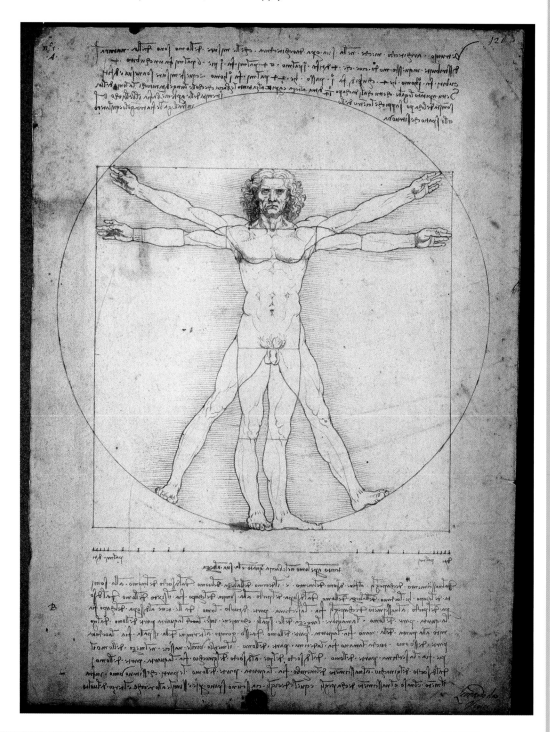

Leonardo da Vinci.
Vitruvian Man c. 1490. Ink,
approx. 13 ½ × 9 ⅝″
(34.3 × 24.5 cm). Galleria
dell'Accademia, Venice

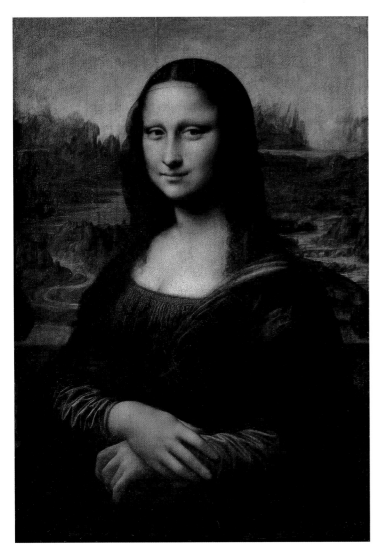

13–3 Leonardo da Vinci. *Mona Lisa.* c. 1503–1506. Oil on panel, 30 ¼″ × 21″ (76.8 × 53.3 cm). Musée du Louvre, Paris

On one level, Leonardo painted a narrative, showing the moment when Jesus tells his companions that one of them will betray him. They react with shock, disbelief, and horror, presenting a study of human emotions. On another level, the *Last Supper* is replete with timeless symbolism. The disciples are arranged in four groups of three around the stable, pyramidal form of Jesus, who sits calmly in the middle of the general commotion. Leonardo placed Judas in the first triad to the left of Jesus, along with the young John the Evangelist and the elderly Peter. Judas, Peter, and John were each to play essential roles in Jesus's mission: Judas, to set in motion the events leading to the Crucifixion; Peter, to lead the Church after Jesus's death; and John, the visionary, to foretell the Second Coming of Christ and the Last Judgment in the Apocalypse. By arranging the disciples and architectural elements in four groups of three, Leonardo referred to traditional Christian numerical symbolism involving the numbers three (divine) and four (earthly), the three persons of the Trinity, the three Theological Virtues, the four Cardinal Virtues, the four elements (earth, air, fire, and water), and earthly time plus space in the four seasons and four directions.

The composition enhances the meaning of the painting. The scene is set in a stagelike space defined by the horizontals of table and coffered ceiling; the one-point linear perspective is emphasized by the tapestries on the side walls. The orthogonals converge on the head of Jesus behind which three windows (another group of three) form a natural halo of light. Leonardo modeled the figures in a rich **chiaroscuro** (light and shadow), which has been obscured by the deterioration of the experimental medium, but is more visible after a recent restoration.

In 1498, Leonardo left Milan and resettled in Florence. There he painted his renowned portrait *Mona Lisa* (fig. **13–3**), between about 1503 and 1506. The subject may have been 24-year-old Lisa Gherardini del Giocondo, the wife of a prominent Florentine merchant. (Mona was a respectful title, madonna). The solid, pyramidal form of her half-length figure was once framed by columns (lost when thieves cut the painting from its frame). It is silhouetted against distant mountains, whose desolate grandeur reinforces the mysterious atmosphere of the painting. To achieve this atmosphere and to help unify his compositions, Leonardo partly covered his paintings with a thin, lightly tinted varnish, which helped create the effect of an overall smoky haze, or **sfumato**. Because early evening light is likely to produce a similar effect naturally, he considered dusk the finest time of day, and recommended that painters set up their studios in a courtyard with black walls and a linen sheet stretched overhead to reproduce the effects of twilight.

Mona Lisa's facial expression has been called "enigmatic" because her gentle smile is not accompanied by the warmth one would expect to see in her eyes. The contemporary fashion for plucked eyebrows and a shaved hairline to increase the height of the forehead adds to her arresting appearance. Perhaps most unsettling is the bold way her gaze has shifted toward the right to look straight out at the viewer. The implied challenge of her direct stare, contrasting with her apparent serenity, has made the *Mona Lisa* one of the most studied and written about, and best-known, paintings in the history of art.

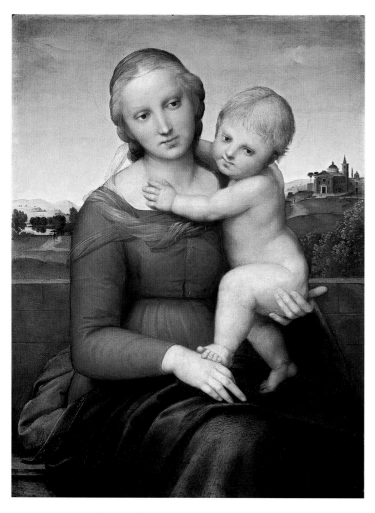

13–4 Raphael. *The Small Cowper Madonna.* c. 1505. Oil on panel, 23 3/8" × 17 3/8" (59.4 × 44.1 cm). National Gallery of Art, Washington, D.C.

Leonardo returned to Milan in 1508 and lived there until 1513. He also lived for a time in the Vatican at the invitation of Pope Leo X, but there is no evidence that he produced any works of art during his stay. In 1516, he accepted the French king Francis I's invitation to relocate to France as an adviser on architecture. He lived there until his death in 1519 (see page 366).

In 1504—at just about the time that Leonardo was working on the *Mona Lisa*—Raphael arrived in Florence. He had come from his native Urbino after studying in Perugia with the leading artist of that city, Perugino. Raphael soon achieved success in Florence. His paintings of the Virgin and Child, such as *The Small Cowper Madonna* (named for a modern owner) of about 1505 (fig. **13–4**), brought him fame and attracted patrons. The monumental, pyramidal form of the Virgin and Child, the naturalistic draperies, and the rich, concentrated colors show that Raphael must have studied the work of Leonardo. However, the clear, even light that softly but solidly models the figures contrasts with the *sfumato* favored by Leonardo. *The Small Cowper Madonna* recalls instead the atmospheric clarity and lovely colors of Perugino's paintings (see page 328). In the distance on a hilltop, Raphael has painted a scene he knew well from his childhood, the domed Church of San Bernardino, two miles outside Urbino. The church

contains the tombs of the dukes of Urbino, Federico and Guidobaldo da Montefeltro, and their wives (see fig. 12–29). Bramante, who worked in Urbino before settling in Rome in 1499, may have designed the church (see "Saint Peter's Basilica," page 352).

Raphael's greatest achievements came during a dozen years spent in Rome, where he arrived around 1509. As the fortunes of the ruling families of Florence and Milan fluctuated sharply because of political struggles, Rome rose to become the most active Italian artistic and intellectual center. Pope Julius II began a campaign to rebuild Rome and the Vatican, and he put Raphael to work almost immediately decorating the papal apartments. In the Pope's library, Raphael painted the four branches of knowledge as conceived in the sixteenth century: theology (the *Disputa*, depicting the discussions concerning the true presence of Christ in the Host Communion bread), philosophy (the *School of Athens*), poetry and the arts (*Parnassus,* home of the Muses), and law, or jurisprudence (the *Cardinal Virtues under Justice*).

Raphael's most outstanding achievement in these rooms was the *School of Athens* (fig. **13–5**), painted during 1510–1511. The painting seems to summarize the ideals of the Renaissance papacy in its grand conception of harmoniously arranged forms and rational space, as well as the calm dignity of the figures.

The shape of the walls and vault of the room itself inspired the composition of the paintings. The viewer gazes at the scene through an illusionistic arch. The classical Greek philosophers Plato and Aristotle command center stage. At the left, Plato gestures toward the heavens as the ultimate source of his philosophy, while Aristotle, his outstretched hand palm down, seems to emphasize the importance of gathering empirical knowledge from observing the natural world. Looking down from niches in the walls are Minerva (on the right), the Roman goddess of wisdom, and Apollo (holding a lyre), the Greek and Roman god of sun, rationality, poetry, and music. Around Plato and Aristotle are mathematicians, naturalists, astronomers, geographers, and other philosophers. For all their serene idealism, the figures within the paintings break classical conventions in their foreshortened **contrapposto** poses. The scene, flooded with light from a single source, takes place in an immense barrel-vaulted interior possibly inspired by the new design for Saint Peter's, which was being rebuilt on a plan by the architect Bramante. The grandeur of the building is matched by the monumental dignity of the philosophers themselves and the sweeping arcs of the composition, which dramatically unify the composition.

Like many artists, Raphael had mastered several arts. In 1515–1516 he provided cartoons (paintings to serve as models for the proposed finished works) on themes from the Acts of the Apostles to be made into tapestries to cover the wall below the fifteenth-century wall paintings of the Sistine Chapel (see fig. 13–9). For the production of tapestries, which were woven in workshops in France and Flanders and were extremely expensive, the artist made charcoal drawings, then painted over them with glue-based colors for the weavers to match. The first tapestry in Raphael's series was the *Miraculous Draft of Fishes on the Sea of Galilee* (Matthew 4:18-22) (fig. **13–6**). The fisherman Simon, whom Christ called to be his first apostle, Peter, became the cornerstone on which the papal claims to authority rested. Andrew, James, and John would also

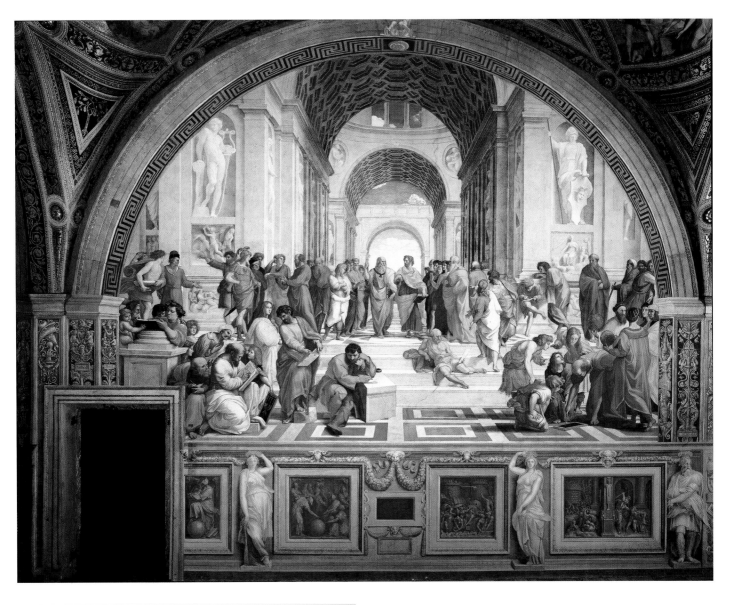

13–5 Raphael. *School of Athens,* Stanza della Segnatura, Vatican, Rome. 1510–1511. Fresco, 19′ × 27′ (5.79 × 8.24 m)

Raphael gave many of the figures in his imaginary gathering of philosophers the features of his friends and colleagues. Plato, standing immediately to the left of the central axis and pointing to the sky, was said to have been modeled after Leonardo da Vinci; Euclid, shown inscribing a slate with a compass at the lower right, was a portrait of Raphael's friend, the architect Donato Bramante. Michelangelo, who was at work on the Sistine Ceiling only steps away from the stanza *(room) where Raphael was painting his fresco, is shown as the solitary figure at the lower left center, leaning on a block of marble and sketching, in a pose reminiscent of the figures of sibyls and prophets on his great ceiling. Raphael's own features are represented on the second figure from the front group at the far right, as the face of a young man listening to a discourse by the astronomer Ptolemy.*

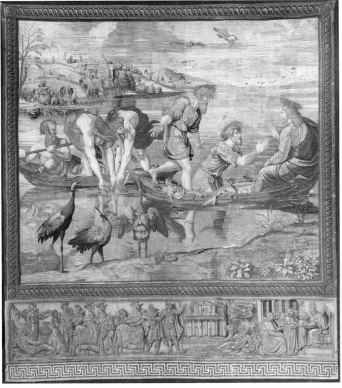

13–6 Shop of Pieter van Aelst, Brussels, after cartoons by Raphael and assistants. *Miraculous Draft of Fishes,* from the nine-piece set, the Acts of the Apostles series; lower border, two incidents from the life of Giovanni de' Medici, later Pope Leo X. 1515–1516. Woven 1517, installed 1519 in the Sistine Chapel. Wool and silk with silver-gilt wrapped threads, 16′1″ × 21′ (590 × 640 cm). Musei Vaticani, Pinacoteca, Rome

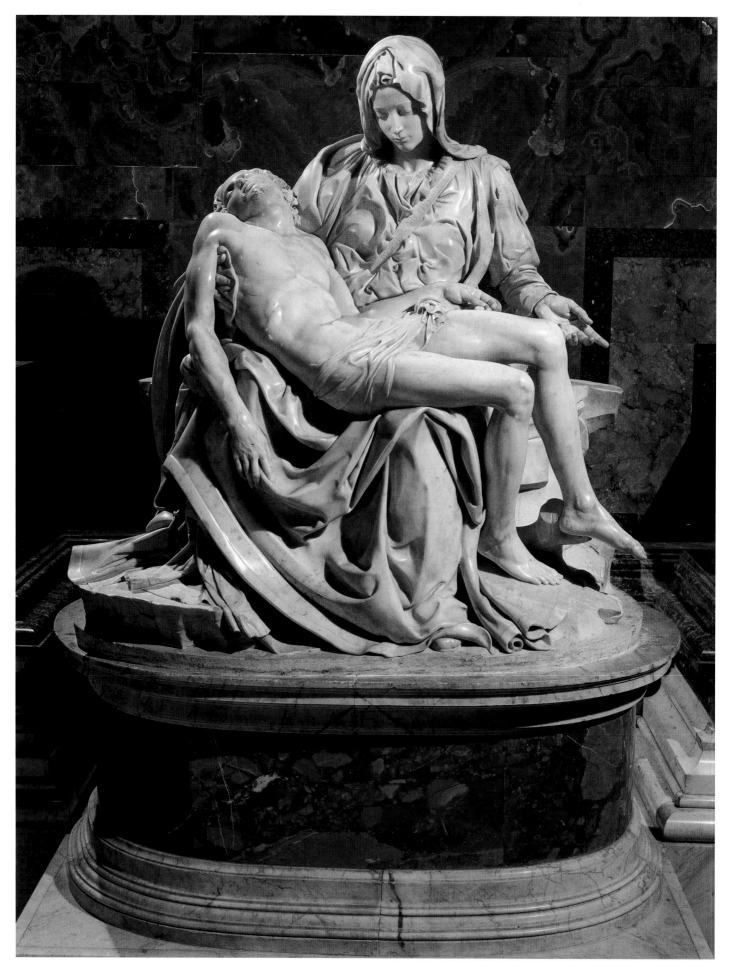

13–7 Michelangelo. *Pietà,* from Old Saint Peter's. c. 1500. Marble, height 5′8 1/2″ (1.74 m). Saint Peter's, Vatican, Rome

become apostles. Their huge straining figures remind us that Raphael felt himself in clear competition with Michelangelo, whose Sistine ceiling had been completed only three years earlier.

The two boats establish a frieze-like composition. The panoramic landscape behind the fishermen includes a crowd on the shore and the city of Rome with its walls and churches. In the foreground the three cranes are not a simple pictorial device; in the sixteenth century, they symbolized the ever-alert and watchful pope, a timely addition because when the tapestries were first displayed in the Sistine Chapel on December 26, 1519, papal authority was already being challenged by reformers including Martin Luther.

Raphael died after a brief illness in 1520. After a state funeral, he was buried in the ancient Roman Pantheon, originally a classical temple to the gods of Rome, but then a Christian church dedicated to the Virgin Mary (see fig. 6–22). In the view of many art historians, Raphael's death marks the end of the classical phase of the High Renaissance.

Michelangelo Buonarroti (1475–1564), like Raphael, spent part of his early career in Florence and later worked for Pope Julius II in Rome. Born in the Tuscan town of Caprese, Michelangelo grew up in Florence and was apprenticed at age 13 to the painter Domenico Ghirlandaio. He soon joined the household of Lorenzo de' Medici, the Magnificent, where he studied sculpture with Bertoldo di Giovanni, a pupil of Donatello. Bertoldo worked primarily in bronze, and Michelangelo later claimed that he had taught himself to carve marble by studying the Medici collection of classical statues.

Michelangelo's major early work, at the turn of the century, was a pietà, commissioned by a French cardinal and installed as a tomb monument in Old Saint Peter's in the Vatican (fig. 13–7). Pietàs—works in which the Virgin supports and mourns the dead Jesus—had long been popular in Northern Europe but were rare in Italian art at the time. Italians generally preferred the Lamentation, which includes all of Christ's followers. Michelangelo's Virgin is a very young, sweet-faced woman of heroic stature holding the smaller, smoothly modeled body of her grown son. The artist's compelling vision of beauty is meant to be seen up close at the statue's own level, so that the viewer can look into Jesus's face. Michelangelo carved his name prominently on the strap across the Virgin's breast. The 25-year-old artist is said to have done this after the statue was finished, stealing into the church at night to provide the answer to the many questions about its creator.

Michelangelo traveled to the marble quarries at Carrara in central Italy to select the block from which to make this large work, a practice that he was to follow for nearly all his sculpture. The choice of the stone was important to him because he envisioned his sculpture as already existing within the marble and needing only his tools to "set it free."

In 1501, Michelangelo accepted a commission for a statue of the biblical hero David (fig. 13–8) for an exterior buttress of the Florence Cathedral. When it was finished in 1504, the David was so admired that the Florentine city council placed it in the prin-

cipal city square, next to the Palazzo della Signoria, the building housing the city's government. Although the statue embodies the antique ideal of the athletic, nude male, the emotional power of the facial expression and concentrated gaze is new. Unlike Donatello's bronze David (see fig. 12–20), this is not a triumphant hero with the head of the giant Goliath under his feet. Slingshot over his shoulder and a rock in his right hand, Michelangelo's David frowns and stares into space, seemingly preparing himself psychologically for the danger ahead. No match for his opponent in experience, weaponry, or physical strength, David represents the power of right over might. He was a perfect emblematic figure for the Florentines, who twice drove out the powerful Medici and reinstituted short-lived republics in the early years of the sixteenth century.

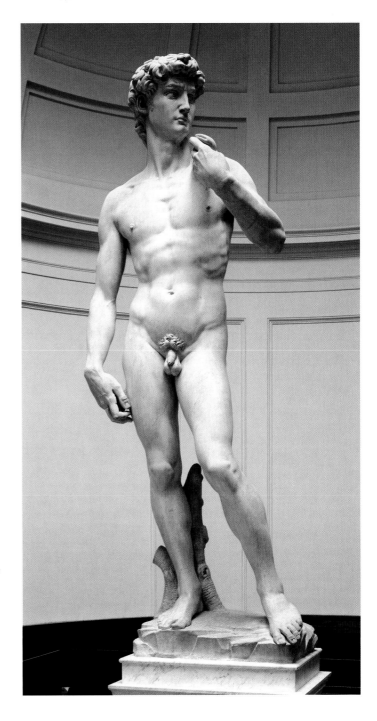

13–8 Michelangelo. *David.* 1501–1504. Marble, height 17′ (5.18 m). Galleria dell'Accademia, Florence

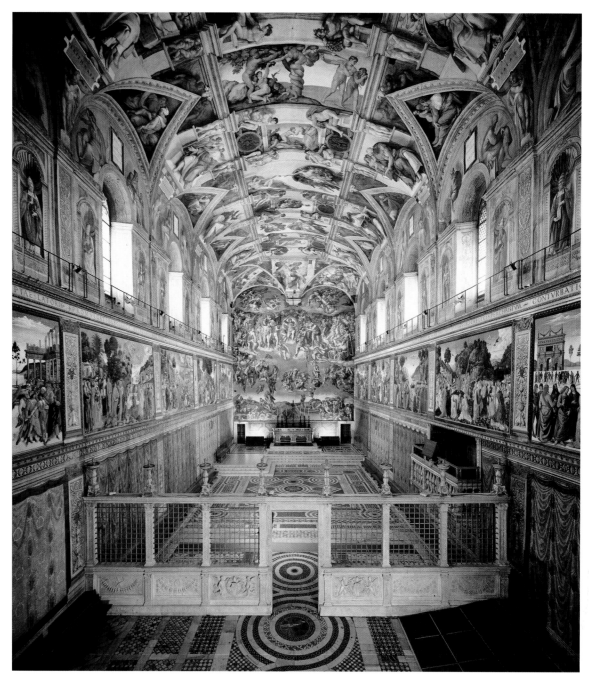

13–9 Interior, Sistine Chapel, Vatican, Rome. Built 1475–1481. Ceiling painted 1508–1512; wall behind altar painted 1536–1541

Named after its builder, Pope Sixtus (Sisto) IV, the chapel is slightly more than 130 feet long and about 43¹/₂ feet wide, approximately the same measurements recorded in the Old Testament for the Temple of Solomon. The floor mosaic was recut from stones used in the floor of an earlier papal chapel. The plain walls were painted in fresco between 1481 and 1483 with scenes from the life of Moses and the life of Christ by Perugino, Botticelli, Ghirlandaio, and others. Below these are trompe l'oeil painted draperies, where Raphael's tapestries illustrating the Acts of the Apostles once hung. Michelangelo's famous ceiling frescoes begin with the lunette scenes above the windows (see fig. 13–10). On the end above the altar is his Last Judgment, *finished in 1541 (see fig. 13–11). The left side of Perugino's painting, page 328, can be seen at the right side of the photograph in the series on the life of Christ.*

Michelangelo had a contract to make other statues for the cathedral, but in 1505 Pope Julius II arranged for him to come to Rome. The sculptor's first undertaking there was the pope's future tomb, but Julius set this commission aside in 1506 and ordered Michelangelo to redecorate the ceiling of his private chapel in the Vatican, the Sistine Chapel (fig. **13–9**). Julius's initial directions for the ceiling specified a simple architectural decoration; later he added the Twelve Apostles. When Michelangelo objected to the limitations of Julius's plan, the pope told him to paint whatever he liked. This Michelangelo presumably did, although he may have had advice from a theologian.

THE SISTINE CEILING RESTORATION

The cleaning of frescoes on the walls of the Sistine Chapel, done in the 1960s and 1970s, was so successful that in 1980 a single lunette from Michelangelo's ceiling decoration was cleaned as a test. Underneath layers of soot and dust was found color so brilliant and so different from the long-accepted dusky appearance of the ceiling that conservators summoned their courage and proposed a major restoration of the entire ceiling. The work was completed in the winter of 1989, and

the *Last Judgment* over the altar was completed in the spring of 1994.

Although the restorers proceeded with great caution and frequently consulted with other experts in the field, the cleaning created serious controversy. The greatest fear was that the work was moving ahead too rapidly for absolute safety. Another concern was that the ceiling's final appearance might not resemble its original state. Some scholars, convinced that Michelangelo had reworked the sur-

face of the fresco after it had dried to tone down the colors, feared that cleaning would remove those finishing touches. In the end, the breathtaking colors that the cleaning revealed forced scholars to thoroughly revise their understanding of Michelangelo's art and the development of sixteenth-century Italian painting. We will never know for certain if some subtleties were lost in the cleaning, and only time will tell if the restoration prolonged the life of Michelangelo's great work.

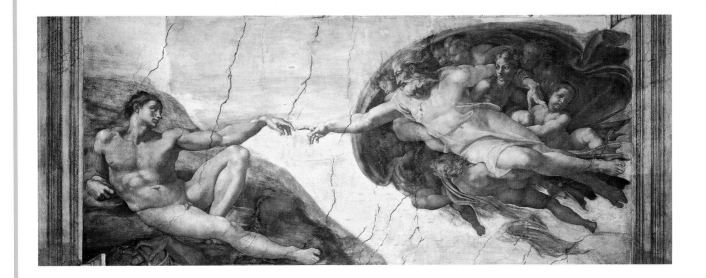

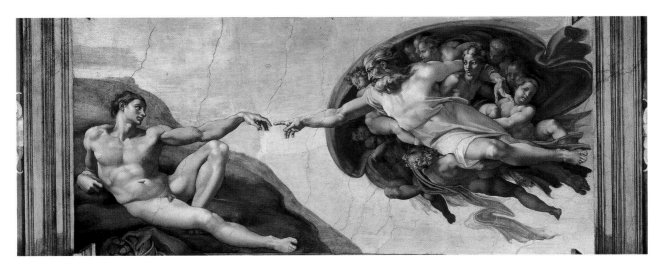

Michelangelo. *Creation of Adam,* the Sistine Chapel, the Vatican, Rome. Above: the fresco before cleaning; below: as it appears today.

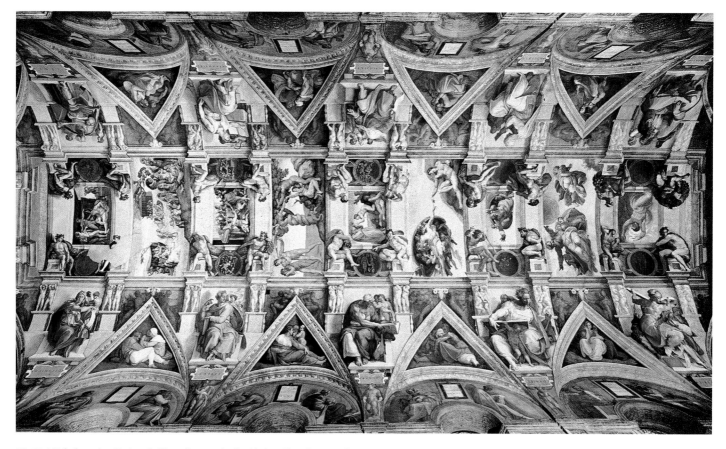

13–10 Michelangelo. *Sistine Ceiling,* frescoes in the Sistine Chapel. Top to bottom: Expulsion (center);
Creation of Eve with Ezekiel (left) and Cumaean Sibyl (right); Creation of Adam; God Gathering the Waters,
with Persian Sibyl (left) and Daniel (right); and God Creating the Sun, Moon, and Planets. 1508-1512.
The spandrels and lunettes depict the ancestors of Jesus.

Michelangelo's design for the Sistine Ceiling consists of an underlying architectural structure, filled with individual figures and narrative scenes. In this fictive imaginary architecture, pilasters seem to support a cornice and ribs of a vault are flattened. This structure is all an illusion, meant to be seen from afar (fig. **13–10**). Figures of nude young men *(ignudi)* sit in a variety of poses on pedestals above the fictive cornice. Rising behind the youths, the equally fictive ribs of the vault divide the ceiling into nine compartments. The scenes in these compartments include depictions of the Creation of Adam and Eve, their disobedience and expulsion from Paradise, and the story of Noah and the Flood, as told in Genesis. Eight triangular compartments over the windows contain paintings of the ancestors of Jesus. Flanking these and below the cornice are ten large seated figures of Old Testament prophets and classical sibyls (female prophets), who were believed to have foretold Jesus's birth.

Near the ceiling's center is the *Creation of Adam,* in which Michelangelo depicts the moment when God charges the languorous Adam with the spark of life. As if to echo the biblical text, Adam's heroic body, outstretched arm, and profile almost mirror those of God, in whose image he has been created. Directly below Adam, one of the *ignudi* grasps a bundle of oak leaves and giant acorns, symbols that refer to Julius's family name (della Rovere, or "of the oak"), and possibly also to a passage in the Old Testament prophecy of Isaiah (61:3): "They will be called oaks of justice, planted by the Lord to show his glory."

A quarter of a century after finishing the ceiling, Michelangelo again went to work in the Sistine Chapel, this time on the *Last Judgment,* painted some time between 1536 and 1541 on the large end wall behind the altar (fig. **13–11**). Michelangelo, now entering his sixties, had complained of feeling old for years, yet he accepted this important and demanding task, which took him two years to finish. He painted a writhing swarm of resurrected humanity, with the saved dragged from their graves and pushed up into a vortex of figures around Christ. Despite the efforts of several saints to save them at the last minute, the damned plunge toward hell on the right. To the right of Christ's feet is Saint Bartholomew, who in legend was martyred by being skinned alive, holding his flayed

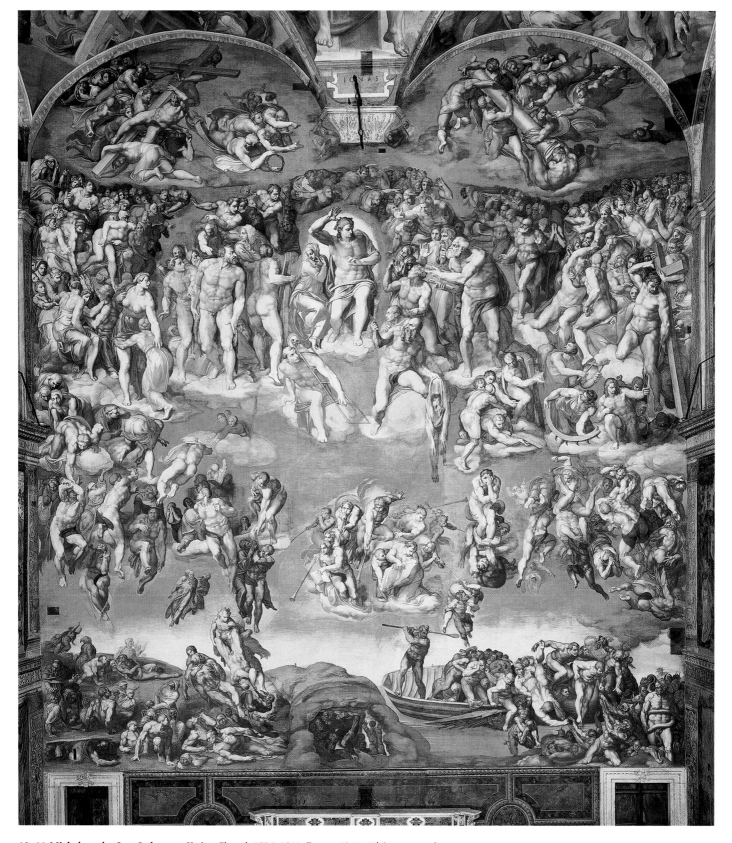

13–11 Michelangelo. *Last Judgment,* Sistine Chapel, 1536–1541. Fresco, 48 × 44′ (encompassing approx. 190 square meters or 2,100 square feet of surface)

Dark, rectangular patches left by the restorers (visible, for example, in the upper left and right corners) contrast with the vibrant colors of the chapel's frescoes. These dark areas show just how dirty the wall had become over the centuries before its recent cleaning.

ELEMENTS OF **Architecture**

Saint Peter's Basilica

The original church of Saint Peter's was built in the fourth century CE by Constantine, the first Christian Roman emperor, to mark the grave of the apostle Peter, the first bishop of Rome and therefore the first pope. Constantine's architect erected a basilica with a nave, flanking side aisles set off by colonnades, and an apse. To allow large numbers of clergy and pilgrims to approach the shrine, they also added a transept. The rest of the church was, in effect, a covered cemetery, carpeted with the tombs of believers who wanted to be buried near the grave of the apostle. In front of the church was a walled atrium. When it was built, Constantine's basilica was one of the largest buildings in the world [interior length 368 feet (112.17 m); width 190 feet, (57.91 m)], and for more than a thousand years it was the most important pilgrimage site in Europe.

That anyone, even a pope, would pull down such a venerated building is an indication of the extraordinary sense of assurance of the age—and of Pope Julius II himself. The deaths of both the pope and the architect Bramante in 1513–1514 put a temporary halt to the project. Successive plans by Raphael and others changed the Greek-cross plan to a Latin-cross plan in order to provide the church with a full-length nave. However,

when Michelangelo was appointed architect in 1546, he returned to the Greek-cross plan and simplified Bramante's design to create a single, unified space. The dome was finally completed (1588–1590) some years after Michelangelo's death by Giacomo della Porta, who retained Michelangelo's basic design but gave the dome a taller and slimmer profile and changed the shape of its openings.

By the early seventeenth century, the need for the basilica had changed. During the Counter-Reformation, the Church emphasized congregational worship, so more space was needed for people and processions. Moreover, it was felt that the new church should more closely resemble Old Saint Peter's and should extend over roughly the same area, including the ground covered by the original atrium. In 1606, Pope Paul V commissioned the architect Carlo Maderno to change Michelangelo's Greek-cross plan back once again to a Latin-cross plan. Maderno extended the nave to its final length of slightly more than 636 feet and added a Baroque façade (see fig. 14–3), thus completing Saint Peter's as it is today. Later in the seventeenth century, the sculptor and architect Gianlorenzo Bernini monumentalized the square in front of the basilica by surrounding it with a great colonnade.

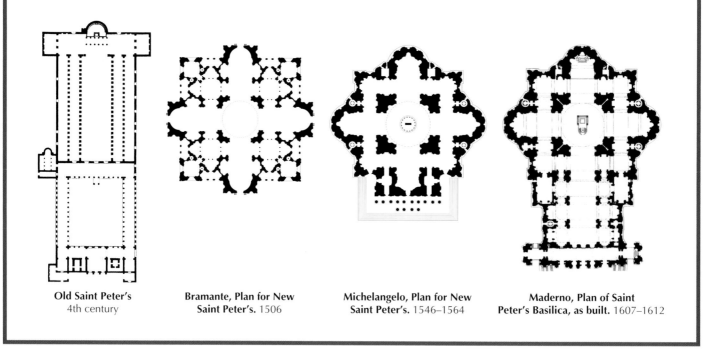

| Old Saint Peter's | Bramante, Plan for New | Michelangelo, Plan for New | Maderno, Plan of Saint |
| 4th century | Saint Peter's. 1506 | Saint Peter's. 1546–1564 | Peter's Basilica, as built. 1607–1612 |

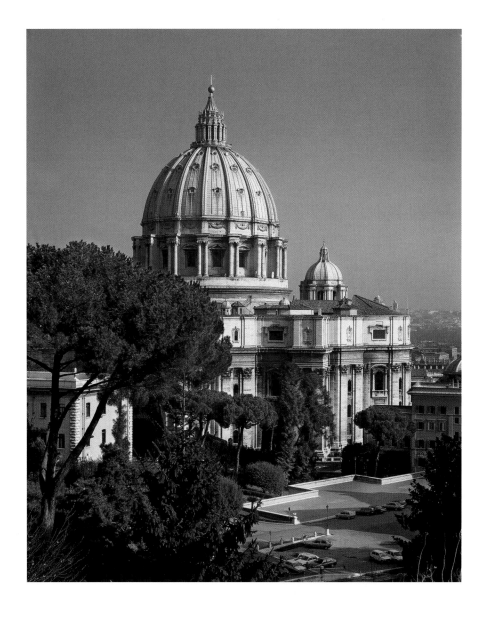

13–12 Michelangelo. Saint Peter's Basilica, Vatican, Rome. c. 1546–1564 (dome completed 1590 by Giacomo della Porta). View from the southwest

skin, the distorted face of which is painted with Michelangelo's own features. On the lowest level of the mural, directly above the altar, is the gaping, fiery mouth of Hell, toward which the demonic boatman Charon propels his craft on the River Styx, which encircles the underworld. The painting is a grim and constant reminder to the celebrants of the Mass—the pope and his cardinals—that ultimately they will be judged for their deeds.

Besides being a sculptor and painter, Michelangelo was also an architect of genius. After the completion of the *Last Judgment*, the artist took on his most important building commission: the rebuilding of Saint Peter's in Rome. The project had begun in 1506, when Pope Julius II made the astonishing decision to demolish the venerable but crumbling Constantinian basilica over Saint Peter's tomb (see fig. 7–6). To design and build the magnificent new church, the pope appointed the architect Donato Bramante (1443/4–1514), who, like Raphael, came from Urbino. Bramante envisioned the new Saint Peter's as a central-plan building, a Greek cross (a cross with four arms of equal length) crowned with an enormous dome (see "Saint Peter's Basilica," opposite). The design was intended to continue the

ancient Roman tradition of domed temples and round tombs called *martyria*; in Renaissance thinking, the central plan and dome also symbolized the perfection of God.

Ultimately, Michelangelo transformed the building into a central-plan church of magnificent proportions and superhuman scale (fig. **13–12**). Seventeenth-century additions and renovations dramatically changed the original plan of the church and the appearance of its interior (see fig. 14–2). However, Michelangelo's Saint Peter's can still be seen in the contrasting forms of the flat and angled walls and the three **hemicycles** (semicircular structures). Within this arrangement, the colossal pilasters (engaged columnar elements extending through two or more stories), **blind windows** (having no openings), and niches form the sanctuary of the church. How Michelangelo would have built the great dome is not known; most scholars believe that he would have made it hemispherical. The dome that was actually erected retains Michelangelo's basic design; it is a segmented dome with regularly spaced ribs, resting on a high drum with pedimented windows between paired columns, and surmounted by a tall lantern shaped like a circular temple.

Over the course of his lengthy career, Michelangelo continued to explore his art's expressive potential. In his late work, he discovered new stylistic directions that would inspire succeeding generations of artists. Michelangelo was an intense man who believed that his art was divinely inspired and who alternated between periods of depression and frenzied activity. He was difficult and often arrogant, yet he was devoted to his friends and helpful to young artists. Later in life, he became deeply absorbed in religion and dedicated himself chiefly to religious works. In his late work, Michelangelo subverted Renaissance ideals of human perfectibility and denied his own youthful idealism, uncovering new forms that mirrored the tensions in Europe during the second half of the sixteenth century.

Venice and the Veneto

In the last quarter of the fifteenth century, Venice emerged as a major artistic center. Venetian painters embraced the oil medium earlier than most other Italian artists, working with oil on both panel and canvas from the late 1470s on where walls crack and mildew. The use of oil glazes permitted the brilliant color and lighting effect desired by Venice's most famous sixteenth-century painters: Bellini, Titian, Tintoretto, and Veronese.

Giovanni Bellini (c. 1430–1516), amazed and attracted patrons with his artistic virtuosity for almost 60 years. Giovanni's career spanned the second half of the fifteenth century, but he produced many of his greatest paintings in the early years of the sixteenth, when his work matured into a grand, simplified, idealized style. In the San Zaccaria Altarpiece the Virgin and Child, four Saints, and an angelic musician appear in an ambiguous spatial setting—part church with a glittering gold mosaic semi-dome; part loggia open to the natural world of trees and cloudy sky (fig. 13–13). The architecture of the altarpiece frame continues in the arches and pilasters of the painting. Light streams in from the left, the north side in a church, counter to the laws of nature. The figures bow their heads, reading and meditating; a single line of music breaks the stillness.

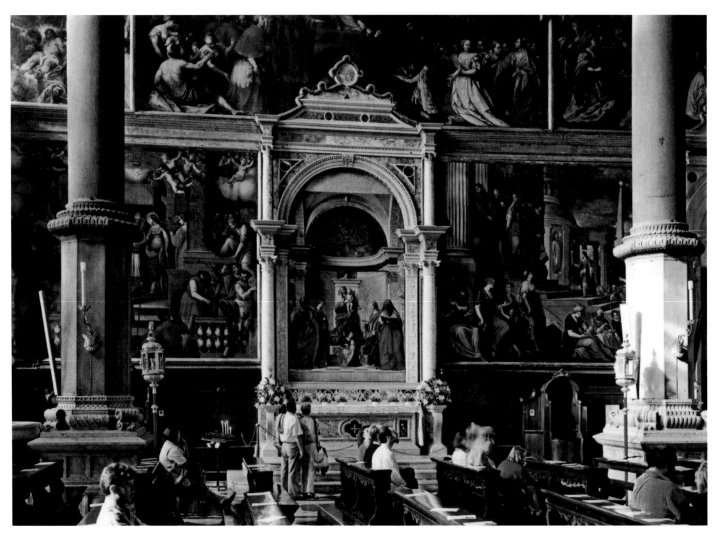

13–13 Giovanni Bellini, *The Virgin and Child Enthroned with Saints,* 1505. Altarpiece in the Church of San Zaccaria, as photographed, in context, by Thomas Struth in his monumental photograph, San Zaccaria, Venice, 1995. The painting: oil on panel, transferred to canvas. Photograph: 5′10″ × 7′6″

The church has become a museum filled with people who have come to study and admire the painting rather than worship at the altar.

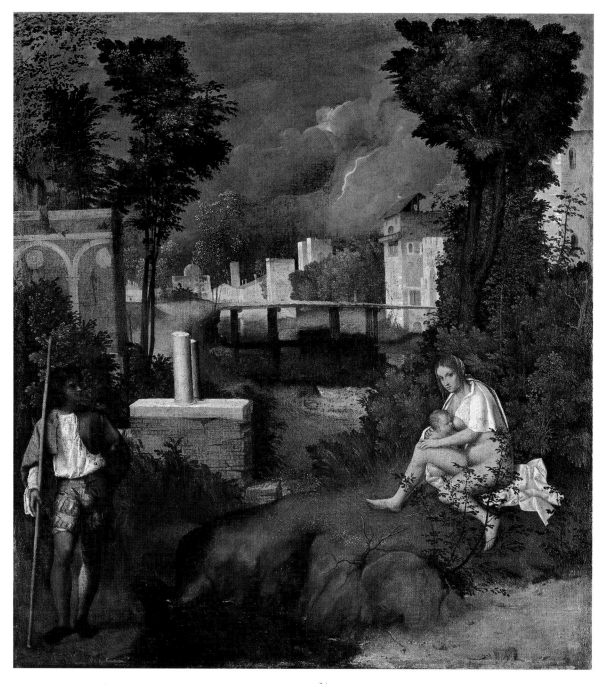

13–14 Giorgione. *The Tempest.* 1505–1510. Oil on canvas, 31″ × 28³⁄₄″ (79.4 × 73 cm). Galleria dell'Accademia, Venice

Art historians have given a special name, *sacra conversazione* ("holy conversation"), to this type of composition showing saints, angels, and sometimes even the painting's donors in the same pictorial space with the enthroned Virgin and Child. Despite the name, no conversation or other interaction among the figures takes place in a literal sense. Instead, the individuals portrayed are joined in a mystical and eternal communion occurring outside of time, in which the viewer is invited to share.

Another Venetian artist of the time, Giorgio da Castelfranco, called Giorgione (c. 1477–1510), created portraits, altarpieces, and frescoes. Giorgione also made a few paintings that show figures placed in mysterious, intensely observed landscapes. The meaning of these works is uncertain, and scholars have theorized that Giorgione approached his work as many modern-day artists do, by selecting subjects in response to personal, private impulses, which he then expressed through his paintings.

Giorgione's career was brief—he died from the plague—and most scholars accept only four or five paintings as entirely by his hand. Nevertheless, his importance to Venetian painting is critical, as he introduced enigmatic pastoral themes, sensuous nude figures, and, above all, an appreciation of nature in landscape painting, which played an increasingly important role in sixteenth-century painting. Giorgione's early life and training are undocumented, but his work suggests that he studied with Giovanni Bellini. Perhaps Leonardo's subtle lighting system and mysterious, intensely observed landscapes also inspired him.

Giorgione's most famous work, called today *The Tempest* (fig. **13–14**), was painted shortly before his death. Simply trying to understand what is happening in the picture piques our interest. At the right, a woman is seated on the ground, nude except for the end of a long white cloth thrown over her shoulders. Her nudity seems maternal rather than erotic as she nurses the baby at her side. Across the dark, rock-edged spring stands a man wearing the uniform of a German mercenary soldier. His head is turned toward the woman, but he appears to have paused for a moment before continuing to turn toward the viewer. X-rays of the painting show that Giorgione altered his composition while he was still at work on it—the woman on the right was originally balanced by another nude woman on the left. The spring between the figures feeds a lake surrounded by substantial houses, and in the far distance a bolt of lightning splits the darkening sky. Indeed, the artist's attention seems focused on the landscape and the unruly elements of nature rather than on the figures.

In 1507, Giorgione took on a new assistant, Tiziano Vecellio, who is better known to us today as Titian (c. 1488–1576). The painting called *Pastoral Concert* (fig. **13–15**) is dated to a few years after this time. Perhaps Giorgione began the painting and Titian

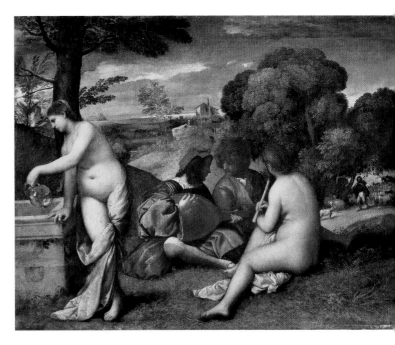

13–15 Titian (formerly attributed to Giorgione). *Pastoral Concert.*
c. 1509–1510. Oil on canvas, 43 1/4″ × 54 3/8″ (109.9 × 132.1 cm).
Musée du Louvre, Paris

WOMEN PATRONS OF THE ARTS

I n the sixteenth century, many wealthy women—both from the aristocracy and from the merchant class—were enthusiastic patrons of the arts. Two English queens, the Tudor half-sisters Mary I and Elizabeth I, glorified their reigns with the aid of court artists, as did most sovereigns of the period. And the Habsburg princesses Margaret of Austria and Mary of Hungary presided over brilliant Humanist courts when they were regents. But perhaps the Renaissance's greatest woman patron of the arts was Isabella d'Esté, Marchesa of Mantua, (1474–1539), who gathered painters, musicians, composers, writers, and literary scholars around her. Married to Francesco II Gonzaga at age 15, she had great beauty, great wealth, and a brilliant mind that made her a successful diplomat and administrator. A true Renaissance woman, her motto was the epitome of rational thinking: "Neither Hope nor Fear." An avid reader and collector of manuscripts and books, she sponsored an edition of Virgil while still in her twenties. She also collected ancient art and objects, as well as works by contemporary Italian artists such as Botticelli, Mantegna, Perugino, Correggio, and Titian. Her *grotto*, or cave, as she called her study in the Mantuan palace, was a veritable museum for her collections. The walls above the storage and display cabinets were painted in fresco by Mantegna, and the carved-wood ceiling was covered with mottoes and visual references to Isabella's impressive literary interests.

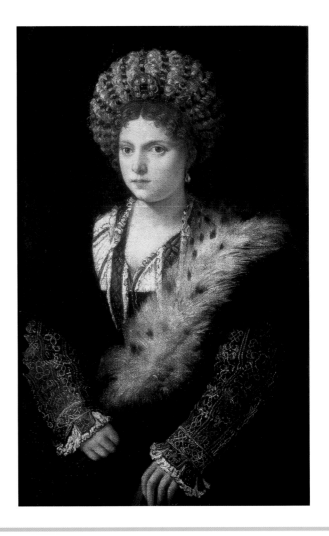

Titian. *Isabella d'Esté.* 1534–1536. Oil on canvas, 40 1/6″ × 25 1/4″
(102 × 64.1 cm). Kunsthistorisches Museum, Vienna

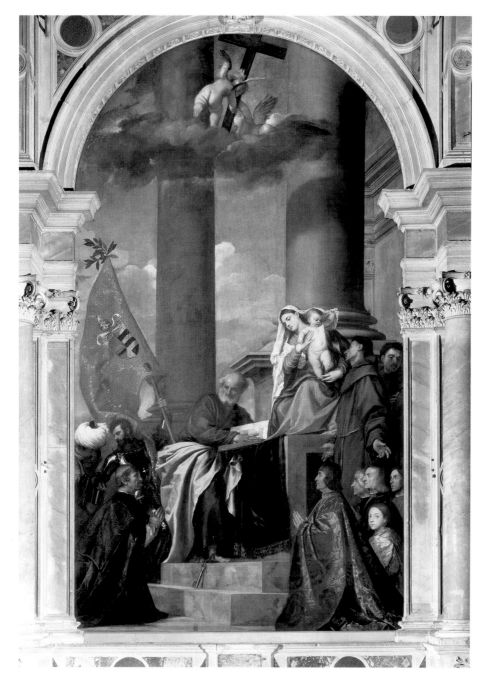

13–16 Titian. *Pesaro Madonna.* 1519–1526. Oil on canvas, 15′11″ × 8′10″ (4.85 × 2.69 m).
Pesaro Chapel, Santa Maria Gloriosa dei Frari, Venice

completed it after Giorgione's death, or Titian, inspired by Giorgione, may have painted it alone. In this puzzling picture, two young men, one richly dressed, the other a barefoot peasant, relax in a verdant landscape. They seem almost oblivious to the two nude women beside them and the shepherd tending his flock in the background. While the meaning of the juxtaposition of the nude and clothed figures is obscure, in a general sense this scene of an outdoor concert evokes the romantic ideal of a lost golden age, some misty time in remote antiquity when people led a carefree pastoral life, a theme much loved by classical and early Renaissance poets. The subject also permitted Titian to display his incomparable talent for painting female nudes. The flesh seems to glow with an incandescent light. The relaxed pose of the seated woman with the pipe contrasts with the complicated stance of the woman at the well. The tightly crossed legs and swiveling body of the standing woman are

impractical if her aim is to fill the glass pitcher but function admirably to focus the viewer's attention on the swelling forms of her stomach and thighs. The sensuous quality of this work suggests that Titian was as inspired by flesh-and-blood beauty as by any source from poetry or art.

The early life of Titian is obscure. He supposedly began an apprenticeship as a mosaicist and then studied painting under Gentile and Giovanni Bellini before working with Giorgione. In 1516, he became official painter to the Republic of Venice. Three years later, the powerful Pesaro family commissioned him to paint an altarpiece in Venice for the Franciscan Church of Santa Maria Gloriosa dei Frari—a Madonna and Child surrounded by members of the Pesaro family (fig. **13–16**). In the left foreground of the so-called *Pesaro Madonna,* Jacopo Pesaro, Bishop of Paphos, kneels directly in front of the Virgin. No doubt he

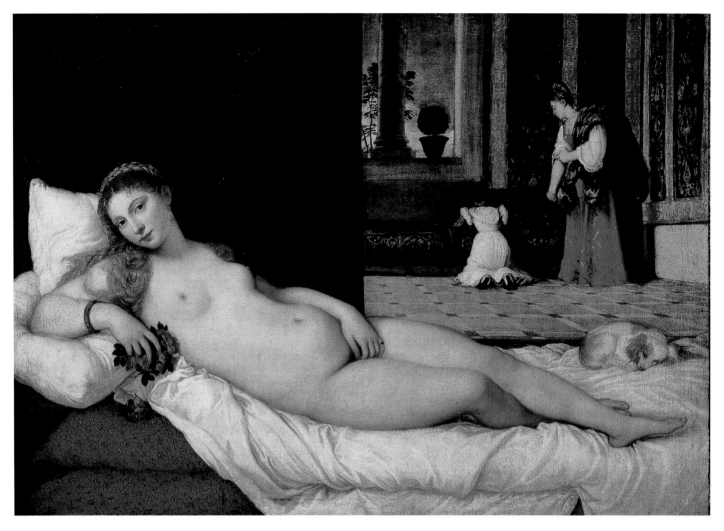

13–17 Titian. *Venus of Urbino.* c. 1538. Oil on canvas, 3′11″ × 5′5″ (1.19 × 1.65 m).
Galleria degli Uffizi, Florence

merited this honored spot because he had led a Venetian army in victory over the Turks in 1502. A turbaned Turkish captive stands behind him, and a knight holds a banner incorporating the arms of Jacopo Pesaro and Pope Alexander VI. Saint Peter, a monumental figure with the key of heaven at his feet, looks approvingly at Jacopo, while Saint Francis, at right, gazes upward at the Christ Child. The grandeur of the scene, with its massive columns and marble staircase, enhances the power and glory of the Pesaros. No photograph can convey the vibrancy of the paint surfaces, which Titian built up in layers of pure colors, chiefly red, white, yellow, and black. The powerful intersecting diagonals of the composition reach from Jacopo Pesaro to the Virgin (innovatively placed off-center), and from the family at the lower right to the tilting banner at the upper left.

Titian's skill as a portrait painter led the most powerful and distinguished people of the time, including Emperor Charles V, to seek him out. Titian skillfully represented his sitters as they wanted to be remembered, at their best. The great Humanist and patron of the arts, Isabella d'Esté, was 60 years old when Titian

painted her portrait, but he had studied an earlier portrait of the lady in order to capture her youthful beauty (see "Women Patrons of the Arts," page 356).

Paintings of nude reclining women became especially popular in sophisticated court circles, where male patrons could enjoy and appreciate the "Venuses" under the cloak of respectable classical mythology. Typical of such paintings is the Venus that Titian painted about 1538 for the duke of Urbino (fig. **13–17**). Here, a beautiful Venetian courtesan—whose gestures seem deliberately provocative—stretches languidly on her couch in a spacious palace, with white sheets and pillows setting off her glowing flesh and golden hair. She holds a bunch of roses, flowers associated with Venus. A spaniel, symbolic of fidelity, sleeping at her feet and maids assembling her clothing in the background lend a comfortable domestic air. The *Venus of Urbino* inspired artists, including Édouard Manet much later (see fig. 18–16).

Paolo Caliari (1528–1588), called Veronese after his hometown of Verona, carried on Titian's vision of the glories of both Venice and the Church. Like Titian, Veronese employed

According to the New Testament, Jesus revealed his impending death to his disciples during a *seder*, a meal celebrating the Jewish festival of Passover. This occasion, known to Christians as the Last Supper, and which, according to the Gospels, took place the evening before the Crucifixion, was a popular subject in sixteenth-century European art. But in 1573, when the painter Veronese delivered an enormous canvas of this subject to fulfill a commission (fig. **13–18**), the patron was shocked. Some people were offended by the grandiose pageantry of the scene. Others protested the impiety of surrounding Jesus with a man picking his teeth, scruffy dogs, and

foreign soldiers. As a result of the furor, Veronese was called before the Inquisition. There he justified himself first by asserting that the picture actually depicted not the Last Supper, but rather the Feast in the House of Simon, a small dinner held shortly before Jesus's final entry into Jerusalem. He also noted that artists customarily invent details in their pictures and that he had received a commission to paint the piece "as I saw fit." His argument fell on unsympathetic ears, and he was ordered to change the painting. Later he sidestepped the issue by changing its title to that of another banquet, one given by the tax collector Levi, whom Jesus had called to follow him (Luke 5:27–32).

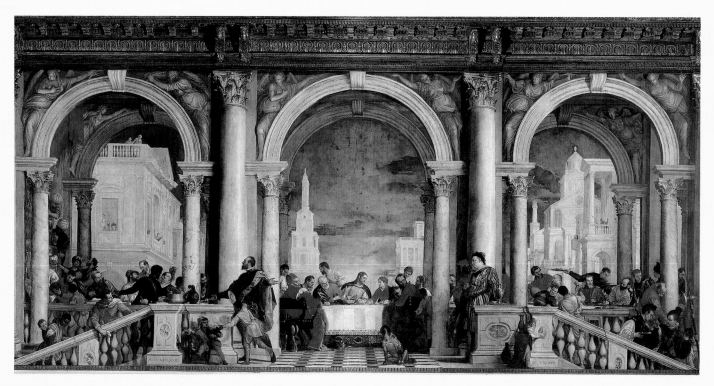

13–18 Veronese. *Feast in the House of Levi,* from the Monastery of Santi Giovanni e Paolo, Venice. 1573. Oil on canvas, 18'3″ × 42' (5.56 × 12.8 m). Galleria dell'Accademia, Venice

elaborate architectural settings and costumes for religious images, but he also added still lifes, anecdotal vignettes, and other details unconnected with the main subject that proved immensely appealing to Venetian patrons. One of Veronese's most famous works is the painting now called *Feast in the House of Levi* (fig. **13–18**), painted for the Dominican Monastery of Santi Giovanni e Paolo, Venice. At first glance the true subject of this painting seems to be

architecture, with the inhabitants of the space secondary to it. Beyond the enormous loggia, entered through colossal triumphal arches, an imaginary city of white marble gleams in the distance. The size of the canvas allowed Veronese to make his figures realistically proportional to the architectural setting without losing their substance. His painting *The Triumph of Venice* in the Ducale Palace of Venice (see Introduction, fig. 15) is equally glorious.

Jacopo Robusti (1518–1594), called Tintoretto ("little dyer") after his father's trade, carried Venetian Renaissance painting in another direction. He is said to have been an apprentice in Titian's shop, where he proclaimed as his goal the combination of his master's color with the drawing of Michelangelo. The speed with which Tintoretto drew and painted was the subject of comment in his own time and of legends thereafter. He may have seemed to paint so rapidly because he employed a large workshop, which included other members of his family. Of his eight children, four became artists. His oldest child, Marietta Robusti, worked with him as a portrait painter, and two or perhaps three of his sons also joined the shop. Another daughter, famous for her needlework, became a nun. Marietta, in spite of her fame and many commissions, stayed in her father's shop until she died, at the age of 30. So skillfully did she capture her father's style and technique that today art historians cannot be certain which paintings are hers.

Tintoretto often developed a composition by creating a small-scale model like a miniature stage set, which he populated with wax figures. He then adjusted the positions of the figures and the lighting until he was satisfied with the entire scene. Using a grid of horizontal and vertical threads placed in front of this model, he could easily sketch the composition onto squared paper for his assistants to recopy onto a large canvas. His assistants also primed the canvas and blocked in the areas of dark and light.

The artist himself finished the painting, having time to concentrate on the more difficult passages.

With his dynamic technique, strong colors, and bright highlights, Tintoretto created a pictorial mood of intense spirituality. The *Last Supper* (fig. **13–19**), one of his last paintings, is filled with the kind of everyday details that Veronese also included, such as a servant kneeling by a basket of provisions, which is inspected by a curious cat. But these realistic elements are transformed by the plunging, off-center perspective and by the brilliant, otherworldly light emanating from Jesus and the disciples, which takes the place of traditional halos. Bands of angels swoop in from above as the supernatural and secular worlds become one. Compared with the timeless, rigorous geometry of Leonardo da Vinci's *Last Supper* (see fig. 13–2), Tintoretto's composition is all sweeping motion and twisting, gesturing figures. The spectator is drawn irresistibly inward, caught up in the sacred drama.

Tintoretto painted the *Last Supper* and a companion painting, the *Gathering of Manna*, for the walls of the sanctuary of the church of San Giorgio Maggiore in Venice, designed by the architect Andrea Palladio (Andrea di Pietro, 1508–1580). Palladio began his career as a stonecutter in Padua, but became one of the foremost architects in Italy. After moving to Vicenza (in a region ruled by Venice), he became the protégé of a Humanist scholar and amateur architect, Giangiorgio Trissino, with whom

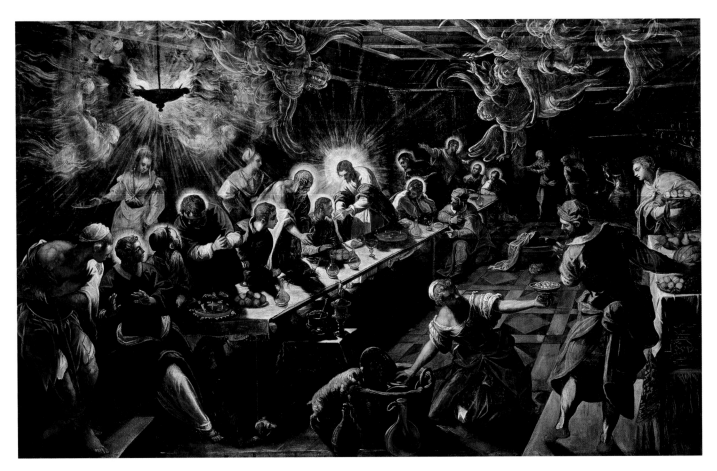

13–19 Tintoretto. *Last Supper.* 1592–1594. Oil on canvas, 12′ × 18′8″ (3.7 × 5.7 m). Church of San Giorgio Maggiore, Venice

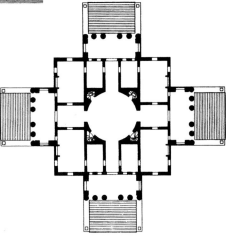

13–20 Andrea Palladio. Villa Rotonda (Villa Capra), Vicenza, Italy. Begun 1550

he made three trips to Rome. During these trips he made drawings of the ancient Roman remains.

Palladio became a scholar and an architectural theorist as well as a designer of buildings. His famous and influential *Four Books of Architecture (I quattro libri dell'architettura)*—published in 1570—provided ideal plans for country estates, using proportions derived from ancient Roman structures. Despite their theoretical bent, his writings were often more practical than earlier treatises. Perhaps his early experience as a stonemason provided him with the knowledge and self-confidence to approach technical problems and discuss them as clearly as he did theories of ideal proportion and uses of the classical orders. In the early eighteenth century, an important Palladian revival began in Venice and Palladio's *Four Books of Architecture* was one of the works often included in the library of an educated person of the time.

Palladio's ability can best be seen in numerous villas (country houses) built early in his career. Around 1550 he started his most famous villa, just outside Vicenza (fig. **13–20**), completed in 1569. Although the term *villa* implies a working farm, Palladio designed this one as a retreat for relaxation, literally a party house. To afford views of the countryside, he placed an Ionic-order porch and a wide staircase on each face of the cubical building. Called the Villa Rotonda because it had been inspired by another round building, the Roman Pantheon (see fig. 6–22), the Rotonda became known as the Villa Capra after its purchase in 1591 by the Capra family. The plan (fig. **13–21**) shows the geometrical clarity of Palladio's conception: a circle inscribed in a small square inside a larger square, with symmetrical rectangular

13–21 Andrea Palladio. Plan of the Villa Rotonda

rooms and identical rectangular porticoes and staircases projecting from each of its faces.

The use of a central dome on a domestic building was a daring innovation that effectively secularized the dome. The Villa Rotonda was the first of what was to become a long tradition of domed palaces and houses, particularly in England and the United States, including Monticello, Thomas Jefferson's country house in Virginia (see fig. 17–10). Jefferson was one of the first people in colonial America to have a copy of Palladio's writings (in English). Interestingly, in the original Italian edition, Palladio himself had described the setting for the Villa Rotonda as "sopra un monticello" (on a small hill).

Mannerism

Italy

A new style, Mannerism, arose in Florence and Rome in the 1520s. The term *Mannerism* comes from the Italian *maniera*, a word used in the sixteenth century to suggest intellectually intricate subjects, highly skilled techniques, and art concerned with beauty for its own sake. Any attempt to define Mannerism as a single style is futile, but certain characteristics occur regularly: extraordinary virtuosity; sophisticated, elegant compositions; and fearless manipulations or distortions of accepted formal conventions. Artists created irrational spatial effects and figures with elongated proportions, exaggerated poses, and enigmatic gestures and expressions. Some artists favored obscure, unsettling, and often erotic imagery; unusual colors and juxtapositions; and unfathomable secondary scenes.

Mannerist sculpture—which is often small in size and made from precious metals—exaggerates body forms and displays extraordinary technical skill. The designs of Mannerist architecture defy uniformity and rationality as well as the conventional use of classical orders.

The first Mannerist painters worked in Florence in the 1520s. The frescoes and altarpiece created by Jacopo da Pontormo (1494–1557) between 1525 and 1528 for the 100-year-old Capponi Chapel in the Church of Santa Felcità in Florence are clearly Mannerist in style (fig. **13–22**). Open on two sides, Brunelleschi's chapel creates the effect of a loggia in which frescoes on the right-hand wall (in the photograph) depict the Annunciation and tondos (circular paintings) under the cupola represent the four Evangelists. The altarpiece on the adjoining wall depicts the Deposition. In the Annunciation the Virgin accepts the angel's message but also seems to have a vision of her future sorrow as, in

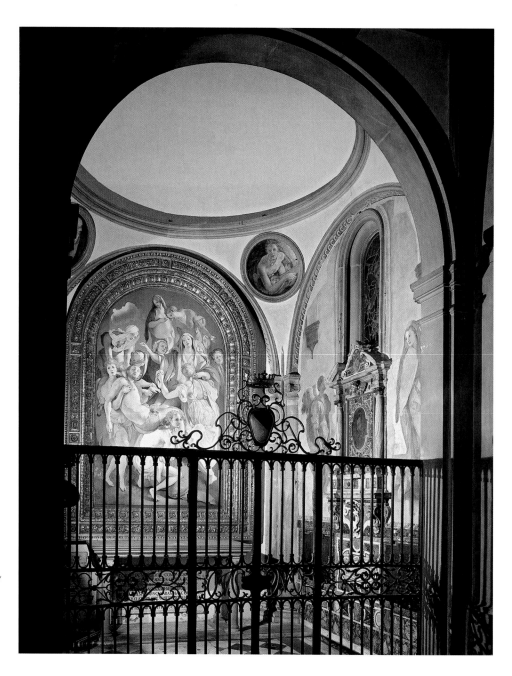

13–22 Capponi Chapel, Church of Santa Felicità, Florence. Early Renaissance Chapel by Filippo Brunelleschi. 1419–1423; Pontormo, tondos with the four evangelists and mural painting of the Annunciation, on the window wall, 1525–1528, fresco; altarpiece, Pontormo, The Deposition, oil on panel, 1525–1527

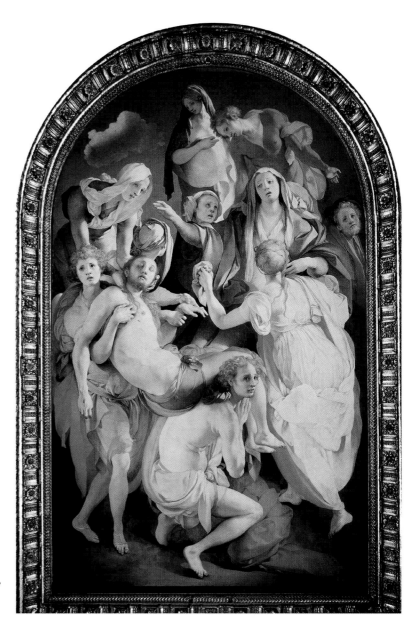

13–23 Jacopo da Pontormo. *Deposition.* 1525–1527. Oil on panel, 10′3″ × 6′4″ (3.12 × 1.93 m). Capponi Chapel, Church of Santa Felcità, Florence

the adjoining painting, she sees her son's body lowered from the Cross (fig. **13–23**). In this Deposition Pontormo's ambiguous composition enhances the visionary quality of the painting. The rocky ground and cloudy sky give little sense of location in space, and some figures press into the viewer's space, while others seem to levitate or stand on a ring of boulders. Pontormo chose a moment just after Jesus's removal from the cross, when the youths who have lowered him have paused to regain their hold. The emotional atmosphere of the scene is expressed in the odd poses and drastic shifts in scale, but perhaps most poignantly in the use of secondary colors and of colors shot through with contrasting colors, like iridescent silks. The palette is predominantly blue and pink with accents of olive green, gray, scarlet, and creamy white. The overall tone of the picture is set by the color treatment of the crouching youth, whose skintight bright pink shirt is shaded in iridescent, pale gray-green.

Pontormo's assistant at this time was Agnolo Bronzino (Agniolo di Cosimo di Mariano Tori, 1503–1572), whose nickname *Bronzino* means "Copper-Colored" (just as we might call someone "Red"). In 1540, Bronzino became the Medici court painter. Although he was a versatile artist who produced altarpieces, frescoes, and tapestry designs over his long career, he is best known today for his portraits in the courtly Mannerist style. Bronzino's virtuosity in rendering costumes and settings creates a rather cold and formal effect, but the self-contained demeanor of his subjects admirably conveys their haughty personalities. The *Portrait of a Young Man* (fig. **13–24**) demonstrates Bronzino's characteristic portrayal of his subjects as intelligent, aloof, elegant, and self-assured. The youth toys with a book, suggesting his scholarly interests, but his walleyed stare creates a slightly unsettling effect and seems to associate his face with the carved masks on the furniture.

Many sixteenth-century Italian artists continued to be inspired by the great leaders of the earlier generation—Leonardo, Raphael, and Michelangelo—instead of adopting the current Mannerist principles. In 1557, the father of a gifted portrait painter from Cremona, Sofonisba Anguissola (1528–1625), consulted Michelangelo about his daughter's artistic talents. He asked Michelangelo for a drawing that she might copy and hoped the master would critique her work. Michelangelo obliged. Sofonisba

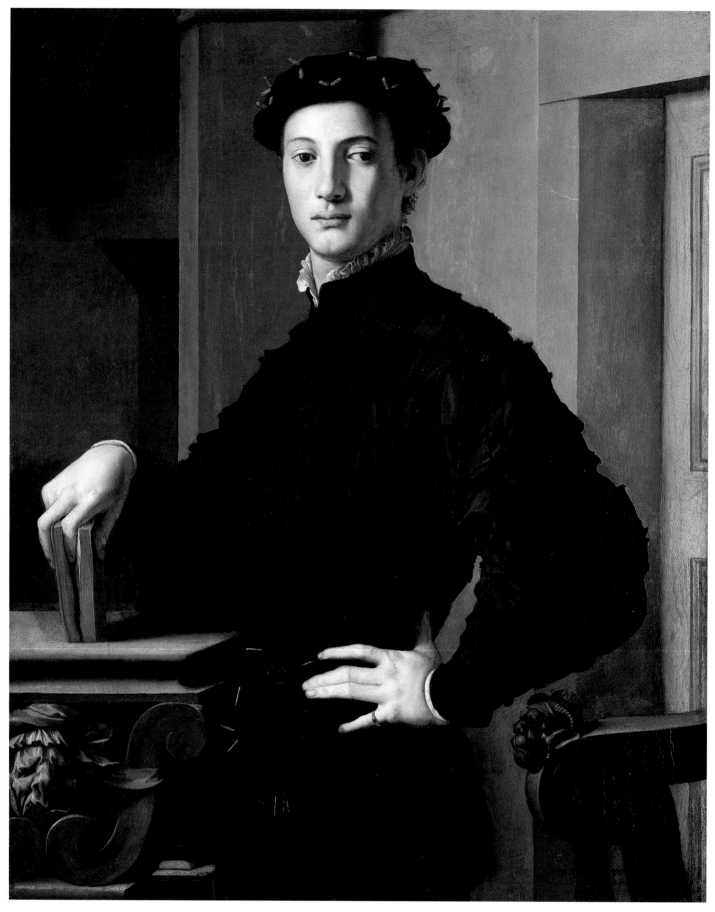

13–24 Agnolo Bronzino. *Portrait of a Young Man.* c. 1540–1545. Oil on wood panel, 37⅝″ × 29½″
(95.5 × 74.9 cm). The Metropolitan Museum of Art, New York

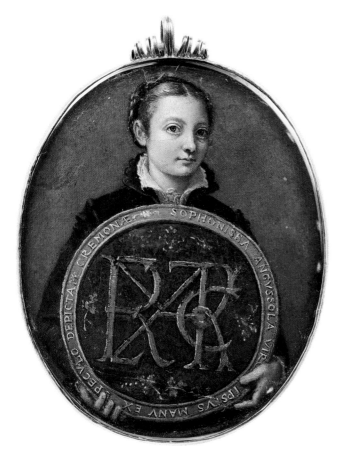

13–25 Sofonisba Anguissola. *Self-Portrait.* c. 1552. Oil on parchment on cardboard, $2\frac{1}{2}'' \times 3\frac{1}{4}''$ (6.4 × 8.3 cm). Museum of Fine Arts, Boston

Sofonisba was not the only talented Anguissola daughter. Her sisters Elena, Lucia, Minerva, Europa, and Anna were all painters, too. Only their brother, Asdrubale, evidently lacked the family talent, but as a member of the city council of Cremona he may have had a political career.

Anguissola was also a skilled miniaturist, an important kind of painting in the sixteenth century, when people had few means of recording the features of a lover, friend, or family member. She painted herself holding a medallion, the border of which spells out her name and hometown, Cremona (fig. **13–25**). The interlaced letters at the center of the medallion are a riddle; they seem to form a monogram with the first letters of her sisters' names: Minerva, Europa, Elena—names that reflect the enthusiasm for the classics in Renaissance Italy.

In 1560, Sofonisba accepted the invitation of the queen of Spain to become a lady in waiting and court painter, a post she held for 20 years. Unfortunately, most of her Spanish works were lost in a seventeenth-century palace fire. After her years at court, she returned to Sicily (a Spanish territory), where she died at the age of 92. Anthony Van Dyck met Sofonisba in Palermo in 1624, where he sketched her and noted that she was then 96 years old. He wrote that she advised him on positioning the lights for her portrait. She said that she did not want the light to be placed too high because the strong shadows would bring out her wrinkles. Clearly she was a lively woman and a realist to the end.

Another northern Italian, Lavinia Fontana (1552–1614), also learned to paint from her father, who was a Bolognese follower of Raphael. By the 1570s, she was a highly respected painter of narratives as well as of portraits, the more usual field for women artists of the time. Her success was so well rewarded, in fact, that her husband, the painter Gian Paolo Zappi, gave up his own career to care for their large family and to help Lavinia by building frames for her paintings. This situation was unusual even in Bologna, which boasted some two dozen women painters as well as a number of women scholars who lectured at the university on a variety of subjects, including law.

In 1581, while still in her twenties, Lavinia painted a *Noli Me Tangere* (fig. **13–26**), illustrating the biblical story of Christ revealing himself for the first time to Mary Magdalen following his Resurrection (Mark 16:9, John 20:17). The Latin title of the painting means "Do not touch me," Christ's words when the Magdalen moved to embrace him, explaining to her that he now existed in a new form somewhere between physical and spiritual. According to the Gospel of John, Mary Magdalen at first mistook Christ for a gardener, so Lavinia represented him with a broad-brimmed hat and spade.

In 1603, Lavinia moved to Rome as an official painter to the papal court. She also soon came to the attention of the Habsburgs, who paid large sums for her work. In 1611, she was honored with a commemorative medal portraying her in a bust as a dignified, elegantly coiffed woman on one side and as an intensely preoccupied artist with rolled-up sleeves and wild, uncombed hair on the other.

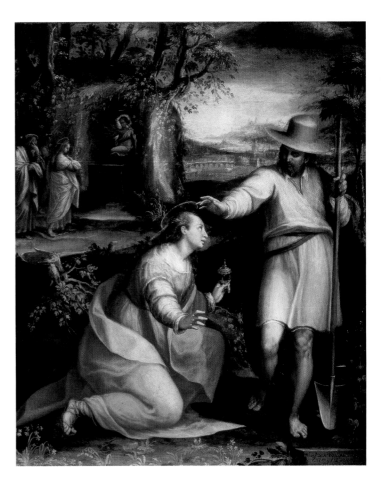

13–26 Lavinia Fontana. *Noli Me Tangere.* c. 1581. Oil on canvas, $47\frac{3}{8}'' \times 36\frac{5}{8}''$ (120.3 × 93 cm). Galleria degli Uffizi, Florence

France

Painters from Italy carried the Mannerist style to France, where King Francis I (ruled 1515–1547) was an important patron of the arts and enthusiastic supporter of the Italian Renaissance style. Francis even persuaded Leonardo to join him at Amboise in the Loire Valley of France, where the artist spent the last two years of his life.

Having chosen as his primary residence a medieval hunting lodge at Fontainebleau, Francis began transforming it in 1526 into a grand country palace, or **château**. In 1530, the king appointed a Florentine artist, the Mannerist painter Rosso Fiorentino (1495–1540), as the first artistic director of the project. After Rosso died, he was succeeded by his Italian colleague Francesco Primaticcio (1504–1570), who spent the rest of his career at Fontainebleau working on the decoration of the château from 1532 until his death. During that time, he also commissioned and imported a large number of copies and casts made from original Roman sculpture, including the *Apollo Belvedere* in the Vatican gardens, the newly discovered *Laocoön* (see Introduction, figs. 27 and 28), and even the relief decoration on the Column of Trajan. These works provided an invaluable visual resource for the northern artists employed on the project.

Among Primaticcio's first projects at Fontainebleau was the redecoration, in the 1540s, of the chambers of the king's official mistress, Anne, Duchess of Étampes (fig. **13–27**). The artist combined the arts of woodworking, stucco relief, and fresco painting in his complex but lighthearted and graceful interior design. The lithe figures of his stucco nymphs recall Pontormo's painting style (see fig. 13–23), with their elongated bodies and small heads. Their spiraling postures and the bits of clinging drapery are playfully sexual. The wall surface is almost overwhelmed with garlands, mythological figures, and Roman architectural

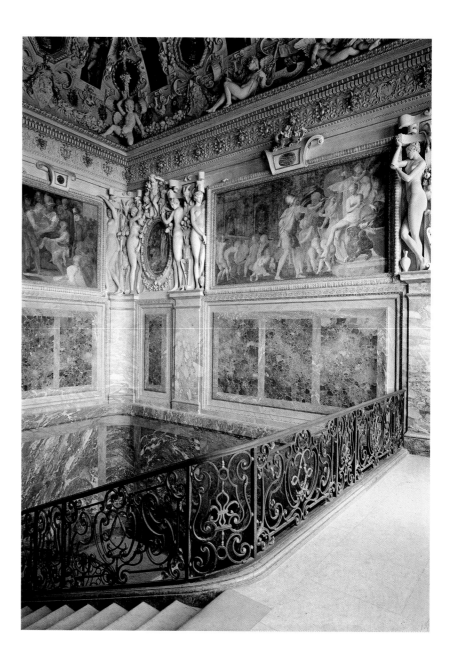

13–27 Primaticcio. Stucco and wall painting. Chamber of the duchess of Étampes, Château of Fontainebleau. 1540s

ornament, and the total visual effect is extraordinarily confident and joyous. The first School of Fontainebleau, as this Italian phase of the palace decoration is called, established a tradition of Mannerism in painting and interior design that spread to other centers in France and the Netherlands.

In the second half of the sixteenth century, probably the most influential sculptor in Italy was Jean de Boulogne (1529–1608), better known as Giambologna (a shortened form of his Italian name, Giovanni da Bologna). Born in Flanders, he settled by 1557 in Florence, where both the Medici family and the sizable Netherlandish community there were his patrons. He not only influenced a later generation of Italian sculptors, he also spread the Mannerist style to the north through artists who came to study his work. Although greatly influenced by Michelangelo, Giambologna was generally more concerned than his predecessor with graceful forms and poses, as in his gilded-bronze *Astronomy,* or *Venus Urania* (fig. **13–28**), of about 1573. The figure's identity is suggested by the astronomical device on the base of the plinth. Designed with a classical prototype of Venus in mind, the sculptor twisted Venus's upper torso and arms to the far right and extended her neck in the opposite direction so that her chin is over her right shoulder, straining the limits of the human body. Consequently, Giambologna's statuette may be seen from any viewpoint. The elaborate coiffure of tight ringlets and the detailed engraving of drapery texture contrast strikingly with the smooth, gleaming flesh of Venus's body. Following the common practice for cast-metal sculpture, the artist replicated this statuette several times for different patrons.

13–28 Giovanni da Bologna, called Giambologna. *Astronomy,* **or** *Venus Urania.* c. 1573. Bronze gilt, height 15 1/4″ (38.8 cm). Kunsthistorisches Museum, Vienna

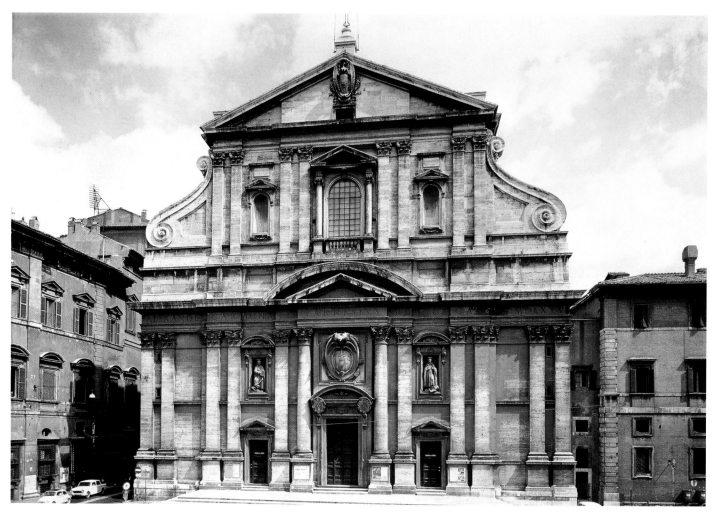

13–29 Giacomo da Vignola and Giacomo della Porta. Façade of the Church of Il Gesù , Rome.
Begun on Vignola's design in 1568; completed by della Porta c. 1575–84

Mannerist Architecture

The architect Giacomo Barozzi (1507–1573), called Vignola after his native town, worked with Primaticcio in France from 1541 to 1543. On his return to Italy, his work seems more expressive of Italian Renaissance than French Mannerist ideals. In Rome he designed the headquarters church for the Society of Jesus (the Jesuit Order), the Church of Il Gesù (Jesus). As conceived by Vignola, the church fit compactly into a city block, its interior essentially a hall for preaching, with shallow side chapels (fig. **13–29**). Even the traditional Christian desire for an east-west-oriented building gave way to the practical considerations of theatrical oratory and urban space. After Vignola's death, Giacomo della Porta, who also completed the dome on Saint Peter's, completed the church in 1584. The simplicity and practical planning of the building, united with della Porta's dignified façade, influenced church design for more than a century.

German Art

German sculptors of the sixteenth century worked in every medium, and they produced some of their finest and most original work in the wood of the linden (limewood) tree, which grew abundantly in the central and southern Germanic lands. Tilman Riemenschneider (active 1483–1531) directed the largest sculpture workshop in Würzburg; he was also politically active in the city's government. Riemenschneider's work attracted patrons from other cities, and in 1501 he signed a contract for one of his major creations, the *Altarpiece of the Holy Blood*, for the Church of Saint James in Rothenburg, which housed an important relic: a drop of what was believed to be Jesus's blood. The altarpiece was to be nearly 30 feet high. A specialist in carving shrines began work on the frame in 1499, and Riemenschneider created the figures. The relative value that the patrons placed on the contributions can be judged from the fact that the frame carver received 50 florins and Riemenschneider only a little more—60 florins.

ELEMENTS OF **Architecture**
Parts of the Church Façade

Giacomo da Vignola and Giacomo della Porta's façade for Il Gesù, of about 1575–1584—like many Renaissance and Mannerist buildings—is firmly grounded in the clean articulation and vocabulary of classical architecture. Il Gesù's façade employs the colossal order, an order in which the columns run through more than one story, and uses huge volutes to aid the transition from the wide lower stories to the narrow upper level. Verticality is also emphasized by the large double pediment that rises from the wide entablature and pushes into the transition zone between stories; by the repetition of triangular pedimental forms (above the aedicula window and in the crowning gable); by the rising effect of the volutes; and, most obviously, by the massing of upward-moving forms at the center of the façade. Cartouches, cornices, and niches provide concave and convex rhythms across the middle zone.

The façade (see fig. 13–29), planned by Vignola but altered by della Porta during construction, followed a design established by Renaissance architects. Paired colossal orders visually unite the first and second stories, while a second order is superimposed on the third story. Large volutes (scroll forms) ease the transition between the wide lower levels and the narrow third level by masking the sloping roofs of the side aisles (see below). The central axis of the building is stressed by gradually moving the orders on the lower level forward, from the relatively flat pilasters at the corners to the engaged half-columns at the center; by crowning the central door with a double pediment (a triangle inside a semicircle) that intrudes into the story above; and by enlarging the central window on the upper level.

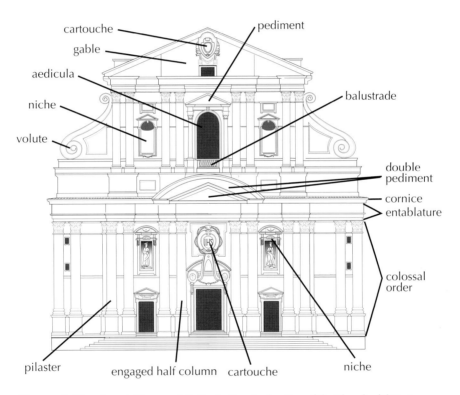

Giacomo da Vignola and Giacomo della Porta. Façade elevation of the Church of Il Gesù.
Rome. c. 1575–1584

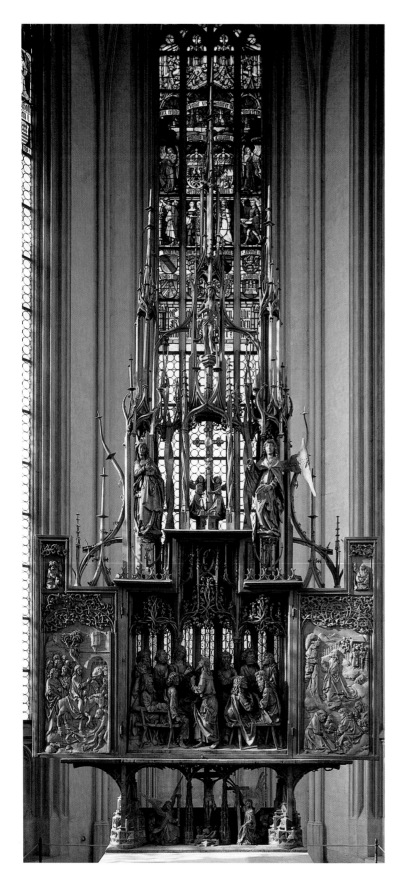

The main panel of the altarpiece represents the *Last Supper* (fig. **13–30**). Like his Italian contemporary Leonardo (see fig. 13–2), Riemenschneider depicted the moment of Jesus's revelation that one of his disciples would betray him. Unlike Leonardo, however, Riemenschneider composed his group with Jesus off-center at the left and the disciples crowded around him. Judas, at center stage, holds a money bag as a symbol of the thirty pieces of silver he received for his treachery. Jesus extends a morsel of food to Judas, signifying that he is the one destined to set in motion the events that will lead to Jesus's death (John 13:21–30). One apostle (John) points down toward the altar where the relic of the Holy Blood would have been displayed.

Rather than creating individual portraits, Riemenschneider repeated a limited number of types. His figures have large heads, prominent features, and elaborate hair treatments with thick wavy locks and deeply drilled curls. The muscles, tendons, and raised veins of hands and feet are especially lifelike, as are the pronounced cheekbones, sagging jowls, and baggy eyes. Voluminous draperies cover the slim figures; the deep folds and active patterning create strong highlights and dark shadows that unify the narrative and the intricate carving of the framework. Although earlier sculpture had been painted and gilded, Riemenschneider introduced the use of a natural wood finish. The scene is set in a stagelike space with real windows in the back wall glazed with bull's-eye glass. Natural light from the church's windows illuminates the sculpture with constantly changing effects, according to the time of day and the weather.

In 1525, Riemenschneider supported the peasants, who, because of economic and religious oppression, rose up against their feudal overlords in the Peasants' War. His involvement led to his being fined and imprisoned. Riemenschneider survived, but created no more sculpture and died just six years later.

Painting and Prints

In painting, two very different artists, Matthias Gothardt, known as Matthias Grünewald (c. 1480–1528), and Albrecht Dürer dominated the first decades of sixteenth-century German art. Grünewald continued the long tradition of German mysticism and emotionalism, while Dürer's intense observation of the natural world represented new interests in empirical observation, linear perspective, and a northern ideal of the human figure.

13–30 Tilman Riemenschneider. *Altarpiece of the Holy Blood. Last Supper* (center); *Entry into Jerusalem* (left wing); *Agony in the Garden* (right wing); *The Annunciation* (upper figures), *The Resurrected Christ* (top-most figure). 1499–1505. Limewood, glass. Height of tallest figure 39″ (99.1 cm). Height of altar 29′6″ (9 m). Sankt Jakobskirche, Rothenburg ob der Tauber, Germany.

The altarpiece stands in a soaring Gothic gallery built over the chapel of the Holy Blood at the west end of the church (1453–1471). A local woodworker, Erhart Harschner, created the elaborate frame.

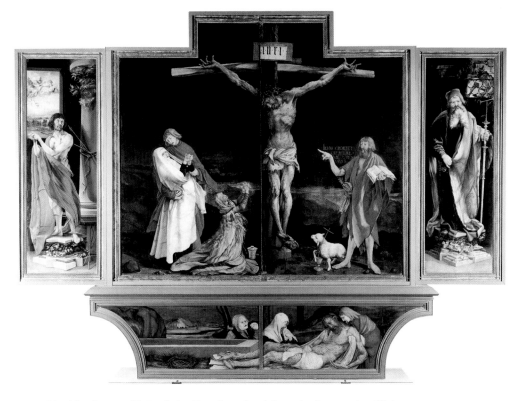

13–31 Matthias Grünewald. *Isenheim Altarpiece,* closed, from the Community of Saint Anthony, Isenheim, France. *Crucifixion* (center panel); *Lamentation* (predella); Saints Sebastian and Anthony Abbot (side panels). c. 1510–1515. Oil on panel, center panels 9′9″ × 10′9″ (2.97 × 3.28 m); each wing 8′2″ × 3′ 1/2″ (2.49 × 0.93 m); predella 2′ 5 1/2″ × 11′2″ (0.75 × 3.40 m). Musée d'Unterlinden, Colmar, France

Grünewald is best known today for the wings he painted between 1510 and 1515 to protect the carved image of Saint Anthony in the *Isenheim Altarpiece* (fig. **13–31**). The altarpiece had been made for the Community of Saint Anthony in Isenheim whose hospital specialized in diseases of the skin, including plague and leprosy. The altarpiece was thought to have healing properties, and viewing it was part of the treatment given to patients who entered the hospital. Made with both fixed and movable wings, the altarpiece was displayed in different configurations depending upon the Church calendar. On normal weekdays, when it was closed, as illustrated here, viewers saw a shocking image of the Crucifixion in a darkened landscape, a Lamentation below, and lifesize figures of Saints Sebastian and Anthony Abbot standing like statues on pedestals at the sides. Grünewald represented, in the most horrific detail, the tortured body of Jesus covered with gashes from being beaten and pierced by the thorns used mockingly to form a crown for his head. Not only do the figure's ashen color, open mouth, and blue lips indicate that he is dead, but he also appears to be already decaying, an effect enhanced by the palette of putrescent greens, yellows, and purplish red. A ghostlike Virgin Mary has collapsed in the arms of an emaciated John the Evangelist, and Mary Magdalen has fallen in anguish to her knees. In the predella, or supporting platform, below, Jesus's bereaved mother and friends prepare his body for burial, a scene that must have been familiar indeed in the hospital. The saints on the wings serve as models for a life of Christian devotion and as intercessors for the sick and dying.

Grünewald's personal identification with the struggles of the peasants in the 1520s led him to actively support them. And like Riemenschneider, Grünewald's involvement damaged his artistic career. The artist left Mainz and spent his last years in Halle, whose ruler was the chief protector of Martin Luther and a long-time patron of Grünewald's contemporary, Albrecht Dürer.

Albrecht Dürer (1471–1528), the leading German Renaissance artist, was the son of a Nuremberg goldsmith and served apprenticeships in painting, stained-glass design, and printmaking. He became familiar with the latest developments in Italian Renaissance art during two trips to the Italian peninsula, in 1494–1495 and 1505–1506. He seems to have resolved to reform the art of his own country by publishing theoretical writings and manuals that discussed Renaissance problems of perspective, ideal human proportions, and the techniques of painting.

compulsively interested in the pleasures of the flesh. These four human temperaments are symbolized here by the melancholy elk, the choleric cat, the phlegmatic ox, and the sensual rabbit. The scurrying mouse is an emblem of Satan, and the parrot may symbolize false wisdom, since it can only repeat mindlessly what it hears. Dürer's pride in his engraving can be seen in the prominence of his signature—a placard bearing his full name and date hanging on a branch of the Tree of Life.

The Reformation and the Arts

Against a backdrop of broad dissatisfaction with financial abuses and lavish lifestyles among the clergy, religious reformers began to challenge specific practices and beliefs of the Catholic Church, especially the sale of indulgences (forgiveness of sins and insurance of salvation in return for a financial contribution). From their protests, the reformers came to be called Protestants, and their insistence on church reform gave rise to a movement called the Reformation. Two of the most important reformers in the early sixteenth century were themselves Catholic priests and trained theologians: Desiderius Erasmus of Rotterdam (1466?–1536), a Dutchman; and Martin Luther (1483–1546), a

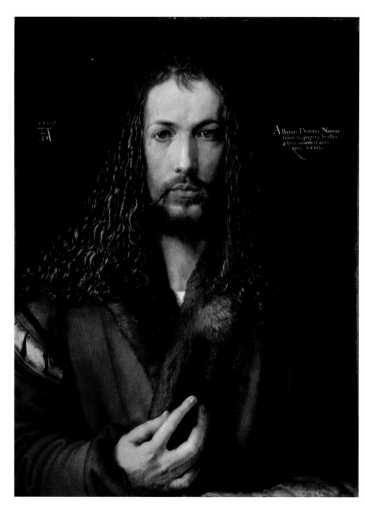

13–32 Albrecht Dürer. *Self-Portrait.* 1500. Oil on wood panel, $25\frac{5}{8}$" × $18\frac{7}{8}$" (65.1 × 48.2 cm). Alte Pinakothek, Munich

Dürer's first Italian trip clearly imparted to him both the idealism associated with art there and the concept of the artist as an independent creative genius. In his self-portrait of 1500 (fig. **13–32**), he represents himself as an idealized, even Christlike, figure in a severely frontal pose, meeting the viewer's eyes like an icon. His rich fur-lined robes and flowing locks of curly hair create a monumental equilateral triangle, a timeless symbol of unity.

Dürer's early interest in Italian art and theoretical investigations continued in his 1504 engraving of *Adam and Eve* (fig. **13–33**). These figures represent his first documented use of a canon of ideal human proportions. The nudes may have been based on Roman copies of Greek statues, probably known to him through prints or small sculpture in the antique manner. Although Dürer idealized the human figures, he recorded the flora and fauna of their setting with typically northern microscopic detail. Embedded in the landscape are symbols of the four humors; it was believed that after Adam and Eve disobeyed God, they and their descendants became vulnerable to imbalances in body fluids that altered human temperament. An excess of black bile from the liver produced melancholy, despair, and greed; yellow bile caused anger, pride, and impatience; phlegm in the lungs resulted in lethargy, disinterest, and a lack of emotion; and an excess of blood made a person unusually optimistic but also

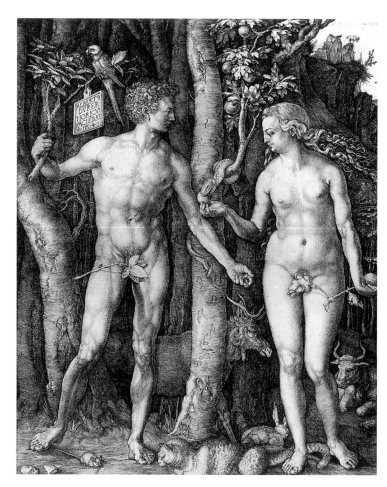

13–33 Albrecht Dürer. *Adam and Eve.* 1504. Engraving $9\frac{7}{8}$" × $7\frac{5}{8}$" (25.1 × 19.4 cm). Philadelphia Museum of Art
PURCHASED: LISA NORA ELKINS FUND

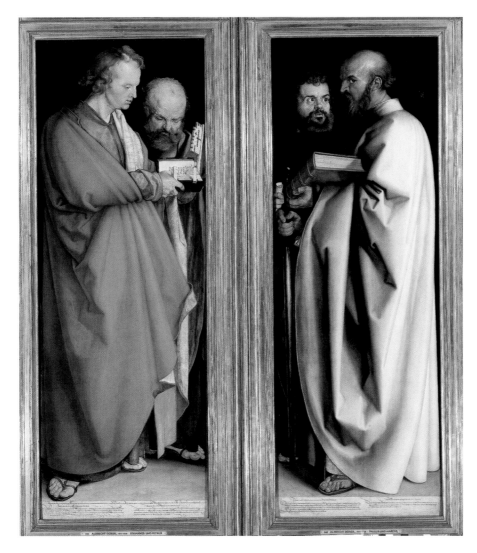

13–34 Albrecht Dürer.
Four Apostles. 1526. Oil on
panel, each panel $7'\,^1/_2''\times 2'6''$
(2.15 × 0.76 m). Alte
Pinakothek, Munich

German. The two men questioned official Church teachings and the pope's supremacy, and they emphasized individual faith and turned to the Bible as the ultimate religious authority.

The growing use of the printing press since the invention of movable metal type in the mid-fifteenth century made books and other printed materials—including pamphlets such as Luther's *On Christian Liberty* (1520)—available to laypeople. Improved communications resulting from such materials gave scholars throughout Europe easier access to each other's work and added to the debates on religious matters. In 1521 the Pope condemned Luther, who, in hiding, began his translation of the Bible into German.

The Reformation had widespread results. The growing availability of Bibles and other texts (in languages other than Latin) eventually led to an increasingly literate public. The Protestants, who failed to reform the practices of the Catholic Church, broke away from Rome. This, in turn, prompted Rome to launch a Counter-Reformation: At the Council of Trent (1545–1563), the Roman Catholic hierarchy formulated a program that included the Inquisition, with its special tribunals to root out heresy.

The effects of the Reformation on art were also significant and sometimes even violent. Some Protestants considered religious imagery to be idolatrous and in some areas actually destroyed religious art and whitewashed church interiors. As a result, many artists turned to portraiture and other secular subjects to make their livings. In Catholic regions, people still venerated traditional images of Christ and the saints, but officials from the Church scrutinized works of art for heretical or profane subject matter.

Martin Luther, himself, never supported the destruction of religious art, and Dürer, who admired Luther's writings, may have painted a pair of large panels commonly referred to as the *Four Apostles* (fig. **13–34**) in order to demonstrate that Protestant imagery was possible. The paintings depict John, Peter, Paul, and Mark. On the left panel, the elderly Saint Peter, the first pope, seems to shrink behind the young Saint John, Luther's favorite evangelist. On the right panel, the Evangelist Mark is nearly hidden behind Saint Paul, whose teachings and epistles were greatly admired by the Protestants. Dürer presented the panels, painted in 1526, to the city of Nuremberg, which had already adopted Lutheranism (then almost synonymous with Protestantism) as its official religion.

Landscape, with or without figures, was an important new category of imagery after the Reformation. Among the most accomplished German landscape painters of the period was Albrecht Altdorfer (c. 1480–1538). In 1505 he became a citizen of the city of Regensburg, in the Danube River Valley, where he remained for the rest of his life and whose portrayal became his

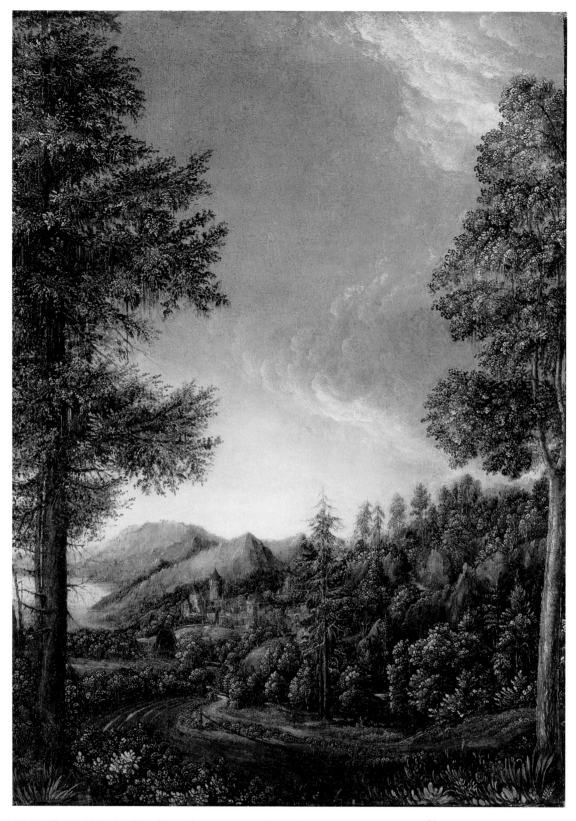

13–35 Albrecht Altdorfer. *Danube Landscape.* c. 1525. Oil on vellum on wood panel, 12″ × 8 ¹/₂″ (30.5 × 22.2 cm). Alte Pinakothek, Munich

specialty. His *Danube Landscape* of about 1525 (fig. **13–35**), a fine example of pure landscape painting—one without a narrative subject or human figures—is unusual for the time. A small work on vellum laid down on a wood panel, the *Landscape* seems to be a minutely detailed view of the natural terrain, but the low mountains, gigantic lacy pines, neatly contoured shrubberies, and

fairyland castle with red-roofed towers are more poetic and mysterious then real. The eerily glowing yellow-white horizon below rolling gray and blue clouds in a sky that takes up more than half the composition suggests something otherworldly.

The successors of Grünewald and Dürer often had to compromise and to take drastic measures to navigate the radically

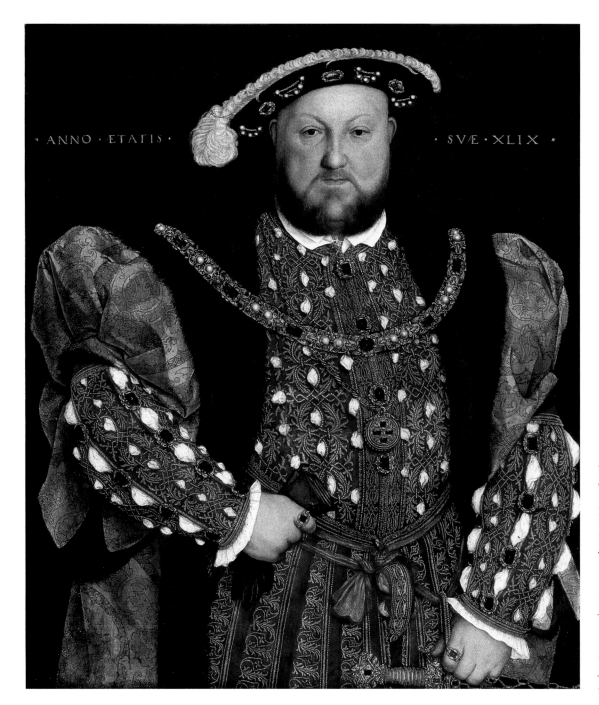

ANNO · ETATIS ·　　　　　　SVÆ · XLIX ·

13–36 Hans Holbein the Younger. *Henry VIII.* 1540. Oil on wood panel, 32 1/2″ × 29 1/2″ (82.6 × 75 cm). Galleria Nazionale d'Arte Antica, Rome

Holbein used the English king's great size to advantage for this official portrait, enhancing Henry's majestic figure with embroidered cloth, fur, and jewelry to create one of the most imposing images of power in the history of art. Henry is dressed for his wedding to his fourth wife, Anne of Cleves, on April 5, 1540.

changed German social and political scene. Some artists, like Tilman Riemenschneider, found their careers at a standstill because of their sympathies for rebels and reformers. Others left their homes to seek patronage abroad because of their support for the Roman Catholic Church. Hans Holbein the Younger (1497–1543), born in Augsburg, spent much of his early career in Basel, Switzerland, but worked in Antwerp and London from 1526 to 1528 to escape religious turmoil. Although he had officially become a Protestant by 1532, harassment from reformers sent him once again to England, where he served as court painter to the Tudor monarch Henry VIII (ruled 1509–1547).

One of Holbein's official portraits of Henry (fig. **13–36**) was painted about 1540. Although the inscription states that Henry is

49, Holbein worked from earlier sketches of the king's features. Henry's huge frame—he was well over 6 feet tall and had a 54-inch waist in his maturity—is covered by the latest style of dress, a short puffed-sleeved cloak of heavy brocade trimmed in dark fur, a narrow, stiff white collar fastened at the front, and a doublet slit to expose his silk shirt and encrusted with gemstones and gold braid. Henry was so fascinated by the elegant French king Francis I that he attempted to emulate and even surpass him in appearance. After Francis set a new style by growing a beard, Henry also grew one, as shown in this portrait. Just as Henry looked abroad, so too the later Tudors favored Netherlandish, German, and French artists. In fact, a vigorous native school of painters did not emerge in England until the eighteenth century.

Netherlandish and Spanish Art

Politically, the Netherlands (a region that at the time included Holland and Belgium) and Spain were united under the Habsburg Empire during the sixteenth century. The art made by Netherlandish and Spanish artists, however, followed several different directions. Some artists continued the styles of the late fifteenth century; others looked back to even earlier Flemish painters for models. Some became Mannerists in the Italian mode. A few, such as the Netherlanish artist Hieronymus Bosch, were such individualists that they must be considered unique.

Hieronymus Bosch (c. 1450–1516) created a world of fantastic imagery, often associated with medieval art, in paintings such as the *Garden of Earthly Delights* (fig. 13–37). There are many interpretations of the triptych. The subject seems to be based on the Christian belief in humanity's natural state of sinfulness. The imagery begins with the Creation of the World (on the wing exteriors, not shown), continues with the Creation of Adam and Eve on the left wing, and ends with the Last Judgment on the right. The fact that only the damned and not the saved are shown in the Judgment scene suggests that Bosch might have meant to suggest that damnation is the natural outcome of a life lived in ignorance and folly. The central panel illustrates the activities engaged in that condemn humanity, where seemingly harmless diversions such as games, romance, and music turn into sins such as lust, gluttony, and sloth. Luscious fruits—strawberries, cherries, grapes, and pomegranates—appear everywhere in the *Garden*, serving as food, as shelter, and in one instance even as a boat. Herbalists believed these fruits enhanced desire and fertility. In the painting the fruits also suggest that life is as fleeting and insubstantial as the taste of a strawberry.

The works of Bosch were so popular that the painter Pieter Bruegel the Elder (c. 1525–1569), nearly half a century later, began his career by imitating Bosch's work. Fortunately, Bruegel's talents went far beyond those of a copyist, and he soon developed his own style and themes. Working first in Antwerp and then in Brussels, he produced artfully composed works that reflected contemporary social, political, and religious conditions. Between 1551 and 1554, Bruegel traveled through the Alps to Rome, Naples, and all the way to Sicily. Unlike many Renaissance artists,

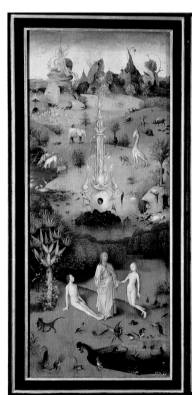
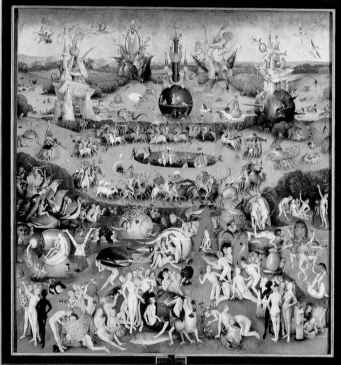
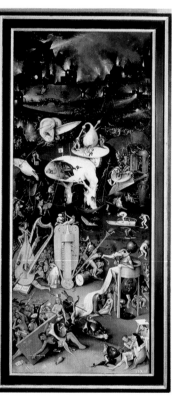

13–37 Hieronymus Bosch. *Garden of Earthly Delights* (center); *Creation* (left wing); *The Damned* (right wing). c. 1505–1515. Oil on wood panel, center panel 7′2¹⁄₂″ × 6′4³⁄₄″ (2.20 × 1.95 m), each wing 7′2¹⁄₂″ × 3′2″ (2.20 × 0.97 m). Museo del Prado, Madrid

This work was commissioned by an aristocrat for his Brussels townhouse, and the artist's choice of a triptych format, which suggests an altarpiece, may have been an understated irony. As a secular work, the Garden of Earthly Delights *may well have inspired lively discussion and even ribald comment, much as it does today in its museum setting. Despite—or perhaps because of—its bizarre subject matter, the triptych was copied in 1566 in tapestry versions, one (now in El Escorial, Madrid) for a cardinal and another for Francis I. At least one painted copy was made as well. Bosch's original triptych was sold at the onset of the Netherlands' revolt and sent in 1568 to Spain, where it entered the collection of Philip II.*

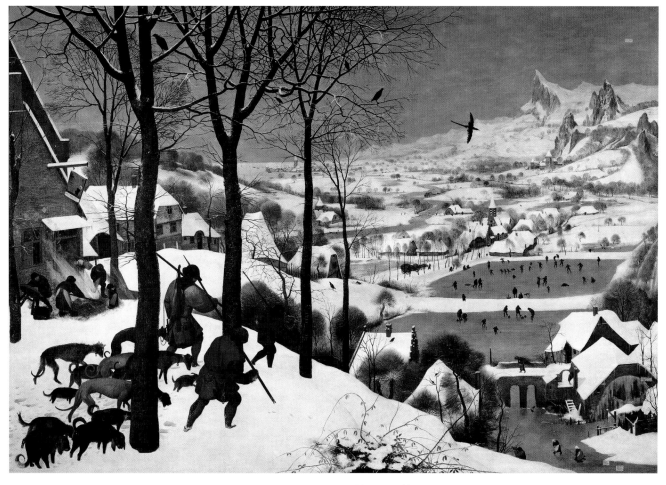

13–38 Pieter Bruegel the Elder. *Hunters in the Snow.* 1565. Oil on panel, 3′10¹⁄₂″ × 5′3³⁄₄″
(1.18 × 1.61 m). Kunsthistorisches Museum, Vienna

*Bruegel's inspiration came in part from visits to country fairs, where he sketched the farmers
and townspeople who became the focus of both his religious and secular painting.*

he did not record the ruins of ancient Rome or the wonders of the Italian cities. Instead he seems to have been fascinated by the landscape, particularly the formidable jagged rocks and sweeping panoramic views of Alpine valleys, which he recorded in detailed drawings. Back home in his studio, he made an impressive leap of the imagination as he painted the flat and rolling lands of Flanders as broad panoramas, even adding imaginary mountains on the horizon.

Cycles, or series, of paintings on a single allegorical subject such as the Times of Day, the Seasons, or the Five Senses became popular decorations in Flemish upper-class homes. Bruegel's *Hunters in the Snow* (fig. **13–38**) of 1565—from a cycle of six panels, in which each represents a pair of months—describes November and December. The artist captures the damp, cold winter weather much as his compatriots the Limbourgs did 150 years earlier (see fig. 12–2). In contrast to much Renaissance and Mannerist art, the subject matter in this painting appears neutral and realistic. The hunters slog stoically by, trailed by their dogs, while workers at an inn singe a pig in a fire before they finish the

butchering. The viewer's eye, plunging across the wide valley toward the distant peaks, is deliberately slowed by the careful balance of the vertical tree trunks and the horizontal rectangles of frozen water.

As a depiction of Flemish life, this scene of the Hunters represents a relative calm before the storm. Two years after it was painted, the northern Netherlandish provinces, which would eventually become the independent country of the Netherlands, began their struggle for independence from Spain. But even during the long years of political and social turmoil, which divided the region along religious lines, people found the resources to patronize artists.

In paintings that reflect Renaissance roots in their quiet realism, Caterina van Hemessen (1528–1587) of Antwerp developed an illustrious international reputation. She learned to paint from her father, with whom she collaborated on large commissions. Her portraits typically depict a subject in three-quarter view, carefully including background elements that could be shown perspectively, such as the easel in her

Self-Portrait (fig. **13–39**). In delineating her own features, Caterina presented a serious young person without personal vanity yet seemingly already self-assured about her artistic abilities. The inscription on the painting reads: "I Caterina van Hemessen painted myself in 1548. Her age 20."

Early in van Hemessen's career, she became a favored court artist of Mary of Hungary, sister of Emperor Charles V and regent of the Netherlands. When Mary ceased to be regent in 1556, the artist accompanied her to Spain, where Flemish painting had been popular since the fifteenth century. They arrived at the outset of the long reign of Philip II (ruled 1556–1598). Caterina married Chretien de Morien, the organist of Antwerp Cathedral, and at the death of their patron, Mary of Hungary, in 1558, the couple received a lifetime pension. Now financially secure, Caterina seems to have given up her painting career.

Philip II had been a serious art collector from an early age, supporting Spanish artists and others throughout his realm. He did not, however, appreciate the works of the man who (in the 20th century) became one of Spain's most famous painters. This was the Greek painter Kyriakos (Domenikos) Theotokopoulos (1541–1614), who arrived in Spain in 1577 after working for ten years in Italy. El Greco ("the Greek"), as he was called, began his career as a Byzantine icon painter in his native Crete. He entered Titian's shop in Venice about 1566, but he soon moved to Rome.

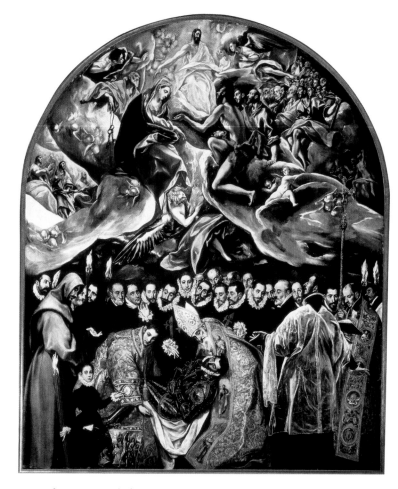

13–40 El Greco. *Burial of Count Orgaz,* Church of Santo Tomé, Toledo, Spain. 1586. Oil on canvas, 16′ × 11′10″ (4.88 × 3.61 m)

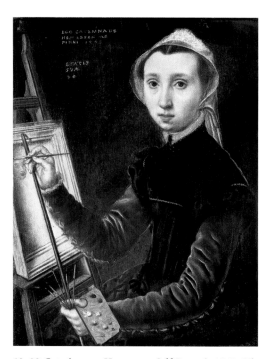

13–39 Caterina van Hemessen. *Self-Portrait.* 1548. Oil on panel, 12¼″ × 9¼″ (31.1 × 23.5 cm). Öffentliche Kunstsammlung, Basel, Switzerland

This self-portrait of the artist at work provides a glimpse into an artist's studio and working methods. The panel on the easel already has its frame, against which the painter leans her painting stick—an essential painter's tool used to steady the hand while doing fine, detailed work. She holds a small rectangular palette, five brushes, and the painting stick in her left hand and, bracing her right hand on the stick, she sketches a head in the upper left hand corner of the panel.

His mature style united the intense emotionalism seen in Byzantine religious art (see fig. 7–27) with rich color and loose brushwork reminiscent of Tintoretto. This pictorial vision ideally suited the needs of patrons in late-sixteenth-century Spain, which was undergoing a fervent religious revival.

In 1586, the artist was commissioned by the Orgaz family to paint a large canvas illustrating a local legend, the *Burial of Count Orgaz* (fig. **13–40**). The fourteenth-century count had been a great benefactor of the Church, and at his funeral Saints Augustine and Stephen were said to have appeared and lowered his body into his tomb, while his soul was seen ascending to heaven. In El Greco's painting, an angel in the center lifts Orgaz's tiny ghostly soul as the miraculous burial takes place below. Portraits of local aristocrats and religious notables fill the background of the picture, which is painted, in the Mannerist tradition, without specific reference to the spatial setting (see fig. 13–23). El Greco placed his eight-year-old son at the lower left next to Saint Stephen and signed the painting on the boy's white kerchief. He may have put his own features on the man above Saint Stephen's head, the only one who looks straight out at the viewer.

El Greco distinguished between earth and heaven in this painting by elongating the heavenly figures and by creating a separate light source above in the figure of Christ, who sheds an otherworldly luminescence quite unlike the natural light below. The dramatic lighting effects and emotionalism of El Greco's work would be echoed by an increasing number of painters in the early seventeenth century, as European art entered the Baroque era.

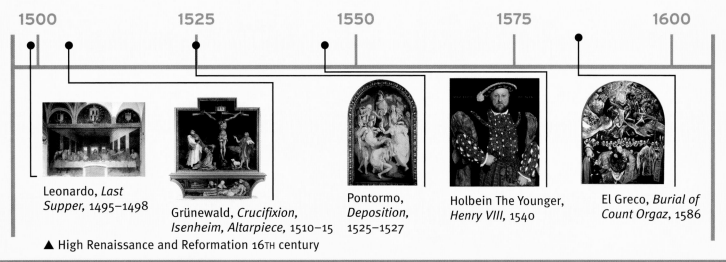

1500   1525   1550   1575   1600

Leonardo, *Last Supper,* 1495–1498

Grünewald, *Crucifixion, Isenheim, Altarpiece,* 1510–15

Pontormo, *Deposition,* 1525–1527

Holbein The Younger, *Henry VIII,* 1540

El Greco, *Burial of Count Orgaz,* 1586

▲ High Renaissance and Reformation 16TH century

LOOKING BACK

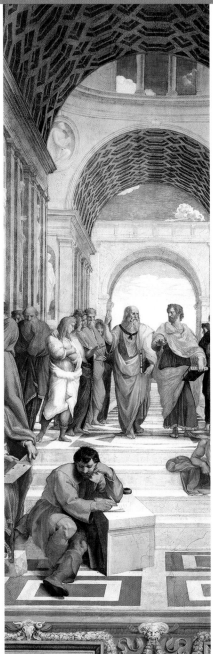

In the fifteenth and sixteenth centuries in Europe, artists and scholars began to explore the natural world with the kind of intensity that their medieval predecessors had devoted to heaven and hell. Of course they continued theological debates as well, but they also studied human and animal anatomy, botany and geology, astronomy and mathematics, and many other subjects. In their desire to incorporate this new knowledge into their art, artists turned to and refined a realistic style that had last been popular during the Roman Republic. In this endeavor, Italian artists followed a theoretical, almost mathematical, bent, while Flemish, French, and other artists followed a more intuitive approach.

Printed books began to replace manuscripts in the mid-fifteenth century, a process that by the sixteenth century created an information explosion comparable to the revolution brought about by computer technology in recent times. An increasingly literate public gained access not only to practical information but also to new ideas. The examination of natural phenomena, for example, led to widespread questioning of authority and eventually to the movement both within and outside the established Church known as the Protestant Reformation. In turn, the Catholic Church and leading conservative elements in national governments attempted to control information, and individuals, during the Counter-Reformation. And the most extreme Protestants declared much of the arts to be wasteful, frivolous, and even idolatrous.

Even so, artists of the time could express as much through painted, sculptural, and architectural forms as poets could with words or musicians with melody. In fact, during this period, people came to believe that the conception of a painting, sculpture, or work of architecture was a liberal—rather than a manual—art, and thus one that required education in the classics and mathematics. Few women, however, had access to the Humanistic education necessary to handle the sophisticated, often esoteric, subject matter used in many paintings or to the studio practice necessary to draw nude figures in foreshortened poses. Furthermore, most artists could not achieve international status without traveling extensively and frequently relocating to follow commissions. Still, despite all these obstacles, talented and successful women artists were active in Europe in the fifteenth and sixteenth centuries, even if many of their names—and much of their work—is not as well known today as those of their male counterparts. During the Renaissance, a myth arose—the myth of divinely inspired creative genius. It appears that this myth, which is still with us today, is equally valid for members of either sex.

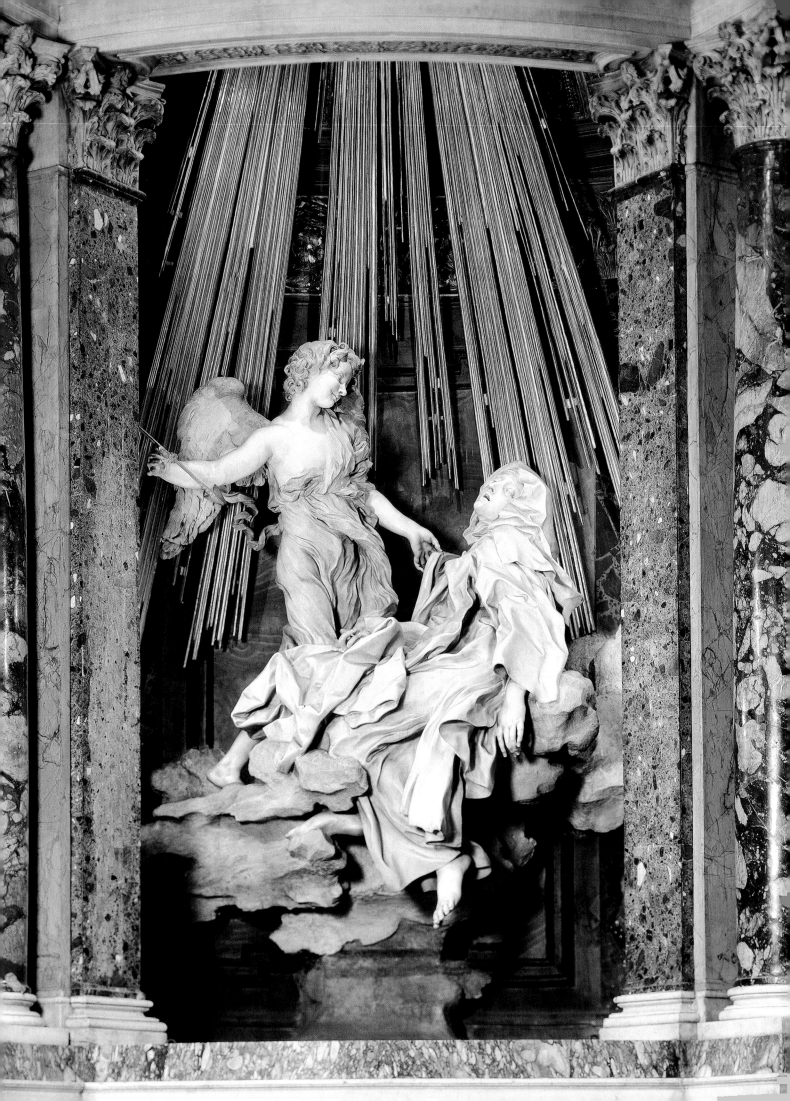

14
Baroque and Rococo Art

I n the Church of Santa Maria della Vittoria in Rome, the sixteenth-century Spanish mystic Saint Teresa of Ávila (1515–1582, canonized 1622) swoons in ecstasy on a bank of billowing clouds (fig. 14–1). A youthful angel plucks open her robe, aiming a gilded arrow at her breast. Gilt bronze rays of supernatural light descend, even as actual light illuminates the figures from a hidden window above. This dramatic scene, created by Gianlorenzo Bernini (1598–1680) between 1645 and 1652, represents a famous vision described with startling, physical clarity by Teresa, in which an angel pierced her body repeatedly with an arrow, transporting her to a state of ecstatic oneness with God.

The sculpture is an exquisite example of the emotional, theatrical style perfected by Bernini in response to the religious and political climate in Rome during the period of spiritual renewal known as the Counter-Reformation. The Protestant Reformation of the previous century had been seen by many as an outgrowth of Renaissance Humanism with its emphasis on rationality and independent thinking. In response, the Catholic Church turned to the authoritarian position of the Middle Ages, a reaction supported by the new Society of Jesus founded by Ignatius Loyola (d. 1556, canonized 1622). In the "spiritual exercises" (1522–1523) initiated by Saint Ignatius, Christians were enjoined to use all their senses to achieve appropriate emotional states as they reenacted (in their imaginations) the events on which they were meditating. They were to feel the burning fires of hell or the bliss of heaven, the lashing of the whips and the flesh-piercing crown of thorns. Art became an instrument of propaganda whose emotional appeal could lead the spectator to reinvigorated Christian belief.

Of course, the arts have often been used to convince or educate, but nowhere more effectively than by the Catholic Church in the seventeenth century. To serve the educational mission of the revitalized and conservative Church, paintings and sculpture had to depict events and people accurately and clearly. Throughout Catholic Europe, painters such as Rubens, Caravaggio, and Gaulli as well as sculptors created brilliant religious art. And although today viewers find this sculpture of Saint Teresa charged with sexuality, the Church—which prohibited lascivious thoughts and nude figures (other than martyrs)—approved of the depictions of such supernatural mystical visions. In fact, to help worshipers achieve the emotional state of religious ecstasy, religious art of the time frequently depicted ecstatic states enhanced by light and miraculous masses of swirling clouds.

14–1 Gianlorenzo Bernini. *Saint Teresa of Ávila in Ecstasy.* 1645–1652. Marble, height of the group 11′6″ (3.5 m). Cornaro Chapel, Church of Santa Maria della Vittoria, Rome

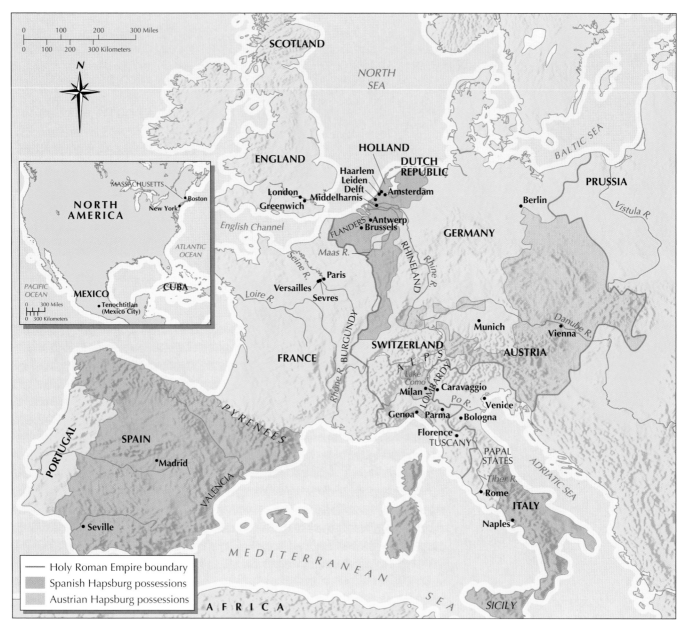

Map 14–1 Baroque and Rococo Periods in Europe and North America

The intellectual and political forces set in motion by the Renaissance and Reformation of the fifteenth and sixteenth centuries intensified in the seventeenth century. Religious wars continued, although gradually the Protestant forces gained control, especially in the north where Spain recognized the independence of the Dutch Republic in 1648. In Rome an energized papacy, aided by the new Jesuit Order, maintained the primacy of Catholicism in southern Europe, the Holy Empire, and France. Rulers kept up a semblance of power and patronage of the arts even as their economic strength slipped away. By the end of the century the Spanish king had to declare bankruptcy, and other rulers were not much better off. Nevertheless artists continued to find patrons in the church and the secular state and in the newly confident and prosperous urban middle class. The artists created a style known as the Baroque, a term of unknown derivation, perhaps related to *barocco*, a jeweler's word for an irregularly shaped pearl—that is, something both beautiful and strange.

Bernini's *Saint Teresa of Ávila in Ecstasy* is one of the great works of the Baroque, the prevailing artistic style in much of Europe in the seventeenth and early eighteenth centuries. Baroque features include the deliberate evocation of intense emotional responses in the viewer; the creation of dramatically lit, often theatrical compositions; the use of diverse media such as bronze and marble within a single artwork; and a spectacular technical virtuosity. The Baroque period also has its own version of classicism, a more emotional and dramatic variant of Renaissance ideals and principles. Baroque classicism featured idealization based on observation of the material world; balanced (though often asymmetrical) compositions; the sense of diagonal movement in space; rich, harmonious colors; and the inclusion of visual references to ancient Greece and Rome. Many Baroque artists achieved their ends through naturalism, the true-to-life depiction of the world that led to the popularity of portraiture, genre paintings (scenes from everyday life), still life (paintings of

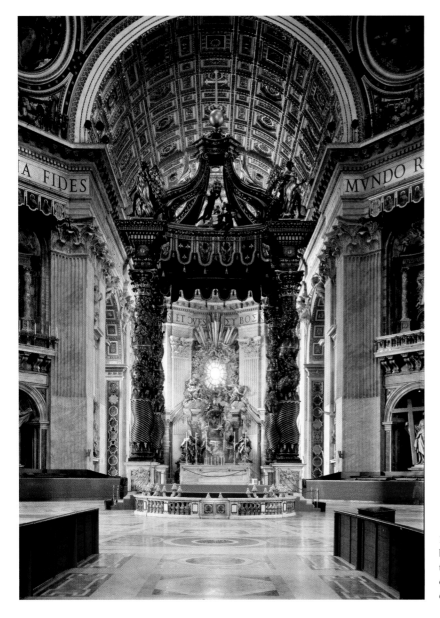

14–2 Gianlorenzo Bernini. *Baldacchino.* 1624–1633. Gilt bronze, height 100′ (30.48 m). Chair of Saint Peter (visible at the back) 1657–1666. Gilt bronze, marble, stucco, and glass. Pier decorations. 1627–1641. Gilt bronze and marble. Located in the crossing of Saint Peter's Basilica, Vatican, Rome

inanimate objects such as food, fruit, or flowers), and religious paintings featuring ordinary people and settings. Intense emotional involvement, naturalistic rendering, and classicism or classical references may exist in the same work. And many of the best examples of Baroque art combine all these elements.

Late in the period, a refined Baroque manner known as the Rococo emerged. Developing in Italy at the beginning of the eighteenth century, this style soon spread into France, central Europe, and even Russia. The Rococo style, characterized by fanciful architectural decoration, a light palette, and often a mood of playful melancholy, remained popular along with earlier Baroque styles until the rise of Neoclassicism in the third quarter of the eighteenth century.

Art for the Counter-Reformation Church: Italy

The patronage of the Church and the aristocratic Roman families—such as the Borghese, the Barberini, and the Farnese—allied with the papacy dominated Italian art from the late sixteenth to the late seventeenth century. A major program of the Counter-Reformation (the official Catholic reaction to the rise of Protestantism, see Chapter 13) included the use of art as propaganda. Churches, whose splendid architecture was embellished with painting, helped convince the faithful of the power of traditional religion. In Rome, Pope Paul V (Borghese, 1605–1621) ordered the expansion and modernization of the new Saint Peter's Basilica. As congregational worship again became important for both Catholics and Protestants, more space was needed in the church. In 1606, he commissioned the architect Carlo Maderno (1556–1629) to add a longer nave and a new façade to Michelangelo's Greek-cross building, only a half century old (see "Saint Peter's Basilica," page 352).

When Urban VIII (Barberini, 1623–1644) was elected pope in 1623, he unhesitatingly gave the young Bernini the task of designing an enormous bronze baldachin, or canopy, for the main altar of Saint Peter's. The resulting *Baldacchino* (fig. **14–2**), which stands about 100 feet high, exemplifies the Baroque tendency toward grandiose displays. Winding bronze grapevines

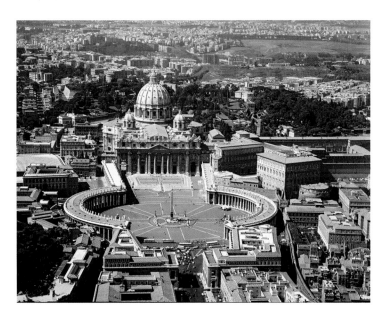

14–3 Gianlorenzo Bernini. Saint Peter's Basilica and Square. Vatican, Rome. Carlo Maderno, façade 1607–1615; Bernini, square designed c. 1656–1657

Perhaps only a Baroque artist of Bernini's talents could have unified the many styles that come together in Saint Peter's Basilica. The visitor today does not see a piecing together of parts made by different builders at different times, starting with Bramante's original design for the building in the sixteenth century, but rather encounters a triumphal unity of all the parts in one coherent whole.

These elements surround a stained-glass window that now depicts the dove of the Holy Spirit. The actual sunlight and the flickering candles, reflected and multiplied by the polished bronze, are a calculated part of the sculpture. Here Bernini has combined nature and art just as he did in the image of *Saint Teresa of Ávila in Ecstasy* (see fig. 14–1).

When Maderno died in 1629, Saint Peter's Basilica was complete as we know it today. However, Bernini, Maderno's collaborator of five years, later designed and supervised the building of a colonnade to enclose the square in front of the church (fig. **14–3**). The space that Bernini had to work with was irregular and already contained an Egyptian obelisk (moved there in 1586) and a fountain (to the right, made by Maderno in 1613), which had to be incorporated into the overall plan. In a remarkable design, Bernini framed the square with two enormous, curved covered walkways using giant Doric columns. These connect with two straight but diverging porticoes that lead up a slight incline to the two ends of Maderno's church façade. Later, in 1675, Bernini added a second matching fountain at the left of the obelisk, which serves to further define and balance the vast space.

Bernini spoke of his conception as representing the "motherly arms of the church" reaching out to the world. He intended to build a third section of the colonnade closing the open side so

decorate twisted columns inspired by columns supposed to have come from Solomon's Temple in Jerusalem. Grapevines are an ancient symbol of the wine of the Eucharist. Thus, the columns combine symbolism from Judaism and Christianity; and in the view of Christian scholars, Solomon's Temple supports the Christian Church just as the Old Testament leads to the New. Crowning the structure is an orb and a cross representing the universe and the reign of Christ. The angels and putti, as well as the tasseled panels imitating textiles on the entablature, are all made of bronze. The work marks the tomb of Saint Peter but also serves as a tribute to Urban VIII and his family, the Barberini, whose emblems—honeybees, suns, and laurel leaves—are prominently displayed.

Visible through the *Baldacchino* is the reliquary containing the throne of Saint Peter, an ancient wooden chair, encased in bronze. The complex structure is known as the Chair of Saint Peter. It symbolizes the direct descent of Christian authority from the apostle Peter to the reigning pope. This belief was rejected by many Protestants and therefore deliberately emphasized in Counter-Reformation Catholicism. The chair is lifted upward by four theologians amid a surge of gilded clouds toward an explosion of angels, putti, and gilded rays of glory.

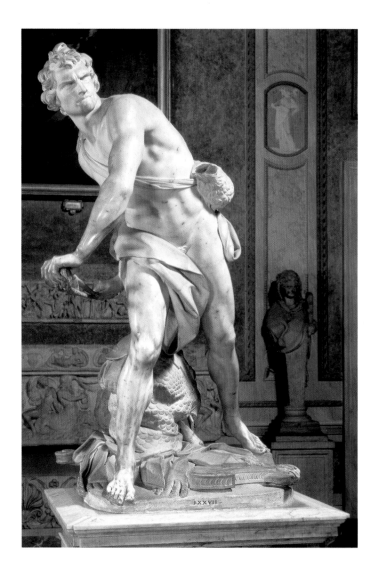

14–4 Gianlorenzo Bernini. *David.* 1623. Marble, height 5'7″ (1.7 m). Galleria Borghese, Rome

that pilgrims, after crossing the Tiber River bridge and passing through the narrow streets, would suddenly emerge into the enormous open space in front of the church. Encountered this way, the great church, colonnade, and square, with its towering obelisk and monumental fountains, would have been an even more awe-inspiring sight.

Bernini began his career as a sculptor not as an architect, and he continued to work in that medium throughout his career for both the papacy and private clients. His sculpture of *David* (fig. **14–4**), made for the nephew of Pope Paul V in 1623, introduced a new type of three-dimensional composition that intrudes forcefully on the viewer's space. The young hero bends at the waist and twists far to one side, ready to launch the fatal rock at Goliath who seems to be standing behind the viewer. The viewer enters the space of the sculpture and becomes part of the work of art. Unlike Donatello's introspective adolescent (see fig. 12–20) or Michelangelo's composed youth (see fig. 13–8),

this more mature David, with his lean, sinewy body, is all tension and determination. His tightly clenched mouth and straining muscles echo his frame of mind, and the energetic figure activates its surrounding space by implying the presence of an unseen adversary.

Even after Bernini's appointment as Vatican architect in 1629, his large workshop enabled him to accept outside commissions, such as the decoration of the funerary chapel of Cardinal Federigo Cornaro in the Church of Santa Maria della Vittoria (fig. **14–5**). For this project, carried out from 1642 to 1652, Bernini covered the walls of the tall, shallow chapel with colored marble panels and created the sculptural group of *Saint Teresa of Ávila in Ecstasy* (see fig. 14–1) for an oval niche above the altar. On the chapel's back wall, the curved ceiling surrounding the window appears to dissolve into a painted vision of clouds and angels, and on the side walls, kneeling against what appear to be balconies, are portrait statues of members of the Cornaro family.

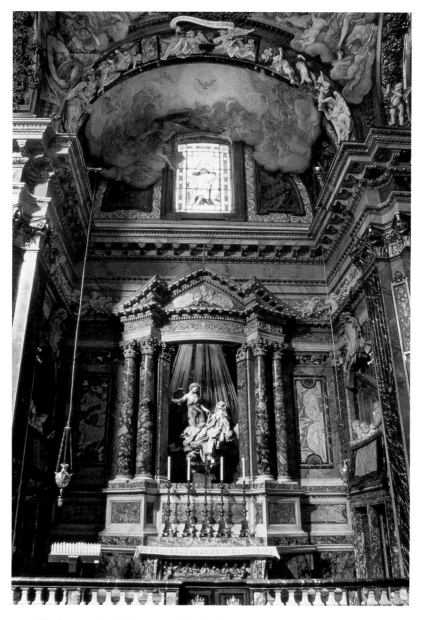

14–5 Gianlorenzo Bernini. Cornaro Chapel, Church of Santa Maria della Vittoria, Rome. 1642–1652

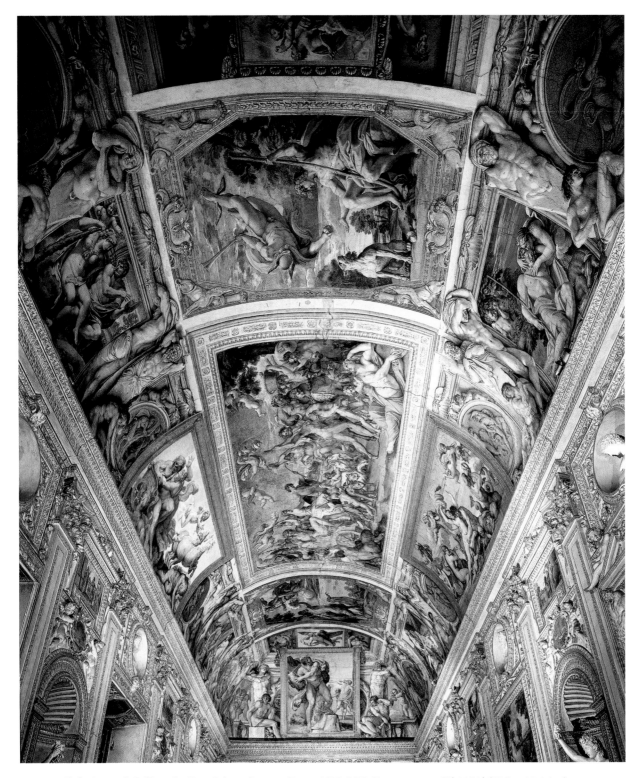

14–6 Annibale Carracci. Ceiling of gallery, Palazzo Farnese, Rome. 1597–1601. Fresco, approx. 68′ × 21′ (20.7 m × 6.4 m)

Two are reading from their prayer books; others converse; and one leans out from his seat, apparently to look at someone entering the chapel. Bernini's complex, theatrical interplay of the various levels of illusion in the chapel was imitated by sculptors throughout Europe.

Baroque illusionism reached its peak in ceiling decorations for churches, civic buildings, palaces, and villas. Many ceilings were covered entirely by *trompe l'oeil* ("fool the eye") painting, but some were complex constructions combining architecture, painting, and stucco sculpture. A ceiling painted by Annibale Carracci (1560–1609) in the Roman palace of the powerful

Farnese family is considered the major monument of early Baroque classicism. Commissioned to celebrate the wedding of Duke Ranuccio Farnese of Parma, it presents an exuberant mythological tribute to earthly love (fig. **14–6**). Annibale, cofounder with his family of an art academy in Bologna, was assisted by his brother Agostino (1557–1602) on this spectacular project, painted at the turn of the century (1597–1601). The ceiling painting creates the illusion of framed paintings, stone sculpture, bronze medallions, and nude youths in an architectural framework, clearly inspired by Michelangelo's Sistine Ceiling (see figs. 13–9 and 13–10). But instead of Michelangelo's

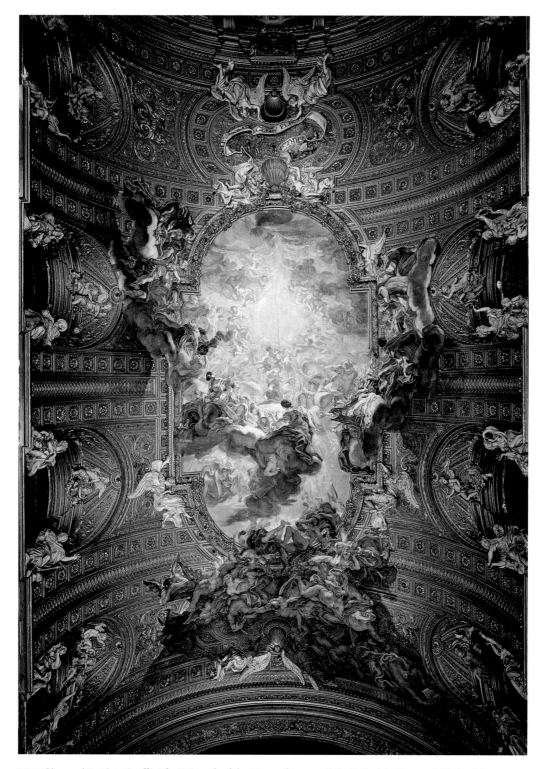

14–7 Giovanni Battista Gaulli. *The Triumph of the Name of Jesus and the Fall of the Damned.* Vault of the Church of Il Gesù, Rome. 1672–1685. Fresco with stucco figures

cool illumination and intellectual detachment, the Farnese Ceiling glows with a warm light that recalls the work of the Venetian painters Titian and Veronese. The primary image, set in the center of the vault, is *The Triumph of Bacchus and Ariadne*, a joyous procession celebrating the wine god's love for Ariadne, a mortal princess. The ceiling became famous almost immediately.

The Farnese family, proud of the gallery, were generous in allowing young artists to sketch the figures there, so that Annibale's great work influenced Italian art well into the seventeenth century. The classicism practiced at the academy and demon-strated in the Farnese palace ceiling produced a strong classical strain in Italian Baroque art, exemplified by the painting of Il Guercino (see Introduction, fig. 18).

Closer in spirit and style to Bernini's art, and the ultimate illusionistic Baroque ceiling, is the *Triumph of the Name of Jesus* (fig. **14–7**), which fills the vault of the nave of the Church of Il Gesù, mother church of the Society of Jesus (the Jesuits), in Rome (see fig. 13–29). The vault of Il Gesù had remained unpainted in the seventeenth century. Giovanni Battista Gaulli (1639–1709), also called Baciccio, created the ceiling we see today between 1676 and 1679. The artist had worked in his youth for Bernini, from whom he absorbed a Baroque taste for drama and spectacle. Gaulli's astonishing creation went beyond anything that had preceded it. Architecture, sculpture, and painting combine to produce the illusion that clouds and angels have floated down through an opening in the church's vault. The whole composition focuses off-center on the golden aura around the letters IHS (barely visible in figure 14–7), a Greek abbreviation for "Jesus," the holy name and symbol of the Jesuits. In Gaulli's interpretation of the Last Judgment, the elect rise toward the name of God and the damned plummet through the ceiling toward the nave floor. The unified visual effect of sculpted angels, actual architectural moldings, and overlapping painted panels extends the frescoed images from the central vault, creating a powerful and exciting appeal to the viewer's emotions.

Not all Roman Baroque art was meant to overwhelm the viewer by sheer spectacle. Michelangelo Merisi (1571–1610), known as Caravaggio after his birthplace in northern Italy, introduced an intense new realism and a dramatic use of light and gesture to Italian Baroque art. After his arrival in Rome in 1592, Caravaggio at first painted for a small circle of sophisticated patrons. His subjects from the 1590s include still lifes and scenes featuring fortunetellers, cardsharps, and street urchins dressed as musicians or mythological figures. Most of his commissions after 1600 were for religious art, and reactions to these paintings were mixed. On occasion his powerful, sometimes brutal, naturalism was rejected by patrons as unsuitable to the subject's dignity. However, this very realism was closely allied with Counter-Reformation ideas of spirituality, including the meditations, or *Spiritual Exercises,* of Saint Ignatius Loyola (1491–1556), the

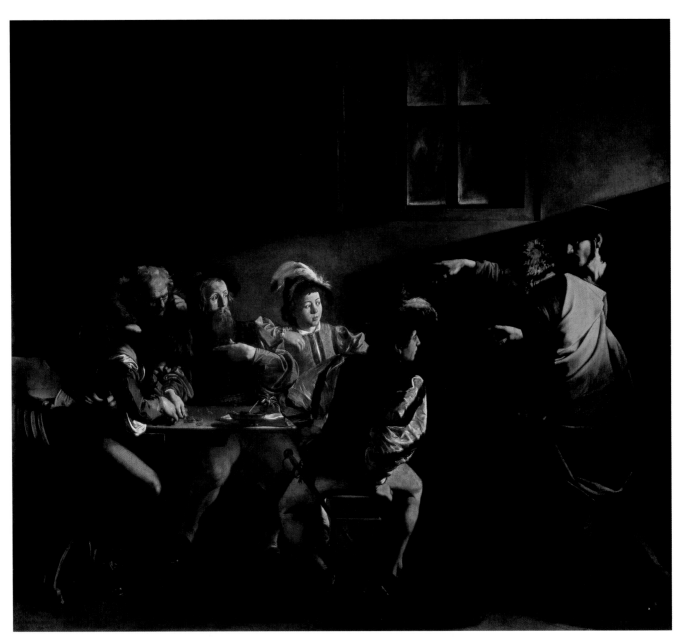

14–8 Caravaggio. *The Calling of Saint Matthew.* 1599–1600. Oil on canvas, 10′ 7 1/2″ × 11′ 2 ″ (3.24 × 3.4 m). Contarelli Chapel, Church of San Luigi dei Francesi, Rome

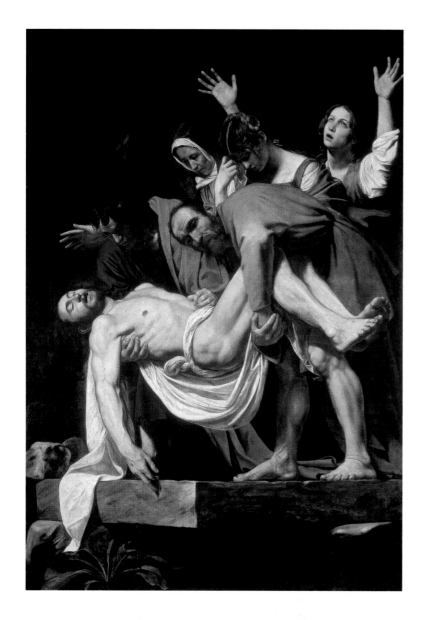

14–9 Caravaggio. *Entombment,* from the Vittrici Chapel, Church of Santa Maria in Vallicella, Rome. 1603–1604. Oil on canvas, 9′ 10 1/8″ × 6′ 7 15/16″ (3 × 2.03 m). Musei Vaticani, Pinacoteca, Rome

The Entombment *was one of many paintings confiscated from Rome's churches and taken to Paris during the French occupation by Napoleon's troops, and it was one of the few to be returned after 1815. Pope Pius VII and his agents were assisted in the negotiations by the sculptor Antonio Canova. The decision was made not to return the artworks to their original churches and chapels but instead to assemble them in a gallery where the general public could enjoy them. Today, Caravaggio's painting is one of the most important in the collections of the Vatican Museums.*

founder of the Jesuit order. It was also connected to the populist theology of the preacher Filippi Neri, later canonized as Saint Philip Neri (1515–1595), who consciously strove to make Christian history and doctrine meaningful to common people.

Caravaggio painted one of his earliest religious commissions, *The Calling of Saint Matthew* (fig. **14–8**), during the years 1599–1600 for the private chapel of the Cointrel family (Contarelli in Italian) in the French community's church in Rome. The painting depicts the moment recorded in the Gospels when Jesus called the tax collector Levi to become one of his apostles (Mark 2:14, Matthew 9:9). Nearly hidden behind the beckoning Saint Peter, the gaunt-faced Jesus dramatically points toward Levi—who will become Saint Matthew but who is now surrounded by young men in plumed hats, velvet doublets, and satin shirts. For all the naturalism of these figures, Caravaggio also used antique and Renaissance sources. Jesus's outstretched arm, for example, recalls God giving life to Adam in Michelangelo's *Creation of Adam* on the Sistine Ceiling (although the hand is a reverse image of Adam's) (see page 349). The future Saint Matthew responds by pointing to himself in surprise, a gesture emphasized by the stream of light entering the painting

from a high, unseen source at the right. The dramatic contrast of light and dark is a heightened variant of chiaroscuro known as tenebrism, an invention of Caravaggio.

The emotional power of Baroque naturalism combines with a solemn, classical monumentality in Caravaggio's *Entombment* (fig. **14–9**), painted in 1603–1604 for a chapel in Santa Maria in Vallicella, the church of St. Philip Neri's Congregation of the Oratory. With almost physical force, the size and immediacy of this painting strikes the viewer. The figures form a large off-center triangle, with the young John the Evangelist at the apex. Angular elements are repeated: the projecting edge of the stone slab; Jesus's bent legs; the akimbo arm, bunched coat, and knock-kneed stance of the bending man on the right. The Virgin and Mary Magdalene barely intrude on the scene, which, through the careful placing of the light, focuses on the body of Christ.

Despite the esteem in which Caravaggio was held as an artist, his violent temper repeatedly got him into trouble. During the last decade of his life, he was frequently arrested, generally for minor offenses: throwing a plate of artichokes at a waiter, carrying arms illegally, street brawling. By 1606, he had to flee from Rome. From then on he was on the run, supporting himself

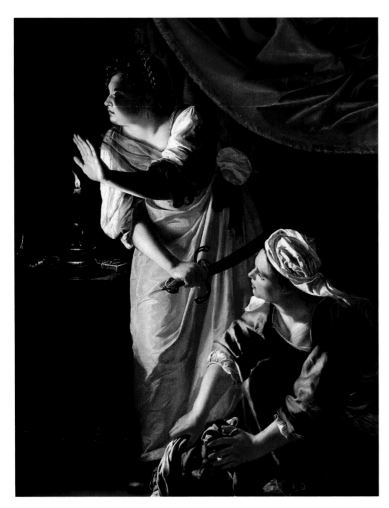

14–10 Artemisia Gentileschi. *Judith and Her Maidservant with the Head of Holofernes.* c. 1625. Oil on canvas, 72 $\frac{1}{2}$" × 55 $\frac{3}{4}$" (184.2 × 141.6 cm). The Detroit Institute of Arts, Detroit Michigan

GIFT OF LESLIE H. GREEN

The beautiful Jewish widow Judith saved her people from the Assyrian army by entering the enemy camp and enticing the general Holofernes to eat and drink until he fell into a stupor. She cut off his head and escaped, carrying off the head as evidence of her heroic act.

Art in the Habsburg Empire

The leaders of the Church lived like princes, but they were not the only patrons of the arts in seventeenth-century Europe. With the growth of nation-states and absolute monarchies, kings and nobles realized that impressive buildings and splendid portraits could secure and enhance their status by surrounding them with an aura of power. Spain's Habsburg kings Philip II, Philip III, Philip IV, and Charles II saw the political and economic decline of the Spanish part of their empire. But one would not guess it from the art. What had seemed an endless flow of gold and silver from the Americas diminished, and Protestant England and the Dutch Republic were an increasingly serious threat to Spanish trade and colonial possessions. Agriculture, industry, and trade all suffered, and there were repeated local rebellions, culminating in 1640, when Portugal reestablished its independence.

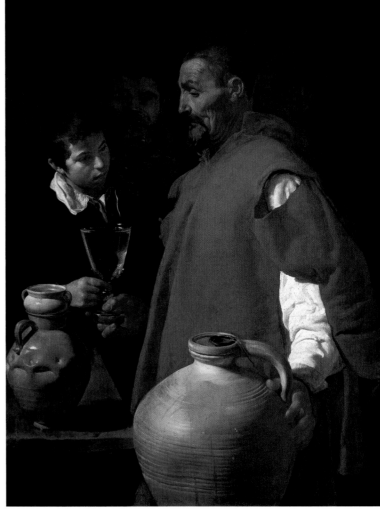

14–11 Diego Velázquez. *Water Carrier of Seville.* c. 1619. Oil on canvas, 41 $\frac{1}{2}$" × 31 $\frac{1}{2}$" (105.3 × 80 cm). Wellington Museum, London

V & A PICTURE LIBRARY

In the oppressively hot climate of Seville, Spain, where this painting was made, water vendors walked the streets selling their cool liquid from large clay jars like the one in the foreground. In this scene, the clarity and purity of the water are proudly attested to by its seller, who offers the customer a sample poured into a glass goblet. The jug contents were usually sweetened by the addition of a piece of fresh fruit or a sprinkle of aromatic herbs.

by painting. He died of a fever on July 18, 1610, just short of his thirty-ninth birthday.

Caravaggio inspired an entire generation of painters with his tenebrist technique and intense realism. One of Caravaggio's most successful Italian followers was Artemisia Gentileschi (1593–c. 1652/3), whose international reputation helped spread the Caravaggesque style beyond Rome. Born in Rome, Artemisia first studied and worked under her father, a follower of Caravaggio. In 1616 she moved to Florence, where she was elected to the Florentine Academy of Design. As a resident of Florence, Artemisia was well aware of the city's identification with the Jewish hero David and heroine Judith (subjects of sculpture by Donatello and Michelangelo). In one of several versions of Judith triumphant over the Assyrian general Holofernes (fig. **14–10**), Artemisia brilliantly uses Baroque naturalism and tenebrist effects, dramatically showing Judith still holding the bloody sword and hiding the candle's light as her maid stuffs the general's head into a sack. Throughout her life, Artemisia painted images of heroic and abused women, including Judith, Susanna, Bathsheba, and Esther.

Spain

In spite of economic decline, Spanish artists and writers created a "Golden Age," which included one of the most brilliant painters of any age: Diego Rodriguez de Silva y Velázquez (1599–1660). Velázquez entered the painters' guild of Seville in 1617. Like many artists in Spain and Spanish-ruled Naples in the early seventeenth century, at the beginning of his career he was profoundly influenced by Caravaggio. As a young artist, Velázquez, who worked from life, painted tavern, market, and kitchen scenes, showing ordinary people amid still lifes of various foods and kitchen utensils. The model for the *Water Carrier of Seville* (fig. **14–11**), a painting of about 1619, was a well-known character in that city. The objects and figures in the painting, arranged with an almost mathematical rigor, allowed the artist to exhibit his virtuosity in rendering sculptural volumes and contrasting textures such as pottery, glass, and fabrics. All the elements in the picture are illuminated by dramatic natural light in Velázquez's version of Caravaggio's tenebrism.

In 1623, Velázquez moved to Madrid, where the young artist became a courtier and the official painter for the young Habsburg monarch Philip IV (ruled 1621–1665), a powerful position that he maintained until his death in 1660. Visits to Italy in 1629–1631 and again in 1649–1651—where Velázquez studied narrative paintings with complex figural compositions—influenced the evolution of the artist's style.

Perhaps Velázquez's most striking and enigmatic work is the enormous multiple portrait known as *Las Meninas*, or *The Maids of Honor*, painted in 1656, near the end of the artist's life (fig. **14–12**). Here, Velázquez draws the spectator directly into the scene. The viewer seems to stand in the space occupied by King Philip and his queen, whose reflections can be seen in the large mirror on the back wall. Velázquez himself is also present, brushes and palette in hand, beside a huge canvas. However, the central focus of the painting is the royal couple's five-year-old daughter, the Infanta (Princess) Margarita. She is surrounded by attendants, all of whom are identifiable portraits. In a bravura style of painting that fascinated the French Impressionist painters of the nineteenth century (see fig. 18–21), Velázquez built up his forms with layers of loosely applied paint and finished off the surfaces with dashing highlights in white, lemon, and pale orange. His technique captures the appearance of light on surfaces, while on close inspection his forms dissolve into a complex maze of individual strokes of paint. Throughout his life, Velázquez had sought respect and acclaim for himself and for the art of painting. In *Las Meninas*, dressed as a courtier and wearing the noble Order of Santiago on his chest and the keys of the palace in his sash, Velázquez proclaimed the dignity and importance of painting as one of the liberal arts.

Velázquez's younger colleague from Seville, Bartolomé Esteban Murillo, was one of the most popular painters of his day. Known for his rich colors and skillful technique, Murillo

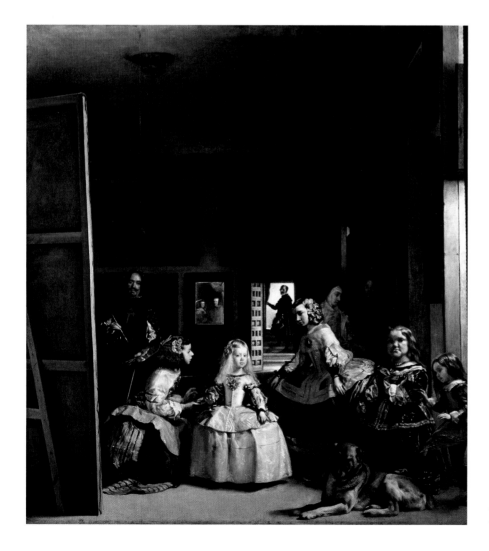

14–12 Diego Velázquez. *Las Meninas (The Maids of Honor).* 1656. Oil on canvas, 10′5″ × 9′½″ (3.18 × 2.76 m). Museo del Prado, Madrid

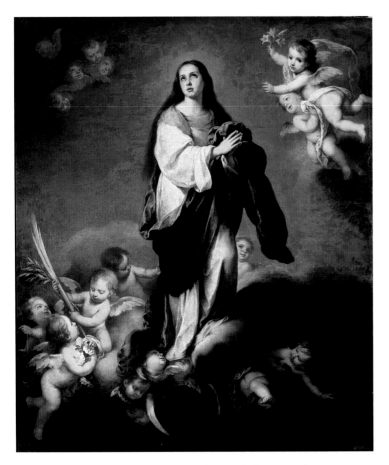

14–13 Bartolomé Esteban Murillo. *The Esquilache Immaculate Conception.* c. 1645–1650. Oil on canvas, 7′8″ × 6′5″ (2.35 × 1.96 m). State Hermitage Museum, St. Petersburg, Russia

Counter-Reformation authorities had provided specific instructions for artists who painted the Virgin: Mary was to be dressed in blue and white, hands folded in prayer, and standing on a crescent moon as she is carried upward by angels surrounded by an unearthly light ("clothed in the sun"). Angels often carry palms and symbols of the Virgin, such as a mirror, fountain, roses, and lilies. They also vanquish Satan, who is represented as a serpent.

Murillo's home, Seville, was a center for trade with the Spanish colonies, and the Church exported many paintings by the artist to the New World. When the native population began to visualize the Christian story, paintings such as Murillo's provided the imagery. The Spanish colonization of the Americas dates to 1519, when Hernan Cortes arrived off the coast of Mexico. Within two years, after forging alliances with enemies of the dominant Aztec people, Cortes succeeded in taking the Aztec capital, Tenochtitlan (on the site of present-day Mexico City). Over the next several years, Spanish forces established Mexico as a colony of Spain. In the wake of the conquest, the European conquerors suppressed local beliefs and practices and imposed Roman Catholicism throughout Spanish America.

Converts in Mexico gained their own patron saint after the Virgin Mary appeared to an Indian, Juan Diego, in 1531. Mary is said to have asked that a church be built on a hill where the goddess Coatlicue had once been worshiped. As evidence of this vision, Juan Diego brought the archbishop flowers that the Virgin had caused to bloom. He carried the flowers wrapped in his cloak, and when he opened his bundle, the cloak bore the image of a dark-skinned Mary in the guise of the Virgin of the Immaculate Conception. An eighteenth-century work by the painter Sebastian Salcedo depicts Mary and the story of Juan Diego (fig. **14–14**). The site of the vision was renamed Guadalupe, after Our Lady of Guadalupe in Spain, and became a venerated pilgrimage center. In 1754, the pope declared the Virgin of Guadalupe to be the patron saint of the Americas.

specialized in religious art and especially in paintings of the Immaculate Conception (fig. **14–13**), the controversial idea that Mary was born free from original sin. Devotion to Mary became widespread during the seventeenth and eighteenth centuries.

ELEMENTS OF **Architecture**

The Baroque Façade

In the seventeenth and eighteenth centuries European architects reinterpreted the classical vocabulary of the Renaissance in ways that emphasized the power and grandeur of the church and state. Vigorously projecting and receding walls, columns and pediments in the elevation, and an overall profusion of sculptural ornament create an arresting theatrical display. Portals become special focal points where the vertical composition of doors and windows can become a lavish sculptural creation. Elaborate late-Baroque styles spread throughout the Habsburg territories and even reached the American colonies.

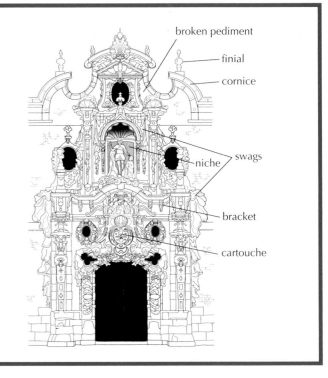

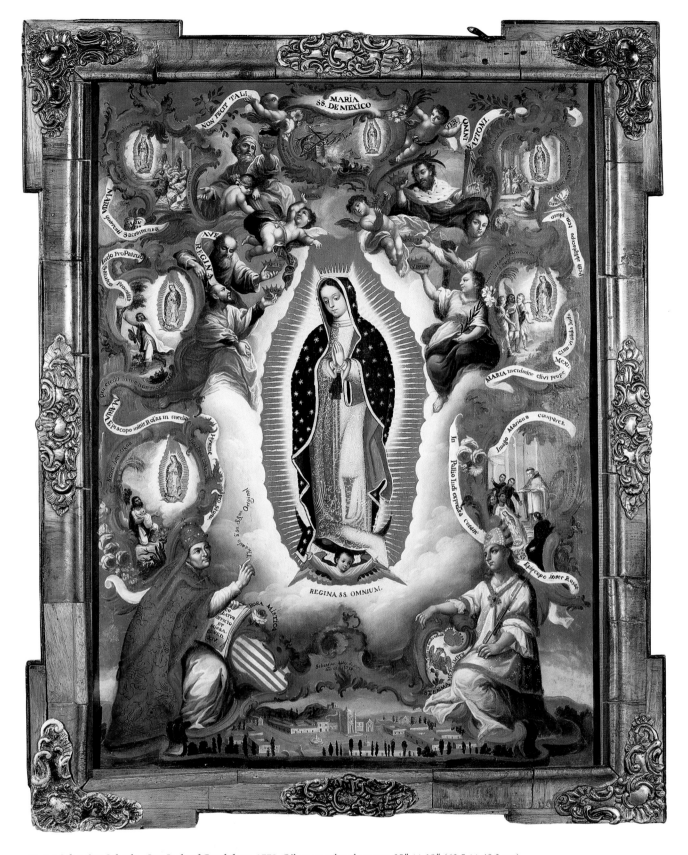

14–14 Sebastian Salcedo. *Our Lady of Guadalupe.* 1779. Oil on panel and copper, 25″ × 19″ (63.5 × 48.3 cm).
Denver Art Museum

COLLECTION, FUNDS CONTRIBUTED BY MR. AND MRS. GEORGE G. ANDERMAN AND AN ANONYMOUS DONOR, (1976–56)

At the bottom right is the female personification of New Spain (Mexico) and at the left is Pope Benedict XIV, who in 1754 declared the Virgin of Guadalupe to be the patron of the Americas. Between the figures, the sanctuary of Guadalupe in Mexico can be seen in the distance. The four small scenes circling the Virgin represent the story of Juan Diego, and at the top, three scenes depict Mary's miracles. The six figures above the Virgin represent Old Testament prophets and patriarchs and New Testament apostles and saints.

Flanders

The Spanish Habsburgs also held Flanders during most of the Baroque period. After a period of relative autonomy under Habsburg regents from 1598 to 1633, the region came under direct and often oppressive Spanish rule. In spite of the shift in political climate, however, artists of great talent flourished in Antwerp, a cultural capital and major art center, where the Spanish were enthusiastic patrons of the arts.

The art of Peter Paul Rubens (1577–1640), who worked for the Habsburgs and other rulers, has become nearly synonymous with the Flemish Baroque style. Rubens was accepted into the Antwerp painters' guild at the age of 21, and shortly thereafter, in 1600, he left for Italy, where he obtained a post with the duke of Mantua. Other than designs for court entertainment and occasional portraits, the duke never acquired a single original work of art by Rubens. Instead, he had him copy famous paintings in collections all over Italy to add to the ducal collection, and so inadvertently provided the young painter with an excellent education.

Rubens returned in 1608 to Antwerp, where he accepted employment from the Habsburg governors of Flanders, the Spanish princess Isabel Clara Eugenia (the daughter of Philip II) and her husband, Archduke Albert. His first major commission was a large canvas triptych for the main altar of the Church of Saint Walpurga, *The Raising of the Cross* (fig. **14–15**), painted in 1609–1610. Unlike many earlier triptychs, in which the wings contain related but independent images—as seen, for example, in Grünewald's Isenheim Altarpiece (fig. 13–31)—Rubens extended the action and landscape of the central scene across all three sections. At the center, Herculean figures strain to haul upright the wooden cross with Jesus already stretched upon it. The followers of Jesus mourn at left, and indifferent soldiers on the right supervise the execution. In his paintings Rubens merges the drama and intense emotion of Caravaggio with the virtuoso technique of Annibale, but he transforms these qualities into a distinctive personal style. The heroic nude figures, dramatic lighting effects, dynamic diagonal composition, and intense emotions show the artist's debt to Italian art, but the rich colors and the realism of the varied textures and surfaces reflect his native Flemish tradition.

Rubens's intelligence, courtly manners, and personal charm made him a valuable and trusted courtier to royal patrons, including Philip IV of Spain, Marie de' Medici of France, and Charles I of England. In fact, he became the first international superstar of the art world. In 1621, Marie de' Medici, widow of King Henri IV and regent for her young son, Louis XIII, asked Rubens to paint the story of her life. In 21 paintings, Rubens glorified her role in ruling France and also commemorated the founding of the Bourbon dynasty, which began with Henri IV. In Rubens's paintings, the lives and political careers of Marie and Henri appear as one continuous triumph overseen by the Roman gods. In the painting depicting the royal engagement (fig. **14–16**),

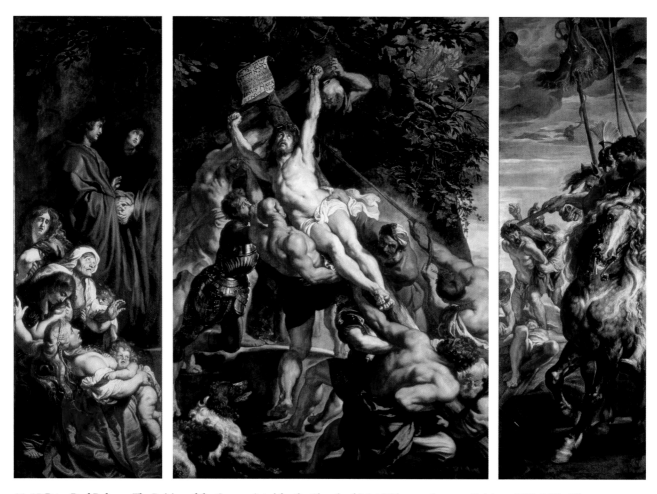

14–15 Peter Paul Rubens. *The Raising of the Cross,* painted for the Church of Saint Walpurga, Antwerp, Belgium. 1609–1610. Oil on canvas, center panel: 15′1⅞″ × 11′1½″ (4.62 × 3.39 m); each wing: 15′1⅞″ × 4′11⅞″ (4.62 × 1.52 m). Cathedral of Our Lady, Antwerp

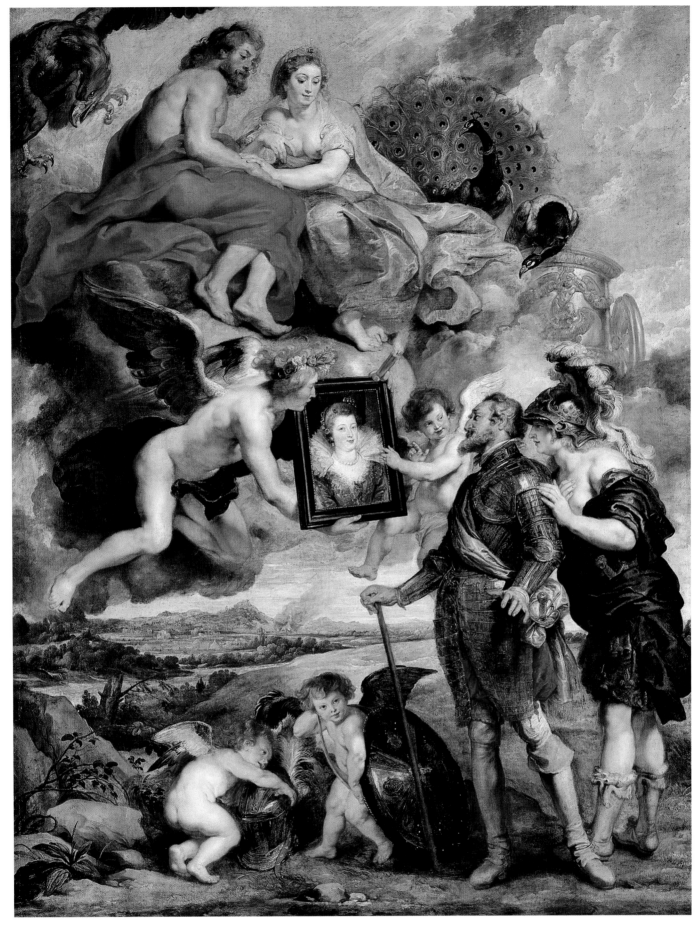

14–16 Peter Paul Rubens. *Henri IV Receiving the Portrait of Marie de' Medici.* 1621–1625. Oil on canvas, 12′11 1/8″ × 9′8 1/8″ (3.94 × 2.95 m). Musée du Louvre, Paris

Of the five paintings in the series of the allergories on *Senses*, painted for the Habsburg rulers, *Sight* (fig. **14–17**) is the most splendid. It is almost an illustrated catalog of the ducal collection. Gathered in a huge vaulted room are paintings, sculpture, furniture, objects in gold and silver, and scientific equipment—all under the magnificent double-headed eagle emblem of the Habsburgs (at the top of the chandelier). The viewer is encouraged to explore the painting *Sight* inch by inch, as if reading a book or a palace inventory. There on the table are Brueghel's copies of Rubens's portraits of Archduke Albert and Princess Isabel Clara Eugenia; another portrait of the duke is on the floor. Besides the portraits, we can find Rubens's *Daniel in the Lions' Den* (upper left corner), *The Lion and Tiger Hunt* (top center), and *The Drunken Silenus* (lower right), as well as the popular subject *Madonna and Child in a Wreath of Flowers* (far right), for which Rubens painted the Madonna and Brueghel created the wreath. Brueghel also included Raphael's *Saint Cecilia* (behind the globe) and Titian's *Venus and Psyche* (over the door).

In the foreground, the classical goddess Venus attended by Cupid (both painted by Rubens) has put aside her mirror to contemplate Jan Brueghel's painting *Christ Healing the Blind*. Venus is surrounded by the equipment needed to see and to study: the huge globe (the earth) at the right and the armillary sphere with its gleaming rings (the heavens) at the upper left symbolize the extent of Humanistic learning. In symbolism that speaks to viewers of our time as clearly as it did to those during Rubens's and Brueghel's day, the books and prints, ruler, compasses, magnifying glass, and the more complex astrolabe, telescope, and eyeglasses refer to those who look but do not see, that is, to spiritual blindness.

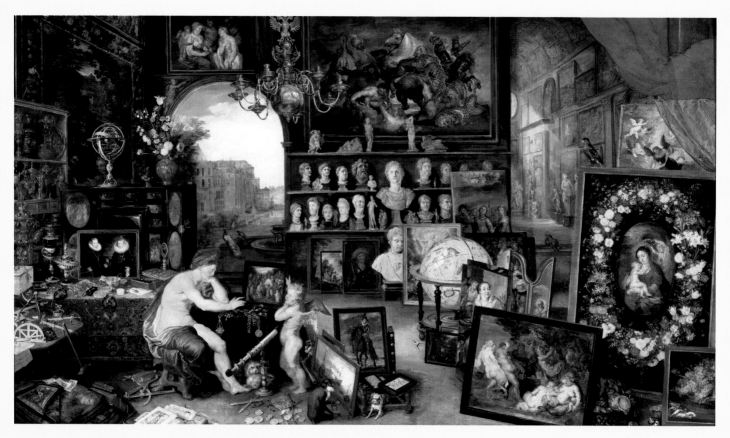

14–17 Jan Brueghel and Peter Paul Rubens. *Sight,* one of the allegorical series ***The Five Senses.*** c. 1617–1618. Oil on panel, 25 5/8″ × 43″ (65 × 109 cm). Museo del Prado, Madrid

Henri IV falls in love with Marie as he gazes at her portrait, shown to him by Cupid and the god of marriage, Hymen. The supreme Roman god, Jupiter, and his wife, Juno, look down approvingly from the clouds. Henri, silhouetted against a landscape in which the smoke of battle lingers, is encouraged by a personification of France to abandon war for love, as putti frolic below with pieces of his armor. The sustained visual excitement of these enormous canvases makes them not only important works of art but political propaganda of the highest order.

Rubens, who accepted commissions from all over Europe, employed dozens of assistants as specialists in the painting of portraits, textiles, landscapes, and even fruits and flowers. Using workshop assistants was standard practice among major artists, but Rubens was particularly efficient and created something close to a painting factory. Working from his detailed sketches, his assistants completed giant canvases suitable for palatial rooms. Among these assistants were two artists who became, important painters in their own right: Jan Brueghel and Anthony van Dyck.

Jan Brueghel (1568–1625), the grandson of Pieter Bruegel (see fig. 13–38) (Jan added the "h" to the family name), was Rubens's neighbor in Antwerp. The two artists frequently collaborated, with Rubens painting the figures and Brueghel creating allegorical settings for them. About 1617 Rubens and Brueghel painted a series of allegories on the theme of the senses for the rulers of the Habsburg Netherlands, Princess Isabel Clara Eugenia and Archduke Albert, who were enthusiastic patrons of the arts and sciences. Indeed, it was their vast collection that inspired the painting allergory on *Sight* (fig. **14–17**).

Another of Rubens's collaborators, Anthony van Dyck (1599–1641), had an illustrious independent career as a portraitist. A precocious student at ten, he had his own studio and a roster of pupils at age 16, although he did not become a member of the Antwerp painters' guild until 1618, the year after he began his association with Rubens as a painter of heads. Later in his career, Van Dyck became court painter to Charles I of England, by whom he was knighted and given a studio, a large salary, and a summer home.

In *Charles I at the Hunt* (fig. **14–18**) of 1635, Van Dyck was able, by clever manipulation of the setting, to portray the king truthfully and yet as a quietly imposing figure. Dressed casually for the hunt and standing on a bluff overlooking a distant view, Charles, who was in fact a very small person, is shown as being taller than his pages and even than his horse, since the animal has lowered its head and its heavy body is partly off the canvas. The viewer's gaze is directed to the king's pleasant features, framed by his jauntily cocked hat. As if in decorous homage, the tree branches bow gracefully toward him, echoing the circular lines of the hat. Contrary to the appearance suggested by Van Dyck's portrait, Charles was not destined to rule his country successfully. As we shall see in the next section, he was a better patron of the arts than politician and king.

Protestant England

England and Scotland had been joined under a Stuart monarch since the death of the imposing Queen Elizabeth I (ruled 1558–1603), when James VI of Scotland ascended the English throne as James I (ruled 1603–1625). Charles I, who ruled from 1625 to 1649, was James's son.

In 1615 King James I had appointed the architect Inigo Jones (1573–1652) to be surveyor-general and commissioned him to design a residence for the queen in Greenwich and a banqueting house at the royal palace of Whitehall in London. Jones, whose architectural style was based on the work of the Renaissance architect Andrea Palladio (see Chapter 13), introduced Renaissance classicism to England. Jones owned a copy of the Italian architect's famous treatise, the *Four Books of Architecture*.

14–18 Anthony van Dyck. *Charles I at the Hunt.*
1635. Oil on canvas, 9′ × 7′ (2.75 × 2.14 m)
Musée du Louvre, Paris

The Whitehall Banqueting House, constructed in 1619–1622 to replace an earlier building destroyed by fire, exemplifies the understated elegance of Jones's interpretation of Palladian design (fig. **14–19**). The Banqueting House was used for court entertainments and ceremonies. The building is one large hall with a balcony on the upper level, and antechambers at each end, one of which contains an entrance. Ionic pilasters suggest a colonnade but do not impinge on the ideal, double-cube space.

In 1630, Charles I commissioned Peter Paul Rubens to decorate the ceiling. Unlike the unified space created by Italian painters like Gaulli (fig. 14–7), Jones divided the flat surface of the ceiling into nine compartments. Rubens painted canvases glorifying the reign of James I, centered around a classical apotheosis of the king and the Stuart dynasty that recalls Veronese's glorification of Venice (Introduction, fig. 15). So proud was Charles of the pictures installed in 1635 that, rather than allow

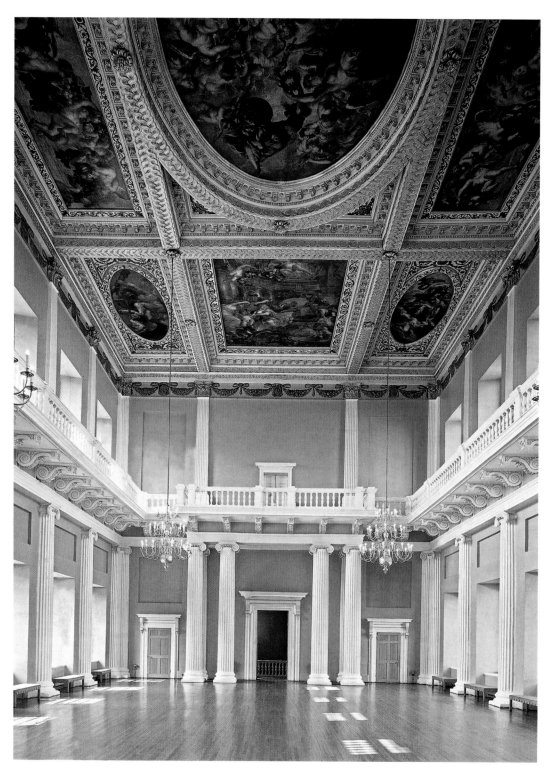

14–19 Inigo Jones. Banqueting House, Whitehall Palace, Interior. Ceiling paintings by Peter Paul Rubens: the *Apotheosis of King James* and *The Glorification of the Stuart Monarchy.* 1630–1635

the smoke of candles and torches to darken them, he moved the evening entertainments to an adjacent pavilion.

Religious and political tensions, particularly a conflict between Charles and the religious reformers known as Puritans, resulted in a series of civil wars, beginning in 1642. Charles lost his throne, and his head, in 1649. Once in power, the Puritans, led by Oliver Cromwell as lord protector, stifled artistic expression. However, austerity did not last, and in 1660, the restoration of the Stuart dynasty under Charles II brought renewed patronage of foreign artists, especially portrait painters. The next century would see the rise of art and architecture in the British Isles and the American colonies that we call *Georgian*, after the Hanoverian kings, George I, II, and III.

The Protestant Netherlands

Spain recognized the sovereignty of the northern Netherlands in 1648. Even before this official recognition, the Dutch Republic—as the United Northern Provinces of the Low Countries was officially known—managed not only to maintain its hard-won freedom but to also prosper. Dutch artists found many eager patrons among the prosperous middle-class citizens of Amsterdam, Leiden, Haarlem, Delft, and Utrecht. Group portraiture that documented the membership of corporate organizations became a Dutch specialty. These large canvases, filled with many individuals who shared the cost of the commission, challenged painters to present a coherent, interesting composition that also gave equal attention to each individual portrait.

Frans Hals (c. 1581/85–1666), the leading painter of Haarlem, developed a style grounded in the Netherlandish love of realism and inspired by the Caravaggesque style. Yet like Velázquez, he tried to re-create the optical effects of light on the shapes and textures of objects. He painted boldly, with slashing strokes and angular patches of paint; when seen at a distance, the colors merge into solid forms over which a flickering light seems to move. Hals's dynamic composition turned the group portrait, such as his *Officers of the Haarlem Militia Company of Saint Adrian* (fig. **14–20**) of about 1627, into a lively social event, even while maintaining a strong underlying geometry of diagonal lines—gestures, banners, and sashes—balanced by the stabilizing

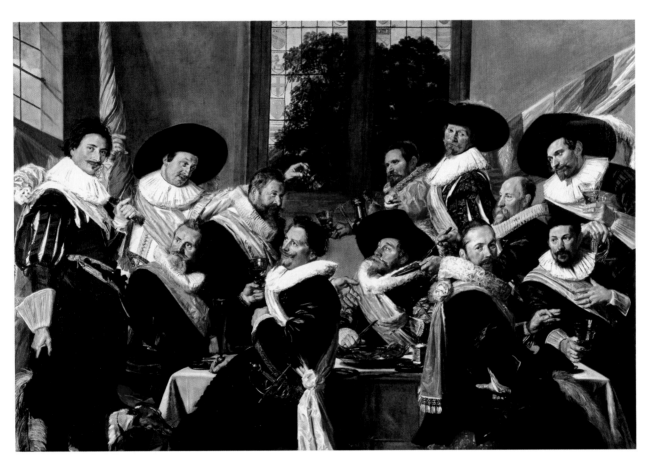

14–20 Frans Hals. *Officers of the Haarlem Militia Company of Saint Adrian.* c. 1627. Oil on canvas, 6′ × 8′8″ (1.83 × 2.67 m). Frans Halsmuseum, Haarlem

Hals painted several group portraits of civic-guard organizations, including two for the Company of Saint Adrian. The company, made up of several guard units, was charged with the protection of Haarlem. Officers came from the upper-middle class and held their commissions for three years, whereas the ordinary guards were tradespeople and craftsmen. Each company was organized like a guild, under the patronage of a saint. When the men were not on alert, the company functioned as a fraternal order, holding archery competitions, taking part in city processions, and maintaining an altar in the local church.

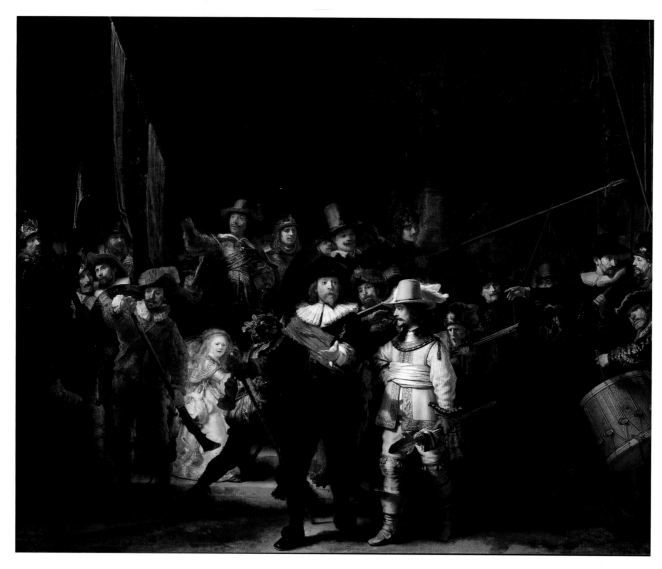

14–21 Rembrandt van Rijn. *Captain Frans Banning Cocq Mustering His Company (The Night Watch).*
1642. Oil on canvas (cut down from the original size), 11′11″ × 14′4″ (3.63 × 4.37 m). Rijksmuseum, Amsterdam

horizontal and vertical perpendiculars of table, window, tall glass, and striped banner. The black suits and hats make the white ruffs and sashes of rose, white, and blue even more brilliant.

The most important painter working in the Netherlands in the seventeenth century was Rembrandt van Rijn (1606–1669). After studying painting in Amsterdam and Leiden and working as an artist in both cities, Rembrandt established a busy studio in Amsterdam. He continued his studies with close observation of the art of his predecessors, such as his analysis of Leonardo's *Last Supper* (see Introduction, figs. 21 and 22, and fig. 13–2) as well as intense observation of the world around him. His repertoire included paintings and etchings of mythological subjects, religious scenes, and landscapes, but like many Dutch artists of the time his primary source of income was portraiture.

In 1640 a civic guard company commissioned Rembrandt to create a large group portrait of its members for its new meeting hall. *Captain Frans Banning Cocq Mustering His Company* (fig. **14–21**) was traditionally known as *The Night Watch*

because in the nineteenth century a layer of dirt and old varnish obscured its colors so that viewers thought the subject was a night scene. After recent cleaning and restoration, the painting glows with a natural golden light that sets afire the palette of rich colors—browns, blues, olive green, orange, and red—around a central core of lemon yellow. As the company takes up its ranks, the crowd, including children, mill around. The surprising image of the running girl carrying a chicken with claws *(klauw* in Dutch) prominently displayed may be a pun on the name of the guns *(klover)* that gave the name Kloveniers to the company. The complex interactions of the figures and the vivid, individualized likenesses of the militiamen make this painting one of the greatest group portraits in European art.

Rembrandt also created profoundly moving religious art. His etchings and drypoints (see "Etching and Drypoint," on page 404) were sought after, widely collected, and brought high prices even in his lifetime. As he grew older, Rembrandt seems to have experienced a deepening religious commitment. In his print

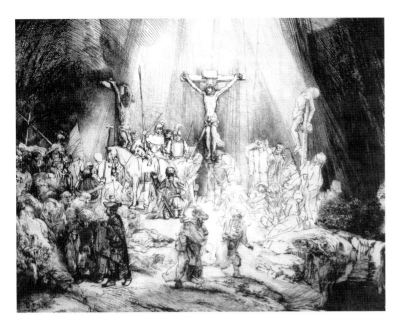

14–22 Rembrandt van Rijn. *The Three Crosses* (first state). 1663. Drypoint and etching, 15 1/6″ × 17 3/4″ (38.5 × 45 cm). Rijksmuseum, Amsterdam

In The Three Crosses, *Rembrandt defined the mystery of Jesus's sacrifice not in realistic terms but as something beyond rational explanation. In Rembrandt's late works, his realism relates to spiritual inner meanings, not to surface details. The eternal battles of dark and light, doom and salvation, evil and good all seem to be waged anew.*

The Three Crosses, Rembrandt tried to capture the moment during the Crucifixion, as described in the gospels, when Jesus cried out, "Father, into your hands I commend my spirit" (Luke 23:46). We can follow Rembrandt's intellectual process through four successive stages, from the relatively anecdotal depiction of the crosses and the surrounding crowd in the first state (fig. **14–22**) to the haunting blackness of the fourth and final state. As Jesus cries out, a mystical light illuminates the darkened scene. Mary, the apostles, and the Roman soldiers are captured and immobilized by the blinding light. Here Rembrandt has depicted the miracle of redemption and the power of God.

Rembrandt painted many self-portraits. These images became more searching as the artist aged and, like many of his paintings, expressed a personal, internalized spirituality new in the history of art. In a self-portrait of 1658 (fig. **14–23**), the half-length figure and the setting merge in a rich, luminous chiaroscuro, with the face and clasped hands emerging out of the darkness. A few well-placed brushstrokes suggest the physical tension in the fingers and the weariness of the soul in the deepset eyes. Mercilessly analytical, the portrait depicts the furrowed brow, sagging flesh, and prematurely aged face (he was only 53) of one who has suffered deeply but retained his dignity.

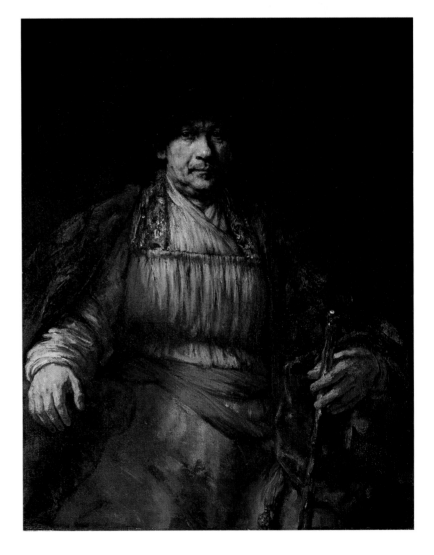

14–23 Rembrandt van Rijn. *Self-Portrait.* 1658.
Oil on canvas, 52 5/8″ × 40 7/8″ (133.6 × 103.8 cm).
The Frick Collection, New York

More typical of Dutch painters, Judith Leyster (c. 1609–1660) painted boisterous genre scenes categorized in their own time by descriptive titles such as "merry company" or "garden party." In her lively *Self-Portrait* (fig. **14–24**), Leyster displays on her easel the type of work on which her popularity was based. The subject, a man playing a violin, may also be a visual pun on the painter's instruments, the palette and brush. To let the viewer immediately see the difference between her painted portrait and the painted painting, she varied her technique, executing the image on her easel more loosely. The narrow range of colors sensitively dispersed in the composition and the warm spotlighting are typical of Leyster's mature style.

The art produced in the Netherlands during the seventeenth century shows that the Dutch delighted in depictions not only of themselves, but also of their country's landscape, cities, and domestic concerns. *The Drawing Lesson* by Jan Steen (see Introduction,

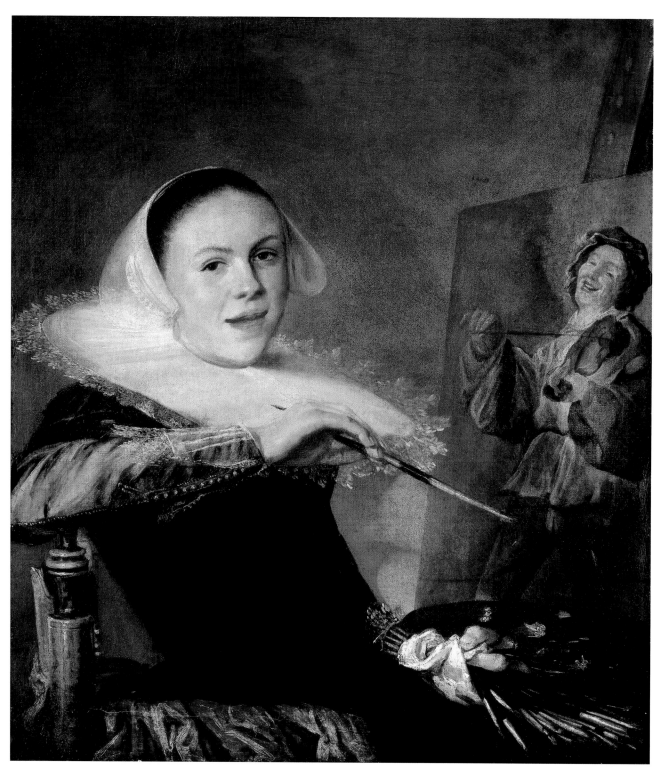

14–24 Judith Leyster. *Self-Portrait.* c. 1630. Oil on canvas, 29 3/8″ × 25 5/8″ (74.6 × 45.1 cm). National Gallery of Art, Washington, D.C.

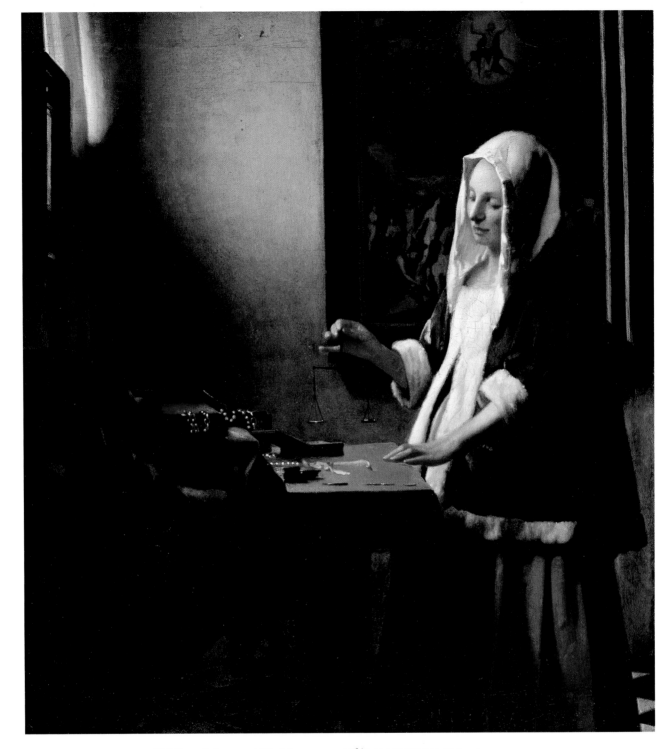

14–25 Jan Vermeer. *Woman Holding a Balance.* c. 1664. Oil on canvas, $16^3/_4''$ × 15″ (42.5 × 38.1 cm).
National Gallery of Art, Washington, D.C.

The artist's shift of viewpoint slightly to one side has created an interesting spatial composition,
and strong contrasts of light and shade add drama to the simple interior.

fig. 20) is typical of the beautifully painted scenes of daily life (genre paintings) that appealed to middle-class patrons of the arts.

Perhaps the greatest Dutch painter of contemporary life was Jan (Johannes) Vermeer of Delft (1632–1675). Vermeer produced few works. Many are enigmatic scenes of women in domestic settings, occupied with some cultivated activity such as writing, reading letters, or making music. Scholars have noted that many works by Vermeer, like other Dutch genre paintings, contain apparently symbolic elements that suggest underlying meanings. The artist, a Catholic in a Protestant country, sometimes added a sobering religious reference to his work. Vermeer's *Woman Holding a Balance* (fig. **14–25**), painted about 1664, can be understood straightforwardly as an exquisitely painted genre scene in which every object is carefully placed to achieve an overall balance and is illuminated by the clear, even light. However, the painting on the wall behind the

Technique

Etching and Drypoint

Rembrandt was the first artist to popularize etching as a major form of artistic expression. In the etching process, a metal plate is coated on both sides with an acid-resistant resin that dries hard without being brittle. Then, instead of laboriously cutting the lines of the desired image directly into the plate, the artist draws through the resin with a sharp needle to expose the metal. The plate is then immersed in acid, which eats into the metal exposed by the drawn lines. By controlling the time the acid stays on different parts of the plate, the artist can make fine, shallow lines or heavy, deep ones. The resin covering the plate is removed before an impression is taken. If a change needs to be made, the lines can be "erased" with a sharp metal scraper. Not surprisingly, a complex image with a wide range of tones requires many steps.

Another technique for registering images on a metal plate is called drypoint, in which a sharp needle is used to scratch lines in the metal. In drypoint, however, the burr, or metal pushed up by the drypoint needle, is left in place. Unlike engraving, in which the burr is scraped off, both the burr and the groove hold the ink. This creates a printed line with a rich black appearance that is impossible to achieve with engraving or etching alone. Unfortunately, drypoint burr is fragile, and only a few prints—a dozen or fewer—can be made before it flattens and loses its character. Rembrandt's earliest prints were entirely etched, but later he added drypoint to achieve greater tonal richness.

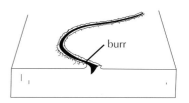

young woman depicts the Last Judgment, suggesting that the empty balance in the woman's hand is more than a casual inclusion. Also, the jewelry and coins on the table and the mirror on the wall are traditional elements in paintings that deal with the theme of *vanitas* (the vanity of earthly things), which stress the fleeting nature of beauty, youth, and riches.

Another type of genre painting that achieved great popularity in the Baroque period is the architectural interior. These views seem to have been painted for their own special beauty, just as were exterior views of the land, cities, and harbors. Emanuel de Witte (c. 1617–1692) specialized in architectural painting in Delft and in Amsterdam. Many of his interiors are

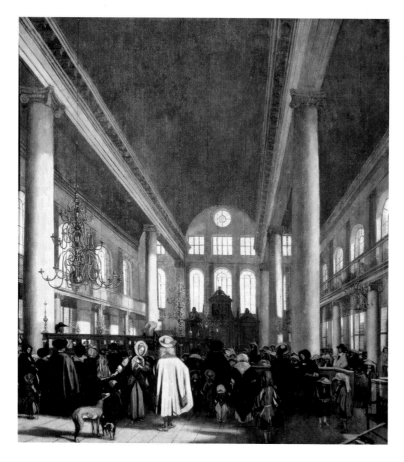

14–26 Emanuel de Witte. *Portuguese Synagogue, Amsterdam.* 1680. Oil on canvas, 43 $\frac{1}{2}$″ × 39″ (110.5 × 99.1 cm). Rijksmuseum, Amsterdam

depictions of actual buildings, such as his *Portuguese Synagogue, Amsterdam* (fig. **14–26**). Today this painting is interesting not only as a work of art, but also as a record of seventeenth-century synagogue architecture and as evidence of Dutch religious tolerance in an age when Jews were often persecuted. The building is a rectangular hall with women's galleries on both sides, roofed by three wooden barrel vaults and lit by large glass windows. In de Witte's painting, the elegant couple in the foreground, the crowd, and the dogs suggest the size and popularity of the synagogue. Fund-raising for a new synagogue began in 1670, with a pledge of 40,000 guilders (the finished building cost 164,365 guilders, excluding the land), and in 1671 Elias Bouman won the building competition. The Sephardi community (Portuguese and Spanish Jews) in Amsterdam had about 2,300 members, most of whom were well-to-do merchants. Their new synagogue, with its classical architecture, Brazilian jacaranda—

wood furniture, and 26 brass chandeliers, was considered to be one of the notable sights of the city. The building was spared by the Nazis during World War II because the Germans planned to turn it into a museum of Jewish culture.

The Dutch loved the peaceful, orderly beauty of their civilized countryside. In his painting *Avenue at Middelharnis*, Meindert Hobbema (1638–1709) records the rational art of a country physically constructed by reclaiming the land from the sea (fig. **14–27**). In contrast to the broad horizontal sweep of the land, Hobbema's compelling demonstration of one-point perspective draws the viewer into the picture and down the rutted, sandy road toward the distant village of Middelharnis. The Dutch love of nature is also apparent in their still-life paintings. Pictures of artfully arranged everyday objects or flowers were a much-admired specialty in the Netherlands in the seventeenth and eighteenth centuries. Such paintings were almost never straightforward

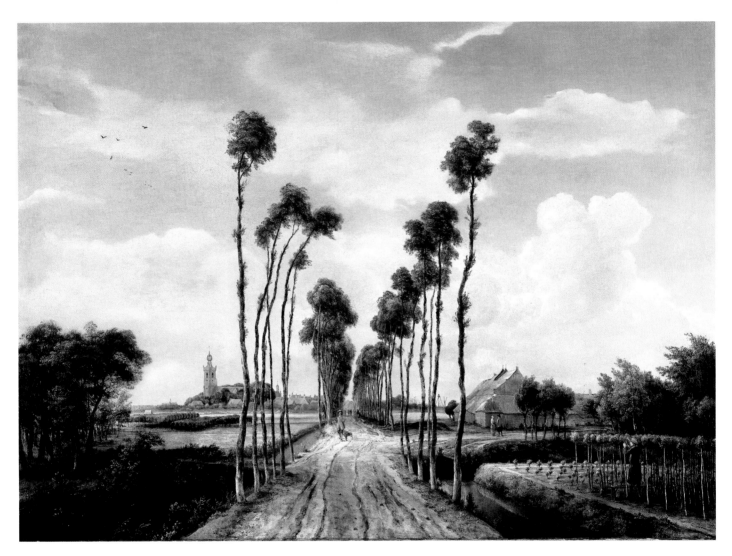

14–27 Meindert Hobbema. *Avenue at Middelharnis.* 1689. Oil on canvas, 40$\frac{3}{4}$″ × 55$\frac{1}{2}$″ (104 × 141 cm). The National Gallery, London

The power of nature is challenged by people who have captured their land not from human rivals but from the sea itself. They are constantly aware of the mighty forces of wind and water ever ready to reclaim their country.

depictions of actual fresh flowers. Instead, artists made color sketches of fresh examples of each type of flower and studied scientifically accurate color illustrations in botanical publications (see "Art and Science," page 413). Using their sketches and notebooks, in the studio they could compose bouquets of perfect specimens of a variety of flowers that did not bloom at the same time. *The Flower Piece with Curtain* by Adrien van der Spelt and Frans van Mieris (see Introduction, fig. 2) is characteristic of such work. The Dutch were so proud of their artists' still-life paintings that they presented one to the French queen Marie de' Medici when she made a state visit to Amsterdam.

Art for the State: France

Patronage of the arts in Europe became expected of an absolute monarch, and following the example of King Louis XIV of France, rulers built and rebuilt their palaces, planted vast gardens, and spent fortunes on paintings, sculpture, and the decorative arts. Nevertheless, the early seventeenth century was a difficult period in France, marked by almost continuous foreign and civil wars. King Henry IV was assassinated in 1610, and the country endured a long regency during the youth of Henry's nine-year-old heir, Louis XIII (ruled 1610–1643).

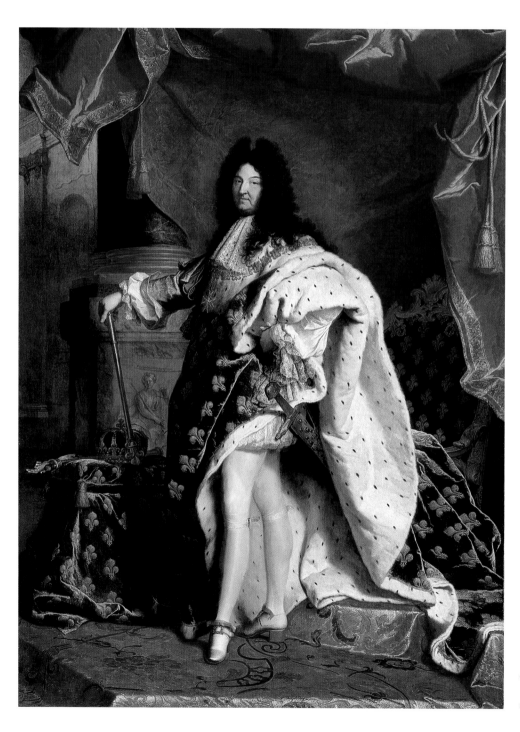

14–28 Hyacinthe Rigaud. *Louis XIV.* 1701. Oil on canvas, 9′2″ × 7′10¹⁄₂″ (2.79 × 2.40 m). Musée du Louvre, Paris

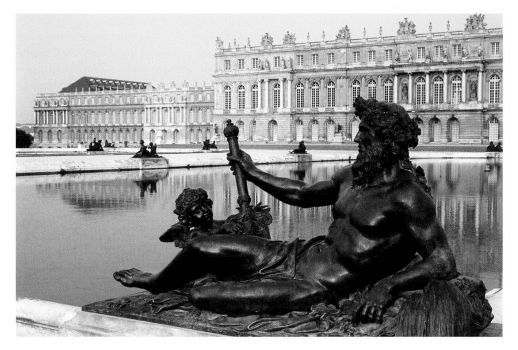

14–29 Louis Le Vau and Jules Hardouin-Mansart. The Garden Façade, Palais de Versailles. Gardens: Andre le Notre, 1668-85

Louis XIV (ruled 1643–1715) also inherited the throne as a youth, and began his personal rule only in 1661. An absolute monarch whose reign was the longest in European history, Louis XIV became known as *le Roi Soleil* ("the Sun King"). He was sometimes glorified in art through parallels drawn between him and the classical sun god, Apollo. In a 1701 portrait by the French court painter Hyacinthe Rigaud (1659–1743), the richly costumed monarch is revealed by an unseen hand pulling aside a billowing curtain (fig. **14–28**). Showing off his elegant legs, of which he was proud, the sixty-three-year-old Louis XIV poses in a blue robe trimmed with gold fleurs-de-lis and lined with white ermine and wears the high-heeled shoes he invented to compensate for his shortness. Despite the commanding pose and magnificent surroundings, the directness of the king's gaze and the realism of his aging face make him movingly human and testify to Rigaud's genius for portraiture.

Under Louis XIV's lavish patronage of the arts, the French court became the envy of every ruler in Europe. The Royal Academy of Painting and Sculpture, founded in 1648, maintained strict national control over the arts, and membership ensured an artist lucrative royal and civic commissions. Although the French Academy was not the first in Europe, none before it had exerted such dictatorial authority—an authority that lasted in France until the late nineteenth century (see "Grading the Old Masters," page 409). Classicism enjoyed particular favor in the academy and permeated French Baroque painting, sculpture, and architecture. When the Royal Academy of Architecture was founded in 1671, its members developed guidelines for architectural design based on the belief that mathematics was the true basis of beauty, with Vitruvius (see "The Vitruvian Man," page 342) and Palladio (see fig. 13–21) as their models.

In 1668, Louis XIV turned his attention to enlarging a small hunting lodge, a château built by Louis XIII at Versailles. The changes Louis XIV commanded consumed the energy of France's greatest painters, sculptors, designers, and architects for decades. For both political and sentimental reasons, the old Versailles château was left standing, and the new building went up around it under the direction first of Louis Le Vau (1612–1670) beginning in 1668, and then after his death, of Jules Hardouin-Mansart (1646–1708) (fig. **14–29**). The three-story elevation has a lightly rusticated ground floor, a main floor lined with enormous arched windows separated by Ionic pilasters, an attic level whose rectangular windows are also flanked by pilasters, and a flat, terraced roof. The overall design of the palace is a sensitive balance of horizontals and verticals relieved by a restrained overlay of regularly spaced projecting blocks with open, colonnaded porches. Concurrently, André Le Nôtre (1613–1700), who planned the gardens, turned the terrain around the palace into an extraordinary work of art, destined to have a powerful influence on urban as well as garden design. Neatly contained expanses of lawn and broad, straight vistas seem to stretch to the horizon, while the formal gardens, pools, fountains, and sculpture immediately behind the palace are an exercise in precise geometry. From these gardens, terraces descend to shaped, wooded areas and the mile-long Grand Canal. Classically harmonious and restful in their symmetrical, geometric design, the Versailles gardens are Baroque in their vast size and extension into the surrounding countryside. Like Bernini's piazza for St. Peter's, Le Nôtre's gardens dwarf the viewer and challenge the imagination.

Residents and visitors to the château could admire the gardens from an arcaded rear terrace designed by Le Vau. In his renovations, Hardouin-Mansart enclosed this previously open space, turning it into an immense gallery known as the Hall of Mirrors (fig. **14–30**). He lit the hall, which is about 240 feet long (73.15 m), with seventeen immense arched windows, lining the opposite wall with Venetian glass mirrors—enormously expensive in the seventeenth century—of exactly the same size and shape. The mirrors reflect the natural light from the windows and give the impression of an even larger space. In a tribute to Annibale's Farnese Ceiling (see fig. 14–6), the painter Charles Le Brun (1619–1690), a founding member of the Royal Academy of Painting and Sculpture, decorated the vaulted ceiling with paintings glorifying the reign of Louis XIV. The underlying theme for the design and decoration of the palace was the glorification of the king as the sun god Apollo.

French seventeenth-century painting was much affected by developments in Italian art. The important painter Nicolas Poussin (1594–1665) worked for French patrons but pursued his career in Italy. As a dedicated classicist, he did not paint the landscape as he saw it but instead organized nature, buildings, and figures into idealized compositions. Thus, Poussin's *Landscape with Saint John on Patmos* (fig. **14–31**), from 1640, appears orderly and admirably arranged. The artist has created a

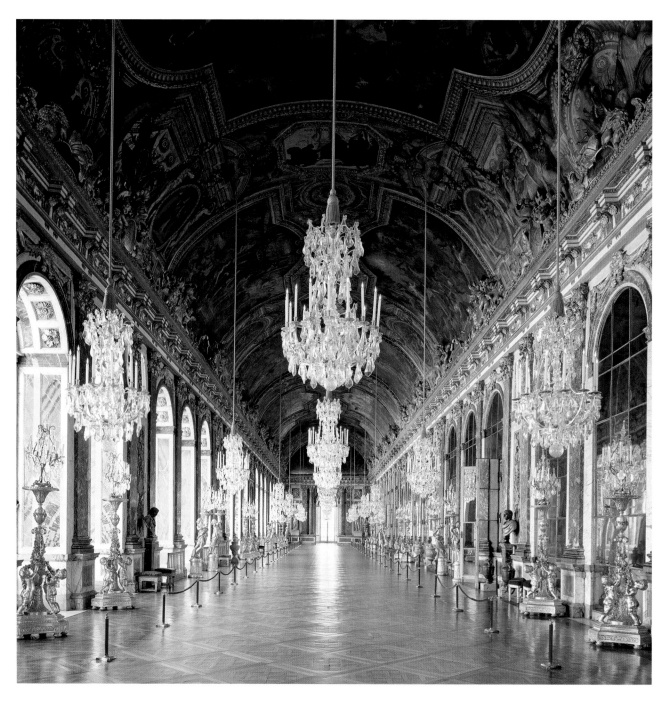

14–30 Jules Hardouin-Mansart (architecture) **and Charles Le Brun** (painting), Palais de Versailles 1668-85, Hall of Mirrors begun 1678

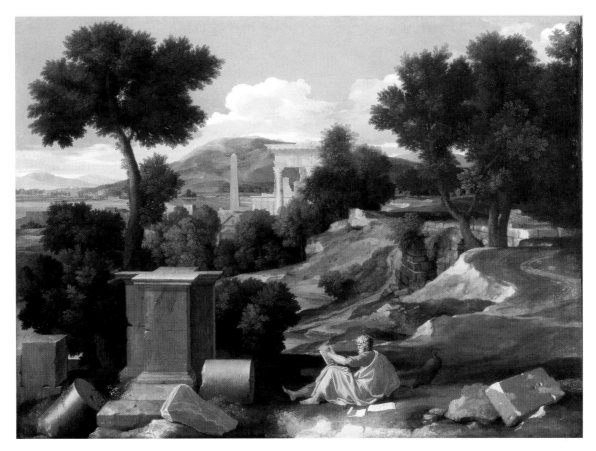

14–31 Nicolas Poussin. *Landscape with Saint John on Patmos.* 1640. Oil on canvas,
39$\frac{1}{2}$" × 53$\frac{3}{4}$" (100.3 × 136.4 cm). The Art Institute of Chicago

GRADING THE OLD MASTERS

The members of the French Royal Academy of Painting and Sculpture considered ancient classical art the standard by which contemporary art should be judged. By the 1680s, however, younger artists began to argue that modern art might equal and even surpass the art of the ancients. A debate also arose over the relative merits of drawing and color in painting. The conservatives argued that drawing was superior because it appealed to the mind, while color appealed to the senses. They saw the work of Nicolas Poussin as perfectly embodying the classical principles of subject and design. The young artists, who admired the vivid colors of Titian, Veronese, and Rubens, claimed that

painting should deceive the eye, and since color achieves this deception more convincingly than drawing, color should be valued over drawing. The two factions were called the *poussinistes* (in honor of Poussin) and the *rubénistes* (for Rubens).

The portrait painter and critic Roger de Piles (1635–1709) published his views in a series of pamphlets in which he took up the cause of the *rubénistes*. In *The Principles of Painting*, de Piles evaluated the most important painters on a scale of 0 to 20. He gave no score higher than 18, since no mortal could possibly achieve perfection. Caravaggio received the lowest grade, a 0 in expression and 6 in drawing, while Michelangelo and Leonardo both got a 4 in color and Rem-

brandt a 6 in drawing. Top grades (18) went to Titian for color, Rubens for composition, and Raphael for drawing and expression.

If we work out the "grades" using the traditional scale of 90% = A, 80% = B, and so forth, many important painters don't do very well. Raphael and Rubens get A's; but no one seems to get a B, although Van Dyck is close with a C plus. Poussin and Titian earn solid C's, while Rembrandt slips by with a C minus. Leonardo gets a D, and Michelangelo, Dürer, and Caravaggio all are resounding failures in de Piles's view. Tastes change, and someday our ideas may seem just as misguided as those of the academicians.

consistent perspective progression from the picture plane back into the distance through a clearly defined foreground, middle ground, and background. These zones are marked by alternating sunlight and shade, as well as by architectural elements in the Roman or Renaissance styles. Some of Poussin's landscapes are of identifiable sites, but this scene incorporates both real and imaginary buildings. In the middle distance are a ruined temple and an obelisk, while the round building set down in the distant city is Hadrian's tomb from Rome (barely visible here). Precisely placed trees, hills, mountains, water, and even clouds have a solidity of form that suggests architecture. The reclining Saint John, and his symbol, the eagle (dark and to the right of him), seem almost incidental to this perfect landscape. The subject of Poussin's painting is in effect the balance and order of nature rather than the story of the saint. Poussin's classical style became the basis of French academic art.

The Rococo Style

The Rococo mode may be seen partly as a reaction at all levels of society, even among kings and bishops, against the Grand Manner of Baroque art, identified with the formality and rigidity of seventeenth-century court life. The Rococo style is characterized by pastel colors, delicately curving forms, dainty figures, and an apparently lighthearted mood. The tendency toward a lighter, more delicate style appeared in Italian painting and pastels about 1700. By the end of Louis XIV's reign in 1715, the Rococo style dominated French architectural decoration, and it quickly spread across Europe.

In France, the Rococo first appeared in the furnishings and decoration of the elegant Parisian townhouses that are known in French as *hôtels*. The Salon de la Princesse in the Hôtel de Soubise in Paris (fig. **14–32**), designed by Germain Boffrand

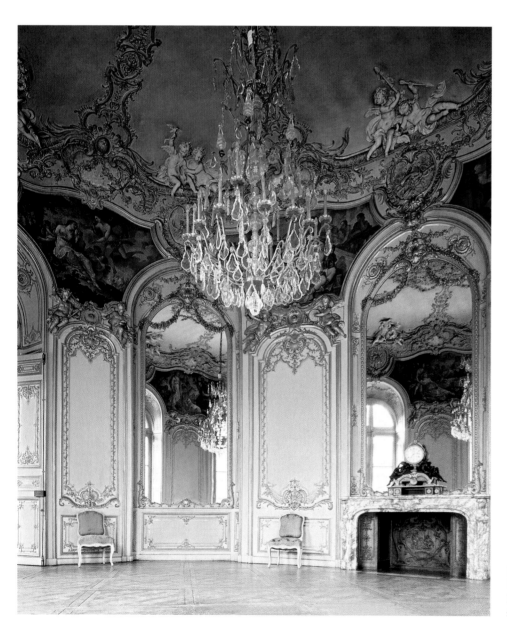

14–32 Germain Boffrand. *Salon de la Princesse,* Hôtel de Soubise, Paris, France. Begun 1732

beginning in 1732, is typical of French Rococo *hôtel* design of the 1730s. The glitter of silver or gold against expanses of white or pastel color, the visual confusion of mirror reflections, delicate ornament in sculpted stucco, carved wood panels called *boiseries,* and inlaid wood designs on furniture and floors were all part of the new look. In residential settings, pictorial themes were often taken from classical love stories, and sculpted ornaments were rarely devoid of putti, cupids, and clouds. In these elegant rooms, Parisian intellectuals gathered for conversation and entertainments presided over by accomplished, educated women of the upper class.

In painting, the Rococo style emerged with the career of the French artist Jean-Antoine Watteau (1684–1721). Watteau worked for a time as a decorator of interiors. In 1717 he was elected to membership in the Royal Academy of Painting and Sculpture on the basis of a painting for which there was no established category. The academicians created a new classification for it, called the *fête galante,* or elegant outdoor entertainment. The work Watteau submitted, *The Pilgrimage to Cythera* (fig. **14–33**), depicts a dreamworld in which an assortment of beautifully dressed couples depart for, or perhaps take their leave from, the mythical island of love. The lush landscape, which has no more reality than a painted theater backdrop, would never soil the characters' exquisite satins and velvets, nor would a summer shower ever threaten them. This idyllic vision, with its overtones of wistful melancholy, had a powerful attraction in early-eighteenth-century Paris and soon charmed the rest of Europe.

Jean-Honoré Fragonard (1732–1806) carried the French Rococo fantasies that Watteau pioneered into the second half of the eighteenth century. Fragonard's most memorable work is a group of fourteen canvases commissioned about 1771 by

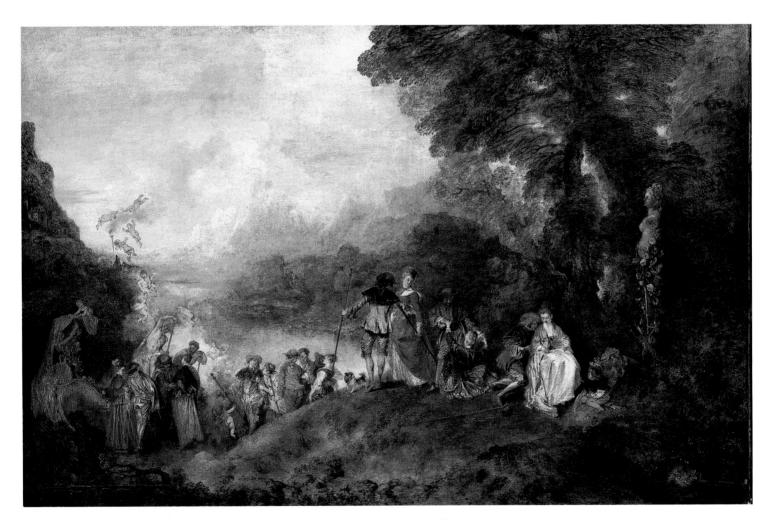

14–33 Jean-Antoine Watteau. *The Pilgrimage to Cythera.* 1717. Oil on canvas, 4′3″ × 6′4¹⁄₂″ (1.3 × 1.9 m). Musée du Louvre, Paris

Madame du Barry, Louis XV's mistress. *The Meeting* (fig. **14–34**) shows a secret encounter between a young man and his sweetheart, who looks back anxiously over her shoulder to be sure she has not been followed while clutching the letter arranging the tryst. These marvelously free and seemingly spontaneous visions of lovers seem to explode in color and luxuriant vegetation. The rapid brushwork that distinguishes Fragonard's technique is at its freest and most lavish here. However, Madame du Barry rejected the paintings and commissioned another set in the newly fashionable Neoclassical style (see Chapter 17). Her view of Fragonard's ravishing visions as passé showed that the Rococo world was, indeed, at its end.

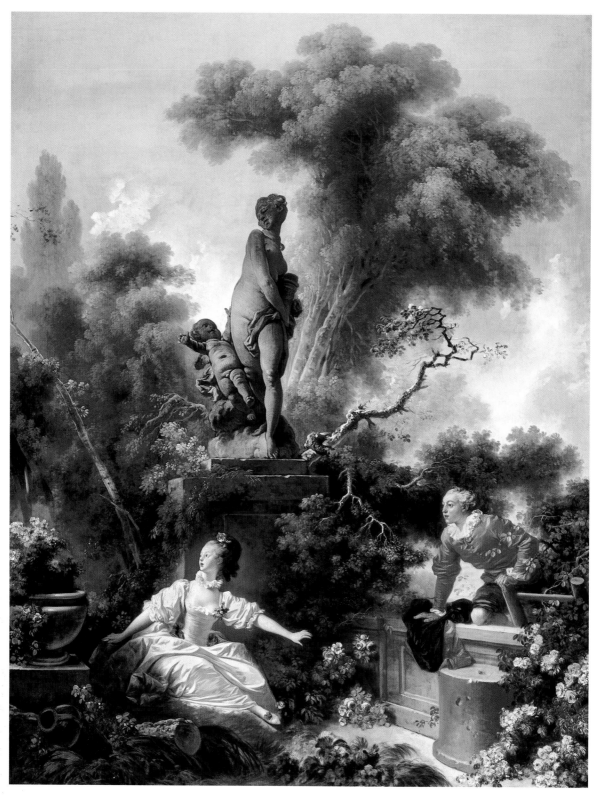

14–34 Jean-Honoré Fragonard. *The Meeting* from *The Progress of Love.* 1771–1773. Oil on canvas, 10′5 1/4″ × 7′5/8″ (3.18 × 2.15 m). The Frick Collection, New York

Art and Science

Artists who worked with scientists (see "Science and the Changing Worldview," below) or carried on scientific investigations in their own right heralded the future. Before the invention of photography, scientists relied on painters to illustrate their work. Artist and scientist were seldom the same person, but Anna Maria Sibylla Merian (1647–1717) contributed to botany and entomology both as a researcher and as an artist. German by birth and Dutch by training, Merian was once described by a Dutch contemporary as a painter of worms, flies, mosquitoes, spiders, "and other filth." In 1699, Amsterdam subsidized Merian's research on plants and insects in the Dutch colony of Surinam in South America. She spent two years exploring the jungle and recording the insects there. On her return to the Dutch Republic, she published the results of her research as *Dissertation in Insect Generations and Metamorphosis in Surinam*, illustrated with 72 large plates engraved after her watercolors (fig. **14–35**).

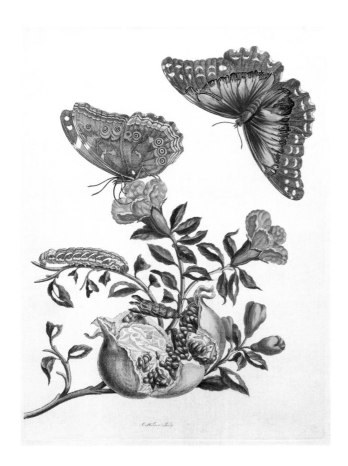

14–35 Anna Maria Sibylla Merian. *Plate 9* from *Dissertation in Insect Generations and Metamorphosis in Surinam.* 1719 (printed posthumously). Bound volume of 72 hand-colored engravings (second edition), $18^7/_8''$ × $13''$ (47.9 × 33 cm). National Museum of Women in the Arts, Washington, D.C.
GIFT OF WALLACE AND WILHELMINA HOLLAD

SCIENCE AND THE CHANGING WORLDVIEW

During the seventeenth and eighteenth centuries, some of the new discoveries of the natural world brought a sense of the grand scale of the universe without, while others focused more precisely on the complexity of the world within. And artists found new ways to mirror these changing perspectives in their own works.

The writings of philosophers Francis Bacon (1561–1626) in England and René Descartes (1596–1650) in France helped establish a new method of studying the world by insisting on scrupulous objectivity and logical reasoning. Bacon argued that the only significant knowledge came from the natural world, and he proposed that facts be gathered and studied systematically. Descartes, who was also a mathematician, is credited with inventing analytic geometry and the modern scientific method.

In 1543, the Polish scholar Nicolaus Copernicus (1473–1543) published *On the Revolutions of the Heavenly Spheres*, which contradicted the long-held view that Earth is the center of the universe (the Ptolemaic theory) by arguing instead that Earth and other planets revolve around the Sun. The Church viewed the Copernican theory as a challenge to its doctrines and in 1616 put Copernicus's work on its Index of Prohibited Books.

At the beginning of the seventeenth century, Johannes Kepler (1571–1630), court mathematician and astronomer to Holy Roman Emperor Rudolf II, demonstrated that the planets revolve around the Sun in elliptical orbits. Kepler noted a number of interrelated dynamic geometric patterns in the universe, the overall design of which he believed was an expression of divine order.

Galileo Galilei (1564–1642), an astronomer, philosopher, and physicist, was the first to develop a tool for observing the heavens: the telescope. As the first person to see moons traveling around Jupiter, his findings provided further confirmation of the Copernican theory. After the Church prohibited the teaching of that theory, Galileo was tried for heresy by the Inquisition. Under duress, he publicly rejected his views, although at the end of his trial, according to legend, he muttered, *Eppur si muove!* ("Nevertheless it [Earth] does move").

The new seventeenth-century science turned to the study of the very small as well as to the vast reaches of space. This included the development of the microscope, developed by the Dutch lensmaker and amateur scientist Anton van Leeuwenhoek (1632–1723). Leeuwenhoek perfected grinding techniques and increased the power of his lenses far beyond what was required for a simple magnifying glass. Ultimately, he was able to study the inner workings of plants and animals and even see microorganisms. For further study and publication, early scientists learned to draw or depended on artists to draw the images revealed by the microscope and in the world around them. This practice would continue until the discovery of photography in the nineteenth century.

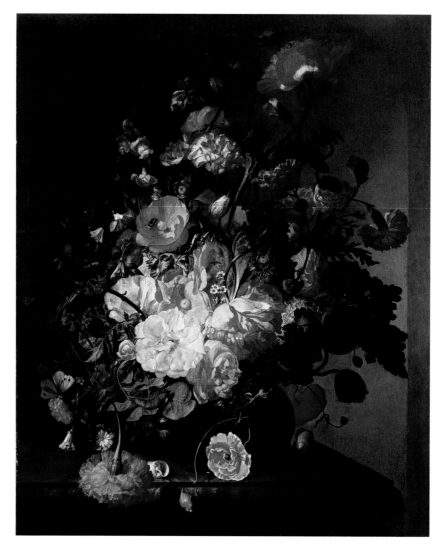

14–36 Rachel Ruysch. *Flower Still Life.* After 1700. Oil on canvas, 30″ × 24″ (76.2 × 61 cm). The Toledo Museum of Art, Ohio

Ruysch created an asymmetrical arrangement of pale oranges, pinks, and yellows rising from the lower left to the top right of the picture, offset by the strong diagonal of the table edge.

For all her meticulous scientific accuracy, Merian carefully arranged her depictions of exotic insects and elegant fruits and flowers to create pleasing compositions.

One of the most sought-after and highest-paid still-life painters in Europe during the Baroque era was Rachel Ruysch (1663–1750), who worked in Amsterdam. During her 70-year career, she specialized in still-life paintings, consisting predominantly of cut-flower arrangements. Her works were highly prized for their sensitive, free-form arrangements and their unusual and beautiful color harmonies (fig. **14–36**). Perhaps less daring than some of her peers but also "scientific" in her outlook, she made every flower in her still-life paintings a botanical study. Ruysch had learned botany as a girl, for her father was a profes-sor of anatomy and botany in Amsterdam. Although married with ten children, Ruysch never stopped painting. She achieved such fame in her lifetime that her paintings often brought high-er prices than did work by Rembrandt. Ruysch often enlivened her compositions with reptiles or insects—in this case, two snail shells and a large gray moth—that contribute an unsettling feel-ing to her paintings. In addition, besides appreciating the beauty of such a composition, viewers may have seen the flaming tulip (the most expensive variety) as a warning against the vanity of pride and greed, just as the short life of the cut flowers may have reminded them of the fleeting nature of beauty and human life. In the Protestant Netherlands, even art informed by science car-ried a moral message in the Baroque and Rococo periods.

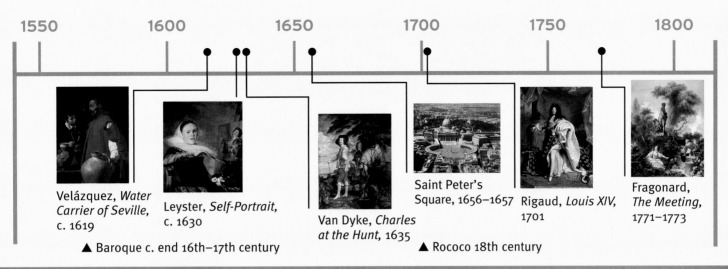

1550   1600   1650   1700   1750   1800

Velázquez, *Water Carrier of Seville,* c. 1619

Leyster, *Self-Portrait,* c. 1630

Van Dyke, *Charles at the Hunt,* 1635

Saint Peter's Square, 1656–1657

Rigaud, *Louis XIV,* 1701

Fragonard, *The Meeting,* 1771–1773

▲ Baroque c. end 16th–17th century   ▲ Rococo 18th century

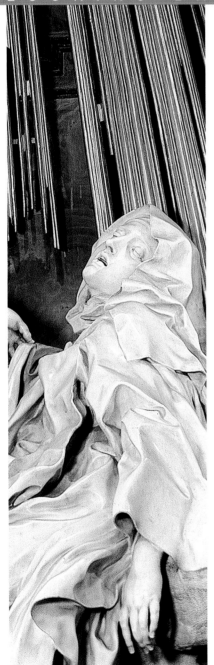

Sometimes Baroque art seems strangely familiar. In the 17th century—as today—many artists and their patrons were concerned with the uses of art, with "viewer response," and with different approaches to, and theories of, art. Artists like Bernini and Rubens produced dramatic theatrical effects, often using their skills to create what we would today call visual propaganda for the established church and monarchy. At a time when political and religious factions attacked each other with lethal fanaticism and enlisted art—as well as God—on their side, works of art could play an important role in capturing the imagination and swaying the emotions of viewers.

Spectacular visions, brilliant state portraits, grandiose palaces and churches proclaimed the power of the church and state. Some artists became international superstars; Rubens, whose home was in Antwerp, enjoyed the patronage of the kings of Spain, France, and England. Other artists, such as Caravaggio, played the role of disruptive, even violent, outsider, even though they too sought the patronage of the establishment. Patronage expanded to include not only the aristocracy and the Catholic Church but also the newly affluent middle class. In places like the Dutch Republic, art was democratized to such extent that the acquisition and collecting of works of art spread through all levels of society, from millers and tavern-keepers to bankers and civic guardsmen.

Many artists abandoned Renaissance ideals of beauty and grace as they strove to capture naturalistic effects. But others, like today's post-modernists, delighted in self-conscious references to the past. Artists and patrons turned to the art and architecture of ancient Rome for grand themes and images as well as decorative details. The ancient world provided the historical context and the "critical theory" for both works of art and the education of artists in official academies, especially the French Academy in Rome.

Trained in both traditional workshops and in the art academies, artists claimed mastery of every medium and control of every resource and technique, from the extreme, even brutal realism of Caravaggio to the cool perfection of Vermeer. In their art they combined simulated textures with skillfully manipulated effects of light to give an illusion of reality—of the tangible mundane world—transformed by supernatural powers. From Rembrandt's dramatic shadow world to Hobbema's sun-washed landscapes and Ruysch's flower pieces, artists re-created the world of nature on their canvases. Seeking a new relationship with the world and influenced by the scientific interests of the day, they added new subjects from this mundane world, including landscape, still life, and scenes of daily life.

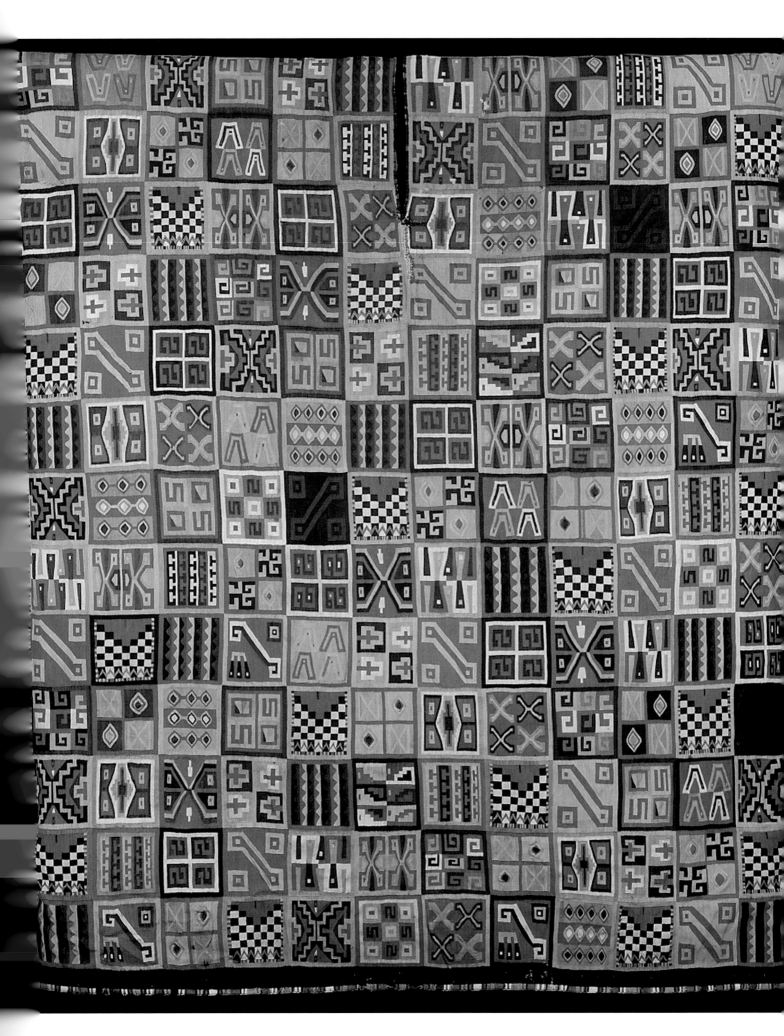

15
Art of the Americas

The remarkable art and architecture of the Americas surprised the Spanish explorers when they arrived in Mexico in 1519 and in Peru in 1532. They found an especially high quality of urban planning, stonework, fiber arts, metalwork, and ceramics. The skill of Inca weavers, for example, continues to amaze experts today (fig. **15–1**). In Inca society, fine textiles had both religious and political significance. Cloth was not only deemed a worthy gift to the gods, but was used to create the images of gods and to wrap images made of precious metals. Cloth was also equated with wealth and power.

Felipe Guaman Poma de Ayala described the conquest, indigenous population, and customs of the Inca in a handwritten and illustrated book written sometime before 1615. One of the 400 full-page illustrations shows the Inca king and his generals and officials dressed in knee-length tunics with checkerboard designs. The colorful tunics were more than mere clothing. Patterns may have signified rank, family, or a geographic location and seem to have been standardized throughout the Inca Empire. Although the Incas never developed a writing system, a kind of symbolic language is indicated by the abstract design of the elaborate royal tunic seen here. The checkerboard pattern is made up of miniature tunics, conveying the ruler's domination over wearers of other types of tunics.

Inca textiles prove to be an interesting study of the effect of official policy, centralized power, and standardization of the fine arts. Weavers and other artists who worked for the state followed the official requirements of design, quality, and quantity. Individual creativity expressed itself within traditional uses of simple, repeated geometric patterns arranged symmetrically. Patterns and colors identified a wearer's status and family or group membership; consequently, textiles played an important role in governing and identifying people in a far-flung empire. Heraldic trappings had a similar place in Western Europe in the Middle Ages and Renaissance. And throughout the world today, school or team colors, mascots, and banners continue to identify and inspire loyalty in sports fans and other groups.

15–1 Tunic, from Peru. Inca, c. 1500 CE.
Wool and cotton, $35\frac{7}{8}'' \times 30''$
(91.1 × 76.2 cm). Dumbarton Oaks
Research Library and Collections,
Washington, D.C.

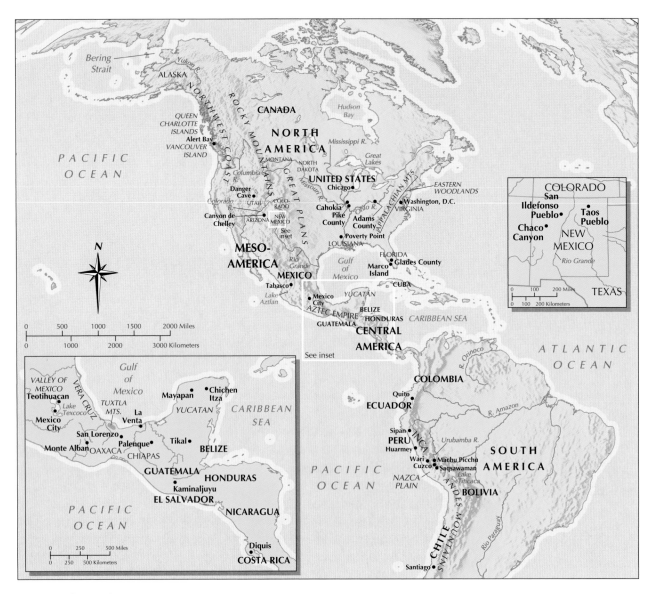

Map 15–1 The Americas

Human beings first arrived in North and South America during the last Ice Age, when glaciers trapped enough of the world's water to lower the level of the oceans and expose a land bridge between Asia and North America. Sometime before about 12,000 years ago, perhaps as early as 20,000 to 30,000 years ago, Paleolithic hunter-gatherers crossed over this land bridge and began to spread out into two vast, uninhabited continents.

Between 10,000 and 12,000 years ago, bands of hunters roamed most of North America; a few even reached as far as the southern end of South America. Although contact between Siberia and Alaska continued after the ice had retreated and rising oceans had flooded the Bering Strait, the people of the Western Hemisphere were essentially cut off from those of Africa and Eurasia until they were overrun by European invaders beginning in the late fifteenth century CE.

In this isolation, the people of the Americas experienced transformations similar to those that followed the end of the Paleolithic era elsewhere. In many regions, they developed an agricultural way of life. A trio of native plants—corn, beans, and squash—was especially important, but people also cultivated potatoes, tobacco, cacao (chocolate), tomatoes, and avocados. As elsewhere, the shift to agriculture in the Americas was accompanied by population growth and, in some places, the rise of hierarchical societies and the appearance of ceremonial centers and towns with monumental architecture. Cities such as Teotihuacan in the Basin of Mexico rivaled those of Europe in size and splendor. The people of Mesoamerica—the region that extends from central Mexico to northern Central America—developed writing, a complex and accurate calendar, and a sophisticated system of mathematics. Central and South American peoples developed an advanced metallurgy and produced exquisite gold, silver, and copper jewelry. In the American Southwest, Native American people built multistoried, apartment-like villages and cliff dwellings, as well as elaborate irrigation systems with canals.

The sudden incursion of Europeans from the fifteenth century onward had a dramatic and lasting impact on Native American people and their art. In some areas, highly advanced civilizations, such as those of the Aztec and Inca, were destroyed. In other regions, such as the North American plains, indigenous groups lost much of their land and saw their populations decimated, yet they retained their traditions and still exist as distinct cultural entities today.

Mesoamerica

Ancient Mesoamerica encompassed the area from north of the Basin of Mexico (the location of Mexico City) to modern Belize

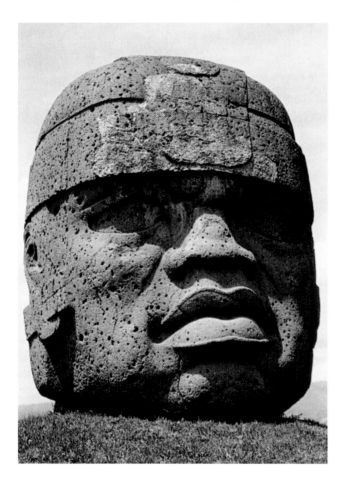

15–2 Colossal Head. Olmec culture. La Venta, Mexico. c. 1100-900 BCE. Basal, height 65″ (2.26 m).
© WERNER FORMAN/ART RESOURCE, NY

The naturalistic colossal heads found at La Venta and San Lorenzo measure about 8 feet in diameter. They are carved from basalt boulders that were transported to the Gulf Coast from the Tuxtla Mountains, more than 60 miles inland.

and included parts of Honduras and El Salvador in Central America. The people of this environmentally geographically diverse region, which included tropical rain forests and semiarid mountain plateaus, were linked by cultural similarities and trade. Among the shared features of the civilizations that arose in Mesoamerica were a ritual ball game with religious and political significance, aspects of monumental ceremonial building construction, and a complex system of multiple calendars including a 260-day ritual cycle and a 365-day agricultural cycle. Mesoamerican society was also sharply divided into elite and commoner classes.

Archaeologists have traditionally divided Mesoamerican history into three broad periods: the Formative or Preclassic (1500 BCE–250 CE), the Classic (250–900 CE), and the Postclassic (900–1521 CE). The Classic period brackets the time during which the Maya erected dated stone monuments. The term reflects the view of early scholars that the Classic period was a kind of golden age, the equivalent of the Classical period in ancient Greece (see Chapter 4). Although this view is no longer current—and the periods are only roughly applicable to other parts of Mesoamerica—the terminology has endured.

The Olmecs

The earliest known major Mesoamerican civilization, that of the Olmecs, emerged during the Preclassic period along the Gulf of Mexico. In the swampy coastal areas of the modern Mexican states of Veracruz and Tabasco, the Olmecs cleared farmland, drained fields, and raised earth mounds on which they constructed religious and political centers. They created monumental works of basalt sculpture, such as colossal heads (see fig. **15–2**), altars, and seated figures. The huge basalt blocks for the large works of sculpture were quarried at distant sites and transported to San Lorenzo, La Venta, and other centers. The colossal heads range in height from 5 to 12 feet and weigh from 5 to more than 20 tons. They are portraits of rulers, adult males wearing close-fitting caps with chin straps and large, round earplugs (cylindrical earrings that pierce the earlobe). The fleshy faces have almond-shaped eyes, flat broad noses, thick protruding lips, and downturned mouths. Each face is different, suggesting that they may represent specific individuals. Twelve heads were found at San Lorenzo. All had been mutilated and buried about 900 BCE, about the time the site went into decline. At La Venta, 102 basalt monuments were found. The Olmecs also established trade contacts throughout Mesoamerica, importing goods not found in the Gulf region, such as obsidian, iron ore, and jade. Writing and calendrical systems first appeared around 600 to 500 BCE in areas with strong Olmec influence.

By 200 CE, forests and swamps began to reclaim Olmec sites, but Olmec civilization had spread widely throughout Mesoamerica and was to have an enduring influence on its successors. As the Olmec centers of the Gulf Coast faded, the great Classic period centers at Teotihuacan in the Basin of Mexico as well as in the Maya region were beginning their ascendancy.

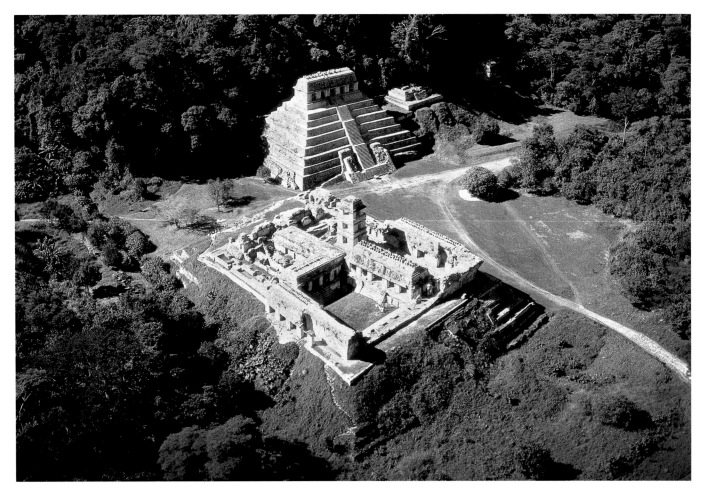

15–3 Palace (foreground) and Temple of the Inscriptions (tomb pyramid of Lord Pakal). Palenque,
Mexico. Maya culture, late 7th century CE

The Maya

The homeland of the Maya people is in southern Mesoamerica, which includes the Yucatán peninsula and the lands of several present-day countries, including Guatemala, Belize, and the western parts of Honduras and El Salvador. The Maya built imposing pyramids, temples, palaces, and administrative structures in densely populated cities. They developed the most advanced hieroglyphic writing in Mesoamerica and the most sophisticated version of the Mesoamerican calendrical system. In addition, they studied astronomy and the natural cycles of plants and animals, and they developed the mathematical concepts of zero and place value before such concepts were used in Europe.

An increasingly detailed picture of the Maya has emerged from recent archaeological research and progress in deciphering their writing. It shows a society divided into competing centers, each with a hereditary ruler and an elite class of nobles and priests supported by a far larger class of farmer-commoners. Rulers established their legitimacy, maintained links with their divine ancestors, and venerated the gods through elaborate rituals, including ball games, bloodletting ceremonies, and human sacrifice. A complex pantheon of deities, many with several manifestations, presided over the Maya universe.

The Maya civilization, which had emerged during the late Preclassic period (250 BCE–250 CE), reached its peak in the southern lowlands of Guatemala during the Classic period (250–900 CE), and shifted to northern Yucatán during the Postclassic period (900–1521 CE). In Palenque, a prominent city of the Classic period, the major buildings are grouped on high ground. A central group of structures includes the so-called Palace (possibly an administrative and ceremonial center as well as a residential structure), the Temple of the Inscriptions, and two other temples (fig. **15–3**). Most of the structures in the three building complexes were commissioned by a powerful ruler, Lord Pakal (Maya for "shield"), who ruled from 615 to 683 CE, and his two sons, who succeeded him.

The Temple of the Inscriptions is a nine-level pyramid that rises to a height of about 75 feet. The consecutive layers probably reflect the belief, current among the Aztec and the Maya at the time of the Spanish Conquest, that the underworld had nine levels. Priests would climb the steep stone staircase on the exterior to reach the temple on top, which recalls the kind of pole-and-thatch houses the Maya still build in parts of Yucatán today. The roof of the temple was topped with a crest known as a **roof comb**, and its façade still retains much of its stucco sculpture. Inscriptions line the back wall of the outer chamber, giving the temple its name.

In 1948 a Mexican archeologist cleared the rear chamber of the summit shrine and entered the corbel-vaulted stairwell that zig-zagged 80 feet down to the tomb of King Pakal. After four years of work, the undisturbed tomb of the king was revealed. The king, covered in jade ornaments, lay in a monumental sarcophagus with a lid carved in low relief that shows him balanced between the underworld and the earth. A stucco portrait of Lord Pakal found with the sarcophagus depicts him as a young man wearing a diadem of jade and feathers (fig. **15–4**). His features reveal the characteristics of the Maya ideal of beauty: a sloping forehead and elongated skull (babies had their heads bound to produce this shape), a large curved nose (enhanced by an added ornamental bridge, perhaps of latex), and full lips. Traces of pigment indicate that this portrait, like much Maya sculpture, was colorfully painted.

As the focus of Maya civilization shifted northward in the Postclassic period, a northern Maya group called the Itzá rose to prominence. Their principal center, Chichén Itzá, which means "at the mouth of the well of the Itzá," flourished from the ninth to the thirteenth century CE, eventually covering about 6 square miles.

One of Chichén Itzá's most conspicuous structures is a massive, nine-level pyramid in the center of a large plaza with a stairway on each side leading to a square temple on the pyramid's summit (fig. **15–5**). Sculptured Feathered Serpent heads embellish the base of the stairway. This structure is known today as the Castillo (Spanish for "castle"). At the spring and fall equinoxes, the rising sun casts an undulating, serpentlike shadow on the stairway balustrades that forms a body for the serpent heads. Sculpture at Chichén Itzá includes half-reclining figures known as **chacmools** (fig. 15–5), which have the sturdy forms, proportions, and angularity of architecture. The chacmools probably represent fallen warriors and were used to receive sacrificial offerings. They once typified Pre-Columbian sculpture for many Westerners.

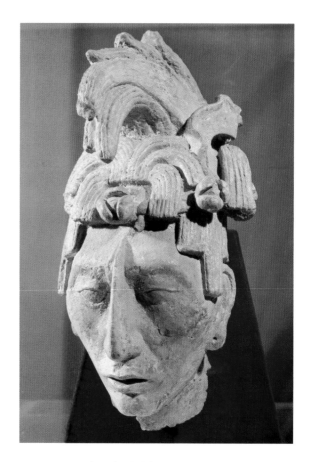

15–4 Portrait of Lord Pakal, from his tomb, Temple of the Inscriptions. Late 7th century CE. Stucco, height 16⅞″ (43 cm). Museo Nacional de Antropologia, Mexico City

This portrait of the youthful Lord Pakal might have been placed in his tomb as an offering, or it might have formed part of the original exterior decoration of the Temple of the Inscriptions.

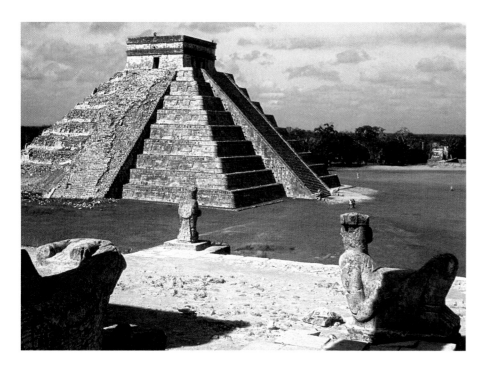

15–5 Castillo with Chacmool in foreground, Chichén Itzá, Yucatán, Mexico. 9th–13th century
SWAAN PHOTOGRAPH COLLECTION. (96.P.21)

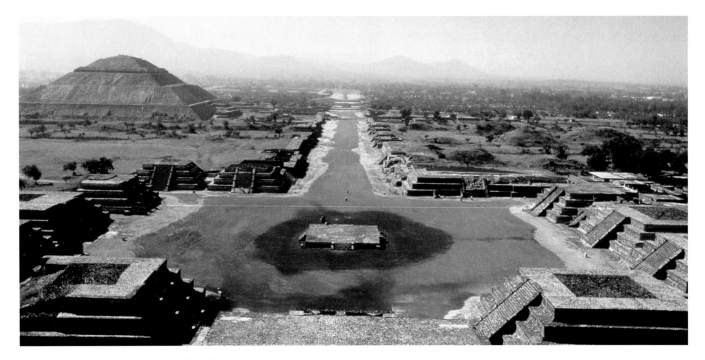

15–6 Ceremonial center of the city of Teotihuacan, Mexico. Teotihuacan culture, c. 500 CE

View from the Pyramid of the Moon down the Avenue of the Dead to the Ciudadela and the Temple of the Feathered Serpent. The Pyramid of the Sun is at the middle left.

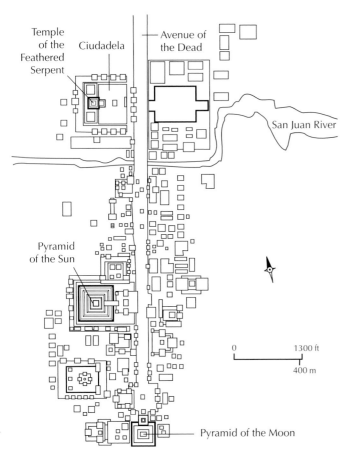

15–7 Plan of the ceremonial center of Teotihuacan

Teotihuacan

Located some 30 miles northeast of present-day Mexico City, Teotihuacan experienced a period of rapid growth early in the first millennium CE. By 200 CE, it had emerged as a significant center of commerce and manufacturing, the first large city-state in the Americas. At its height, between 350 and 650 CE, Teotihuacan covered nearly 9 square miles and had a population of some 150,000, making it one of the largest cities in the world at that time (figs. **15–6, 15–7**). One reason for its dominance was its control of the market for high-quality obsidian. This volcanic stone, made into tools and vessels, was traded for luxury items such as the green feathers of the quetzal bird, used for priestly headdresses, and the spotted fur of the jaguar, used for ceremonial garments.

The name *Teotihuacan* is an Aztec word meaning "The City (gathering place) of the Gods." The people of Teotihuacan worshiped many deities that were recognizably similar to those worshiped by later Mesoamerican people, including the Aztecs, who dominated central Mexico at the time of the Spanish Conquest. Among these are the Rain or Storm God (god of fertility, war, and sacrifice), known to the Aztecs as Tlaloc, and the Feathered Serpent, known to the Maya as Kukulcan and to the Aztecs as Quetzalcoatl.

Teotihuacan's principal structures included the Pyramid of the Sun, the Pyramid of the Moon, and the Ciudadela, a vast sunken plaza surrounded by temple platforms. The city's principal religious and political center, the Ciudadela could accommodate an assembly of more than 60,000 people. Its focal point was the pyramidal Temple of the Feathered Serpent (fig. **15–8**).

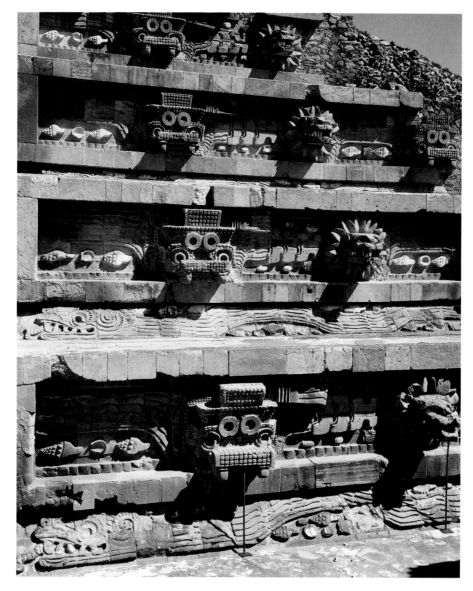

15–8 Temple of the Feathered Serpent, the Ciudadela, Teotihuacan, Mexico. Teotihuacan culture, c. 350 CE

This seven-tiered structure exhibits the ***talud-tablero*** construction that is a hallmark of the Teotihuacan architectural style. The sloping base, or *talud*, of each platform supports a vertical *tablero*, or entablature, which is surrounded by a frame and filled with sculptural decoration. The Temple of the Feathered Serpent was enlarged several times, and—as was characteristic of Mesoamerican pyramids—each completed enlargement enclosed the previous structure, like the concentric layers of an onion. Archaeological excavations of earlier-phase *tableros* and a stairway balustrade have revealed painted heads of the Feathered Serpent, the goggle-eyed Rain or Storm God (or Fire God, according to some), and reliefs of aquatic shells and snails. The flat, angular, abstract style, typical of Teotihuacan art, is in marked contrast to the curvilinear style of Olmec art. The Rain God features a squarish, stylized head or headdress with protruding upper jaw, huge, round eyes originally inlaid with obsidian, and large, circular earspools. The fanged serpent heads, perhaps composites of snakes and other creatures, emerge from an aureole of stylized feathers. The Rain God and the Feathered Serpent may be symbols of regeneration and cyclical renewal, perhaps representing the alternating wet and dry seasons.

The Aztecs

Maya civilization was in decline by the time of the Spanish Conquest; by the end of the fifteenth century, a people known as the Aztecs controlled much of Mexico. The rise to power of the Aztecs had been recent and swift. Only 400 years earlier, according to their own legends, they had been a nomadic people living on the shores of a mythical island called Aztlan somewhere to the northwest of the Basin of Mexico, where present-day Mexico City is located. They called themselves the Mexica, hence the name *Mexico*. The term *Aztec* derives from the word *Aztlan*.

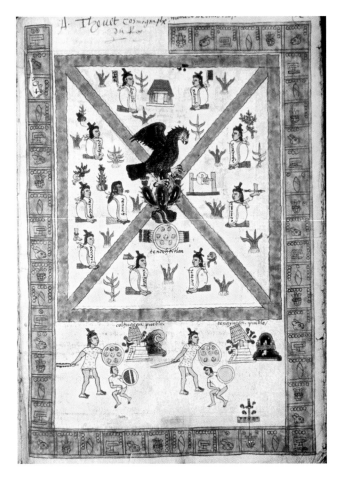

15–9 The Founding of Tenochtitlan, page from *Codex Mendoza*. Aztec, 1540s CE. Ink and paint on paper, 8 7/16″ × 12 3/8″ (21.4 × 31.4 cm). The Bodleian Library, Oxford

MS. ARCH SELDEN. A.1.FOL. 2R

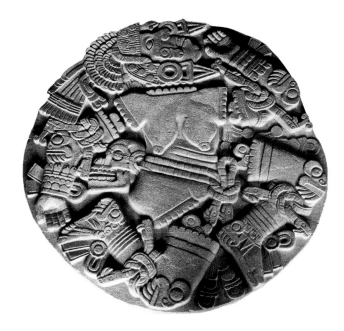

15–10 The Moon Goddess, Coyolxauhqui. Aztec, late 15th century CE. Stone, diameter 11′6″ (3.5 m)

This disk was discovered accidentally in 1978 by workers from a utility company who were excavating at a street corner in downtown Mexico City.

After a period of migration, the Aztecs arrived in the Basin of Mexico in the thirteenth century. There they eventually settled on an island in Lake Texcoco, where they had seen an eagle perching on a prickly pear cactus *(tenochtli)*, a sign that Huitzilopochtli, their patron god, told them would mark the end of their wandering. They called the place Tenochtitlan (meaning "the prickly pear cactus on a stone"). The city was situated on a collection of islands linked by human-made canals.

In the fifteenth century, the Aztecs—joined by allies in a triple alliance—began an aggressive campaign of expansion. The tribute they exacted from all over Central Mexico transformed Tenochtitlan into a glittering capital. As the Spanish conquistador Hernando Cortés approached Tenochtitlan in November 1519, he and his soldiers marveled at the stone buildings, towers, and temples that seemed from a distance to rise from the water like a mirage.

Most Aztec books were destroyed in the wake of the Spanish invasion, but the work of Aztec scribes appears in several **codices** (manuscripts) created after the conquest. The first page of the *Codex Mendoza*, prepared for the Spanish viceroy in the 1540s, can be interpreted as an idealized representation of the city of Tenochtitlan (fig. **15–9**). An eagle perched on a prickly pear cactus—the symbol of the city—fills the center of the page.

Waterways surround the city and divide it into four quarters, which are further subdivided into wards, as represented by the seated figures. The victorious warriors at the bottom of the page represent early Aztec conquests over nearby cities.

Tenochtitlan had a sacred precinct, possibly symbolized in figure 15–9 by the structure (a temple or house) at the top of the page. The focal point of the precinct was the Great Temple, a 130-foot-high stepped pyramid with dual temples on top, one of which was dedicated to Huitzilopochtli (an Aztec patron-god associated with the sun and warfare) and the other to Tlaloc, the Mesoamerican god of rain and fertility. The Great Temple was an important site for ritual sacrifice. Victims climbed stairs on the exterior to the Temple of Huitzilopochtli at the summit, where several priests threw them over a stone and another quickly cut open their chests and offered their hearts to the gods. The bodies were then rolled down the stairs and dismembered. Hundreds of severed heads were said to have been kept on a skull rack in the plaza of the sacred precinct.

The Aztecs believed that human actions, including bloodletting and human sacrifice, were vital to the continued existence of the universe. Huitzilopochtli, son of the Earth Mother Coatlicue, was thought to require sacrificial victims so that he could, in a re-creation of the events surrounding his birth, drive the stars and the moon from the sky at the beginning of each day. The stars were his half brothers, and the moon, Coyolxauhqui, was his half sister. According to the myth, when Coatlicue conceived Huitzilopochtli by placing a ball of feathers in her bosom as she was sweeping, Huitzilopochtli's jealous siblings conspired to kill her. When they attacked, Huitzilopochtli emerged from her body fully grown and armed, drove off his brothers, and destroyed his half sister, Coyolxauhqui. Aztec rituals re-created the mythic events surrounding his birth.

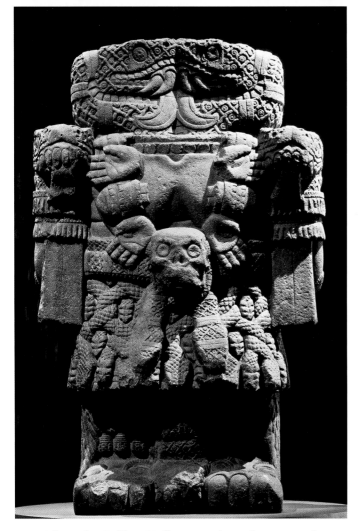

15–11 *The Mother Goddess, Coatlicue.* Aztec, late 15th century CE. Stone, height 8′6″ (2.59 m). Museo Nacional de Antropologia, Mexico City

A huge circular relief of Coyolxauhqui once lay at the foot of the Huitzilopochtli shrine, as if the enraged and triumphant god had cast her there like a sacrificial victim (fig. **15–10**). Her torso is in the center, surrounded by her decapitated head and dismembered limbs. The rope belt around her waist is attached to a skull buckle. She wears bells on her cheeks, a magnificent feather headdress, and distinctive ear ornaments composed of disks, rectangles, and triangles. The sculpture is two-dimensional in concept, with a deeply cut background. Inside the Temple of Huitzilopochtli, an imposing statue of Coatlicue (fig. **15–11**), mother of Huitzilopochtli, stood high above the vanquished Coyolxauhqui. One of the conquistadors who arrived at the site in 1520 described seeing such a statue covered with blood. Coatlicue means "she of the serpent skirt," and this broad-shouldered figure with clawed hands and feet wears a skirt of twisted snakes. A pair of serpents, symbols of blood, rise from her neck to form a head. Around her neck hangs a necklace of sacrificial offerings—hands, hearts, and a dangling skull pendant. Despite its intricate surface, the sculpture's simple, bold, and blocky form creates a single unified whole. The colors with which it was originally painted would no doubt have heightened its dramatic impact. The Spanish conquerors built their own capital, Mexico City, over the ruins of Tenochtitlan and built a cathedral on the site of Tenochtitlan's sacred precinct. The statue of Coatlicue was found near the cathedral during excavations there in 1792.

Central America

Unlike their neighbors in Mesoamerica who lived in complex hierarchical societies, the people of Central America generally lived in extended family groups led by chiefs. A notable example of these small chiefdoms was the Diquis culture (located in present-day Costa Rica), which lasted from about 700 CE to about 1500 CE.

The Diquis occupied fortified villages without monumental architecture or sculpture and seem to have engaged in constant warfare with one another. They produced fine featherwork, ceramics, textiles, and gold objects. (The name Costa Rica, which means "rich coast" in Spanish, probably reflects the value the Spanish placed on the gold they found there.)

Metallurgy and the use of gold and copper-gold alloys were widespread in Central America. The technique of lost-wax casting probably first appeared in present-day Colombia between 500 and 300 BCE (see Starter Kit, "Lost-Wax Casting"). From there it spread north to the Diquis. The small, exquisite pendant shown in figure **15–12** illustrates the sophisticated design and technical facility of Diquis goldwork. The pendant depicts a male figure wearing bracelets, anklets, and a belt with a snake-headed penis sheath. He plays a drum while holding the tail of a snake in his teeth and its head in his left hand. The wavy forms with serpent heads emerging from his scalp suggest an elaborate headdress, and the creatures emerging from his legs suggest some kind of reptile costume. The inverted triangles on the headdress probably represent birds' tails.

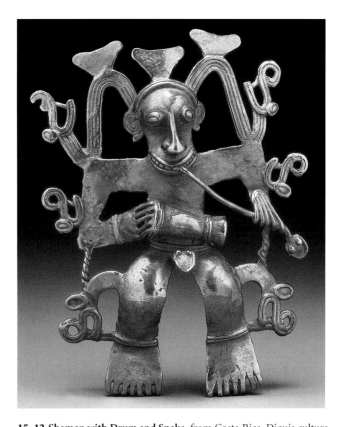

15–12 Shaman with Drum and Snake, from Costa Rica. Diquis culture, c. 13th–16th century CE. Gold, 4¼″ × 3¼″ (10.8 × 8.2 cm). Museos del Banco Central de Costa Rica, San José, Costa Rica

In Diquis mythology, serpents and crocodiles inhabited a lower world; humans and birds a higher one. Diquis art depicts animals and insects as fierce and dangerous. Perhaps the man in the pendant is a shaman transforming himself into a composite serpent-bird or performing a ritual snake dance surrounded by serpents or crocodiles. The scrolls on the sides of his head may represent the shaman's power to hear and understand the speech of animals. Whatever its specific meaning, the pendant evokes a ritual of mediation between earthly and cosmic powers involving music, dance, and costume.

Whether gold figures of this kind were protective amulets or signs of high status, they were certainly more than personal adornment. Shamans and warriors wore gold to inspire fear, perhaps because gold was thought to capture the energy and power of the sun. This energy was also thought to allow shamans to leave their bodies and travel into cosmic realms.

South America: The Central Andes

Like Mesoamerica, the central Andes of South America—primarily present-day Peru and Bolivia—saw the development of complex hierarchical societies with rich and varied artistic traditions. The area is one of dramatic contrasts. The narrow coastal plain sandwiched between the Pacific Ocean and the soaring Andes is one of the driest deserts in the world. Life here depends on the rich marine resources of the Pacific and the rivers that descend from the Andes. The Andes themselves are a region of snowcapped peaks, fertile river valleys, and high plateaus that support llama, alpacas, vicuña, and guanacos. The lush eastern slopes of the Andes descend to the tropical rain forest of the Amazon basin.

In the central Andes, the earliest evidence of monumental architecture dates to the third millennium BCE. Sites with ceremo-nial mounds and plazas were discovered near the sea, while early centers in the highlands consisted of multiroomed, stonewalled structures with sunken central fire pits in which ritual offerings were burned. Large, U-shaped ceremonial complexes with circular sunken plazas were built from the second millennium BCE. Some of the most enigmatic monumental constructions in Peru are the earthworks, or **geoglyphs**, first created by the people of the Nazca culture, who dominated the south coast of Peru from about 100 BCE to 700 CE. On great stretches of desert, the people literally drew in the earth. By removing a layer of dark gravel, they exposed the lighter underlying soil, then edged the resulting lines with stones. In this way, they created gigantic images, visible only from the air, including a hummingbird (fig. **15–13**), a killer whale, a monkey, a spider, a duck, and other birds, plants, geometric patterns and straight, parallel lines that extend for up to 12 miles. The beak of the hummingbird in figure 15–13 consists of two parallel lines, each 120 feet long. Despite numerous theories, the purpose of these geoglyphs, which dwarf even the most ambitious modern environmental sculpture, is not known. Animals and plants in a similar style appear on a much smaller scale on multicolored pottery made by Nazca artisans.

The Moche Culture

The Moche culture dominated the north coast of what is now Peru, from the Piura Valley to the Huarmey Valley—a distance of some 370 miles—between about 200 BCE and 600 CE. Moche lords ruled each valley in this region from a ceremonial-administrative center. The largest of these, in the Moche Valley (from which the culture takes its name), contained the so-called Pyramids of the Sun and the Moon. Both pyramids were built entirely of adobe bricks. The Pyramid of the Sun, the largest

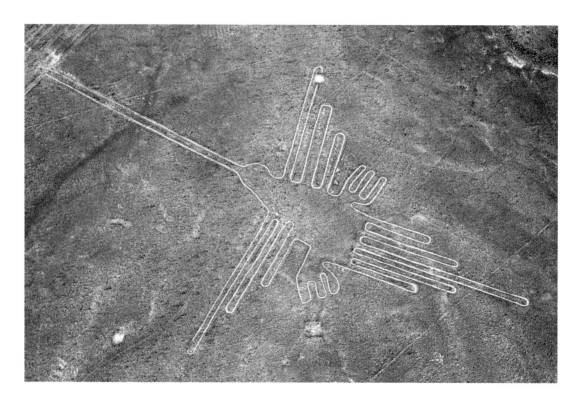

15–13 Geoglyph of a hummingbird, Nazca Plain, southwest Peru. Nazca culture c. 100 BCE–700 CE. Length approx. 450′ (137 m); wingspan approx. 200′ (60.9 m)

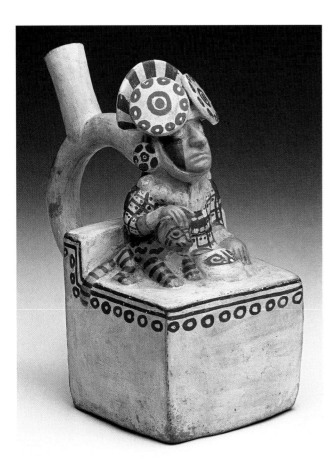

15–14 *Moche Lord with a Feline,* from Moche Valley, Peru. Moche culture, c. 100 BCE–500 CE. Painted ceramic, height 7 1/2" (19 cm). Art Institute of Chicago

Behind the figure is the distinctive stirrup-shaped handle and spout. Vessels of this kind, used in Moche rituals, were also treasured as special luxury items and were buried with individuals of high status.

on many high-quality Moche vessels. Paintings indicate that vessels of this type were used in Moche rituals.

A central theme in Moche iconography is the sacrifice ceremony, in which prisoners captured in battle are sacrificed and several elaborately dressed figures drink their blood. Archaeologists have labeled the principal figure in the ceremony as the Warrior Priest and other important figures as the Bird Priest and the Priestess. The recent discovery of a number of spectacularly rich Moche tombs indicates that the sacrifice ceremony was an actual Moche ritual and that Moche lords assumed the roles of the principal figures. The occupant of a tomb at Sipan was buried with the regalia of a warrior priest. In a tomb at the site of San José de Moro, just south of Sipan, an occupant was buried with the regalia of a priestess.

Among the riches accompanying the Warrior Priest at Sipan was a pair of exquisite gold-and-turquoise earspools, each of which depicts three Moche warriors (fig. **15–15**). The central figure is made of beaten gold and turquoise. He and his companions are adorned with tiny gold-and-turquoise earspools. They wear spectacular gold-and-turquoise headdresses topped with delicate sheets of gold that resemble the crescent-shaped knives used in sacrifices. The crests, like feathered fans of gold, would have swayed in the breeze as the wearer moved. The central figure has a crescent-shaped nose ornament and carries a gold club and shield. A necklace of owl's-head beads strung with gold thread hangs around his shoulders. Many of the figure's anatomical features have been rendered in painstaking detail.

ancient structure in South America, was originally a cross-shaped structure 1,122 feet long by 522 feet wide that rose in a series of terraces to a height of 59 feet. This site had been thought to be the capital of the entire Moche realm, but evidence is accumulating that the Moche were not so centralized.

The Moche were exceptional potters and metalsmiths. They developed ceramic molds, which allowed them to mass-produce some forms. Vessels were made in the forms of naturalistically modeled human beings and animals, as well as in the form of architectural structures. They also created realistic portrait vessels and recorded mythological narratives and ritual scenes in intricate fine-line painting. Similar scenes were painted on the walls of temples and administrative buildings. Moche smiths, the most sophisticated in the central Andes, developed several innovative metal alloys.

The ceramic vessel in figure **15–14** shows a Moche lord sitting in a structure associated with high office. He wears an elaborate headdress and large earspools and strokes a cat or perhaps a jaguar cub. The so-called stirrup, or U-shaped spout, appears

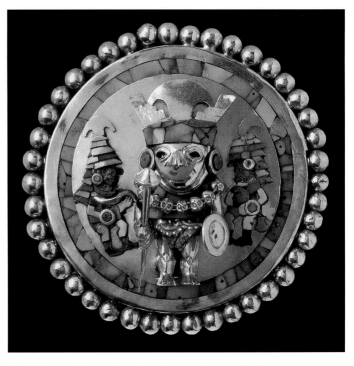

15–15 Earspool, from Sipan, Peru. Moche culture, 2nd–5th century CE. Gold, turquoise, quartz, and shell, diameter approx. 5" (12.7 cm). Bruning Archaeological Museum, Lambayeque, Peru

The Inca Empire

The largest state in the Andes region in the Pre-Columbian era was the Inca Empire. It extended for more than 2,600 miles along western South America, encompassing most of modern-day Ecuador, Peru, Bolivia, and northern Chile. The Inca called their empire the Land of the Four Quarters. At its center was their capital, Cuzco, "the navel of the world," located high in the Andes Mountains. The early history of the Inca people is obscure. The Cuzco region had been under the control of the earlier Wan Empire, and the Inca state was probably one of many small competing kingdoms that emerged in the highlands in the wake of the Wari collapse. In the fifteenth century, the Inca, like the Aztecs in the Basin of Mexico, began suddenly and rapidly to expand. Through conquest, alliance, and intimidation, they subdued most of their vast domain by 1500. To hold together the linguistically and ethnically diverse empire, the Inca relied on an overarching state religion, a hierarchical bureaucracy, and various forms of labor taxation, satisfied by a set amount of time spent performing tasks for the state. To speed transport and communication, the Inca built nearly 25,000 miles of roads, with more than a thousand lodgings spaced a day's journey apart and a relay system of waiting runners to carry messages. In common with other Native American civilizations, the Inca had no draft animals or wheeled vehicles for transportation. Travelers went on foot, and llamas were used as pack animals.

Inca builders created stonework structures of great refinement and durability (see "Inca Masonry," right). The most spectacular surviving example is Machu Picchu (fig. **15–16**). At 9,000 feet above sea level, the site straddles a ridge between two high peaks in the eastern slopes of the Andes. Machu Picchu's location, near the eastern limits of the empire, was the ruler's summer home. Its temples and carved sacred stones imply it may also have had an important religious function.

The production of textiles is an ancient art in the Andes (see fig. 15–1). Inca textiles suggest that they were the products of a complex society. The production of the cloth required a settled agricultural community where wool (alpaca and vicuña) and cotton could be produced, cleaned, dyed, and spun into yarn. The weavers worked on simple back-strap looms using a wool weft on a cotton warp. Both men and women worked as weavers for the central government, and the finished cloth was collected and stored in warehouses throughout the empire. The people in effect paid taxes in textiles. As one of the primary forms of wealth for the Inca, cloth was a fitting offering for the gods. Fine garments were draped around golden statues, and complex images were woven of cloth. Garments also carried important symbolic messages. Their patterns and designs indicated, among other things, a

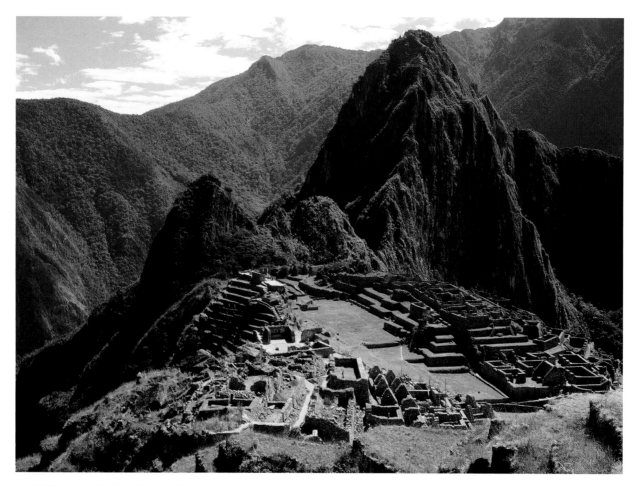

15–16 Machu Picchu, Peru. Inca, 15th–16th century CE

Inca Masonry

Working with the simplest of tools—mainly heavy stone hammers—and using no mortar, Inca builders created superb stonework, built terraces for growing crops, and made structures both simple and elaborate, including roads that linked the empire together. At Machu Picchu (see fig. 15–16), all buildings and terraces within its 3-square-mile extent were made of granite, the hard stone indigenous to the site. Commoners' houses and some walls were constructed of irregular stones and religious structures were erected using squared-off, smooth-surfaced stones laid in even rows. At a few Inca sites, the stones were boulder-size—up to 27 feet tall.

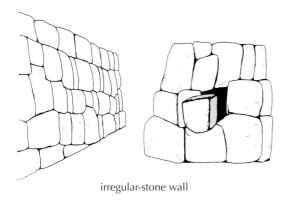

irregular-stone wall

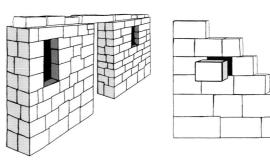

smooth-surfaced wall

person's ethnic identity and social rank. Each square in the tunic represents a miniature tunic, but the meaning of the individual patterns is not yet completely understood. The checkerboard pattern designated military officers and royal escorts. The four-part motifs may refer to the Land of the Four Quarters.

The Aftermath of the Spanish Conquest

Hernando Cortés arrived off the eastern coast of Mexico from the Spanish colony in Cuba in 1519. He forged alliances with the Aztecs' enemies and, within two years, took control of Tenochtitlan. Over the next several years, Spanish forces subdued much of the rest of what is today Mexico and established it as a colony of Spain. In 1532, Francisco Pizarro, following Cortés's example, led an expedition to South America. He and his men seized the Inca ruler, Atahualpa, held him for a huge ransom in gold, and then treacherously strangled him. They marched on to Cuzco and seized it in 1533.

The Spanish who conquered the Inca Empire were obsessed with amassing gold and silver. They melted down whatever they could find to enrich themselves and the royal coffers of Spain. The Inca, in contrast, valued gold and silver not as precious metals in themselves, but as symbols of the sun and the moon. Only a few small figures, buried as offerings, escaped the invaders' treasure hunt. A small llama was found near Lake Titicaca (fig. **15–17**). To the Inca, the llama had a special connection with the sun, rain, and fertility. In Cuzco, a llama was sacrificed to the sun every morning and evening. Dressed in a red tunic and

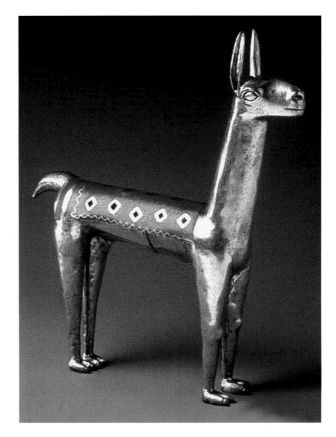

15–17 Llama, from Bolivia or Peru, found near Lake Titicaca, Bolivia. Inca, 15th century CE. Cast silver with gold and cinnabar, 9″ × 8½″ × 1¾″ (22.9 × 21.6 × 4.4 cm)

wearing gold jewelry, this llama would be paraded through the streets during April celebrations. According to Spanish commentators, these processions also included life-size gold and silver images of people and gods.

Native American populations in Mexico and Peru declined sharply after the conquest because of the exploitative policies of the conquerors and the ravages of smallpox and other diseases, against which the indigenous people had no immunity. European missionaries suppressed local beliefs and practices and worked to spread Roman Catholicism throughout the Americas. And increasing numbers of Europeans began to settle the land.

North America

Compared with the densely inhabited agricultural regions of Mesoamerica and South America, much of North America remained sparsely populated before the arrival of Europeans in the late fifteenth century. In the Northeast, people lived primarily by hunting, fishing, and gathering edible plants. In the Southeast and in the lands drained by the Mississippi and Missouri river systems, agriculture emerged, and nomadic hunting and gathering gave way to more settled communities by 1000 BCE or possibly even earlier. Toward the end of the first millennium BCE, people in the Southwest of the present-day United States also began to adopt an agricultural way of life.

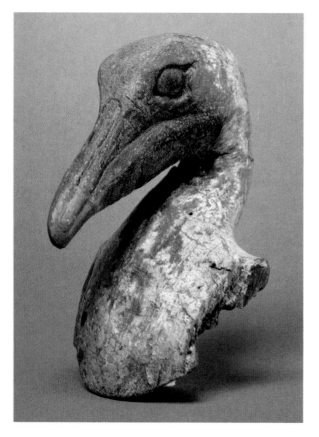

15–18 Pelican figurehead, Key Marco, Florida. Glades culture, c. 1000 CE. Wood and paint, $4^{3}/_{8}'' \times 2^{3}/_{8}'' \times 3^{1}/_{8}''$ (11.2 × 6 × 8 cm). The University Museum of Archaeology and Anthropology, Philadelphia
(T4.303)

The Southeast

The culture of the southeast in North America (especially in the area the Spanish later called "La Florida") is only beginning to be understood. Archaeologists have shown that people lived in communities formed around a central earthen mound—a platform that probably supported a chief's house, the shrines of ancestors, and a place for a sacred fire, tended by special guardians. Posts carved with birds and animals have been found preserved in swamps, and the large mound called Fort Center in Glades County, Florida, gives the culture its name: Florida Glades.

In 1895, excavators working in submerged mud and shell mounds off Key Marco on the west coast of Florida made a remarkable discovery. Painted wooden animal and bird heads, a human mask, and the figure of a kneeling cat-human were found in circumstances that suggested a ruined shrine. Recently carbon-14 dating of these items has confirmed a date of about 1000 CE. Although the heads are simplified, the artists show a remarkable power of observation in reproducing the creatures they saw around them, such as the pelican (fig. **15–18**). The surviving head, neck, and breast of the pelican are made of carved wood painted black, white, and gray (other pieces also included pink and blue). The bird's outstretched wings were found nearby, but the wood shrank and disintegrated as it dried. Carved wooden wolf and deer heads were also found. Archaeologists think the heads might have been attached to ceremonial furniture or posts. Such images suggest the existence of a bird and animal cult or perhaps the use of birds and animals as clan symbols.

The Mound Builders

In the fertile lands near the Ohio, Illinois, Mississippi, and Missouri rivers, the people of the Adena, Hopewell, and Mississippian cultures cultivated maize (corn) and other crops. They began building monumental **earthworks** and burying their leaders with valuable grave goods sometime before 1000 BCE. Objects discovered in these burials show that the people of the Mississippi and Ohio Valleys traded widely with other regions. For example, burials of the mound-building Adena (1000 BCE–200 CE) and Hopewell (c. 100 BCE–500 CE) cultures contained jewelry made with copper imported from the Upper Peninsula of present-day Michigan and silhouettes cut in sheets of mica from the Appalachian Mountains.

The Hopewell people also made pipes of fine-grain pipestone carved with realistic representations of forest animals and birds, sometimes with inlaid eyes and teeth of freshwater pearls and bone. A pearl-eyed beaver crouching on a platform forms the bowl of a pipe found in present-day Illinois (fig. **15–19**). As in a modern pipe, the bowl—a hole in the beaver's back— could be filled with dried leaves (the Hopewell may not have grown tobacco), the leaves lighted, and smoke drawn through a hole in the stem. A second way to use these pipes was to blow smoke inhaled from another vessel through the pipe to envelop the animal carved on it. Hopewell pipes and pipestone have been found from Lake Superior to the Gulf of Mexico.

The people of the Mississippian culture (900–600 CE) continued the mound-building tradition of the Adena, Hopewell, and other early southeastern cultures. One of the most impressive Mississippian-period earthworks is the Great Serpent Mound, nearly ¼-mile long, in present-day Ohio (fig. **15–20**). Carbon-14 dating of wood charcoal samples from the mound suggests that the earthwork was built about 1070 CE. It was probably the work of the people of the Fort Ancient culture (900–1600 CE), a Mississippian group of the Ohio Valley. There have been many interpretations of the twisting snake form, especially the "head" at the highest point, an oval enclosure that some see as opening its jaws to swallow a huge egg formed by a heap of stones.

The Mississippian peoples built a major urban center known as Cahokia near the juncture of the Illinois, Missouri, and Mississippi rivers (now East St. Louis, Illinois). Although the site may have been inhabited as early as c. 3000 BCE, Cahokia, as we know it, was begun about 900 CE, and most construction took place between about 900 and 1500. At its height, the city had a

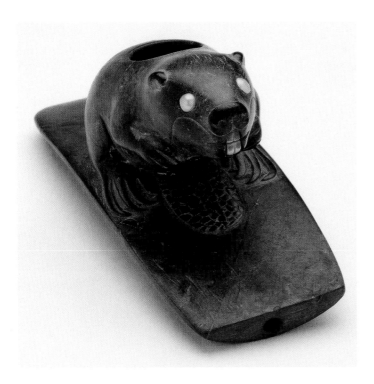

15–19 Beaver effigy platform pipe, from Bedford Mound Pike County, Illinois. Hopewell culture, c. 100–200 CE. Pipestone, river pearl eyes, and bone teeth, length 4½″ (11.4 cm). Gilcrease Museum, Tulsa, Oklahoma

Pipes made by people of the Hopewell culture may have been used for smoking hallucinatory plants, perhaps during rituals involving the animal carved on the pipe bowl. The beaver's shining pearl eyes suggest an association with the spirit world.

15–20 Great Serpent Mound, Adams County, Ohio. c. 1070 CE. Length 1,254′ (328.2 m)
COURTESY OF CAHOKIA MOUNDS STATE HISTORIC SITE.

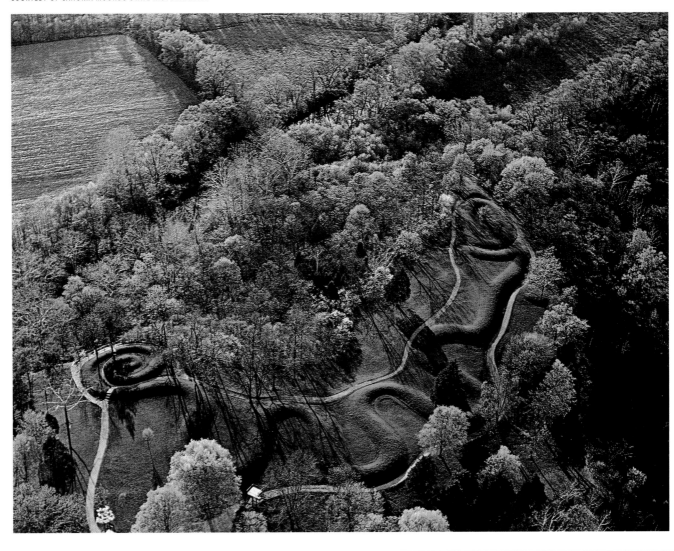

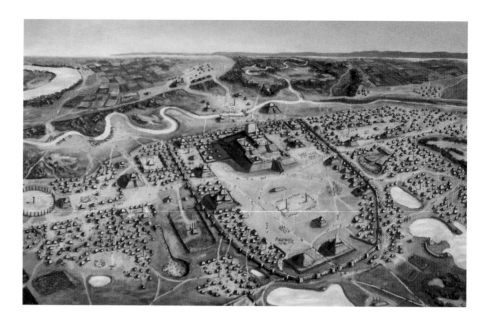

15–21 Reconstruction of central Cahokia, East St. Louis, Illinois. Mississippian culture, c. 1150 CE. Earth mounds and wooden structures; east-west length approx. 3 miles (4.84 km), north-south length approx. 2 1/4 miles (3.63 km); base of great mound, 1,037′ × 790′ (316 × 241 m), height approx. 100′ (30 m). Painting by William R. Iseminger

population of between 10,000 and 20,000 people, with another 10,000 in the surrounding countryside (fig. **15–21**).

The most prominent feature of Cahokia is an enormous 100-foot earth mound called Monk's Mound covering 15 acres. A small, conical platform on its summit originally supported a wooden fence and a rectangular temple or house. Smaller rectangular and conical mounds in front of the principal mound surrounded a large, roughly rectangular plaza. The city's entire ceremonial center was protected by a stockade, or fence, of upright wooden posts—a sign of increasing warfare. In all, the walled enclosure contained more than 500 mounds, platforms, wooden enclosures, and houses. The various earthworks functioned as tombs and as bases for palaces and temples, and also served to make astronomical observations. One conical burial mound was located next to a platform that may have been used for sacrifices.

The Southwest

Farming cultures were slower to arise in the arid Southwest. The Hohokam culture, centered in the central and southern parts of present-day Arizona, emerged around 200 BCE and endured until sometime after 1200 CE. The Hohokam built large-scale irrigation systems; they constructed deep and narrow canals to reduce evaporation and lined the canals with clay to reduce seepage. In what is now called the Four Corners region—where Colorado, Utah, Arizona, and New Mexico meet—this irrigation technology was adopted to produce food for settled communities. Around 900 CE they began building elaborate, multistoried structures with many rooms for specialized purposes, including communal food storage and rituals. The Spaniards called the Rio Grande communities "pueblos," or towns. The descendants of these people, including the Hopi and Zuni, still occupy these pueblos and other nearby areas. An early photographer, Timothy O'Sullivan, recorded pueblos ruins in the Canyon de Chelley, in Arizona, while accompanying a geological expedition in 1873.

The largest known pueblo center is Pueblo Bonito in Chaco Canyon, New Mexico, which was built between c. 900 and 1300 CE (fig. **15–22**). This remarkable, D-shaped structure covered more than three acres. Some 800 rooms—including thirty kivas (subterranean circular rooms used as ceremonial centers)—rose four or five stories high. The outer perimeter wall was 1,300 feet long. The sandstone masonry walls on the ground floor were 4 feet thick, and trunks of ponderosa pines transported 50 miles were used for roof beams. As new rooms were added over time, older rooms lost access to natural light. Amazingly, all aspects of construction—including quarrying, timber cutting, and transport—were done without draft animals, wheeled vehicles, or metal tools.

Pueblo Bonito stood at the center of a trading network of wide, straight roads, in some places with curbs and paving. The builders made no effort to avoid topographic obstacles; when they encountered cliffs, they ran stairs up them. This practice suggests that the roads served as processional routes in addition to practical thoroughfares.

Women were the potters in pueblo society. In the eleventh century, these potters perfected a functional, aesthetically pleasing, coil-built earthenware, a ceramic fired at a low temperature. The wide-mouthed seed jar shown in figure **15–23** is painted with complex black-and-white dotted squares and zigzag patterns that conform to the body of the jar and, in spite of their angularity, enhance its curved shape. The intricate and inventive play of positive and negative space—represented by dark and light areas—suggests lightning flashing over a grid of irrigated fields.

The Pueblo people of the southwest still make fine ceramics in the traditional way using traditional designs. One of the best-known twentieth-century Pueblo potters is Maria Montoya Martinez (1881–1980) of San Ildefonso Pueblo. Inspired by prehistoric **blackware** pottery that was unearthed at nearby archaeological excavations, she and her husband, Julian Martinez (1885–1943), developed a distinctive new ware decorated with **matte** (non-gloss) black designs on a lustrous black background

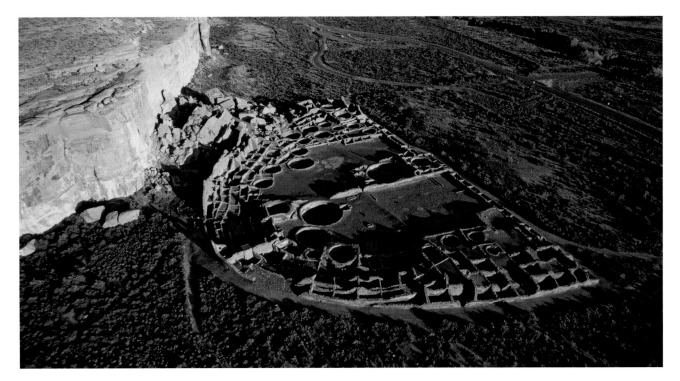

15–22 Pueblo Bonito, Chaco Canyon, New Mexico, the ancestral home of the Pueblo people. 850-1250 CE

(fig. **15–24**). Their decorative patterns were inspired by both traditional Pueblo imagery and the then-fashionable Euro-American Art Deco.

Other traditional practices also survive today (see "Basketry," page 435). Some contemporary Pueblo villages, like those of their Anasazi forebears, consist of multistoried, apartment-like dwellings built of adobe brick rather than stone. One of these, Taos Pueblo, shown here in a 1947 photograph (fig. **15–25**), is located in north-central New Mexico. The northernmost of the surviving Pueblo communities, Taos once served as a trading center between Plains and Pueblo peoples. It burned in 1690 but was rebuilt about 1700 and has since been often modified. Two complexes of great multifamily houses stand on either side of Taos Creek, rising up to five stories in a stepped fashion to form a series of roof terraces, where people could cook as well as view the ceremonies in the plaza below.

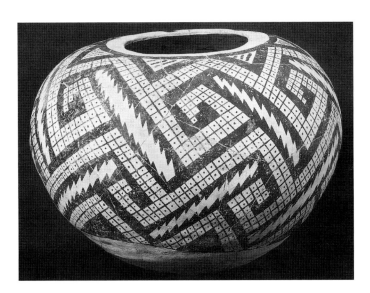

15–23 Seed jar. Pueblo culture, c. 1150 CE. Earthenware and black-and-white pigment, diameter 14 $\frac{1}{2}$″ (36.8 cm). The St. Louis Art Museum, St. Louis, Missouri

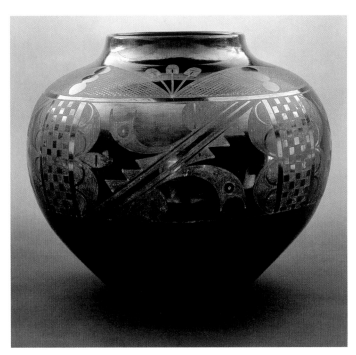

15–24 Maria Montoya Martinez and **Julian Martinez. Storage jar,** c. 1942. San Ildefonso, Pueblo, New Mexico. Black on black ceramic, height 18 $\frac{3}{4}$″ (47.6 cm), diameter 22 $\frac{1}{2}$″ (57.1 cm). Museum of Indian Arts and Culture/Laboratory of Anthropology, Museum of New Mexico, Santa Fe

(CATALOG #31959/12)

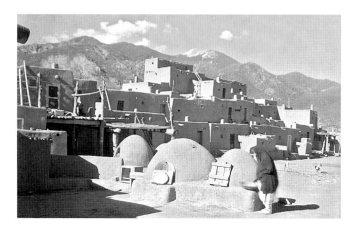

15–25 Taos Pueblo, Tewa, Taos, New Mexico. Photographed by Laura Gilpin in 1947, Amon Carter Museum, Fort Worth, Texas
LAURA GILPIN COLLECTION (NEG. # P1979.208.698)

The Eastern Woodlands and the Great Plains

When European settlement began in earnest in North America around the late 1500s to early 1600s, forests stretched from the Hudson Bay to the Gulf of Mexico and from the Atlantic coast to the Mississippi River and Missouri River watersheds. Between this Eastern Woodlands region and the Rocky Mountains to the west lay an area of prairie grasslands now known as the Great Plains.

In the Eastern Woodlands, Native American peoples supported themselves by a combination of hunting and agriculture. Living together in villages, they cultivated corn, squash, and beans. They used waterproof birchbark to construct their homes and to make the watercraft known as the canoe. In the sixteenth century, one Eastern Woodlands group, the Iroquois, formed a powerful confederation of northeastern Native American nations that played a prominent military and political role until after the American Revolution.

On the Great Plains, two differing ways of life developed, one nomadic—dependent on the region's great migrating herds of buffalo for food, clothing, and shelter—and the other sedentary and agricultural. Horses (which had become extinct in North America), reintroduced by Spanish explorers in the sixteenth century, and later, firearms, made buffalo hunting vastly more efficient than before and attracted more people to the nomadic way of life.

As European settlers on the eastern seaboard began to turn forests into farms, they put increasing pressure on the Eastern Woodlands peoples, seizing their lands and forcing them westward. The resulting interaction of Eastern Woodlands artists with one another and with Plains artists led to the emergence of a Prairie style among numerous groups.

One distinctively Eastern Woodlands medium that found its way to the Plains was **quillwork** embroidery. Quillwork involved soaking porcupine and bird quills to soften them, then dyeing them, and working them into rectilinear, ornamental surface patterns on deerskin clothing and on birchbark artifacts like baskets and boxes. A Lakota legend recounts how a mythical ancestor, Doublewoman ("double" because she was both beautiful and ugly, benign and dangerous) appeared to a Lakota woman in a dream and taught her the art of quillwork. As this legend suggests, quillwork was a woman's art form. The Sioux baby carrier shown in figure **15–26** is richly decorated with symbols of protection and well-being, including bands of antelopes in profile and mythical thunderbirds with their heads turned and their tails outspread. The thunderbird was an especially beneficent symbol, thought to be capable of providing protection against both human and supernatural adversaries. In some areas beadwork replaced quillwork in the nineteenth century, when the women began to acquire colored glass beads through trade with Europeans. At first they imitated the patterns of quillwork, but by mid-century they began to incorporate European floral designs into their work.

The nomadic Plains peoples developed a light, portable dwelling known as a **tepee** (fig. **15–27**), which was sturdily constructed to withstand the wind, dust, and rain of the prairies. Hides (later, canvas) covered a framework of poles to form an almost conical structure that leaned slightly in the direction of the prevailing wind. The flap-covered door and smoke hole (the opening at the

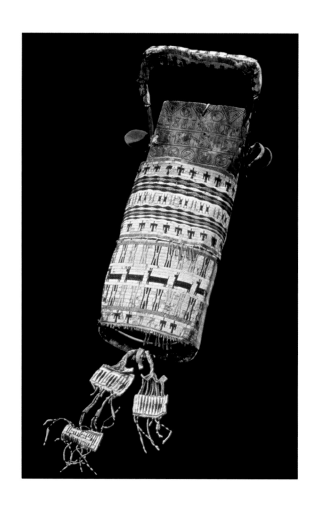

15–26 Baby carrier, from the Upper Missouri River area. Eastern Sioux, 19th century. Board, buckskin, porcupine quill, length 31″ (78.7 cm). Smithsonian Institution, Washington, D.C.

Technique

Basketry

Basketry involves weaving reeds, grasses, or other materials to form containers. The three principal basket-making techniques are coiling, or sewing together a spiraling foundation of rods with some other material; twining, or sewing together a vertical warp of rods; and plaiting, which involves weaving strips over and under each other. In North America the earliest evidence of basketwork, found in Danger Cave, Utah, dates to as early as 8400 BCE. Over the subsequent centuries basket makers developed basketry into an art form that combined utility with great beauty.

The coiled basket shown here was made by the Pomo of northern California. According to Pomo legend, the earth was dark until their ancestral hero stole the sun and brought it to earth in a basket. He hung the basket first just over the horizon, but, dissatisfied with the light it gave, he kept suspending it in different places across the dome of the sky. He repeats this process every day, which is why the sun moves across the sky from east to west. In the Pomo basket, the structure of coiled willow and bracken fern root produces a spiral surface into which the artist worked sparkling pieces of clamshell, trade beads, and the soft tufts of woodpecker and quail feathers. Such baskets were treasured possessions, often cremated with their owners at death.

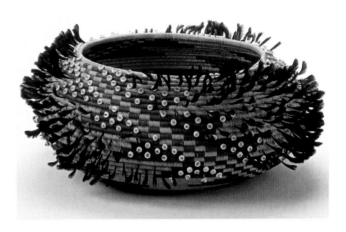

Feathered Bowl Wedding Basket. c. 1877. Pomo. Willow, bracken fern root, clamshell, trade beads, woodpecker and quail feathers, height 5 ½" (14 cm), diameter 12" (30.5 cm). Philbrook Museum of Art, Tulsa, Oklahoma

GIFT OF CLARK FIELD (1948.39.37)

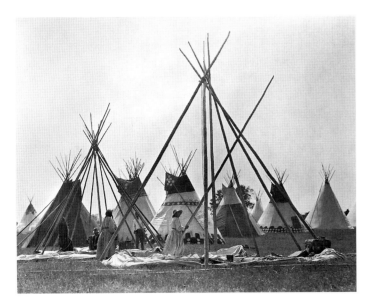

15–27 Blackfoot women raising a tepee. Photographed c. 1900. Montana Historical Society, Helena

When packed to be dragged by a horse, the tepee served as a platform for transporting other possessions as well. Tepees were the property and responsibility of women. Blackfoot women could set up their tepees in less than an hour.

top above the central hearth) usually faced away from the wind. Designed and built by women, the typical tepee required about 18 buffalo hides, the largest about 38. An inner lining covered the lower part of the walls and part of the floor to protect the occupants from drafts. Women painted, embroidered, quilled, and beaded tepee linings, backrests, clothing, and equipment. Plains men recorded their exploits in symbolic and narrative form in paintings on tepee linings and covers and also on buffalo-hide robes.

The earliest known painted buffalo-hide robe illustrates a battle fought in 1797 by the Mandan (of what is now North Dakota) and their allies against the Sioux (fig. **15–28**). The painter, trying to capture the full extent of a conflict in which five nations took part, shows a party of warriors in 22 separate episodes. The party is armed with bows and arrows, lances, clubs, and flintlock rifles. Their leader appears with a pipe and wears an elaborate eagle-feather headdress. The lively stick figures of the warriors have rectangular torsos and tiny round heads. The figures stand out clearly against the light-colored background of the buffalo hide; to make them, the painter pressed lines into the hide, then added black, red, green, yellow, and brown pigments. A strip of colored porcupine quills runs down the spine. The robe would have been worn draped over the shoulders of the powerful warrior whose deeds it commemorates. As he moved, the painted

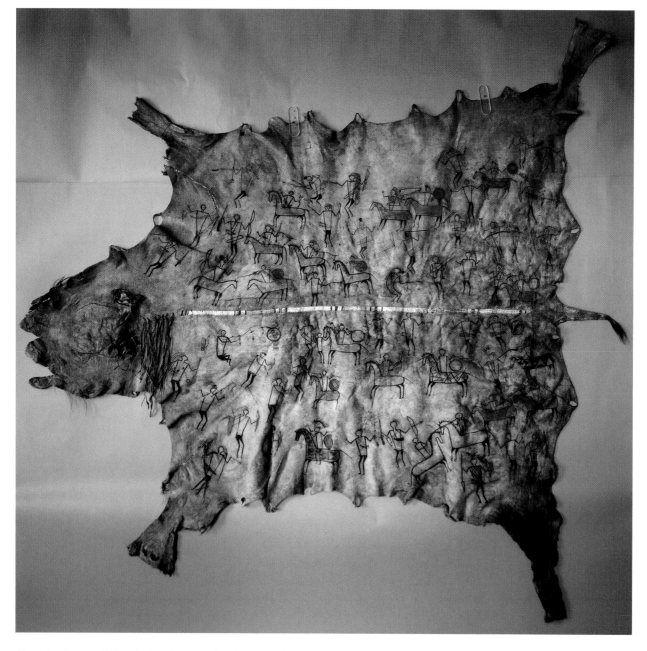

15–28 Battle-scene hide painting, from North Dakota. Mandan, 1797–1800. Tanned buffalo hide, dyed porcupine quills, and black, red, green, yellow, and brown pigment, 7′10″ × 8′6″ (2.44 × 2.65 m). Peabody Museum of Archaeology, Harvard University, Cambridge, Massachusetts (99-12-10/53121)

This painted hide was collected in 1804 by Meriwether Lewis and William Clark on their 1804–1806 expedition into western lands acquired by the United States in the Louisiana Purchase, making it the earliest documented example of Plains painting. Lewis and Clark presented it to President Thomas Jefferson, who displayed the robe in the entrance hall of Monticello, his home in Virginia.

horses and warriors would appear to come alive, transforming him into a living representation of his exploits. Life and art on the Plains changed abruptly in the 1870s and 1880s after the transcontinental railway was completed and increasing numbers of settlers killed off the buffalo and took over more and more of the land, thereby destroying the Native American way of life.

The Northwest Coast

Before the arrival of European explorers, the Native American peoples composing the First Nations of the Northwest Coast—among them the Tlingit (of southern Alaska), the Haida (of southern Alaska and the Queen Charlotte Islands), and the

During the harsh winter season, when spirits are thought to be most powerful, many northern people seek spiritual renewal through their ancient rituals—including the potlatch and the initiation of new members into the prestigious Hamatsa Society. With snapping beaks and cries of *"Hap! Hap! Hap!"* ("Eat! Eat! Eat!"), Hamatsa, the people-eating spirit of the north, and his three assistants—horrible masked monster birds—begin their wild ritual dance (fig. **15–29**). The dancing birds threaten and even attack the Kwakwaka'wakw (Kwakiutl) people who gather for the Winter Ceremony. At this time, youths are captured, taught the Hamatsa lore, and then—in a spectacular theater-dance performance—are "tamed" and brought back into civilized life.

Afterward, the masked bird dancers appear—first Raven-of-the-North-End-of-the-World, then Crooked-Beak-of-the-End-of-the-World, and finally the untranslatable Huxshukw, who cracks open skulls with its beak and eats the brains of its victims. Snapping their beaks, these masters of illusion enter the room backward, their masks pointed up as though the birds are looking skyward. They move slowly counterclockwise around the floor. At each change in the music they crouch, snap their beaks, and let out wild cries of *"Hap! Hap! Hap!"* Essential to the ritual dances are the huge carved and painted wooden masks, articulated and operated by strings worked by the dancers. Among the finest masks are those by Willie Seaweed (1873–1967), a Kwakwaka'wakw chief (see fig. **15–30**). Their brilliant colors and exuberantly decorative carving style determined the direction of twentieth-century Kwakwaka'wakw sculpture.

The Canadian government, abetted by missionaries, outlawed the Winter Ceremony and potlatches in 1885, claiming the event was injurious to health, encouraged prostitution, endangered children's education, damaged the economy, and was cannibalistic. But the Kwakwaka'wakw refused to give up their "oldest and best" festival—one that spoke powerfully to them in many ways, establishing social rank and playing an important role in arranging marriages. By 1936 the government and the missionaries, who called the Kwak-

waka'wakw "incorrigible," gave up. But not until 1951 could the Kwakwaka'wakw people gather openly for Winter Ceremonies, including the initiation rites of the Hamatsa Society.

The photographer Edward S. Curtis (1868–1952) devoted 30 years to documenting the lives of Native Americans and First Nations peoples. This 1914 photograph shows participants in a film he made about the Kwakwaka'wakw. For the film, his assistant, Richard Hunt (a member of the Kwakwaka'wakw), borrowed family heirlooms and commissioned many new pieces from the finest Kwakwaka'wakw artists. Most of the pieces are now in museum collections. The photograph shows carved and painted posts, masked dancers (including those representing people-eating birds), a chief at the left (holding a speaker's staff and wearing a cedar neck ring), and spectators at the far right.

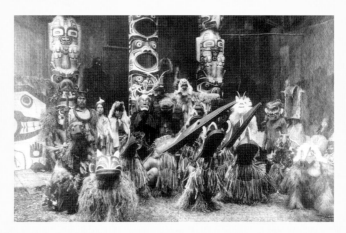

15–29 Hamatsa dancers, Kwakwaka'wakw (Kwakiutl). Canada. Photographed in 1914 by Edward S. Curtis

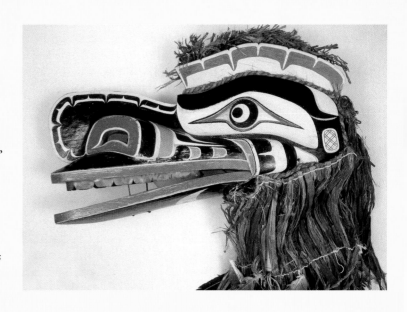

15–30 Attributed to Willie Seaweed. Kwakwaka'wakw (Kwakiutl) bird mask, from Alert Bay, Canada. Prior to 1951. Cedar wood, cedar bark, feathers, and fiber, 10″ × 72″ × 15″ (25.4 × 183 × 38.1 cm). Collection of the Museum of Anthropology, Vancouver, Canada

The name Seaweed is an Anglicization of the Kwakwaka'wakw name Siwid, meaning "Paddling Canoe," "Recipient of Paddling," or "Paddled to"—referring to a great chief whose guests paddle from afar to attend potlatches. Willie Seaweed was not only a sculptor; he was the chief of his clan and a great orator, singer, and tribal historian who kept the tradition of the potlatch alive during years of government repression.

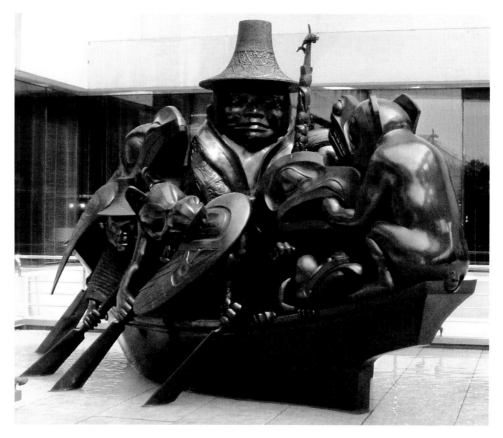

15–31 Bill Reid. *The Spirit of Haida Gwaii.* Haida, 1991. Bronze, approx. 13′ × 20′ (4 × 6 m). Canadian Embassy, Washington, D.C.

Kwakwaka'wakw (formerly spelled Kwakiutl, of the central Canadian coast and Alert Bay)—lived on the Pacific coast of North America from what is today southern Alaska to as far south as what is today northern California. Their major food source was salmon from the region's many rivers. Harvested and dried, the fish could sustain large populations throughout the year.

People lived in extended family groups in large, elaborately decorated communal houses made of massive timbers and thick planks. Family groups claimed descent from a mythic animal or animal-human ancestor. Chiefs, who were in the most direct line of descent from the ancestor, validated their status and garnered prestige for themselves and their families by holding ritual feasts known as potlatches during which they gave valuable gifts to their guests. Shamans, who were sometimes also chiefs, mediated between the human and spirit worlds.

The participants who danced in the Winter Ceremony of the Kwakwaka'wakw wore striking costumes and gigantic carved and painted masks (see "Closer Look," fig. 15–30). Among the most elaborate masks were those used by the elite Hamatsa society in their dances. Transformed into supernatural creatures, the dancers searched for "victims". By using strings inside the masks, they could snap the beaks open and shut with spectacular effect.

Northwest Coast painters preferred a color scheme of black, white, and red—later adding yellow and blue-green. Their designs are very complex and difficult to interpret. The images consist of two basic elements: the ovoid (a slightly bent rectangle with rounded corners) and the **formline** (a continuous, shape-defining line).

The contemporary Haida artist Bill Reid (1920–1998) sought to sustain and revitalize the traditions of his Haida ancestors' art in his work. Trained as a wood carver, painter, and jeweler, Reid revived the art of carving dugout canoes and totem poles in the Haida homeland of Haida Gwaii ("Islands of the People"), known today as the Queen Charlotte Islands. Late in life he began to create large-scale sculpture in bronze. With their black patina, these works recall traditional Haida carvings in argillite, a shiny black stone. One of them, *The Spirit of Haida Gwaii*, now stands outside the Canadian Embassy in Washington, D.C. (fig. 15–31). This sculpture, which Reid viewed as a metaphor for modern Canada's multicultural society, depicts a collection of figures from the natural and mythic worlds of the First Nations struggling to paddle forward in a canoe. The dominant figure in the center is a shaman wearing a spruce-root basket hat and Chilikat blanket. He holds a speaker's pole—a staff that gives him the right to speak with authority. In the prow, the place reserved for the chief in a war canoe, is the Bear. The Bear faces backward rather than forward, however, and is bitten by the Eagle, with formline-patterned wings. The Eagle, in turn, is bitten by the Seawolf. In the stern, steering the canoe, is the Raven, the trickster in Haida mythology. The Raven is assisted by Mousewoman, the traditional guide and escort of humans in the spirit realms. According to Reid, the work represents a "mythological and environmental lifeboat," where "the entire family of living things . . . whatever their differences, . . . are paddling together in one boat, headed in one direction."

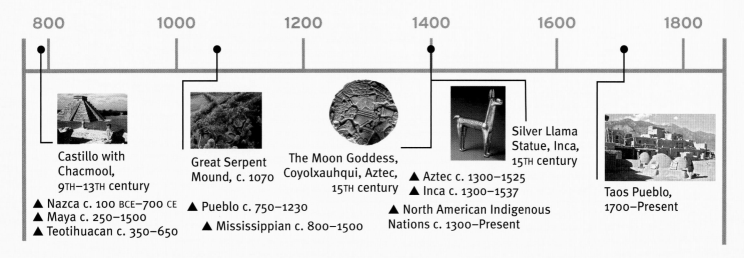

800   1000   1200   1400   1600   1800

Castillo with
Chacmool,
9TH–13TH century

▲ Nazca c. 100 BCE–700 CE
▲ Maya c. 250–1500
▲ Teotihuacan c. 350–650

Great Serpent
Mound, c. 1070

▲ Pueblo c. 750–1230
  ▲ Mississippian c. 800–1500

The Moon Goddess,
Coyolxauhqui, Aztec,
15TH century

Silver Llama
Statue, Inca,
15TH century

▲ Aztec c. 1300–1525
▲ Inca c. 1300–1537

▲ North American Indigenous
Nations c. 1300–Present

Taos Pueblo,
1700–Present

LOOKING BACK

Changing taste and broadening interests have moved indigenous American art out of the basements of natural history and anthropology museums and into art galleries. Now a museum for American Indian art and culture stands with other Smithsonian Institutions on the Mall in Washington D.C. True recognition at last!

Although art was central to their lives, the indigenous peoples of the Americas designated no special objects as "works of art." Some pieces were essentially utilitarian and others had ritual uses and symbolic associations, but people drew no distinction between art and other aspects of material culture or between the fine arts and the decorative arts.

American Indian art must be seen in the cultural context in which it was made, a context that has in many cases been lost to time or to the disruption of European conquest in the fifteenth and sixteenth centuries. Fortunately, art history, anthropology, and archeology have helped to recover at least some of that lost context. We have learned from archeological research conducted during the past century. Far from being the wilderness described by early invaders and travelers, the continents had large, complex cities such as Teotihuacan in Mexico and ceremonial centers like Cahokia in Illinois. Elaborate individual architectural structures dominated the landscape, whether the jungles around Palenque in Mexico or the mountains of Machu Picchu in Peru. Without wheeled vehicles or metal tools, people quarried stone, cut timber, and transported these building materials, often to distant sites. In the Andes mountains of Peru and radiating out from Chaco Canyon and elsewhere in the North American Southwest, scholars have traced road networks extending over hundreds of miles. The archeological record shows that people traded not only luxury items and materials but also food and other essentials over great distances.

In Mesoamerica, monumental sculpture covered buildings and, in the form of gods and goddesses, loomed over the devotees. In the river valleys of North America people shaped the earth into huge serpents, bears, and eagles, while in the Nazca Plain in Peru people engraved images of birds and insects into the surface of the earth. The arts could be small and fragile as well as large and enduring. The textiles of the Incas have been preserved in the desert climate, while in North America only relatively modern basketry, quillwork, and hide paintings survive. As we have seen in many cultures, ceramics outlast the damage of time and climate. Even when they are found in damaged condition, they tell their story of the makers' development of technology and design skill.

Having survived first as "curiosities" then as tourist souvenirs, the arts of the indigenous peoples of the Americas are at last recognized for their own qualities.

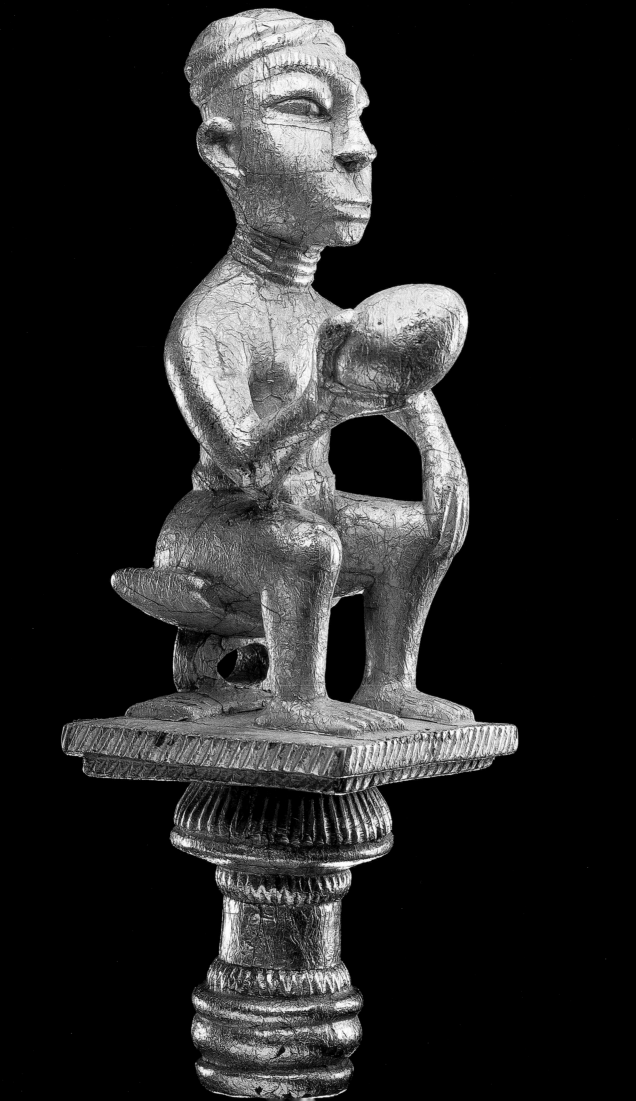

African Art

Astaff or rod is a nearly universal symbol of authority and leadership. In ancient Egypt, 5,000 years before Kojo Bonsu carved this Asante speaker's staff, a sculptor depicted King Narmer holding a mace (a weighted club, see fig. 2–14). The mace's symbolism emphasized the king's role as the mighty ruler who brought order to the lands watered by the Nile. Today in many colleges, a ceremonial mace is carried by the leader of an academic procession and placed in front of the speaker's lectern. Asante speakers who carry their image-topped staffs are part of this widespread tradition.

As in other societies throughout the world, art in Africa identifies those who hold important positions. Art validates their right to kingship, or their authority as representatives of the family or community, and communicates the rules for moral behavior that must be obeyed by all members of the society. This luxurious gold-covered finial of a spokesperson's staff (fig. 16–1) belongs to the royal culture of one of the Akan kingdoms of Ghana, in West Africa. The Akan admire elegant speech. One of their adages is, "We speak to the wise man in proverbs, not in plain speech." Consequently, their governing system includes the special post of Ruler's Spokesperson. Since about 1900 these advisers have carried staffs of office. This finial of a carved figure holding an egg illustrates an Akan parable: "Political power is like an egg. Grasp it too tightly and it will shatter in your hand; hold it too loosely and it will slip from your fingers."

Since the fifteenth century when the first Europeans explored Africa, quantities of African artworks have been shipped back to Western museums of natural history or ethnography, where the works were first exhibited as curious artifacts of "primitive" cultures. Toward the end of the nineteenth century, however, profound changes in Western thinking about art gradually led more and more people to appreciate the inherent aesthetic qualities of these objects and at last to embrace them fully as art. In recent years, scholars have further enhanced the world's appreciation and understanding of traditional African arts by exploring their rich meaning from the point of view of the people who made and used them. To attempt to fully understand artwork such as this finial, it is necessary to consider the vital role in the continuity of human life for which it was created.

16–1 Kojo Bonsu (attributed). Finial of a spokesperson's staff *(okyeame poma),* from an Akan kingdom, Ghana. Asante culture, 20th century. Wood and gold, height 11 $\frac{1}{4}$" (28.57 cm). Gold of Africa Museum, Cape Town

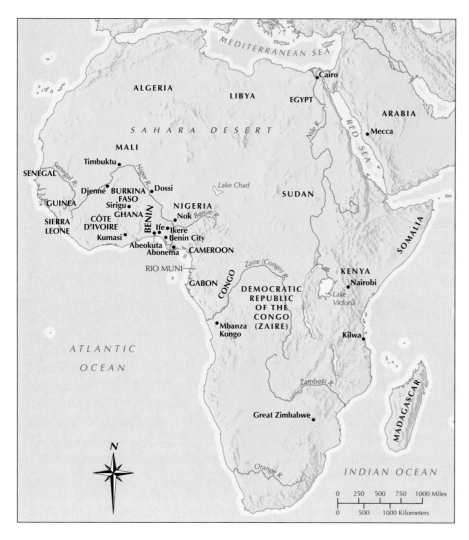

Map 16–1 The African Continent

Africa is a continent of enormous diversity. Geographically, it ranges from vast deserts to tropical rain forests, from flat grasslands to spectacular mountains and dramatic rift valleys. Human diversity in Africa is equally impressive. More than 1,000 major languages have been identified, representing a seemingly infinite variety of cultures, each with its own history, customs, and art forms. Africa is the site of one of the great ancient civilizations, that of Egypt (see Chapter 2), and North Africa later contributed prominently to the development of Islamic art and culture.

The history of African art begins in the Paleolithic era. Like prehistoric people around the world, early Africans painted and inscribed an abundance of images on the walls of caves and over-hanging rocks. The mountains of the central Sahara have especially fascinating examples of rock art, with the earliest images dating from at least 8000 BCE. At that time, the Sahara was a great grassy plain, perhaps much like the game-park areas of modern East Africa. Vivid images of hippopotamuses, elephants, giraffes, antelope, and other animals incised into rock surfaces testify to the abundant wildlife that roamed the region.

By 4000 BCE, hunting had given way to herding as the Saharan climate became more arid. Remarkably lifelike paintings on rock surfaces from the herding period show scenes of cattle and the people who tended them. The desiccation of the Sahara coincided with the rise of Egyptian civilization along the Nile Valley to the east. As the Saharan grasslands dried up, some of their inhabitants may have migrated to the Nile Valley region in search of arable land and pasture. Perhaps this migration, by greatly

expanding the population of the valley, contributed to the tensions that resulted in the emergence of complex forms of social organization there.

Saharan people presumably migrated southward as well, into the Sudan, the broad belt of grassland that stretches across Africa south of the Sahara desert, bringing with them knowledge of agriculture and animal husbandry. Agriculture reached the Sudan by at least 3000 BCE, and knowledge of ironworking spread across the area toward the middle of the first millennium BCE.

Some of the earliest evidence of iron technology in sub-Saharan Africa comes from the so-called Nok culture, which arose in the western Sudan (present-day Nigeria), as early as 500 BCE. The Nok people were farmers who grew grain and oil-bearing seeds; they were also smelters, using the technology for refining ore. In addition, they created the earliest known sculpture of sub-Saharan Africa, producing accomplished terra-cotta figures of human and animal subjects between about 500 BCE and 200 CE.

The Nok head shown here (fig. 16–2), slightly larger than life-size, originally formed part of a complete figure. The triangular or D-shaped eyes are characteristic of Nok style and appear in Nok animal sculptures. Each large bun of the elaborate hairstyle is pierced with a hole that may have held ornamental feathers. Other Nok figures boast large quantities of beads and other prestige ornaments. Since the original context for these pieces is unknown—none of these sculptures were excavated by archaeologists—it is difficult to hypothesize what their original meaning and function might have been.

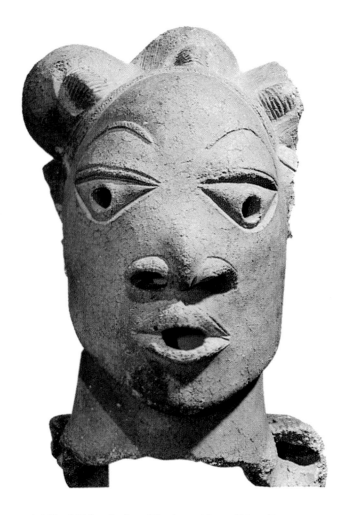

16–2 Head. Nok style, from Nigeria. c. 500 BCE–200 CE. Terra cotta, height 14 ¹³/₁₆″ (36 cm). National Museum, Lagos, Nigeria

The city of Ife, a sacred site for the Yoruba people, arose in the southern, forested part of present-day Nigeria by about 800 CE, several centuries after the last Nok terra cottas were produced. Yoruba myth tells how at Ife the gods descended from heaven on iron chains to create the world. Remarkable, naturalistic works of sculpture were created in this sacred city between about 1050 CE and 1400 CE.

A life-size bronze head of an *oni* (king) shows the extraordinary artistry achieved by Ife sculptors (fig. **16–3**). The modeling of the flesh is extremely sensitive, especially around the nose and mouth. The eyes are strikingly similar in shape to those of some modern Yoruba, and the face is covered with decorative parallel scarification patterns (decorations made by scarring the skin). Holes along the scalp apparently permitted the attachment of hair, a crown, or perhaps a beaded veil. The head might possibly have been attached to a wooden mannequin using the large holes at the base of the neck. If so, the mannequin may have been dressed in a deceased *oni's* robe used for display during his memorial services. Some historians speculate that the heads might have held the sacred crowns of the oni during a vacancy of the throne.

Ife was the artistic parent of the great city-state of Benin, which arose some 150 miles to the southeast. According to oral histories, the earliest kings of Benin belonged to the Ogiso, or Skyking, dynasty. After a long period of misrule, however, the Edo people of Benin asked the oni of Ife for a new ruler. The oni

sent Prince Oranmiyan, who founded a new dynasty in 1170 CE. Some two centuries later, the fourth king, or *oba*, of Benin decided to start a tradition of memorial sculpture like that of Ife. He sent to Ife for master metal casters, and the practice of casting memorial heads for the shrines of royal ancestors of Benin is still in the hands of their descendants to this day.

Benin brass heads range from small, thinly cast, naturalistic images to large, thickly cast, highly stylized representations. The dating of these works is controversial, but many scholars have concluded that the smallest, most naturalistic heads were created during a so-called Early Period (1400–1550 CE), when Benin artists were still heavily influenced by those of Ife. The memorial heads grew increasingly stylized during the Middle Period (1550–1700 CE), becoming very large and heavy during the ensuing Late Period (1700–1897 CE), with angular, stylized

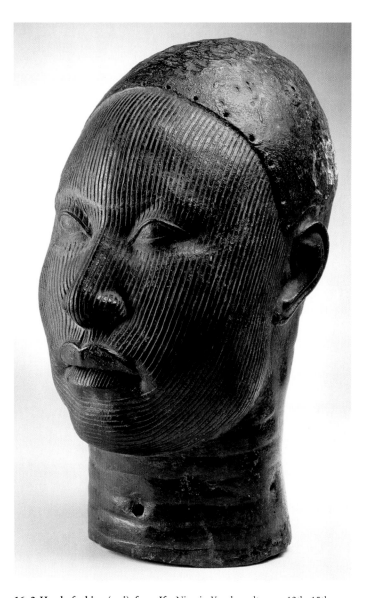

16–3 Head of a king (oni), from Ife, Nigeria. Yoruba culture, c. 12th–15th century. Bronze, height 11 ⁷/₁₆″ (29 cm). Museum of Ife Antiquities, Ife, Nigeria

The proportions of the few known full figures are characteristically African, with the head making up as much as one-quarter of the total height. These proportions probably reflect a belief in the head's importance as the abode of the spirit and the focus of individual identity.

features and an elaborate beaded crown (fig. **16–4**). A similar crown is still worn by the present-day *oba*.

All the Benin heads include representations of coral-bead necklaces, which have been part of the royal costume from earliest times to the present day. In Late Period sculpture, the necklaces form a tall, cylindrical mass that obscures the chin and greatly adds to the weight of the sculpture. The increase in size and weight of Benin memorial heads over time may reflect the growing power and wealth of the *oba* deriving from Benin's expanding trade with Europe. Benin traded with Portugal from the late fifteenth century, first in ivory and forest products and later, tragically, in slaves. Commerce between Benin and Europe flourished until 1897, when, in reprisal for the massacre of a party of trade negotiators, British troops sacked and burned the royal palace of Benin, sending the *oba* into an exile from which he did not return until 1914.

The Benin kings also commissioned important works in ivory. One example is a beautiful pendant that represents an *iyoba*, or queen mother (fig. **16–5**). As the mother of the king, the *iyoba* ranked as one of the senior members of the court. This

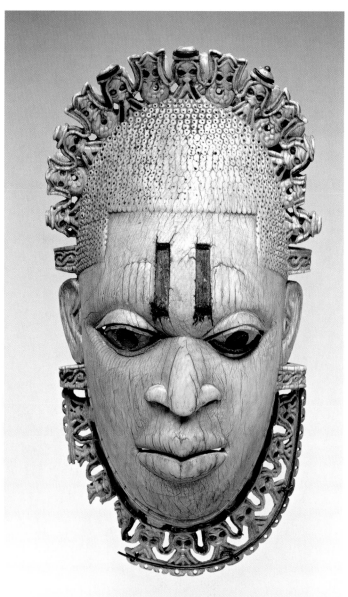

16–5 Pendant representing an *iyoba*, from Benin, Nigeria. Edo culture, c. 1550 CE. Ivory, iron, and copper, height 9 ¼″ (23.4 cm). The Metropolitan Museum of Art, New York

THE MICHAEL C. ROCKEFELLER MEMORIAL COLLECTION, GIFT OF NELSON A. ROCKEFELLER, 1972 (1978.412.323)

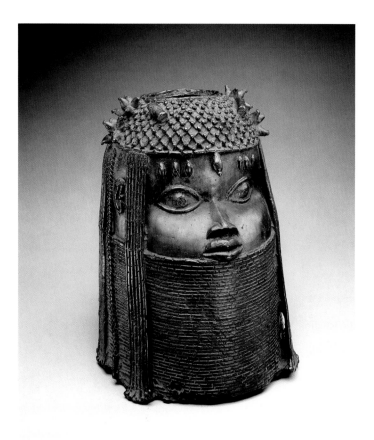

16–4 Head of an *Oba* (King), from Benin, Nigeria. Edo culture, 18th century. Brass, height 13″ (33 cm). The Metropolitan Museum of Art, New York

GIFT OF MR. AND MRS. KLAUS G. PERLS, 1991. (1991.17.2). PHOTOGRAPH © 1991 THE METROPOLITAN MUSEUM OF ART

Almost all Benin metal sculpture was made by the lost-wax casting process (see Starter Kit). Although Benin sculptures are popularly referred to as "bronze," other copper alloys such as brass were more common.

pendant may represent Idia, the first and best-known *iyoba*. She is particularly remembered for raising an army and using her magical powers to help her son Esigie (ruled 1504–1550 CE) defeat his enemies.

The pendant, a belt or hip ornament, was probably worn at the *oba's* waist. There were originally iron inlays in the pupils and in the scarification patterns on the forehead. The *iyoba's* necklace represents heads of Portuguese soldiers with beards and flowing hair. (The Portuguese also helped Esigie expand his kingdom.) In her crown, more Portuguese heads alternate with figures of mudfish, which in Benin iconography symbolize Olokun, the Lord of the Great Waters. Mudfish lived on the riverbanks, mediating between water and land, just as the *oba*, who was viewed as sacred, mediated between the human world and the supernatural world of Olokun.

Ife and Benin were but two of the many cities that arose in ancient Africa. At a site near Djenné known as Old Djenné, excavations (by both archaeologists and looters) have uncovered hundreds of terra-cotta figures dating from the thirteenth to the sixteenth centuries. The figures were polished, covered with a red clay slip, and fired at a low temperature. A horseman, armed with quiver and arrows and a dagger, is an impressive example (fig. **16–6**). Man and horse are formed of rolls of clay on which details of faces, clothing, and harness are carved, engraved, and painted. The rider has a long oval head and jutting chin, pointed oval eyes set in multiple framing lids, and a long straight nose. He wears short pants and a helmet with a chin strap, and his horse has an ornate bridle. Such elaborate military equipment suggests that the horseman could be a guardian figure, hero, or even a deified ancestor. Similar figures have been found in sanctuaries. Over time, urban life declined, and so did the arts. In the fifteenth and sixteenth centuries, when rivals began to raid these African cities, the long tradition of ceramic sculpture came to an end.

In southeastern Africa, another important African city flourished: Great Zimbabwe. Zimbabwe was part of an extensive trade network along the Zambezi, Limpopo, and Sabi Rivers. It funneled gold, ivory, and exotic skins to coastal trading towns of the Swahili peoples between 1000 and 1500 CE. It is estimated that at the height of its power in the fourteenth century, Great Zimbabwe and its surrounding environs housed a population of more than 10,000 people. A large cache of goods found there containing items such as Portuguese medallions, Persian pottery, and Chinese porcelain testifies to the extent of trade at Great Zimbabwe.

The word *Zimbabwe* derives from the Shona term for "venerated houses" or "houses of stone," and, indeed, much of Great Zimbabwe was built of stone. Scholars agree that the stone structures were constructed by the ancestors of the present-day Shona people, who still live in the region. Construction at the site took advantage of the enormous boulders abundant in the vicinity. Masons used the uniform granite blocks that split naturally from the boulders to build a series of tall enclosing walls. As the artisans

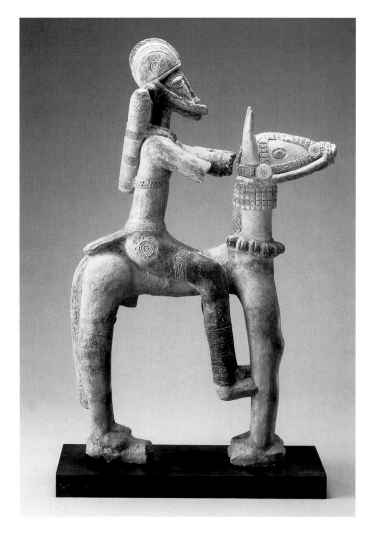

16–6 *Horseman,* from Old Djenné, Mali. 13–15th century. Terra cotta, height 27 3/4″ (70.5 cm). The National Museum of African Art, Smithsonian Institution, Washington, D.C.
MUSEUM PURCHASE, (86–12–2)

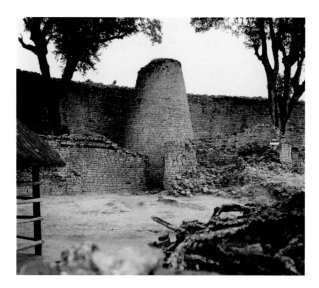

16–7 Conical Tower, Great Zimbabwe. Before 1450 CE

capped with three courses of ornamental stonework. Resembling a large version of a present-day Shona granary, it may have represented the good harvest and prosperity for which the ruler of Great Zimbabwe was held responsible.

Archaeologists have determined that the city was established by the third century CE and that by the middle of the ninth century it had become a major urban center. Also by the ninth century, Islam was becoming an economic and religious force in West Africa, North Africa, and the northern terminals of the trans-Saharan trade routes.

When Koi Konboro, the twenty-sixth king of Djenné, converted to Islam in the thirteenth century, he transformed his palace into the first of three successive mosques in the city. Like the two that followed, the first mosque was built of adobe brick. With its great surrounding wall and tall towers, it was said to have been more beautiful and more lavishly decorated than the Kaaba, the central shrine of Islam, at Mecca. In the early nineteenth century, the mosque was razed and a far more humble structure erected on a new site. This second mosque was in turn replaced by the current grand mosque, constructed between 1906 and 1907 on the ancient site and in the style of the original.

The mosque's eastern, or "marketplace," façade boasts three tall towers; the center of the façade contains the mihrab (fig. 16–8). The finials, or crowning ornaments, at the top of each tower bear ostrich eggs, symbols of fertility and purity. The façade and sides of the mosque are distinguished by tall, narrow, engaged columns, which act as buttresses. These columns are characteristic of West African mosque architecture, and their cumulative rhythmic effect is one of great verticality and grandeur. The most unusual features of West African mosques are the torons, wooden beams projecting from the walls. Torons provide permanent supports for the scaffolding erected each year so that the exterior of the mosque can be replastered.

grew more skillful, they used dressed, or smoothly finished, stones and laid them in fine, level courses. Each enclosure defined a ritual space or surrounded dwellings made of adobe (a sun-dried mixture of clay and straw) with conical thatched roofs.

The largest building complex at Great Zimbabwe is located in a broad valley below the hilltop enclosures. Known today as Imba Huru, or the Big House, it was probably a royal residence as well as a religious center. It is ringed by a massive masonry wall constructed without mortar. This wall is more than 800 feet long, 32 feet high, and 17 feet thick at the base. Inside the outer wall are numerous smaller stone enclosures and adobe platforms. A fascinating structure known simply as the Conical Tower (fig. 16–7) is some 18 feet in diameter and 30 feet high, and the tower was originally

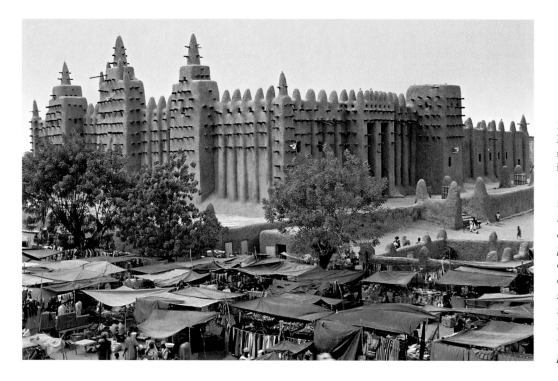

16–8 Great Friday Mosque, Djenné, Mali, showing the eastern and northern façades. Rebuilding of 1907 in the style of 13th-century original

The plan of the mosque is not quite rectangular. Inside, nine rows of heavy adobe columns, 33 feet tall and linked by pointed arches, support a flat ceiling of palm logs. An open courtyard on the west side is enclosed by a great double wall only slightly lower than the walls of the mosque itself. The main entrances to the prayer hall are in the north wall (to the right in the photograph).

During the twentieth century, African sculptures—wood carvings of astonishing formal inventiveness and power—have found admirers around the world. Wood decays rapidly, however, and little wood sculpture from lands south of the Sahara remains from before the nineteenth century. As a result, much of ancient Africa's artistic heritage has been irretrievably lost. Yet the beauty of ancient African creations in such durable materials as terra cotta, stone, and bronze bear eloquent witness to the skill of ancient African artists and the splendor of the civilizations in which they worked.

African Art in the Modern Era: Living Traditions and New Trends

European exploration and subsequent colonization of the African continent brought Africa's flourishing and diverse societies into sudden and traumatic contact with the "modern" world. European ships first visited sub-Saharan Africa in the fifteenth century, and for the next several hundred years, European contact with Africa was almost entirely limited to coastal areas,

AFRICAN FURNITURE AND THE ART DECO STYLE

In some African cultures, elaborate stools or chairs were created not only to indicate their owners' status but also to serve as altars for their souls after death. Thrones and other important seats in Africa are often carved from a single block of wood. This is the case with a chair taken from the Ngombe people, who live along the Congo River. The back is cantilevered out from the seat, which is in turn supported by four massive, braced legs. The rich surface decoration consists of European brass carpet tacks and darker iron tacks arranged in parallel lines and diamond patterns. The use of the imported tacks indicates that the owner had access to the

extensive trade routes linking people of the inland forest to people of the coast. Both copper and iron were precious materials in central Africa; they were used as currency long before contact with Europe, and they were associated with both high social status and spirituality. The chair was thus an object of both beauty and power.

France began to colonize Africa in the late nineteenth century, and African objects were brought to France by soldiers, administrators, and adventurers. Exhibitions held in France in 1919 and 1923 displayed trophies from the newly vanquished territories, including household objects and art works from African courts.

Just as painters and sculptors such as Picasso and Matisse were inspired by the formal power of African masks, the French designer Pierre Legrain (1889–1929) recognized the aesthetic excellence of African sculpture and furniture. Legrain's Africa-inspired pieces appeared in the 1925 design exhibition "International Exposition of Modern Decorative and Industrial Arts," where the term *style moderne* was given to describe the new geometric simplicity that characterized many of the objects displayed there. The Exhibition helped launch a popular commercial style called *Art Deco* (a label coined in the late 1960s).

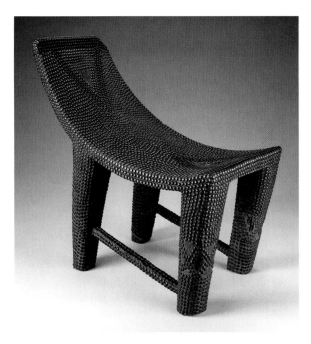

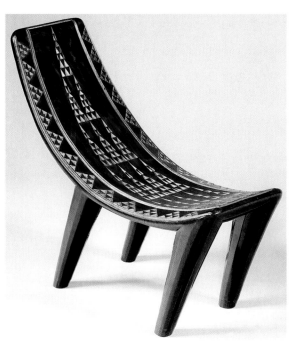

Chair, from Democratic Republic of Congo. Ngombe culture, 20th century. Wood, brass, and iron tacks, height at tallest point 25⅝″ (65.1 cm). National Museum of African Art, Washington, D.C.

Pierre Legrain. *Tabouret.* c. 1923. Lacquered wood, horn, gilding, length 20½″ × 10½″ × 25¼″ (52 × 26.6 × 64.1 cm). Virginia Museum of Fine Arts, Richmond

where trade, including the devastating slave trade, was carried out. During the nineteenth century, however, as the trade in slaves to the West was gradually eliminated, European explorers and Christian missionaries, such as Stanley Livingston, began to investigate the unmapped African interior. Drawn by the potential wealth of Africa's natural resources, European governments began to seek territorial concessions from African rulers. Diplomacy soon gave way to force, and, toward the end of the century, competition among rival European powers fueled the so-called scramble for Africa, when European leaders raced to lay claim to whatever portion of the continent they were powerful enough to seize. By 1914, virtually all of Africa was under colonial rule. In the years following World War I, nationalistic movements arose across the continent; from 1945 through the mid-1970s, one colony after another gained its independence.

The tower at Great Zimbabwe and the mosque of Djenné are monumental public architecture. Traditional West African houses—which resemble the mosque on a small scale—are also distinctive. Adobe walls, reinforced by buttresses, rise above the roofline in conical turrets, emphasizing the entrance. Rooms open inward onto a courtyard. Extended upper walls mask a flat roof terrace that gives more space for work and living.

The farming communities of the Nankani people in the border area between Burkina Faso and Ghana, in West Africa, have also developed a distinctive painted adobe architecture. The mud and adobe buildings of their walled compounds are low and single storied with either flat roofs that form terraces or conical roofs. Some buildings are used only by men, others by women. The Nankani men control an ancestral shrine by the entrance, a corral for cattle, a granary, and they have rectangular houses. The inner courtyards, outdoor kitchen, and round houses are the women's areas (fig. **16–9**). Men build the compound; women paint the buildings inside and out. The women decorate the walls with horizontal molded ridges called *yidoor*, meaning both "rows in a cultivated field" and "long eye" (long life) to express good wishes for the family. They paint the walls with rec-

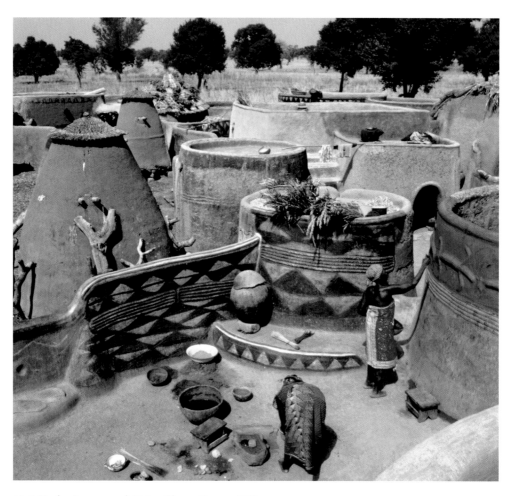

16–9 Nankani compound, Sirigu, Ghana. Houses. 1972

Among the Nankani people, creating living areas is a cooperative but gender-specific project. Men build the structures, women decorate the surfaces. The structures themselves are also gender-specific. The round dwellings shown here are women's houses located in an interior courtyard; men occupy rectangular flat-roofed houses. The bisected lozenge design on the dwelling to the left is called zalanga, *the name for the braided sling that holds a woman's gourds and most treasured possessions.*

tangles and squares cut diagonally to create triangular patterns, a rectilinear surface decoration that contrasts with the curving walls. The painted patterns are called "braided sling," "broken pottery," and "broken gourd," and since the triangular motifs can be seen as pointing up or down, they are sometimes called "filed teeth." The same geometric motifs are used on pottery and baskets, and for scarification of the skin. When people decorate themselves, their homes, and their possessions with the same patterns, art is serving to enhance a cultural identity.

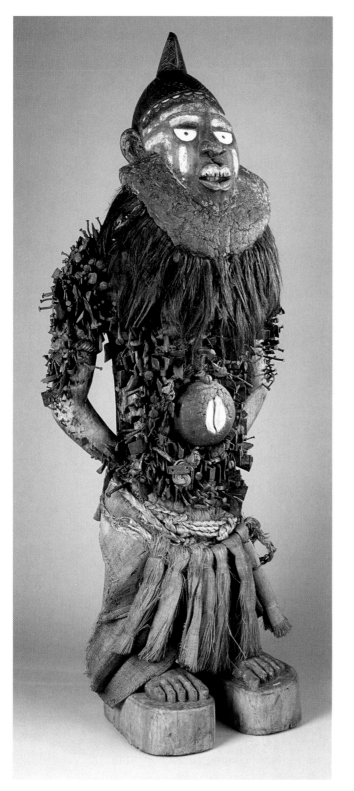

Art and the Spirit World

Much traditional African art is devoted to dealings with the spirit world. Spirits are believed to inhabit the fields that produce crops, the rivers that provide fish, the bush and forests that are home to game, and the land that must be cleared in order to build a new village. A family, too, includes spirits—those of its ancestors as well as those of children yet unborn. In the blessing or curse of these myriad spirits lies the difference between success and failure in life. To communicate with these all-important spirits, some African societies usually rely on a specialist in ritual—a person known as a diviner who opens the lines of communication between the supernatural and human worlds (see Introduction, page 8). Diviners use such techniques as prayer, sacrifice, offerings, magic, divination, and even the creation of images that give spirits a physical form.

Excellent examples of works made for centuries in central Africa are the *minkisi* (singular, *nkisis*) of the Kongo and Songye peoples of the Democratic Republic of the Congo (formerly Zaire). These pieces enforce ethical behavior and regulate power. The best-known of *minkisi* are the large wooden *minkonde* (singular, *nkonde*) figures, which bristle with nails, pins, blades, and other sharp objects (fig. **16–10**). A *nkisi nkonde* begins its life as a simple, unadorned wooden figure. It may be purchased from a carver at a market or commissioned by a diviner who is adept at diagnosing supernatural ills on behalf of a client or clients. Drawing on vast knowledge, the diviner prescribes certain magical/medicinal ingredients, called *bilongo*, that will help solve the client's problem. These *bilongo*, which may include human hair, nail clippings, and other animal, plant, or mineral ingredients, are added to the figure, either mixed with white clay and plastered directly onto the body or held in a packet suspended from the neck or waist.

16–10 Power figure *(nkisi nkonde),* from the Democratic Republic of the Congo (formerly Zaire). Kongo culture, 19th century. Wood, nails, pins, blades, and other materials, height 44″ (111.7 cm). The Field Museum, Chicago

(# A109979AC)

The sculpture provides a dramatic example of the ways in which works of African art are transformed by use. When first carved, the figure is "neutral," with no particular significance or use. Magical materials applied by a diviner transform the figure into a powerful being, at the same time modifying its form. While the object is empowered, nails may also be removed as part of a healing or oath-taking process. And when the figure's particular powers are no longer needed, then additions may all be stripped away to be replaced with different magical materials that give the same figure a new function. The result is that many hands play a role in creating the work of art we see in a museum. The person we are likely to label as the "artist" is only the initial creator. Many others modify the work, and in their hands the figure becomes a visual document of the history of the conflicts that have threatened the community.

In many West African cultures, fired ceramics are made exclusively by women. Among the Mande-speaking people of Mali, Burkina Faso, Guinea, and Ivory Coast, potters are *numumusow*, female members of *numu* lineages. Their husbands, fathers, and sons are the sculptors and blacksmiths of the Mande. Women from these families hold an important place in society. In addition to being potters, they may resolve disputes and initiate girls.

Numumusow make a wide selection of vessels, including huge storage jars (fig. **16–11**). The form of a pot reflects its intended use. Additional types include wide bowls and cooking pots, narrow-necked stoppered water bottles, and small eating dishes. The *numumusow* form the soft and sticky clay by coiling and modeling with their fingers. They decorate their vessels by burnishing (polishing), engraving, or adding pellets or coils of clay, or coloring with slip (a wash of colored clay). The vessels are fired at low temperatures in a shallow pit or in the open; this produces a ware that can be used to cook over an open fire without breaking.

Even though most urban Africans use metal and plastic dishes and cookware today, large earthenware jars still keep water cool and clean in areas where refrigeration is expensive. In the past, water-storage jars were public display pieces, standing near the entrance to the house, where a guest would be offered a drink of cool water as an essential part of hospitality. Mande vessels for drinking water are often decorated with incised lines and molded ridges. On older wares, such as this example, raised images of figures or lizards may refer to Mande myths or philosophical concepts.

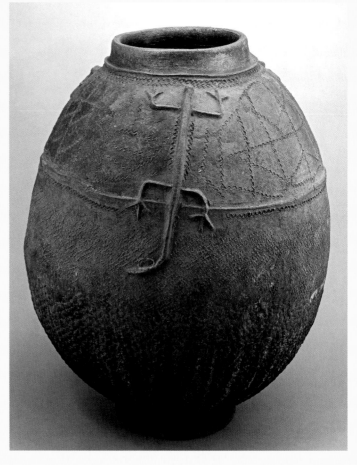

16–11 Jar, from Mali. Bamana culture, 20th century. Earthenware, 23 1/2″ × 18 3/4″ (59.7 × 47.6 cm). The Nelson-Atkins Museum of Art, Kansas City, Missouri
PURCHASE: THE GEORGE H. AND ELIZABETH O. DAVIS FUND

The *bilongo* transform the *nkonde* into a living being with frightful powers, ready to attack the forces of evil on behalf of a human client. Each *bilongo* ingredient has a specific role in activating the figure. For example, the Kongo people admire the quickness and agility of a particular species of mouse. Tufts of this mouse's hair included in the *bilongo* ensure that the *nkisi nkonde* will act rapidly when its powers are activated.

To mobilize the figure's powers, clients drive a nail or other pointed object into the *nkisi nkonde*, which may serve many private and public functions. Two warring villages might agree to end their conflict by swearing an oath of peace in the presence of the *nkonde* and then driving a nail into it to seal the agreement. A mother might invoke the power of the *nkonde* to heal her sick children. Two merchants might agree to a partnership by driving two small nails into the figure side by side and then make their pact binding by wrapping the nails together with a stout cord.

Another ongoing artistic tradition is found among the Baule people of the Ivory Coast. They believe that each of us lived in the spirit world, a parallel realm, before we were born. While there, we had a spirit spouse, whom we left behind when we entered this life. A person who has difficulty assuming his or her gender-specific role as an adult Baule—a man who has not married, for example, or a woman who has not borne children—may dream of his or her spirit spouse. For such a person, the diviner may prescribe the carving of an image of the spirit-spouse (fig. **16–12**)—either a female figure *(bloto bla)* for a man or a male figure *(bloto bian)* for a woman. The figures display the most admired and desirable marks of beauty so that the spirit spouses may be encouraged to enter and inhabit them. The owner keeps the figure in his or her room, dressing it in beautiful textiles and jewelry, washing it, anointing it with oil, feeding it, and caressing it. The Baule hope that pleasing their spirit spouse (by caring for the sculpture) will restore balance to their human life.

Art and Power

Works of art in Africa, as in other continents, can be used to signify power in this world as well as power in the spirit world. In an Akan kingdom of Ghana or the Ivory Coast, for example, the spokesperson's staff indicates the eminence of the ruler's special advisers. In the finial of the staff in fig. 16–1, an allegorical carving of a man holding an egg, was probably made in the 1960s or 1970s by Kojo Bonsu. The son of a famous carver, Osei Bonsu, Kojo Bonsu lives in the Asante city of Kumasi and continues to carve prolifically. He decorated the staff with **gold leaf**, a sign of the object's importance. Gold was a major source of power for the Asante, who traded it for centuries, first across the Sahara to the Mediterranean world, and then directly to Europeans on the West African coast.

Yoruba kings manifested their power through the large, complex palaces in which they lived. In the traditional palace plan, the principal rooms once opened onto a veranda, where elaborate figured posts supported the roof. Dense, highly descriptive figure carvings also covered the doors. Perhaps the finest architectural sculptor of modern times was Olówè of Isè, who carved doors and veranda posts for rulers of the Ekiti-Yoruba kingdoms in southwestern Nigeria.

The door of the royal palace in Ikéré illustrates Olówè's artistry (fig. **16–13**). Its asymmetrical composition combines narrative and symbolic scenes in horizontal, rectangular panels. Tall bodies carved in profile are topped with heads that face out to confront the viewer. Long necks and elaborate hairstyles make the figures appear even taller, unlike typical Yoruba sculpture, which uses shorter, more static figures. The figures—which move energetically against an underlying decorative pattern—are carved in such high relief that the upper portions are actually carved in the round. The entire surface of the door is also painted.

Olówè seems to have worked from the early 1900s until his death in 1938. He was famous throughout Yorubaland and called upon by patrons as distant as 60 miles from his home, though few written records of his activities remain. The art historian Philip Allison wrote of meeting Olówè and watching him work, and (echoing the praises of the Yoruba themselves) described Olówè carving the iron-hard African oak "as easily as [he would] a calabash [gourd]." Olówè also carved the divination bowl illustrated in the Introduction (see page 8).

Woven textiles, called **kente**, still signal status in the Akan kingdoms of Ghana (fig. **16–14**). The pattern of the Asante kente cloth here, known as *oyokoman ogya da mu*—meaning "there is a fire between two factions of the Oyoko clan"—refers to the civil war that followed the death of the Asante king Osei Tutu in about 1730. Traditionally, only the king of the Asante was allowed to wear this pattern. Other patterns were reserved for members of the royal family or the court. Commoners who dared to wear a restricted pattern were severely punished.

Kente cloth is made on small, light looms that produce long, narrow strips of fabric. Asante weavers begin by laying out the long **warp** (vertical) threads in a brightly colored pattern. Today the threads are likely to be rayon. Formerly, however, they were silk, which the Asante produced by unraveling Chinese cloth obtained through European trade. **Weft** threads woven through the warp produce complex patterns, including double weaves in which the front and back of the cloth display different patterns. The long strips produced on the loom are then cut to size and sewn together to form large rectangles of finished *kente* cloth. In present-day Ghana, the wearing of *kente* and other traditional

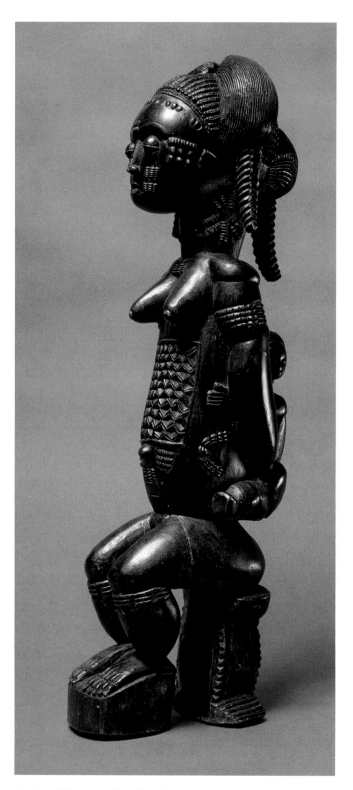

16–12 Spirit-spouse (bloto bla), from Ivory Coast. Baule culture, early 20th century. Wood, height 17⅛″ (43.5 cm)

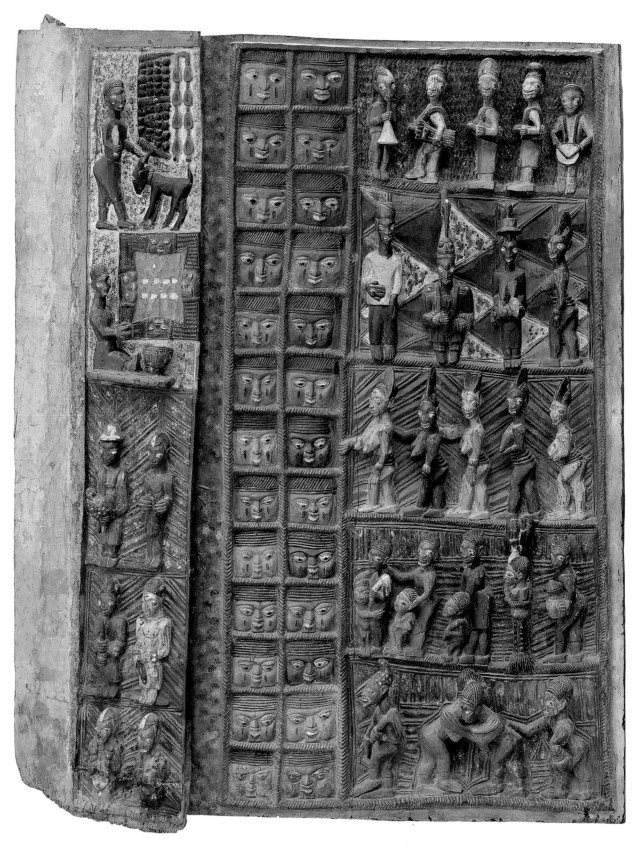

16–13 Olówè of Isè. Door from Yoruba royal palace in Ikéré, Nigeria. c. 1925. Wood, pigment, height 6′2⁷⁄₈″ (1.9 m). The Detroit Institute of the Arts

Carvings illustrate scenes from palace life. At the left are scenes of divination and the use of a divination bowl. On the right side, the second register depicts the principal figures: a guard, the Ogoga (king) wearing his crown, and his principal wife wearing a European top hat and nursing a child.

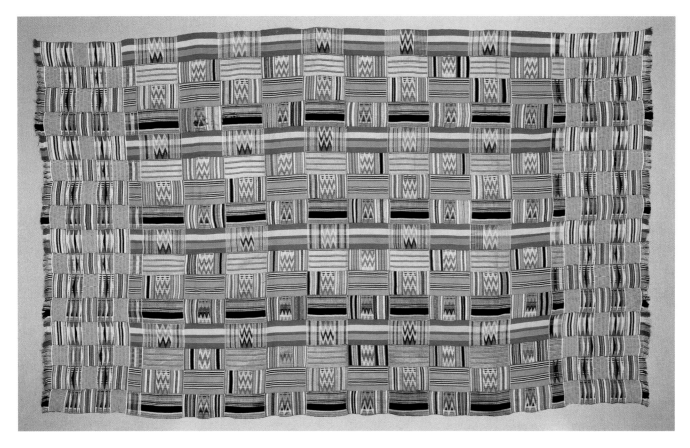

16–14 *Kente* **cloth, from Ghana.** Asante culture, 20th century. Silk, $6'10\frac{9}{16}'' \times 4'3\frac{9}{16}''$ (2.10 × 1.31 m). National Museum of African Art and National Museum of Natural History, Washington, D.C.

PURCHASED WITH FUNDS PROVIDED BY THE SMITHSONIAN COLLECTIONS ACQUISITION PROGRAM, 1983–85, EJ 10583

textiles is encouraged, and patterns are no longer restricted to a particular person or group.

The Masquerade

Perhaps the best-known works of African art are masks. In many communities, masquerades no longer occur, and Kongo peoples rarely dance with masks today. However, the Bwa people of central Burkina Faso still use masks to depict spirits in seasonal ceremonies. When young Bwa men and women are initiated into adulthood following the onset of puberty, they are taught about the world of nature spirits and about the wooden masks that represent them.

The initiates are first separated from younger playmates by older relatives who "kidnap" them and explain their disappearance in the community by saying that they have been devoured by wild beasts. The initiates are stripped of their clothing and made to sleep on the ground without blankets. Isolated from the community, they are taught about the spirit world invoked by the masks. Although they have seen these masks all their lives, they learn for the first time that they are made of wood and have been worn by their older brothers and cousins. They learn of the spirit each mask represents, and they memorize the story of each spirit's encounter with the founding ancestors of the clan. Returning to the community, the initiates display their new knowledge in a public ceremony. Each boy performs with one of the masks, in a dance that expresses the character and personality that the mask represents. The girls, who are not allowed to wear the masks, sing the songs that accompany each one. At the end of the ceremony, the young men and women rejoin their families as adults, ready to marry, start farms, and begin families of their own.

Most Bwa masks depict spirits in human or animal shapes. Among the most spectacular masks, however, are abstract examples crowned with a tall, narrow plank, which represent spirits that have taken neither animal nor human form (fig. **16–15**). The patterns of these abstract masks convey a message about the proper moral conduct of life. The white crescent at the top represents the quarter moon, under which initiations are held. The large central X represents the scar that every initiated Bwa wears. The horizontal zigzags represent the path of ancestors and symbolize adherence to traditional ways. The hooked shape that projects above the face is said to represent the beak of the hornbill, a bird associated with the supernatural world and believed to be an intermediary between the living and the dead.

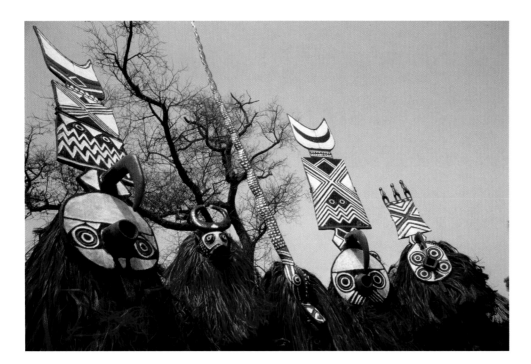

16–15 Two masks in performance, from Dossi, Burkina Faso. Bwa culture, 1984. Wood, mineral pigments, and fiber, height approx. 7′ (2.13 m)

When the Bwa became targets of slave raiders, they developed a new art form in response to the threat; they created imposing wooden masks like these as a more powerful means of communicating with protective spirits. (The new masks replaced earlier ones made of leaves.)

Africa also has a rich tradition of funerary art—that of Egypt is probably the best known in the West (see Chapter 2). All over Africa, when death comes, special ceremonies and rituals help the community mourn. The death of a child is a particularly traumatic event. The Yoruba people of Nigeria have one of the highest rates of twin births in the world. The birth of twins is a joyful occasion, yet it is troubling as well, for twins are more delicate than single babies, and one or both may die. When a Yoruba twin dies, the parents consult a diviner, who may tell them that an image of a twin, or *ere ibeji*, must be carved.

The mother cares for the "birth" of this image by sending the artist food while the image is being carved and gifts when it is finished. Then she dances home, carrying the figure as she would a living child, accompanied by the singing of neighborhood women. She places the figure in a shrine in her bedroom and lavishes care upon it, feeding it, dressing it richly, and anointing it with cosmetic oils. The Yoruba believe that the spirit of a dead twin thus honored may bring its parents wealth and good luck.

The female *ibeji* figures, which may be the work of the Yoruba artist Akiode (d. 1936), radiate health and well-being (fig. **16–16**). Their beautiful, glossy surfaces and rings of fat indicate that they are well fed; breasts and other attributes signal the mature adulthood that they might one day have achieved. They represent hope for survival, for the future, and for prosperity. Figures such as these reflect the enduring cycle of life that is such a vital part of African art.

Many African artists today have come of age in a postcolonial culture that mingles American, European, and African elements. Drawing on these diverse influences, they have established a place in the lively international art scene along with their European, American, and Asian counterparts, and their work is shown as readily in Paris, Tokyo, and Los Angeles as it is in the African cities of Abidjan, Kinshasa, and Dakar.

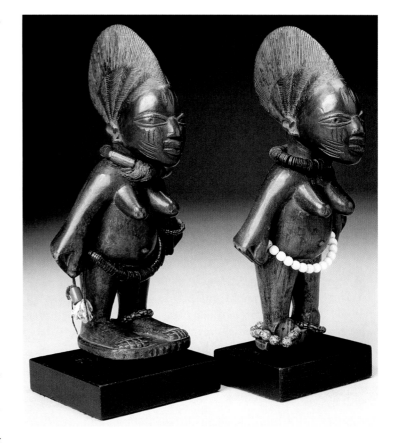

16–16 Twin figures *(ere ibeji),* from Nigeria. Yoruba culture, 20th century. Wood, height 7⅞″ (20 cm). The University of Iowa Museum of Art, Iowa City

As with other African sculpture, patterns of use result in particular signs of wear. The facial features of ere ibeji *are often worn down or even obliterated by repeated feedings and washings. Camwood powder applied as a cosmetic builds to a thick crust in areas that are rarely handled, and the blue indigo dye regularly applied to the hair eventually builds to a thin layer.*

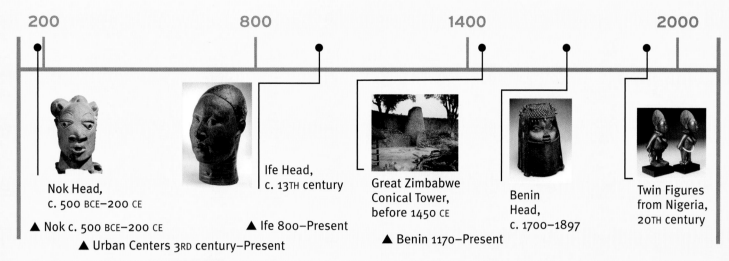

200	800	1400	2000

Nok Head,
c. 500 BCE–200 CE

Ife Head,
c. 13TH century

Great Zimbabwe
Conical Tower,
before 1450 CE

Benin
Head,
c. 1700–1897

Twin Figures
from Nigeria,
20TH century

▲ Nok c. 500 BCE–200 CE   ▲ Ife 800–Present

▲ Urban Centers 3RD century–Present   ▲ Benin 1170–Present

L O O K I N G   B A C K

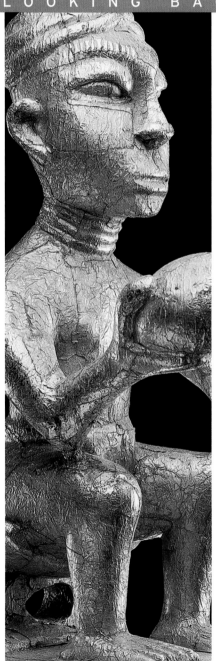

In many world cultures, the distinction between "fine art" and "craft" does not exist. The traditional Western academic hierarchy of materials—in which marble, bronze, oil, and fresco are valued more than terra cotta and watercolor—and the equally artificial hierarchy of subjects in which history painting, including religious history, stands supreme are irrelevant to non-Western art.

The indigenous peoples of Africa, the Americas, and the Pacific did not produce objects as works of art. In their eyes, all pieces were utilitarian objects, adorned in ways necessary for their intended purposes. A work was valued for its effectiveness and for the role it played in society. Some, like a West African water jar, ease the burden of daily life. And like art in all cultures, many pieces have had great spiritual or magical power. Such works of art cannot be fully comprehended or appreciated when they are seen only on pedestals or encased in glass boxes in museums or galleries. They must be imagined, or better yet seen, as acting in their societies. How powerfully might our minds and emotions be engaged if we saw Kwakwaka'wakw or Bwa masks functioning in religious drama, changing not only the outward appearance, but also the very essence of the individual.

At the beginning of the twentieth century, European and American artists broke away from the academic bias that extolled the classical heritage of Greece and Rome. They found new inspiration in the art—or craft, if you will—of many different non-European cultures. Artists explored a new freedom to use absolutely any material or technique that effectively challenged outmoded assumptions and opened the way for a free and unfettered delight in, and understanding of, Native American, African, and Pacific Island art. The intellectual community as well as collectors, dealers, and critics have come to appreciate the non-Western aesthetics and to treasure forgotten and ignored arts on their own terms. And the later twentieth- and twenty-first centuries' conception of art as a multimedia adventure has helped validate works of art once seen only in ethnographic collections and in the homes of private collectors. Today objects once called "primitive" are recognized as great works of art and acknowledged to be an essential dimension of a twenty-first-century worldview. The line between "art" and "craft" seems more artificial and less relevant than ever before.

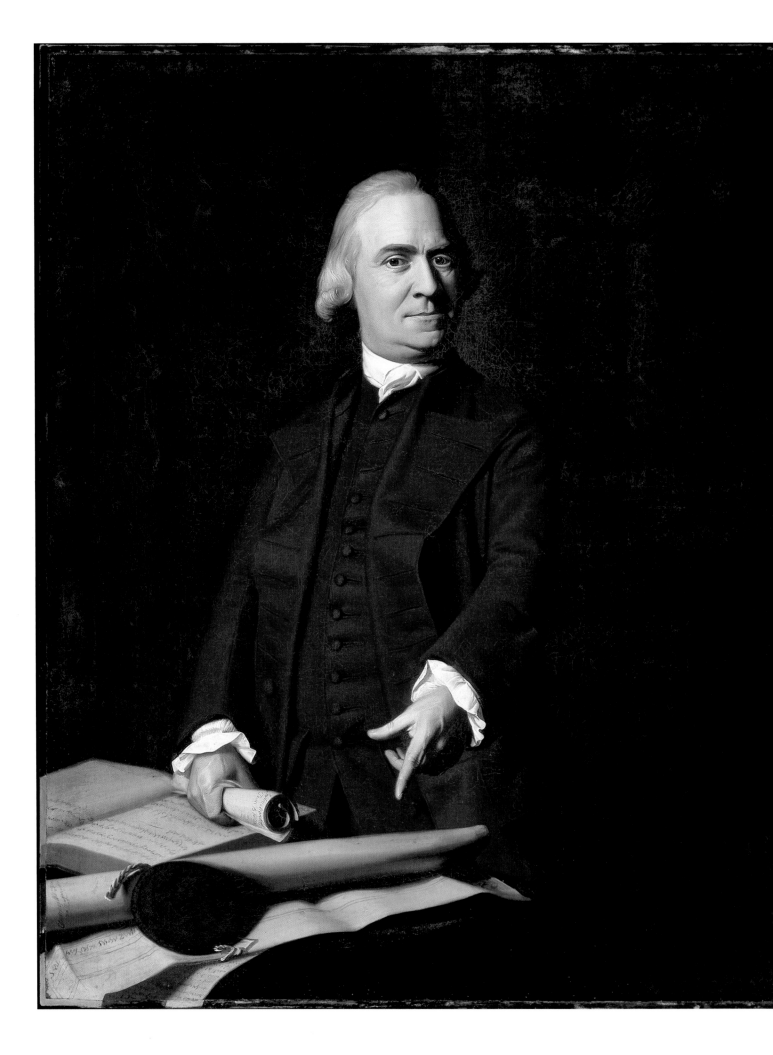

Neoclassicism, Romanticism, and Realism

LOOKING FORWARD

On March 5, 1770, a street fight broke out between several dozen residents of Boston and a squad of British soldiers. The British fired into the crowd, killing three men and wounding eight others, two of whom later died. Dubbed the Boston Massacre by anti-British patriots, the event was one of many that led to the Revolutionary War of 1775–1783, which won independence from Britain for the 13 American colonies.

The day after the Boston Massacre, Samuel Adams, a member of the Massachusetts legislature, demanded that the royal governor, Thomas Hutchinson, expel British troops from the city—a confrontation that Boston painter John Singleton Copley immortalized in oil paint (fig. **17–1**). Adams, conservatively dressed in a brown suit and waistcoat, stands before a table and looks sternly out at the viewer, who occupies the place of Governor Hutchinson. With his left hand, Adams points to the charter and seal granted to Massachusetts by King William and Queen Mary; in his right, he grasps a petition prepared by the aggrieved citizens of Boston.

The vivid realism of Copley's style makes the life-size figure of Adams seem almost to be standing before us. Adams's head and hands, dramatically lit, surge out of the darkness with a sense of immediacy appropriate to the urgency of his errand. The legislator's defiant stance and emphatic gesture convey the moral force of his demands, which are impelled not by emotion but by reason. The charter to which he points insists on the rule of law, and the faintly visible classical columns behind him connote ancient Roman virtue and rationality—important values of the Enlightenment, the major philosophical movement of eighteenth-century Europe as well as of Colonial America. Enlightenment political philosophy—ideas that Adams ardently supported—provided the ideological basis for both the American and the French Revolutions. Enlightenment thinkers were generally optimistic that men and women, when set free from their political and religious shackles, could be expected to act both rationally and morally. Thus, in pursuing their own happiness, they would promote the happiness of others.

17–1 John Singleton Copley. *Samuel Adams.*
c. 1770–1772. Oil on canvas, 50″ × 40″ (127 × 102.2 cm).
Museum of Fine Arts, Boston

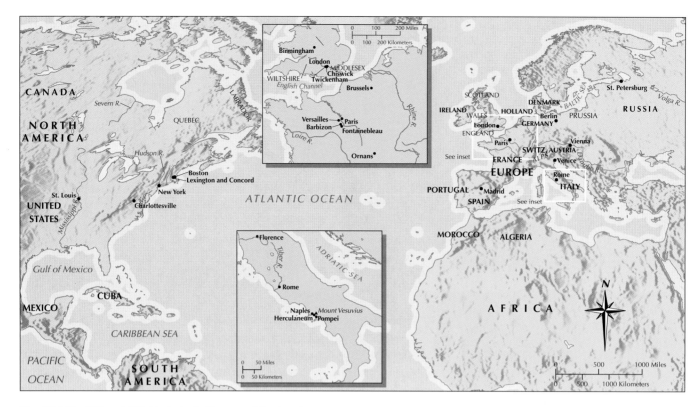

Map 17–1 The 18th and 19th Centuries in Europe and the Americas

Cultural historians call the eighteenth century the Age of Enlightenment or the Age of Reason. Reason became the touchstone for evaluating nearly every civilized endeavor, including philosophy, art, and politics. By extension, nature, which was thought to embody reason, was invoked to corroborate the correctness—and goodness—of everything from political systems to architectural designs (see Map 17–1, above).

An optimistic and even reverential attitude toward scientific inquiry developed in the West during the eighteenth century, and this enthusiasm for scientific inquiry (the epitome of reason) extended to historical and archaeological studies. Partly as a result of this new awareness of their history and partly stimulated by new discoveries in the excavations of Pompeii (see Chapter 6) and Herculaneum—two Roman cities buried by the first-century eruption of Mount Vesuvius—Neoclassicism emerged as the dominant style in art in the later years of the eighteenth century. Neoclassicism in art is characterized by subject matter borrowed from ancient Greece and Rome, stylistic dependence on antique sources, heroic nudity in sculpture and sometimes painting, classical orders in architecture, and the dominance of drawing over painterly effects in the visual arts. Also, a persuasive moralism exalted virtues popularly attributed to Republican Rome: moral incorruptibility, patriotism, and courage. Playful Rococo tendencies gave way to a general longing for noble and serious modes of expression.

Concurrent with Neoclassicism was a mode of expression called Romanticism. Romantic painting and sculpture often feature fantastic or literary themes, perhaps set in a remote time or place and infused with a spirit of poetic fancy or melancholy. But Romanticism was less a specific style than an imaginative approach to art, centered in the strong subjective feelings of the artist. Many artworks at the end of the eighteenth century combine elements of Neoclassicism and Romanticism.

The nineteenth century, in turn, has been called the Positivist Age. In the visual arts, the positivist spirit appears in the widespread rejection of Romantic subjectivism and imagination in favor of the accurate and apparently objective description of the ordinary, observable world. A new emphasis on descriptive accuracy, or **realism**, had its roots in naturalism, an approach to art in use since ancient times. At first, naturalist art that carried a socialist political message was described as realism. But by 1860, the term *realism* lost its political meaning and had become for most artists and critics simply a synonym for naturalism. In fact, the terms *realism* and *naturalism* are often used interchangeably.

Neoclassicism and Its Heritage

Eighteenth-century Italy, with its wealth of antique ruins, was the birthplace of the Neoclassic movement, led by Antonio Canova (1757–1822), the foremost Neoclassic sculptor in Europe. Born into a family of stonemasons near Venice, Canova

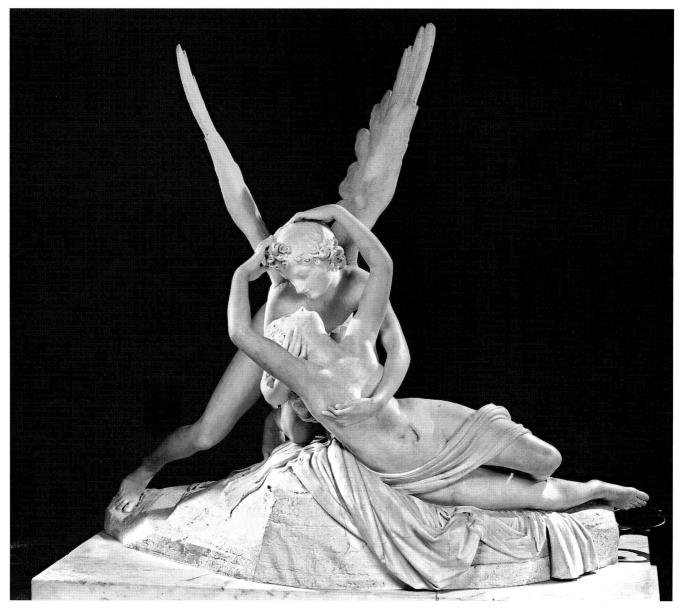

17–2 Antonio Canova. *Cupid and Psyche.* 1787–1793. Marble, 5′1″ × 5′8⅛″ (1.55 × 1.73 m). Musée du Louvre, Paris

settled in Rome in 1781, rapidly achieving such renown that critics compared him with Michelangelo. One of Canova's most admired works is the erotic mythological subject *Cupid and Psyche* (fig. **17–2**). Condemned to a deathlike sleep by a jealous Venus, Psyche revives at Cupid's kiss. Here Canova combined a Romantic interest in emotion with a more typically Neoclassical appeal to the senses of sight and touch. Cupid's wings offset the rounded forms of the two linked bodies, and the lustrous finish of the off-white marble skin is played against the textures of drapery and rocks. Although carved fully in the round, the figures are meant to be seen in an almost two-dimensional way, as a symmetrical series of interlocking triangles and ovals. The piece also recalls the ancient classical sculpture that attracted so many artists and scholars to Rome.

A trip through Europe—known as the "Grand Tour"—and a prolonged stay in Rome became an important part of the education of many well-to-do Westerners. In fact, many countries established academies in Rome, most of which still flourish today as centers of study and research. The academies promoted classical principles in the arts, and artists and architects of the time readily adopted this new classicism.

Portrait Painting

In France a strong reaction against the Rococo had solidified during the 1760s, and many French artists began to work in a classicizing mode. For some years they expressed their new sobriety through their choice of subject matter, while still retaining

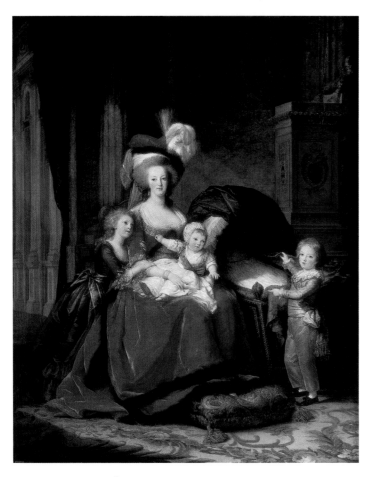

who concluded that men and women should conform to the roles assigned to them by nature (i.e., biology), with women tending to the home and raising children, and men practicing learned professions, governing the state, and taking other active roles in public life.

Vigée-Lebrun (1755–1842) was one of the most famous portraitists in France in the last quarter of the eighteenth century. In 1783 she was elected to one of the four places in the French Academy available to women (see "Art Academies in the Eighteenth Century," page 462). Elected at the same time was Adélaïde Labille-Guiard (1749–1803), who in 1790 successfully petitioned to end the restriction on entry for women. Labille-Guiard's commitment to education and promoting the interests of women painters is reflected in her *Self-Portrait with Two Pupils* (fig. 17–4). Exhibited in 1785 at the **Paris Salon**, the biennial exhibition open to members of the French Academy, this monumental image of the artist at her easel was also meant to answer sexist rumors that her paintings had been painted by men. In a witty role reversal, the only male to be seen is her father, whose portrait bust is at her side. Labille-Guiard's self-portrait, like many other paintings produced in France just before the Revolution, is relaxed, elegant, and urbane.

17–3 Marie-Louise-Élisabeth Vigée-Lebrun. *Portrait of Marie Antoinette with Her Children.* 1787. Oil on canvas, 9′ ¹⁄₄″ × 7′ ⁵⁄₈″ (2.75 × 2.15 m). Château, de Versailles et de Trianon

As the favorite painter to the queen, Vigée-Lebrun escaped from Paris with her daughter on the eve of the Revolution in 1789 and fled to Rome. After a very successful self-exile working in Italy, Austria, Russia, and England, the artist finally resettled in Paris in 1805 and again became popular with Parisian art patrons. Over her long career, she painted about 800 portraits in a vibrant style that changed very little over the decades.

Rococo forms and coloring. Marie-Louise-Élisabeth Vigée-Lebrun's portrait of the French queen, Marie Antoinette, and her children falls into this mode (fig. 17–3). Painted two years before the outbreak of the French Revolution, which spelled the end of the Bourbon monarchy, the painting is a flagrant piece of propaganda. The court had hoped that the queen's depiction as a devoted mother would counter her public image as immoral, extravagant, and conniving. Marie Antoinette's youngest son squirms on her lap, and her daughter leans affectionately against her. In a poignant touch, the older son points to the empty cradle of a recently deceased sibling. The image of Marie Antoinette as a loving mother surrounded by her children represented the ideal expounded by Enlightenment philosophers, especially the influential French-Swiss theorist Jean-Jacques Rousseau (1712–1778),

Forty Years of Revolution: 1775–1815	
1775	First skirmishes of the American Revolution, Lexington and Concord, Massachusetts
1776	American Declaration of Independence
1781	Victory of the Americans over the British at Yorktown, New York
1787	Constitution of the United States signed
1789	Storming of the Bastille in Paris and beginning of the French Revolution; George Washington, first president of the United States, 1789–1797
1793	Execution of Louis XVI and Marie Antoinette in Paris
1799	Napoleon takes over French government
1801	Thomas Jefferson, third president of the United States (1801–1809)
1802	Napoleon becomes life consul; emperor, 1804
1808	Spanish War of Independence (1808–1814)
1812	Napoleon defeated in Russia; British-American War of 1812
1814	Napoleon abdicates and is exiled
1815	Return of Napoleon; defeat at Waterloo, second exile; Congress of Vienna divides up Europe

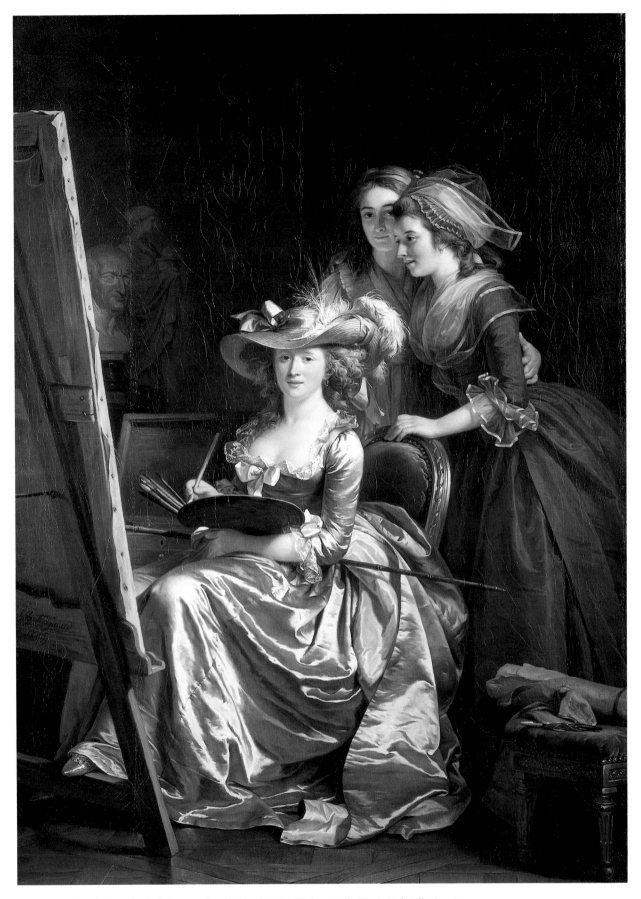

17–4 Adélaïde Labille-Guiard. *Self-Portrait with Two Pupils, Mademoiselle Marie Gabrielle Capet (1761–1818) and Mademoiselle Carreaux de Rosemond (d. 1788).* 1785. Oil on canvas, 6′11″ × 4′11 ½″ (2.11 × 1.51 m). The Metropolitan Museum of Art, New York

ART ACADEMIES IN THE EIGHTEENTH CENTURY

During the seventeenth century, the French government founded royal academies for the instruction and encouragement of artists and architects, writers, scientists, musicians, and dancers. In 1667 the Royal Academy of Painting and Sculpture began to mount occasional exhibitions of members' recent work. These exhibitions came to be known as the Salons because they were held in the Salon d'Apollon (Hall of Apollo) in the Palais du Louvre. From 1737, the Salons were mounted every other year, with a jury of members selecting the works that would be shown. As the only public art exhibitions of any importance in Paris, the Salons were enormously influential in establishing officially approved styles and in molding public taste.

In England, the Royal Academy of Arts was different in that it was a private institution independent of any interference from the Crown. Founded in 1768, it had only two functions: to operate an art school and to hold two annual exhibitions, one of art of the past and the other of contemporary art, which was open to any exhibitor on the basis of merit alone. The Royal Academy continues to function in this way today.

Besides the influential French and British academies, other art academies, public and private, sprang up throughout Europe in the eighteenth century. They primarily welcomed male artists; the number of women members was often restricted or women were welcomed only as honorary members. In France only seven women were awarded the title of academician (full member) between 1648 and 1706. By 1770, four women had been admitted to the French Royal Academy but when the men again became worried that women members would become "too numerous"—the academy declared that four women would be the limit at any one time. Women were not admitted to the academy's school or allowed to compete for academy prizes, both of which were nearly indispensable for professional success.

Women fared even worse at the British Royal Academy in London. After the Swiss painters Angelica Kauffmann and Mary Moser were named founding members in 1768, no other women were elected until 1922, and then only as associates. In a 1771–1772 portrait of the London Academicians, Johann Zoffany showed the men grouped around two nude male models. Propriety prohibited the presence of women in this setting, so Zoffany painted the portraits of the female members hanging on the wall.

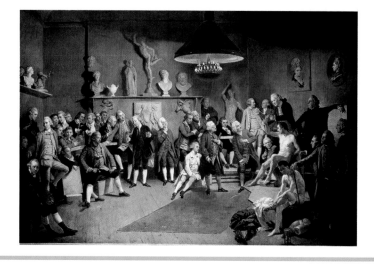

Johann Zoffany. *Academicians of the Royal Academy.*
1771–1772. Oil on canvas, 47 $\frac{1}{2}$" × 59 $\frac{1}{2}$" (120.6 × 151.2 cm).
The Royal Collection, Windsor Castle, New Windsor, England

In England at this time Thomas Gainsborough (1727–1788) achieved great success with paintings such as his *Portrait of Mrs. Richard Brinsley Sheridan* (fig. **17–5**), which shows the professional singer and wife of the celebrated playwright seated informally outdoors. The distant landscape view and the use of a tree to frame the sitter's head recall Van Dyck (see fig. 14–18) but the formula is updated with feathery brushwork and a lighter palette. Gainsborough seems to identify the woman with the landscape, matching her windblown hair to the foliage of the tree overhead. The work illustrates one of the new values of the Enlightenment: the emphasis on nature and the natural as the sources of goodness and beauty.

In Colonial America, the taste of the settlers was generally conservative, and styles often lagged behind the European mainstream. John Singleton Copley (1738–1815), the stepson of an English immigrant painter-engraver, grew up to be North America's first painter of genius. Copley's sources of inspiration were meager, but his work was already drawing attention by the time he was 15. Copley's clients valued not only his excellent technique, but also his ability to dignify them while recording their features with unflinching realism. In his portrait of *Sam Adams* (see fig. 17–1), Copley seems to be personifying the spirit of Puritan New England.

Copley's talents so outdistanced those of his colonial contemporaries that he decided to travel abroad to enhance his career. In June 1774, he sailed for Europe, where he visited London, Paris, and Italy. The next year he settled in London where he spent the rest of his life. For more than a century, many of the most talented artists of the young United States followed in Copley's footsteps, going to Europe to obtain the best training and to forward their careers.

Moralized Genre Painting

Members of the growing middle class, made up of newly prosperous merchants and professionals who had money to commission portraits, helped fuel the market for a type of painting known as

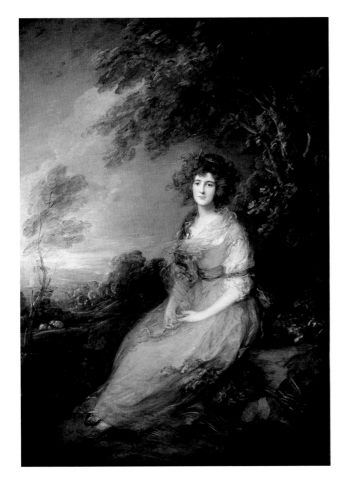

17–5 Thomas Gainsborough. *Portrait of Mrs. Richard Brinsley Sheridan.* 1785–1787. Oil on canvas, $86\frac{5}{8}''$ × $60\frac{5}{8}''$ (220 × 154 cm). National Gallery of Art, Washington, D.C.

moralized genre painting. In fact, reformers argued that art should promote and support public virtue and integrity.

British patrons tended to favor amusing and easily understandable satirical and moralizing scenes over high-minded history paintings with subjects drawn from mythology, the Bible, or classical literature. By doing so, they contradicted art theorists of their time and earlier, who had long considered **history painting** the highest form of artistic endeavor. Following the discontinuation of government censorship in 1695, there emerged in Britain a flourishing culture of literary satire, directed at a variety of political and social targets. The first artist inspired by the work of these novelists and essayists was William Hogarth (1697–1764). Hogarth believed art should contribute to the improvement of society, so about 1730, he began illustrating moralizing tales of his own invention in sequences of four to six paintings. He then reproduced the canvases as sets of prints for sale to the public, both to maximize his profits and to influence as many people as possible.

Hogarth's *Marriage à la Mode* series (1743–1745) was inspired by an essay written by the English essayist and poet Joseph Addison promoting the concept of marriage based on love. The opening scene, *The Marriage Contract* (fig. **17–6**), shows the gout-ridden Lord Squanderfield pointing proudly to his family tree as he arranges for his son to marry the daughter of a wealthy merchant. The merchant gains entry for his family into the aristocracy, while the lord gets the money he needs to complete his Palladian house, which is visible through the window. Sitting back to back are the loveless couple, who will be sacrificed

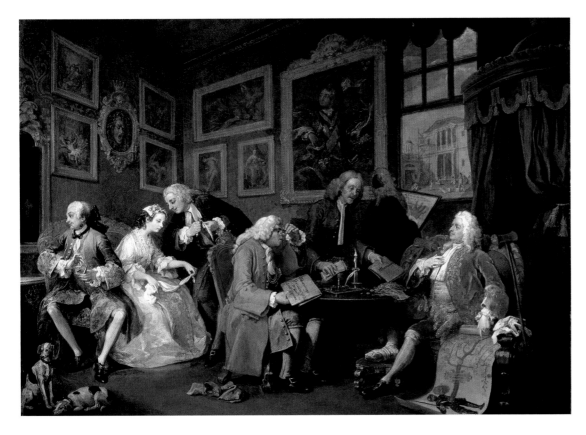

17–6 William Hogarth. *The Marriage Contract,* from *Marriage à la Mode.* 1743–1745. Oil on canvas, 28″ × 36″ (71.7 × 92.3 cm). The National Gallery, London

for their fathers' pride and greed. The young Squanderfield admires himself in the mirror, while the lawyer Silvertongue whispers to the unhappy fiancée. The five additional scenes show the progressively disastrous results of such a union, culminating in murder and suicide. Stylistically, Hogarth's paintings combine the anecdotal realism of seventeenth-century Dutch genre painters (see Introduction, fig. 20) with the nervous elegance of the Rococo style. His work became so popular that in 1745 he was able to give up portrait painting altogether, an art that he considered a deplorable form of vanity, and he devoted his time to moralizing satires.

The Italian-trained Swiss artist Angelica Kauffmann (1741–1807), a leading Neoclassical history painter, had been invited to Britain in 1766 by a wealthy client, and by 1768 she was one of only two women artists named among the founding members of the Royal Academy in London (see "Art Academies in the Eighteenth Century," page 462). In her painting *Cornelia Pointing to Her Children as Her Treasures* (fig. **17–7**), Kauffmann illustrated both an incident from ancient Republican Rome and a moral lesson. A woman visitor had been showing Cornelia her jewels and then requested to see those of her hostess. In response, Cornelia gestured to her children and stated, "These are my jewels." The setting is classically simple, and the figures are based loosely on those found in Roman wall paintings. The sentiment, however—the glorification and idealization of the good mother—belongs unmistakably to the eighteenth century.

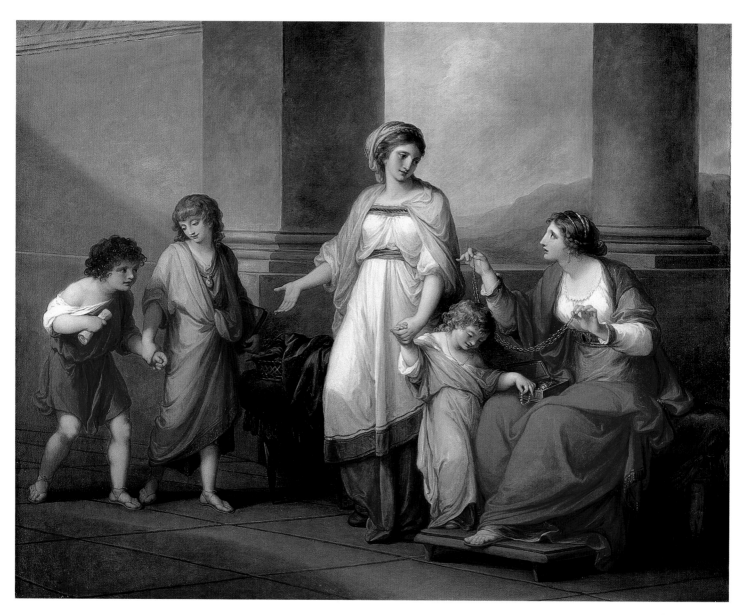

17–7 Angelica Kauffmann. *Cornelia Pointing to Her Children as Her Treasures.* 1785. Oil on canvas, 40″ × 50″ (101.6 × 127 cm). Virginia Museum of Fine Arts, Richmond, Virginia
THE ADOLPH D. AND WILKINS C. WILLIAMS FUND

An Enlightenment concern with developments in the natural sciences is seen in the dramatic depiction of *An Experiment on a Bird in the Air-Pump* (fig. **17–8**) by Joseph Wright of Derby (1734–1797). Trained as a portrait painter, Wright made the Grand Tour in 1773–1775 and then returned to the English Midlands to paint local society. Many of those he painted were the self-made entrepreneurs of the first wave of the Industrial Revolution, which was centered there in towns such as Birmingham. Wright belonged to the Lunar Society, a group of industrialists (including Josiah Wedgwood), mercantilists, and progressive nobles who met in Derby. As part of the society's attempts to popularize science, Wright painted a series of "entertaining" scenes of scientific experiments, including this work.

The eighteenth century was an age of rapid technological advances and the development of the air pump was among the most innovative scientific developments of the time. Although it was employed primarily to study the property of gases, it was also widely used to promote the public's interest in science because of its dramatic possibilities. In the experiment shown here, air was pumped out of the large glass bowl until the small creature inside, a bird, collapsed from lack of oxygen; before the animal died, air was reintroduced by a simple mechanism at the top of the bowl. In front of an audience of adults and children, a lecturer is shown on the verge of reintroducing air into the glass receiver. Near the window at the right, a boy stands ready to lower a cage when the bird revives. (The moon visible out the window is a reference to the Lunar Society.) By delaying the reintroduction of air, the scientist has created considerable suspense, as the reactions of the two girls indicate. Their father, a voice of reason, attempts to dispel their fears.

The dramatic lighting not only underscores the life-and-death issue of the bird's fate but also suggests that science brings light into a world of darkness and ignorance. The lighting adds a spiritual dimension as well. During the Baroque era, such intimate lighting effects had been used for religious scenes (see fig. 14–8). Here science replaces religion as the great light and hope of humanity. This theme is emphasized through the devout expressions of some of the observers.

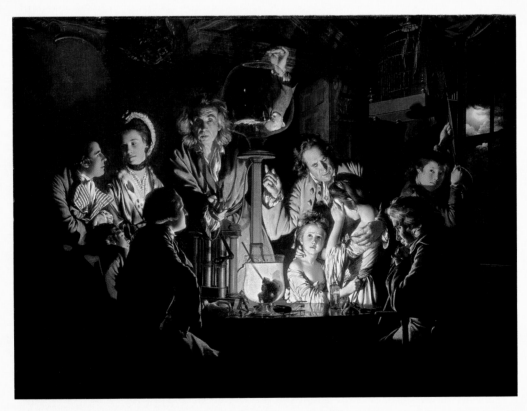

17–8 Joseph Wright. *An Experiment on a Bird in the Air-Pump,* 1768. Oil on canvas, 6′ × 8′ (1.83 × 2.44 cm). The National Gallery, London

Neoclassical Architecture in England and North America

While the Rococo style remained popular in continental architecture, a group of British professional architects and wealthy amateurs took a stance against what they saw as the immoral extravagance of the Italian Baroque. They advocated a return to the austerity and simplicity they saw in the architecture of Andrea Palladio. They studied in Italy and then returned home to build magnificent Palladian villas set in extensive gardens on their country estates.

In the art of garden design, the British could claim true originality. They created a style that contrasted sharply with the rigid formality of seventeenth-century gardens and with the classicism of their stately homes. Known throughout Europe as the English landscape garden, the sweeping lawns, winding paths, irregularly shaped pools and streams, and asymmetrically placed groves of trees imitated the appearance of the natural rural landscape, carefully and discreetly "improved" by human intelligence and skill.

An especially innovative British Neoclassical architect was the Scottish architect and interior designer Robert Adam (1728–1792). When he made the Grand Tour in 1754–1758, Adam largely ignored the great Roman civic architecture and focused instead on the applied ornament of Roman domestic architecture. When he returned to London to set up an architectural firm with his two younger brothers, he brought with him drawings and prints that provided a complete inventory of ancient decorative motifs, which he then modified to create his own elegant style. His designs proved ideally suited both to the evolving taste of wealthy clients and to the imperial aspirations of the new British king, George III, whose reign began in 1760.

Adam achieved worldwide fame for his interior designs, such as the renovations he carried out between 1760 and 1769 for the Duke of Northumberland at his country estate, Syon House, near London. The opulent colored marbles, gilded relief panels, classical statues, spirals, garlands, rosettes, and gilded moldings are luxuriously profuse yet are restrained by the strong geometric order imposed on them (fig. **17–9**). Adam's preference for bright pastel colors and small-scale decorative elements

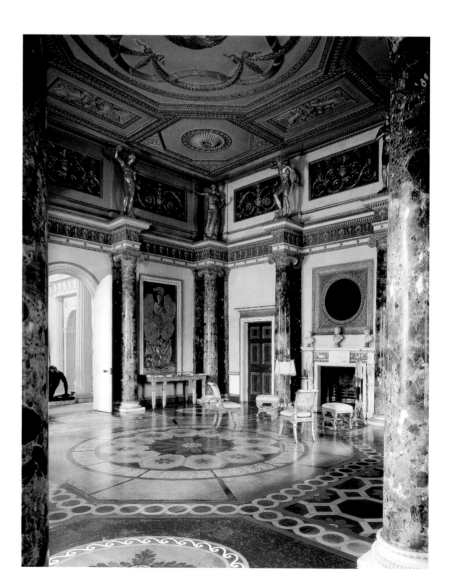

17–9 Robert Adam. Anteroom, Syon House, Middlesex, England. 1760–1769

Adam's conviction that it was acceptable to modify details of the classical orders was generally opposed by the British architectural establishment. As a result of that opposition, Adam was never elected to the Royal Academy.

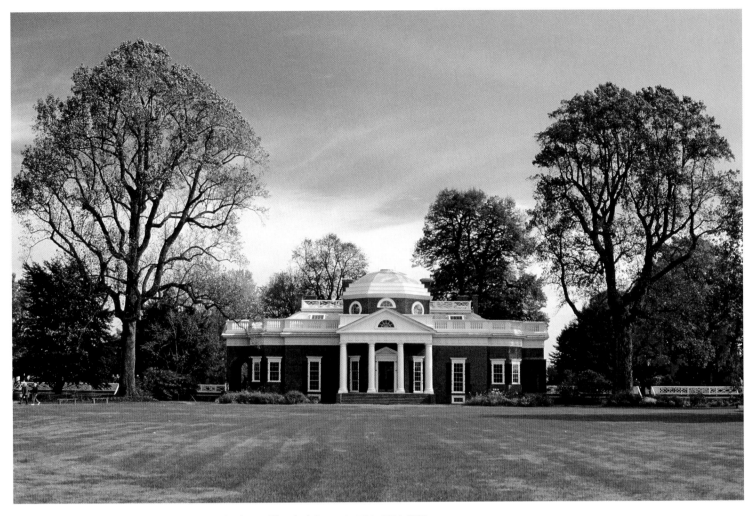

17–10 Thomas Jefferson. Monticello, near Charlottesville, Virginia. 1770–1784, 1796–1808

lightens the effect. Such interiors were designed partly as settings for the art collections of British aristocrats, which included antiquities as well as a range of Neoclassical painting, sculpture, and decorative arts.

Despite mounting hostilities with Britain from 1775 to 1781, American domestic architecture remained tied to developments in England. Neoclassicism became the dominant style in the United States during the Federal Period (1783–1830) that followed the colonies' victory in their War of Independence.

Thomas Jefferson (1743–1826), an enthusiastic amateur architect, designed his Virginia residence, Monticello, in a style influenced by British Palladian villas. His first house, built in the 1770s, was based on a design in Palladio's *Four Books of Architecture*. In 1785, Jefferson went to Paris as the American ambassador to France. There he discovered an elegant domestic architecture that made his home seem very provincial. When he returned in 1793, he completely redesigned Monticello, using French doors and tall narrow windows (fig. **17–10**) and a balustrade above the

unifying cornice to mask the second floor. Despite these French elements and his stated rejection of the British Palladian mode, the building's simplicity and combination of temple front and dome remain closer to English than to French buildings. Monticello is less grand than English stately homes because of its humbler building materials (brick with wooden trim, and columns formed of stuccoed and painted bricks) and its extended lowlying profile.

Neoclassical Painting in France

In the 1770s, the French history painter Jacques-Louis David (1748–1825) developed a truly Neoclassical painting style. In 1774 David had won the Prix de Rome, a competitive scholarship for study in Italy awarded to the top graduating students from the French Academy's art school. During six years in Rome, David studied the art of Raphael and Michelangelo, the Baroque classicism of Poussin and the Carracci, and above all, ancient

During the Georgian period, wealthy British families filled their homes with objects made of fine silver. The utensils and vessels that they collected were not simply practical articles but also statements of high social status.

Gentlefolk employed finely crafted silver vessels to serve and consume punch and drank from cups or goblets such as the simple yet elegant goblet by Ann and Peter Bateman, which has a gilded interior to protect the silver from the acid present in alcoholic drinks. (Hester Bateman's double beaker, also with a gilded interior, was made for use while traveling.) The punch was served with a ladle such as the one shown here, by Elizabeth Morley, which has a twisted whalebone handle that floats, making it easy to retrieve from the punch bowl. Filled goblets would be offered on a flat salver like the one made by Elizabeth Cooke. Gentlemen also used silver containers to carry snuff, a pulverized tobacco that was inhaled by well-to-do members of both sexes. The flat snuffbox, by Alice and George Burrows, has curved sides for easy insertion into the pockets of a gentleman's tight-fitting trousers.

All the objects shown here bear the marks of silver shops run either wholly or partly by women, who played a significant role in the production of Georgian silver (fig. **17–11**).

While some women served formal apprenticeships and went on to become members of the goldsmiths' guild (which included silversmiths), most women became involved with silver through their relation to a master silversmith—typically a father, husband, or brother—and they frequently specialized in a specific aspect of the craft, such as engraving, **chasing**, or polishing. The widows of silversmiths often took over their husbands' shops and ran them with the help of journeymen or partners.

Hester Bateman (1708–1794), the most famous woman silversmith in eighteenth-century Britain, inherited her husband's small spoonmaking shop at the age of 52 and transformed it into one of the largest silver manufactories in the country. Adapting new technologies of mass production to the manufacture of silver, Bateman marketed her well-designed, functional, and relatively inexpensive wares to the newly affluent middle class, making no attempt to compete with those silversmiths who catered to the monarchy or the aristocracy. She retired when she was 82 after training her daughter-in-law Ann and her sons and grandson to carry on the family enterprise. Both Hester's double beaker and Ann and Peter's goblet show the restrained elegance characteristic of Bateman silver.

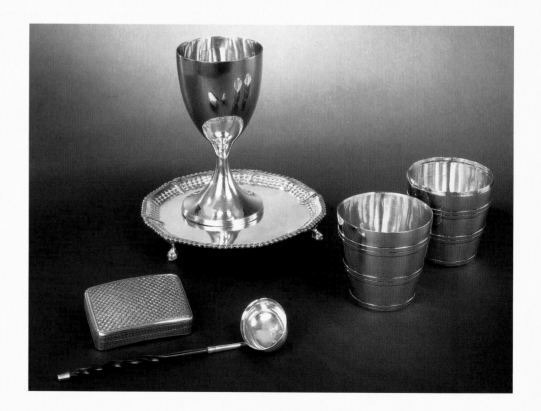

17–11 Elizabeth Moerley, *George III toddy ladle,* 1802; **Alice and George Burrows,** *George III snuffbox,* 1802; **Elizabeth Cooke,** *George III salver,* 1767; **Ann and Peter Bateman,** *George III goblet,* 1797; **Hester Bateman,** *George III double beaker,* 1790. National Museum of Women in the Arts, Washington, D.C.

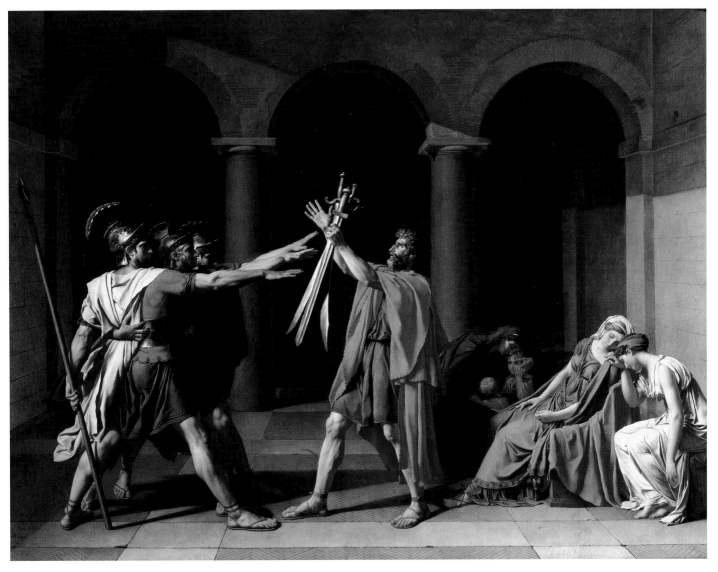

17–12 Jacques-Louis David, *Oath of the Horatii.* 1784–1785. Oil on canvas, 10′8 3/8″ × 14′ (3.26 × 4.27 m). Musée du Louvre, Paris

Roman sculpture and frescoes. After his return to Paris, he produced a series of severe classical paintings that extolled the antique virtues of moral incorruptibility, stoicism, courage, and patriotism. The first of these, painted as a royal commission, was the *Oath of the Horatii* of 1784–1785 (fig. **17–12**).

David's painting was inspired by Pierre Corneille's seventeenth-century drama *Horace.* Somewhat surprisingly, however, David chose to depict an incident that is not part of the story in any known source: the Horatii taking an oath to fight to the death for Rome. The young men's father, Horace, standing at the center, administers the oath to his sons. To the right of him, Horace's daughter Camillia, who is betrothed to one of the Curatii, and his daughter-in-law Sabina, a Curatii herself, weep, knowing that whatever the outcome of the battle, they will inevitably lose someone dear to them. The energetic young men with their glittering swords are a powerful contrast to the swooning women already mourning the tragedy to come. The message of the

finished painting—the value of putting patriotic duty above personal interests and even family obligations—is expressed with such clarity and power that it created a sensation when David exhibited it in Rome and Paris in early 1785.

David's *Oath* became an emblem of the French Revolution of 1789. Its harsh lesson in republican citizenship effectively captured the mood of the new leaders of the French state who came to power in 1793—especially the Jacobins, egalitarian democrats who abolished the monarchy and presided over the Reign of Terror in 1793–1794. (The Reign of Terror was unprecedented for its murderous vengence. During one particularly bloodthirsty stretch, 1,376 individuals were guillotined in 47 days.)

The initial French Republic ended in 1799 when the government was reorganized under Napoleon Bonaparte, a popular and successful general. After Napoleon was named emperor in 1804, David became his court painter. Even before that time, David produced canvases that turned Napoleon into a larger-than-life

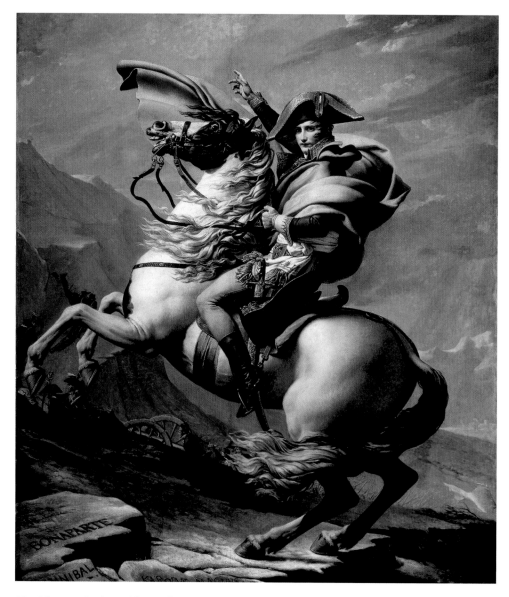

17–13 Jacques-Louis David. *Napoleon Crossing the Saint-Bernard.* 1800–01. Oil on canvas, 8′11″ × 7′7″ (2.7 × 2.3 m). Musée National du Chateau de la Malmaison, Rueil-Malmaison

David flattered Napoleon by reminding the viewer of two other great generals from history who had accomplished this difficult feat—Charlemagne and Hannibal—by carving the names of all three on the rock in the lower left.

figure. *Napoleon Crossing the Saint-Bernard* (fig. **17–13**), painted during 1800–1801, is an idealized vision of a military campaign. David shows the future emperor leading his troops across the Alps into Italy. Although Napoleon actually made the crossing on a donkey, here he charges up the mountain on a rearing horse, past rocks incised with his name and the names of his heroic predecessors, Hannibal and Charlemagne. With its sweeping diagonals and flowing draperies, this painting of a contemporary event owes as much to the idealized Grand Manner of the Baroque as it does to Neoclassicism. David's career had become so closely linked with Napoleon that when Napoleon fell from power in 1814, David moved to Brussels, where he died in 1825.

As the leading force in French painting during the Revolutionary and Napoleonic eras, David trained many young artists. Jean-Auguste-Dominique Ingres (1780–1867) was one of David's most talented pupils; he thoroughly absorbed his teacher's Neoclassical vision yet interpreted it in a new manner. Inspired by Raphael rather than by antique art, Ingres emulated the Renaissance artist's graceful lyricism, precise drawing, and idealized forms. Ingres won the Prix de Rome and lived in Italy from 1806 to 1824. In 1835, he returned to Italy to serve as director of the French Academy in Rome until 1841. As a teacher and theorist, Ingres became the most influential European artist of his time.

Although Ingres, like David, fervently desired acceptance as a history painter, his paintings of literary subjects and contemporary events were less successful than his female nudes and erotically charged portraits of women, especially his numerous representations of the odalisque (a woman living in the woman's quarter of an *oda*, a Turkish house). The odalisque appealed to patrons because of its exotic, non-Western source. In the *Large Odalisque* (fig. **17–14**) of 1814, the look the woman levels at her master, while turning her naked body away from what we assume is his gaze, makes her simultaneously erotic and aloof. The cool blues of the couch and the curtain at the right heighten the effect of the woman's warm skin, while the tight angularity of the crumpled sheets accentuates the languid, sensual contours of her form. Line here is the undisputed means of definition; in fact, we are hardly aware of the physical medium of paint.

Although Ingres's commitment to fluid line and elegant postures was grounded in his Neoclassical training, he treated a number of Romantic themes (such as this odalisque) in a highly personal, almost Mannerist fashion. Note the elongation of the woman's back (she seems to have several extra vertebrae);

the widening of her hip; and her tiny, seemingly boneless feet. All appear anatomically incorrect but they are aesthetically compelling. As a teacher and theorist, Ingres established the taste of a generation and helped ensure the dominance of classicism over a strong subcurrent of Romanticism in France well into the nineteenth century.

Romanticism

Romanticism, already anticipated in French painting during Napoleon's reign, did not gain wide public acceptance until after 1830. In general, Romantic painting featured loose, fluid brushwork, strong colors, complex compositions, dramatic contrasts of light and dark, and expressive poses and gestures—all suggesting a revival of the more dramatic aspects of the Baroque. French Romantic artists not only drew upon literary sources but also added a new dimension of social criticism.

The Romantic style became identified with a type of social commentary in which the dramatic presentation was intended to stir public emotions, especially in the work of its chief exponents: Théodore Géricault (1791–1824) and Eugène Delacroix (1798–1863).

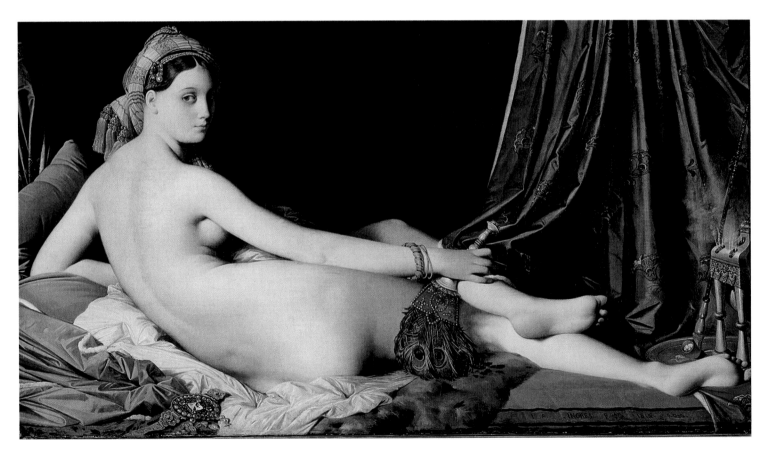

17–14 Jean-Auguste-Dominique Ingres. *Large Odalisque.* 1814. Oil on canvas, approx. 35″ × 64″ (88.9 × 162.5 cm). Musée du Louvre, Paris

© REUNION DES MUSÉES NATIONAUX/ART RESOURCE, NY

During Napoleon's campaigns against the British in North Africa, the French discovered the exotic Near East. Upper-middle-class men were particularly attracted to the patriarch institutions they encountered abroad, perhaps in part as a reaction against the demands for equality being made by French women inspired by the revolutions of the eighteenth century.

Géricault began his career painting works inspired by Napoleonic military campaigns. During a brief stay in Rome between 1816 and 1817, he studied the work of Michelangelo. Géricault returned to Paris determined to make a great painting of a contemporary event, and finally decided to treat the scandalous and sensational shipwreck of the *Medusa* (fig. **17–15**). In 1816 a ship of colonists headed for Madagascar ran aground near its destination; its captain was an incompetent aristocrat appointed by the newly restored monarchy for political reasons. Because there were insufficient lifeboats, the captain ordered 152 passengers and crew onto a small raft, which tossed about on stormy seas for nearly two weeks before it was found. The 15 survivors had subsisted for the last days of their horrific voyage on human flesh.

Géricault decided to show the moment when the survivors first spotted their rescue ship, but survival was not yet assured. The artitst's academic training underlies the painting's organization, which is constructed as a series of interlocking triangles. The outstretched arms of the victims lead the viewer's eyes to the upper right, where the climactic figure of an African is held aloft by other men. This figure waves a cloth to attract the attention of a ship that is still only a speck on the horizon. The work master-fully illustrates this human tragedy—and communicates the injustice that caused it—with indignant compassion.

At the Salon of 1819, Géricault showed his painting under the neutral title *A Shipwreck Scene*, perhaps to downplay its politically inflammatory aspects and to encourage appreciation of its larger philosophical theme—of the eternal and tragic struggle of humanity against the elements. Most contemporary French critics, however, interpreted the painting as a political commentary; liberals praised it, and royalists condemned it. Because the monarchy understandably refused to buy the canvas, Géricault exhibited *The Raft of the "Medusa"* commercially on a two-year tour of Ireland and England. The London exhibition attracted more than 50,000 paying visitors.

Eugène Delacroix, who modeled for one of the nude victims on the raft, followed Géricault as the inspirational leader of the Romantic movement. The contrast in styles between Ingres's *Large Odalisque* (see fig. 17–14) and Delacroix's *Women of Algiers* (fig. **17–16**) points out the difference between the clear, linear, sculptural Neoclassical style and the diffuse, colorful, painterly, almost Baroque Romantic mode. Although Delacroix generally supported liberal political aims, his visit in 1832 to

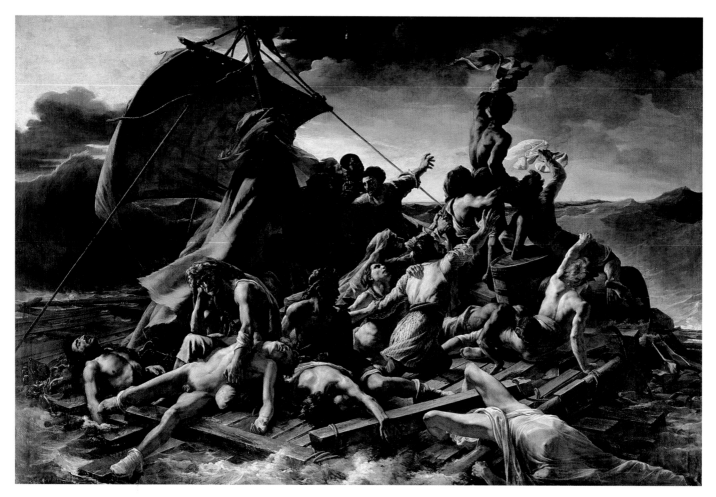

17–15 Théodore Géricault. *Raft of the "Medusa."* 1818–1819. Oil on canvas, 16′1″ × 23′6″ (4.9 × 7.16 m).
Musée du Louvre, Paris

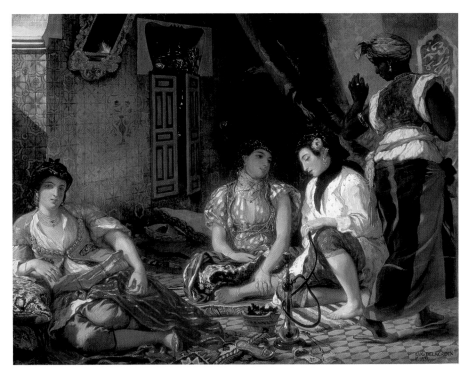

17–16 Eugène Delacroix. *Women of Algiers.* 1834. Oil on canvas, 5'10⅞" × 7'6⅛" (1.8 × 2.29 m). Musée du Louvre, Paris

Morocco seems to have stirred his more conservative side. As enthralled as Delacroix was with the brilliant color and dignified inhabitants of North Africa, his attraction to the patriarchal political and social system is also evident in *Women of Algiers* and other paintings. This image of hedonism and passivity countered the contemporaneous demands of many French women for property reform, more equitable child-custody laws, and other egalitarian initiatives.

In Spain, Francisco Goya y Lucientes (1746–1828), an artist who defies classification, became a major figure in the Romantic movement. Goya began his career painting portraits and genre scenes, the latter used as tapestry designs by the Royal Manufactory in Madrid. By the turn of the century, however, his study of Velázquez and Rembrandt began to be manifest in his work in freer brushwork, richer colors, and dramatic presentation.

In 1799 Goya published *Los Caprichos (The Caprices)*, the first of several suites of etchings he created. These prints exhibit a bitter outlook that is absent from his earlier genre paintings and tapestry cartoons. Setting the tone for the 80 etchings is the print originally intended as its **frontispiece**, *The Sleep of Reason Produces Monsters* (fig. **17–17**). Although the text published with

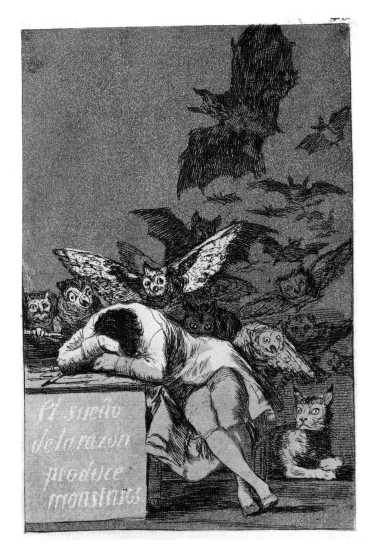

17–17 Francisco Goya. *The Sleep of Reason Produces Monsters,* from *Los Caprichos (The Caprices).* 1796–1798. Series published 1799. Etching and aquatint, 8½" × 6" (21.6 × 15.2 cm)

After printing about 300 sets of this series, Goya offered them for sale in 1799. He withdrew them from sale two days later without explanation. Historians believe that he was probably warned by the Church that if he did not he might have to appear before the Inquisition because of the unflattering portrayal of the Church in some of the etchings.

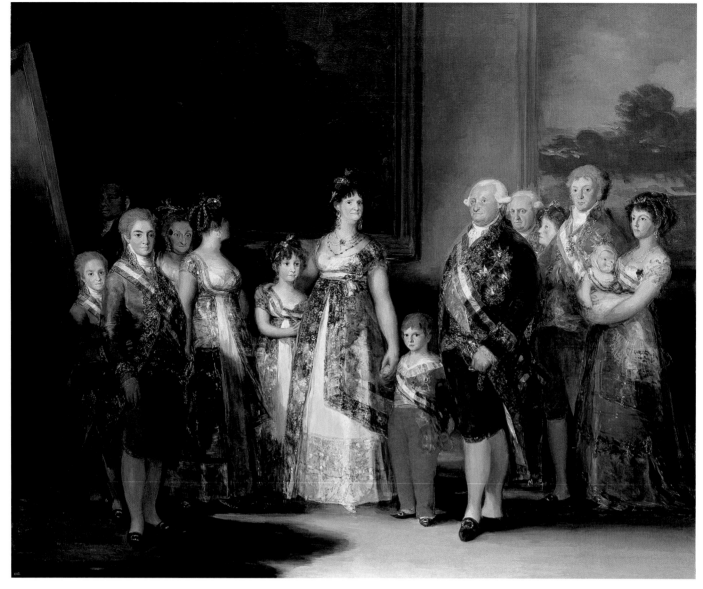

17–18 Francisco Goya. *Family of Charles IV.* 1800. Oil on canvas, 9'2" × 11' (2.79 × 3.36 m). Museo del Prado, Madrid

the print sounds a hopeful note ("Imagination abandoned by reason produces impossible monsters; united with her, she is the mother of the arts and the source of their wonders"), the images are an angry attack on contemporary Spanish manners and morals that make Hogarth's satire (see fig. 17–6) seem tame.

The print shows a slumbering personification of Reason, behind whom lurk the dark creatures of the night—owls, bats, and a cat—that are let loose when Reason sleeps. The rest of the *Caprichos* enumerate the specific follies of Spanish life. Goya hoped that the series would show Spanish people the errors of their ways and reawaken them to reason. Although the premise is hopeful, Goya's portrait of human folly and cruelty is disturbing. The artist did not share the Enlightenment faith in the ultimate rationality and goodness of humanity, and he believed that the violence, greed, and foolishness of his society had to be examined mercilessly if it were to be changed in any way.

Goya's large portrait of the *Family of Charles IV* (fig. **17–18**) openly acknowledges the influence of Velàzquez's *Las Meninas* (see fig. 14–12). Goya even places himself behind the easel on the left, just as Velàzquez had in his painting. Unlike *Las Meninas*, however, Goya's painting is realistic rather than flattering—some see the painting as a cruel exposé of the royal family as common, ugly, and inept. Considering Goya's position as the principal court painter at the time of this royal commission, it is difficult to imagine the artist deliberately mocking his patrons. In fact, Goya made preparatory sketches for the painting, which the family apparently approved. Viewers who first saw the painting in 1800 may have found it striking not because it was demeaning but because its candid representation was refreshingly modern.

In 1808 Napoleon conquered Spain and placed his brother Joseph Bonaparte on its throne. Many Spaniards, including Goya, at first welcomed the French because they hoped for liberal reforms, but the government soon turned despotic. On May 2, 1808, a rumor spread in Madrid that the French planned to kill the royal family. The populace rose up and a day of bloody street fighting ensued. Hundreds of Spanish people were executed the following morning. The fighting soon spread to the countryside, and for the next six years the Spanish conducted guerilla warfare against the French occupying forces, events recorded by Goya in another print series, *The Horrors of War.*

After the war, Goya made a pair of paintings to commemorate the events of May 2 and May 3. The more famous of the two paintings shows a French firing squad executing helpless Spanish prisoners in the predawn hours of May 3 (fig. **17–19**). The violent gestures of the terrified rebels and the mechanical efficiency of the firing squad are like scenes from a nightmare. The man in the white shirt, confronting his faceless killers with outstretched arms suggesting the crucified Jesus, is an image of particular horror and pathos. When asked why he painted such a brutal scene, Goya responded: "To warn men never to do it again."

The Enlightenment's faith in reason and empirical knowledge was countered by Romanticism's celebration of the emotions and subjective forms of experience, as dramatized in Goya's *The Sleep of Reason Produces Monsters* (see fig. 17–17). This rebellion against reason led Romantic artists such as the Swiss painter John Henry Fuseli (1741–1825) to glorify the irrational side of human nature that the Enlightenment sought to deny. Fuseli was raised in an intellectual household where originality, freedom of expression, and the imaginative power of the irrational were celebrated. His family and friends were inspired by

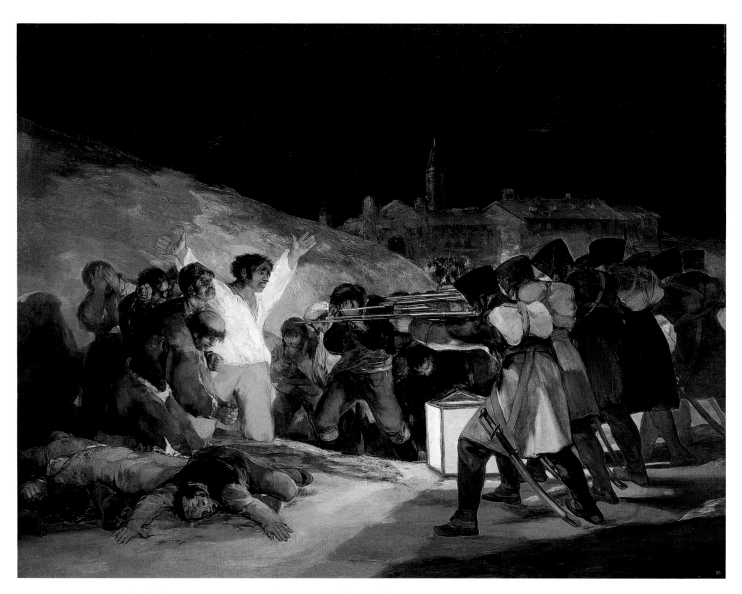

17–19 Francisco Goya. *Third of May, 1808.* 1814–1815. Oil on canvas, 8′9″ × 13′4″ (2.67 × 4.06 m). Museo del Prado, Madrid

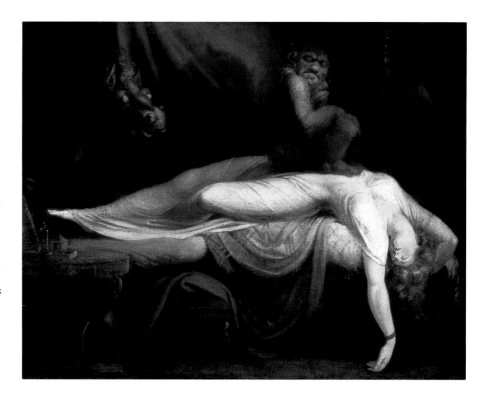

17–20 John Henry Fuseli. *The Nightmare.* 1781. Oil on canvas, $39\frac{3}{4}''\times49\frac{1}{2}''$ (101 × 126 cm). The Detroit Institute of Arts

The Austrian psychoanalyst Sigmund Freud, who believed that dreams were manifestations of the dreamer's repressed desires, had a reproduction of The Nightmare *in his office. Romantic escape was as appealing in the eighteenth and nineteenth centuries as it is at the beginning of the twenty-first century.*

British poetry, including the works of Shakespeare. Fuseli also admired Rembrandt and Caravaggio for their expressiveness. After studying in Rome (1770–1778), where he focused on Michelangelo rather than ancient classical art, Fuseli settled permanently in London. By the early 1780s, with works such as *The Nightmare* (fig. **17–20**), he began to make a reputation as a painter of the irrational and the erotic. Since Romantic art is often highly personal, concerned as it is with emotions and subjective experience, it is not surprising that *The Nightmare* may include autobiographical elements. On the back of one of the versions of the painting, Fuseli sketched the portrait of Anna Landolt, a woman he loved and lost.

Romantic Landscape Painting

Romantic taste in England found a major outlet in landscape painting. By the early nineteenth century, Romantic landscape painting generally took one of two forms—the naturalistic or the dramatic. The naturalistic style entailed closely observed representations of tranquil nature, meant to communicate reverence for the landscape as a spiritual precinct and to counteract the effects of industrialization and urbanization that were rapidly transforming it. The other—the dramatic—emphasized turbulent or fantastic natural scenery, often shaken by natural disasters such as storms and avalanches, and aimed to stir viewers' emotions and arouse a feeling of the **sublime**. John Constable

(1776–1837), one of the two great landscape painters in England, specialized in naturalistic scenes of rural stability. The other, Joseph Mallord William Turner (1775–1851), focused on mood and drama.

The son of a successful miller, Constable claimed that the landscape of his youth in southern England had made him a painter before he ever picked up a brush. In spite of his training at the Royal Academy, where landscape was considered an inferior art, he was greatly impressed by the work of seventeenth-century Dutch landscape artists, and theirs was the example he followed. *The White Horse* (fig. **17–21**) of 1819 draws on Constable's intense observation of every facet of the natural landscape, recorded in sketches he made on walking tours. Although he composed his paintings in his studio, he used sketches made on-site, insisting that art should be an objective record of things actually seen. As a storm passes away to the right, a farmer and his helpers ferry a workhorse across a river. Sunlight glistens off the water and foliage, an effect Constable achieved through tiny dabs of white paint.

The naturalistic stylistic current to which Constable's pastoral idylls belong is sometimes referred to as Romantic naturalism, although Constable detested what he called "cold, trumpery stuff" and "bravura," by which he meant Romantic effects of drama and grandeur. Constable also made no reference to rural England's ongoing economic depression and civil unrest, or to the blight attending England's industrialization.

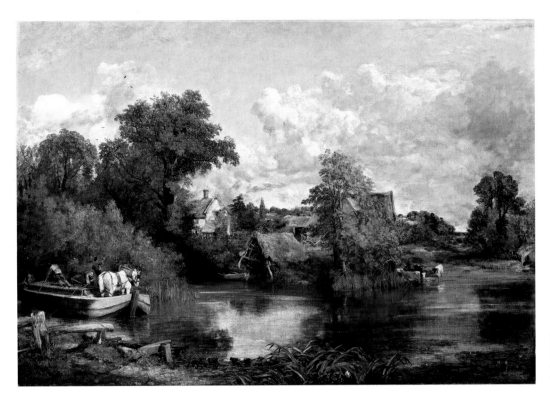

17–21 John Constable. *The White Horse.* 1819. Oil on canvas, 4′3³⁄₄″ × 6′2¹⁄₈″ (1.31 × 1.88 m). The Frick Collection, New York

"AM I NOT A MAN AND A BROTHER?"

For two centuries the name Wedgwood has been synonymous with fine English ceramics, especially tableware. But there was another side to Josiah Wedgwood. He was active in the international effort to halt the African slave trade and abolish slavery. To publicize the abolitionist cause, he asked the sculptor William Hackwood to design an emblem for the British Committee to Abolish the Slave Trade, formed in 1787. The compelling image created by Hackwood had the likeness of an African man kneeling in chains, with the legend, "Am I Not a Man and a Brother?" Wedgwood sent copies of the medallion to Benjamin Franklin, who was the president of the Philadelphia Abolition Society, and to others in the movement. In the nineteenth century, the women's suffrage movement in the United States adapted the image by representing a woman in chains with the motto, "Am I Not a Woman and a Sister?"

A work of art as explicitly political as this was unusual in the eighteenth century. Nevertheless, artists in both Europe and America responded to the tumultuous social changes and political events with powerful and courageous works of art.

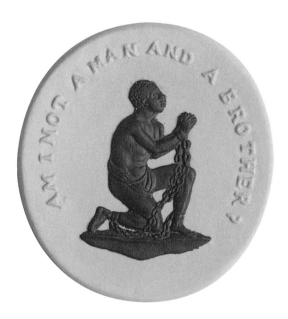

William Hackwood, for Josiah Wedgwood. *"Am I Not a Man and a Brother?"* 1787. Black-and-white jasperware, 1³⁄₈″ × 1³⁄₈″ (3.5 × 3.5 cm). Wedgwood Museum Trust Limited, Barlaston, Staffordshire, England

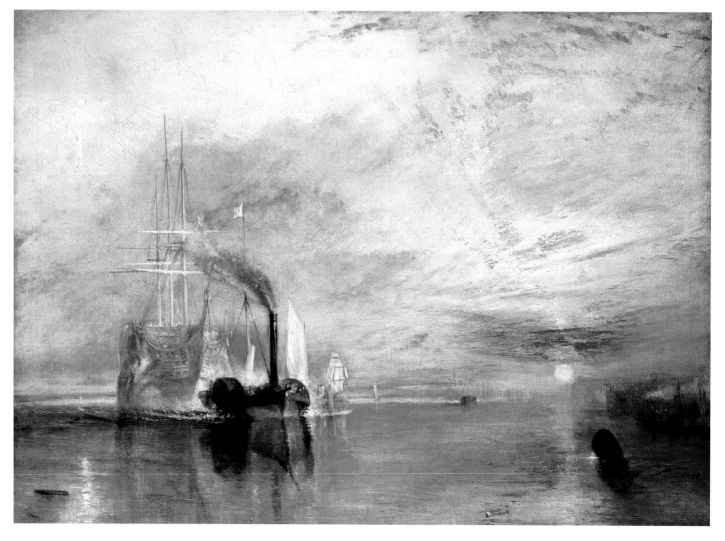

17–22 Joseph Mallord William Turner. *The Fighting "Téméraire," Tugged to Her Last Berth to Be Broken Up.* 1838. Oil on canvas, 35 $\frac{1}{4}$" × 48" (89.5 × 121.9 cm). The National Gallery, London

Turner, Constable's contemporary, imbued his early works with a pleasant, picturesque quality not far removed from Constable's, and he rapidly won public acclaim. At 27, Turner was elected a full member of the Royal Academy, and later he became a professor at the Royal Academy school. As Turner's personal style matured, the phenomena of colored light and misty atmosphere became the true subjects of his paintings. To the academicians, his works increasingly looked like sketches or preliminary underpainting of unfinished canvases, but to his admirers, including Constable, they were "golden visions, glorious and beautiful," painted with "tinted steam."

The Fighting "Téméraire," Tugged to Her Last Berth to Be Broken Up (fig. **17–22**) of 1838 is both a painting of a contemporary event and a study in the optical effects of the setting sun over water. The "*Téméraire*" had been the second-ranking British ship at the Battle of Trafalgar in 1805, a great British naval victory over the combined fleets of Spain and Napoleon's France. Some 33 years later, however, the ship was ready for the scrap heap, and Turner watched as it was towed away to be destroyed. Some have interpreted the scene as a symbol of the passing of the old order, the sailing ship literally and figuratively destroyed by the steam-engine-driven tug. The broad and painterly treatment of the sky, which Turner laid down largely with a palette knife, foreshadows the abstraction of his late works of the 1840s, in which land, sea, and sky dissolve into vaporous bursts of color and light.

Early Photography

The development of photography in the early nineteenth century was a prime expression of the new, positivist interest in descriptive accuracy. Since the Renaissance, Westerners had been seeking a mechanical method for recording a scene. One early device was the **camera obscura** (Latin for "dark chamber"). It consisted of a darkened room or box with a lens on one side through which light passed and projected onto the opposite side an upside-down image of the scene, which an artist could then trace. Photography was developed as a way to "fix"—that is, to make permanent—the visual impressions produced by a camera obscura, or camera, on light-sensitive material.

The first person to achieve this goal was the "gentleman inventor" Joseph-Nicéphore Niépce (1765–1833). Using metal-and-glass plates covered with a kind of light-sensitive asphalt called bitumen, and a camera, he succeeded around 1826 in making the first positive-image photographs. Later, Niépce met Louis-Jacques-Mandé Daguerre (1787–1851), who, working with a lens maker, developed an improved camera.

After Niépce's death in 1833, Daguerre, in 1835, discovered that an exposure to light of only 20 to 30 minutes would produce a latent image on a silver plate treated with iodine fumes, which could then be made visible through an after-process involving mercury vapor. By 1837 he had developed a method of fixing the image by bathing the plate in a strong solution of common salt after exposure. Daguerre's first picture of this type (**daguerreotype**), a still life of plaster casts and a framed drawing (fig. **17–23**), makes the earliest claim for photography as an art form through its specifically "artistic" subject matter.

The 1839 announcement of Daguerre's invention prompted the English scientist William Henry Fox Talbot (1800–1877) to publish the results of his own work on what he called the **calotype** (from the Greek term for "beautiful image"). Beginning in the mid-1830s, Fox Talbot had made negative copies of engravings, pieces of lace, and leaves by placing them on paper impregnated with silver chloride and exposing them to light. By the summer of 1835, he was using this chemically treated paper in both large and small cameras. Then, in 1840, he discovered, independently of Daguerre, that latent images resulting from exposure to the sun for short periods of time could be developed chemically. Applying the technique he had earlier used with engravings and leaves, Fox Talbot was able to make positive prints from the calotype negatives. Fox Talbot's process, even more than Daguerre's, became the basis of modern photography because, unlike Daguerre's—which created a single, positive image—Talbot's calotype process produced a negative image from which an unlimited number of positives, or prints, could be made.

Fox Talbot's book *The Pencil of Nature* (issued in six parts, 1844–1846) was the first book to be illustrated with photographs. The subjects of the photographs were often rural. In *The Open Door* (fig. **17–24**) the photographer evoked an agrarian way of life that was fast disappearing. A traditional, handcrafted broom—of a type that mass production was beginning to make obsolete—rests against the doorway of a timeworn cottage. In an attempt at artfulness, the photographer carefully positioned the broom's handle to parallel the shadows on the upper right of the door.

In 1851, Frederick Scott Archer, a British sculptor and photographer, took the final step in the development of early photography. Archer found that silver nitrate would adhere to glass if it was mixed with collodion, a combination of guncotton, ether, and alcohol used in medicinal bandages. When wet, this

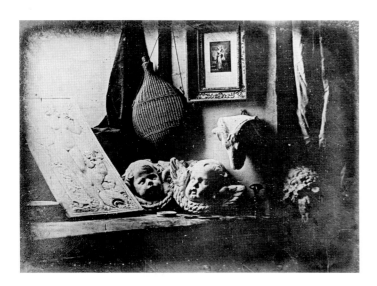

17–23 Louis-Jacques-Mandé Daguerre. *The Artist's Studio.* 1837. Daguerreotype, $6\frac{5}{8} \times 8\frac{5}{8}''$ (17 × 22 cm). Société Française de Photographie, Paris

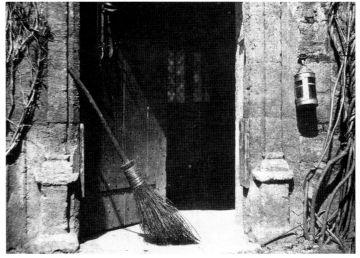

17–24 William Henry Fox Talbot. *The Open Door.* 1843. Salt-paper print from a calotype negative. Science Museum, London
FOX TALBOT COLLECTION

A camera is essentially a lightproof box with a hole, called an aperture (a), which is usually adjustable in size and regulates the amount of light that strikes the film (b). The aperture is covered with a lens (c), which focuses (d) the image on the film, and a shutter (e), a kind of door that opens for a controlled amount of time to regulate the length of time that the film is exposed to light—usually a small fraction of a second. In the example illustrated, the shutter is open, exposing the film to light. Modern cameras with viewfinders (f) and small single-lens reflex cameras are generally used at eye level, permitting the photographer to see virtually the same image that the film will capture.

In modern black-and-white photography, silver halide crystals (silver combined with iodine, chlorine, or other halogens) are suspended in a gelatin base to make an emulsion that coats the film (in early photography, before the invention of plastic, a glass plate was coated with a variety of emulsions). The film is then exposed. Light reflected off objects enters the camera and strikes the film. Pale objects reflect more light than do dark ones. The silver in the emulsion collects most densely where it is exposed to the most light, producing a "negative" image on the film. Later, when the film is placed in a chemical bath (developed), the silver deposits turn black, as if tarnishing. The more light the film receives, the denser the black tone created. A positive image is created from the negative in a darkroom—the film negative is placed over a sheet of paper that, like the film, has been treated to be light-sensitive, and light is directed through the negative onto the paper. Thus, a multiple number of positive prints can be generated from a single negative.

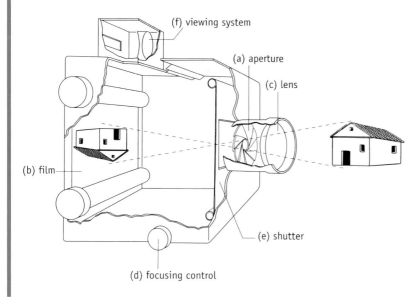

(f) viewing system
(a) aperture
(c) lens
(b) film
(e) shutter
(d) focusing control

---

collodion–silver nitrate mixture needed only a few seconds' exposure to light to create an image. The result was a glass negative, from which countless positive proofs with great tonal subtleties could be made.

Once this practical photographic process had been invented, the question became how to make use of it. For some, photography was a convenience, replacing a live model; for others, it was a cheap substitute for, and therefore a threat to, the profession of painting, especially portraiture. Those in the sciences agreed on its value for recording data, but artists were less certain how to take advantage of it. Julia Margaret Cameron (1815–1879) was one of the pioneers of photography as an art form in its own right. Cameron's principal subjects were the great men of British arts, letters, and sciences, many of whom had long been family friends.

Cameron's portrait of the famous British historian Thomas Carlyle is deliberately slightly out of focus (fig. **17–25**). By blurring details Cameron sought to call attention to the light that suffused her subjects—an artistic metaphor for creative genius.

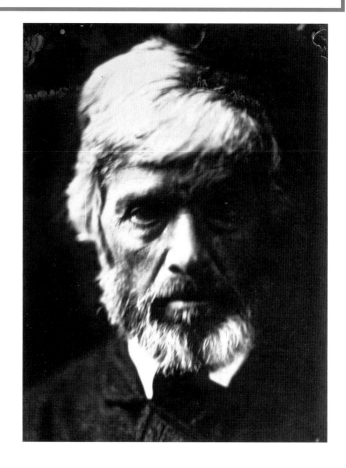

17–25 Julia Margaret Cameron. *Portrait of Thomas Carlyle.* 1863. Silver print, 10″ × 8″ (25.4 × 20.3 cm). The Royal Photographic Society, London

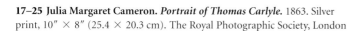

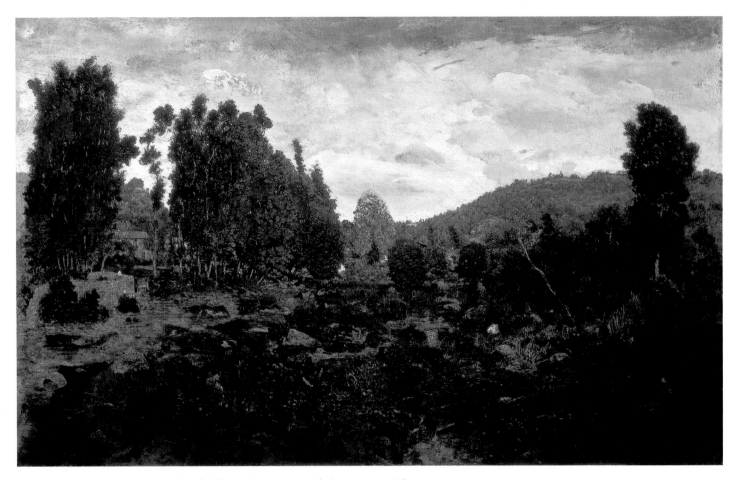

17–26 Théodore Rousseau. *The Valley of Tiffauges (Marais en Vendée).* 1837–1844. Oil on canvas, 25¹⁄₂″ × 40¹⁄₂″ (64.7 × 103 cm). Cincinnati Art Museum

GIFT OF EMILIE L. HEINE IN MEMORY OF MR. AND MRS. JOHN HAUCK (1940.1202)

The Paris Salon, held every fall to showcase contemporary artists, established the accepted official style. The organizers of the Salon turned down Rousseau's painting so many times that the artist came to be known as "le grand refuse" (the great refused one).

Carlyle's concentrated expression is so intense that the dramatic lighting of his hair, face, and beard almost seems to emanate from within. With regard to her medium Cameron said: "My aspirations are to ennoble Photography and to secure for it the character and uses of High Art by combining the real and ideal."

Naturalism and Realism in Europe

Painting of all types, whether academic or avant-garde, increasingly shared with photography an allegiance to factual accuracy. As we have seen, in the second quarter of the nineteenth century, innovative English artists such as Constable pioneered a naturalist credo that art should faithfully record ordinary life. In France this naturalistic current was represented in the 1830s and 1840s by a group of painters who became known as the Barbizon School—so called because a number of the painters lived and worked around the quiet village of Barbizon. Academic jurors and conservative critics initially attempted to bar

such naturalistic landscapes and rural scenes from the Salons, but after about 1850 the critical fortunes of the members of the Barbizon School soared. To those living in a rapidly urbanizing Europe, the image of a peaceful and contented country life began to grow in appeal.

One member of the Barbizon School was Théodore Rousseau (1812–1867). Rousseau began painting landscapes around 1830, inspired by the works of Constable and seventeenth-century Dutch landscapes. Although his paintings—with their informal composition and loose paint handling—look as if they might have been painted directly on the spot, Rousseau in fact composed them in his studio and worked on them over several years (fig. **17–26**). Not until the rise of Impressionism a generation later would artists routinely execute pictures on this scale outdoors, directly in front of the subject.

Although Rousseau's first submission to the Salon in 1831 was accepted, his modest canvases for the French countryside were systematically refused between 1836 and 1841 because they were not

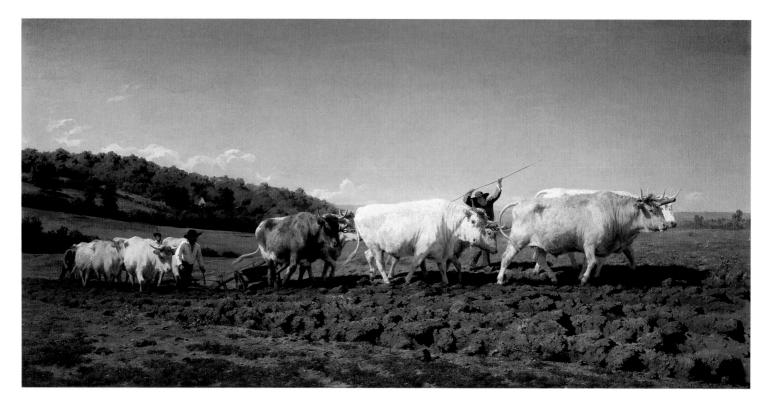

17–27 Rosa Bonheur. *Plowing in the Nivernais: The Dressing of the Vines.* 1849. Oil on canvas, 5′9″ × 8′8″ (1.75 × 2.64 m). Musée d'Orsay, Paris

Bonheur was often compared with Georges Sand, a contemporary woman writer who adopted a male name as well as male dress. Sand devoted several of her novels to the humble life of farmers and peasants. Critics at the time noted that Plowing in the Nivernais *may have been inspired by a passage in Sand's novel* The Devil's Pond *(1846) that begins: "But what caught my attention was a truly beautiful sight, a noble subject for a painter. At the far end of the flat ploughland, a handsome young man was driving a magnificent team [of] oxen."*

idealized, were not peopled with biblical or classical figures, and seemed too sketchy and "unfinished." Like most works by Rousseau and his colleagues, *The Valley of Tiffauges* invites the spectator to experience the soothing tranquility of unspoiled nature.

Rosa Bonheur (1822–1899), though not a member of the Barbizon School, was one of the most popular French painters to address the taste for rural scenes. Bonheur's success in what was then a male domain owed much to the socialist convictions of her parents, who belonged to a radical utopian sect that believed in the equality of women. In order to achieve realistic depictions of the farm animals she loved, she read zoology books and made detailed studies in the countryside and in slaughterhouses. In fact, to gain access to all-male preserves, Bonheur had to get police permission to dress in men's clothing.

Although Bonheur received some critical praise for her animal portraits in the 1840s, her success dates from the Salon of 1848, where she showed eight paintings and won a first-class medal. As a result, the government commissioned a work from her, *Plowing in the Nivernais: The Dressing of the Vines* (fig. **17–27**). In this monumental painting, powerful beasts and workers offer a reassuring image of the continuity of agrarian life. The stately movement of men and animals reflects the kind of carefully balanced compositional schemes taught in the academy and echoes scenes of processions found in classical art. The painting's compositional harmony—the shape of the hill is answered by and continued in the general profile of the oxen and their handler on the right—as well as its smooth illusionism and conservative theme were very appealing to popular taste in England, the United States, and France. Bonheur became so famous that in 1865 she received France's highest award, membership in the Legion of Honor, becoming the first woman to be awarded its Grand Cross.

A defining moment in Realism as we understand it today grew out of the Revolution of 1848 in France. In February of that year, Parisian workers overthrew the monarchy and established the Second Republic (1848–1851), whose founders' socialist goals, including collective ownership of the means of production and distribution, were abandoned when conservative factions won elections that summer. Fear of further disruptions continued to trouble many, while others, including the painter Gustave Courbet (1819–1877), became converts to the radicals' visions of social change.

Courbet was inspired by the events of 1848 to turn his attention to poor and ordinary people. Born and raised in Ornans near the Swiss border and largely self-taught as an artist, he moved to Paris in 1839. The street fighting of 1848 seems to have radicalized him. Courbet proclaimed his new political commitment in three large paintings he submitted to the Salon of 1850–1851. One of these, *A Burial at Ornans* (fig. **17–28**), is a monumental canvas commemorating (but not actually recording) the funeral of Courbet's grandfather Oudot, who had died in 1847. Instead of arranging figures in a conventional pyramid that would indicate a hierarchy of importance, Courbet lined them up in rows across the picture plane—an arrangement he considered more democratic. The artist's respect and affinity for the people is expressed in the vast scale of the work—a size ordinarily reserved for the depiction of major historical events. It is also

shown in the way the mourners' genuine sorrow is contrasted with the apparent indifference of the two Church officials dressed in red behind the officiating priest. Conservative critics hated the work for its focus on common people and its disrespect for traditional composition and standards of beauty.

Partly for convenience, Bonheur, Courbet, and the other country-life naturalists and Realists who emerged in the 1850s are sometimes referred to as the generation of 1848 (named for the year of the Revolution). Because he had liberal political views and sympathized with working-class people, the somewhat older Honoré Daumier (1808–1879) is grouped with this generation. Daumier believed that art and architecture must invent new forms and subject matter to speak to the realities of contemporary life (see Introduction, fig. 16). He helped to usher in the new taste for realism [generic realism] through biting satires of academic art and its upper-middle-class audience. Daumier used the new medium of lithography and the popular press to express his ideas in images that recall the power of Goya.

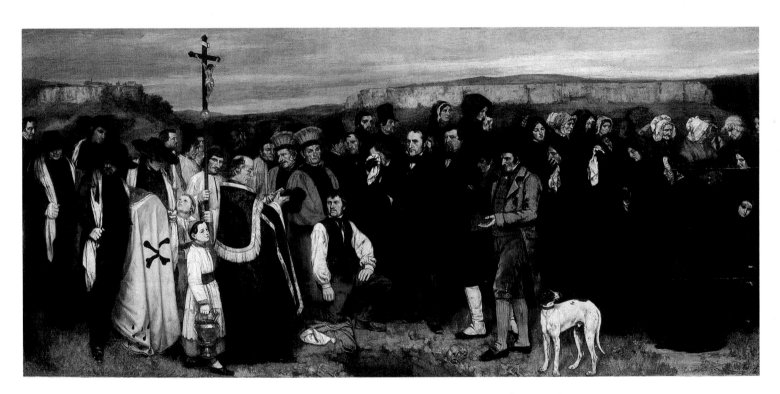

17–28 Gustave Courbet. *A Burial at Ornans.* 1849. Oil on canvas, 10′2″ × 21′8″ (3.1 × 6.6 m). Musée d'Orsay, Paris
© REUNION DES MUSÉES NATIONAUX/ART RESOURCE, NY

A Burial at Ornans was inspired by the 1848 funeral of Courbet's maternal grandfather, Jean-Antoine Oudot, a veteran of the Revolution of 1793. The painting is not meant as a record of that particular funeral, however, since Oudot is shown alive in profile at the extreme left of the canvas, his image adapted by Courbet from an earlier portrait. The two men to the right of the open grave, dressed in late-eighteenth-century clothing, are also revolutionaries of Oudot's generation, and their proximity to the grave suggests that one of their peers is being buried. Courbet's picture may be interpreted as linking the revolutions of 1793 and 1848, both of which sought to advance the cause of democracy in France.

Artists of other Western nations also embraced Realism in the period after 1850. In Russia, for example, the plight of the peasantry captured the attention of painters. In 1861 the czar abolished serfdom, emancipating Russia's peasants from the virtual slavery they had endured on the large estates of the aristocracy. Two years later, a group of painters inspired by the emancipation declared their allegiance to the peasant cause and to freedom from the St. Petersburg Academy of Art, which had controlled Russian art since 1754. Rejecting what they considered the escapist "art for art's sake" aesthetics of the academy, the members of the group, calling themselves the Wanderers, dedicated themselves to bringing a socially relevant art to the people in traveling exhibitions.

Ilya Repin (1844–1930), who attended the St. Petersburg Academy and won a scholarship to study in Paris, joined the Wanderers on his return to Russia in 1878. He had painted a series of works illustrating the social injustices then prevailing in his homeland, the first and most famous of which was *Bargehaulers on the Volga* (fig. **17–29**). The painting features a group of wretched peasants condemned to the brutal work of pulling ships up the Volga River. In order to heighten our sympathy for these workers, Repin placed a youth in the center of the group, a young man who will soon look as old and tired as his companions unless something is done to rescue him. In this way, the painting is a cry for action.

Painting in the United States

While Europe suffered through the Napoleonic Wars (1799–1815), the United States was entering an era of great optimism and expansion. The new country emerged from its war for independence from Britain with sufficient resources, technology, and entrepreneurs to move into the forefront of the industrialized world. Many nineteenth-century American painters, sculptors, and architects looked to Europe for their inspiration, but others found everything they needed in their native landscape and took pride in the American scene. These artists and their patrons tended to favor a detailed Realism and local interests over high-minded Neoclassical scenes drawn from ancient history.

America's foremost Romantic landscape painter in the first half of the nineteenth century was Thomas Cole (1801–1848). Cole emigrated from England to the United States at 17 and by 1820 was working as an itinerant portrait painter. On trips outside New York City, he sketched and painted the landscape, which quickly became his chief interest, and his paintings launched what became known as the Hudson River School. Cole painted *The Oxbow* (fig. **17–30**)—which he considered one of his "view" paintings—for exhibition at the National Academy of Design in

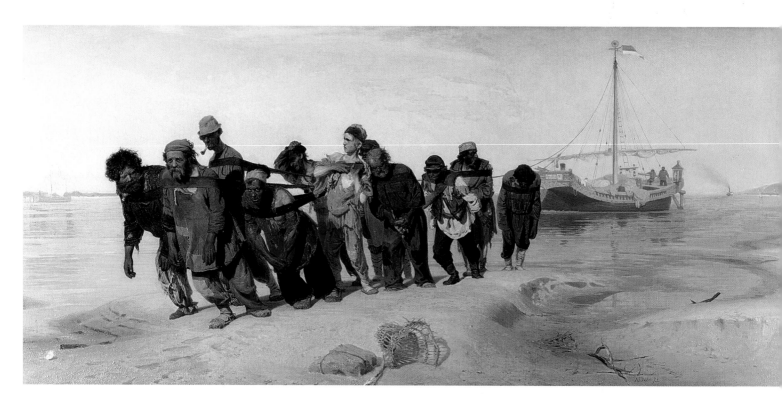

17–29 Ilya Repin. *Bargehaulers on the Volga.* 1870–1873. Oil on canvas, 4′3 1/16″ × 9′2 5/8″ (1.3 × 2.81 m). Russian State Museum, St. Petersburg

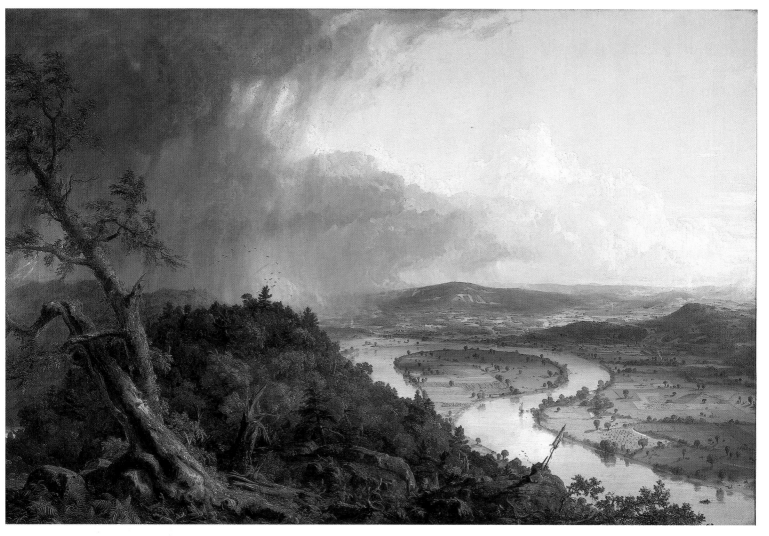

17–30 Thomas Cole. *The Oxbow.* 1836. Oil on canvas, 52 ¹/₂″ × 76″ (1.31 × 1.94 m).
The Metropolitan Museum of Art, New York

New York. The monumental scale suits the dramatic view from the top of Mount Holyoke in western Massachusetts across a spectacular oxbow-shaped bend in the Connecticut River. To Cole, such ancient geological formations constituted America's "antiquities." Along a great sweeping arc produced by the departing dark clouds and the edge of the mountain, Cole contrasts two sides of the American landscape: dense, stormy wilderness and congenial pastoral valleys. The fading storm perhaps suggests that the wild will eventually give way to the civilized.

Along with such images of native scenery, pictures of everyday American life were also popular in the mid-nineteenth century. A leading American genre painter was the Missouri artist George Caleb Bingham (1811–1879). The first major painter to live and work in the western half of the coun-

try, Bingham sketched and painted scenes of everyday life along the Mississippi River.

With *Fur Traders Descending the Missouri* (fig. **17–31**), painted about 1845, Bingham began an association with the newly formed American Art Union in New York. As a way to promote American painters, the Union purchased works for a flat fee, then reproduced prints of the paintings to be sold by subscription. *Fur Traders Descending the Missouri*, which Bingham sold to the Union for $25, is an idyllic scene of a French trapper and his son with their pet bear cub in a dugout canoe. As they glide through the early-morning stillness, the sun tinges the clouds with rosy gold and morning mists shroud the river landscape in mystery. Despite the peacefulness of the scene, there is an underlying ominous feeling. Branches and rocks stick out of

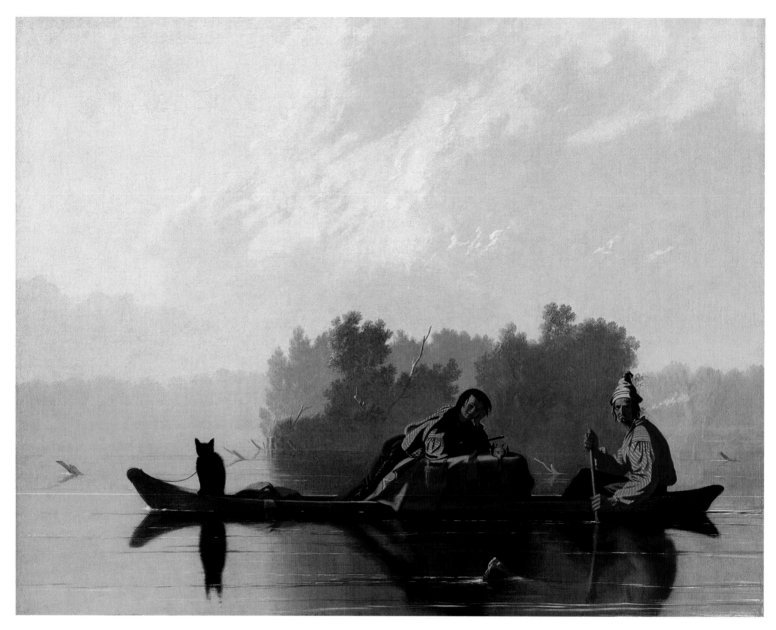

17–31 George Caleb Bingham. *Fur Traders Descending the Missouri.* c. 1845. Oil on canvas,
29″ × 36 ½″ (73.7 × 92.7 cm). The Metropolitan Museum of Art, New York

the water, reminders of the hazards the boatmen faced, and the mysterious black shape of the chained bear cub mirrored in the glassy water surface produces an eerie effect reminiscent of the demon in Fuseli's painting *The Nightmare.* Bingham's scene seems not only idealized but also nostalgic, for by the time it was painted the independent French voyageurs who had opened the fur trade using canoes had been replaced by trading companies using larger, more efficient craft. Bingham's painting records a vanished way of life and celebrates the early stages of commerce on the frontier.

Bingham's idyllic visions of life in the West appeared just as America's open spaces began to face threats from industrial development and urbanization. The Industrial Revolution, the flurry of technological progress and mechanization that began in Europe in the mid-eighteenth century, reached the United States by the early nineteenth century. A transcontinental railroad was completed in 1869, and by the 1890s the American frontier had all but disappeared. In the second half of the nineteenth century, both the United States and Europe would experience a new art and a new modern age.

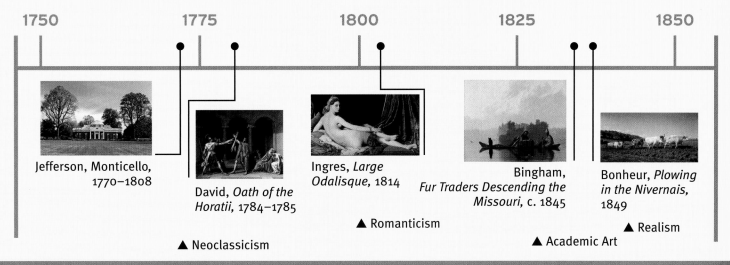

1750	1775	1800	1825	1850

Jefferson, Monticello, 1770–1808

David, *Oath of the Horatii*, 1784–1785

Ingres, *Large Odalisque*, 1814

Bingham, *Fur Traders Descending the Missouri*, c. 1845

Bonheur, *Plowing in the Nivernais*, 1849

▲ Romanticism

▲ Realism

▲ Neoclassicism

▲ Academic Art

L O O K I N G   B A C K

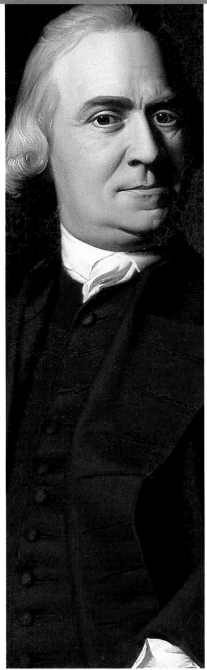

The eighteenth century marks a great divide in Western history. When the century opened, wealthy aristocrats owned or controlled the land worked by the largest and poorest class, the farmers. By the end of the century, the situation had changed dramatically. A new source of wealth—industrial manufacturing—created an expanded affluent middle class and powerful entrepreneurs. This Industrial Revolution provided better living conditions for the middle class but suffering for many poorer families. A new philosophy that conceived of all white men (some "radical" thinkers included women and other races) as deserving of equal rights and opportunities spurred a revolution in politics. And both rapid urbanization and mass migration of workers seeking better economic opportunities disrupted the old order.

Developments in politics and economics were themselves manifestations of a broader philosophical revolution known as the Enlightenment. Early-eighteenth-century thinkers generally held the optimistic view that humanity and its institutions could be reformed, if not perfected. Rejecting conventional notions that men and women were here to serve God or the ruling class, philosophers insisted that humans were born to serve themselves, to pursue their own happiness and fulfillment. By the nineteenth century, such idealism had been challenged by the rise of capitalist societies. Socialists condemned the exploitation of workers, and radical communists called for the abolition of private property.

Four artistic styles prevailed during the period: Rococo, Neoclassicism, Romanticism, and Realism. The Neoclassical style arose in reaction to the dominant Rococo style of the early eighteenth century (see Chapter 14). Neoclassical artists presented mythological or historical subjects in a style derived from classical sources. In its didactic manifestations, Neoclassicism was an important means for conveying Enlightenment ideals. Romanticism represented a continuation of the elements of Neoclassicism. While the terms Rococo and Neoclassicism identify distinct artistic styles—the one complex and sensuous, the other simple and restrained—Romanticism describes not only a style but also an attitude. Romanticism is chiefly concerned with imagination and the emotions, and it is often understood as a reaction against the Enlightenment focus on rationality. Romanticism celebrates the individual and the subjective rather than the universal and the objective. Many works of art of the later eighteenth and early nineteenth centuries combined elements of both Neoclassicism and Romanticism. Realism, in turn, was a reaction against all three earlier styles. It favored the accurate portrayal of the natural world and grew out of a nineteenth-century belief in close observation and the supposed objectivity of the scientific method.

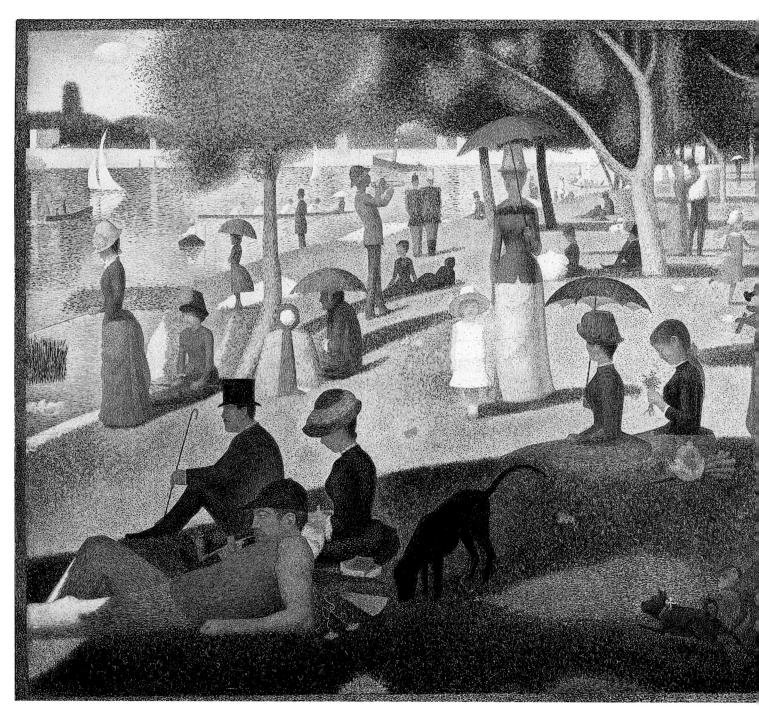

18–1 Georges Seurat. *A Sunday Afternoon on the Island of La Grande Jatte.*
1884–1886. Oil on canvas, 6′9 $\frac{1}{2}$″ × 10′1 $\frac{1}{4}$″ (2.07 × 3.08 m).
The Art Institute of Chicago

Later Nineteenth-Century Art in Europe and the United States

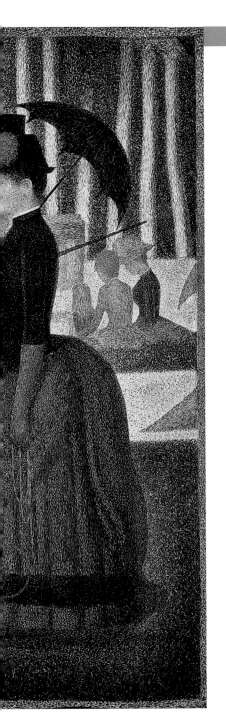

In his painted evocation *A Sunday Afternoon on the Island of La Grande Jatte*, Georges Seurat (1859–1891) took a typical Impressionist subject, weekend leisure activities, and gave it an entirely new interpretation (fig. **18–1**). An avid reader of scientific color theory, Seurat applied his paint in small dots of pure color in the belief that when they are "mixed" in the eye—as opposed to being mixed on the palette—the resulting colors would be more luminous. He used upward moving lines (seen in the angle of the coastline, a tree branch and elsewhere) and warm bright colors, since according to another theory current at the time these elements created "happy" paintings. During the months Seurat spent visiting the island, he studied the individuals he found there and also the way the light fell on the people and the landscape. Each character in the final painting—even the woman with the monkey—was based on detailed observations made at the original site.

The technique of painting that Seurat developed, known as pointillism, was an aspect of the Neo-Impressionist style—just one example of a variety of techniques and styles that became popular at the end of the nineteenth century in both Western Europe and the United States. These various styles—often consciously at odds with one another—are nevertheless grouped by writers and critics under a common label: "modernism."

In may ways modernism is an attitude, not a look. The process of making a work of art, including the materials and their handling, assumed an important role at this time, an approach that led to abstract and nonrepresentational art in the twentieth century. Some artists focused on self-expression, while other tried to suppress human feeling. Many artists saw the need to communicate deep-felt social concerns; at the same time others looked on the world with unbridled utopianism, often in direct counterpoint to the political and social crises of the age. Some artists saw the artwork as a unique experience in which the materials and process of painting, or carving, or printmaking were primary, and subject matter became almost irrelevant.

Surely Seurat's Parisians felt as much rain and cold as sun, and the popular island of La Grand Jatte must have been littered with picnic refuse by the time the crowds left on Sunday. But in his painting, Seurat makes it seem an island of perpetual tranquility and a place to escape from messy worldly problems. It is a perfect lazy day, and that feeling of relaxation is conveyed through the vivid warm colors and a composition of horizontals and verticals receding gently into the background. Is Seurat presenting his vision of an ideal society in his carefully calculated and formal representation of people in a sunny landscape? Or is he simply engaged in an intellectual exercise in the method of painting?

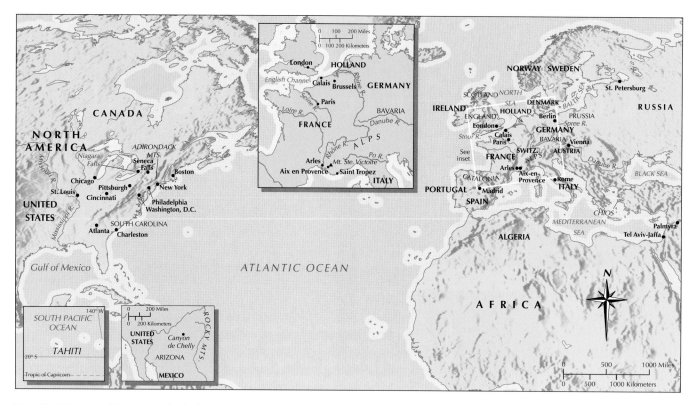

Map 18–1 Europe and North America in the Late Nineteenth Century

The Enlightenment set in motion powerful forces that would dramatically transform life in Europe and the United States during the nineteenth century (see Map 18–1, above). Great advances in manufacturing, transportation, and communications created new products for consumers and new wealth for entrepreneurs, fueling the rise of urban centers and improving living conditions for many. Animating these developments was the widespread belief in "progress" and the ultimate perfectibility of human civilization—a belief rooted deeply in Enlightenment thought. But this so-called Industrial Revolution also condemned masses of workers to poverty and catalyzed new political movements that sought to reform society.

Technological developments in agriculture and manufacturing displaced many owners of small farms and cottage industries—as well as their employees—forcing people to move to new factory and mining towns in search of employment. Increasing numbres of industrial laborers suffered miserable working and living conditions. Socialist movements, in turn, condemned the exploitation of laborers by capitalist factory owners and advocated communal or state ownership of the means of production and distribution. The most radical of these movements was Communism, which called for the abolition of private property. In 1848 Karl Marx and Friedrich Engels published the *Communist Manifesto*, which predicted the violent overthrow of the property-holding bourgeoisie (middle class) by the proletariat (working class) and the creation of a classless society.

Also in 1848, the Americans Lucretia Mott and Elizabeth Cady Stanton held the country's first women's rights convention, in Seneca Falls, New York. In their fight to improve the status of women, they called for the equality of women and men before the law, property rights for married women, the acceptance of women into institutions of higher education, the admission of women to all trades and professions, equal pay for equal work, and women's suffrage (achieved only in 1920).

American suffragists were also active in the abolitionist movement, which sought to end slavery, but slavery in the United States was only finally eliminated as a result of the devastating Civil War (1861–1865). After this battle between the states, the United States became a major industrial power, and the American Northeast underwent rapid urbanization, fueled by millions of immigrants from Europe seeking economic opportunities.

The second half of the nineteenth century has been called the "positivist age," an age of faith in the positive consequences of close observation of the natural world and validation through scientific inquiry. Some scientific discoveries of the time challenged traditional religious beliefs and affected social philosophy. Contrary to the biblical account of creation, Charles

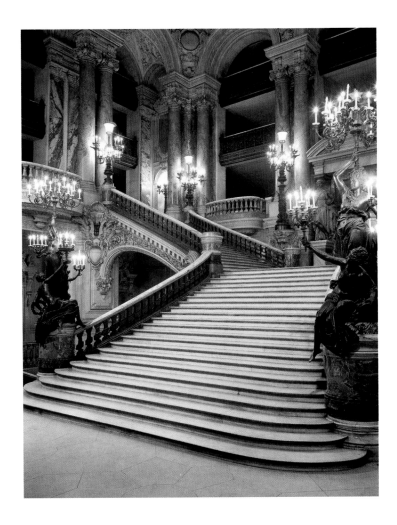

18–2 Charles Garnier. Opera, Grand Staircase. Paris. 1861–1874

The bronze figures holding the lights on the staircase are by Marcello, the pseudonym used by Adele d'Affry, the duchess Castiglione Colonna (1836–1879), as a precaution against the male chauvinism of the contemporary art world.

Darwin proposed that all life evolved from a common ancestor and changed through genetic mutation and natural selection, so that the best-adapted species survive while others become extinct. Religious conservatives attacked Darwin's account of evolution, which treated the human being as just another natural animal and thus seemed to deny the divine creation of humans and even the existence of God. The scientific method—observe and collect evidence, analyze and evaluate data, propose and test hypotheses, and only then accept or reject the results—describes the approach of many artists just as aptly as it characterizes the orientation of scientists and leaders of business and industry.

In the visual arts, the positivist spirit may be most obvious in the widespread rejection of Romanticism in favor of the accurate and apparently objective description of the ordinary, observable world. Positivist thinking is evident in the full range of artistic developments of the period after 1850—from photography, capable of recording nature with unprecedented accuracy, to the highly descriptive style of academic art, to Impressionism's quasi-scientific emphasis on the optical properties of light and color. In architecture, the application of new technologies also led gradually to the abandonment of historical styles and ornamentation in favor of allowing the basic structures and materials themselves to more directly or "realistically" express a designer's intentions.

The late-nineteenth-century emphasis on realism did not go unchallenged, however, as artists in both Europe and the United States turned to radically new abstract art forms to express their personal feelings about their subjects or to evoke states of mystery or spirituality. Like the Romantic artists before them, they shunned the depiction of ordinary, modern life in favor of exploring the realms of myth, fantasy, and imagination.

Architecture

Major works of public architecture in the nineteenth century tended to be based on historic models—a practice called **historicism**, which is the application of decorative motifs and styles from the past. The conventions of historicism were taught at the architecture school of the École des Beaux-Arts (School of Fine Arts) in Paris, an important training ground for European and American architects.

The Paris Opera House (fig. **18–2**), designed by Charles Garnier (1825–1898), resembles no recognizable historical style. Garnier called it "Napoleon III" after France's current political leader, although "neo-Baroque" might be an equally suitable name. Opulent ornamentation, in conjunction with the building's primary function as a place of entertainment, was intended to celebrate the devotion to wealth and pleasure that characterized the period. Heavy, gilded decoration, neo-Baroque sculpture, and a

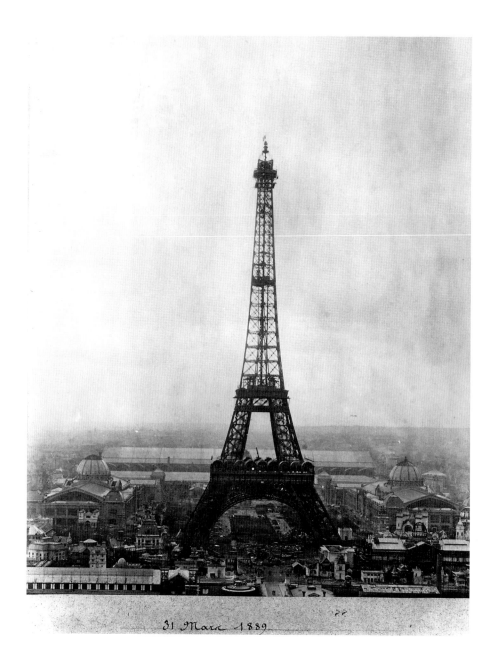

18–3 Gustave Eiffel. Eiffel Tower, Paris. 1887–1889. Height 984′ (300 m)

The Eiffel Tower embodies the nineteenth-century belief in progress through science and technology. The exposed structure creates a new kind of beauty derived from modern engineering rather than traditional architectural forms. The tower became a symbol of technological innovation and human aspiration.

lavish mix of expensive, polychrome materials cover the interior, and—the highlight of the interior was not so much the spectacle on-stage as the one on the great, sweeping Baroque staircase, where members of the Paris elite—from old nobility to newly wealthy industrialists—could display themselves. As Garnier himself said, the purpose of the Opera was to fulfill the most basic of human desires: to hear, to see, and to be seen.

While historicism and revival styles were popular, modern conditions and materials had an increasing impact on construc-tion. Building techniques introduced in the late eighteenth and first half of the nineteenth centuries ultimately led to an empha-sis on structure and the abandonment of dependence on historic styles. It was engineers rather than architects who had pioneered the use of the most important new building materials: cast iron, wrought iron, and steel. (In England in 1776–1779, Abraham Darby III had built the first cast-iron bridge at an industrial site known as Coalbrookdale.) The skeletal structure desired by builders since the twelfth century was at last possible, enabling

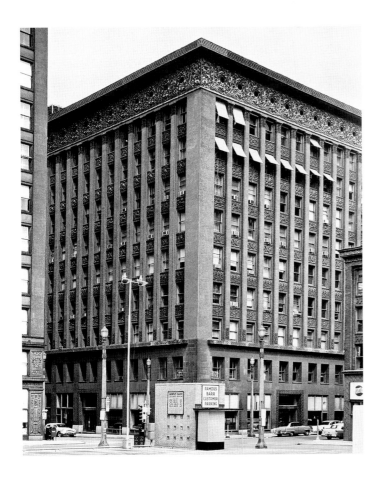

18–4 Louis Sullivan. Wainwright Building. St. Louis, Missouri. 1890–1891

the qualities of light, space, and movement to be incorporated into building designs.

The Eiffel Tower dominated the skyline of the new Paris as the towers of Notre-Dame, had the old (fig. **18–3**). Gustave Eiffel (1832–1923), a civil engineer, built his famous tower for the Paris Universal Exposition of 1889. He won a competition for the design of a monument that would symbolize French industrial progress. Composed of iron latticework, the tower stands on four huge legs reinforced by trussed (braced) arches similar to those used in railway bridges. Passenger elevators allowed fairgoers to ascend to the top of what was then, at 300 meters (984 feet), the tallest structure in the world. The French public loved the tower, but most architects, artists, and writers found it completely lacking in beauty—"monstrous," "ugly," and "useless" were but a few of the words they used to describe it. They dolefully predicted that it would have a brutalizing effect on the future of architecture in Paris. (One response to this concern was the birth of Art Nouveau, a style stressing flowing curves and organic forms that attempted to be modern without losing a preindustrial sense of beauty. See page 499.)

Iron-framed buildings, however, have a fatal susceptibility to fire. Exposed to intense heat, iron will warp, buckle, collapse, or melt altogether. The immediate solution was to encase the internal iron supports in fireproof materials and return to masonry sheathing. In the early 1860s, the perfection of a technique for making inexpensive steel (an alloy of iron and carbon that is stronger and lighter than pure iron) introduced new architectural possibilities. Steel's light weight combined with strength made taller buildings feasible, as did the introduction of passenger elevators, the first of which was installed in the United States in 1857.

Steel was first used for buildings in 1884 by young Midwestern architects who are now grouped under the label "the Chicago School." Equipped with the new technologies and eager to escape from Beaux-Arts historicism, the Chicago School architects produced a new kind of building: the skyscraper. An early example of their work, and evidence of its rapid spread throughout the Midwest, is the Wainwright Building in St. Louis, Missouri (fig. **18–4**), built by Louis Sullivan (1856–1924). Sullivan adapted the formal vocabulary and basic compositional rules of the Beaux-Arts tradition, dividing the ten-story office building into three parts—base, body, and crowning cornice—but he gave the building an entirely new vertical emphasis. The Wainwright Building is taller than it is wide, and its vertical elements emphasize this; corner piers rise in uninterrupted lines to the cornice, their verticality echoed and reinforced between the windows by small piers, designed to suggest the steel framing beneath them. The Chicago School had found an American alternative to the Beaux-Arts tradition—an end to historicism and the invention of a new architectural style appropriate to the modern age.

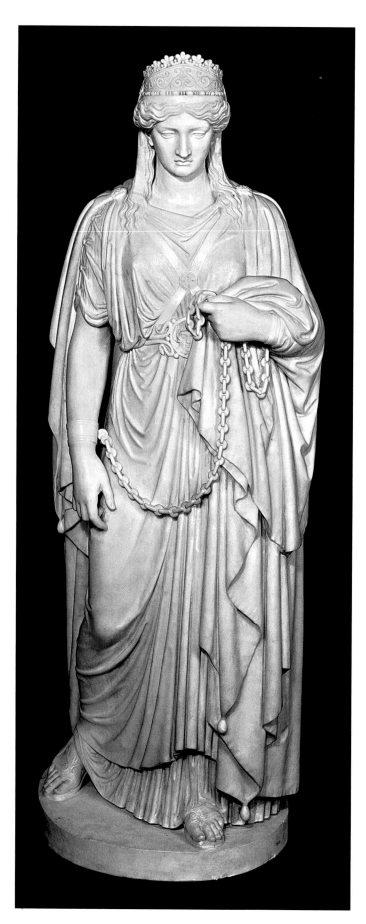

18–5 Harriet Hosmer. *Zenobia in Chains.* 1859. Marble, height 4′ (1.21 m).
Wadsworth Atheneum, Hartford, Connecticut

GIFT OF MRS. JOSEPHINE M. J. DODGE

Academic Art

Historicism in nineteenth-century architecture had its counterpart in academic art: painting and sculpture that followed the conservative principles of the French Academy, which continued to exert enormous influence over artistic matters. Students at the École des Beaux-Arts and other academic institutions began their training by copying prints and plaster casts of classical and Renaissance sculpture; then they studied live models posed like classical sculpture. When, in the opinion of their teachers, they had developed sufficient technical skill and detailed knowledge of the human form to make actual paintings or works of sculpture, they were expected to recall their earlier immersion in classical art and "correct" ordinary nature to conform to classicism's higher ideal.

As a sequel to study at the Academy, or sometimes as an alternative to it, young artists, and sculptors in particular, often visited or settled in Italy. Italy remained the wellspring of inspiration for artists (and for sculptors it was also the source of the materials and skilled workers needed to work the white marble, the material associated with classical sculpture). By the second half of the nineteenth century bustling artists' colonies in Rome and Florence even included women, whom the American author Henry James dubbed the "white, marmorean [marble] flock."

The most prominent of these women, Harriet Hosmer (1830–1908), had moved to Rome in 1852. Hosmer rapidly mastered the Neoclassical mode and began producing major exhibition pieces such as *Zenobia in Chains* (fig. **18–5**). Neoclassical in form but Romantic in content, the sculpture represents an exotic historical subject calculated to appeal to the viewer's emotions. Zenobia, the heroic third-century queen of Palmyra, was defeated by the Romans and forced to march through the streets of Rome in chains. Hosmer presents her as a noble figure, resolute even in defeat. "I have tried to make her too proud to exhibit passion or emotion of any kind," wrote Hosmer of Zenobia, "not subdued, though a prisoner; but calm, grand, and strong within herself." Zenobia embodies an ideal of womanhood strikingly modern in its defiance of Victorian conventions of female submissiveness.

Edmonia Lewis (c. 1845–after 1911) also moved to Rome to become a sculptor. Born in New York State to a Chippewa mother and an African-American father, Lewis was orphaned at the age of four and raised by her mother's people. With the help of abolitionists, she attended Oberlin College, the first college in the United States to grant degrees to women, and then moved to Boston. Her highly successful busts and medallions of abolitionist leaders and Civil War heroes financed her move to Rome in 1867, where she was welcomed into Hosmer's circle.

In Rome, Lewis continued to dedicate herself to the causes of human freedom, especially those involving women: "I have a strong sympathy for all women who have struggled and suffered," she said. *Hagar in the Wilderness* (fig. **18–6**), for example, tells the story of the Egyptian concubine of the biblical patriarch Abraham, given to him by his childless wife, Sarah, so that he might have a son. Hagar bore a son, Ishmael, but later the elderly Sarah also bore a son, Isaac. The jealous Sarah demanded that Abraham abandon Hagar and Ishmael and drive them out into

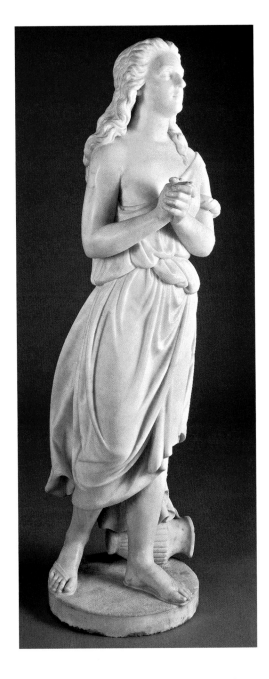

18–6 Edmonia Lewis. *Hagar in the Wilderness.* 1875.
Marble, $52\frac{5}{8}'' \times 15\frac{1}{4}'' \times 17''$ (133.6 × 38.7 × 43.2 cm).
Smithsonian American Museum, Smithsonian Institution,
Washington, D.C.

the wilderness. When Hagar and Ishmael were dying from thirst in the desert, an angel provided water (Genesis 16:1–16; 21:9–21). Because of Hagar's African origins, the story represented for Lewis the plight and the hope of her entire race.

Naturalism

Neoclassical idealism remained a powerful force in both sculpture and painting well into the nineteenth century, but a new taste for descriptive accuracy was gradually emerging that reflected the positivist values of the times. Photography, with the camera's extraordinary ability to create an accurate record, may also have contributed to this shift in taste. The bankers and businesspeople who came to dominate European and North American society and politics in the years in the second half of the nineteenth century were, as patrons, generally less interested in art that idealized than in art that brought the ideal down to earth.

And although the national academies throughout Europe continued to control both the teaching and the display of art, increasing numbers of artists rejected their precepts in favor of the naturalist credo that art should faithfully record ordinary life. Soon even the national academies embraced this new desire for highly detailed depiction of physical forms, and, by the 1860s, the terms *Realism* and *naturalism* had lost their socialist political meanings (see page 482). Even painters who treated subjects remote from contemporary life showed a growing interest in realistic detail. With a reporter's concern for the facts, Sir Lawrence Alma-Tadema (1836–1912) carefully researched Greek history and archaeology for his 1868 painting, *Phidias and the Frieze of the Parthenon, Athens* (see Intro fig. 26), even recording the color applied to the sculpture frieze in defiance of earlier Neoclassical artists' delight in pure white marble. Compared with Neoclassical artists such as Jacques-Louis David (see fig. 17–12), Sir Lawrence and his contemporaries began to think of history as a set of objective facts rather than as something from which to learn moral lessons.

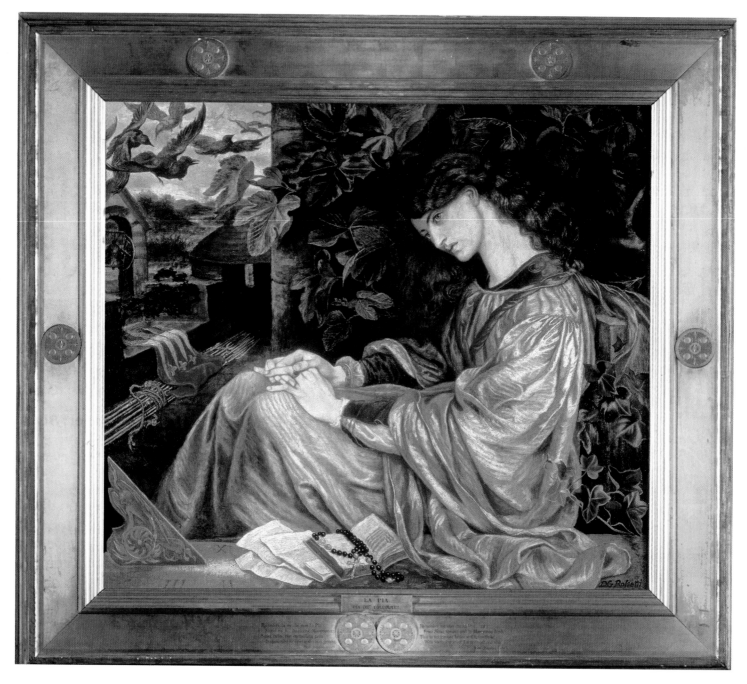

18–7 Dante Gabriel Rossetti. *La Pia de' Tolomei.* 1868–1869. Oil on canvas,
41 ½″ × 47 ½″ (105.4 × 119.4 cm). Spencer Museum of Art, The University of Kansas, Lawrence

In addition to his work as a painter and poet, Rossetti created innovative and beautiful designs for picture frames, book bindings, wallpaper, and furniture, as well as architectural sculpture and stained glass. The gilded frames he designed for his pictures were intended to enhance their decorative effect and make their meaning clearer through inscriptions and symbols. The massive frame surrounding La Pia de' Tolomei *features simple moldings on either side of broad, sloping boards, into which are set a few large roundels. The title of the painting is inscribed above the paired roundels at the lower center. On either side of them appear four lines from Dante's* Purgatory *spoken by the spirit of La Pia, in Italian at the left and in Rossetti's English translation at the right, which reads: "Remember me who am La Pia,—me/From Siena sprung and by Maremma dead./This in his inmost heart well knoweth he/With whose fair jewel I was ringed and wed."*

Reactions Against the Academy

In England, reaction against academic art began building at mid-century. Even young artists formed the Pre-Raphaelite Brotherhood in 1848 to counter what they considered the misguided practices of contemporary British art. Instead of the idealized Raphaelesque conventions taught at the Royal Academy, they advocated the naturalistic, descriptive approach to the human body and to nature used by earlier Northern Renaissance masters. They also advocated moralizing subject matter in keeping with a long tradition in Britain, exemplified by Hogarth (see fig. 17–6), and they filled their paintings with the type of symbolism found in medieval art.

Dante Gabriel Rossetti (1828–1882), a leading member of the Pre-Raphaelite Brotherhood, looked to the Middle Ages for a spiritual beauty and meaning he found lacking in his own time. His painting *La Pia de' Tolomei* (fig. **18–7**) had personal relevance for the artist while at the same time illustrating a story from Dante's *Purgatory*. La Pia (the Pious One), wrongly accused of infidelity and locked up by her husband in a castle, is dying. The rosary and prayer book at her side refer to the piety from which she takes her name, while the sundial and ravens apparently allude to passing time and her impending death. La Pia's continuing love for her husband, whose letters lie under her prayer book, is also symbolized by the evergreen ivy behind her. The painting is not simply an idealized transcription of a text however; the luxuriant fig leaves that surround the figure are traditionally associated with lust and the Fall of Man and have no source in Dante's tale. Jane Burden, who was Rossetti's model for this and many other paintings, was the wife of Rossetti's friend William Morris, but she had become Rossetti's lover. Note that La Pia (Jane) fingers her wedding ring, a captive not so much of her husband as of her marriage. Thus the subject of the painting is also a metaphor for Rossetti's own unhappy situation.

William Morris (1834–1896) was less interested in painting than in design. His interest developed in the context of a widespread reaction against gaudy and shoddy industrially produced goods, and he intended to provide a handcrafted alternative to them. After marrying Jane Burden in 1859, Morris set out to decorate their new home. Unable to find satisfactory furnishings, Morris, with the help of some friends, designed and made the furniture himself. He then founded a decorating firm to produce a full range of medieval-inspired pieces. Although many of the furnishings offered by Morris & Company were expensive, one-of-a-kind items, others, such as the rush-seated chair illustrated here (fig. **18–8**), were relatively inexpensive. Concerned with creating a "total" environment in which architecture and décor were styled in harmony, Morris and his colleagues designed not only furniture but also stained glass, tiles, wallpaper, and fabrics such as the Peacock and Dragon curtain seen behind the Sussex chair in figure 18–8.

A socialist, Morris saw the pre-industrial era as a model for both economic and social reform, and he recognized a wholesome social component in the skilled craftwork needed to produce handcrafts. He sought to eliminate industrialization not

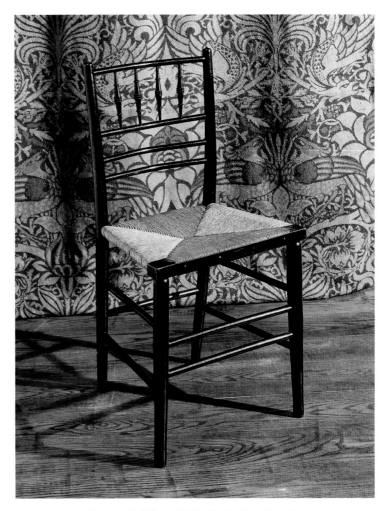

18–8 *(foreground in photo)* **Philip Webb (?). Single chair from the Sussex range.** In production from c. 1865. Ebonized wood with rush seat, $32\frac{5}{8}'' \times 19\frac{3}{8}''$ (83.8 × 35.6 cm). Manufactured by Morris & Company. William Morris Gallery (London Borough of Waltham Forest)

(background) **William Morris. Peacock and Dragon curtain.** 1878. Handloomed jacquard-woven woolen twill, $12'10\frac{1}{2}'' \times 11'5\frac{1}{8}''$ (3.96 × 3.53 m). Manufactured at Queen Square and later at Merton Abbey. Victoria and Albert Museum, London

Morris and his principal furniture designer, Philip Webb (1831–1915), adapted the Sussex range from traditional rush-seated chairs of the Sussex region. The handwoven curtain in the background is typical of Morris's fabric designs in its use of flat patterning that affirms the two-dimensional character of the textile medium. The pattern's prolific organic motifs and soothing blue and green hues—the decorative counterpart to those of naturalistic landscape painting—were meant to provide relief from the stresses of modern urban existence.

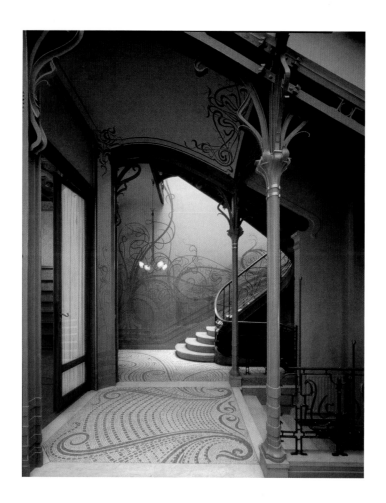

18–9 Victor Horta. Stairway, Tassel House, Brussels. 1892–1893

only because he found factory-made products ugly but also because of mass production's deadening influence on the worker. Thus his aim was to benefit not just a few wealthy clients but all of society. With craftwork, he maintained, the laborer would acquire as much satisfaction from creating a fine piece as the consumer did using it. Morris's work and ideas inspired what became known as the Arts and Crafts Movement.

Not all those who participated in the revival of the decorative arts were motivated by a commitment to improving the conditions of modern life. Many, including the American expatriate James Abbott McNeill Whistler (1834–1903), simply saw the Arts and Crafts revival as a means to satisfy a taste for beauty and beautiful things. Whistler had been one of the first to collect Japanese art when it became available in curio shops in London and Paris after the 1853 reopening of that nation to the West. The new vogue for Japanese art had fueled in him a growing dissatisfaction with naturalism, and in 1859 he moved from Paris to London, in part to distance himself from artists such as Gustave Courbet.

The simplified, elegant forms and subtle chromatic harmonies of Japanese art (see Chapter 9) had a profound influence on Whistler's art. In 1864 he exhibited three paintings that signaled this new direction. One of them, *Rose and Silver: The Princess from the Land of Porcelain* (see Intro fig. 24, left wall), shows a Caucasian woman dressed in a Japanese robe and posed amid a collection of Asian artifacts. The work is Whistler's answer to the medieval costume pieces of the Pre-Raphaelites.

As the work's title—*Rose and Silver*—declares, Whistler attempted to create a formal, coloristic harmony. Thus, delicate organic shapes are shown against a rich orchestration of colors featuring silver and rose. By leaving his wet brushmarks visible, Whistler emphasized the paint itself over the depicted subject. Whistler's growing commitment to "art for art's sake," or an art of purely aesthetic values, culminated in the dining room decoration he called *Harmony in Blue and Gold: The Peacock Room*, a showcase of his painting *Rose and Silver*.

Art Nouveau

Whistler's commitment to "art for art's sake" anticipated a popular style known as Art Nouveau (New Art). The practitioners of Art Nouveau such as Victor Horta (fig. **18–9**) rejected the values of modern industrial society and sought new aesthetic forms that would recapture a pre-industrial sense of beauty. Their ideas and style permeated all aspects of European art at the end of the nineteenth century. They applied fluid linear arabesques and organic forms to all aspects of design, drawing inspiration from ancient Celtic art and from nature—vines, snakes, flowers, and winged insects—whose delicate and sinuous forms were the basis of their graceful and attenuated linear designs. Following from this commitment to organic principles, they also sought to harmonize all aspects of design into a beautiful whole, as found in nature itself. In Italy this movement was known as *Stile Floreale* (Floral Style) and *Stile Liberty* (after the Liberty department store in London); in Germany and Austria, as *Jugendstil* (Youth Style); in Spain, as *modernista* (modernist); in France it had a number of names, including *moderne*. The name most used today came from a shop, La Maison de l'Art Nouveau (The House of New Art), which opened in Paris in 1895.

A leader in the Art Nouveau style of the 1890s was a Belgian architect, Victor Horta (1861–1947). In 1892 Horta received his first independent commission, to design Tassel House, a private residence in Brussels. The result, especially the house's entry hall and staircase, was strikingly original. Horta laid out the wall decoration, floor tile, and ironwork (used instead of stone or wood) in an intricate series of long, graceful curves to integrate interior design and architecture into an exquisite and unified whole.

Almost ten years before Horta's decorative ironwork at the Tassel House in Brussels, the Catalan architect Antoní Gaudí (1852–1926) was creating spectacular examples of Art Nouveau in Barcelona. Unlike his contemporaries, Gaudí attempted to introduce the organic principle into the very structure of his buildings. Much of his work, such as his residential complexes and churches in Spain, reflects his concern for integrating natural forms into daily life and for combining architecture, sculpture, and craft arts. In Güell Park *(Parc Güell)*, the ideal community he designed on the outskirts of Barcelona, a continuous, serpentine bench serves as a boundary wall for the public plaza (fig. **18–10**). Like a strange flowering vine, the surface of the bench-wall glitters with a mosaic of broken pottery and tiles in homage to the long tradition of Moorish ceramic art in Spain. This is a national as well as a personal alternative to academic historicism and modern industrialization, reflecting Gaudí's affinity for the Iberian traditions as well as his concern for organic and harmonious surroundings.

Art in the United States

In the United States, in contrast to the late Neoclassicism prevalent in sculpture, factual naturalism had an unbroken tradition in painting stretching back to Colonial portrait painters

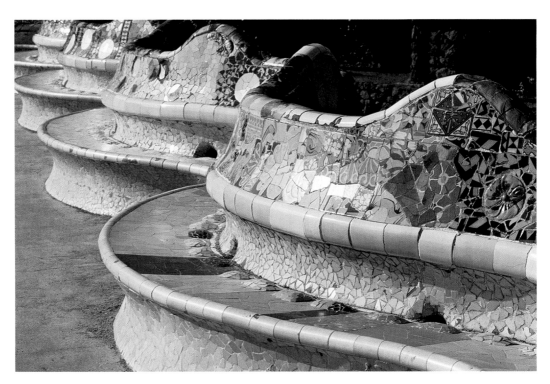

18–10 Antoní Gaudí. *Serpentine bench,* Güell Park, Barcelona. 1900–1914

(see fig. 17–1). The advocates of realism had long considered it distinctly American and democratic, and the Civil War (1861–1865) brought increasing attention to that most naturalistic of media—photography. The work of photographers came to public attention when Mathew B. Brady (1823–1896) gained permission from government officials to take a team and a darkroom wagon to the field of battle. Among his assistants was Timothy O'Sullivan (1840–1882), whose photographs of Western landscapes rival the finest paintings.

O'Sullivan (1840–1882) accompanied Western survey expeditions to make what were ostensibly documentary photographs; however, images like *Ancient Ruins in the Cañon de Chelley, Arizona* (fig. **18–11**) are infused with a Romantic sense of awe before the grandeur of nature. The 700-foot canyon wall fills the composition, giving the viewer no clear vantage point

and scant visual relief. The bright, raking sunlight across the rock face reveals little but the cracks and striations formed over eons. The image suggests not only the immensity of geological time but also humanity's insignificant place within it. Like the classical ruins that were a popular theme in European Romantic art and poetry, the Native American ruins suggest the inevitable passing of all civilizations. The four puny humans on the left, standing in this majestic yet barren place, reinforce the theme of human futility and insignificance, and the overall melancholic sensibility of the work may reflect the emotional impact of the Civil War.

Another artist who made his name recording the Civil War for the press was Winslow Homer (1836–1910). Homer believed that unadorned realism was the appropriate style for a democratic people. Prior to the war, Homer had produced illustrations

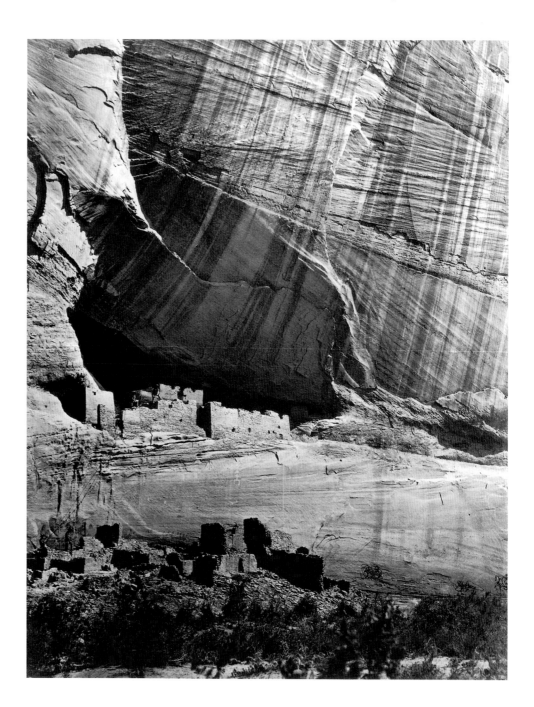

18–11 Timothy O'Sullivan. *Ancient Ruins in the Cañon de Chelley, Arizona.* 1873. Albumen print. National Archives, Washington, D.C.

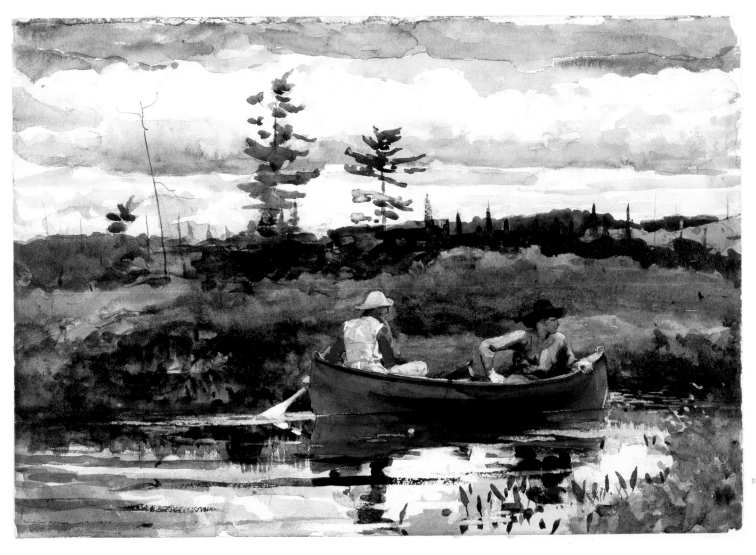

18–12 Winslow Homer. *The Blue Boat.* 1892. Watercolor over graphite, 15″ × 21 ½″ (38.5 × 54.7 cm). Museum of Fine Arts, Boston

for books as well as popular weekly magazines. In his role as both reporter and illustrator for *Harper's Weekly*, Homer produced works that are considered to be among the finest pictorial reporting of the Civil War. In 1866–1867 he spent ten months in France, where the naturalist art he saw may have inspired the rural subjects that he painted when he returned.

In the 1870s, Homer became a master of the difficult watercolor medium (fig **18–12**). In watercolor, pigments suspended in water are laid down with rapid, sure brushstrokes on white paper, and the image cannot be successfully corrected or reworked. Colors are almost translucent with whites, including highlights, produced by leaving the paper bare. Watercolor had become a popular medium for rapid sketching outdoors.

Homer used the medium to produce finished works of art that capture fleeting impressions of sparkling sunlight, wind-blown foliage, and water. His watercolors often have a great freshness and spontaneity, as well as a distinct luminosity and saturation of color.

The most uncompromising American naturalist of the era was Thomas Eakins (1844–1916). Following an academic training in Philadelphia and Paris, the artist spent six months in Spain, where he encountered the profound realism of Diego Velázquez (see fig. 14–11) and other seventeenth-century masters. After returning to Philadelphia in 1870, Eakins began painting frank portraits, often in everyday settings, whose lack of conventional charm generated little popular interest. One painting, *The Gross Clinic* (fig. **18–13**), did attract attention, but of a negative kind. It was severely criticized and was refused exhibition space at the 1876 Philadelphia Centennial. The large work shows Dr. Samuel David Gross performing an operation while young medical students look on. Beams of light highlight the representatives of science—a young medical student, the doctor, and his assistants. The light is not meant to stir emotions but to make a point: amid the darkness of ignorance and fear, modern science is the light of knowledge.

For a time, Eakins taught at the Pennsylvania Academy of Fine Arts. Among his students were women and African-Americans—both groups who were often excluded from art schools. One of his most brilliant pupils was Henry Ossawa Tanner (1859–1937) who, from 1879 to 1885, absorbed Eakins's lessons of truthful representation and focus on ordinary subjects. In 1891, after working as a photographer and teacher in Atlanta, Tanner moved to Paris where his painting received favorable critical attention. In the 1890s he painted scenes from African-Amer-

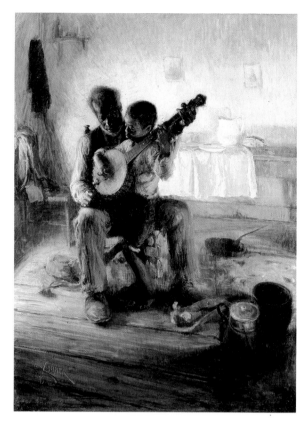

18–14 Henry O. Tanner. *The Banjo Lesson.* c. 1893. Oil on canvas, 48″ × 35″ (121.9 × 88.9 cm). Hampton University Museum, Hampton, Virginia

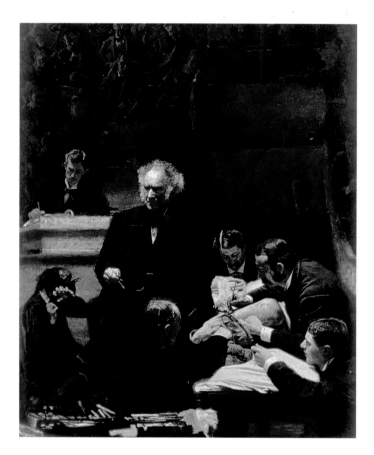

18–13 Thomas Eakins. *The Gross Clinic.* 1875. Oil on canvas, 8′ × 6′5″ (2.44 × 1.96 m). Jefferson Medical College of Thomas Jefferson University, Philadelphia

In the shadows along the right-hand side of The Gross Clinic, *Eakins included a self-portrait, testimony to his personal knowledge of the subject. Eakins had studied anatomy, an interest that led him to photography, which he used both as an aid for painting and as a tool for studying the body in motion.*

ican and rural French life in a style that combined the realism of Eakins with the delicate brushwork he had learned from the Impressionists. With strong sympathetic images like the *The Banjo Lesson* (fig. **18–14**), he hoped to counter the caricatures of African-American life created by other artists. Ultimately Tanner dedicated himself to biblical subjects, believing that art should serve religion.

Impressionism

By the mid-1860s the painter Édouard Manet (1832–1883) had become the unofficial leader of a group of progressive artists and writers who gathered at the Café Guerbois in the Montmartre district of Paris. These artists, who matured in the 1860s and 1870s, pushed the French Realist tradition into new territory. Instead of treating themes that had engaged Courbet and the Barbizon painters—the working classes and rural life—they generally painted the upper-middle class, the city, and leisure activities. And although many of them also painted the countryside, their point of view was usually that of a city person on holiday.

Among the artists who frequented the café were Claude Monet, Edgar Degas, and Pierre Auguste Renoir, who would soon exhibit together as the Impressionists. With the exception of Degas—who, like Manet, remained a studio painter—these artists began to paint outdoors, *en plein air* ("in the open air"), in an effort to record directly the fleeting effects of light and atmos-

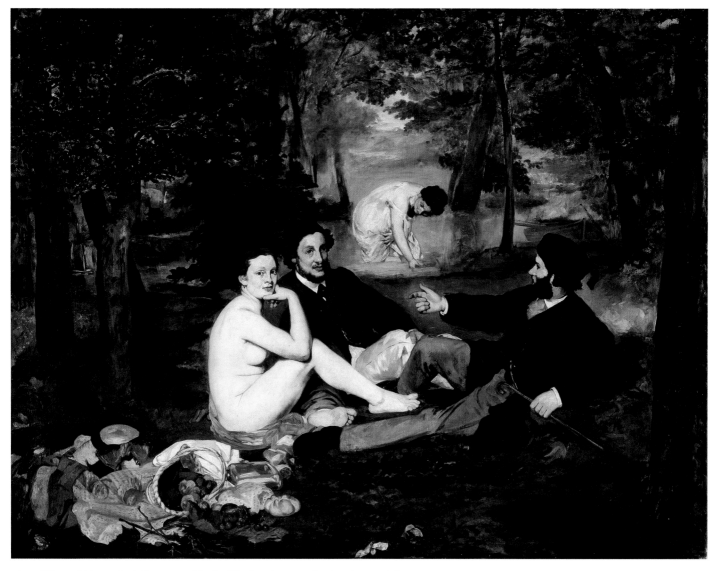

18–15 Édouard Manet. *Le Déjeuner sur l'herbe (The Luncheon on the Grass).* 1863. Oil on canvas,
7′ × 8′8″ (2.13 × 2.64 m). Musée d'Orsay, Paris

phere. (*Plein air* painting was greatly facilitated by the invention in 1841 of portable tin tubes filled with premixed oil paint.)

The poet Charles Baudelaire, a close friend of Manet, called for an artist to be the painter of contemporary manners, "the painter of the passing moment and of all the suggestions of eternity that it contains." Manet seems to have responded by painting *Le Déjeuner sur l'herbe (The Luncheon on the Grass)* (fig. **18–15**). When the jury for the official Salon of 1863 turned down nearly 3,000 works, including Manet's, a storm of protest erupted, prompting the French emperor Napoleon III to order an exhibition of the refused works called the Salon des Refusés (Salon of the Rejected Ones). In that exhibition, *Le Déjeuner sur l'herbe* provoked a critical avalanche that was a mixture of shock and bewilderment. Manet had ignored the basic tenets of academic painting. To a viewer used to traditional perspective and the rounded modeling of forms using gradations of shadow, the figures were jarring. Nor did critics understand why Manet had chosen the scandalous subject of well-dressed men relaxing

with scantily clad women, although the artist had thought that his basic intent would be fairly obvious to viewers. After all, he based his painting on the Venetian "Old Masters" like Titian (see fig. 13–15).

Today some critics see Manet as a painter of modern alienation; his figures are distant in both their physical and their psychological relationships. The man on the left in *Le Déjeuner sur l'herbe* gazes off absently while the nude turns her attention away from her companions and toward the viewer. Moreover, her gaze makes us conscious of our role as outside observers—we, too, are estranged. Manet's rejection of warm colors for a scheme of cool blues and greens plays an important role, as do his flat, sharply outlined figures, which seem starkly lit because of the near absence of modeling. The figures are not integrated with their natural surroundings, as in the paintings that inspired Manet, but seem to stand out sharply against them, as if they are cutouts seated before a painted backdrop (see "Artistic Allusions in Manet's Art," page 504).

ARTISTIC ALLUSIONS IN MANET'S ART

Manet had in his studio a copy of *The Pastoral Concert*, a work in the Louvre then attributed to Giorgione and now attributed to both Titian and Giorgione (see fig. 13–XX). Manet's *Le Dejeuner sur l'herbe* (see fig. 18–15) was clearly inspired by *The Pastoral Concert*, a modern reply to its theme of people at ease in nature. Manet also adapted for his composition a group of river gods and a nymph from an engraving by Marcantonio Raimondi based on Raphael's *Judgment of Paris*—an image that, in turn, looked back to classical reliefs (fig. **18–16**). Manet's allusion to the engraving was apparent to some observers at the time, such as the critic Ernest Chesneau, who specifically noted this borrowing and objected to it.

With its deliberate allusions to Renaissance artworks, Manet's painting addresses not just the subject of figures in a landscape. Manet surveys the history of art and Manet's relationship to it by encouraging the viewer to compare his painting with those that inspired it. To a viewer who has in mind the traditional perspective and the sculptural modeling of forms used in Renaissance works, the stark lighting of Manet's nude and the flat, cutout quality of his figures become all the more shocking. Thus, by openly referring to these exemplary works of the past, Manet emphasized his own radical innovations.

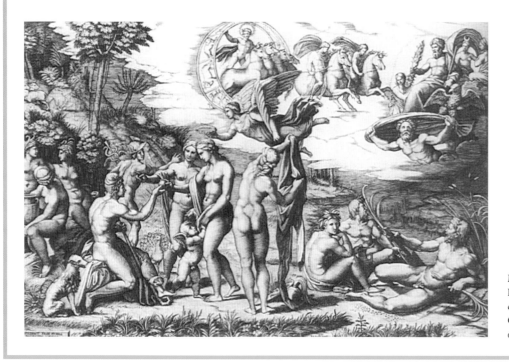

Marcantonio Raimondi, after Raphael's *The Judgment of Paris*. c.1520. Engraving. Yale University Art Gallery, New Haven

GIFT OF EDWARD B. GREENE, YALE 1990

Shortly after completing *Le Déjeuner sur l'herbe*, Manet painted *Olympia* (fig. **18–16**), whose title alluded to a socially ambitious prostitute of the same name in a novel and play by Alexandre Dumas *fils* (the son). Like *Le Déjeuner sur l'herbe*, *Olympia* was based on a painting by Titian (see fig. 13–17). At first glance, Manet appears to pay homage to the work's Venetian source in subject matter and composition; however, Manet has made his modern counterpart the very antithesis of Titian's Venus. Whereas Titian's woman is curvaceous and softly rounded, Manet's is angular and flattened. Whereas Venus looks lovingly at the male spectator, Olympia appears coldly indifferent. Manet has subverted the entire tradition of the accommodating female nude, for Olympia stares down on us, indicating that she is in the position of power. This relationship between viewer and subject is underscored by the reaction of the cat, who arches its back and seems to hiss. Not surprisingly, conservative critics heaped scorn on the painting when it was displayed at the Salon of 1865.

In April 1874, Monet, Degas, Renoir, Berthe Morisot, Paul Cézanne, and others exhibited together in Paris as the Société Anonyme des Artistes Peintres, Sculpteurs, Graveurs, etc. (Corporation of Artists Painters, Sculptors, Engravers, etc.), usually shortened to Société Anonyme. While the exhibition received some positive reviews, it was attacked by conservative critics. Louis Leroy, writing in the comic journal *Charivari*, seized on the title of a painting by Monet—*Impression, Sunrise* (1872) (fig. **18–17**)—and dubbed the entire exhibition *Impressionist*. While Leroy used the word to attack the paintings, Monet and many of his colleagues were pleased to accept the label, which spoke to their concern for capturing an instantaneous impression of a scene in nature. Seven more Impressionist exhibitions followed between 1876 and 1886, with the contributors varying slightly on each occasion. By the end of the century, these independent exhibitions effectively ended the French Academy's centuries-old stranglehold on the display of art and thus on the artistic standards associated with them.

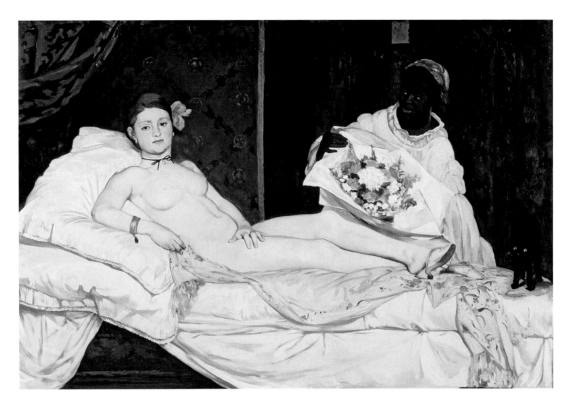

18–16 Édouard Manet. *Olympia.* 1863. Oil on canvas, 4′3″ × 6′2¼″ (1.31 × 1.91 m).
Musée du Louvre, Paris

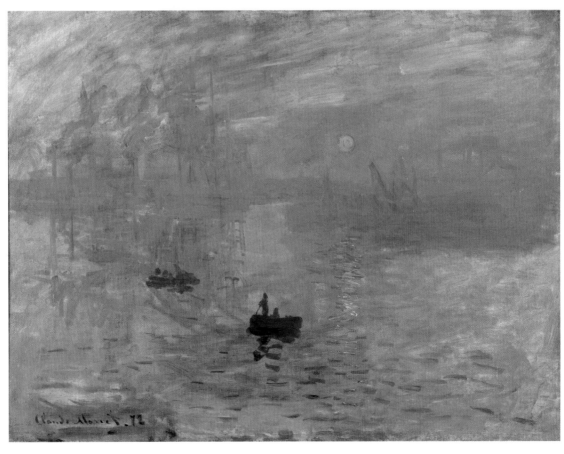

18–17 Claude Monet. *Impression, Sunrise.* 1872. Oil on canvas, 19½″ × 25½″ (49.5 × 64.7 cm).
Musée Marmottan, Paris, France

Claude Monet (1840–1926), after some early efforts at *plein air* painting near his family home along the Normandy coast, developed his own technique of painting with strokes and touches of pure color, intended to describe flowers, leaves, and waves, but also to register simply as marks of paint on the surface of the canvas. Monet's fully Impressionist pictures of the 1870s and 1880s—such as *Impression, Sunrise* and *Boulevard des Capucines, Paris* (fig. **18–18**)—are made up almost entirely of flecks of color (Leroy sneeringly called them "tongue-lickings"). Using these discrete marks of paint, Monet recorded the shifting play of light on the surface of objects and the effect of that light on the eye, rather than the physical character of the objects. His decision to paint the street scene from an upper window enabled him to combine the high vantage point that he admired in Japanese prints with the direct observation of life associated with Impressionism.

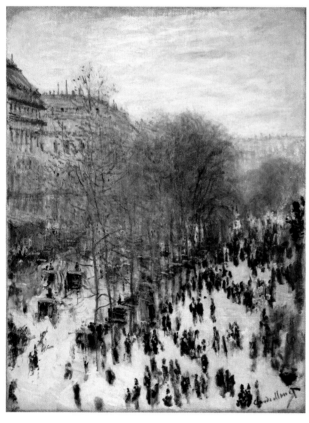

18–18 Claude Monet. *Boulevard des Capucines, Paris.* 1873–1874. Oil on canvas, 31 ¼″ × 23 ¼″ (79.4 × 59.1 cm). The Nelson-Atkins Museum of Art, Kansas City, Missouri

PURCHASE: THE KENNETH A. AND HELEN F. SPENCER FOUNDATION ACQUISITION FUND (F72–35).

Monet painted this picture from the balcony of Nadar's photography studio at 35 Boulevard des Capucines, the site of the first Impressionist exhibition. In an appreciative review, critic Ernest Chesnau wrote: "The extraordinary animation of the public street, the crowd swarming on the sidewalks, the carriages on the pavement, and the boulevard's trees waving in the dust and light—never has movement's elusive, fugitive, instantaneous quality been captured and fixed in all its tremendous fluidity as it has in this extraordinary, marvelous sketch."

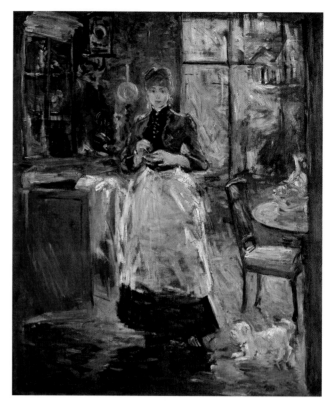

18–19 Berthe Morisot. *In the Dining Room.* 1886. Oil on canvas, 24 ⅛″ × 19 ¾″ (61.3 × 50.2 cm)

NATIONAL GALLERY OF ART, WASHINGTON, D.C., CHESTER DALE COLLECTION, 1963.10.185.(1849)/PA

The American painter Lilla Cabot Perry (1848–1933) recalled Monet telling her, "When you go out to paint, try to forget what objects you have before you—a tree, a house, a field, or whatever. Merely think, here is a little square of blue, here an oblong of pink, here a streak of yellow, and paint it just as it looks to you, the exact color and shape, until it gives your own naive impression of the scene before you." Two important ideas are expressed here. One is that a quickly painted oil sketch provides the most accurate record, a view that had been a part of academic training since the late eighteenth century. Sketches had been considered merely part of the preparation for the final work, and as a result, viewers did not see Monet's paintings as "finished." The second idea—that art benefits from a naive vision untainted by intellectual preconceptions—was a part of the naturalist and Realist traditions from which Monet's work evolved.

Monet's fellow Impressionist Berthe Morisot (1841–1895), who participated in seven of the Impressionists' eight exhibitions, had met Édouard Manet in 1868, and she married his brother, Eugene, in 1874. Unlike most women painters of the time who married—and gave up their art to devote themselves to domestic duties—Morisot continued painting after she wed, although she took as her subject the lives of bourgeois women. Her technique became increasingly loose and painterly over the course of the 1870s. In fact, her vigorous and varied brushwork in *In the Dining Room* (fig. **18–19**) calls attention to the act of painting itself. The palette of pastel colors and her lavish use of white are characteristic of her work. In her painting, Morisot sought an equality for women that she felt men refused to cede. Late in life she commented: "I don't think there has ever been a man who treated a

JAPONISME

A fascination with Japan and its culture swept across the West in the last half of the nineteenth century. The vogue began shortly after the U.S. Navy forcibly opened Japan to Western trade and diplomacy in 1853. Soon, Japanese lacquers, fans, bronzes, hanging scrolls, kimonos, ceramics, illustrated books, and *ukiyo-e* (prints of the "floating world," the realm of geishas and popular entertainment) began to appear in western European specialty shops, art galleries, and even some department stores. French interest in Japan and its arts reached such proportions by 1872 that the art critic Philippe Burty gave this enthusiasm a name: **japonisme**.

Japanese art (see Chapter 9) profoundly influenced Western painting, printmaking, applied arts, and eventually architecture. The tendency toward simplicity, flatness, and the decorative evident in much painting and graphic art in the West between roughly 1860 and 1900 is probably the most characteristic result of that influence. Nevertheless, its impact was extraordinarily diverse. What individual artists took from the Japanese depended on their own interests. Thus, Whistler found encouragement for his decorative conception of art, while Edgar Degas discovered both realistic subjects and interesting compositional arrangements (see fig. 18–20), and those interested in the reform of late-nineteenth-century industrial design found in Japanese objects both fine craft and a smooth elegance lacking in the West. Some artists, including Vincent van Gogh, saw in the spare harmony of Japanese art evidence of an idyllic society, which he considered a model for the West.

woman as an equal, and that's all I would have asked, for I know I'm worth as much as they" (Higonnet, page 19).

Unlike Morisot, not all the painters who are grouped with the Impressionists (because they participated in some or all of the exhibitions organized by Monet and his friends) truly worked in an Impressionist style. The artist whose work most severely tests the Impressionist label is Edgar Degas (1834–1917). His friendship with Manet, whom he met in 1862, and with the Realist critics in his circle, led him gradually toward the depiction of contemporary life. After a period of painting psychologically probing portraits of friends and relatives, Degas turned in the

1870s to such Paris amusements as the music hall, opera, ballet, circus, and racetrack. Degas began to think of art less as a mirror held up to the world than as a lofty form of entertainment that employed realistic elements.

Degas was especially drawn to the ballet. From carefully observed studies of rehearsals and performances, he arranged his own visual choreography. *The Rehearsal of the Ballet on Stage* (fig. **18–20**) is not a factual record of something seen but a careful composition, inspired partly by Japanese prints, intended to delight the eye (see "Japonisme," above). The rehearsal is viewed as if from an opera box close to the stage, creating an abrupt

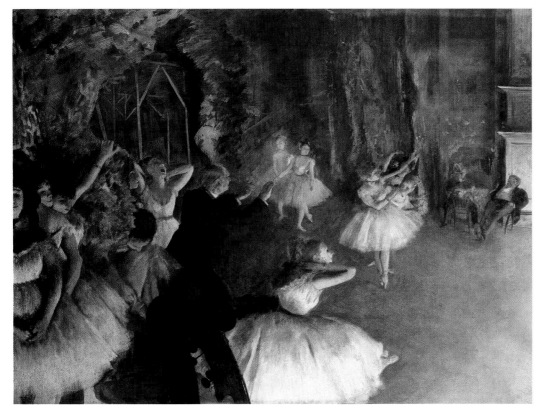

18–20 Edgar Degas. *The Rehearsal of the Ballet on Stage.* c. 1874. Pastel over brush-and-ink drawing on thin, cream-colored wove paper, laid on bristol board, mounted on canvas, 21″ × 28½″ (53.3 × 72.3 cm). The Metropolitan Museum of Art, New York

BEQUEST OF MRS. H. O. HAVEMEYER COLLECTION, GIFT OF HORACE HAVEMEYER, 1929 (29.160.26).

In the right background of Degas's picture sit two well-dressed, middle-aged men, each probably a "protector" of one of the dancers. Because ballerinas generally came from lower-class families and exhibited their scantily clad bodies in public—something that "respectable" bourgeois women did not do—they were widely assumed to be sexually available, and they often attracted the attentions of wealthy men willing to support them in exchange for sexual favors. Several of Degas's ballet pictures include one or more of the dancers' mothers, who would accompany their daughters to rehearsals and performances in order to safeguard their virtue.

foreshortening of the scene emphasized by the dark scroll of the bass viol that juts up from the lower left.

It could be argued, based on such carefully arranged works as *The Rehearsal of the Ballet on Stage*, that Degas never truly adopted an Impressionist style. Other artists passed through an Impressionist phase and went on to explore other ideas. In the years after 1880, in particular, a number of artists began to reconsider their earlier approaches or make important adjustments to them. Manet, for instance, had embraced his younger colleagues' brighter palette about 1870, but his late paintings, such as *A Bar at the Folies-Bergère* (fig. **18–21**), contradict the happy aura of works such as Monet's boulevard or country scenes.

Manet's painting revolves around one of the barmaids at the Folies-Bergère, a large nightclub with a series of bars arranged around a vaudeville theater. A performer on a trapeze, whose legs can be seen at the upper left, entertains the crowd reflected in the mirror behind the bar. On the marble bartop Manet has spread a glorious still life of liquor bottles, tangerines, and flowers, associated not only with the pleasures for which the Folies-Bergère was famous but also (formally) with the barmaid herself, whose wide hips, strong neck, and closely combed golden hair are echoed in the champagne bottles. The barmaid's demeanor, however, refutes these associations. Manet puts the viewer directly in front of her, in the position of her customer. From the front, the woman appears self-absorbed and downcast, but her mirrored reflection and that of her customer suggest a different story. In the reflection she leans toward the patron, whose intent gaze she appears to meet; the physical and psychological distance between them has vanished. Exactly what Manet meant to suggest by this juxtaposition has been much debated. One possibility is that he wanted to contrast the longing for happiness and intimacy with the disappointing reality of everyday existence.

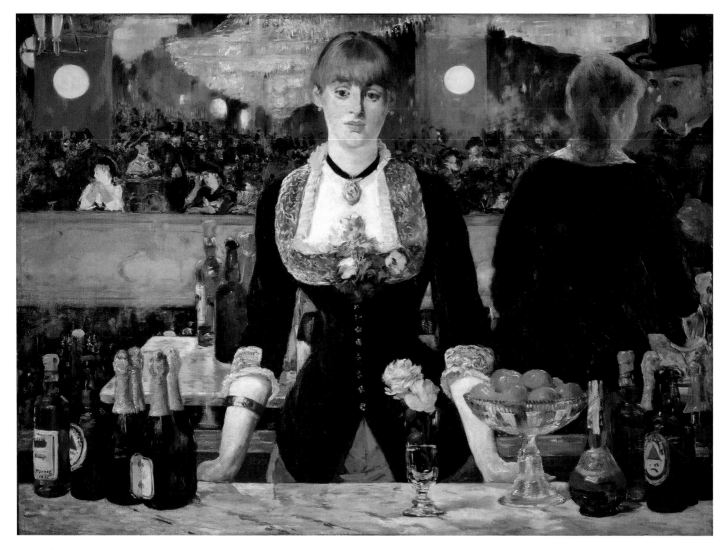

18–21 Édouard Manet. *A Bar at the Folies-Bergère.* 1881–1882. Oil on canvas, 37³/₄″ × 51¹/₆″ (95.9 × 130 cm). Courtauld Institute of Art Gallery, London

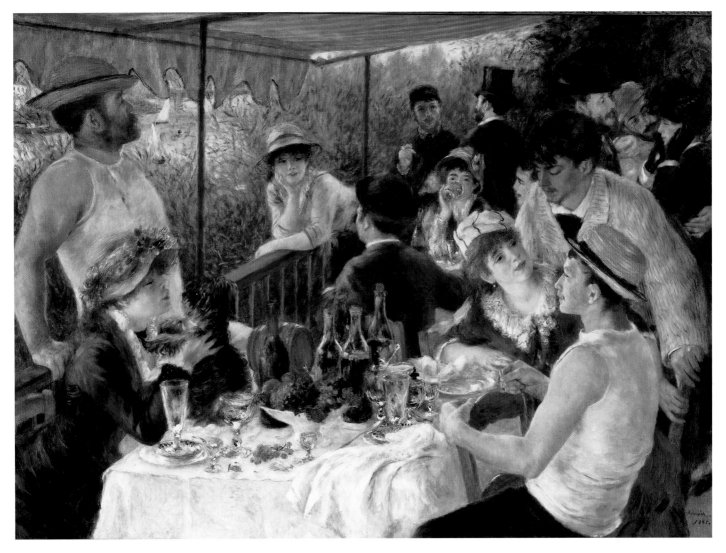

18–22 Pierre-Auguste Renoir. *Luncheon of the Boating Party.* 1881. Oil on canvas, 4′3″ × 5′8″ (1.29 × 1.73 m). The Phillips Collection, Washington, D.C.

Later Impressionism

In the years after 1880, Impressionism underwent what historians have termed a "crisis," as many artists grew dissatisfied with their attempts to capture momentary perceptions through spontaneous brushwork and casual compositions. In response, artists began to select subjects more carefully, work longer on their pictures, and develop styles that lent their imagery a greater sense of permanence and seriousness.

The artist most strongly affected by this crisis was Renoir, whose exposure to the paintings of Raphael and other Old Masters on a trip to Italy in 1881 caused him to reconsider his commitment to painting fleeting impressions of modern life. Consequently, although he continued to use sensual brushwork and lush color, he began to present firmly modeled figures and relatively traditional compositions. In *Luncheon of the Boating*

Party, a variation on the traditional pyramidal structure advocated by the academies underlies the apparent informality of the summer scene (fig. **18–22**). A small triangle whose apex is the woman leaning on the rail is set within a larger, somewhat looser pyramid that culminates in the two men at the rear. Thus, instead of a moment quickly scanned in passing (an impression), Renoir composed a more stable and permanent grouping. Renoir has glamorized his young artist friends and their models, showing them in attitudes of relaxed congeniality, smiling, chatting, and flirting. This idyllic image of a carefree age of innocence, a kind of paradise, nicely encapsulates Renoir's essential notion of art; he said, "For me a picture should be a pleasant thing, joyful and pretty."

Mary Cassatt (1845–1926), who, like Renoir, exhibited with the Impressionists, also moved toward a firmer handling of form and more classic subjects in the period after 1880. In the

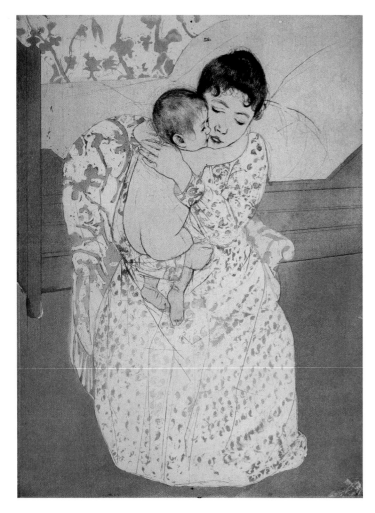

Maternal Caress (fig. **18–23**), one of the many colored prints she produced in her later career, Cassatt offers a sensitive, modern response to the tradition of the Madonna and Child. The plump infant, apparently fresh from the bath, shares a tender moment with its adoring mother. The flat decorative patterns, simple contours, and sharply sloping floor derive from Japanese prints (see "Japonisme," page 507). Cassatt, like Degas, remained a studio painter, but her distaste for what she called the tyranny of the Salon jury system made her one of the staunchest supporters of the Impressionists.

By the early twentieth century, of the original group of artists designated as Impressionists, Monet remained closest to the roots of the style, with its flickering brushstrokes designed to capture the passing moment. During the last two decades of his life (he died in 1926), Monet found endless enjoyment painting his gardens and his water-lily pond at Giverny, his country home. In most of his paintings of the pond, there is neither a horizon line nor a place for the viewer to stand. We are in the midst of the pool, between water and sky, adrift among floating blossoms and reflections of leaves and clouds (fig. **18–24**). Indeed, the largest of these water-lily canvases seem to envelop the viewer completely.

Post-Impressionism

The English critic Roger Fry coined the term *Post-Impressionism* in 1910 to identify a broad reaction against Impressionism in painting of the late nineteenth and early twentieth centuries. Art historians recognize Paul Cézanne, Georges Seurat, Paul Gauguin, Vincent van Gogh, and Paul Signac as the principal Post-Impressionist artists; some also add Henri de Toulouse-Lautrec. Each of these painters moved through an Impressionist phase and continued to use in his mature work the bright Impressionist palette. But each also came to reject Impressionism's emphasis on the spontaneous recording of light and color and instead sought to create art with a greater degree of formal order and structure. This goal led the Post-Impressionists to develop more abstract styles that would prove highly influential for the development of modernist painting in the early twentieth century.

18–23 Mary Cassatt. *Maternal Caress.* 1891. Drypoint and soft-ground etching, and aquatint. $14\frac{3}{4}'' \times 10\frac{3}{4}''$ (37.5 × 27.3 cm). (Mathews and Shapiro 1989 12.vi/vi). Chester Dale Collection.

18–24 Claude Monet. *Water Lilies.* c. 1920. Oil on canvas, $6'5\frac{1}{2}'' \times 19'7\frac{1}{2}''$ (1.97 × 5.98 m). The Museum of Modern Art, New York

Paul Cézanne's (1839–1902) radical stylistic innovations were instrumental in paving the way for twentieth-century **abstraction**. Yet he was ignored or misunderstood in his own day by all but a few perceptive collectors and fellow artists. In the 1870s Cézanne discovered Impressionism and began the objective transcription of what he called his "sensations" of nature. Unlike the Impressionists, however, Cézanne did not seek to capture transitory effects of light and atmosphere but rather to create a sense of order in nature through a careful and methodical application of color that merged drawing and modeling into a single process. His professed aim was to "make of Impressionism something solid and durable, like the art of the museums."

Cézanne's tireless pursuit of his goal is exemplified in his paintings of Mont Sainte-Victoire, which he could view near his home in Aix-en-Provence. The mountain (fig. **18–25**) rises above the valley, which is dotted with houses and trees and is traversed at the far right by an aqueduct. Framing the scene at the left is an evergreen tree, which echoes the contours of the mountain, creating harmony between the two principal elements of the composition. The even lighting, still atmosphere, and absence of human activity in the landscape communicate a sense of timeless endurance, at odds with the Impressionists' interest in capturing a momentary aspect of the ever-changing world. Cézanne's handling of paint is more deliberate and constructive than the Impressionists' spontaneous and sometimes random brushwork. His strokes, which vary from short, parallel hatchings to sketchy lines to broader swaths of flat color, weave every element of the landscape together into a unified surface design. That surface design coexists with the effect of spatial recession that the composition simultaneously creates, generating a fruitful tension between the illusion of three dimensions "behind" the picture plane and the physical reality of its two-dimensional surface.

Although it is tempting to see in *Mont Sainte-Victoire* evidence of Cézanne's ultimate rejection of Impressionist **aesthetics** for an interest in solid form, this and works like it remain firmly grounded in the understanding of the individual brush

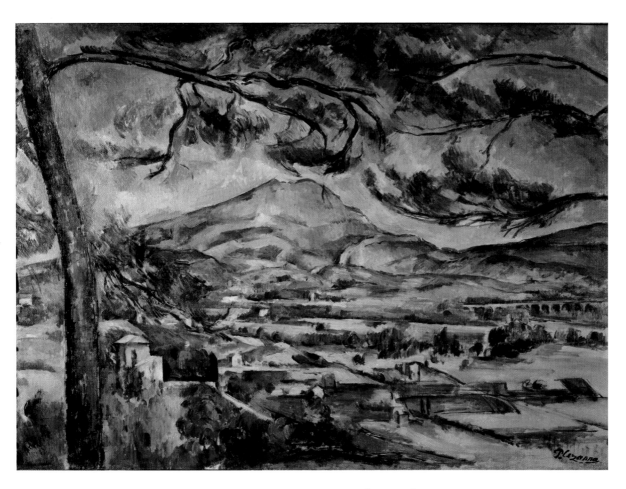

18–25 Paul Cézanne. *Mont Sainte-Victoire.* c. 1885–1887. Oil on canvas, 26.29″ × 36.34″ (66.8 × 92.3 cm). Courtauld Institute of Art Gallery, London

On the one hand, recession into depth is suggested by elements such as the foreground tree that helps draw the eye into the valley, and by the gradual transition from the intense greens and orange-yellows of the foreground to the softer blues and pinks in the distant mountain range, which create an effect of atmospheric perspective. On the other hand, this illusion of consistent recession into depth is challenged by the inclusion of blues, pinks, and reds in the foreground foliage, which relate the foreground forms to the background mountain and sky, and by the tree branches in the sky, which follow the contours of the mountain, making the peak appear nearer and binding it to the foreground plane.

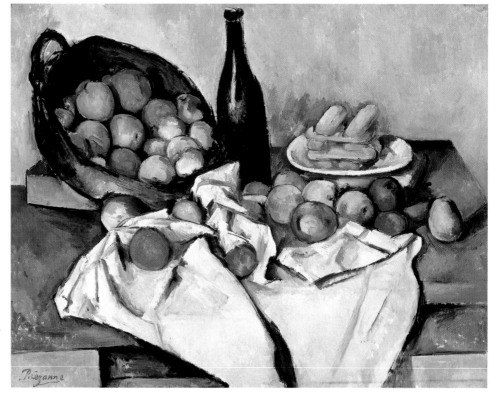

18–26 Paul Cézanne. *Still Life with Basket of Apples.*
1890–1894. Oil on canvas, $24\frac{3}{8}'' \times 31''$
(61.9 × 78.7 cm). The Art Institute of Chicago

mark as a record of the artist's immediate "sensation" of nature. In the middle section of the composition, for example, the solid rectangular strokes, generally applied according to a rigid grid of vertical and horizontal lines, nevertheless form dynamic and irregular contours. Cézanne used the **"passage technique"** in which shapes closed on one side are open on another so that they can merge with adjacent shapes (see "Cubism," pages 531–535). The merging of shapes along with the juxtaposition of warm and cool colors creates a spatial tension. The passage technique is heightened by the contradiction between the presumed depth of the landscape and the flat painted surface of the canvas that the viewer actually sees, a contradiciton that allowed Cézanne to explore and communicate the essential tension in nature between permanence and change.

Spatial ambiguities of a different sort appear in Cézanne's late still lifes, in which many of the objects seem incorrectly drawn. In *Still Life with Basket of Apples* (fig. **18–26**), for example, an apparently conventional studio arrangement of fruit, pastries, and wine bottle is, on closer examination, on the verge of collapse. As Cézanne shifts his viewpoint to capture multiple aspects of the objects, the bottle seems to tilt precariously on a tabletop whose right and left sides do not match. The folds of the white cloth add considerably to the work's instability; only the small tucks in the fabric seem to prevent the apples from cascading to the floor. Such apparent inaccuracies are not evidence of any incompetence, however; they reflect, instead, the artist's willful disregard for the rules of traditional scientific perspective. Perspective mandates that the eye of the artist (and hence the viewer) occupy a fixed point relative to the scene being observed, but Cézanne studies different objects in a painting from slightly different positions. The composition as a whole, assembled from multiple sightings, is thus more complex and dynamic. Instead of a faithful reproduction of objects, Cézanne was re-creating, or reconstructing, nature.

The Post-Impressionists Seurat and Gauguin held beliefs different from those of Cézanne; they saw art as a force for social commentary and even change. The name that came into general use to describe such art was **avant-garde**. Originally a military term for an advance unit, it was used in 1825 by a French socialist, the Comte de Saint-Simon, to refer to those artists whose visual expression would prepare people to accept the social changes he and his colleagues envisioned. The idea of producing a socially revolutionary art had briefly attracted such artists as Courbet, but the real popularity of this notion dates from the Post-Impressionist era.

Seurat was apparently one of the first in his generation to think of himself as an avant-garde artist (see "Looking Forward," page 489). He devoted his energies to "correcting" Impressionism, which he found too intellectually shallow and too improvisational. In the mid-1880s he gathered around him a circle of young artists who became known as the Neo-Impressionists. (Neo-Impressionism refers primarily to a type of technique and theory involving vision and color, while Post-Impressionism refers mostly to a time frame or era. Artists such as Seurat and Paul Signac fall into both categories.)

Seurat belonged to a group of artists, intellectuals, and amateur scientists who were studying theories of vision, light, and color. Seurat applied their theories to his painting in a technique he called "divisionism" or "pointillism". The work that became the centerpiece of the new movement and made Seurat's reputation was *A Sunday Afternoon on the Island of La Grande Jatte* (see fig. 18–1). Seurat first exhibited *La Grande Jatte* at the eighth and final Impressionist exhibition in 1886. The theme of weekend leisure is typically Impressionist, but the rigorous divisionist technique, the stiff formality of the figures, and the highly calculated geometry of the composition produce a solemn, abstract effect quite at odds with the casual naturalism of earlier Impressionism.

From its first appearance, the painting, with its curiously formal and stylized figures, gave rise to a number of conflicting interpretations. Contemporary accounts of the island indicate that on Sundays it was noisy, littered, and chaotic. By painting the island the way he did, Seurat may have intended to represent an ideal image of middle-class life and leisure—a model of how tranquil the island—and perhaps life—*should* be. On the other hand, some art historians see this and other works by Seurat as satirizing the habits and attitudes of the growing Parisian middle class, and they have spent much time attempting to unlock and interpret the many perceived "symbols" present in this and other compositions.

Certainly for one artist, the desire to escape modern life in Paris was a clear goal; the French painter Paul Gauguin (1848–1903) moved first to Brittany and then to Panama. At the age of 37, he had given up a conventional existence as a Paris stockbroker and left his wife and five children to pursue a full-time painting career. In 1888, he spent two months with van Gogh in Arles, and sailed for Tahiti in the South Pacific in 1891.

Before Gauguin left for the South Pacific, he had found inspiration in the simplified drawing, flattened space, and anti-natural color of medieval stained glass, Breton folk art, and Japanese prints. He rejected Impressionism (although he had exhibited in the last four Impressionist exhibitions, 1880–1886) because it neglected subjective feelings. Gauguin called his anti-Impressionist style *synthetism*, because it synthesized observation of the subject in nature with the artist's feelings about that subject, expressed through abstracted line, shape, space, and color.

A product of such synthesis is *Mahana no atua (Day of the God)* (fig. **18–27**), which, despite its Tahitian subject, was painted in France during Gauguin's return after two years in the South Pacific. Gauguin had gone to Tahiti hoping to find an unspoiled, pre-industrial paradise. He had imagined the Tahitians to be childlike and close to nature, but what he discovered, instead, was a thoroughly colonized country whose native culture was rapidly disappearing under the pressures of Westernization. In his paintings, Gauguin chose to ignore this reality and to depict the Edenic ideal of his imagination.

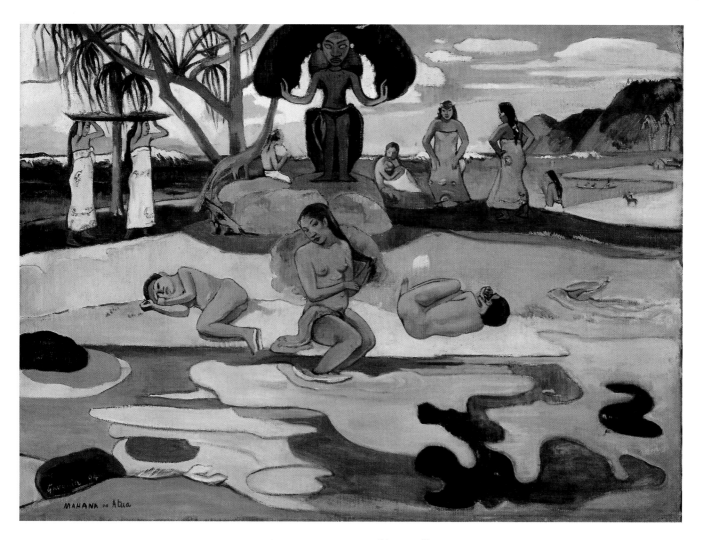

18–27 Paul Gauguin. *Mahana no atua (Day of the God)*. 1894. Oil on canvas, $27\frac{3}{8}''\times 35\frac{5}{8}''$ (69.5 × 90.5 cm).
The Art Institute of Chicago

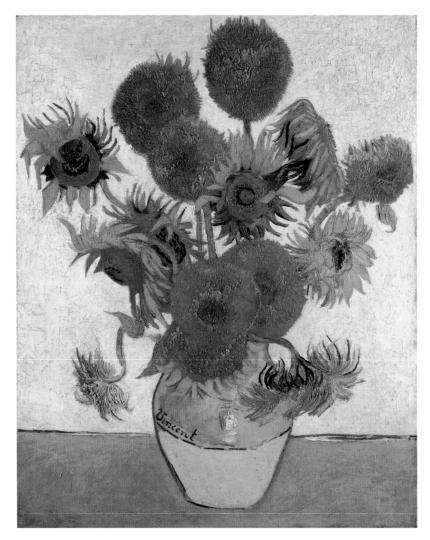

18–28 Vincent van Gogh. *Sunflowers.* 1888. Oil on canvas, $36\frac{1}{4}''\times 28\frac{3}{4}''$ (92.1 × 73 cm). The National Gallery, London

Gauguin divided *Mahana no atua* into three horizontal zones in styles of increasing abstraction. The upper zone, painted in the most realistic manner, centers on the statue of a god, behind which extends a beach landscape populated by Tahitians. In the middle zone, directly beneath the statue, three figures occupy a beach divided into several bands of antinaturalistic color. The central female bather dips her feet in the water and looks out at the viewer, while on either side of her two figures recline in fetus-like postures—perhaps the three women symbolize birth, life, and death. Filling the bottom third of the canvas is a strikingly abstract pool whose surface offers a dazzling array of bright colors, arranged in a puzzlelike pattern of flat, curvilinear shapes. By reflecting a strange and unexpected reality exactly where we expect to see a mirror image of the familiar world, this magic pool seems the perfect symbol of Gauguin's desire to evoke "the mysterious centers of thought."

Among the artists in Gauguin's circle before his departure for Tahiti was the Dutch painter Vincent van Gogh (1853–1890). Van Gogh had moved to Paris in 1886, where at first he came under the influence of the Impressionists and Neo-Impressionists. Soon he departed radically from Seurat's divisionist technique and applied his paint freely in multidirectional dashes of thick pigment, giving his pictures a greater sense of physical energy and a palpable surface texture.

Van Gogh shared Gauguin's desire for a simple, pre-industrial life, and the two planned to move to the south of France and establish a commune of like-minded artists. In the spring of 1888, van Gogh moved to Arles, where the radiant sun and lush farmland prompted him to create such dazzling images as his famous series of *Sunflowers* (fig. **18–28**), painted in anticipation of his friend's arrival. When Gauguin finally joined van Gogh, their constant quarrels soon led to violent confrontation and

Gauguin's departure. Only a few close friends and his brother Theo stood by van Gogh to the end. After a series of psychological crises that led to his hospitalization, van Gogh shot himself in July 1890.

The paintings van Gogh produced during the last year and a half of his life testify to his heightened emotional state. At the same time, they contributed significantly to the emergence of the expressionistic tradition, in which the intensity of an artist's feelings overrides fidelity to the actual appearance of things. One of the earliest examples of **expressionism** is *The Starry Night*

(fig. **18–29**), which van Gogh completed near the asylum of Saint-Rémy. The sky, pulsating with exploding stars high above the quiet town, is clearly more a record of what van Gogh felt than of what he saw. The painting may give expression to the then-popular idea that after death people journeyed to a star, where they continued their lives. Van Gogh wrote: "Just as we take the train to get to Tarascon or Rouen, we take death to reach a star." In the painting, a cypress tree, a traditional symbol of both death and eternal life, dramatically links the terrestrial world and the heavens.

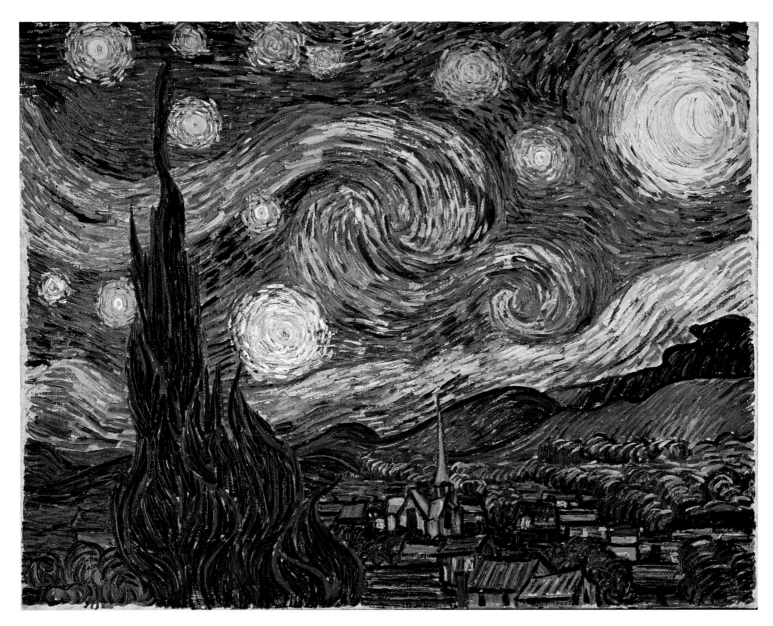

18–29 Vincent van Gogh. *The Starry Night*. 1889. Oil on canvas, 28 3/4″ × 36 1/4″ (73 × 92 cm).
The Museum of Modern Art, New York

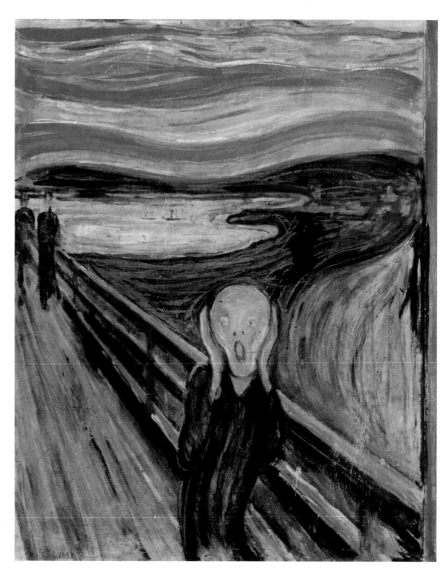

18–30 Edvard Munch. *The Scream.* 1893. Tempera and casein on cardboard, 36″ × 29″ (91.3 × 73.7 cm). Nasjonalgalleriet, Oslo

Munch derived his anxious, compelling visions from observation of the real world—the red and yellow lights in the sky actually occur in northern lands—however he transformed the visual record using acid colors, crude forms, and rough surface textures.

A more frightening image of the night sky can be seen in the painting of the Norwegian Edvard Munch (1863–1944). Munch had encountered the work of Gauguin and his Scandinavian followers before he painted his famous work, *The Scream* (fig. **18–30**). This unforgettable image of modern alienation merges Symbolist suggestiveness with expressionist intensity of feeling. Munch recorded the painting's genesis in his diary: "one evening I was walking along a path; the city was on one side, and the fjord below. I was tired and ill. … I sensed a shriek passing through nature. … I painted this picture, painted the clouds as actual blood." The overwhelming anxiety that sought release in this primal scream was chiefly a dread of death, as the sky and the figure's skull-like head suggest, but the setting of the picture also suggests a fear of open spaces. The expressive abstraction of form and color in the painting foreshadows the anxieties that will plague life in the twentieth and twenty-first centuries.

Expressionism was one way to communicate the psychological impact of the modern world. Another artistic response was to capture the emotive energy of modern life, a tactic followed by Henri de Toulouse-Lautrec (1864–1901) in his paintings and prints (see "Lithography," opposite). From the late 1880s,

Toulouse-Lautrec chronicled life in Montmartre, a part of Paris devoted to entertainment and inhabited by many people who lived on the fringes of society.

Toulouse-Lautrec designed lithographic posters as advertisements for popular night spots and entertainers between 1891 and 1901. His portrayal of the café dancer *Jane Avril* (fig. **18–31**) demonstrates the remarkable originality that he brought to an essentially commercial project. The composition juxtaposes the dynamic figure of the dancer onstage with the cropped image of a bass viol player and the scroll of his instrument. The bold foreshortening of the stage and the prominent placement of the bass in the foreground both suggest the influence of Degas (see fig. 18–20); however, Toulouse-Lautrec has extended the bass viol's head into a curving frame that surrounds Avril and connects her visually with her musical accompaniment. The radical simplification of form, suppression of modeling, flattening of space, and integration of blank paper into the composition all suggest the influence of Japanese woodblock prints (see "Japonisme," page 507). The emphasis on curving lines and the harmonization of the lettering with the rest of the design also connect the poster with Art Nouveau.

Technique

Lithography

Aloys Senefelder invented **lithography** in Bavaria, Germany, in 1796 and registered for an exclusive right to the process the following year. Lithography is a planographic process—that is, the printing is done from a flat surface. It was the first wholly new printing process to be introduced since the fifteenth century, when the **intaglio**, or **incising**, process was developed.

Lithography, still popular today, is based on the natural antagonism between oil and water. The artist draws on a flat surface—traditionally, fine-grained stone—with a greasy, crayonlike instrument. The stone's surface is flooded with water, over which an oil-based ink is rolled. The ink adheres to the greasy areas but not to the damp ones. A sheet of paper is placed face-down on the inked stone. Blankets are placed over the paper to protect it from the scraper. The stone, paper, and protective blankets are then passed through a flatbed press. A scraper applies light pressure from above as the stone and paper pass under it, transferring ink from stone to paper, thus making lithography a direct method of creating a printed image. Francisco Goya, Honoré Daumier, and Toulouse-Lautrec exploited the medium to great effect.

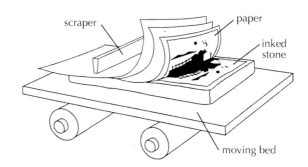

Although often energetic and colorful, many of Toulouse-Lautrec's images depict the sad reality of the festivities at the popular dance halls, and—like Manet's paintings—they reveal the artist's sensitivity to a new kind of loneliness: the modern feeling of alienation.

Paul Signac (1863–1935) moved in the avant-garde intellectual and art circles of Paris, but he became enchanted by the landscape of the Mediterranean coast of France. An enthusiastic sailor, he divided his time between Paris and the coast, eventually acquiring a house in Saint-Tropez on the French Riviera. There he painted the harbor with its old houses and sailboats and occasionally he painted the people, too.

Signac emerged as the leading theorist in the Neo-Impressionist circle of the 1880s and 1890s, a group that included the critic Félix Fénéon (1861–1944) and the eccentric amateur scientist Charles Henry (1859–1926). In Fénéon's view, great art "sacrifices anecdote to arabesque, analysis to synthesis, fugitive to permanent" (Ferretti-Bocquillon, page 161). And this is precisely what Signac has done in his *Place des Lices, Saint-Tropez* (see "Closer Look," page 518). The work—to which Signac gave the alternate musical title of *Opus 242*—is an homage to the light and color of the south—and to the rhythms of the swaying plane trees.

Signac was fascinated by other painters' experiments with color and became close to people who (in retrospect) became leading Post-Impressionists and expressionists—van Gogh, Gauguin, Toulouse-Lautrec, and Henri Matisse (see Chapter 19). In 1887 Signac had befriended van Gogh in Paris and introduced him to the scientific study of color—especially the interaction of contrasting colors—and he later visited van Gogh in Arles. He also encouraged Matisse to come to the south (see pages 526–527).

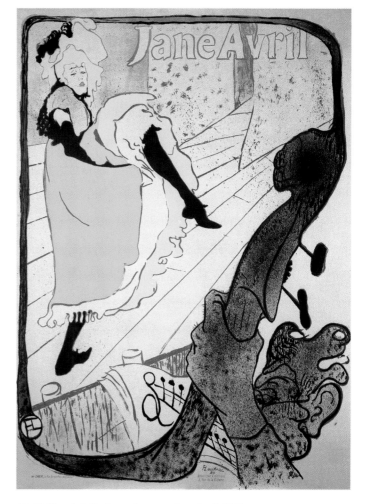

18–31 Henri de Toulouse-Lautrec. *Jane Avril.* 1893.
Lithograph, 50 ½″ × 37″ (129 × 94 cm). San Diego Museum of Art
THE BALDWIN M. BALDWIN COLLECTION

In the center of a park in Saint-Tropez, a man sits, framed by the undulating branches of the rows of plane trees (European sycamores) and the horizontal lines of the bench, the distant wall, and red-roofed buildings (fig. **18–32**). The trees defy the regularity of the rows in which they were planted and seem to dance rhythmically. Signac's painting reflects the avant-garde artist's interests in the abstract, decorative quality of Japanese prints and in the scientific study of light and perception. The subtle asymmetrical composition of dark branches against the setting sun recalls Hokusai's views of Mount Fuji (see fig. 9–26), and the brilliant contrasting purple/blue and yellow/orange paint, applied using the divisionist technique, reflects color theories being discussed in intellectual circles in Paris.

Artists like Seurat and Signac, whom in 1886 the critic Félix Fénéon dubbed Neo-Impressionists, knew Michel-Eugene Chevreul's "Law of the simultaneous contrast of colors" (1839). Chevreul (1786–1889) argued that not only do contrasting colors enhance each other's intensity, but that adjacent objects cast reflections of their own color onto their neighbors. Fénéon described the phenomenon: "Two adjacent colors exert a mutual influence, each imposing its own complementary on the other; for green a purple, for red a blue green, for yellow an ultramarine, for violet a greenish yellow, for orange a cyan blue." (Ferretti-Bocquillon, page 160).

The backlit trees, sun-dappled leaves, and areas of dazzling light breaking up the shadows on the ground show that Signac, Seurat, and other Neo-Impressionists did not feel constrained to apply Chevreul's law systematically. They listened to people like the intellectual Charles Henry, too, who in 1889 devised a color wheel, which he called a chromatic circle. In works (illustrated by Signac), Henry studied the exact gradations of contrasting colors that—when placed side by side—not only intensify each other's effect but, when used in small dots, also "blend in the eye of the beholder." This phenomenon, known as optical mixture, creates a shimmering effect in the viewer's vision. Painters put this theory into practice, setting down hues in dots of pure color, one next to another, in what came to be known by various names: divisionism (the term preferred by Seurat), pointillism, and simply Neo-Impressionism. In theory, these juxtaposed dots would merge in the viewer's eye to produce the impression of other colors, more luminous and intense than if they had been mixed on the palette. In fact, this optical mixture is never complete, for the dots of color tend to remain separate, giving Neo-Impressionist paintings a speckled appearance.

In addition to illustrating Henry's *Chromatic Circle*, which was published as a monograph in 1890, Signac wrote his own book, *From Delacroix to Neo-Impressionism* (1899), in which he articulated the Neo-Impressionist aesthetic theory. The work is considered a landmark both in the study of color and in the appreciation of Delacroix.

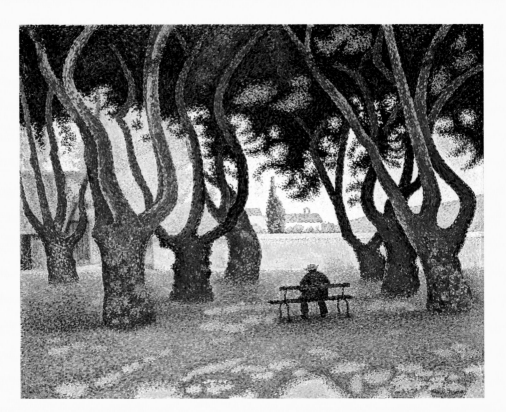

18–32 Paul Signac. *Place des Lices, Saint-Tropez.* 1893. Oil on canvas, $25^{3}/_{4}'' \times 32^{3}/_{16}''$ (65.4 × 81.8 cm). Carnegie Museum of Art, Pittsburgh

Signac was even one of the artists represented in the first exhibition held in the shop that gave its name to the Art Nouveau movement (see page 499).

Late-Nineteenth-Century French Sculpture

The most successful and influential sculptor of the Post-Impressionist era was Auguste Rodin (1840–1917). His status as a major sculptor was confirmed in 1884, when he won the competition for a monument, commissioned by the city of Calais, to commemorate an event from the Hundred Years' War—the *Burghers of Calais* (fig. **18–33**). In 1347 King Edward III of England lay siege to Calais, but he offered to spare the city if six leading citizens (burghers) would surrender themselves to him for execution. Rodin shows the six volunteers—dressed in sackcloth with rope halters and carrying the keys to the city—marching out to what they assume will be their deaths. (Impressed by their courage, the king spared them.)

The officials in modern Calais were upset to find that their chosen sculptor produced not calm, idealized heroes but ordinary men in various attitudes of resignation and despair. Rodin expressively lengthened their arms, greatly enlarged their hands and feet, and swathed them in heavy fabric. He showed not only how they may have looked but also how they must have felt as they forced themselves to take one difficult step after another. Rodin's willingness to stylize the human body for expressive purposes was a revolutionary move that opened the way for the more radical innovations of later sculptors. He also planned to place the figures on a low base, almost at street level, to suggest to viewers that ordinary people like themselves were capable of noble acts. Rodin's removal of public sculpture from a high pedestal to a low base would lead, in the twentieth century, to the elimination of the pedestal itself and to the presentation of sculpture in the "real" space of the viewer.

Camille Claudel (1864–1943), an assistant in Rodin's studio who worked on the *Burghers of Calais*, was an accomplished

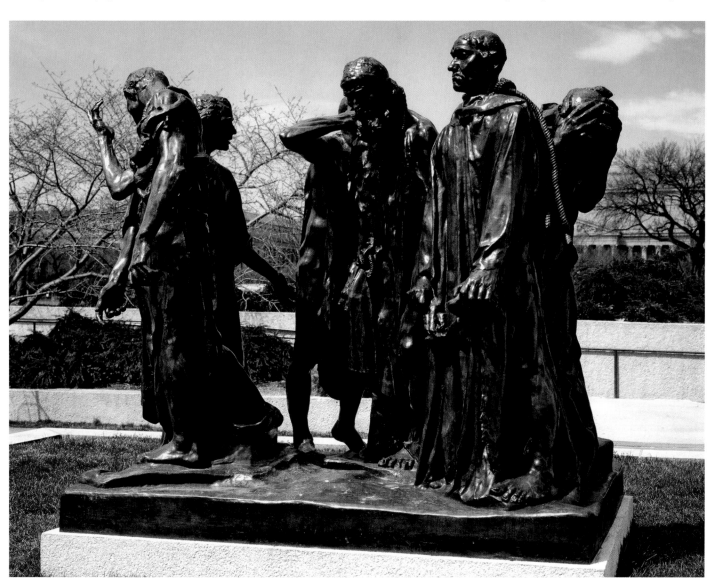

18–33 Auguste Rodin. *Burghers of Calais.* 1884–1886. Bronze, 6′ 10$\frac{1}{2}$″ × 7′11″ × 6′6″
(2.1 × 2.4 × 2.0 m). Hirshhorn Museum and Sculpture Garden, Smithsonian Institution, Washington, D.C.

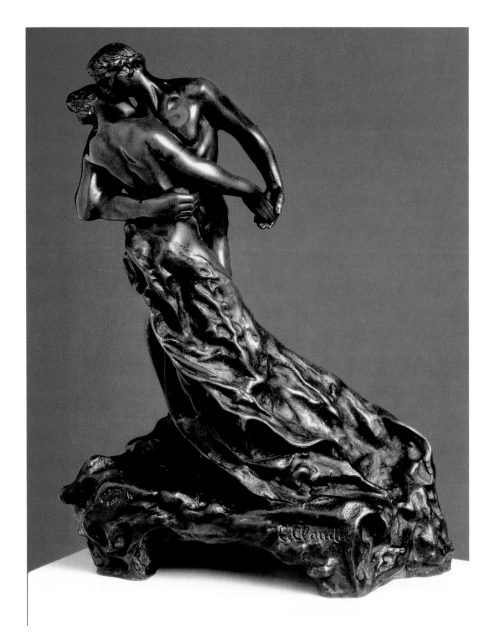

18–34 Camille Claudel. *The Waltz.* 1892–1905. Bronze, height $9^{7}/_{8}"$ (25 cm). Neue Pinakothek, Munich.

French composer Claude Debussy, a close friend of Claudel, displayed a cast of this sculpture on his piano. Debussy acknowledged the influence of art and literature on his innovative musical compositions.

sculptor whose work was overshadowed by the dramatic story of her life. Claudel formally began to study sculpture in 1879 and became Rodin's pupil four years later. After she started working in his studio, she also became his mistress—an often stormy relationship that lasted 15 years. Both during and after her association with Rodin, Claudel enjoyed independent professional success, but she also suffered from psychological problems that eventually overtook her, and she spent the last 30 years of her life in an asylum.

Among Claudel's most celebrated works is *The Waltz* (fig. **18–34**). The sculpture depicts a dancing couple, the man unclothed and the woman seminude, her lower body enveloped in a long, flowing gown. In Claudel's original conception, both figures were entirely nude, but she had to add drapery to the female figure after an inspector from the Ministry of the Beaux-Arts declared the piece to be indecent. The swirling drapery—which recalls the fluid lines of Art Nouveau—proved to be a fortunate addition, for it conveys an illusion of fluent motion as the dancing partners whirl in space. Despite the closeness of the dancers there is little actual physical contact between them, and their facial expressions reveal no passion or sexual desire. After violating decency standards with her first version of *The Waltz*, Claudel perhaps sought in this new rendition to portray love as a union more spiritual than physical.

| 1850 | 1860 | 1870 | 1880 | 1890 | 1900 |

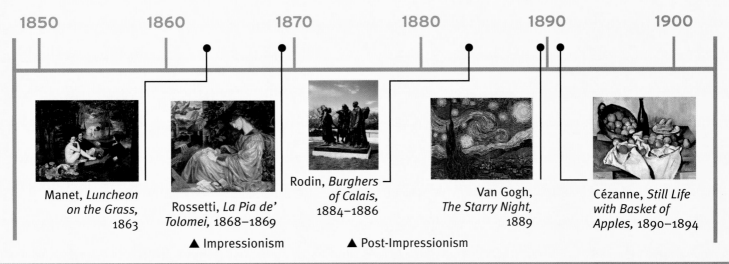

Manet, *Luncheon on the Grass,* 1863

Rossetti, *La Pia de' Tolomei,* 1868–1869

Rodin, *Burghers of Calais,* 1884–1886

Van Gogh, *The Starry Night,* 1889

Cézanne, *Still Life with Basket of Apples,* 1890–1894

▲ Impressionism   ▲ Post-Impressionism

LOOKING BACK

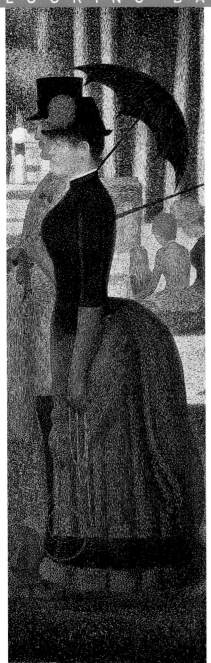

The Enlightenment and the Industrial Revolution transformed the intellectual and material life in Europe and the United States during the nineteenth-century. The ideal of political and religious freedom and boundless faith in individual ability to meet intellectual and economic challenges and achieve personal goals underlay the era's apparent self-confidence. Life in the new urban centers, it was thought, would lead to better living conditions than the old agrarian system had provided. With this self confidence came a belief in the superiority of the European culture, intense nationalism, and the rise of imperialism. To secure access to cheap raw materials and cheap labor, European nations established colonies in most of Africa and nearly a third of Asia, and the United States did the same in the Pacific. Economic expansion also led to cultural exchange.

The economic situation of artists changed as the ability of the church and the secular nobility to patronize the arts declined. Newly wealthy bourgeoisie, as well as national governments and academies became major patrons of the arts. Large annual exhibitions in European and American cultural centers took on increasing importance as a means for artists to show their work, win prizes, attract buyers, and gain commissions. Art criticism proliferated in mass-printed periodicals, helping both to make and to break artistic careers. And, in the later decades of the century, commercial art dealers gained in importance as marketers of both old and new art.

The arts lost some of their importance in the culture to science and technology. The examination of the material world, begun in the fifteenth-century in the West, led to a continuous stream of new approaches to many activities, including the arts. In the second half of the nineteenth century, positivist thinking influenced by objective, scientific inquiry is evident not only in the rejection of Romanticism and the growth of Realism in art but also in the highly descriptive style of academic art, the application of new technologies in architecture, and finally in the Impressionist and Post-Impressionist painters' emphasis on light and the phenomenon of perception. In the late nineteenth century, some painters claimed to follow quasi-scientific methods; they responded only to visual stimulation, as objective organs of sight in order simply to record the light and color. Then, in reaction, Post-Impressionists, such as Paul Cézanne, sought to reproduce solid forms or, like Vincent van Gogh, to capture emotional states.

Artists were committed to being part of a cultural avant-garde, to innovation, to being modern—not just to keeping up-to-date but to leading a revitalized art community into the next century. Today, crowds of visitors to exhibitions of Impressionist painting attest to the enduring popularity of late nineteenth century "modern" art.

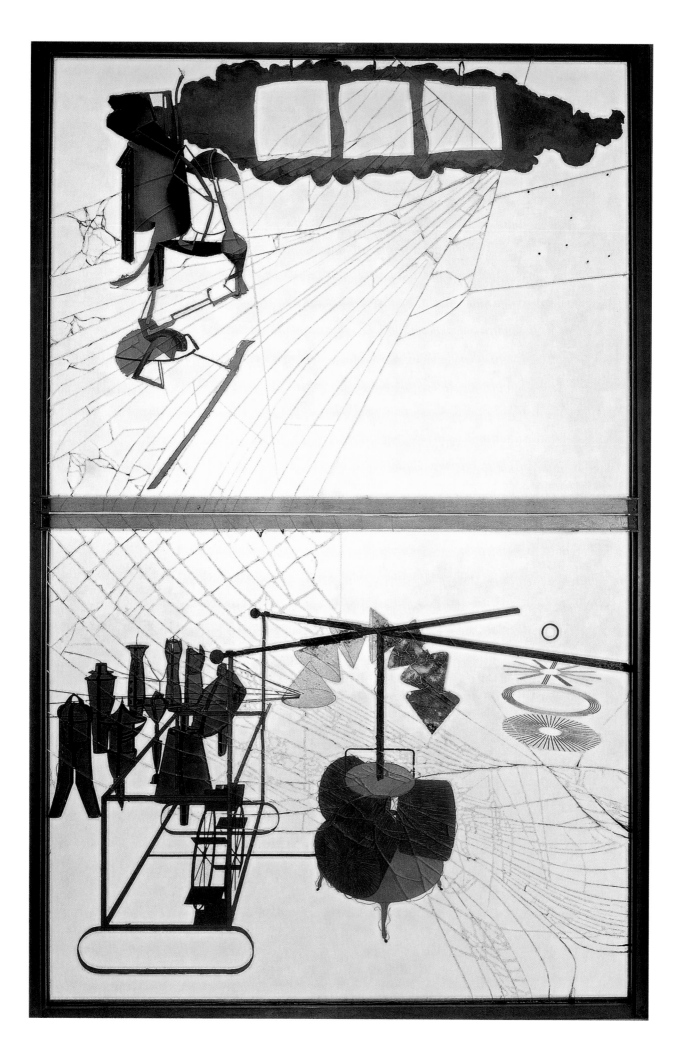

19

Modern Art: Europe and North America in the Early Twentieth Century

LOOKING FORWARD

Marcel Duchamp (1887–1968) said that he wanted to "put painting once again at the service of the mind." As he stressed the intellectual process of making art, Duchamp valued the ideas behind the art object more than the art object itself, and this new way of thinking about art also liberated the creative process. Duchamp loved to use wordplay—including poetry and puns—more than straightforward means of communication, and he undermined the very idea of unique art objects with his "readymades." Readymades are found objects, ordinary manufactured items such as a bicycle wheel, snow shovel, or urinal (which he called *Fountain*; see fig. 19–18), that became art simply because an artist selected them. Duchamp's radical concepts about art surfaced in all his works, especially his masterwork, *The Bride Stripped Bare by Her Bachelors, Even*, also known as *The Large Glass* (fig. **19–1**). Although Duchamp worked on the piece for eight years, he only considered it finished after the nine-foot panel of glass, paint, and wire was accidentally shattered in 1926 and then put back together in 1936.

The complex clues to understanding this work and its title seem to be as equally important to Duchamp as the random accident that completed it. The Bride in the upper half of the glass controls the nine Bachelors below. Duchamp's notes on the piece, written between 1912 and 1915, leave paths to meaning as well as enigmas. "The Bride is basically a motor," Duchamp wrote, who runs on "love gasoline." Thus she is also an image of female sexual desire. The Bride sends forth a cloud across the glass that Duchamp called "the Halo of the Bride" and her "Cinematic Blossoming," and she issues her "commands, orders, authorizations, etc." through the three squares of clear glass. Later critics suggested that the Bride is emitting a lovesick sigh.

In contrast, the Bachelors' portion of the glass (bottom half) contains recognizable objects drawn in linear perspective. Nine "malic" (Duchamp's word for "male-like") pieces at the left dangle from wires attached to seven cones that arch over a chocolate grinder. The pieces are ready to be set in motion by a rectangular frame on elliptical gliders powered by a water wheel. Both water wheel and scissor-like rods are also linked to the chocolate grinder. At the right the three circular test patterns used by eye doctors hover as "Oculist Witnesses" to the thwarted consummation.

As Calvin Tonkins wrote in his biography *Duchamp* (page 12): "Duchamp has come to be considered a forerunner of Conceptual art, as well as Pop art, Minimal art, Performance art, Process art, Kinetic art, anti-form and Multimedia art, and virtually every postmodern tendency." Duchamp believed that art was whatever the artist said it was and that the viewer was as important as the artist.

19–1 Marcel Duchamp. *The Bride Stripped Bare by Her Bachelors, Even (The Large Glass).* 1915–1923. Oil, varnish, lead foil, lead wire, and dust on two glass panels, 9′1¼″ × 5′9¼″ (2.77 × 1.76 m). Philadelphia Museum of Art

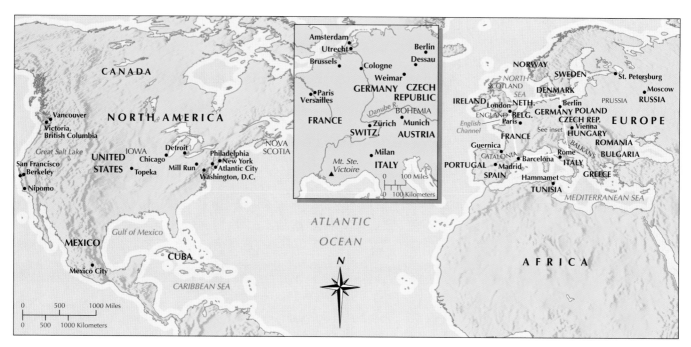

Map 19–1 Europe and North America in the Early Twentieth Century

The backdrop of politics, war, and technological change is critical to understanding twentieth-century art. As that century dawned, many Europeans and Americans believed optimistically that human society would "advance" through the spread of democracy, capitalism, and technological innovation. However, the competitive nature of colonialism, nationalism, and capitalism created great instability in Europe, and countries joined together in rival political alliances. World War I erupted in August 1914, initially pitting Britain, France, and Russia (the Allies) against Germany and Austria (the Central Powers). The United States entered the war in 1917 and contributed to an Allied victory the following year (see Map 19–1, above).

World War I significantly transformed European politics and economics, especially in Russia, which became the world's first Communist nation in 1917, when a popular revolution brought the Bolshevik (meaning "Majority") Communist party of Vladimir Lenin to power. In 1922 the Soviet Union, a Communist state encompassing Russia and neighboring areas, was created.

American and Western European economies soon recovered from the war (with the exception of Germany, whose economy was weakened by reparations that the Allies demanded), but the 1929 New York stock market crash plunged much of the world into the Great Depression. In 1933 U.S. President Franklin D. Roosevelt responded with the New Deal, an ambitious welfare program meant to provide jobs and stimulate the American economy. Britain and France instituted state welfare policies during the 1930s as well. Elsewhere in Europe, the economic crisis brought to power right-wing totalitarian regimes: Benito Mussolini in Italy, Adolf Hitler in Germany, and General Francisco Franco in Spain. Meanwhile, in the Soviet Union, Joseph Stalin succeeded Lenin in 1924.

German aggression toward Poland in 1939 led to the outbreak of World War II. The most destructive war in history, World War II claimed the lives of millions of soldiers and civilians from Asia, North America, and Europe, including 6 million European Jews who perished in the Nazi Holocaust. It ended in Europe in May 1945 and in the Pacific that August.

During the two great wars of the twentieth century, technological innovations resulted in such deadly devices as the fighter bomber and the atom bomb. Yet dramatic scientific developments and improvements in medicine, agriculture, communications, and transportation also transformed the daily life of millions of people, especially in Europe and North America. The first analog and digital computers, designed to process huge amounts of data and perform advanced calculations, were also introduced in the 1930s.

Accompanying the momentous changes in politics, economics, and science were equally revolutionary developments in art and culture, which scholars have gathered under the label of "modernism." Although *modern* simply means "up-to-date," the term *modernism* connotes a rejection of conventions and a commitment to radical innovation. Like scientists and inventors, modern artists engaged in a process of experimentation and discovery, exploring new possibilities of creativity and expression in a rapidly changing world.

Early Modern Art in Europe

After 1900 the pace of artistic innovation increased, producing a dizzying succession of movements, or "isms," including Fauvism, Cubism, Futurism, Dadaism, and Surrealism. Each movement had a charismatic leader or group who promoted the movement's unique philosophy, often through written declarations of princi-

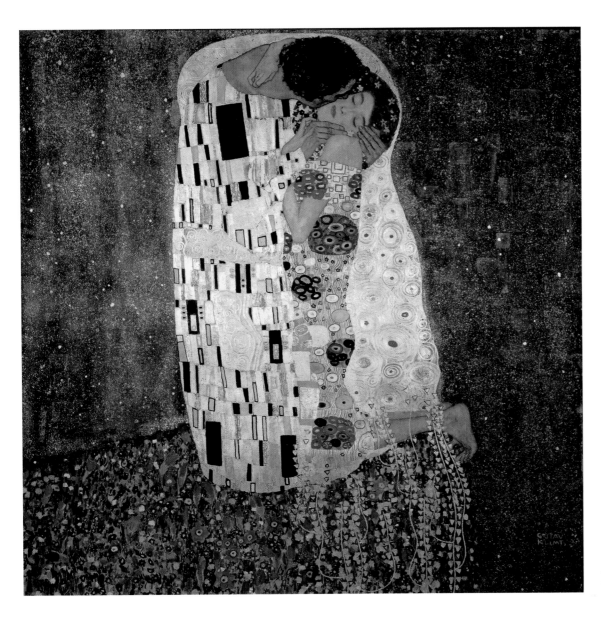

19–2 Gustav Klimt. *The Kiss.*
1907–1908. Oil on canvas,
5′10³/₄″ × 6′ (1.8 × 1.83 m).
Österreichische
Nationalbibliothek, Vienna

ples called manifestoes. Although modernism is characterized by tremendous aesthetic diversity, several broad tendencies mark many modernist artists. Foremost is a tendency toward abstraction, even going as far as nonrepresentational art, which communicates exclusively through such formal means as line, shape, color, and texture. A second feature of modernism is a tendency to emphasize physical processes—for example, through visible brushstrokes or chisel marks. A third feature is modernism's continual exploration of the nature of art itself through the adoption of new techniques and materials—including ordinary, "nonartistic" materials—that break down distinctions between art and everyday life.

The rise of European and American modernism in the early twentieth century was driven by such exhibitions as the 1905 Salon d'Automne ("Autumn Exhibition") in Paris, which launched the Fauve movement; the first Der Blaue Reiter exhibition in Munich in 1911; and the 1913 New York Armory Show, the first large-scale introduction of European modernism to

American audiences. The Museum of Modern Art opened in New York in 1929; and state-supported museums dedicated to modern art also opened in major European capitals, such as Paris, Rome, and Brussels, signaling the transformation of modernism from an embattled fringe movement to an officially recognized component of "high culture."

Expressionist Movements

From the Post-Impressionist period onwards, a great many artists believed that the chief function of making art was to express their intense feelings to the world. In *The Kiss* (fig. **19–2**), Gustav Klimt (1862–1918)—the president of the Vienna Secession, an Austrian Art Nouveau group—depicts a world filled with ominous foreboding. Not evident at first glance is the tension in the couple's physical relationship, most noticeable in the way that the woman's head is forced uncomfortably against her

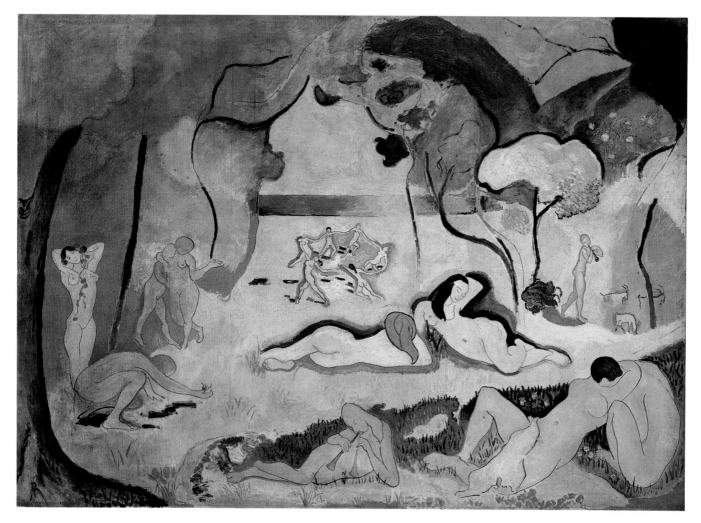

19–3 Henri Matisse. *The Joy of Life.* 1905–1906. Oil on canvas, 5'8$\frac{1}{2}$" × 7'9$\frac{3}{4}$" (1.74 × 2.38 m). The Barnes Foundation, Merion, Pennsylvania

The Joy of Life was originally owned by the brother and sister Leo and Gertrude Stein, important American patrons of European avant-garde art in the early twentieth century. They hung their collection in their Paris apartment, where they hosted an informal salon that attracted many leading literary, musical, and artistic figures, including Matisse and Picasso. In 1913 Leo moved to Italy while Gertrude remained in Paris, pursuing a career as a modernist writer and continuing to host a salon with her companion, Alice B. Toklas

shoulder. That they kneel dangerously close to the edge of a precipice further unsettles the initial impression for those who look beyond the beautiful surface.

The Vienna Secession was part of a generational revolt expressed in art, politics, literature, and the sciences. The Viennese physician Sigmund Freud, founder of psychoanalysis, may be considered part of this larger cultural movement, one of whose major aims was, according to the architect Otto Wagner, "to show modern man his true face." On the other hand, artists such as Klimt also wanted to create a richly decorative art and architecture that would offer an escape from the drab, ordinary world.

Les Fauves

In the 1880s and 1890s, Munch, van Gogh, Paula Modersohn-Becker, Käthe Schmidt Kollwitz, and others developed their personal visions in the 1880s and 1890s. Then, in the years just before World War I, many artists in France, Germany, and Russia turned to Expressionist styles, formed groups of like-minded artists, and finally came to the notice of the critics and the public. The first of these groups emerged in France around 1905. Henri Matisse (1869–1954) and his friends combined the dynamic brushwork of van Gogh with bold primary colors, often applied directly from the tube. The effect was explosive— "like sticks of dynamite," the painter André Derain said—and won the style's practitioners the label *Les Fauves* (French for "the wild beasts," a derogatory name given by the critic Louis Vauxcelles). Dynamic brushwork heightened the energy of the brilliant colors, conveying a new intensity of visual experience.

The Joy of Life (fig. **19–3**) by Matisse treats hedonistic pursuits in a pastoral realm animated by a bouquet of luscious colors. Naked revelers dance, make love, commune with nature, or simply stretch out in their idyllic glade by the sea. Colors freed from naturalistic constraints convey the joyous mood, as do the uninhibited figures. The brushwork, too, is softer, more careful,

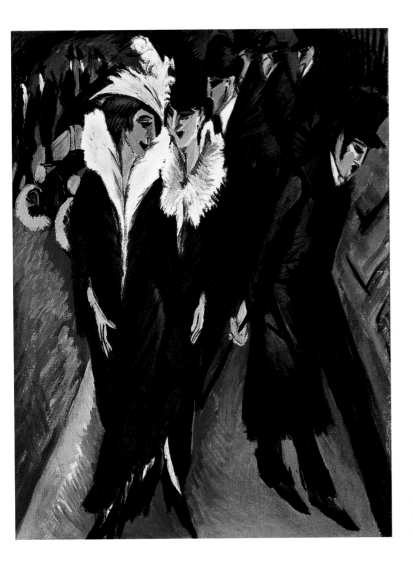

19–4 Ernst Ludwig Kirchner. *Street, Berlin.* 1913. Oil on canvas,
47 1/2″ × 37 7/8″ (120.6 × 91 cm). The Museum of Modern Art, New York

and more subservient to the pure sensuality of the color than in his earlier work. Movement is apparent in the long, flowing curves of the trees and in the sinuous contours of the nude bodies. These undulating rhythms, in combination with the relaxed poses of the two reclining women at the center, establish the quality of "serenity, relief from the stress of modern life," as Matisse characterized his work from this period. In an essay titled "Notes of a Painter," which Matisse published in 1908, he expressed his allegiance to "an art . . . devoid of troubling or depressing subject matter . . . a mental comforter, something like a good armchair in which to rest."

Die Brücke

The German counterpart to Fauvism was Die Brücke ("The Bridge"). In 1905, three architecture students at the Dresden Technical College, including Ernst Ludwig Kirchner (1880–1938), formed what they called a brotherhood. Members of the group admired the writings of the German philosopher Frederich Nietzsche. In *Thus Spoke Zarathustra*, Nietzsche used the metaphor of the bridge to explain how civilization is precariously balanced between two contradictory states of being in the evolutionary process; progress and degeneration, or modernity (the future) and

barbarism (the past). Though tinged with pessimism, Nietzsche's writings emphasize the process of human transformation; they perceive possibilities for rebirth and renewal in "primitive" states such as childhood or in animal instincts.

For Die Brücke artists, both modernity (as symbolized by the metropolis) and the "primitive" held connotations for regeneration—but the two could also signify and lead to regression. The artists associated large urban centers with fresh creativity and new beginnings, yet the modern metropolis tended to breed a competitive climate that recalled a Darwinian struggle for the survival of the fittest. They also believed that just below the surface of polite society seethed a barbarism on the verge of being unleashed. Die Brücke artists were both excited by and wary of this precarious balance.

Kirchner's *Street, Berlin* (fig. **19–4**) captures this dynamic paradox. A crowd of sophisticated urbanites seems to speed toward the foreground. The immediacy of their hurried movement is conveyed through Kirchner's slashing brushstrokes and raw, vibrant colors. Although crowded together physically, the well-dressed men and women seem isolated from one another psychologically; they are inhuman manikins rather than members of a community. Their angular, brittle shapes formally

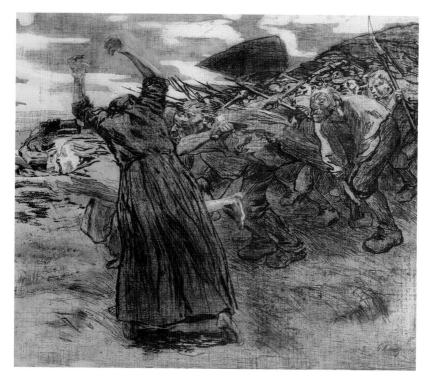

19–5 Käthe Schmidt Kollwitz. *The Outbreak,* from the *Peasants' War* series. 1903. Etching, 20″ × 23⅓″ (50.7 × 59.2 cm). Staatliche Museen zu Berlin, Preussischer Kulturbesitz, Kupferstichkabinett

underscore the message about modern alienation caused by the stress and friction of city living. In Kirchner's painting, the metropolis has become an emblem of the conflicting nature of modernity; it is new and energetic, but it also can evoke the savagery masked by civilized behaviors.

More deeply involved with the ills of society in the early modern period is Käthe Schmidt Kollwitz (1867–1945). Raised in a socialist household, she studied at the Berlin School of Art for Women and at a similar school in Munich. In 1891 she married a doctor who shared her leftist political views, and they settled in a working-class neighborhood in Berlin. Art for her was a political tool, and to reach as many people as possible, she became a printmaker.

Kollwitz hoped to win sympathy for working-class people. Between 1902 and 1908, she produced the *Peasants' War* series, seven etchings that depict events of the sixteenth-century peasant rebellion in a stark graphic style. In *The Outbreak* (fig. **19–5**), Kollwitz takes full advantage of etching techniques to express the peasants' emotive energy exploding against their oppressors. Raw and jagged lines scratched into the plate communicate the peasants' built-up fury from years of mistreatment. In the front, with her back to us, is Black Anna, the leader of the revolt. Kollwitz said that she modeled the figure of Anna after herself.

One artist of the time who found inspiration in Gauguin's formal simplicity and Edenic themes was Paula Modersohn-Becker (1876–1907). Living in the rustic village of Worpswede, an artist's colony in Germany, she became dissatisfied with the pre-vailing naturalist style. She made four trips to Paris between 1900 and her death in 1907 to see the latest developments in art. Her *Self-Portrait with an Amber Necklace* (fig. **19–6**), painted in 1906, testifies to her assimilation of the innovations she saw in France. The basic shapes and simple outlines of the self-portrait—with its prominent eyes as well as its nudity, her body decorated only with flowers and a necklace—suggest that she may have seen African sculpture as well as Post-Impressionist painting. Standing before a screen of flowering plants and tenderly holding two small blooms, she shows herself at one with nature.

Der Blaue Reiter

The last major pre–World War I Expressionist group to come out of the crucible of late-nineteenth-century painting formed in Munich around the Russian painter Vasily Kandinsky (1866–1944). In 1895, after seeing a Monet painting whose color moved him deeply, Kandinsky decided to devote himself to art. He left Moscow to study in Munich because of the research being done there on the effects of color and form on the human psyche. In 1911 Kandinsky organized Der Blaue Reiter ("The Blue Rider" or "The Blue Knight"), a group of nine artists who shared his interest in the power of color. "The Rider" or "The Knight" was the popular Russian name for the image of Saint George, mounted on a horse and slaying a dragon that appeared on the Moscow city emblem. The horseman was blue because Kandinsky considered that color to represent spirituality and the male principle.

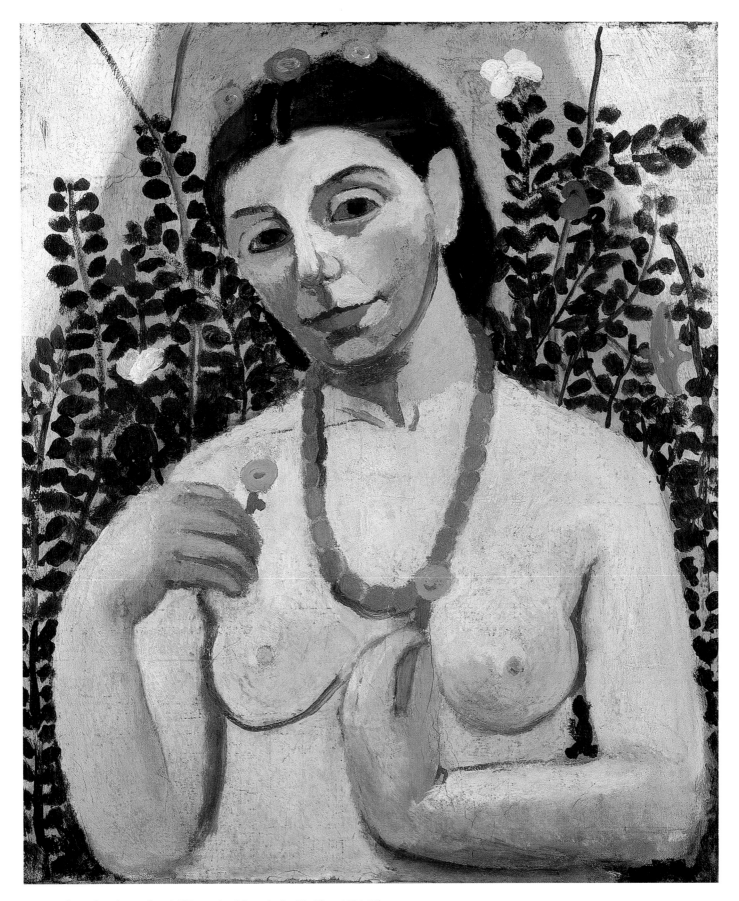

19–6 Paula Modersohn-Becker. *Self-Portrait with an Amber Necklace.* 1906. Oil on canvas, 24″ × 19 3/4″ (61 × 50 cm). Öffentliche Kunstsammlung, Kunstmuseum, Basel, Switzerland

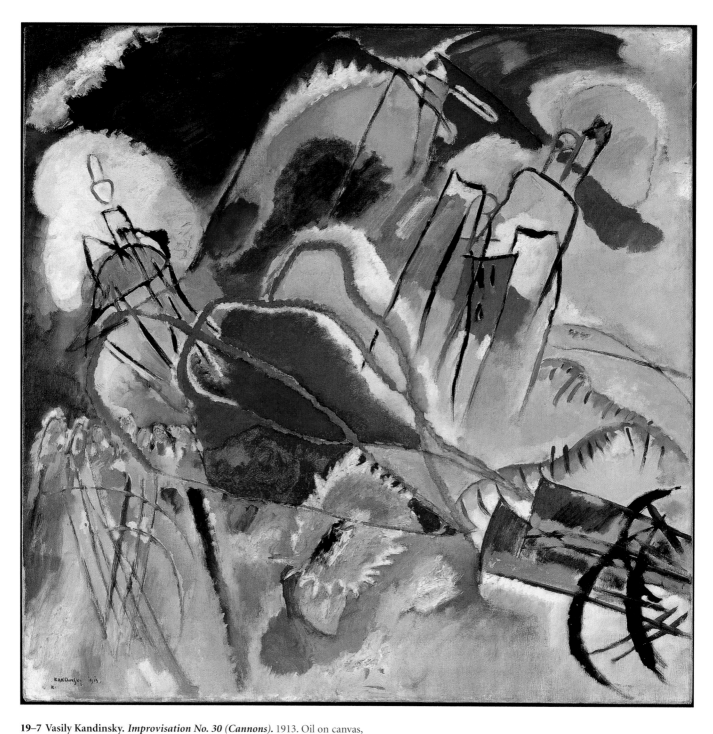

19–7 Vasily Kandinsky. *Improvisation No. 30 (Cannons).* 1913. Oil on canvas,
43 $\frac{1}{4}$″ × 43 $\frac{1}{4}$″ (109.9 × 109.9 cm). The Art Institute of Chicago

Millennial and apocalyptic imagery appeared often in
Kandinsky's art in the years just prior to World War I. According to
an ancient Russian tradition, revived around 1900, Moscow would
be the capital of the world during the millennium, the thousand
years of Christ's reign on Earth that would follow the Apocalypse,
as prophesied by Saint John the Evangelist. In *Improvisation No. 30
(Cannons)* (fig. **19–7**), the firing cannons in the lower right combine with the intense reds, a blackened sky, and precariously leaning buildings and mountains to suggest a scene from the end of the
world. Although sometimes thought to reflect fear of the coming
war, the painting may instead be an ecstatic vision of the destructive prelude to the Second Coming of Christ. Kandinsky never
expected his viewers to understand the symbolism of his forms,
which at times intentionally border on the nonrepresentational.
Instead, he intended to awaken their spirituality through the sheer
force of color that explodes dramatically across the canvas.

The Swiss-born Paul Klee (1879–1940) is among the
best-known artists associated with Der Blaue Reiter, but his

involvement with the group was never more than tangential. A 1914 trip to Tunisia inspired Klee's interest in the expressive potential of color. On his return, he painted a series of watercolors based on his memories of North Africa, among them *Hammamet with Its Mosque* (fig. **19–8**). The play between geometric composition and irregular brushstrokes in this watercolor is reminiscent of Cézanne's work, which Klee had recently seen. The luminous colors and delicate washes (applications of diluted watercolor) result in a gently shimmering effect. Like a careful arrangement of pleasing musical sounds, the subtle modulations of red shapes across the bottom, seem especially melodic.

Klee, who played the violin and belonged to a musical family, seems to have wanted to use color the way a musician would use sound, not to describe appearances but to evoke subtle nuances of feeling. The theory that painting could be nonrepresentational like music was a prevailing idea among many European modernists, especially Expressionists like Klee and Kandinsky. If notes and melodies could evoke an emotive response, so too could pure forms, shapes, colors, and lines.

Cubism

Both the splintered shapes in Kirchner's *Street, Berlin* (see fig. 19–4) and the flattened space and geometric blocks of color in Klee's *Hammamet with Its Mosque* reflect the influence of Cubism, one of the most talked-about "isms" of twentieth-century art. Cubism was the joint invention of Pablo Picasso and Georges Braque.

Picasso (1881–1973), born in Spain and educated in art academies in Barcelona and Madrid, began to make frequent extended visits to Paris, where he moved in 1904. Initially drawn to the socially conscious tradition in French painting that included artists such as Daumier (see Introduction, fig. 16) and Toulouse-Lautrec (see fig. 18–31), Picasso went through an extraordinary and complex transformation between early 1905 and the winter of 1906–1907. Wanting to produce art of greater formal and psychological strength, he began to study classical sculpture at the Louvre. In 1906 the Louvre installed a newly acquired collection of sculpture from Iberia (Spain and Portugal) that dated to the sixth and fifth centuries BCE. These archaic figures

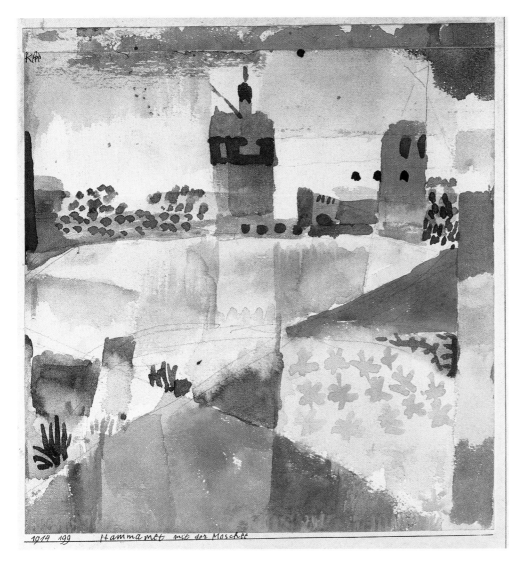

19–8 Paul Klee. *Hammamet with Its Mosque.* 1914. Watercolor and pencil on two sheets of laid paper mounted on cardboard, $8\frac{1}{8}$″ × $7\frac{5}{8}$″ (20.6 × 19.4 cm). The Metropolitan Museum of Art, New York

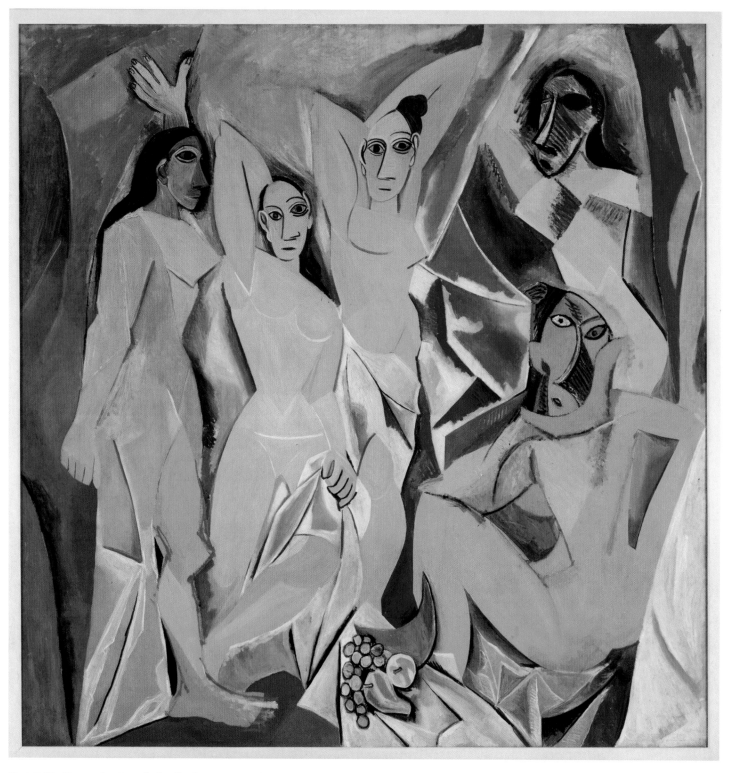

19–9 Pablo Picasso. *Les Demoiselles d'Avignon.* 1907. Oil on canvas, 8′ × 7′8″ (2.43 × 2.33 m).
The Museum of Modern Art, New York

became the chief influence on his work for the next year. His interest in abstraction was reinforced by visits to Spain, where he saw Catalan medieval art (see fig. 10–30), and also by African sculpture (see Chapter 16), which he saw in the ethnographic museum in Paris.

Picasso's wide-ranging studies culminated in 1907 in *Les Demoiselles d'Avignon* (fig. **19–9**). The simplified features and wide, almond-shaped eyes of the three figures on the left reflect the Iberian influence, while the two figures at the right were inspired by African masks. The painting is Picasso's response to *The Joy of Life* by Matisse (see fig. 19–3), exhibited the year before, and to the French classical tradition, which to Picasso was embodied in Ingres's paintings of odalisques (see fig. 17–14). Picasso, however, substituted a bordello for a harem.

The term *demoiselles* was a euphemism for prostitutes, and *Avignon* refers not to the French town but to a street in the red-light district of Barcelona.

Picasso makes the viewer an uneasy participant in the painting. The fruit in the foreground rests on a surface that tilts boldly into the viewer's space at an angle that contradicts the angle at which the female figures are rendered. The women pose for and look directly at us, but they hardly present a conventional picture of yielding femininity. The artist flattened the figures and transformed the entire space into a turbulent series of sharp curves and angles, conveying what one art historian called "a tidal wave of aggression." Two women raise their arms in a traditional gesture of accessibility but contradict it with their hard, piercing gazes and firm mouths. Women, Picasso suggests, are not the gentle and passive creatures men would like them to be.

Picasso's friends were horrified by his new work. Matisse, for example, accused Picasso of making a joke of modern art and threatened to break off their friendship. Only one artist, the French painter Georges Braque (1882–1963), responded positively, and he saw in *Les Demoiselles d'Avignon* a potential that Picasso probably had not fully intended. Picasso was not consciously trying to break with the traditional Western means of depicting space. Yet it was his formal innovation in this area that Braque responded to in this proto-Cubist work; Picasso, Braque observed, had flattened space, incorporated multiple perspectives within a single picture plane, and taken liberties with form much as Cézanne had in his late paintings (see fig. 18–26).

Braque carried the experiment further during 1908. In his landscape painting, he reduced nature's complexity to its essential colors and basic geometric shapes. Matisse remarked on Braque's "little cubes," and the critic Louis Vauxcelles picked up the phrase and wrote that Braque "reduced everything to cubes." Thus the name *Cubism* was born. Braque's painting also pointed Picasso in a new direction, and soon the two artists began an intimate working relationship that lasted until Braque went off to war in 1914.

The move toward abstraction and ultimately to nonrepresentation continued in a series of still-life paintings Braque and Picasso produced over the next two-and-a-half years. In Braque's *Violin and Palette* (fig. **19–10**), the gradual elimination of traditional pictorial space and the reduction of clearly recognizable subject matter is well under way. The still-life items are not arranged on a table with the traditional illusion of depth, but are placed in a shallow space parallel to the picture plane. None of the lines converge at a single point on an established "horizon." Using the passage technique developed by Cézanne (see page 512), Braque knit the various elements together into a single shifting surface of forms, a process he continued to use until he moved toward the complete disintegration of subject matter. Such paintings have been called Analytic Cubism because of the way the artists broke objects into parts as if to analyze them.

The works of 1911 and early 1912 by Picasso and Braque reflect a different approach to the breaking up of forms and the flattening of pictorial space. Instead of simply fracturing an object, they pick it apart and rearrange its elements. Remnants of

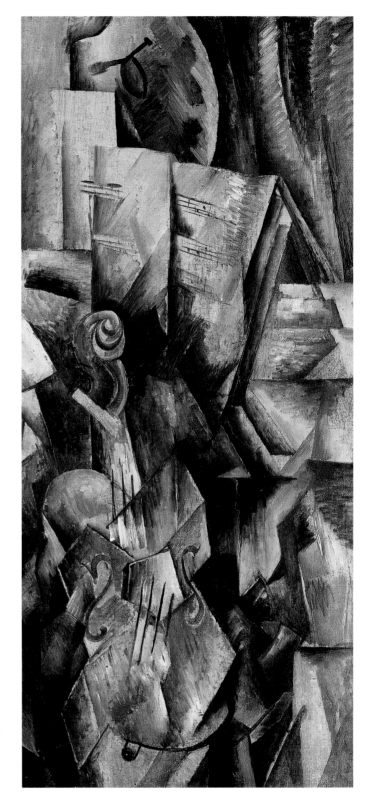

19–10 Georges Braque. *Violin and Palette.* 1909–1910. Oil on canvas, $36\frac{1}{8}''$ × $16\frac{7}{8}''$ (91.8 × 42.9 cm). Solomon R. Guggenheim Museum, New York

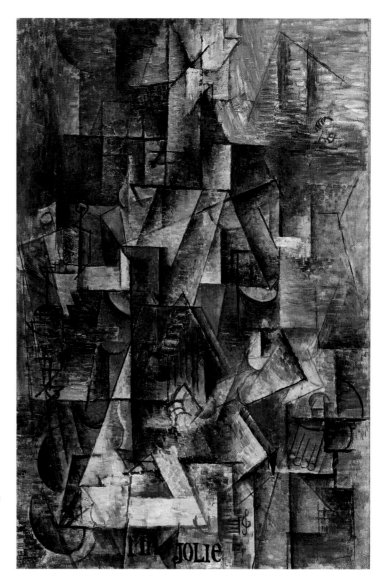

19–11 Pablo Picasso. *Ma Jolie.* 1911–1912. Oil on canvas, 39⅜″ × 25¾″ (100 × 65.4 cm). The Museum of Modern Art, New York

In 1923 Picasso said, "Cubism is no different from any other school of painting. The same principles and the same elements are common to all. The fact that for a long time Cubism has not been understood . . . means nothing. I do not read English, [but] this does not mean that the English language does not exist, and why should I blame anyone . . . but myself if I cannot understand [it]?

the subject are evident throughout Picasso's *Ma Jolie* (fig. **19–11**), for example, but any attempt to reconstruct the image of a woman with a stringed instrument would be misguided because the subject provided only the raw material for a formal composition. *Ma Jolie* is not a representation of a woman, a place, or an event; it is simply "pure painting." Picasso included a musical analogy—a treble clef and the words *Ma Jolie* ("My Pretty One"), a popular song—suggesting that the viewer should approach the painting the way one would a musical composition, either by simply enjoying the arrangement of its elements or by analyzing it, but not by asking what it represents.

A subtle tension between order and disorder is maintained throughout the painting. For example, the shifting effect of the surface, a delicately patterned texture of grays and browns, is regularized through the use of short, horizontal brushstrokes that firmly establish a grid and effectively counteract the surface flux. What at first may seem a random assemblage of lines and muted colors is in fact a well-organized composition. The aesthetic satisfaction of such a work is thus heightened by the way chaos seems to resolve itself into order.

Works like *Ma Jolie* brought Picasso and Braque to the brink of nonrepresentation, but in the spring of 1912 they changed course and began to create works that suggested more clearly discernible subjects. This second major phase of Cubism is known as Synthetic Cubism because of the way the artists created motifs by combining simpler elements, as in a chemical synthesis. Picasso's *Glass and Bottle of Suze* (fig. **19–12**), like many of the works he and Braque created from 1912 to 1914, is a **collage** (from *coller*, "to glue" in French), a technique in which paper or other material is pasted onto another surface. At the center, newsprint and construction paper suggest a tray or round table supporting a glass and a bottle of liquor with an actual label. In true Cubist mode, multiple perspectives are at work. We see simultaneously the top of the blue table, tilted toward us, and the side of a cup. The bottle stands on the table, its label facing us, while we can also see the round top of the bottle and the top of its cork, which are parallel with the angle of the table. Around this arrangement Picasso pasted larger pieces of newspaper and wallpaper. The elements together evoke not only a place, a bar, but also an activity: the viewer alone with a newspaper, enjoying a quiet drink.

The refuge from daily bustle that both art and quiet bars can provide was a central theme in the Synthetic Cubist works of Braque and Picasso. The two artists, however, used different types of newspaper clippings. Braque's clippings deal almost entirely with musical and artistic events, whereas Picasso often included references to political events that would soon shatter the peaceful pleasures these works evoke. In *Glass and Bottle of Suze,* the newspaper clippings deal with the First Balkan War of 1912–1913, which led to World War I.

Responses to Cubism

As the various phases of Cubism emerged from the studios of Braque and Picasso, it became clear to the art world that something of great significance was happening. The radical innovations upset the public and most critics, but members of the avant-garde saw in them the future of art. Even Matisse, the great lyrical colorist and Fauve, took a hard look at the new concept of space and form inaugurated by Picasso and Braque.

Orphism

In the radical painting of Robert Delaunay (1885–1941) and Sonia Delaunay-Terk (1885–1979), there is a greater emphasis on color.

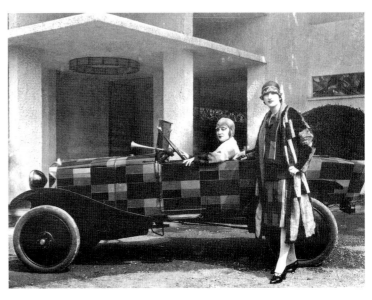

19–13 Sonia Delaunay-Terk. Clothes and customized Citroën B-12. From *Maison de la Mode*, 1925

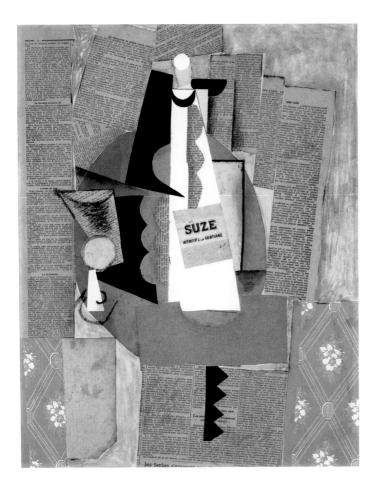

19–12 Pablo Picasso. *Glass and Bottle of Suze.* 1912. Pasted paper, gouache, and charcoal, $25\frac{3}{4} \times 19\frac{3}{4}''$ (65.4 × 50.2 cm). Washington University Gallery of Art, St. Louis, Missouri

Beginning in 1910, the year they married, the couple took Cubism into a new, wholly different direction. They began to fuse Fauvist color with Analytic Cubist form in works dedicated to the modern city and modern technology. The critic and poet Guillaume Apollinaire labeled the style *Orphism* (from Orpheus, the legendary Greek musician), implying an analogy between music and the new abstract style of painting. The Delaunays preferred to think of their work in terms of "simultaneity," a complicated concept connoting the collapse of spatial distance and temporal sequence into a simultaneous "here and now," and the creation of harmonic unity out of discordant elements.

Delaunay-Terk became a distinguished textile and fashion designer. Her greatest critical success came in 1925 at the International Exposition of Modern Decorative and Industrial Arts, for which she decorated a Citroën sports car to match one of her textile designs (fig. **19–13**). Her bold geometric patterns seem to express the new modernity of the automobile age. Moreover, the small three-seater Citroën was specifically designed to appeal to the "new woman," who, like Delaunay-Terk, was more mobile, less tied to home and family, and less dependent on men than her predecessors.

Futurism

In Italy, Cubism led to Futurism, which emerged on February 20, 1909, when a Milanese literary magazine editor, Filippo Marinetti, published his "Foundation and Manifesto of Futurism" in a Paris newspaper. An outspoken attack against everything old, dull, "feminine," and safe, Marinetti's manifesto promoted the supposedly exhilarating "masculine" experiences of warfare and reckless speed to liberate Italy from its outworn past.

Among the artists and poets who gathered around Marinetti was Umberto Boccioni (1882–1916), whose major sculptural

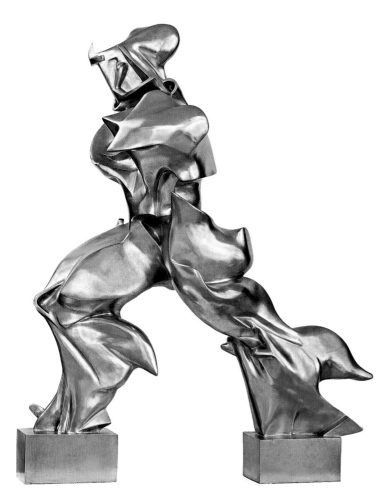

ian artists who adopted French styles with some ambivalence. Among her creations were costumes and sets that she designed for the impresario Sergei Diaghilev's famed Ballets Russes, including the performances of *Le Coq d'or* (1914) *Night on Bald Mountain* (1923), and the 1926 revival of Stravinsky's *Firebird*.

Goncharova and her lifelong companion, Mikhail Larionov (1881–1964), were torn between the desire to develop a native, characteristically Russian art and the wish to keep up with Western European developments. Exposed to French and Italian art and also the Slavophile (pro-Russian) movement in Moscow, they created a new Russian style known as Cubo-Futurism. In her *Electric Light* (fig. **19–15**), Goncharova combines two styles, simplified Cubist shapes and a dynamic Futurist composition. Brilliant electric light bulbs almost explode into yellow discs and rays, energized by their swinging, snake-like cords and switches. The painting is at the same time a study in contrasting enhanced colors and a potent symbol of technological advance - of Russia's modernity.

Suprematism

After Goncharova and Larionov left for Paris in 1915, their colleague Kazimir Malevich (1878–1935) emerged as the leading figure of the Moscow avant-garde. Indeed, Malevich was the first Russian to go beyond Cubo-Futurism, and he did so spectacularly and unforgettably. Malevich is recognized as the modernist artist who produced the first truly nonrepresentational work of

19–14 Umberto Boccioni. *Unique Forms of Continuity in Space.* 1913. Bronze, $43\frac{7}{8}''\times34\frac{7}{8}''\times15\frac{3}{4}''$ (111.4 × 88.6 × 40 cm). The Museum of Modern Art, New York

Boccioni and the Futurist architect Antonio Sant'Elia were both killed in World War I. The Futurists had ardently promoted Italian entry into the war on the side of France and England. After the war Marinetti's movement, still committed to nationalism and militarism, supported the rise of Fascism under Benito Mussolini, although a number of the original members of the group rejected this direction.

work, *Unique Forms of Continuity in Space* (fig. **19–14**), seems to epitomize a revitalized Italy. Cubist figure studies, which Boccioni saw in Paris in 1911, inspired the exaggerated muscular curves and counter-curves of this powerful sculpture, the stretched and inflated forms of which express the figure's force and speed. The work personifies the new Italian man envisioned by the Futurists, a strong figure rushing headlong into the brave new Futurist world.

Since the time of Peter the Great (ruled 1682–1725), the Russian upper classes had turned to Western Europe for cultural models. Knowledge of Analytic Cubism and Futurism arrived in Moscow almost simultaneously, and since the two had some superficial similarities, Russian artists tended to link them. Natalia Goncharova (1881–1962) was one of many Russ-

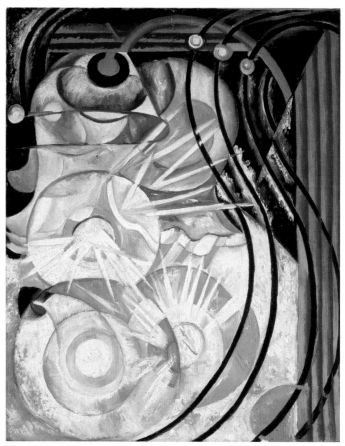

19–15 Natalia Goncharova. *Electric Light.* 1913. Oil on canvas, $41\frac{1}{2}''\times32''$ (1055 × 81.3 cm). Musee National d'Art Moderne. Centre National d'Art et de Culture. George Pompidou. Art Resource

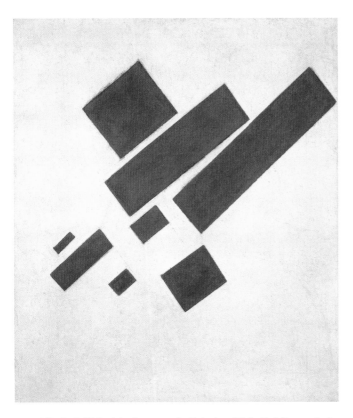

19–16 Kazimir Malevich. *Suprematist Painting (Eight Red Rectangles).* 1915. Oil on canvas, 22$\frac{1}{2}$″ × 18$\frac{7}{8}$″ (57 × 48 cm). Stedelijk Museum, Amsterdam

flapped when he moved his arms. Dressed in this manner, he slowly and solemnly recited the poem, which consisted entirely of nonsense sounds. By retreating into sound alone, he avoided language, which he believed had been spoiled by the lies and excesses of journalism and advertising. Ball wanted to introduce the healthy play of children back into restricted adult lives, and—as was typical of Dada—his performance also had a playful element.

The flexibility of interpretation inherent in Dada extended to its name, too. In German, the term signifies "baby talk"; in French, it means "hobbyhorse"; and in Russian, "yes, yes." The name, and the movement, could be defined as the individual wished.

The Dada movement first spread from Zürich to New York and Barcelona, and then to Berlin (1918), Cologne, and Paris. The leading figure in the New York group was the French artist Marcel Duchamp (1887–1968), who had moved to New York in 1915. Duchamp and his friends maintained that art should appeal to the mind rather than to the senses. This cerebral approach is exemplified in Duchamp's **readymades,** which were ordinary manufactured objects transformed into artworks simply through their selection by the artist. The most notorious

art. According to his later reminiscences, "in the year 1913, in my desperate attempt to free art from the burden of the object, I took refuge in the square form and exhibited a picture which consisted of nothing more than a black square on a white field." Malevich exhibited 39 works in this radically new mode in St. Petersburg in the winter of 1915–1916. One work, *Suprematist Painting (Eight Red Rectangles)* (fig. **19–16**), consists simply of rectangles arranged diagonally on a white painted ground. Malevich called this art "Suprematism," short for "the supremacy of pure feeling in creative art." By eliminating traditional subject matter and focusing entirely on formal issues, Malevich freed twentieth-century artists to explore the previously untapped potential of nonrepresentational works of visual art.

Dada

The Dada movement, which began with the opening of the Cabaret Voltaire in Zürich, Switzerland, on February 5, 1916, was a remarkable manifestation of the disillusioned mood of the times. The cabaret's founders, the German actor and artist Hugo Ball (1886–1927) and his companion, Emmy Hennings, a nightclub singer, attracted a circle of avant-garde writers and artists who shared in Ball's and Hennings's disgust with bourgeois culture.

Ball's performance while reciting one of his sound poems, "Karawane" (fig. **19–17**), reflects the spirit of the cabaret. Ball encased his legs and body in blue cardboard tubes, and wore on his head a white-and-blue "witch-doctor's hat," as he called it. The huge gold-painted cardboard collar over his shoulders

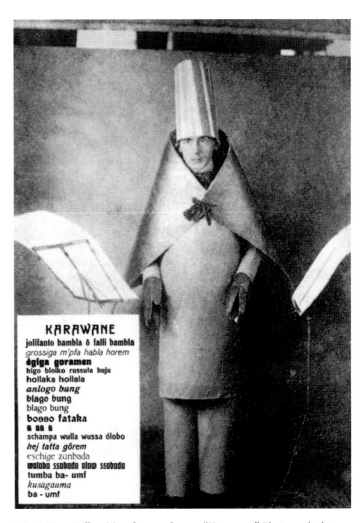

19–17 Hugo Ball reciting the sound poem "Karawane." Photographed at the Cabaret Voltaire, Zürich, 1916

ELEMENTS OF **Architecture**
The Skyscraper

The skyscraper depended on the development of these essentials: metal beams (or girders) and columns for the structural-support skeleton; the separation of the building-support structure from the enclosing layer (the cladding); fireproofing materials and measures; elevators; and plumbing, central heating, artificial lighting, and ventilation systems. First-generation skyscrapers, built between about 1880 and 1900, were concentrated in the Midwest, especially Chicago. Second-generation skyscrapers, with more than 20 stories, date from 1895.

At first the tall buildings were freestanding towers, sometimes with a base. New York City's Building Zone Resolution of 1916 introduced mandatory setbacks—recessions from the ground-level building line—to ensure light and ventilation of adjacent sites. Built in 1931, the 1,250-foot, setback-form Empire State Building, diagrammed here, is thoroughly modern in having a streamlined exterior that conceals the great complexity of the internal structure and mechanisms that make its height possible. The Empire State Building is still one of the tallest buildings in the world.

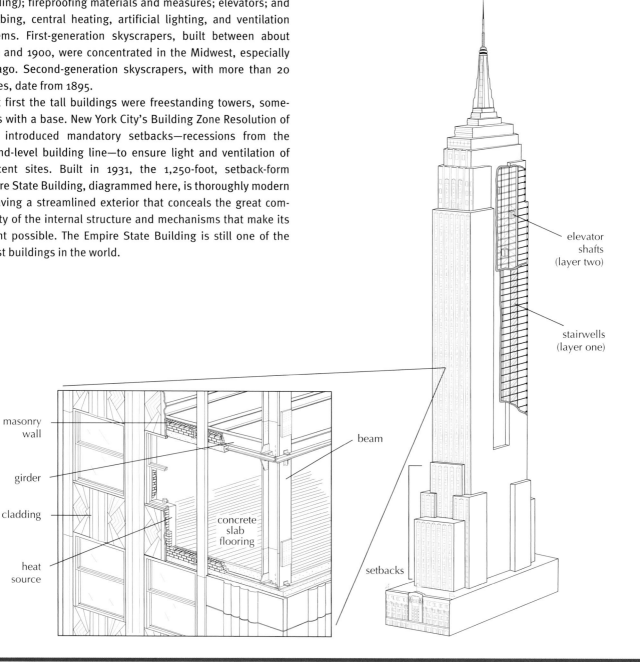

elevator
shafts
(layer two)

stairwells
(layer one)

masonry
wall

girder

cladding

heat
source

beam

concrete
slab
flooring

setbacks

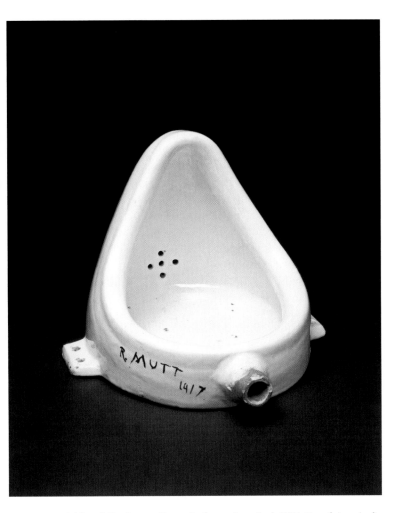

19–18 Marcel Duchamp. *Fountain (second version).* 1950. Porcelain urinal, 12″ × 15″ × 18″ (30.5 × 38.1 × 45.7 cm). Readymade: Glazed Sanitary China with Black Paint. Philadelphia Museum of Art

GIFT (BY EXCHANGE) OF MRS. HERBERT CAMERON MORRIS. © 2006 ARS ARTISTS RIGHTS SOCIETY, NY

An ordinary plumbing fixture signed by Duchamp with the pseudonym "R. Mutt" and presented as a "readymade" work of art, the original Fountain *mysteriously disappeared shortly after it was rejected by the jury of the American Society of Independent Artists exhibition in 1917. The appearance of this lost original is known only from a photograph by Alfred Stieglitz. The second version of* Fountain, *illustrated here, was selected in Paris by the art dealer Sidney Janis at Duchamp's request for an exhibition in New York in 1950. In 1964, Duchamp supervised the production of a small edition of replicas of the original* Fountain *based on the Stieglitz photograph. One of these replicas sold at auction in 1999 for $1.76 million, setting a record for a work by Duchamp.*

readymade was *Fountain* (fig. **19–18**), a porcelain urinal turned 90 degrees and signed with the pseudonym "R. Mutt," a play on the name of the fixture's manufacturer. Duchamp submitted *Fountain* anonymously in 1917 to the first exhibition of the American Society of Independent Artists, open to anyone who paid a $6 entry fee. Duchamp, a founding member of the society, entered the found object partly as a test. A majority of the society's directors declared that the *Fountain* was not a work of art, and, moreover, was indecent, so the piece was refused. Duchamp immediately resigned from the society.

Duchamp wrote, "The only works of art America has given are her plumbing and bridges." In a more serious vein, he added: "Whether Mr. Mutt with his own hands made the fountain or not has no importance. He CHOSE it. He took an ordinary article of life, placed it so that its useful significance disappeared under the new title and point of view—created a new thought for that object." Duchamp's philosophy of the readymade, succinctly expressed in these words, had a tremendous impact on later twentieth-century artists.

Duchamp's most intellectually challenging work is *The Bride Stripped Bare by Her Bachelors, Even* (see fig. 19–1). Notes that Duchamp made while working on the piece confirm that it operates on several intellectual and aesthetic levels. Most fundamentally it is a pessimistic statement of the insoluble frustrations of male-female relations. Loaded with layers of irony, the work is also a statement about the role of chance in the creative process. For example, after the piece sat in storage for several years, some of the dust that had collected on its surface was glued permanently into place.

Modern Art Comes to the United States

At the end of the nineteenth century, American artists, led by the artist and teacher Robert Henri (1865–1929), sought a purely "American" style, free from both European academic conventions and the then dominant Impressionist style. In 1908, Henri organized an exhibition of paintings by artists who came to be called "The Eight," five of whom became known as members of the Ashcan School because of their interest in depicting scenes of gritty urban life in New York City.

An outspoken opponent of the Ashcan School was the photographer Alfred Stieglitz (1864–1946), who chose a different approach in photographing the quintessentially modern city of New York (see fig. **19–19**). In 1905 Stieglitz opened a New York gallery where he exhibited contemporary art and photography, hoping to break down the artificial barrier between the two. Located at 291 Fifth Avenue, the Little Galleries of the Photo-Secession was soon simply called 291. In collaboration with another American photographer, Edward Steichen (1879–1973), who then lived in Paris, Stieglitz arranged exhibitions unlike any seen before in the United States, showing works by Cézanne, Toulouse-Lautrec, Rodin, Picasso, Braque, Matisse, and the Rumanian sculptor Constantin Brancusi.

The event that climaxed Stieglitz's pioneering efforts on behalf of European modernism (although he did not arrange it) was the so-called Armory Show, an "International Exhibition of Modern Art," which was held in 1913 at the 69th Regiment Armory in New York City. The aim of the exhibition was to demonstrate how outmoded the views of the National Academy of Design were. The Armory Show also demonstrated how old-fashioned the American realistic approach to painting was.

Of the more than 1,300 works in the show, only about a third were by Europeans, but it was to these works that primary attention was paid. Critics claimed that Matisse, Kandinsky, Braque, and others were the agents of "universal anarchy." The American academic painter Kenyon Cox called them mere "savages." When a selection of works from the show were exhibited in Chicago, civic leaders there called for a morals commission to investigate the exhibition.

A number of younger artists, however, responded positively to the new art. Marsden Hartley's modernist painting

Portrait of a German Officer (fig. **19–20**) does not literally represent its subject but speaks symbolically through the use of numbers, letters, and fragments of German military paraphernalia and insignia. Hartley mourned the death of his close friend, a young Prussian lieutenant, Karl von Freyburg, through the act of painting. References to Freyburg include his initials ("Kv.F"), his age (24), his regiment number (4), epaulettes, lance tips, and the Iron Cross he was awarded the day before he was killed. The cursive E may refer to Harley himself, whose given name was Edmund. Even the seemingly abstract, geometric patterns have symbolic meaning: the blue-and-white diamond pattern comes from the Bavarian flag; the black-and-white stripes represent the Prussian flag; and the red, white, and black bands constitute the flag of the German Empire, adopted in 1871. Note also the black-and-white checkerboard pattern, which commemorates Freyburg's love of chess.

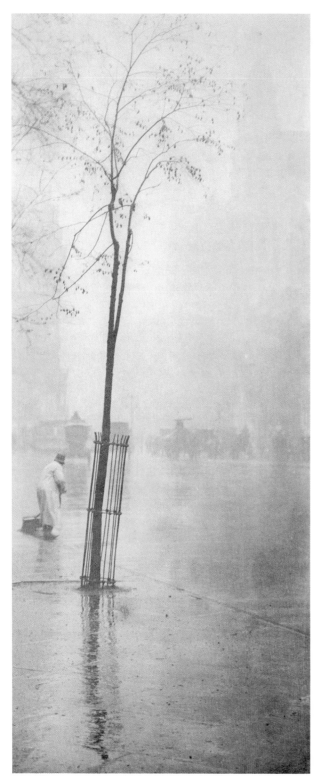

19–19 Alfred Stieglitz. *Spring Showers.* 1902. (30 × 12.6 cm).
The Alfred Stieglitz Collection, The Art Institute of Chicago
1949.849

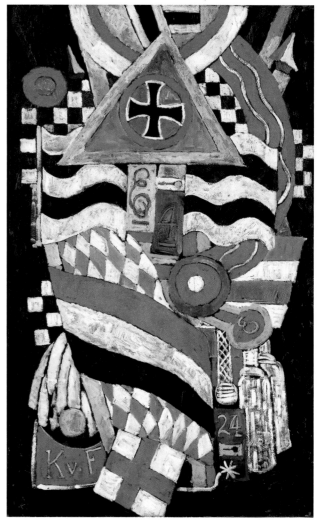

19–20 Marsden Hartley. *Portrait of a German Officer.*
1914. Oil on canvas, 68$\frac{1}{4}$″ × 41$\frac{3}{8}$″ (1.78 × 10.5 m).
The Metropolitan Museum of Art, New York

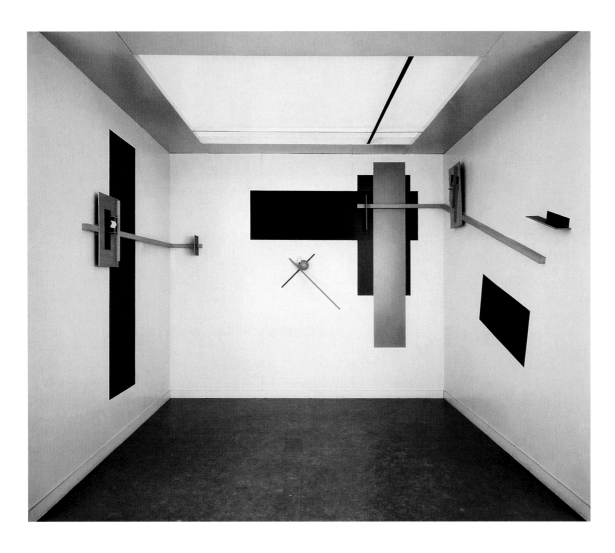

19–21 El Lissitzky. Proun space created for a Berlin art exhibition. 1923, reconstruction 1965. Stedelijk Van Abbemuseum, Eindhoven, the Netherlands

Art Between the Wars

The wars that ravaged Europe in the first half of the twentieth century had a profound effect on Western artists and architects. The dizzying array of "isms" that fragmented the European art world before World War I offered many formal options to postwar innovators. After the Great War, as World War I was then known, members of artists' groups such as the Dutch de Stijl and the German Bauhaus sought the basis for a new society in severely rational beauty and order. The Surrealists, in contrast, celebrated subjectivity, intuition, and chance. In the United States, many artists retreated from European-inspired modernism into a focus on the American scene. Only in the late 1930s and 1940s did artists and architects fleeing Hitler's Europe renew American interest in nonrepresentational art. Abstract Expressionism, the first modernist painting style of international importance developed in the United States, emerged during World War II and the immediate postwar period (see Chapter 20).

The Armory Show of 1913 had marked an important turning point in the history of art in the United States. In the ten years after the exhibition, American artists began to assimilate the most recent developments in European art and for the first time in their history, they began to break free from their provincial status. In the United States, many artists retreated from European-inspired modernism into a focus on the American scene.

Europe

Constructivism

In Russia, the most dynamic artistic achievements of the period immediately following World War I came from avant-garde artists who enthusiastically supported the Russian Revolution, during which the czar was overthrown in March 1917. After this, the Bolsheviks (radical Socialists) rose to power under Vladimir Lenin in November 1917.

Artists of the Russian Revolution known as Constructivists were committed to the notion that the artist should leave the studio and "go into the factory, where the real body of life is made." They envisioned politically engaged artists devoted to creating useful objects and promoting the aims of collective society.

One of the members of this socially visionary movement was an engineer, El Lissitzky (1890–1941). After the revolution, he taught architecture and graphic arts and soon came under the influence of Malevich, who was a fellow professor. By 1919 El Lissitzsky was using Malevich's formal vocabulary for propaganda posters and for artworks he called *Prouns,* an acronym for "Project for the Affirmation of the New." He made a Proun space for an exhibition in Germany (fig. **19–21**), the engineered look of which is meant not merely to celebrate industrial technology but to encourage precise thinking among the viewers.

De Stijl

In the Netherlands the counterpart to the inspired **formalism** of El Lissitzky was the De Stijl ("The Style") movement, led by Piet Mondrian (1872–1944). De Stijl was grounded in the conviction that there are two kinds of beauty: a sensual or subjective one and a higher, rational, objective, "universal" kind. In his mature works, Mondrian sought the essence of the second kind, eliminating representational elements because of their subjective associations and curves because of their sensual appeal.

In paintings such as *Composition with Red, Blue, and Yellow* (fig. **19–22**), he restricted his formal vocabulary to the three **primary colors** (red, yellow, and blue), the three neutrals (black, gray, and white), and horizontal and vertical lines. The two linear directions are meant to symbolize the harmony of a series of opposites, including male versus female, individual versus society, and spiritual versus material. For Mondrian the essence of higher beauty was "dynamic equilibrium," which he achieved through the precise arrangement of color areas of different visual weight. For example, in fig. 19–22, the heavier weight of the large red area threatens to tip the painting to the right, but the placement of the smaller rectangle of blue at the lower left prevents this imbalance by balancing the red's weight. Mondrian

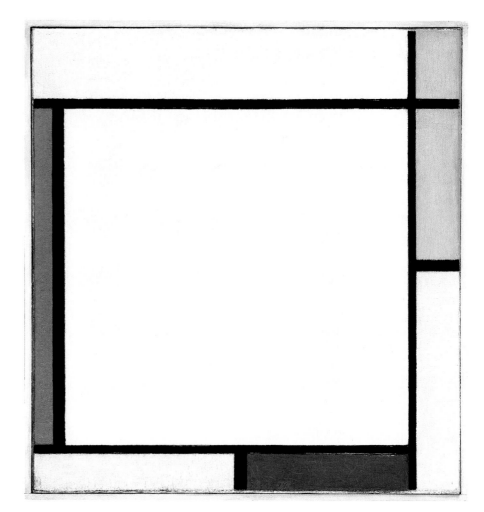

19–22 Piet Mondrian. *Composition with Red, Blue, and Yellow.* 1930. Oil on canvas, $18\frac{1}{8}$" × $18\frac{1}{8}$" (46.038 × 46.038 cm). The Menil Collection, Houston

© 2004 MONDRIAN/HOLTZMAN TRUST

Mondrian so disliked the sight of nature, whose irregularities he held largely accountable for humanity's problems, that when seated at a restaurant table with a view of the outdoors, he would ask to be moved.

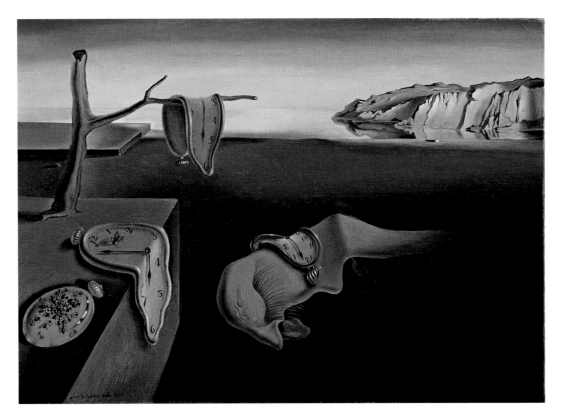

19–23 Salvadore Dalí. *The Persistence of Memory.* 1931. Oil on canvas, $9\frac{1}{2}''$ × 13″ (24.1 × 33 cm). The Museum of Modern Art, New York

and his colleagues hoped that this method of composition, based on ideas of balance and the resolution of conflict, would help stabilize the viewer as well, "purifying" humankind's chaotic natural instincts.

Surrealism

The intellectual successor to the Dada movement of the teens was Surrealism, a movement founded by the French writer André Breton (1896–1966). Breton sought to free human behavior from the constrictions of reason and bourgeois morality. In 1924 he published his *Manifesto of Surrealism,* outlining his own view of Freud's theory that the human psyche is a battleground where the rational forces of the conscious mind struggle against the irrational, instinctual urges of the unconscious. Breton and his followers employed a number of techniques for liberating the individual unconscious, including dream analysis, free association, **automatic writing**, word games, and hypnotic trances. Their aim was to help people discover the larger reality, or "surreality," that lay beyond conventional notions of what was real.

Among the writers and artists around Breton was the Spanish painter and printmaker Salvador Dalí (1904–1989). Dalí contributed the "paranoiac-critical method" to Surrealist practice.

In this approach, the sane man or woman cultivates the ability of the paranoiac to misread ordinary appearances in order to free himself or herself from the shackles of conventional thought. Dalí demonstrated his method in *The Persistence of Memory* (fig. **19–23**) by placing limp timepieces in a very realistic view of the Bay of Rosas near his birthplace in Catalonia.

According to Dalí, the idea of the soft watches came to him one evening after dinner while he was meditating on a plate of ripe Camembert cheese. One of the limp watches drapes over an amoeba-like human head, its shape inspired by a large rock on the coast. The head, which Dalí identified as a self-portrait, appeared in several paintings and, in combination with the limp watches, may express the anxiety Dalí felt concerning his own sexuality. Another image of anxiety in the work is the ant-covered watchcase at the lower left, inspired by Dalí's childhood memories of seeing dead animals swarming with ants. The absurd yet compelling image of ants feeding on a metallic watch typifies the Surrealist interest in unexpected juxtapositions of disparate realities. Dalí's choice of a highly realistic style makes his irrational world seem more convincing and more unsettling.

Building on Duchamp's earlier found objects, the Swiss artist Meret Oppenheim (1913–1985) produced disquieting assemblages such as *Object* (*Le Dejeuner en fourrure*) (fig. **19–24**). Oppenheim was one of the few female participants in the Surrealist movement. Consisting of a cup, saucer, and spoon covered with the fur of a Chinese gazelle, Oppenheim's work transforms implements normally used for drinking tea into a hairy ensemble that simultaneously attracts and repels the viewer.

In contrast, a blithe and playful spirit animates the painting of Joan Miró (1893–1983), another Catalan artist who exhibited on numerous occasions with the Surrealists, but who never officially joined the group or shared its theoretical interests. In *Dutch Interior I* (fig. **19–25**), Miró imaginatively paraphrased a seventeenth-century Dutch painting of a lute player serenading a young woman with a dog and cat on the floor. Miró playfully translated these elements into a **biomorphic** language of curving shapes and lines that evoke organic forms and seem to mutate before the viewer's eyes. The animated forms and cheerful colors create a giddy effect, counterbalanced by the crisply delineated shapes and tightly structured composition that reveal a high degree of formal control.

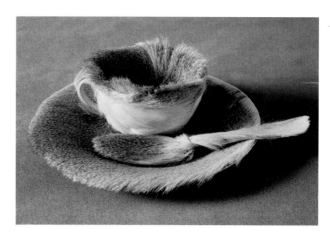

19–24 Meret Oppenheim. *Object* (*Le Dejeuner en fourrure*) */ Luncheon in Fur.* 1936. Fur-covered cup, diameter $4\frac{3}{8}''$ (10.9 cm); fur-covered saucer, diameter $9\frac{3}{8}''$ (23.7 cm); fur-covered spoon, length $8''$ (20.2 cm); overall height, $2\frac{7}{8}''$ (7.3 cm). The Museum of Modern Art, New York

Oppenheim's Object *was inspired by a café conversation with Picasso about her designs for jewelry made of fur-lined metal tubing. When Picasso remarked that one could cover just about anything with fur, Oppenheim replied, "Even this cup and saucer."*

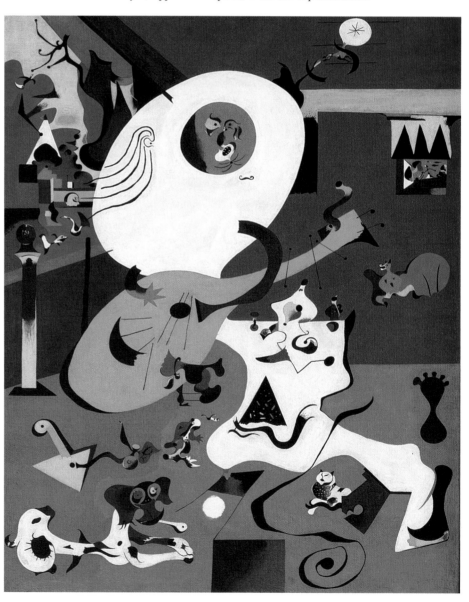

19–25 Joan Miró. *Dutch Interior, I.* 1928. Oil on canvas, $36\frac{1}{8}'' \times 28\frac{3}{4}''$ (91.8 × 73 cm). The Museum of Modern Art, New York

Sculpture

Constantin Brancusi (1876–1957) took a different approach as he sought to portray "the essence of things." Brancusi arrived in Paris from his native Romania in 1904. By 1907 he was an assistant to Rodin (fig. 18–33) but he soon rejected Rodin's modeling method for the technique of direct carving. In his mature sculpture, such as the *Torso of a Young Man* (fig. **19–26**), he emphasized formal and conceptual simplicity, distilling his subject into smooth and purified forms. He has turned this fragment of the human body into three cylinders, which he balances on two cubes and two trapezoids. Motivating this change was Brancusi's interest in the ancient Greek philosophy of Plato, who held that all worldly objects and beings are imperfect imitations of their perfect models, or ideas, which exist only in the mind. Like Plato, Brancusi sought timeless essence, and he tried to capture the higher world of ideas through elegantly simplified forms.

In most of his own works of the 1920s and 1930s, Henry Moore (1898–1986) practiced direct carving in stone and wood as a way of pursuing the ideal of "truth to material." A central subject in Moore's art is the reclining female figure, such as *Recumbent Figure* (fig. **19–27**), whose massive, simplified forms recall Pre-Columbian art. The carving reveals Moore's sensitivity to the inherent qualities of the stone, whose natural striations harmonize with the sinuous surfaces of the design. While certain elements of the body are clearly defined, such as the head and breasts, supporting elbow, and raised knee, other parts flow together into an undulating mass more suggestive of a hilly landscape than of a human body. An open cavity penetrates the torso, emphasizing the relationship of solid and void fundamental to Moore's art. The sculptor wrote in 1937, "A hole can itself have as much shape-meaning as a solid mass."

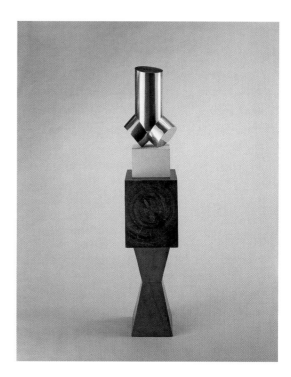

19–26 Constantin Brancusi, *Torso of a Young Man.* 1924. Bronze on stone and wood bases; combined fig. and bases $40\frac{3}{8}'' \times 20'' \times 18\frac{1}{4}''$ (102.4 × 50.5 × 46.1 cm). Hirshhorn Museum and Sculpture Garden, Smithsonian Institution.

GIFT OF JOSEPH H. HIRSHHORN, 1966

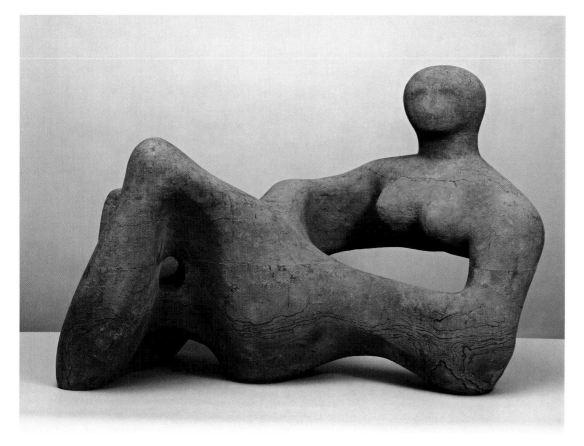

19–27 Henry Moore. *Recumbent Figure. 1938. Hornton stone, length 55″ (141 cm). Tate Gallery, London

© HENRY MOORE ESTATE. TATE GALLERY, LONDON/ART RESOURCE, NY

Originally carved for the garden of the architect Serge Chermayeff in Sussex, Moore's sculpture was situated next to a low-lying modernist building with an open view of the gently rolling landscape. "My figure looked out across a great sweep of the Downs, and her gaze gathered at the horizon," Moore later recalled. "The sculpture had no specific relationship to the architecture. It had its own identity and did not need to be on Chermayeff's terrace, but it so to speak enjoyed being there, and I think it introduced a humanizing element; it became a mediator between modern house and ageless land." (Marcel)

ven artists such as Pablo Picasso, who was not actually part of the Surrealist group, profited from the
approaches and techniques pioneered by the Surrealists. The expressive forms of *Guernica* (fig. **19–28**)—
fragmented, distorted, and evocative of much more than
words can say—would not have been possible without the
lessons of Surrealism.

The Spanish Civil War between Republicans and Fascists
had begun in 1936. In April 1937, German pilots of the famous
Condor Legion—flying for the Spanish fascist leader General
Francisco Franco—bombed the Basque city of Guernica,
killing more than 1,600 men, women, and children. Countries
all over the globe were shocked by the world's first aerial
bombing of civilians, which some historians, in retrospect,
see as a prelude to World War II.

Pablo Picasso, who was living in Paris at the time, reacted to the massacre by creating a monumental painting that
has become a symbol of the brutality of war and humanity's
struggle for freedom from oppression. A damning indictment
of the Fascists, *Guernica* is a stark, hallucinatory nightmare,

focusing on its victims. Picasso restricted his palette to
black, gray, and white—the **tones** of the newspaper photographs that publicized the atrocity. Expressively distorted
women, one holding a dead child and another in a burning
house, wail in desolation at the carnage. The suffering Spanish Republic takes the form of a screaming horse, an image
also taken to represent betrayed innocence. To the left is a
bull, thought to symbolize either Franco or Spain. An electric
light and a woman holding a lantern suggest Picasso's desire
to reveal the event in all its horror.

The painting, commissioned by the short-lived Spanish
Republican government for the Spanish pavilion at the
world's fair in Paris in 1937, became a famous symbol of the
inhumanity of fascism and war. That same summer Hitler
held the infamous exhibition of "degenerate art" in Munich
(see "Suppression of the Avant-Garde in Germany," page
538). During World War II, which Picasso spent in Paris, a
Nazi officer showed him a reproduction of *Guernica* and
asked, "Is that you who did that?" Picasso is said to have
replied, "No, it is you."

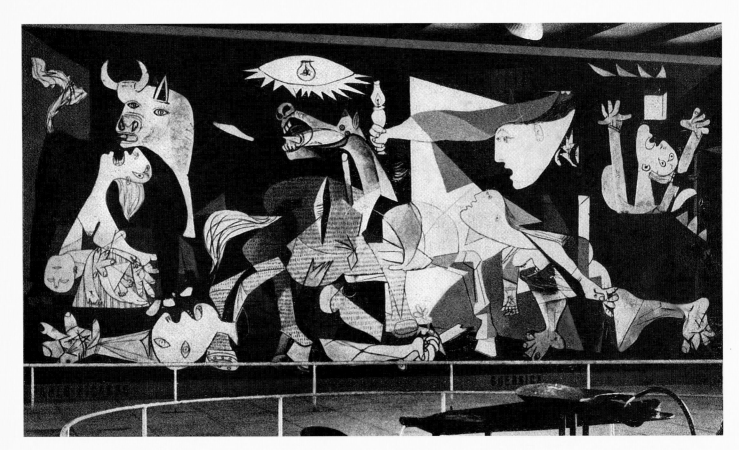

19–28 Pablo Picasso. *Guernica*. 1937. Oil on canvas, 11′6″ × 25′8″ (3.5 × 7.8 m). Museo Nacional Centro de Arte Reina Sofia, Madrid. On permanent loan
from the Museo del Prado, Madrid. Shown installed in the Spanish Pavilion of the Paris Exposition, 1937. In the foreground: Alexander Calder's *Fontaine de
Mercure*. Mercury, sheet metal, wire rod, pitch, and paint, 44″ × 115″ × 77″ (122 × 292 × 196 cm). Fundacio Joan Miró, Barcelona

Art in North America

The United States

The American sculptor and engineer Alexander Calder (1898–1976) made contact with members of the Dada and Surrealist groups on visits to Paris in the 1920s and 1930s. He also visited Mondrian's studio, where he was impressed by the rectangles of colored paper that Mondrian had tacked up everywhere on the walls. What would it be like, he wondered, if the flat shapes were moving freely in space, interacting in not just two but three dimensions? The experience inspired Calder to begin creating mobiles, sculptures like his *Lobster Trap and Fish Tail* (fig. **19–29**) in which the individual parts float and bob in response to shifting currents of air. At first, this mobile seems almost nonrepresentational, but Calder's title works on our imagination, helping us to find the oval trap awaiting unwary crustaceans at the right and the delicate wires at the left that suggest the backbone of a fish. The term *mobile,* which in French means both "moving body" and "motive," or "driving force," came from Calder's friend Marcel Duchamp, who no doubt relished the double meaning of the word.

In the early decades of the twentieth century, American artists like Calder had to go to Europe if they wanted to keep abreast of developments in contemporary art. Alfred Stieglitz's gallery at 291 was one of the few places where they could see the more radical manifestations of contemporary European art and the work of pioneering American modernists such as Georgia O'Keeffe (1887–1986).

In her drawings and paintings, O'Keeffe—who lived with Stieglitz starting in 1920—adopted the formal qualities of

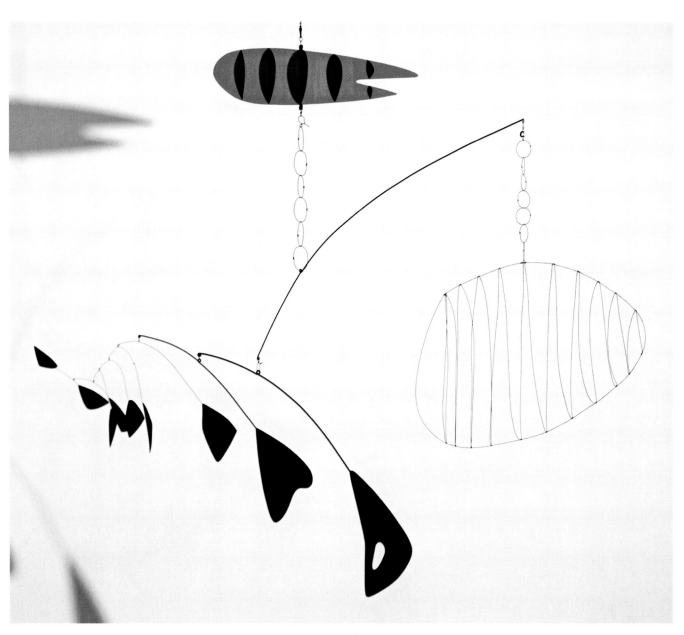

19–29 Alexander Calder. *Lobster Trap and Fish Tail.* 1939. Hanging mobile of painted steel wire and sheet aluminum, height 8′6″ (2.6 m). The Museum of Modern Art, New York

Cubism and the energy of Futurism to her own personal vision. Beginning in 1924, the year of her marriage to Stieglitz, O'Keeffe's paintings of flowers (see Introduction, fig. 4), gigantic and distorted through her use of camera-like close-up views, recall Surrealism in their suggestion of female sexuality. O'Keeffe worked with abstract patterns and sharp linear qualities while at the same time paying homage to the American tradition of realism. This intense scrutiny of nature combined with the use of the close-up also inspired the work of photographer Edward Weston (see Introduction, fig. 3).

After World War I, the United States entered a period of isolationism that would last until the Japanese bombing of Pearl Harbor in 1941. Struggling through the economic distress of the Great Depression and the agricultural catastrophe of the Dust Bowl, Americans turned their attention inward. In the 1920s and 1930s, the majority of American artists returned to realism and to paintings that chronicled American life. Urban and industrial subjects attracted new realists who were inspired by photogra-

phy, which during these same decades often took the clean, abstract geometries of the factory and skyscraper as its subject. Only in the late 1930s and 1940s would artists and architects fleeing Hitler's Europe renew American interest in modernism.

A group of painters calling themselves Precisionists worked with simplified forms, crisply defined edges, smooth brushwork, and unmodulated colors. Although they shared important thematic and formal similarities with O'Keeffe's work, she never claimed to be part of the group. The leading Precisionist artist was Charles Sheeler (1883–1965), who often based his paintings on his own photographs, many of which were made on commercial assignment. In 1927 Sheeler photographed the new Ford Motor Company plant at River Rouge, outside Detroit, Michigan. Three years later, he used the background of one of these photographs to make *American Landscape* (fig. **19–30**), a panoramic scene of the river, a boat slip, ore storage bins, and a cement plant. The painting illustrates the transformation of raw materials into industrial goods, and its title suggests that Sheeler

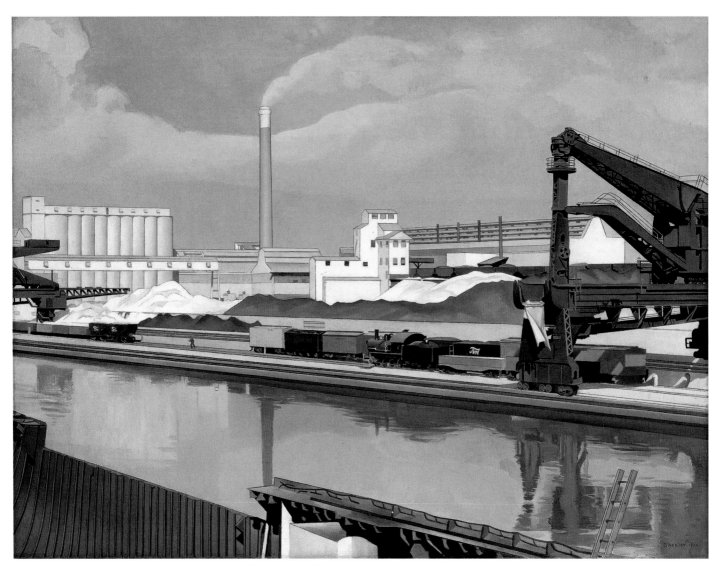

19–30 Charles Sheeler. *American Landscape.* 1930. Oil on canvas, 24″ × 31″ (61 × 78.7 cm). The Museum of Modern Art, New York

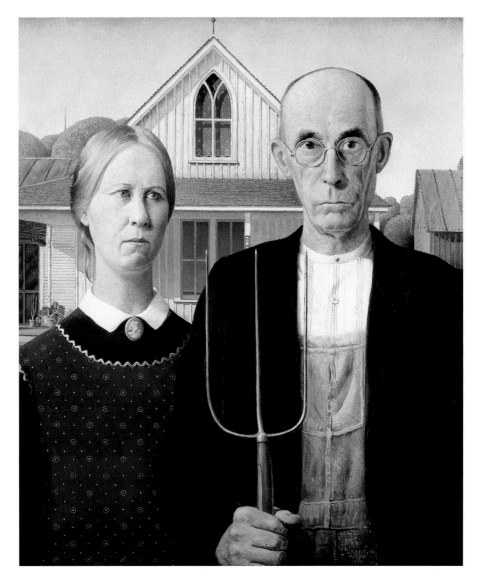

19–31 Grant Wood. *American Gothic.* 1930. Oil on beaverboard, 29$\frac{7}{8}$″ × 24$\frac{7}{8}$″ (74.3 × 62.4 cm).
The Art Institute of Chicago

was responding to the popular viewpoint that such factories demonstrated America's optimism in mechanization and belief in a better future. That he painted the work a year after the great stock-market crash of 1929, which began the Great Depression, suggests that the painting may be a testament to Sheeler's continuing faith in American industry and in its fundamental stability.

Sheeler's focus on a recognizable American subject, painted in a realistic style, allies his work to a broader tendency known as American Scene Painting, which flourished during the Great Depression. These artists energetically documented the lives and circumstances of the American people and the American landscape. While some produced images that confronted the depressed conditions of the present, others celebrated the myths and traditions of the American past or crafted optimistic images to provide hope for the future.

One group of American Scene painters from the Midwest are called Regionalists. A generally optimistic attitude pervades the work of the group, whose leading exponent was Grant Wood (1891–1942).

Wood, from Iowa, focused on the farms and small-town life of the American heartland. His *American Gothic* (fig. **19–31**) is usually thought to be a picture of a husband and wife, but it was actually meant to show an aging Iowa farmer and his unmarried daughter (Wood's dentist and sister were the models). Wood pictures the stony-faced pair standing in front of their house, built in a Victorian style known as "Carpenter Gothic," which suggests the importance of religion in their lives. The farmer's pitchfork signifies his occupation while giving him a somewhat menacing air. The woman is associated with potted plants, seen behind her right shoulder, which symbolize traditionally feminine domestic and horticultural skills. Wood considered the painting to be a sincerely affectionate portrayal of the small-town Iowans he had grown up with—conservative, provincial, religious Midwesterners, descendants of the pioneers.

In spite of the largely positive visions of the Regionalists, the economic hardships of the Great Depression meant that many farmers faced bankruptcy, and rural regions suffered great poverty. In 1935, a newly established government agency, the Farm Securities Administration (FSA), began to hire photographers to document the problems of farmers and migrant workers. Dorothea Lange (1895–1965) played a major role in the formation of the FSA photography program. As a freelance photographer in San Francisco, Lange was touched by the struggles of the city's poor and unemployed, and she began to photograph their plight. In 1934 she collaborated on a report on migrant farm laborers in California, which helped persuade state officials to build migrant labor camps. Her photographs influenced the federal government to include a photographic unit in the FSA, and in 1935 Lange was hired as one of the unit's first photographers. Her most famous photograph is *Migrant Mother, Nipomo, California* (fig. **19–32**). The woman in the picture is Florence Thompson, a 32-year-old mother of ten children. Drawn and prematurely aged, she gazes past the viewer into an uncertain future. The fears of all disenfranchised people, perpetually shunted to the margins of society, seem crystallized in her worried face.

The Harlem Renaissance

During World War I thousands of African-Americans left the rural South for jobs in northern defense plants. The Great Migration, as it is known, created racial tensions over housing and employment that in turn fostered a concern for the rights of African Americans. African-American writers, artists, and musicians explored black experience and identity in what became known as the Harlem Renaissance.

The intellectual Alain Locke, an influential voice in the 1920s Harlem Renaissance, encouraged younger black artists and writers to seek their contemporary cultural identity in their African and African-American heritage. In a 1925 essay titled "The New Negro" Locke urged for the transformation from older and negative models of the American black to one embracing a "new psychology" and "new spirit."

The first black artist to answer Locke's call was Aaron Douglas (1898–1979), a native of Topeka, Kansas, who moved to New York City in 1925 and rapidly developed an abstract style influenced by African art as well as by the contemporary, hard-edged aesthetic of Art Deco. Douglas limited his palette to a few subtle hues, varying in value from light to dark and sometimes organized abstractly into concentric bands that suggest musical rhythms or spiritual emanations. In paintings such as *Aspects of Negro Life: From Slavery Through Reconstruction* (fig. **19–33**), he used schematic figures, silhouetted in profile with the eye rendered frontally as in ancient Egyptian art.

This work, painted for the 135th Street branch of the New York Public Library under the sponsorship of the Public Works of Art Project, was intended to awaken in African Americans a sense of their place in history. At the right, they celebrate the

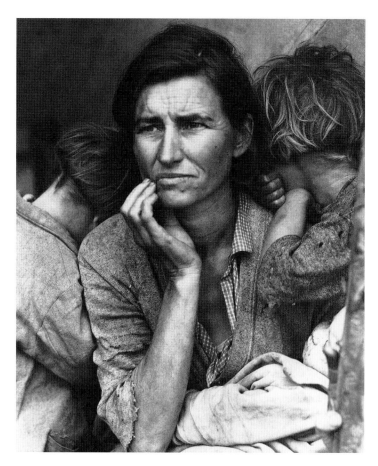

19–32 Dorothea Lange. *Migrant Mother, Nipomo, California.*
February 1936. Gelatin-silver print. Library of Congress, Washington, D.C.

Emancipation Proclamation of 1863, which freed the slaves. Concentric circles issue from the Proclamation, which is read by a figure in the foreground. At the center of the composition, an orator, symbolizing black leaders of the Reconstruction era, urges black freed men, some still picking cotton, to cast their ballots, while he points to a silhouette of the U.S. Capitol on a distant hill. Concentric circles highlight the ballot in his hand. In the background, the fearsome Ku Klux Klan, hooded and on horseback, invades from the left while at the right a jazz trumpeter heralds freedom. The heroic orator at the center of Douglas's panel remains the focus of the composition, inspiring contemporary viewers to continue the struggle for equality.

Like Douglas, photographer James VanDerZee (1886–1983) created positive images, as opposed to stereotypes, of African Americans that conveyed the sense of racial pride and social empowerment promoted by the "New Negro" movement. The largely self-taught VanDerZee maintained a studio in Harlem for nearly 50 years and specialized in portraits of the neighborhood's middle- and upper-class residents. His best-known photograph, *Couple Wearing Raccoon Coats with a Cadillac, Taken on West 127th Street, Harlem, New York* (fig. **19–34**), depicts the ideal "New Negro" man and woman: prosperous, confident, and cosmopolitan, thriving and living glamorously even in the midst of the Depression.

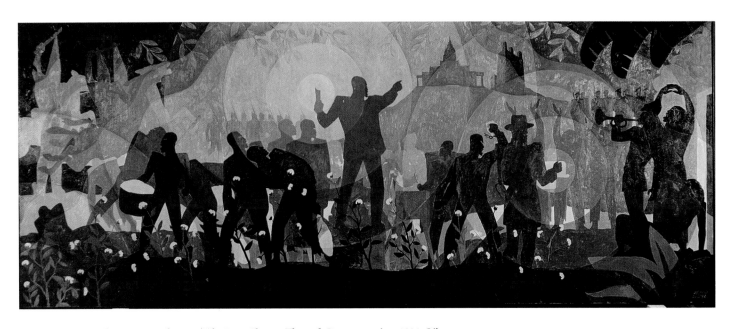

19–33 Aaron Douglas. *Aspects of Negro Life: From Slavery Through Reconstruction.* 1934. Oil on canvas, 5′ × 10′8″ (1.5 × 3.25 m). Schomburg Center for Research in Black Culture, New York Public Library, Astor, Lenox, and Tilden Foundations/Art Resource, NY

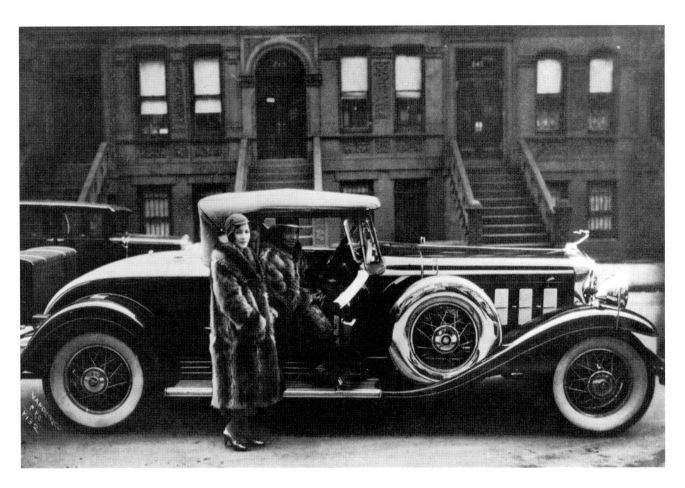

19–34 James VanDerZee. Detail of *Couple Wearing Raccoon Coats with a Cadillac, Taken on West 127th Street, Harlem, New York.* 1932. Gelatin silver print

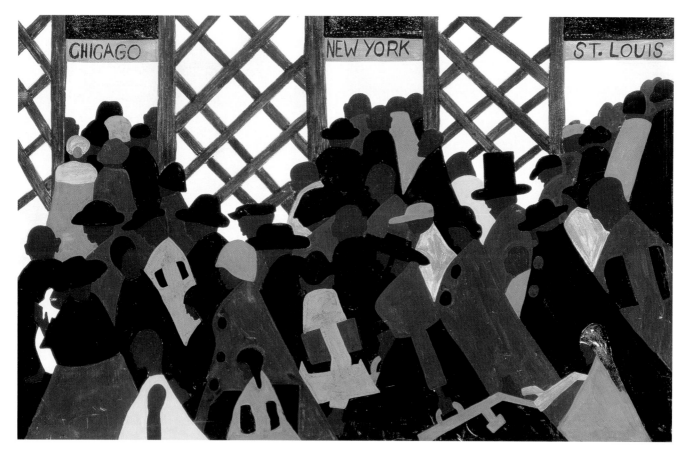

19–35 Jacob Lawrence. *During the World War There Was a Great Migration North by Southern Negroes,* panel 1 from *The Migration of the Negro.* 1940–1941. Tempera on masonite. 12″ × 18″ (30.5 × 45.7 cm). The Phillips Collection, Washington. D.C.

This is the first image in Lawrence's 60-panel cycle that tells the story of the migration of Southern African Americans to the industrialized North in the decades between the two world wars. Edith Halpert exhibited the entire series the same year at her Downtown Gallery, which also represented such prominent white artists as Charles Sheeler (see fig. 19–30). Thus, at age 23 Lawrence became the first African-American artist to gain acclaim in the segregated New York art world. The next year, the Migration series was jointly acquired by the Phillips Collection in Washington, D.C., and the Museum of Modern Art in New York, each of which purchased 30 paintings.

Influenced by Aaron Douglas, the younger Harlem artist Jacob Lawrence (1917–2000) devoted much of his early work to the depiction of black history, in dozens of small panels, each accompanied by a text. In 1940–1941, Lawrence created his best-known series, *The Migration of the Negro,* the sixty panels of which chronicled the great twentieth-century exodus of African Americans from the rural South to the urban North—an exodus that had brought Lawrence's own parents from South Carolina to Atlantic City, New Jersey, where he was born. The first panel (fig. **19–35**), depicts a train station filled with black migrants who stream through portals labeled with the names of Northern and Midwestern cities. The bold abstract style, with its simple shapes and bright, flat colors, suggests the influence of both Cubism and African-American folk art.

Mexico

Artists in Mexico and Canada followed the same pattern as they focused on local scenes and problems. Prominent in the new Mexican mural movement of the 1930s was Diego Rivera

(1886–1957). Rivera had lived in Paris, painting in the Synthetic Cubist style, and in 1920–1921 he traveled to Italy to study the great frescoes of the Renaissance. On his return to Mexico, he painted a series of monumental murals for Mexican government buildings, inspired by both Italian Renaissance art and the Pre-Columbian art of Mexico. In 1932 the Rockefeller family commissioned Rivera to paint a mural for the lobby of the RCA Building in Rockefeller Center in New York City on the theme "Man at the Crossroads Looking with Hope and High Vision to the Choosing of a New and Better Future." When Rivera, a Communist, provocatively included a portrait of Lenin in the mural, the Rockefellers canceled his commission, paid him his fee, and had the unfinished mural destroyed. In response to what he called an "act of cultural vandalism," Rivera re-created the mural in the Palacio de Bellas Artes in Mexico City, under the new title *Man, Controller of the Universe* (fig. **19–36**).

At the center of the mural, a figure in overalls represents Man, who symbolically controls the universe through technology. Crossing behind him are two great ellipses that represent,

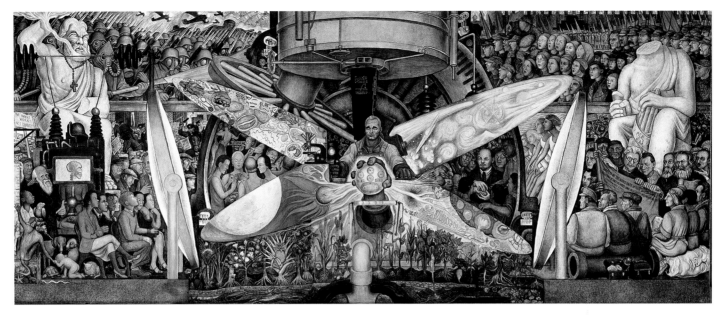

19–36 Diego Rivera. *Man, Controller of the Universe.* 1934. Fresco, 15'9$\frac{1}{8}$" × 37'2$\frac{1}{2}$" (4.85 × 11.45 m).
Museo del Palacio de Bellas Artes, Mexico City

respectively, the microcosm of living organisms as seen through the microscope at Man's right hand, and the macrocosm of outer space as viewed through the giant telescope above his head. Below, fruits and vegetables rise from the earth as a result of his agricultural efforts. To the viewer's right, Lenin joins the hands of several workers of different races; at the left, decadent capitalists debauch themselves in a nightclub. Rivera vengefully included in this section a portrait of the bespectacled John D. Rockefeller, Jr. At the sides of the mural, Rivera contrasts the peaceful Socialist workers with the militarism and labor unrest of the capitalist world.

While Rivera and other muralists painted public messages, other Mexican artists made more private, introspective statements through the medium of easel painting. André Breton claimed Frida Kahlo (1910–1954) to be a natural Surrealist, although she herself said: "I never painted dreams. I painted my own reality." That reality included her mixed German and Mexican ancestry. In *The Two Fridas* (fig. **19–37**), Kahlo presented her two ethnic selves: the European one, in a Victorian dress; and the Mexican one, wearing a traditional Mexican skirt and blouse. The painting also reflects her stormy relationship with Diego Rivera. The two married in 1929 but were in the process of

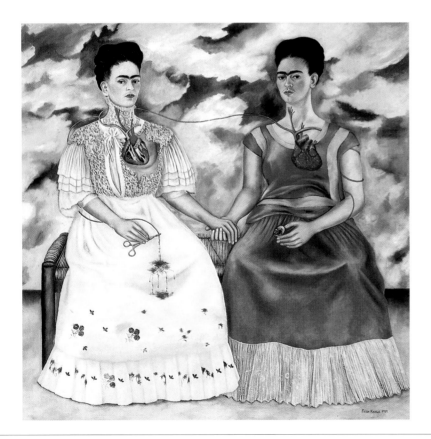

19–37 Frida Kahlo. *The Two Fridas.* 1939. Oil on canvas, 5'8$\frac{1}{2}$" × 5'8$\frac{1}{2}$" (1.74 × 1.74 m). Museo de Arte Moderno, Instituto Nacional de Bellas Artes, Mexico City

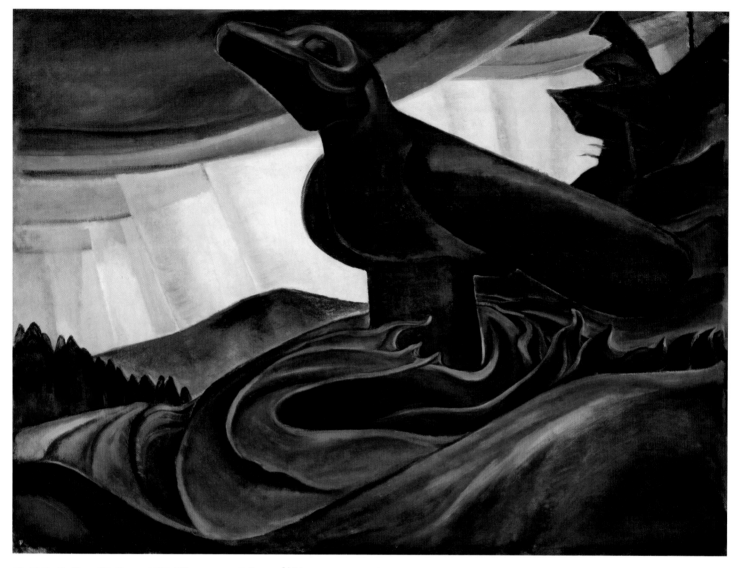

19–38 Emily Carr. *Big Raven.* 1931. Oil on canvas, 34″ × 44⅝″ (87.3 × 114.4 cm).
The Vancouver Art Gallery, Canada

obtaining a divorce when Kahlo was painting *The Two Fridas* in 1939. She told an art historian at the time that the European image was the Frida whom Diego loved and the Mexican image was the Frida he did not. The two Fridas join hands and are linked by an artery running between them. The artery begins at a miniature of Rivera as a boy held by the Mexican Frida and ends in the lap of the Europeanized Frida, who attempts without success to stem the flow of blood.

Canada

The artist Emily Carr (1871–1945) lived in Vancouver, British Columbia, where she taught art and became a founding member of the British Columbia Society of Art. On a 1907 trip to Alaska, she first saw the monumental carved poles of Northwest

Coast Native Americans and resolved to document these "real art treasures of a passing race." Over the next 23 years Carr visited more than 30 native village sites across British Columbia, making drawings and watercolors, which became the basis for oil paintings.

As her art matured, Carr developed a dramatic and powerfully sculptural style full of dark and brooding energy. An impressive example of such work is *Big Raven* (fig. **19–38**), which Carr painted in 1931, based on a watercolor she made in 1912 in an abandoned village in the Queen Charlotte Islands. She had discovered a carved raven raised on a pole, the surviving member of a pair that had marked a mortuary house. In her autobiography Carr described the raven as "old and rotting," but in her painting the bird appears strong and majestic, thrusting

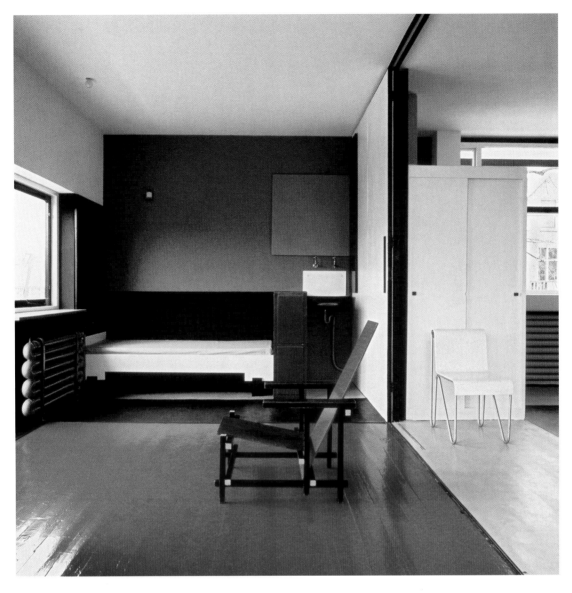

19–39 Gerrit Rietveld. Interior, Schröder House, with Red and Blue Chair. Utrecht, the Netherlands. 1924

dynamically above the swirling vegetation, a symbol of enduring spiritual power. Through its focus on a Native American artifact set in a recognizably northwestern Canadian landscape, Carr's *Big Raven* may be interpreted as an assertion of national pride comparable to the paintings of the Mexican muralists and the Harlem Renaissance.

Architecture

Europe

Gerrit Rietveld (1888–1964) became the major architect and designer of the de Stijl movement. His famous Red-Blue Chair is shown here in the bedroom of the Schröder House (fig. **19–39**) in Utrecht. Rietveld applied Mondrian's design aesthetic—the

dynamic symmetry of rectangular planes of color—to the entire house and its built-in furnishings. Sliding partitions on the interior, the idea of the house's owner Truus Schröder-Schrader, allowed modifications in the spaces used for sleeping, working, and entertaining. A wealthy woman, Schröder-Schrader wanted her home to suggest an elegant austerity, with the basic necessities sleekly integrated into a meticulously restrained whole.

Like the Dutch proponents of de Stijl, followers of a movement known as Purism, which developed in France, firmly believed in the power of art to change the world. The leading Purist figure was the Swiss-born Charles-Édouard Jeanneret (1887–1965), a largely self-taught architect and designer who moved to Paris in 1917. Three years later, Jeanneret, partly to demonstrate his faith in the ability of individuals to remake

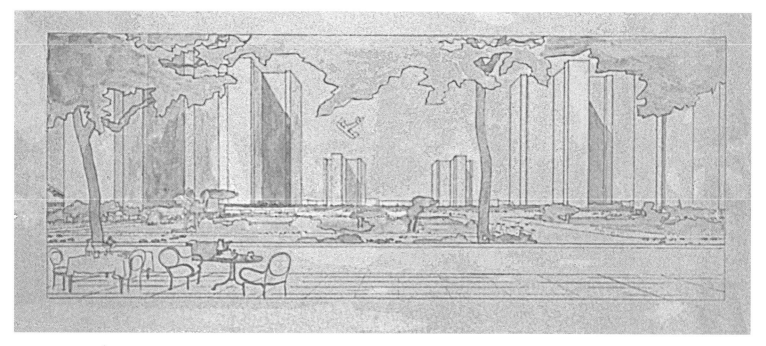

19–40 Charles-Édouard Jeanneret (Le Corbusier). Plan for a Contemporary City of Three Million Inhabitants. 1922. (From *Oeuvre complete*, 1910–29)

The skyscrapers Le Corbusier planned for the center of his city were intended to house offices, not residences. Residences would be in smaller suburban terraces of five-story houses around the periphery of the city. In 1925 Le Corbusier devised a similar plan for Paris, convinced that the center of the city needed to be torn down and rebuilt to accommodate automobile traffic. The Parisian street was a "Pack-Donkey's Way," he said. "Imagine all this junk . . . cleared off and carried away and replaced by immense clear crystals of glass, rising to a height of over six hundred feet!"

themselves, renamed himself Le Corbusier, a play on the French word for crow (*corbeau*).

One of Le Corbusier's first major projects was his Plan for a Contemporary City of Three Million Inhabitants (fig. **19–40**), which he exhibited in Paris in 1922. Le Corbusier envisioned for the future a city of uniform style, laid out on a grid and dominated by skyscrapers, with wide traffic arteries that often passed below ground level. Large expanses of parkland would surround strictly functional buildings. The result, Le Corbusier thought, would be a new, clean, and efficient city filled with light, air, and greenery—a vision that had a profound effect on later city planning, especially in the United States. His ideas formed the basis of the International Style (see "Elements of Architecture," page 538).

The Bauhaus

The German counterpart to the total, rational planning envisioned by de Stijl and Le Corbusier was carried out at the Bauhaus school (loosely translated as "House of Building"). The Bauhaus (1919–1933) was the brainchild of Walter Gropius (1883–1969), one of the founders of modernist architecture.

Gropius, who belonged to several utopian groups, admired the spirit of the medieval building guilds, or *Bauhütten*, that had erected the great German cathedrals. He sought to revive their cooperative spirit and bring together modern art and industry by combining the schools of art and craft in the German city of Weimar into a single institution.

At first the Bauhaus school had no formal training program in architecture. Gropius felt that students needed to demonstrate proficiency in workshop courses before going on to study architecture. The workshops—which included classes in pottery, metal-work, textiles, stained glass, furniture making, carving, and wall painting—were intended to teach both specific technical skills and basic design, based on the principle of learning through doing. Gropius believed that art should serve a socially useful function, and in 1922 he implemented a new emphasis on industrial design.

The next year the Hungarian-born Laszlo Moholy-Nagy (1895–1946) reoriented the Bauhaus workshops toward the creation of sleek, functional designs suitable for mass production. The elegant tea and coffee service by Marianne Brandt (1893–1983),

SUPPRESSION OF THE AVANT-GARDE IN GERMANY

The 1930s in Germany witnessed a serious political reaction against avant-garde art and, eventually, a concerted effort to suppress it. One of the principal targets was the Bauhaus, the art and design school founded in 1919 by Walter Gropius, where Mies van der Rohe, Klee, Kandinsky, Josef Albers, and many other luminaries taught. Through much of the 1920s, the Bauhaus had struggled against an increasingly hostile and reactionary political climate. As early as 1924 conservatives had accused the Bauhaus of being not only educationally unsound but also politically subversive. To avoid having the school shut down by the opposition, Gropius moved it to Dessau in 1925, at the invitation of Dessau's liberal mayor, but left soon after the relocation. His successors faced increasing political pressure, as the school was a prime center of modernist practice, and the Bauhaus was again forced to move in 1932, this time to Berlin.

After Adolf Hitler came to power in 1933, the Nazi party mounted an aggressive campaign against modern art. In his youth Hitler himself had been a mediocre academic painter, and he had developed an intense hatred of modernism and the avant-garde. During the first year of his regime, the Bauhaus was forced to close for good. A number of the artists, designers, and architects who had been on its faculty—including Gropius, Mies, and Albers—immigrated to the United States.

The Nazis also launched attacks against the painters, whose often intense depictions of German soldiers defeated in World War I and the economic depression following the war were considered unpatriotic. Most of all, the treatment of the human form in these works, such as the expressionistic exaggeration of facial features, was deemed offensive. The works of these and other artists were removed from museums, while the artists themselves were subjected to public ridicule and often forbidden to buy canvas or paint.

As a final move against the avant-garde, the Nazi leadership organized in 1937 a notorious exhibition of banned works. The "Degenerate Art" exhibition was intended to erase modernism once and for all from the artistic life of the nation. Seeking to brand all the advanced movements of art as sick and degenerate, it presented modern artworks as specimens of human pathology; the organizers printed derisive slogans and comments to that effect on the gallery walls (see archival photograph, below). The 650 paintings, sculpture, prints, and books confiscated from German public museums were viewed by 2 million people in the four months the exhibition was on view in Munich and by another million during its subsequent three-year tour of German cities.

By the time World War II broke out, the German authorities had confiscated countless works from all over the country. Most were publicly burned, though the Nazi officials sold much of the looted art at public auction in Switzerland to obtain foreign currency. Among the many artists crushed by the Nazi suppression was Ernst Ludwig Kirchner, whose *Street, Berlin* (see fig. 19–4) was included in "Degenerate Art." The state's open animosity was a factor in Kirchner's suicide in 1938.

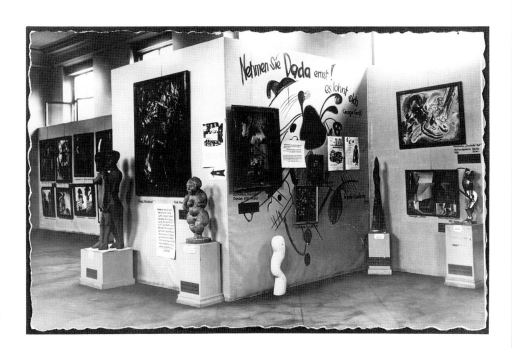

The Dada Wall in Room 3 of "Degenerate Art" (Entartete Kunst) Exhibition, Munich, 1937

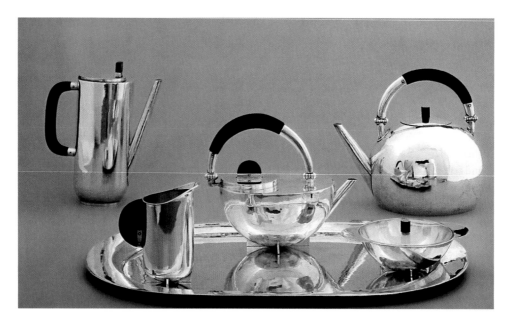

19–41 Marianne Brandt. *Tea and Coffee Service.* 1924. Silver and ebony, with Plexiglas cover for sugar bowl. Bauhausarchiv-Museum fur Gestaltung, Berlin, Germany

The lid of Marianne Brandt's sugar bowl is made of Plexiglas, reflecting the Bauhaus's interest in incorporating the latest advances in materials and technology into the manufacture of utilitarian objects.

for example (fig. **19–41**), though handcrafted in silver, was a prototype for mass production in a cheaper metal such as nickel silver. Several of Brandt's designs went into mass production, earning much-needed revenue for the school. After Gropius and Moholy-Nagy left the school in 1928, Brandt directed the metal workshop. As a woman holding her own in the otherwise all-male metals workshop, Brandt was an exceptional figure at the Bauhaus. Although women were admitted to the school on an equal basis with men, Gropius opposed their education as architects and channeled them into pottery and textile workshops, which he deemed appropriate for their gender.

When the Bauhaus moved to the German city of Dessau in 1925, Gropius designed the new building, built in 1925–1926 (fig. **19–42**). The structure frankly acknowledges the reinforced concrete, steel, and glass of which it is built. Gropius made no attempt to cover or decorate his building materials. Modern engineering methods made it possible to replace walls as massive structural supports with glass panels and to create light, airy spaces. Even the sans serif (without serifs) letters of the Bauhaus sign announce the functional ideals of the group.

Beginning in 1930, the Bauhaus was directed by the architect Ludwig Mies van der Rohe (1886–1969). Mies had a passion for realizing the subtle perfection of structure, proportion, and detail, using sumptuous materials such as travertine, richly veined marbles, tinted glass, and bronze. The school remained under his direction until 1933; when the Nazi party came to power that year, they closed the school (see "Suppression of the Avant-Garde in Gemany," page 538).

Business leaders embraced modernism in architecture. The so-called International Style seemed to epitomize the efficiency, standardization, and impersonality that had become synonymous with the modern corporation itself. But other architects and critics called for an architecture that would provide spiritual nourishment to those starved by the severity of the International-al Style. As early as 1900, Frank Lloyd Wright (1867–1959) advocated an "organic" approach that integrated architecture with nature. When asked what could be done to improve the modern industrial city, he bluntly responded: "Tear it down."

Wright's most famous architectural expression of his conviction that buildings ought to be a part of nature—in it, not

ELEMENTS OF **Architecture**
The International Style

After World War I, increased exchanges between modernist architects led to the development of a common formal language, transcending national boundaries, which came to be known as the International Style. The term gained wide currency as a result of a 1932 exhibition at the Museum of Modern Art in New York, "The International Style: Architecture Since 1922," organized by the architectural historian Henry-Russell Hitchcock and the architect and curator Philip Johnson. Hitchcock and Johnson identified three fundamental principles of the style.

The first principle was "the conception of architecture as volume rather than mass." The use of a structural skeleton of steel and concrete made it possible to eliminate load-bearing walls on both the exterior and interior. Thus the building could be wrapped in a skin of glass, metal, or masonry, creating an effect of enclosed space (volume) rather than dense material (mass). And interiors could feature open, free-flowing plans providing maximum flexibility in the use of space.

The second principle was "regularity rather than symmetry as the chief means of ordering design." Regular distribution of structural supports and the use of standard building parts promoted rectangular regularity rather than the balanced axial symmetry of classical architecture. The avoidance of classical balance also encouraged an asymmetrical disposition of the building's components.

The third principle was the rejection of "arbitrary applied decoration." The new architecture depended upon the intrinsic elegance of its materials and the formal arrangement of its elements to produce harmonious aesthetic effects.

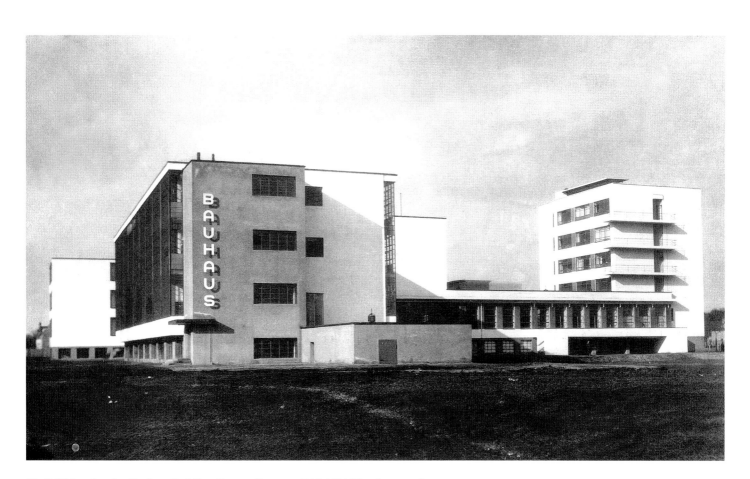

19–42 Walter Gropius. Bauhaus Building, Dessau, Germany. 1925–1926. View from northwest

One of the enduring contributions of the Bauhaus was graphic design. The sans serif letters of the building's sign not only harmonize with the architecture's clean lines but also communicate the Bauhaus commitment to modernity. Sans serif typography (that is, a typeface without serifs, the short lines at the end of the stroke of a letter) had been used since the early nineteenth century. Many new sans serif typefaces were created in the 1920s.

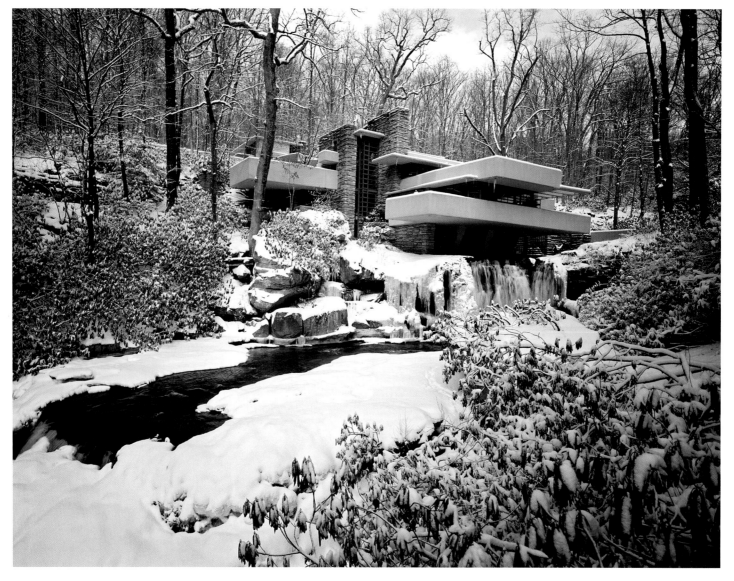

19–43 Frank Lloyd Wright. Edgar Kaufmann House / Fallingwater, Mill Run, Pennsylvania. 1935–1937

simply on it—is Fallingwater, in rural Pennsylvania (fig. **19–43**). The site of this country house was notable for its waterfall and pool where the owners, the Edgar Kaufmann family, escaped to play and swim in the summer. Wright decided to build the house into the cliff over the pool, allowing the water to flow around and under the house. In a daring engineering move, he cantilevered a series of broad terraces out from the house, echoing the great slabs of natural rock. The rocks on which the family had once lounged by the waterfall became the hearthstone of the fireplace. Wright effectively incorporated long bands of windows and glass doors into the structure in order to offer spectacular views, uniting woods, water, and house.

Architects like Frank Lloyd Wright, Le Corbusier, and Walter Gropius and his Bauhaus associates kept a visionary idealism alive through the military and economic disasters, with the accompanying social and political upheavals, of the first half of the twentieth century.

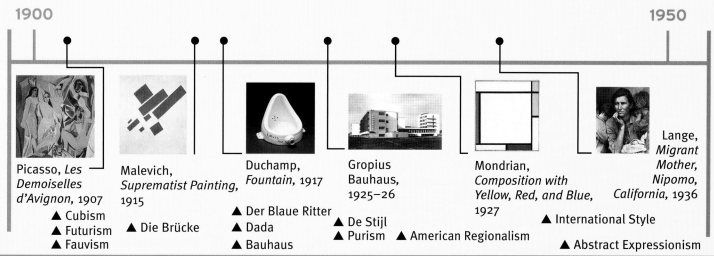

Picasso, *Les Demoiselles d'Avignon*, 1907
▲ Cubism
▲ Futurism
▲ Fauvism

Malevich, *Suprematist Painting*, 1915
▲ Die Brücke

Duchamp, *Fountain*, 1917
▲ Der Blaue Ritter
▲ Dada
▲ Bauhaus

Gropius Bauhaus, 1925–26
▲ De Stijl
▲ Purism ▲ American Regionalism

Mondrian, *Composition with Yellow, Red, and Blue*, 1927
▲ International Style

Lange, *Migrant Mother, Nipomo, California*, 1936
▲ Abstract Expressionism

LOOKING BACK

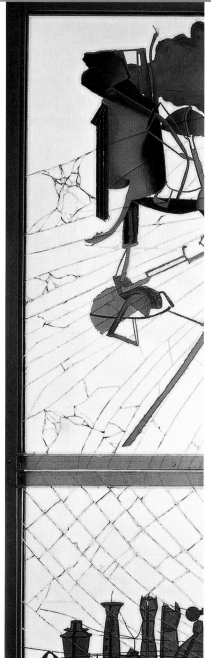

Three disasters—two wars and an economic depression—defined Western culture during the first half of the twentieth century. Beginning with a decade of optimism that in retrospect seems like smug self-satisfaction, by 1914 European nations were so entangled in economic and political competition that war became inevitable. By 1917 the United States was drawn into the conflict, turning the European battles into World War I. The joy of victory for the United States, England, and France—and the despair in Germany and the former Habsburg Empire—soon turned to misery during a period of American and European economic collapse, followed by a worldwide depression and World War II, which spread from Europe to the United States, North Africa, and Asia. When that war ended in 1945, the United States and the USSR had supplanted the European nations as the world's two super powers.

Such traumatic upheavals in society profoundly influenced cultural institutions, destroying their philosophical and economic underpinning. In Socialist and Communist states, artists lost their privileged positions as part of the cultural elite and became workers for the state. Meanwhile, the Great Depression forced capitalist governments to provide many artists with a livelihood by offering work on public projects.

The story of twentieth-century art reads like the title of Aldous Huxley's 1928 novel *Point Counter Point*. Artists and art movements reacted to each other with accelerating speed and vigor, as artistic innovation and public taste swung back and forth—a pattern that had begun in the nineteenth century between the poles of Rococo and Neoclassicism, Romanticism and Realism, and then Impressionism and Post-Impressionism. This point-counterpoint relationship appears on a personal level, too, for example between Braque and Picasso, two artists who challenged and inspired each other to create Cubist paintings, prints, and collages. Their relationship exemplifies the way in which artists often propose, test, and revise their ideas and techniques.

New technology of the time also had a profound impact on how people made and saw art. Futurism sought to capture the energy—the speed and light—of the technological age, while Dada mocked and denied the validity of the work of art. Surrealist artists turned in on themselves as they explored a universal, symbolic dreamworld, while other artists glorified external appearances in Regionalism. Decades of technological innovation also underlay amazing achievements in architecture as engineering and aesthetic practice combined to permit architects to create new architectural forms, from private homes to skyscrapers.

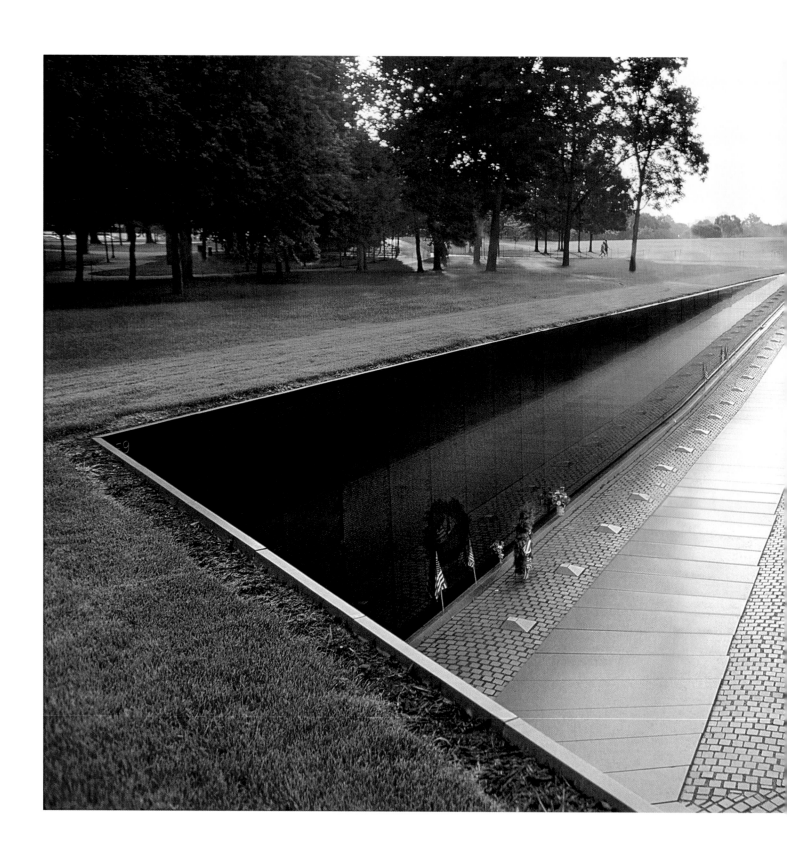

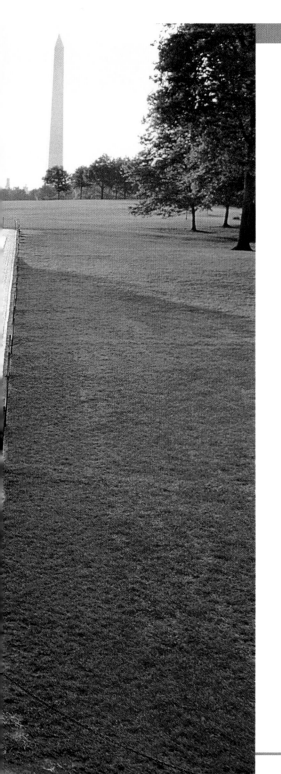

20
Art Since 1945

" **C**attle die. Kinfolk die. We all die. Only fame lasts," said the Vikings. Names remain. Flat, polished stone walls inscribed with thousands of names reflect back the images of the living as they contemplate the memorial to the Vietnam War's (1965–1973) dead and missing veterans (fig. **20–1**). The idea is brilliant in its simplicity. The artist, Maya Ying Lin (b. 1960), combined two basic ideas: the minimal grandeur of long, black granite walls and row upon row of engraved names—the abstract and the intimate conjoined. The power of Lin's monument lies in its understatement. The wall is a statement of loss, sorrow, and the futility of war, and the names are so numerous that they lose individuality and become a surface texture. It is a timeless monument to suffering humanity, faceless in sacrifice. Maya Ying Lin said, "The point is to see yourself reflected in the names."

The walls also reflect more than visitors. One wall faces and reflects the George Washington Monument (constructed 1848–1884). Robert Mills, the architect of many public buildings at the beginning of the nineteenth century, chose the obelisk, a time-honored Egyptian sun symbol, for his memorial to the nation's founder. The other wall leads the eye to the Neoclassical-style Lincoln Memorial. By subtly incorporating the Washington and Lincoln monuments into the design, Lin's *Vietnam Veterans Memorial* reminds the viewer of sacrifices made in defense of liberty throughout the United States' history.

Until the modern era, most public art celebrated and commemorated political and social leaders and aspects of war: officers and soldiers—both victorious and slain—in large, freestanding monuments. The motives of those who have commissioned public art have ranged from civic pride and the wish to honor heroes to political propaganda and social intimidation. Lin's memorial in Washington, D.C., to the American men and women who died in or never returned from the Vietnam War is among the most visited works of public art of the twenty-first century and certainly among the most affecting war monuments ever conceived. As art critic Michael Kimmelman wrote in *The New York Times* (January 13, 2002, page 37), "Good art outlasts the events that prompted the artists to make it."

20–1 Maya Ying Lin. *Vietnam Veterans Memorial.* 1982. Black granite, length 500′ (152 m). The Mall, Washington, D.C.

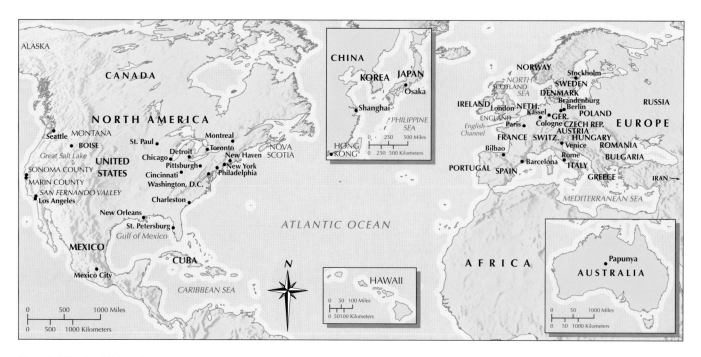

Map 20–1 The World since 1945

The United States and the Soviet Union emerged from World War II as the world's most powerful nations and soon were engaged in the Cold War. The Soviets set up Communist governments in Eastern Europe (the Eastern bloc) and supported the development of Communism elsewhere. A second huge Communist nation emerged in 1949 when Mao Tse-tung established the People's Republic of China. Meanwhile the United States, through financial aid and political support, sought to contain the spread of Communism.

While the Soviet Union and the United States vied for world leadership, the old European states gave up their empires. The British led the way by withdrawing from India in 1947. Other European nations gradually granted independence to colonies in Asia and Africa.

In the 1980s, the Communist stronghold in Eastern Europe began to crumble and was virtually gone by 1990, effectively ending the Cold War. Formerly Communist republics turned to capitalism and many sought democratic reforms on social, economic, and political levels. This global capitalism increased the economic interdependence among nations, and wealthy countries like the United States saw increasing prosperity. Despite this growth, the world today seems smaller, thanks to remarkable advances in transportation and communication, including the Internet. And with enhanced global communication has come increased awareness of the many grave problems that confront us in the twenty-first century.

The "Mainstream" Crosses the Atlantic

The United States' stature after World War II as the most powerful democratic nation was soon reflected in the arts. American artists and architects assumed leadership in artistic innovation, and by the late 1950s the dominance of their work was acknowledged across the Atlantic, even in Paris. This dominance endured until around 1970, when the belief in the existence of an identifiable mainstream, or single dominant line of artistic development, began to wane (see "The Idea of the Mainstream," page 569).

Although realism dominated American art in the period between the two world wars, some artists of the period maintained an interest in abstract and nonrepresentational styles of art. In the 1930s groundbreaking exhibitions at the Museum of Modern Art in New York promoted European avant-garde art and so helped to pave the way for Abstract Expressionism, the dominant style of the late 1940s and 1950s in the United States.

America's living link with the modernist tradition in Europe was Hans Hofmann (1880–1966), a German-born teacher and painter who had come to the United States before World War II. The rise of Fascism in Europe and the outbreak of World War II stranded people like Hofmann and led a number of prominent European artists and writers to move to the United States. By 1940 André Breton, Salvador Dalí, and Piet Mondrian were all living in New York. Although many of the émigrés kept to themselves, their very presence provoked fruitful discussions among American artists.

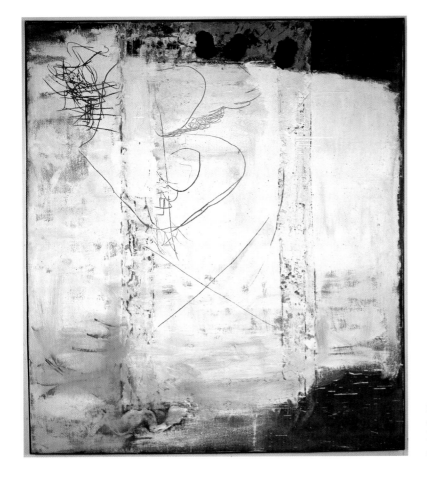

20–2 Antoni Tapies. *White with Graphism*. 1957. Mixed media on canvas, 6′3⅞″ × 5′8¾″ (1.93 × 1.75 m). The Mildred Lane Kemper Art Museum, Washington University, St. Louis, Missouri

GIFT OF MR. AND MRS. RICHARD WEIL, 1963

After the war, in Europe the most distinctive approach to painting was called *art informel* ("formless" art) or Lyrical Abstraction or *tachisme* (*tache*, "spot" or "stain"). The artists argued that since the two world wars had discredited all notions of humanity as reasonable, they as artists had the duty to invent a new and more "authentic" concept of our species. They believed they were able to do so by returning to the origins of art as expressed in the simple, honest mark.

One of the many artists who participated in this movement was the Catalan painter Antoni Tapies (b. 1923). In works such as *White with Graphism* (fig. **20–2**), he attempted to recover the primordial language of art with crudely drawn and incised marks on a white ground that recalled a prehistoric cave wall. Tapies did not mean to communicate a particular message but rather to record the fundamental urge for self-expression. In 1953, when Tapies visited New York, he found that American artists were taking similar approaches to their art.

Deeply affected by the ideas of Surrealism and the teaching of Hans Hofmann, New York artists began working in a style collectively called Abstract Expressionism. This term designates a wide variety of work produced between 1940 and roughly 1960. By the late 1940s, two major approaches to nonrepresentational art emerged: action painting, or gesturalism, characterized by active paint handling; and Color Field painting, distinguished by broad sweeping fields of color. Because not all Abstract Expres-sionist work was either abstract or expressionistic, some art historians prefer to refer to the work of these artists simply as the New York School.

The Abstract Expressionists took from the Surrealists both a commitment to examining the unconscious and techniques for doing so. But whereas the European Surrealists had derived their notion of the unconscious from Sigmund Freud, many of the Americans subscribed to the thinking of Swiss psychoanalyst Carl Jung (1875–1961). His theory of the "collective unconscious" holds that beneath one's private memories is a storehouse of feelings and symbolic associations common to all humans.

A leading Jung-inspired Abstract Expressionist was the action painter Jackson Pollock (1912–1956). Undergoing Jungian analysis between 1939 and 1941, the alcoholic and self-destructive artist made little progress with his personal problems. The sessions greatly affected his work, however, giving him a new vocabulary of signs and symbols and a belief in the therapeutic role of art in society.

In the mid-1940s, Pollock replaced Jungian painted symbols with freely applied paint, working on large canvases spread out on the floor. He began to employ enamel house paints along with conventional oil paints in the winter of 1946–1947, dripping them onto his canvases with sticks and brushes using a variety of fluid arm and wrist movements. The result over the next four years was a series of graceful linear abstractions such as

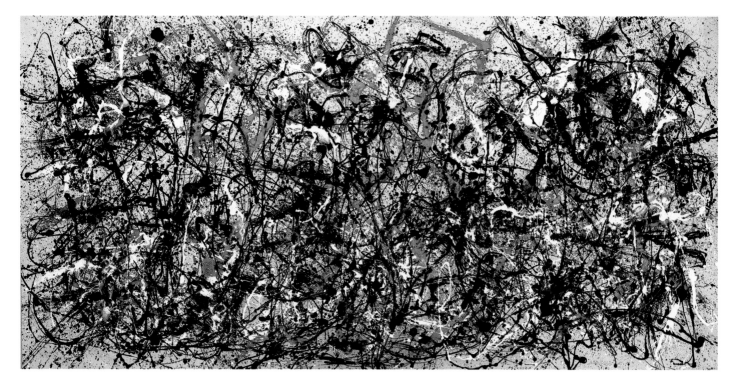

20–3 Jackson Pollock. *Autumn Rhythm (Number 30).* 1950. Oil on canvas, 8′9″ × 17′3″ (2.66 × 5.25 m). The Metropolitan Museum of Art, New York

Autumn Rhythm (Number 30) (fig. **20–3**). Delicate skeins of paint effortlessly loop over and under one another in a mesmerizing pattern that spreads across the surface of the canvas. As the title of this and other Pollock paintings suggest, the artist seems to have felt that in the free, unself-conscious act of painting he was giving vent to primal, natural forces.

In 1945 Pollock married Lee Krasner (1908–1984), an original member of the so-called New York School and Hofmann's student. When Krasner had first begun living with Pollock in 1942, she had virtually stopped painting (in order to devote herself to the conventional role of a supportive wife). But she soon resumed painting, and despite marital problems caused, at least in part, by Pollock's alcoholism, continued to create significant works. After Pollock's death in an automobile crash in 1956, Krasner took over his studio and during the next year and a half produced a dazzling group of monumental gestural paintings (fig. **20–4**), painted in bold sweeping curves that express not only her grief but also her identification with the forces of nature suggested by the bursting rounded forms.

In contrast to Pollock, who said that he found "pure harmony" when at work on his drip paintings, his contemporary Willem de Kooning (1904–1997) insisted, "Art never seems to make me peaceful or pure." De Kooning was born in the Netherlands and immigrated to the United States in 1926. After a period of painting in a nonrepresentational mode, he shocked the New York art world in the early 1950s by returning to the figure with a series of paintings of women. The first of the series, *Woman I* (fig. **20–5**), took him almost two years to finish. DeKooning's wife, the artist Elaine de Kooning (1918–1989), said that he painted it, scraped it, and repainted it at least several dozen times. Part of de Kooning's dissatisfaction stemmed from the way his subject, a figure inspired by conventionally pretty images of women seen in American advertising, kept veering away from those models. What emerges in *Woman I* is not the elegant companion of advertising fantasy but a powerful adversary, more dangerous than alluring. Only the soft pastel colors and luscious paint surface give any hint of de Kooning's original sources, and these qualities are nearly lost in the furious slashing of the paint.

De Kooning was committed to the high level of aesthetic achievement historically set by great Western painters, and his works were a carefully orchestrated buildup of interwoven strokes and planes of color based largely on the example of Analytic Cubism (see figs. 19–10 and 19–11). "Liquefied Cubism" is the way one art historian described them. The deeper roots of de Kooning's work, however, lie in the coloristic tradition of artists such as Titian and Rubens, who superbly transformed flesh into paint.

During the 1950s, de Kooning dominated the avant-garde in New York. Among the handful of modernist painters who resisted his influence was Mark Rothko (1903–1970), a pioneering **Color Field** painter who used large rectangles of color to evoke transcendent emotional states. In works such as *Brown, Blue,*

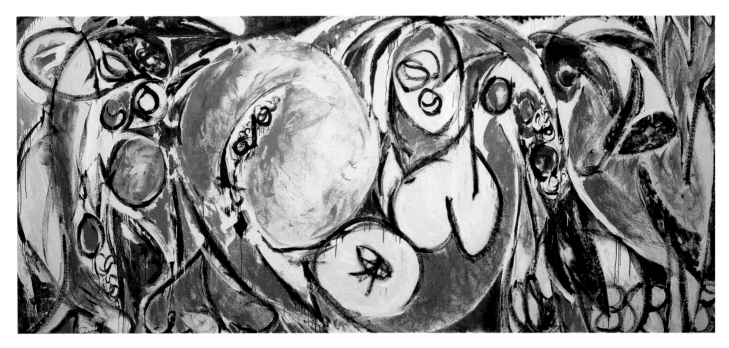

20–4 Lee Krasner. *The Seasons.* 1957. Oil on canvas, 7′8 3/4″ × 16′11 3/4″ (2.36 × 5.18 m). Whitney Museum of Art, New York

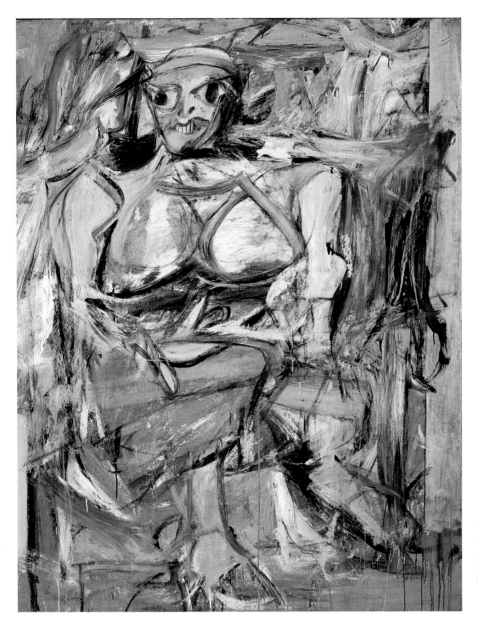

20–5 Willem de Kooning. *Woman I.* 1950–1952. Oil on canvas, 6′3 7/8″ × 4′10″ (1.93 × 1.47 m). The Museum of Modern Art, New York

20–6 Mark Rothko. *Brown, Blue, Brown on Blue.*
1953. Oil on canvas, 9′7³⁄₄″ × 7′7¹⁄₄″ (2.97 × 2.34 m).
The Museum of Contemporary Art, Los Angeles

Brown on Blue (fig. **20–6**), Rothko consciously sought a profound harmony between the two divergent human tendencies that German philosopher Friedrich Nietzsche (1844–1900) called the Dionysian (after the Greek god of wine, the harvest, and inspiration) and the Apollonian (after the Greek god of light, music, and truth). The painting's rich color is its Dionysian element, the emotional and instinctive side of human nature, while the simple compositional structure underlying the coloristic virtuosity is its rational and disciplined Apollonian counterpart. Together they form a deeply satisfying unity, which hints at a momentary resolution of our fundamental human duality.

Elements from Color Field paintings like Rothko's intermingled with the gesturalism of action painting in the work of Helen Frankenthaler (b. 1928). Frankenthaler, like Pollock, worked on the floor, drawn to what she described as Pollock's "dancelike use of arms and legs." She produced a huge canvas, *Mountains and Sea* (fig. **20–7**), in this way, working from watercolor sketches she had made in Nova Scotia. Instead of using thick, full-bodied paint, as Pollock did, Frankenthaler thinned her oil paints and applied them in washes that soaked into the raw canvas, producing an effect that resembles watercolor but also evokes Color

Field painting. A few delicate contour lines suggest not only the mountains of the painting's title but also less translatable, dream-inspired Surrealistic forms.

The New York School also included talented sculptors such as David Smith (1906–1965). Smith learned metalworking as a welder and riveter at an automobile plant in his native Indiana. During the last five years of his life, Smith turned to formalism—a shift partly inspired by his discovery of stainless steel as a medium. Smith explored both the relative lightness and the beauty of steel's polished surfaces in the Cubi series, monumental combinations of geometric units inspired by and offering homage to the formalism of Cubism. Like the Analytic Cubist works of Braque and Picasso, *Cubi XIX* (see Intro, fig. 5) presents a finely tuned balance of elements that, though firmly welded together, seem ready to collapse at the slightest provocation. The viewer's aesthetic pleasure depends on this tension and on the dynamic curvilinear patterns formed by the play of light over the sculpture's burnished surfaces. The Cubi works were meant to be seen outdoors, not only because of the effect of sunlight but also because of the way natural shapes and colors complement their inorganic form.

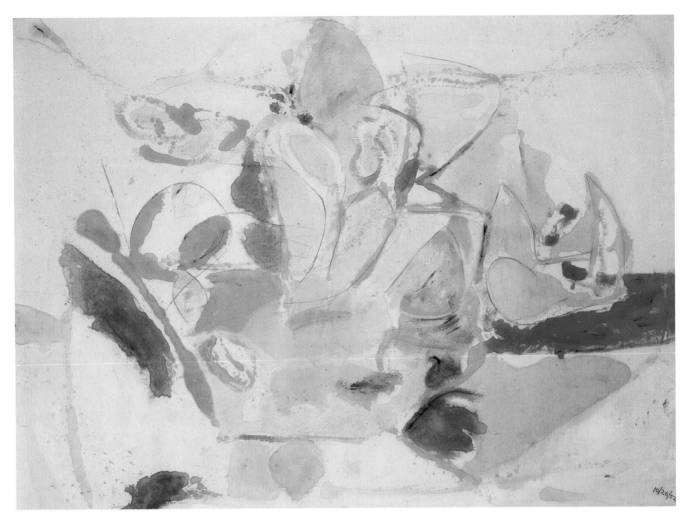

20–7 Helen Frankenthaler. *Mountains and Sea.* 1952. Oil on canvas, 7′2 3/4″ × 9′8 1/4″ (2.20 × 2.95 m).
Collection of the artist on extended loan to the National Gallery of Art, Washington, D.C.

THE IDEA OF THE MAINSTREAM

A central conviction of modernist artists, critics, and art historians has been the existence of an artistic mainstream, the notion that some artworks are more central and important than others—not only by virtue of their aesthetic quality but because they participate in the progressive unfolding of some larger historical purpose. This type of art has been extolled as representative of "high culture." According to this view, the overall evolutionary pattern is what confers value, and any art that does not fit within it, regardless of its appeal, can be for the most part ignored (see "The High/Low Myth of Modernism," page 547).

The first significant discussions of what constitutes the modernist mainstream emerged after World War II, shaped by the critical writings of Clement Greenberg (1909–1994). Greenberg argued that modern art since Édouard Manet (see Chapter 18) involved the progressive disappearance of narrative, figuration, and pictorial space because art itself—regardless of what artists may have thought they were doing—was undergoing a "process of self-purification" in reaction to a deteriorating civilization.

Greenberg was famous for identifying Abstract Expressionism as the dominant style of the late 1940s and 1950s; he championed the New York School of painting. Inspired in part by Hofmann's teaching, he demanded close analysis of the work of art and judgments based on visual perception alone—a methodology called formalism or formal analysis. Belief in the concept of the mainstream gradually eroded, however, and a reaction against Greenberg's ideas began in the 1970s. Because Greenbergian formalism omitted so much of the history of recent art, observers began questioning whether a single, dominant mainstream had ever existed. The extraordinary proliferation of art styles and trends after the 1960s greatly contributed to those doubts.

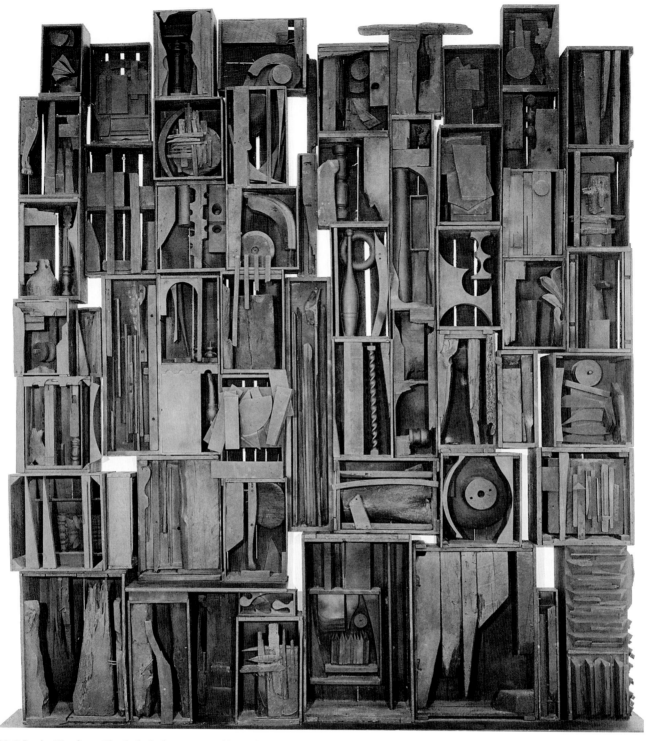

20–8 Louise Nevelson. *Sky Cathedral.* 1958. Assemblage of wood construction painted black,
11′3 1/2″ × 10′ 1/4″ × 18″ (3.44 m × 3.05 m × 45.7 cm). The Museum of Modern Art, New York

Assemblage

By the end of the 1950s, many artists and critics were ready for a change from Abstract Expressionism. One alternative path was **assemblage**, that is, putting together disparate elements to construct a work of art. By 1950 Louise Nevelson (1899–1988) had developed a Cubist-inspired version of assemblage that prefigured the Minimalist (stripped to essentials) focus on formal concerns. Prowling the streets of downtown Manhattan, she collected discarded packing boxes in which she would carefully arrange chair legs, broom handles, cabinet doors, spindles, and other wooden refuse. She painted her assemblages a matte black, both to obscure the identity of the individual elements and to integrate them formally.

After stacking several of these boxes together against a studio wall, Nevelson realized that the resulting accumulation made

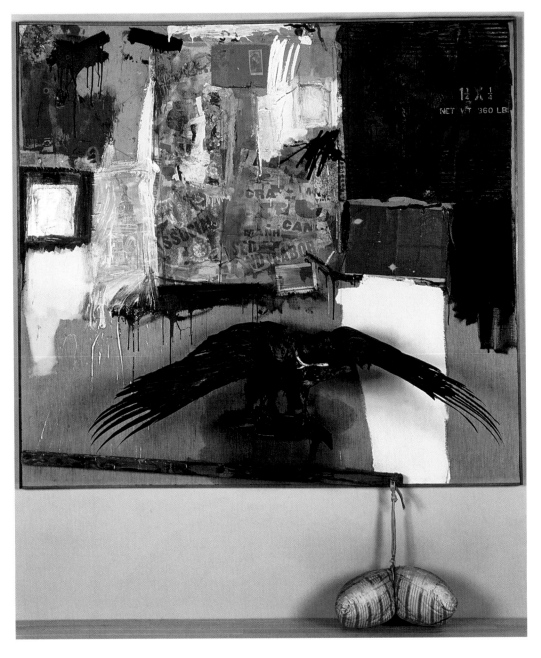

20–9 **Robert Rauschenberg.** *Canyon.* 1959. Combine painting with oil, pencil, paper, metal, photograph, fabric, wood, on canvas, plus buttons, mirror, stuffed eagle, cardboard box, pillow, paint tube 6′1″ × 5′6″ × 2′3/4″ (1.85 × 1.68 × 0.63 m)

Avant-garde critics were not bothered by the fact that much of Rauschenberg's and the other assemblers' materials were drawn from popular culture. Many of the early-twentieth-century collagists, including Picasso and Braque, had worked with similar materials. However, critics such as Hilton Kramer (at the New York Times*) and Thomas Hess (at* Artnews*) pointed out that whereas earlier artists had aesthetically coordinated such elements, transforming the crude materials of life into the finer ones of art, Rauschenberg and his associates left them in their raw, "unpurified" condition. In this view, such works as this one were not art at all.*

a more powerful effect than the individual units. One of her first monumental wall assemblages was *Sky Cathedral* (fig. **20–8**). What she particularly liked about the new schema was the way it could transform ordinary space just as the prosaic elements she worked with were transformed into a work of art. In order to complete this process, and to add a poetic dimension, Nevelson first displayed *Sky Cathedral* bathed in soft blue light, recalling moonlight. An equally evocative use of assemblage can be seen in James Hampton's *Throne of the Third Heaven of the Nations' Millennium General Assembly,* see Intro, fig. 12.

Robert Rauschenberg (b. 1925) developed a distinctive style of assemblage by chaotically mixing painted and found elements in artworks he called "combines." *Canyon* (fig. **20–9**), one of these combines, features an assortment of old family pho-

tographs (the boy with the upraised arm is Rauschenberg's son), public imagery (the Statue of Liberty), fragments of political posters (in the center), and various objects salvaged from the trash (the flattened steel drum at upper right) or even purchased or donated by friends (the stuffed eagle). The artist meant his work to be open to various readings, choosing material that each viewer might interpret differently. Cheerfully accepting the chaos and unpredictability of modern urban experience, he tried to find artistic metaphors for it. "I only consider myself successful," Rauschenberg said, "when I do something that resembles the lack of order I sense."

In 1961 the Museum of Modern Art organized an exhibition titled "The Art of Assemblage." Rauschenberg was one of two major American artists included in the show; the other was his close friend Jasper Johns (b. 1930). Inspired by the example of Marcel Duchamp (see fig. 19–18), Johns produced conceptually challenging works that seemed to bear on issues raised in contemporary art. For instance, art historians and critics had praised the "nonhierarchical" or "all-over" quality of so much Abstract Expressionist painting, particularly the late work of Pollock. The target in *Target with Four Faces* (fig. **20–10**), an emphatically hierarchical, organized image, can be seen as a response and a rebuttal to this position.

Target also has a psychological dimension that may stem from the artist's own anxieties and fears. Above the target are four faces, casts taken at different times from the same model. Cut off below eye level and thus made anonymous, they are as blank and empty as the target itself. The viewer can complete the process of depersonalization by closing the hinged flap over the faces, obliterating the human presence. The work of Johns had a powerful effect on the artists who matured around 1960, and Johns' interest in Duchamp helped elevate that artist to a place of importance previously reserved for Picasso.

Not since Dada had the art world seen creations like the assemblages and kinetic sculptures of Jean Tinguely (1925–1991). In his *Homage to New York* (see fig. 20–11), Tinguely, an anarchist, wanted to free the machine, to let it play. "Art hasn't been fun for a long time," he said. Like the creations of his Dada forebears, Tinguely's work was implicitly critical of an overly restrained and practical bourgeois mentality.

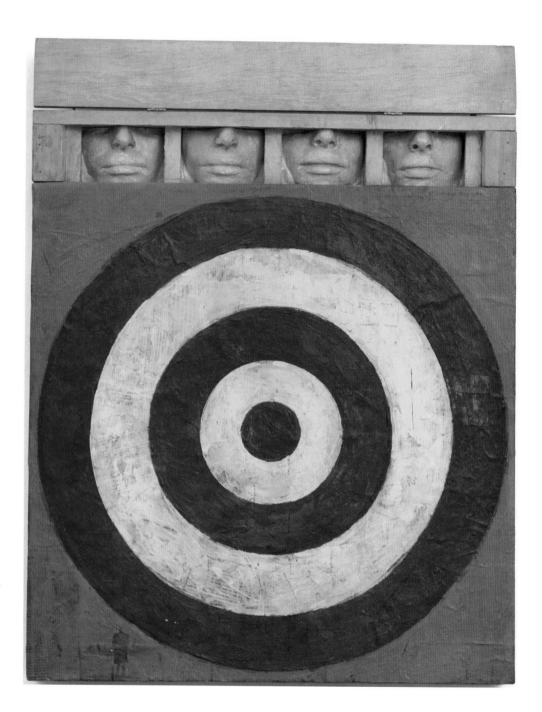

20–10 Jasper Johns. *Target with Four Faces.* 1955. Assemblage: encaustic on newspaper and cloth over canvas, surmounted by four tinted plaster faces in wood box with hinged front; overall, with box open, $33\frac{5}{8}'' \times 26'' \times 3''$ (85.4 × 66 × 7.6 cm). The Museum of Modern Art, New York

On the evening of March 17, 1960, a distinguished group of guests, including Governor Nelson Rockefeller of New York, gathered in the sculpture garden of the Museum of Modern Art in New York City. Awaiting them was an unlikely construction titled *Homage to New York* (fig. **20–11**) by the Swiss-born artist Jean Tinguely (1925–1991). The work was assembled from yards of metal tubing, several dozen bicycle and baby-carriage wheels, a washing-machine drum, an upright piano, a radio, several electric fans, a noisy old Addressograph machine (a forerunner of computer addressing), a bassinet, numerous small motors, two motor-driven devices that produced abstract paintings by the yard, several bottles of chemical inks, and various noisemakers. White paint covered everything except the crowning element—an inflated orange meteorological balloon.

The machine, designed to destroy itself when activated, was plugged in as the expectant guests watched. Smoke poured out of the machinery and covered the crowd, and parts of the contraption broke free and scuttled off in various directions, sometimes threatening onlookers. A device meant to douse the burning piano—which repeatedly played three notes—failed to work, and firefighters had to be called in. The firefighters extinguished the blaze and finished the work's destruction to boos from the crowd, which, with the exception of the museum officials present, had been delighted by the spectacle.

This new kind of art, dramatic but transitory, prefigured a question and answer raised by musician and philosopher John Cage (see page 578). Surveying art and music in 1961, he asked, "Where do we go from here," and his answer was, "Towards theater." Such questions about what art is and what role it plays in society have marked the richly innovative period since 1960.

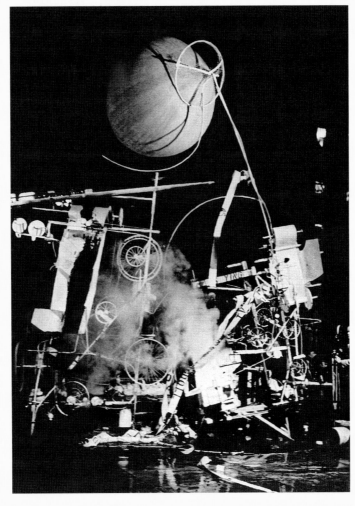

20–11 Jean Tinguely. Fragment from *Homage to New York*. 1960.
Painted metal, wood, and cloth, 6'8$\frac{1}{4}$" × 29$\frac{5}{8}$" × 7'3$\frac{7}{8}$"
(203.7 × 75.1 × 223.2 cm). Self-destroying sculpture in the garden of the
Museum of Modern Art, New York. Gift of the artist (227.1968)

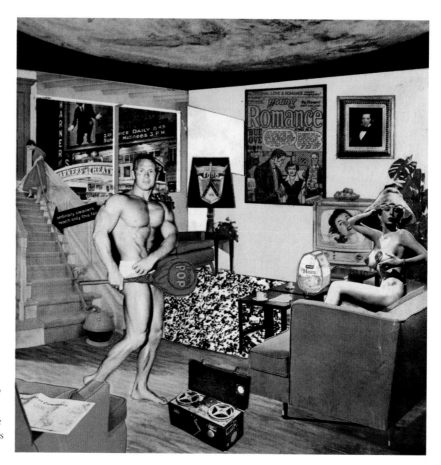

20–12 Richard Hamilton. *Just What Is It That Makes Today's Homes So Different, So Appealing?* 1956. Collage, 10$\frac{1}{4}$" × 9$\frac{1}{4}$" (26 × 23.5 cm). Kunsthalle, Tübingen, Germany. Hamilton's collage was part of a 1956 London exhibition titled "This Is Tomorrow."

Pop Art

Pop art, as its name suggests, took its style and subject matter from popular culture: its sources were comic books, advertisements, movies, and television. Many critics were alarmed by Pop, fearful that open acknowledgment of the powerful commercial culture would threaten the survival of both modernist art and high culture—meaning a civilization's most sophisticated, not its most representative, products (see "The High/Low Myth of Modernism", below).

Pop art originated in London in the work of the Independent Group (IG), formed in 1952 by a few members of the Institute of Contemporary Art (ICA). One of the IG's most prominent figures was the London-born artist Richard Hamilton (b. 1922) whose collage *Just What Is It That Makes Today's Homes So Different, So Appealing* (1959) satirizes modern life and especially American materialism (fig. **20–12**). American advertisements, whose utopian vision of a future of contented people with ample leisure time to enjoy cheap and plentiful material goods, was very appealing to people living amid the austerity of post-war Britain. Products of the American mass media and commercial culture—including Hollywood movies, Madison Avenue advertising, science fiction, and pop music—soon became the central subject matter of British Pop art.

THE HIGH/LOW MYTH OF MODERNISM

One of the prevailing ideals of the modernist avant-garde was to distance itself intellectually and aesthetically from the banalities of everyday, middle-class life—what was sometimes referred to as "lowbrow" culture.

"Lowbrow" and "kitsch" are labels applied to the habits, tastes, artifacts (mostly mass-produced), and amusements of ordinary, popular culture—that is, any cultural expression that falls outside the parameters of what was considered elite, or "high" culture (see "The Idea of the Mainstream," page 569). The term *kitsch* derives from the German word *verkitschen* (to make cheap). Mass-produced consumer goods have generally been given this label—a categorization that often has a pejorative connotation when such goods are compared to "high," or fine, art. (Kitsch is often considered a mark of vulgarity and "bad," or uneducated, taste.)

Boundaries between "high" and "low" began to blur when the Pop artists (see pages 574–576) of the early 1960s began to champion imagery culled from popular culture by putting it into the context of "high" art—similar to what Marcel Duchamp did when he exhibited a urinal as a work of art in 1917 and titled it *Fountain* (see fig. 19–18). Postmodern artists continue to question and obscure distinctions between "high" and "low" as a way of repudiating and/or critiquing modernism.

Rauschenberg, with his conceptually intriguing use of subjects from ordinary life, had helped open the way for Pop art. Even more attuned to popular culture, Roy Lichtenstein (1923–1997), used imagery he found in cartoons and advertisements. He adopted the print medium's heavy outlines and imitated the **Benday dots** used in offset printing. Although many people assume that he merely copied from the comics, in fact he made numerous subtle, important formal adjustments that tightened, clarified, and strengthened the final image. *Oh, Jeff . . . I Love You, Too . . . But . . .* (fig. **20–13**) compresses into a single frame the soap opera story of two people who fall in love, face a crisis that temporarily threatens their relationship, and then live happily ever after. Lichtenstein reminds the grown-up viewer, however, that this plot is only an adolescent fiction; real-life relationships end with the "But . . ."

Another Pop artist who veiled personal meditations behind the impersonal veneer of American popular imagery was Andy Warhol (1928?–1987). A successful commercial illustrator in New York City during the 1950s, Warhol grew envious of Rauschenberg's and Johns's emerging "star status" and decided in 1960 to pursue a career as an artist. His decision to focus on popular culture was more than a careerist move, however; it also allowed him to celebrate the middle-class social and material values he had absorbed growing up amid the hardships of the Great Depression. In the *Marilyn Diptych* (fig. **20–14**), Warhol even celebrates its industrial mode of production.

The painting, produced in Warhol's studio called the Factory, is one of the first in which Warhol turned from hand painting to the assembly-line technique of silk-screening photographic images onto canvas, allowing him to produce many versions of a single subject. Like so many people,

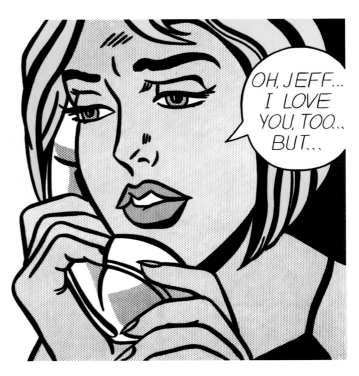

20–13 Roy Lichtenstein. *Oh, Jeff . . . I Love You, Too . . . But . . .* 1964. Oil on Magna on canvas, 4′ × 4′ (1.22 × 1.22 m). Private collection
© ESTATE OF ROY LICHTENSTEIN

Warhol was fascinated by American movie stars such as Marilyn Monroe. The strip of pictures in this work suggests the sequential images of film. Even the face Warhol portrays, taken from a publicity photograph (see "Appropriation," below), is not that of Monroe the person but of Monroe the

APPROPRIATION

During the late 1970s and 1980s, appropriation (the presentation of a preexisting image as one's own) became a popular technique among Postmodernists (see page 585) in both the United States and Western Europe. The borrowing of figures or compositions has been an essential technique throughout the history of art, but the emphasis had always been on changing or personalizing the source. A copy or reproduction was not considered a legitimate work of art until Marcel Duchamp changed the rules with his readymades (see fig. 19–18), insisting that the quality of an artwork depends not on formal invention but on the ideas that stand behind it.

Duchamp's own appropriations inspired the Pop artists Warhol and Roy Lichtenstein (see figs. 20–13 and 20–14), whose reuse of imagery from popular culture, high art, ordinary commerce, and the tabloids helped point the way for the artists of the 1970s and 1980s.

Critics and historians now use the term *appropriation* to describe the activities of two distinct groups. To the first belong artists such as Betye Saar (see fig. 20–25) and Jaune Quick-to-See Smith (see fig. 20–31), who combine and shape their borrowings in personal ways. These artists, along with earlier ones such as Rauschenberg (see fig. 20–9), might be called **collage** appropriators. "Straight

appropriators," on the other hand, are those who simply repaint or rephotograph imagery from commerce or the history of art and present it as their own.

The work of appropriators is grounded in the ideas of the French literary critics known as the Post-Structuralists. In his essay "The Death of the Author" (1968), for example, Roland Barthes (1915–1980) argued that the meaning of a work of art depends not on what the author meant but on what the reader understands. Furthermore, he questioned the modernist notion of originality, of the author as a creator of an entirely new meaning; according to Barthes, the author merely recycles meanings from other sources.

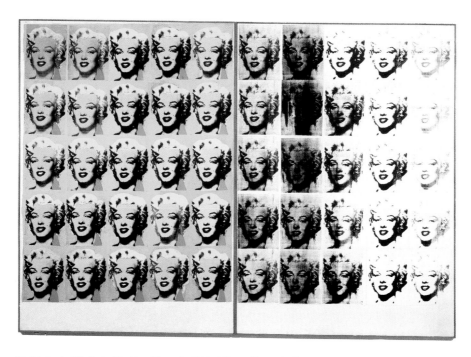

20–14 Andy Warhol. *Marilyn Diptych.* 1962. Oil, acrylic, and silk screen on enamel on canvas, 6′8⅞″ × 4′8⅝″ (2.05 × 1.44 m). Tate Gallery, London

Warhol assumed that all Pop artists shared his affirmative view of ordinary culture. In his account of the beginnings of the Pop movement, he wrote: "The Pop artists did images that anybody walking down Broadway could recognize in a split second—comics, picnic tables, men's trousers, celebrities, shower curtains, refrigerators, Coke bottles—all the great modern things that the Abstract Expressionists tried so hard not to notice at all."

star; Warhol was interested in her public mask, not in her personality or character. He borrowed the diptych format from the Byzantine icons of Christian saints he saw at the Greek Orthodox church services he attended every Sunday. By symbolically treating the famous actress as a saint, Warhol shed light on his own fascination with fame. He implies that fame not only brings wealth and transforms the ordinary into the beautiful, but it also confers, like holiness for a saint, a kind of immortality.

Unlike Warhol and Lichtenstein swedish-born Claes Oldenburg (b. 1929) used elements from popular culture to criticize society. Oldenburg's humor—fundamental to his goal to reanimate a dull, lifeless culture—is clearly evident in such large-scale public projects as his Lipstick Monument for his alma mater, Yale University (fig. **20–15**). The late 1960s were marked by student demonstrations against the Vietnam War. By mounting a giant lipstick tube on tracks from a Caterpillar tractor, Oldenburg suggested a missile rising from a tank and simultaneously subverted the warlike reference by casting the missile in the form of a feminine cosmetic with erotic overtones. Oldenburg thus urged his audience, in the vocabulary of the time, to "make love, not war." The university, offended by the work's irreverent humor, made Oldenburg remove it. In

1974 he reworked *Lipstick (Ascending) on Caterpillar Tracks* in fiber-glass, aluminum, and steel and donated it to the university, which this time accepted it.

Minimalism/Post-Minimalism and Op Art

In contrast to the emphasis on image-based content in Pop art, other styles that emerged in the wake of Abstract Expressionism focused on stripping all extra-artistic meanings from artworks and reducing them to technical essentials. The most intense investigation of perception occurred in "optical art," popularly known as Op art, a kind of nonobjective art that used precisely structured patterns of lines and colors to affect visual perception. The painting *Current* (fig. **20–16**) by the British artist Bridget Riley (b. 1931) consists of tightly spaced, parallel, curved lines that produce an effect of fluctuating motion. As with many Op art works, staring at the pattern may produce discomfort.

Other artists, including the sculptor Donald Judd (1928–1994), turned to a style known as Minimalism. Convinced that Abstract Expressionism had deteriorated into a set of techniques for faking both the subjective and the transcendent, around 1960 Judd began to search for an art free of falsehood. He decided that sculpture offered a better medium than painting for

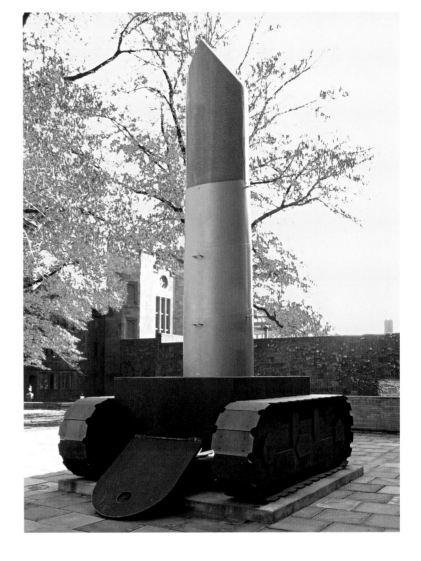

20–15 Claes Oldenburg. *Lipstick (Ascending) on Caterpillar Tracks.*
1969, reworked 1974. Painted steel body, aluminum tube, and
fiberglass tip, 21′ × 19′5 ½″ × 10′11″ (6.70 × 5.94 × 3.33 m).
Installed at Beinike Plaza, Yale University, New Haven, Connecticut.
Yale University Art Gallery

GIFT OF COLOSSAL KEEPSAKE CORPORATION

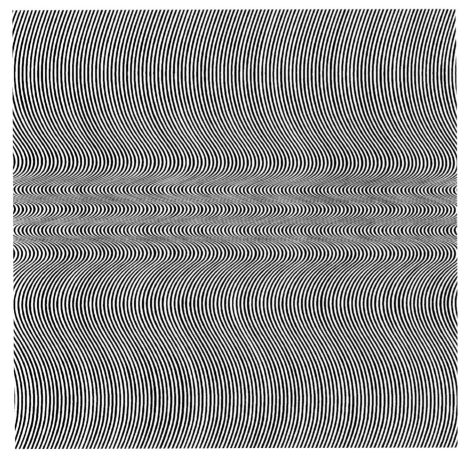

20–16 Bridget Riley. *Current.* 1964. Synthetic
polymer on board, 58⅜″ × 58⅞″(148 × 149 cm).
The Museum of Modern Art, New York

While the American popular media loved Op art,
most avant-garde critics detested it. Lucy Lippard,
for example, called it "an art of little substance,"
depending "on purely technical knowledge of color
and design theory which, when combined with a
conventional geometric … framework, results in
jazzily respectable jumping surfaces, and nothing
more." For Lippard and like-minded New York
critics, Op art was too involved with investigating
the processes of perception to qualify as serious art.

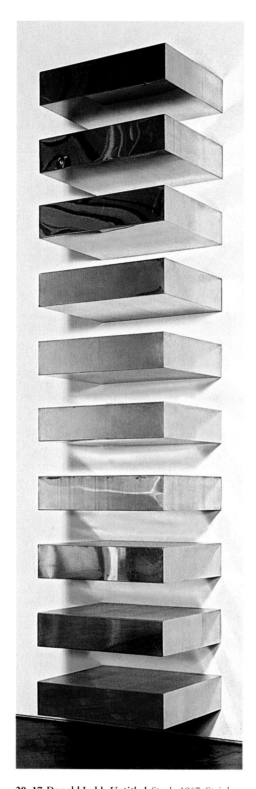

20–17 Donald Judd. *Untitled.* Stack. 1967. Stainless steel and Plexiglas, each of the ten units measures 6 ″ × 27 ″ × 24 ″(15.2 × 68.6 × 61 cm). Spencer Museum of Art, University of Kansas, Lawrence

creating literal, matter-of-fact art. Rather than *depicting* shapes, which Judd thought smacked of illusionism and therefore fakery, he produced *actual* shapes. In search of simplicity and clarity, he soon evolved a formal vocabulary featuring identical rectangular units arranged in rows and constructed of industrial materials, especially anodized aluminum and Plexiglas. *Untitled* (fig. **20–17**) is a typical example of Judd's mature work.

Approaches to Minimalism varied. Eva Hesse (1936–1970) countered the rigid prefabricated forms of Judd's Minimalism by incorporating malleable techniques such as sewing, lacing, and bandaging into her work. Instead of sleek surfaces, her work shows the actual process of art-making. Her *Rope Piece* (fig. **20–18**), for example, takes on a different shape and different dimensions each time it is installed. The work consists of several sections of rope, which Hesse and her assistant dipped in latex, knotted and tangled, and then hung from wires attached to the ceiling. The resulting linear web or "drawing in space" resembles a three-dimensional version of a poured painting by Jackson Pollock, and, like Pollock's work, it achieves a sense of structure despite its chaotic appearance. In the face of the severe exactitude of Minimalism, Hesse provided an alternative in her choice of materials and in their inherent capacity for movement and change.

Conceptual and Performance Art

While Hesse and other Post-Minimalists made artworks whose mutability challenged the idea of the art object as static and durable, the artists who came to be known as Conceptualists pushed Minimalism to its logical extreme by eliminating the art object itself. This shift away from the aesthetic object toward the pure idea was largely inspired by the growing reputation of Marcel Duchamp and his assertion that making art should emphasize mental, rather than physical activity.

The most prominent American Conceptual artist of his generation was Joseph Kosuth (b. 1945), who abandoned painting in 1965 and began to work with language. His *One and Three Chairs* (fig. **20–19**) presents an actual chair, a full-scale black-and-white photograph of the same chair, and a dictionary definition of the word chair. The work thus leads the viewer from the physical chair to the purely linguistic ideal of "chairness" and invites the question, "Which is the most real?"

Some Conceptual artists used their bodies as an art medium and engaged in activities or performances that they considered works of art. Many of these artists had fallen under the spell of the musician and philosopher John Cage (1912–1992) in the 1950s. Cage turned to everyday experience and pure chance in creating his compositions, and furthermore advocated the unity of the arts—including theater, music, and dance as well as the visual arts. Friends of Cage such as Allan Kaprow (b. 1927) gave up painting for loosely scripted, multimedia events they called **Happenings**. Meanwhile in Japan a group of artists produced dramatic displays they called **Performance Art**—for example, in a work called *Hurling Colors*, they smashed bottles of paint on a canvas on the floor. In Paris, Yves Klein (1928–1962)—who after 1957 worked only in blue, which he considered the most spiritual color—produced *Anthropometries of the Blue Period* in 1960.

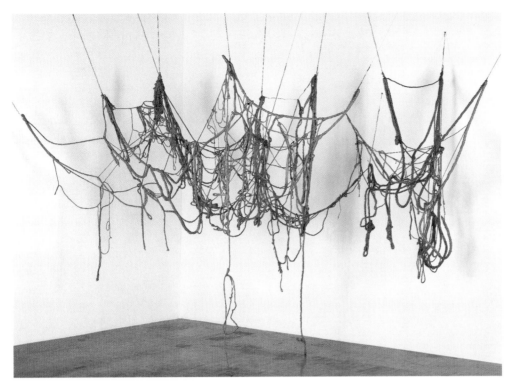

20–18 Eva Hesse. *Rope Piece.*
1969–1970. Latex over rope, string
and wire; two strands, dimensions
variable. Whitney Museum of
American Art, New York

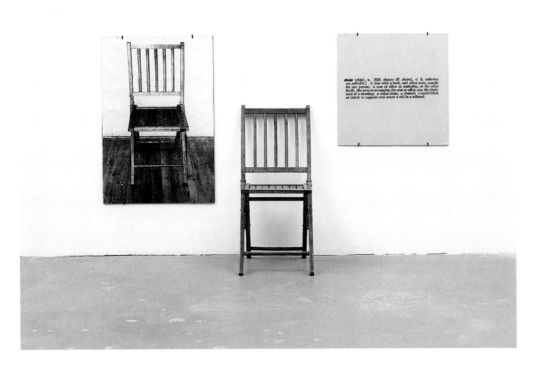

20–19 Joseph Kosuth. *One and Three Chairs.* 1965. Wood folding chair, photograph of chair,
and photographic enlargement of dictionary definition of chair; chair, $32\frac{3}{8}''$ × $14\frac{7}{8}''$ × $20\frac{7}{8}''$
(82.2 × 37.8 × 53 cm); photo panel, $36''$ × $24\frac{1}{8}''$ (91.4 × 61.3 cm); text panel,
$24\frac{1}{8}''$ × $24\frac{1}{2}''$ (61.3 × 62.2 cm). The Museum of Modern Art, New York

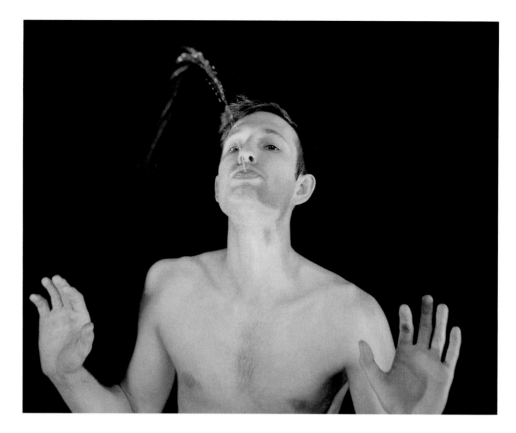

20–20 Bruce Nauman. *Self-Portrait as a Fountain.* 1966–1967. Color photograph, $19\frac{3}{4}''\times 23\frac{3}{4}''$ (50.1 × 60.3 cm)

COURTESY LEO CASTELLI GALLERY, NEW YORK

Regarding his works of the later 1960s, Nauman observed, "I was using my body as a piece of material and manipulating it. I think of it as going into the studio and being involved in some activity. Sometimes it works out that the activity involves making something, and sometimes the activity itself is the piece."

He covered three nude female models with blue paint and pressed them against large sheets of paper in an attempt to capture the spirit within the flesh. Klein's *Monotone Symphony*—20 minutes of single notes followed by 20 minutes of silence—accompanied the performance.

In 1966–1967, the American artist Bruce Nauman (b. 1941) made a series of 11 color photographs based on wordplay and visual puns. In *Self-Portrait as a Fountain* (fig. **20–20**), for example, the bare-chested artist tips his head back, spurts water into the air, and, in the spirit of Duchamp, designates himself a work of art.

Earthworks and Site-Specific Art

In the late 1960s and 1970s, sculptors began to create art never intended for display in a gallery or museum and not intended for sale. They worked outdoors, using what they found at the site to fashion **earthworks**, a new kind of artwork called **site-specific** sculpture.

Robert Smithson (1938–1973) sought to illustrate what he called the "ongoing dialectic" in nature between the constructive forces that build and shape form and the destructive forces that destroy it. *Spiral Jetty* (fig. **20–21**), a 1,500-foot spiraling stone and earth platform extending into the Great Salt Lake in Utah, reflects these ideas. To Smithson, the salty water and the algae of the lake suggested the primordial ocean where life began, and the abandoned oil rigs dotting the lake shore brought to mind both prehistoric dinosaurs and a vanished civilization. He used the spiral because it is an archetypal shape that appears throughout the natural world, from galaxies to seashells. (The spiral attracted Frank Lloyd Wright for similar reasons [see fig. 20–32]). Also, unlike modernist squares, circles, and straight lines, it is a "dialectical" shape, one that opens and closes, curls and uncurls endlessly. More than any other shape, it suggested to him the perpetual "coming and going of things." Part of Smithson's intention was that the algae living in the lake would turn the water into a display of ephemeral colors, and that eventually the action of the water would cause the earthwork to erode and disappear.

Strongly committed to the realization of temporary, site-specific artworks in both rural and urban settings are Christo and Jeanne-Claude, both born on June 13, 1935. Christo Javacheff (who uses only his first name) emigrated from his native

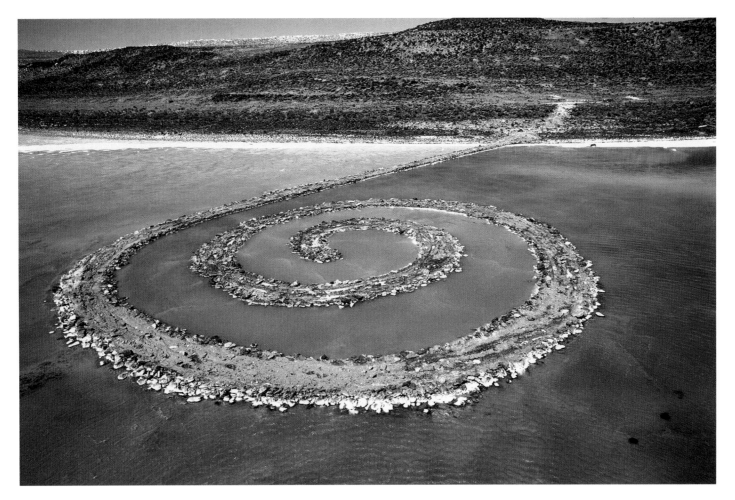

20–21 Robert Smithson. *Spiral Jetty.* 1969–1970. Black rock, salt crystal, and earth spiral, length 1,500′ (457 m). Great Salt Lake, Utah

© ESTATE OF ROBERT SMITHSON/LICENSED BY VAGA, NEW YORK. COURTESY JAMES COHAN GALLERY, NEW YORK. COLLECTION: DIA CENTER FOR THE ARTS, NEW YORK. PHOTO BY GIANFRANCO GORGONI

Bulgaria to Paris in 1958, where he met Jeanne-Claude de Guillebon. They began their artistic collaboration in 1961. The couple's interest in "wrapping" places or things in swaths of fabric soon became an obsession, and they began wrapping progressively larger items. One of their best-known works, *Running Fence* (fig. **20–22**) consisted of a 24 $\frac{1}{2}$-mile-long, 18-foot-high nylon "fence" that crossed two counties in northern California. The artists chose the location in Sonoma and Marin counties for aesthetic reasons, as well as to call attention to the link between urban, suburban, and rural spaces. In all their work, Christo and Jeanne-Claude reveal the joy and beauty in both natural and built space. At the same time, given the nature of their work, collaborations between the two artists and various social groups are usually necessary before a project can proceed beyond the planning stages. Such collaborations sometimes lead to conflicts over a proposed project and thus also serve to prompt public discussion and draw attention to their efforts and ideas. To realize their massive projects, Christo and Jeanne-Claude usually rely on a diverse and devoted community of supporters and assistants, including college students, local citizens, and fellow artists. Recently they filled Central Park in New York with "gates".

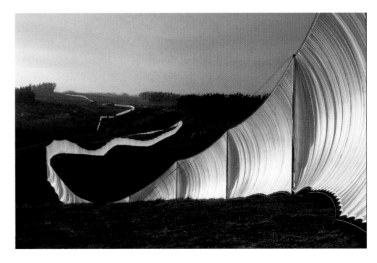

20–22 Christo and Jeanne-Claude. *Running Fence.* 1972–1976. Nylon fence, height 18′ (5.5 m), length 24 $\frac{1}{2}$ miles (40 km). Sonoma and Marin Counties, California

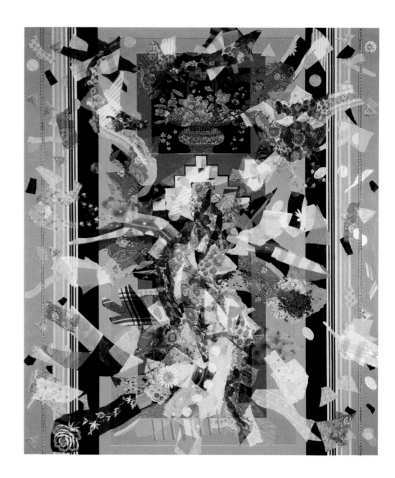

20–23 Miriam Schapiro. *Personal Appearance #3.* 1973. Acrylic and fabric on canvas, 60 × 50″ (152.4 × 127 cm). Private collection

Feminist Art

The 1970s also saw the rise of the feminist movement in the United States. In August 1970 (the fiftieth anniversary of the adoption of the Nineteenth Amendment to the Constitution, which guaranteed women the right to vote), women assessed their progress in various fields since 1920. They were disappointed by what they found. In the arts, women constituted about half the nation's practicing artists, but only 18 percent of commercial New York galleries carried any work by women. And of the 151 artists whose works were in the 1969 Whitney Annual—one of the country's most important exhibitions of the work of living artists—only eight were women. Few women served as museum directors, and few achieved the rank of full professor in art history departments.

To focus more attention on women in the arts, feminist artists began organizing women's cooperative galleries. Feminist art historians, such as Eleanor Tufts in her groundbreaking book *Our Hidden Heritage* (1974) and Linda Nochlin in essays, wrote about women artists. In 1971, Miriam Schapiro (b. 1923) and Judy Chicago (b. 1939) established the Feminist Art Program, dedicated to training women artists, at the California Institute of the Arts (CalArts).

Schapiro championed the theory that women have a distinct artistic sensibility that can be distinguished from that of men, and hence a specifically feminine aesthetic. During the late 1950s and 1960s she made explicitly female versions of the dominant mod-ernist styles, including reductive, hard-edged abstractions of the female form: large X-shapes with openings at their centers. In 1973 she created *Personal Appearance #3* (fig. **20–23**), using underlying hard-edged rectangles and overlaying them with a collage of fabric and paper. She called her new technique *fem mage* (from *female* and *collage).* Combining painting and fabrics, the works celebrate traditional women's craftwork. A founder of the P and D (Pattern and Decoration) movement, Schapiro said, "I dovetail my feminism with decoration" (cited in Gouma-Peterson, page 29). The formal and emotional richness of her work were meant to counter the Minimalist aesthetic of the 1960s, which Schapiro and other feminists considered typically male.

Judy Chicago assumed a leading role in the 1970s, and her work *The Dinner Party* (fig. **20–24**) is perhaps the best-known work of feminist art created that decade. In 1970 she adopted the surname Chicago (from the city of her birth) to free herself from "all names imposed upon her through male social dominance." At CalArts, Chicago and Schapiro led a collective of twenty-one women students in the creation of *Womanhouse* (1971–1972), a collaborative art environment, and from *Womanhouse* emerged *The Dinner Party* (1974–1979). A complex, mixed-media installation that fills an entire room, the work speaks powerfully of the accomplishments of women throughout history. Five years of collaborative effort went into the creation of the work, involving hundreds of women and several men who volunteered their talents as ceramists, needleworkers, and china painters to realize Chicago's designs.

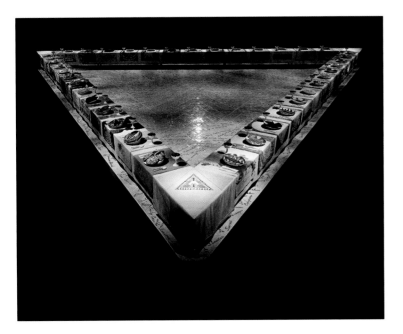

20–24 Judy Chicago. *The Dinner Party.* 1979. White tile floor inscribed in gold with 999 women's names; triangular table with painted porcelain, sculpted porcelain plates, and needlework. Mixed-media, 48″ × 42″ × 3′ (122.9 × 42 × 91 cm)

COLLECTION OF THE BROOKLYN MUSEUM OF ART. GIFT OF THE ELIZABETH A. SACKLER FOUNDATION THROUGH THE FLOWER, NM © 2007 JUDY CHICAGO/ARTISTS RIGHTS SOCIETY (ARS), NEW YORK

The Dinner Party is composed of a large, triangular table, each side stretching 48 feet, which rests on a triangular platform covered with 2,300 triangular porcelain tiles. Chicago saw the equilateral triangle as a symbol of the equalized world sought by feminism and also identified it as one of the earliest symbols of the feminine. The porcelain "Heritage Floor" bears the names of 999 notable women from myth, legend, and history. Along each side of the table's three sides, thirteen place settings each represent a famous woman. The 39 women honored include some that we have covered in this book, including the ancient Egyptian pharaoh Hatshepsut (see fig. 2–25); the French poet and scholar Christine de Pizan (see Introduction, fig. 23); the Renaissance art patron Isabella d'Esté (see page 356); and the painters Artemesia Gentileschi (see fig. 14–10) and Georgia O'Keeffe (see Introduction, fig. 4). Chicago emphasized china painting and needlework in *The Dinner Party* to celebrate craft mediums traditionally practiced by women and to argue that they should be considered "high" art forms equivalent to painting and sculpture. This argument complemented her larger aim of raising awareness of the many contributions women have made to history, thereby fostering women's empowerment in the present.

Typical of those who achieved widespread recognition only with the arrival of the feminist movement is the Los Angeles–based artist Betye Saar (b. 1926). Saar made both collages and constructions. Her best-known work, *The Liberation of Aunt Jemima* (fig. **20–25**) is a box constructed of found objects. It appropriates the derogatory stereotype of the cheerfully servile domestic servant and transforms it into an icon of militant black feminist power. Aunt Jemima holds a broom and pistol in one hand and a rifle in the other and stands behind a large clenched fist, a symbol of "black power." Saar's armed Jemima liberates herself not only from racial oppression but also from traditional gender roles that had long relegated black women to subservient positions.

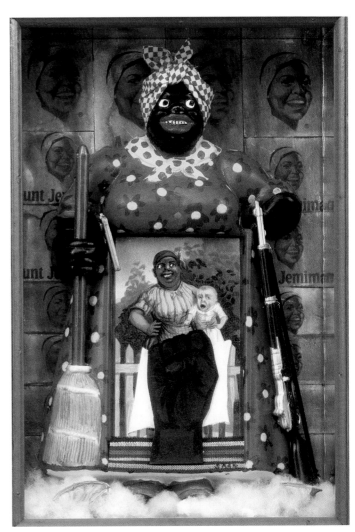

20–25 Betye Saar. *The Liberation of Aunt Jemima.* 1972. Mixed media, 8″ × 11¾″ × 2¾″ (20.3 × 29.8 × 6.9 cm). University Art Museum, University of California, Berkeley

PURCHASED WITH THE AID OF FUNDS FROM THE NATIONAL ENDOWMENT OF ARTS (SELECTED BY THE COMMITTEE FOR THE ACQUISITION OF AFRO-AMERICAN ART)

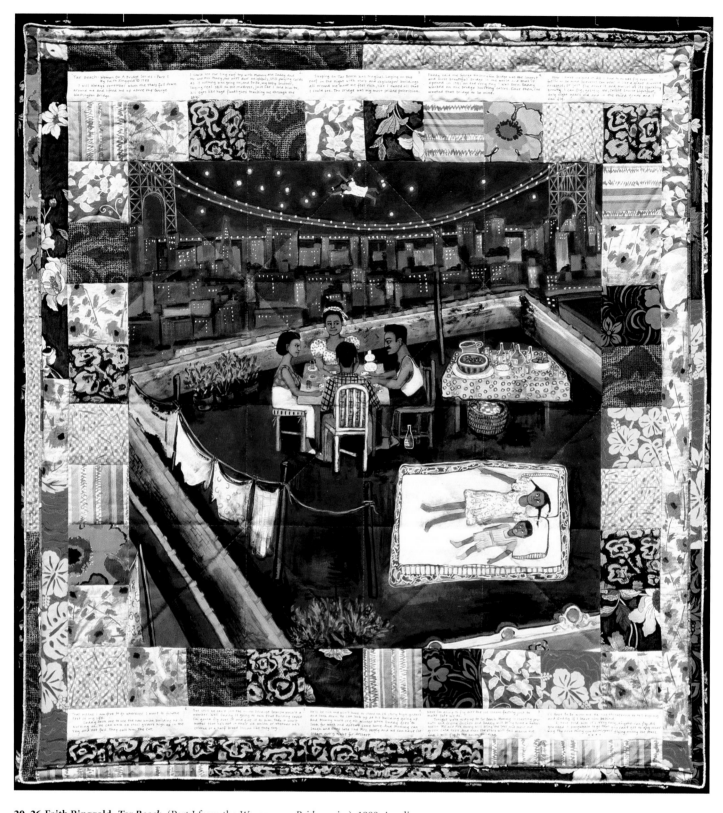

20–26 Faith Ringgold. *Tar Beach.* (Part I from the *Woman on a Bridge* series). 1988. Acrylic on canvas, bordered with printed, painted, quilted, and pieced cloth, $74\frac{5}{8}''\times 68\frac{1}{2}''$ (190.5 × 174 cm). Solomon R. Guggenheim Museum, New York

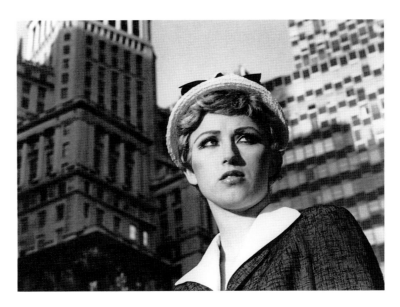

20–27 Cindy Sherman. *Untitled Film Still.* 1978. Black-and-white photograph, 8″ × 10″ (20.3 × 25.4 cm)

COURTESY CINDY SHERMAN AND METRO PICTURES, NEW YORK

In the early 1970s, Faith Ringgold (b. 1930), another African-American artist, began to paint on soft fabrics rather than stretched canvases and to frame her images with decorative quilted borders. In 1977 Ringgold began writing an autobiography, which she combined with her quilts to create her signature medium—the story quilt. Ringgold's story quilts are always narrated by women, and usually address themes related to women's lives. A splendid example is *Tar Beach* (fig. **20–26**) based on the artist's childhood memories of growing up in Harlem. The "Tar Beach" of the title is the roof of the apartment building where Ringgold's family slept on hot summer nights. The little girl, Cassie, describes sleeping on Tar Beach as a magical experience. She dreams that she can fly and that she owns everything she passes over. Ringgold's colorful painting in the center of the quilt shows Cassie and her brother lying on a blanket at the lower right while their parents and two neighbors play cards at a table at center. Directly above the adults appears a second Cassie, flying over the George Washington Bridge against a star-dotted sky. Cassie's childish fantasy of achieving the impossible is charming but also delivers a serious message by reminding the viewer of the real social and economic limitations that African-Americans have faced throughout their history.

In 1977 a leader among second-generation feminists, Cindy Sherman (b. 1954), began work on a series of black-and-white photographs of herself in various assumed roles. The images simulate stills from B-movies of the 1940s and 1950s. In one of these photographs, Sherman plays a perplexed young innocent apparently recently arrived in a big city, its buildings looming threateningly behind her (fig. **20–27**). The image suggests a host of films in which a similar character is overwhelmed by dangerous forces and is rescued by a hero. While Sherman's motives are complex, many observers have suggested that in these works she indicts Hollywood's stereotypical images of women and femininity by showing how one can "invent" oneself in a variety of roles.

Late Modernism/Postmodernism

Many Minimalists, inspired by the theories of art critics such as Greenberg (see "The Idea of the Mainstream," page 569), believe that art represents a pure realm outside ordinary existence and that the history of art followed a coherent, progressive trajectory culminating in modernism and abstraction. To most of the artists who came after them, by contrast, the concepts of artistic purity and the mainstream seemed naive. Critics and artists recognized that they lived in the midst of artistic **pluralism**, the acceptance of a variety of artistic intentions and styles.

The generation that grew to maturity around 1970 had been the first to accept pluralism in its own right as a manifestation of our culturally heterogeneous age. The decline of the concept of modernism in the various arts was neither uniform nor sudden. Its gradual erosion occurred over a long period and was the result of many individual transformations. The various approaches to art that emerged at the end of the twentieth century are designated by the catchall term *postmodernism*. Although there is no universal agreement on exactly what the term *postmodern* means, it involves rejection of the concept of the mainstream and recognition of artistic pluralism.

Neo-Expressionism

Much contemporary art (from c. 1970–present) implicitly acknowledges the exhaustion of the old modernist faith in modern innovation—and in what it implied about the "progressive" course of history—by reviving older styles. The names assigned

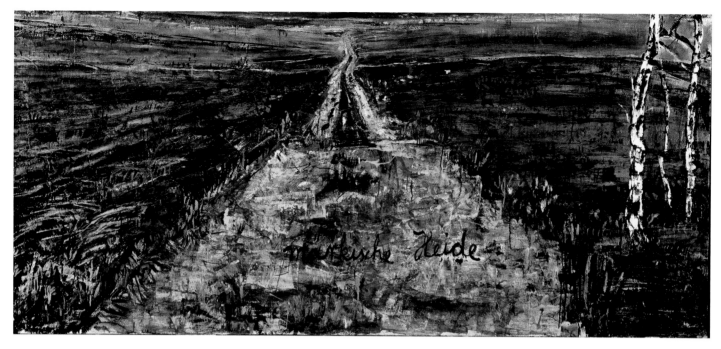

20–28 **Anselm Kiefer.** *Märkische Heide.* 1974. Oil, acrylic, and shellac on burlap, 3′10¹⁄₂″ × 8′4″ (1.18 × 2.54 m). Stedelijk Van Abbemuseum, Eindhoven, the Netherlands

Kiefer often incorporates words and phrases into his paintings that amplify their meaning. Here, the words Märkische Heide ("Heath of the Brandenburg March"—a march is a territory like a county) evoke an old patriotic tune of the Brandenburg region, "Märkische Heide, Märkische Sand."

to these styles often begin with the prefix *neo*, denoting a new form of something that already exists, a typical postmodern position. Leading New York art galleries in 1980 signaled the emergence of Neo-Expressionism, the first of these revival styles. About the same time, various European artists working in a similar vein gained critical recognition in the United States. One is the German artist Anselm Kiefer (b. 1945). In his work, Kiefer, who was born in the last weeks of World War II, revisits his country's Nazi past and the events of World War. The burned and barren landscape in *Märkische Heide* (The Heath of the Brandenburg March) (fig. **20–28**) evokes the ravages of war that the Brandenburg area, near Berlin, experienced. The road that lures us into the landscape, a standard device used in landscape paintings since the seventeenth century, invites us into the region's dark past. Kiefer's works compel viewers to ponder troubling historical and social realities, "in order," he said, "to understand the madness."

The Persistence of Modernism

Despite declarations of the death of modernism by postmodern artists and critics, many artists remained committed to its central values of formal innovation and personal expression. A leading modernist painter is Elizabeth Murray (b. 1940), whose artistic breakthrough came in the late 1970s, when she began to work on irregularly shaped canvases. During the 1980s Murray's canvases, stretched over thick plywood supports, became increasingly complex and three-dimensional physical presences over whose swelling surfaces she painted abstract figures and familiar objects. *Chaotic Lip* (fig. **20–29**) is an enormous, organically shaped can-

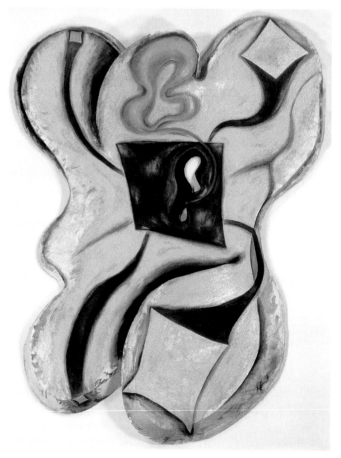

20–29 **Elizabeth Murray.** *Chaotic Lip.* 1986. Oil on canvas, 9′9¹⁄₂″ × 7′2¹⁄₂″ × 1′ (3.01 × 2.22 × 0.31 m). Spencer Museum of Art, The University of Kansas, Lawrence

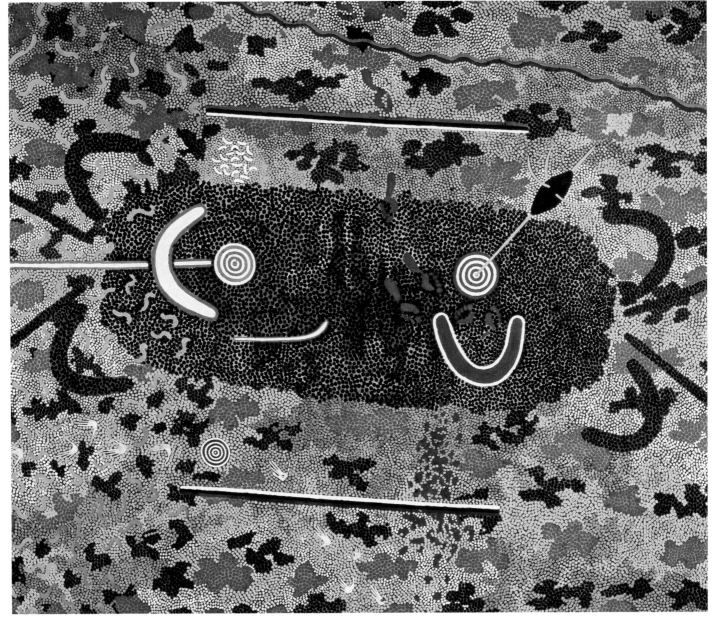

20–30 Clifford Possum Tjapaltjarri. *Man's Love Story.* 1978. Papunya, Northern Territory, Australia. Synthetic polymer paint on canvas, 6'11¾" × 8'4¼" (2.13 × 2.55 m). Art Gallery of South Australia, Adelaide

VISUAL ARTS BOARD OF THE AUSTRALIA COUNCIL CONTEMPORARY ART PURCHASE GRANT, 1980

vas with rounded lobes that radiate out in several directions. The artist's bold and colorful style is inspired simultaneously by "high" modernist art and "low" popular culture; she employs Cubist-style fragmentation, Fauvist color, Surrealist **biomorphism**, and gestural Abstract Expressionist paint handling, while also drawing inspiration from cartoons and animated films.

The techniques and mediums popularized by modern American and European artists have spread around the world. In Australia, for example, Aborigine artists adopted canvas and acrylic paint for rendering traditional imagery once associated with more ephemeral mediums such as bark, sand, and body painting. In 1971, aborigines who were experts in sand painting—an ancient ritual art form that involves creating large colored designs on the ground—formed an art cooperative in Papunya, in central Australia, and painting soon became an economic mainstay in the region.

After a 1988 exhibition of his paintings, Clifford Possum Tjapaltjarri (c. 1932–2002), a founder of the Papunya cooperative, gained an international reputation. As in the technique of sand painting, he works with his canvas on the floor, using traditional patterns and colors (principally red and yellow ochers). His paintings may at first seem entirely nonrepresentational, but they actually carefully convey complex myths, traditions, and social rules through stories. For example, *Man's Love Story* (fig. **20–30**) involves two mythical ancestors. One man came to Papunya in search of honey ants; the white U-shape on the left represents the man seated in front of a water hole with an ants' nest, represented by concentric circles. His digging stick lies to his right and white sugary leaves lie to his left. The straight white "journey line" represents his trek from the west. A second man, represented by the brown-and-white U-shaped form, came from the north, leaving footprints, and sat down by another water

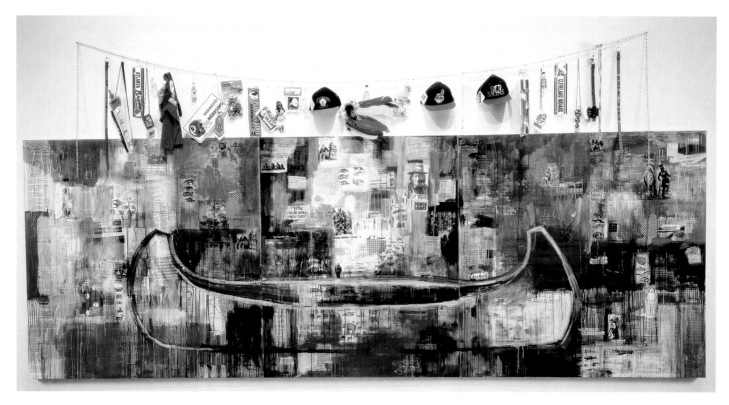

20–31 Jaune Quick-to-See Smith. *Trade (Gifts for Trading Land with White People).* Salish-Cree-Shoshone, 1992. Oil and collage on canvas, 5′ × 14′2″ (1.52 × 4.32 m). Chrysler Museum of Art, Norfolk, Virginia

hole nearby. He began to spin a string made of human hair on a spindle (the form leaning toward the upper right of the painting), but he thought about the woman he loved, who belonged to a kinship group into which he could not marry. Distracted by her approach, he let his hair string blow away (represented by the brown flecks below him) and so lost all his work. Then four women (the dotted U-shapes) from the group into which he could marry came with their digging sticks and sat around the two men. A rich food supply surrounds them—wiggly shapes representing caterpillars and dots representing seeds. Thus, what seems to be a richly decorative surface pattern is in fact a visual record of the ephemeral impressions left on the earth by the figures—their tracks, direction lines, and the U-shaped marks they left when sitting. Dot by dot the artist has captured the vast expanse and shimmering light of the arid landscape.

Later Art with Social Impact

As a major form of communication, the arts have always been used to drive home ideas, and since the nineteenth century artists have expressed their own ideas as well as those of their patrons. Roger Shimomura (b. 1939) turned painting and prints into powerful statements in a series based on his grandmother's diary. In his 1978 painting *Diary* (see Introduction, fig. 17), he depicts his grandmother's record of the family's experience in an internment camp in Idaho. (U.S. citizens of Japanese ancestry were forcibly confined in internment camps during World War II.) Shimomura painted his grandmother writing while he (the

toddler) and his mother stand by an open door—a door that opens out to a barbed-wire-enclosed compound. Shimomura combined two formal traditions—the Japanese art of color woodblock prints (see figs. 9–25 and 9–26) and American Pop art—to create a personal style that expresses his own dual heritage as it makes a powerful political statement.

Jaune Quick-to-See Smith (b. 1940), who was born on the Confederated Salish and Kootenai Reservation in western Montana and is enrolled there, also combines traditional and contemporary forms to convey political and social messages. During the United States's quincentennial celebration of Columbus's arrival in what came to be called the Americas (see Chapter 15), Quick-to-See Smith created paintings and collages that confronted viewers with their own, perhaps unwitting, stereotypes. In *Trade (Gifts for Trading Land with White People)* (fig. **20–31**) a stately canoe floats over a richly colored and textured field, which on closer inspection proves to be a dense collage of clippings from Native American newspapers. On a chain above the painting hangs a collection of fake Indian trinkets (chicken feather headdresses, beaded belts, keyholders, necklaces) and demeaning mascot images for teams with names like the Atlanta Braves, the Washington Redskins, and the Cleveland Indians. Surely, the painting suggests, Native Americans could trade these goods to retrieve their lost lands, just as European settlers traded trinkets to acquire those lands in the first place. As Gerrit Henry wrote in *Art in America* (November 2001), Smith "looks at things Native and national through bifocals of the old and the new, the sacred and the profane, the divine and the witty."

Many artists since the 1980s have had an interest in the theory of Deconstruction developed by the French philosopher Jacques Derrida (1930–2004). Concerned mostly with the analysis of verbal texts, Derridean deconstruction holds that no text possesses a single, intrinsic meaning but rather its meaning is always "intertextual"—a product of its relationship to other texts—and is always "decentered," or "dispersed" along an infinite chain of linguistic signs whose meanings are themselves unstable. Deconstructivist art and architecture is, consequently, often "intertextual" in its use of design elements from other traditions, including modernism, and "decentered" in its denial of unified and stable forms.

Installation and Electronic Art

The issue of art's potential social mission and the desire to make art meaningful to a larger public took on a new prominence by the 1990s. Contemporary artists experimented with new media, such as video monitors, to connect with modern audiences living in a media-oriented culture. Beginning in the early 1980s, Jenny Holzer (b. 1950) turned to some of advertising's more pervasive tools, including electronic signage, to reach out to people who do not usually go to galleries and museums. For example, using the Spectacolor board then in use in New York City's Times Square, she flashed a series of short, provocative messages. Holzer phrased her messages as one-liners suited to the reading habits of Americans raised on advertising sound bites. And her use of signage as a medium emphasizes the postmodern outlook that art consists of layers of "texts" (or meanings) that can be "read" (see "Deconstruction," above).

In a spectacular installation in 1989–1990, Holzer wrapped her signboards in a continuous loop around the multilevel spiraling interior of Frank Lloyd Wright's Guggenheim Museum (fig. 20–32). The words moved and flashed in red, green, and yellow colored lights, surrounding the visitor with Holzer's unsettling declarations ("You are a victim of the rules you live by") and disturbing commands ("Scorn Hope," "Forget Truths," and "Don't Try to Make Me Feel Nice"). The installation also included, on the ground floor and in a side gallery, spotlighted granite benches carved with more of Holzer's texts. The juxtaposition of

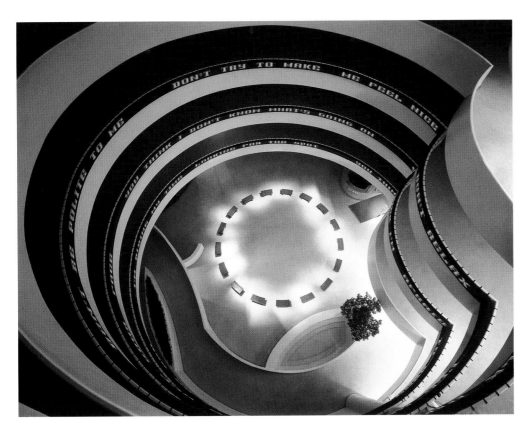

20–32 Jenny Holzer. *Untitled (Selections from Truisms, Inflammatory Essays, The Living Series, The Survival Series, Under a Rock, Laments, and Mother and Child Text).* 1989. Extended helical tricolor LED electronic-display signboard; site-specific dimensions, $16\frac{1}{2}'' \times 162' \times 6''$ (41.9 cm × 49 m × 15.2 cm)

SOLOMON R. GUGGENHEIM MUSEUM, NEW YORK (89.326). PARTIAL GIFT OF THE ARTIST, 1989 cutting-edge technology, lights, and motion with the static, hand-carved benches, evocative of antiquity and mortality, created a striking contrast fundamental to the expressive effect of the whole.

Installation artists often work with video, either using the video monitor itself as a visible part of their work or projecting video imagery onto walls, screens, or other surfaces. A pioneer video artist is the Korean-born, New York-based Nam June Paik (b. 1931), who proclaimed that just "as collage technique replaced oil paint, the cathode ray tube will replace the canvas." He began working with modified television sets in 1963 and bought his first video camera in 1965. Since then, Paik has worked with live, recorded, and computer-generated images displayed on video monitors of varying sizes, which he often combines into sculptural ensembles such as *Electronic Superhighway: Continental U.S.* (fig. **20–33**) (recently acquired by the Smithsonian, Alaska, Hawaii American Art Museum). Stretching across an entire wall, the work features a map of the continental United States outlined in neon and backed by video monitors perpetually flashing with color and movement and accompanied by sound. The monitors within the borders of each state displayed images reflecting that state's culture and history, both distant and recent. The only exception was New York State, whose monitors displayed live, closed-circuit images of the gallery visitors, placing them in the artwork and transforming them from passive spectators into active participants.

Paik often uses rapid cuts and fast motion to evoke the ceaseless flow of images and information carried by electronic communication systems. By contrast, the California-based video artist Bill Viola (b. 1951) may employ extreme slow motion to

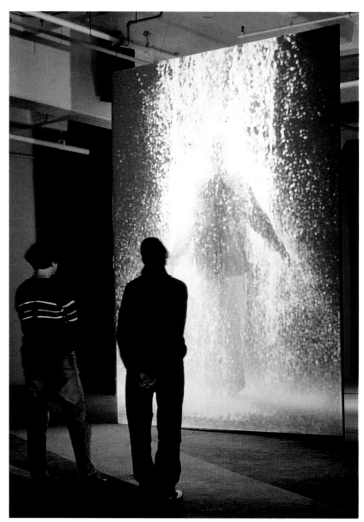

20–34 Bill Viola. *The Crossing.* 1996. Video/sound installation with two channels of color video projected onto 16-foot-high screens, 10 ½ minutes. View of one screen at 1997 installation at Grand Central Market, Los Angeles. Bill Viola Studio

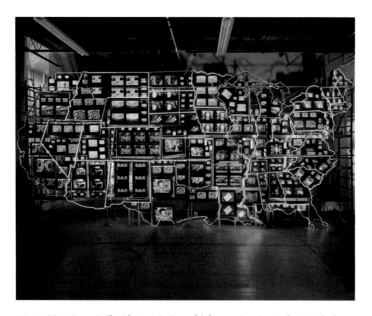

20–33 Nam June Paik. *Electronic Superhighway: Continental U.S.*, **Alaska, Hawaii.** 1995. Installation: multiple television monitors, laser disk images, and neon, 15′ × 32′ (4.57 × 9.75 m). The Smithsonian American Art Museum, Washington, D.C.

heighten sensory awareness and induce a state of contemplation at odds with the fast-paced images of the mass media. Inspired by both Eastern and Western religions, Viola frequently addresses themes relating to birth, death, and spirituality. In *The Crossing* (fig. **20–34**), two videos, projected simultaneously on either side of a 16-foot-high screen, show a casually dressed pale man on a dark set, approaching in slow motion. When his body almost fills the screen, he stops and stands impassively, facing the viewer. On one side of the screen, a small flame appears at the man's feet and gradually spreads to consume his entire body. On the other side, a trickle of water starts falling on his head, steadily increasing into a torrent that inundates him. Meanwhile, the amplified sounds of fire and water increase to a mighty roar. When the flames die down and the water subsides, the man has disappeared. What is perhaps most remarkable about this (illusionistic) annihilation is that the man does not physically resist but calmly accepts being engulfed by the elements, even stretching out his arms as if to

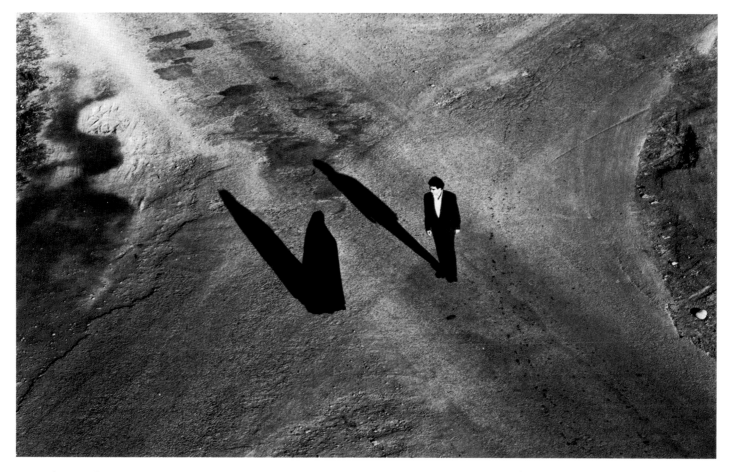

20–35 Shirin Neshat. Production still from *Fervor*. 2000. Video/sound installation with two channels of black-and-white video projected onto two screens, 10 minutes

welcome them. Viola's work dramatizes, among other things, the shared belief of many world religions—including Hinduism, Judaism, and Christianity—in the power of fire and water to purge and purify the human mind and soul.

While Viola's works resonate within a wide variety of cultural traditions, the photographic and video artist Shirin Neshat (b. 1957) addresses universal themes within the specific context of modern-day Islamic society. Neshat was studying art in California when revolution shook her native Iran in 1979. Returning to Iran in 1990, the artist was shocked by the extent to which fundamentalist Islamic rule had transformed her homeland, particularly through the strict rules forbidding women to appear in public without the traditional *chador*, a covering that veils women from head to foot. Upon her return to the United States, Neshat began using the black *chador* as the central motif of her work.

In the late 1990s Neshat began to make visually arresting and poetically structured videos that offer subtle critiques of Islamic society. *Fervor* (fig. **20–35**), in Neshat's words, "focuses on taboos regarding sexuality and desire" in Islamic society that

"inhibit the contact between the sexes in public. A simple gaze, for instance, is considered a sin. . . ." Composed of two separate video channels projected simultaneously on two large, adjoining screens, *Fervor* presents a simple narrative. In the opening scene, a black-veiled woman and jacket-wearing man, viewed from above, cross paths in an open landscape. Later, they meet again while entering a public ceremony where men and women are divided by a large curtain. On a stage before the audience, a bearded man fervently recounts (in Farsi, without subtitles) a story of seduction, passionately urging his listeners to resist such sinful desires. As the audience begins to chant in response to his exhortations, the male and female protagonists grow increasingly anxious, and the woman eventually rises and exits hurriedly. *Fervor* ends with the man and woman passing each other in an alley, again without verbal or physical contact. Neshat concentrates on dualisms and divisions—between East and West, male and female, individual desire and collective law.

The rapid development of computers in recent decades has provided artists with increasingly powerful tools. A rich creative alternative that soon developed was the digitization of scanned drawings, photographs, and video images, the tones of which were broken down into individual units (pixels) and the lines of which were translated into sine curves. These elements, rendered as sets of digits, could then be manipulated by the computer. Jennifer Steinkamp's (b. 1958) work *Jimmy Carter* (fig. **20–36**) is an impressive demonstration of digital art, the term used to identify the wide variety of art made with the help of digital computer technology.

Since the mid-1980s, the digital manipulation of scanned photographs and video images has become increasingly common in avant-garde art, and since the advent of the World Wide Web in the mid-1990s, an increasing number of digital works have been placed online, where they are accessible to anyone with an Internet connection and the appropriate software. Many online digital works are interactive, inviting the viewer to navigate them or otherwise act on them, often by contributing information or data that changes the form of the work and thereby directly involves the viewer in the creative process.

American Craft Art

Only since the Renaissance have Western critics and art historians generally maintained a distinction between the so-called "high" or fine arts—architecture, sculpture, painting, the graphic arts, and, more recently, photography—and the so-called "minor" or decorative arts such as ceramics, textiles, glass, metalwork, furniture, and jewelry, which typically serve either a practical or an ornamental function. In the postwar decades of the twentieth century, however, a number of artists began to push traditional craft mediums in new directions that blurred the conventional distinctions between fine and decorative arts. Their work might best be called craft art.

A major innovator in the clay medium was the Montana-born Peter Voulkos (1924–2002), who came under the influence of de Kooning and other gestural painters in 1953. The radical American break from European and Asian traditions, sometimes called the "clay revolution," began with the ruggedly sculptural ceramic works Voulkos produced in the mid-1950s. By the late 1950s Voulkos had abandoned the pot form altogether and was making large ceramic works spontaneously assembled from numerous wheel-thrown and slab-built elements, their surfaces often covered with bright, freely applied glazes or epoxy paint. In the early 1960s, Voulkos returned to traditional ceramic forms but rendered them nonfunctional by tearing, gouging, and piercing them in the gestural fashion derived from Abstract Expressionism (fig. **20–37**).

A comparable revolution in glass was initiated by Harvey Littleton (b. 1922), a professor at the University of Wisconsin. In 1963, Littleton established at the university the nation's first hot-glass studio program, and other glass programs soon sprang up around the country. Many of these programs were led by Littleton's former students, including Dale Chihuly who established the famous Pilchuck Glass School in Seattle in 1971 (see Introduction, fig. 19).

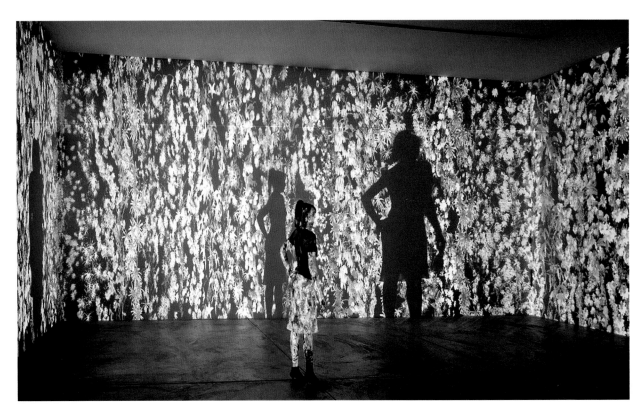

20–36 Jennifer Steinkamp. *Jimmy Carter.* 2002. Site-specific computer-generated light projection installation with 3 projectors and 3 Mac G3 computers. 35′ × 18′ × 14′ (10.6 × 5.5 × 4.3 m)

COURTESY ACME

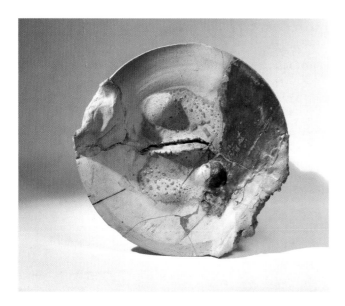

20–37 Peter Voulkos. *Untitled Plate.* 1962. Gas-fired stoneware with glaze, diameter 16¼″ (41.3 cm). The Oakland Museum of California

Like ceramics and glass, the use of traditional woodworking techniques by artists also broke down the barriers between decorative and fine arts. Crafts or mediums traditionally associated with "domesticity" have also been elevated into a "high" art status by artists such as Wendell Castle, who created both wood sculptures and sculptural furniture. Wendell Castle (b. 1932), during the 1960s, made highly original laminated wood furniture in an organic, sculptural style. In the late 1970s he changed direction and began carving technically demanding *trompe l'oeil* sculpture also in wood. Related to the style known as Superrealism, Castle's carvings represent everyday objects placed on or draped over furniture that he has built using traditional techniques. The impressively crafted *Ghost Clock* (fig. **20–38**), which imitates an eighteenth-century clock, is covered by a *trompe l'oeil* sheet carved out of bleached mahogany. The sculpture's power comes not only from its astonishing illusionism but also its haunting imagery, evoking an anthropomorphic presence forever hidden beneath a shroud.

His impressive woodworking skills link his sculpture to the contemporary American craft art movement. A master of the medium of wood is Martin Puryear (b. 1941). Puryear had an early interest in biology that would shape his mature aesthetic. Puryear's *Plenty's Boast* (fig. **20–39**), while not representational, suggests any number of things, including a strange sea creature or a fantastic musical instrument. Perhaps the most obvious reference is to the horn of plenty evoked in the sculpture's title. But the cone is empty, implying an "empty boast"—another reference to

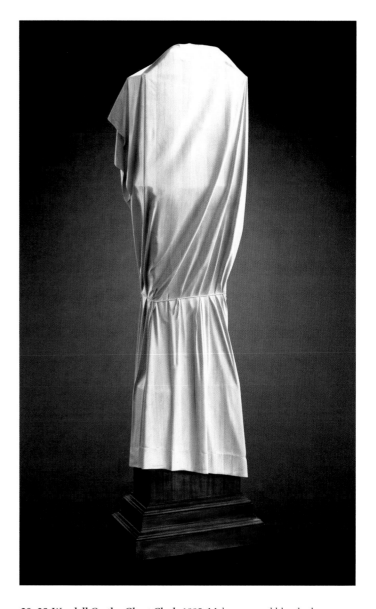

20–38 Wendell Castle. *Ghost Clock.* 1985. Mahogany and bleached Honduras mahogany, 7′2¼″ × 2′1½″ × 1′3″ (2.19 × 0.62 × 0.38 m). Renwick Gallery, Smithsonian American Art Museum, Washington, D.C.

20–39 Martin Puryear. *Plenty's Boast.* 1994–1995. Red cedar and pine, 5′8″ × 6′11″ × 9′10″ (1.73 × 2.11 × 1.35 m). The Nelson-Atkins Museum of Art, Kansas City, Missouri

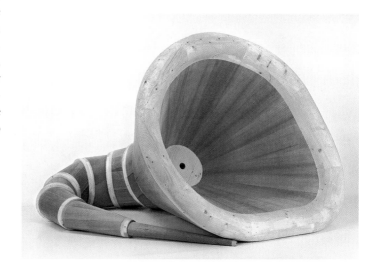

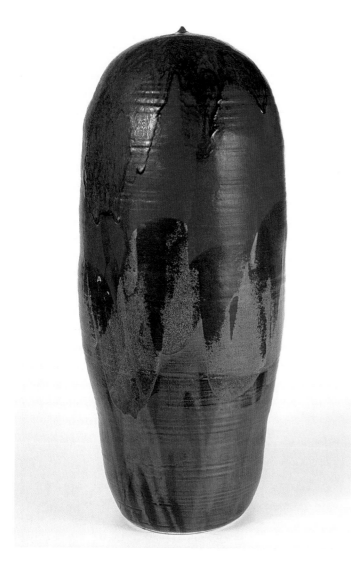

Architecture

Modernism endured in architecture until about 1970. The stripped-down, rectilinear industrial vocabulary pioneered by such architects as Gropius (see fig. 19–42) and Le Corbusier (see fig. 19–40) and known as the International Style dominated new urban construction in much of the world after World War II (see "Elements of Architecture: The International Style," page 559). Many of the finest examples of International Style architecture were built in the United States by Bauhaus architects (see Chapter 19), including Ludwig Mies van der Rohe (1886–1969), who escaped Nazi Germany and assumed prestigious positions at American schools of architecture and design.

Mies designed apartments, schools, and office buildings, including the Seagram Building in New York City (fig. **20–41**), which he designed with Philip Johnson (1906–2005). Mies's buildings are distinguished by his attention to detail. Because he had a large budget for the Seagram Building, he used custom-made bronze instead of standardized steel on the exterior. New York building codes required that the steel supports for the structure be encased in concrete, so the bronze beams are only ornamental stand-ins for the functional girders inside. Tall,

20–40 Toshiko Takaezu. *Large Form.* c. 1995. Stoneware, glaze, 32″ × 12″ × 12″ (82 × 31 × 31 cm). Museum of Arts and Design, New York

PROMISED GIFT OF SANDY AND LOU GROTTA

Like many craft artists, Takaezu feels a strong physical and emotional connection to her medium: "One of the best things about clay is that I can be completely free and honest with it. When I make it into a form, it is alive, and even when it is dry, it is still breathing! I can feel the response in my hands, and I don't have to force the clay. The whole process is an interplay between the clay and myself and often the clay has much to say."

the title. The richness of the sculpture lies not only in its multiple metaphorical references (a postmodern trait), but also in its superbly crafted idiosyncratic yet elegant forms.

In contrast to the evocative art of Wendell Castle and Martin Puryear are the self-contained ceramic forms of Toshiko Takaezu (b. 1922), who was born in Hawaii to Japanese parents. Since the late 1950s she has closed the tops of her vessels (leaving only a pinhole opening for the hot air to escape during firing), rendering them nonfunctional and emphasizing their status as abstract sculptural forms rather than utilitarian objects. A virtuoso colorist, she employs a rich variety of glazes to create sensuous hues and surface effects. Among her favorite colors are deep blues, purples, and blacks—seen, for example, in *Large Form* (fig. **20–40**)—which evoke for the artist the beauty of her native Hawaii.

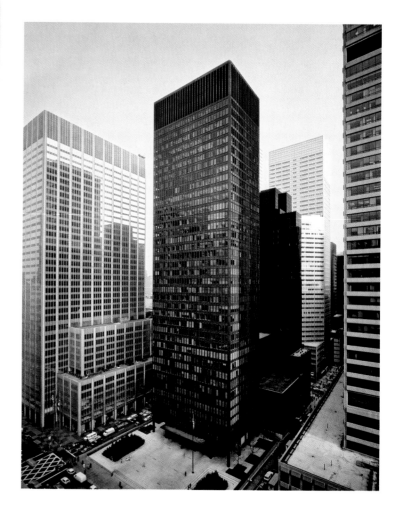

20–41 Ludwig Mies van der Rohe, Seagram Building, New York, 1956–1958. Commissioned by Joseph E. Seagram and Sons Corporation, under the advisement of Phyllis Bronfman Lambert

CRITICAL THEORY

Since the ancient Greek Polykleitos wrote his canon (see page 110), theories of art and the creative process have abounded. Leon Alberti (1404–1472) wrote on art and architecture in the Renaissance (see page 322), and Roger de Piles (1635–1709) established criteria for judging the masters in the seventeenth century (see page 409). Heinrich Wölfflin (1864–1945) called his formulations *Principles of Art History* (Box 409), and in the mid-twentieth century Erwin Panofsky (1892–1968) sought meaning beyond and behind the surface image through iconography and iconology. But these theorists did not divorce critical theory from works of art and the creative process.

Contemporary critical theory evolved out of linguistics and literary theory. At the beginning of the twentieth century, the linguist Saussure developed the "science of signs" (semiotics). He wrote of language and words, but by equating images with words, his theories and terminology were applied to works of art. The "signifier" and "signified" allowed texts (works of art) to be decoded in a complex system of shifting meanings (see fig. 20–19). The Post-Structuralists—like Roland Barthes, who wrote *The Death of the Author* (1968)—argued that meaning lies not in the intention of the artist but in the understanding of the viewer (see "Appropriation", page 575). And in the theoretical position known as Deconstruction (see "Deconstruction", page 589), developed by Jacques Derrida (1930–2004), meaning is suggested through pairings of opposites—light/dark, male/female—and becomes diffused, always related to other texts/signs, which are equally fluid or "decentered."

Theorists also looked at the social implications of art. Inspired by Marxist social theory and concerned with class struggle, some critics eliminated such elite ideas as aesthetic quality. They treated art as a commodity, not as an act of creative genius that conveyed spiritual values, and viewed art patronage as a vehicle of class oppression. Walter Benjamin (1892–1940), in *The Work of Art in the Age of Mechanical Reproduction* (1936), foresaw the "commodification" of art. As the arts became "visual culture," any and all objects became equal, and unlike the "old art history," this new history of images avoids the very idea of masterpieces.

Meanwhile, Sigmund Freud's theories of the irrational mind, the Oedipus Complex, and sexual fetishism, further developed by Jacques Lacan (1901–1981), form the basis of psychoanalytic theories of art. Feminist and gender theorists (page 582), and recent Post-colonial studies, further extend the analysis into the cultural politics of male-dominated societies and cultures formerly colonized by Western powers.

Critical theory became so divorced from the traditional concept of the creative process that some artists and historians began to see the work of art as simply "cooked up." Michael Aurbach (sculptor, and past president of the College Art Association) created a Duchampian machine (see fig. 19–1) that he called *The Critical Theorist*. In this playful but biting satire, the "Essence of Derrida" and the "Extract of Foucault" are cooked up in a big pot and then processed. Color and fragrance are added, and the mix goes into two stainless steel strainers ("Fact Removers") and then into commercial condiment dispensers with freely spinning cranks (the "Spin Cycle of scholarly hype"). After passing by a meat cleaver (the "Cutting Edge") and through a teapot ("Art Evaporator") and a garbage disposal ("Object Disposal"), the product comes out on a conveyor belt as a book on critical theory. The book, however, proves to be only a wooden block; Aurbach's machine has gone to a lot of trouble over nothing.

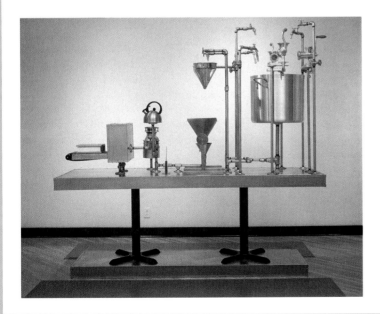

Michael Aurbach. *The Critical Theorist.* 2002. mixed media (cooking equipment). 7.5′ × 6.5′ × 8′ (2.29 × 1.98 × 2.44 m)
COLLECTION OF THE ARTIST

narrow windows with discreet dark glass emphasize the skyscraper's height. Set back from the street, the building rises quickly and impressively off piers (metal or concrete columns that raise a building above ground level) from a sunlit plaza with reflecting pools, fountains, and, originally, beech trees.

Postmodernism manifested itself first in architecture in the work of Robert Venturi (b. 1925). In the pioneering publication *Complexity and Contradiction in Architecture* (1966), Venturi argued that the problem with Mies and other International Style architects was their impractical unwillingness to accept the modern city for what it is: a complex, contradictory, and heterogeneous collection of "high" and "low" architectural forms (see "The High/Low Myth of Modernism," page 574). Taking these ideas further in the book *Learning from Las Vegas* (1972), he suggested that rather than turning their backs in disdain on ordinary commercial buildings, architects should get in "the habit of looking nonjudgmentally" at them. "Main Street is almost all right," Venturi observed.

A reaction to mid-century modernism in architecture, known as *High Tech*, is characterized by the expressive use of advanced building technology and industrial materials, equipment, and components. Among the most spectacular examples of High Tech architecture is the Hong Kong & Shanghai Bank (fig. **20–42**) by the English architect Norman Foster (b. 1935). Invited by his client to design the most beautiful bank in the world, Foster spared no expense in the creation of this futuristic 47-story skyscraper. The rectangular plan features service towers at the east and west ends, eliminating the central service core typical of earlier skyscrapers such as the Seagram Building. The load-bearing steel skeleton, composed of giant masts and girders, is on the exterior. The individual stories hang from this structure, allowing for uninterrupted facades and open working areas filled with natural light.

The Toronto-born, California-based postmodernist Frank Gehry (b. 1929) achieved his initial fame in the late 1970s and 1980s with his inventive use of vernacular forms and inexpensive materials set into unstable and conflicted arrangements. Then in the 1990s Gehry developed a new powerfully organic, sculptural style, most famously exemplified in his dramatic Guggenheim Museum in the Basque city of Bilbao, Spain (fig. **20–43**). In Bilbao he reconciled the client's needs for a museum and critic monument with his own interest in sculptural form. The commission for the Guggenheim Museum Bilbao provided him with an extraordinary opportunity. The Solomon R. Guggenheim Museum in New York had become one of the most famous museums in the world, as much for Frank Lloyd Wright's innovative architecture (see Intro, fig. xx and fig. 20–32) as for its collection of abstract art. Like Wright's spiraling design, Gehry's sprawling, organic plan resembles a living organism, like some gigantic metallic flower growing along the bank of the river. Gehry covered the building's complex steel skeleton with a thin skin of silvery titanium that shimmers gold or silver depending on the natural light and climatic conditions. From many vantage points, however, the building also resembles a giant ship, a reference to the shipbuilding and port facilities so important to the economy of the northern Spanish city. Inside, the museum features a giant atrium, which both pays homage to Wright's famous design and attempts to outdo it in size and effect (fig. **20–44**). In competing with Wright, Gehry said he meant to provide for the needs of the artists. "Artists want to be in great buildings," he claimed. In an early installation photo Claes Oldenburg's huge white shuttlecock feathers droop over the second floor balcony/observation platform, further animating the space of the atrium.

Public Memory and Art: The Memorial

Art in public places often engages our intellect, educating or reminding us of significant events in history. Yet the most effective memorials also appeal to our emotions. Public memorials—art forms themselves—can be both a universal and intimate experience, addressing subjects that have entered our collective conscious as a nation, yet remain highly personal. In recent years, art designed for public spaces rather than for museum walls or private collectors' homes has provoked many sensational controversies involving public funding, censorship, and individual rights.

The *Vietnam Veterans Memorial* (see fig. 20–1), now widely admired as a fitting and moving testament to the Americans who died in that conflict, was originally a lightning rod for contention. The request for proposals for the design of the monument stipulated that the memorial be without political or mili-

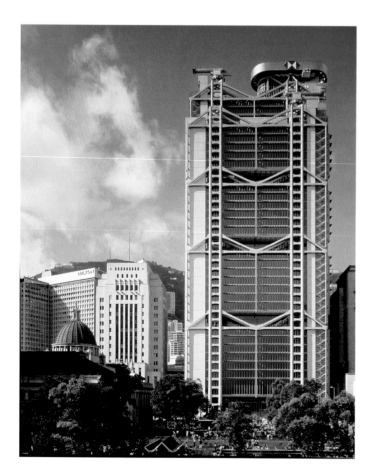

20–42 Norman Foster. Hong Kong & Shanghai Bank, Hong Kong. 1979–1986

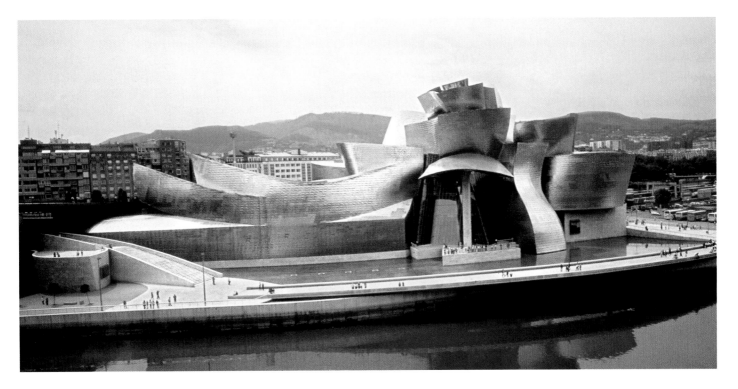

20–43 **Frank O. Gehry. Guggenheim Museum, Bilbao,** Spain. 1993–1997

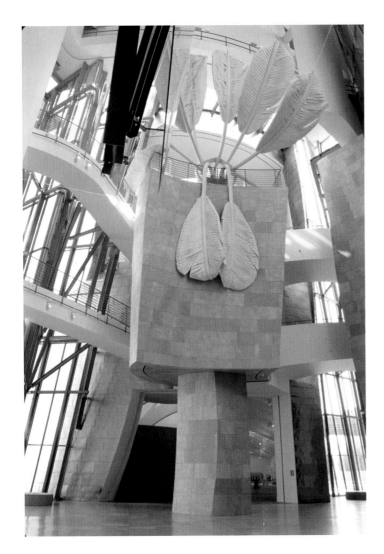

20–44 **Atrium, Guggenheim Museum, Bilbao,** Spain. 1997

Claes Oldenburg's gigantic feathers enliven the space of the atrium. Through the far door a glimpse can be had of the gallery housing Richard Serra's 102-foot-long Cor-Ten steel snake.

tary content, that it be reflective in character, that it harmonize with its surroundings, and that it include the names of the more than 58,000 dead and missing. In 1981 the Vietnam Veterans Memorial Fund awarded the commission to Maya Ying Lin, then an undergraduate in the architecture department at Yale University. Her Minimalist-inspired design called for two 200-foot-long walls (later expanded to almost 250 feet), set into rising ground. The names of the dead were to be incised into the walls in the order in which they died.

Controversies over appropriate memorials continue. Soon after the Twin Towers of the World Trade Center in New York City were destroyed on September 11, 2001, artists, architects, government officials, and ordinary citizens sought to create a meaningful testament that would serve as a global statement against terrorism. Conceived and executed during the Cold War (see page 564), the World Trade Center reflected the United States' confidence in itself as a global power. The Twin Towers stood 110 stories tall, dominating the Manhattan skyline. While their simplistic and brute form was not well received by some critics, their sheer size left all in awe of this major engineering accomplishment.

The World Trade Center site had to be rebuilt—as a memorial, as a symbol, and as a functional group of buildings. In February 2003, the Polish-born American architect Daniel Libeskind (b. 1946) won an international competition to design the site. Libeskind's plans are centered around a sunken field incorporating the foundations of the destroyed twin towers and the concrete slurry wall that prevented the Hudson River from

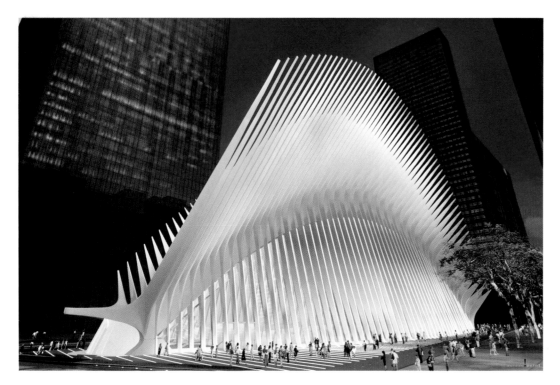

20–45 Santiago Calavatra. World Trade Center, Transportation Hub.
Digital three-dimensional model. 2006–2009. New York City
PORT AUTHORITY OF NEW YORK AND NEW JERSEY

flooding the site—a metaphor, to Libeskind, of tenacity and survival. This area also includes a memorial to the more than 2,500 people who died there. A skyscraper soaring to the patriotic height of 1776 feet would contain gardens which Libeskind calls "a constant affirmation of life." Libeskind sees the tower rising triumphant from the disaster of September 11, "an affirmation of vitality in the face of danger, an affirmation of life in the aftermath of tragedy."

As part of the the World Trade Center site, the Spanish architect Santiago Calatrava has designed a subway and train station, *The World Trade Center Transportation Hub* (fig. **20–45**). The steel and glass terminal, scheduled for completion in 2009, will comfortably handle 80,000 travelers a day. In designing and then illustrating his ideas Calatrava uses digital three-dimensional modeling. Calatrava, known as a master of linear design in building, has created a light, airy structure whose retractable roof can turn a hall into an open courtyard. Calatrava intends that the building be positioned on the site to reflect the place of the sun at the time of the tragedy. Calatrava has begun the process of creating a new city and new symbols for the twenty-first century.

Shanghai-born Wenda Gu (b. 1955) dedicates his art to bringing people together. In 1993 he began his United Nations series, consisting of installations made of human hair pressed, into bricks, carpets, and curtains. Many of his "monuments"—such as *United Nations—Babel of the Millennium* (fig. **20–46**)—incorporate invented scripts that, by frustrating viewers' ability to read them, evoke the limitations of human knowledge. Wenda Gu, joins the fundamental quest of artists throughout history to extend the boundaries of human perception, feeling, and thought and to express humanity's deepest wishes and most powerful dreams.

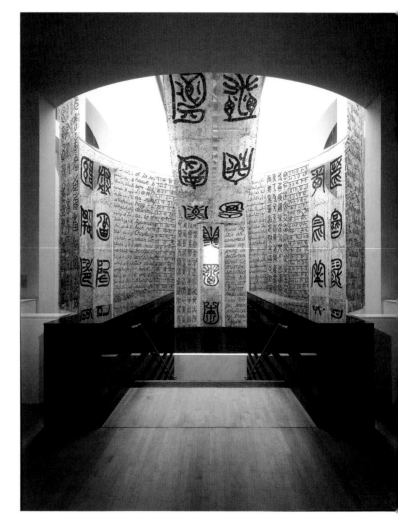

20–46 Wenda Gu. *United Nations—Babel of the Millennium.* 1999.
Site-specific installation made of human hair, height 75′ (22.9 m), diameter 34′ (10.4 m). San Francisco Museum of Modern Art
FRACTIONAL AND PROMISED GIFT OF VIKI AND KENT LOGAN

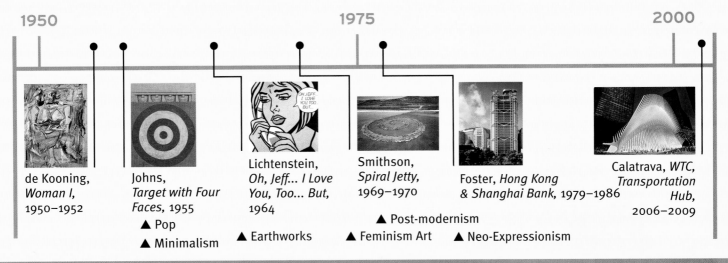

1950 · 1975 · 2000

de Kooning,
Woman I,
1950–1952

Johns,
*Target with Four
Faces,* 1955

▲ Pop

▲ Minimalism

Lichtenstein,
*Oh, Jeff... I Love
You, Too... But,*
1964

▲ Earthworks

Smithson,
Spiral Jetty,
1969–1970

▲ Post-modernism

▲ Feminism Art

Foster, *Hong Kong
& Shanghai Bank,* 1979–1986

▲ Neo-Expressionism

Calatrava, *WTC,
Transportation
Hub,*
2006–2009

LOOKING BACK

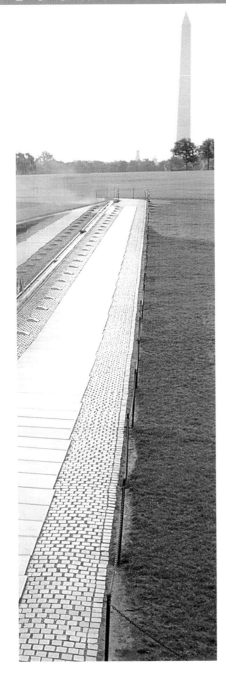

Heirs to the turmoil of the twentieth century, people in the twenty-first century face great opportunities—for unprecedented well-being or potential disaster. Economic gains, including increased agricultural production, together with improved medicine enhance both the quality and length of life. At the same time the threat of nuclear warfare and more insidious problems of global warming, pollution, fresh-water depletion, soil erosion and deforestation threaten human existence. The boon of widespread education has led to appreciation of other cultures but is offset by increased intolerance of ethnic and religious differences. Artists have responded by challenging cultural institutions and the traditional arts and by questioning the meaning of life and art.

By the second half of the twentieth century, the United States had become the world's leader in the arts, and New York replaced Paris as the principal international art capital. In the 1940s and 50s, Jackson Pollock, Willem de Kooning, and others led a movement known as Abstract Expressionism (or Action Painting), but they were soon challenged by artists who glorified popular culture in the so-called Pop art of the 1960s. In the 1970s and 80s, innovation in art and architecture became a global phenomenon. New technology also had a profound impact on artists, as photography and cinema, video, and computers changed the way people visualized and understood the world. Art that was at least as much conceptual as it was visual came to the fore. Artists produced happenings, and then performances, and then eliminated the tangible work of art altogether. Some artists became active participants in highly non-traditional methods, even turning themselves into works of art. Postmodern artists could play with any and every style and medium—including the elimination of the physical object—while also maintaining an ironic distance. But even arguing factions could agree that in the modern and postmodern eras nearly every point of view has value.

Even when artists have seemed to be more interested in intellectual exercises than in tangible works of art, the general public has demonstrated an enduring love of beautifully made objects. Attendance at museums and galleries is high, especially for exhibitions of ancient Egyptian works; Impressionist and Post-Impressionist painting; the crafts of glass, gold, or fiber; and art attached to intriguing personalities such as Leonardo or Vermeer, Andy Warhol, or Frida Kahlo. Our appreciation of the work of art as a superbly crafted object—as well as our desire for an intellectually challenging encounter and an aesthetically rewarding visual experience—continues.

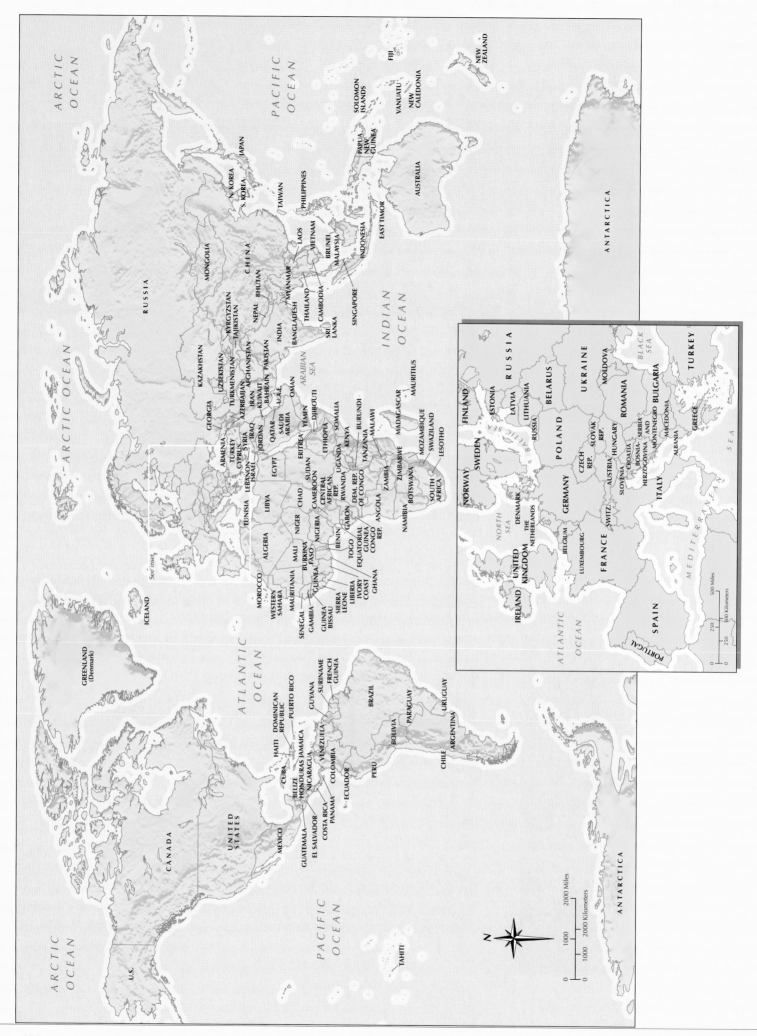

Glossary

abacus The flat slab at the top of a **capital,** directly under the **entablature.**

abstract, abstraction Any art that does not represent observable aspects of nature or transforms visible forms into a pattern resembling the original model. Also: the formal qualities of this process.

academy, academician An institutional group established for the training of artists. Most academies date from the Renaissance and after; they were particularly powerful state-run institutions in the seventeenth and eighteenth centuries. In general, academies replaced **guilds** as the venue where students learned the craft of art and were also provided with a complete education, including art theory and artistic rules. The academies helped artists to be seen as trained specialists, rather than as craftspeople, and promoted the change in the social status of the artist. An academician is an official academy-trained artist.

acanthus A leafy plant whose foliage inspired architectural ornamentation, used in the **Corinthian** and **Composite** orders and in the **relief** scroll known as the *rinceau.*

acropolis The citadel of an ancient Greek city, located at its highest point and consisting of temples, a treasury, and sometimes a royal palace. The most famous is the Acropolis in Athens, where the ruins of the Parthenon can be found.

adobe Sun-baked blocks made of clay mixed with straw. Also: the buildings made with this material.

aedicula (aediculae) A decorative architectural frame, usually found around a **niche,** door, or window. An aedicula is made up of a **pediment** and **entablature** supported by **columns or pilasters.**

aesthetics The philosophy of beauty.

aisle Passage or open corridor of a church, hall, or other building that parallels the main space, usually on both sides, and is delineated by a row, or **arcade,** of **columns** or **piers.** Called **side aisles** when they flank the **nave** of a church.

album A book consisting of blank pages (**album leaves**) on which typically an artist may sketch, draw, or paint.

allegory In a work of art, an image (or images) that illustrates an **abstract** concept, idea, or story, often suggesting a deeper meaning.

altar A tablelike structure where religious rites are performed. In Christian churches, the altar is the site of the rite of the **Eucharist.**

altarpiece A painted or carved panel or **winged** structure placed at the back of or behind and above an **altar.** Contains religious imagery, often specific to the place of worship for which it was made.

ambulatory The passage (walkway) around the **apse** in a **basilican** church or around the central space in a **centrally planned building.**

amphora An ancient Greek jar for storing oil or wine, with an egg-shaped body and two curved handles.

aniconic A representation without images of human figures.

animal interlace Decoration made up of interwoven animals or serpents, often found in Celtic and early northern European art. See **ribbon interlace.**

animal style A type of imagery used in Europe and western Asia during the ancient and medieval periods, characterized by animals or animal-like **forms** arranged in intricate patterns or combats.

apotheosis Deification of a person or thing. In art, often shown as an ascent to heaven or glory, borne by an eagle, angels, or **putti.**

apprentice A student artist or craftsperson in training. In a traditional system of art and craft training established under the **guilds** and still in use today, master artists took on apprentices (students) for a specific number of years. The apprentice was taught every aspect of the artist's craft, and he or she participated in the master's workshop or **atelier.**

appropriation Term used to describe an artist's practice of borrowing from another source for a new work of art. While in previous centuries artists often copied one another's figures, **motifs,** or **compositions,** in modern times the sources for appropriation extend from material culture to works of art.

apse, apsidal A large semicircular or polygonal (and usually vaulted) **niche** protruding from the end wall of a building. In a Christian church, it contains the **altar.** Apsidal is an adjective describing the condition of having such a semicircular or polygonal space.

aquatint A type of **intaglio** printmaking developed in the eighteenth century that produces an area of even **tone** without laborious **cross-hatching.** The aquatint is made by using a porous resin coating on a metal plate, which, when immersed in acid, allows an even, allover biting of the plate. The resulting printed image has a granular, textural effect.

aqueduct A trough to carry flowing water, if necessary, supported by **arches.**

arabesque A type of **linear** surface decoration based on foliage and **calligraphic forms,** usually characterized by flowing lines and swirling shapes.

arcade A series of arches, carried by **columns** or **piers** and supporting a common wall or **lintel.** In a **blind** arcade, the arches and supports are engaged (attached to the background wall) and have a decorative function.

arch In architecture, a curved structural element that spans an open space. Built from wedge-shaped stone blocks called **voussoirs,** which, when placed together and held at the top by a trapezoidal **keystone,** form an effective weight-bearing unit. Requires **buttresses** at either side to contain outward thrust caused by the weight of the structure. **Corbel arch:** arch or **vault** formed by **courses** of stones, each of which projects beyond the lower course until the space is enclosed; usually finished with a **capstone. Horseshoe arch:** an arch of more than a half-circle, often used in western Islamic architecture. **Ogival arch:** a pointed arch created by S-curves. **Relieving arch:** an arch built into a heavy wall just above a **post-and-lintel** structure (such as a gate, door, or window) to help support the wall above. Relieves some of the weight on the lintel by transferring the load to the side walls.

Archaic smile The curved lips of an ancient Greek statue, usually interpreted as an attempt to animate the features.

architrave The bottom element of an **entablature,** beneath the **frieze** and the **cornice.**

archivolt Curved **molding** formed by the **voussoirs** making up an **arch.**

ashlar See **dressed stone.**

assemblage An artwork created by gathering and manipulating two- and/or three-dimensional found objects.

atelier The studio or workshop of a master artist or craftsperson, often including junior associates and **apprentices.**

atmospheric perspective See **perspective.**

atrium An unroofed interior courtyard in a Roman house, sometimes having a pool. Also: the open courtyard in front of a Christian church, or an entrance area in modern architecture.

attic story The top story of a building. In **classical** architecture, the level above the **entablature,** often decorated or carrying an inscription.

attribute The symbolic object or objects that identify a particular deity, saint, or personification in art.

automatism A technique whereby the usual intellectual control of the artist over his or her brush or pencil is forgone. The artist's aim is to allow the subconscious to create the artwork without rational interference. Also called **automatic writing.**

avant-garde A term derived from the French military word meaning "before the group," or "vanguard." Avant-garde denotes those artists or concepts of a strikingly new, experimental, or radical nature for the time.

axis mundi A concept of an axis of the world, which denotes important sacred sites and provides a link between the human and celestial realms. For example, in Buddhist art, the *axis mundi* can be marked by monumental free-standing decorated pillars.

background Within the depicted space of an artwork, the area of the image at the greatest distance from the **picture plane.**

bailey The outermost walled courtyard of a castle.

baldachin A canopy (whether suspended from the ceiling, projecting from a wall, or supported by **columns**) placed over an honorific or sacred space such as a throne or church **altar.**

balustrade A low barrier consisting of a series of short circular posts (called balusters), with a rail on top.

baptistry A building used for the Christian ritual of baptism. It is usually separate from the main church and often octagonal or circular in shape.

barrel vault See **vault.**

base Any support. Masonry supporting a statue or the **shaft of a column.**

basilica A large rectangular building. Often built with a **clerestory, side aisles** separated from the center **nave** by **colonnades,** and an **apse** at one or both ends. Roman centers for administration, later adapted to Christian church use. Constantine's architects added a transverse aisle at the end of the nave called a **transept.**

bay A unit of space defined by architectural elements such as **columns, piers,** and walls.

beehive tomb A **corbel** vaulted tomb, conical in shape like a beehive, and covered by an earthen mound.

bell krater An ancient Greek bell-shaped vessel for mixing wine and water.

Benday dots In modern printing and typesetting, the dots that make up lettering and images. Often machine- or computer-generated, the dots are very small and closely spaced to give the effect of density and richness of **tone.**

biomorphic Adjective used to describe forms that resemble shapes found in nature. Also, a **style** in art characterized by biomorphic shapes is called **Biomorphism.**

bird's-eye view A view from above.

black-figure A style of ancient Greek pottery in which black figures are painted on a red clay ground.

blackware A ceramic technique that produces pottery with a primarily black surface. Blackware has both matte and glossy patterns on the surface of the wares.

blind window See **blind.**

blind Decorative elements attached to the surface of a wall, with no openings.

block printing A printed image, such as a **woodcut** or wood engraving, made from a carved wooden block.

bodhisattva A deity that is far advanced in the long process of transforming itself into a buddha. While seeking enlightenment or emancipation from this world (nirvana), bodhisattvas help others attain this same liberation.

Book of Hours A private prayer book, having a calendar, services for the canonical hours, and sometimes, special prayers.

bracket, bracketing An architectural element that projects from a wall and that often helps support a horizontal part of a building, such as beams or the eaves of a roof.

bronze A metal made from copper alloy, usually mixed with tin. Also: any sculpture or object made from this substance.

burin A metal instrument used in **engraving** to cut lines into the metal plate. The sharp end of the burin is trimmed to give a diamond-shaped cutting point, while the other end is finished with a wooden handle that fits into the engraver's palm.

buttress, buttressing An architectural support, usually consisting of massive masonry built against an exterior wall to brace the wall and counter the thrust of the **vaults.** Transfers the weight of the vault to the ground. **Flying buttress:** An **arch** built on the exterior of a building that transfers the thrust of the roof vaults at important stress points through the wall to a detached buttress **pier** leading to the wall buttress.

cairn A pile of stones or earth and stones that served both as a prehistoric burial site and as a marker of underground tombs.

calligraphy The art of highly ornamental handwriting.

calotype The first photographic process utilizing negatives and paper positives. It was invented by William Henry Fox Talbot in the late 1830s.

came (cames) A lead strip used in the making of leaded or **stained-glass** windows. Cames have an indented vertical groove on the sides into which the separate pieces of glass are fitted to hold the design together.

camera obscura An early cameralike device used in the Renaissance and later for recording images of nature. Made from a dark box (or room) with a hole in one side (sometimes fitted with a lens), the camera obscura operates when bright light shines through the hole, casting an upside-down image of an object outside onto the inside wall of the box.

canon Established rules or standards.

canon of proportions A set of ideal mathematical ratios in art based on measurements of the human body.

cantilever A beam or structure that is anchored at one end and projects horizontally beyond its vertical support, such as a wall or **column.** It can carry loads throughout the rest of its unsupported length. Or a bracket used to carry the **cornice** or extend the eaves of a building.

capital The sculpted block that tops a **column.** According to the conventions of the orders, capitals include different decorative elements. See **order.** Also: a historiated capital is one displaying a narrative.

capstone The final, topmost stone in a **corbel** arch or **vault,** which joins the sides and completes the structure.

cartoon A full-scale drawing used to transfer the outline of a design onto a surface (such as a wall, canvas, or panel) to be painted, carved, or woven.

cartouche A frame for a **hieroglyphic** inscription formed by a rope design surrounding an oval space. Used to signify a sacred or honored name. Also: in architecture, a decorative device or plaque used for inscriptions or epitaphs.

caryatid A sculpture of a draped female figure acting as a **column** supporting an entablature.

catacomb An underground burial ground consisting of tunnels on different levels, having **niches** for urns and **sarcophagi** and often incorporating rooms (**cubiculae**).

cathedral The principal Christian church in a diocese, built in the bishop's administrative center and housing his throne (*cathedra*).

cella The principal interior room in a Greek or Roman temple within which the cult statue was usually housed. Also called the **naos.**

centering A temporary structure that supports a masonry **arch and vault** or **dome** during construction until the mortar is fully dried and the masonry is self-sustaining.

central-plan building Any structure designed with a primary central space surrounded by symmetrical areas on each side. For example, **Greek-cross plan** (equal-armed cross).

ceramics Wares made of baked clay.

chacmool In Mayan sculpture, a half-reclining figure probably representing an offering bearer.

chasing

château (châteaux) A French country house or residential castle. A château fort is a military castle incorporating defensive works such as towers and battlements.

cherub (cherubim) The second-highest order of angels. Popularly, an idealized small child, usually depicted naked and with wings.

chevet In a French church the space beyond the **transepts** consisting of **apse, ambulatory,** and radiating chapels.

chevron A decorative motif made up of repeated inverted Vs; a zigzag pattern.

chiaroscuro An Italian word designating the contrast of dark and light in a painting, drawing, or print. Chiaroscuro creates spatial depth and **volumetric** forms through gradations in the intensity of light and shadow.

choir The section of a Christian church reserved for the clergy or the religious, either between the **crossing** and the **apse** or in the **nave** just before the crossing, screened or walled and fitted with stalls (seats). Also an area reserved for singers.

churrigeresque An elaborate style of Baroque architecture and ornament seen in Spain, Portugal, and Latin America, named after the Spanish architect José Benito de Churriguera (1665–1725).

Classical A term referring to the art and architecture of ancient Greece between c. 480–320 BCE.

classical, classicism Any aspect of later art or architecture reminiscent of the rules, **canons,** and examples of the art of ancient Greece and Rome. Also: in general, any art aspiring to the qualities of restraint, balance, and rational order exemplified by the ancients. Also: the peak of perfection in any period.

clerestory The topmost zone of a wall with windows in a **basilica** extending above the **aisle** roofs. Provides direct light into the central interior space (the nave).

cloisonné An enamel technique in which metal wire or strips are affixed to the surface to form the design. The resulting areas (cloisons) are filled with **enamel** (colored glass).

cloister An open space, part of a monastery, surrounded by an **arcaded** or **colonnaded** walkway, often having a fountain and garden, and dedicated to nonliturgical activities and the secular life of the religious. Members of a cloistered order do not interact with outsiders.

codex (codices) A book, or a group of manuscript pages (folios), held together by stitching or other binding on one side.

coffer A recessed decorative panel that is used to reduce the weight of and to decorate ceilings or **vaults.** The use of coffers is called coffering.

coiling A technique in basketry. In coiled baskets a spiraling structure is held in place by another material.

collage A technique in which cutout paper forms (often painted or printed), and/or found materials, are pasted onto another surface. Also: an image created using this technique.

colonnade A row of **columns,** supporting a straight **lintel** (as in a porch or **portico**) or a series of **arches** (an **arcade**).

colonnette A small **column** attached to a pier or wall.

colophon The data placed at the end of a book listing the book's author, publisher, **illuminator,** and other information related to its production.

Color Field

colossal order See **order.**

column An architectural element used for support and/or decoration. Consists of a rounded vertical **shaft** placed on a **base** topped by a decorative **capital.** May follow the rules of one of the architectural **orders.** Although usually freestanding, columns can be attached to a wall (engaged).

column statue A column carved to depict a human figure.

complementary color The primary and secondary colors across from each other on the color wheel (red and green, blue and orange, yellow and purple). When juxtaposed, the intensity of both colors increases.

Composite order See **order.**

composition The arrangement of **formal elements** in an artwork.

compound pier A **pier** or large **column** with **shafts, pilasters, or colonnettes** attached to it on one or all sides.

conch A half-**dome.**

concrete A building material developed by the Romans, made primarily from lime, sand, cement, and rubble mixed with water. Concrete is easily poured or **molded** when wet and hardens into a particularly strong and durable stonelike substance.

cone mosaic An early type of surface decoration created by pressing colored cones of baked clay into prepared wet plaster.

connoisseurship A term derived from the French word *connoisseur,* meaning "an expert," and signifying the study and evaluation of art based on formal, visual, and stylistic analysis. A **connoisseur** studies the **style** and technique of an object to deduce its relative quality and possible maker. This is done through visual association with other, similar objects and styles. See also **contextualism.**

content When discussing a work of art, the term can include all of the following: its subject matter; the ideas contained in the work; the artist's intention; and even its meaning for the beholder.

contextualism A methodological approach in art history that focuses on the cultural background of an art object. Contextualism utilizes the literature, history, economics, and social developments (among other things) of a period, as well as the object itself, to explain the meaning of an artwork. See also **connoisseurship.**

contrapposto A twisting body position. Also: a way of representing the human body so that its weight appears to be borne on one leg.

corbel, corbeling A roofing and arching technique in which each course of stone projects inward and slightly beyond the previous layer (a corbel) until the uppermost corbels meet. Results in a high, nearly pointed **arch or vault.** A corbel table is a table supported by corbels.

corbel arch See **arch.**

corbeled vault See **vault.**

Corinthian order See **order.**

cornice The uppermost section of a **Classical entablature.** More generally, a horizontally projecting element found at the top of a building wall or **pedestal.** A raking cornice is formed by the junction of two slanted cornices, most often found in **pediments.**

course A horizontal layer of stone used in building.

crenellation Alternating high and low sections of a wall, giving a notched appearance and creating permanent defensive shields in the walls of fortified buildings.

cross-hatching A technique primarily used in printmaking and drawing, in which a set of parallel lines (hatching) is drawn across a previous set, but from a differing (usually right) angle. Cross-hatching gives a great density of **tone** and allows the artist to create the illusion of shadows efficiently.

cross vault See **vault.**

crossing The juncture of the **nave** and the **transept** in a church, often marked on the exterior by a tower or **dome.**

cruciform A term describing anything that is cross-shaped, as in the cruciform plan of a church.

cubiculum (cubicula) A small private room for burials in the **catacombs.**

cuneiform writing An early form of writing with wedge-shaped marks; impressed into wet clay with a **stylus,** primarily by ancient Mesopotamians.

curtain wall A wall in a building that does not support any of the weight of the structure. Also: the free-standing outer wall of a castle, usually encircling the inner **bailey** (yard) and **keep** (primary defensive tower).

cycle A series of images depicting a story or theme intended to be displayed together, and forming a visual narrative.

cyclopean construction A method of building utilizing huge blocks of rough-hewn stone. Any large-scale, **monumental** building project that impresses by sheer size. Named after one-eyed giants of legendary strength from Greek myth.

cylinder seal A small cylindrical stone decorated with **incised** patterns. When rolled across soft clay or wax, the resulting raised pattern or design (relief) served as an identifying signature.

dado (dadoes) The lower part of a wall, differentiated in some way (by a **molding** or different color) from the upper section.

daguerreotype An early photographic process named for Louis-Jacques Mondé Daguerre. A daguerreotype was a positive print made on a light-sensitized copper plate.

Daoism A Chinese philosophy that emphasizes the close relationship of humans and nature.

desert varnish In southwestern North America, a substance that turned cliff faces into dark surfaces. Neolithic artists would draw images by scraping through the dark surface.

diptych Two panels of equal size, usually decorated with paintings or **reliefs,** and hinged together.

dolmen A prehistoric structure made up of two or more large (often upright) stones supporting a large, flat, horizontal slab or slabs.

dome A round **vault,** usually over a circular space. Consists of a curved masonry vault of shapes and cross sections that can vary from hemispherical to bulbous to ovoidal. May use a supporting vertical wall (drum), from which the vault springs, and may be crowned by an open space (**oculus**) and/or an exterior **lantern.** When a dome is built over a square space, an intermediate element is required to make the transition to a circular drum. There are two types: A dome on **pendentives** (spherical triangles) incorporates **arched,** sloping intermediate sections of wall that carry the weight and thrust of the dome to heavily **buttressed** supporting **piers.** A dome on **squinches** uses an arch built into the wall (squinch) in the upper corners of the space to carry the weight of the dome across the corners of the square space below. A half-dome or conch may cover a semicircular space.

Doric order See **order.**

dressed stone Highly finished, precisely cut blocks of stone laid in even **courses,** creating a uniform face with fine joints. Often used as a facing on the visible exterior of a building, especially as a **veneer** for the **façade.** Also called **ashlar.**

drillwork The technique of using a drill for the creation of certain effects in sculpture.

drum The wall that supports a **dome.** Also: a segment of the circular **shaft of a column.**

drypoint An **intaglio** printmaking process by which a metal (usually copper) plate is directly inscribed by means of a pointed instrument (stylus). The resulting design of scratched lines is inked, wiped, and printed. Also: the print made by this process.

earthworks Artwork and/or sculpture, usually on a large scale, created by manipulating the natural environment. Also: the earth walls of a fort.

echinus A cushion-like circular element found below the **abacus** of a **Doric** capital. Also: a similarly shaped **molding** (usually with egg-and-dart **motifs**) underneath the **volutes** of an **Ionic** capital. Egg-and-dart is a **motif** used in decorative **molding,** and is made up of an alternating pattern of round (egg) and downward-pointing, tapered (dart) elements.

edition A single printing of a book or print. An edition includes only what is printed at a particular moment, usually pulled from the same press by the same publisher.

elevation The arrangement, proportions, and details of any vertical side or face of a building. Also: an architectural drawing showing an exterior or interior wall of a building.

embroidery The technique in needlework of decorating fabric by stitching designs and figures with threads. Also: the material produced by this technique.

enamel A technique in which powdered glass is applied to a metal surface in a decorative design. After firing, the glass forms an opaque or transparent substance that is fixed to the metal background. Also: an object created with enamel technique. See **cloisonné.**

enamelwork See **enamel.**

engaged column See **column.**

engraving An **intaglio** printmaking process of inscribing an image, design, or letters onto a metal or wood surface from which a print is made. An engraving is usually drawn with a sharp implement (**burin**) directly onto the surface of the plate. Also: the print made from this process.

entablature In the **Classical orders,** the horizontal elements above the **columns** and **capitals.** The entablature consists of, from top to bottom, a **cornice, frieze,** and **architrave.**

entasis A slight swelling of the **shaft** of a Greek **column.** The optical illusion of entasis makes the column appear from afar to be straight.

etching An **intaglio** printmaking process in which a metal plate is coated with acid-resistant resin and then inscribed with a **stylus** in a design, revealing the plate below. The plate is then immersed in acid, and the design of exposed metal is eaten away by the acid. The resin is removed, leaving the design etched permanently into the metal and the plate ready to be inked, wiped, and printed.

Eucharist The central rite of the Christian Church, from the Greek word "thanksgiving." Also known as the Mass or Holy Communion, it is based on the Last Supper. According to traditional Catholic Christian belief, consecrated bread and wine become the body and blood of Christ; in Protestant belief, bread and wine symbolize the body and blood.

exedra (exedrae) In architecture, a semicircular **niche.** On a small scale, often used as decoration, whereas larger exedrae can form interior spaces.

expressionism Terms describing a work of art in which forms are created primarily to evoke subjective emotions rather than to portray objective reality.

façade The face or front wall of a building.

fête galante A subject in painting depicting well-dressed people at leisure in a park or country setting. It is most often associated with eighteenth-century French Rococo painting.

finial A knoblike architectural decoration usually found at the top point of a spire, **pinnacle,** canopy, or **gable.** Also found on furniture.

flower piece Any painting with flowers as the primary subject; a **still life** of flowers.

flying buttress See **buttress.**

folio A large sheet of paper, which, when folded and cut, becomes four separate or **parchment** pages in a book. Also: a page or leaf in a **manuscript** or book; more generally, any large book.

foreground Within the depicted space of an artwork, the area that is closest to the **picture plane.**

foreshortening The illusion created on a flat surface in which figures and objects appear to recede or project sharply into space. Accomplished according to the rules of **perspective.**

form In speaking of a work of art or architecture, the term refers to purely visual components: line, color, shape, texture, mass, spatial qualities, and **composition—all** of which are called **formal elements.**

formalism, formalist An approach to the understanding, appreciation, and valuation of art based almost solely on considerations of **form.** This approach tends to regard an artwork as independent of its time and place of making.

formline In Native American works of art, a line that defines a space or **form.**

forum A Roman town center; site of temples and administrative buildings and used as a market or gathering area for the citizens.

fresco A painting technique in which water-based pigments are applied to a surface of wet plaster (called *buon fresco). Fresco a secco* is created by painting on dried plaster. **Murals** made by both these techniques are called frescoes.

frieze The middle element of an **entablature,** between the **architrave** and the **cornice.** Usually decorated with sculpture, painting, or **moldings.** Also: any continuous flat band with **relief** sculpture or painted decorations.

frontispiece An illustration opposite or preceding the title page of a book. Also: the primary **façade** or main entrance **bay** of a building.

fusuma Sliding doors covered with paper, used in an East Asian house. *Fusuma* are often highly decorated with paintings and colored **backgrounds.**

gable The triangular wall space found on the end wall of a building between the two sides of a pitched roof. Also: a triangular decorative panel that has a gablelike shape.

gallery In church architecture, the story found above the side aisles of a church, usually open to and overlooking the **nave.** Also: in secular architecture, a long room, usually above the ground floor in a private house or a public building, used for entertaining, exhibiting pictures, or promenading. Also, *galleria.*

genre A type or category of artistic form, subject, technique, **style,** or **medium.**

genre scene A term used to loosely categorize paintings depicting scenes of everyday life, including (among others) domestic interiors, parties, inn scenes, and street scenes.

geoglyphs Earthen designs on a colossal scale, often created in a landscape as if to be seen from an aerial viewpoint.

geometric A period in Greek art from about 1100 to 600 BCE; the art is characterized by patterns of rectangles, squares, and other **abstract** shapes. Also: any **style** or art using primarily these shapes.

gesso A ground made from glue, gypsum, and/or chalk forming the ground of wood panel or the priming layer of a canvas. Provides a smooth surface for painting.

gesturalism Painting and drawing in which the brushwork or line visibly records the artist's physical gesture at the moment the paint was applied or the lines laid down. Associated especially with expressive styles, such as Zen painting and Abstract Expressionism.

gilding The application of paper-thin gold leaf or gold pigment to an object made from another **medium** (for example, a sculpture or painting). Usually used as a decorative finishing detail.

giornata (giornate) Adopted from the Italian term meaning "a day's work," a *giornata* is the section of a fresco plastered and painted in a single day.

glazing An outermost layer of vitreous liquid (glaze) that, upon firing, renders ceramics waterproof, and forms a decorative surface. In painting, a technique particularly used with oil **mediums** in which a transparent layer of paint (glaze) is laid over another, usually lighter, painted or glazed area.

gold leaf Paper-thin sheets of hammered gold that are used in **gilding.**

graffiti Decorative drawings scratched on rocks, walls, or objects. Also: drawings and/or text of an obscene, political, or violent nature.

Grand Manner A grand and elevated **style** of painting popular in the eighteenth century in which the artist looked to the ancients and to the Renaissance for inspiration.

granulation A technique for decorating gold in which tiny balls of the precious metal are fused to the main surface in a pattern.

graphic arts A term referring to those arts that are drawn or printed and that utilize paper as primary support.

graphic design A concern in the visual arts for shape, line, and two-dimensional patterning, often especially apparent in works including typography and lettering.

Greek-cross plan See **central-plan building.**

grid A system of regularly spaced horizontally and vertically crossed lines that gives regularity to an architectural **plan.** Also: in painting, a **grid** enables designs to be enlarged or transferred easily.

Grisaille A painting executed primarily in shades of gray.

groin vault See **vault.**

groundline The solid baseline that indicates the ground plane on which the figure stands. In ancient representations, such as those of the Egyptians, the figures and the objects are placed on a series of groundlines to indicate depth (space in registers).

grout A soft cement placed between the **tesserae** of a **mosaic** to hold the design together. Also used in tiling.

guild An association of craftspeople. The medieval guild had great economic power, as it controlled the selling and marketing of its members' products, and it provided economic protection, political solidarity, and training in the craft to its members. The painters' guild was usually dedicated to Saint Luke, their patron saint.

half-barrel vault See **vault.**

Hand-scroll A long, narrow, horizontal painting or text (or combination thereof) common in Chinese and Japanese art and of a size intended for individual use. A hand-scroll is stored wrapped tightly around a wooden pin and is unrolled for viewing or reading.

hanging scroll In Chinese and Japanese art, a vertically oriented painting or text mounted within sections of silk. At the top is a semicircular rod; at the bottom is a round dowel. Hanging scrolls are kept rolled and tied except for special occasions, when they are hung for display, contemplation, or commemoration.

haniwa Pottery forms (cylinders, human figures, and buildings) that were placed on top of Japanese tombs or burial mounds.

Happening An art form developed in the 1960s incorporating performance, theater, and visual images. A happening was organized without a specific narrative or intent; with audience participation, the event proceeded according to chance and individual improvisation.

hemicycle A semicircular interior space or structure.

henge A circular area enclosed by stones or wood posts set up by Neolithic peoples. It is usually bounded by a ditch and raised embankment.

hieratic In painting and sculpture, a formalized **style** for representing rulers or sacred or priestly figures.

hieratic scale The use of different sizes for significant or holy figures and those of the everyday world to indicate importance. The larger the figure, the greater the importance.

hieroglyphs Picture writing; words and ideas rendered in the form of pictorial symbols.

high relief See **relief sculpture.**

historicism The strong consciousness of and attention to the institutions, themes, **styles,** and forms of the past, made accessible by historical research, textual study, and archeology.

history painting Paintings based on historical, mythological, or biblical narratives. Once considered the noblest form of art, history paintings generally convey a high moral or intellectual idea and are often painted in a grand pictorial **style.**

hollow-casting See **lost-wax casting.**

horizon line A horizontal "line" formed by the implied meeting point of earth and sky. In **linear perspective,** the **vanishing point** or points are located on this "line."

horseshoe arch See **arch.**

house-church A Christian place of worship located in a private home.

house-synagogue A Jewish place of worship located in a private home.

hue Pure color. The saturation or intensity of the hue depends on the purity of the color. Its **value** depends on its lightness or darkness.

hydria A large ancient Greek and Roman jar with three handles (horizontal ones at both sides and one vertical at the back), used for storing water.

hypostyle hall A large interior room characterized by many closely spaced **columns** that support its roof.

icon An image in any material representing a sacred figure or event in the Byzantine, and later the Orthodox, Church. Icons were venerated by the faithful, who believed them to have miraculous powers to transmit messages to God.

iconoclasm The banning or destruction of **icons** and religious art. Iconoclasm in eighth- and ninth-century Byzantium and sixteenth- and seventeenth-century Protestant territories arose from differing beliefs about the power, meaning, function, and purpose of imagery in religion.

iconography The study of the significance and interpretation of the **subject matter** of art.

idealization A process in art through which artists strive to make their **forms** and figures attain perfection, based on pervading cultural values or their own mental image of beauty.

illumination A painting on paper or **parchment** used as illustration and/or decoration for **manuscripts** or **albums.** Usually done in rich colors, often supplemented by gold and other precious materials. The illustrators are referred to as illuminators. Also: the technique of decorating manuscripts with such paintings.

illusionism, illusionistic An appearance of reality in art created by the use of certain pictorial means, such as **perspective and foreshortening.** Also: the quality of having this type of appearance.

impost, impost block A block, serving to concentrate the weight above, imposed between the **capital of a column** and the springing of an **arch** above.

impression Any single printing of an **intaglio** print (**engraving, drypoint, or etching**). Each and every impression of a print is by nature different, given the possibilities for variation inherent in the printing process, which requires the plate to be inked and wiped between every impression.

incising A technique in which a design or inscription is cut into a hard surface with a sharp instrument.

ink painting A monochromatic **style** of painting developed in China using black ink with gray **washes.**

inlay A decorative process in which pieces of one material are set into the surface of an object fashioned from a different material.

intaglio Term used for a technique in which the design is carved out of the surface of an object, such as an engraved seal stone. In the **graphic arts,** intaglio includes **engraving, etching, and drypoint**—all processes in which ink transfers to paper from **incised,** ink-filled lines cut into a metal plate.

interlace A type of **linear** decoration in which ribbonlike bands are **illusionistically** depicted as if woven under and over one another.

intuitive perspective See **perspective.**

Ionic order See **order.**

iwan A large, **vaulted** chamber with a **monumental arched** opening on one side.

jamb In architecture, the vertical element found on both sides of an opening in a wall, and supporting an **arch or lintel.**

japonisme A **style** in nineteenth-century French and American art that was highly influenced by Japanese art.

joined-wood sculpture A method of constructing large-scale wooden sculpture developed in Japan. The entire work is constructed from smaller hollow blocks, each individually carved and assembled when complete. The joined-wood technique allowed the production of larger sculpture, as the multiple joints alleviate the problems of drying and cracking found with sculpture carved from a single block.

kente A woven cloth made by the Ashanti peoples of Africa. Kente cloth is woven in long, narrow pieces in complex and colorful patterns, which are then sewn together.

key block A key block is the master block in the production of a colored **woodcut,** which requires different blocks for each color. The key block is a flat piece of wood with the entire design carved or drawn on its surface. From this, other blocks with partial drawings are made for printing the areas of different colors.

keystone The topmost **voussoir** at the center of an arch, and the last block to be placed. The pressure of this block holds the arch together. Often of a larger size and/or decorated.

keep Principal tower in a castle.

kiln An oven designed to produce the high temperature for the baking, or firing, of clay.

kinetic art Artwork that contains parts that can be moved either by hand, air, or motor.

kore (korai) An archaic Greek statue of a young woman.

kouros (kouroi) An archaic Greek statue of a young man or boy.

kylix A shallow Greek vessel or cup, used for drinking, with a wide mouth and small handles near the rim.

lacquer A hard, glossy surface varnish. Lacquer can be layered and manipulated or combined with pigments and other materials for various decorative effects.

lancet A tall, narrow window crowned by a sharply pointed **arch,** typically found in Gothic architecture.

lantern A turretlike structure situated on a roof, **vault, or dome,** with windows that allow light into the space below.

Latin-cross plan A cross-shaped building plan, incorporating a long arm (nave) and three shorter arms.

linear, linearity An emphasis on line, as opposed to mass or color.

linear perspective See **perspective.**

lintel A horizontal element of any material carried by two or more vertical supports to form an opening.

literati painting A style of painting that reflects the taste of the educated class of East Asian intellectuals and scholars. Aspects include an appreciation for the antique, small scale, and an intimate connection between maker and audience.

lithograph A print made from a design drawn on a flat stone block with greasy crayon. Ink is applied to a wet stone and, when printed, adheres only to the greasy areas of the design.

loggia Italian term for a covered open-air **gallery.** Often used as a corridor between buildings or around a courtyard, loggias usually have **arcades** or **colonnades.**

lost-wax casting A method of casting metal, such as bronze, by a process in which a wax mold is covered with clay and plaster, then fired, melting the wax and leaving a hollow form. Molten metal is then poured into the hollow space and slowly cooled. When the hardened clay and plaster exterior shell is removed, a solid metal form remains to be smoothed and polished.

low-relief See **relief sculpture.**

lunette A semicircular wall area, framed by an **arch** over a door or window. Can be either plain or decorated.

madrasa An Islamic institution of higher learning, where teaching is focused on theology and law.

majolica Pottery painted with a tin **glaze** that, when fired, gives a lustrous and colorful surface.

mandorla An almond-shaped area in which a sacred figure, such as Christ, is represented.

Mannerist A sophisticated, elegant style characterized by elongated **forms,** irrational spatial relationships, unusual colors and lighting effects, and exquisite craft. These traits are associated with the style called Mannerism of the sixteenth century.

manuscript A handwritten book or document.

martyrium (martyria) In Christian architecture, a church, chapel, or shrine built over the grave of a martyr or the site of a great miracle.

mastaba A flat-topped, one-story building with slanted walls over an ancient Egyptian underground tomb.

mathematical perspective See **perspective.**

matte A smooth surface without shine or luster.

mausoleum A monumental building used as a tomb. Named after the tomb of Mausolos erected at Halikarnassos around 350 BCE.

medallion Any round ornament or decoration. Also: a large medal.

medium (mediums) In general, the material from which any given object is made. In painting, the liquid substance in which pigments are suspended.

megaron A "great room" or large audience hall in a Mycenaean Greek ruler's residence.

menorah A Jewish lamp-stand with seven or nine branches; the nine-branched menorah is used during the celebration of Hanukkah. Representations of the seven-branched menorah, once used in the Temple of Jerusalem, became a symbol of Judaism.

metope The carved, painted, or plain rectangular spaces between the **triglyphs** of a **Doric frieze.**

middle ground Within the depicted space of an artwork, the area that takes up the middle distance of the image. See also **foreground.**

mihrab A recess or **niche** that distinguishes the wall oriented toward Mecca (qibla) in a mosque.

minaret A tall slender tower on the exterior of a mosque from which believers are called to prayer.

minbar A high platform or pulpit in an Islamic mosque.

modeling In painting, the process of creating the illusion of three-dimensionality on a two-dimensional surface by the use of light and **shade.** In sculpture, the process of **molding** a three-dimensional form out of a malleable substance.

module A basic unit of construction.

molding A shaped or sculpted strip with varying contours and patterns. Used as decoration on architecture, furniture, frames, and other objects.

monolith A single stone, often very large.

monumental A term used to designate a project or object that, whatever its physical size, gives an impression of grandeur.

mosaic Images formed by small colored stone or glass pieces (tesserae), affixed to a hard, stable surface.

mosque An edifice used for communal Muslim worship.

motif Any recurring element of a design or composition. Also: a recurring theme or subject in artwork.

mudra A symbolic hand gesture in Buddhist art that denotes certain behaviors, actions, or feelings.

mullion A slender vertical element or **colonnette** that divides a window into subsidiary sections.

multiple-point perspective See **perspective.**

muqarna The transition between decorative flat and rounded surfaces; usually found on the **vault** of a **dome.**

mural Wall-like. A large painting or decoration, created either directly on the wall, or created separately and affixed to the wall.

naos The principal room in a temple or church. In ancient architecture, known as the **cella.** In a Byzantine church, known as the **nave** and **sanctuary.**

narthex The vestibule or entrance porch of a church.

naturalism, naturalistic A style of depiction in which the physical appearance of the rendered image in nature is the primary inspiration. A naturalistic work appears to record the visible world.

nave The central **aisle of a basilica,** two or three stories high and flanked by aisles, and defined by the nave **arcade** or nave **colonnade.**

necropolis A large cemetery or burial area, literally a city of the dead.

niche A hollow or recess in a wall or other solid architectural element. Niches can be of varying size and shape, and may be intended for many different uses, from display of objects to housing of a tomb.

niello A metal technique in which a black sulfur alloy is rubbed into fine lines **engraved** into a metal (usually gold or silver). When heated, the alloy becomes fused with the surrounded metal and provides contrasting detail.

nonrepresentational Abstract art that does not attempt to reproduce the appearance of objects, figures, or scenes in the natural world. Also called **nonobjective art.**

obelisk A tall, four-sided stone **shaft,** hewn from a single block, that tapers at the top and is completed by a pyramidion. A sun symbol erected by the ancient Egyptians in ceremonial spaces (such as entrances to temple complexes). Today used as a commemorative monument.

oblique perspective See **perspective.**

oculus (oculi) In architecture, a circular opening. Oculi are usually found either as windows or at the apex of a **dome.** When at the top of a dome, an oculus is either open to the sky or covered by a decorative exterior **lantern.**

ogival arch See **arch.**

oil painting Any painting executed with the pigments floating in a **medium** of oil. Oil paint has particular properties that allow for greater ease of working (among others, a slow drying time, which allows for corrections, and a great range of relative opaqueness of paint layers, which permits a high degree of detail and luminescence).

one-point perspective See **perspective.**

openwork Decoration, such as **tracery,** with open spaces incorporated into the pattern.

orant The representation of a standing figure praying with outstretched and upraised arms.

order A system of proportions in **Classical** architecture that includes every aspect of the building's **plan, elevation,** and decorative system. **Composite:** a combination of the Ionic and the Corinthian orders. The **capital** combines **acanthus** leaves with **volute** scrolls. **Corinthian:** the most ornate of the orders, the Corinthian includes a **base,** a fluted column **shaft** with a capital elaborately decorated with acanthus leaf carvings. Its **entablature** consists of an **architrave** decorated with **moldings, a frieze** often containing sculptured **reliefs, and a cornice** with dentils. **Doric:** the column shaft of the Doric order can be fluted or smooth-surfaced and has no base. The Doric capital consists of an undecorated **echinus** and **abacus.** The Doric entablature has a plain architrave, a frieze with **metopes** and **triglyphs,** and a simple cornice. **Ionic:** the column of the Ionic order has a base, a fluted shaft, and a capital decorated with volutes. The Ionic entablature consists of an architrave of three panels and moldings, a frieze usually containing sculpted relief ornament, and a cornice with dentils. **Tuscan:** a variation of Doric characterized by a smooth-surfaced column shaft with a base, a plain architrave, and an undecorated frieze. A **colossal order** is any of the above built on a large scale, rising through several stories in height and often raised from the ground by a **pedestal.**

orthogonal Any line running back into the represented space of a picture perpendicular to the imagined **picture plane.** In **linear perspective,** all orthogonals converge at a single **vanishing point** in the picture and are the basis for a **grid** that maps out the internal space of the image. An orthogonal **plan** is any plan for a building or city that is based exclusively on right angles, such as the grid plan of many modern cities.

pagoda An East Asian **reliquary** tower built with successively smaller, repeated stories. Each story is usually marked by an elaborate, projecting roof.

painterly A **style** of painting which emphasizes the techniques and surface effects of brushwork (also color, light, and shade).

palette A handheld support used by artists for the storage and mixing of paint during the process of painting. Also: the choice of a range of colors made by an artist in a particular work, or typical of his or her style.

palmette A fan-shaped petal design used as decoration on classical Greek vases.

panel painting Any painting executed on a wood support. The wood is usually planed to provide a smooth surface. A panel can consist of several boards joined together.

parapet A low wall at the edge of a balcony, bridge, roof, or other place from which there is a steep drop, built for safety. A parapet walk is the passageway, usually open, immediately behind the uppermost exterior wall or battlement of a fortified building.

parchment A writing surface made from treated skins of animals. Very fine parchment is known as **vellum.**

Paris Salon The annual display of art by French artists in Paris during the eighteenth and nineteenth centuries. Established in the seventeenth century as a venue to show the work of members of the French Academy, the Salon and its judges established the accepted official style of the time.

passage In painting, passage refers to any particular area within a work, often those where **painterly** brushwork or color changes exist.

passage grave A prehistoric tomb under a **cairn,** reached by a long, narrow, slab-lined access passageway or passageways.

passage technique A term used to describe Paul Cezanne's technique of blending adjacent shapes in which shapes closed on one side are open on another so that they can merge.

patron The group or person who commissions or supports a work of art.

pedestal A platform or **base** supporting a sculpture or other monument. Also: the block found below the base of a **classical column** (or **colonnade**), serving to raise the entire element off the ground.

pediment A triangular **gable** found over major architectural elements such as **Classical** Greek **porticoes,** windows, or doors. Formed by an **entablature** and the ends of a sloping roof or a raking **cornice.** A similar architectural element is often used decoratively above a door or window, sometimes with a curved upper **molding.** A broken pediment is a variation on the traditional pediment, with an open space at the center of the topmost angle and/or the horizontal **cornice.**

pendentive The concave triangular section of a **vault** that forms the transition between a square or polygonal space and the circular base of a **dome.**

performance art An artwork based on a live, sometimes theatrical performance by the artist.

peristyle A surrounding **colonnade** in Greek architecture. A peristyle building is surrounded on the exterior by a colonnade. Also: a peristyle court is an open colonnaded courtyard, often having a pool and garden.

perspective A system for representing three-dimensional space on a two-dimensional surface. **Atmospheric perspective:** A method of rendering the effect of spatial distance by subtle variations in color and clarity of representation. **Intuitive perspective:** A method of giving the impression of recession by visual instinct, not by the use of an overall system or program. **Oblique perspective:** An intuitive spatial system in which a building or room is placed with one corner in the picture plane, and the other parts of the structure recede to an imaginary **vanishing point** on its other side. Oblique perspective is not a comprehensive, mathematical system. **One-point** and **multiple-point perspective** (also called **linear, scientific,** or **mathematical perspective**): A method of creating the illusion of three-dimensional space on a two-dimensional surface by delineating a **horizon line** and multiple **orthogonal** lines. These recede to meet at one or more points on the horizon (called vanishing points), giving the appearance of spatial depth. Called scientific or mathematical because its use requires some knowledge of geometry and mathematics, as well as optics. **Reverse perspective:** A Byzantine perspective theory in which the orthogonals or rays of sight do not converge on a vanishing point in the picture, but are thought to originate in the viewer's eye in front of the picture. Thus, in reverse perspective the image is constructed with orthogonals that diverge, giving a slightly tipped aspect to objects.

pictograph A highly stylized depiction serving as a symbol for a person or object. Also: a type of writing utilizing such symbols.

picture plane The theoretical spatial plane corresponding with the actual surface of a painting.

picturesque A term describing the taste for the familiar, the pleasant, and the pretty, popular in the eighteenth and nineteenth centuries in Europe. When contrasted with the **sublime,** the picturesque stood for all that was ordinary but pleasant.

pier A masonry support made up of many stones, or rubble and concrete (in contrast to a column **shaft,** which is formed by a single stone or a series of **drums**), often square or rectangular in plan and capable of carrying very heavy architectural loads. See also **compound pier.**

pietà A devotional subject in Christian religious art. After the Crucifixion the body of Jesus was laid across the lap of his grieving mother, Mary. When others are present the subject is called the Lamentation.

pilaster An engaged **columnar** element that is rectangular in format and used for decoration in architecture.

pinnacle In Gothic architecture, a steep pyramid decorating the top of another element such as a **buttress.** Also: the highest point.

plaiting In basketry, the technique of weaving strips of fabric or other flexible substances under and over each other.

plan A graphic convention for representing the arrangement of the parts of a building.

plinth The slablike base or pedestal of a column, statue, wall, building, or piece of furniture.

pluralism A social structure or goal that allows members of diverse ethnic, racial, or other groups to exist within the society while continuing to practice the customs of their own divergent cultures. Also: an adjective describing the state of having many valid contemporary styles available at the same time to artists.

podium A raised platform that acts as the foundation for a building, or as a platform for a speaker.

polychrome The multicolored painted decoration applied to any part of a building, sculpture, or piece of furniture.

polyptych An **altarpiece** constructed from multiple panels, sometimes with hinges to allow for movable wings.

porcelain A type of extremely hard and fine ceramic made from a mixture of kaolin and other minerals. Porcelain is fired at a very high heat, and the final product has a translucent surface.

portal A grand entrance, door, or gate, usually to an important public building, and often decorated with sculpture.

portico In architecture, a projecting roof or porch supported by **columns,** often marking an entrance.

post-and-lintel construction An architectural system of construction with two or more vertical elements (posts) supporting a horizontal element (lintel).

predella The lower zone, or base, of an **altarpiece,** decorated with painting or sculpture related to the main **iconographic** theme of the altarpiece.

primary colors Blue, red, and yellow, the three colors from which all others are derived.

pronaos The enclosed vestibule of a Greek or Roman temple, found in front of the cella and marked by a row of **columns** at the entrance.

proscenium The stage of an ancient Greek or Roman theater. In modern theater, the area of the stage in front of the curtain. Also: the framing **arch** that separates a stage from the audience.

provenance The history of ownership of a work of art from the time of its creation to the present.

punchwork Decorative designs that are stamped onto a surface, such as metal or leather, using a punch (a handheld metal implement).

putto (putti) A plump, naked little boy, often winged. In classical art, called a cupid; in Christian art, a **cherub.**

pylon A massive gateway formed by a pair of tapering walls of oblong shape. Erected by ancient Egyptians to mark the entrance to a temple complex.

qibla The mosque wall oriented toward Mecca indicated by the **mihrab.**

quadrant vault See **vault.**

quillwork A Native American decorative craft technique. The quills of porcupines and bird feathers are dyed and attached to material in patterns.

raku A type of ceramic pottery made by hand, coated with a thick, dark **glaze,** and fired at a low heat. The resulting vessels are irregularly shaped and glazed and are highly prized for use in the Japanese tea ceremony.

readymade An object from popular or material culture presented without further manipulation as an artwork by the artist.

realism A term first used in Europe around 1850 to designate a kind of **naturalism** with a social or political message, which soon lost its didactic import and became synonymous with naturalism.

red-figure A style of ancient Greek vase painting made in the sixth and fifth centuries BCE. Characterized by red-clay-colored figures on a black **background.**

register A device used in systems of spatial definition. In painting, a register indicates the use of differing **groundlines** to differentiate layers of space within an image. In sculpture, the placement of self-contained bands of **reliefs** in a vertical arrangement. In printmaking, the marks at the edges used to align the print correctly on the page, especially in multiple-block color printing.

relic See **reliquary.**

relief sculpture A sculpted image or design whose flat background surface is carved away to a certain depth, setting off the figure. Called high or low (bas) relief depending upon the extent of projection of the image from the background. Called sunken relief when the image is modeled below the original surface of the background, which is not cut away.

relieving arch See **arch.**

reliquary A container, often made of precious materials, used as a repository for sacred **relics** (venerated objects associated with a saint or martyr).

renaissance

repoussé A technique of hammering metal from the back to create a protruding image. Elaborate **reliefs** are created with wooden armatures against which the metal sheets are pressed and hammered.

representational Any art that attempts to depict an aspect of the external, natural world in a visually understandable way.

reverse perspective See **perspective.**

ribbon See **ribbon interlace.**

ribbon interlace A linear decoration made up of interwoven bands.

rib vault See **vault.**

roof comb In a Mayan building, a masonry wall along the apex of a roof that is built above the level of the roof proper. Roof combs support the highly decorated false **façades** that rise above the height of the building at the front.

rose window A round window, often filled with **stained glass,** with **tracery** patterns in the form of wheel spokes. Large, elaborate, and finely crafted, rose windows are usually a central element of the **façade** of French Gothic cathedrals.

rosette A round or oval ornament resembling a rose.

rotunda Any building (or part thereof) constructed in a circular (or sometimes polygonal) shape, usually producing a large open space crowned by a **dome.**

roundel Any element with a circular format, often placed as a decoration on the exterior of architecture.

rustication In building, the rough, irregular, and unfinished effect deliberately given to the exterior facing of a stone edifice. Rusticated stones are often large and used for decorative emphasis around doors or windows or across the entire lower floors of a building.

sacristy In a Christian church, the room in which the priest's robes and the sacred vessels are housed. Sacristies are usually located close to the **sanctuary** and often have a place for ritual washing.

sanctuary A sacred or holy enclosure used for worship. In ancient Greece and Rome, consists of one or more temples and an **altar.** In Christian architecture, the space around the altar in a church called the chancel or presbytery.

sarcophagus (sarcophagi) A rectangular stone coffin. Often decorated with **relief** sculpture.

scientific perspective See **perspective.**

scriptorium (scriptoria) A room in a monastery for writing or copying **manuscripts.**

sculpture in the round Three-dimensional sculpture that is carved free of any background or block.

sfumato In painting, the effect of haze in an image. Resembling the color of the atmosphere at dusk, *sfumato* gives a smoky effect.

sgraffito A decoration produced by scratching through plaster or glaze.

shade Any area of an artwork that is shown through various technical means to be in shadow.

shading The technique of making such an effect.

shaft The main vertical section of a **column** between the **capital** and the **base,** usually circular in cross section.

shikhara In the architecture of northern India, a conical (or pyramidal) structure found atop a Hindu temple.

side aisle See **aisle.**

site-specific sculpture A sculpture commissioned and designed for a particular spot.

slip A mixture of clay and water applied to a ceramic object as a final decorative coat. Also: a solution that binds different parts of a vessel together, such as the handle and the main body.

spandrel The area of wall adjoining the exterior curve of an **arch** between its springing and the **keystone,** or the area between two arches, as in an **arcade.**

squinch An **arch** or **lintel** built over the upper corners of a square space. Allows a circular or polygonal **dome** to be more securely set above the walls, and converts the space to an octagon.

stained glass Molten glass is given a color that becomes intrinsic to the material. Additional colors may be fused to the surface (flashing). Stained glass is most often used in windows, for which small pieces of differently colored glass are precisely cut and assembled into a design, held together by **cames.** Additional painted details may be added to create images.

stele (stelae) A stone slab placed vertically and decorated with inscriptions or **reliefs.** Used as a grave marker or memorial.

still life A type of painting that has as its subject inanimate objects (such as food, dishes, fruit, or flowers).

stringcourse A continuous horizontal band, such as a **molding,** decorating the face of a wall.

stucco A mixture of lime, sand, and other ingredients into a material that can be easily molded or modeled. When dry, produces a very durable surface used for covering walls or for architectural sculpture and decoration.

stupa In Buddhist architecture, a bell-shaped or pyramidal religious monument, made of piled earth or stone and containing sacred **relics.**

style A particular manner, **form,** or character of representation, construction, or expression typical of an individual artist or of a certain school or period.

stylization; stylized A manner of representation that conforms to an intellectual or artistic idea rather than to **naturalistic** appearances.

stylobate In **Classical** architecture, the stone foundation on which a temple stands.

stylus An instrument with a pointed end (used for writing and printmaking), which makes a delicate line or scratch. Also: a special writing tool for **cuneiform** writing with one pointed end and one triangular wedge end.

subject matter See **content.**

sublime A concept, thing, or state of exceptional and awe-inspiring beauty and moral or intellectual expression. The sublime was a goal to which many nineteenth-century artists aspired in their artworks. See **picturesque.**

sunken relief See **relief sculpture.**

swag A decorative device in architecture or interior ornament (and in paintings) in which a loosely hanging garland is made to look like flowers or gathered fabric.

talud-tablero A design characteristic of Mayan architecture at Teotihuacan in which a sloping *talud* at the base of a building supports a wall-like *tablero,* where ornamental painting and sculpture are usually placed.

tempera A painting **medium** made by blending egg or egg yolks with water, pigments, and occasionally other materials, such as glue.

tenebrism The use of strong **chiaroscuro** and artificially illuminated areas to create a dramatic contrast of light and dark in painting.

tepee A portable dwelling constructed from hides (later canvas) stretched on a structure of poles set at the base in a circle and leaning against one another at the top. Tepees were typically found among the nomadic Native Americans of the North American plains.

terracotta **A medium** made from clay fired over a low heat and sometimes left unglazed. Also: the orange-brown color typical of this medium.

tessera (tesserae) The small piece of stone, glass, or other object that is pieced together with many others to create a **mosaic.**

tint The dominant color in an object, image, or pigment.

tondo A painting or **relief** of circular shape.

tone The overall degree of brightness or darkness in an artwork. Also: saturation, intensity, or **value** of color and its effect.

torana In Indian architecture, an ornamented gateway **arch** in a temple, usually leading to the **stupa.**

tracery The stone or wooden bars in a window, screen, or panel, that support the structure and often create an elaborate decorative pattern.

transept The arm of a **cruciform** church, perpendicular to the **nave.** The point where the nave and **transept** cross is called the **crossing.** Beyond the crossing lies the **sanctuary,** whether **apse, choir,** or **chevet.**

triforium The element of the interior **elevation** of a church, found directly below the **clerestory** and consisting of a series of arched openings. The triforium can be made up of openings from a passageway or **gallery** or can be a plain or decorated wall.

triglyph Rectangular blocks between the **metopes** of a **Doric frieze.** Identified by the three carved vertical grooves, which approximate the appearance of the ends of wooden beams.

triptych An artwork made up of three panels. The panels may be hinged together so the side segments (wings) fold over the central area.

triumphal arch A freestanding, massive stone gateway with a large central **arch,** built as urban ornament and/or to celebrate military victories (as by the Romans).

trompe l'oeil A manner of representation in which the appearance of natural space and objects is re-created with the express intention of fooling the eye of the viewer, who may be convinced that the subject actually exists as three-dimensional reality.

trumeau **A column, pier,** or **post** found at the center of a large **portal** or doorway, supporting the **lintel.**

tunnel vault See **vault.**

Tuscan order See **order.**

twining A basketry technique in which short rods are sewn together vertically. The panels are then joined together to form a vessel.

tympanum In **Classical** architecture, the vertical panel of the **pediment.** In medieval and later architecture, the area over a door enclosed by an **arch and a lintel,** often decorated with sculpture or **mosaic.**

typology In Christian **iconography,** a system of matching Old Testament figures and events and even some **classical** and other secular sources to New Testament counterparts to which they were seen as prefigurements.

ukiyo-e A Japanese term for a type of popular art that was favored from the sixteenth century, particularly in the form of color **woodblock** prints. *Ukiyo-e* prints often depicted the world of the common people in Japan, such as courtesans and actors, as well as landscapes and myths.

undercutting A technique in sculpture by which the material is cut back under the edges so that the remaining form projects strongly forward, casting deep shadows.

underglaze Color or decoration applied to a ceramic piece before glazing.

value The darkness or lightness of a color (hue).

vanishing point **In a perspective** system, the point on the **horizon line** at which **orthogonals** meet. A complex system can have multiple vanishing points.

vanitas An image, especially popular in Europe during the seventeenth century, in which all the objects symbolize the transience of life. *Vanitas* paintings are usually of **still lifes** or **genre** subjects.

vault An **arched** masonry structure that spans an interior space. **Barrel** or **tunnel vault:** an elongated or continuous semicircular vault, shaped like a half-cylinder. **Groin or cross vault:** a vault created by the intersection of two barrel vaults of equal size which creates four side compartments of identical size and shape. **Quadrant** or **half-barrel vault:** as the name suggests, a half-barrel vault. **Rib vault:** ribs (extra masonry) demark the junctions of a groin vault. Ribs may function to reinforce the groins or may be purely decorative. **Corbeled vault:** a vault made by projecting courses of stone. See also **corbeling.**

vellum A fine animal skin prepared for writing and painting. See **parchment.**

veneer In architecture, the exterior facing of a building, often in decorative patterns of fine stone or brick. In decorative arts, a thin exterior layer of finer material (such as rare wood, ivory, metal, and semiprecious stones) laid over the form.

verism **A style** in which artists concern themselves with capturing the exterior likeness of an object or person, usually by rendering its visible details in a finely executed, meticulous manner.

volumetric A term indicating the concern for rendering the impression of three-dimensional volumes in painting, usually achieved through **modeling** and the manipulation of light and shadow **(chiaroscuro).**

volute A spiral scroll, as seen on an **Ionic capital.**

votive figure An image created as a devotional offering to a god or other deity.

voussoirs The oblong, wedge-shaped stone blocks used to build an **arch.** The topmost voussoir is called a **keystone.**

wall painting See **mural.**

ware A general term designating pottery produced and decorated by the same technique.

warp The vertical threads in a weaver's loom. Warp threads make up a fixed framework that provides the structure for the entire piece of cloth, and are thus often thicker than weft threads. See also **weft.**

wash A diluted watercolor or ink. Washes may be applied to drawings or prints to add **tone** or touches of color.

weft The horizontal threads in a woven piece of cloth. Weft threads are woven at right angles to and through the warp threads to make up the bulk of the decorative pattern. In carpets, the weft is often completely covered or formed by the rows of trimmed knots that form the carpet's soft surface. See also **warp.**

westwork The monumental, west-facing entrance section of a Carolingian, Ottonian, or Romanesque church. The exterior consists of multiple stories between two towers; the interior includes an entrance vestibule, a chapel, and a series of **galleries** overlooking the **nave.**

wing A side panel of a **triptych** or **polyptych** (usually found in pairs), which was hinged to fold over the central panel. Wings often held the depiction of the donors and/or subsidiary scenes relating to the central image.

woodblock print A print made from a block of wood that is carved in **relief** or **incised.**

woodcut A type of print made by carving a design into a wooden block. The ink is applied to the plate with a roller. As the ink remains only on the raised areas between the carved-away lines, these carved-away areas and lines provide the white areas of the print. Also: the process by which the woodcut is made.

x-ray style In Aboriginal art, a manner of representation in which the artist depicts a figure or animal by illustrating its outline as well as essential internal organs and bones.

ziggurat In Mesopotamia, a tall stepped tower of earthen materials, often supporting a shrine.

Selected Bibliography

General

Adams, Laurie Schneider. *Art across Time*. 2nd ed. New York: McGraw-Hill, 2002.

Anderson, Richard L. *Art in Small-Scale Societies*. 2nd ed. Englewood Cliffs, N.J.: Prentice Hall, 1989.

Andrews, Malcolm. *Landscape and Western Art*. Oxford History of Art. Oxford: Oxford Univ. Press, 1999.

Bearden, Romare. *A History of African American Artists: From 1792 to the Present*. New York: Pantheon, 1993.

Berlo, Janet Catherine, and Lee Ann Wilson. *Arts of Africa, Oceania, and the Americas: Selected Readings*. Englewood Cliffs, N.J.: Prentice Hall, 1993.

Brownston, David M., and Ilene Franck. Timelines of the Arts and Literature. New York: HarperCollins, 1994.

Chadwick, Whitney. *Women, Art, and Society*. 3rd rev. & exp. ed. New York: Thames and Hudson, 2002.

Chipp, Herschel Browning. *Theories of Modern Art: A Source Book by Artists and Critics*. California Studies in the History of Art. Berkeley: Univ. of California Press, 1984.

Cole, Bruce, and Adelheid Gealt. *Art of the Western World: From Ancient Greece to Post-Modernism*. New York: Summit, 1989.

Crouch, Dora P. *A History of Architecture: Stonehenge to Skyscrapers*. New York: McGraw-Hill, 1985.

Dictionary of Art, The. 34 vols. New York: Grove's Dictionaries, 1996.

Encyclopedia of World Art. 17 vols. New York: McGraw-Hill, 1972–87.

Ferguson, George Wells. *Signs and Symbols in Christian Art*. New York: Oxford Univ. Press, 1967.

Fleming, John, Hugh Honour, and Nikolaus Pevsner. *The Penguin Dictionary of Architecture*. 5th ed. New York: Penguin, 1998.

Gardner, Helen. *Gardner's Art through the Ages*. 12th ed. Eds. Richard G. Tansey and Fred S. Kleiner. Fort Worth: Harcourt Brace College, 2005.

Griffiths, Antony. *Prints and Printmaking: An Introduction to the History and Techniques*. 2nd ed. London: British Museum Press, 1996.

Hall, James. *Dictionary of Subjects and Symbols in Art*. Rev. ed. New York: Harper & Row, 1979.

Harris, Ann Sutherland, and Linda Nochlin. *Women Artists: 1550–1950*. Los Angeles: Los Angeles County Museum of Art, 1976.

Harrison, Charles, and Paul Wood, eds. *Art in Theory, 1900–1990: An Anthology of Changing Ideas*. New ed. Cambridge, Mass.: Blackwell, 2003.

Heller, Nancy G. *Women Artists: An Illustrated History*. 4th ed. New York: Abbeville, 2003.

Holt, Elizabeth Gilmore, ed. *A Documentary History of Art*. 3 vols. New Haven: Yale Univ. Press, 1986.

Honour, Hugh, and John Fleming. *The Visual Arts: A History*. 6th ed. New York: Abrams, 2002.

Hornblower, Simon, and Antony Spawforth. *The Oxford Classical Dictionary*. 3rd ed. rev. Oxford: Oxford University Press, 2003.

Hughes, Robert. *American Visions: The Epic History of Art in America*. New York: Alfred Knopf, 1997.

Hults, Linda C. *The Print in the Western World: An Introductory History*. Madison: Univ. of Wisconsin Press, 1996.

Janson, H. W., and Anthony F. Janson. *History of Art: the Western Tradition*. Rev. 6th ed. New York: Abrams, 2004.

Jeffrey, Ian. *Photography: A Concise History*. London: Thames and Hudson, 1981.

Jones, Lois Swan. *Art Information and the Internet: How To Find It, How to Use It*. Phoenix: Oryx Press, 1999.

Kemp, Martin. *The Oxford History of Western Art*. Oxford: Oxford Univ. Press, 2000.

Kostof, Spiro. *A History of Architecture: Settings and Rituals*. 2nd ed. rev. Greg Castillo. New York: Oxford Univ. Press, 2000.

Langer, Suzanne. *Feeling and Form*. Upper Saddle River, N.J.: Prentice Hall, 1990.

Lewer, Debbie. *Post-Impressionism to World War II*. Malden, Mass.: Blackwell, 2006.

Livingstone, E. A. *The Concise Oxford Dictionary of the Christian Church*. Oxford: Oxford Univ. Press, 2000.

McConkey, Wilfred J. *Klee as in Clay: A Pronunciation Guide*. 3rd ed. Lantham, Md.: Madison Books, 1992.

Minor, Vernon Hyde. *Art History's History*. Upper Saddle River, N.J.: Prentice Hall, 2001.

Nelson, Robert S. and Richard Shiff, eds. *Critical Terms for Art History*. 2nd ed. Chicago: Univ. of Chicago Press, 2003.

Pohl, Frances. Framing America: *A Social History of American Art*. New York: Thames and Hudson, 2002.

Preble, Duane, Sarah Preble, and Patrick Frank. *Artforms: An Introduction to the Visual Arts*. 7th ed. rev. Dudley, Mass.: Pearson Education, 2004.

Roberts, Helene, ed. *Encyclopedia of Comparative Iconography: Themes Depicted in Works of Art*. 2 vols. Chicago: Fitzroy Dearborn, 1998.

Roth, Leland M. *Understanding Architecture: Its Elements, History, and Meaning*. New York: Icon Editions, 1993.

Rothberg, Robert I., and Theodore K. Rabb, eds. *Art and History: Images and Their Meaning*. Cambridge: Cambridge Univ. Press, 1988.

Sed-Rajna, Gabrielle. *Jewish Art*. Trans. Sara Friedman and Mira Reich. New York: Abrams, 1997.

Slatkin, Wendy. *Women Artists in History: From Antiquity to the Present*. 4th ed. Upper Saddle River, N.J.: Prentice Hall, 2001.

Stangos, Nikos. *The Thames and Hudson Dictionary of Art and Artists*. Rev. exp. & updated ed. World of Art. New York: Thames and Hudson, 1994.

Steer, John, and Antony White. *Atlas of Western Art History: Artists, Sites and Movements from Ancient Greece to the Modern Age*. New York: Facts on File, 1994.

Stokstad, Marilyn, in collaboration with David Cateforis. *Art History*. Rev. 2nd ed. New : Upper Saddle River, N.J.: Prentice Hall, 2005.

Sutton, Ian. Western *Architecture: From Ancient Greece to the Present*. World of Art. New York: Thames and Hudson, 1999.

Thacker, Christopher. *The History of Gardens*. Berkeley: Univ. of California Press, 1979.

Trachtenberg, Marvin, and Isabelle Hyman. *Architecture, from Prehistory to Postmodernity*. 2nd ed. New York: Abrams, 2002.

Tufts, Eleanor. *Our Hidden Heritage: Five Centuries of Women Artists*. New York: Paddington, 1974.

Walker, John A. *Design History and the History of Design*. London: Pluto, 1989.

West, Shearer, ed. *The Bulfinch Guide to Art History: A Comprehensive Survey and Dictionary of Western Art and Architecture*. Boston: Little, Brown and Co., 1996.

Wilkins, David G., Bernard Schultz, and Katheryn M. Linduff. *Art Past/Art Present*. 5th ed. Upper Saddle River, N.J.: Prentice Hall, 2005.

Chapter 1 Art Before the Written Word

Bahn, Paul G. *The Cambridge Illustrated History of Prehistoric Art*. Cambridge: Cambridge Univ. Press, 1998.

Bataille, Georges. *The Cradle of Humanity: Prehistoric Art and Culture*. Ed. Stuart Kendall; trans. Michelle Kendall and Stuart Kendall. New York: Zone Books; Cambridge: MIT Press, 2005.

Blocker, H. Gene. *The Aesthetics of Primitive Art*. Lantham, Md.: Univ. Press of America, 1994.

Castleden, Rodney. *The Making of Stonehenge*. London: Routledge, 1993.

Chauvet, Jean-Marie, Eliette Brunel Deschamps, and Christian Hillaire. *Dawn of Art: The Chauvet Cave*. New York: Abrams, 1996.

Chippindale, Christopher. *Stonehenge Complete*. New York: Thames and Hudson, 1994.

Clegg, John. *Aesthetics and Rock Art*. Eds. Thomas Heyd, John Clegg. Aldershot, Hampshire, England; Burlington, Vt.: Ashgate, 2005.

Flood, Josephine. *Archaeology of the Dreamtime: The Story of Prehistoric Australia and Its People*. Rev. ed. New Haven: Yale Univ. Press, 1990.

Kenrick, Douglas Moore. *Jomon of Japan: The World's Oldest Pottery*. London and New York: Kegan Paul International, 1995.

Laing, Lloyd Robert, and Jennifer Laing. *Ancient Art: The Challenge to Modern Thought*. Dublin: Irish Academic, 1993.

Layton, Robert. *Australian Rock Art: A New Synthesis*. New York: Cambridge Univ. Press, 1992.

Leroi-Gourhan, André. *The Dawn of European Art: An Introduction to Paleolithic Cave Painting*. Trans. Sara Champion. Cambridge: Cambridge Univ. Press, 1982.

Lhote, Henri. *The Search for the Tassili Frescoes: The Story of the Prehistoric Rock-Painting of the Sahara*. 2nd ed. Trans. Alan Houghton Brodrick. London: Hutchinson, 1973.

Lloyd, Seton, and Hans Wolfgang Muller. *Ancient Architecture*. New York: Rizzoli, 1986.

Oliphant, Margaret. *The Atlas of the Ancient World: Charting the Great Civilizations of the Past*. New York: Simon & Schuster, 1992.

Price, T. Douglas, and Gray M. Feinman. *Images of the Past*. 3rd ed. Mountain View, Calif.: Mayfield, 2000.

Ruspoli, Mario. *The Cave of Lascaux: The Final Photographs*. New York: Abrams, 1987.

Sanders, N. K. *Prehistoric Art in Europe*. 2nd ed. Pelican History of Art. New Haven: Yale Univ. Press, 1995.

Sura Ramos, Pedro A. *The Cave of Altamira*. Ed. Antonio Beltran. New York: Abrams, 1999.

Wilcox, A. R. *The Rock Art of Africa*. London: Croon Helm, 1984.

Chapter 2 The Art of Mesopotamia and Egypt

Aldred, Cyril. *Egyptian Art in the Days of the Pharaohs, 3100–320 B.C.* World of Art. London: Thames and Hudson, 1980.

Amiet, Pierre. *Art of the Ancient Near East*. Trans. John Shepley and Claude Choquet. New York: Abrams, 1980.

Andrews, Carol. *Ancient Egyptian Jewelry*. New York: Abrams, 1991.

Arnold, Dieter. *Temples of the Last Pharaohs*. New York: Oxford Univ. Press, 1999.

Bierbrier, Morris. *Tomb-Builders of the Pharaohs*. London: British Museum, 1982.

Bottero, Jean. *Mesopotamia: Writing, Reasoning, and the Gods*. Trans. Zainab Bahrani and Marc Van De Mieroop. Chicago: Univ. of Chicago Press, 1992.

Collon, Dominique. *Ancient Near Eastern Art*. Berkeley: Univ. of California Press, 1995.

Egyptian Art in the Age of the Pyramids. New York: Metropolitan Museum of Art, 1999.

Egyptian Book of the Dead, The: The Book of Going Forth by Day: Being the Papyrus of Ani (Royal Scribe of the Divine Offerings). Trans. Raymond O. Faulkner. San Francisco: Chronicle, 1994.

Frankfort, Henri. *The Art and Architecture of the Ancient Orient*. 5th ed. Pelican History of Art. New Haven: Yale Univ. Press, 1996.

Haywood, John. *Ancient Civilizations of the Near East and the Mediterranean*. London: Cassell, 1997.

James, T. G. H., and W. V. Davies. *Egyptian Sculpture*. Cambridge: Harvard Univ. Press, 1983.

Kozloff, Arielle P., and Betsy M. Bryan. *Egypt's Dazzling Sun: Amenhotep III and His World*. Cleveland: Cleveland Museum of Art, 1992.

Lehner, Mar. *The Complete Pyramids*. New York: Thames and Hudson, 1997.

Malek, Jaromir. *Egyptian Art*. Art & Ideas. London: Phaidon, 1999.

———. *Egypt: 4,000 Years of Art*. London: Phaidon, 2003.

Martin, Geoffrey Thorndike. *The Hidden Tombs of Memphis: New Discoveries from the Time of Tutankhamun and Ramesses the Great*. London: Thames and Hudson, 1991.

Mellaart, James. *The Earliest Civilization of the Near East*. London: Thames and Hudson, 1965.

Menu, Bernadette. *Ramesses II: Greatest of the Pharaohs*. Discoveries. New York: Abrams, 1999.

Montet, Pierre. *Everyday Life in Egypt in the Days of Ramesses the Great*. Trans. A. R. Maxwell-Hysop and Margaret S. Drower. Philadelphia: Univ. of Pennsylvania Press, 1981.

Reeves, C. N. *The Complete Tutankhamun: The King, the Tomb, the Royal Treasure*. London: Thames and Hudson, 1990.

Roaf, Michael. *Cultural Atlas of Mesopotamia and the Ancient Near East*. New York: Facts on File, 1990.

Robins, Gay. *The Art of Ancient Egypt*. Cambridge: Harvard Univ. Press, 1997.

Saggs, H. W. F. *Civilization before Greece and Rome*. New Haven: Yale Univ. Press, 1989.

Smith, William Stevenson. *The Art and Architecture of Ancient Egypt*. 3rd ed. Rev. William Kelly Simpson. Pelican History of Art. New Haven: Yale Univ. Press, 1998.

Tiarditti, Francesco, and Araldo De Luca. *Egyptian Treasures from the Egyptian Museum in Cairo*. New York: Abrams, 1999.

Wilkinson, Richard H. *Reading Egyptian Art: A Hieroglyphic Guide to Ancient Egyptian Painting and Sculpture*. London: Thames and Hudson, 1992.

Winstone, H. V. F. *Howard Carter and the Discovery of the Tomb of Tutankhamun*. London: Constable, 1991.

Wolkstein, Dianne, and Samuel Noah Kramer. *Inanna: Queen of Heaven and Earth*. New York: Harper & Row, 1983.

Chapter 3 Early Asian Art

Arts of China. 3 vols. Tokyo: Kodansha International, 1968–70.

Barnhart, Richard M. *Three Thousand Years of Chinese Painting*. New Haven: Yale Univ. Press, 1997.

Berkson, Carmel. *Elephanta: The Cave of Shiva*. Princeton, N.J.: Princeton Univ. Press, 1983.

Chandra, Pramod. *The Sculpture of India, 3000 B.C.–1300 A.D.* Washington, D.C.: National Gallery of Art, 1985.

Clunas, Craig. *Art in China*. Oxford History of Art. Oxford: Oxford Univ. Press, 1997.

Craven, Roy C. *Indian Art: A Concise History*. Rev. ed. World of Art. New York: Thames and Hudson, 1997.

Ebrey, Patricia Buckley. *The Cambridge Illustrated History of China*. Cambridge: Cambridge Univ. Press, 1996.

Eck, Diana L. *Darsan: Seeing the Divine Image in India*. 3rd ed. Chambersburg, Pa.: Anima, 1998.

Elisseeff, Danielle, and Vadime Elisseeff. *Art of Japan*. Trans. I. Mark Paris. New York: Abrams, 1985.

Errington, Elizabeth, and Joe Cribb, eds. *The Crossroads of Asia: Transformation in Image and Symbol in the Art of Ancient Afghanistan and Pakistan*. Cambridge, Eng.: Ancient India and Iran Trust, 1992.

Fong, Wen, ed. *The Great Bronze Age of China: An Exhibition from the People's Republic of China*. New York: Metropolitan Museum of Art, 1980.

Harle, James C. *The Art and Architecture of the Indian Subcontinent*. 2nd ed. Pelican History of Art. New Haven: Yale Univ. Press, 1994.

Kurata, Bunsaku. Horyu-ji, *Temple of the Exalted Law: Early Buddhist Art from Japan*. New York: Japan Society, 1981.

Lee, Sherman E. *A History of Far Eastern Art*. 5th ed. New York: Abrams, 1994.

_____. *China, 5,000 Years: Innovation and Transformation in the Arts*. New York: Solomon R. Guggenheim Museum, 1998.

Martynov, Anatolii Ivanovich. *Ancient Art of Northern Asia*. Urbana: Univ. of Illinois Press, 1991. Mason, Penelope. *History of Japanese Art*. New York: Abrams, 1993.

Paine, Robert Treat, and Alexander Soper. *Art and Architecture of Japan*. 3rd ed. Pelican History of Art. Harmondsworth, Eng.: Penguin, 1981.

Pearson, Richard. *Ancient Japan*. Washington, D. C.: Sackler Gallery, 1992.

Sickman, Lawrence, and Alexander Soper. *Art and Architecture of China*. Pelican History of Art. Harmondsworth, Eng.: Penguin, 1971.

Stanley-Baker, Joan. *Japanese Art*. Rev. & exp. ed. World of Art. New York: Thames and Hudson, 2000.

Sullivan, Michael. *The Arts of China*. 4th ed. exp. & rev. Berkeley: Univ. of California Press, 1999.

Thorp, Robert L., and Richard Ellis Vinograd. *Chinese Art and Culture*. New York: Abrams, 2001.

Tregear, Mary. *Chinese Art*. Rev. ed. World of Art. New York: Thames and Hudson, 1997.

Varley, H. Paul. *Japanese Culture*. 4th ed. updated & exp. Honolulu: Univ. of Hawaii Press, 2000.

Watanabe, Yasutada. *Shinto Art: Ise and Izumo Shrines*. Trans. Robert Ricketts. Heibonsha Survey of Japanese Art, vol. 3. New York: Weatherhill, 1974.

Weiner, Sheila L. *Ajanta: Its Place in Buddhist Art*. Berkeley: Univ. of California Press, 1977.

Whitfield, Roderick, and Anne Farrer. *Caves of the Thousand Buddhas: Chinese Art from the Silk Route*. London: British Museum, 1990.

Chapter 4 Art of Greece and the Aegean World

Adam, Robert. *Classical Architecture: A Comprehensive Handbook to the Tradition of Classical Style*. New York: Abrams, 1991.

Ashmole, Bernard. *Architect and Sculptor in Classical Greece*. Wrightsman Lectures. New York: New York Univ. Press, 1972.

Avery, Catherine, ed. *The New Century Handbook of Greek Mythology and Legend*. New York: Appleton-Century Crofts, 1972.

Barber, R. L. N. *The Cyclades in the Bronze Age*. Iowa City: Univ. of Iowa Press, 1987.

Beard, Mary, and John Henderson. *Classical Art: From Greece to Rome*. Oxford History of Art. Oxford: Oxford Univ. Press, 2001.

Biers, William. *The Archaeology of Greece: An Introduction*. 2nd ed. Ithaca: Cornell Univ. Press, 1996.

Boardman, John. *Greek Art*. 4th ed. rev. and exp. World of Art. London: Thames and Hudson, 1997.

_____. Greek Sculpture: *The Archaic Period, A Handbook*. World of Art. New York: Oxford Univ. Press, 1991.

_____. Greek Sculpture: *The Classical Period, A Handbook*. London: Thames and Hudson, 1985.

Cartledge, Paul, ed. *The Cambridge Illustrated History of Ancient Greece*. Cambridge Illustrated History. Cambridge: Cambridge Univ. Press, 1998.

Fitton, J. Lesley. *Cycladic Art*. 2nd ed. London: British Museum, 1999.

Francis, E. D. *Image and Idea in Fifth-Century Greece: Art and Literature after the Persian Wars*. London: Routledge, 1990.

Fullerton, Mark. D. *Greek Art*. Cambridge: Cambridge Univ. Press, 2000.

Higgins, Reynold. *Minoan and Mycenean Art*. Rev. ed. World of Art. New York: Thames and Hudson, 1997.

Hurwit, Jeffrey M. *The Art and Culture of Early Greece 1100–480 B.C.* Ithaca, N.Y.: Cornell Univ. Press, 1985.

_____. *The Athenian Acropolis: History, Mythology, and Archaeology from the Neolithic Period to the Present*. Cambridge: Cambridge Univ. Press, 1999.

Jenkins, Ian. *The Parthenon Frieze*. Austin: Univ. of Texas Press, 1994.

Lagerlof, Margaretha Rossholm. *The Sculptures of the Parthenon: Aesthetics and Interpretation*. New Haven: Yale Univ. Press, 2000.

Lawrence, A. W. *Greek Architecture*. 5th ed. rev. R. A. Tomlinson. Pelican History of Art. New Haven: Yale Univ. Press, 1996.

Osborne, Robin. *Archaic and Classical Greek Art*. Oxford History of Art. Oxford: Oxford Univ. Press, 1998.

Pedley, John Griffiths. *Greek Art and Archaeology*. 3rd ed. London: Laurence King, 2002.

Preziosi, Donald and Louise Hitchcock. *Aegean Art and Architecture*. Oxford History of Art. Oxford: Oxford Univ. Press, 1999.

Spivey, Nigel. *Greek Art. Art & Ideas*. London: Phaidon Press, 1997.

Stewart, Andrew F. *Greek Sculpture: An Exploration*. 2 vols. New Haven: Yale Univ. Press, 1990.

Chapter 5 The Spread of Greek Art and Culture

Aruz, Joan, ed. *The Golden Deer of Eurasia: Scythian and Sarmatian Treasures from the Russian Steppes*. New Haven: Yale Univ. Press, 2000.

Brendel, Otto J. *Etruscan Art*. 2nd ed. Pelican History of Art. New Haven: Yale Univ. Press, 1995.

De Grummond, Nancy T., and Brunilde S. Ridgway. *From Pergamon to Sperlonga: Sculpture in Context*. Berkeley: Univ. of California Press, 2000.

Ferrier, R. W., ed. *Arts of Persia*. New Haven: Yale Univ. Press, 1989.

Fildes, Alan. *Alexander the Great: Son of the Gods*. Los Angeles: J. Paul Getty Museum, 2002.

Kunze, Max. *The Pergamon Altar: Its Rediscovery, History, and Reconstruction*. Berlin: Staatliche Museen zu Berlin, Antikensammlung, 1991.

Pang, Tina. *Treasures of the Eurasian Steppes: Animal Art from 800 B.C. to 200 A.D.* New York: Ariadne Galleries, 1998.

Pollitt, J. J. *Art in the Hellenistic Age*. Cambridge: Cambridge Univ. Press, 1986.

Porada, Edith. *The Art of Ancient Iran: Pre-Islamic Cultures*. Art of the World. New York: Crown, 1965.

Reeder, Ellen D., ed. *Scythian Gold: Treasures from Ancient Ukraine*. New York: Abrams in association with the Walters Art Gallery and the San Antonio Museum of Art, 1999.

Roux, Georges. *Ancient Iraq*. 3rd ed. London: Penguin, 1992.

Smith, R. R. R. *Hellenistic Sculpture: A Handbook*. World of Art. New York: Thames and Hudson, 1991.

Spivey, Nigel. *Etruscan Art*. World of Art. New York: Thames and Hudson, 1997.

Sprenger, Maja, and Gilda Bartolini. *The Etruscans: Their History, Art, and Architecture*. New York: Abrams, 1983.

Webster, T. B. L. *The Art of Greece: The Age of Hellenism*. Art of the World. New York: Crown, 1966.

Chapter 6 Roman Art

Bianchi Bandinelli, Ranuccio. *Rome: The Centre of Power: Roman Art to A.D. 200*. Trans. Peter Green. Arts of Mankind. London: Thames and Hudson, 1970.

Breeze, David John. *Hadrian's Wall*. 4th ed. London: Penguin, 2000.

Brown, Peter. *The World of Late Antiquity: A.D. 150–750*. New York: Norton, 1989.

Christ, Karl. *The Romans: An Introduction to Their History and Civilization*. Berkeley: Univ. of California Press, 1984.

D'Ambra, Eve. Roman Art. Cambridge: Cambridge Univ. Press, 1998.

Dunabin, Katherine M. D. *Mosaics of the Greek and Roman World*. Cambridge: Cambridge Univ. Press, 1999.

Elsner, Jas. Imperial *Rome and Christian Triumph: The Art of the Roman Empire, A.D. 100–450*. Oxford History of Art. Oxford: Oxford Univ. Press, 1998.

Gabucci, Ada. *Ancient Rome: Art, Architecture, and History*. Eds. Stefano Peccatori and Stephano Zuffi. Trans. T. M. Hartman. Los Angeles: J. Paul Getty Museum, 2002.

Gabucci, Ada, ed. *The Colosseum*. Los Angeles: J. Paul Getty Museum, 2002.

Grant, Michael. *Art in the Roman Empire*. London: Routledge, 1995.

Guilland, Jacqueline, and Maurice Guilland. *Frescoes in the Time of Pompeii*. New York: Potter, 1990.

Heintze, Helga von. Roman Art. New York: Universe, 1990.

L'Orange, Hans Peter. *The Roman Empire: Art Forms and Civic Life*. New York: Rizzoli, 1985.

MacDonald, William L. *The Architecture of the Roman Empire: An Introductory Study*. Rev. ed. 2 vols. Yale Publications in the History of Art. New Haven, Conn.: Yale Univ. Press, 1982.

_____. *The Pantheon: Design, Meaning, and Progeny*. Cambridge: Harvard Univ. Press, 1976.

MacDonald, William, and John A. Pinto. *Hadrian's Villa and Its Legacy*. New Haven: Yale Univ. Press, 1995.

Packer, James E., et al. *The Forum of Trajan in Rome: A Study of Its Monuments*. 2 vols., portfolio and microfiche. California Studies in the History of Art; 31. Berkeley: Univ. of California Press, 1997.

Pollitt, J. J. *The Art of Rome, c. 753 B.C.–337 A.D.: Sources and Documents*. Englewood Cliffs, N.J.: Prentice Hall, 1966.

Ramage, Nancy H., and Andrew Ramage. *Roman Art: Romulus to Constantine*. 4th ed. Upper Saddle River, N.J.: Prentice Hall, 2005.

Stewart, Peter. *Roman Art*. Oxford: Oxford University Press, 2004

Strong, Donald. *Roman Art*. 2nd. rev. & annotated ed. Pelican History of Art. New Haven: Yale Univ. Press, 1995.

Vitruvius, Pollio. *Ten Books on Architecture*. Trans. Ingrid D. Rowland. Cambridge: Cambridge Univ. Press, 1999.

Chapter 7 Jewish, Early Christian, and Byzantine Art

Age of Spirituality: *Late Antique and Early Christian Art, Third to Seventh Century*. New York: Metropolitan Museum of Art, 1979.

Cioffarelli, Ada. *Guide to the Catacombs of Rome and Its Surroundings*. Rome: Bonsignori, 2000.

Cormack, Robin. *Byzantine Art*. Oxford History of Art. Oxford: Oxford Univ. Press, 2000.

Cutler, Anthony. *The Hand of the Master: Craftsmanship, Ivory, and Society in Byzantium (9th–11th Centuries)*. Princeton: Princeton Univ. Press, 1994.

Demus, Otto. *Mosaic Decoration of San Marco, Venice*. Ed. Herbert L. Kessler. Chicago: Univ. of Chicago Press, 1988.

Evans, Helen C., and William D Wixon, eds. *The Glory of Byzantium*. New York: Abrams, 1997.

Kleinbauer, W. Eugene. *Saint Sophia at Constantinople: Singulariter in Mundo*. Dublin, N.H.: William L. Bauhan, 1999.

Krautheimer, Richard. *Early Christian and Byzantine Architecture*. 4th ed. Pelican History of Art. Harmondsworth, Eng: Penguin, 1986.

Lowden, John. *Early Christian and Byzantine Art. Art & Ideas*. London: Phaidon, 1997.

Mainstone, R. J. Hagia Sophia: *Architecture, Structure and Liturgy of Justinian's Great Church*. London: Thames and Hudson, 1988.

Manicelli, Fabrizio. *Catacombs and Basilicas: The Early Christians in Rome*. Florence: Scala, 1981.

Mark, Robert, and Ahmet S. Cakmak. *Hagia Sophia from the Age of Justinian to the Present*. Cambridge: Cambridge Univ. Press, 1992.

Matthews, Thomas F. *The Art of Byzantium*. London: Calmann and King Ltd., 1999.

Milburn, R. L. P. *Early Christian Art and Architecture*. Berkeley: Univ. of California Press, 1988.

Rutgers, Leonard Victor. *Subterranean Rome: In Search of the Roots of Christianity in the Catacombs of the Eternal City*. Leuven: Peeters, 2000.

Simson, Otto Georg von. *Sacred Fortress: Byzantine Art and Statecraft in Ravenna*. Chicago: Univ. of Chicago Press, 1948.

Snyder, James. *Medieval Art: Painting, Sculpture, Architecture, 4th–14th Century*. New York: Abrams, 1989.

Stevenson, James. *The Catacombs: Rediscovered Monuments of Early Christianity*. Ancient Peoples and Places. London: Thames and Hudson, 1978.

Stokstad, Marilyn. *Medieval Art*. 2nd ed. Boulder, Colo.: Westview Press, 2004.

Teteriatnikov, Natalia. *Mosaics of Hagia Sophia, Istanbul: The Fossati Restoration and the Work of the Byzantine Institute*. Washington, D.C.: Dumbarton Oaks Research Library and Collection, 1998.

Vio, Ettore, and Eunio Concina. *The Basilica of St. Mark in Venice*. New York: Riverside, 1999.

Webb, Matilda. *The Churches and Catacombs of Early Christian Rome: A Comprehensive Guide*. Brighton, Eng.: Sussex Academic Press, 2001.

Weitzmann, Kurt. *Late Antique and Early Christian Book Illumination*. New York: Braziller, 1977.

Chapter 8 Islamic Art

Asher, Catherine B. *Architecture of Mughal India*. New York: Cambridge Univ. Press, 1992.

Atasoy, Nurhan. *Splendors of the Ottoman Sultans*. Ed. and trans. Tulay Artan. Memphis, Tenn.: Lithograph, 1992.

Atil, Esin. *The Age of Sultan Suleyman the Magnificent*. Washington, D.C.: National Gallery of Art, 1987.

Beach, Milo Cleveland. *Mughal and Rajput Painting*. New York: Cambridge Univ. Press, 1992.

Blair, Sheila S., and Jonathan M. Brown. *The Art and Architecture of Islam 1250–1800*. New Haven: Yale Univ. Press, 1994.

Brend, Barbara. *Islamic Art*. Cambridge: Harvard Univ. Press, 1991.

Dodds, Jerrilynn D., ed. Al-Andalus: *The Art of Islamic Spain*. New York: Metropolitan Museum of Art, 1992.

Dye, Joseph M. *The Arts of India*. Richmond: Virginia Museum of Fine Arts/Philip Wilson Publishers, 2001.

Frishman, Martin, and Hasan-Uddin Khan. *The Mosque: History, Architectural Development and Regional Diversity*. London: Thames and Hudson, 1994.

Grabar, Oleg. *The Alhambra*. Cambridge: Harvard Univ. Press, 1978.

_____. *The Mediation of Ornament*. A. W. Mellon Lectures in the Fine Arts. Princeton, N.J.: Princeton Univ. Press, 1992.

_____. *Mostly Miniatures: An Introduction to Persian Painting*. Princeton, N.J.: Princeton Univ. Press, 2000.

Grabar, Oleg, and Richard Ettinghausen. *The Art and Architecture of Islam, 650–1250*. Penguin History of Art. New Haven: Yale Univ. Press, 2001.

Irwin, Robert. *Islamic Art in Context: Art, Architecture, and the Literary World*. Perspectives. New York: Abrams, 1997.

Khatibi, Abdelkebir, and Mohammed Sijelmassi. *The Splendour of Islamic Calligraphy*. Rev. and exp. ed. New York: Thames and Hudson, 1996.

Koran, The. Rev. ed. Trans. N. J. Dawood. London: Penguin, 1993.

Nou, Jean-Louis. *Taj Mahal*. Text by Amina Okada and M. C. Joshi. New York: Abbeville, 1993.

Pal, Pratapaditya. *Court Paintings of India, 16th–19th Centuries*. New York: Navin Kumar, 1983.

Pal, Pratapaditya, et al. *Romance of the Taj Mahal*. Los Angeles: Los Angeles County Museum of Art, 1989. *Palace and Mosque: Islamic Art from the Near East*. Ed. Tim Stanley. London: Victoria and Albert Museum, Abrams, 2004.

Schimmel, Annemarie. *Calligraphy and Islamic Culture*. New York: New York Univ. Press, 1983.

Welch, Stuart Cary. *The Emperors'Album: Images of Mughal India*. New York: Metropolitan Museum of Art, 1987.

_____. *India: Art and Culture, 1300–1900*. New York: Metropolitan Museum of Art, 1985.

Chapter 9 Later Asian Art

Addiss, Stephen. *The Art of Zen: Painting and Calligraphy by Japanese Monks, 1600–1925*. New York: Abrams, 1989.

Andrews, Julia Frances. *Painters and Politics in the People's Republic of China, 1949–79*. Berkeley: Univ. of California Press, 1994.

Barnhart, Richard M. *Painters of the Great Ming: The Imperial Court and the Zhe School*. Dallas, Tex.: Dallas Museum of Art, 1993.

Billeter, Jean François. *The Chinese Art of Writing*. New York: Skira/Rizzoli, 1990.

Blurton, T. Richard. *Hindu Art*. Cambridge: Harvard Univ. Press, 1993.

Clunas, Craig. *Pictures and Visualities in Early Modern China*. Princeton, N.J.: Princeton Univ. Press, 1997.

Eight Dynasties of Chinese Painting: The Collections of the Nelson Gallery-Atkins Museum, Kansas City, and the Cleveland Museum of Art. Cleveland: Cleveland Museum of Art; Bloomington: Indiana University Press, 1980.

Fang, Jing Pei. *Treasures of the Chinese Scholar: Form, Function, and Symbolism*. Ed. J. May Lee Barrett. New York: Weatherhill, 1997.

Fisher, Robert E. *Buddhist Art and Architecture*. World of Art. New York: Thames and Hudson, 1993.

Fong, Wen C. and James C. Y. Watt. *Possessing the Past: Treasures from the National Palace Museum, Taipei*. New York: Metropolitan Museum of Art, 1997.

Forrer, Matthi. *Hokusai*. New York: Rizzoli, 1988.

Guth, Christine. *Art of Edo Japan: The Artist and the City, 1615–1868*. Perspectives. New York: Abrams, 1996.

Hayashiya, Tatsusaburo, Masao Nakamura, and Seizo Hayashiya. *Japanese Arts and the Tea Ceremony*. Trans. and adapted by Joseph P. Macadam. Heibonsha Survey of Japanese Art, vol. 15. New York: Weatherhill, 1974.

Hickman, Money L. *Japan's Golden Age: Momoyama*. New Haven: Yale Univ. Press, 1996.

Khanna, Balraj, and Aziz Kurtha. *Art of Modern India*. London: Thames and Hudson, 1998.

Liu, Laurence G. *Chinese Architecture*. New York: Rizzoli, 1989.

Losty, Jeremiah P. *The Art of the Book in India*. London: British Library, 1982.

Merritt, Helen and Nanako Yamada. *Guide to Modern Japanese Woodblock Prints, 1900–1975*. Honolulu: Univ. of Honolulu Press, 1995.

Mitchell, George. *The Royal Palaces of India*. London: Thames and Hudson, 1994.

Munroe, Alexandra. *Japanese Art after 1945: Scream Against the Sky*. New York: Abrams, 1994.

Murase, Miyeko. *Iconography of the Tale of Genji: Genji Monogatari Ekotoba*. New York: Weatherhill, 1983.

_____. *Masterpieces of Japanese Screen Painting: The American Collections*. New York: Braziller, 1990.

Ng, So Kam. *Brushstrokes: Styles and Techniques of Chinese Painting*. San Francisco: Asian Art Museum of San Francisco, 1993.

Rowland, Benjamin. *Art and Architecture of India: Buddhist, Hindu, Jain*. Pelican History of Art. Harmondsworth, Eng.: Penguin, 1977.

Seo, Audrey Yoshiko. *The Art of Twentieth-Century Zen: Paintings and Calligraphy by Japanese Masters*. Boston: Shambhala, 1998.

Sullivan, Michael. *Art and Artists of Twentieth-Century China*. Berkeley: Univ. of California Press, 1996.

_____. *Symbols of Eternity: The Art of Landscape Painting in China*. Stanford: Stanford Univ. Press, 1979.

Thompson, Sarah E., and H. D. Harootunian. *Undercurrents in the Floating World: Censorship and Japanese Prints*. New York: Asia Society Gallery, 1992.

Till, Barry. *The Arts of Meiji Japan, 1868–1912: Changing Aesthetics*. Victoria, B.C.: Art Gallery of Victoria, 1995.

Tillotson, G. H. R. *The Rajput Palaces: The Development of an Architectural Style, 1450–1750*. New York: Oxford Univ. Press. 1999.

Vainker, S. J. Chinese *Pottery and Porcelain: From Prehistory to the Present*. London: British Museum, 1991.

Watson, William. *The Arts of China, 900–1620*. Pelican History of Art. New Haven: Yale Univ. Press, 2000.

Weidner, Marsha, ed. *Latter Days of the Law: Images of Chinese Buddhism, 850–1850*. Lawrence: Spencer Museum of Art, Univ. of Kansas, 1994.

Yu, Zhuoyun, comp. *Palaces of the Forbidden City*. Trans. Ng Mau-Sang, Chan Sinwai, and Puwen Lee. New York: Viking, 1984.

Chapter 10 Early Medieval and Romanesque Art

Alexander, J. J. G. *Medieval Illuminators and Their Methods of Work*. New Haven: Yale Univ. Press, 1992.

Andrews, Francis B. *The Mediaeval Builder and His Methods*. New York: Barnes & Noble, 1993.

Backhouse, Janet, D. H. Turner, and Leslie Webster. *The Golden Age of Anglo-Saxon Art, 966–1066*. Bloomington: Indiana Univ. Press, 1984.

Bandmann, Günter. *Early Medieval Architecture as Bearer of Meaning*. Trans. Kendall Wallis. New York: Columbia University Press, 2005.

Benton, Janetta Rebold. *Art of the Middle Ages*. World of Art. New York: Thames and Hudson, 2002.

Branner, Robert. *Manuscript Painting in Paris during the Reign of Saint Louis: A Study of Styles*. California Studies in the History of Art. Berkeley: Univ. of California Press, 1977.

Braunfels, Wolfgang. *Monasteries of Western Europe: The Architecture of the Orders*. Trans. Alistair Laing. New York: Thames and Hudson, 1993.

Brown, Michelle. *Understanding Illuminated Manuscripts: A Guide to Technical Terms*. Malibu, Calif.: J. Paul Getty Museum in association with the British Library, 1994.

Cahn, Walter. *Romanesque Bible Illumination*. Ithaca, N.Y.: Cornell Univ. Press, 1982.

_____. *Romanesque Manuscripts: The Twelfth Century*. 2 vols. Survey of Manuscripts Illuminated in France. London: H. Miller, 1996.

Calkins, Robert C. *Medieval Architecture in Western Europe: From A.D. 300–1500*. Iv. + laser optical disc. New York: Oxford Univ. Press, 1998.

_____. *Monuments of Medieval Art*. New York: Dutton, 1979.

Conant, Kenneth John. *Carolingian and Romanesque Architecture, 800–1200*. 3rd ed. Pelican History of Art. Harmondsworth, Eng.: Penguin, 1973.

Diebold, William J. *Word and Image: An Introduction to Early Medieval Art*. Boulder, Colo.: Westview Press, 2000.

Dodwell, C. R. *Pictorial Arts of the West, 800–1200*. Pelican History of Art. New Haven: Yale Univ. Press, 1993.

Duby, Georges. *Sculpture: The Great Art of the Middle Ages from the Fifth to the Fifteenth Century*. New York: Skira/Rizzoli, 1990.

Evans, Angela Care. *The Sutton Hoo Ship Burial*. Rev ed. London: British Museum, 1994.

Farr, Carol. *The Book of Kells: Its Function and Audience*. London: British Library, 1997.

Fitzhugh, William W., and Elisabeth I. Ward, eds. *Vikings: The North Atlantic Saga*. Washington, D.C.: Smithsonian Institution Press, 2000.

Forsyth, Ilene H. *The Throne of Wisdom: Wood Sculptures of the Madonna in Romanesque France*. Princeton, N.J.: Princeton Univ. Press, 1972.

Grape, Wolfgang. *The Bayeux Tapestry: Monument to a Norman Triumph*. New York: Prestel, 1994.

Harbison, Peter. *The Golden Age of Irish Art: The Medieval Achievement, 600–1200*. London: Thames and Hudson, 1998.

Hubert, Jean, Jean Porcher, and W. F. Volbach. *Carolingian Renaissance. Arts of Mankind*. New York: Braziller, 1970.

Kennedy, Hugh. *Crusader Castles*. Cambridge: Cambridge Univ. Press, 1994.

Kenyon, John. *Medieval Fortifications*. Leicester: Leicester Univ. Press, 1990.

Kubach, Hans Erich. *Romanesque Architecture*. History of World Architecture. New York: Electa/Rizzoli, 1988.

Labarge, Margaret Wade. *A Small Sound of the Trumpet: Women in Medieval Life*. London: Hamilton, 1990.

Laing, Lloyd. *Art of the Celts*. World of Art. New York: Thames and Hudson, 1992.

Megaw, Ruth, and Vincent Megaw. *Celtic Art: From Its Beginnings to the Book of Kells*. Rev. and exp. ed. New York: Thames and Hudson, 2001.

Mentre, Mirelle. *Illuminated Manuscripts of Medieval Spain*. New York: Thames and Hudson, 1996.

Myer-Harting, Henry. *Ottonian Book Illumination: An Historical Study*. 2 vols. 2nd rev. ed. London: Harvey Miller, 1999.

Nees, Lawrence. *Early Medieval Art*. Oxford History of Art. Oxford: Oxford Univ. Press, 2003.

Nordenfalk, Carl Adam Johan. *Early Medieval Book Illumination*. New York: Rizzoli, 1988.

Petzold, Andreas. *Romanesque Art*. Perspectives. New York: Abrams, 1995.

Radding, Charles M., and William W. Clark. *Medieval Architecture, Medieval Learning: Builders and Masters in the Age of Romanesque and Gothic*. New Haven: Yale Univ. Press, 1992.

Schapiro, Meyer. *Romanesque Art*. New York: Braziller, 1977.

Sekules, Veronica. *Medieval Art*. Oxford History of Art. Oxford: Oxford Univ. Press, 2001.

Stalley, R. A. *Early Medieval Architecture*. Oxford History of Art. Oxford: Oxford Univ. Press, 1999.

Stoddard, Whitney. *Art and Architecture in Medieval France: Medieval Architecture, Sculpture, Stained Glass, Manuscripts*. The Art of the Church Treasuries. New York: Harper & Row, 1972.

Stokstad, Marilyn. *Medieval Art*. 2nd ed. Boulder, Colo.: Westview Press, 2004.

Stones, Alison, Jeanne Krochalis, Paula Gerson, and Annie Shaver-Crandell. *The Pilgrim's Guide: A Critical Edition*. 2 vols. London: Harvey Miller, 1998.

Wieck, Roger S. *Time Sanctified: The Book of Hours in Medieval Art and Life*. New York: Braziller, 1988.

Williams, John. *The Illustrated Beatus: Corpus of the Illumination of the Commentary on the Apocalypse*. London: Harvey Miller, 1994.

Wilson, David M. *Anglo-Saxon Art: From the Seventh Century to the Norman Conquest*. London: Thames and Hudson, 1984.

_____. _The Bayeux Tapestry: The Complete Tapestry in Color._ New York: Random House, 1985.

Wilson, David M., and Ole Klindt-Jensen. _Viking Art._ 2nd ed. Minneapolis: Univ. of Minnesota Press, 1980.

Year 1200, The. 2 vols. New York: Metropolitan Museum of Art, 1970.

Zarnecki, George. _The Art of the Medieval World: Architecture, Sculpture, Painting, the Sacred Arts._ New York: Abrams, 1975.

Chapter 11 Gothic Art

Andrews, Francis B. _The Medieval Builder and His Methods._ New York: Dover Publications, 1993.

Armi, C. Edson. _The "Headmaster" of Chartres and the Origins of "Gothic" Sculpture._ University Park: Pennsylvania State Univ. Press, 1994.

Bony, Jean. _French Gothic Architecture of the 12th and 13th Centuries._ California Studies in the History of Art. Berkeley: Univ. of California Press, 1983.

Borsook, Eve, and Fiorella Superbi Gioffredi. _Italian Altarpieces, 1250–1550: Function and Design._ Oxford: Clarendon, 1994.

Camille, Michael. _The Medieval Art of Love: Objects and Subjects of Desire._ New York: Abrams, 1998.

_____. _Gothic Art: Glorious Visions._ Perspectives. New York: Abrams, 1996.

_____. _The Gothic Idol: Ideology and Image Making in Medieval Art._ Cambridge New Art History and Criticism. Cambridge: Cambridge Univ. Press, 1989.

Chelazzi Dini, Giulietta, Alessandro Angelini, and Bernardina Sani. _Sienese Painting: From Duccio to the Birth of the Baroque._ New York: Abrams, 1997.

Chiellini, Monica. _Cimabue._ Trans. Lisa Pelletti. Florence: Scala, 1988.

Coldstream, Nicola. _Medieval Architecture._ Oxford History of Art. Oxford: Oxford Univ. Press, 2002.

Cole, Bruce. _Giotto and Florentine Painting, 1280–1375._ New York: Harper & Row, 1975.

Crosby, Sumner McKnight. _The Royal Abbey of Saint-Denis from Its Beginnings to the Death of Suger, 475–1151._ Yale Publications in the History of Art. New Haven: Yale Univ. Press, 1987.

Erlande-Brandenburg, Alain. _Gothic Art._ Trans. I. Mark Paris. New York: Abrams, 1989.

_____. _Notre Dame de Paris._ New York: Abrams, 1998.

Favier, Jean. _The World of Chartres._ Trans. Francisca Garvie. New York: Abrams, 1990.

Frankl, Paul. _Gothic Architecture._ Rev. ed. New Haven: Yale University Press, 2000.

Grodecki, Louis. _Gothic Architecture._ Trans. I. Mark Paris. History of World Architecture. New York: Electa/Rizzoli, 1985.

Grodecki, Louis, and Catherine Brisac. _Gothic Stained Glass, 1200–1300._ Ithaca, N.Y.: Cornell Univ. Press, 1985.

O'Neill, John Philip., ed. _Enamels of Limoges, 1100–1350._ Trans. Sophie Hawkes, Joachim Neugroschel, and Patricia Stirneman. New York: Metropolitan Museum of Art, 1996.

Panofsky, Erwin. _Abbot Suger on the Abbey Church of St. Denis and Its Art Treasures._ 2nd ed. Ed. Gerda Panofsky-Soergel. Princeton, N.J.: Princeton Univ. Press, 1979.

_____. _Gothic Architecture and Scholasticism._ Latrobe, Penn.: Archabbey, 1951.

Pevsner, Nikolaus, and Priscilla Metcalf. _The Cathedrals of England._ 2 vols. Harmondsworth, Eng.: Viking, 1985.

Sauerlander, Willibald. _Gothic Sculpture in France, 1140–1270._ Trans. Janet Sandheimer. London: Thames and Hudson, 1972.

Scott, Kathleen L. _Later Gothic Manuscripts, 1390–1490._ 2 vols. A Survey of Manuscripts Illuminated in the British Isles; 6. London: Harvey Miller, 1996.

Simson, Otto Georg von. _The Gothic Cathedral: Origins of Gothic Architecture and the Medieval Concept of Order._ 3rd ed. Bollingen Series. Princeton, N.J.: Princeton Univ. Press, 1988.

Smart, Alastair. _The Dawn of Italian Painting, 1250–1400._ Ithaca, N.Y.: Cornell Univ. Press, 1978.

White, John. _Art and Architecture in Italy, 1250 to 1400._ 3rd ed. Pelican History of Art. Harmondsworth, Eng.: Penguin, 1993.

_____. _Duccio: Tuscan Art and the Medieval Workshop._ New York: Thames and Hudson, 1979.

Williamson, Paul. _Gothic Sculpture, 1140–1300._ Pelican History of Art. New Haven: Yale Univ. Press, 1995.

Wilson, Christopher. _The Gothic Cathedral: The Architecture of the Great Church, 1130–1530._ New York: Thames and Hudson, 1990.

Chapter 12 Early Renaissance Art

Adams, Laurie Schneider. _Italian Renaissance Art._ Boulder, Colo.: Westview Press, 2001.

Ainsworth, Maryan Wynn. _Petrus Christus: Renaissance Master of Bruges._ New York: Metropolitan Museum of Art, 1994.

Ahl, Diane Cole, ed. _The Cambridge Companion to Masaccio._ New York: Cambridge Univ. Press, 2002.

Alexander, J. J. G. _The Painted Page: Italian Renaissance Book Illumination, 1450–1550._ New York: Prestel, 1994.

Ames, Lewis Francis. _The Intellectual Life of the Early Renaissance Artist._ New Haven: Yale Univ. Press, 2000.

Baxandall, Michael. _Painting and Experience in Fifteenth-Century Italy: A Primer in the Social History of Pictorial Style._ Oxford: Clarendon, 1972.

Campbell, Lorne. Renaissance _Portraits: European Portrait-Painting in the 14th, 15th, and 16th Centuries._ New Haven: Yale Univ. Press, 1990.

Cavallo, Adolph S. _The Unicorn Tapestries at the Metropolitan Museum of Art._ New York: The Metropolitan Museum of Art; Abrams, 1998.

Chastell, Andre. _French Art: The Renaissance, 1430–1620._ Paris: Flammarion, 1995.

Christiansen, Keith. _Andrea Mantegna: Padua and Mantua._ New York: Braziller, 1994.

Christiansen, Keith, Laurence B. Kanter, and Carl Brandon Strehlke. _Painting in Renaissance Siena, 1420–1500._ New York: Metropolitan Museum of Art, 1988.

Circa 1492: Art in the Age of Exploration. Washington, D.C.: National Gallery of Art, 1991.

Cole, Bruce. _Italian Art, 1250–1550: The Relation of Renaissance Art to Life and Society._ New York: Harper & Row, 1987.

_____. _Masaccio and the Art of Early Renaissance Florence._ Bloomington: Indiana Univ. Press, 1980.

Cuttler, Charles D. _Northern Painting from Pucelle to Bruegel: Fourteenth, Fifteenth and Sixteenth Centuries._ New York: Holt, Rinehart and Winston, 1973.

Freeman, Margaret B. _The Unicorn Tapestries._ New York: Metropolitan Museum of Art, 1976.

Hartt, Frederick, and David G. Wilkins. _History of Italian Renaissance Art: Painting, Sculpture, Architecture._ 5th ed. New York: Abrams, 2003.

Heydenreich, Ludwig Heinrich. _Architecture in Italy, 1400 to 1600._ Rev. Paul Davies. Pelican History of Art. New Haven: Yale Univ. Press, 1996.

Huizinga, Johan. _The Autumn of the Middle Ages._ Trans. Rodney J. Payton and Ulrich Mammitzsch. Chicago: Univ. of Chicago Press, 1996.

Krautheimer, Richard. _Ghiberti's Bronze Doors._ Princeton, N.J.: Princeton Univ. Press, 1971.

Lane, Barbara G. _The Altar and the Altarpiece: Sacramental Themes in Early Netherlandish Painting._ New York: Harper & Row, 1984.

McCorquodale, Charles. _The Renaissance: European Painting, 1400–1600._ London: Studio Editions, 1994.

Pacht, Otto. _Early Netherlandish Painting: From Rogier van der Weyden to Gerard David._ Ed. Monika Rosenauer.m Trans. David Britt. London: Harvey Miller, 1997.

_____. _Van Eyck and the Founders of Early Netherlandish Painting._ Ed. Maria Schmidt-Dengler. Trans. David Britt. London: Miller, 1994.

Panofsky, Erwin. _Early Netherlandish Painting: Its Origins and Character._ 2 vols. Cambridge: Harvard Univ. Press, 1966.

Paolucci, Antonio. _The Origins of Renaissance Art: The Baptistry Doors, Florence._ New York: George Braziller, 1996.

Rosenberg, Charles. _Art and Politics in Late Medieval and Early Renaissance Italy, 1250–1500._ South Bend, Ind.: Univ. of Notre Dame Press, 1990.

Saalman, Howard. _Filippo Brunelleschi: The Buildings._ University Park: Pennsylvania State Univ. Press, 1993.

Snyder, James. _Northern Renaissance Art: Painting, Sculpture, and the Graphic Arts from 1350 to 1575._ 2nd ed. Upper Saddle River, N. J.: Prentice Hall, 2005.

Verdon, Timothy, and John Henderson, eds. _Christianity and the Renaissance: Image and Religious Imagination in the Quattrocento._ Syracuse, N.Y.: Syracuse Univ. Press, 1990.

Welch, Evelyn S. _Art and Society in Italy, 1350–1500._ Oxford History of Art. Oxford: Oxford Univ. Press, 1997.

Chapter 13 Art of the High Renaissance and Reformation

Aikema, Bernard, ed. _Renaissance Venice and the North: Crosscurrents in the Time of Bellini, Dürer, and Titian._ New York: Rizzoli, 2000.

Algranti, Gilberto, ed. _Titian to Tiepolo: Three Centuries of Italian Art._ New York: Rizzoli/St. Martin's Press, 2002.

Andrews, Lew. _Story and Space in Renaissance Art: The Rebirth of Continuous Narrative._ New York: Cambridge Univ. Press, 1995.

Bambach, Carmen. _Drawing and Painting in the Italian Renaissance Workshop: Theory and Practice, 1300–1600._ Cambridge: Cambridge Univ. Press, 1999.

Baxandall, Michael. _The Limewood Sculptors of Renaissance Germany._ New Haven: Yale Univ. Press, 1980.

Bier, Justus. _Tilman Riemenschneider, His Life and Work._ Lexington: Univ. of Kentucky Press, 1989.

Blunt, Anthony. _Art and Architecture in France: 1500–1700._ 5th ed. Rev. Richard Beresford. Pelican History of Art. New Haven: Yale Univ. Press, 1999.

Boucher, Bruce. _Andrea Palladio: The Architect in His Time._ New York: Abbeville, 1994.

Brown, Jonathan. _Painting in Spain, 1500–1700._ Pelican History of Art. New Haven: Yale Univ. Press, 1998.

Brown, Patricia Fortini. _Art and Life in Renaissance Venice._ Perspectives. New York: Abrams, 1997.

Burroughs, Charles. _The Italian Renaissance Palace Facade: Structures of Authority, Surfaces of Sense._ Cambridge: Cambridge Univ. Press, 2002.

Cole, Alison. _Virtue and Magnificence: Art of the Italian Renaissance Courts._ Perspectives. New York: Abrams, 1995.

Dixon, Annette, ed. _Women Who Ruled: Queens, Goddesses, Amazons in Renaissance and Baroque Art._ London: Merrell; Ann Arbor: Univ. of Michigan Museum of Art, 2002.

Emison, Patricia A. _Low and High Style in Italian Renaissance Art._ New York: Garland Publishing, 1997.

Farago, Claire J. _Reframing the Renaissance: Visual Culture in Europe and Latin America, 1450–1650._ New Haven: Yale Univ. Press, 1995.

Field, Judith Veronica. _The Invention of Infinity: Mathematics and Art in the Renaissance._ Oxford: Oxford Univ. Press, 1997.

Freedberg, S. J. _Painting in Italy, 1500 to 1600._ 3rd ed. Pelican History of Art. New Haven: Yale Univ. Press, 1993.

Graham-Dixon, Andrew. _Renaissance._ Berkeley: Univ. of California Press, 1999.

Grössinger, Christa. _Picturing Women in Late Medieval and Renaissance Art._ New York: St. Martin's Press, 1997.

Harbison, Craig. _The Mirror of the Artist: Northern Renaissance Art in Its Historical Context._ Perspectives. New York: Abrams, 1995.

Hayum, André. _The Isenheim Altarpiece: God's Medicine and the Painter's Vision._ Princeton Essays on the Arts. Princeton, N.J.: Princeton Univ. Press, 1989.

Heydenreich, Ludwig H. _Leonardo: "The Last Supper."_ Art in Context. London: Allen Lane, 1974.

Huizinga, Johan. _Waning of the Middle Ages: A Study of the Forms of Life, Thought, and Art in France and the Netherlands in the XIVth and XVth Centuries._ Garden City, N.Y.: Doubleday, 1954.

Jacobs, Fredrika Herman. _Defining the Renaissance Virtuosa: Women Artists and the Language of Art History and Criticism._ Cambridge: Cambridge Univ. Press, 1997.

Jestez, Bertrand. _The Art of the Renaissance._ Trans. Mark Paris. New York: Abrams, 1995.

Landau, David, and Peter Parshall. _The Renaissance Print: 1470–1550._ New Haven: Yale Univ. Press, 1994.

Lotz, Wolfgang. _Architecture in Italy, 1500–1600._ Rev. Deborah Howard. Pelican History of Art. New Haven: Yale Univ. Press, 1995.

Manca, Joseph. _Moral Essays on the High Renaissance: Art in Italy in the Age of Michelangelo._ Lanham, Md.: Univ. Press of America, 2001.

Mann, Nicolas, and Luke Syson, eds. _The Image of the Individual: Portraits in the Renaissance._ London: British Museum Press, 1998.

Martineau, Jane, and Charles Hope, eds. _The Genius of Venice, 1500–1600._ New York: Abrams, 1984.

McHam, Sarah Blake, ed. _Looking at Italian Renaissance Sculpture._ Cambridge: Cambridge Univ. Press, 1998.

Murray, Linda. _The High Renaissance and Mannerism: Italy, the North, and Spain, 1500–1600._ World of Art. London: Thames and Hudson, 1995.

Murray, Peter. _Renaissance Architecture._ History of World Architecture. Milan: Electa, 1985.

Olson, Roberta J. M. _Italian Renaissance Sculpture._ World of Art. New York: Thames and Hudson, 1992.

Paoletti, John T., and Gary M. Radke. _Art in Renaissance Italy._ 2nd ed. New York: Abrams, 2002.

Partridge, Loren W. _The Art of Renaissance Rome, 1400–1600._ New York: Abrams, 1996.

Perlingieri, Ilya Sandra. *Sofonisba Anguissola: The First Great Woman Artist of the Renaissance*. New York: Rizzoli, 1992.
Pietrangeli, Carlo, et al. *The Sistine Chapel: The Art, the History, and the Restoration*. New York: Harmony, 1986.
Poeschke, Joachim. *Michelangelo and His World: Sculpture of the Italian Renaissance*. Trans. Russell Stockman. New York: Abrams, 1996.
Pope-Hennessy, Sir John. *Italian High Renaissance and Baroque Sculpture*. 4th ed. Oxford: Phaidon, 1996.
Rosand, David. *Painting in Cinquecento Venice: Titian, Veronese, Tintoretto*. Rev. ed. Cambridge: Cambridge Univ. Press, 1997.
Rowland, Ingrid D. *The Culture of the High Renaissance: Ancients and Moderns in Sixteenth-Century Rome*. Cambridge: Cambridge Univ. Press, 1998.
Shearman, John. *Mannerism*. Harmondsworth, Eng.: Penguin, 1967.
Tavernor, Robert. *Palladio and Palladianism*. World of Art. New York: Thames and Hudson, 1991.
Tinagli, Paola. *Women in Italian Renaissance Art: Gender, Representation, and Identity*. New York: St. Martin's Press, 1997.
Turner, Richard. *Renaissance Florence: The Invention of a New Art*. Perspectives. New York: Abrams, 1997.
Vasari, Giorgio. *The Lives of the Artists*. Trans. Julia Conaway Bondanella and Peter Bondanella. New York: Oxford Univ. Press, 1991.
Williams, Robert. *Art, Theory, and Culture in Sixteenth-Century Italy: From Techne to Metatechne*. Cambridge: Cambridge Univ. Press, 1997.
Wohl, Hellmut. *The Aesthetics of Italian Renaissance Art: A Reconsideration of Style*. Cambridge: Cambridge Univ. Press, 1999.

Chapter 14 Baroque and Rococo Art

Ackley, Clifford S. *Printmaking in the Age of Rembrandt*. Boston: Museum of Fine Arts, 1981.
Age of Caravaggio, The. New York: Metropolitan Museum of Art, 1985.
Alpers, Svetlana. *The Making of Rubens*. New Haven: Yale Univ. Press, 1995.
Berger, Robert W. *Versailles: The Chateau of Louis XIV*. Monographs on the Fine Arts. University Park: Pennsylvania State Univ. Press, 1985.
Blunt, Anthony, et al. *Baroque and Rococo Architecture and Decoration*. New York: Harper & Row, 1982.
Boucher, Bruce. *Italian Baroque Sculpture*. World of Art. New York: Thames and Hudson, 1998.
Brown, Christopher. *Scenes of Everyday Life: Dutch Genre Painting of the Seventeenth Century*. London: Faber & Faber, 1984.
Brown, Jonathan. *The Golden Age of Painting in Spain*. New Haven: Yale Univ. Press, 1991.
Brown, Jonathan, and Carmen Garrido. *Velasquez: The Technique of Genius*. Hew Haven: Yale Univ. Press, 1998.
Earls, Irene. *Baroque Art: A Topical Dictionary*. Westport, Conn.: Greenwood Press, 1996.
Franits, Wayne E., ed. *The Cambridge Companion to Vermeer*. Cambridge: Cambridge Univ. Press, 2001.
Haak, Bob. *The Golden Age: Dutch Painters of the Seventeenth Century*. Trans. and ed. Elizabeth Willems-Treeman. New York: Abrams, 1984.
Held, Julius Samuel, and Donald Posner. *17th- and 18th-Century Art: Baroque Painting, Sculpture, Architecture*. Library of Art History. New York: Abrams, 1971.
Kiers, Judikje, et al. *Glory of the Golden Age: Dutch Art of the 17th Century*. Amsterdam: Waanders, Rijksmuseum, 2000.
Kiers, Judikje, and Fieke Tissink. *Golden Age of Dutch Art: Painting, Sculpture, Decorative Art*. London: Thames and Hudson, 2000.
Kubler, George, and Martin Soria. *Art and Architecture in Spain and Portugal and Their American Dominions, 1500–1800*. Pelican History of Art. Harmondsworth, Eng.: Penguin, 1959.
Lagerlof, Margaretha Rossholm. *Ideal Landscape: Annibale Caracci, Nicolas Poussin, and Claude Lorrain*. New Haven: Yale Univ. Press, 1990.
Liedtke, Walter, Michael C. Plomp, and Axel Rüger. *Vermeer and the Delft School*. New York: Metropolitan Museum of Art, New Haven: Yale Univ. Press, 2001.
McTighe, Sheila. *Nicolas Poussin's Landscape Allegories*. Cambridge: Cambridge University Press, 1996.
Minor, Vernon Hyde. *Baroque and Rococo: Art & Culture*. New York: Abrams, 1999.
Norberg-Schulz, Christian. *Baroque Architecture*. New York: Rizzoli, 1986.
Olson, Todd. *Poussin and France: Painting, Humanism, and the Politics of Style*. New Haven: Yale Univ. Press, 2002.
Pizzamiglio, Gilberto and Manlio Brusatin., eds. *The Baroque in Central Europe: Places, Architecture, and Art*. Venice: Marsilio, 1992.
Plax, Julie Anne. *Watteau and the Cultural Politics of 18th-Century France*. New York: Cambridge Univ. Press, 2000.
Slive, Seymour. *Dutch Painting 1600–1800*. Pelican History of Art. New Haven: Yale Univ. Press, 1995.
Stratton-Pruitt, Suzanne L., ed. *Cambridge Companion to Velasquez*. Cambridge: Cambridge Univ. Press, 2002.
Sutton, Peter. *The Age of Rubens*. Boston: Museum of Fine Arts, 1993.
Tomlinson, Janis. *From El Greco to Goya: Painting in Spain, 1561–1828*. New York: Abrams, 1997.
Vergara, Alexander. *Rubens and His Spanish Patrons*. Cambridge: Cambridge Univ. Press, 1999.
Vlieghe, Hans. *Flemish Art and Architecture, 1585–1700*. Pelican History of Art. New Haven: Yale Univ. Press, 1998.
Welu, James A., and Pieter Biesboer, eds. *Judith Leyster: A Dutch Master and Her World*. New Haven: Yale Univ. Press, 1993.
Westerman, Mariët. *Art and Home: Dutch Interiors in the Age of Rembrandt*. Denver, Colo.: Denver Art Museum; Netherlands: Waanders, 2001.
_____. *A Worldly Art: The Dutch Republic, 1585–1718*. Perspectives. New York: Abrams, 1996.
White, Christopher. *Rembrandt as an Etcher: A Study of the Artist at Work*. 2nd ed. New Haven: Yale Univ. Press, 1999.
White, Christopher, and Quentin Buvelot. *Rembrandt by Himself*. London: National Gallery Publications, 1999.
Wine, Humphrey. *Claude: The Poetic Landscape*. London: National Gallery Publications, 1994.
Wintermute, Alan. *Watteau and His World: French Drawing from 1700–1750*. New York: Rizzoli/St. Martin's Press, 1999.
Wittkower, Rudolf. *Art and Architecture in Italy, 1600 to 1750*. 3 vols. 6th ed. Rev. Joseph Conners and Jennifer Montagu. Pelican History of Art. New Haven: Yale Univ. Press, 1999.

Chapter 15 Art of the Americas

Archuleta, Margaret, and Rennard Strickland. *Shared Visions: Native American Painters and Sculptors in the Twentieth Century*. Phoenix: Heard Museum, 1991.
Benson, Elizabeth P., and Beatriz de la Fuente, eds. *Olmec Art of Ancient Mexico*. Washington, D. C.: National Gallery of Art, 1996.
Berlo, Janet Catherine, and Ruth B. Phillips. *Native North American Art*. Oxford History of Art. Oxford: Oxford Univ. Press, 1998.
Bringhurst, Robert. *The Black Canoe: Bill Reid and the Spirit of Haida Gwaii*. Seattle: Univ. of Washington Press, 1991.
Broder, Patricia Janis. *Earth Songs, Moon Dreams: Paintings by American Indian Women*. New York: St. Martin's Press, 1999.
Coe, Michael D., et al. *The Olmec World: Ritual and Rulership*. Princeton, N.J.: Princeton Univ. in association with Abrams, 1995.
Coe, Ralph. *Lost and Found Traditions: Native American Art, 1965–1985*. Ed. Irene Gordon. Seattle: Univ. of Washington Press, 1986.
Crandall, Richard C. *Inuit Art: A History*. Jefferson, N.C.: McFarland, 2000.
Fane, Diane. *Converging Cultures: Art and Identity in Spanish America*. New York: Brooklyn Museum in association with Abrams, 1996.
Feest, Christian F. *Native Arts of North America*. Updated ed. World of Art. New York: Thames and Hudson, 1992.
Grimes, John B., Christian F. Feest, and Mary Lou Curran, eds. *Uncommon Legacies: Native American Art from the Peabody Essex Museum*. New York: American Federation and the Univ. of Washington Press, 2002.
Jonaitis, Aldona, ed. *Chiefly Feast: The Enduring Kwakiutl Potlatch*. Seattle: Univ. of Washington Press, 1991.
Krumnine, Mary Louise Elliot, and Susan C. Scott, eds. *Art and the Native American: Perceptions, Reality, and Influences*. University Park: Pennsylvania State Univ., 2001.
MacDonald, George F. *Haida Art*. Seattle: Univ. of Washington Press, 1996.
McQuinton, Don. *Visions of the North: Native Art of the Northwest Coast*. San Francisco: Chronicle Books, 1995.
Mauer, Evan M. *Visions of the People: A Pictorial History of Plains Indian Life*. Minneapolis: Minneapolis Institute of Arts, 1992.
Meuli, Jonathan. *Shadow House: Interpretations of Northwest Coast Art*. Amsterdam: Harwood Academic Publishing, 2001.
Mexico: Splendors of Thirty Centuries. New York: Metropolitan Museum of Art, 1990.
Miller, Mary Ellen. *The Art of Mesoamerica: from Olmec to Aztec*. 3rd ed. World of Art. London: Thames and Hudson, 2001.
Monroe, Dan L., et al. *Gifts of the Spirit: Works of Nineteenth-Century and Contemporary Native American Artists*. Salem, Mass.: Peabody Essex Museum, 1996.
Pasztory, Esther. *Pre-Columbian Art*. New York: Cambridge Univ. Press, 1998.
_____. *Aztec Art*. New York: Abrams, 1983.
Penny, David. *Native Arts of North America*. Trans. Peter Snowden. Paris: Terrail, 1998.
_____. *Art of the American Indian Frontier: The Chandler-Pohrt Collection*. Detroit: Detroit Institute of the Arts,1992.
Rasmussen, Waldo, Fatima Bercht, and Elizabeth Ferrer. *Latin American Artists of the Twentieth Century*. New York: Museum of Modern Art, 1993.
Reno, Dawn E. *Contemporary Native American Artists*. Brooklyn: Alliance Publishing, 1995.
Schobinger, Juan. *The Ancient Americans: A Reference Guide to the Art, Culture, and History of Pre-Columbian North and South America*. Trans. Carys Evans Corrales. Armonk, N.Y.: Sharp Reference, 2001.
Trimble, Stephen. *Talking with the Clay: The Art of Pueblo Pottery*. Santa Fe: School of American Research Press, 1987.
Vincent, Gilbert Tapley. *Masterpieces of American Indian Art: From the Eugene and Clare Thaw Collection*. New York: Abrams, 1995.
Wood, Nancy C. *Taos Pueblo*. New York: Knopf, 1989.

Chapter 16 African Art

Abiodun, Rowland, Henry J. Drewal, and John Pemberton III, eds. *The Yoruba Artist: New Theoretical Perspectives on African Arts*. Washington, D.C.: Smithsonian Institution, 1994.
Adler, Peter, and Nicholas Barnard. *African Majesty: The Textile Art of the Ashanti and Ewe*. New York: Thames and Hudson, 1992.
Astonishment and Power. Washington, D.C.: National Museum of African Art, Smithsonian Institution, 1993.
Bacquart, Jean-Baptiste. *The Tribal Arts of Africa*. New York: Thames and Hudson, 1998.
Bargna, Ivan. *African Art*. Trans. Jacqueline A. Cooperman. Rev. Michael Thompson. (Milano), Italy: Jaca Book; Wappingers' Falls, N.Y.: Antique Collector's Club, 2000.
Barley, Nigel. *Smashing Pots: Feats of Clay from Africa*. London: British Museum, 1994.
Bassani, Ezio. *African Art and Artifacts in European Collections: 1400–1800*. Ed. Malcolm McLeod. London: British Museum, 2000.
Beckwith, Carol and Angela Fisher. African Ark: People and Ancient Cultures of Ethiopia and the Horn of Africa. New York: Abrams, 1990.
Ben-Amos, Paula. *The Art of Benin*. Rev. ed. Washington, D.C.: Smithsonian Institution Press, 1995.
Biebuyck, Daniel P. *Lega Culture: Art, Initiation, and Moral Philosophy among a Central African People*. Berkeley: Univ. of California Press, 1973.
Blauer, Ettagale. *African Elegance*. New York: Rizzoli, 1999.
Blier, Suzanne Preston. *Ritual Arts of Africa: The Majesty of Form*. Perspectives. New York: Abrams, 1998.
Cole, Herbert M. *Icons: Ideals and Power in the Art of Africa*. Washington, D.C.: National Museum of African Art, Smithsonian Institution, 1989.
D'Azevedao, Warren L. *The Traditional Artist in African Societies*. Bloomington: Indiana Univ. Press, 1989.
Drewal, Henry, and John Pemberton III. *Yoruba: Nine Centuries of African Art and Thought*. New York: Center for African Art, 1989.
Garlake, Peter S. *Early Art and Architecture of Africa*. Oxford History of Art. Oxford: Oxford Univ. Press, 2002.
_____. *The Hunter's Vision: The Prehistoric Art of Zimbabwe*. Seattle: Univ. of Washington Press, 1995.
Gilfoy, Peggy S. *Patterns of Life: West African Strip-Weaving Traditions*. Washington, D.C.: National Museum of African Art, Smithsonian Institution, 1992.
Harris, Michael D. *Transatlantic Dialogue: Contemporary Art In and Out of Africa*. Chapel Hill: Univ. of North Carolina; Seattle: Univ. of Washington Press, 1999.
Kasfir, Sidney Littlefield. *Contemporary African Art*. World of Art. London: Thames and Hudson, 2000.
Magnin, André. *African Art Now: Masterpieces from the Jean Pigozzi Collection*. New York: Merrell, Houston: in association with the Museum of Fine Arts, 2005.

Mark, John, ed. *Africa, Arts and Cultures*. London: British Museum, 2000.
Martin, Phyllis, and Patrick O'Meara, eds. *Africa*. 3rd ed. Bloomington: Indiana Univ. Press, 1995.
Mbiti, John S. *African Religions and Philosophy*. 2nd ed. Oxford: Heinemann, 1990.
McNaughton, Patrick R. *The Mande Blacksmiths: Knowledge, Power and Art in West Africa*. Bloomington: Indiana Univ. Press, 1988.
McClusky, Pamela. *Art from Africa: Long Steps Never Broke a Back*. Seattle: Seattle Art Museum; Princeton, N.J.: Princeton Univ. Press, 2002.
Meyer, Laure. *Art and Craft in Africa: Everyday Life, Ritual, and Court Art*. Paris: Terrail, 1995.
Murray, Jocelyn, ed. *Cultural Atlas of Africa*. New York: Facts on File, 1998.
Neyt, François. *Luba: To the Sources of the Zaire*. Trans. Murray Wyllie. Paris: Editions Dapper, 1994.
Perrois, Louis, and Marta Sierra Delage. *The Art of Equatorial Guinea: The Fang Tribes*. New York: Rizzoli, 1990.
Phillips, Tom. *Africa: The Art of a Continent*. London: Prestel, 1996.
Roy, Christopher D. *Art and Life in Africa: Selections from the Stanley Collection*. Iowa City: Univ. of Iowa Museum of Art; Seattle: Univ. of Washington Press, 1992.
Schildkrout, Enid, and Curtis A. Keim. *African Reflections: Art from Northeastern Zaire*. Seattle: Univ. of Washington Press, 1990.
Schuster, Carl, and Edmund Carpenter. *Patterns That Connect: Social Symbolism in Ancient & Tribal Art*. New York: Abrams, 1996.
Sieber, Roy. *African Furniture and Household Objects*. Bloomington: Indiana Univ. Press, 1980.
Sieber, Roy, and Roslyn Adele Walker. *African Art in the Cycle of Life*. Washington, D.C.: National Museum of African Art, Smithsonian Institution, 1987.
Stepan, Peter. *Africa*. Trans. John Gabriel and Elizabeth Schwaiger. London: Prestel, 2001.
Thompson, Robert Ferris. *Face of the Gods: Art and Altars of Africa and the African Americas*. New York: Museum for African Art; Munich: Prestel, 1993.
Visonà, Monica Blackmun, et al. *A History of Art in Africa*. New York: Abrams, 2000.
Vogel, Susan. *Africa Explores: 20th Century African Art*. New York: Center for African Art, 1991.
Walker, Roslyn A. *Olówè of Isè: A Yoruba Sculptor to Kings*. Washington, D.C.: National Museum of African Art, Smithsonian Institution, 1998.
Whittington, Michael E. *Earth, Fire, and Spirit: African Pottery and Sculpture*. Charlotte, N.C.: Mint Museum of Art, 1998.
Willett, Frank. *African Art: An Introduction*. New ed. World of Art. New York: Thames and Hudson, 2003.

Chapter 17 Neoclassicism, Romanticism, and Realism

Barger, M. Susan, and William B. White. *The Daguerreotype: Nineteenth-Century Technology and Modern Science*. Washington, D.C.: Smithsonian Institution, 1991.
Berger, Martin A. *Man Made: Thomas Eakins and the Construction of Gilded Age Manhood*. Berkeley: Univ. of California Press, 2000.
Boime, Albert. *Magisterial Gaze: Manifest Destiny and American Landscape Painting*. Washington, D.C.: Smithsonian Institution Press, 1991.
_____. *Art in an Age of Bonapartism, 1800–1815*. Chicago: Univ. of Chicago Press, 1990.
Brown, David Blayney. *Romanticism*. London: Phaidon, 2001.
Clark, T. J. *The Absolute Bourgeois: Artists and Politics in France, 1848–1851*. Berkeley: Univ. of California Press, 1999.
_____. *Image of the People: Gustave Courbet and the 1848 Revolution*. Berkeley: Univ. of California Press, 1999.
Clarke, Graham. *The Photograph*. Oxford History of Art. Oxford: Oxford Univ. Press, 1997.
Conrads, Margaret C. *Winslow Homer and the Critics: Forging a National Art in the 1870s*. Princeton, N.J.: Princeton Univ. Press in association with the Nelson-Atkins Museum of Art, 2001.
Cooper, Wendy A. *Classical Taste in America 1800–1840*. Baltimore: Baltimore Museum of Art, 1993.
Denis, Rafael Cordoso, and Colin Trodd. *Art and the Academy in the Nineteenth Century*. New Brunswick, N.J.: Rutgers Univ. Press, 2000.
Des Cars, Laurence. *The Pre-Raphaelites: Romance and Realism*. New York: Abrams, 2000.
Eisenman, Stephen. *Nineteenth-Century Art: A Critical History*. 2nd ed. London: Thames and Hudson, 2002.
Grinsby, Darcy Grimaldo. *Extremities: Painting Empire in Post-Revolutionary France*. New Haven: Yale Univ. Press, 2002.
Hemingway, Andrew, and William Vaughn. *Art in Bourgeois Society, 1790–1850*. Cambridge: Cambridge Univ. Press, 1998.
Irwin, David. *Neoclassicism*. London: Phaidon, 1997.
Johns, Christopher, M. S. *Antonio Canova and the Politics of Patronage in Revolutionary and Napoleonic Europe*. Berkeley: Univ. of California Press, 1998.
Lucie-Smith, Edward. *American Realism*. New York: Abrams, 1994.
Malpas, James. *Realism*. Cambridge: Cambridge Univ. Press, 1997.
Manners and Morals: Hogarth and British Painting, 1700–1760. London: Tate Gallery, 1987.
Mitchell, Timothy. *Art and Science in German Landscape Painting, 1770–1840*. New York: Oxford Univ. Press, 1993.
Monneret, Sophie. *David and Neoclassicism*. Trans. Chris Miller and Peter Snowdon. Paris: Terrail, 1999.
Needham, Gerald. *19th-Century Realist Art*. New York: Harper & Row, 1988.
Nesterova, Yelena. *The Itinerants: The Masters of Russian Realism: Second Half of the 19th and Early 20th Centuries*. Trans. Paul Williams and Jovan Nicolson. Bournemouth: Parkstone; St. Petersburg: Aurora, 1996.
Newhall, Beaumont. *The History of Photography: From 1839 to the Present*. 5th ed. rev. New York: Museum of Modern Art, 1997.
Novotny, Fritz. *Painting and Sculpture in Europe, 1780–1880*. 2nd ed. Pelican History of Art. New Haven: Yale Univ. Press, 1995.
Prettejohn, Elizabeth. *Rossetti and His Circle*. New York: Stewart, Tabori & Chang, 1998.
Pultz, John. *Body and the Lens: Photography, 1839 to the Present*. Perspectives. New York: Abrams, 1995.
Ribeiro, Aileen. *Ingres in Fashion: Representations of Dress and Appearance in Ingres's Images of Women*. New Haven: Yale Univ. Press, 1999.
Roberts, John. *The Art of Interruption: Realism, Photography, and the Everyday*. Manchester, N.Y.: Manchester Univ. Press, 1998.
Rosenblum, Naomi. *A World History of Photography*. 3rd ed. New York: Abbeville Press, 1997.
Rosenblum, Robert, and H. W. Janson. *19th-Century Art*. Rev. and updated ed. Upper Saddle River, N. J.: Pearson Prentice Hall, 2005.
Roworth, Wendy Wassyng. *Angelica Kauffman: A Continental Artist in Georgian England*. London: Reaktion, 1992.
Rykwert, Joseph, and Anne Rykwert. Robert and James Adam: *The Men and the Style*. New York: Rizzoli, 1985.
Schaaf, Larry J. *Out of the Shadows: Herschel, Talbot and the Invention of Photography*. New Haven: Yale Univ. Press, 1992.
Sewell, Darrel. *Thomas Eakins*. Philadelphia: Philadelphia Museum of Art in association with Yale Univ. Press, 2001.
Stoichita, Victor, and Anna Maria Coderch. *Goya: The Last Carnival*. London: Reaktion, 1999.
Taylor, Joshua C., ed. *Nineteenth-Century Theories of Art*. Berkeley: Univ. of California Press, 1987.
Todd, Pamela. *Pre-Raphaelites at Home*. New York: Watson-Guptill, 2001.
Toman, Rolf, ed. *Neoclassicism and Romanticism: Architecture, Sculpture, Painting, Drawing, 1750–1848*. Trans. Paul Aston, Peter Barton, and Eileen Martin. Cologne: Könemann, 2000.
Valkenier, Elizabeth Kridl. *Ilya Repin and the World of Russian Art*. New York: Columbia Univ. Press, 1990.
Vaughan, William. *Romanticism and Art*. World of Art. New York: Thames and Hudson, 1994.
Vaughan, William, and Françoise Cachin. *Arts of the 19th Century*. 2 vols. New York: Abrams, 1998.
Viscomi, Joseph. *Blake and the Idea of the Book*. Princeton, N.J.: Princeton Univ. Press, 1993.
West, Alison. *From Pigalle to Préault: Neoclassicism and the Sublime in French Sculpture, 1760–1840*. Cambridge: Cambridge Univ. Press, 1998.
Wolf, Bryan Jay. *Romantic-Revision: Culture and Consciousness in Nineteenth-Century American Painting and Literature*. Chicago: Univ. of Chicago Press, 1986.

Chapter 18 Later Nineteenth-Century Art in Europe and the United States

Adams, Steven. *The Barbizon School and the Origins of Impressionism*. London: Phaidon, 1994.
Adler, Kathleen. *Impressionism*. New Haven: Yale Univ. Press, 1999.
Baudelaire, Charles. *The Painter of Modern Life, and Other Essays*. 2nd ed. Trans. and ed. Jonathan Mayne. London: Phaidon, 1995.
Berger, Klaus. *Japonisme in Western Painting from Whistler to Matisse*. Trans. David Brit. Cambridge Studies in the History of Art. Cambridge: Cambridge Univ. Press, 1992.
Bocquillon-Ferretti, Marina. *Signac, 1863–1935*. New York: Metropolitan Museum of Art; New Haven: Yale Univ. Press, 2001.
Boime, Albert. *The Academy and French Painting in the Nineteenth Century*. London: Phaidon, 1971.
Bretell, Richard R. *Modern Art, 1851–1929: Capitalism and Representation*. Oxford History of Art. Oxford: Oxford Univ. Press, 1999.
Broude, Norma. *World Impressionism: The International Movement, 1860–1920*. New York: Abrams, 1990.
_____. *Impressionism: A Feminist Reading: The Gendering of Art, Science, and Nature in the Nineteenth Century*. New York: Rizzoli, 1991.
Butler, Ruth. *Rodin: The Shape of Genius*. New Haven: Yale Univ. Press, 1993.
Callen, Anthea. *The Art of Impressionism: Painting Technique and the Making of Modernity*. New Haven: Yale Univ. Press, 2000.
Clark, T. J. *The Painting of Modern Life: Paris in the Time of Manet and His Followers*. Rev. ed. Princeton, N.J.: Princeton Univ. Press, 1999.
Cumming, Elizabeth, and Wendy Caplan. *Arts and Crafts Movement*. World of Art. New York: Thames and Hudson, 1991.
Denvir, Bernard. *Chronicle of Impressionism: A Timeline History of Impressionist Art*. Boston: Little, Brown, 1993.
_____. *Post-Impressionism*. World of Art. New York: Thames and Hudson, 1992.
_____. *The Impressionists First Hand*. World of Art. New York: Thames and Hudson, 1991.
_____. *The Thames and Hudson Encyclopedia of Impressionism*. World of Art. New York: Thames and Hudson, 1990.
Dorra, Henri., ed. *Symbolist Art Theories: A Critical Anthology*. Berkeley: University of California Press, 1994.
Duncan, Alastair. *Art Nouveau*. World of Art. New York: Thames and Hudson, 1994.
Garb, Tamar. *Bodies of Modernity: Figure and Flesh in Fin-de-Siècle France*. New York: Thames and Hudson, 1998.
Gibson, Michael. *Symbolism*. Cologne (Köln): Taschen, 1995.
Hamilton, George Heard. *Painting and Sculpture in Europe, 1880–1940*. 6th ed. Pelican History of Art. New Haven: Yale Univ. Press, 1993.
Hargrove, June, ed. *The French Academy: Classicism and Its Antagonists*. Newark: Univ. of Delaware Press, 1990.
Herbert, Robert L. *Impressionism: Art, Leisure, and Parisian Society*. New Haven: Yale Univ. Press, 1988.
_____. *Seurat: Drawings and Paintings*. New Haven. Yale Univ. Press, 2001.
Higonnet, Anne. *Berthe Morisot's Images of Women*. Cambridge: Harvard Univ. Press, 1992.
Hornberg, Cornelia. *Vincent van Gogh and the Painters of the Petit Boulevard*. New York: St. Louis Art Museum/Rizzoli, 2001.
Kelder, Diane. *The Great Book of French Impressionism*. 2nd ed. New York: Artabras, 1997.
Machotka, Pavel. *Cezanne: Landscape into Art*. New Haven: Yale Univ. Press, 1996.
Medina, Joyce. *Cezanne and Modernism: The Poetics of Painting*. Albany, N.Y.: State Univ. of New York Press, 1995.
Nochlin, Linda. *Representing Women*. New York: Thames and Hudson, 1999.
Nord, Phillip. *Impressionists and Politics: Art and Democracy in the Nineteenth Century*. London: Routledge, 2000.
O'Gorman, James F. *Three American Architects: Richardson, Sullivan, and Wright, 1865–1915*. Chicago: Univ. of Chicago Press, 1991.
Post-Impressionism: Cross-currents in European and American Painting, 1880–1906. Washington, D.C.: National Gallery of Art, 1980.
Roos, Jane Mayo. *Early Impressionism and the French State, 1866–1874*. Cambridge: Cambridge Univ. Press, 1996.
Rubin, James Henry. *Impressionism*. London: Phaidon, 1999.
Schapiro, Meyer. *Impressionism: Reflections and Perceptions*. New York: George Braziller, 1997.
Smith, Paul. *Seurat and the Avant-Garde*. New Haven: Yale Univ. Press, 1997.
_____. *Impressionism: Beneath the Surface*. Perspectives. New York: Abrams, 1995.
Stansky, Peter. *Redesigning the World: William Morris, the 1880s, and the Arts and Crafts*. Princeton, N.J.: Princeton Univ. Press, 1985.

Thomson, Belinda. *Impressionism: Origins, Practice, Reception*. New York: Thames and Hudson, 2000.

_____. *Post-Impressionism*. Cambridge: Cambridge Univ. Press, 1998.

Walther, Ingo F. *Vincent van Gogh: The Complete Paintings*. New York: Taschen, 1997.

_____. *Impressionist Art, 1860–1920*. Trans. Michael Hulse. New York: Taschen, 1997.

West, Shearer. *Fin-de-Siècle: Art and Society in an Age of Uncertainty*. Woodstock, N.Y.: Overlook Press, 1993.

Chapter 19 Modern Art: Europe and North America in the Early Twentieth Century

Alcantara, Isabel, and Sandra Egnolff. *Frida Kahlo and Diego Rivera*. New York: Prestel, 1999.

Antliff, Mark. *Cubism and Culture*. London: Thames and Hudson, 2001.

Arnason, H. H., Peter Kalb revision author. *History of Modern Art: Painting, Sculpture, Architecture, Photography*. 5th ed. Upper Saddle River, N. J.: Prentice Hall, 2004.

Art into Life: Russian Constructivism, 1914–32. New York: Rizzoli, 1990.

Barron, Stephanie, ed. *Degenerate Art: The Fate of the Avant-Garde in Nazi Germany*. Los Angeles: Los Angeles County Museum of Art, 1991.

Behr, Shulamith. *Expressionism*. New York: Cambridge Univ. Press, 1999.

Blake, Peter. *No Place Like Utopia: Modern Architecture and the Company We Kept*. New York: Knopf, 1993.

Bois, Yves Alain. *Matisse and Picasso*. Paris: Flammarion, 1998.

Brown, Milton W. *The Story of the Armory Show: The 1913 Exhibition That Changed American Art*. 2nd ed. New York: Abbeville, 1988.

Castleman, Riva, ed. *Art of the Forties*. New York: Museum of Modern Art, 1991.

Caws, Mary Ann, ed. *Surrealist Painters and Poets: An Anthology*. Cambridge: MIT Press, 2001.

Corn, Wanda. *The Great American Thing: Modern Art and National Identity, 1915–1935*. Berkeley: Univ. of California Press, 1999.

Craven, Wayne. *American Art: History and Culture*. Rev. 1st ed. New York: McGraw Hill, 2003.

Curtis, James. *Mind's Eye, Mind's Truth: FSA Photography Reconsidered*. Philadelphia: Temple Univ. Press, 1989.

Curtis, Penelope. *Sculpture, 1900–1945: After Rodin*. Oxford History of Art. Oxford: Oxford Univ. Press, 1999.

Dachy, Marc. *The Dada Movement, 1915–1923*. New York: Skira/Rizzoli, 1990.

Droste, Magdalena. *Bauhaus, 1919–1939*. Cologne (Köln): Tachen, 1990.

Dube, Wolf-Dieter. *Expressionists*. Trans. Mary Whittall. World of Art. New York: Thames and Hudson, 1998.

Elger, Dietmar. *Expressionism: A Revolution in German Art*. Cologne (Köln): Taschen, 1998.

Ferrier, Jean Louis. *The Fauves: The Reign of Color*. Paris: Terrail, 1995.

Ferrier, Jean Louis, ed. *Art of Our Century: The Chronicle of Western Art, 1900 to the Present*. New York: Prentice Hall, 1989.

Folgarait, Leon. *Mural Painting and Social Revolution in Mexico, 1920–1940: Art of the New Order*. New York: Cambridge Univ. Press, 1998.

Freeman, Judi. *The Fauve Landscape*. Los Angeles: Los Angeles County Museum of Art, 1990.

Giedion, Sigfried. *Walter Gropius: Work and Teamwork*. New York: Dover, 1992.

Golding, John. *Paths to the Absolute: Mondrian, Malevich, Kandinsky, Pollock, Newman, Rothko, and Still*. Princeton, N.J.: Princeton Univ. Press, 2000.

Gray, Camilla. *Russian Experiment in Art, 1863–1922*. Rev. and enl. ed. by Marian Burleigh-Motley. New York: Thames and Hudson, 1986.

Green, Christopher. *Picasso's Les demoiselles d'Avignon*. Cambridge: Cambridge Univ. Press, 2001.

_____. *Art in France, 1900–1940*. Pelican History of Art. New Haven: Yale Univ. Press, 2000.

Greenough, Sarah et al. *Modern Art and America: Alfred Stieglitz and His New York Galleries*. Washington, D.C.: National Gallery of Art; New York: Bullfinch, 2000.

Haiko, Peter, ed. *Architecture of the Early XX Century*. Trans. Gordon Clough. New York: Rizzoli, 1989.

Hammacher, A. M. *Modern Sculpture: Tradition and Innovation*. Enl. ed. New York: Abrams, 1988.

Harrison, Charles, Francis Frascina, and Gill Perry. *Primitivism, Cubism, Abstraction: The Early Twentieth Century*. New Haven: Yale Univ. Press, 1993.

Haskell, Barbara. *The American Century: Art and Culture, 1900–1950*. New York: Whitney Museum of American Art, 1999.

Herbert, James D. *Fauve Painting: The Making of Cultural Politics*. New Haven: Yale Univ. Press, 1992.

Hunter, Sam, John Jacobus, and Daniel Wheeler. *Modern Art: Painting, Sculpture, Architecture*. 3rd ed. rev. and exp. Upper Saddle River, N.J.: Prentice Hall, 2004.

Lane, John R., and Susan C. Larsen. *Abstract Painting and Sculpture in America 1927–1944*. Pittsburgh: Museum of Art, Carnegie Institute, 1984.

Levine, Neil. *The Architecture of Frank Lloyd Wright*. Princeton, N.J.: Princeton Univ. Press, 1996.

Lewis, Samella S. *African American Art and Artists*. Rev. and exp. ed. Berkeley: Univ. of California Press, 2003.

Lloyd, Jill. *German Expressionism: Primitivism and Modernity*. New Haven: Yale Univ. Press, 1991.

Murray, Joan. *Canadian Art of the Twentieth Century*. Toronto: Dundurn, 1999.

Naumann, Francis M. *Making Mischief: Dada Invades New York*. New York: Whitney Museum of Art in association with Abrams, 1996.

Nesbitt, Peter T., and Michelle DuBois. *Over the Line: The Art and Life of Jacob Lawrence*. Seattle: Univ. of Washington Press, 2000.

Neumann, Eckhard, ed. *Bauhaus and Bauhaus People*. New York: Van Nostrand Reinhold, 1993.

Overy, Paul. *De Stijl*. World of Art. New York: Thames and Hudson, 1991.

Patton, Sharon. *African-American Art*. Oxford History of Art. Oxford: Oxford Univ. Press, 1998.

Powell, Richard. *Black Art and Culture in the Twentieth Century*. New York: Thames and Hudson, 1997.

Rickey, George. *Constructivism: Origins and Evolutions*. Rev. ed. New York: George Braziller, 1995.

Rosenblum, Robert. *Cubism and Twentieth-Century Art*. Rev. ed. New York: Abrams, 2001.

Rubin, William. *Picasso and Braque: Pioneering Cubism*. New York: Museum of Modern Art, 1989.

Spector, Jack. *Surrealist Art and Writing, 1919–1939*. New York: Cambridge Univ. Press, 1997.

Stich, Sidra. *Anxious Visions: Surrealist Art*. New York: Abbeville, 1990.

Tomkins, Calvin. *Duchamp: A Biography*. New York: H. Holt, 1996.

Udall, Sharyn Rohlfsen. *Carr, O'Keeffe, Kahlo: Places of Their Own*. New Haven: Yale Univ. Press, 2000.

Weiss, Jeffrey S. *The Popular Culture of Modern Art: Picasso, Duchamp, and Avant-Gardism*. New Haven: Yale Univ. Press, 1994.

Whitfield, Sarah. *Fauvism*. World of Art. New York: Thames and Hudson, 1996.

Whitford, Frank. *The Bauhaus: Masters and Students by Themselves*. Woodstock, N.Y.: Overlook Press, 1993.

Woodham, Jonathan M. *Twentieth-Century Design*. Oxford History of Art. Oxford: Oxford Univ. Press, 1997.

Chapter 20 Art Since 1945

Anfam, David. *Abstract Expressionism*. World of Art. New York: Thames and Hudson, 1990.

Alberro, Alexander and Blake Stimson. *Conceptual Art: A Critical Anthology*. Cambridge: MIT Press, 1999.

Archer, Michael. *Art Since 1960*. 2nd ed. New York: Thames and Hudson, 2002.

Atkins, Robert. *Artspeak: A Guide to Contemporary Ideas, Movements, and Buzzwords*. 2nd ed. New York: Abbeville, 1997.

Batchelor, David. *Minimalism*. New York: Cambridge Univ. Press, 1997.

Bolton, Richard, ed. *Culture Wars: Documents from the Recent Controversies in the Arts*. New York: New Press, 1992.

Broude, Norma, and Mary D. Garrard. *The Power of Feminist Art: The American Movement of the 1970s, History and Impact*. New York: Abrams, 1994.

Deepwell, Katy. *Women Artists and Modernism*. New York: St. Martin's Press, 1998.

Dormer, Peter. *Design Since 1945*. World of Art. New York: Thames and Hudson, 1993.

Ferguson, Russell, ed. *Discourses: Conversations in Postmodern Art and Culture*. Documentary Sources in Contemporary Art. Cambridge: MIT Press, 1990.

Fineberg, Jonathan. *Art since 1940: Strategies of Being*. Rev. ed. New York: Abrams, 2000.

Goldberg, Rose Lee. *Performance Art: From Futurism to the Present*. Rev. ed. London: Thames and Hudson, 2001.

Gouma-Peterson, Thalia, and Miriam Schapiro. *Shaping the Fragments of Art and Life*. New York: Abrams, 1999.

Hanhardt, John G. *The Worlds of Nam June Paik*. New York: Guggenheim Museum, 2000.

Hays, K. Michael, and Carol Burns, eds. *Thinking the Present: Recent American Architecture*. New York: Princeton Architectural, 1990.

Hertz, Richard. *Theories of Contemporary Art*. 2nd ed. Englewood Cliffs, N.J.: Prentice Hall, 1993.

Hoffman, Katherine. *Explorations: The Visual Arts since 1945*. New York: HarperCollins, 1991.

Kingsley, April. *The Turning Point: The Abstract Expressionists and the Transformation of American Art*. New York: Simon & Schuster, 1992.

Kuspit, Donald B. *Clement Greenberg, Art Critic*. Madison: Univ. of Wisconsin Press, 1979.

Livingstone, Marco. *Pop Art: A Continuing History*. New York: Abrams, 1990.

Lucie-Smith, Edward. *Art in the Eighties*. Oxford: Phaidon, 1990.

Madoff, Steven Henry. *Pop Art: A Critical History*. Berkeley: Univ. of California Press, 1997.

McCarthy, David. *Pop Art*. New York: Cambridge Univ. Press, 2000.

Meyer, James, ed. *Minimalism*. New York: Cambridge Univ. Press, 1997.

Morgan, Robert C. *Conceptual Art: An American Perspective*. Jefferson, N.C.: McFarland, 1994.

Phillips, Lisa. *The American Century: Art and Culture, 1950–2000*. New York: Whitney Museum of American Art, 2000.

Rosen, Randy, and Catherine C. Brawer, comps. *Making Their Mark: Women Artists Move into the Mainstream, 1970–85*. New York: Abbeville, 1989.

Ross, Clifford. *Abstract Expressionism: Creators and Critics, An Anthology*. New York: Abrams, 1990.

Rush, Michael. *New Media in Late 20th-Century Art*. World of Art. New York: Thames and Hudson, 1999.

Rushing, Jackson W. III. *Native American Art in the Twentieth Century: Makers, Meanings, and Histories*. London: Routledge, 1999.

Sandler, Irving. *American Art of the 1960's*. New York: Harper & Row, 1988.

_____. *The New York School: The Painters and Sculptors of the Fifties*. New York: Harper & Row, 1978.

Sayre, Henry M. *The Object of Performance: The American Avant-Garde Since 1970*. Chicago: Univ. of Chicago Press, 1989.

Shapiro, David, and Cecile Shapiro. *Abstract Expressionism: A Critical Record*. New York: Cambridge Univ. Press, 1990.

Smith, Jaune Quick-to-See, and Harmony Hammond. *Women of Sweetgrass: Cedar and Sage*. New York: American Indian Center, 1984.

Taylor, Paul, ed. *Post-Pop Art*. Cambridge: MIT Press, 1989.

Wagner, Anne Middleton. *Three Artists (Three Women): Modernism and the Art of Hesse, Krasner, and O'Keeffe*. Berkeley: Univ. of California Press, 1996.

Waldman, Diane. *Collage, Assemblage, and the Found Object*. New York: Abrams, 1992.

Weaver, Mike, ed. *The Art of Photography, 1939–1989*. London: Royal Academy of Arts, 1989.

Wheeler, Daniel. *Art since Mid-Century: 1945 to the Present*. Englewood Cliffs, N.J.: Prentice Hall, 1991.

Word as Image: American Art, 1960–1990. Milwaukee: Milwaukee Art Museum, 1990.

Index

Credits

Credits and Copyrights

Introduction
01 Roger Wood, London; Corbis/Bettmann; 02 The Art Institute of Chicago; 03 University of Arizona, Museum of Art; 04 University of Arizona, Museum of Art; 05 Art Resource, N.Y.; 06 Art Resource, N.Y.; 07 Museo Nacional del Prado; 08 Spencer Museum of Art; 09 E. G. Schempf/The Nelson-Atkins Museum of Art; 10 VAGA; 11 John Decopoulos; 12 Art Resource, N.Y.; 13; Philip A. Charles/National Gallery of Art, Washington D.C.; 14 Franko Khoury/National Museum of African Art/Smithsonian Institution; 15 Sisterland Art Resource, N.Y.; 16 Giraudon/Art Resource, N.Y.; 17 Spencer Museum of Art; 18 Mel McLean/The Nelson-Atkins Museum of Art; 19 Claire Garoutte/Spencer Museum of Art; 20 The J. Paul Getty Museum; 21 Ghigo Roli/Index Ricerca Iconografica; 22 The Metropolitan Museum of Art; 23 British Library; 24 Freer Gallery of Art/Smithsonian Institution; 25 David Heald/The Solomon R. Guggenheim Museum; 26 Birmingham Museums and Art Gallery; 27 M. Sari/Musei Vaticani/Art Resource, N.Y.; 28 Hirmer Fotoarchiv; 29 SCALA/Art Resource, N.Y. 30 Victoria and Albert Museum, London/Art Resource, N.Y.

Chapter 1
1–1 Ministere de la Culture et des Communications; 1–2 K. H. Augustin, Esslingen/Ulmer Museum; 1–3 Sisse Brimberg/National Geographic Image Collection; 1–4 Erich Lessing/Art Resource, N.Y.; 1–6 Sisse Brimberg/National Geographic Image Collection; 1–7 Yvonne Vertut; 1–8 Sisse Brimberg National Geographic Image Collection; 1–10 Institut Amatller de Arte Hispanico; 1–11a Erich Lessing Art Resource, N.Y.; 1–11b Erich Lessing/Art Resource, N.Y.; 1–13 Mick Sharp Photography; 1–14 The Heritage Service; 1–15 Aerofilms; 1–17 Nationalmuseet Danske Afdeling; 1–19; Succec/Craig Law

Chapter 2
2–1 The Egyptian Museum; 2–02 Erich Lessing/AKG London Ltd; 2–2a Erich Lessing/Art Resource, N.Y.; 2–2b Erich Lessing/Art Resource, N.Y.; 2–4 Corbis/Bettmann; 2–5 The Oriental Institute Museum; 2–6 Nationalmuseet Danske Afdeling; 2–7 The Metropolitan Museum of Art; 2–8 University of Pennsylvania Museum of Archaeology and Anthropology; 2–9 Herve Lewandowski/Art Resource/Musée du Louvre; 2–10 D. Arnaudet/Louvre, Paris France/RMN; Art Resource/Musée du Louvre; 2–12 The Metropolitan Museum of Art; 2–13 The British Museum Great Court Ltd; 2–14a SCALA/Art Resource, N.Y.; 2–14b SCALA/Art Resource, N.Y.; 2–15 CORBIS- NY; 2–17 Araldo de Luca/The Egyptian Museum, Cairo/Index Ricerca Iconografica; 2–18 Harvard University-MFA Expedition/Museum of Fine Arts, Boston; 2–19 Peter M. Wilson/CORBIS- NY; 2–20 Semitic Museum, Harvard University/Harvard University Semitic Museum; 2–21 Yvonne Vertut; 2–22 E. G. Schempf/The Nelson-Atkins Museum of Art; 02–23 Araldo da Luca/The Metropolitan Museum of Art; 2–24 The Metropolitan Museum of Art; 2–25 Petera A. Clayton; 2–28 Yann Arthus-Bertrand/Corbis/Bettmann; 2–30 Yvonne Vertut; 2–31 Guillermo Aldana/The Getty Conservation Institute; 2–32 Bildarchiv Preussischer Kulturbesitz, Berlin, Germany/Art Resource; 2–33 Art Resource/Bildarchiv Preussischer Kulturbesitz; 2–34 Art Resource, N.Y.; 2–35 Araldo de Luca Studio/Index Ricerca Iconografica; 2–36 The British Museum; 2–37 The British Museum Great Court Ltd; BOX Herve Lewandowski/Art Resource/Musée du Louvre

Chapter 3
3–1 National Geographic Image Collection; 3–2a, b Giraudon/The Bridgeman Art Library International; 3–3 Archaeological Museum, Sarnath/Archive Jean-Louis Nou Paris; 3–4 Richard Todd/National Museum of New Delhi; 3–5 University of Michigan Museum of Art; 3–6 Richard Todd/National Museum of New Delhi; 3–7 Government Museum of Mathura; 3–8 Benoy K. Behl; 3–9 University of Michigan Museum of Art; 3–10 University of Michigan Museum of Art; 3–11 George Gerster/Photo Researchers, Inc.; 3–12 Institute of History and Philology, Academia Sinica; 3–13 Cultural Relics Publishing House; 3–14 Cultural Relics Publishing House; 3–15 The Nelson-Atkins Museum of Art; 3–16 Wolfgang Kaehler; CORBIS- NY; 3–17 Cultural Relics Publishing House; 3–18 Cultural Relics Publishing House; 3–19 Cultural Relics Publishing House; 3–20 Collection of the Tokyo National Museum/DNP Archives.Com Co., Ltd; 3–22 Japan National Tourist Organization; 3–23 Carmen Redondo/Corbis/Bettmann; 3–24 Japan National Tourist Organization; BOX National Palace Museum, Taipei, Taiway/The National Palace Museum

Chapter 4
4–1 Greek National Tourism Organization; 4–2 Hellenic Republic Ministry of Culture; 4–3 McRae Books Srl; 4–4 Petros M. Nomicos/The Archaeological Society at Athens; 4–5, 4–6, 4–7 Archeological museum, Iraklion, Crete/Studio Kontos Photostock; 4–8 Nimatallah/Art Resource, N.Y.; 4–10 Dagli Orti/Picture Desk, Inc./Kobal Collection; 4–11 Studio Kontos Photostock; 4–12 Deutches Arch. Inst./Deutsches Archaologisches Institut, Athens; 4–13 The Metropolitan Museum of Art; 4–14 The Metropolitan Museum of Art; 4–15 Erich Lessing/Art Resource, N.Y.; 4–18 Gian Beerta Vanni/Archaeological Museum, Korkyra (Corfu)/Art Resource, N.Y.; 4–19 The Metropolitan Museum of Art; 4–20 Acropolis Museum, Athens, Greece/Studio Kontos Photostock; 04–21 Chateau-Musée, Boulogne-su-Mer, France/Devos; 4–23 Bildarchiv Preussischer Kulturbesitz/Art Resource/Bildarchiv Preussischer Kulturbesitz; 4–24 Museum of Fine Arts, Boston; 4–25 Nimatallah/Art Resource, N.Y.; 4–26 Archeological Museum, Delphi/Studio Kontos Photostock; 4–27a SCALA/Art Resource, N.Y.; 4–27b SCALA/Museo Archeologico Naz, Italy/Art Resource, N.Y.; 4–29 Royal Ontario Museum; 4–29a, b, c The British Museum Great Court Ltd; 4–30 Baghdad Museum/The British Museum Great Court Ltd; 4–31 The Bridgeman Art Library International; 4–32 Wolfgang Kaehler/CORBIS- NY; 4–34 (c) Archaeological Receipts Fund/Hellenic Republic Ministry of Culture; 4–35 Canali

Photobank; 4–36 Scala/Alinari/Art Resource, N.Y.; 4–37 Erich Lessing/Art Resource, N.Y.

Chapter 5
5–1 Art Resource/Musée du Louvre; 5–2; SCALA/Alinari/Art Resource, N.Y.; 5–3 Studio Kontos Photostock; 5–4 Marvin Trachtenberg; 5–6 Musées des Louvre/Art Resource; 5–7 The Metropolitan Museum of Art; 5–8a Musei Capitolini; 5–8b COR-BIS- NY; 5–9 Tourist Organization of Greece; 5–10 Art Resource, N.Y.; 5–11 The Oriental Institute Museum; 5–12 Bildarchiv Preussischer Kulturbesitz; 5–15 Corbis/Bettmann; 5–16 The Oriental Institute Museum; 5–17 Museo Nazionale di Villa Giulia, Italy/Canali Photobank; 5–18 Soprintendenza alle Antichita' Firenze; 5–19 SCALA/Art Resource, N.Y.; 5–20 Soprintendenza Archeologica per l'Etruria Meridionale; 5–21 Villa Giulia; 5–22 Erich Lessing/Art Resource, N.Y.; BOX Ashmolean Museum

Chapter 6
6–1 Musei Vaticani; 6–2 American Numismatic Society of New York; 6–3 Canali Photobank; 6–4 Vincenzo Pirozzi; 6–6 Danita Delimont Photography; 6–7 SuperStock, Inc.; 6–8 L. Giordano/Musei Vaticani; 6–9 Foto Vasari/Index Ricerca Iconografica; 6–10 SCALA/Art Resource, N.Y.; 6–11 Kunsthistorisches Museum Wien; 6–13 Pedicini/Index Ricerca Iconografica; 6–14 Fitzwilliam Museum; 6–15 SCALA/Art Resource, N.Y.; 6–16 Villa of the Mysteries, Pompeii/Canali Photobank; 6–17 Jean Pragen/Getty Images Inc./Stone Allstock; 6–18 Canali Photobank; 6–19 A. Vasari/Index Ricerca Iconografica; 6–21 American Academy in Rome; 6–22 Canali Photobank; 6–23 Danita Delimont Photography; 6–25; Biran Brake/John Hilleison Agency; 6–26 IKONA/Foto Vasari Roma; 6–27a, b Araldo de Luca Archives; 6–28 Museo Archeologico Nazionale, Naples/Gemeinnutzige Stiftung Leonard von Matt; 6–29 Canali Photobank; 6–30 Araldo De Luca/Musei Capitolini, Rome, Italy/Index Ricerca Iconografica; 6–31 IKONA; 6–33 Capitoline Museum/Canali Photobank; 6–34 Araldo de Luca Archives; BOX National Museum of Ireland

Chapter 7
7–1 Index Ricerca Iconografica; 7–2 Villa Torlonia, Rome/Canali Photobank; 7–3 Erich Lessing/Art Resource, N.Y.; 7–4 David Harris/Israel Museum Jerusalem; 7–5 SCALA/Art Resource, N.Y.; 7–7 Vincenzo Pirozzi; 7–8 Nimatallah/Index Ricerca Iconografica; 7–9 Canali Photobank; 7–10 Canali Photobank; 7–11 Achim Bednorz; 7–13 Marvin Trachtenberg; 7–15 SCALA/Art Resource, N.Y.; 7–16 SCALA/Art Resource, N.Y.; 7–17 SCALA/Art Resource, N.Y.; 7–18 Bildarchiv der Osterreichische Nationalbibliothek; 7–19; Donato Pineider, Florence/Biblioteca Medicea Laurenziana Firenze; 7–20 Studio Kontos Photostock; 7–21 Carrieri Fotografo; 7–22 Galleria Dell'Accademia, Venice/Cameraphoto Arte di Codato G.P. & C. snc; 7–24 Cameraphoto Arte di Codato G.P. & C. snc; 7–25, 7–26 Bruce White/The Metropolitan Museum of Art; 7–27 Wim Swaan Photograph Collection/The Getty Research Institute for the History of Art and the Humanities; 7–28 Sovfoto/Eastfoto

Chapter 8
8–1 Smithsonian Institution, Washington, DC/Freer Gallery of Art; 8–2 The Metropolitan Museum of Art; 8–3 A.F. Kersting; 8–4 Said Nuseibeh Photography; 8–6 Roger Wood/Corbis/Bettmann; 8–7 Raffaello Bencini Fotografo; 8–8; Benini/Raffaello Bencini Fotografo;8–09 Art Resource/Reunion des Musées Nationaux; 8–10 Werner Forman Archive Ltd; 8–11 The Metropolitan Museum of Art; 8–12; Ronald Sheridan/The Ancient Art & Architecture Collection Ltd; 8–13 John and Lisa Merrill/CORBIS- NY; 8–14 Peter Sanders Photography; 8–15 Freer Gallery of Art/Smithsonian Institution; 8–16 The Metropolitan Museum of Art; 8–18 SCALA/Art Resource, N.Y.; 8–19 Sonia Halliday Photographs; 8–20 The Metropolitan Museum of Art; BOX Z. Perkins/James F. Ballard Collection/The Saint Louis Art Museum; BOX2 The New York Public Library, Research Libraries/Art Resource; BOX3 Library of Congress

Chapter 9
9–1 Mike Yamashita. All Rights Reserved./Woodfin Camp & Associates; 9–3 University of Michigan Museum of Art; 9–4 National Museum of India/Henri Stierlin; 9–5 Museum of Fine Arts, Boston; 9–6 Katherine Wetzel/Virginia Museum of Fine Arts; 9–7 Dave G. Houser/CORBIS- NY; 9–9 The National Palace Museum; 9–10 Robert Newcombe/The Nelson-Atkins Museum of Art; 9–11 Percival David Foundation; 9–12 Asian Art Museum Foundation of San Francisco; 9–13 The National Palace Museum; 9–14 Robert Newcombe (4/1991)/The Nelson-Atkins Museum of Art; 9–16 Wan-go/H. C. Weng; 9–17 Nimtallah/AKG London NY; 9–18 Japan National Tourist Organization; 9–19 Freer Gallery of Art/Smithsonian Institution; 9–20 The Tokugawa Reimeikai Foundation; 9–21 The Cleveland Museum of Art; 9–22 Japan National Tourist Organization; 9–23 Sunritz Hattori Museum of Arts; 9–25 Philadelphia Museum of Art; 9–26 Tibor Franyo/Honolulu Academy of Arts

Chapter 10
10–1 Bayerische Staatsbibliothek; 10–2 Kit Weiss/Nationalmuseet Danske Afdeling; 10–3 The British Museum Great Court Ltd; 10–6 Achim Bednorz; 10–7 Bibliothèque Nationale, Paris/Art Resource/Reunion des Musées Nationaux; 10–8 Erich Lessing/Art Resource, N.Y.; 10–10 Bibliothèque Nationale, Paris/Art Resource, N.Y.; 10–11 Art Resource/The Pierpont Morgan Library; 10–12 Oronoz Archivo; 10–13 The Metropolitan Museum of Art; 10–14 Frank Tomio/Bildarchiv Foto Marburg; 10–15 Achim Bednorz; 10–16 Hessisches Landes- und Hochschulebibliothek; 10–17 Erich Lessing/Art Resource, N.Y.; 10–18 Leonard Von Matt/Gemeinnutzige Stiftung Leonard von Matt; 10–19 Marvin Trachtenberg; 10–21 Achim Bednorz; 10–23 Achim Bednorz; 10–24 SCALA/Art Resource, N.Y.; 10–25 A.F. Kersting; 10–26 Ghigo Roli/Index Ricerca Iconografica; 10–27 Vanni/Art Resource, N.Y.; 10–28 Jean Roubier, Paris/French Embassy Washington DC; 10–29 Dagli Orti/Picture Desk, Inc./Kobal Collection; 10–30 Calveras/Merida/Sagrista/Museu Nacional d'Art de Catalunya; 10–31 Corpus Christi College; 10–32 Ursula Seitz-Gray, Ffm./Thuringer Universitats-und Landesbibliothek Jena; 10–33 Paderborn Diocesan Museum; 10–34 The Metropolitan Museum of Art

Chapter 11
11–1 Sonia Halliday Photographs; 11–3 French Embassy Washington DC; 11–4 Herve Champollion/Agence Photographique TOP; 11–5 Francios Lauginie/Caisse Nationale

des Monuments Historique et des Sites; 11–7 Laura Lushington/Sonia Halliday Photographs; 11–8 Jean Bernard Photographe/Bordas Publication; 11–9 Sonia Halliday & Bryan Knox (Arps)/Sonia Halliday Photographs; 11–10 Corbis/Bettmann; 11–11 Paul Almasy/CORBIS- NY; 11–12 Foto Marburg/Art Resource, N.Y.; 11–13 Achim Bednorz; 11–14 Jean Bernard/Jean Bernard Photographe/Bordas Publication; 11–15 The Pierpont Morgan Library/Art Resource, N.Y.; 11–16 The Metropolitan Museum of Art; 11–17 M. Beck-Coppola/Louvre, Paris/Art Resource/Musée du Louvre; 11–18 The Walters Art Museum; 11–19 London Aerial Photo Library/CORBIS- NY; 11–21 Aerofilms; 11–22 The Pierpont Morgan Library/Art Resource/The Pierpont Morgan Library; 11–23 The Metropolitan Museum of Art; 11–24 Achim Bednorz; 11–25 Avery Architectural and Fine Arts Library; 11–26 SCALA/Art Resource, N.Y.; 11–27 Nicola Pisano/Canali Photobank; 11–28 Canali Photobank; 11–29 Cimabue (Cenni di Pepi)/Index Ricerca Iconografica; 11–30 Galleria degli Uffizi; 11–31 Alinari/Art Resource, N.Y.; 11–32 ALINARI/Art Resource, N.Y.

Chapter 12
12–1 Frick Collection; 12–2 Musée Conde, Chantilly, France/Art Resource, N.Y.; 12–3 The Metropolitan Museum of Art; 12–4 National Gallery of Art, Washington D.C.; 12–5 The National Gallery Company Ltd.; 12–6 National Gallery del Prado; 12–7 The Metropolitan Museum of Art; 12–8 Galleria degli Uffizi; 12–9 The Metropolitan Museum of Art; 12–10 John Rylands University Library of Manchester; 12–11 The Metropolitan Museum of Art; 12–12 Cincinnati Art Museum; 12–13 Art Resource, N.Y.; 12–15, 12–16 SCALA/Art Resource, N.Y.; 12–17 Cantarelli/Index Ricerca Iconografica; 12–18 ALINARI/Art Resource, N.Y.; 12–19 The Walters Art Museum; 12–20 Nimatallah/Art Resource, N.Y.; 12–21 Codato/Canali Photobank; 12–22, 12–23 SCALA/Art Resource, N.Y.; 12–24, 12–25 Studio Mario Quattrone; 12–26 Erich Lessing/Art Resource, N.Y.; 12–27 The National Gallery Company Ltd.; 12–28 SCALA/Art Resource, N.Y.; 12–29 Art Resource, N.Y.; 12–30 Art Resource, N.Y.

Chapter 13
13–1 Musei Vaticani; 13–2 Studio Mario Quattrone; 13–3 Lewandowski/LeMage/Art Resource/Musée du Louvre; 13–4 National Gallery of Art, Washington D.C.; 13–5, 13–6 Musei Vaticani; 13–7 Index Ricerca Iconografica; 13–8 Index Ricerca Iconografica; 13–9 Zigrossi Bracchetti/Vatican Musei/IKONA; 13–10 AKG London Ltd; 13–11 Archivo Musei Vatican/Musei Vaticani; 13–12 Canali Photobank; 13–14 Cameraphoto/Art Resource, N.Y.; 13–15 Erich Lessing/Art Resource/Musée du Louvre; 13–16 Embassy of Italy; 13–17 Summerfield/Galleria degli Uffizi, Florence/Index Ricerca Iconografica; 13–18 ALI-NARI/Art Resource, N.Y.; 13–19 Cameraphoto/Art Resource, N.Y.; 13–20 Canali Photobank; 13–22 Index Ricerca Iconografica; 13–23 Capponi Chapel, Church of Santa Felicita, Italy/Canali Photobank; 13–24 The Metropolitan Museum of Art; 13–25 Giraudon/The Bridgeman Art Library International; 13–28 Kunsthistorisches Museum Wien; 13–29 SCALA/Art Resource, N.Y.; 13–30 Erich Lessing/Art Resource, N.Y.; 13–32 SCALA/Alte Pinakothek, Munich/Art Resource, N.Y.; 13–33 Philadelphia Museum of Art; 13–34, 13–35 Alte Pinakothek; 13–36 Index Ricerca Iconografica; 13–37 Oronoz/Museo Nacional del Prado; 13–38 Kunsthistorisches Museum Wien; 13–39 Martin Buhler; Kunstmuseum Basel; 13–40 SCALA/Art Resource, N.Y.; BOX1 AKG London Ltd; BOX2 Cameraphoto/AKG London Ltd; BOX3 AKG London Ltd

Chapter 14
14–1 Canali Photobank; 14–2 SCALA/Art Resource, N.Y.; 14–3 Corbis/Bettmann; 14–4 SCALA/Art Resource, N.Y.; 14–5 Adros Studio Fotografia; 14–6 Canali Photobank; 14–7 SCALA/Art Resource, N.Y.; 14–8, 14–9 Canali Photobank; 14–10 Detroit Institute of Arts; 14–11 Wellington Museum, London/V & A Images; 14–12 SCALA/Art Resource, N.Y.; 14–13 The State Hermitage Museum; 14–14 Denver Art Museum; 14–15 Institut Royal du Patrimoine Artistique (IRPA-KIK); 14–16 Art Resource/Art Resource, N.Y.; 14–17 SCALA/Art Resource, N.Y.; 14–18 Art Resource/Musée du Louvre; 14–19 Inigo Jones/Historic Royal Palaces Enterprises Ltd; 14–20 Frans Hals Museum De Hallen; 14–21, 14–22 Rijksmuseum; 14–23 Frick Collection; 14–24 National Gallery of Art, Washington D.C.; 14–25 Richard Carafelli/National Gallery of Art, Washington D.C.; 14–26 Rijksmuseum; 14–27 The National Gallery Company Ltd.; 14–28 Herve Lewandowski/Art Resource/Musée du Louvre; 14–29 William Swaan Photograph Collection/The Getty Research Institute for the History of Art and the Humanities; 14–30 The Ancient Art & Architecture Collection Ltd.; 14–31 The Art Institute of Chicago; 14–32 Wim Swaan/The Getty Research Institute for the History of Art and the Humanities; 14–33 Art Resource/Musée du Louvre; 14–34 Frick Collection; 14–35 National Museum of Women In the Arts; 14–36 The Toledo Museum of Art

Chapter 15
15–1 Justin Kerr/Dumbarton Oaks Research Library & Collections; 15–3 Art Resource/The Museum of Modern Art; 15–4 SCALA/Art Resource, N.Y.; 15–5 Wim Swaan Collection/The Getty Research Institute for the History of Art and the Humanities; 15–6 Elizabeth Barrows Rogers/Mexican Government Tourism Office; 15–8 Picture Desk, Inc./Kobal Collection; 15–9 University of Oxford/Bodleian Library; 15–10 Enrique Franco Torrijos, Mexico City/Embassy of Mexico; 15–11 Werner Forman/Art Resource, N.Y.; 15–12 John Bigalow Taylor; 15–13 Kevin Schafer/CORBIS- NY; 15–14 The Art Institute of Chicago; 15–16 Dagli Orti/Picture Desk, Inc./Kobal Collection; 15–17 John Bigelow Taylor, NY/American Museum of Natural History; 15–18 University of Pennsylvania Museum of Archaeology and Anthropology; 15–19 Gilcrease Museum; 15–20 Tony Linck; 15–21 Cahokia Mounds State Historic Site; 15–22 Richard A. Cooke/CORBIS- NY; 15–23 The Saint Louis Art Museum; 15–24 Museum of Indian Arts & Culture; 15–25 Amon Carter Museum; 15–26 Smithsonian National Museum of Natural History; 15–27 Montana Historical Society; 15–28 Peabody Museum, Harvard University; 15–29 Smithsonian Institution Archives; 15–30 Museum of Anthropology; 15–31 Embassy of Canada; BOX The Philbrook Museum

Chapter 16
16–1 Sarah DaVanzo Collection; 16–2 Port Authority of New York & New Jersey; 16–3 Museum of Ife Antiquities, Nigeria/Dirk Bakker; 16–4, 16–5 The Metropolitan Museum of Art; 16–6 Franko Khoury/National Museum of African Art/Smithsonian Institution; 16–7 Getty Images Inc./Image Bank; 16–8 Casement

Creative Services Inc.; 16–9 Margaret Courtney-Clarke/Corbis/Bettmann; 16–10 The Field Museum; 16–11 The Nelson-Atkins Museum of Art; 16–12 University of Pennsylvania Museum of Archaeology and Anthropology; 16–13 Detroit Institute of Arts; 16–14 Franko Khoury/National Museum of African Art/Smithsonian Institution; 16–15 Charles & Josette Lenars/CORBIS- NY; 16–16 The University of Iowa Museum of Art; BOX1 Ron Jennings/Virginia Museum of Fine Arts; BOX2 National Museum of African Art/Smithsonian Institution

Chapter 17
17–1 Museum of Fine Arts, Boston; 17–2 Art Resource/Musée du Louvre; 17–3 Caisse Nationale des Monuments Historique et des Sites; 17–4 The Metropolitan Museum of Art; 17–5 National Gallery of Art, Washington D.C.; 17–6 The National Gallery of Art; 17–7 Virginia Museum of Fine Arts; 17–8 The National Gallery Company Ltd.; 17–9 Richard Bryant/Arcaid; 17–10 (c) David R. Frazier Photolibrary, Inc./Alamy Images; 17–11 National Museum of Women In the Arts; 17–12, 17–13 Art Resource/Reunion des Musées Nationaux; 17–14, 17–15 Herve Lewandowski/Art Resource/Musée du Louvre; 17–16 Art Resource/Musée du Louvre; 17–17 The Hispanic Society of America; 17–18 Erich Lessing/Art Resource, N.Y.; 17–19 Oronoz-Nieto/Museo Nacional del Prado; 17–20 Detroit Institute of Arts; 17–21 Frick Collection; 17–22 The National Gallery Company Ltd.; 17–23 Societe Francaise de Photographie; 17–24 Archives of American/Smithsonian Institution; 17–25 Science & Society Picture Library; 17–26 Cincinnati Art Museum; 17–27 Erich Lessing/Art Resource/Musée d'Orsay; 17–28 Herve Lewandowski/Art Resource/Musée d'Orsay; 17–29 The State Russian Museum/CORBIS- NY; 17–30, 17–31 The Metropolitan Museum of Art; BOX The Wedgwood Museum

Chapter 18
18–1 The Art Institute of Chicago; 18–2 Giraudon/Art Resource, N.Y.; 18–4 Library of Congress; 18–5 Wadsworth Atheneum; 18–6; National Museum of American Art, Washington, DC/Art Resource, N.Y.; 18–7 Spencer Museum of Art; 18–8 William Morris Gallery; 18–9 Ch. Bastin & J. Evrard; 18–10 Corbis/Bettmann; 18–11 Timothy O'Sullivan/National Archives and Records Administration/Presidential Library; 18–12 Museum of Fine Arts, Boston; 18–13 The Bridgeman Art Library International; 18–14 Hampton University Museum; 18–15 Art Resource/Musée d'Orsay; 18–16 Erich Lessing/Art Resource, N.Y.; 18–18 Robert Newcombe (1/1998)/The Nelson-Atkins Museum of Art; 18–19 National Gallery of Art, Washington D.C.; 18–20 The Metropolitan Museum of Art; 18–21 Courtauld Institute of Art; 18–22 The Phillips Collection; 18–23 Dean Beasom/National Gallery of Art, Washington D.C.; 18–24 Art Resource/The Museum of Modern Art; 18–25 Courtauld Institute of Art; 18–26 The Art Institute of Chicago; 18–27 The Art Institute of Chicago; 18–28 The National Gallery Company Ltd.; 18–29 Art Resource/The Museum of Modern Art; 18–30 J. Lathion/Nasjonalmuseet for Kunst/Nasjonalgalleriet; 18–31 San Diego Museum of Art; 18–32 Carnegie Museum of Art; 18–33 Hirshhorn Museum and Sculpture Garden/Smithsonian Institution; 18–34 Artothek; BOX Yale University Art Gallery

Chapter 19
19–1 Philadelphia Museum of Art; 19–2 Bildarchiv der Osterreichische Nationalbibliothek; 19–3 Barnes Foundation; 19–4 Art Resource/The Museum of Modern Art; 19–5 Art Resource/Bildarchiv Preussischer Kulturbesitz; 19–6 Martin Buhler/Kunstmuseum Basel; 19–7 The Art Institute of Chicago; 19–8 The Metropolitan Museum of Art; 19–9 Art Resource/The Museum of Modern Art; 19–10 The Solomon R. Guggenheim Museum; 19–11 Art Resource, N.Y.; 19–12 Washington University Gallery of Art; 19–13 L & M Services; 19–14 Art Resource, N.Y.; 19–16 Stedelijk Museum; 19–17 Kunsthaus Zurich; 19–18 Graydon Wood, 1998/Philadelphia Museum of Art; 19–20 The Metropolitan Museum of Art; 19–21 Van Abbemuseum; 19–22 Hickey-Robertson/The Menil Collection; 19–23, 19–24, 19–25 Art Resource/The Museum of Modern Art; 19–26 Hirshhorn Museum and Sculpture Garden/Smithsonian Institution; 19–27 Tate; 19–28 The New York Public Library Photographic Services/Art Resource; 19–29 Art Resource/The Museum of Modern Art; 19–30 Art Resource, N.Y.; 19–31 The Art Institute of Chicago; 19–32 Library of Congress; 19–33 Schomburg Center for Research in Black Culture/Art Resource, N.Y.; (c) Donna VanDerZee. All Rights Reserved/James Van Der Zee; 19–35 Artists Rights Society, Inc.; 19–36 Schalkwijk/Art Resource, N.Y.; 19–37 Art Resource, N.Y.; 19–38 Trevor Mills/Vancouver Art Gallery; 19–39 James Linders Fotografie; 19–40 A.D.A.G.P.- Societe des Auteurs dans les Arts Graphiques et Plastiques; 19–41 Fred Kraus/Bauhausarchiv-Museum fur Gestaltung; 19–42 Walter Gropius/Art Resource/The Museum of Modern Art; 19–43 Corbis/Bettmann; BOX Adk, Berlin, George Grosz-Archiv/Stiftung Archiv der Akademie der Kunste

Chapter 20
20–1; Wally McNamees/CORBIS- NY; 20–2 Washington University Gallery of Art; 20–3 The Metropolitan Museum of Art; 20–4 Geoffrey Clements/Whitney Museum of American Art; 20–5 Art Resource/The Museum of Modern Art; 20–6 Valerie Walker/Museum of Contemporary Art, Chicago; 20–8 Art Resource, N.Y.; 20–9 Sonnabend Gallery; 20–10 SCALA/Art Resource, N.Y.; 20–12 John Bigalow Taylor/The Museum of Modern Art; 20–13 Estate of Roy Lichtenstein; 20–14 Art Resource, N.Y.; 20–15 Yale University Art Gallery; 20–16 Art Resource/The Museum of Modern Art; 20–17 Spencer Museum of Art; 20–18 Whitney Museum of American Art; 20–19 Art Resource/The Museum of Modern Art; 20–20 Eric Pollitzer/Leo Castelli Gallery, New York; 20–21 Gianfranco Gorgoni/James Cohan Gallery; 20–22 Christo and Jeanne-Claude; 20–23 Robert Hickerson; 20–24 Through the Flower; 20–25 Benjamin Blackwell/Berkeley Art Museum; 20–26 Faith Ringgold, Inc.; 20–27 Cindy Sherman/Metro Pictures; 20–28 Van Abbemuseum; 20–29 Paula Cooper Gallery/Elizabeth Murray; 20–30 Art Gallery of South Australia; 20–31 Chrysler Museum of Art; 20–32 David Heald (c) SRGF, NY/The Solomon R. Guggenheim Museum; 20–33 Art Resource/Smithsonian American Art Museum; 20–34 Fotoworks-Benny Chan/James Cohan Gallery; 20–35 Larry Barns/Barbara Gladstone Gallery; 20–36 ACME/Jennifer Steinkamp; 20–39 Robert Newcombe/The Nelson-Atkins Museum of Art; 20–40 Museum of Arts & Design; 20–41 Andrew Garn; 20–42 Ian Lambot/Foster and Partners; 20–43 AP Wide World Photos; 20–44 Guggenheim Museum Bilbao; 20–45 Port Authority of New York & New Jersey